Frommer's®

England
& the Best of Wales

22nd Edition

by Nick Dalton & Deborah Stone

WILEY

John Wiley & Sons, Inc.

Published by:
JOHN WILEY & SONS, INC.

Copyright © 2012 John Wiley & Sons Ltd, The Atrium, Southern Gate, Chichester,
West Sussex PO19 8SQ, UK
Telephone (+44) 1243 779777
Email (for orders and customer service enquiries): cs-books@wiley.co.uk. Visit our Home Page on www.
wiley.com

Publisher: Kelly Regan
Project Manager: Daniel Mersey
Editor: Mark Henshall
Project Editor: Hannah Clement
Cartography: Andrew Murphy
Photo Editor: Cherie Cincilla, Richard H. Fox, Jill Emeny
Front cover photo: Sunrise, ocean and coastline, Cornwall, England/© David Noton Photography / Alamy
Images
Back Cover photo: Welsh pony in typical Welsh mountain landscape in Snowdonia, Wales/© Tim Graham /
Alamy Images

Wiley also publishes its books in a variety of electronic formats and by print-on-demand. Some content
that appears in standard print versions of this book may not be available in other formats. For more information about Wiley products, visit us at www.wiley.com.

For information on our other products and services or to obtain technical support, please contact our
Customer Care Department within the U.S. at 877/762-2974, outside the U.S. at 317/572-3993 or fax
317/572-4002.

British Library Cataloguing in Publication Data
A catalogue record for this book is available from the British Library
ISBN 978-1-118-28767-5 (pbk)
ISBN 978-1-118-33371-6 (ebk)
ISBN 978-1-118-33485-0 (ebk)
ISBN 978-1-118-33137-8 (ebk)

Typeset by Wiley Indianapolis Composition Services

Printed and bound in the United States of America

5 4 3 2 1

CONTENTS

19 NORTH WALES 721

20 PLANNING YOUR TRIP 747

LIST OF MAPS

ABOUT THE AUTHORS

Nick Dalton and Deborah Stone work as a team (generally helped on research trips by children Georgia and Henry). Using the knowledge garnered from writing about England and Wales for newspapers, magazines, and books, they were lead writers here, uniting a team despatched to the countries' far reaches.

They co-wrote Kent, Surrey & Sussex, Cambridge & East Anglia, and Cardiff & South Wales, along with Suggested Itineraries, and much of The Best of ..., In Depth (in which history graduate Deborah revelled in the "Today" and "Making of..." sections), and Planning Your Trip.

Together they have written Frommer's *Wales With Your Family*, and have worked on Frommer's editing projects for destinations from Vienna to Iceland.

Nick writes on travel for U.K. newspapers such as the *Daily Telegraph*, the *Times* and the *Daily Express*. He also, for his sins, covers skiing and cruises worldwide, and is a regular visitor to the U.S., where he has written travel guides for Colorado and other states. He has also written Frommer's *Salzburg Day By Day*.

Deborah has written prolifically for the *Daily Telegraph* and *Daily Express*, on U.K. and family travel, having spent her childhood camping all over Britain, but particularly in East Anglia and Wales. She is a leading cruise writer, and is Online Gardening Editor at the Daily and *Sunday Express*.

Donald Strachan is a Scottish journalist, writer, and editor who has lived most of his life "down south" in England. He has written about the country, and wider European travel, for newspapers worldwide, including the *Sydney Morning Herald* and the *Guardian*, and is a U.K. *Sunday Telegraph* contributor on travel-related new technology. He's also authored or co-authored several recent guidebooks to European destinations, including Frommer's *London 2013* and Frommer's *Florence, Tuscany & Umbria*. Donald was responsible for the sections on London, North Wales, Hampshire, Dorset, Wiltshire, and southern Somerset.

Rhonda Carrier, who hails from the East Midlands, has lived in London, Paris, Vienna and Hong Kong, and is now based in Manchester, writes widely about travel in the U.K. and abroad for Frommer's and frommers.com, Rizzoli, takethefamily.com, *The Guardian* and *The Observer*, *The Mail Online*, P&O Ferries and others. A family travel expert, she has authored three editions of Frommer's *London with Kids* as well as the guidebooks Frommer's *Brittany With Your Family* and Frommer's *Normandy With Your Family*, and edited several other titles in the 'With Your Family' series. Rhonda wrote the chapters East Midlands, The Northwest, and Yorkshire & the Northeast.

Louise McGrath is a freelance travel writer and editor. Born in England, she lived in the U.S., Colombia and Spain before moving to Northern Ireland in 2006. Since 2000 she has worked as an editor for Whatsonwhen (now Frommer's Unlimited) writing destination guides, and has authored several guide books, including Frommer's *Lisbon Day by Day*, Frommer's *Lake District Day by Day* and Frommer's *England and the Best of Wales 2012*, for which she worked on the Lake District chapter. Louise speaks Spanish and Portuguese, has an MA in Latin American Literature & Culture and is currently studying for the CIM Diploma in Digital Marketing.

Christi Daugherty has written for newspapers and wire services around the world on subjects ranging from politics to murder. She's also written numerous books for Frommer's, including Frommer's *Ireland 2011* and Frommer's *Ireland Day by Day*. Her first novel, Night School, will be published in 2012. She lives in a small town in southeast England, where she wrote the Devon chapter for this book.

Rebecca Ford is an award-winning travel writer and journalist who contributes to a wide range of national newspapers and magazines, writing about subjects as varied as wildlife watching in Peru and walking in Italy. She has authored and co-authored many guidebooks, including ones to U.K. destinations such as Scotland, Wales and London, as well as *Frommer's England and the Best of Wales 2012*. Rebecca wrote the chapter on Cornwall – which is fitting as she's part Cornish and has been visiting this fascinating corner of the country since she was a child.

Stephen Keeling is an award-winning journalist and writer who lives in New York but returns to his native England several times a year. He spent 7 years working in Asia as a financial journalist and editor before writing his first travel guide in 2006, and has since authored numerous titles including *Frommer's Italy* and *Frommer's Tuscany & Umbria*. Stephen was responsible for the sections on Bristol, Bath, the Cotswolds, the Heart of England, and the Thames Valley and Chilterns.

HOW TO CONTACT US

In researching this book, we discovered many wonderful places—hotels, restaurants, shops, and more. We're sure you'll find others. Please tell us about them, so we can share the information with your fellow travelers in upcoming editions. If you were disappointed with a recommendation, we'd love to know that, too. Please email frommers@wiley.com or write to:

Frommer's England and the Best of Wales, 22nd Edition
John Wiley & Sons, Inc. • 111 River St. • Hoboken, NJ 07030-5774

ADVISORY & DISCLAIMER

Travel information can change quickly and unexpectedly, and we strongly advise you to confirm important details locally before traveling, including information on visas, health and safety, traffic and transport, accommodation, shopping and eating out. We also encourage you to stay alert while traveling and to remain aware of your surroundings. Avoid civil disturbances, and keep a close eye on cameras, purses, wallets and other valuables.

While we have endeavored to ensure that the information contained within this guide is accurate and up-to-date at the time of publication, we make no representations or warranties with respect to the accuracy or completeness of the contents of this work and specifically disclaim all warranties, including without limitation warranties of fitness for a particular purpose. We accept no responsibility or liability for any inaccuracy or errors or omissions, or for any inconvenience, loss, damage, costs or expenses of any nature whatsoever incurred or suffered by anyone as a result of any advice or information contained in this guide.

The inclusion of a company, organization or Website in this guide as a service provider and/or potential source of further information does not mean that we endorse them or the information they provide. Be aware that information provided through some Websites may be unreliable and can change without notice. Neither the publisher or author shall be liable for any damages arising herefrom.

FROMMER'S STAR RATINGS, ICONS & ABBREVIATIONS

Every hotel, restaurant, and attraction listing in this guide has been ranked for quality, value, service, amenities, and special features using a **star-rating system.** In country, state, and regional guides, we also rate towns and regions to help you narrow down your choices and budget your time accordingly. Hotels and restaurants are rated on a scale of zero (recommended) to three stars (exceptional). Attractions, shopping, nightlife, towns, and regions are rated according to the following scale: zero stars (recommended), one star (highly recommended), two stars (very highly recommended), and three stars (must-see).

In addition to the star-rating system, we also use **seven feature icons** that point you to the great deals, in-the-know advice, and unique experiences that separate travelers from tourists. Throughout the book, look for:

special finds—those places only insiders know about

fun facts—details that make travelers more informed and their trips more fun

kids—best bets for kids and advice for the whole family

special moments—those experiences that memories are made of

overrated—places or experiences not worth your time or money

insider tips—great ways to save time and money

great values—where to get the best deals

The following **abbreviations** are used for credit cards:

AE	American Express	DISC	Discover	V	Visa
DC	Diners Club	MC	MasterCard		

TRAVEL RESOURCES AT FROMMERS.COM

Frommer's travel resources don't end with this guide. Frommer's website, **www.frommers. com**, has travel information on more than 4,000 destinations. We update features regularly, giving you access to the most current trip-planning information and the best airfare, lodging, and car-rental bargains. You can also listen to podcasts, connect with other Frommers.com members through our active-reader forums, share your travel photos, read blogs from guidebook editors and fellow travelers, and much more.

THE BEST OF ENGLAND & WALES

by Nick Dalton & Deborah Stone

England and Wales are full of delights. From London's happening streets, to historic corners where the last big happenings were centuries ago, these are places and things that we love. The list is almost endless, but here we try to give you a sample of what excites us. There are things that are brand new and lots of things that aren't, yet they all send a shiver down our spines and make us want to return. From Hadrian's Wall and Stonehenge to London's looming Shard (Europe's tallest building) and the new Harry Potter studio tour, these are experiences that you will never forget.

CITIES & TOWNS Start with **London,** treasure of treasures, where there is now the biggest sight of all—the Shard, 310-m (1,017-ft.) tall. There will be a hotel and a viewing platform but for now it's simply a sight that fills the sky from so many viewpoints. You can see it best from classic sights (the Tower of London, St. Paul's Cathedral). London is also full of free museums and galleries, such as the **British Museum,** expansive parks, and even more expansive shopping. In 2013 it's the 150th anniversary of London's Tube network, and plans are underway for steam trains to return to the tunnels for special events. Then move on to places such as **Manchester,** the cradle of industry; **Liverpool,** with its docks and Beatles history; and small, more esoteric cities such as classical **Bath,** quaint **Chichester,** and tiny **St. Davids** in the west of Wales. Each will inspire you in a different way.

THE COUNTRYSIDE For a relatively small place, England and Wales have an awful lot of contrasts, from the mountains of the **Peak District** and **Snowdonia** to the flat fenlands of the **East Coast,** from the rolling hills of the **South Downs** (which in spring 2011 became England's newest National Park) to the fantastic scenery of the **Lake District.** Amid all that are 13 National Parks, taking in the undulating openness of the **North York Moors** and the ancient woodlands of the **New Forest.** And the backdrop changes quickly; a day's journey can take you across several different landscapes.

EATING & DRINKING   The food is something that you couldn't have dreamed about 20 years ago. There are now more than 130 restaurants (including more than a dozen pubs) with the esteemed **Michelin star.** What is important, though, is that Britons are respecting their food again. Whether it's a top **London** restaurant, somewhere modest in the **countryside,** or, increasingly, a place at the seaside, chefs fall over themselves to serve local, often organic, seasonal produce; fresh seafood or estate-reared game; just-picked vegetables; even salt dried from buckets of seawater (at the **Sportsman** at Whitstable in Kent). And beer has never been better, with small breweries producing top ales, while English vineyards (and even one just outside the Welsh capital, Cardiff) produce decent wines.

THE COAST   This might only be a small island, but the variety of coastal experiences is extraordinary. You'll find beautiful sandy beaches (**West Wittering** in Sussex, **Newgale** in Pembrokeshire, whole swathes of **North Norfolk**), strangely bleak stretches (**Dungeness** in Kent), looming white cliffs (much of England's south coast, from **Dover** to **Devon**), estuaries in **Essex,** and countless little bays around **Wales.**

THE most unforgettable
TRAVEL EXPERIENCES

- **Conquering Snowdon (Wales):** And, even better, finding it's so clear a day that you can see the sea both to the west and, in the haze, to the north. It's the highest mountain in England and Wales, and feels like it. You might have walked up, but you probably took the clattery steam cog railway. Walking down the grassy, rocky slopes will take several hours, but it's worth it. See p. 725.

- **Getting that view of Buckingham Palace (London):** Enter The Mall under Admiralty Arch and you can see the palace shimmering at the end of The Mall; the grandeur of the Queen's home increases step by step until it fills your vision, dotted with the bright red tunics of the ceremonial guardsmen. See p. 88.

- **Having a pint:** Maybe at Oxford's medieval Turf Tavern (where Bill Clinton drank as a student), a stone pub on the Yorkshire Moors, or a little place in the backstreets of London; a famous inn or an unassuming gem in any town or city. But there's nothing that helps you appreciate the scenery quite like a glass of good British beer.

- **Viewing the sea for the first time:** Coming over the crest of a hill, or around a bend, and finding that great, twinkling expanse, fringed by beaches, maybe cliffs: Everyone has their own perfect memory, but the excitement never fades. You'll pull over, stroll onto the sands … and you can do it all around the country.

- **Looking over London from the top of St. Paul's:** You really can climb up to the very top, via hidden steps in the glorious dome, for 360-degree views over the capital, giving the feeling that you're at the heart of where modern London began. If that's uplifting, the view down is deliciously dizzying. See p. 112.

- **Riding an old train:** Waiting for the whistle and the blast of steam is magical. There are dozens of "heritage lines" around the country, more than 20 in Wales alone. Old locomotives chug across idyllic countryside, along the coast, and up Welsh mountains. The National Railway Museum in York (p. 646) pays homage.

THE most unforgettable
CITY EXPERIENCES

o **Finding yourself in the city of the Beatles (Liverpool):** The childhood homes of Paul and John might be underwhelming (in a nice way), but there's still the Magical Mystery Tour (taking in Penny Lane), the Beatles Story (full of memorabilia), a reborn Cavern Club, and the Beatle Week in August. And the city is still celebrating the 50th anniversary, in 2012, of the Mop Tops' formation; See p. 583.

o **Having a bath in Bath (Somerset):** The stunning, steaming Roman Baths are there to visit, with lunch in the Pump Room restaurant; then you can sample the waters at the modern Thermae Bath Spa with its open-air pool and views across the Georgian, UNESCO World Heritage site rooftops. See p. 336.

o **Seeing the backstreets of Manchester:** Britain's inner-city regeneration is summed up by Castlefield, a once-blighted area of warehouses and canals that is now full of restaurants, bars, museums, and art galleries. The world's first railway station, from 1830, is the free Museum of Science & Industry. See p. 566.

o **Crisscrossing the Tyne (Newcastle):** Sixties art-rockers The Nice once performed the *Five Bridges Suite* to celebrate the city crossings, but there's now also the Millennium Footbridge, a curving, modernistic affair that looks like a blinking eye when it tilts to let boats past. On one side are the city streets, on the other the arts venues of Gateshead. See p. 664.

o **Wandering across London:** Sure, it's a big place. But there's no better way to see it than on foot. Start, maybe, in Kensington and meander across Hyde Park, down Piccadilly, into Soho and Covent Garden, up Fleet Street, past St. Paul's, and into the City, spotting tiny churches and other gems on the way. See p. 68.

o **Wondering whether you're actually in a city (South Wales):** Yes, you are; it's St. Davids, Britain's smallest city, in the far west. It's hardly a small town but the population of barely 2,000 is bolstered by the thousands of tourists who come for the nearby countryside and beaches, and the elegant cathedral. See p. 714.

THE most unforgettable
FOOD & DRINK EXPERIENCES

o **Tasting snail porridge at the Fat Duck (Berkshire):** Nothing shows England's emergence as a culinary innovator more than this multi-Michelin-starred restaurant, a window into the singularly creative mind of chef Heston Blumenthal. The earthy porridge (snails, oats, ham, almonds) is genius, and dishes such as salmon poached in licorice gel are a whimsical treat. See p. 203.

o **Dining with a celebrity chef:** Try Restaurant Gordon Ramsay in Chelsea (p. 141), or a whole menu of the outrageous chef's other places (including gastropubs) in London; at the seaside in Cornwall you'll find Rick Stein, Jamie Oliver, and Nathan Outlaw (p. 420), while other up-and-coming names can be found across the country.

o **Sampling oysters in Whitstable (Kent):** Slurp on a single bivalve as you walk the seafront, or have a dozen in a relaxed waterside restaurant. This old fishing town has transformed itself into the home of the oyster, and the quayside is awash with stalls, takeout options, and a fish market. See p. 251.

- **Browsing at Borough Market (London):** The sight and smell of fresh produce (and grilling meat) are heaven at this focal point for the real food movement. Tucked under the railway near London Bridge Station, there's a feel of the past, combined with the eco-friendly ethics that are so very now. See p. 153.
- **Giving yourself up to a restaurant with rooms:** They're all the rage in Wales, where you can spend a weekend in boutique luxury while eating splendid food. Tyddyn Llan (p. 746), off the beaten track in Denbighshire in the north, won a Michelin star in 2010, while Patricks with Rooms (p. 706) is a family delight facing the sea in Mumbles, near Swansea.
- **Going bulb crazy at the Garlic Farm (Isle of Wight):** The U.K.'s leading garlic grower is a pungent paradise, with a shop selling many varieties, including smoked garlic, as well as garlic to grow, and a restaurant serving dishes featuring the farm's own game, produce, and, of course, garlic. See p. 308.

THE most unforgettable
LOCAL EXPERIENCES

- **Heading into Pig country (Hampshire):** The Pig, in a delightful New Forest setting, is one of the new breed of socially conscious hotels. At least 80% of the menu is sourced from within 25 miles, there are daily contributions from the kitchen garden, and yet more items are foraged seasonally. See p. 306.
- **Following the Thames (Surrey):** No sooner do you get out of London than you're in a leafy, countryside idyll, little craft put-putting past and grass underfoot as you tread the Thames Path, passing local communities. There are riverside pubs, historic sites, and the disbelief that the city is just a 20-minute train ride away. See p. 286.
- **Taking the cliff train from Lynmouth (Devon):** When the old pulleys creak and the big tanks fill, this century-old, water-powered train climbs 183m (600 ft.) from the North Devon fishing village up to cliff-top Lynton. The views are extraordinary, but the experience is both breathtaking and kind of scary. See p. 368.
- **Sipping homemade wine in the countryside (Isle of Wight):** You'll often find locals at the Rosemary Vineyard on the edge of Ryde, sitting on the terrace outside the Vineleaf cafe, enjoying views across the fields and hills, with a glass of wine, or maybe even a blackberry liqueur. See p. 308.
- **Stumbling over a field of bluebells (Surrey):** The flowers herald spring all over the place, but there's nowhere finer than Surrey Hills (p. 282). Potter about the little roads that dive into the woods, see a footpath sign, and just walk. Or aim for Leith Hill (p. 283), with one of the best spots near the parking areaat the bottom.
- **Finding a bargain at London's best street market:** A jumble of open-air stalls and warrens of indoor arcades combine to make Portobello Road the quintessential West London market. Haggle hard and you'll likely get 15% off the asking price. Saturday is the best day, when even the crowds can't ruin the fun. See p. 154.

THE best FAMILY
EXPERIENCES

- **Playing Harry Potter (Hertfordshire):** The tour of the studios where the movies were made only opened in spring 2012 but it is already one of the country's biggest family attractions. Once you've walked through Hogwarts and other extravagant sets you'll see why. See p. 238.

○ **Sitting on Southwold beach (Suffolk):** This is old-school seaside in a nicely genteel way, with ice creams and good waves (and not far to walk to get to them). And for grown-ups, there's a pub (the Lord Nelson) to slip off to at the top of the steps, and beguiling individual shops not much farther. See p. 523.

○ **Reliving the Industrial Revolution (Shropshire):** It was born on the River Severn in the early 1700s, and is commemorated by a string of enlightening, interactive, child-friendly museums (particularly Blists Hill Victorian Town) set around Iron-bridge Gorge, with the world's first bridge made of iron. See p. 488.

○ **Riding the coasters (Surrey):** Chessington World of Adventures is a theme park that proves England can do it as well as the U.S. Scare yourself silly on the big roller coasters, but there are also rides for youngsters, as well as nice grassy areas, and a zoo full of animals (*real* ones such as lions and tigers). See p. 285.

○ **Being a right Charlie (Buckinghamshire):** There's nothing quite like painting your own diddly design onto a phizz-whizzing plate. The Roald Dahl Museum, in the village where the late author lived and wrote *Charlie and the Chocolate Factory* and other children's classics, is as irreverent as his books. See p. 231.

○ **Going back in time (Warwickshire):** The crashing and banging of ancient battles fought turns Warwick Castle from simply a castle into a whole medieval theme park. You'll find yourself on a quest to fit everything in amid the princesses, kings, towers, dungeons, gardens, and more. See p. 463.

THE best HISTORIC EXPERIENCES

○ **Lording it at Highclere (Hampshire):** This is one of England's finest stately homes, and the setting for transatlantic hit TV show *Downton Abbey*. See where Emmy and Golden Globe nominated actress Elizabeth McGovern rules the roost as Lady Cora and get the feeling for how life was (or should have been).

○ **Taking time out for Greenwich (London):** This elegant Thames-side enclave with its rich seafaring past was granted Royal Borough status in 2012 as part of the Queen's Diamond Jubilee celebrations. It's also a World Heritage Site for its National Maritime Museum Old Royal Naval College, and Royal Observatory. See p. 121.

○ **Walking in King Harold's footsteps (East Sussex):** There's something quite eerie but exciting about walking on the grassy spot where English history changed for-ever. The hillside site of the Battle of Hastings, and the Norman Conquest, is quietly impressive. See p. 260.

○ **Standing on Hadrian's Wall (Northumberland):** It leaves you speechless, the breathtaking scale of this Roman monument, which weaves off in either direction, across hill and dale, coast to coast. Walking all 73 miles is the ultimate achieve-ment, but pop into the remains of its forts if you can't. See p. 672.

○ **Marveling at Stonehenge (Wiltshire):** Okay, it might be hemmed in by roads, but this monolithic stone circle will still be here when the traffic is history. With stones weighing 45 tonnes (50 tons) and more than 2 millennia old, it really does give you a creepy feeling in this windswept spot. See p. 328.

○ **Exploring Welsh castles:** There's a whole hatful here, and they're all different. Don't miss Conwy (p. 740) with its eight towers; rugged Harlech (p. 727); Caernarfon (p. 732), overlooking the Isle of Anglesey; and Pembroke (p. 711), with its huge town walls. And the wild fantasy of Cardiff Castle (p. 682) is a must.

THE best OUTDOOR EXPERIENCES

○ **Circumnavigating Wales:** If you've got a few weeks to spare you can, since the Wales Coast Path opened in May 2012, walk the length of the coastline, some 850 miles. The path takes in beaches, cliffs, riverbanks, and town promenades as it makes its way; if you don't have time, there are plenty of short sections with free maps available. See p. 715.

○ **Taking the Ullswater Steamer (Cumbria):** There's nothing like being huddled up against the mist as the little Victorian boat sails the length of the Lake District's pristine showpiece. Stand on deck, taking photos as the scenery changes around every bend, and hop off halfway back for a hike. See p. 630.

○ **Getting lost on Dartmoor (Devon):** The landscape in the National Park constantly changes, rising to steep hills, then plunging into deep gorges. The roads are narrow and winding, and often unmarked. It's when you get lost that you'll end up alone at the top of a hill as a herd of wild ponies runs by, a storm hard on their heels. Heaven. See p. 377.

○ **Heading for the coast:** Britain's beaches are incredibly varied, whether the vast expanse of Watergate Bay in Cornwall (see p. 418), the dreamy spots on the Isles of Scilly (see p. 412), cliff-fringed Mwnt in west Wales (see p. 717), or the fun-palace feel of Blackpool (see p. 595).

○ **Hiking the South Downs Way (Hampshire/West Sussex):** Fill your lungs as you follow the chalk downland that sweeps along the south coast some 99 miles. It crosses windswept cliffs, climbs open hills, and ducks into valleys and then up again. It's a week's experience for serious hikers, although you can dip in for a Sunday afternoon stroll. See p. 277.

○ **Gardening at Wisley (Surrey):** Gardens bloom across the country but you have to start somewhere, and this home of the Royal Horticultural Society (less frenetic than London's Kew Gardens) is the biggest and the best. There are flowers, woods, hills, a cathedral-like glasshouse, show gardens, plant trials, and good food. See p. 280.

THE best FREE EXPERIENCES

○ **All the museums:** The major collections in England and Wales are free to enter. Biggest and best is London's British Museum (see p. 85), which has artifacts from around the world, including Greece's Elgin Marbles and a wealth of Egyptian treasures, but there are many others, from the grandeur of the National Museum of Wales in Cardiff (see p. 682) to the little Fishermen's Museum in Hastings (see p. 263).

○ **Entering another world in Richmond Park (Surrey):** Go through big gates in high walls and you find deer grazing in flank-high ferns and swans lording it over a host of other waterbirds on the Pen Ponds. This great Royal Park's hills, woods, and grassland look as they might have in Henry VIII's time. Go in spring to see Isabella Plantation in bloom with azaleas and rhododendrons. See p. 286.

- **Waking at the foot of Scafell Pike (Cumbria):** It's a summer's morn and you leave your tent to conquer England's highest peak. The stone steps are seemingly endless, but you forget the thigh-burn as you take in the panoramic views of Wastwater behind you, then push onto the peak-top plateau for a satisfying 360-degree view of mountains and tarns below. See p. 608.

- **Doing the National Gallery (London):** One of the world's greatest collections of Western art, packed with artists from da Vinci to Rembrandt to Picasso. It's also incredibly well thought out, and so straightforward to navigate the areas in chronological order. As if that's not enough, next door is the National Portrait Gallery, featuring works by everyone from Warhol to Rossetti to George Bernard Shaw. See p. 90.

- **Cycling the Mawddach Trail (North Wales):** The scenery is breathtaking as you leave the seaside town of Barmouth, in the shadow of Snowdon; this path on an old rail line crosses the Mawddach Estuary then follows the waters along the beautiful, deep valley to Dolgellau, almost 10 miles. See p. 727.

THE best CONTEMPORARY EXPERIENCES

- **Ogling the Olympic sites (London):** With the 2012 Games done and dusted, the Olympic Park has become a beautifully planted public space dotted with iconic venues (the Olympic Stadium, the Velodrome, the Aquatics Centre). It's a whole new place to explore and marvel at. See Chapter 4.

- **Seeing the light with Turner (Kent):** Turner Contemporary, which opened in 2011, is a stunning white building on the seafront of fast-rejuvenating Margate, on the spot where J. M. W. Turner used to paint his mesmeric seascapes (see p. 250). In March 2012 another seafront gallery opened, just around the coast at Hastings, East Sussex. The Jerwood displays a private collection of modern art and classics. See p. 263.

- **Getting fresh air on Cardiff Bay (South Wales):** It's hard to believe this was once the grubby docks. The quay is a riot of restaurants and bars under the eye of the Wales Millennium Centre, a copper-roofed arts complex, while the extraordinary Barrage protects the now calm Bay. The Pont y Werin (People's Bridge) over the River Ely completes a 6.5-mile circular foot and cycle path. See p. 684.

- **Feeling small in Tate Modern (London):** Enter this former power station on the Thames and your jaw drops at the size of the cathedral-like piston hall, which usually houses outrageous art installations, from twisting metal slides to monstrous spiders. Delve deeper and you find a wealth of Dalis, Warhols, Picassos, and a restaurant with one of London's best views. See p. 110.

- **Finding a hidden garden (Cornwall):** The Eden Project is not quite what you'd expect in a lush Cornish valley. The huddle of huge geodesic domes looks like a moonbase—and well it could be: It's a garden of the future, an Amazon rain forest under glass. See p. 404.

- **Heading for space (Leicestershire):** Calling Houston: We have a rival. A futuristic tower signals the National Space Centre, which has space rockets, moon rock, a landing simulator, interactive displays, and a galaxy of jaw-dropping facts. All that in a place where they really do study comets—Leicester. See p. 558.

THE best ARTS EXPERIENCES

o **Being enchanted by Cornwall's artistic side:** St. Ives (p. 415) is a little fishing village with exquisite light that has attracted artists for more than a century, and which is home to the Tate St. Ives gallery and the Barbara Hepworth Museum & Sculpture Garden. Newlyn, near Penzance, was also a painters' haven; see important works at Penzance's Penlee House museum. See p. 408.

o **Going to a music festival:** They're big business, attract all ages, and feature everyone from the latest acts to venerable megastars playing Glastonbury (see p. 359) and the Isle of Wight (see p. 308) as well as lesser-known gems such as Guilfest in Surrey (see p. 281).

o **Seeing Shakespeare in his hometown (Warwickshire):** Well, seeing one of his plays, anyway. The Royal Shakespeare Theatre in Stratford-upon-Avon is the place for powerful, up-to-the-minute interpretations, and you'll have the chance to visit all the Shakespeare sights, including his birthplace. See p. 452.

o **Learning to love panto:** England's traditional Christmas fare, pantomime is great slapstick fun, often with top TV names and, increasingly, U.S. stars: In the past several seasons, Wimbledon Theatre has had Henry (The Fonz) Winkler, David Hasselhoff, and even Pamela Anderson, all dressed up and falling over.

o **Reveling on the South Bank (London):** England's arts quarter takes in both the 1950s' beauty of the Royal Festival Hall (RFH) and the brutal modernism of the National Theatre. Street theatre rubs shoulders with classic productions, and there's usually something free in the grand foyer of the RFH. See chapter 4.

o **Discovering Another Place (Lancashire):** A hundred figures cast in iron from sculptor Antony Gormley's own body rise from the sand for 2 miles along the coast at Crosby between Formby and Liverpool, and gaze eerily out to sea. See p. 589.

ENGLAND & WALES IN DEPTH

by Nick Dalton & Deborah Stone

The past few years have seen England and Wales reborn. The countries have become at ease with their past as never before, while moving forward to be cutting-edge destinations. England's now a world culinary leader, which is something no one would have believed a generation ago. Everyone's fiercely proud of their history and artistic achievements, as visitors will see in new museums, galleries, and attractions. The castles, palaces, and stately homes continue to present world-beating experiences as tradition and innovation combine to cultivate national life. And the countryside, ever changing and often stunning, increasingly offers challenging activities for those who love the outdoors. You'll also find hotels, restaurants, and tourist facilities are better equipped to offer the comfort, ambience, and all-round excellence that the visitor deserves.

Exploring England and Wales is like climbing a mountain—you always want to carry on to see what's over the next peak or around the next corner. The character of every region is as diverse as its countryside. The north of England has more dramatic scenery than the gently rolling south, and west Wales is green and hilly while East Anglia is flat with big skies. Yet every region is connected with the whole, and once you've explored one you can't help wanting to experience another. It's addictive, and there's no shame in carrying around a sightseeing wishlist—as long as you take your time ticking things off. England and Wales may not be big countries but they're crammed full of incredible sights. And not just historic sights, either. Sport, music, theatre, fashion, and even food here are among the best in the world. You might be visiting a region for the first time but be warned: Once you've seen one part of England and Wales you'll want to see more.

ENGLAND & WALES TODAY

You can see the pinnacle of England's bright new future shining across London. The Shard is Western Europe's tallest building, a shimmering, pointed, glassy tower nearing completion near London Bridge. It soars 310m (1,017 ft.) above the city and provides a fitting backdrop for both the medieval Tower of London and the Victorian masterpiece of Tower Bridge. It is England pushing forward, regaining her crown as one of the world's major powers and destinations, while looking over her sovereign past.

The Shard, by architect **Renzo Piano,** is the high point, literally, of the postmodern architecture that has swept Britain. Other examples in London include the **Lloyd's building** by **Richard Rogers,** 30 St. Mary Axe, dubbed the **"Gherkin"** by Sir Norman Foster, and **Canary Wharf Tower (One Canada Square),** by **César Pelli.**

Post-modernist architecture is not the only way that England and Wales have changed dramatically in recent years. Uninspiring hotels used to be matched by the food, but the invention and imagination—always evident in art, music, and design—have now spread into where visitors stay and what they eat. The U.K.'s first luxurious Shangri-La hotel will be opening on floors 34 to 52 in The Shard, and it will look down over Borough Market, London's trendiest spot dealing in posh, organic, locally sourced food. The hotel, due to open in 2013, will also have views over the City, the country's financial heart, which is still beating strongly despite having caused more than a few heartaches for its role in the continuing global financial nightmare.

The economic downturn has seriously affected employment, lifestyle, and attitudes. The government, a coalition between the right-wing Conservatives and the marginally less-so Liberal Democrats, is cutting services, from health to road-mending, while increasing taxes. In early 2012 unemployment reached its highest level for 17 years, the news coming as anti-capitalist protesters who had camped outside St Paul's Cathedral throughout the winter were ordered to be evicted.

The vibrant cultural life in Britain is being pressurized as, for example, the arts, humanities, and education struggle for funding. The

The Shard

English and Welsh are practical people—empiricists; however, as the cuts bite, their frustration at how this affects their daily life, infrastructure, and creative freedom is beginning to manifest itself. Meanwhile, the previous political governing party is happy to lie low, given that Prime Minister David Cameron is never going to be popular and could lead his party out of power as soon as the next election (likely to be in May 2015).

The riots in England of August 2011 have been the cause of much national soul-searching but seem unlikely to change the way the country is run. News International's phone-hacking scandal—forcing the closure of the *News of the World* after 168 years—could prove more far reaching, and alter the political and media landscape.

Abnormal weather in parts of the world on which Britain depends for staples, such as flour and grain, has pushed shop prices higher. And the cost of gas (petrol), already at record levels because of huge levels of taxation (more than $5 for a U.S. gallon), is soaring due to unrest in the Middle East.

But life goes on, and 2012 was a momentous year for the country. Britain put on the greatest sporting event the nation has ever seen, the Olympic Games, which focused the eyes of the world here. The Games came at a time when the nation was also celebrating the Queen's Diamond Jubilee (60 years as monarch). It was also a year when Britain reveled in its literary past, with movies and TV adaptations celebrating the 200th anniversary of the birth of Charles Dickens.

There also continues to be a lot to shout about, as a dynamic cultural milieu of independent thinking, eccentricity, and verve mean that talent is often appreciated.

OUR LOVE OF A royal WEDDING

The English, or let's say a great many of the English, adore a royal wedding. Prince Charles and Lady Diana Spencer were married at St. Paul's Cathedral in London on July 29, 1981, a ceremony watched by an estimated global television audience of 750 million. The fairytale wedding came 5 months after Charles, 32, had presented Diana with a memorable sapphire and diamond engagement ring. The wedding day was declared a national holiday and 600,000 people lined the wedding procession route to see 20-year-old Diana arrive for the ceremony in the royal family's glass coach with her father, Earl Spencer. Diana's wedding dress was a fashion hit, made from ivory taffeta and antique lace with a spectacular 7.62-m (25-ft.) train. After the drive to Buckingham Palace in an open-topped State Landau the couple appeared on the palace balcony to the cheers of thousands.

Prince William was born less than a year later, on June 21, 1982, and Prince Harry came along on September 15, 1984. However, 9 years later Charles and Diana had separated, and they divorced in August 1996.

Tragically, Diana died after a car crash in Paris on August 31, 1997. Her death prompted an unprecedented public outpouring of grief, which many say has changed the British national psyche forever. The Queen and Prince Charles came under unaccustomed public criticism, accused of not caring about Diana's death.

Around 1 million people were on the streets to see the funeral cortege on its way to Westminster Abbey on September 6, and many watched it continue to the Spencer family's estate at Althrop in Northamptonshire, where Diana was buried. An award-winning exhibition at the stately home displays Diana's wedding dress and many childhood mementos.

Now there is a new generation: Prince William gave Diana's sapphire and diamond engagement ring to his fiancée, Kate Middleton (now known as Catherine) when they became engaged in 2010. They were married at Westminster Abbey on April 29, 2011, in a ceremony viewed by an estimated 2 billion people around the world. The public, it seems, never tires of royal weddings.

From the Academy-award winning *The King's Speech* and Adele's record breaking second album *21* to Carol Ann Duffy becoming the first woman Poet Laureate and Hilary Mantel's critically acclaimed historic novel *Wolf Hall,* these are lands that revel in diversity. And the record-breaking Harry Potter novels which became record-breaking movies have now become what will surely be a record-breaking visitor attraction, The Making of Harry Potter at the Warner Brothers studios, still packed with giant sets, where the films were made, just outside London.

Britain began believing it was great again in the 1990s. It was the decade of Cool Britannia. A wave of music—Britpop—from bands such as Blur, Oasis, and Pulp, was followed by the optimism prompted by the 1997 landslide General Election victory by Tony Blair's New Labour Party. After nearly 20 years of Conservative governments it felt like a new era of opportunity. In London, the Millennium Dome opened in 1999 and thousands visited the Millennium Experience, a modern-day Festival of Britain. It is now a concert venue called the O2—although to most people it is still the Dome. The **Tate Modern** (p. 110) art museum opened in May 2000 in a former power station, and the **London Eye** (p. 108) was also built to celebrate the new millennium.

Lots was also happening elsewhere. Manchester was transformed after the 1996 IRA bombing; **Birmingham's Bull Ring shopping center** (p. 469) was rebuilt in sensational style in 2003, and the city's regeneration continues. Newcastle, Liverpool, Cardiff, and most recently Swansea have all benefited from major overhauls.

But care has been taken with this 21st-century makeover, and England and Wales continue to offer an unbeatable mix of beautiful countryside, a culture rich in history, and the arts, plus modern cities that cater to discerning visitors.

THE MAKING OF ENGLAND & WALES

Prehistory & the Romans (3600 B.C.–ca. A.D. 400)

England and Wales have several prehistoric sites, but the most famous is **Stonehenge** near Salisbury (p. 328), which experts believe was a temple, possibly started in 3600 B.C. and added to over subsequent centuries. Hadrian's Wall is the most dramatic piece of architecture to survive from the Roman period, although there are also **Roman baths** at Bath (p. 340) and the remains of Roman walls, villas, temples, and forts elsewhere.

England, Wales, and the rest of the British Isles became detached from continental Europe at the end of the Ice Age when sea levels rose and the English Channel and Irish Sea were formed. The islands have been inhabited for 500,000 years. It was the prehistoric inhabitants who built Stonehenge and the Britons were joined by the Celtic tribes who arrived in about 800 B.C. from mainland Europe. These tribes brought variants of the Welsh, Cornish, and Celtic languages still spoken by a minority in the U.K. today.

There were constant clashes between the tribes over territory, which is why they failed to unite to prevent the first Roman invasion by Julius Caesar, the Roman governor of Gaul (France and Belgium), in 55 B.C.

Bad weather damaged Caesar's ships, and trouble in France meant he returned to the mainland despite landing at Deal, in Kent. But he returned the next year and defeated the Britons, imposing trade treaties and tax-like tributes. He didn't stay long,

England's Historical Highlights

| 0 | | 50 mi |
| 0 | | 50 km |

SCOTLAND

Northumberland
National Park

NORTHUMBERLAND

Hadrian's Wall
TYNE
& WEAR

Belfast

NORTHERN
IRELAND

CUMBRIA

COUNTY DURHAM

Lake District
National Park

North York Moors
National Park

NORTH
SEA

Yorkshire Dales
National Park

NORTH
YORKSHIRE

Isle of Man

IRISH
SEA

LANCASHIRE

WEST
YORKSHIRE

EAST RIDING
OF YORKSHIRE

MERSEYSIDE

GREATER
MANCHESTER

SOUTH
YORKS.

ISLE OF
ANGLESEY

CONWY

FLINTS.

CHESHIRE

Peak District
National Park

LINCOLNSHIRE

The Wash

Snowdon

GWYNEDD

DENB.

WREX

DERBYS.

NOTTS.

Snowdonia
National Park

SHROPSHIRE

ENGLAND

Cardigan
Bay

POWYS

STAFFS.

LEICS.

RUTLAND

NORFOLK

The Broads
National Park

WALES

WEST
MIDLANDS

NORTHANTS.

CAMBS.

East
Anglia

CEREDIGION

HEREFORD-
SHIRE

WORCS.

WARKS.

SUFFOLK

PEMBROKESHIRE

Brecon Beacons
National Park

BEDS

Pembrokeshire Coast
National Park

CARMARTHEN-
SHIRE

GLOUCS.

BUCKS.

HERTS.

ESSEX

NEATH
PT. TALBOT

MER.
TYDFIL

MONM.

BL. GWENT

TORFAEN

CAERPHILLY

OXON.

SWANSEA

RH.
CY. TAF.

NEWPORT

BRISTOL

BERKSHIRE

LONDON

GREATER
LONDON

BRIDGEND

VALE OF
GLAM.

Cardiff

WILTSHIRE

SURREY

KENT

Bristol Channel

Exmoor
National Park

SOMERSET

HAMPSHIRE

WEST
SUSSEX

EAST
SUSSEX

Strait of Dover

DEVON

DORSET

New Forest
National Park

South Downs
National Park

Dartmoor
National Park

ISLE OF
WIGHT

CORNWALL

English Channel

FRANCE

Channel Is.

① Stonehenge

⑥ Pembroke Castle

② Hastings

⑦ Plymouth

③ Runnymede

⑧ Ironbridge

④ Tower of London

⑨ The Big Pit

⑤ Windsor Castle

⑩ Home of the Beatles

and the tribal Britons continued fighting among themselves without any Roman Legions to keep order.

That all changed in A.D. 43–44, when Emperor Claudius invaded, pushing farther than the south coast and capturing the Southeast's capital, present-day Colchester. You can still see parts of the Roman walls in **Colchester** (p. 517) and the castle that was built with bricks taken from the Roman temple that lies beneath it. Although Colchester remained the capital for a while, by A.D. 47 the Romans had founded Londinium as a garrison with a trading settlement. Remains of Roman London are still being discovered as new developments are built, and you can see part of London's original Roman wall near the **Tower of London** (p. 112).

There was little resistance to the Roman fighting machine, although there was one well-known uprising, led by Queen Boudicca of the Iceni tribe who ruled parts of East Anglia. The Romans had tried to force their will on Boudicca by publicly whipping her, and she subsequently led a rebellion that razed Colchester. Then she marched on London (there's a statue of Boudicca in Parliament Square) and rampaged through St. Albans, then known as Verulamium—70,000 people were killed.

The Romans moved north and west, conquering tribes as they went, but they were stopped by the ferocious Picts in Scotland, and did not get far into Wales because of the mountainous countryside, although a Roman Legion was stationed at **Caerleon,** where the remains of an impressive amphitheatre and baths can still be seen (p. 685). In A.D. 122, **Hadrian's Wall** was built across northern England from Wallsend on the east coast to Bowness-on-Solway, on the west coast (p. 672); meantime, the Welsh tribes—well, they were just left to their fighting. Then, after 350 years of rule, the Romans went home, abandoning the Romano-Britons.

By 410, the Germanic Saxons, Jutes, and Angles had carved out settlements in southern and eastern England, and the Saxons went on to dominate all but the far north and Wales, where the Romano-Britons were forced to flee. The Saxons had neatly divided England into Northumbria in the north, East Anglia in the east, Wessex in the south, and Mercia in the west and Midlands by the 600s. Subsequently, King Offa of Mercia had the 177-mile **Offa's Dyke** earthworks built (p. 695) from **Chepstow** in South Wales to **Prestatyn** in North Wales, to keep the Celtic Welsh tribes out of England in 787.

The Saxon kings reigned supreme until the Vikings, forced from their settlements in Scandinavia, started taking an interest in England. They were driven from southern England by King Alfred the Great of Wessex, whose headquarters were at **Winchester** (p. 290), but the Vikings remained in the north and east, evidenced by astonishing burial mounds at **Sutton Hoo** in Suffolk (p. 525). The Vikings were even stronger in the Northeast, as the **Jorvik Viking Centre** in York (p. 646) illustrates. By 924, the rest of England was united behind King Athelstan of Wessex, but this

Anglo-Saxon period of peace was ruptured by the Viking King Sweyn and his son Cnut, who were given gold—Danegeld in fact—to leave the Anglo-Saxons alone.

By 1013 Sweyn had thrown out King Ethelred (the Unready), and even when Ethelred returned from Normandy King Sweyn remained in charge. Several Viking (or Danish) kings followed, hence the influx of Viking words into what became the English language. Tuesday, Wednesday, Thursday, and Friday are all named after Viking gods, and the Viking word for village, "by," led to names such as **Grimsby** and **Whitby** (p. 652).

The Saxons maintained control of some southern regions, which is why the Saxon king Edward the Confessor assumed the throne in 1042. Childless, he promised the crown to William, Duke of Normandy. Later his adviser, Harold Godwinson, swore to support William's claim to the throne. When Edward died in 1066 and Harold succeeded him, he surely knew trouble lay ahead. William invaded **Pevensey,** in Sussex, while Harold was fighting a Viking invasion in the northeast. He had to march south to meet the Normans at **Battle,** near **Hastings,** in Sussex. Harold lost and died—the end of an era.

Norman rule was to change everything in England and Wales, but already the tribal rivalries that still trouble Great Britain—between the Celts in Wales, Scotland, and Ireland, and the Anglo-Saxons in England—were well established.

The Middle Ages (1066–1599)

Among the most impressive legacies of these unstable ages are the medieval castles and cathedrals, which have stood the test of time. See William the Conqueror's Tower of London with its sublime White Tower (p. 112).

Other examples are the impregnable Conwy and Caernarfon castles in Wales. Visit remarkable Ely Cathedral near Cambridge and the incomparable Canterbury Cathedral.

White Tower, London

 Essential Histories

Historian Simon Schama's BBC series *A History of Britain* (available on DVD) begins around 3100 B.C., finishing in 1965. There are three BBC books from the series, all called *A History of Britain,* subtitled *At the Edge of the World?: 3000 B.C.–A.D. 1603; The British Wars: 1603–1776;* and *The Fate of Empire: 1776–2000.* Journalist and television broadcaster Andrew Marr has produced a DVD called *A History of Modern Britain* as well as the book *The Making of Modern Britain,* while broadcaster David Dimbleby has written a book to accompany his BBC documentary series *Seven Ages of Britain.* Also excellent is Terry Deary's series of *Horrible Histories* children's books, with all the facts plus some delightful gore.

The Normans descended from another branch of the Viking tribes who had left the cold, wet, infertile islands of Scandinavia to seek a better life. Although they had changed their name, they hadn't changed their ways. They quickly colonized England and, unlike the Romans, tamed the more fertile (and therefore profitable) parts of South Wales.

William's success came partly from his building impregnable castles wherever they were needed. In 1078, for example, he built the White Tower at the Tower of London and used it as a palace and fortress, and he built the original castle at Windsor (p. 199).

William was crowned King William I at **Westminster Abbey** (p. 103) in 1067, and his supporters went on to build simple motte and bailey castles on the land William gave them. The mottes—mounds of earth—still survive in many places; some were incorporated into the stone castles that replaced the original wooden baileys, or keeps.

William is also remembered for The Domesday (or Doomsday) Book of 1086, a survey of all his newly conquered land and possessions. The feudal system of the time meant that the King owned all the land but divided it between the Church and his supporters. The Domesday survey was an efficient way to assess the financial and military resources available to him, as well as enabling him to levy taxes and ensure an oath of allegiance from all landlords and tenants. It was known as The Domesday Book because—like Judgment Day—there was no escape from it. The original is still kept in the National Archives, and it's been used to settle property arguments and trace family trees for centuries.

The Normans are also renowned for their religious architecture, with **Ely Cathedral** in Cambridgeshire (p. 507) among the most glorious examples of their work, although the abbey and original church was founded by a Saxon princess.

The French Gothic style of architecture invaded in the late 12th century, trading rounded arches for pointy ones—an engineering discovery that freed churches from the heavy Norman walls and allowed ceilings to soar and windows to proliferate. The style can be divided into three overlapping periods: Early English (1150–1300), Decorated (1250–1370), and Perpendicular (1350–1550). The best example of Early English is **Salisbury Cathedral** (p. 327). The first to use pointy arches was **Wells Cathedral** (p. 357).

William died in 1087, succeeded by his son William II who died in a hunting accident in 1100. The next significant king was Henry II, the first of the Plantagenet family, who came to the throne in 1154. This French nobleman had made strategic marriages and, when he married Eleanor of Aquitaine, he owned more of France than the French king. Eleanor was a formidable character, as portrayed in the 1968 film *The Lion in Winter*. Together they had eight children, among them Richard the Lionheart and his younger brother King John.

Salisbury Cathedral

What They Say

"When a man is tired of London, he is tired of life; for there is in London all that life can afford."
—Samuel Johnson

"There'll always be an England ... even if it's in Hollywood."
—Bob Hope

Richard I, who came to the throne in 1189, is regarded as a romantic hero in the stories of Robin Hood and his merry men, who were said to have lived in **Sherwood Forest** near Nottingham. Hollywood films have portrayed Richard as much loved by his subjects—ironic because he didn't like cold, wet England and preferred to fight for Christianity in the Crusades. When he died in 1199, John succeeded him, but Bad King John was so unpopular that the Norman barons, whose families had been given their land by William I after the conquest, forced him to sign the Magna Carta in 1215 to limit his power. The Magna Carta gave all freemen (barons) rights and liberties, but, more importantly, meant English monarchs were no longer above the law. This became the basis of the English Constitution, and later the American Bill of Rights.

The Plantagenets ruled for the next 200 years, with King John's son Henry III succeeding him in 1216, aged 9, and setting up the first English Parliament in 1258. He rebuilt **Westminster Abbey** and built the first Palace of Westminster where Parliament still sits today (p. 100). This was the period when the nobility started to consider themselves English rather than French, although they still spoke French. (Only the Saxon peasants spoke English.) Henry III died in 1272, and his son Edward I was a much stronger monarch. He marched into Wales, defeated Llewelyn ap Gruffydd, the Prince of Wales, and incorporated Wales into England in 1284.

He built the superb Welsh medieval castles of **Beaumaris,** on Anglesey (p. 736); **Conwy,** which still has its town walls (p. 740); **Caernarfon** (p. 732), which is where Prince Charles was invested as the present Prince of Wales in 1969; and **Harlech** (p. 727). All were built as a response to the second Welsh rebellion of 1282 and were significantly more imposing than the castles at **Aberystwyth** (p. 717), Flint, and Rhuddlan, which followed the first rebellion a decade before.

In 1307 Edward II came to the throne, but, an ineffectual king, he was deposed by his wife Eleanor of Castille in 1327. She put their 14-year-old son, Edward, on the throne so she could in effect rule the country. When he turned 18, though, Edward III took control and tried to claim the French throne. When he was rebuffed, he started what turned out to be the Hundred Years' War in 1337. This kept him, his son the Black Prince, and successive monarchs occupied abroad until 1453.

At home, the ordinary people were having a hard time. The Black Death, or plague, which had ravaged Europe reached England in 1348. It killed one-third of the European population and half of the people of England and Wales, and returned in 1361, 1374, and regularly thereafter until about 1670. Richard II, aged 10, succeeded his grandfather, Edward III, and became one of the most unpopular kings. His poll tax of 1381 sparked the Peasants' Revolt. Richard met leaders Wat Tyler and Jack Straw in London and agreed to the abolition of serfdom, but then joined in the suppression of the revolts.

One of Richard's courtiers was Geoffrey Chaucer, who wrote *The Canterbury Tales*—stories told by a group of pilgrims as they journeyed from London to Canterbury where Thomas Becket, Henry II's Archbishop, had been murdered by Henry's knights. The *Tales* were written in English, unusual at the time because Latin and French dominated the written word. At about the same time John Wycliffe translated the Bible into English. Both were signs of social unrest, and in 1399 Richard II was deposed by his cousin Henry of Bolingbroke. Richard died in captivity at Pontefract Castle, Yorkshire, in 1400 while Bolingbroke was crowned Henry IV and made a coronation speech in English.

Henry IV was the first of a new dynasty called the House of Lancaster and spent much of his reign fighting off rebellious nobles, such as Owain Glyndwr, the last native Prince of Wales. The Welsh nobles were still sympathetic to Richard II, and Glyndwr led a rebellion against Henry IV helped by his cousins the Tudors. Henry IV, having failed to defeat the rebellion, decreed that the Welsh could not hold public office or marry anybody English. Not surprisingly, this didn't garner him any support in Wales, which by 1404 was mostly controlled by Glyndwr, who held a Parliament at Machynlleth and made alliances with France and Scotland.

England gradually regained control of Wales. Henry V, crowned in 1417, restored land and titles to the nobility who had fought his father, ensuring relative domestic peace. He was successful in the continuing Hundred Years' War, notably at the Battle of Agincourt, and ended up owning much of France. He died in 1422, when his heir was 9 months old. Although his son succeeded him, he wasn't crowned Henry VI until 1429. Two years later, he also became the King of France. Henry VI's poor choice of advisers left him vulnerable to power struggles. He lost all of France (except Calais), much of it to Joan of Arc, and in 1453 he had a breakdown.

By 1455 there was civil war—the War of the Roses—between Henry VI's House of Lancaster and the House of York. It was messy: In 1461 the dead Duke of York's son crowned himself Edward IV, causing Henry VI to flee—but he returned, was captured, and then restored to the throne in 1471. Then it was Edward's turn to flee, but he returned to destroy the Lancastrian army at Tewkesbury and Henry was murdered shortly afterward.

Edward IV appointed his brother Richard to be Protector when he was succeeded by his 12-year-old son, Edward V, in 1483. It was a bad decision. Richard put the boy king and his younger brother (also Richard) in the Tower of London and crowned himself Richard III. The Princes in the Tower, as they became known, were murdered. But things didn't work out well for Richard III, either. In 1485 Henry Tudor, born in **Pembroke Castle** (p. 711) and part of the House of Lancaster, killed Richard in the Battle of Bosworth Field, between Coventry and Leicester, and claimed the throne to become Henry VII, the first of the Tudor dynasty.

The Tudors (1485–1603)

There's now a Bosworth **Battlefield Heritage Centre** (p. 556) at the spot where Henry VII won the crown. But it's fair to say Henry Tudor is responsible for far more of England's and Wales's heritage than that. His reign is considered to be the close of the Middle Ages, and he ended rivalry between the Houses of Lancaster and York by marrying Elizabeth of York, the eldest child of King Edward IV.

He was a clever king: Avoiding costly wars, forging trade alliances to create more wealth, setting up councils in Wales and the north to bring them into the administrative fold, and reforming the judicial system by introducing the Court of Star

Chamber. Flamboyant Henry VIII inherited a fortune from his father in 1509, and a wife from his elder brother Arthur. Arthur had married the King of Spain's eldest daughter, Catherine of Aragon, at London's old St. Paul's Cathedral in 1501, but the sickly heir to the throne died 5 months later. Catherine came with a huge dowry so Henry VII petitioned the Pope to have the marriage annulled so that his new heir, Henry, could marry her and keep the money.

The marriage went forth and Catherine gave birth to several children, but only daughter Mary survived—and Henry wanted a son. By now he also wanted Anne Boleyn, born at **Blickling Hall** in Norfolk (p. 527) and a member of his wife's court. The 2008 film *The Other Boleyn Girl* portrays Henry's affair with Anne's sister Mary, but Anne was more ambitious and demanded to be queen.

Henry petitioned the Pope in 1530 for an annulment to his marriage with Catherine, but the Pope didn't want to upset the Spanish king. A few years later, Anne gave in to Henry's lust, and when she became pregnant, he secretly married her in 1533. When the Pope declared the marriage invalid, Henry announced himself Head of the Church of England, confirmed by an Act of Parliament in 1534. The English Reformation had begun.

Henry still considered himself a Catholic and persecuted Protestants, but he was also suspicious of those loyal to the Pope, particularly monks and nuns. So in 1535 he executed several as a warning to others, then sent out officials to investigate the monasteries. In 1538 he was excommunicated from the Catholic Church and eventually closed all monasteries and nunneries and sold off their land.

By this time Henry had already executed Anne Boleyn for alleged adultery and, within days, married Anne's lady-in-waiting Jane Seymour. Anne had given birth to a girl—Elizabeth—but Jane finally gave Henry a male heir, Prince Edward, then died shortly afterward.

Henry was advised to marry a Protestant princess to create a new alliance against the Catholic monarchs, so artist Hans Holbein was sent to Saxony to paint a portrait of Anne of Cleves. Henry married her in January 1540 on the strength of the painting but later found he didn't like her much. The marriage was annulled in July 1540, and he subsequently married Catherine Howard, cousin of Anne Boleyn. That didn't end well either: 2 years later she was executed for having lovers *before* their marriage (and the three alleged lovers were executed with her).

The sixth and final wife of Henry VIII was Katherine Parr, a well-educated widow who had hoped to marry Jane Seymour's brother Thomas. However, she was obliged to marry Henry, at **Hampton Court Palace** (p. 122) in 1543. She nursed Henry through various ailments, though he died in 1547 and was buried in St. George's Chapel at **Windsor Castle** (p. 199) next to Jane Seymour.

If Henry's life was dramatic, what happened next was extraordinary. His sickly son succeeded him as Edward VI, aged 10. During Edward's 5-year reign, the Church of England finally became Protestant and adopted an English Book of Common Prayer. Although Edward was devout, he obviously couldn't have made those decisions himself, and the atmosphere of religious fervor intensified when Edward was succeeded by his Catholic elder sister in 1553.

Before Mary I gained the crown, though, there was an attempt to put Lady Jane Grey on the throne. Jane was Henry VIII's niece, and married to the Duke of Northumberland's son. The Duke was fiercely Protestant and a powerful adviser to Edward VI. When it was obvious Edward was dying, Northumberland made the king denounce his half-sisters as illegitimate and declare Jane his heir. Jane was queen for 9 days, until Mary arrived in London to take the throne.

Mary was supported over Lady Jane Grey because she promised not to challenge the religious status quo, and she did not have Jane executed—at least not initially. That came when Mary started reintroducing Catholicism, which didn't please many of the noble families now living on monastery land. After another attempt to put Jane on the throne, Mary had her beheaded in 1554.

Mary also reintroduced Catholic bishops, revived heresy laws, and pronounced Protestantism a treasonable offense punishable by death. And that was just the start. She had 300 Protestants burned at the stake during her 4-year reign. That's 75 a year, compared with the 81 people in 38 years that her father had burned! It's no wonder she was called Bloody Mary.

Her marriage to Catholic Philip II of Spain had already made her unpopular, and she lost England's last French possession—Calais—when Spain dragged England into a war with France. Not surprisingly, few mourned her death in 1558.

Her sister Elizabeth was under house arrest at **Hatfield House** in Hertfordshire (p. 238) when the news of Mary's death arrived. She was crowned Queen in 1559 at Westminster Abbey. The Virgin Queen had many suitors but, sensibly, managed to play one against another so she could retain her own power.

Elizabeth reversed Mary's Catholic laws and worked with Parliament to create an Anglican form of Protestantism that tolerated Catholicism, but she was often the target of Catholic plots, many involving her cousin Mary Queen of Scots. Mary was forced to abdicate by Scotland's nobility and her 1-year-old son, James VI, was put on the Scottish throne. She escaped to England, only to be imprisoned by Elizabeth for nearly 20 years and eventually executed, in 1587.

The most famous Catholic plot against Elizabeth was the King of Spain's attempt to invade England to claim his dead wife's—Mary I's—throne. King Philip II of Spain sent the Spanish Armada of 130 ships in July 1588 to invade England. When it was spotted off Cornwall, beacons were lit all the way to London to warn of the danger. Enter one of England's greatest heroes—Sir Francis Drake—who was in Plymouth (p. 393) when the alarm went up.

The English Navy followed the Armada, which was on its way to Spanish-owned Netherlands to pick up troops. The Armada anchored at Gravelines, in France—the nearest suitable port to the troops—and at nightfall Drake sent eight burning ships into the middle of the wooden fleet. With the route to the English Channel blocked by Drake's ships, the Spanish were forced to sail through storms around Scotland to Ireland, where they stopped for supplies. But the Irish thought they were being invaded and drove them off. Only about half the Armada returned to Spain.

It added to Drake's heroic reputation—and to Elizabeth's image as a strong, unbeatable leader. Drake had already been knighted and lived comfortably at **Buckland Abbey** in Devon (p. 378), today owned by the National Trust, and made his fortune by attacking and looting Spanish bullion ships on their way from South America back to Europe.

Elizabeth's reign was also a time of major exploration, mainly to find a new route to the East to break the Spanish hold on the lucrative spice trade. The attempted colonization of Newfoundland, by Sir Martin Frobisher, and North Carolina, by Sir Walter Raleigh, laid the foundation for the British Empire.

Elizabeth I died in 1603, aged a remarkable 69. Ironically, she was succeeded by Mary Queen of Scots' son, who became James I of England and Wales while remaining James VI of Scotland. Although he hadn't been much help to his mother when she was alive, one of the first things he did was have the remains of Mary Queen of Scots moved to **Westminster Abbey** (p. 103), to an exceptionally fine tomb, which is still there today.

This was also a time of some of England's finest literature. Shakespeare (1564–1616) was creating his vast body of work, with his plays being performed in London at the Globe theatre, which opened on the south bank of the Thames in 1599. A re-creation today sits just along the river (p. 165). Also at work was Ben Jonson (1572–1637)—a playwright, poet, and actor, and a competitor to Shakespeare, best known for his satirical plays such as *Volpone*.

The Stuarts (1603–88)

James I was the first of the Stuart kings, but although he effectively united the crowns of England and Scotland, they still had separate governments and were not politically united until 1707 (interestingly in May 2011 a Scottish National Party—SNP—parliamentary majority election result means a Scottish independence referendum in the next few years is possible). James I was welcomed to England because people did not want continued fighting over the crown, but he broke promises to be lenient to Catholics and upset some Protestants by not introducing the more extreme rules of Scottish Presbyterianism.

The Gunpowder Plot, in 1605, was the most dramatic consequence: Disaffected Catholics plotted to blow up the House of Lords while James I was in it, neatly disposing of him and the pro-Protestant nobility, clergy, and judges at the same time. Guy Fawkes, a Catholic convert who had fought for the Spanish in the Netherlands, was put in charge of the explosives. However, the plot was leaked, and Guy Fawkes was discovered in the building's cellar. He was tortured until he betrayed his co-conspirators, and was executed at the **Tower** (p. 112).

Bonfire Night is still celebrated on November 5 with effigies of Guy Fawkes burned on fires throughout the land, often in people's backyards. There are large events, too, where the town turns out for parades, public bonfires, and fireworks.

James I is also remembered for ordering a definitive English translation of the Bible. The *Authorized King James Bible* of 1611 remained the standard text until it was revised in the 1880s. When James died in 1625 he was succeeded by his son Charles I, who attempted to bypass Parliament, taxed people to the hilt, and—his worst mistake—favored high-church Anglicanism (closely aligned to his French wife's Catholicism) while remaining deeply suspicious of Puritan Protestants. He alienated politicians and subjects of every persuasion. Then he tried to take control of the army. No wonder civil war broke out.

The English Civil War was in fact a series of wars from 1642–46, with the Royalist supporters mainly in the north and west, and the Parliamentary supporters in the south and east. Ironically, the Parliamentarians also had the backing of the Scots because of Charles I's anti-Puritanism. Charles eventually tried to make an alliance with the Scots, but they handed him to the Parliamentarians who decided the only way to prevent more war was to execute him. In 1649 he was beheaded outside the Banqueting House in London's **Whitehall** (p. 84).

The Civil War is often referred to as the English Revolution. Certainly the following 11 years make up the only period in which England and Wales have been republics. The decision to execute Charles came after "purging" Parliament of his sympathizers, but it shocked the public and many of the nobility—in fact it shocked most of Europe.

Oliver Cromwell, a Member of Parliament and gentleman farmer from Cambridgeshire, had created a New Model Army during the Civil War and remained at the head of the new Commonwealth's army. He crushed all rebellions, notably in Ireland. The Scottish were furious with England for executing their king, and when his son Charles arrived from Europe, they crowned him Charles II and sent him with an army to invade England. Charles II got all the way to **Worcester** (p. 478) before Cromwell defeated his troops, but Charles famously escaped by hiding in a hollow tree and fleeing to France.

Many people in England and Wales wanted Charles as their king, too, but in 1653 Cromwell dismissed Parliament and became Lord Protector, a military dictator with puritan leanings. He shut theatres, closed inns to discourage drinking, and banned most sports—outlawing them completely on Sundays. He is even accused of "killing Christmas" by sending soldiers out to prevent celebrations involving raucous eating and drinking.

So it was a relief to most people when Cromwell died in 1658, even though his son Richard succeeded him. Richard didn't last long, though, and by 1660 Charles II was king of England and Wales, as well as Scotland. One of the first things he did was order that Cromwell should be dug up and his corpse put on trial. It was found guilty and hanged, with his head cut off and put on display.

The Restoration (1660–89)

Among the still-extant legacies of Cromwell's Commonwealth are a deep-seated unease about military rule and a religious tolerance colored by a suspicion of extremism. But the Restoration was notable primarily for its revelry, and at times shocking, licentiousness.

Sports and theatres were high on Charles's agenda. He had a house built in **Newmarket** (p. 504) so he could live there during the racing season, as did his most famous mistress, the actress Nell Gwynne. He was also patron of two theatre companies, and Restoration comedy became known for its bawdy plots and use of satire, poking fun at political figures and topical events. William Wycherley's 1675 play *The Country Wife* is often performed today.

This was also a period of scientific expansion. Mathematician Isaac Newton studied the composition of light, invented a reflecting telescope, and, most famous of all, set out his theory of gravity and the laws of motion in 1687—2 years after Charles II's death.

Architect Christopher Wren was also a mathematician, and in 1661 was made Professor of Astronomy at Oxford University. His knowledge of physics and engineering led to his being commissioned to design the **Sheldonian Theatre** in Oxford (p. 219) in 1664. But it was the Great Fire of London in 1666 that really gave him the opportunity to shine.

London at the time was still a medieval city of half-timbered buildings, which had grown from the walled Roman city. Shops and houses were built very close together in a maze of alleys and narrow streets. The city was filthy, with open sewers and little access to clean water, and plague was a recurring problem. The Great Plague of 1665 was spread by rats' fleas, although nobody knew that at the time. By July, during a hot summer, more than 1,000 Londoners were dying every week. Theatres, markets, and taverns were closed by order of the Privy Council, and the king and his entourage moved to **Salisbury** (p. 325).

Possibly the most famous plague village in England is Eyam, in Derbyshire (p. 535), where about 260 of 350 villagers died. The clergyman had persuaded them to remain in quarantine, helping to stop the spread of the disease. Now the victims are remembered each year with a church service on Plague Sunday, the last Sunday in August.

Back in London, in 1666 the plague continued to pick off occasional victims, but in September a fire started at the king's baker's shop in Pudding Lane, in the old city. The baker's ovens had not been put out properly overnight, sparks escaped, and fire spread through the wooden buildings. It was so intense that the lead roof of the old St. Paul's Cathedral melted before the building burned down along with 84 other churches.

The fire is commemorated by the **Monument** (p. 111), a 61.5-m (202-ft.) tower topped by an urn of golden flames. It was designed by Sir Christopher Wren, and if you climb the 311 spiral steps you can see many of the other buildings Wren built after the fire, when modern London was created. Wren's greatest triumph was the new **St. Paul's Cathedral** (p. 112). But Wren also designed 51 other new churches, as well as the **Royal Observatory** at Greenwich (p. 122), through which the Prime Meridian line runs. This is the internationally agreed official starting point for each day, year, and millennium, and the longitude of every place on earth is measured from here, as explained in the Dava Sobel novel *Longitude* (Walker & Co.). Wren also designed the Royal Hospital for retired soldiers, where the RHS Chelsea Flower Show takes place each May, and **Trinity College Library** in Cambridge (p. 499).

Charles II was succeeded by his brother James II in 1685, an unpopular heir because he was openly Catholic (Charles was a secret Catholic). He appointed Catholics to key posts and dismissed Parliament so he could rule without interference. In 1688 his wife gave birth to a son, which was the last straw for England's Protestant nobility. They invited James's Protestant daughter from his first marriage and her Dutch husband William of Orange to take the throne.

Glorious Revolution (1689)

William of Orange arrived with a small army and was supported by the English military chiefs whom James had alienated, marching on London in what became known as the Glorious Revolution. James fled, and a new Parliament declared his abdication in 1689, leaving the throne free for the joint monarchs William III and Mary II. Their reign brought the end of a monarch's divine right to rule England and Wales. Parliament passed the Bill of Rights, preventing the throne from passing laws or raising taxes without Parliament's consent, so a monarch could never dismiss Parliament. The Bill also prevented Catholics from taking the throne.

Mary died of smallpox in 1694 and William died in 1702. They had no surviving children so Mary's sister, Anne, succeeded William. Anne attended Parliament regularly, restored the income from tithes to the Church, and it was during her reign that England and Wales became politically united with Scotland to create the United Kingdom of Great Britain with the 1706 Act of Union.

One of the greatest legacies of Anne's reign was architecture. Queen Anne buildings are particularly notable, and among the best known is **Blenheim Palace** (p. 227) in Woodstock, Oxfordshire. It was built for the Churchill family by Queen Anne to reward the first Duke of Marlborough (John Churchill) for leading British troops to victory over the French in the 1704 Blenheim Battle (part of the Spanish Succession wars). Sir Winston Churchill was born there in 1874.

Anne had 17 children but only one survived birth—and he died at age 11. Parliament had already passed the Act of Succession to ensure the Protestant heirs of Sophia of Hanover (James I's granddaughter) could claim the throne, rather than James II's Catholic heirs, so Anne was succeeded by George of Hanover in 1714.

The Georgians (1714–1830)

George I and his son George II never learned to speak English, sticking to their native German. Unsurprisingly they were disliked by the people. George III was the first English-born king in the Hanover line, and although he is chiefly remembered for losing the American colonies and going mad (as portrayed in Alan Bennett's 1991 play and the subsequent film *The Madness of King George*), at least he could speak English.

Georgian England was a cruel and lawless period. This was the era of Dick Turpin, the highway robber who brought terror to Essex until his death in 1739. It was also a time of piracy: Blackbeard was born in Bristol in 1718 and looted ships off North Carolina. There were at least 200 hanging offenses—from murder to stealing fish—while bear-baiting, badger-baiting, cock fights, and goose-riding were regarded as entertainment.

The Georgians were pretty stylish, though, as we can see from the period's architecture. In London, architect John Nash was responsible for **Regent Street** and remodeled **Buckingham Palace** (p. 88). The London churches of Nicholas Hawksmoor are also revered—and, according to Peter Ackroyd's 1985 novel *Hawksmoor,* built under the influence of Freemasonry—while architect John Soane designed the Bank of England in the City. The churches (and Jack the Ripper) also feature in Alan Moore's graphic novel *From Hell,* and the subsequent film of the same name starring Johnny Depp. Ackroyd, a poet, novelist, and biographer, is London to the core; his retelling of novels and history with gripping new conclusions makes him one of British literature's finest forces.

George I overcame a rebellion by supporters of the Catholic descendants of James II (Jacobites) but left most of the governing of England, Wales (and now Scotland) to Parliament. He was succeeded by George II in 1727, who overcame a second Jacobite rebellion—this time led by Bonnie Prince Charlie, last of the Stuart line—in 1745.

George II was the last British king to lead his troops into battle, taking on the French in 1743. However, it was William Pitt, essentially foreign affairs minister, who masterminded Britain's victory in the Seven Years' War (1756–63), a series of colonial conflicts between Britain, France, and Spain that left Britain with control over India and North America.

Ten years after George III came to the throne in 1760, Captain Cook claimed Australia for Britain during his HMS *Endeavour* voyage to find the fabled southern continent. He claimed parts of New Zealand in 1769 before reaching Australia, and his story is told at the **Captain Cook Memorial Museum** (p. 652), in his hometown of Whitby in Yorkshire.

The 1801 Act of Union led to the creation of the United Kingdom of Britain and Ireland, with far-reaching consequences. Irish Catholics were promised equality with Protestants by Prime Minister William Pitt, but George III was against Catholic emancipation and appointed another prime minister. Equality did not come until 1829 and by then civil war in Ireland was a constant threat.

George III's more famous ill-advised policy was to tax excessively the North American colonies to pay for his grandfather George II's wars. This, of course, led to war

THE GEORGIAN arts SCENE

The arts flourished during the Georgian era: *Robinson Crusoe* author Daniel Defoe visited the east of England and wrote about **East Anglia** (p. 492) in *Tour Through the Eastern Counties of England 1722*, noting Colchester's "fair and beautiful" streets. In 1726 *Gulliver's Travels* was published by Jonathan Swift, an Anglo-Irish clergyman, and the artist William Hogarth created satirical illustrations of the country's low morals. Among his most famous work was *A Rake's Progress*, a series of eight prints based on paintings now at **Sir John Soane's Museum** in London (p. 93). They track a wealthy young man's descent from a life of pleasure to debtor's prison and madness. His work was in sharp contrast to the genteel portraits by Joshua Reynolds and Thomas Gainsborough, which are in London's **Tate Britain** (p. 102).

William Blake, born in 1757, brought a vision of heaven and hell with his illustrations and engravings for books and poetry, and his epic *Jerusalem*. John Constable, born in the flat Suffolk countryside in 1776, was starting to make waves with his landscapes, which he continued to produce until his death in 1837. J. M. W. Turner was a landscape painter, whose work flourished well into the Victorian era. His depictions of light, particularly at the east coast, are remarkable; the new **Turner Contemporary Museum** opened at Margate in Kent, where he spent time, in 2011 (p. 250).

The mid-18th century to the early 19th century was also a time for the Romantic Poets, generally regarded as Percy Bysshe Shelley, Lord Byron, John Clare, Samuel Taylor Coleridge, and William Wordsworth (as well as William Blake). Wordsworth's *Daffodils* is perhaps the most oft-quoted for its simple sentiments, but much of the group's work combined a romantic view of England with a social conscience.

with America in 1771 and defeat in 1781. The loss of the American colonies ruined the king's health, and from 1811 his son the Prince Regent took control. He was crowned George IV in 1820.

The **Regency style** covers the years 1811 to 1820, the period before the Prince Regent's became king. It is best illustrated in Brighton's **Royal Pavilion** (p. 266), the Prince's exotic India-inspired summer house on England's South Coast. Many of Bath's beautiful Georgian buildings were also Regency haunts.

Bath became the most fashionable city outside London during the **Regency period** thanks to its ancient spa. Novelist Jane Austen included the city's Assembly Rooms (p. 338) in two of her novels—*Persuasion* and *Northanger Abbey*. There's now a Jane Austen Centre at the handsome **Royal Crescent** (p. 340), built between 1767 and 1774 and regarded as the pinnacle of Palladian architecture in Britain. The whole city is a UNESCO World Heritage site.

With the British defeat of Napoleon at Waterloo in 1815, Britain was emerging as the most powerful country in Europe. The Industrial Revolution had started around the town of Ironbridge in Staffordshire, where the award-winning **Ironbridge Gorge**

Royal Crescent, Bath

How the Georgians became Victorians

George IV died in 1830 and was succeeded by his brother, William IV, who ruled during a time of social unrest caused by the appalling working conditions of the Industrial Revolution. Although he tried for social reforms at the start of his reign, he had second thoughts during the riots before the 1832 Reform Act was passed. This gave the vote to male householders where the house was worth more than £10, which did nothing for the angry working classes and left the popularity of the monarchy dangerously low. William had 10 illegitimate children by his mistress but no surviving children with his wife Queen Adelaide, so when he died in 1837 his crown (and the resentment of the increasingly vocal industrial workers) was inherited by his niece, **Victoria.**

Museum can be found (p. 488), and the world's first steam-driven passenger railway was opened between Stockton and Darlington in 1825. A carriage from the line is on display at the **National Railway Museum Shildon,** in County Durham (p. 29), and the **National Railway Museum** in York has possibly the world's greatest railways collection (p. 646).

The Victorians (1837–1901)

England and Wales are still largely defined by the Victorian Age. Britain became the most industrialized country in the world, fueled mainly by coal from Wales and Northeast England. You can see these old mines work at the **Blaenavon World Heritage site** (p. 693) near Abergavenny (p. 694), where there are iron works, workers cottages, a heritage railway, and the elevator below ground at the fantastic Big Pit.

Alexander Cordell wrote about Blaenavon in his novels, notably his trilogy *Rape of the Fair Country* (1959), *The Hosts of Rebecca* (1960), and *Song of the Earth* (1969). These moving accounts of working life in the 19th century dealt with the social unrest at the time, much arranged by the Chartist Movement, which held protests in many industrial towns. Chartism shaped modern politics, despite it being rejected over the next 60 years. Workers won the right to vote in elections (previously only a landowner's privilege).

In 1848, when there were revolutions all over Europe, the Chartist Movement was waning because political rights in England and Wales were ahead of other countries. Employment was rising and living standards improving, thanks partly to the building of railways, which provided work and transported agricultural products to towns and manufactured products to ports for export. Many of the industrial railways are now heritage lines popular with tourists, for instance the Llanberis Lake Railway, which takes visitors to the **National Slate Museum** in Snowdonia (p. 724).

The most influential Victorian writer was Charles Dickens who knew from firsthand experience the misery of poverty: His father's financial problems landed them in a debtor's prison in 1824. By Victoria's time he had established himself as a journalist and wrote *Oliver Twist* (1837–39), *David Copperfield* (1849–50), and *Great Expectations* (1860–61) in monthly installments. Go to Kent to find out more about Dickens's life in **Rochester** (p. 247), which in 2012 celebrated the 200th anniversary of his birth. Families would enjoy **Dickens World,** in Chatham (p. 248).

Another major writing talent of the Victorian age was Oscar Wilde. Although he was born and educated in Dublin, Ireland, he won a scholarship to **Magdalen**

College, Oxford (p. 217), and moved to London after graduation to write poetry. He eventually became a journalist and published children's stories such as *The Happy Prince,* producing his only novel, *The Picture of Dorian Gray,* in 1891. He is best known, though, for his plays: *Lady Windermere's Fan, A Woman of No Importance, An Ideal Husband,* and *The Importance of Being Earnest.* Wilde was jailed for homosexuality in 1895 and sentenced to hard labor at Reading Gaol (the subject of his 1898 poem *The Ballad of Reading Gaol*). He died, impoverished and broken, in Paris, in 1900.

The Pre-Raphaelite movement transformed painting in the Victorian era. There are fabulous collections at **Tate Britain** in London (p. 102) and the **Birmingham Museum & Art Gallery** (p. 470). The art critic John Ruskin had greatly promoted the work of the Pre-Raphaelite Brotherhood (notably its founders William Holman Hunt, John Everett Millais, and D. G. Rossetti), but he was also a poet, conservationist (influencing the founders of the National Trust), and social revolutionary—campaigning for free schools and libraries. His home, **Brantwood,** near Coniston in the Lake District (p. 620) was visited by luminaries such as Charles Darwin.

The fairytale version of the Middle Ages by the Pre-Raphaelite painters led to Gothic Revival architecture. Gothic "Revival" is a bit misleading, as its practitioners usually applied Gothic features at random. The best example is the **Houses of Parliament** in London (1835–52). **Charles Barry** designed the wonderful seat of government and his clock tower, usually called **Big Ben** after its biggest bell, has become an icon.

Victoria was only 18 when she became queen in 1837, and married her cousin Prince Albert of Saxe-Coburg-Gotha 3 years later. Contrary to Victoria's image as a gloomy killjoy, she was lively and independent when young, and very much in love with Albert. The couple was not popular, though, until Prince Albert began to win public recognition for his work on behalf of Britain.

His most impressive triumph was the Great Exhibition of 1851 in the huge glass-built Crystal Palace in London's **Hyde Park** (p. 95). This showcased Britain's industrial and technological achievements, but exhibits from colonized countries were invited to make it an even more important global event. The exhibition's profits funded the construction of the **Natural History Museum** (p. 101), **Science Museum** (p. 102), and **Victoria & Albert Museum** (p. 103) in London. Albert was finally given a title, Prince Consort, in 1857 in recognition of his growing popularity. Tragically, 4 years later he was dead from typhoid.

Victoria never recovered from his death and retired to their favorite family home, **Osborne House** on the Isle of Wight (p. 309), which is still full of the personal presents they bought each other. She wore black for the rest of her life, and withdrew

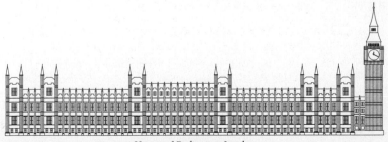

Houses of Parliament, London

RULE OF THE railways

There are more "heritage railways" in Wales (well over 20) than in any other country in the world, and England is not far behind. These nostalgic train trips were all working railway lines once. Some are former passenger railways, but many were used by industries such as coal and slate mines to transport materials to iron and steelworks, factories, or the docks. The railways were a product of the Industrial Revolution and ensured that Britain's manufacturing industries led the world. Many were narrow-gauge tracks that ran through valleys and around mountains where there were no roads. In some places, that's still the case, so you're seeing countryside that might only otherwise be accessible to hardened walkers.

James Watt invented the rotary steam engine in 1783. By 1804 Richard Trevithick had built the first steam locomotive to run on rails for the Pennydarren Ironworks in Merthyr Tydfil, South Wales. The Brecon Mountain Railway now runs from Merthyr along the old **Brecon and Merthyr Railway Line** (p. 702), opened in 1859 and closed in 1964. There are views of Pen-y-Fan, the highest peak in South Wales, and the Taf Fechan Reservoir. By 1811, 150 miles of rail track had

been built in South Wales, the powerhouse of the Industrial Revolution.

George Stephenson, son of a colliery fireman in Northumberland, became an engineer after working on James Watt's engine. He was appointed engineer of the Liverpool to Manchester Line in 1826—the first passenger railway line in Britain. Stephenson's locomotive—The Rocket—reached 30mph, and the line was opened for business in 1830. You can still see **Stephenson's Rocket** in London's Science Museum (p. 102).

By the 1840s, railway lines were built by private companies all over the country. There were 8,000 miles of track in Britain by 1855, which allowed the iron and coal industries to expand. Ports grew to deal with exports and fishing towns benefited from being able to sell to a wider market. The same was also true of agricultural products, increasing the farmers' markets and making food cheaper for people in urban areas. Manufactured goods also reached their markets more easily, bringing down prices and increasing demand and therefore creating jobs.

Railways helped to shape the national character: Trains led to nationwide developments such as newspapers, trade unions, and even a time zone. Previously,

from public life. Her increasing unpopularity was only reversed by her new interest in the British Empire—particularly India.

By the beginning of the 20th century Britain had the world's largest empire, a booming economy, and a growing middle class.

The Edwardians (1901–10)

The end of the Victorian era coincided with the start of the 20th century. Victoria died in 1901 and was succeeded by her son Edward VI who, now 60, had spent most of his adult life as the leading light of London society. He married Princess Alexandra of Denmark in 1863 but had many mistresses, notably the actress Lily Langtry. The Edwardian era was a glittering period of modernization: **Harrods** department store (p. 160) moved into its building in Knightsbridge in 1901, and the American-inspired **Selfridges** (p. 160) opened in Oxford Street.

every region had a slightly different time, based on the local sunrise and sunset. Now everybody in Britain kept the same time, so that rail timetables would work.

After World War I, there were 120 rail companies in Britain, which were reduced to 4: the Great Western Railway; London, Midland, and Scottish Railway (LMS); London and North Eastern Railway (LNER); and the Southern Railway. This created an efficient, golden age of rail travel. The LNER's Mallard still holds the world steam speed record, reaching 126mph in 1938. This beautiful blue engine is now at **Locomotion: The National Railway Museum** at Shildon (www.nrm.org.uk; ✆ 01388/777 999), where you can see many other historic trains including the streamlined Duchess of Hamilton—a 1938 Art Deco masterpiece.

The railways were nationalized in 1948, including industrial lines such as the Ffestiniog Railway in North Wales. You can travel on the **Ffestiniog** (p. 730) **and Welsh Highland Railways** (p. 733) from the coast at Porthmadog to Blaenau Ffestiniog (where you can visit the **Llechwedd Slate Caverns;** p. 726) or from Porthmadog to **Caernarfon** (with its mighty castle; p. 732). Both branches take you past Snowdonia's spectacular scenery.

By 1955 the railways were losing so much money that the network was "modernized." Steam trains had largely already been replaced by diesel engines, and now some lines were electrified. But it was the 1963 report by Dr. Richard Beeching, chairman of the British Railways Board, that changed the rail network forever. He recommended closing 5,000 miles of line and more than 2,000 stations—throwing thousands out of work and cutting off remote areas. Among the lines that went was the **West Somerset Railway** (p. 361). Before it closed in 1971 it was used to film the train carriage scenes in the Beatles' film *A Hard Day's Night*. Reopened by enthusiasts in 1976, it is now the longest heritage railway in Britain.

Another victim was the Severn Valley Railway, which is now a heritage line. Its Bradley Manor station appeared in the 2005 movie *The Chronicles of Narnia: The Lion, the Witch and the Wardrobe*, while Keighley and Worth Valley Railway in West Yorkshire was where 1970's *The Railway Children* was filmed. The line now has steam trains and Railway Children events. For details of more than 250 rail museums and tourist lines, see the **Heritage Railway Association** website www.heritagerailways.com.

Since the 1880s Art Nouveau had been gaining popularity and was the forerunner of Art Deco, which emerged in about 1908 to crystallize the modern style of the 20th century. London's **Victoria & Albert Museum** (p. 103) and Eltham Palace in south London are among the best examples of Art Deco interiors in England.

Although Britain was booming, the struggle for social equality continued, not least by the Suffragette Movement—or Women's Social and Political Union—founded by Emmeline Pankhurst in 1903 to win the right to vote for women. By the time Edward VII was succeeded by his son George V in 1910, the movement was known for women chaining themselves to railings and going on hunger strikes in jail. However, with the advent of World War I, the Suffragettes threw themselves behind the war effort—many women did men's jobs in munitions factories. They were rewarded in 1918, when Parliament gave women property owners over the age of 30 the vote.

On April 10, 1912, RMS *Titanic* left Southampton and 5 days later sunk after hitting an iceberg in the Atlantic. Most of those on board died, including many of the crew from Southampton, in Hampshire. The city's **Maritime Museum,** a 15th-century wool warehouse (p. 302), tells their story and has one of the world's best collections of maritime history.

In 1913, news arrived of the death of Captain Scott of Antarctica in his bid to reach the South Pole. He and his team had reached the pole on January 18, 1912, only to find a Norwegian team led by Roald Amundsen had beaten them to it. On the way back to their ship, Captain Oates—suffering from frostbite and virtually unable to carry on—left their tent and walked to his death so he would no longer be a burden, uttering the immortal words: "I am just going outside and may be some time." Scott and the rest of his team were discovered in their tent in November 1912, with the last entry in Scott's diary dated March 29. The **Scott Polar Research Institute** in Cambridge (p. 501) has Scott's letters home and many other exhibits from his expeditions.

World Wars I & II (1914–45)

Britain joined World War I in August 1914 when Germany refused to withdraw from Belgium. Among the soldiers who chronicled the horror of trench warfare was Rupert Brooke, a Cambridge graduate who wrote the 1912 war poem *The Old Vicarage, Grantchester.* Many people visit **Grantchester** (p. 498) to see the village church mentioned in his poem, where the clock has been stopped at "ten to three"—and where there's honey still for tea.

The coalition wartime prime minister was Liberal Party leader Lloyd George, who was put in charge of the war effort and given much of the credit for the Allies' military success. Lloyd George said he wanted to create "a land fit for heroes," but recession following the war delivered only unemployment—particularly in the industrial heartlands, which had produced coal, iron, steel, and ships for the war.

In 1926 the coal miners walked off the job because pit owners wanted to increase hours and reduce wages. It led to a General Strike, but there was significant opposition owing to a fear of Communism after the 1917 Russian Revolution. It was a time of social unrest, particularly in Ireland. In 1916 the Easter Week Rebellion in Dublin by republicans started a civil war, which ended in 1922 with an Irish Free State breaking away from Northern Ireland and the U.K. after Prime Minister Lloyd George signed the Irish Agreement in 1921.

Work started in 1922 on the Stadium of the British Empire Exhibition, which was to take place in 1924, but the first event at what was to be called simply **Wembley Stadium** was the 1923 Football Association Cup—or FA Cup—between West Ham and Bolton. It was dubbed the White Horse Cup Final when police on horses had to control the 200,000-plus spectators who had forced their way into the stadium, which had a capacity of 127,000. Bolton won 2–0 and the FA Cup was held there every year until 2000, when the stadium was demolished and a new one built.

The Wall Street Crash of 1929 ushered in an even more chaotic decade, with the Great Depression causing massive unemployment in the old industrial areas, although the Midlands and the Southeast were less affected. There were high points, though, despite the Depression. Sir Malcolm Campbell beat his own world land speed record at Daytona Beach in Florida in 1932, driving his distinctive Bluebird car at 241.773mph. You can see the Bluebird at the **National Motor Museum** in

Beaulieu, Hampshire (p. 304), as well as other famous exhibits including several James Bond vehicles and the flying Ford Anglia from *Harry Potter and the Chamber of Secrets.*

King George V died in 1936, and was succeeded by Edward VIII. But Edward's plan to marry divorced American Wallace Simpson caused a constitutional crisis. As head of the Church of England he could not marry a divorcée, so he abdicated after 327 days and the crown passed to his brother George VI.

By September 1939, Britain was at war again, and Oscar-winning film *The King's Speech* tells the story of how George VI announced the start of World War II. However, the emerging national hero was Winston Churchill (knighted by the present Queen Elizabeth in 1953). As prime minister, Churchill became the symbol of Britain's fighting spirit during World War II. In May and June 1940, during the Dunkirk evacuation, 338,000 British and allied troops were rescued against all odds from the beaches of Normandy in northern France and brought safely back to England. They were saved by hundreds of little boats as well as Royal Navy ships as the nation famously "pulled together." It prompted one of Churchill's most famous Parliamentary speeches: "We shall fight on the beaches, we shall fight on the landing grounds, we shall fight in the fields and in the streets, we shall fight in the hills. We shall never surrender." The **Churchill War Rooms** (p. 100) in London's King Charles Street brings the conflict to life for visitors of all ages.

In June 1940 Churchill announced: "… the Battle of France is over. I expect that the Battle of Britain is about to begin." France surrendered 4 days later and by July German fighter planes were attacking shipping in the English Channel and coastal towns. By August, RAF airfields were under attack and in September London and other important cities were targeted. There are several Battle of Britain museums in England, but by far the most important is the **Imperial War Museum Duxford** (p. 506) near Cambridge. The fight for air supremacy was over by fall 1940 with the RAF on top. "Never in the field of human conflict, was so much owed by so many to so few," was Churchill's famous tribute. However, the Luftwaffe continued to bomb British cities until the end of the war.

These blitzes were aimed at factories and transport but inevitably hit residential areas and historic buildings too. In London 30,000 people were killed and countless buildings bombed. Birmingham, Liverpool, Manchester, Sheffield, Southampton, and Hull were among the major targets, as was Coventry where the medieval **St. Michael's Cathedral** (p. 466) was destroyed in 1940. The ruins remain, but a new cathedral was built after the war as a symbol of hope, and it has attracted tourists ever since its consecration in 1962.

For a better idea of how the people of England and Wales coped from 1939 to 1945, you can also visit the **Imperial War Museum** in London (p. 108) and **Imperial War Museum North** in Manchester (p. 571). The hospital in tunnels at Dover Castle in Kent (p. 254) is also a revelation.

 Classic Authors for a Taste of England

Graham Greene	Sir Arthur Conan Doyle
W. Somerset Maugham	Charles Dickens
H. G. Wells	Jane Austen
C. P. Snow	George Orwell

Postwar England & Wales (1945–Present Day)

The war ended in Europe in May 1945, with Britain heavily in debt and the economy ruined. Many towns and cities needed to be rebuilt. Rationing, introduced in 1940, became even stricter. It wasn't completely lifted until 1954.

One of the bright spots of the 1940s was Princess Elizabeth's wedding to Prince Philip of Greece and Denmark, who had served in the Royal Navy during the war as a lieutenant. The couple became secretly engaged in 1946, and Philip had to give up his Greek citizenship and title to become a British citizen. He used the surname Mountbatten, a version of his mother's German family name Battenburg. The couple were married at **Westminster Abbey** (p. 103) in November 1947, and moved into Clarence House at St. James's Palace in London, now the official residence of Prince Charles.

After the war, the British Empire became the Commonwealth of Nations. One of the most significant events was the partition of India and Pakistan into two countries in 1947, when the king's title of Emperor of India ceased. Many other countries were granted independence in the following decades.

The postwar break-up of the British Empire was reflected in domestic social reforms. Free secondary school education had only been introduced in 1944, and after the war the Labour Party won the 1945 General Election by a landslide vote. It nationalized the coal industry in 1947, and in 1948 the National Health Service (NHS) was established to provide free hospital and medical provision.

The 1948 Olympic Games were held in London, the first since the Berlin Games of 1936, and were known as the "Austerity Games" because rationing was still in force. The Olympics took place largely in the old Wembley Stadium, with 59 nations participating. The new Wembley Stadium was a venue for the 2012 Olympic Games, and tours are available. You can also see international sport and the world's biggest bands there.

George Orwell's novel *Nineteen Eighty-Four* was published in 1949, warning about the perils of centralized government and coining the phrase "Big Brother," but the 1950s brought a new optimism. The 1951 Festival of Britain celebrated British industry, arts, and sciences on London's **South Bank** (p. 76), a bomb site from World War II. The Royal Festival Hall is now a concert hall with regular free foyer events. It is part of the South Bank Centre, which includes the Queen Elizabeth Hall music venue, the Hayward Gallery, the British Film Institute's BFI Southbank, and the National Theatre.

King George VI died unexpectedly of lung cancer in 1952 and Queen Elizabeth came to the throne, the symbol of a new era. This new era was symbolized by the "kitchen sink" novels of the period focusing on the new social mobility. John Braine's 1957 novel, *Room at the Top,* about a young man's attempt to escape the working class, became the first of Britain's "New Wave" films in 1959. Braine was one of a dozen or so writers and novelists labeled "angry young men" after the 1956 John Osborne play *Look Back in Anger,* which was filmed in 1959. Find out more at the **National Media Museum** in Bradford (p. 639).

The Great Train Robbery of 1963, when £2.6 million was stolen in used bank notes from the Glasgow-to-London mail train, is as much a part of English folklore now as the Hole in the Wall gang of the American Wild West. Numerous books and television documentaries have been made about the robbery, including the 1988 film *Buster,* starring Phil Collins and Julie Walters.

A Great British Top 10

"England Swings"
Roger Miller (1965)
"Scarborough Fair"
Simon and Garfunkel (1966)
"Penny Lane/Strawberry Fields Forever" The Beatles (1967)
"Waterloo Sunset"
The Kinks (1967)
"Streets of London" Ralph McTell (1969)

"Grantchester Meadows"
Pink Floyd (1970)
"Solsbury Hill"
Peter Gabriel (1977)
"(I Don't Want To Go To) Chelsea"
Elvis Costello and the Attractions (1978)
"London Calling" The Clash (1979)
"(Waiting For You and) England to Return" Stackridge (2009)

Also in 1963, the Profumo Affair (Secretary of War John Profumo's affair with model Christine Keeler, a friend of a Soviet naval attaché) caused a scandal. Assignations took place at Lord Astor's **Cliveden House** in Taplow, Buckinghamshire. It was once the home of high society and visited by British monarchs since the early 18th century. It's now a hotel, but the grandiose gardens and beautiful woodlands, owned by the National Trust, are open year-round (p. 207).

The rock-and-roll music of the 1950s was falling out of fashion by the mid-1960s, but motor bike-riding rockers were still going strong and in 1964 they fought with gangs of mods (style-conscious youngsters who listened to ska and English, rather than American, music) at south-coast seaside resorts such as **Margate** (p. 249) and **Brighton** (p. 265) during the May public holiday weekend. Movies such as 1979's *Quadrophenia,* starring Sting, capture the mood of the era.

By contrast, Churchill's death in 1965 at the age of 90 seemed to herald the end of an era. His funeral at St. Paul's Cathedral was attended by heads of state from all over Europe. He was buried at the parish church in Bladon, near his **Blenheim** estate (p. 227) in Woodstock, Oxfordshire. At one stage, the public line to file past his coffin was more than 1 mile long.

The 1966 Football World Cup final was won by England, in a 4–2 victory over West Germany at Wembley Stadium. It's an achievement that has never been repeated, although the nation lives in hope. The warm glow of this summer success was swept away that October, however, with one of the most heart-breaking disasters ever to affect these islands. A coal-tip slide at Aberfan near Merthyr Tydfil in South Wales engulfed the village school and nearby houses, killing 144 people, including 116 children. *Cider With Rosie* novelist Laurie Lee visited the village in 1967 and was moved to write about "The Village That Lost Its Children" in his 1975 collection of essays, *I Can't Stay Long.*

Meanwhile, Francis Chichester sailed into Plymouth, in Devon (p. 393) in May 1967 to become the first man to sail single-handedly around the world—an incredible achievement in an age before electronic navigation systems. Aged 65, he had stopped only at Sydney on his epic voyage, and was rewarded with a knighthood from the Queen a few months later, in a public ceremony at the Royal Naval College in Greenwich. The college was designed by Christopher Wren and built between 1696 and 1712. It is now part of the UNESCO World Heritage site of **Maritime Greenwich** (p. 121).

The 1970s was a troubled decade of shortages and strikes. The oil crisis of 1973–74 led to regular power cuts and the 3-day working week to save fuel. In February

SWINGING sixties

In the 1960s, England was at the heart of the world. Recovering from the battering it had received during World War II, a new generation was emerging: Youngsters, who hadn't seen war, and who wanted something new. They craved music, and found it, mostly, through the R 'n' B and soul records imported for American servicemen who were still based here. **The Beatles** weren't the first homegrown act to entrance teenagers (they'd already had Adam Faith and Cliff Richard), but they were the first with a new attitude, and who wrote their own music. Others followed, **The Rolling Stones, The Zombies, Downliners Sect, The Pretty Things, The Kinks, The Yardbirds, The Who** ... the list was endless. The Beatles, with their lovable moptops, had their first number 1, "Please Please Me," in 1963. The Beatles and Merseybeat conquered the world but there were more and more bands from the south. The Stones were marketed as the bad boys of cool, with their first show at London's Marquee Club in 1962. Meanwhile Tom Jones, son of a miner from Pontypridd in South Wales, had his first number 1 in 1965 with "It's Not Unusual." Other outsiders moved in, such as American Jimi Hendrix who, between 1968 and 1969, lived in a flat on Brook Street, next door to the house occupied by composer Handel in 1723–59 (it's now the **Handel House Museum;** p. 89). Venues like the Marquee (now closed) and the 100 Club hosted gigs and parties that have become legendary. As the decade wore on, psychedelic and progressive acts emerged: Cambridge's **Pink Floyd,** Canterbury's **Soft Machine,** and many others.

Clothing was an essential ingredient in the '60s' mix. The mod fashions and miniskirts of designer **Mary Quant** defined the era. Models **Jean Shrimpton** (b. 1942) and **Twiggy** (b. 1949) were the faces of Swinging London. Chelsea's **King's Road** (p. 152) and **Carnaby Street** (p. 151) were the places to be.

Many films define the era. *Performance,* starring The Rolling Stones' lead singer Mick Jagger, the Beatles' *Hard Day's Night,* and Michelangelo Antonioni's *Blowup* (with a live cameo by the Yardbirds) all capture the spirit of the era.

1974 an all-out strike by the National Union of Miners was enough to bring Prime Minister Edward Heath's Conservative government down, and by March there was a new Labour government led by Harold Wilson. A recession from 1975 prompted years of strike and unrest, culminating in the Labour government's Winter of Discontent in 1978, when the country ground to a halt, a combination of public services strikes and heavy snow. Punk music, a response to the decade's dire prospects, peaked in 1977 with the release of the Sex Pistols' notorious "God Save the Queen," a record that was re-released in summer 2012 to tie in with the Queen's Diamond Jubilee.

The Tate Gallery (now **Tate Britain;** p. 102) hit the headlines in February 1976 with its brick sculpture by American artist Carl Andre. The sculpture, 120 firebricks laid out in a two-deck oblong, had been bought more than 3 years before but caught the public imagination when the Tate's director refused to say how much the sculpture had cost.

In 1977 the nation's most-loved racehorse, Red Rum, won the **Grand National** at Aintree (p. 41) for an unprecedented third time. The **National Horseracing Museum** at Newmarket (p. 505) near Cambridge has items associated with Red Rum, as well as other legendary racehorses and jockeys.

A General Election put Margaret Thatcher and the Conservatives into power in 1979, and her economic policies divided the nation as unemployment dramatically increased. Her popularity was only assured by the 1982 Falklands "War" (officially only a "conflict") and victory, when Britain defended its South Atlantic islands against Argentina. Thatcher's political success was cemented by free-market agreements with the United States, and her domestic success was underlined by the growing prosperity of Britain's new homeowners and shareholders after council houses were sold off and nationalized industries were privatized.

The 1984 miners' strike, over the closure of pits that were no longer producing enough coal to be economic, was a bitter struggle and did much to cause the hostility toward Mrs. Thatcher, which still exists today in the areas where job losses were severe. The movie *Billy Elliot*, released in 2000 and now a West End musical, is set in 1984–85 with the strike as its backdrop. By the late 1980s, divisions within the Conservatives led to a leadership challenge, and Mrs. Thatcher resigned in 1990 to make way for Conservative leader John Major to become prime minister. But among her lasting legacies is the **Docklands** area of East London (p. 77), where London's love affair with high-rise buildings began.

"New Labour" took power in 1997, under the leadership of the youngest prime minister in over 180 years, Tony Blair (43 years old). This was an age of optimism and Blair became Labour's longest-serving prime minister, but his tenure in the U.K. became increasingly shrouded by his support for the "War on Terror" and actions in Iraq. Gordon Brown succeeded his long-term sparring partner Blair in 2007 but by 2010 he had resigned as prime minister and leader of the Labour Party and a new Conservative-Liberal Democrat coalition was ushered in.

Compared to Thatcher's '80s, today, despite the economic climate, the country is a very different place. Compare some of the gloomy New Town Brutalist architecture that seemed to symbolize Thatcher's government with contemporary architecture's refreshing new buildings: Eric Parry's extension to the Holburne Museum in Bath, the Hepworth Wakefield museum in West Yorkshire, and the Turner Contemporary museum in Margate, Kent. It also *feels* different, an invigorating environment where a cutting-edge cultural environment exists happily alongside the ever-present pop culture of the past.

The '60s still rule, as shown by the 2010 movie *Brighton Rock*, Graham Greene's 1950s' gangster tale reset in the following decade. The music from that era (and from the 1970s) is acquiring a new lease of life, as the stars are treated with the reverence that used to be accorded old bluesmen; **Paul McCartney** has never been bigger and younger generations are as keen to watch him at a festival as they are the latest girl sensations, Adele, who won six 2012 Grammys, and Jessie J. **Robert Plant** is more successful than ever and one of the biggest draws is Damon Albarn's post-Blur electro-pop extravaganza **Gorillaz,** which features two ex-members of The Clash, comic book artwork, and a host of stars from down the years.

The first U.K. rock festival was on the **Isle of Wight** (p. 306) in 1968, and starred Marc Bolan's band Tyrannosaurus Rex. Bob Dylan played in 1969 and **Jimi Hendrix** (who'd made his home in Britain) in 1970, although that was the last **Isle of Wight Festival** until it was revived in 2002. The **Glastonbury Festival** (p. 359) in Somerset took up the baton in 1970. Both are still going strong.

Yet there is still an irrepressible surge of new bands; some explode swiftly while others stay the course. Of the latter, the **Editors, Kasabian, White Lies,** and **Arctic Monkeys** are some of the best known. Ollie Murs, a runner up in reality TV show

What They Say

"Now that I own the BBC/What am I supposed to make of this thing/All this power/All this glory/All these DJs/And all these lorries."

—Sparks, *Now That I Own The BBC* (1994)

The X Factor, is the idol of teenage girls, Ed Sheeran has even made singer-songwriters popular again, and even the very sensible Coldplay topped the charts in 2012.

Wales has long had its own music: The infectious rock 'n' roll of **Andy Fairweather Low** (once the singer in '60s chart toppers Amen Corner, a long-time guitarist in Eric Clapton's band, and now splendidly solo) and **Dave Edmunds,** and the experimental angst of the Velvet Underground's **John Cale** (still playing major shows), while more recent acts such as **Duffy** with her rich soul music, and art rockers **Super Furry Animals** (and their solo frontman **Gruff Rhys**) are major stars.

Comic books used to be a particularly American thing, but a host of Brits have crossed the Atlantic and many have their work made into big-budget films, not least **Neil Gaiman** (the novels *Coraline* and *Stardust*) and **Alan Moore** (*Watchmen, V For Vendetta, League of Extraordinary Gentlemen, From Hell*).

Literature in Britain has never been stronger. Erudite fantasy has become big-selling reality for Philip (*Golden Compass*) Pullman and J.K. (Harry Potter) Rowling, but there are far more esoteric novels that have become bestsellers. Read almost anything by A. S. Byatt, Hilary Mantel, Ian McEwan (whose *Atonement* was turned into the movie starring Keira Knightley), Martin Amis, Jeanette Winterson, Zadie Smith, and Will Self and it is possible to see the anger, introspection, and inventiveness of modern Britain, with some, such as Byatt and Winterson, spilling over into young people's fiction. Meanwhile, author Niall Griffiths' edgy novels have put Aberystwyth on the map as much as Irvine Welsh and Ian Rankin's books did for Edinburgh.

Stage plays are also another British success story, with a wealth of learned offerings, often dealing with difficult subjects, from Alan Bennett, David Hare, Harold Pinter, Tom Stoppard, Michael Frayn, and others.

British movies are still taking on the world, such as *The King's Speech,* which won four 2011 Oscars, including best film. One of the biggest films of 2012 was *War Horse,* Steven Spielberg's adaptation of British children's author Michael Morpurgo's novel, which had already spawned an award-winning stage play. And the timeless qualities of Charles Dickens have been shown in *Great Expectations,* starring Helena Bonham Carter and Ralph Fiennes, in celebration of the bicentennial of the author's birth in 2012.

Yet it is not just the arty films that are crossing the Atlantic successfully; Simon Pegg and Nick Frost are now U.S. stars with their films *Shaun of the Dead, Hot Fuzz,* and *Paul*. British directors (who are often also writers) are also big business: Shakespearean heavy hitter Kenneth Branagh (*Thor*), Paul Greengrass (*Green Zone, The Bourne Ultimatum*), Christopher Nolan (*Batman Begins, The Dark Knight,* plus 2012's *The Dark Knight Rises,* as well as the story for 2013's Superman rebirth *Man of Steel*), Stephen Daldry (*The Reader,* for which Kate Winslet won the best actress Oscar, and the 2012 drama *Extremely Loud and Incredibly Close,* starring Sandra Bullock and Tom Hanks), Edgar Wright (*Shaun of the Dead, Scott Pilgrim vs. the World*), and Andrea Arnold, whose 2009 movie *Fish Tank* was named Outstanding British Film in the BAFTA awards. And TV just grows, with perhaps more choice on dozens of cable and satellite channels than even in the U.S., a far cry from the dark days of 1982 when the country celebrated the launch of its fourth TV station, Channel 4. Yet still the BBC reigns supreme, the world's greatest broadcaster, feted for its news reporting, its drama, and its comedy. And on U.S. TV, one of the biggest stars for the past few years has been Englishman Hugh Laurie, a veteran of BBC comedy and drama series, in *House*, the medical drama that ended in spring 2012. Andrew Garfield, Peter Parker in 2012's *Amazing Spider-Man*, might have been born in LA but was brought up and learnt his trade in England (he has an English mother); he also starred in *The Social Network*.

EATING & drinking

There are now more than 100 restaurants in England with one Michelin star. There are another dozen-plus with two stars, and four with that ultimate accolade of three stars. One of them is the home of Gordon Ramsay, who seems to be on American TV more than President Obama; another, the Fat Duck at Bray, is the masterwork of another TV star, Heston Blumenthal and his molecular cooking style. There are now also more than a dozen pubs with Michelin stars, which is the ultimate accolade for pub grub. Oh, and a handful of restaurants in Wales also have stars.

It says a lot about British cuisine, once so derided, where an emphasis on locally sourced produce is now king. Even high-street chain restaurants are largely of a decent standard (you can never go wrong with a Pizza Express), and you'd have to be extremely unlucky not to stumble on a good curry house. Add to that the plethora of Chinese, Thai, and Italian places, plus growing numbers of French and Spanish tapas restaurants, as well as all those fish and chip shops and coffee shops (a Starbucks is as much an English institution now as a chippie), and you'll never want for food.

There are few things visitors won't be familiar with these days, as even the most remote U.S. brewpub, Canadian bar, or New Zealand eatery sometimes features a menu heavy in Englishness (cottage pie, bangers and mash). What you will find is increasingly good pub grub, with gastropubs offering fare that would outstrip that of many restaurants.

Not surprising since master chef Marco Pierre White now owns a string of inns in Norfolk, and the outspoken Gordon Ramsay has several London pubs. There are seafood delights around the country (Morecambe Bay prawns, Whitstable oysters, Cromer crabs, jellied eels in London's East End, kippers and other smoked fish around the land). Local lamb, estate-raised beef and venison, eclectic gourmet sausages and pies are all increasingly on the menu. Wales has all these, too, plus its own treats … flat, sugary Welsh cakes, and (more of an acquired taste) laverbread, a type of seaweed.

In the 1960s and 1970s real ale was being replaced with trouble-free gassy kegs of Watney's Red Barrel; a people's revolution followed with small brewers popping up, traditional methods being praised, and something that was declared dead reborn, better than ever before. The revolution even swept America, brewpubs appearing in every town offering dark beers instead of the pale yellow fizz that was the norm.

Nowadays in Britain there's a regional variety of beers, from the divine Hop Back from Salisbury, Wiltshire, with its award-winning White Lightning to the Whitstable Brewery, making Oyster Stout, in a shed in the Kent seaside town. But England and Wales have wine, too. There's a number of vineyards in southern England, including the Adgestone on the Isle of Wight, and in a valley outside Cardiff there's even the successful Llanerch vineyard.

Wales is making its mark in the entertainment world, with BBC Wales producing the revamped *Dr. Who* science fiction series (now becoming a transatlantic hit, with some filming in the U.S. and with Neil Gaiman among the writers), along with hard-hitting, alien-hunting spin-off *Torchwood* (the Miracle Day series even being a trans-atlantic co-production). Welsh comedy is on the up, too, with performers such as Rob Brydon, and the award-winning BBC series *Gavin and Stacey*. Welsh actor Rhys Ifans (*Notting Hill, Enduring Love, Mr Nice, Harry Potter and the Deathly Hallows*) played villain Dr. Curt Connors/the Lizard in The Amazing Spider-Man. He and compatriot Michael Sheen (*Wilde, Frost/Nixon, The Twilight Saga: New Moon,* and even *Dr. Who*) are male leads in the footsteps of Anthony Hopkins and Richard Harris. Even Mr. Fantastic in the *Fantastic Four* movies is Welshman Ioan Gruffudd, while Hopkins plays Norse god Odin in *Thor*.

WHEN TO GO
Climate

You don't come to England and Wales for the weather, but it's nowhere near as bad as many visitors expect. You can't be an island on the edge of the Atlantic Ocean without experiencing some rain brought over by westerly winds, but while the west coast of Wales and England get the worst of this you'll enjoy warm, sunny, summer days all over England and Wales (and mild, wet ones).

Like all countries, mountainous areas can have local cloud and drizzle so North Wales, the Lake District, and other rugged areas in the north have their own weather trends. Particularly enjoyable are the light summer evenings, when daytime stretches until at least 10pm at the summer solstice in June (although in winter it can be dark before 4pm). Rain is most likely in the latter part of the year, but there's no "dry season" here, hence Wimbledon's famous tennis in late June and early July being regularly disrupted.

Daytime temperatures can range from 30° to 95°F (-1° to 35°C), but they rarely stay below 36°F (2°C) or above 79°F (26°C) for too long. Evenings are usually cool,

DATELINE

55 B.C. Julius Caesar invades England.

A.D. 43 Romans conquer England.

410 Jutes, Angles, and Saxons form small kingdoms in England.

470 Romans found Londinium.

500–1066 Anglo-Saxon kingdoms fight off Viking warriors.

1066 William, Duke of Normandy, invades England, defeating Harold II at the Battle of Hastings.

1154 The Plantagenets launch their rule (which lasts until 1399) with the crowning of Henry II.

1215 King John signs the Magna Carta at Runnymede.

1215 Hadrian's Wall is built.

1337 Hundred Years' War between France and England begins.

1485 Battle of Bosworth Field ends the Wars of the Roses between the houses of York and Lancaster; Henry VII launches the Tudor dynasty.

1534 Henry VIII brings the Reformation to England and dissolves the monasteries.

even in summer, but hot July and August days can be muggy—particularly on London's Tube network (also known as the Underground), which is not air-conditioned. Note that the British like to keep hotel thermostats about 10°F (6°C) below the American comfort level.

London's Average Daytime Temperatures & Rainfall

	JAN	FEB	MAR	APR	MAY	JUNE	JULY	AUG	SEPT	OCT	NOV	DEC
Temp. (°F)	39	39	45	48	55	61	61	64	59	52	46	43
Temp. (°C)	4	4	7	9	13	16	16	18	15	11	8	6
Rainfall (in.)	2.1	1.6	1.5	1.5	1.8	1.8	2.2	2.3	1.9	2.2	2.5	1.9

Cardiff's Average Daytime Temperatures & Rainfall

	JAN	FEB	MAR	APR	MAY	JUNE	JULY	AUG	SEPT	OCT	NOV	DEC
Temp. (°F)	40	40	43	46	52	57	61	61	57	52	44	42
Temp. (°C)	4	4	6	8	11	14	16	16	14	11	7	6
Rainfall (in.)	4.2	3.0	2.9	2.5	2.7	2.6	3.1	4.0	3.8	4.6	4.3	4.6

CURRENT WEATHER CONDITIONS The best place to head online for a detailed weather forecast is www.bbc.co.uk/weather.

WHEN YOU'LL FIND BARGAINS In short, summer's warmer weather gives rise to many outdoor music and theatre festivals. But winter offers savings pretty much across the board.

The cheapest time to fly to Britain is usually during the off season: from late October to mid-December and from January to mid-March. In the last few years, the long-haul airlines in particular have offered some irresistible fares during these periods. Remember that weekday flights are often cheaper than weekend fares.

Rates generally increase between March and June, then hit their peak in high travel seasons between late June and September, and in December for the run-up to Christmas and New Year. July and August are also when most Europeans take their holidays, so besides higher prices, there are more crowds and more limited availability of the best hotel rooms.

1558 The accession of Elizabeth I ushers in an era of exploration and a renaissance in science and learning.

1588 Spanish Armada defeated.

1603 James VI of Scotland becomes James I of England, thus uniting the crowns of England and Scotland.

1620 Pilgrims sail from Plymouth on the *Mayflower* to found a colony in the New World.

1629 Charles I dissolves Parliament, ruling alone.

1642–49 Civil war between Royalists and Parliamentarians; the Parliamentarians win.

1649 Charles I beheaded, and England is a republic.

1653 Oliver Cromwell becomes Lord Protector.

1660 Charles II restored to the throne with limited power.

1665–66 Great Plague and Great Fire decimate London.

1688 James II, a Catholic, is deposed, and William and Mary come to the throne, signing a bill of rights.

continues

You can avoid crowds, to some extent, by planning trips for November or January through March. Sure, it may be rainy and cold—but the country doesn't shut down when the tourists thin out (although many countryside attractions such as National Trust properties do close for the winter). Often you'll find city arts festivals during the off season, and hotel prices can drop by 20%. By arriving after the winter holidays, you can also take advantage of post-Christmas sales, which these days start on December 26 or 27. There's usually another major sales period in stores in mid-summer.

Calendar of Events

JANUARY

London's **New Year's Day Parade** crowns the capital's festive season with 3 hours of pomp and frivolity. More than 10,000 dancers, acrobats, cheerleaders, musicians, and performers assemble in the heart of the city every year for a "celebration of nations." Over 400,000 people regularly descend on central London to admire the floats and entertainers that appear in the parade—be sure to arrive early to secure a good space. www.londonparade.co.uk.

London's large Chinese community welcomes the **Chinese New Year** with a colorful bang. Discover cultural events throughout the city center and catch splendid lion dances and performances in Trafalgar Square and Leicester Square. The New Year celebrations are one of the biggest in the world outside of China and as dusk sets on the day the crowds descend on Chinatown to continue the celebrations into the night. www.chinatownlondon.org.

FEBRUARY

York, most often associated historically with the Romans, was in fact ruled by Viking kings as Jorvik between A.D. 866 and A.D. 952. These age-old leaders are remembered each year during the **Jorvik Viking Festival.** Would-be adventurers and wannabe Vikings from all over the world gather in the city to watch Norse warriors fight to the (mock) death with their enemies, the Saxons, as well as to enjoy dozens of arts, music, drama, and action events throughout the city. www.jorvik-viking-centre.co.uk.

As a preview to its annual **Food and Drink Festival,** Chester hosts its famous **Cheese Rolling Championships.** Locals cheer on the Cheshire team as they take on their

1727	George I, the first of the Hanoverians, assumes the throne.
1756–63	In the Seven Years' War, Britain wins Canada from France.
1775–83	Britain loses its American colonies.
1795–1815	The Napoleonic Wars lead, finally, to the Battle of Waterloo and the defeat of Napoleon.
1837	Queen Victoria begins her reign as Britain reaches the zenith of its empire.
1901	Victoria dies, and Edward VII becomes king.
1914–18	England enters World War I and emerges victorious on the Allied side.
1936	Edward VIII abdicates to marry an American divorcée.
1939–45	In World War II, Britain stands alone against Hitler from the fall of France in 1940 until the U.S. enters the war in 1941. Dunkirk is evacuated in 1940; bombs rattle London during the Blitz.
1945	Germany surrenders. Churchill is defeated; the Labour government introduces the welfare state and begins to dismantle the Empire.

Lancashire and Stilton rivals over a creative obstacle course, in what has become a charmingly curious celebration of Chester's cheese-making tradition. www.visitchester.com.

MARCH

The **Newcastle Science Festival** sees venues throughout the city fizzle with amazing robots, incredible inventions, and the occasional fireball. With plenty of activities for children and adults, it appeals to aspiring academics and skeptic scientists alike. www.newcastlesciencefest.co.uk.

St. Patrick's Day may have started in Ireland but nowadays it's celebrated throughout the world, not least in Manchester which hosts one of Europe's biggest celebrations of all things Irish. Lasting roughly 2 weeks, the **Manchester Irish Festival** pays tribute to the Emerald Isle with parties, music, comedy, theatre, sport, and dance throughout the city. It all culminates in the city's own St. Patrick's Day parade, which regularly attracts crowds of up to 150,000 people. www.irishfestival.co.uk.

APRIL

It's not just the pretty timber-framed houses that lure tourists to Stratford-upon-Avon. As Shakespeare's birthplace this small town carries real cultural clout, and the Royal Shakespeare Company celebrates "the Bard" with performances of his works throughout the year. It's in April, the month of Shakespeare's birth (and death), that the **Shakespeare Season** begins afresh. www.rsc.org.uk.

More than just a sporting event, the **London Marathon** is the world's longest street party. Roads along the route come alive with bands, cheering crowds, entertainers, and 36,000 pairs of feet hitting the tarmac along the 26.2 mile course. www.virginlondonmarathon.com.

The **Grand National** at Aintree Racecourse in Liverpool is widely regarded as the greatest steeplechase in the world. The atmosphere is compelling, with punters exchanging tips and form and almost as much to see off track as on it. Scan the stands and look out for the ladies who make up Liverpool's high society and soccer (football) players' wives sorority—their attire has a reputation for being reliably lavish, frequently lurid, and occasionally ludicrous. www.aintree.co.uk.

The **Oxford and Cambridge University Boat Race,** in London on a Saturday in early April, is another great tradition. Rowers battle it out on the Thames between Putney and Chiswick bridges with the riverbanks in between taking on a festival atmosphere. www.theboatrace.org.

1952 Queen Elizabeth II ascends the throne.

1973 Britain joins the European Union.

1979 Margaret Thatcher becomes prime minister.

1982 Britain defeats Argentina in the Falklands conflict.

1990 Thatcher is ousted; John Major becomes prime minister.

1991 Britain fights with Allies to defeat Iraq.

1992 Royals are jolted by fire at Windsor Castle and marital troubles of their two sons. Britain joins the European Single Market.

Deep recession signals the end of the booming 1980s.

1994 England is linked to the Continent by rail via the Channel Tunnel, or Chunnel. Tony Blair elected Labour Party leader.

1996 The IRA breaks a 17-month cease-fire with a truck bomb at the Docklands that claims two lives. Charles and Diana divorce.

1997 London swings again. The Labour Party ends 18 years of Conservative rule with a landslide election victory. The death of Diana, Princess of Wales.

continues

MAY

The **Hay Festival** is among the largest literary get togethers in the English-speaking world. The event annually attracts up to 50,000 people to Hay-on-Wye in Wales for almost 2 weeks of interviews, lectures, readings, and performances featuring distinguished authors. This is a festival that will leave you flushed with enthusiasm and brimming with inspiration rather than stressed out and exhausted. www.hayfestival.com.

Bohemian, beach-front Brighton comes into its own every summer and not just due to the much-anticipated good weather. In May, the city's **Brighton Festival** returns with 3 weeks of energetic arts-themed performances and eclectic occurrences, the development of which is heavily influenced by whichever illustrious creative is Guest Artistic Director. www.brightonfestival.org.

London's **Chelsea Flower Show** is Europe's premier gardening event. Some of the greatest exponents of the art exhibit imaginative garden designs over an 11-acre site at the Royal Hospital in Chelsea, creating a floral wonderland for the public to explore. Visitors can roam through scores of gardens and exhibitions, with the displays showcasing some of the world's finest examples of horticultural excellence. www.rhs.org.uk/chelsea.

The country house of Glyndebourne, near Lewes, East Sussex, draws crowds to its manicured lawns and pristine interiors with the **Glyndebourne Festival.** A celebration of opera, its productions can range from Mozart to modern but some things retain a cute, anachronistic flourish. Gentlemen typically gather for performances in tuxedos, while ladies in evening dresses sip champagne. www.glyndebourne.com.

JUNE

The Queen celebrated her Golden Jubilee in 2012 but June 2, 2013, is the anniversary of her coronation. Celebrations will continue around the country and the BBC has said that it will commemorate the event with an evening of live TV, just as it did at the time.

The Royal Academy of Arts' **Summer Exhibition** in London is the world's largest open contemporary art exhibition. Paintings, sculptures, drawings, and models by many distinguished artists jostle with works by unknown and emerging artists. The exhibition is spread over themed rooms, with separate spaces for invited artists and open submissions, so visitors can easily deduce if a canvas of blotched figures or indistinguishable squiggles is from a supposed master or overenthusiastic novice. www.royalacademy.org.uk.

1998	Prime Minister Tony Blair launches "New Britain"—young, stylish, and informal.
1999	England rushes toward the 21st century with the Millennium Dome at Greenwich.
2000	London presides over millennium celebration; gays allowed to serve openly in the military.
2002	Queen Elizabeth, the Queen Mother, dies at age 101.
2005	Suicide bomb attacks devastate London.
2007	Tony Blair steps down; Gordon Brown becomes prime minister.
2009	England suffers economic slowdown.
2010	Conservative David Cameron narrowly becomes prime minister thanks to a coalition with the Liberal Democrats.
2011	Prince William marries Kate Middleton.
2012	Summer Olympic Games in London.

Trooping the Colour is a quintessentially English experience of pomp and ceremony that celebrates Queen Elizabeth II's birthday and sees central London bedecked in flags and regaled by pageantry. Troupes of troops form a procession along St. James's Park and the Queen herself can be glimpsed enjoying the spectacle at the head of the parade—by those lucky enough to secure a good viewing spot. www.royal.gov.uk.

The town of Ascot becomes the focal point of horseracing each June with the return of the **Royal Ascot** meeting. The most famous meeting in the series is the **Gold Cup,** which takes place on Thursday. The Queen herself occasionally enters horses in the race but betting isn't limited to the action on course. Bookies also routinely take bets on what color hat Her Majesty will wear on the day. www.ascot.co.uk.

Whether Londoners are right to claim it as the world's greatest tennis tournament is one thing, but the top-seed players, traditional strawberries and cream, and the infamous rain delays definitely distinguish **Wimbledon** from other Grand Slams. Some of the greatest matches of all time have been fought on Centre Court, 8 miles from central London. www.wimbledon.org.

Glastonbury is the festival-goers' festival. It started in 1970 and features stars now whose *parents* weren't even born then, as well as the likes of Paul McCartney and U2. The Somerset site becomes a city, which is as much effete slumming as hippie chic. And there's usually mud. www.glastonbury festivals.co.uk.

JULY

The Proms concerts take over London's classical musical calendar every summer and, with some justification, can claim to be the greatest classical music festival in the world. Over 8 weeks, the majestic Royal Albert Hall resounds to the sound of dozens of perhaps unexpectedly experimental concerts, all amid a staple diet of symphony orchestra performances. www.bbc.co.uk/proms.

The **Cardiff Festival** features the best in street theatre, live music, family entertainment, funfairs, and drama uniting other bashes such as the International Food & Drink Festival and the Harbour Festival. Events take place throughout the city, mostly at weekends, and many events are free. www.cardiff-festival.com.

Dozens of performances in venues throughout Birmingham attract thousands of visitors each year to the **Birmingham International Jazz Festival.** The event includes impromptu performances and lively sessions hosted everywhere from department stores to parks and restaurants, and winds down with late-night, lounge-style performances from top jazz stars in cozy venues. www.bigbearmusic.com/bijf.

In Suffolk, the **Maverick** festival is Europe's leading country and roots music get together uniting top and trendy names on July 4 weekend from both sides of the Atlantic (such as U.S. actress and *Downton Abbey* star Elizabeth McGovern and her band Sadie and the Hot Heads) for concerts in the barns and paddocks of Easton Farm Park amid a chorus of ducks and geese. www.maverickfestival.co.uk

AUGUST

Liverpool's **International Beatle Week** celebrates the music and lives of one of the most innovative, inspirational, and influential pop groups of all time: The Beatles. Although the band broke up decades ago, they're still proudly celebrated in Liverpool, and here you can see tribute bands from around the world on open-air stages and in all-night marathons. www.beatlesfestival.co.uk.

Around a million people throng the pastel-hued streets of west London for the **Notting Hill Carnival,** Europe's biggest carnival. Fabulous floats make a dazzling circuit of the area and sound systems blast out music all day. Sample delicious Caribbean jerk chicken as you sink into a soundtrack of calypso, soul, funk, and reggae. www.nottinghill-carnival.co.uk.

Manchester stages one of the biggest **Pride** events in Europe, a host of parties, parades, and celebrations as the city sways in a fiesta of fun. The events vary immensely but are reliably chaotic, and endearingly cheeky—much like Manchester itself. www.manchester pride.com.

SEPTEMBER

It's absolutely vital to get your quiff and sideburns just right at the **Porthcawl Elvis Festival** in Wales, the largest Elvis event in Europe. There are official concerts celebrating the King of Rock 'n' Roll but plenty more fun to be had at the fringe festival in 20-plus venues around town. www.elvies.co.uk.

More typically Welsh is the **Llandovery Sheep Festival** (late September), which includes sheep being driven through town, sheep shearing, sheep dog trials, rare breeds auction, and lots of other less-sheepy fun, all fuelled by lots of lamb roasts. llandoverysheepfestival.co.uk

Gentle giants fill the sky over Ashton Court Estate for Bristol's **International Kite Festival.** The aerial extravaganza is the U.K.'s leading showcase for designers, operators, and manufacturers of inflatables, play structures, and air sculptures. www.kite-festival.org.uk.

Peek inside some 700 of the English capital's most famous buildings and best-kept architectural secrets at **London Open House Weekend.** Explore the Foreign Office, Bank of England, and other landmark buildings normally hidden from public view. www.londonopenhouse.org.

OCTOBER

Exemplifying just how provocative and precocious the British art world can be, the **Turner Prize** is awarded to a British artist under 50 and can be relied upon to court controversy and collect commendations year after year. Previous winners have included Chris Ofili and Martin Creed. The works of the nominees are displayed at London's Tate Britain gallery. www.tate.org.uk.

NOVEMBER

Foiled in his attempt to blow up London's Houses of Parliament and murder King James I on November 5, 1605, Guy Fawkes was executed and the safety of the king celebrated with the lighting of bonfires throughout the country. The tradition continues to this day with crowds across the land celebrating **Bonfire Night** around November 5. As darkness descends families gather around a blazing pyre, with a smouldering effigy of Fawkes on top. Huge events occur in towns and cities with thousands of people watching spectacular fireworks displays that end the evening, but there are also plenty of smaller events.

DECEMBER

The **New Year** celebrations in the village of Allendale are more adrenaline-fuelled than most. In the approach to midnight, costumed men balance flaming whisky barrels filled with hot tar—and weighing up to 15kg (33 lb)—on their heads and then toss them onto an unlit bonfire. The bonfire explodes into flames, and at the stroke of midnight everyone joins to dance around the fire and sing "Auld Lang Syne." www.visitnorthumberland.com. London is also increasingly becoming the place to be, with one of the world's biggest fireworks displays lighting up the Thames against a backdrop of Big Ben and the London Eye. www.london.gov.uk.

Public Holidays

England has **eight public holidays:** New Year's Day (Jan 1); Good Friday/Easter Monday (usually Apr); May Public Holiday (first Mon in May); Spring Public Holiday (last Mon in May, or first in June); August Public Holiday (last Mon in Aug); Christmas Day (Dec 25); Boxing Day (Dec 26). If a date such as Christmas Day falls on a Saturday or Sunday, the public holiday rolls over to Monday.

RESPONSIBLE TOURISM

It's difficult to talk about the rights and wrongs of tourism if you're flying several thousand miles to get somewhere. However, there are everyday things you can do to minimize the impact—and especially the carbon footprint—of your travels. Remove chargers from cellphones, PSPs, laptops, and anything else that draws from the mains, once the gadget is fully charged. Turning off all hotel room lights (plus the TV and air-conditioning) can have a massive effect; it really is time all hotels had room card central power switches.

If you're shopping, consider buying seasonal fruit and vegetables or local cheeses from farmers' markets rather than produce sourced by supermarkets from the far side of the globe. Tap water in Britain is always drinkable, and far preferable to a plastic bottle of water that has been pumped out of the earth hundreds of miles away and transported by truck; and although we all need bottled water occasionally when we travel, it makes sense to reuse the bottle. British supermarkets still offer free grocery bags, but are encouraging customers to reuse them, or bring their own bags. Use public transportation to get around cities. And don't rent a car any bigger than you need (apart from anything else, gas/petrol is so expensive in England these days that as well as saving fossil fuel, you'll also be saving yourself from bankruptcy).

Green trips also extend to where you eat and stay. Vegetarian foods tend to have a much smaller impact on the environment because they eschew energy- and resource-intensive meat production. Most hotels now offer you the choice to use your towels for more than 1 night before they are re-laundered—laundry makes up around 40% of an average hotel's energy use. Turning down the air-conditioning whenever you go out obviously also makes a difference. The **Green Tourism Business Scheme** (www.green-business.co.uk) was set up in 1997 and covers the whole of the U.K. It awards grades to hotels that meet various sustainability criteria—businesses that are "actively engaged in reducing the negative environmental and social impacts of their tourism operations." Gold, silver, and bronze award-winners are expected to manage energy effectively, promote public transport and green spaces, and support local cultural activities—and are listed on their website. Properties are assessed every 2 years against strict criteria covering areas such as energy efficiency, waste minimization and recycling, use of local produce, and support of public transport. Green Tourism Week (www.greentourismweek.co.uk) each June pays tribute to the best performers.

For environmentally sensitive hotels try **It's a Green Green World** (www.itsagreengreenworld.com), which lists places, including "eco cottages" powered by the wind and sun. **Responsible Travel** (www.responsibletravel.com, www.responsiblevacation.com in U.S.) is an environmentally aware travel agent. It offers "green holidays" across the U.K., including London. Newspaper green travel sections such as www.telegraph.co.uk/travel/hubs/greentravel and www.guardian.co.uk/travel/green are good places to keep up with the issues and get inspiration. **Vision on Sustainable Tourism** (www.tourism-vision.com) is another excellent news hub. Carbon offsetting (not uncontroversial) can be arranged through, among others, **ClimateCare** (www.climatecare.org). In the U.K., **Tourism Concern** (www.tourismconcern.org.uk) works to reduce social and environmental problems connected with tourism. Visit Britain (www.visitbritain.com) also has its own accreditation scheme for businesses and places to stay.

For flexible **volunteering** opportunities that you can build into your city itinerary, see "Voluntourism & Slow Travel," p. 50.

Getting Back to Basics

There are more than three dozen places in England that have been designated as areas of natural beauty; England also has 10 national parks, 12 national trails, and a protected coastline that stretches for miles and miles, including all of Cornwall. If you're looking for green spaces, there are rolling hills, moorland, vast parks (such as the Peak District in Derbyshire), and even huge green areas in London and other cities. For general information, go to www.enjoyengland.com or call ✆ **020/7678-1400.** Wales also has three National Parks (Brecon Beacons, Snowdonia, and Pembrokeshire Coast) and for summer 2012 the completed Wales Coast Path, which stretches 870 miles, was opened.

If you'd like to explore the National Parks in particular, the best source of information is the **Association of National Park Authorities,** 126 Bute St., Cardiff CF10 5L3, in Wales (www.nationalparks.co.uk; ✆ **029/2049-9966**). It provides information for both Wales and England, from the Yorkshire Dales to Snowdonia in the north of Wales. A trio of National Parks in Wales covers around 20% of the land mass of the country. With the addition of the South Downs (which in 2010 became England's 10th National Park), 10% of the landmass in England and Wales will be part of the National Park system.

Leave No Trace (www.lnt.org) has drawn up a code for outdoor visitors to unspoiled landscapes, such as those found in the English countryside. Park officials can also offer advice on hiking and camping and steer you to festivals or special events being staged.

Those who want to further reduce the size of their carbon footprint can travel on bike. For details on cycling through England (including escorted tours), contact the U.K.'s **National Cyclists Organisation** at CTC, Parklands, Railton Road, Guildford, Surrey GU2 9JX (www.ctc.org.uk; ✆ **0844/736-8450**). Membership is £37.

Organic Holidays (www.organicholidays.co.uk; ✆ **01943/870791**) is a good website that unites like-minded offerings, much involving smart places to stay with an organic food element, although it stretches to putting your own tent up in a field on a certified organic permaculture farm. **Natural Matters** (www.naturalmatters.net; ✆ **01566/781688**) also offers eco-friendly holidays, including the rental of a cottage made of straw bales and using renewable energy.

If you don't want to explore green England on your own, you can take part in an eco-friendly tour. Ranging from canoeing to kayaking, mountain climbing to archeological digs, the best clearing house for adventure trips is **Specialty Travel Index** (www.specialtytravel.com; ✆ **888/624-4030**).

The **Association of Independent Tour Operators** (www.aito.co.uk) is a group of specialist operators leading the field in making U.K. holidays sustainable. The **Association of British Travel Agents** (ABTA; www.abta.com) acts as a focal point for the U.K. travel industry, and is one of the leading groups spearheading responsible tourism in Britain.

SPECIAL INTEREST TOURS

Cycling

The **National Cycle Network** ★★ covers 10,000 miles, running from Dover on the south coast to Inverness in the Scottish Highlands. Most routes use old railway lines, canal towpaths, and riversides. The **C2C (Coast to Coast or Sea to Sea) Cycle Route** runs 140 miles from the Irish Sea to the North Sea across the Pennines, Dales, and Lake District. The **Essex Cycle Route** covers 250 miles of countryside, through some of England's most charming villages. The **Devon Coast to Coast Route** runs 90 miles across the southwest peninsula, skirting Dartmoor. The **West Country Way** links the Cornish coast to Bath and Bristol for 248 miles. And the

Severn & Thames Cycle Route runs 100 miles linking two of Britain's major rivers.

Sustrans (www.sustrans.org.uk; ☎ **0845/113-0065**) has full information and free online maps of the Network. The **Cyclists Touring Club** (www.ctc.org.uk; ☎ **0844/736-8450**) can suggest routes and provide information and maps. Membership in the U.K. costs £39 a year and includes a bi-monthly magazine, maps, and cycle shop discounts. For a free copy of *Britain for Cyclists,* with information on routes, call the **British Tourist Authority** (☎ **800/462-2748** in the U.S., or 888/847-4885 in Canada), or contact U.S. operator **Euro-Bike & Walking Tours** (www.eurobike.com; ☎ **800/575-1540** in the U.S. and Canada).

Fishing

Fly-fishing was born here, and it's an art form. Local fishing guides are available to lead you to waters that are well stocked with trout, perch, grayling, sea bream, Atlantic salmon, and such lesser-known species as rudd and roach. The **Salmon & Trout Association,** Fishmonger's Hall, London Bridge, London EC4R 9EL (www.salmon-trout.org; ☎ **020/7283-5838**), has information about British fishing regulations.

Golf

Golf has been around in Britain since Edward VII first began stamping over the greens of such courses as Royal Lytham & St. Annes, in the Northwest, and Royal St. Georges, near London. Yet, despite its huge popularity, golf in Britain remains a clubby sport where some of the most prestigious courses are reserved for members. Rules at most British golf courses tend to be stricter in matters of dress code and protocol than their equivalents in the United States.

Golf International, 14 E. 38th St., New York, NY 10016 (www.golfinternational.com; ☎ **800/833-1389** or 212/986-9176), can open doors with packages from 7 to 14 days, including as much or as little golf, on as many different courses, as a participant wants. **Adventures in Golf,** 22 Greeley St., Ste. 7, Merrimack, NH 03054 (www.adventures-in-golf.com; ☎ **877/424-7320** or 603/424-7320), and **Jerry Quinlan's Celtic Golf,** 1129 Rte. 9 South, Cape May Courthouse, NJ 08210 (www.celticgolf.com; ☎ **800/535-6148** or 609/465-0600), also arrange tours, during which you can stay anywhere from guesthouses to manor houses.

Sailing

Britain has a rich maritime heritage and there are plenty of opportunities to get afloat. There are sailing schools and charter operations all round the coast, as well as on inland lakes and rivers. **The Royal Yachting Association,** RYA House, Ensign Way, Hamble, Hants SO31 4YA (www.rya.org.uk; ☎ **023-8060-4100**), can provide a list of suitable companies. There is also a wealth of advice and instruction among the books published by Wiley Nautical (www.wileynautical.com).

Hiking, Walking & Other Activities

England and Wales alone have some 100,000 miles of trails and footpaths. The **Ramblers' Association,** Camelford House, 87–90 Albert Embankment, 2nd Floor, London SE1 7TW (www.ramblers.org.uk; ☎ **020/7339-8500,** or 029/2064-4308 in Wales), has several books and maps on hiking and walking in Great Britain. Prices range from free to £15.

Visit Wales has a comprehensive file of active options on www.visitwales.co.uk/active, from fishing to climbing, caving to rappelling (abseiling), plus alternative activities such as bushcraft and archery. In Wales there are many companies offering activities, such as Adventure Britain (www.adventurebritain.com; ✆ 01639/700388), offering caving, gorge walking, canyoning, canoeing, coasteering, and climbing in and near Brecon Beacons National Park.

There are many companies across England and Wales with tours focused on an individual area. For the mountain terrain of Wales's Snowdonia National Park, **Pathfinder,** Clynnog Fawr, Tan-yr-allt, Caernarfon, Gwynedd LL54 5NS, in North Wales (www.pathfindersnowdonia.co.uk; ✆ 01286/660202), offers walks of the summits, as well as rock climbing, kayaking, and rafting, among other activities.

Drover Holidays (www.droverholidays.co.uk; ✆ 01497/821144) has introduced electric bikes alongside its regular models in the Brecon Beacons, arranging both guided and self-guided tours. A guided tour with electric bike starts at about £220 for a weekend, with B&B, luggage transfers, and rail station pickup. Drover also has walking tours.

Walking Holidays (www.bathwestwalks.com; ✆ 01761/233807) has guided tours through the West Country and the Cotswolds, taking in such attractions as the Wiltshire Downs and the Mendip Hills, as well as the coastal scenery of Exmoor.

One of Britain's leading specialist companies, **Headwater** (www.headwater.com; ✆ 01606/720199) has several self-guided tours, with classy places to stay. There's Wye Valley cycling, which includes bikes and baggage transfers between hotels (including a Regency coaching inn in Hay-on-Wye) for 5 nights, while you crisscross between England and Wales. There are also 5-night independent walking tours, in the Cotswolds and from Oxford to Stratford-upon-Avon, which again include luggage transfers and luxury hotels and inns. The tours cost about £500.

Discovery Travel (www.discoverytravel.co.uk; ✆ 01904/632226) has a number of self-guided walking holidays in England and Wales. **Wilderness Travel** (www.wildernesstravel.com; ✆ 800/368-2794 or 510/558-2488) has treks and inn-to-inn hiking tours, including a 2-week coast-to-coast ramble across England.

English Lakeland Ramblers (www.ramblers.com; ✆ 800/724-8801 or 703/680-4276) offers 7- or 8-day walking tours for the average active person in places such as the Lake District. A minibus takes hikers and sightseers daily to trails and sightseeing points. Experts tell you about the area's culture and history and highlight its natural wonders. There are also tours of the Cotswolds, as well as inn-to-inn tours and privately guided tours.

Country Walkers (www.countrywalkers.com; ✆ 800/464-9255 or 802/244-1387) has "walking vacations" that last 7 days in the Cotswolds and the Lake District.

For a refreshingly different take on hiking the countryside, the website www.walkinganddrinkingbeer.blogspot.com, by American writer Rich Grant, features engaging features for walkers who hope to encounter good English beer around every corner. **Beer Tours** (www.beertoursuk.com; ✆ 01829/250502) offers 3- to 5-day tours starting in Chester and visiting breweries in the North, Midlands, and North Wales, along with pubs from the quirky to the grand. There's also a beer-tasting and a beer-matched dinner. The website www.visitabrewery.co.uk lists almost 30 breweries in the Cask Masque beer excellence scheme and gives details of their tours.

The **British Activity Holiday Association** (www.baha.org.uk; ✆ 01244/301342) has details of activity camps, family holidays, day camps, and adult breaks.

Horseback Riding

There are a number of companies in Britain offering horse-riding holidays. **Equestrian Escapes** (www.equestrian-escapes.com; ✆ **01829/781133**) is a good example, with breaks including beach riding in Cornwall, spa and ride in the Brecon Beacons (both from 2 nights), to family holidays in Berkshire, just an hour from London.

Various U.S. companies, such as **Equitour** (www.ridingtours.com; ✆ **800/545-0019** or 307/455-3363), offer horseback-riding package tours of Britain. Two types of 7-day trips can be arranged: One based at a stable beside the Bristol Channel, or on the fields of Dartmoor, with instruction in jumping and dressage, and tours in Wales, with a 7-day trek. On the latter, riders spend nights at different B&Bs or inns and keep their mount at nearby stables.

Eastern Trekking Associates (✆ **888/836-6152** or 706/541-2450) leads small groups of around six riders each on tours of the Exmoor region, arguably the most beautiful district of England. Horseback-riding trips are also arranged in Wales.

Literary Tours

Lynott Tours (www.lynotttours.com; ✆ **800/221-2474**) has a number of tours, including "Jane Austen, Beatrix Potter, and the Brontës" (taking in the Lake District and Yorkshire) and "Literary Cotswolds." Hotels, guide, and most meals are included. The **British Connection** (www.thebritishconnection.com; ✆ **404/373-1420**) offers literary tours with a focus on Shakespeare, Jane Austen, Agatha Christie, and even mystery writers.

Rail Tours

Great Rail Journeys (www.greatrail.com; ✆ **01904/734154**) offers luxury escorted tours by rail (mostly aboard steam train and all involving steam journeys) throughout England and Wales. **UK Railtours** (www.ukrailtours.com; ✆ **01438/715050**) has a large number of day trips on railways, mostly historic, although some involving modern trains on unusual goods routes, which include travel from several stops en route. The **Railway Touring Company** (www.railwaytouring.co.uk; ✆ **01553/661500**) puts together wonderful days out on steam trains (the Cumbrian Mountain Express, the Sussex Belle), which set off from various points around the U.K.

University Study Programs

You can study British literature at renowned universities such as Oxford and Cambridge during the week and then take weekend excursions to the countryside of Shakespeare, Austen, Dickens, and Hardy. While doing your coursework, you can live in dormitories with other students and dine in elaborate halls or the more intimate Fellows' clubs. Studies in England are not limited to the liberal arts, or to high school or college students. Some programs are designed specifically for teachers and seniors.

Affiliated with Richmond College in London, the **American Institute for Foreign Study** (www.aifs.com; ✆ **866/906-2437** or 203/399-5000) offers 4 weeks or more for high-school students, as well as internships and academic programs for college students. There are also courses leading to an MBA.

The **Institute of International Education (IIE)** (www.iie.org; ✆ **212/883-8200**) administers a variety of academic, training, and grant programs for the U.S. Information Agency (USIA), including Fulbright grants. It is especially helpful in arranging enrollment for U.S. students in summer school programs. **Worldwide**

Classrooms, P.O. Box 1166, Milwaukee, WI 53201 (www.worldwide.edu; ✆ 414/224-3476), produces an extensive listing of schools offering study-abroad programs in England.

Escorted Tours

Escorted tours are structured group tours, with a group leader. The price usually includes everything from airfare to hotels, meals, tours, admission costs, and local transportation.

Abercrombie & Kent (www.abercrombiekent.com; ✆ 800/554-7016) offers extremely upscale escorted tours that are loaded with luxury. **Martin Randall Travel** (www.martinrandall.com; ✆ 800/988-6168) features cultural tours led by expert lecturers in archeology, architecture, art, history, music, and so on. Its tours focus on everything from English country houses and gardens to Hadrian's Wall to the Welsh National Opera in Cardiff. It also has all-inclusive classical music holidays timed for international festivals.

Other U.S. contenders in the upscale package-tour business include **Maupintour** (www.maupintour.com; ✆ 800/255-4266) and **Tauck World Discovery** (www.tauck.com; ✆ 800/788-7885).

But not all escorted tours are pricey. One of the U.K.'s leading tour operators, **Shearings** (www.shearings.com; ✆ 0844/824-6351), has a number of tours lasting between 5 and 10 days, including decent hotels and most meals. The trips available from www.coachholidays.com (✆ 0845/330-3747) bring together more than 80 operators, often with discount prices.

U.S.-based **Trafalgar Tours** (www.trafalgartours.com; ✆ 866/544-4434) offers affordable packages, with lodgings in unpretentious hotels. Seven-day itineraries start from a little over $1,000, not including flights. One of Trafalgar's leading competitors, with similar tours, is **Globus & Cosmos Tours** (www.globusandcosmos.com; ✆ 866/755-8581).

There are a number of companies within the U.K. offering tours. **Travelsphere** (www.travelsphere.co.uk; ✆ 0844/567-9960) is one of the leading escorted operators, putting together trips that take in castles and gardens, and particularly scenic railways in England and Wales.

For more information on escorted tours, see www.frommers.com/planning.

Voluntourism & Slow Travel

If you have an interest in giving something back, try volunteering while you're here. Conservation charity **BTCV** (www.btcv.org; ✆ 020/7278-4294) is always looking for people to help with projects such as clearing ponds and coppicing woodland. Anyone can volunteer via the website, and it's free to take part. There are many sessions that are part of the charity's Green Gym, which makes sure you stay fit as you help. It's also worth keeping an eye on **Timebank** (www.timebank.org.uk). This online resource helps you match your location and availability with volunteering opportunities nearby—although most are more suited to a long stay or residency.

Volunteering England (www.volunteering.org.uk; ✆ 020/7520-8900) is a charity that works with groups such as Friends of the Earth to find volunteers for projects; many of them are conservation-minded, although it also works in other areas, and was involved in finding volunteer helpers for London's 2012 Olympics Games. Before you commit to voluntary work, it's important to make sure of its aims, who will benefit, and whether the work will suit you. **Volunteer International**

(www.volunteerinternational.org) has a helpful list of questions to ask to determine the intentions and nature of a project.

USEFUL TERMS & LANGUAGE

There are dialects and language variations across England and Wales, far too many to give a full breakdown (and language changes rapidly these days), but here are a selection of words that you might encounter, and which pretty much transcend local barriers.

bangers sausages; usually paired with mashed potato for "bangers and mash"

banging good; usually applied to music

barking crazy or mad; coined from a former asylum in London's eastern suburb of Barking

barney an argument or disagreement

bedlam madness; as in "the roads are bedlam today"; a corruption of "Bethlehem," an asylum formerly at the corner of Moorgate and London Wall, in the City

black cab an official black taxi, as opposed to a private hire "minicab"; only black cabs are permitted to tout for fares curbside

butcher's a look (from Cockney "butcher's hook"); as in "can I have a butcher's?"

BYO short for "bring your own"; a restaurant that doesn't have a license to sell alcoholic drinks but will happily open any you bring along, sometimes for a small corkage fee

circus a (usually circular) coming together of streets, as at Piccadilly Circus and Finsbury Circus in London

clink a prison; after the former Clink Prison, on London's South Bank

damage the cost or bill; as in "what's the damage?"

dodgy not to be trusted, suspect; as in "that £20 note looks dodgy"

dosh money; also "bread" or "dough"

gaff home; "back to my gaff" means "back to my place"

G 'n' T gin and tonic; served with "ice and a slice," i.e. an ice cube (two if you're lucky) and a lemon wedge

greasy spoon a basic cafe known for fried food

gutted extremely disappointed; as in "I'm gutted that Arsenal beat Spurs last night"

lager straw-hued, fizzy beer such as Budweiser and Foster's, served colder than traditional ales (although it's a myth that English beers are served "warm," lager should appear at cool cellar temperature)

naff cheap looking, or unfashionable

Porter type of dark, strong ale; London brewers Fuller's and Meantime both brew contemporary versions

pint both a measure of beer and a general term for having a drink; as in "do you fancy going for a pint later?"

quid one pound; "10 quid" or "a tenner" is £10

subway pedestrian underpass; London's underground railway is "the Tube"

How to Speak Welsh

To the novice, it's quite extraordinary just how *Welsh* Wales is. Signs, addresses, place names, and menus are mostly in both Welsh and English, which can be baffling in itself. Road signs are in both languages, which leads the unwary to suspect there are two different towns ahead. And then sometimes there's a lone sign that's just Welsh, making you think you've missed the road to Cardiff. Because, unlike many other languages, there's rarely a translation obvious to the untrained eye. Pembrokeshire becomes Dyfed while Cardigan comes in slightly closer as Cerdigion. *Llan* (which seems to be the start of half the place names) means "church," while *aber* (which seems to start the other half) is "river mouth."

Several words it is handy to know are *gwesty* (hotel), *siôp* (shop), *gorsaf* (station), *traeth* (beach), *ffordd* (road), and *cawl cennin* (leek soup).

And while we're on the subject we shouldn't forget the classic Llanfairpwllgwyngyllgogerychwyrndrobwllllantysiliogogogoch, the village in Anglesey, which (roughly) is translated as: "The Church of St. Mary by the pool with the white hazel near the rapid whirlpool by St. Tysilio's church and the red cave." On the road signs you'll see it as Llanfair PG, which isn't half as much fun.

aber	river mouth	**ffordd**	road
afon	river	**gorsaf**	station
araf	slow	**gwesty**	hotel
bach/fach	small	**heddlu**	police
bont/pont	bridge	**llan**	church lands
bwlch	gap, pass	**llyn**	lake
carreg	stone	**llwybr cyhoeddus**	public footpath
cefn	ridge	**lôn**	lane
coed	wood	**marched**	ladies
croes/groes	cross	**mynydd**	mountain
cwm	valley	**pen**	top
dim	no	**rhyd**	ford
dim mynediad	no entry	**siôp**	shop
dinas	fort, city	**Swyddfa'r Post**	Post Office
dynion	gentlemen	**toiledau**	toilets
eglwys	church	**traeth**	beach
fawr/mawr	big	**ysbyty**	hospital
felin/melin	mill		

SUGGESTED ITINERARIES

by Nick Dalton & Deborah Stone

T he trick is in the planning. Don't just start your trip and expect it to all come together. Plan ahead and you can get much more out of your time. Here are some suggestions for trips, using both road and rail. They might look rushed but they're realistic. The first is general interest and the second homes in on a fascinating region; the others are for those with special interests: gardens and families. They're designed for a week but you can take longer, or you could fit two together for a fun-packed fortnight. What they do is show just how compact England and Wales are, and how much you can fit in. Have fun!

3

REGIONS IN BRIEF

England is a part of the United Kingdom, which comprises England, Wales, Scotland, and Northern Ireland. Only 50,327 sq. miles—about the size of New York State—England has an amazing amount of countryside and wilderness and an astonishing regional, physical, and cultural diversity. See the map in the insert at the beginning of this book for the regions outlined below.

England

LONDON   Around 7 million Londoners live here, although "London" extends to cover more than 609 sq. miles. The City of London is rather different, just 1 sq. mile. The rest is the city (as opposed to the City, the financial hub), which gives way to towns and boroughs. London's outlying areas are described in chapter 4. A new attraction to the east of the City is the Olympic Park, heart of the 2012 Games, with the Olympic stadium, wave-shaped Aquatics Centre, and the futuristic Velodrome.

THE THAMES VALLEY   England's most famous river continues westward from Kew to its source in the Cotswolds. A land of meadows, woodlands, attractive villages, market towns, and rolling hillsides, this is one of England's most gently scenic areas. Highlights include **Windsor Castle** (Elizabeth II's chosen residence) and nearby **Eton College,** founded by a young Henry VI in 1440. **Henley-on-Thames,** site of the Royal Regatta, is one of the best Thames-side towns; and at the university city of **Oxford,** you can tour the colleges.

THE SOUTHEAST (KENT, SURREY & SUSSEX)   This is the land of Admiral Nelson and Virginia Woolf, Sir Winston Churchill and J. M. W. Turner. The area of Kent around Chatham and Rochester is also Charles Dickens territory, where he lived and where he set many stories—and which was at the heart of 2012 celebrations on the 200th anniversary of his birth. The Southeast is where you'll find the boisterous seaside city of **Brighton;** and **Canterbury,** famed for its religious pilgrimages and cathedral. Kent has many castles and stately homes (exquisite **Leeds Castle, Chartwell,** where Churchill lived) and also the dockyards that Nelson sailed from. Sussex has many coastal beauty spots (such as West Wittering beach) and lovely towns, including Chichester, as well as the South Downs Way, a wild walk across chalk hills just inland. Surrey, on the edge of London, is often overlooked, yet has Thames-side towns, the Surrey Hills (with Leith Hill, the highest point in the Southeast), the city of Guildford, and forest and heathland that offers splendid walks.

HAMPSHIRE & WILTSHIRE   Southwest of London, these counties possess two of England's greatest **cathedrals,** Winchester and Salisbury, and Europe's most significant prehistoric monument, **Stonehenge.** Hampshire is bordered on its western side by the woodlands and heaths of the **New Forest.** The towns of **Portsmouth** and **Southampton** loom large in naval heritage; the former's historic dockyard is where you can see Nelson's flagship, HMS *Victory.* The **Isle of Wight,** once Queen Victoria's favorite retreat, is a seaside haven trapped in time. Wiltshire is the beginning of the **West Country;** here you'll find Wilton House, the 17th-century home of the earls of Pembroke, and Old Sarum, the remains of what is believed to have been an Iron Age fortification.

THE SOUTHWEST (DORSET, SOMERSET, DEVON & CORNWALL)   This is the area most associated with summer getaways, with miles of beautiful coastline—England's first natural World Heritage Site encompasses the coast of Dorset and East Devon, known as the Jurassic Coast for its geology and fossils. Dorset, Thomas Hardy country, is a land of rolling downs, rocky headlands, well-kept villages, and rich farmlands. Somerset offers such magical spots as **Glastonbury** (with the country's greatest music festival) and beaches galore. Devon has both **Exmoor** and **Dartmoor national parks,** and its northern and southern coastlines are peppered with grand resorts and pretty villages. In Cornwall, you're never more than 20 miles from the rugged coastline, which terminates at **Land's End.** This is also were King Arthur is said to have lived, at **Tintagel Castle.** Among the cities worth visiting in the region are **Bath,** with its impressive Roman baths and Georgian architecture; **Plymouth,** the departure point of the *Mayflower;* and **Wells,** the site of a great cathedral.

THE COTSWOLDS   This area features classic English countryside encompassing parts of Oxfordshire, Gloucestershire, Somerset, Wiltshire, Warwickshire, and Worcestershire. Limestone villages sit amongst green hills, a scene that's barely changed in hundreds of years. Here you'll find lovely pubs and market towns, glorious gardens and stately homes. Names such as Broadway, Bourton-on-the-Water, Lower and Upper Slaughter, Snowshill, and Stow-on-the-Wold are all worth dropping in on. **Cirencester** is the uncrowned capital of the Cotswolds, and **Cheltenham** is an elegant Regency spa town.

STRATFORD & WARWICK   This is Shakespeare country and the heart of England, in a region that was to be the birthplace of the Industrial Revolution. **Stratford-upon-Avon** is Shakespeare's home town, filled with historic sites and a fabulous riverside theatre. **Warwick Castle,** one of England's great castles, is a huge tourist experience, and the ruins of **Kenilworth Castle** are worth seeing too.

BIRMINGHAM & THE WEST MIDLANDS   **Birmingham** is Britain's largest city after London. This sprawling metropolis was once known for its overpass jungles and grubby suburbs, but is becoming the heart of new Britain with its urban makeover. The English marshes cut through **Shropshire** and **Herefordshire.** The **Ironbridge Gorge** was at the heart of the Industrial Revolution (and should be on everyone's must-see list), and the famous **Potteries** are in Staffordshire.

EAST ANGLIA (ESSEX, CAMBRIDGESHIRE, NORFOLK & SUFFOLK)   This area comprises the flatlands that start to the east of London and stretch all the way to the sea, a place that once was a kingdom in itself. You'll find **Constable Country** (the gentle landscapes that fill John Constable's paintings), but also the **Fens,** drained and fertile plains of a beguiling starkness out of which looms **Ely Cathedral. Cambridge,** with its colleges, is a big attraction, and everyone should have a go at punting on the River Cam. The coast of Essex is startlingly attractive, while farther north is Suffolk (with the genteel seaside town of Southwold), and Norfolk, where the north-facing coast is windswept, bleak, and beautiful.

THE EAST MIDLANDS (DERBYSHIRE, LEICESTERSHIRE, LINCOLNSHIRE, NORTHAMPTONSHIRE & NOTTINGHAMSHIRE)   Derbyshire's Peak District is one of Britain's rugged charms; here you'll find **Chatsworth House,** the seat of the dukes of Devonshire. Northamptonshire has **Sulgrave Manor,** the ancestral home of George Washington, and **Althorp House,** the childhood home of Diana, Princess of Wales. **Lincoln** has one of England's great cathedrals. **Nottingham** recalls Robin Hood, though Sherwood Forest is not what it was in the outlaw's heyday.

THE NORTHWEST   Here you'll find the magnificent port city of Liverpool, once a major gateway to the U.S., and childhood home to the most famous pop group of all, the Beatles. There's also Manchester, Britain's one-time industrial heart, and now a hip, happening place. Along with those you've got the charming walled Roman city of **Chester,** and the brash but unmissable seaside resort of **Blackpool** with its cheap and cheerful fun by the sea.

THE LAKE DISTRICT   Here is some of England's most dramatic scenery: A lake around every bend, hemmed in by ominous peaks (snow-tipped until early summer), with tiny roads and little towns. It's a place of poetry and literature, home to, among others, Wordsworth, Samuel Taylor Coleridge, John Ruskin, and Beatrix Potter. **Windermere** is perhaps the best location for touring the area, but there are many other charming towns, including **Grasmere** and **Ambleside.**

YORKSHIRE & NORTHUMBRIA   Yorkshire is the setting for stories by the Brontës and vet James Herriot. **York,** with its immense cathedral and medieval streets, is one of England's most magnificent ancient cities. Northumbria takes in **Northumberland, Cleveland, Durham,** and **Tyne and Wear** (the area around **Newcastle,** a city that's now a throbbing arts and culture destination). **Hadrian's Wall,** built by the Romans to keep out marauding Scots, is staggering. Durham cathedral is one of Britain's finest examples of Norman architecture, **Fountains Abbey** is among the country's greatest ecclesiastical ruins, while **Castle Howard** is a great country home.

Wales

CARDIFF & SOUTHERN WALES   The capital of Wales, **Cardiff** is a city reborn, the docks where coal and slate were once shipped out turned into Cardiff Bay, a tourist attraction of arts, food, watersports, and leisure. In the old heart are the vast

National Museum of Wales, with everything from a huge collection of Impression-ist paintings to an animatronic woolly mammoth, as well as the quite astonishing Victoria decorative arts delight of **Cardiff Castle.** It's only a short journey to the **Big Pit,** with its mining history (and mine tour). Southern Wales is full of other delights, from the mountainous beauty of **Brecon Beacons National Park** to the wild coast-line of Pembrokeshire and the west. West of Cardiff is **Swansea,** birthplace of Dylan Thomas; you'll also find places he lived as you travel farther west.

NORTH WALES   This is where you'll find Snowdonia National Park, a massive area of mountains, rivers, lakes, and rugged coast; at its heart is Snowdon, the highest point in England and Wales at 1,085m (3,560 ft.). Once you've done this, it's time to move on to see historic castles such as **Harlech, Caernarfon,** and especially **Conwy Castle,** ordered by Edward I and a masterpiece of medieval architecture. The playful Italianate coastal village of Portmeirion is a delight, and you'll find more historic railways than you could do in one trip.

ENGLAND HIGHLIGHTS (1 WEEK)

If you're coming to England for a short time, you want to make the most of it. And our week-long tour does just that. It might seem packed, but that's what you're here for. If you'd like to slow down for a bit then feel free to drop a place or two to save a day to relax. This tour gives you a good dip into London **(the Tower of London, British Museum),** and then takes you on an edited highlights trip of all those places you could name without hardly thinking **(Windsor Castle, Stratford-upon-Avon, Oxford, Hampton Court).**

Days 1 & 2: London Calling

Start on the banks of the Thames, the mighty river that flows through London. A ride on the **London Eye** (p. 108), near Westminster Bridge, the world's larg-est observation wheel, is the way to get your bearings. The ride takes 30 min-utes. Afterwards, check out Westminster Bridge with its wonderful view of the **Houses of Parliament** and the clock tower **Big Ben** (although the name is actually that of the bell; p. 100). Walk past them and you're immediately at **Westminster Abbey** (p. 103), where most of England's queens and kings have been crowned and where they lie at rest. Check out the fan-vaulted Henry VII's Chapel (one of the loveliest in all of Europe), the shrine to Edward the Confes-sor, and Poets' Corner, where the literati (Chaucer, Dickens, Tennyson) are buried. Allow 1 hour here.

Now it's time for a stroll up **Whitehall,** passing **10 Downing Street,** the official residence of the prime minister (you can join the crowd gawking at the gates), to **Trafalgar Square** (p. 93). Towering over the pedestrianized square is Nelson's Column, a tribute to Admiral Nelson. It's the thing to have your photo taken in front of one of the stone lions at the base. On one side of the square is the **National Gallery** (p. 90), where you can do a highlights tour of the gallery's 30 must-see paintings, which include Van Gogh's sunflowers and works by Gainsborough, Monet, and Vermeer. You could easily spend 1½ hours here, but it's worth nipping next door to the **National Portrait Gallery** (p. 91) with everything from Old Masters to pop art by David Oxtoby and Andy Warhol.

Suggested England Itineraries

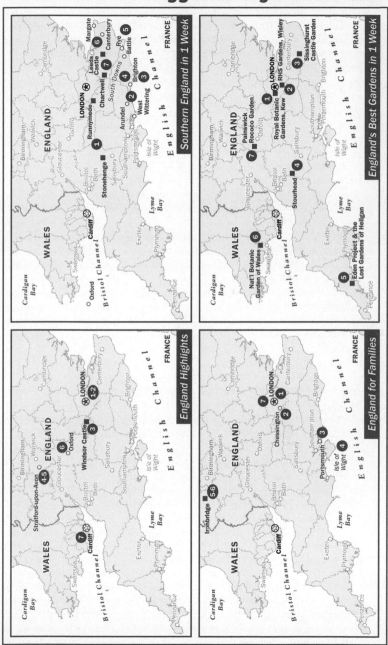

Head up Long Acre to **Covent Garden** (p. 154), the former fruit and vegetable market, now full of shops, cafes, sandwich bars, and, often, street entertainers. Treat yourself to a swift lunch break.

Wander along the **Strand** back to Trafalgar Square, and straight across and up the **Mall** all the way to **Buckingham Palace** (p. 88). Stare at the guardsmen, and maybe even pose with one for a photo. Turn around and head into St. James's Park where you can walk by the lake, coming out near Parliament Square. Head across Westminster Bridge again, and walk along the river, past the London Eye, and onto the South Bank arts area. Here is the 1950s grand **Royal Festival Hall** where you may be able to pick up good-priced tickets for a play (which is likely to feature top stars). Whether you do or not, there may well be free music in the foyer (which has a bar), or there are a number of other places, mostly with outside tables, where you can relax with a glass of wine.

On **Day 2,** start at the world's most impressive city castle, the **Tower of London** (p. 112). There's an hour-long guided tour by a Yeoman (a "Beefeater") plus exhibitions of Royal treasures, so allow 2 hours here. Afterward, walk out onto Tower Bridge and marvel at the Victorian engineering feat. Turn back and head down onto the embankment, past the Tower Hotel, and into St. Katherine Docks. The old dock is now full of yachts and gin palaces, plus coffee houses and restaurants. From St. Katherine's Pier hop aboard a river bus for the short ride past the Tower, the South Bank, and the Savoy Hotel to Embankment Pier. Hop off and walk up Charing Cross Road, full of old bookshops, and to the **British Museum** (p. 85). This is the mammoth home of one of the world's greatest treasure-troves—much of it plundered from other parts of the globe when Britannia ruled the waves. The most exciting of these treasures are the Elgin Marbles, taken from Greece, and the Rosetta Stone, taken from Egypt. You'll need at least 2 hours for the most cursory of visits.

Now walk east along Holborn and veer off into London's legal quarter, taking in placid Lincoln's Inn Fields. Drop down onto Fleet Street, once home to Britain's newspaper industry, which has gorgeous views of St. Paul's Cathedral up Ludgate Hill. This whole walk may take an hour. To bolster your energy levels, pop into El Vino, a dark, old wine bar, once the Fleet Street haunt of journalists, who are now outnumbered by lawyers. **St. Paul's,** masterpiece of architect Sir Christopher Wren, is your next stop (p. 112). And you can get up to the dome, for London views and nerve-jangling looks down to the ground.

Your work's almost done. Just wander down the footpath to the river and onto the Millennium Bridge, a narrow footbridge, which has terrific views up and down the river. On the other side is the **Tate Modern** (p. 110), a vast, brick power station converted into one of the world's most exciting art museums. If you have the energy you can have a walk around (it's free); if not, just poke your nose in and retire to the riverfront cafe-bar for a drink, or maybe to the seventh-floor restaurant for dinner with one of the best views in London.

Day 3: Windsor Castle

This is a perfect day trip, and calmer than the previous 2 days. Windsor and **Windsor Castle** (p. 199) are just half an hour's train ride from London's Waterloo or Paddington stations. Windsor is a place the Queen loves, and she spends lots of time here. There's pageantry to rival the Changing of the Guard ceremony at Buckingham Palace, from April to July, Monday to Saturday at 11am (off-season hours differ slightly—see p. 200). Wander through **St.**

George's Chapel, where some monarchs are entombed; and stroll through **Jubilee Gardens.** You'll need at least 2 hours, and maybe a bit more as you should have a quick look around the riverside town.

Head back to London, probably in the late afternoon, and you might want to have a quiet walk in **Hyde Park** (p. 95). It's a tranquil spot at any time of year, with the long lake, the Serpentine, cutting across the middle like a rural river. It's an easy walk into **Kensington Gardens** (basically it's the same park, the other side of the road) for a look at the Albert Memorial, Queen Victoria's monumental tribute to her late husband. Now you're in the Kensington/Knightsbridge area and it's not finding a restaurant that's the problem, it's the choosing.

Days 4 & 5: Stratford-upon-Avon

From Paddington Station, you can be in the lovely riverside town of **Stratford-upon-Avon** in 2 hours. After checking into a hotel for 2 nights, head for the **Shakespeare Birthplace Trust** (p. 454), which owns five Shakespeare-related properties, and buy a global ticket. Start with **Shakespeare's Birthplace** (p. 457); pop into **Holy Trinity Church** (p. 456), where he's buried; and then move onto **Hall's Croft** (p. 456), where his daughter Susanna lived. At some point you might want a spot of lunch—the riverside terrace at the **Royal Shakespeare Theatre** (p. 454) is a good spot. While at the theatre, see if there are tickets available for tomorrow. Later, for dinner, you don't need to head farther than the **Black Swan,** generally called the **Dirty Duck** (p. 459). The old riverside pub is the place for a drink, and you can either eat in the bar or in its Conservatory restaurant.

On the morning of **Day 5,** continue with the Shakespeare theme, visiting **Anne Hathaway's Cottage** (p. 456), the thatched, childhood home of his wife, and **Mary Arden's House (Glebe Farm) & Palmer's Farm** (p. 456), his mother's childhood home.

Don't stop for lunch; instead, grab a sandwich, and get the train to Warwick, 8 miles away. Here is **Warwick Castle** (p. 463), one of England's most perfect castles. It's now a full-fledged medieval theme zone, but walking around the place is a singular experience itself.

Return to Stratford, where the glass-walled, Art Deco-tinged rooftop restaurant in the 1930s' Royal Shakespeare Theatre serves pre-performance dinners beginning at 4:30pm. Then you can see the Shakespeare production we know you managed to get tickets for …

Day 6: Oxford

You can get to Oxford by train in a little over 1½ hours, changing at Banbury or Leamington Spa, so you'll be at the university city by mid-morning. Head straight for the **Oxford Tourist Information Centre** (p. 214), a 5-minute walk from the station, and sign up for one of the regular 2-hour walking tours. You'll get a knowledgeable view of the city, and often your small group will go inside otherwise-closed college gates.

Have lunch at the 17th-century **Turf Tavern** (p. 224), tucked away down an alleyway; it's where Bill Clinton used to drink while at university.

Refreshed, walk around the corner to the **Ashmolean** (p. 215), one of Britain's finest museums, which rivals the British Museum in its hoard of ancient things; its Egypt galleries reopened in 2011, the latest phase of a huge revamp. Around the corner again is the quirky **Pitt Rivers Museum** (p. 217), based around the collection of early archeologist and anthropologist General Pitt-Rivers.

Relax over dinner at the **Cherwell Boathouse** (p. 220), a summertime punt station on the Cherwell, and an acclaimed year-round restaurant with terrace.

Day 7: Cardiff

It may seem unlikely, but heading off to Wales for the day can be done; the hourly train takes only 1¾ hours (changing at Didcot, in the Cotswolds). You'll arrive mid-morning and should walk straight to the **National Museum and Gallery** (p. 683), where you can get a nice coffee in the foyer cafe before browsing the collection of Impressionists, archeological finds, and geographical exhibits. Don't spend too long because you need to dart around the corner to **Cardiff Castle** (p. 682). This isn't a sensible castle at all but a Victorian Arts & Crafts folly on a medieval base, the work of a Welsh coal baron—the richest man in the world—who could pretty much do as he wished. Have a bite at the cafe, with views from the terrace across the grounds and up at the castle on its mound while you're waiting for your tour to start.

Afterward, it's time to hop on the Baycar bendy-bus outside to nip over to **Cardiff Bay** (p. 684); it only takes a few minutes. Once there, you can see how much time you've got, and how late you feel like getting back to London. You'll find yourself by Roald Dahl Plass, the big open space, with iconic water sculpture, between the copper-topped Wales Millennium Centre and the Bay. The brand new **Dr. Who Experience** (p. 686) exhibition in its purpose-built home is great fun, and take a wander out past the old Pierhead Building, the Senedd (the Welsh parliament), and back. Treat yourself to one of the country's best ice creams at **Cadwaladers Ice Cream Café** (p. 687) on the waterfront, and think about getting the train back.

SOUTHERN ENGLAND IN 1 WEEK

It's all very well tearing around a country, but sometimes there are great bits on your doorstep that you ignore, or don't even know about. Southern England can be a bit like that. It doesn't quite have the scenery of farther-flung locales but, make no mistake, this is a place that will fill your time more than adequately. This tour, which requires a car, is delightful in itself, a relaxing swing through the byways and along the coast, but it also makes a perfect second week after you've seen England's iconic highlights (see itinerary, above).

Day 1: Runnymede & Stonehenge

You're heading for Stonehenge, but first an added attraction: Drive out of London heading west onto the M3, turn on the M25, then come off at junction 13 onto the A308. On the rural banks of the Thames (6 miles from the frenetic activity of Windsor) is **Runnymede** (p. 205). It was in a meadow here in 1215 that King John sealed the Magna Carta, the document that made all men equal under the law. There is an impressive monument erected by the American Bar Association, and you can walk through the meadows, take the Thames Path, and even go on a boat ride. There's a little cafe here facing the river, or you might want to plan ahead and bring a picnic.

Get back onto the M3 and head southwest, turning onto the A303. If you're lucky with the traffic you may get to **Stonehenge** (p. 328) in 90 minutes. The monumental stone circle in the middle of Salisbury Plain is a must-see site, even though, with main roads running past, it can be a disappointment. You walk around the circle, at a distance, on paths, so while you'll be glad to have done it, you won't spend as long here as you might have anticipated. You can get up close to the stones at **Avebury** (p. 334), the biggest stone circle in the world (although not as striking as Stonehenge), about 25 miles north, and you can visit for free (although the museum is worth paying for). You can get in until dusk, so try and catch a sunset. There are many country hotels near here, particularly in picturesque **Marlborough** several miles away.

Day 2: West Wittering & Arundel

Head south past Salisbury, and southeast past Southampton and Portsmouth to **Chichester** (p. 274); you might do it in a couple of hours. This is a pretty town—stop if you have time—but you're looking for signs to The Witterings, then **West Wittering** (p. 277), several miles away. This is one of Britain's most divine beaches, privately owned and splendidly maintained. The pure sands, backed by dunes, stretch into the distance and there are views across to the **Isle of Wight** (p. 306). This is a place that's as loved by adults as by children: There are walks onto East Head, a sand dune spit that protects Chichester harbor. There's a cafe, ice-cream shop, and the big grassy parking lot behind the dunes doubles as a picnic and games area.

A few miles east of Chichester is **Arundel** (p. 274), an ancient Sussex town on the River Arun. Have a wander (outside town there are walks through the water meadows), but concentrate on **Arundel Castle** (p. 275). Take an hour or so to explore the rooms filled with paintings by Old Masters, the walled gardens, and grounds. You don't want to be too late leaving as you'll have surely booked in at **Amberley Castle** (p. 278), a real castle several miles away that is now a luxury hotel. Here you can explore among the medieval weaponry, the clipped yew hedges, the gardens, lawns, and ponds knowing that at the end of the day the portcullis comes down with you inside.

Day 3: Brighton

You won't want to leave Amberley, but less than half an hour away is Brighton, the capital of the south coast, a city by the sea. You'll want to stay on the sea-front, and the **Hilton Metropole** (p. 273) is a good choice, a grand hotel from the past that's part of the resort's history. Check in, then hit the seafront; you've got the day so you can relax. Head toward the pier; you can walk above the beach, or you can drop down to beach level where, under the arches, there are pubs, seafood bars, shops, cafes, and other seaside fun. Close together are the **Fishing Museum** (p. 269) and **Brighton Smokehouse** (p. 269), where you can join the line for a hot mackerel sandwich. Head onto the pier for views back onto the Regency seafront.

Opposite the pier is the **SeaLife Centre** (p. 269), the world's oldest aquarium, and worth an hour's visit. A few minutes' walk away is the **Royal Pavilion,** a royal holiday home from the Regency era, a must-see extravagance of Oriental design. In the grounds is **Brighton Museum** (p. 266), a decidedly modern collection of furniture, art, and local history; it's free, so pop in at the very least to see Salvador Dali's *Lips* sofa, which is near the entrance.

For lunch, head down to the seafront near your hotel, to the **Regency** (p. 271), a superb fish restaurant with little fanfare; get an outside table and a whole crab salad, or grilled Dover sole, or the wonderful fish and chips.

The rest of the day you can wander the streets. **The Lanes** and **North Laine** are little streets filled with quirky designer shops, which cross the main shopping area that is full of mainstream brands.

For the evening, have a drink at the traditional **Fortune of War** pub (p. 269), spilling out from the beachfront arches. There are plenty of restaurants in the area, too. The **Windsor** (p. 273) in the Hilton Metropole—big, white, chandeliered, and with huge seaview windows—is very refined.

Day 4: The South Downs

A short drive east and you come to **Charleston** (p. 268), the farmhouse home of Vanessa Bell, sister of Virginia Woolf, and Duncan Grant. The house is a place to love whether you're into the Bloomsbury Set of arty intellectuals or not; it's imaginatively, even crazily decorated from walls to furniture to garden. Aim to spend an hour or so here (the garden is particularly striking) before getting your walking boots on. The farmhouse is in the lee of the **South Downs,** the rolling hills that follow the coast, and just off the **South Downs Way** (p. 277), the phenomenal walk that goes from Eastbourne to Winchester. If you've set off promptly this morning, you should still have a good half-day's hike, topping bare, windy Firle Beacon (217m/712 ft.) in one direction, or passing through the pretty village of Alfriston in the other. There are plenty of inns and hotels in the area.

Day 5: Battle & Rye

Just along the coast is a place that was at the turning point of British history. In the Battle of Hastings, King Alfred was defeated by the Normans, marking the end of English rule and the start of French. The battlefield is still an emotional spot and now the site of an award-winning exhibition. It's easy to spend the morning here, looking round **Battle** (p. 261), the market town that grew up around the Abbey that William the Conqueror founded to celebrate his victory. There are various options for lunch in the medieval streets. For the afternoon, **Rye** is a charming spot. This town used to be a leading sea port until the harbor silted up; it's now several miles from the sea but still has a river and hostelries that reflect its history as a place where smugglers gathered. Rye is a place to walk around and appreciate (you don't come here for any specific attraction). You could end your day at **The George** (p. 264), one of southern England's most charming hotels.

Day 6: Margate & Canterbury

Follow the coast around to Dover, and keep going until you reach **Margate** (p. 249), one of England's easternmost points. It may take around 1½ hours. This is a classic English seaside town, a place that fell into disrepair as people went abroad for their holidays, but which is now back on its feet. Explore the seafront and jolly beach, but you're here for the **Turner Contemporary** (p. 250), the country's newest major art museum. The stark, white building on the seafront celebrates J. M. W. Turner, whose iconic seascapes were painted at this very spot when there was a lodging house here. Grab a coffee and a snack at one of the trendy places on the **Harbour Arm** pier, and then make the 30-minute drive to

Canterbury (p. 240). Check into your hotel and then head for the **cathedral; St. Augustine's Abbey** next door; and the fascinating, subterranean **Roman Museum.** You might even fancy **The Canterbury Tales** (p. 243), a lively, garish attraction devoted to Chaucer's classic tale. There are a number of good places for dinner but the **Goods Shed** (p. 245), a farmers' market and restaurant, showcases the food of this area, known as the Garden of England.

Day 7: Leeds Castle & Chartwell

You've got less than an hour's drive to get to **Leeds Castle** (p. 259), England's most perfect castle, which is in the middle of a serene lake, in rolling grounds. Some castles you can get away with simply looking around the outside, but this one, with its royal apartments, demands to be explored further. The gardens are an attraction in themselves.

Half an hour away, just off the M25 (your route back to London), is **Chartwell** (p. 256), the long-time home of war-time prime minister Winston Churchill. Not only do you get to see his papers, you also see the gardening work he did in his spare time. From here, allow 2 hours to get to London.

ENGLAND FOR FAMILIES

England's offerings may appeal as much to your children as to you. Let them experience sights they've seen on TV, great buildings, and history. London can be quite tiring, so this tour begins and ends there, cutting a happy swath across the countryside in between.

Day 1: London

The heart of England's history and culture is the **Tower of London** (p. 112), and this is the place to start. The megafortress is not only a splendid castle, but also has enough *Horrible Histories* about it to please the pickiest youngster: Traitors' Gate, where miscreants were unloaded from barges, never to be seen again until their heads popped up on spikes at London Bridge, is one example. The tour, led by a Yeoman, has an air of timelessness about it. Allow 2 hours.

Afterward, cross Tower Bridge and take a stroll from here to the South Bank, passing the warship HMS *Belfast*. From London Bridge, take the Tube to Hampstead (the journey is less than 30 min.), a village-like northern suburb that opens onto **Hampstead Heath.** This vast area of open space has ponds, woods, and hills, not least Parliament Hill with its views across the City, with St. Paul's Cathedral looking like a toy below.

Day 2: Chessington

A big trip isn't just about ticking off the sights; it's about relaxing and having fun. Drive the few miles to London's southwestern outskirts and check into the Holiday Inn Chessington, a big, stylishly modern hotel with a safari lodge theme at **Chessington World of Adventures** (p. 285), one of the country's top theme parks; you get free entry if you stay. Head straight into the park, which has rides for all ages, from tots to teenagers, and is the only park to have an impressive collection of animals, too. It started as a zoo, and still has tigers and lions in big, grassy, junglelike enclosures (which you can see from all sides), along with gorillas, birds of prey, and the new Wanyama Reserve safari-like area with zebras, gazelles, and giraffes roaming. The reserve is right near the hotel, so you can look at the animals from the terrace of the African-themed Zafari Bar and Grill. The large indoor pool has views of monkeys and birds. The family rooms are cool (and that's our children's view) with a separate sleeping area and their own TV.

Day 3: Portsmouth

Chessington is not far from the A3, which will take you all the way to Portsmouth in 1½ hours. Here the **Historic Dockyard** (p. 297) is a fantastic place for youngsters. It's home to Admiral Nelson's flagship, **HMS *Victory,*** which you can walk around. They'll also love HMS *Warrior,* from 1860, the iron-hulled, steam-powered warship, which also involves ladders, hatches, and other gymnastics. There are docks to run around on, boat rides, and exhibitions. Just across the road is the ferry to the Isle of Wight; it's a tiny ship that takes less than half an hour, and has great views of both the island and Portsmouth. You dock in Ryde and it's a 15-minute drive to **Seaview,** and the **Seaview hotel** (p. 311), a boutique family hotel, where the food (including inventive children's menus) is excellent.

Day 4: The Isle of Wight

Drive to the island's south coast (about 20 min.), and the resort of **Sandown.** This is one of the best areas for finding fossils, which pour out of the chalk cliffs, and the modern **Dinosaur Isle Museum** (p. 308), on the coast road, has a collection going back almost 2 centuries, plus lots of child-friendly fun. Join one of the museum's fossil walks out onto the beach and under the cliffs—children love the combination of fossil-hunting and splashing in rock pools. Then spend the afternoon swimming and playing. Plan to leave around teatime, as your next stop, the following day, is a bit of a journey to an exceptional place. Plan to stay near **Oxford.** Take the ferry back to Ryde, and get onto the M27 heading west for about 15 miles. Follow the A33 to Winchester then the A34 all the way to Oxford.

Days 5 & 6: Ironbridge

It's about 80 miles (2 hr.) by car from Oxford to **Ironbridge** (p. 487), site of the world's first iron bridge. It was at the heart of the Industrial Revolution, at one time a raging place of foundries and smoke. Now, however, it is a family delight, which needs to be explored over 2 days. Start with the gorge itself, where children love running across the bridge and throwing sticks into the River Severn below; just up the hill is **Enginuity** (p. 488), a hands-on science and energy museum. Ironbridge's little high street has cute stores and coffee shops, and there are plenty of pretty places to stay locally.

On the following day, head about a mile out of town to **Blists Hill Victorian Town,** a collection of old buildings turned into a townscape on the site of old blast furnaces. It's a wealth of industrial history turned into a world of wonder and fun with a steam train, shops, horse and cart rides, a fairground, and an old-time fish and chip shop. There's a carnival atmosphere, and its hillside setting means country walks and clambering along the Hay Incline Plane, a fantastical contraption that lowered barges to river level. When you've finished, drive down the river to the **Tar Tunnel,** a spot where natural bitumen was collected and used for pitch; children love donning hard hats for the short, dark exploration. Then walk across the footbridge and along the river to **Jackfield Tile Museum,** where even youngsters find the Edwardian extravagance interesting.

Day 7: London

Head for London (several hr.), but stop off at **The Making of Harry Potter,** a new extravaganza (p. 238) at Warner Brothers Studios, near Watford (it's just a short detour north to junction 19 after the M40 reaches London's M25 ring road). The walking tour takes you onto sets (including Hogwarts' Great Hall), displays a wealth of props (the triple-decker Knight Bus), and reveals the special effects secrets of the movie series. From here it's an easy drive into London and your hotel.

ENGLAND'S BEST GARDENS IN 1 WEEK

England's gardens grow beautifully, and in some cases they have been doing so for centuries. This tour takes you to those that are at the very pinnacle of horticulture and beauty. You'll need a car, and your travels will take you across some wonderful countryside. You might naturally expect this to be a summer tour, but although these gardens are at their best from June to September, they are designed to be year-round spectacles, with winter foliage, spring bulbs, and rich late-season hues.

Day 1: Royal Botanic Gardens, Kew

London's great garden, **Kew** (p. 124), is a fantastic world tucked away behind high walls, one that has been developing for 250 years and which lays claim to containing more than one in eight of all known plant species. You can generally find parking, but there is a Kew Gardens stop on the District Line Tube. This is a full day out at any time of year as there are 300 acres, which vary from clipped formal gardens to wild woodland areas. The ornate Palm House is massive and dates from the 1840s, while the Princess of Wales Conservatory is modernistic. Kew was long a prim, traditional garden but now boasts the Rhizotron (an underground look at tree roots) and the Xstrata Treetop Walkway, which runs 18m (60 ft.) high through the tops of oaks and other trees. There are also museums, an art gallery, a Chinese pagoda (from 1762), and the Orangerie, a lovely restaurant that serves everything from sandwiches to table-service meals. There is a gate directly on the Thames, so this is also a good excuse for a riverside walk, or you can cross Kew Bridge to the pubs at Strand on the Green (the Bell & Crown, Bull's Head, and City Barge) for a post-Kew riverside drink.

Day 2: RHS Gardens, Wisley

Off the A3 (itself a picture in spring, lined with gorse bushes), just past the M25, is **Wisley** (p. 280), the home of the Royal Horticultural Society. Whereas Kew is first and foremost a scientific institution, Wisley is just as concerned with the nuts and bolts of everyday gardening. You'll find fields where there may be dozens of varieties of sweet peas on trial, or vegetables, and there are vast areas of fruit trees. But that's beyond the extravagantly planted borders, the exquisite rose garden, the wild gardens (where you'll find toads the size of dinner plates croaking madly in the summer), woodland and lake, and the modern, cathedral-like Glasshouse, with its tropical and temperate collections. Like Kew, this is very much a destination, with its sophisticated Conservatory restaurant (which also does afternoon teas), less formal Conservatory cafe, and the little Orchard Cafe, where you'll find the Honest Sausage selling posh hot dogs. The county town of Guildford is nearby and a good place to stay; you might also be able to fit in a walk in the formal gardens in the castle grounds or in Stoke Park.

Day 3: Sissinghurst Castle Garden

An hour or so from Guildford, across the heart of Surrey into Kent, is **Sissinghurst** (p. 259). This is perhaps the most romantic garden of your tour, and a contrast to your previous days. Set in the grounds of a ruined Elizabethan manor, Sissinghurst was created by garden designer and writer Vita Sackville-West and her husband, novelist and diplomat Harold Nicholson, in the 1930s. The pair turned around 300 years of neglect and created a year-round delight; the dreamlike White Garden, with its silver and white foliage, is perhaps the highlight, but there's also a spring garden full of daffodils and a vegetable garden that shows how it should be done, in style and execution, all with the surviving tower looming over them. It's a good several-hour drive to your next stop, but a charming one, and for much of it you can use the A272 directly west, which follows the line of the chalky South Downs to Winchester.

Day 4: Stourhead

Stourhead (p. 335) is near Salisbury in Wiltshire. The huge lake, which reflects the temples, grottos, and trees lining its banks, leaves you breathless, but it is only the heart of the 2,650-acre estate. This landscaped garden is much the same as when it was created in 1740; flowering shrubs are everywhere (try for the rhododendrons in late spring) and rare trees thrive. There are endless walks to enjoy, and the restaurant serves vegetables from the walled garden, and beef from the estate. The next couple of days are hectic, but worth it. It's a significant drive (3–4 hr.) to Cornwall, so we recommend traveling this evening and staying in the St. Austell or St. Mawes area at Hotel Tresanton or Idle Rocks Hotel.

Day 5: Eden Project & the Lost Gardens of Heligan

These two gardens are different again from anything you've seen so far, and both a great contrast to one another. The **Lost Gardens of Heligan** (p. 404), near the fishing village of Mevagissey, were part of a Victorian estate that fell into disrepair over 70 years. Rediscovered in 1990, the sub-tropical jungle that has been protected by Cornwall's warm climate has been restored. Equally extraordinary is the **Eden Project** (p. 404), a former clay mine in a lush Cornish valley that's been covered with a series of huge geodesic domes, like something from a science-fiction film. Inside are more than a million plants from around the world, including the planet's largest "captive" rainforest. Afterward, hit the road for 3 or so hours and you can be in Wales for dinner, in a little hotel just across the Severn Bridge.

Day 6: National Botanic Garden of Wales

From your hotel it should take less than 2 hours to get to this relatively new garden (opened 2000), near **Swansea.** The **National Botanic Garden** (p. 705), created on 400-year-old parkland, has at its heart the Great Glasshouse, a low dome that seems a continuation of the hill (and which features warmth-loving plants from many locations, including California); around the edge are woods and parkland; and in between are lawns and formal gardens. Lunch should be taken in the **Seasons** restaurant, in an old stable block, which uses produce from the walled garden and lamb and beef from the garden's own organic farm. Stay in one of the many little hotels that dot the countryside.

Day 7: Painswick Rococo Garden

The drive here shouldn't take more than a couple of hours, as it's almost all motorway (M4/M5). **Painswick** (p. 438), near Stroud, in the Cotswolds, is a great example of gardens at their most ornate. It was created in the early 1700s and rescued late last century. The garden's flamboyance (including a maze) is in contrast to the views across the valley in which it sits. The **Coach House** restaurant uses produce from the kitchen garden and is a nice spot for lunch before your drive back to London, which will take a little over 2 hours.

LONDON

by Donald Strachan

London never seems to get tired. It's the greatest quality of this city with 2 millennia of history, that it stays forever young and energetic. Britain's capital is home to the great art collections of the National Gallery, architectural icons like Westminster Abbey, and a rich royal heritage, but it also spawns underground design and musical innovation. It is a city of independent villages—Chelsea or Greenwich has little in common with Shoreditch or Soho—and a conurbation of grand parks as well as great buildings.

4

SIGHTSEEING   The old sits alongside the new—nowhere more than at Wren's great baroque dome of **St. Paul's Cathedral,** framed by 21st-century skyscrapers—and London is rightly famed for its museums. Prized collections, ancient and contemporary—from Bloomsbury's **British Museum** to the South Bank's **Tate Modern**—share top billing with eccentric spaces like the **Sir John Soane's Museum** that could only exist here. Ride the **London Eye** observation wheel to get to grips with the city's layout.

EATING & DRINKING   Whatever your favorite flavor, you'll find it somewhere here. As London's center of gravity moves east, so does the dining scene: **Viajante** is the most creative restaurant to grace an eastside hotel. West End institutions **Rules** and **J. Sheekey** are as good as ever, as are the high-toned French dining rooms in **Mayfair.** Areas with lower rents continue to attract skillful chefs to cool cafes and a new breed of tapas bar, and you'll find local craft microbrews complementing gastropub cooking in most London neighborhoods.

SHOPPING   The sheer variety of shops and shopping districts can be bewildering, even for a regular visitor. **Knightsbridge** and **Chelsea** have the chi-chi boutiques, **Mayfair** the finest men's tailors, and the latest in street-style springs up from the hip stores and pop-up shops of **Shoreditch** and the East End. This is a city that has something for every taste or budget, and best buys remain collectables, vintage fashions, and accessories. Street markets as diverse as **Columbia Road** and **Portobello** are also experiencing a mini-renaissance.

ENTERTAINMENT & NIGHTLIFE   If you do your relaxation after dark, you've chosen the right city. When the sun sets, historic monuments and grand museums fade into the inky night, and a whole new London comes to life. The **West End's** bright lights draw the crowds with mega-musicals and big-name dramas. **Soho** is still buzzing—and the streets of **Shoreditch, Hoxton,** and **Dalston** are jumping well into the small hours.

THE best LONDON TRAVEL EXPERIENCES

○ **Taking afternoon tea at the Ritz Palm Court:** The traditional tea ritual lives on in 21st-century London. The pomp and circumstance of the British Empire continue at the Ritz—only the Empire is missing these days. See p. 149.

○ **Hanging out on the hip streets of the "New" East End:** London's fashionable folk haunt the streets and alleyways of "New" East London. Shop the designer boutiques and vintage stores of Shoreditch, dine out on French cuisine at Les Trois Garçons (p. 145), drink elegant cocktails at Nightjar (p. 168), and dance till the small hours at Plastic People (p. 175).

○ **Spending an evening at a West End theatre:** London is the theatrical capital of the world. The live stages of Theatreland, around Covent Garden and Soho, offer a unique combination of variety, accessibility, and economy—and programs have everything from serious drama to marquee musicals. See p. 163.

○ **Watching the sunset from Waterloo Bridge:** This famous river crossing is perfectly positioned to watch the embers of the day dissipate behind the Houses of Parliament. The view is so memorable that it moved the Kinks to write a chart-topping song in 1967: "As long as I gaze on / Waterloo sunset / I am in paradise." See p. 76.

○ **Walking in the footsteps of Sir Christopher Wren:** The architect who rebuilt so much of London after the Great Fire of 1666 is best known for his churches. Walk from St. Bride's, on Fleet Street, past his icon, St. Paul's Cathedral, to St. Mary-le-Bow and beyond to appreciate his genius. See "Saints & the City," p. 114.

ORIENTATION

Arriving

BY PLANE

London's flagship airport for arrivals from across the globe is **London Heathrow** (LHR; www.heathrowairport.com), 17 miles west of the center and boasting five hectic, bustling terminals (named imaginatively, Terminals 1 to 5, although Terminal 2 is closed until 2014). This is the U.K. hub of most major airlines, including British Airways, Virgin Atlantic, Qantas, and the North American carriers. **London Gatwick** (LGW; www.gatwickairport.com) is the city's second major airport, with two terminals (North and South), 31 miles south of central London in the Sussex countryside.

Increasingly, however, passengers are arriving at London's smaller airports—particularly since the proliferation of budget airlines, which now dominate short-haul domestic and international routes. **London Stansted** (STN; www.stanstedairport.com), 37 miles northeast of the center, is the gateway to short-haul destinations in the U.K., Continental Europe, and parts of the Middle East. It's also a hub for Ryanair. **London Luton** (LTN; www.london-luton.co.uk) anchors a similarly diverse short-haul network, and lies 34 miles northwest of the center. Ryanair and easyJet are regular visitors. **London City** (LCY; www.londoncityairport.com), the only commercial airport actually in London itself, is frequented mainly by business travelers from nearby Docklands and the City, but does have some key intercity links with regular direct flights to New York, Edinburgh, Florence, and Madrid. British Airways and Cityjet are its two major airlines. **London Southend** (SEN; www.southendairport. com), 40 miles east of the center, became a secondary base for easyJet short-haul services in 2012.

For information on getting into London from each of the major airports, see p. 747.

BY CAR

To anyone thinking of arriving in the capital by car, our most important piece of advice would be: "Don't." Roads in and around the city are clogged with traffic, and the M25 highway that rings the city is prone to major traffic jams at any time of day—but especially between 7:30 and 9am, or 4 and 7pm on weekdays, and on Sundays from mid-afternoon till late in the evening. On top of that, and despite the complaints and grumbles of Londoners, the public transportation system is pretty efficient.

From the north, roads converge at London's **North Circular Road** (the A406), then proceed in a slow but orderly fashion into the center, with the occasional bottle-neck and inevitable jam. It's horribly clogged at peak traffic hours, but otherwise a reasonable route into the north of the city. From the west, both the M40/A40 and M4/A4 routes into the city are slightly more efficient. (Remember, we're talking in *relative* terms here; no one averse to sitting in stationary traffic should attempt any of these routes at peak times.) From Kent and the Channel ports, such as Dover, the A2 usually clips along satisfactorily outside rush hour, although a bottleneck at the Black-wall Tunnel creates long lines every weekday. From the southwest, it's usually quicker to head clockwise around the M25 to enter London via the M4 or M40 (see above), unless you're heading for a southwestern suburb like Richmond or Kew.

BY TRAIN

Precisely which of London's many mainline stations you arrive at depends on where you started your journey. **Paddington Station** serves Heathrow Airport and destinations west of London—including Oxford, Reading, Bristol, and South Wales. **Marylebone Station** is used mostly by commuters, but also serves Warwick. **Euston Station** serves North Wales and major cities in northwest England, including Liverpool and Manchester; trains also depart from here to the Lake District and Glasgow, Scotland, via the West Coast Mainline. **King's Cross Station** is the end-point of the East Coast Mainline—trains arrive here from York, Newcastle, and Edinburgh. **Liverpool Street Station** is the City's main commuter hub, but also links London with Stansted Airport, Cambridge, and Norwich. The City's other main-line stations—Cannon Street, Moorgate, Blackfriars, and Fenchurch Street—are also heavily used by commuters from the neighboring counties of Hertfordshire, Essex, Kent, Surrey, and Sussex, as is **Charing Cross Station,** close to Trafalgar Square. **Waterloo Station** serves the southwest of England: Trains from Devon, Dorset, and Hampshire terminate here, as do Salisbury services. **Victoria Station** serves Gat-wick Airport, as well as cities and towns across southern England, including Brighton. South of the River Thames, **London Bridge Station** is another busy commuter hub, and also serves Brighton and Gatwick Airport. Each of London's mainline stations is connected to the city's vast bus and Tube networks (see below), and each has phones, sandwich bars, fast-food joints, luggage storage areas, and somewhere to ask for transport information.

Missing from the list above is **St. Pancras Station,** the London hub for high-speed Eurostar services to Paris and Brussels, as well as some domestic services to the East

Follow London on Twitter

@secret_london   @londonist
@glplondon   @qypedoeslondon
@TelegraphLondon   @visitlondonweb
@ldn

Midlands and South Yorkshire. Restored and reopened in 2007, it connects England with Belgium and France through the multibillion-pound **Channel Tunnel.**

Visitor Information

The official **Visit London** online home is the excellent www.visitlondon.com. You can download PDF brochures and maps, or have them mailed to a U.K. or U.S. address, or ask any question about the city by filling out the online contact form at www.visitlondon.com/contact-us.

Once in the city, the **Britain and London Visitor Centre,** 1 Lower Regent St., London SW1 4XT (✆ **08701/566-366;** Tube: Piccadilly Circus), can help you with almost anything, from the superficial to the most serious queries. Located just downhill from Piccadilly Circus, it deals with procuring accommodations in all price categories through an on-site travel agency, and you can also book bus or train tickets throughout the U.K. It's open year-round Monday 9:30am to 6pm, Tuesday to Friday 9am to 6pm, and Saturday and Sunday 9am to 4pm. Between April and September, weekday closing is a half-hour later. There are further central information points at: **King's Cross St. Pancras,** LUL Western Ticket Hall, Euston Road (Mon–Sat 7:15am–9:15pm, Sun 8:15am–8:15pm); **Holborn station,** Kingsway (Mon–Fri 8am–6pm); **Victoria rail station,** opposite Platform 8 (Mon–Sat 7:15am–9:15pm, Sun 8:15am–8:15pm); **Piccadilly Circus Underground station** (daily 9:15am–7pm); **Liverpool Street Underground station** (Mon–Sat 7:15am–9:15pm, Sun 8:15am–8:15pm); **Euston rail station,** opposite Platform 8 (Mon–Fri 7:15am–9:15pm, Sat 8:15am–6:15pm, Sun 8:15am–6:15pm); **Greenwich,** 2 Cutty Sark Gardens (✆ **0870/608-2000;** daily 10am–5pm).

The Square Mile (see below) has its own visitor information center, the **City of London Tourist Information Centre,** St. Paul's Churchyard (✆ **020/7332-1456**). Opening hours are Monday to Saturday 9:30am to 5:30pm, Sunday 10am to 4pm.

London is such a web-savvy city that almost as soon as we recommend a news source or blog, it is immediately matched or superseded by another. However, there are some phenomenally useful London resources on the Internet. You'll find the latest local news and weather at www.bbc.co.uk/london and www.thisislondon.co.uk. LDN (www.ldn.in) aggregates information about all kinds of events, deals, and trivia. The **Visit London Blog** (http://blogs.visitlondon.com) manages to combine the official line with an eye for the unusual, but if you want to head off-piste and under the city's skin, bookmark blogs like the magnificent **Great Wen** (www.greatwen.com). **Londonist** (http://londonist.com) remains the best source for street-level coverage of arts, events, food, drink, and London trivia, and **I Know a Great Little Place...** (www.greatlittleplace.com) is often updated with bar openings, club nights, dining ideas, and unusual tours. For the latest on London's theatre scene, consult www.officiallondontheatre.co.uk. If you wish to attend Christian worship, www.cityevents.org.uk has a regularly updated calendar of services at all the City's churches. The

Museum of London's **Streetmuseum** app (iPhone and Android) uses augmented reality and the inbuilt camera to superimpose historic images of London onto a view of the modern streets. For regular features and updates, visit www.frommers.com/destinations/London.

London's Neighborhoods in Brief

WEST END

Bloomsbury & Fitzrovia Bloomsbury, a world within itself, is bounded roughly by Euston Road to the north, Tottenham Court Road to the west, New Oxford Street to the south, and Clerkenwell to the east. It is, among other things, the academic heart of London. The mighty **British Museum** (p. 85) lies at its center, to the north of which are several colleges, including University College London, one of the main branches of the University of London. Writers such as Virginia Woolf, who lived in the area, have fanned the neighborhood's reputation as a place devoted to liberal thinking, arts, and "sexual frankness." However, Bloomsbury is a now fairly staid neighborhood of neat garden squares.

The heart of Bloomsbury is **Russell Square,** where the outlying streets are lined with moderately priced to expensive hotels and B&Bs. It's a noisy but central place to stay. Hotel prices have risen here in the past decade but are still nowhere near the levels of those in Mayfair and St. James's, and there are still bargains to be found, particularly on busy Gower Street. At its southern doorstep lie the restaurants and nightclubs of Soho, the theatre district, and the markets of Covent Garden. If you stay here, it's a 5-minute Tube ride to the heart of the West End.

To the west across Tottenham Court Road is **Fitzrovia,** a rather forgotten stretch of the West End, somewhat overshadowed by its more glamorous neighbors. To those in the know it offers a respite from the crowds and madness along Oxford Street, with good shops and dining, particularly on Charlotte Street.

Covent Garden & the Strand The flower, fruit, and "veg" market is long gone (since 1970), but memories of Professor Higgins and his "squashed cabbage leaf," Eliza Doolittle, linger on. Covent Garden contains the city's busiest group of restaurants, pubs, and cafes outside of Soho, as well as hip shops, particularly around Neal Street and Seven Dials. The restored market buildings here represent one of London's more successful examples of urban recycling. The main building is now home to shops, as well as an arts and crafts market, while the former flower market holds the **London Transport Museum** (p. 90).

The area attracts professional street performers, who do their juggling and unicycling on the piazza by **St. Paul's Church** in front of thronging crowds in summer—and just a few shivering souls in winter. Appropriately enough, London's theatre district starts around Covent Garden and spills westward over to Leicester Square and Piccadilly Circus (see below).

You'll probably come to the Covent Garden area for the theatre or dining rather than for a hotel room. There are only a few hotels—although among those few are some of London's smartest. We recommend our favorites on p. 181.

Running east from Trafalgar Square, parallel to the River Thames, the Strand forms the southern border of Covent Garden. Most of the grand mansions and fine houses that once lined its length have—with the honorable exceptions of **Somerset House** and the **Savoy Hotel** (p. 181)—been replaced by nondescript offices and chain restaurants.

Leicester Square & Piccadilly Piccadilly Circus and Leicester Square are two of the capital's most famous locations, and yet you can't help feeling that if all London's attractions were of this quality, the city wouldn't receive any visitors at all. A barely-there square, **Piccadilly Circus** is more the confluence of major streets—Regent Street, Shaftesbury Avenue, and Piccadilly—than it is a venue in its own right. It is a small, partly pedestrianized junction with relentless traffic and crowds; some interesting, if rather overshadowed Regency architecture (which can be seen to better effect on Regent Street); and one small, albeit undeniably pretty statue known to most Londoners as Eros (although trivia fans should note that it was meant to be his brother, Anteros, the Greek god of requited love).

Leicester Square, just to the east, is larger and fully pedestrianized, and has a bit more going on, but is perhaps even more tawdry, dominated by huge cinemas and mainstream nightlife and eating options. During the day the square is somewhat of a poor man's Covent Garden, with various low-rent buskers belting out the standards. At night, particularly on weekends, it's a bit too crowded to be pleasant. An ongoing £18 million redevelopment by Westminster Council has had little effect so far. Some of the new arrivals—notably the **St. John Hotel** (p. 182)—have hinted at a more upmarket future, while others (M&Ms World) have pulled in the other direction, leaving the square more or less where it was. It's convenient for those who want to be at the center of the action. The downside is the expense, the noise, congestion, and pollution.

Much more inviting than either is **Piccadilly** itself, the grand avenue running west from Piccadilly Circus, which was once the main western road out of London. It was named for the "picadil," a ruffled collar created by Robert Baker, a 17th-century tailor. If you want to do some shopping with a bit of added grandeur, retreat to a Regency promenade of exclusive shops, the **Burlington Arcade** (p. 151), designed in 1819.

Soho & Chinatown Just south of the international brands and off-the-peg glamour of Oxford Street—the capital's über-high street—is somewhere altogether more distinctive: Soho, London's louche dissolute heart. It's a place where high and low living have gone hand in hand since the 19th century, and where today the gleaming offices of international media conglomerates and Michelin-starred restaurants sit next to tawdry clip joints and sex shops. In the '50s and '60s, its smoky clubs helped give birth to the British jazz and rock 'n' roll scenes. There are dozens of great places to eat, drink, and hang out, ranging from chic, high-end gastrofests to cheap, late-opening stalwarts like **Bar Italia** (p. 150). Many of the best are found on Dean, Frith, and Greek Streets.

Soho is bordered by Regent Street to the west, Oxford Street to the north, Charing Cross Road (lined with bookstores) to the east, and the Theatreland of Shaftesbury Avenue to the south. Close to its southern edge is Old Compton Street, the longtime home of the capital's gay scene. Carnaby Street—a block from Regent Street—was the epicenter of the universe during the swinging '60s. It's recently become a bit of a schlocky tourist trap, although some quality independent stores have emerged again.

South of Shaftesbury Avenue is London's **Chinatown** … although "town" is a slightly grand way of describing what essentially amounts to two or three streets lined with restaurants. The main street, Gerrard Street, is rather kitsch, with giant oriental-style gates and pagoda-esque phone boxes. However, this is a genuine, thriving community, and one of the most dependable areas for Chinese food.

Marylebone & Oxford Street Pretty much every town in the country has a high street, a collection of shops and businesses aimed at the surrounding community. **Oxford Street** could be regarded as London's high street, where the biggest chains have flagship branches and where several of the capital's most prestigious department stores, including Selfridges and John Lewis, are found. It can be a brutal place, particularly on weekends and the weeks before Christmas, when it is choked with people, traffic, and noise—not to mention pickpockets.

North of Oxford Street, the district of **Marylebone** (pronounced *Mar*-lee-bone) was once the poor relation of Mayfair to the south, but has become much more fashionable of late—certainly more so than when it was the setting for public executions at the

Tyburn gallows (although those did at least attract the crowds). The last executions took place here in the late 18th century. Marylebone has emerged as a major "bedroom" district for London. It's not as convenient as Bloomsbury, but the hub of the West End's action is virtually at your doorstep if you stay here. Once known only for its town houses turned into B&Bs, the district now offers accommodations in all price ranges.

Mayfair Once a simple stretch of fields outside the main part of the city where an annual party was held at the start of summer (the "May Fair" that gave the area its name), this is now one of the most exclusive sections of London, filled with luxury hotels, Georgian town houses, expensive restaurants, and swanky shops—hence its status as the most expensive property on the U.K. version of the board game *Monopoly*. Sandwiched between Regent Street and Hyde Park, it's convenient for London's best shopping and reasonably close to the West End theatres, yet removed from the peddlers and commerce of Covent Garden and Soho.

One of the curiosities of Mayfair is **Shepherd Market,** a micro-village of pubs, two-story inns, restaurants, and book and food stalls, nestled within Mayfair's grandness.

St. James's The neighborhood begins at Piccadilly Circus and moves southwest, incorporating the south side of Piccadilly, Pall Mall, The Mall, St. James's Park, and Green Park. Often called "Royal London," St. James's basks in its associations with everybody from the "merrie monarch" King Charles II to the current Queen Elizabeth II. Be sure to stop in at **Fortnum & Mason,** on Piccadilly itself, the grocer to the Queen. Hotels in this neighborhood tend to be expensive, but if the Queen should summon you to "Buck House," you won't have far to walk.

Trafalgar Square (p. 93) lies at the opposite end of The Mall to Buckingham Palace, marking the district's eastern boundary. Its north side is taken up by the neoclassical facade of the **National Gallery** (p. 90), while in the middle stands Nelson's Column, erected in honor of the country's victory over Napoleon at the Battle of Trafalgar, in 1805.

WEST LONDON

Kensington The Royal Borough lies west of Kensington Gardens and Hyde Park and is traversed by two major shopping streets, Kensington High Street and Kensington Church Street. Since 1689, when asthmatic William III fled Whitehall Palace for Nottingham House (where the air was fresher), the district has enjoyed royal associations. In time, Nottingham House became **Kensington Palace** (p. 95), and the royals grabbed a chunk of Hyde Park to plant their roses. Kensington Palace was home to the late princesses Margaret and Diana, and in 2013 will be the new home of Prince William and Kate, the Duchess of Cambridge. With all those royal associations, Kensington is a wealthy neighborhood with some very well-to-do hotels and shops. Although it can feel like you've left central London behind on its quiet residential streets, it's just a few Tube stops from High Street Kensington Station to the heart of the action.

Paddington & Bayswater Paddington radiates out from Paddington Station, north of Hyde Park and Kensington Gardens. It's one of the major B&B centers in London, attracting budget travelers who fill the lodgings along Sussex Gardens and Norfolk Square. Just south of Paddington, north of Hyde Park, and abutting more fashionable Notting Hill to the west, is **Bayswater,** also filled with budget B&Bs. The eastern boundary of both, Edgware Road runs north from Marble Arch, was first laid out by the Romans, and is now one of the capital's major centers of Middle Eastern culture, lined with Lebanese restaurants and *shisha* cafes.

Paddington and Bayswater are "in-between" areas. Stay here for moderately priced lodgings (there are expensive hotels, too) and for convenience to **Hyde Park** (p. 95) and transportation. Pick your hotel with care; you'll find our favorites starting on p. 187.

Notting Hill Fashionable Notting Hill is bounded on the east by Bayswater and on the south by Kensington. Hemmed in on the north by the elevated road known as the Westway and on the west by the Shepherd's Bush roundabout, it has many turn-of-the-20th-century mansions and small houses sitting on quiet, leafy, recently gentrified streets, plus a number of hot restaurants and bars. In the 1950s the area welcomed a significant influx of Caribbean immigrants, whose cultural heritage is vibrantly celebrated each year at the **Notting Hill Carnival,** Europe's largest street party. Hotels are few, but often terrifyingly chic. Notting Hill is also home to **Portobello Road,** the site of London's most famous street market (p. 154). Adjacent **Holland Park,** an expensive residential neighborhood spread around the park of the same name, is a little more serene, but also more staid. Just to the west, the increasingly fashionable area of **Shepherd's Bush** is attracting a slew of artists and photographers, and in their wake a number of trendy new hangouts, while Europe's largest shopping center—upscale **Westfield**—can be found on the northeastern flank of Shepherd's Bush Green.

SOUTHWEST LONDON

Westminster Westminster has been the seat of first English, then British, government since the days of Edward the Confessor (1042–66). Dominated by the Houses of Parliament and **Westminster Abbey** (p. 103), the area runs along the Thames to the east of St. James's Park. Whitehall is the main thoroughfare, linking Trafalgar Square with Parliament Square.

Westminster also encompasses Victoria, an area that takes its name from bustling Victoria Station. Many B&Bs and hotels have sprouted up here because of the neighborhood's proximity to the rail station, which provides the main fast link with Gatwick Airport. If you've arrived without a hotel reservation, you'll find decent pickings on the streets off Belgrave Road; we've selected our local favorites starting on p. 188. Things are a bit pricier to the southwest in **Pimlico,** the area bordering the river, which is filled with fine Regency squares.

Belgravia South of Knightsbridge, this area has long been one of the main aristocratic quarters of London, rivaling Mayfair in grandeur. Scattered with grand, formal, and often startlingly expensive hotels, Belgravia is a haven of upmarket tranquility. If you

lodge here, no one will ever accuse you of staying on the "wrong side of the tracks."

Chelsea Beginning at Sloane Square, this stylish Thames-side district lies south and to the west of Belgravia. The area has always been a favorite of writers and artists, including Oscar Wilde, George Eliot, J. M. W. Turner, Henry James, and Thomas Carlyle. The main drawback to Chelsea as a base is inaccessibility. Except for Sloane Square, there's a dearth of Tube stops, and unless you like to take a lot of buses or expensive taxis, you may find getting around a chore.

Chelsea's major boulevard is **King's Road,** where Mary Quant launched the miniskirt in the 1960s, Vivienne Westwood devised the punk look in the 1970s, and where today Charles Saatchi's eponymous **Saatchi Gallery** (p. 102) makes the running in the contemporary art world.

Knightsbridge & Brompton One of London's swankiest neighborhoods, Knightsbridge is a top residential, hotel, and shopping district just south of Hyde Park. Its defining feature and chief attractions are **Harrods** (p. 160) on the Brompton Road, "the Notre Dame of department stores," and nearby Beauchamp Place (pronounced *Bee*-cham), a Regency-era, boutique-lined street with a scattering of restaurants. Staying here will come at a price.

South Kensington If you want to be in the vicinity of the shops, boutiques, and restaurants of Knightsbridge and Chelsea, but don't have the resources for a hotel there, head for South Kensington, where the accommodations are more moderately priced. Southeast of Kensington Gardens, primarily residential South Kensington is often called "museumland" because it's dominated by a complex of museums and colleges, including the **Natural History Museum** (p. 101), **Victoria and Albert (V&A)** (p. 103), and **Science Museum** (p. 102). South Kensington boasts some fashionable restaurants and town-house hotels, and is just a couple of stops along the Tube's Piccadilly Line from Green Park.

Earl's Court Earl's Court lies south of Kensington and just west of South

Kensington. For decades the favored haunt of visiting Australians (hence its nickname, "Kangaroo Valley"), the area is still home to many immigrants—mainly eastern Europeans these days—and is also a popular base for budget travelers, thanks to its wealth of B&Bs, inexpensive hotels, and hostels, and its convenient access to central London: A 15-minute Tube ride takes you into the heart of the West End. Littered with fast-food joints, pubs, and cafes, it provides a cheap, cheerful base, but little in the way of refinement and no major sights.

SOUTH BANK

Lying south across the Thames from Covent Garden, this is where you'll find the **London Eye** (p. 108), **National Theatre** (p. 165), and **Southbank Centre** (p. 167; the largest arts center in Western Europe, and still growing). Although the area's time as a top hotel district may yet come, that day hasn't arrived yet. A few interesting accommodations aside, the South Bank is, however, a popular evening destination for culture and dining. To the east the South Bank bleeds into Bankside, the site of **Tate Modern** (p. 110), **Shakespeare's Globe** (p. 109), and **HMS Belfast** (p. 106), and today the two areas are generally regarded as forming a single zone linked by a cheery riverside path taking you all the way—via inland detours at London Bridge—from Westminster Bridge to Tower Bridge. The area is accessible as never before, reached from its eastern end by **London Bridge Station,** and from its central stretch by the new southside entrance to **Blackfriars Station.** Also now boasting a revamped north side entrance, Blackfriars has become the first London station to span the Thames.

THE CITY

The Square Mile When Londoners speak of "the City," they mean the original Square Mile that's now Britain's main financial district. The City was the original site of "Londinium," the first settlement of the Roman conquerors. Although it retains some of its medieval character, much of the City was swept away by the Great Fire of 1666, the Blitz of 1940, and the zeal of modern developers. Landmarks include Sir Christopher Wren's masterpiece, **St. Paul's Cathedral**

(p. 112), which stood virtually alone in the surrounding rubble after the Blitz, and the curvy glass skyscraper 30 St. Mary Axe, better known as the "Gherkin." Some 2,000 years of history unfold at the City's **Museum of London** (p. 111). Most of the hotels are set up for business travelers, not sightseers. However, that can sometimes mean weekend bargains at upscale establishments; see p. 193 for our favorites.

Holborn & the Inns of Court The old borough of Holborn (pronounced *Ho*-burn), which abuts the Square Mile southeast of Bloomsbury, and Temple, south of Holborn across the Strand, represents the heart of legal London—here you'll find barristers, solicitors, and law clerks, operating out of four Inns of Court (legal associations that are part college, part club, and part hotel): Gray's Inn, Lincoln's Inn, Middle Temple, and Inner Temple. Still Dickensian in spirit, the Inns are otherworldly places to explore, away from the traffic, with ancient courtyards, mazy passageways, and gas lamps.

Clerkenwell This neighborhood, north and a little west of the City, was the site of London's first hospital, and is the home of several early churches. In the 18th century, Clerkenwell declined into a muck-filled cattle yard, home to cheap gin distilleries and little else. A handful of hot restaurants and clubs have sprung up, and art galleries line St. John's Square and the fringe of Clerkenwell Green. The area is a good base for young and fashionable visitors, close to the bars and clubs of Hoxton and Shoreditch, and a short walk from the Square Mile itself.

EAST LONDON

The East End, Hoxton & Dalston A multitude of slums formed east of the old city walls during the intense industrialization and urbanization of the 19th century, many of which were bombed out of existence during World War II. Cheap rents have attracted a certain type of young, design-savvy entrepreneur to some parts, and you'll now find lots of trendy bars, clubs, restaurants, and vintage clothing outlets. Much of the most fashionable life is found just north of the Square Mile, around **Hoxton Square** and its periphery, including the "Shoreditch Triangle," formed by Old Street, Great Eastern Street, and Shoreditch High Street. The area is also leading the way in new technology; the glut of web-based and tech companies based around the interchange of Old Street and City Road has led to it being dubbed "Silicon Roundabout." There's always plenty going on, making it a place to base yourself if you want to take advantage of the intense, fluid nightlife, but perhaps a little hectic if you prefer your 8 hours and an early start. Options for accommodations have grown (p. 194) and there are good, affordable places to eat, particularly in **Shoreditch** and **Dalston.**

Immediately east of the City, the redeveloped Spitalfields area boasts a number of great (and historic) markets, including a craft market still trading in the old **Spitalfields Market** (p. 154) building.

Brick Lane is the heart of London's Bangladeshi community, and still a great place for a curry. Farther east, the shiny stadia of **Olympic Park** in Stratford represent the area's biggest development for a generation.

Docklands In 1981, in the most ambitious scheme of its kind in Europe, the London Docklands Development Corporation (LDDC) was formed to redevelop the then-moribund dockyards of Wapping, the Isle of Dogs, the Royal Docks, and Surrey Docks. The area is bordered roughly by Tower Bridge to the west and London City Airport to the east. Despite some early setbacks and a couple of ill-timed recessions, the plan was ultimately successful. Many businesses have moved here; Thames-side warehouses have been converted to Manhattan-style lofts and museums, entertainment complexes, shops, and an ever-growing list of restaurants have popped up at this river-city in the making.

Canary Wharf, on the Isle of Dogs, is the heart of Docklands. This 69-acre site is dominated by a 240-m (787-ft.) tower, One Canada Square, which was the tallest building in the U.K. until the "Shard" was completed at London Bridge.

NORTH & NORTHWEST LONDON

King's Cross & St. Pancras Long a seedy area on the fringe of central London, King's Cross is in the midst of a massive

card is **Hampstead Heath** [...] 791 acres of meadows [...] land; it maintains [...] despite being s[...]

Highgate [...] gate i[...] d[...]

[...] Paris [...] architecture [...] a huge [...] world [...] [...], and Gothic [...] Today the glamorous and restored station is a dazzling entry point into Britain, its grand architecture further enhanced by the 2011 reopening of the 19th-century Midland Railway Hotel as the **St. Pancras Renaissance London** (p. 180).

Camden London's alternative heart lies just east of Regent's Park. Since the 1960s, its thicket of clubs and pubs have been at the forefront of a succession of—usually short-lived—musical scenes: Punk, Brit-pop, alt-folk, the embers of which often continue smoldering here some time after the wider blaze has died down. Camden's various sprawling markets (p. 154), which occupy a number of venues north of the Tube stop and sell a vast abundance of arts, crafts, and fashions, have turned the area into one of London's major tourist destinations, with tens of thousands pitching up here each weekend. It's a noisy, vibrant, and crowded place, and for all those reasons, perhaps not the best area to base yourself unless you're here to party. In any case, Camden doesn't really have much of a hotel scene, although there are some good restaurants. Adjacent **Primrose Hill** is a pretty urban village of Victorian terrace houses rolling up a hill on the north side of Regent's Park. From the hill, some 78m (256 ft.) up, you have a panoramic sweep of central London.

Hampstead This residential suburb of north London, beloved by Keats and Hogarth, is a favorite excursion. Everyone from Sigmund Freud and D. H. Lawrence to Anna Pavlova and John Le Carré have lived here, and it's still one of the most desirable districts in the city. It has some hotels and B&Bs, although it is quite a few Tube stops from central London. Hampstead's calling

p. 117), nearly
ponds, and wood-
its rural atmosphere
rrounded by cityscapes.

Along with Hampstead, High-
another choice north London resi-
ntial area, particularly on or near Pond
Square and along Highgate High Street.
Once celebrated for its "sweet salutarie
airs," Highgate has long been a desirable
place for Londoners to live. Today most visitors come to see **Highgate Cemetery**
(p. 117), the final resting place of Karl Marx
and George Eliot.

SOUTHEAST LONDON—GREENWICH
In the southeast of London, this suburb,
which contains the prime meridian—"zero"

for the reckoning of terrestrial longitudes—
enjoyed its first heyday under the Tudors.
King Henry VIII and both of his daughters,
Queens Mary I and Elizabeth I, were born
here. Greenwich Palace, Henry's favorite, is
long gone, though, replaced by a hospital
for sailors during its second great age,
which saw it emerge in the 18th and 19th
centuries as one of the country's main naval
centers. Today's visitors come to this port
village for nautical sights, including the
National Maritime Museum (p. 121), which
sports a new £20 million wing, and some
niche shopping opportunities (p. 155).

GETTING AROUND
By Public Transportation

The first London word that any visitor needs to learn is "Oyster." The **Oyster Card**
is a plastic smartcard that is your gateway to pretty much every form of London public
transport. You can still pay to use all these services with cash, but an Oyster offers big
savings on just about every journey. The pay-as-you-go card costs £5 for adults from
any Tube or major rail station—a charge that's refundable if you return the card after
use. As well as these discounts, your daily bill for using an Oyster is capped at the
price of an equivalent 1-Day Travelcard (see below), so there's no longer any need to
calculate in advance whether to buy a discounted multi-trip travel ticket. Basically, if
you're staying more than a day or so, and plan to use London's public transport network, then investing in an Oyster is a no-brainer. It saves you time and money.

To use an Oyster, simply touch it against the yellow card-reader that guards the
entry/exit gates at Tube and rail stations. The gates will open. You should always swipe
your Oyster card as you leave the station, even if the gate is open, otherwise you will
get charged maximum fare next time you use your card because you haven't "completed" your previous journey. On the bus you'll find the reader next to the driver. If
you're caught traveling without having swiped your Oyster, you're liable for an on-the-
spot fine.

You can order an Oyster in advance, preloaded with as much credit as you like,
from www.tfl.gov.uk/oyster. Postage to the U.K. is free, but worldwide delivery costs
£4.25. It's cheaper for overseas residents to wait and purchase from the first Tube
station they enter—activation is immediate. To top-up your balance, use cash or a
credit card at any Oyster machine, which you'll find inside most London rail stations,
at any of a network of around 4,000 newsstands (newsagents) citywide (see http://
ticketstoplocator.tfl.gov.uk), or online if you register your card in advance.

THE TUBE & DOCKLANDS LIGHT RAILWAY The **"Tube"** is the quickest and
easiest way to move around the capital. All Tube stations are marked with a red circle
and blue crossbar. There are 10 extensive lines, plus the short Waterloo & City line

linking Waterloo and Bank, all of which are conveniently color-coded and clearly mapped on the walls of every Tube station. The Tube generally operates Monday to Saturday 5am to 12:30am, Sunday 7:30am to 11:30pm. The above-ground extension of the Tube that links the City with points around the East End and Docklands, including London City Airport, is known as the **Docklands Light Railway,** or "DLR." This metro rail system is essentially integrated with the Tube.

Tickets for the Tube operate on a system of nine fare zones. The fare zones radiate in concentric rings from the central Zone 1, which is where most visitors spend the majority of their time. Zone 1 covers the area from Liverpool Street in the east to Notting Hill in the west, and from Waterloo in the south to Baker Street, Euston, and King's Cross in the north. Tube maps should be available at any Tube station. You can also download one before your trip from the excellent Transport for London (TfL) website, at www.tfl.gov.uk/assets/downloads/standard-tube-map.pdf or download one of the many London Tube apps from your smartphone's app store. A 24-hour information service is also available at © **0843/222-1234.** The best planning tool is the TfL Journey Planner, online at www.tfl.gov.uk/journeyplanner.

If you don't have an Oyster (see above), you can get your ticket at a vending machine or a ticket window. But note the prices: The cash fare for travel across up to three zones is £4.30, rising to £5.30 to travel across six zones. A journey from anywhere in zones 1 or 2 to anywhere else in zones 1 or 2 using Oyster pay-as-you-go costs £2 outside peak hours, £2.70 before 9:30am. Oyster will get you across all six zones for £2.90 after 9:30am. On all ticketed journeys, you can transfer as many times as you like as long as you stay on the Tube or DLR network.

THE BUS NETWORK   London's buses can be a delightful way to navigate the city. Not only are they regular, efficient, and—late nights aside—comfortable, but also cheap compared to the Tube system. Buses also allow you to see where you're going—no need for an open-topped bus tour when you can ride the upper deck of an old-fashioned heritage **Routemaster** from Knightsbridge to Trafalgar Square on route no. 9, or Regent Street to St. Paul's and the Tower on the no. 15. Other excellent "sightseeing" routes include the no. 8 (from Oxford Circus to the Bank of England) and the no. 11 (from Victoria, past Parliament, and through Trafalgar Square to Bank).

Unfortunately, the bewildering array of services and routes deters many visitors—and even some locals. There are online route maps and downloadable area maps available at www.tfl.gov.uk/tfl/gettingaround/maps/buses. If you have Internet access, you could also try Busmapper.co.uk: Simply click your start and end points on an embedded Google Map and the site will suggest the best routes and tip you off about forthcoming departures. It's also available as an iPhone and Android app. **When's My Bus** (http://whensmybus.tumblr.com) is a handy service for Twitter users: Tweet your bus number and location to @whensmybus and it tweets back the next departure.

Unlike on the Tube, fares do not vary according to distance traveled—but if you transfer buses, you must pay again. A single journey from anywhere to anywhere costs £2.30 with cash, £1.35 with an Oyster Card. You can travel on buses all day with an Oyster for £4.20.

Buses generally run from 5am to just after midnight. Some run 24 hours, but other popular routes are served by **night buses,** running once every half-hour or so during the night, and with service numbers prefixed by an "N." For **open-top bus tours** of the city, see "Special Interest Tours," p. 46.

Central London

4 | LONDON | Getting Around

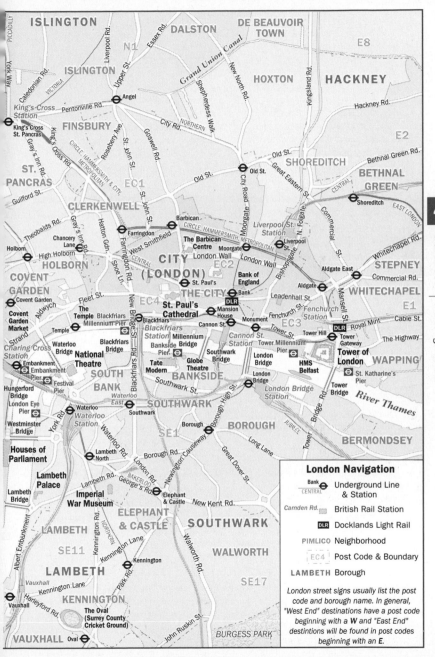

London Navigation

Bank ⊖ CENTRAL	Underground Line & Station
Camden Rd. ▫▫▫	British Rail Station
DLR	Docklands Light Rail
PIMLICO	Neighborhood
EC4	Post Code & Boundary
LAMBETH	Borough

London street signs usually list the post code and borough name. In general, "West End" destinations have a post code beginning with a W and "East End" destinations will be found in post codes beginning with an E.

4

Getting Around

LONDON

THE OVERGROUND & OTHER RAIL SERVICES The remarkable improvements in London's surface rail network have been the big transport story of recent years. Especially useful for visitors to North and Southeast London is the **London Overground** (marked in orange on most transport maps). The Overground connects Kew in southwest London with Highbury in North London, Stratford in East London adjacent to the 2012 Olympic Park, as well as Whitechapel and Wapping in the East End, and then points south of the river to Crystal Palace and beyond. The new, air-conditioned carriages and upgraded track ensure an efficient, comfortable ride. Oyster Cards are valid on Overground services. See www.tfl.gov.uk/overground for more. Oyster Cards are also valid on the remainder of London's surface rail network—encompassing a vast web of commuter and local services.

TRAVELCARDS For the **1-Day Off-Peak Travelcard,** valid for travel anywhere within zones 1 and 2 after 9:30am, the cost is £7 for adults or £3.20 for children aged 5 to 15. **One-Week Travelcards** cost adults £29.20 for travel in zones 1 and 2. For more Travelcard prices, visit www.tfl.gov.uk/tickets.

By Taxi

London "black cab" taxi drivers must pass a series of tests known as "the Knowledge," and cabbies generally know every London street within 6 miles of Charing Cross. You can pick up a taxi either by heading for a cab rank—stations, marquees of West End hotels and department stores, and major attractions all have them—or by hailing one in the street. The taxi is available if the yellow taxi sign on its roof is lit. Cabs are among the best designed in the world, and seat up to five passengers. Standard vehicles are wheelchair friendly.

Black-taxi meters start at £2.20, with increments of £2 or more per mile thereafter, based on distance and elapsed time. Surcharges are imposed after 8pm and on weekends and public holidays. Expect a mile-long journey to average around £6 to £8, a 2-mile journey around £8 to £13, and so on. There's no need to tip, although you may like to round the fare upward if you receive friendly service. To book, phone **One-Number Taxi** on ☎ 0871/871-8710. There's a £2 booking fee.

Minicabs are also plentiful, and are useful when regular taxis are scarce, as is often the case in the suburbs or late at night. These cabs are often meterless, so do discuss the fare in advance. If you text CAB to ✆ **60835,** TfL's Cabwise service will text you back with the telephone number of the nearest two licensed minicab offices. Premium minicab operator **Addison Lee** also has taxi booking apps for smartphone platforms including iPhone, Android, and Blackberry; see www.addisonlee.com/discover/mobile. **Kabbee** (www.kabbee.com) is an Android and iPhone app that compares minicab prices and lets you book from your handset.

By Boat

Once London's watery highway, the River Thames is these days more suited to a sightseeing trip than an A-to-B journey. However, it is used by some Docklands commuters, and that commuter service is as fun a way as any to get to the maritime sights of Greenwich (p. 121). **Thames Clippers** (www.thamesclippers.com) runs a year-round fleet of catamarans between the London Eye Pier and North Greenwich Pier, stopping at Embankment Pier, Bankside Pier, Tower Millennium Pier, Canary Wharf Pier, and Greenwich Pier, among others. Services run every 20 to 30 minutes for most of the day; journey time from Embankment to Greenwich is 35 minutes. An adult single costs £5.50, £5 with an Oyster Card, £3.70 if you hold a valid Travelcard, and £2.80 for children aged 5 to 15. A **River Roamer,** allowing unlimited travel between 9am and 9pm—or all-day at weekends—costs £12.60, £8.40 for Travelcard holders, and £6.30 for children. A Family River Roamer costs £26.50. Buy online, on board, or at any of the piers. There's also a separate **Tate-to-Tate** service that connects Tate Modern, in Bankside, with Tate Britain, in Pimlico. Tickets cost £5, and boats depart at least hourly, between 10am and 5pm.

For trips upriver to Hampton Court and Kew, see "River Cruises On the Thames," p. 125.

By Bicycle

The **Barclays Cycle Hire scheme** (www.tfl.gov.uk/barclayscyclehire) was launched in 2010. Anyone can rent a so-called "Boris Bike"—jocularly named after mayor at the time, Boris Johnson—from any of the hundreds of docking stations dotted around the center from Bow and Hackney to Olympia, and Regent's Park to the Oval. There's no need to return the bike to the same docking station you collected it from, making the scheme ideal for short-range, spontaneous tourism. Charges are made up of a fixed access fee—£1 per day or £5 per week—and a usage fee—it's free to rent a bike for 30 minutes, £1 for an hour, £6 for 2 hours. Buy access with a credit or debit card at the docking station or join online. Bikes are suited to anyone aged 14 or over.

You should always ride London's roads with extreme care. For more on cycling in London, see www.tfl.gov.uk/cycling.

[FastFACTS] LONDON

Area Codes The country code for Great Britain is **44.** The area code for London is **020** (omit the initial "0" if calling from overseas). The full telephone number is then usually eight digits long. As a general rule, businesses and homes in central London have numbers beginning with a **7;** those farther out begin with an **8.** You may also come across numbers beginning with a **3.**

Doctors If you need a non-emergency doctor, your hotel can recommend one, or you can contact your embassy or consulate. Failing that, try the G.P. (General Practitioner) finder at www.nhsdirect.nhs.uk. North

American members of the **International Association for Medical Assistance to Travelers** (IAMAT; www.iamat.org; ☎ **716/754-4883,** or 416/652-0137 in Canada) can consult that organization for lists of local approved doctors. *Note:* U.S. and Canadian visitors who become ill while they're in London are eligible only for free *emergency* care. For other treatment, including follow-up care, you'll be asked to pay.

Emergencies Dial ☎ **999** for police, fire, or ambulance. Give your name and state the nature of the emergency. Dialing ☎ **112** also connects you to the local emergency services anywhere in the E.U.

Hospitals There are 24-hour, walk-in Accident & Emergency departments at the following central hospitals: **University College London Hospital,** 235 Euston Rd., London NW1 2BU (www.uclh.nhs.uk; ☎ **020/3456-7890;** Tube: Warren St.); **St. Thomas' Hospital,** Westminster Bridge Road (entrance on Lambeth Palace Rd.), London SE1 7EH (www.guysandstthomas.nhs.uk; ☎ **020/7188-7188;** Tube: Westminster or Waterloo). The **NHS Choices** website (www.nhs.uk) has a search facility that enables you to locate your nearest Accident & Emergency department wherever you are in the U.K. In a medical emergency, you should dial ☎ **999.**

Maps If you plan to explore London in any depth, you'll need a detailed street map with a street index. We use and recommend the **London A to Z,** available in various sizes at newsagents and bookstores citywide.

Police London has two official police forces, the City of London police (www.cityoflondon.police.uk) whose remit covers the "Square Mile" and its 8,600 residents; and the Metropolitan Police ("the Met"), which covers the rest of the capital and is split into separate borough commands for operational purposes. Non-emergency contact numbers and opening hours for all the Met's local police stations are listed at www.met.police.uk/local. In a non-emergency, you can contact your local police station from anywhere by dialing ☎ **101.** Losses, thefts, and other criminal matters should be reported at the nearest police station immediately. You will be given a crime number, which your travel insurer will request if you make a claim against any losses. Dial ☎ **999** or 112 if the matter is serious.

EXPLORING LONDON

In the listings below, children's prices generally apply to those 15 and under. To qualify for a senior discount, you must be 60 or older. Students must present a student ID to get discounts. In addition to closing on public holidays, many attractions close between Christmas and New Year, so always check ahead if visiting at that time. All museums are closed Good Friday, December 25 and 26, and New Year's Day.

The West End

Banqueting House ★ HISTORIC HOME   This sumptuous dining chamber is the only remaining part of the once-mighty Whitehall Palace. Its commission in the early 17th century by James I marked both the arrival of Renaissance architecture in England and a particular high point for the Stuart Dynasty, which had just become the first royal family to rule both England and Scotland. However, just a few decades later, in 1649, Banqueting House would provide the setting for the dynasty's lowest ebb when James's successor, Charles I, fresh from his defeat in the English Civil Wars, was executed in front of the building.

Today the main attraction of this great feasting hall is not the food—which you won't be able to sample unless you're a visiting head of state—but the

Our London Top 10 Attractions

British Museum (below): The history and wonders of human civilization packed into one glorious neoclassical building.

Hampstead Heath (p. 117): London's finest open space—with views, ponds, woodland, grassland, kite-flying, bird-watching, and wilderness galore.

National Gallery (p. 90): More than 2,000 masterpieces grace one of the world's great art museums.

Natural History Museum (p. 101): For youngsters, it's all about the dinosaurs, but this "cathedral of nature" provides an engaging overview of life in all its forms.

Royal Botanic Gardens, Kew (p. 124): The ultimate garden for a nation of gardeners.

St. Paul's Cathedral (p. 112): Wren's masterpiece is packed with views, inside and out.

Tate Modern (p. 110): Bankside's hymn to the "shock of the new" just sprouted a new extension.

Tower of London (p. 112): This formerly fearsome fortress is now a family-fun favorite.

Victoria and Albert Museum (p. 103): Always evolving and growing, this houses perhaps the world's finest collection of decorative arts.

Westminster Abbey (p. 103): Britain's great monument to itself, where nearly every monarch of the past 1,000 years has been crowned.

ceiling paintings by Rubens, which imagine James I crowned amid a swirling mass of cherubic flesh. The house often closes on short notice for official events, so it's best to call in advance. *Insider tip:* Classical concerts are held here on the first Monday evening of each month (Aug excepted). The website lists the upcoming program; book by calling © **020/3166-6153.**

Whitehall Palace, Horse Guards Ave., SW1. www.hrp.org.uk/banquetinghouse. © **0844/482-7777.** Admission £5 adults, £4 seniors and students, free children 15 and under. Mon–Sat 10am–5pm (last admission 4:30pm). Tube: Westminster or Embankment.

British Museum ★★★ ☺ MUSEUM The "BM" was born in the age of Enlightenment and Empire, the progeny of two great British desires—the desire for knowledge and the desire for other people's possessions. In the 18th and 19th centuries, the British upper classes traveled the globe, uncovering the artifacts of distant civilizations, packing them in crates, and shipping them home. Their acquisitions formed the basis of the museum's collection, which has since been built into one of the world's largest and finest.

The collection is arranged along roughly geographical lines, so you could order your tour accordingly, taking in the **Rosetta Stone** from Egypt (the object that finally enabled scholars to decipher hieroglyphics), the **Elgin (or Parthenon) Marbles** from Ancient Greece, or the treasures of a 7th-century Saxon ship burial from **Sutton Hoo,** in Suffolk. But there's so much more—Babylonian astronomical instruments, giants heads from Easter Island, totem poles from Canada, mummies from Egyptian tombs, Chinese sculptures, Indian texts, Roman statues, African art ... the list goes on. In fact, the museum has more objects in storage than it ever does on display.

And if that wasn't enough, the BM hosts a succession of blockbuster temporary exhibitions, which are often staged in the **Reading Room,** the former home of the British Library. It lies at the center of the **Great Court,** the building's central

Attractions, Hotels & Restaurants in the West End

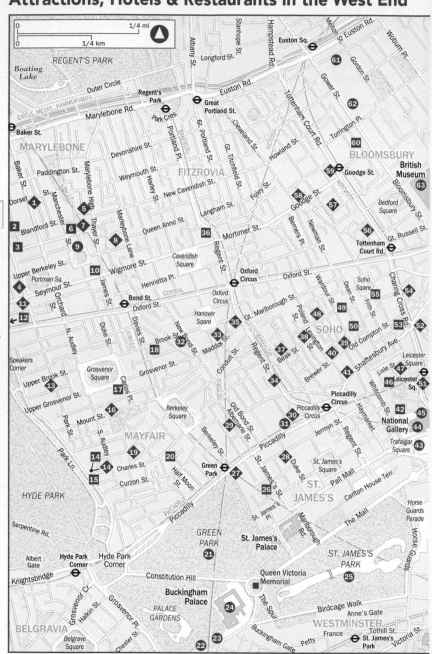

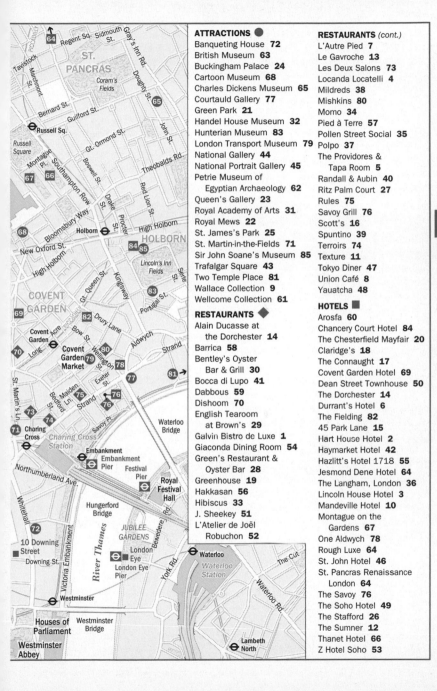

ATTRACTIONS ●

Banqueting House **72**
British Museum **63**
Buckingham Palace **24**
Cartoon Museum **68**
Charles Dickens Museum **65**
Courtauld Gallery **77**
Green Park **21**
Handel House Museum **32**
Hunterian Museum **83**
London Transport Museum **79**
National Gallery **44**
National Portrait Gallery **45**
Petrie Museum of
  Egyptian Archaeology **62**
Queen's Gallery **23**
Royal Academy of Arts **31**
Royal Mews **22**
St. James's Park **25**
St. Martin-in-the-Fields **71**
Sir John Soane's Museum **85**
Trafalgar Square **43**
Two Temple Place **81**
Wallace Collection **9**
Wellcome Collection **61**

RESTAURANTS ◆

Alain Ducasse at
  the Dorchester **14**
Barrica **58**
Bentley's Oyster
  Bar & Grill **30**
Bocca di Lupo **41**
Dabbous **59**
Dishoom **70**
English Tearoom
  at Brown's **29**
Galvin Bistro de Luxe **1**
Giaconda Dining Room **54**
Green's Restaurant &
  Oyster Bar **28**
Greenhouse **19**
Hakkasan **56**
Hibiscus **33**
J. Sheekey **51**
L'Atelier de Joël
  Robuchon **52**

RESTAURANTS (cont.)

L'Autre Pied **7**
Le Gavroche **13**
Les Deux Salons **73**
Locanda Locatelli **4**
Mildreds **38**
Mishkins **80**
Momo **34**
Pied à Terre **57**
Pollen Street Social **35**
Polpo **37**
The Providores &
  Tapa Room **5**
Randall & Aubin **40**
Ritz Palm Court **27**
Rules **75**
Savoy Grill **76**
Scott's **16**
Spuntino **39**
Terroirs **74**
Texture **11**
Tokyo Diner **47**
Union Café **8**
Yauatcha **48**

HOTELS ■

Arosfa **60**
Chancery Court Hotel **84**
The Chesterfield Mayfair **20**
Claridge's **18**
The Connaught **17**
Covent Garden Hotel **69**
Dean Street Townhouse **50**
The Dorchester **14**
Durrant's Hotel **6**
The Fielding **82**
45 Park Lane **15**
Hart House Hotel **2**
Haymarket Hotel **42**
Hazlitt's Hotel 1718 **55**
Jesmond Dene Hotel **64**
The Langham, London **36**
Lincoln House Hotel **3**
Mandeville Hotel **10**
Montague on the
  Gardens **67**
One Aldwych **78**
Rough Luxe **64**
St. John Hotel **46**
St. Pancras Renaissance
  London **64**
The Savoy **76**
The Soho Hotel **49**
The Stafford **26**
The Sumner **12**
Thanet Hotel **66**
Z Hotel Soho **53**

The Guard Doesn't Change Every Day

The ceremony begins at 11:30am sharp every day between May and July, and on alternate days for the rest of the year—in theory, anyway. However, it's often canceled in bad weather, which shows just what an unnecessary ceremony it is. If it looks like it's going to rain, it's probably best to head somewhere else instead.

courtyard, which is topped by a giant glass roof designed by Foster and Partners, and boasts various cafes and picnic areas.

Of course you could always take the easy option, and let someone else decide what you should see. Free half-hour "Eye Opener Tours" to different sections of the museum are given every 15 to 30 minutes from 11am to 3:45pm.

Great Russell St., WC1. www.britishmuseum.org. © 020/7323-8299. Free admission. Sat–Thurs 10am–5:30pm; Fri 10am–8:30pm. Tube: Holborn, Tottenham Court Rd., Goodge St., or Russell Sq.

Buckingham Palace ★ ☺ ✋ PALACE   The first house to stand on the site of what is now the principal London home of the monarch was built by the Duke of Buckingham in 1702. It was acquired by George II in 1761 and expanded and renovated throughout the 19th century, first by the flamboyant John Nash for George IV, and later by the more dour Edward Blore (dubbed "Blore the Bore") for Victoria. A new facade—including the famous balcony from which the royal family waves to the masses on major royal occasions—was added in 1913.

Although the exterior is rather boxy and uninspiring, the interior has more going on. For 8 weeks in August and September, while the royals are elsewhere, you can look for yourself. Tours visit a small selection of the palace's 600-plus rooms, including the Grand Staircase, the Throne Room, the Picture Gallery (which displays masterpieces by Van Dyck, Rembrandt, Rubens, and others), and the lavish State Rooms, where the Queen entertains heads of government with grand formal banquets. You can also take a walk along a 3-mile path through 40 acres of landscaped gardens.

Outside of the summer months, the only parts of the palace open to the public are the **Queen's Gallery** (p. 92) and the **Royal Mews** (p. 92).

Buckingham Palace is also the setting for a daily dose of public pageantry, **Changing of the Guard.** Pretty much every guidebook says the same thing about the ceremony—it's terribly British and a bit dull, and who are we to buck the trend? The needlessly elaborate ceremony for changing the 40 men guarding Buckingham Palace with another contingent from Wellington Barracks only exists for the benefit of visitors these days. It's actually interesting for about 5 minutes—with bearskin-wearing, red-coated soldiers, music from the marching band, shouted orders, complicated marching patterns. The trouble is the whole thing lasts for around 40 minutes—and if you want a decent vantage point, you'll need to turn up at least 1 hour early.

A much more accessible piece of pageantry can be seen at nearby **Horse Guards Parade** (p. 100) in Whitehall.

At end of The Mall. www.royalcollection.org.uk. © 020/7766-7300. Palace tours £18 adults, £16.50 seniors and students, £10.25 children 5–16, £47 family ticket, free for ages 4 and under; Changing of the Guard free. Aug 1–Sept 25 (dates can vary), and additional dates may be added. Daily 9:45am–6pm. Changing of the Guard daily May–July at 11:30am and alternating days for the rest of the year. Tube: St. James's Park, Green Park, or Victoria.

Cartoon Museum ★★ 📖 MUSEUM This is the capital's first and only museum dedicated to the great British traditions of cartooning, caricaturing, and comics. Displays are arranged chronologically, beginning in the early 18th century with the first British attempts at the new art form of *caricatura*, recently imported from Italy. From here it traces the development of the great cartoonists of the age, such as William Hogarth and George Cruikshank, whose work helped shine a light on the political and social hypocrisies of the day. The displays then take in the great magazine boom of the 19th and 20th centuries, which saw publications such as *Punch* setting the standard for political cartooning, and onto the works of modern satirists, including Steve Bell and Gerald Scarfe. The small shop by the entrance (free to enter) is a good source of graphic novels and collections of historic cartoons.

35 Little Russell St., WC1. www.cartoonmuseum.org. © **020/7580-8155.** Admission £5.50 adults, £4 seniors, £3 students, free for children 17 and under. Tues–Sat 10:30am–5:30pm; Sun noon–5:30pm. Tube: Tottenham Court Rd. or Holborn.

Charles Dickens Museum ★ MUSEUM This is the great novelist's only surviving London address, whose period-style rooms are filled with Dickensiana. Although he lived here for just a few years, from 1837 until 1840, this most prolific of authors still found the time to churn out several classics, including *Nicholas Nickleby, Oliver Twist, Pickwick Papers, The Old Curiosity Shop,* and *Barnaby Rudge*. Revamped and expanded to celebrate the bicentenary of Dickens' birth in 2012, the museum's reconstructed interiors contain his study, manuscripts, and personal effects.

48 Doughty St., WC1. www.dickensmuseum.com. © **020/7405-2127.** Admission £7 adults, £5 students and seniors, £3 children, £15 family ticket. Daily 10am–5pm. Tube: Russell Sq., Chancery Lane, or Holborn.

Courtauld Gallery ★ ART MUSEUM Like a mini-National Gallery, the Courtauld is one of the capital's finest small art museums. It holds an intense collection of works, covering all periods from the Renaissance to the 20th century, although the focus is very much on **Impressionism** and **Post-Impressionism** with works by Monet, Renoir, Gaugin, Van Gogh (including his *Self-Portrait with Bandaged Ear*), and Manet (it holds his final painting, *A Bar at the Folies-Bergère*). The Kandinskys on the top floor are also well worth seeking out. *Insider tip:* If money is a bit tight, try to visit on Monday morning when entry is free (until 2pm; excludes public holidays); if you stick around there's also a free 15-minute lecture about the collection at 1:15pm.

Somerset House, Strand, WC2. www.courtauld.ac.uk. © **020/7872-0220.** Admission £6 adults, £4.50 seniors and international students, free for children 17 and under, U.K. students, and for all Mon till 2pm. Daily 10am–6pm. Tube: Covent Garden, Temple, or Waterloo.

Green Park ★ ☺ PARK/GARDEN This most basic of London's great Royal Parks has an almost zen-like simplicity to it. There are no statues, water features, or adventure playgrounds here, just acres of rolling green lawns and tall trees—plus, in summer, local workers sunning their lunch hour away on the grass, or on the stripy **deckchairs** (£1.50) that are the park's only formal facility. In spring the park's color scheme broadens slightly, when hosts of daffodils bloom.

Piccadilly, SW1. www.royalparks.org.uk/parks/green-park. © **030/0061-2350.** Free admission. Open 24 hr. Tube: Green Park.

Handel House Museum ★ HISTORIC HOME Two musicians, separated by a couple of hundred years, and with profoundly different approaches to their art—albeit both hugely influential in their own way—made their homes on Brook Street, in the heart of Mayfair. The first was George Frederic Handel (1685–1759), the

German composer who moved to Britain aged 25 and settled at this address in 1723. He remained here for the rest of his life, creating the scores for many of his most famous works, including *Messiah* and *Music for the Royal Fireworks*. He was followed in 1968 by the American guitarist, **Jimi Hendrix,** who lived (some of the time) next door at number 23 with his English girlfriend until his death in 1970.

Both properties are now owned by the Handel House Museum, although only Handel's former home is currently open to the public. It's been meticulously restored to its Georgian prime with period fixtures, fittings, and fabrics. Exhibits include two antique harpsichords, various scores, and a canopied bedroom from 1720.

Classical recitals are given every Thursday (plus the occasional Tues or Sun), between 6:30 and 7:30pm and cost £9 (£5 for students). The program is mainly Handel favorites played by harpsichordists, baroque quartets, and the like, although Hendrix tunes (done in a classical style) crop up occasionally.

25 Brook St., W1. www.handelhouse.org. ©**020/7495-1685.** Admission £6 adults, £5 students and seniors, £2 children 5–15. Free for children 4 and under, and all children on Sat and Sun. Tues–Sat 10am–6pm (until 8pm Thurs); Sun noon–6pm. Tube: Bond St.

Hunterian Museum ★ MUSEUM   The shiny cases and cabinets of the Hunterian may give it a superficially modern, antiseptic feel, but this is a collection with its roots firmly in the past—and gore very much at its heart. It's made up of medical oddities and curiosities, most of them assembled in the late 18th century by John Hunter, the physician to "mad" King George III, for the purposes of instructing medical students. Bizarre highlights include various body parts pickled in jars (both human and animal), gruesome-looking teaching models (such as the lacquered systems of arteries and veins stuck onto wooden boards), skeletons of "dwarfs" and "giants," and some horror-inducing items of surgical equipment. Its grimly fascinating stuff. Free guided tours of the collection take place every Wednesday at 1pm.

Royal College of Surgeons, 35–43 Lincoln's Inn Fields, WC2. www.rcseng.ac.uk/museums. ©**020/7869-6560.** Free admission. Tues–Sat 10am–5pm. Tube: Holborn.

London Transport Museum ★★ ☺MUSEUM   Arranged more or less chronologically, this museum, housed in the swish glass-and-iron confines of Covent Garden's former flower market, traces the history of the capital's transport network from the days of steam and horse power to the green technologies of today. There are some wonderful old contraptions on display, including a reconstruction of an 1829 horse-drawn omnibus, a steam locomotive that ran along the world's first underground railway, and London's first trolleybus.

In addition to all the impressive hardware, the museum has displays on the often-overlooked aesthetics of public transport, particularly the signs, posters, and logos that together provided London Transport with such a clear graphic sensibility in the early 20th century.

There's lots of great stuff for children here, too, including a hands-on section where they can climb aboard miniature buses, trams, trains, and tubes, and trails to pick up at the front desk. *Insider tip:* The £13.50 entrance fee entitles you to unlimited visits over a 12-month period—hang on to your ticket.

Covent Garden Piazza, WC2. www.ltmuseum.co.uk. ©**020/7379-6344.** Admission £13.50 adults, £10 seniors and students, free for children 15 and under. Sat–Thurs 10am–6pm; Fri 11am–6pm (last admission 5:15pm). Tube: Covent Garden.

National Gallery ★★★ ☺ART MUSEUM   The National's collection of more than 2,300 paintings provide a comprehensive overview of the development of

Western art from the mid-1200s to 1900, rivaling any of Europe's great art galleries, such as the Louvre, the Prado, or the Uffizi. It's certainly more impressive than the original collection, founded by the British Government in 1824, which had just 38 works.

The layout is chronological. Passing through the sturdy neoclassical facade on Trafalgar Square, you turn left to find the gallery's oldest works, housed, by way of contrast, in its newest section, the 1990s-built **Sainsbury Wing.** It covers the period from 1250 to 1500, including paintings by such Renaissance and pre-Renaissance greats as Giotto, Piero della Francesca, Botticelli, Leonardo da Vinci, and Van Eyck (including his famed *Arnolfini Portrait*).

The chronology then moves onto the West Wing, covering 1500 to 1600 and filled with European Old Masters, such as Titian, Raphael, El Greco, and Hans Holbein. Next in line is the North Wing (1600–1700), where highlights include a Rembrandt self-portrait and works by Caravaggio and Velázquez, with things culminating in the East Wing (1700–1900), with a celebrated selection of Impressionist and Post-Impressionist paintings, including various water lilies by Monet, Van Gogh's *Sunflowers,* and Renoir's *Les Parapluies* (The Umbrellas)—some of the most popular (not to say most valuable) paintings in the collection.

If you can't decide where to begin, try joining a free 1-hour taster tour of the collection given every day at 11:30am and 2:30pm. Children's trails are available for £1 from the front desk (or can be downloaded for free in advance from the website).

Trafalgar Sq., WC2. www.nationalgallery.org.uk.✆ **020/7747-2885.** Free admission; fee charged for temporary exhibitions. Sat–Thurs 10am–6pm; Fri 10am–9pm. Tube: Charing Cross or Leicester Sq.

National Portrait Gallery ★★ ☺ ART MUSEUM   Most museums acquire their collections according to some notion of quality, with the aim of displaying the finest works of a particular artist, movement, or period. Not so the "NPG," where the collection is based not so much on ability as identity. Pictures have been chosen on the basis of who the subject is, not how well they've been captured by the artist. As a result, the works vary hugely in quality, and have been rendered in a great mishmash of styles and mediums, including oil paintings, sculptures, photographs, and LCD screens. The result is jolly and exuberant, like a giant scrapbook of the nation.

You'll pass Tudor kings and queens (including a study of Henry VIII by Holbein), great writers and thinkers (look out for Shakespeare sporting a natty gold earring, a portly looking Samuel Johnson by Sir Joshua Reynolds, and the Brontë sisters as captured by their brother, Bramwell), as well as the musicians, movie stars, politicians, and sporting royalty of today. However, if you need a little help working out who's who, free "Portrait of the Day" talks are given most Saturdays and some Wednesdays at noon. This is a great place to hang out on Thursdays and Fridays, when the gallery (as well as its cafe, bar, and restaurant) stays open till 9pm, laying on art talks and concerts—typically classical, jazz, or blues. *Insider tip:* The NPG's **Portrait Restaurant** has one of London's great "secret" views, out over Trafalgar Square toward the Houses of Parliament.

St. Martin's Place, WC2. www.npg.org.uk.✆ **020/7306-0055.** Free admission; fee charged for temporary exhibitions. Sat–Wed 10am–6pm; Thurs–Fri 10am–9pm. Tube: Charing Cross or Leicester Sq.

Petrie Museum of Egyptian Archaeology ★ 🏛 MUSEUM   Part of the University College London campus, this dusty, delightful collection of miniature treasures from Ancient Egypt makes the perfect companion exhibition to the rather larger and grander items on display in the Egyptian galleries of the nearby British

Museum (p. 85). Built up by the famed 19th-century Egyptologist, Flinders Petrie, the museum boasts a wonderfully evocative array of finds from the land of the pharaohs, including jewelry, pots, papyrus documents, frescoes, carvings, and some of the world's oldest-surviving cloth. Pick up a torch from the front desk and get exploring—the lighting is kept to a minimum to help conserve the delicate items.

University College London, Malet Place, WC1. www.ucl.ac.uk/museums/petrie. © **020/7679-2884.** Free admission. Tues–Sat 1–5pm. Tube: Goodge St. or Euston Sq.

Queen's Gallery ★ART MUSEUM   This 19th-century chapel is the only part of Buckingham Palace (aside from the Royal Mews, p. 92) that welcomes visitors year round. Today it's a gallery dedicated to rotating exhibitions of the wide-ranging treasure trove that is the **Royal Collection.** You'll find special showings of paintings, prints, drawings, watercolors, furniture, porcelain, miniatures, enamels, jewelry, and more. At any given time, you may see such artistic peaks as Van Dyck's equestrian portrait of Charles I; a dazzling array of gold snuffboxes; paintings by Monet; studies by Leonardo da Vinci; or perhaps even the recent and less-than-flattering portrait of the current Queen, by Lucian Freud.

Buckingham Palace, Buckingham Palace Rd., SW1. www.royalcollection.org.uk. © **020/7766-7301.** Admission £7.50 adults, £6.75 students and seniors, £3.75 children 5–16, free for children 4 and under. Daily 10am–5:30pm (last admission 4:30pm). Tube: Victoria.

Royal Academy of Arts ★ART MUSEUM   Established in 1768, the country's first professional art school counted painters Sir Joshua Reynolds and Thomas Gainsborough among its founding members. Each member has had to donate a work of art, and so, over the years, the Academy has built up a sizable collection. Ever-changing highlights are displayed in the **John Madejski Fine Rooms,** which can be visited as part of a free guided tour at 1pm on Tuesday, 1 and 4pm Wednesday to Friday, and 11:30am on Saturday. The Academy's annual **Summer Exhibition** has been held for more than 200 years. Today, however, the main focus of the gallery, and the principal draw for visitors, is its temporary exhibitions (costing upward of £12), which are usually blockbuster affairs—"Degas and the Ballet" and "David Hockney RA: A Bigger Picture" have been some of the recent hits.

Burlington House, Piccadilly, W1. www.royalacademy.org.uk. © **020/7300-8000.** Admission for temporary shows varies from £3 to £15.50. Free admission to guided tours of John Madejski Fine Rooms depending on the exhibition. Sat–Thurs 10am–6pm (last admission 5:30pm); Fri 10am–10pm (last admission 9:30pm). Tube: Piccadilly Circus or Green Park.

Royal Mews HISTORIC SITE/MUSEUM   This is where the British royal family's grandest forms of road transport are stored, including their fleet of Rolls Royces, their carriages, and the horses that pull them, who enjoy luxurious stables adorned with tile walls and gleaming horse brasses. Pride of place goes to the **Gold State Coach,** built in 1761. Decorated with a riotous assortment of gold leaf, painted panels, and sculptures of cherubs, lions' heads, and dolphins, it's the sort of thing that only a monarch could get away with. It's also absolutely huge—3.6m (12 ft.) high, 7m (23 ft.) long, weighing 4 tonnes (4.4 tons), and requiring eight horses to pull it. Also here is the 1902 **State Landau,** the coach in which both princess Diana and princess Kate rode following marriages to their respective princes.

Buckingham Palace, Buckingham Palace Rd., SW1. www.royalcollection.org.uk. © **020/7766-7302.** Admission £8 adults, £7.25 seniors and students, £5 children 5–17, free for children 4 and under, £21.25 family ticket. Daily Apr–Oct 10am–5pm; Nov–Dec 10am–4pm. Closed during state visits, royal events, and from Christmas through New Year. Tube: Victoria.

St. James's Park ★★ ☺ PARK/GARDEN   With its scenic central pond, tended flowerbeds, and picnic-friendly lawns, it's difficult to believe that this Royal Park was once a swamp near a leper colony. Today it's as elegant a green space as London can muster, and one of the best places in the center of town to watch wildfowl. Its pond is home to more than 20 species, including ducks, geese, and even four pelicans—the descendants of a pair presented to Charles II by a Russian ambassador in 1662— which are all fed daily between 2:30 and 3:30pm.

The Mall, SW1. www.royalparks.org.uk/parks/st-jamess-park.☏ **030/0061-2350.** Free admission. Open 24 hr. Tube: St. James's Park.

St. Martin-in-the-Fields ★ CHURCH   Although its setting at the edge of one of London's busiest squares makes the church's name seem almost willfully ironic, St. Martin's was indeed surrounded by fields when first founded in the 13th century. But these had already long gone by the time the current grand 18th-century building was constructed, the work of James Gibbs, a disciple of Christopher Wren. Today, following a £36 million makeover, it looks as good as ever, with an interior adorned with fine Italian plasterwork. A full program of classical concerts (plus the odd bit of jazz) is laid on here. Those performed at lunchtime are free (although a £3.50 donation is "suggested"), while evening tickets cost £7 to £26.

Inside, the excellent **Café in the Crypt** enjoys one of the most atmospheric locations in London, its floor made up numerous gravestones (including highwayman Jack Sheppard and Nell Gwynne, Charles II's mistress). The crypt is also home to the **London Brass Rubbing Centre** ★ ☺, where children can rub a wide selection of replica brasses (from £4.50), open Monday to Wednesday 10am to 7pm, Thursday to Saturday 10am to 10pm, and Sunday noon to 7pm.

Trafalgar Sq., WC2. www.smitf.org.☏ **020/7766-1100.** Free admission. Mon–Fri 9am–6pm; Sat– Sun 8:45am–7:30pm as long as no service is taking place. Concerts Mon, Tues, and Fri 1pm; Tues and Thurs–Sat 7:30pm. Tube: Charing Cross.

Sir John Soane's Museum ★★ MUSEUM   Perhaps the finest small museum in London, the building is both a repository for a fascinating collection of curios— Egyptian sarcophagi, Greek marbles and bronzes, Roman jewelry, medieval sculptures, Renaissance paintings, and more—and an enchanting demonstration of architectural ingenuity. Both are the work of the eponymous Sir John (1753–1837), one of London's foremost architects and collectors. Soane clearly saw no point in acquiring something if it couldn't be displayed, and so adorned every wall and surface, and even the ceilings of his home with artifacts and artworks. The result is a wonderfully stylish clutter. The museum plans to restore and open up Soane's (and Mrs Soane's) private apartments on the second floor by 2014.

Insider's tip: On the first Tuesday evening of every month, this most evocative of collections ups the ante by giving visitors the chance to explore its labyrinthine confines by candlelight. Expect to wait in line for at least 1 hour.

13 Lincoln's Inn Fields, WC2. www.soane.org.☏ **020/7405-2107.** Free admission (donations invited). Tues–Sat 10am–5pm; 1st Tues of each month also 6–9pm. Tours given Sat at 11am; £5 tickets distributed at 10:30am, first-come, first-served (group tours by appointment only). Tube: Holborn.

Trafalgar Square ★ SQUARE   Though undoubtedly London's best known square, boasting illustrious landmarks—including the **National Gallery** (p. 90), **St. Martin-in-the-Fields** (see above), and at its center, **Nelson's Column,** a granite column topped with a statue of Horatio Viscount Nelson (1758–1805), one of the country's celebrated naval heroes—Trafalgar was until recently a congested, unpleasant place. Remodeling over the past decade has seen its northern stretches pedestrianized and the pigeons sent on their way, significantly improving the ambience. Look out for a few unusual attractions, including an equestrian statue of Charles I, from where all distances from London are measured; the **world's smallest police station**—it has room for just one, rather lonely officer; and an empty plinth, the "**Fourth Plinth**" (the other three bear statues) on which temporary artworks are displayed.

Trafalgar Sq., WC2. www.london.gov.uk. Free admission. Open 24 hr. Tube: Charing Cross.

Two Temple Place ★ART MUSEUM   Opened in 2011 to host temporary exhibitions of publicly owned art from the U.K.'s regional collections, the latest addition to the capital's art scene enjoys a grand setting in a Gothic Revival mansion built in the late 19th century by William Waldorf Astor (founder of the famous New York Hotel that bears his name). Behind the Portland stone facade, the interior has a strange Victoriana-meets-Disney vibe, with the otherwise fairly straightforwardly opulent rooms (lots of marble and mahogany) adorned with bizarre details, such as the statues of characters from *The Three Musketeers* (Astor's favorite book) on the banisters of the main staircase. A gilded frieze in the Great Hall shows 54 seemingly random characters from history and fiction, including Pocohontas, Machiavelli, Bismarck, Anne Boleyn, and Marie Antoinette.

Temple Place, WC2. www.twotempleplace.org. ✆ **020/7836-3715.** Free admission. Mon and Wed–Sat 10am–4:30pm; Sun noon–5pm. Tube: Temple.

Wallace Collection ★★ART MUSEUM   Located in the palatial town house of the late Lady Wallace, this collection, built up over 2 centuries by one of London's leading aristocratic families, is a contrasting array of art and armaments. (The collection is similar in many ways to those of the Frick Museum in New York and the Musée Jacquemart-André in Paris.) The artworks include such classics as Frans Hals's *Laughing Cavalier* and Rembrandt's portrait of his son Titus. The paintings of the Dutch, English, Spanish, and Italian schools are outstanding. It's best visited on one of the free "Highlights" tours given at 1pm Monday and Friday; 2:30pm Tuesday and Thursday; and 11:30am and 2:30pm Wednesday, Saturday, and Sunday.

Manchester Sq., W1. www.wallacecollection.org. ✆020/7563-9500. Free admission (some exhibits charge). Daily 10am–5pm. Tube: Bond St. or Baker St.

Wellcome Collection ★ ☺ MUSEUM   The capital's finest museum of medicine was born out of the personal compulsion of Sir Henry Wellcome, a renowned 19th-century pharmacist and collector of historical medical artifacts from around the world. It's divided into two sections. The first, "Medicine Man," comprises Henry's original collection, and is wonderfully strange, an extraordinary assortment of medical oddities, including Ancient Egyptian canopic jars, Roman phallic amulets, South American mummies, a medieval leper clapper, and "secondhand" guillotine blades, as well as a number of "celebrity" items, such as Napoleon's toothbrush, Nelson's razor blade, and Darwin's walking stick. The second section, "Medicine Now" is slightly less bonkers, but no less interesting, focusing on modern medical trends and developments, with plenty of hi-tech stuff on genomes, vaccines, nanotechnology, and the like. Free tours of the museum are given on Saturdays (11:30am and 2:30pm) and Sundays (2:30pm).

183 Euston Rd., NW1. www.wellcomecollection.org. ✆ **020/7611-2222.** Free admission. Tues–Wed and Fri–Sat 10am–6pm; Thurs 10am–10pm; Sun 11am–6pm. Tube: Euston Sq., Euston, or Warren St.

West London

Hyde Park ★★★ **& Kensington Gardens** ★★ ☺ PARK/GARDEN   Once a favorite deer-hunting ground of Henry VIII, Hyde Park is central London's largest park. With the adjoining Kensington Gardens it forms a single giant open space, made up of 608 acres of velvety lawns interspersed with ponds, flowerbeds, trees, meadows, playgrounds, and more. The two parks are divided by a 42-acre lake known as the **Serpentine.** Paddleboats and rowboats can be rented from the **boathouse** (open Easter–Oct) on the north side (© **020/7262-1330**) costing £10 per hour for adults, £5 per hour for children. Part of the Serpentine has also been set aside for use as a **lido** (© **020/7706-3422**), where you can swim, provided you don't mind the often "challenging" water temperature. It costs £4 for adults, £3 for children.

Near the Serpentine bridge is the **Princess Diana Memorial Fountain,** the somewhat (perhaps appropriately) troubled monument to the late princess. When first opened in 2004, its slippery granite surfaces proved unsuited for something intended as a swimming and paddling venue, leading to its almost instant closure. It has since reopened with additional safety features.

At the northeastern tip of Hyde Park, near Marble Arch, is **Speakers' Corner,** where people have the right to speak (and more often shout) about any subject that takes their fancy. In the past you might have heard Karl Marx, Lenin, or George Orwell trying to convert the masses; today's speakers tend to be less well known, if no less fervent, and heckling is all part of the fun.

Blending with Hyde Park to the west of the Serpentine, and bordering the grounds of Kensington Palace (see below), are the well-manicured **Kensington Gardens.** They contain numerous attractions including the **Serpentine Gallery** (p. 96), a famous statue of **Peter Pan** erected by J. M. Barrie himself (secretly, in the middle of the night), and the **Diana, Princess of Wales Memorial Playground,** a pirate-themed fun area that has proved a more successful tribute to the late Princess of Wales than Hyde Park's fountain. At the park's southern edge is the **Albert Memorial,** a gloriously over-the-top, gilded monument erected by Queen Victoria in honor of her late husband.

Hyde Park, W2. www.royalparks.org.uk/parks/hyde-park. © **030/0061-2000.** Free admission. Hyde Park daily 5am–midnight. Kensington Gardens daily 6am–dusk. Tube: Hyde Park Corner, Marble Arch, or Lancaster Gate.

Kensington Palace ★ PALACE   The palace started life as a simple (relatively speaking) Jacobean mansion, but was turned into something much grander by Sir Christopher Wren on the orders of William III, who acquired it in the late 17th century. Since then it's been the home of various royals, including Victoria, Princess Margaret (the late sister of the current queen), and perhaps most famously, Diana, Princess of Wales—it was at the palace's gates that the great carpet of flowers was laid in the weeks following her death in 1997.

In 2012, the palace emerged from the initial stages of its most significant revamp in a generation, with new cafes, courtyards, and educational facilities, and the palace gardens connected to **Kensington Gardens** (see above) for the first time since the 19th century. In time the interior will be organized into exhibition areas focusing on the lives of four sets of royals: William III, Mary II, and Anne; George II; Victoria; and the princesses Margaret and Diana. The first of these, "Victoria: love, duty and loss," provides an overview of Victoria's life from the day the 17-year-old princess was awakened in her room in Kensington Palace to be told her uncle, William IV, had died and that she was now queen, to her later life as Empress of India and figurehead of an age. Renovation of the palace's private quarters will also take place by 2013, when Prince William and the Duchess of Cambridge move into the rooms formerly occupied by Princess Margaret. The palace's magnificent 18th-century **Orangery** (see p. 149) is a fine venue for afternoon tea.

The Broad Walk, Kensington Gardens, W8. www.hrp.org.uk/KensingtonPalace. ℂ **0844/482-7777.** Admission £12.50 adults, £11 seniors and students, £6.25 children 5–15, £34 family ticket. Mar–Oct daily 10am–6pm; Nov–Feb daily 10am–5pm. Tube: Queensway or Notting Hill Gate; High St. Kensington on south side.

Museum of Brands, Advertising & Packaging ★ ▮MUSEUM A museum dedicated not so much to things, as the packets the things come in. These days people are pretty savvy as to the value and appeal of packaging. However, back when the museum's founder, Robert Opie, began his collection—according to legend, in 1963 at the age of 16 with a chocolate wrapper—the idea of appreciating packaging for its own sake was in its infancy (that great art hymn to packaging, Andy Warhol's *Campbell's Soup Cans* had been produced the year before). The collection has since grown to vast proportions, comprising some 12,000 items from the past 120 years, including everything from magazine advertisements and washing powder boxes to cereal packets and milk bottles, as well as assorted toys and household appliances.

2 Colville Mews, Lonsdale Rd., W11. www.museumofbrands.com. ℂ **020/7908-0880.** Admission £6.50 adults, £4 seniors and students, £2.25 children 5–15, £15 family ticket. Tues–Sat 10am–6pm; Sun 11am–5pm. Closed Fri–Mon last weekend in August. Tube: Notting Hill Gate.

Serpentine Gallery ★ ART MUSEUM Just southwest of the Serpentine (see above), from which it takes its name, Kensington Gardens' Serpentine Gallery is one of London's leading contemporary art spaces—not to mention a good place to retire to should the British weather curtail your plans for a day of sunbathing or boating. It plays host to a rolling succession of shows, each displayed for a couple of months. Notable exhibitions have featured Henry Moore, Andy Warhol, and Damien Hirst. Over the past decade the Serp has perhaps become best known for commissioning a temporary **pavilion** each summer from one of the world's leading architects (in the Jean Nouvel, Frank Gehry, Daniel Libeskind league)—the more avant-garde and "out there," the better.

A new offshoot of the museum, the **Serpentine Sackler Gallery** opened in 2012, just to the north across the lake in Hyde Park. It's housed in the Magazine Building, a 19th-century ammunition depot, which has been remodeled by the architect Zaha Hadid, who was also responsible for the aquatic park at the London 2012 Olympic Games. With the addition of a transparent extension for a cafe-restaurant and an outdoor playspace, the new venue is dedicated to putting on rotating displays of new art.

Kensington Gardens, W2. www.serpentinegallery.org. ℂ **020/7402-6075.** Free admission. Daily 10am–6pm. Tube: Knightsbridge or Lancaster Gate.

Southwest London

Chelsea Physic Garden ★ GARDEN This is the second-oldest surviving botanical garden in England after Oxford's, founded by the Worshipful Society of Apothecaries in 1673 for the purpose of growing plants for medicinal study. To this end, plant specimens, including trees, began arriving from all over the world, many to grow in English soil for the first time. Some 7,000 plants still survive here, including

Attractions, Hotels & Restaurants in West London

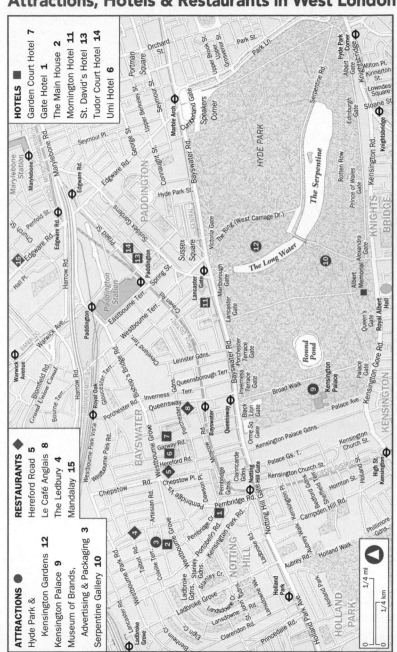

HOTELS ■

Garden Court Hotel **7**
Gate Hotel **1**
The Main House **2**
Mornington Hotel **11**
St. David's Hotel **13**
Tudor Court Hotel **14**
Umi Hotel **6**

RESTAURANTS ◆

Hereford Road **5**
Le Café Anglais **8**
The Ledbury **4**
Mandalay **15**

ATTRACTIONS ●

Hyde Park &
Kensington Gardens **12**
Kensington Palace **9**
Museum of Brands,
Advertising & Packaging **3**
Serpentine Gallery **10**

Attractions, Hotels & Restaurants in Southwest London

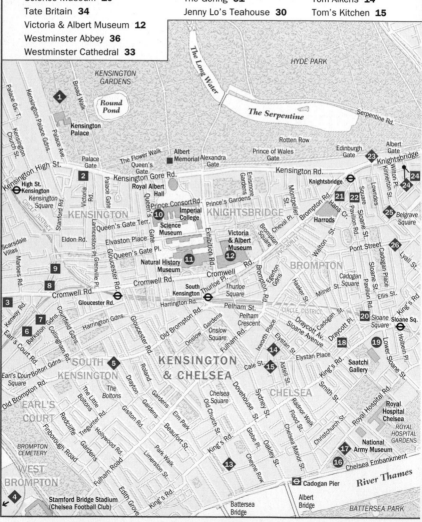

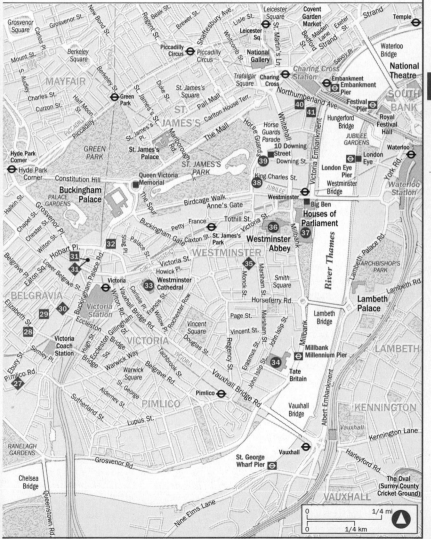

HOTELS ■

B&B Belgravia **29**
Base2Stay **7**
The Berkeley **24**
The Capital **21**
Corinthia Hotel London **40**
Draycott Hotel **20**

Easyhotel **8**
41 Hotel **32**
The Goring **31**
Henley House **6**
The Milestone **2**
Morgan House
Hotel **28**

Parkcity Hotel **9**
The Rockwell **3**
Royal Horseguards
Hotel **41**
San Domenico
House **18**
30 Pavilion Road **22**

everything from pomegranate to exotic cork oak. After such a buildup, you might be expecting something rather grand and sweeping in the Kew mold. But the Chelsea Physic is a rather small, crowded little place, albeit packed with botanical interest.

66 Royal Hospital Rd., SW3. www.chelseaphysicgarden.co.uk. © **020/7352-5646.** Admission £8 adults, £5 children 5–15 and students. Apr–Oct Wed–Fri noon–5pm (Jul–Aug Wed till 10pm), Sun and public holiday Mon noon–6pm. Tube: Sloane Sq.

Churchill War Rooms ★★ HISTORIC SITE   These cramped subterranean rooms were the nerve center of the British war effort during the final years of World War II, where Winston Churchill and his advisors planned what they hoped would be an Allied victory. In August 1945, with the conflict finally won, the rooms were abandoned exactly as they were, creating a time capsule of the moment of victory.

You can see the **Map Room** and its huge wall maps; the Atlantic map is a mass of pinholes (each hole represents at least one convoy). Next door is Churchill's bedroom-cum-office, which has a bed and a desk with the two BBC microphones on it via which he tried to rally the nation. Other rooms include Churchill's kitchen and dining room, and the Transatlantic Telephone Room that is little more than a broom closet housing the scrambler phone with which Churchill conferred with U.S. President Roosevelt.

Also in the war rooms is the **Churchill Museum,** the world's first major museum dedicated to the life of Sir Winston Churchill.

Clive Steps, at end of King Charles St., SW1. www.iwm.org.uk/visits/churchill-war-rooms. © **020/7930-6961.** Admission £16 adults, £13 seniors and students, free for children 15 and under. Daily 9:30am–6pm (last admission 5pm). Tube: Westminster or St. James's Park.

Horse Guards HISTORIC SITE   North of Downing Street, on the site of the guard house of Whitehall Palace (which burned down in 1698), stands the 18th-century Horse Guards building, the headquarters of the **Household Cavalry Mounted Regiment,** whose soldiers have two principal duties: To protect the sovereign and to provide photo opportunities for tourists—their dandy uniforms of bright tunics and plumed helmets take a great shot.

The **ceremony ★** for changing the two mounted guards here is a good deal more accessible than the more famous one down the road at Buckingham Palace. It takes place at 11am and 4pm from Monday to Saturday, and at 10am and 4pm on Sunday, and lasts around 30 minutes. The mounted sentries are relieved every hour.

If you pass through the arch at Horse Guards, you'll find yourself at **Horse Guards Parade,** formerly the tiltyard (jousting area) of Whitehall Palace, which leads onto St. James's Park. It is here that the Household Cavalry help celebrate the Queen's birthday in June with a military pageant known as **"Trooping the Colour"** (p. 43).

Most of the building is usually closed to visitors, although a small section has been turned into the **Household Cavalry Museum** (www.householdcavalrymuseum. co.uk; © 020/7930-3070); admission costs £6 for adults, £4 for children.

Whitehall, SW1. © **020/7414-2479.** Free admission. Tube: Charing Cross, Westminster, or Embankment.

Houses of Parliament & Big Ben ★ ICON   The image of the **Palace of Westminster** (the official name for the building containing the Houses of Parliament) and its clocktower known as **Big Ben** (to everyone except pedants, who will tell you, as I'm doing, that Big Ben is in fact the name of the bell, not the tower) has become an icon of icons. It is the scene most evocative of the capital's timeless nature, and yet all is not as it seems. Although the site has been in use for almost 1,000 years—first as a royal palace, and then from the 16th century onward as the seat of Parliament—most of what you see dates only from the mid-19th century. It was designed in a deliberately medieval-looking, "Gothic Revival" style to replace a structure that burned down in 1834. There are, however, much older sections hidden within, including the 11th-century **Westminster Hall,** which still boasts its 14th-century hammerbeam roof, and the 14th-century **Jewel Tower.**

You can take a guided tour of the buildings on Saturdays throughout the year and during the summer recess (when the politicians are on vacation), which takes in various places of interest in the vast 1,000-room complex, including Westminster Hall, the Royal Gallery, and the Queen's Robing Room, where the monarch gets ready for her speeches to parliament. You are also allowed to pop into the **House of Commons** chamber itself, where the country's 650 elected MPs (Members of Parliament) come to argue over the latest legislation, as well as the secondary chamber, the **House of Lords.** To see British democracy in (for want of a better word) action, will probably involve a fair bit of waiting around. When the House is sitting—Monday to Thursday and some Fridays during the parliamentary seasons—line up outside the Cromwell Green visitor entrance, usually for a couple of hours (generally less for the Lords). Tickets are allocated on a first-come, first-served basis. Don't go expecting any great rhetorical fireworks, however. Most debates are sparsely attended and jargon-heavy. When parliament is sitting, U.K. visitors can arrange guided tours (of both parliament and Big Ben) by contacting their MP.

Across the street is the **Jewel Tower ★,** Abingdon Street (www.english-heritage. org.uk/daysout/properties/jewel-tower; ✆ **020/7222-2219**), one of only two surviving buildings from the medieval Palace of Westminster. Although originally built in 1365 to house Edward III's treasure-trove, the tower today holds only an exhibition on the history of Parliament. It is open daily from 10am to 5pm April to October, and weekends only 10am to 4pm November to March. Admission is £3.20 for adults, £2.90 for students and seniors, and £1.90 for children.

Old Palace Yard, SW1. www.parliament.uk. House of Commons ✆**020/7219-4272;** House of Lords ✆ **020/7219-3107.** Free admission to debates. Guided tours: £15 adults, £6 children 5–15, £37 family ticket. Tours take place Sat 9:15am–4:30pm; Aug–Sept Mon–Tues and Fri–Sat 9:15am–4:30pm, Wed–Thurs 1:15pm–4:30pm. Tours last 75 min. To attend debates, the House of Commons sits at the following times Mon–Tues 2:30–10:30pm, Wed 11:30am–7:30pm, Thurs 10:30am–6:30pm, and Fri 9:30am–3pm. Join the line at Cromwell Green entrance. Tube: Westminster.

Natural History Museum ★★★ ☺ MUSEUM

It seems fitting that one of London's great museums should be housed in such a grand building, a soaring Romanesque structure that provides a suitably reverent setting for what is often described as a "cathedral of nature." The museum's remit is to cover the great diversity of life on Earth, although that coverage is by no means uniform. One group of life forms gets a lot more attention lavished on it than any others, much to the delight of visiting 8-year-olds—**dinosaurs.** As you arrive, your first vision will be the giant cast of a diplodocus looming down above you. If you want to see more of these great prehistoric beasts—but with added rubbery skin and jerky movements—then turn left where you'll find a hall filled with fossils and finds, as well as displays of animatronic dinosaurs permanently surrounded by wide-eyed children.

The dinosaurs form part of the Blue Zone, one of the four color-coded sections that make up the museum. This zone is primarily concerned with animals, both past and present, and has plenty of other showstoppers, including a 40-m (90-ft.) model of a blue whale hanging from the ceiling, a saber-tooth tiger skeleton, and an adult-size model of a fetus.

The Green Zone's galleries focus on the environment, evolution, and ecology. Highlights include giant models of insects (in the Creepy Crawlies gallery) and a collection of precious stones in the museum's new section, the **Vault.**

The Earth's interior processes are explored in the Red Zone, where you can try and stay upright on an earthquake simulator, and see plastercasts of victims preserved in ash by the volcanic eruption at Pompeii.

The final zone, the Orange Zone, is the museum's latest pride and joy, comprising the eight-story glass-and-steel **Darwin Centre,** the most significant addition to the museum since it opened in 1881. Constructed in 2008 for the 150th anniversary of Darwin's *Origin of the Species,* the center is primarily a research institute, but also boasts hi-tech attractions for the public. The museum offers resources for younger visitors, including free discovery guides, explorer backpacks, and family workshops.

Cromwell Rd., SW7. www.nhm.ac.uk. © **020/7942-5000.** Free admission. Daily 10am–5:50pm. Tube: South Kensington.

Saatchi Gallery ★ ART MUSEUM   If British contemporary art is a balloon, then the Saatchi is the hot air that's been keeping it aloft for the past 20 years. Having occupied various premises, the collection of the British advertising mogul and mega-collector Charles Saatchi has now taken over a grand three-story former military school. The constantly changing displays of new "challenging" art are free to view, a welcome rarity for a non-publicly funded museum. Expect plenty of controversy—at least one big one a year or it's not really doing its job.

Duke of York's Headquarters, King's Rd., SW3. www.saatchi-gallery.co.uk. © **020/7811-3070.** Free admission. Daily 10am–6pm. Tube: Sloane Sq.

Science Museum ★★★ ☺ MUSEUM   Founded in the 1850s in the wake of—and largely with left over contraptions from—the Great Exhibition, the "Museum of Patents," as it was originally known, has grown to become the country's preeminent museum of science. It's also one of the capital's great interactive experiences, filled with buttons to press, levers to pull, and experiments to absorb you. There's plenty of impressive hardware on display, beginning, just after the entrance, in the **Energy Hall,** where you can meet the great clunking behemoths of the Industrial Revolution, including steam locomotives and giant beam engines. Beyond, the **Making the Modern World** exhibition celebrates 150 of most of the most significant icons of industrial progress from the past 250 years, including Charles Babbage's "Difference Engine," the first automatic calculator, Watson and Crick's model of the structure of DNA, and the Apollo 10 command module. On the same floor is the **Legend of Apollo 4-D Cinema,** offering viewers a computer-simulated round-trip to the moon, complete with stirring music and a portentous voiceover.

And that's just the start of the museum. Elsewhere you'll find galleries dedicated to medicine, telecommunications, computers, and flight—the last now with state-of-the-art flight simulators—as well as the ever popular **Launchpad,** where there are more than 50 hands-on experiments for youngsters to try, as well as an IMAX cinema showing spectacular nature- and space-related reels on a giant screen.

Exhibition Rd., SW7. www.sciencemuseum.org.uk. © **0870/870-4868.** Free admission. Daily 10am–6pm. Closed Dec 24–26. Tube: South Kensington.

Tate Britain ★★★ ART MUSEUM   Fronting the Thames near Vauxhall Bridge, the Tate looks like a smaller and more graceful relation of the British Museum.

Within is the country's finest collection of domestic art, dating from the 16th century to the present, with most of the country's leading artists represented, including such notables as Gainsborough, Reynolds, Stubbs, and Constable, William Hogarth and the incomparable William Blake, as well as such modern greats as Stanley Spencer, Francis Bacon, and David Hockney. The collection of works by J. M. W. Turner is the Tate's largest by a single artist, spread over seven rooms. Turner himself willed most of his paintings and watercolors to the nation.

And, just to show the young ones that it can still swing with the best of them, Tate Britain is also the host each autumn of the annual **Turner Prize,** the media-baiting, controversy-seeking competition for the best contemporary British art.

Free tours of parts of the collection are offered Monday to Friday (at 11am, noon, 2pm, and 3pm) and on Saturdays and Sundays at noon and 3pm, and the first Friday of each month sees the "Late at Tate" event, which involves extended opening hours (till 10pm) and free events, such as talks, film screenings, or live music.

If you want to make an art-filled day of it, the **Tate to Tate boat service** departs from just out front to **Tate Modern** all day (see p. 110).

Millbank, SW1. www.tate.org.uk/britain. © **020/7887-8888.** Free admission; special exhibitions incur a charge of £5–£15. Daily 10am–6pm (last admission 5:15pm). Tube: Pimlico.

Victoria and Albert Museum ★★★ ☺ MUSEUM   The V&A (as it's usually known) could justly claim to be the world's greatest collection of applied arts, comprising seven floors and 150 galleries, in which are displayed, at a rough estimate, around four million items of decorative art from across the world and throughout the ages—sculptures, jewelry, textiles, clothes, paintings, ceramics, furniture, architecture, and more. Many of the collections are among the finest of their type. The V&A has the largest collection of Renaissance sculptures outside Italy, the greatest collection of Indian art outside India (in the Nehru Gallery), and the country's most comprehensive collection of antique dresses (in the Fashion Gallery). The Photography Gallery can draw on some 500,000 individual images, the recently added William & Judith Bolling Gallery holds one of the world's largest (and most glittering) collections of European jewelry, while the British Galleries can offer perhaps the greatest diversity of British design available anywhere, with all the great names of the past 400 years represented, including Chippendale, Charles Rennie Mackintosh, and William Morris.

To help you plot your path, your first stop should be the front desk where you can pick up leaflets, floor plans, and themed family trails. If you'd rather somebody else made the decisions for you, free guided tours leave from the grand entrance daily, hourly between 10:30am and 3:30pm. Art-based drop-in events are laid on for families on weekends.

Cromwell Rd., SW7. www.vam.ac.uk. © **020/7942-2000.** Free admission. Temporary exhibitions often £12.50. Sun–Thurs 10am–5:45pm; Fri 10am–10pm. Tube: South Kensington.

Westminster Abbey ★★★ CHURCH   The Abbey is not just one of the finest examples of ecclesiastical architecture in Europe, it's also the shrine of the nation where monarchs are anointed before God and memorials to the nation's greatest figures fill every corner. From the outside, it's a magnificently earnest-looking structure, its two great square towers and pointed arches the very epitome of medieval Gothic, while the inside is a cluttered mass of symbols and statuary. The building was begun in 1245 under the reign of Henry II and finally completed in the early 16th century. This replaced an earlier structure commissioned in 1045 by Edward the Confessor (which itself had replaced a 7th-century original) and consecrated in 1065, just in time to host Edward's funeral and (following a brief tussle in Hastings) the coronation of William the Conqueror. It has been, with a couple of exceptions, the setting for every coronation since, and it was here on April 29, 2011, that Prince William married Kate Middleton.

More or less at the center of the Abbey stands the shrine of Edward the Confessor, while scattered around are the tombs of various other royals, including Henry V, Elizabeth I, and Richard III—all rather overshadowed by the Renaissance tomb of Henry VII. Nearby is the surprisingly shabby **Coronation Chair,** on which almost every monarch since Edward II, including the current one, has sat during their coronation.

In **Poet's Corner** you'll find a great assortment of memorials to the country's greatest men (and a few women) of letters, clustered around the grave of Geoffrey Chaucer, who was buried here in 1400. These include a statue of Shakespeare, his arm resting on a pile of books, Jacob Epstein's bust of William Blake, as well as tributes to Jane Austen, Coleridge, John Milton, Dylan Thomas, and D. H. Lawrence.

Statesmen and men of science—Disraeli, Newton, Charles Darwin—are also interred in the Abbey or honored by monuments. Near to the west door is the 1965 memorial to Sir Winston Churchill and the tomb of the **Unknown Warrior,** commemorating the British dead of World War I.

Broad Sanctuary, SW1. www.westminster-abbey.org. © **020/7222-5152.** Admission £16 adults, £13 students and seniors, £6 children 11–18, £32 family ticket, free for children 10 and under. Mon–Tues and Thurs–Fri 9:30am–4:30pm (last admission 3:30pm); Wed 9:30am–7pm (last admission 6pm); Sat 9:30am–2:30pm (last admission 1:30pm). Tube: Westminster or St. James's Park.

Westminster Cathedral ★ CATHEDRAL This spectacular brick-and-stone church (1903) is the headquarters of the Roman Catholic Church in Britain. Adorned in retro-Byzantine style, it's massive: 108m (354 ft.) long and 47m (154 ft.) wide. One hundred different marbles compose the richly decorated interior, and mosaics emblazon the chapels and the vaulting of the sanctuary. If you take the elevator to the top of the 82-m (269-ft.) campanile, you'll be rewarded with sweeping views that stretch from the Houses of Parliament to the "Gherkin." The cathedral's renowned choir usually performs daily: Download a timetable from the website.

Ashley Place, SW1. www.westminstercathedral.org.uk. © **020/7798-9055.** Cathedral free admission. Tower £5 adults, £2.50 seniors, students, and children. Cathedral services Mon–Sat 7am–7pm; Sun 8am–8pm. Tower Mon–Sat 9:30am–5pm; Sat–Sun 9:30am–6pm. Tube: Victoria.

The South Bank

Florence Nightingale Museum ★ ☺ MUSEUM The museum celebrates the life and work of one of the great Victorian British women, best known for nursing soldiers during the Crimean War (1853–56). However, you'll learn that the greatest achievement of the "lady with the lamp" was probably as a statistician. She used then revolutionary techniques for presenting data, such as pie charts, to prove the importance of sanitation and hygiene in lowering the death rate of wounded soldiers.

The museum holds many objects owned or used by Nightingale, including clothes, furniture, letters, and even her pet stuffed owl. There are also audiovisual displays on her life and a reconstruction of a Crimean ward.

The museum is very much slanted toward families and schoolchildren—parties of whom arrive regularly during termtime—and free family events, such as storytellings, art workshops, and trails are staged most weekends.

Westminster Abbey

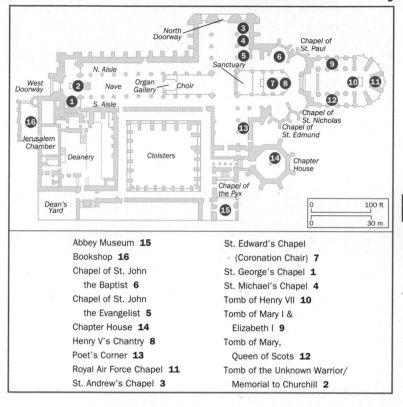

Abbey Museum **15**
Bookshop **16**
Chapel of St. John
  the Baptist **6**
Chapel of St. John
  the Evangelist **5**
Chapter House **14**
Henry V's Chantry **8**
Poet's Corner **13**
Royal Air Force Chapel **11**
St. Andrew's Chapel **3**

St. Edward's Chapel
  (Coronation Chair) **7**
St. George's Chapel **1**
St. Michael's Chapel **4**
Tomb of Henry VII **10**
Tomb of Mary I &
  Elizabeth I **9**
Tomb of Mary,
  Queen of Scots **12**
Tomb of the Unknown Warrior/
  Memorial to Churchill **2**

St. Thomas' Hospital, 2 Lambeth Palace Rd., SE1. www.florence-nightingale.co.uk. © **020/7620-0374.** Admission £5.80 adults, £4.80 seniors, students, children ages 5–15, and persons with disabilities, free for children 4 and under; £16 family ticket. Daily 10am–5pm. Tube: Westminster, Waterloo, or Lambeth North.

Garden Museum ★ MUSEUM   Housed in a small medieval church, St. Mary-Lambeth, this offers a celebration of that most British of pastimes—gardening. Its focus is unashamedly domestic, concentrating less on the Capability Browns of the world with their grand landscaped parks, than on the unsung heroes of suburbia carefully tending backyard plots. Inside is an assortment of antique implements, a collection of gardening-related art, and a treasure trove of gardening memorabilia.

Outside, the museum's own garden is filled with historic plants that thrive in the microclimate within the church's walls. The churchyard contains two notable memorials from the history of horticulture: The tomb of **Captain Bligh,** whose journey aboard the *Bounty* to Tahiti in the late 18th century to obtain breadfruit trees prompted the famous mutiny against him; and the tomb of John Tradescant, a gardener and plant hunter for King Charles II. *Insider tip:* Free guided tours are given on the last Tuesday of each month at 2pm. First come, first served.

Lambeth Palace Rd., SE1. www.gardenmuseum.org.uk. ✆ **020/7401-8865.** Admission £6 adults, £5 seniors, £3 students, free children 15 and under. Sun–Fri 10:30am–5:30pm; Sat 10:30am–4pm. Closed 1st Mon of month (except public holidays). Tube: Lambeth North.

Golden Hinde ☺ HISTORIC SITE   By the river, just around the corner from Southwark Cathedral, is this full-size replica of the ship on which Sir Francis Drake became the first Englishman to circumnavigate the globe in the 16th century. It may seem a touch cozy, but the proportions are accurate—it has even been sailed around the world to prove it. On board it's all very yo-ho-ho, with actors in period costume entertaining you with Tudor maritime tales as you explore the five levels. Understandably, it's very popular with children, and at weekends is usually given over to private birthday parties where everyone dresses up as pirates and buccaneers.

If your children really want to get a feel for life at sea (or rather, in dry dock), you can sign them up for a "Family Overnight Living History Tour," which runs once a month from April to October. Between your arrival (all children must be accompanied by an adult) at 5pm and 10am the next day, you join a crew of Tudor sailors, tending to the ship's needs, eating Tudor food and drink, and sleeping in the cramped lower deck.

Pickford's Wharf, Clink St., SE1. www.goldenhinde.com. ✆ **020/7403-0123.** Admission £6 adults, £4.50 seniors, students, and children 15 and under; £18 family. Mon–Sat 10am–5:30pm; sleepovers cost £39.95 per person—bring sleeping bag. Tube: London Bridge.

Hayward Gallery ART MUSEUM   Opened in 1968, and forming the arts wing of the **Southbank Centre** (p. 167), which also includes the Royal Festival Hall, the Queen Elizabeth Hall, and the Purcell Room, the Hayward is perhaps the epitome of the concrete brutalist style of architecture for which the Southbank is so derided (or occasionally, admired). But, while the outside might not grace that many postcards, the interior is a superior art space that presents a program of major contemporary exhibits.

Belvedere Rd., South Bank, SE1. http://ticketing.southbankcentre.co.uk/find/hayward-gallery-visual-arts. ✆ **020/7960-4200.** Admission varies, but usually £10 adults, £9 seniors, £8 students, £7.50 children 12–17; free for children 11 and under. Sun–Wed 10am–6pm; Thurs–Fri 10am–8pm. Tube: Waterloo or Embankment.

HMS Belfast ★ ☺ HISTORIC SITE   Moored opposite the Tower of London, between Tower Bridge and London Bridge, HMS *Belfast* is an 11,874-tonne (11,684-ton) World War II cruiser, now preserved as a floating museum run by the Imperial War Museum (see below). Always popular with youngsters, who love climbing between its seven levels of clunking metal decks, the *Belfast* has recently been given an interactive makeover. So, in addition to admiring all the hardware on display—including naval guns and anti-aircraft weaponry—it's possible to tackle simulated missions on touchscreen computers in the Interactive Operations Room and place yourself in the midst of a naval battle in the Gun Turret Experience, which uses light, sound, smoke, and even smell effects to tell its story. Incidentally, the ship's guns have a range of 14 miles, which means it could take out Hampton Court Palace (p. 122) if staff felt so inclined. Children aged 15 and under must be accompanied by an adult.

Morgan's Lane, Tooley St., SE1. www.iwm.org.uk/visits/hms-belfast. ✆ **020/7940-6300.** Admission £14 adults, £11.20 seniors and students, £6.50 unemployed, free for children under 16. Mar–Oct daily 10am–6pm (last admission 4pm); Nov–Feb 10am–5pm (last admission 4pm). Tube: London Bridge.

Attractions, Hotels & Restaurants in South Bank & The City

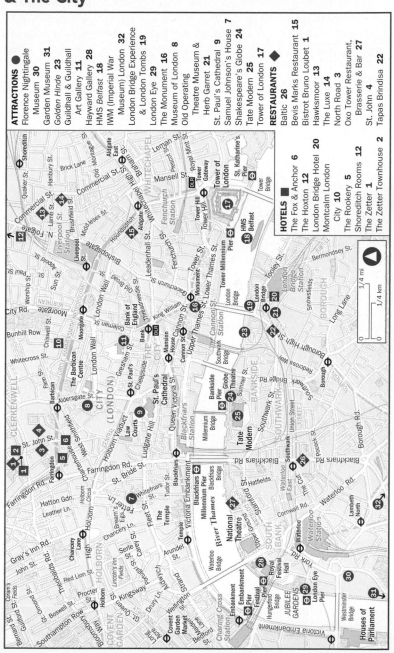

ATTRACTIONS ●
Florence Nightingale Museum **30**
Garden Museum **31**
Golden Hinde **23**
Guildhall & Guildhall Art Gallery **11**
Hayward Gallery **28**
HMS Belfast **18**
IWM (Imperial War Museum) London **32**
London Bridge Experience & London Tombs **19**
London Eye **29**
The Monument **16**
Museum of London **8**
Old Operating Theatre Museum & Herb Garret **21**
St. Paul's Cathedral **9**
Samuel Johnson's House **7**
Shakespeare's Globe **24**
Tate Modern **25**
Tower of London **17**

RESTAURANTS ◆
Baltic **26**
Bevis Marks Restaurant **15**
Bistrot Bruno Loubet **1**
Hawksmoor **13**
The Luxe **14**
North Road **3**
Oxo Tower Restaurant, Brasserie & Bar **27**
St. John **4**
Tapas Brindisa **22**

HOTELS ■
The Fox & Anchor **6**
The Hoxton **12**
London Bridge Hotel **20**
Montcalm London City **10**
The Rookery **5**
Shoreditch Rooms **12**
The Zetter **1**
The Zetter Townhouse **2**

IWM (Imperial War Museum) London ★★★ ☺ MUSEUM From 1814 to 1930, this deceptively elegant, domed building was the Bethlehem Royal Hospital, an old-style "madhouse," where the "patients" formed part of a Victorian freak show—visitors could pay a penny to go and stare at the lunatics. (The hospital's name since entered the language as "Bedlam," a slang expression for chaos and confusion.) Thankfully, civilization has moved on in its treatment of the mentally ill, although as this warfare museum shows, nations are still as capable of cruelty and organized madness as they ever were.

The great, gung-ho 38-cm (15-in.) naval guns parked outside the entrance give an indication of what you can expect in the main hall. This is the boys' toys section with a whole fleet of tanks, planes, and missiles on display (including a Battle of Britain Spitfire, a V2 rocket, and a German one-man submarine), and plenty of interactivity for the youngsters, with cockpits to climb into and touchscreen terminals to explore.

After the initial bombast, however, comes a selection of thoughtful, sobering exhibits, focusing on the human cost of war. These include galleries exploring life during World Wars I and II—both on the battlefield and at home—a new gallery celebrating exploits of supreme valor, "Extraordinary Heroes," and the "Secret War" exhibition which looks at the use of duplicity, subterfuge, and spying in wartime.

On the upper floors, things become more thoughtful still. The third floor provides an intense account of the Holocaust, examining the first attempt to apply modern industrial techniques to the destruction of people. And, just to remind you that this is not an evil that has been permanently consigned to history, the "Crimes against Humanity" exhibition explores modern genocides. Its central exhibit is a harrowing 30-minute film. These two galleries are not recommended for children 13 and under.

Lambeth Rd., SE1. www.iwm.org.uk/visits/iwm-london. ☎ **020/7416-5320.** Free admission. Daily 10am–6pm. Tube: Lambeth North or Elephant and Castle.

London Bridge Experience & London Tombs ☺ MUSEUM Head down beneath the foundations of what has been the capital's prime river crossing for almost two millennia, to find out about the bridge's history and experience a bit of gore—expect heads on spikes, animatronic prisoners, costumed actors playing the roles of Boudicca and William Wallace, and so forth. It bills itself as a "scare attraction" and is big on family fun, if not quite so heavy on intellectual rigor. The admission price rises and falls over the course of the day, and is most expensive between noon and 3pm.

2–4 Tooley St., SE1. www.thelondonbridgeexperience.com. ☎ **0800/043-4666.** Admission £24.50 adults, £22.58 seniors and students aged 15–17, £19 children 5–14. Mon–Fri 10am–5pm; Sat–Sun 10am–6pm. Tube: London Bridge.

London Eye ★★ ☺ OBSERVATION WHEEL The largest observation wheel in Europe, the London Eye has become, in the decade since it opened, a potent icon of the capital, as clearly identified with London as the Eiffel Tower is with Paris. And indeed, it performs much the same function—giving people the chance to observe the city from above. Passengers are carried in 32 glass-sided "pods," each representing one of the 32 boroughs of London (which lucky travelers get Croydon?), that make a complete revolution every half-hour. Along the way you'll see bird's-eye views of some of London's most famous landmarks, including the Houses of Parliament, Buckingham Palace, the B.T. Tower, St. Paul's, the "Gherkin," and of course, the River Thames itself. "Night flights," when you can gaze at the twinkling lights of the city are available in winter. Ticket prices are 10% cheaper if booked online.

Millennium Jubilee Gardens, SE1. www.londoneye.com. ℂ **0871/781-3000.** Admission £18.60 adults, £15 seniors and students, £9.50 children 4–15. Times vary, but the Eye is open daily from 10am, usually till 9pm in summer (9:30pm in July–Aug) and till 8:30pm in winter. Tube: Waterloo or Westminster.

Old Operating Theatre Museum & Herb Garret ★★ ☺MUSEUM

Next time you find yourself moaning about a trip to the family doctor, remember it could be *much* worse, as this antique operating theatre shows. Although less than 200 years old, it might as well be from the Stone Age, such have been the advances in medical science. It was once part of St. Thomas' Hospital, but was sealed over and forgotten about for more than a century when the hospital relocated in 1861. Now restored, it provides a grim window into the past. Its centerpiece is Europe's oldest operating theatre in which operations—mainly amputations—were performed on a wooden table without anesthetic or antiseptic. Patients were bound to prevent them struggling free, a box of sawdust was placed beneath them to collect the blood, and then the surgeon got to work, the aim being to sever the limb as quickly as possible to prevent the patient from bleeding to death. The grisly spectacle was watched by medical students in the surrounding seating—this really was a "theatre"—as you can do every Saturday at 2pm, when a demonstration of 19th-century "Speed Surgery" is staged.

The **Herb Garret,** located above the theatre, was used for drying medicinal plants. It was rediscovered at the same time, and provides a more peaceful, aromatic second act.

9a St. Thomas St., SE1. www.thegarret.org.uk. ℂ **020/7188-2679.** Admission £5.90 adults, £4.90 seniors and students, £3.40 children 15 and under, £13.80 family. Daily 10:30am–5pm. Tube: London Bridge.

Shakespeare's Globe ★ HISTORIC SITE/THEATRE

This is a recent re-creation of one of the most significant public theatres ever built, Shakespeare's Globe, where the Bard premiered many of his most famous plays. The new Globe isn't an exact replica: It seats 1,500 patrons, not the 3,000 who regularly squeezed in during the early 1600s, and this thatched roof has been specially treated with a fire retardant—just as well, as a shot from a stage cannon fired during a performance of *Henry*

 ## London's Best "Bird's-Eye" Views

The **London Eye** (p. 108) is the most obvious of the attractions offering a "bird's-eye" view of the capital, but it's by no means the only vantage point. For centuries, **St. Paul's Cathedral** (p. 112) has been letting Londoners willing to climb its 500 plus steps gaze out over their city, spread out below them like a great 3-D map. Worthy, albeit slightly less elevated, panoramas are also offered from the top of **Westminster Cathedral** (p. 104), the **Monument** (p. 111), the **National Portrait Gallery** restaurant (p. 91), and the **Oxo Tower**—

this last one is particularly recommended, because it's free.

At the time of writing, these were set to be joined by some new views on the block, including a 60-m (200-ft.) **Cable Car** over the Thames between the ExCel Centre and the O2 Arena, the 115-m (377-ft.) **ArcelorMittal Orbit Tower** at Olympic Park, and—towering over them all—the 310-m (1,017-ft.) **Shard,** Western Europe's tallest building. It's 72nd-floor observation deck will be London's highest public space.

VIII provided the ultimate finale, setting the roof alight and burning the original theatre to the ground.

Insider tip: Guided tours of the facility are offered throughout the day in the theatre's winter off season. From May to September, however, Globe tours are only available in the morning. In the afternoon, when matinee performances are taking place, alternative (and cheaper) tours to the scanty remains of the **Rose Theatre,** the Globe's precursor (which was torn down in the early 17th century), are offered instead.

See p. 165 for details on attending a play here.

21 New Globe Walk, SE1. www.shakespearesglobe.com. © **020/7902-1400.** Admission and Globe Tour/Rose Tour £13.50/10 adults, £12/9 seniors, £11/8.50 students, £8/7 children 5–15, free for children 4 and under, £35/29 family ticket. Oct–Apr daily 10am–5pm; May–Sept daily 9am–noon and 12:30–5pm. Tube: Mansion House or London Bridge.

Tate Modern ★★★ ART MUSEUM   Welcoming more than four million visitors a year, Tate Modern is the world's most popular modern art gallery (the free admission helps), and one of the capital's best attractions. From the day it opened in 2000, it has received almost as many plaudits for its setting as for its contents. It's housed in a converted 1940s' brick power station, the brooding industrial functionalism of the architecture providing a fitting canopy for the challenging art within. Through the main entrance you enter a vast space, the **Turbine Hall,** where a succession of giant temporary exhibitions are staged—the bigger and more ambitious, the better.

The permanent collection encompasses a great body of modern art dating from 1900 to the present. Spread over several levels, it covers all the big hitters, including Matisse, Rothko, Pollock, Picasso, Dali, Duchamp, and Warhol, and is arranged according to themes and movements—surrealism, minimalism, cubism, expressionism, and so on. Further explanation—always useful where modern art is concerned—is provided by the free 45-minute guided tours of the collection given daily at 11am, noon, 2pm, and 3pm. Tate Modern stays open late on Friday and Saturday, when events, such as concerts and talks, are often held.

Such has been Tate Modern's success that a new extension has been built, which should be complete by the time this guide hits the shelves. Taking the form of an asymmetrical pyramid, it uses the same type of bricks as the original building, making it look as if the power station has simply sprouted a new, angular growth. It will contain new art spaces, some occupying the massive underground oil tanks that once powered the station's turbines.

Bankside, SE1. www.tate.org.uk/modern. © **020/7887-8888.** Free admission. Sun–Thurs 10am–6pm; Fri–Sat 10am–10pm. Tube: Southwark or London Bridge.

The City

Guildhall & Guildhall Art Gallery ★ HISTORIC SITE/ART MUSEUM   The headquarters of the City of London Corporation, the administrative body that has overseen the City's affairs for the past 800 years, the Guildhall's original medieval framework has endured significant repairs following the 1666 Great Fire and World War II (as well as the addition of a rather incongruous concrete wing in the 1970s). Today its Great Hall has a touch of the medieval theme park about it, filled with colorful livery banners and with a (reconstructed) minstrel's gallery from where 3-m (9-ft.) statues of mythical giants Gog and Magog gaze down on proceedings.

East across Guildhall Yard, the **Guildhall Art Gallery** displays a constantly updated selection from the Corporation's 4,000-plus works relating to the capital. The main attraction (there's certainly no missing it) is John Singleton Copley's *The*

Defeat of the Floating Batteries at Gibraltar, September 1782, which at 42.5 sq m (458 sq ft.) is Britain's largest independent oil painting, and takes up two whole storys. Fridays are the best time to visit, when you can join a free tour of the collection at 12:15, 1:15, 2:15, and 3:15pm.

Head down beneath the art collection to visit the scant remains of **London's Roman amphitheatre,** which dates from the 2nd century A.D., but remained undiscovered until 1988. Images of spectators and missing bits have been added to give visitors a better idea of what it once looked like.

Guildhall Yard, Gresham St., EC2. www.guildhallartgallery.cityoflondon.gov.uk. Ⓒ **020/7332-3700.** Free admission. Mon–Sat 10am–5pm; Sun noon–4pm. Tube: Bank, St. Paul's, or Moorgate.

The Monument ★ ☺ OBSERVATION POINT It's hardly a giant by modern standards, and indeed is these days obscured by the midsized buildings surrounding it, but at 61.5m (202 ft.) this is still the world's tallest free-standing column—a boast that probably has more to do with changing building techniques than anything else. Designed by Sir Christopher Wren, it was erected in the 1670s to commemorate London's revival following the Great Fire of 1666; hence the golden fiery orb at its top. Apparently, if the Monument fell over, it would, providing it fell in the right direction, land on the exact spot in Pudding Lane where the Great Fire started. It's 311 steps to the summit, from where the views are among the finest in the city.

Fish Street Hill, EC3. www.themonument.info. Ⓒ**020/7626-2717.** Admission £3 adults, £2 seniors and students, £1 children. Daily 9:30am–5:30pm. Tube: Monument or London Bridge.

Museum of London ★★ ☺ MUSEUM Although the location is rather grim, in the center of an unappealing roundabout in London's Barbican district, this museum is an absolute joy, particularly since a recent revamp gives visitors a real sense of the drama of London's story unfolding. Exhibits are arranged so that you can begin and end your chronological stroll through 250,000 years at the main entrance to the museum. Upstairs you'll find sections devoted to "London before London" (with flint arrow heads and Bronze Age weapons); Roman London (mosaics, statues, and scale models of the city); Medieval London (Viking battleaxes and knights' armor); and War, Plague, and Fire (models of Shakespeare's Rose Theatre, the Great Fire, and Cromwell's death mask). The recently revamped downstairs galleries bring the story up to date with displays on the "Expanding City: 1666–1850" (including a re-created 18th-century prison and a 240-year-old printing press); "People's City: 1850s–1940s" (walk a replica Victorian street); and "World City: 1950s–Today" (explore an

---

 A money-saving PASS

The **London Pass** provides admission to more than 55 attractions in and around London, "timed" admission at some attractions (bypassing the lines), plus free travel on public transport (buses, Tubes, and trains) and a pocket guidebook. It costs £44 for 1 day, £59 for 2 days, £72 for 3 days, and £95 for 6 days (children aged 5 to 15 pay £29, £44, £49, or £68, respectively), and includes admission to St. Paul's Cathedral, HMS *Belfast,* the Jewish Museum, and the Thames Barrier Visitor Centre—and many other attractions. This rather pricey pass is useful if you're trying to cram 2 days' worth of sightseeing into a single day. But if you're a slow-moving visitor, who likes to stop and smell the roses, you may not get your money's worth. See www.londonpass.com.

interactive model of the Thames), as well as perhaps the museum's most eye-catching exhibit, the **Lord Mayor's Coach,** a gilt-and-scarlet fairytale carriage built in 1757.

London Wall, EC2. www.museumoflondon.org.uk. ℭ **020/7001-9844.** Free admission. Daily 10am–6pm. Tube: St. Paul's or Barbican.

St. Paul's Cathedral ★★★ ☺ CATHEDRAL

London's skyline has changed dramatically during the past three centuries. Buildings have come and gone, architectural styles have waxed and waned, but throughout there has been one constant—the great plump dome of St. Paul's Cathedral gazing beatifically down upon the city. Despite the best intentions of the Luftwaffe and modern skyscraper designers, Sir Christopher Wren's masterpiece is still the defining landmark of the skyline.

The interior is a neck-craningly large space. Dotted around at ground level are tombs and memorials to various British heroes, including the Duke of Wellington, Lawrence of Arabia, and in the South Quire Aisle, an effigy of John Donne, one of the country's most celebrated poets and a former dean of St. Paul's. It's one of the few items to have survived from the previous, medieval cathedral, which was destroyed by the Great Fire in 1666; you can still see scorch marks on its base.

The cathedral offers some of the capital's best views, although you'll have to earn them by undertaking a 500-plus-step climb up to the **Golden Gallery.** Here you can enjoy giddying 360-degree panoramas of the capital, as well as perhaps equally stomach-tightening views down to the floor 111m (364 ft.) below.

Down in the crypt is a bumper crop of memorials, including those of Alexander Fleming, Admiral Lord Nelson, William Blake, and Wren himself—the epitaph on his simple tombstone reads: "Reader, if you seek a monument, look around you."

St. Paul's Churchyard, EC4. www.stpauls.co.uk. ℭ **020/7246-8350.** Cathedral and galleries £14.50 adults, £13.50 seniors and students, £5.50 children 6–18, £34.50 family ticket, free for children 5 and under. Cathedral (excluding galleries) Mon–Sat 8:30am–4pm; galleries Mon–Sat 9:30am–4pm. No sightseeing Sun (services only). Tube: St. Paul's.

Samuel Johnson's House ★ HISTORIC HOME

Poet, lexicographer, critic, biographer, and above all, quotation machine, Dr. Samuel Johnson lived in this Queen Anne house between 1748 and 1759. It was here that he compiled his famous dictionary—not as is commonly supposed, the first of the English language, but certainly the most influential to date. His house has been painstakingly restored to its mid-18th-century prime and is well worth a visit. Guided walks taking in many of the local sites associated with Johnson's life, including Temple Bar and Fleet Street, take place on the first Wednesday of the month, leaving from the entrance of the house at 3pm. They cost £5. No booking is required.

17 Gough Sq., EC4. www.drjohnsonshouse.org. ℭ **020/7353-3745.** Admission £4.50 adults, £3.50 students and seniors, £1.50 children, £10 family ticket, free for children 10 and under. Oct–Apr Mon–Sat 11am–5pm; May–Sept Mon–Sat 11am–5:30pm. Tube: Chancery Lane.

Tower of London ★★★ ☺ CASTLE

On a sunny summer afternoon, the Tower, one of the best preserved medieval castles in the world, can be a cheerful buzzing place, filled with happy swarms of tourists being entertained by costumed actors and historically themed events. At such times it can be easy to forget that beneath all the kitschy tourist trappings lies a castle with a very brutal and bloody history.

The Tower is actually a compound of structures built at various times for varying purposes. The oldest part is the **White Tower,** begun by William the Conqueror in 1078 to keep London's native Saxon population in check. Later rulers added towers,

St. Paul's Cathedral

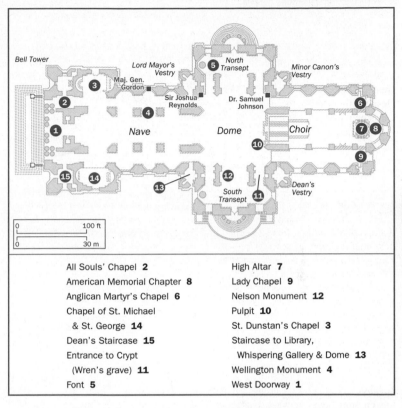

Bell Tower

Lord Mayor's Vestry

Maj. Gen. Gordon

5 North Transept

Minor Canon's Vestry

3

Sir Joshua Reynolds

Dr. Samuel Johnson

6

2

4

1

Nave

Dome

Choir

7 **8**

10

9

15 **14**

13

12

11

Dean's Vestry

South Transept

| 0 | 100 ft |
| 0 | 30 m |

All Souls' Chapel **2**	High Altar **7**
American Memorial Chapter **8**	Lady Chapel **9**
Anglican Martyr's Chapel **6**	Nelson Monument **12**
Chapel of St. Michael	Pulpit **10**
& St. George **14**	St. Dunstan's Chapel **3**
Dean's Staircase **15**	Staircase to Library,
Entrance to Crypt	Whispering Gallery & Dome **13**
(Wren's grave) **11**	Wellington Monument **4**
Font **5**	West Doorway **1**

walls, and fortified gates, until the buildings became like a small town within a city. Although it began life as a stronghold against rebellion, the tower's main role eventually became less about keeping people out, than making sure whoever was inside couldn't escape. It became the favored prison and execution site for anyone who displeased the monarch. Notable prisoners served their last meals here include the "princes in the tower," Lady Jane Grey (who reigned as queen for just 9 days before being toppled by Mary I in 1553), and Anne Boleyn, one of several unfortunates who thought that marrying that most unforgiving of monarchs, Henry VIII, was a good idea. A plaque on Tower Green marks the spot where they met their grisly ends.

Displays on some of the Tower's captives can be seen in the **Bloody Tower,** including a reconstruction of the study of Sir Walter Raleigh, the great Elizabethan adventurer who is generally credited with having introduced tobacco smoking to England. A favorite of Elizabeth I, he was executed by James I, a fervent anti-smoker, having spent 13 years as a prisoner here.

In addition to being a prison, the Tower has also been used as a royal palace, a mint, and an armory. Today, however, it's perhaps best known as the keeper of the **Crown Jewels,** the main ceremonial regalia of the British monarch, which—when not being used—are displayed in the tower's **Jewel House.** It's probably best to

SAINTS & THE city: A WALK

For somewhere so unashamedly dedicated to Mammon, the financial center of London also offers plenty of spiritual comfort (which no doubt comes in handy when stocks start tumbling). Our favorite historic churches can be toured in an afternoon, if you're quick.

Beginning at Temple Tube, turn left out of the station, and head north up Arundel Place. Turn right onto the Strand, and stroll east along Fleet Street till you reach **Prince Henry's Room,** 17 Fleet St. (currently closed), one of London's only surviving houses to pre-date the Great Fire of 1666. Turn right through the stone arch by the house, down Inner Temple Lane to **Temple Church ★**, King's Bench Walk, EC4 (www.templechurch.com; ✆ **020/7353-3470**), a round church founded in the late 12th century by the **Knights Templar,** one of the most powerful religious military orders during the Crusades. Much restored and rebuilt in subsequent centuries, it has enjoyed a resurgence of interest since being featured in *The Da Vinci Code.* Admission is £3, free to seniors and anyone under 21 years. Opening hours are Monday, Tuesday,

Thursday, and Friday 11am to 1pm and 2 to 4pm, and Wednesday 2 to 4pm.

Back on Fleet Street continue east. Take a right down Salisbury Court, then a left onto St. Bride's Passage for **St. Bride's,** Fleet Street, EC4 (www.stbrides. com; ✆ **020/7427-0133**), perhaps the city's oldest church, founded in the 6th century. Rebuilt by Sir Christopher Wren after the Great Fire, its distinctive multi-step spire was said to have inspired the design of modern wedding cakes. It's known as the "Journalists' Church," owing to its proximity to Fleet Street, the old home of the British press. It's free to enter. Hours are Monday through Friday 8am to 6pm, Saturday 11am to 3pm, and Sunday 10am to 1pm and 5 to 7:30pm.

Return to Fleet Street and head east along Ludgate Hill. A diversion north up Old Bailey will take you past the Central Criminal Court (also more commonly known as the **Old Bailey**). If you crane your neck you should just about be able to make out the statue of Lady Liberty holding a sword and a set of scales perched upon its roof. Carry on north, along Giltspur Street and West

tackle this soon after your arrival, as the lines seem to build over the course of the day. You hop aboard a travelator for a slow glide past some of the Queen's top trinkets, including the Imperial State Crown (modeled each year at the State Opening of Parliament), which looks like a child's fantasy of a piece of royal headwear, set with no fewer than 3,000 jewels, including the fourth-largest diamond in the world.

After the jewels, the tower's next most popular draw is probably the **Royal Armory** located in the White Tower, where you can see various fearsome-looking weapons, including swords, halberds, and morning stars, as well as bespoke suits of armor made for kings. The complex also boasts the only surviving medieval palace in Britain, dating back to the 1200s. It stands in the riverside wall above **Traitors' Gate,** through which prisoners were brought to the Tower. Within are reconstructed bedrooms, a throne room, and chapel.

Be sure to take advantage of the free hour-long tours offered by the iconic guards, the Yeoman Warders—more commonly known as **Beefeaters.** They'll regale you with tales of royal intrigue, and introduce you to the Tower's current most famous

Smithfield, bearing right until you reach **St. Bartholomew-the-Great**, 6–9 Kinghorn St., EC1 (www.greatstbarts.com; ☎ **020/7606-5171**). Begun in 1123, this is one of the best examples of large-scale Norman architecture in the city. Admission is £4, and it's open Monday through Friday 8:30am to 5pm, Saturday 10:30am to 4pm, and Sunday 8:30am to 8pm. Opposite, **St. Bartholomew's Hospital** ("Barts") has a small **Hospital Museum** of medical curiosities (North Wing, West Smithfield, EC1; www.bartsandthelondon.nhs.uk; ☎ **020/3465-5798**). It's free, and open Tuesday through Friday 10am to 4pm. Guided tours of the collection are given at 2pm on Fridays (£5).

Retrace your steps back down to Ludgate Hill and continue east until the glorious facade of **St. Paul's Cathedral** ★★★ (p. 112), the city's finest baroque church, looms into view. Pass through the cathedral's churchyard onto New Change, site of a major new shopping center, **One New Change,** then right on Cheapside for **St. Mary-le-Bow** (www.stmarylebow.co.uk; ☎ **020/7248-5139**), otherwise known as the "Cockney

Church"; to be a "true Cockney," you must be born within the sound of its bells. First erected around 1,000 years ago, it was rebuilt by Sir Christopher Wren following the Great Fire and again, in the style of Wren, after World War II. It's open Monday through Friday 6:30am till 6pm; admission is free.

Continue east, then southeast down King William Street, and finally east along Eastcheap and Great Tower Street to **All-Hallows-by-the-Tower** ★, Byward Street, EC3 (www.allhallowsbythetower.org.uk; ☎ **020/7481-2928**), just down the road from (and providing elevated views over) the Tower of London. When the first church was built here in the 7th century, the site had already been in use for several centuries. You can see Roman, Saxon, and medieval remains at its small museum. The famous diarist **Samuel Pepys** supposedly watched the progress of the Great Fire from the church's spire. Admission to the church is free. Museum hours are Monday through Friday 10am to 5:30pm, Saturday 10am to 5pm, and Sunday 1 to 5pm.

From here it's a short walk east to the nearest Tube station, Tower Hill.

residents, the six ravens who live on Tower Gardens. According to legend, if the ravens ever leave the Tower, the monarchy will fall—the birds' wings are kept clipped, just to make sure. The tours take place every half-hour from 9:30am until 3:30pm in summer (2:30pm in winter) and leave from the Middle Tower near the entrance.

Tower Hill, EC3. www.hrp.org.uk/TowerOfLondon. ☎ 0844/482-7777. Admission £20 adults, £17 students and seniors, £10.45 children 5–15, £55 family ticket, free for children 4 and under. Mar–Oct Tues–Sat 9am–5.30pm, Sun–Mon 10am 5:30pm; Nov–Feb Tues–Sat 9am–4:30pm, Sun–Mon 10am–4:30pm. Tube: Tower Hill/DLR: Tower Gateway.

East London

Geffrye Museum ★ MUSEUM   For an insight into how Britain's domestic interiors have developed over 4 centuries, head to this museum housed in a set of restored 18th-century almshouses. It consists of 11 chronologically arranged period rooms where you can follow the changing tastes in furnishings in English middle-class homes over the generations. There are Jacobean, Georgian, and Victorian interiors, as well as 20th-century rooms, where you'll see luxuriant Art Deco styles giving way to the utilitarian designs that followed World War II. Newer galleries showcase

Tickets are cheaper if booked online: £17 for adults, £9 for children. If buying your ticket at the venue, pick them up at the kiosk at Tower Hill Tube Station before emerging above ground—the lines should be shorter. Even so, choose a day other than Sunday—crowds are at their worst then—and arrive as early as you can in the morning, or late in the afternoon.

the decor of the later 20th century. Outside the chronological theme continues with four period gardens dating from the 17th to the 20th centuries. The Geffrye is especially charming around Christmas, when each room is dressed in period festive style.

136 Kingsland Rd., E2. www.geffrye-museum.org.uk.✆ **020/7739-9893.** Free admission to period rooms; £2.50 to Almshouses (free for children 15 and under). Tues–Sat 10am–5pm; Sun and public holidays noon–5pm. Gardens Apr–Oct only. Train: Hoxton.

Museum of London Docklands ★ ☺ MUSEUM   This East London outpost of the Museum of London looks at the history of the capital's river, and in particular the growth and demise of the trading industry that once flourished upon it. Housed in a relic of that industry, a Georgian sugar warehouse, the museum tells the story of the docks from the beginnings of river commerce under the Romans through the glory days of Empire, when London was the world's busiest port, to the closure of the central London docks in the 1970s. It also takes a look at the subsequent regeneration of the area, of which this museum forms a part. The displays focus on both local social aspects—you can walk through "Sailor Town," a reconstructed Victorian community—and the global implications of London's rise as a major trading city. The more shameful aspects of the subject are examined in "London: Sugar and Slavery," and there's also a dedicated hands-on children's section by the entrance, "Mudlarks."

West India Quay, E14. www.museumindocklands.org.uk.✆ **020/7001-9844.** Free admission. Daily 10am–6pm. Tube: Canary Wharf/DLR: West India Quay.

V&A Museum of Childhood ★★ ☺ MUSEUM   A branch of the Victoria and Albert Museum, the U.K.'s national collection of objects relating to childhood contains items dating from the 1600s to the present day, and has had a major recent revamp.

The "Moving Toys" section displays things that can be moved manually (rocking horses, spinning tops, pedal cars, and so on); those powered with springs and cogs (clockwork toys, jack-in-the-boxes); anything with circuits and motors (remote control cars and train sets); and those that create the illusion of movement through special effects (such as magic lanterns, zoetropes, and modern video games). The "Creativity" area aims to show how toys help children to use their imaginations with displays of puppets, toy theatres, dolls from all over the world, and construction sets such as Lego and Meccano. "Childhood" looks at aspects of growing up through toys that have been designed to give children a taste of adult life: toy hospitals, tea sets, even toy guns, as well as perhaps the museum's most celebrated exhibit, a display of elaborate dolls houses from throughout the centuries—the oldest dating back to 1673.

Obviously, the museum is also extremely child-friendly with interactive areas punctuating the static displays, and free arts and crafts activities laid on daily from 2 to 4pm. It's best for children aged up to 12—there's not much aimed at teens.

Cambridge Heath Rd., E2. www.vam.ac.uk/moc.© **020/8983-5200.** Free admission. Daily 10am–5:45pm. Tube: Bethnal Green.

Whitechapel Art Gallery ★★ ART MUSEUM   In 2009 East London's premier art museum reopened following the most significant revamp since its foundation in 1901. Throughout its history the gallery has often played a leading role in the development of artistic movements. In the 1930s, it hosted Britain's first showing of Picasso's *Guernica,* as part of an exhibition protesting the Spanish Civil War. It then shocked postwar audiences by introducing them to Jackson Pollock's abstracts, and championed Pop Art in the 1960s. Expect further revelations in the future. It also offers regular free talks, as well as cheap film screenings and concerts.

77–82 Whitechapel Rd., E1. www.whitechapelgallery.org. © **020/7522-7888.** Free admission. Tues–Sun 11am–6pm. Tube: Aldgate East.

North & Northwest London

British Library ★ MUSEUM   One of the world's great repositories of books, the British Library receives a copy of every single title published in the U.K., which are stored on 400 miles of shelves. In 1996, the whole lot (14 million books, manuscripts, sound recordings, and other items) was moved from the British Museum to the library's new home in St. Pancras. The current building may be a lot less elegant than its predecessor, but the bright, roomy interior is far more inviting than the rather dull, redbrick exterior suggests. Within are a number of permanent galleries, the highlight being the "Treasures of the British Library," where 200 of the library's most precious possessions are displayed, including a copy of Magna Carta (1215), a Gutenberg Bible, and the journals of Captain Cook.

96 Euston Rd., NW1. www.bl.uk.© **0843/208-1144.** Free admission. Mon and Wed–Fri 9:30am–6pm; Tues 9:30am–8pm; Sat 9:30am–5pm; Sun 11am–5pm. Tube: King's Cross or Euston.

Hampstead Heath ★★★ ☺ PARK/GARDEN   This 791-acre expanse of high heath is made up of formal parkland, woodland, heath, meadowland, and ponds. One of the few places in the big city that feels properly wild, it's a fantastic place to lose yourself on a rambling wander. On a clear day, you can see St. Paul's Cathedral, the Houses of Parliament, and even the hills of Kent from the prime viewing spot atop Parliament Hill, 98m (322 ft.) up. For years Londoners have come here to sun-worship, fly kites, fish the ponds, swim, picnic, jog, or just laze about.

Much of the northern end is taken up by the manicured grounds of **Kenwood House,** a great spot for a picnic, where concerts are staged on summer evenings. Along its eastern end are ponds set aside for bathing (there's a ladies' pool, a men's pool, and a mixed pool), sailing model boats, and as a bird sanctuary—the heath is one of London's best **birdwatching** locations.

South of the heath is the leafy, well-to-do **Hampstead Village,** a longtime favorite haunt of writers, artists, architects, musicians, and scientists. Keats, D. H. Lawrence, Shelley, Robert Louis Stevenson, and Kingsley Amis all lived here. The village's Regency and Georgian houses offer a quirky mix of historic pubs, toy shops, and chic boutiques, especially along **Flask Walk.**

Hampstead, NW3. www.cityoflondon.gov.uk. © **020/7482-7073.** Free admission. Open 24 hr. Tube: Hampstead/Train: Hampstead Heath or Gospel Oak.

Highgate Cemetery CEMETERY   A stone's throw east of Hampstead Heath, this beautiful cemetery is laid out around a huge 300-year-old cedar tree and is laced

Attractions, Hotels & Restaurants in East London

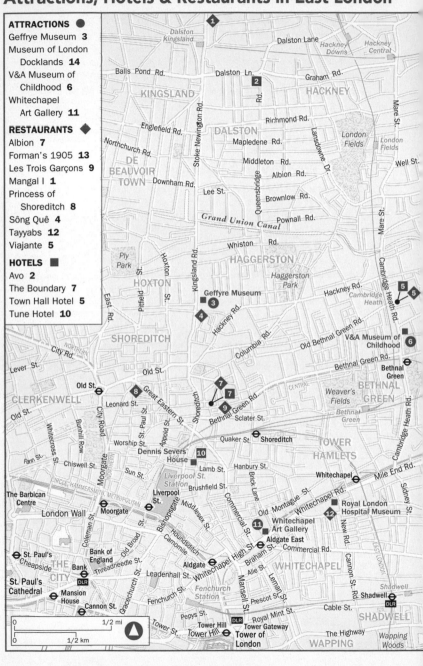

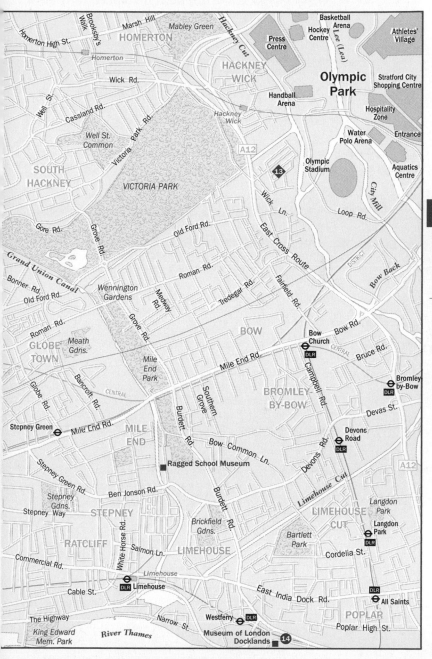

with serpentine pathways. The cemetery was so popular and fashionable in the Victorian era that it was extended on the other side of Swain's Lane in 1857. The most famous grave is that of **Karl Marx,** who died in Hampstead in 1883; his grave, marked by a gargantuan bust, is in the eastern cemetery. In the old western cemetery—accessible only by guided tour—are scientist Michael Faraday and poet Christina Rossetti.

Swain's Lane, N6. www.highgate-cemetery.org. © **020/8340-1834.** Western Cemetery guided tour £7 adults, £5 students, £3 children 8–15 (cash only). Eastern Cemetery admission £3 adults, £2 students, free children 15 and under (cash only). Western Cemetery: Mar–Nov tours Mon–Fri 2pm, Sat–Sun hourly 11am–4pm; Dec–Feb tours Sat–Sun hourly 11am–3pm. Eastern Cemetery: Apr–Oct Mon–Fri 10am–4:30pm, Sat–Sun 11am–4:30pm; Nov–Mar Mon–Fri 10am–3:30pm, Sat–Sun 11am–3:30pm. Both cemeteries closed at Christmas and during funerals. Tube: Archway, then bus 143, 210, 271, or C11.

Jewish Museum ★MUSEUM   Reopened to the public in 2010, following a £10 million improvement, this Camden museum retells the often difficult history of Britain's Jewish communities from the time of the first settlers in 1066 to the present, as well as illuminating aspects of Jewish ritual and belief. Most of the items date from after the English Civil Wars, when Oliver Cromwell changed the law to allow Jews to settle in Britain. You can see a variety of historical artifacts, including a 13th-century *mikvah* (ritual bath) and a 17th-century Venetian synagogue ark, and, in the most affecting section, learn about the Holocaust as experienced by a single Auschwitz survivor, Leon Greenman, whose story is cleverly (and movingly) used to represent the plight of an entire people.

129–131 Albert St., NW1. www.jewishmuseum.org.uk. ©**020/7284-7384.** Admission £7.50 adults, £5.50 seniors and students, £3.50 children 5–15, free for children 4 and under. Sun–Thurs 10am–5pm; Fri 10am–2pm. Tube: Camden Town.

London Zoo (ZSL) ★★ ☺ZOO   When London Zoo—one of the finest big city zoos in the world—was founded back in 1820, it was purely for the purposes of scientific research. Highlights of the modern London Zoo include the "Clore Rainforest Lookout," a steamy indoor replica jungle inhabited by sloths, tamarin monkeys, and lemurs; "B.U.G.S.," which apparently stands for Biodiversity Underpinning Global Survival, but does also contain plenty of bugs, including leaf-cutter ants, brightly colored beetles, and giant, scary bird-eating spiders; and, the current flagship, "Gorilla Kingdom," a moated island resembling an African forest clearing, which provides a naturalistic habitat for gorillas and colobus monkeys. There are always plenty of activities going on here, including keeper talks, feeding times, and "meet the animals" displays. A day-planner is handed out at the front gate, or you can download one from the website.

   Insider tip: Savings of around 10% can be made if you book a family ticket online; these are not available at the front gate.

Outer Circle, Regent's Park, NW1. www.zsl.org/zsl-london-zoo. © **0844/225-1826.** Admission winter season/mid-season/peak season including donation: £18.50/19.50/20.50 adults, £17/18/19 students and seniors, £15.10/15.50/16.50 children 3–15. Mar–Oct daily 10am–5:30pm; Nov–Feb daily 10am–4pm. Tube: Regent's Park or Camden Town/Bus: C2 or 274.

Regent's Park ★★ ☺PARK/GARDEN   Designed by 18th-century genius John Nash to surround a palace for the Prince Regent (the palace never materialized), this is the most classically beautiful of all London's parks, and featured briefly in the film, *The King's Speech.* Its core is a rose garden planted around a small lake alive with waterfowl and spanned by Japanese bridges; in early summer, the rose perfume is heady in the air. Rowboats and sailing dinghies are available from the **Boathouse Café** (✆ 020/7724-4069) for £6.50 per adult and £4.40 per child for 1 hour.

Regent's Park, NW1. www.royalparks.org.uk/parks/the-regents-park. ✆ 030/0061-2300. Free admission. Daily 5am–dusk. Tube: Baker St., Great Portland St., or Regent's Park.

Southeast London—Greenwich

With the great skyscrapers of Canary Wharf to the north, and waves of faceless suburbia to the south, Greenwich seems almost out of place—a royal theme park smuggled into London's backwaters. It makes a great escape from the center of town, with a look and ambience all its own. For the full effect, arrive by **Thames Clipper** boat (p. 125), which shows off the riverside architecture to its best effect.

Cutty Sark ★ ☺ HISTORIC SITE   It's back. The *Cutty Sark,* one of the 19th century's speediest ships, which endured a large (but thankfully not fatal) fire in 2007, has finally been restored to its former grandeur and is once again on display in dry dock at Greenwich. The ship was one of a new breed of super-swift craft—known as clippers—built with the aim of reducing journey times between Britain and the Far East, to aid the burgeoning tea trade. For a couple of decades, clippers ruled the waves, consistently lowering the record for the round-Africa route until the opening of the Suez Canal in 1869 rendered them almost instantly obsolete. The *Cutty Sark* was built that same year, arriving just as the party was coming to an end. Today, she is one of only three surviving ships of her type, and has been on display in Greenwich since the 1950s. The most recent renovation has improved access (elevators have been added) and a new display on the boat's history and construction has been created below the hull.

Greenwich Church St., SE10. www.rmg.org.uk/cuttysark. ✆ 020/8858-2698. Admission £12 adults, £9.50 seniors and students, £6.50 children 5-15. Tuesday to Sunday 10am-5pm (last admission 4pm) DLR: Cutty Sark.

National Maritime Museum ★★ ☺ MUSEUM   The world's largest maritime museum just got a little bigger. The new £20 million **Sammy Ofer Wing** contains several exhibition spaces, including "Voyagers," a cross between a traditional museum display and an art piece. Stories of Britons at sea surround a 20-m (66-ft.) installation, "The Wave," where maritime-themed images and words are projected onto screens.

The rest of the museum is more traditional, dedicated to exploring this island nation's intense relationship with watery surrounds. The cannon, relics, ship models, and paintings tell the story of 1,000 naval battles and 1,000 victories (plus the odd defeat). The lower two floors are divided into themed sections, including "Explorers," "Maritime London," and "Atlantic Worlds," and are filled with nautical oddities— everything from the dreaded cat-o'-nine-tails, used to flog sailors until 1879, to Nelson's Trafalgar coat, with the fatal bullet hole in the left shoulder clearly visible.

Romney Rd., SE10. www.rmg.co.uk/national-maritime-museum. ✆ 020/8858-4422. Free admission. Daily 10am–5pm. DLR: Cutty Sark.

Old Royal Naval College ★ HISTORIC SITE   The great baroque waterfront facade of this wonderfully grand structure offers perhaps the clearest distillation of Greenwich's charms. UNESCO certainly thought so, describing it as the "finest and most dramatically sited architectural ... ensemble in the British Isles." It's the work of England's holy trinity of 17th-century architects—Wren, Hawksmoor, and Vanbrugh (mostly Wren, in truth)—and was designed in 1694 as a hospital for veteran sailors. The pensioners moved out in 1873, when the complex became the Royal Naval

College. The Royal Navy finally ended its association with the building in 1998, since when it has been home to part of the University of Greenwich. Just three sections are open to the public: The Georgian chapel of **St. Peter and St. Paul,** where organ recitals are often given; the magnificent **Painted Hall ★** by Sir James Thornhill, where the body of Nelson lay in state in 1805; and the **Discover Greenwich Centre,** which contains an intriguing and interactive exhibition on the history of Greenwich as well as this royal suburb's tourist information service.

Old Royal Naval College, SE10. www.oldroyalnavalcollege.org. ℭ**020/8269-4747.** Free admission. Daily 10am–5pm. DLR: Cutty Sark.

Royal Observatory ★ ☺ HISTORIC SITE   The home of **Greenwich Mean Time,** the Observatory was designed by Sir Christopher Wren in the early 18th century and boasts the country's largest refracting telescope, as well as displays on timekeeping, a *camera obscura,* and (the only part of the site that's free to visit) an interactive astronomy exhibition. The highlight, however, is the **Planetarium** (the only one in the country), where effects-laden star shows are projected onto its ceiling.

Outside, overlooking Greenwich's serene park, you can enjoy one of London's most popular photo opportunities, standing across the **Prime Meridian,** the line of 0-degree longitude marked in the courtyard, with one foot in the Earth's eastern hemisphere and one foot in the western. At lunch you can set your watch precisely by watching the red **"time ball"** atop the roof, which has dropped at exactly 1pm since 1833, to enable passing shipmasters to set their chronometers accurately.

Blackheath Ave., SE10. www.nmm.ac.uk/places/royal-observatory. ℭ**020/8858-4422.** Admission to Observatory £7 adults, £5 seniors and students, free for children aged 15 and under; Planetarium £6.50 adults, £4.50 children, £17.50 family. Daily 10am–5pm. Train: Greenwich/DLR: Cutty Sark.

Outlying Attractions

Dulwich Picture Gallery ★★ ART MUSEUM   Just 12 minutes by train from Victoria Station, this houses one of the country's most significant collections of European Old Masters from the 17th and 18th centuries. The core of the collection was assembled by a pair of London art dealers in the 1790s on behalf of King Stanislaus Augustus of Poland, who thought a royal art collection would be just the thing to enhance his prestige. Unfortunately, he'd rather overestimated his standing and his kingdom was partitioned out of existence before the shipment could be made, so the paintings remained in London. The dealers bequeathed the collection to the independent school, Dulwich College, which commissioned **Sir John Soane** (p. 93) to create the world's first public art museum to display them; it opened in 1817. Soane's cunningly positioned skylights beautifully illuminate the pieces from such figures as Rembrandt, Rubens, Canaletto, Gainsborough, Watteau, and Poussin. The *Sunday Telegraph* has hailed Dulwich as "the most beautiful small art gallery in the world." Free guided tours of the collection are given at 3pm on Saturdays and Sundays.

Gallery Rd., SE21. www.dulwichpicturegallery.org.uk. ℭ**020/8693-5254.** Admission £5 adults, £4 seniors, free for students, the unemployed, and children 17 and under. Tues–Fri 10am–5pm; Sat–Sun 11am–5pm. Train: W. Dulwich.

Hampton Court Palace ★★★ ☺ PALACE   The 16th-century palace of Cardinal Wolsey can teach us a lesson: Don't try to outdo your boss, particularly if he happens to be Henry VIII. The rich cardinal did just that, and he eventually lost his fortune, power, and prestige, and ended up giving his lavish palace to the Tudor monarch. Henry's additions include an **Astronomical Clock** above Clock Court (still

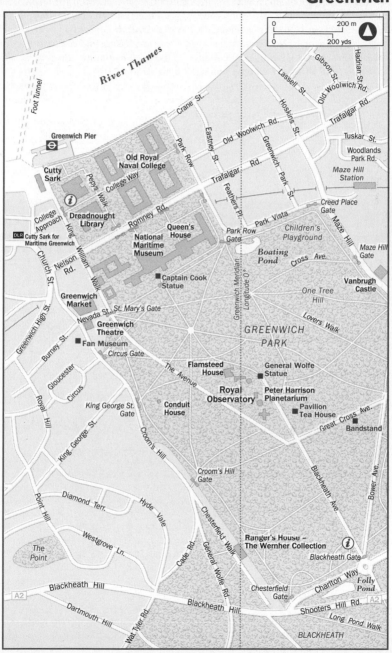

showing the phases of the moon, position of the sun, and signs of the Zodiac), the Great Hall with its hammerbeam roof, a Tiltyard (for jousting competitions), and a "real tennis" court.

Although the palace enjoyed prestige in Elizabethan days, it owes much of its present look to monarchs William and Mary—or rather, to Sir Christopher Wren. You can parade through the apartments today, filled with porcelain, furniture, paintings, and tapestries. The **King's Dressing Room** is graced with some of the best art, mainly paintings by Old Masters on loan from Queen Elizabeth II. Also, be sure to inspect the **Chapel Royal** (Wolsey wouldn't recognize it) and **Henry VIII's Kitchens,** where Tudor feasts are still regularly prepared.

The 59-acre **gardens**—including Tudor and Elizabethan Knot Gardens—are open daily year-round. The most popular section is the serpentine shrubbery **Maze,** also the work of Wren, and accounting for countless lost children every year. A garden **cafe** and restaurant are located in the Tiltyard. *Insider tip:* Tickets are considerably cheaper if bought online.

East Molesey, Surrey. www.hrp.org.uk/HamptonCourtPalace. © **0844/482-7777.** Palace admission £16 adults, £13.20 students and seniors, £8 children 5–15, £43.45 family ticket, free for children 4 and under; gardens admission £5.30 adults, £4.60 students and seniors, free children without palace ticket during summer. Maze: £3.85 adults, £2.75 children 5–15, free children 4 and under. Cloisters, courtyards, state apartments, great kitchen, cellars, and Hampton Court exhibition Mar–Oct daily 10am–6pm; Nov–Feb daily 10am–4:30pm. Gardens year-round daily 7am–dusk (no later than 9pm). Train: Hampton Court (30 min. from Waterloo).

Horniman Museum ★★ ☺MUSEUM   South London's only serious rival to the grand museums north of the river, this charmingly esoteric place is based on the personal collection of Frederick Horniman, a Victorian tea trader. It amounts to 350,000 objects made up of all sorts and everything, from African tribal masks to a gigantic, overstuffed walrus, and from musical instruments (it holds one of the country's most important collections) to oversized model insects, as well as a small aquarium constructed in waterfall-like tiers. It's divided into three broad categories: Natural history; music; and world cultures. There's a full range of events and activities, including storytelling and craft sessions for children. Outside its 16 acres of grounds were revamped in 2011 and now boast a medicinal garden, a food garden, an animal walk (with sheep, goats, and guinea pigs), and a music garden.

100 London Rd., Forest Hill, SE23. www.horniman.ac.uk. © **020/8699-1872.** Free admission except for temporary exhibitions. Museum daily 10:30am–5:30pm. Gardens Mon–Sat 7:30am–dusk; Sun 8am–dusk. Train: Forest Hill (13 min. from London Bridge Station; 24 min. from Shoreditch High St.).

Royal Botanic Gardens, Kew ★★★ ☺ PARK/GARDEN   These world-famous gardens are home to thousands of elegantly arranged plants, but Kew Gardens, as it's more commonly known, is no mere pleasure garden—it's essentially a vast scientific research center that also happens to be extraordinarily beautiful. The gardens' 299-acre site encompasses lakes, greenhouses, walks, pavilions, and museums. Among the 50,000 plants are notable collections of ferns, orchids, aquatic plants, cacti, mountain plants, palms, and tropical water lilies.

No matter what season you visit, Kew always has something to see, with species of shrubs, flowers, and trees from every part of the globe, from the Arctic Circle to tropical rainforests. If the weather's chilly, you can keep warm in the three great hothouses: The **Palm House** (the warmest, with a thick, sweaty mass of jungle plants); the slightly cooler **Temperate House;** and the **Princess of Wales Conservatory,** with 10 climatic zones, from arid to tropical. But when the sun is out, head to the newest attraction, a 200-m (656-ft.) Treetop Walkway taking you up into the canopy, some 20m (59 ft.) in the air, for a stroll through chestnut, lime, and oak trees.

Kew, Surrey. www.rbgkew.org.uk. ✆ **020/8332-5655.** Admission £13.50 adults, £11.50 students and seniors, free for children 15 and under. Apr–Aug Mon–Fri 9:30am–6pm, Sat–Sun 9:30am–7pm; Sept–Oct daily 9:30am–5:30pm; Nov–Jan daily 9:30am–3:45pm; Feb–Mar daily 9:30am–5pm. Tube: Kew Gardens.

Organized Tours
RIVER CRUISES ON THE THAMES

A trip on the river gives you an entirely different angle on London. You'll see how the city grew along and around the Thames, and how many of its landmarks turn toward the water. The Thames was London's first highway.

Thames River Services, Westminster Pier, Victoria Embankment, SW1 (www. westminsterpier.co.uk; ✆ **020/7930-4097;** Tube: Westminster), concerns itself with downriver traffic from Westminster Pier to such destinations as Greenwich, St. Katharine's Dock, and the Thames Barrier. One-way fares are £10 for adults and £5 for children 15 and under. Round-trip fares are £13 for adults, £6.50 for children. A family ticket costs £33.50 round-trip.

A perfectly fine and cheaper, if slightly more functional, option for downriver trips from Embankment Pier to the London Eye, Bankside, the Tower of London, Canary Wharf, and/or Greenwich are the regular, fast water-borne commuter services operated by **Thames Clippers ★**. One-day, unlimited travel roamer passes are available. For details, see p. 83.

Westminster Passenger Service Association (www.wpsa.co.uk; ✆ **020/7930-2062;** Tube: Westminster), which also uses Westminster Pier, offers the only riverboat service upstream to Kew, Richmond, and Hampton Court, with regular daily sailings from just before Easter until the end of October on traditional riverboats with licensed bars. Round-trip tickets to Hampton Court are £22.50 for adults, £15 for seniors, £11.25 for children aged 4 to 14, and £56.25 for a family ticket; one child 3 or younger accompanied by an adult goes free. Round-trip tickets to Kew cost £18, £12, £9, and £45, respectively. Travelcard holders are entitled to a third off quoted ticket prices.

BUS & CYCLE TOURS

For the bewildered first-timer, the quickest way to bring London into focus is probably to take a bus tour—but it isn't cheap. The **Original London Sightseeing Tour** passes by many of the major sights in a couple of hours or so, depending on traffic. The tour—that uses a traditional double-decker bus with live commentary by a guide—costs £26 for adults, £13 for children aged 5 to 15, free for those 4 and younger. A family ticket costs £91 and includes up to three children. The ticket, valid for 48 hours, allows you to hop on or off the bus at any point on any of three different circuits around the city. Your ticket also entitles you to a free riverboat ride and a choice of free 90-minute walking tours.

Tickets can be purchased on the bus or at any of the five start-points—Marble Arch, Trafalgar Square, Woburn Place, Piccadilly Circus, or Grosvenor Gardens—and from the **Original London Visitor Centre,** 17–19 Cockspur St., Trafalgar Square, SW1 (✆ **020/7389-5040;** Tube: Charing Cross). For information or phone purchases, call ✆ **020/8877-1722.** It's also possible to book online at www.theoriginaltour.com. Do so ahead of time, especially in low season, and you may secure significant discounts on the prices quoted above.

A much cheaper alternative is to seek out the two remaining London bus lines where old-fashioned **Routemaster ★** double-decker buses still operate. Only route **9**—which skirts Hyde Park and Green Park, and halts at Piccadilly Circus and Trafalgar Square—and route **15**—linking Monument and St. Paul's with Trafalgar Square and Regent Street—offer this "heritage" service. Although you can't hop on and off at will—unless you've bought a Travelcard (see "Getting Around," p. 78)—you can enjoy your own self-guided London bus tour for £1.35 per person.

For more on navigating London's bus network, see "Getting Around," p. 78.

If you prefer two wheels to four, the **London Bicycle Tour Company** (www. londonbicycle.com; *©* **020/7928-6838**) guides groups around six separate circuits of the capital, originating from its base at Gabriel's Wharf, on the South Bank. The Central London Tour costs £17 and takes approximately 2½ hours, passing Buckingham Palace, Westminster Abbey, and St. Paul's Cathedral en route. It leaves daily at 10:30am; tours of the Royal West and East London run weekends only, and cost £20 for the longer, 3½-hour circuits. Between November and March booking ahead is essential. New tours added in 2012 include the Night Tour (Sat only; booking essential) and a 2½-hour West End tour (daily, in summer only). Hybrid bike and helmet rental is included in all tour prices.

WALKING TOURS

London Walks ★ (www.walks.com; *©* **020/7624-3978**) is the oldest established walking-tour company in London—and still offers the best range of guided walks, departing every day of the week from points around town. Their hallmarks are variety, value, reasonably sized groups (generally under 30), and—above all—superb guides. The renowned crime historian Donald Rumbelow leads the daily **Jack the Ripper walk** (www.jacktheripperwalk.com) on Sundays, and occasional Mondays, Tuesdays, and Fridays; gather outside Tower Hill station before 7:30pm. Other notable themed walks include "Shakespeare's and Dickens' London," "The Beatles Magical Mystery Tour," Harry Potter movie locations, and "Hidden London." Several walks run every day, and all cost £8 for adults, £6 for students and seniors; children 14 and younger go free. Check the website for a schedule, or consult the London walks leaflet that you'll find in almost every information center and hotel in London; no reservations are needed and walks last around 2 hours.

Context ★ (www.contexttravel.com; *©* **020/3318-5637,** or 800/691-6036 in the U.S.) takes a more didactic approach to its walking program, with smaller groups led by engaging docents who are experts and scholars in their fields. Walks such as "London: Portrait of a City" are ideal for visitors who want to dig a little deeper. Prices range from £55 to £70 per person for walks of 2½ to 4 hours' duration. Both London Walks and Context can arrange private guides for individuals or small groups.

Unseen Tours ★ (www.sockmobevents.org.uk; *©* **07514/266-774**) runs guided walks of city neighborhoods led by homeless and former homeless residents. Guides with years of local knowledge garnered on the streets specialize in giving visitors a raw look at their city from a unique angle. Tours cost £8, and are packed with alternative history, anecdotes, and peeks into corners that are too easy to miss. They last 80 to 90 minutes and run Friday through Sunday on five different routes—around Shoreditch, Covent Garden, London Bridge, Brick Lane, and Mayfair. There's no need to book ahead, unless you're in a large group—just gather at the rendezvous points at the times specified on the website. Tours are not suited to young children.

SPECIAL-INTEREST TOURS & EXPERIENCES

If you want to see behind the scenes of the world's most famous broadcasting organization, **BBC Tours** ★ (www.bbc.co.uk/tours; ✆ **0370/901-1227** or **01732/427770**) leads group visits around Television Centre, in White City, and recently renovated, Art Deco Broadcasting House, in the West End. The former focuses on television and includes a visit to the BBC newsroom, while the latter is all about radio and takes in the famous BBC Radio Theatre and the chance to create your own short program. The tours are restricted to visitors aged from 9 and 12 upwards, respectively. There's also an interactive Children's Tour aimed at accompanied youngsters aged 6 to 11. Little ones are able to see inside a real BBC dressing room, hang out on sets of well-known programs, and even make a short TV spot of their own. All tours last between 1½ and 2 hours and cost £10 for adults, £9 seniors, and £8 children. Family tickets for up to four people cost £30. There's something running most days of most weeks; book online or by telephone.

Soccer fans may be interested in an all-areas tour of Arsenal's **Emirates Stadium** (www.arsenal.com/stadiumtours; ✆ **020/7619-5000**). Approximately 1-hour visits around the capital's finest club ground take in the dressing rooms, players' tunnel, and directors' boxes. Tours are self-guided and available between 10:15am and 3:45pm on most non-matchdays, and cost £17.50 for adults, £9 for children aged 5 to 15, and £42 for a family of four. Dedicated Arsenal fans should consider paying extra (£35/£18) to join a tour led by a club legend such as Charlie George or Lee Dixon. These generally run once per day, twice on weekends.

There are hundreds of English cheeses, and you can discover just a few of them at themed, tutored cheese tastings at **Neal's Yard Dairy** ★ (www.nealsyarddairy.co.uk; ✆ **020/7500-7575**). "Classes" are sociable affairs, a mixture of flip-chart science and informative banter, and take place above this top cheesemonger's warehouse opposite Borough Market (see p. 153). There's a range of themes, ranging from "Beer and Cheese" (a favorite of ours) and "Modern Traditionals" to "Cider and Cheese" and "England vs. Spain." Booking is essential; prices are usually £50 per person for a 2-hour evening session.

In fact, whatever your niche interest, you'll probably be able to locate an expert to show you how it's done London-style. **The Intelligence Trail** (www.theintelligence trail.co.uk) runs espionage-themed tours around the city that are ideally suited to modern history and ephemera buffs. Tours cost £20 (less if you pay ahead of time online) and are not suitable for anyone aged 17 and under. **Dragon and Flagon** (www.londonpubtours.weebly.com; ✆ **020/8554-8803**) runs walking and drinking tours of the city's historic pubs. Tours cost £10 per adult. **Walk, Eat, Talk, Eat** (www.walkeattalkeat.com; ✆ **020/7426-0894**) leads foodie walks, packed with insider knowledge, in the eastern part of the city. These Sunday walks cover brunch or lunch, last 2½ hours, and cost £30 to £40 including tastings. Chocolate lovers can take a cocoa-fueled walk around the master chocolatiers of Mayfair and Chelsea with **Chocolate Ecstasy Tours** (www.chocolateecstasytours.com; ✆ **07981/809536**). Daytime tours usually run at weekends, costing £40 to £45 for walks of around 3 hours that include tastings and discounts at some of the world's most creative chocolate stores.

As well as the tours recommended above, you could also check tour and experience aggregators like **Isango!** (www.isango.com), **Viator** (www.viator.com), and **Get Your Guide** (www.getyourguide.com).

WHERE TO EAT

London is one of the world's great dining capitals. Here you can experience a global range of cuisines, anything from a traditional English feast to the regional cooking of countries from Italy to India. The last few years have been momentous for the restaurant scene. Top-end places can no longer rest on their laurels; they are dealing with educated, well-traveled, and opinionated customers who know the value of a meal. Prices have stayed the same and even lowered in some cases, and most major restaurants now offer good-value set meals.

On top of that, the "gastropub" has become a force to be reckoned with. Young chefs have taken over moribund pubs, filled them with odd pieces of furniture, and now offer top cooking at less-than-top prices. Some are in the center, but you'll find many gastropubs in residential neighborhoods outside the usual tourist areas. Another big change in the last few years is the geographic shift from the West End to East London, where new cafes and small restaurants have emerged in what is now a dynamic part of the capital. It's all good news for restaurant-goers: Eating out in London offers more choice, more value, and more fun than ever.

Look to the Internet for occasional impressive discounts on London dining. Websites promoting special deals include **Lastminute.com** and **Squaremeal.co.uk**. It's also worth subscribing to regular newsletters like those e-mailed weekly by **Lovefoodlovedrink.co.uk** and **Travelzoo.com**, and signing up to deals websites like **KGB Deals** (www.kgbdeals.co.uk/london), **LivingSocial** (www.livingsocial.com), or **Groupon** (www.groupon.com). For a top meal at reasonable prices, many destination restaurants offer set-price lunch deals, as well as limited, but top-quality pre- and post-theatre menus; see details in the reviews below.

The West End
MAYFAIR
Very Expensive

Alain Ducasse at the Dorchester ★★★ FRENCH   Alain Ducasse is the name here, but it's talented Jocelyn Herland who earned the recent three Michelin stars. The plush room centers around a circular table for six, hidden behind a translucent curtain and lit with fiber-optic cables. It's better to sit in the pretty front room overlooking Hyde Park. This is French haute cuisine, but with a nod toward London's more relaxed style. The cooking is superb; the quality of the seasonal ingredients shining through in starters such as sautéed lobster, truffled chicken quenelles, and pasta; and a main dish of rich veal from the Limousin region. Desserts are great setpieces, although the cheeseboard is lacking the range such a restaurant should offer. And the wine list? Splendid, but splendidly priced too.

Inside the Dorchester Hotel, Park Lane, W1. www.alainducasse-dorchester.com. © **020/7629-8866.** Reservations required 2 weeks in advance. Set-price 3-course lunch menu £60 inc. 2 glasses of wine, coffee, and water. Set 2 courses £55, 3 courses £78, 4 courses £95, tasting menu 7 courses £115. AE, DC, MC, V. Tues–Fri noon–2pm; Tues–Sat 6:30–10pm. Tube: Green Park, Hyde Park Corner, or Marble Arch.

Hibiscus ★★★ CONTEMPORARY EUROPEAN   The cooking is spectacular—with enough culinary fireworks to satisfy the most adventurous—while the setting is elegant and understated. Claude Bosi made his name and reputation at his Hibiscus restaurant in Ludlow in Shropshire, then came to London in 2007 with his wife Claire, who runs the front of house. His style of cooking includes ingredients that you wouldn't expect in classic French dishes: Crab salad comes with turnip, Kentish sea

4

Where to Eat

LONDON

128

leaves, ginger, and smoked olive oil; Welsh mutton with a walnut crust with white bean and prune parfait. This is one to save for—put yourself into the hands of the master and appreciate an exceptional, and different, eating experience.

29 Maddox St., W1. www.hibiscusrestaurant.co.uk. ℂ **020/7629-2999.** Reservations required. Lunch 3 courses £35–£43; 6-course tasting menu (whole table only) £90, 8-course tasting menu (whole table only, Sat only) £100. A la carte 2 courses £60, 3 courses £80. Fri and Sat evenings 4 courses £77.50, 6 courses £87.50, 8 courses £97.50. AE, DC, MC, V. Mon–Thurs noon–2:30pm and 6:30–10pm; Fri–Sat 6–10pm. Tube: Green Park.

Le Gavroche ★★★ FRENCH   There may be new kids on the block, new cuisines, and new young chefs, but Le Gavroche remains the number-one choice in London for classical French cuisine from Roux, Jr., son of the chef who founded the restaurant in 1966. The famous cheese soufflé is still there, alongside lobster mousse with caviar and a Champagne butter sauce. From the main courses: Grilled scallops with carrots and salad and tarragon mustard sauce or roast veal with creamed morel mushroom sauce and mashed potatoes; and desserts including apricot and Cointreau soufflé. It's beautifully presented and served with style by faultless staff. The wine list is a masterclass in top French wines, and is kind to the purse on lesser- known varieties. It all takes place in a comfortable, conventional basement dining room which may be too old-fashioned for some, but with its Picassos on the walls, perfectly sets the scene for a classic meal.

43 Upper Brook St., W1. www.le-gavroche.co.uk. ℂ **020/7408-0881.** Reservations required as far in advance as possible. Main courses £26.90–£54.80; set lunch £52; *Le Menu Exceptionnel* (whole table) £100. AE, MC, V. Mon–Fri noon–2pm; Mon–Sat 6:30–11pm. Tube: Marble Arch.

Expensive

Greenhouse ★★ CONTEMPORARY EUROPEAN   The secret garden and fountain comes as a surprise to first-time visitors. Tucked away in Mayfair, the Greenhouse's pretty dining room looks out onto the greenery. Lyon-born head chef Antonin Bonnet is an inspired master, producing first-class dishes without destroying the natural flavors of his ingredients. His skill in mixing unusual combinations shines through in dishes like a gutsy cider-marinated mackerel with horseradish foam and pickled black radish, followed by Scottish venison with spiced pear and smoked celeriac. Vegetarians are well treated with a separate menu so tempting it might convert carnivores.

27a Hays Mews, W1. www.greenhouserestaurant.co.uk. ℂ **020/7499-3331.** Reservations required. Set lunch 2 courses £25, 3 courses £29; vegetarian menu £85; tasting menu £90. AE, DC, MC, V. Mon–Fri noon–2:30pm; Mon–Sat 6:30–11pm. Tube: Green Park.

Scott's ★★ SEAFOOD   Scott's is glamorous and glitzy, a seafood restaurant that is on every celebrity's speed dial. Opened as an oyster warehouse in 1851 by a young fishmonger, John Scott, the restaurant moved to Mayfair in 1968. The dining room is drop-dead gorgeous, oak-paneled with art on the walls and a show-stopping crustacean display in the central bar. Meat eaters are taken care of, as are vegetarians and vegans, but fish is the raison d'être; it seems perverse to ignore the freshest of oysters, caviar that starts at £80, octopus carpaccio, smoked haddock with colcannon, or a simple, perfectly cooked sea bass. The owners have opened the **Mount Street Deli** ★, 100 Mount St., W1 (www.themountstreetdeli.co.uk; ℂ **020/7499-6843**) opposite, a perfect place for breakfast, a light lunch, or afternoon tea.

20 Mount St., W1. www.scotts-restaurant.com. ℂ **020/7495-7309.** Reservations required. Main courses £17.50–£42. AE, DC, MC, V. Mon–Sat noon–10:30pm; Sun noon–10pm. Tube: Green Park or Bond St.

Moderate

Momo ★ MOROCCAN/NORTH AFRICAN   Entering, you step into a colorful fantasy of Moroccan life: Stucco walls, wooden screens, rugs, brass lanterns, and low tables take you straight to Marrakech. The menu is pretty authentic as well, built around couscous and tagines bursting with chicken or lamb, preserved lemons, and olives. You might start with a *briouat* of cheese, mint, and potatoes served with quince marmalade, or the chef's specialty of *pastille*—filo pastry parcels filled with sweet-tasting wood pigeon, almonds and cinnamon, and an orange confit. Informal, on-site **Café Mô** serves all-day meze (£4.50 per dish or meze selections £13.50–£21).

25 Heddon St., W1. www.momoresto.com. © **020/7434-4040.** Reservations required. Main courses £17–£36; fixed-price lunch £15–£19; set menu £49. AE, DC, MC, V. Mon–Sat noon–2:30pm and 6:30–11:30pm; Sun 6:30–11pm. Tube: Piccadilly Circus or Oxford Circus.

Pollen Street Social ★★ MODERN BRITISH   Jason Atherton made his name working for Gordon Ramsay, then left to open this amazingly successful restaurant. Casual diners make for the lounge bar and a menu of tapas dishes. Small plates are also on the main restaurant menu, so you can share starters then order a regular main. Scallop ceviche, cucumber and radish with a soy dressing and apple, Cornish crab with pear and a sweet and sour cauliflower and frozen peanut powder, or cauliflower and squid will not take the edge off your appetite. So move on to pork belly with apple, curly kale, mulled blackberries, and cob nut paste or halibut with paella and sprouting broccoli. It's sophisticated cooking in a relaxed, casual venue.

8 Pollen St., W1. www.pollenstreetsocial.com. © **020/7290-7600.** Main courses £22.50–£25. AE, MC, V. Mon–Sat noon–2:30pm and 6–10:30pm. Tube: Oxford Circus.

ST. JAMES'S
Moderate
Green's Restaurant & Oyster Bar ★ SEAFOOD/TRADITIONAL BRITISH   Clubby, comfortable, and definitely part of the Establishment, Green's has been serving its brand of traditional British cooking for over 30 years. Wood-paneled walls hung with cartoons, a central bar, and seemingly soundproof booths with leather banquettes make Green's a safe bet for its political and power-broking customers. This is the place for roasted parsnip soup with apple crisps; the famous salmon fish-cakes; oysters in season; very upscale fish and chips; filet of beef with horseradish; or the occasional discreet foray into contemporary cooking like monkfish with butternut squash ravioli and hazelnut sage butter. Game is a strength, as are the fish dishes, and the wine list is superb. It could all be rather stuffy, but it's not.

36 Duke St., St. James's, SW1. www.greens.org.uk. © **020/7930-4566.** Reservations required. Main courses £17–£42.50. AE, DC, MC, V. Mon–Sat noon–3pm and 5:30–10pm. Tube: Green Park. Also at 14 Cornhill, EC2 (©**020/7220-6300**).

PICCADILLY CIRCUS & LEICESTER SQUARE

All the options below (along with those under "Covent Garden & the Strand" and "Soho," elsewhere in this section) are candidates for dining before or after a show in London's Theatreland.

Expensive
Bentley's Oyster Bar & Grill ★★ SEAFOOD/TRADITIONAL BRITISH   Bentley's is a London institution that opened in 1916 and went through various ups and downs, before being rescued by the highly talented and charming Irish chef, Richard Corrigan. Under his expert guidance, Bentley's (according to its many

fans) now serves the best fish in London. The street-level Oyster Bar, vaguely Arts and Crafts in feel, is a great place for watching the guys shucking oysters behind the bar and dining off the likes of dressed crab, smoked salmon, or smoked eel. In the more formal upstairs Grill, the menu includes stalwarts like the rich Bentley's fish soup, but it's worth being more adventurous and trying dishes such as roast cod with chorizo sausage and rocket. It's all conducted in a genuinely friendly atmosphere, though high-ish prices and occasionally slow service put off some people.

11–15 Swallow St., W1. www.bentleysoysterbarandgrill.co.uk. © **020/7734-4756.** Oyster Bar: Main courses £10.50–£19.50. Grill: Main courses £19–£32. AE, MC, V. Oyster Bar Mon–Sat 7–10am and noon–midnight; Sun noon–10pm. Restaurant Mon–Fri noon–3pm and 6–11pm; Sat 6–11pm. Tube: Piccadilly Circus.

Inexpensive
Tokyo Diner ✦ JAPANESE   This Japanese interloper into prime Chinatown territory is cheap and friendly, refuses tips, takes £1 off dishes between 3 and 6pm, and is open every day of the year from noon to midnight. No wonder it's so popular. Donburi rice dishes pull in students and the impecunious to fill up on beef and onion braised in sweet Japanese sauce with ginger. Others go for their popular bento box set meals: £14.80 gets you a chicken teriyaki box, in which chicken flambéed in teriyaki sauce is served with rice, vegetables, and pickles. Sushi and soup noodles complete the picture.

2 Newport Place, WC2. www.tokyodiner.com. © **020/7287-8777.** Main courses £6.50–£13.50. Bento box set meals £14.50–£20. MC, V. Daily noon–midnight. Tube: Leicester Sq.

COVENT GARDEN & THE STRAND
The restaurants in and around Covent Garden and the Strand are convenient choices for West End theatre-goers.

Very Expensive
L'Atelier de Joël Robuchon ★★★ FRENCH   The London Atelier of Robuchon (who has 26 Michelin stars and restaurants around the world) is based on his concept of an informal restaurant. There are three areas: The first floor, which is the most conventional; the top floor Le Salon bar; and the moody red and black "Atelier." For the most dramatic effect, eat here and book at the counter. Here you can watch the theatre of the chefs producing tapas-style dishes—small bombshells of taste as in beef and foie gras mini-burger; pig's trotter on parmesan toast; and egg cocotte with wild mushroom cream, all wildly inventive and beautifully presented. The a la carte menu follows the conventional three-course approach, using superb ingredients. The pre-theatre menu represents stunning value.

13–15 West St., WC2. www.joel-robuchon.com. © **020/7010-8600.** Reservations essential. Main courses £19–£38; small tasting dishes £11–£19; Menu Découverte 8 courses £125; Vegetarian Découverte 8 courses £80; lunch and pre-theatre 2-course menu £25, 3 courses £29. AE, MC, V. Daily noon–2:30pm and 5:30–10:30pm. Tube: Leicester Sq.

Expensive
J. Sheekey ★★ SEAFOOD   Tucked into a small alleyway off St. Martin's Lane, J. Sheekey has long been a Theatreland favorite for both the famous (Laurence Olivier and Vivien Leigh) and the not-so-famous. It's a charming dining room with pictures of theatrical greats lining the walls. You can opt for the favorites—Atlantic prawns, the famous Sheekey's fish pie—but it's worth trying more unusual dishes. Monkfish and tiger prawn curry comes topped with crispy fried shallots and basmati rice. The more casual **J. Sheekey Oyster Bar,** 33–34 St. Martin's Court

(**020/7240-2565**), is next door, has the same look, and offers Sheekey classics and smaller dishes.

28–32 St. Martin's Court, WC2. www.j-sheekey.co.uk. © **020/7240-2565.** Reservations recommended. Main courses £15–£42. Weekend set lunch menu, 3 courses £26.50. AE, DC, MC, V. Mon–Sat noon–3pm and 5:30pm–midnight; Sun noon–3:30pm and 6–11pm. Tube: Leicester Sq.

Les Deux Salons ★★FRENCH/BRASSERIE   The third venture from Michelin-starred Anthony Demetre and Will Smith is the kind of smart brasserie that will have the French reaching for their smelling salts. It's large, bustling, decorated with the requisite amount of polished brass, mirrors, and dark wood, evokes the Belle Epoque, and offers a standard of cooking that is now rare in Parisian brasseries. The upper floor is more intimate; the ground floor swings along in style. A well-drilled kitchen produces impeccable dishes like snail and Herefordshire bacon pie; ravioli stuffed with veal; bavette of beef; daily specials like rabbit in mustard, plus such tongue-in-cheek desserts as rum baba, and floating islands. Service is spot on; prices are reasonable; Les Deux Salons is a palpable hit.

40–42 William IV St., WC2. www.lesdeuxsalons.co.uk. © **020/7420-2050.** Reservations recommended. Main courses £11–£22.50; 3-course lunch £15.50. AE, MC, V. Mon–Sat noon–11pm; Sun 10am–5pm. Tube: Charing Cross.

Rules ★TRADITIONAL BRITISH   This is the place for a genuine taste of traditional London. Opened in 1798 as an oyster bar, the gorgeous, red plush Edwardian interior with drawings and cartoons covering the walls is much as it was when feeding the great and good of the theatrical and literary world—like Charles Dickens, H. G. Wells, Laurence Olivier, and Clark Gable. What keeps Rules alive today is its devotion to top, traditional British cooking. Native Irish or Scottish oysters; the best game only served in season—wild Highland Red deer, grouse, snipe, pheasant, and woodcock; and beef from the owner's estate, skillfully prepared and cooked. Puddings (not desserts in this most British of restaurants) might be a rib-stickingly good Golden Syrup sponge pudding, a winter blackberry and apple crumble, or even rice pudding, bringing back childhood memories.

35 Maiden Lane, WC2. www.rules.co.uk. © **020/7836-5314.** Reservations recommended. Main courses £19–£32. AE, DC, MC, V. Mon–Sat noon–11:45pm; Sun noon–10:45pm. Tube: Covent Garden.

Savoy Grill ★★★ TRADITIONAL BRITISH   Opened a few months after the glorious Savoy Hotel (p. 181) reclaimed its place among London's icons of discreet luxury, the Savoy Grill, run by Gordon Ramsay, is everything we hoped for. The Art Deco-inspired interior is a real gem, with sparkling chandeliers, walls that gleam a deep amber, and black-and-white photographs of past stars like Bogart and Bacall. The menu balances the classics with a touch of the modern: Cornish crab mayonnaise with apple salad, wild celery, and wafer-thin Melba toast; scallops with leeks and shrimp butter; or go for a grilled venison chop. This is a return to past glories.

In the Savoy Hotel, Strand, WC2. www.gordonramsay.com. © **020/7592-1600.** Reservations required. Main courses £18–£36. AE, DC, MC, V. Mon–Sat noon–3pm and 5:30–11pm; Sun noon–4pm and 6–10:30pm. Tube: Charing Cross.

Moderate
Giaconda Dining Room ★ 🍴 CONTEMPORARY EUROPEAN   Tucked among the guitar shops of Denmark Street, just off Tottenham Court Road, the Giaconda comes as a surprise. Run by husband and wife Australians, Paul and Tracey Merrony, its bistro-like atmosphere, good cooking, and down-to-earth pricing set it

apart. Dishes like salad of baked beetroot and leeks vinaigrette with goat curd to start followed by sautéed duck breast with celeriac purée and beetroot with a cherry sauce have Giaconda regulars purring with pleasure. A reasonably-priced wine list, relaxed atmosphere, and pleasant staff complete an appealing package.

9 Denmark St., WC2. www.giacondadining.com. ℰ **020/7240-3334.** Main courses £6.50–£20.50. AE, MC, V. Tues–Fri noon–2:15pm; Tues–Sat 6–9:15pm. Tube: Tottenham Court Rd.

Mishkins ★ ▮▮JEWISH/AMERICAN   Russell Norman, the genius behind **Polpo** (p. 134) and **Spuntino** (p. 135), has done it again. Who knew a "Jewish deli with cocktails," that would be at home on New York's Lower East Side, was just what London needed? Reuben on rye with pastrami, sauerkraut, and Swiss cheese; chopped chicken liver sandwich; great meatballs; an all-day brunch of dishes like latkes, smoked eel, apple sauce, and sour cream; or all-day supper of meat loaf—how could it be anything but a roaring success?

25 Catherine St., WC2. www.mishkins.co.uk. ℰ**020/7240-2078.** Main courses £6–£12. AE, MC, V. Mon–Fri 11am–midnight; Sun noon–11pm. Tube: Tottenham Court Rd.

Terroirs ★ FRENCH   Hearty rustic French food, good wines (including "natural" unfiltered wine from small artisan growers), and a vibrant atmosphere gives Terroirs the edge over other Covent Garden restaurants. The street-level wine bar is a great meeting place for pre-theatre drinks, charcuterie that takes in pork and pistachio terrine, rillettes, and Bigorre saucisson, properly kept French cheeses, and tapas-style snacks. The basement restaurant is the place for a longer meal, although it has a similar menu of small plates like potted shrimps on toast, herring and warm potato salad, and whole Dorset crab with mayonnaise.

5 William IV St., WC2. www.terroirswinebar.com. ℰ**020/7036-0660.** Reservations recommended. Small plates £3.50–£12. Main courses £6–£17. AE, MC, V. Mon–Sat noon–11pm. Tube: Charing Cross. Also at Brawn, 49 Columbia Rd., E2 (ℰ**020/7729-5629**).

Inexpensive

Dishoom ★ INDIAN   India has provided so much inspiration for London dining that it's difficult to imagine a new experience. Then up pops this wonderful place, modeled on the Bombay cafes of the 1960s. It looks great, with a geometrically tiled floor, marble-topped tables, odd lights and pictures, and its blackboard of rules at the door: "No water to outsiders" and "All castes served." It swings along from breakfasts of sausage or bacon naan rolls through all-day dining on lightly spiced soups, salads, small plates of vegetable or lamb samosas, fish fingers, or calamari to dinner grills of chicken tikka, sheekh kebab, spicy lamb chops, or one-pot biryani dishes. Finish off with *kulfi* (Indian ice cream) on a stick or a lassi.

12 Upper St. Martin's Lane, WC2. www.dishoom.com. ℰ**020/7420-9320.** No reservations. Main courses £5.50–£11.50. AE, MC, V. Mon–Thurs 8am–11pm; Fri 8am–midnight; Sat 10am–midnight; Sun 10am–10pm. Tube: Leicester Sq.

SOHO

Soho's restaurants offer more options for dining before a show at a West End theatre.

Expensive

Hakkasan ★ CHINESE/CANTONESE   Opened by the restaurateur Alan Yau (who has done so much to transform London's dining scene), this sexy, moody, subtly lit basement venue serves top-notch modern Cantonese cuisine. During the day, the dim sum is among the best in London—delicate, exquisitely fresh, and beautifully cooked. In the evening top-end ingredients are cooked with subtle skill. Sweet-and-sour Duke of Berkshire pork with pomegranate takes the concept to new heights; stir-fry ostrich comes in yellow bean sauce; from the seafood section, the Chilean sea bass with Szechuan pepper, sweet basil, and spring onion is perfectly treated, the sauce complementing, not overpowering the fish. Even desserts, often the poor relation in Chinese restaurants, are superb. The wine list is a lesson in matching food and wine.

8 Hanway Place, W1. www.hakkasan.com. ✆ **020/7494-8888.** Reservations recommended. Main courses £10–£29. AE, MC, V. Mon–Sat noon–11:45pm; Sun noon–10:30pm. Tube: Tottenham Court Rd. Also at 17 Bruton St., W1 ✆ **020/7907-1888**).

Moderate

Bocca di Lupo ★★ ITALIAN   The hugely popular "mouth of the wolf" is a smart restaurant with an open kitchen, tiled floors, wooden tables, and large paintings of food on the walls. The downside of its popularity is that it's busy, cramped, and noisy—and you must book in advance. Chef Jacob Kenedy has toured Italy in a search for genuine regional dishes, and the result is a glorious trot around the country. If you want the full tour, go for the small plates and share as many as possible, perhaps blood salami with toast from Tuscany, and the Venetian fried eel, prawns, and squid with polenta. More substantial dishes include roast teal with polenta and *guanciale* (unsmoked bacon from pig's cheek) made with herbs, and Ligurian sea bream baked in salt. The all-Italian wine list offers a good selection by the carafe or the glass, but beware: Drinking will up your bill.

12 Archer St., W1. www.boccadilupo.com.✆ **020/7734-2223.** Reservations recommended. Main courses £7–£27. AE, MC, V. Mon–Sat 12:30–3pm and 5:30–11pm; Sun 12:45–3:45pm and 5–9pm. Tube: Piccadilly Circus.

Randall & Aubin ★ SEAFOOD   Randall & Aubin began as a butcher's shop in 1911 selling top-quality meat from Paris, so it's appropriate that it was turned into a restaurant in 1996 by restaurateurs Ed Baines and James Poulton. It's a lovely setting; marble surfaces, white tiles, and old wooden furniture fit perfectly into its new incarnation as a restaurant—albeit one that specializes in fish and seafood. Caviar might weigh in at £90 to £150 a serving, but it's the well-priced dishes like fried sole with beans and sautéed potatoes (£14), and grilled sea bass with scallions, chives, and rosemary salsa and potatoes (£15.50) that please the crowds of loyal fans. Or do as we like to do: Sit at the bar, order champagne, and toy with an oyster.

16 Brewer St., W1. www.randallandaubin.com. ✆ **020/7287-4447.** No reservations. Main courses £7.50–£29.50. AE, DC, MC, V. Mon–Wed noon–11pm; Thurs–Sat noon–midnight; Sun noon–10pm. Tube: Piccadilly Circus or Leicester Sq.

Inexpensive

Mildreds ★ 🛗 VEGETARIAN   Mildreds may sound like a 1940s' Joan Crawford movie, but it's one of London's most enduring vegetarian and vegan dining spots. The airy room with a bar at the front can get very crowded, and you'll probably find yourself sharing a table. The food always hits the spot, and uses organically grown, seasonal produce. The menu changes daily, but always includes homemade soups, pastas, and salads. There are dishes like sundried tomato and buffalo mozzarella risotto cake; Sri Lankan sweet potato and cashew nut curry; and unusual sides.

45 Lexington St., W1. www.mildreds.co.uk. ✆ **020/7494-1634.** No reservations. Main courses £7.25–£9.75. No credit cards. Mon–Fri 9am–11pm; Sat noon–11pm. Tube: Tottenham Court Rd.

Polpo ★★ 🛗 ITALIAN   Modeled on a *baraco* (Venetian wine bar), the decor here is perfect, with stripped brick walls, Victorian tiles, wooden floors, and leather banquettes. A menu of small dishes of regional specialties includes *cicchetti* (Venetian bar snacks) of asparagus, taleggio cheese, and prosciutto ham or salt cod on grilled polenta, all costing between £1 and £3. Breads are excellent—try the broad bean, ricotta, and mint bruschetta for something different. More substantial tapas-style dishes run from *cotechino* (warm, thick-sliced salami) with lentils and salsa verde to a *fritto misto* (mixed fried fish) or *linguine vongole* (pasta with clams), and there are plenty of vegetarian options too. Alas, a no bookings policy at dinner can mean long waits.

41 Beak St., W1. www.polpo.co.uk. ©**020/7734-4479.** No reservations. Dishes £1–£14. AE, MC, V. Mon–Sat noon–3pm and 5:30–11pm; Sun noon–4pm. Tube: Piccadilly Circus. Also at Da Polpo, 6 Maiden Lane, WC2 (© **020/7836-8448**); and Polpetto, French House, 49 Dean St., W1 (©**020/7734-1969**).

Spuntino ★ 🍴 AMERICAN/BURGER   Spuntino looks the part of a New York speakeasy, with an industrial, artfully scruffy interior. London restaurateur Russell Norman has embraced New York dining ideas, as he did before with Venetian wine bar, **Polpo** (p. 134). Come here for small plates, which such as imaginative sliders (miniburgers) like beef and marrow meatballs and lamb and pickled cucumber. It's all well done—even the peanut butter and jelly sandwich for those after a blast from their past. A no booking policy means queues at peak times, so arrive unfashionably early or even mid-afternoon for a less rushed experience.

61 Rupert St., W1. www.spuntino.co.uk. No phone. No reservations. Main courses £5.50–£10. AE, MC, V. Mon–Sat 11am–midnight; Sun noon–11pm. Tube: Piccadilly Circus.

Yauatcha ★ASIAN   This Asian eatery, describing itself as a modern reinterpretation of the old Chinese teahouse, is the brainchild of Alan Yau, who won Britain's first Michelin star for Chinese cooking at his top-of-the-range restaurant, Hakkasan (see above). At this informal dim sum outlet service is casual, although it's so popular you're sometimes rushed through your meal to make way for new arrivals. The ground floor is quiet; the basement buzzes. Dim sum, among London's finest, is served for both lunch and dinner, and often takes unusual ingredients like scallops, Wagyu beef, venison, or king crab.

15 Broadwick St., W1. www.yauatcha.com. ©**020/7494-8888.** Dim sum £3–£12. Set meal for 2 £28.88. AE, MC, V. Mon–Sat noon–11:45pm; Sun noon–10:30pm. Tube: Oxford Circus.

BLOOMSBURY & FITZROVIA
Very Expensive
Pied à Terre ★★★FRENCH   You could easily walk past the entrance to one of London's best restaurants without a second glance. And once inside, the dark decor is as unassuming as the exterior. But persevere, for Australian chef Shane Osborn has two well-deserved Michelin stars. The set lunch is one of London's greatest bargains. Where else could you get tuna tartare with avocado crème fraîche, quail eggs, and fennel dressing, then roast pork with its braised cheek, potato fondant, and spicy sauce perfectly balanced with pickled apples and apple purée for £27.50? Cheese or dessert (including pre-dessert) might be a smooth mango velouté with coconut mousse and Thai basil for an extra £6. The a la carte dinner menu is more ambitious producing superb dishes that look as beautiful as they taste. Save up for Pied à Terre; you won't regret it.

34 Charlotte St., W1. www.pied-a-terre.co.uk. ©**020/7636-1178.** Set-price 2-course lunch £27.50; set-price 2-course dinner £60 (desserts £14, cheeses £16.50 per person); 10-course dinner £95;

vegetarian £85. AE, MC, V. Mon–Fri 12:15–2:30pm; Mon–Sat 6–11pm. Tube: Goodge St. or Tottenham Court Rd.

Moderate

Dabbous ★ CONTEMPORARY EUROPEAN   Olli Dabbous began at Le Manoir aux Quat' Saison outside Oxford, then worked at Michelin-starred Texture (see below) before setting up on his own in a big two-story industrial space. The basement bar majors in great cocktails with fashionable infusions, plus a good bar menu. The upstairs restaurant buzzes as waitstaff bring small plates of combinations you couldn't imagine would work—until you try them. Try a fennel, lemon balm, and pickled rose petal salad; beef tartare with cigar oil, whiskey, and rye; roast crab with cocoa beans and oyster leaf. It's all very well done, and at great prices.

39 Whitfield St., W1. www.dabbous.co.uk. ✆ **020/7323-1544.** Main courses £11–£14. Tasting menu, 7 courses £49. AE, MC, V. Tues–Sat noon–11:30pm. Tube: Goodge St.

Inexpensive

Barrica ★ SPANISH/TAPAS   Barrica looks the part—blackboards chalked up with daily specials, tiled floor, jars of colored pickled vegetables, Spanish posters, hanging hams, and a wall of wine bottles. This excellent tapas bar has an authentic feeling of Spain. The menu offers a tempting selection of dishes from around the country, served in proper small proportions at proper small prices. Those famous hams are here, of course, but also on offer are pork and oxtail meatballs, ham croquettes, and more, plus a substantial dish of the day. They take their wine list seriously, so try an unusual variety or go for the sherry suggestions.

62 Goodge St., W1. www.barrica.co.uk.✆ **020/7436-9448.** Tapas £2.75–£15. AE, MC, V. Mon–Fri noon–11:30pm; Sat 1–11:30pm. Tube: Goodge St. or Tottenham Court Rd.

MARYLEBONE
Very Expensive

Locanda Locatelli ★★ ☺ ITALIAN   The setting is sexy with beige leather seating and etched-glass dividers—it's a great place for spotting the A-list celebrities who love the restaurant. But chef Giorgio is a family man and children are just as welcome, particularly at Sunday brunch. The cooking is superb and portions are generous with pastas scoring particularly highly. Pan-fried red mullet comes with Parma ham and warm fennel salad; roast partridge with Swiss chard, chestnut, and grape is meltingly tender and gutsy. Panettone bread-and-butter pudding has to be the best in London. The all-Italian wine list is superb, with many bottles under £30 and a Sicilian at £12, surely the best value in town.

8 Seymour St., W1. www.locandalocatelli.com. ✆ **020/7935-9088.** Reservations required. Main courses £9–£31.50. AE, MC, V. Mon–Fri noon–3pm; Sat–Sun noon–3:30pm; Mon–Thurs 6:45–11pm; Fri–Sat 6:45–11:30pm; Sun 6:45–10:15pm. Tube: Marble Arch.

Expensive

L'Autre Pied ★★ CONTEMPORARY EUROPEAN   The younger sister of the successful Pied à Terre (see above), this is the domain of young chef Marcus Eaves, who gained his first Michelin star in 2009 soon after opening. The dark red seating, hand-painted walls, and wooden tables make a cozy ambience, ideal for the well-heeled shoppers of Bond Street. The cooking is skillful, with intense flavors brought to the fore in dishes that range from a starter of ravioli of confit pheasant with savoy cabbage and a nutmeg and chestnut cream, to a deeply satisfying main dish of roasted partridge breast and confit leg coming with its own mini-game pie, *choucroûte,* and a mustard sauce. It's expensive, but the set lunch and pre-theatre dinner is a steal.

5–7 Blandford St., W1. www.lautrepied.co.uk. ℂ **020/7486-9696.** Reservations required. Main courses £16–£28.50; fixed-price lunch or pre-theatre (6–7pm) set menu 2 courses £18.95, 3 courses £22.50; tasting menu £52. AE, MC, V. Mon–Fri noon–2:45pm; Sat noon–2:30pm; Sun noon–3:30pm; Mon–Sat 6–10:45pm (Sun until 9:30pm). Tube: Bond St.

The Providores & Tapa Room ★★ PACIFIC RIM/FUSION   If you've wondered what fusion cooking is all about, book at Peter Gordon's Providores for a sublime example. For more than 10 years, the New Zealander has been showing how combinations of often relatively unknown ingredients can be fused together to produce a truly gourmet experience. It's the masterly combinations that make each dish such a wonderful discovery. Squid with papaya, pickled carrot, and pomelo (Asian citrus fruit) salad with tamarind caramel and coriander is a glorious explosion of sweet and sour tastes. Grilled scallops come with a dumpling of quinoa and crab, purée of celeriac and tomato sambal (chili-based sauce), and lotus crisps. Lunch is a la carte, but dinner is a set menu with the savory dishes starter-sized to encourage you to taste as many as possible. The main **Providores** restaurant is upstairs. The downstairs, low-key **Tapa Room** offers all-day dining, and is a perfect place for breakfast.

109 Marylebone High St., W1. www.theprovidores.co.uk. ℂ **020/7935-6175.** Tapa Room: tapas £2.40–£14.80. The Providores: Main courses lunch £7.80–£25; set dinner 2/3/4/5 courses £33/£47/£57/£63. AE, MC, V. Tapa Room Mon–Fri 9–11:30am and noon–10:30pm; Sat 10am–3pm and 4–10:30pm; Sun 10am–3pm and 4–10pm. The Providores Mon–Fri noon–2:45pm and 6–10pm; Sun noon–2:45pm and 6–9:45pm. Tube: Baker St./Bond St.

Texture ★★ NORDIC   Scandinavian restaurants are relatively rare in London, but they're making a culinary impact. And so with Texture, where Agnar Sverrisson is cooking up a cool storm. The decor is pared down—smart wood and high ceilings with bright art work on the walls. The fireworks come with the cooking, where classic dishes are given an Icelandic touch, using light flavors rather than traditional French cream sauces. Asian influences appear as well: Try Cornish brill with lemon grass quinoa, barley, and cauliflower touches, or three cuts of lamb with swede. The wine list is one of London's best.

34 Portman St., W1. www.texture-restaurant.co.uk. ℂ **020/7224-0028.** Reservations required. Main courses £27.50–£34.50. Set lunch menus: 2 courses £19, 3 courses £24, 7-course tasting menu £76. AE, MC, V. Tues–Sat noon–2:30pm and 6:30–11pm. Tube: Marble Arch.

Moderate

Galvin Bistro de Luxe ★★ FRENCH   The Galvin brothers, Chris and Jeff, opened Galvin Bistro de Luxe in 2005, considered at the time a brave venture because the site had seen off several hopefuls. But their formula of producing some of the best rustic French food to be found in London *and* Paris at reasonable prices in an elegant, buzzing brasserie has proved a winner. Tastes shine through in dishes like fish soup with rouille and cheese; sautéed veal kidneys with chanterelle mushrooms and a mustard sauce; and those staples of bistro cooking, tarte au citron and apple tarte tatin.

6 Baker St., W1. www.galvinrestaurants.com. ℂ **020/7935-4007.** Reservations required. Main courses £18–£25.50; fixed-price menu lunch £19.50, dinner £21.50. AE, MC, V. Mon–Sat noon–2:30pm; Sun noon–3pm; Mon–Wed 6–10:30pm; Thurs–Sat 6–11pm; Sun 6–9:30pm. Tube: Baker St. Also at 35 Spital Sq., E1 (ℂ**020/7299-0400**).

Union Café CONTEMPORARY EUROPEAN   We find this place a real haven after shopping in Oxford Street or Marylebone. The buzzing restaurant, part of the upmarket Brinkley's group, is chic with wooden floors, industrial air vents, and an open kitchen. The menu goes the global path: Deep-fried brie with cranberry jelly; tempting meze plates; linguine with tiger prawns, mussels, and chili; but it's the juicy, tender Union burger with chips that seems to go down best with the punters.

96 Marylebone Lane, W1. www.brinkleys.com/unioncafe.asp. *©* **020/7486-4860.** Reservations recommended. Main courses £14–£24. AE, MC, V. Mon–Fri noon–3:30pm and 6–10:30pm; Sat 11am–4pm and 6:30–11pm; Sun 11am–4pm. Tube: Bond St.

West London
PADDINGTON & BAYSWATER
Moderate
Hereford Road ★★ MODERN BRITISH Once a butcher's shop, now a restaurant in the St. John mode of British no-fuss, no-fancy cooking. Chef Tom Pemberton's time at **St. John Bread & Wine** (p. 145) shows in a menu that takes in potted crab as well as grilled ox heart and roast quail with that most British (but underused) meddler jelly for starters, and moves onto mains of pot-roast duck leg and fennel, or devilled lamb's kidneys and mash. The regulars of Notting Hill have taken this offal-heavy restaurant to their heart.

13 Hereford Rd., W2. www.herefordroad.org. *©* **020/7727-1114.** Reservations recommended. Main courses £10–£14.20; set lunch, 2 courses Mon–Fri £13.60, 3 courses £15.50. AE, MC, V. Mon–Sat noon–3pm and 6–10:30pm; Sun noon–4pm and 6–10pm. Tube: Bayswater.

Inexpensive
Mandalay ⓘ BURMESE This cramped, family-run cafe is still the only Burmese restaurant in London, drawing a mix of students, locals, and those in the know. The menu takes in influences from China, India, and Thailand too, so you can combine shrimp and vegetable spring rolls; samosas and fritters; as well as spicy lamb curry, sweet-and-sour chicken, and shrimps with bamboo shoots. The small kitchen turns out the dishes with remarkable skill, particularly given the size of the menu. The drinks list is short.

444 Edgware Rd., W2. www.mandalayway.com. *©* **020/7258-3696.** Reservations required at dinner. Main courses £3–£8. AE, MC, V. Daily noon–2:30pm and 6–10:30pm. Tube: Edgware Rd.

NOTTING HILL
Expensive
The Ledbury ★★ EUROPEAN Australian-born Brett Graham has now earned two Michelin stars at this sophisticated neighborhood restaurant. With an inventive approach to ingredients and taste combinations that show true Aussie innovation, he produces dishes like flamegrilled mackerel with smoked eel, mustard, and *shiso* (Japanese mint) as a starter and grouse in season cooked in lapsang souchong tea with prunes, walnut milk, and mushrooms for a main dish. This is adventurous stuff—and in lesser hands could be a disaster. Here it is some of the best cooking around, and he's just as good at desserts.

127 Ledbury Rd., W11. www.theledbury.com. *©* **020/7792-9090.** Reservations recommended. Main courses (lunch) £28.50–£30; set lunch Mon–Fri 2 courses £30, 3 courses £35; set dinner £80. Tasting menu £105. AE, MC, V. Tues–Sat noon–2pm, Sun noon–2:30pm. Mon–Sat 6:30–10:15pm; Sun 7–10pm. Tube: Westbourne Park.

Moderate
Le Café Anglais ★★ ☺ MODERN BRITISH This is a grand brasserie in feel with huge windows, high ceilings, and banquette seating, located in Whiteleys shopping center. There's also a glamorous all-day cafe and oyster bar, ideal for those seeking an elegant light snack between buying posh frocks. There are plenty of classics on the

menu, like Parmesan custard and anchovy toast for a starter and any of the excellent game dishes. With its long menu, set menus, children's meals and parties, and friendly welcome, Le Café Anglais works hard to create the atmosphere of a neighborhood restaurant and succeeds; this is a restaurant that pleases everyone.

8 Porchester Gardens, W2. www.lecafeanglais.co.uk. © **020/7221-1415.** Reservations required. Main courses £12.50–£30; set lunch Mon–Fri 2 courses £18.50, 3 courses £22.50; Sun lunch 2 courses £25, 3 courses £30. AE, MC, V. Daily noon–3:30pm; Mon–Thurs 6:30–10:30pm; Fri–Sat 6:30–11pm; Sun 6:30–10pm. Tube: Bayswater or Queensway.

Southwest London
BELGRAVIA
Expensive

Amaya ★★ INDIAN   Theatrical, with its chefs working at the open kitchen and charcoal grill; beautiful, with pink sandstone black granite worktops, chandeliers of cascading crystals, and colorful modern art; and seductive, with its rosewood and red bar—it's not surprising that Amaya is such a hit. And that's before you taste the food. Chef Karunesh Khanna not only has a Michelin star, he also specializes in tapas-style Indian food, so go in a group to share as many of the wonderful array of dishes as possible. Try prawns with tomato and ginger; marinated leg of lamb; lamb seasoned with cardamom, mace, and ginger cooked over charcoal; and a range of vegetarian dishes like tandoor-cooked broccoli in yogurt sauce.

Halkin Arcade, Motcomb St., SW1. www.amaya.biz. © **020/7823-1166.** Reservations required. Main courses £11.50–£24; set-price lunch £19.50–£29, set-price dinner £38.50–£70. AE, DC, MC, V. Mon–Sat 12:30–2:15pm and 6:30–11:30pm; Sun 12:45–2:45pm and 6–10:30pm. Tube: Knightsbridge.

Palm ★ ☺ AMERICAN/STEAK   Walk into the long buzzing bar and you'll find a TV at one end showing North American sports. Two adjacent dining rooms follow the decor of the other Palms in this American group: casual yet smart, with wooden floors and walls covered in caricatures of famous or faithful customers. The menu goes beyond the normal steakhouse, with classic Italian dishes (Palm's founders were Italian immigrants) like veal marsala, and fresh seafood and burgers, but steak is what Palm is all about. It's expensive, but go for the Prime New York Strip—12 oz, for £39.50. The welcome is as big as the portions; there's a good children's menu and a reasonably-priced wine list.

1 Pont St., SW1. www.thepalm.com/london. © **020/7201-0710.** Reservations recommended. Main courses £14–£50. AE, DC, MC, V. Mon–Sat noon–11pm; Sun noon–9pm. Tube: Knightsbridge or Sloane Sq.

KNIGHTSBRIDGE
Very Expensive

Dinner by Heston Blumenthal ★★ TRADITIONAL BRITISH   This restaurant opened in 2011 by one of the world's great chefs, Heston Blumenthal of the Fat Duck in Bray, was one of London's most eagerly expected openings in recent memory. Dishes are based on Britain's culinary past, from savory porridge (ca. 1660) and broth of lamb (ca. 1730) to powdered duck (ca. 1670) and beef royal (ca. 1720). Finish with a sublime dessert—tipsy cake from 1810 perhaps? Don't worry; this is an extremely serious, profoundly satisfying re-rendering of historic recipes with modern cooking techniques. A unique experience in a crowded marketplace.

Inside Mandarin Oriental Hyde Park, 66 Knightsbridge, SW1. www.dinnerbyheston.com. © **020/7201-3833.** Reservations required. Main courses £23–£36; 3-course set lunch Mon–Fri £32. Daily noon–2:30pm and 6:30–10:30pm. AE, DC, MC, V. Tube: Knightsbridge.

Marcus Wareing at the Berkeley ★★★ FRENCH Diners at this claret-colored, cosseting restaurant are treated to all the goodies expected from one of London's top venues. Marcus Wareing began as a protégé of Gordon Ramsay but then took over the restaurant independently and blossomed. The three-course, fixed-price lunch menu at £38 is relatively inexpensive, but the dishes—wood pigeon with tomato, black pudding, and lettuce followed by perhaps chicken with root vegetables—don't stretch the kitchen. So if you can, blow the budget and go a la carte. Start with foie gras with prunes, walnuts, apple, and celery, then follow with sweet Cornish lamb, offset with a pink peppercorn yogurt. Don't expect a quick meal; delicious extras—smooth velouté as a pre-starter, lip-tingling granitas between courses, and pre-desserts keep you guessing as to what might come your way next.

Inside Berkeley Hotel, Wilton Place, SW1. www.marcus-wareing.com.℗ **020/7235-1200.** Reservations required. Lunch menu, 2 courses £30, 3 courses £38; a la carte menu £80; prestige menu or vegetarian menu £98; weekend menus £85 and £120. AE, MC, V. Mon–Fri noon–2:30pm; Mon–Sat 6–11pm. Tube: Knightsbridge.

Moderate

Bar Boulud ★★ FRENCH French-born, U.S.-raised, superstar chef Daniel Boulud opened the doors of his first London venture to universal approval in 2009. It's in the Mandarin Oriental, but with its own entrance, and has an attractive decor of red banquette seating, an open kitchen, and a real buzz. You won't encounter the Michelin three-star cuisine of his New York restaurant, but hearty, rustic cooking. A charcuterie counter rightly takes pride of place—Daniel Boulud was born in Lyon. Feast on classic French bistro fare like a *petit aioli* of seafood and vegetables with a perfect garlic mayonnaise; a coq au vin that had us rushing home to dig out the French recipe books; homemade sausages; and for dessert, a rich dark chocolate and raspberry gâteau. Prices are very reasonable for this part of London and level of glamour.

In the Mandarin Oriental Hyde Park, 66 Knightsbridge, SW1. www.barboulud.com.℗ **020/7201-3899.** Reservations recommended. Main courses £9–£62; 3-course fixed-price menu £23. AE, MC, V. Daily noon–3pm and 5–11pm (10:30pm Sun). Tube: Knightsbridge.

KENSINGTON & SOUTH KENSINGTON
Very Expensive

Tom Aikens ★★★ FRENCH Chef Tom Aikens has a remarkable capacity to shrug aside life's mishaps (an abrupt departure from his first restaurant, Pied à Terre, economic woes, and the rapid closure of one of his recent restaurants). His signature dining room is quietly chic, a discreet background for a meal that delivers real punch. His style is a modern interpretation of haute French cuisine, produced with flourish and skill. A roast scallop soup comes with black pudding and parsnip purée; poached lobster tail with English asparagus and an asparagus mousse. Despite contrasting ingredients, the cooking shows harmony and cohesion, as exemplified by John Dory with chestnut ravioli, chestnut sauce, cabbage, and bacon.

43 Elystan St., SW3. www.tomaikens.co.uk.℗ **020/7584-2003.** Reservations required. Set lunch 2 courses £45; dinner main courses £30–£40; tasting menu £55. AE, DC, MC, V. Mon–Fri noon–2:30pm; Mon–Sat 6:45–11pm. Tube: South Kensington.

Expensive

Cambio de Tercio ★★ CONTEMPORARY SPANISH Vibrantly colored in blood reds, deep pinks, and bright yellows, and adorned with equally vibrant stylized paintings of bull fighting, this is not the place for the shy and retiring. But it is the place for exciting, modern Spanish cooking. The menu has wide appeal. It offers conventional dishes like fried squid; prawns with garlic-parsley oil; and the classic, and beautifully cooked, crisp suckling pig with rosemary. But it also takes you on a different journey. With many of the dishes available tapas size, you'll be tempted to forgo the straight three-course route for a series of small dishes, perhaps foie gras cream with sherry, roast corn, and Manchego cheese; hake with baby squid cooked in its own ink and roast green pepper; and, naturally, superb Iberico pata negra ham.

163 Old Brompton Rd., SW5. www.cambiodetercio.co.uk. © **020/7244-8970.** Main courses £17.50–£23; 7-course tasting menu £37. AE, DC, MC, V. Mon–Fri noon–2:30pm; Sat–Sun noon–3pm; Mon–Sat 7–11:30pm; Sun 7–11pm. Tube: Gloucester Rd. or South Kensington. Also at 174 Old Brompton Rd., SW7 (©**020/7370-3685**); and 108–110 New King's Rd., SW6 (©**020/7371-5147**).

CHELSEA
Very Expensive
Gordon Ramsay ★★★ FRENCH Whatever may be happening in the fiery chef's empire elsewhere, a meal here remains one of London's great pleasures. From the moment you walk in the door, you are cosseted, and made to feel special. The menu is changing under head chef Clare Smyth—a chef to take note of—while retaining the subtlety and delicacy of the master. Try, for example, ravioli of lobster, langoustine, and salmon with a lemongrass and chervil velouté, or sautéed foie gras with roasted veal sweetbreads. The emphasis is on retaining the essential flavors of top ingredients while delivering exquisite tastes. A rare experience.

68 Royal Hospital Rd., SW3. www.gordonramsay.com. ©**020/7352–4441.** Reservations essential (1 month in advance). A la carte menu 3 courses £95; fixed-price 3-course lunch £45, 7-course dinner £125. AE, DC, MC, V. Mon–Fri noon–2:30pm and 6:30–11pm. Tube: Sloane Sq.

Moderate
Pig's Ear ★ 🍴 MODERN BRITISH/GASTROPUB The street-level bar serves excellent traditional beers, and dishes like risotto or roast guinea fowl in the packed back dining room. The Blue Room serves more sophisticated meals: smoked salmon mousse; a good charcuterie plate for starters; wild duck with buttered Savoy cabbage, miso-glazed turnips, and sour cherries as a typical main. It's a posh gastropub, befitting from its posh location in Chelsea, but it's friendly and casual, and you're always made to feel welcome.

35 Old Church St., SW3. www.thepigsear.info. ©**020/7352-2908.** Reservations required in restaurant. Main courses £14–£25. AE, DC, MC, V. Mon–Fri 12.30–3pm and 6–10pm; Sat 12:30–10:30pm; Sun 12:30–9pm. Tube: Sloane Sq.

Tom's Kitchen ★ TRADITIONAL BRITISH High octane, hugely busy, and wildly popular, this former pub has been turned into a brasserie from top chef **Tom Aikens** (p. 140), and is a great all-day venue. The menu is a rundown of all that's good in London's more casual venues: full English breakfast; butternut squash soup; mackerel pâté; excellent pastas and salads; mains like pork belly and lentils; and the show-stopping baked Alaska flamed at the table.

27 Cale St., SW3. www.tomskitchen.co.uk. © **020/7349-0202.** Reservations required. Main courses £7.50–£30. AE, MC, V. Mon–Fri 8–11:45am and noon–3pm; Sat–Sun 10am–4pm; daily 6–11pm (10:30pm on weekends). Tube: South Kensington. Also at Somerset House, Strand, WC2 (©**020/7845-4646**).

WESTMINSTER & VICTORIA
Expensive
Cinnamon Club ★★ INDIAN This former Victorian library is a gorgeous, stately building with wood paneling, high ceilings, and a book-lined gallery. It's a suitably grand setting for the many Members of Parliament who seem to regard it as their

club. And it's a suitably theatrical setting for the exciting Indian cooking from executive chef Vivek Singh. European ingredients, Indian spicing, classical cooking techniques, and Western-style presentation make for a heady mix. Such a balancing act could be disastrous in less skilled hands, but here it produces some of the most innovative Indian cooking you'll find. Try Gressingham duck breast with coconut vinegar sauce; hot sweet king prawns with curry sauce and brown rice; or saddle of lamb with sesame tamarind sauce. Go conventional at breakfast with a perfect, light kedgeree—the dish of fish, rice, eggs, parsley, and cream brought back from the Raj by British colonials.

Old Westminster Library, 30–32 Great Smith St., SW1. www.cinnamonclub.com. ℭ **020/7222-2555.** Main courses £14–£25; set menu pre- and post-theatre 2 courses £22, 3 courses £24; tasting menu £75. AE, DC, MC, V. Mon–Fri 7:30–9:30am, noon–2:45pm, and 6–10:30pm; Sat noon–2:45pm and 6–10:30pm. Tube: St. James's Park or Westminster. Also at Cinnamon Kitchen, 9 Devonshire Sq., EC2 (ℭ **020/7626-5000**).

Moderate
The Orange ★ ☺ GASTROPUB/CONTEMPORARY EUROPEAN The
Orange is a smart gastropub with four delightful rooms for overnight stays. There's a heaving bar downstairs, with a dining room adjoining and a second dining room upstairs. It serves a clever menu that has the wealthy nearby residents of Pimlico coming back again and again. Sautéed wild mushrooms with polenta or soup of the day might start the meal. Wood-fired pizzas, conveniently served in two sizes, are popular with the families who regularly eat here, while mains like sea bream with new potatoes, olives, and anchovies, or house-baked pies satisfy the parents. It's fun, cheerful, and the staff go about their business with great charm.

37–39 Pimlico Rd., SW1. www.theorange.co.uk. ℭ **020/7881-9844.** Main courses £9–£26; set 3-course menu £35. AE, MC, V. Mon–Thurs 8–11:30pm; Fri–Sat 8am–midnight; Sun 8am–10:30pm. Tube: Sloane Sq.

Inexpensive
Jenny Lo's Teahouse 🌶 CANTONESE/SZECHUAN This teahouse is really a
small, fun cafe, ideal for inexpensive lunches. It was opened by Jenny Lo, daughter of the late Ken Lo, the tennis-playing restaurateur whose *Memories of China* brought upper-class Chinese cooking to London. Ken Lo cookbooks contribute to the dining room decor of black refectory tables set with napkins and chopsticks. The menu offers a range of well-cooked dishes like vermicelli rice noodle (noodles topped with grilled chicken breast and Chinese mushrooms). Rounding out the menu are stuffed Peking dumplings; chili-garnished spicy prawns; and wonton soup with slithery dumplings.

14 Eccleston St., SW1. ℭ **020/7259-0399.** Reservations not accepted. Main courses £7.50–£9.50. No credit cards. Mon–Fri noon–2:55pm; Mon–Sat 6–9:55pm. Tube: Victoria.

RICHMOND
Expensive
Petersham Nurseries Café ★★ CONTEMPORARY EUROPEAN In a
greenhouse full of odd furniture, artifacts, and sweet-smelling plants, you'll find Australian chef Skye Gyngell cooking some of the best food in London. The venue and chef—Skye is *Vogue*'s food writer, and has written two bestselling cookbooks, *A Year in My Kitchen* and *My Favorite Ingredients*—may be the height of fashion, but people flock here for her superbly cooked dishes that use ingredients from the Nurseries. The cafe's lunch might include beetroot soup with chervil and crème fraîche; halibut

with clams; and panna cotta with roasted rhubarb. For a less expensive treat try the **Teahouse** and its homemade sandwiches, soups, cakes, and flapjacks.

Church Lane, Richmond. www.petershamnurseries.com. ℭ **020/8605-3527.** Reservations required (as far in advance as possible). Main courses £19.50–£30.50. Set lunch 2/3 courses £24.50/£28.50. AE, DC, MC, V (no credit cards in the Teahouse). Café Tues–Sun noon–3pm. Teahouse Mon–Sat 9am–5pm; Sun 11am–5pm. Closed Jan. Tube: Richmond.

South Bank
BANKSIDE
Expensive
Oxo Tower Restaurant, Brasserie & Bar ★★INTERNATIONAL   The Oxo Tower is one of London's top dining spots—literally, as it's on the eighth floor of Oxo Tower Wharf. Stunning river views make the terrace one of summer's most sought-after venues. Both the Brasserie and the Restaurant share the same chic, 1930s' liner decor, and the same contemporary ethos in the cooking. The **Brasserie** is more casual, offering all the current modish mixes of tastes, spices, and inspirations like chargrilled, Moroccan spiced quail followed by teriyaki salmon with soba noodle salad. Dishes on the **Restaurant** menu use more luxury ingredients: langoustines, foie gras, sea bass that comes with crab, samphire, a truffle beurre blanc, and fennel salad, and wild game in season. It's all seasonally led, with carefully sourced British ingredients to the fore.

22 Barge House St., SE1. www.harveynichols.com/restaurants. ℭ**020/7803-3888.** Reservations recommended. Main courses £21.50–£35; set lunch 2 courses £22.50, 3 courses £35. AE, DC, MC, V. Mon–Fri noon–2:30pm and 6–11pm; Sat noon–2:30pm and 5:30–11pm; Sun noon–3pm and 6:30–10pm. Tube: Blackfriars or Waterloo.

WATERLOO & SOUTHWARK
Moderate
Baltic ★ 🍴EASTERN EUROPEAN   This is our favorite place after a visit to the Old Vic Theatre, particularly if the actors arrive to eat. It's cool in decor (minimalist with roof lights and upholstered chrome chairs), but hot on atmosphere—with a continuous, contented buzz and good jazz. It's owned by Jan Woroniecki who introduced his version of Eastern European cuisine at Kensington's Wódka. Like its sister restaurant, the menu here mixes Polish, Russian, and Hungarian influences to great effect. Gravadlax salmon marinated in vodka with potato latkes; marinated herring; or Polish black pudding for starters, then our favorite to follow: A rich goose leg with beetroot, scallions, and redcurrant is cooked with self-confident skill. There's live jazz on Sundays, and great cocktails from the bar staff, who mix unusual ingredients like rhubarb jam or beetroot with proper Eastern European vodkas.

74 Blackfriars Rd., SE1. www.balticrestaurant.co.uk. ℭ020/7928-1111. Main courses £15–£17; set menu 2 courses £14.50, 3 courses £17.50; Sun 2 courses £16.50, 3 courses £19.50. AE, MC, V. Mon–Fri noon–3pm and 5:30–11:15pm; Sat–Sun noon–4:30 and 5:30–10:30pm. Tube: Southwark.

Tapas Brindisa ★ SPANISH/TAPAS   Borough Market brings a steady stream of customers to the area—folk who regard good food as one of life's necessities—so Tapas Brindisa, which sources its food directly from Spain, is constantly busy. Add to that a no bookings policy and a relatively small dining space, and you'll find yourself with a long wait at popular times. But customers agree that it's worth it, for ambitious plates like leek soup with manchego cheese; pan-fried cuttlefish with green bean salad; and clams with butter beans and bacon. Charcuterie is top class (but beware, it can push up the bill); there's also a selection of cured fish and specialty cheeses you won't find elsewhere. Partner it with a fino sherry or silky Rioja.

18–29 Southwark St., SE1. www.brindisa.com. © **020/7357-8889.** Tapas plates £4–£21.50. AE, MC, V. Mon–Thurs 11am–3pm and 5:30–11pm; Fri–Sat 9–11am, noon–4pm, and 5:30–11pm; Sun 11am–10pm. Also at 46 Broadwick St., W1 © **020/7534-1690**); and 7–9 Exhibition Rd., SW7 © **020/7590-0008**).

The City
SPITALFIELDS
Moderate
Hawksmoor ★ AMERICAN/STEAK With its bare brick walls, wooden tables, and walls covered with photographs, Hawksmoor is every bit the New York steak joint. Its food won't disappoint steakhouse aficionados either. Hawksmoor prides itself on top-quality, perfectly aged, generous portions of beef, sourced from the famous quality London butcher, Ginger Pig, dry-aged for at least 35 days, and cooked exactly to order. All the prime cuts are here: Porterhouse; bone-in prime rib; Chateaubriand; all perfectly seared on the outside, perfectly tender inside. Starters are pretty good too: The potted smoked mackerel with toast goes down well, and the prawn cocktail is a lovely retro number. Talking of cocktails, the bar staff mixes a mean mint julep.

157 Commercial St., E1. www.thehawksmoor.com.© **020/7247-7392.** Main courses £13–£35. AE, MC, V. Mon–Fri noon–3pm and 6–10:30pm; Sat 11am–3pm and 6–10:30pm; Sun 11am–4:30pm. Tube: Liverpool St. Also at 7 Langley St., WC2 © **020/7247-7392**).

The Luxe CONTEMPORARY EUROPEAN John Torode has expanded from his original venture, Smiths of Smithfield, into the revitalized Spitalfields Market, where restaurants sit cheek-by-jowl in the modernized Victorian structure. Torode's Luxe offers a multi-purpose restaurant experience. The noisy street-level cafe buzzes all day, and is a favorite of ours for breakfast or a gourmet lunchtime burger. There's a basement music and cocktail bar and an upstairs dining room, complete with open kitchen, exposed brick walls, and silk wallpaper recalling the area's Huguenot silk-weaving heritage. Start with herb and potato gnocchi with meat sauce, sage, and pecorino then move onto slow roast belly of pork with mash and green sauce.

109 Commercial St., E1. www.theluxe.co.uk. © **020/7101-1751.** Main courses £14–£26.50. AE, MC, V. Restaurant Mon–Fri noon–3pm; Sun noon–4pm; Mon–Sat 6–9:30pm. Cafe-bar Mon–Sat 9am–11:30pm; Sun 9:30am–10pm. Tube: Liverpool St.

CLERKENWELL & FARRINGDON
Moderate
Bistrot Bruno Loubet ★★ FRENCH A collective cheer went up among London's restaurant-goers when Bruno Loubet returned to the capital after 8 years in Australia. And when this star of 1990s' London opened Bistrot Bruno Loubet in the adventurous and funky **Zetter** (p. 193), nobody was disappointed. The all-day bistro hits the spot with a short, gutsy menu. Classic bistro dishes are given a twist in starters like guinea fowl boudin blanc on a pea soup, or terrine of pork and leek with pomegranate dressing, while a main dish of hare with macaroni and spinach gratin, and a classic, perfect bouillabaisse demonstrates that London restaurants are the equal of Paris's best.

St. John's Sq., 86–88 Clerkenwell Rd., EC1. www.thezetter.com/en/restaurant.© **020/7324-4455.** Main courses £15–£20. AE, MC, V. Mon–Fri 7–10:30am, noon–2:30pm, and 6–10:30pm; Sat 7:30–11am, noon–3pm, and 6–10:30pm; Sun 6–10pm. Tube: Farringdon.

North Road ★★ CONTEMPORARY EUROPEAN/SCANDINAVIAN   Nordic cooking is notoriously under-represented in London, but this venture from Danish chef Christoffer Hruskovase should convince Londoners to look north. Suitably Scandinavian and minimal, the restaurant is both welcoming and smart. The Nordic influence comes not so much with the ingredients (which are British), as with the cooking approach, which uses less butter and cream and the *sous-vide* vacuum method (cooking in airtight plastic bags in a water bath) to keep the essentials of ingredients intact. Start with Dorset shrimp and carrot, followed by veal with celeriac, celery, and wild thyme. Norfolk deer with beetroot comes rolled in hay (a Viking preservation technique), giving a smoky taste that's enhanced by smoked bone marrow. Desserts also surprise: Try the *Flavours of Woodland*—birch bark, walnuts, chestnuts, and wild herbs. Vegetables and foraged herbs are used extensively. You'll find the clean, light tastes here refreshingly different.

60–73 St. John St., EC1. www.northroadrestaurant.co.uk. ✆**020/3217-0033.** Reservations recommended. Main courses £18.50–£24. MC, V. Set lunch 2 courses £18, 3 courses £20; 5-course tasting menu £55; 7-course tasting menu £65. Mon–Thurs noon–2:30pm and 6–10:30pm; Fri noon–2:30pm and 6–11pm; Sat 6–11pm. Tube: Barbican or Farringdon.

St. John ★★ MODERN BRITISH   "Nose to tail eating" characterizes Fergus Henderson's no-nonsense approach. All parts of the animal are used—neck, tongue, trotters, tail, liver, and heart—to produce dishes that devotees travel miles for. Smoked sprats with potato and horseradish; potted beef and pickled prunes; or, for the truly dedicated, roast bone marrow and parsley salad. It's a seasonally led menu— in winter Gloucester Old Spot pork chop with bitter chard will keep out the cold. The ingredients are the best; the cooking is superb; the dish is what it says on the menu; the restaurant is a plain, whitewashed room in a former smokery. There's a sister restaurant in Spitalfields, **St. John Bread & Wine** ★, 94–96 Commercial St., E1 (www.stjohnbreadandwine.com; ✆ 020/7251-0848; Tube: Liverpool St.).

26 St. John St., EC1. www.stjohnrestaurant.co.uk. ✆**020/7251-0848.** Reservations required. Main courses £12–£18. AE, DC, MC, V. Mon–Fri noon–3pm; Mon–Sat 6–11pm; Sun 1–3:30pm. Tube: Farringdon.

TOWER HILL
Moderate

Bevis Marks Restaurant ★ JEWISH   Bevis Marks is a surprising venue—a kosher restaurant attached to London's 18th-century synagogue. Stylish and very popular, it's widely recognized as the best kosher restaurant in London. The menu is an interesting mix of traditional Ashkenazi dishes and those with Asian influences. On the starter menu, chicken soup with matzo balls sits happily beside "Bevis Marks" crispy Thai salt-beef, bean shoots, sweet chili, and cilantro. Main dishes continue down the same path: English lamb chops come with new potatoes roasted in rosemary; chicken with lime leaf-scented rice and Thai green curry sauce. There's an interesting selection of Israeli bottles on a pricey wine list.

Bevis Marks, EC3. www.bevismarkstherestaurant.com. ✆**020/7283-2220.** Main courses £16–£26. AE, MC, V. Mon–Thurs noon–3pm and 5:30–10pm; Fri noon–3pm. Tube: Aldgate or Liverpool St.

East London
SHOREDITCH
Expensive

Les Trois Garçons ★ 🏮FRENCH   Walk into Les Trois Garçons and you enter a fantasy, or possibly a nightmare, according to your taste. The interior of this former

Victorian pub is full of glittering, lurid colored and crystal chandeliers, old handbags that hang from the ceiling, stuffed animals, and general bric-a-brac. The three "garçons," Hassan Abdullah, Michel Lassere, and Stefan Karlson opened the restaurant 10 years ago and have not looked back. The menu is equally flamboyant, offering dishes that some find sublime and others over the top. Try their famous foie gras cured in Sauternes and cooked *au torchon* (in a tea towel), or perhaps a perfectly cooked tortellini of crab with bacon crisp offset with lemongrass sauce. This is an expensive restaurant, but fun and a place to go if the culinary world seems drab and predictable.

1 Club Row, E1. www.lestroisgarcons.com. ℭ **020/7613-1924.** Reservations essential. Tasting menu £63.50 (whole table only); set menu 2 courses £40.50, 3 courses £47. AE, MC, V. Mon–Sat 6pm–midnight. Tube: Liverpool St./Train: Shoreditch High St.

Moderate

Princess of Shoreditch ★ MODERN BRITISH/GASTROPUB This handsome old pub close to Old Street has been beautifully transformed. The downstairs bar fills up with City types at lunchtime downing pints of Wandle ale from Battersea brewery, Sambrook, and tucking into soup of the day (£5.50); fish and chips (£11.95); and pies (£10.50). Up the spiral staircase, the dining room is a more serious affair with an extended menu, and attracts more serious diners. Propose the deal over halibut with clam chowder sauce, or lamb rump with celeriac purée and crispy potatoes, then clinch it with apple crumble. At weekends it's popular with families and groups of friends.

76 Paul St., EC2. www.theprincessofshoreditch.com. ℭ **020/7729-9270.** Main courses £11.50–£20, set lunch 2 courses £14, 3 courses £18. AE, MC, V. Mon–Thurs noon–3pm and 6:30–10pm; Fri noon–3pm and 6–10:30pm; Sat–Sun 10am–4:30pm and 6–10:30pm. Tube: Old St.

Inexpensive

Albion TRADITIONAL BRITISH/CAFE Sir Terence Conran's Boundary Project is all-embracing: Within the trendy **Boundary Hotel** (p. 194) there's a smart basement restaurant, summer rooftop terrace bar, and the Albion street-level shop, bakery, and cafe. Don't be fooled by the retro decor with its wood and leather banquettes, industrial lights, and white tiles. Despite its description as a "caff," this is really a posh cafe where the punters wear trendy trainers rather than cloth caps. Being Sir Terence, it's all extremely well done. You can eat all day on good old British classics—omelet, potted shrimps, or devilled kidneys. Free Wi-Fi is the icing on the steamed syrup pudding.

2–4 Boundary St., E2. www.albioncaff.co.uk. ℭ **020/7729-1051.** No reservations. Main courses £4.75–£12.50. AE, MC, V. Daily 8am–11:30pm. Tube: Liverpool St./Train: Shoreditch High St.

Sông Quê VIETNAMESE Kingsland Road remains the headquarters of London's Vietnamese restaurants, so there is plenty of competition in the area. Sông Quê holds its own—although not for its decor, which is more garish cafe than chic London venue. The vast menu includes reliable *pho* noodle soups with the well-flavored, aromatic broth full of meat and herbs. Barbecued quail is another favorite for its deeply satisfying, well-cooked meat. At night the lines are long; the best time to go is at lunch.

134 Kingsland Rd., E2. www.songque.co.uk. ℭ **020/7613-3222.** Main courses £4.50–£14.50. MC, V. Mon–Fri noon–3pm and 5:30–11:30pm; Sat 5:30–11:30pm; Sun 12–11pm. Train: Hoxton.

WHITECHAPEL

Inexpensive

Tayyabs ★ INDIAN This Pakistani/Punjabi-inspired restaurant goes from strength to strength. In a former Victorian pub, it's on two levels and near enough to the City for savvy bankers to make it their local lunch spot. Tayyabs' gutsy food at low prices makes it a welcome change from the more tourist-orientated Brick Lane Indian restaurants. Punjabi meat curries, flavorful kebabs, and their now well-known marinated lamb chops are the staples; or go for the daily specials.

83 Fieldgate St., E1. www.tayyabs.co.uk. ℂ **020/7247-9543.** Main courses £6–£10. AE, MC, V. Daily noon–midnight. Tube: Aldgate East or Whitechapel.

BETHNAL GREEN
Very Expensive

Viajante ★★ CONTEMPORARY EUROPEAN   When he was performing culinary miracles at various East London venues, Portuguese-born Nuno Mendes was the darling of diners desperately seeking the next big thing. Now he's resurfaced inside the **Town Hall Hotel** (p. 195). In a restaurant with a kitchen so open it feels like you're in somebody's living room, this El Bulli-trained chef serves dishes that will either knock your socks off or leave you scratching your head. From the first *amuse bouche* that is sublime—through dishes that pair skate wing topped with crisp yeast and a purée of cauliflower; slow cooked pork and tiger prawns with grated egg, anchovy purée, and deep-fried capers—the surprises keep coming. This is supremely skillful, playful, flawlessly executed cooking. Forget a long, expensive trip to Spain's El Bulli; go to the East End instead.

Inside Town Hall Hotel, Patriot Sq., E2. www.viajante.co.uk. ℂ **020/7871-0461.** Reservations required. Lunch menu 3 courses £28, 6 courses £50, 9 courses £65. Dinner menu 6 courses £65, 12 courses £90. AE, MC, V. Mon–Thurs noon–2pm and 6–9:30pm; Fri–Sun 6–9:30pm. Tube: Bethnal Green.

HACKNEY
Moderate

Forman's 1905 🏠 TRADITIONAL BRITISH/SEAFOOD   You may not have heard of Forman's, but you've perhaps tasted their smoked salmon somewhere in London—maybe at Gordon Ramsay or the Dorchester. Forman's is an established East End smokery (opened in 1905) run by generations of one family. At the moment it's a small, casual venue where salmon reigns supreme, with a few quintessentially British dishes like rump of lamb on offer, and an all-British wine list. The present owner, Lance Forman, is a formidable character who when forced to move from his smokery due to the Olympic Park construction, struck a very good deal and built a new smokery right opposite the Stadium. Also in the large building is a gallery and event space.

Stour Rd., E3. www.formansfishisland.com. ℂ**020/8525-2365.** Main courses £11.50–£19.50. MC, V. Restaurant Thurs–Fri 7–11pm; Sat 10am–2pm and 7–11pm; Sun noon–5pm. Gallery and Bar Thurs–Fri 5–9pm; Sat–Sun noon–5pm. Train: Hackney Wick.

DALSTON
Inexpensive

Mangal I ★ 🔥 TURKISH   You can tell you are in prime territory for *ocakbasi* (open-coal barbecue cooking) in Stoke Newington Road from the aroma of cooking meat that wafts through the air. Follow your nose just off the main road and you come to Mangal I. The kelim-hung room might not be the greatest in looks, but it cooks and serves a succulent mound of meat and vegetables. Feast on the mixed meze while you're waiting for the herbed lamb *sis* or spicy minced kebabs to appear. You should book and expect delays in service at busy times.

10 Arcola St., E8. www.mangal1.com. ℂ **020/7275-8981.** Reservations recommended. Main courses £6–£15. No credit cards. Daily noon–midnight. Train: Dalston Kingsland. Also at 4 Stoke Newington Rd., N16 (ℂ**020/7254-7888**).

North & Northwest London
CAMDEN TOWN
Expensive
York & Albany ★ CONTEMPORARY EUROPEAN   Camden Town is not known as a gastronomic destination, so the locals got very excited when Gordon Ramsay reopened this derelict pub as a fine dining restaurant with rooms. Overseen by Angela Hartnett, whose credentials include Michelin stars at Murano and the Connaught Hotel, it's a relaxed place that offers the best dining in the area. Top seasonal ingredients drive the menu, as in grilled mackerel with red pepper piperade and saffron aioli; or roast partridge with a perfect smoked garlic pomme purée, spinach, and baby artichokes. Steamed treacle sponge and custard for two brings out the greedy; the tiramisu is perfect. The only downsides are the sometimes slapdash service and the noise level when the place is full. The early set supper menu is a bargain. It's a wonderful breakfast place and a small courtyard makes summer dining a treat.

127–129 Parkway, NW1. www.gordonramsay.com/yorkandalbany. ✆ **020/7388-3344.** Reservations recommended. Main courses £17–£22. Set menus and early supper 2 courses £18, 3 courses £21. AE, MC, V. Mon–Fri 7–10:30am, noon–3pm, and 6–11pm; Sat 7–11:30am, noon–3pm, and 6–11pm; Sun noon–8:30pm. Tube: Camden Town.

HAMPSTEAD
Moderate
Wells ★ CONTEMPORARY EUROPEAN/GASTROPUB   Close enough to Hampstead Heath to attract walkers with their dogs and families, this place is also the local for many of Hampstead's decidedly upmarket residents. The old Georgian building is made up of a street-level bar and three rooms in the upstairs restaurant serving the same menus. The decor is chic enough for any smart gastropub; add to that the feel of a country retreat and it's not surprising this is a winner. Dishes like rabbit and mushroom terrine, and seared scallops with pea purée, bacon, and pea shoots sit happily beside rib-eye steak and chips and smoked haddock with champ potato, poached egg, and mustard beurre blanc. It's all very well done in a charming low-key way. Sunday lunch is a family occasion, and good beers are on tap.

30 Well Walk, NW3. www.thewellshampstead.co.uk. ✆ **020/7794-3785.** Reservations recommended. Main courses £11–£24. MC, V. Mon–Fri noon–3pm and 6–10pm; Sat noon–4pm and 7–10pm; Sun noon–4pm and 7–9:30pm. Bar daily noon–11pm. Tube: Hampstead.

Southeast London
GREENWICH
Moderate
Old Brewery MODERN BRITISH   The handsome Old Brewery, owned and run by the Meantime Brewery and supplying some of London's restaurants and pubs with its nectar, is a cafe by day and a restaurant by night. Huge shiny vats full of brewing beer (this is a working brewery) adorn one end; large windows and wooden tables and chairs fill the main space. It has a solid, dependable menu with dishes like devilled whitebait and seared foie gras to start, and Dorset plaice and venison as mains, many coming with recommended beers to try. It's a great place for true beer buffs, who can also book the brewery tour.

Pepys Building, Old Royal Naval College, SE10. www.oldbbrewerygreenwich.com. ✆ **020/3327-1280.** Main courses £11–£21.50. MC, V. Cafe Daily 10am–5pm. Bar: Mon–Sat 11am–11pm; Sun noon–10:30pm. Restaurant Mon–Sat 6–11pm; Sun 6–10:30pm. DLR: Cutty Sark.

Teatime

Formal afternoon tea in London is a relaxing, civilized affair. Elegantly served on delicate china, there are dainty finger sandwiches, fresh-baked scones served with jam and clotted cream, and an array of small cakes and pastries. An attentive waiter is ready to refill your pot of tea. At many places, you can gild the lily with a glass of Champagne. It makes an atmospheric alternative to pre-theatre dining.

Interesting West End alternatives to top London hotels include Momo's **Café Mô** (p. 130), where you're transported to Morocco with mint tea and whichever sweet pastry you might fancy. Or try **Chai Bazaar,** part of Indian restaurant **Chor Bizarre,** 16 Albemarle St., W1 (www.chorbizarre.com; ✆ **020/7629 9802;** Tube: Green Park) for Indian teas matched with Indian desserts. High tea here costs £9.50.

MAYFAIR

English Tearoom at Brown's ★★   Brown's has upped the ante with not one, but two tea sommeliers who will take you through the 17-strong list of teas, and a policy of replenishing any of the delights in front of you at no extra charge. The now requisite, albeit fabulous range of sandwiches on offer in London's top hotels is augmented by some of the best fruit cake you'll find and an assortment of gluten- and nut-free items. It's all elegantly conducted in a wood-paneled room with an open fire.

Brown's Hotel, Albemarle St., W1. www.brownshotel.com. ✆ **020/7518-4155.** Reservations recommended. Afternoon tea £39.50, with champagne £49.50. AE, DC, MC, V. Mon–Fri 3–6pm; Sat–Sun 1–6pm. Tube: Green Park.

ST. JAMES'S

Ritz Palm Court ★★★   This remains the top place for afternoon tea in London—and the hardest to get into without reserving way in advance. It's a spectacular stage setting, complete with marble steps and columns, a baroque fountain, and little wooded gold chairs. Nibble on a smoked salmon sandwich and egg mayonnaise roll then pig out on the chocolate cake. But you're really here to feel like a duchess.

Inside Ritz Hotel, 150 Piccadilly, W1. www.theritzlondon.com. ✆ **020/7493-8181.** Reservations required at least 8 weeks in advance. Jeans and sneakers not accepted; jacket and tie required for men. Afternoon tea £42–£53, with champagne £64. AE, DC, MC, V. 5 seatings daily at 11:30am, 1:30, 3:30, 5:30, and 7:30pm. Tube: Green Park.

KENSINGTON

The Orangery   Just north of, but part of **Kensington Palace** (p. 95), the Orangery is a long, narrow garden pavilion built in 1704 for Queen Anne. Rows of potted orange trees bask in sunlight from soaring windows, and tea is served amid Corinthian columns, Grinling Gibbons woodcarvings, and urns and statuary. The menu includes soups, salads, and sandwiches. But it's afternoon tea that brings out the great aunts. The array of different teas is served with high style, accompanied by fresh scones with clotted cream and jam, and Belgian chocolate cake.

In the gardens of Kensington Palace, W8. ✆ **020/7376-0239.** Reservations not accepted. Afternoon tea £15, with champagne £34. MC, V. Daily noon–5pm. Tube: High St. Kensington.

VICTORIA

The Goring ★★   Still family owned after a century in business, this comfortable hotel offers afternoon tea in the lounge, and in the summer on the sunny terrace overlooking the private garden. It's a clubby sort of place, with regulars propping up the very popular, convivial bar all day long. Straying a little from the format, tea has

COFFEE & A cake

There was a time when the only cup of coffee that could pass muster with a caffeine aficionado was at the splendid survivor in Soho, **Bar Italia** ★, 22 Frith St., W1 (☏ **020/7437-4520**). Then a wave of young, well-trained baristas jetted in, mostly from Australia and New Zealand, and changed the face of London's coffee houses forever. They're all very serious, using top coffee roasts and the best techniques; there are often tasting notes to accompany the brew. Now you can get the best coffee in the world in London. It's no idle boast; try any of these below.

Flat White, 17 Berwick St., W1 (☏ **020/7734-0370**) just off Berwick Street Market, is a magnet for Antipodeans who also make up the staff. Like many, they use superior Square Mile Coffee Roaster beans. Open Monday to Friday 8am to 7pm; Saturday and Sunday 9am to 6pm. Tube: Leicester Square, Tottenham Court Road. The same owners run **Milk Bar** ★ in Soho, at 3 Bateman St., W1 (☏ **020/7287-4796**). Go for the great welcome, coffees, sandwiches, and snacks around £4–£5 and changing art on the walls.

Open Monday to Friday 8am to 7pm; Saturday and Sunday 9am to 6pm. Tube: Tottenham Court Road.

Another Antipodean-owned and -run place, **Kaffeine** ★, 66 Great Titchfield St., W1 (☏ **020/580-6755**) is the place for a Square Mile summer blend espresso in a smart venue. Open Monday to Friday 7:30am to 6pm; Saturday 9am to 6pm. Tube: Oxford Circus.

Monmouth Coffee House, 26 Monmouth St., WC2 (☏ **020/7379-3516**) has been serving top filter coffees for over 30 years. The original Monmouth Street venue is cozy and a great place for cakes from Paul, around £4. Monday to Saturday 8am to 6:30pm. Tube: Covent Garden. Other locations in London.

Prufrock Coffee, 140 Shoreditch High St., E1 (☏ **020/7033-0500**). The U.K.'s first World Barista Champion, Gwylim Davies, is the hero here, serving great flat whites and espressos to go with its cakes and sandwiches. It's inside the menswear shop, Present. Open Monday to Friday 10:30am to 6pm; Saturday 11am to 5pm; Sunday 11am to 4pm. Train: Shoreditch High Street.

Jaffa cakes, and mulled wine and pear jelly with cinnamon cream. It's as suitable for your great aunt as it is for your next romantic interest.

Beeston Place, Grosvenor Gardens, SW1. www.goringhotel.co.uk. ☏**020/7396-9000.** Afternoon tea £35; champagne tea £45. AE, DC, MC, V. Daily 3:30–4:30pm. Tube: Victoria.

SHOPPING

London's shopping scene is an eclectic mix of the thrifty and the luxurious. Shopping here isn't just about the big department stores, the impressive labels, or the obvious high-street chains anymore: It's going local, it's going boutique, and it's getting more personalized, as London develops an affordable charm of its own. The shopping scene today is all about being original, whether you're buying unique glassware on Portobello Road, or haunting the vintage boutiques of the East End. It's about making your shopping personal to you, and buying something that you'll treasure forever. The chances are you've picked it up from a little-known **pop-up shop** that disappeared a week later. They're all over London at the moment—and pop-ups are one trend that seems to be sticking around.

West End

Oxford Street is undeniably the West End's main shopping attraction. Start at Marble Arch—the westernmost end—for designer department store **Selfridges** (p. 160). As you walk the length of the famous street toward Tottenham Court Road, you'll notice that the quality of shops goes downhill, especially east of Oxford Circus. Think bargain basement tat and cheap souvenirs, and you have the idea. **Topshop** (p. 159) remains an Oxford Street must-visit (the branch here is the largest clothes shop in Europe). You're certainly very brave to attempt Oxford Street at the weekend; weekday mornings are best for your sanity.

Oxford Street is also a great starting point for hitting the more interesting shopping areas, such as affluent **Marylebone.** It's impossible not to fall in love with the quaintness of Marylebone's high street. The street's chocolate shops and interiors brands ooze luxury.

Regent Street—home of an **Apple Store**—crosses Oxford Street at Oxford Circus. Regent Street shopping is more toward the high end of "high street," typified by the affordable luxury of chain shops like **Mango** and **French Connection.** Head south from Oxford Circus for the world-famous **Liberty** (p. 160) department store. You're now at the top of **Carnaby Street,** and while it's not quite the '60s-style mecca it once was, you can enjoy a good few hours' shopping here—especially if you veer off into the **Newburgh Quarter.** The area is also home to **Kingly Court,** a gorgeous little piazza of independent shops and vintage boutiques. The area can be overpriced, but it provides a great place to people-watch.

Parallel to Regent Street, the **Bond Street** area connects **Piccadilly** with Oxford Street, and is synonymous with the luxury rag trade. It's not just one street, but a whole area, mainly comprising New Bond Street and Old Bond Street. It's the flagship location for the best designers—you'll find Prada and Gucci here, and **Tiffany** is quite at home nestled among designer jewelry shops. A slew of international hotshots, from Chanel to Versace, have digs nearby. Make sure you stop off at **Dover Street Market** (p. 160)—not a market at all, but actually a designer shop housing all sorts of fashionable folk under one roof.

Burlington Arcade (www.burlington-arcade.co.uk; Tube: Piccadilly Circus), a glass-roofed Regency passage leading off Piccadilly, looks like a period exhibition, and is lined with mahogany-fronted intriguing shops and boutiques. Lit by wrought-iron lamps and decorated with clusters of ferns and flowers, its small, upscale stores specialize in fashion, gold jewelry, Irish linen, and cashmere. If you linger there until 5:30pm, you can watch the **beadles** (the last London representatives of Britain's oldest police force) ceremoniously place the iron grills that block off the arcade until 9am, at which time they remove them to start a new business day. Make sure to catch the clock at **Fortnum & Mason** (p. 160)—it moves on the hour in a rather lovely display.

Nearby **Jermyn Street** (Tube: Piccadilly Circus), on the south side of Piccadilly, is a tiny two-block street populated by high-end men's haberdashers and toiletries shops; many have been doing business for centuries. A bit to the north, **Savile Row** is where you'll find London's finest men's tailors.

The West End theatre district borders two more shopping areas: **Soho** (Tube: Tottenham Court Rd. or Leicester Sq.), where the sex shops are slowly morphing into cutting-edge designer boutiques—check out clothing exchange **Bang Bang** (p. 158) for designer bargains—and **Covent Garden,** a shopping masterpiece stocked with fashion, food, books, and everything else. The original Covent Garden marketplace has overflowed its boundaries and eaten up the surrounding neighborhood; it's fun to shop the narrow streets. Just off trendy **Neal Street** and Seven Dials, **Neal's Yard** is a stunning splash of color on rainy days if you're looking to buy foodstuffs from **Neal's Yard Dairy** (p. 161). **Monmouth Street** is somewhat of a local secret: Many shops here serve as outlets for British designers, selling both used and new clothing. In addition, stores specialize in everything from musical instruments from the Far East to palm readings. Make sure, too, to take in **Charing Cross Road** and get your nose into one of the many bookstores.

South Bank

Apart from somewhat tired **Gabriel's Wharf,** the South Bank isn't really a shopping destination on its own—although the area is slowly getting a facelift. The **Oxo Tower,** Bargehouse Street (✆ **020/7021-1600;** Tube: Waterloo) now has a collection of upscale boutiques on its lower floors, and **Borough Market** (p. 153) brings foodie crowds south in their droves, as does **Tate Modern** (p. 155) with its fabulous shop for artsy visitors and locals. The **Southbank Centre** (p. 167) shop has also had a huge revamp, and now stocks art and design goodies on two floors.

Southwest London

The home of **Harrods** (p. 160), **Knightsbridge** is probably the second-most famous London retail district. (Oxford St. just edges it out.) **Sloane Street** is traditionally regarded as a designer area, but these days it's more "upscale high street," and nowhere near as luxurious as **Bond Street** (see above). This is where you can grab some aromatherapy from **Jo Malone,** 150 Sloane St. (www.jomalone.co.uk; ✆ **0870/192-5121;** Tube: Sloane Sq.), a haven for bespoke perfumes.

Walk southwest on **Brompton Road**—toward the V&A Museum (p. 103)—and you'll find **Cheval Place,** lined with designer resale shops, and **Beauchamp Place** (pronounced *Bee*-cham). It's high end, but with a hint of irony. Expect to see little lapdogs poking their heads out of handbags.

You'll also be near **King's Road** (Tube: Sloane Sq.); another beacon of '60s cool, this is now a haven for designer clothes and homewares. About a third of King's Road is devoted to independent fashion shops, another third houses design-trade showrooms and stores for household wares: Scandinavian designs are prominent, and **Design House Stockholm** (www.designhousestockholm.com; ✆ **020/7352-8403**) is a must. The remaining third are a mix of dress shops and shoe boutiques. The clothes shops tend to suit a more mature customer (with a more mature budget), but you'll have fun shopping here if you remain oblivious to shop assistants who can be on the snooty side.

Finally, don't forget all those museums in nearby **South Kensington.** They have fantastic and exclusive gift shops. If you're looking for jewelry and homewares, the **V&A** (p. 103) and the **Design Museum** are must-visits. The **Science Museum** (p. 102) shop is perfect for inquisitive children. Make sure to view the collections, too. The big names don't charge for entry, and have some world-class exhibits.

West London

If you're heading west, the first place you should find yourself in is **Notting Hill.** Of course, one of the main draws for shopping in West London is **Portobello Market** (p. 154). Every Sunday, the whole of Portobello Road turns into a sea of antiques, cool clothing (and even cooler shoppers), and maybe even a celebrity or three.

Some of the best boutiques in London are also here. The independent shopping scene thrives; this is an area where people want to be unique, but still look expensive and groomed. Expect one-off boutiques housing designer labels you've never heard of, quirky homewares, and plenty of retro record shops. Stick to Portobello for the antiques, but head to **Westbourne Grove** and **Ledbury Road** for the boutiques.

The area is also full of organic and fancy food stores, with **Whole Foods** (p. 162) having its flagship home here. They take their food very seriously in West London: It does come at a price, but the quality is good so make sure you pick up a few bits.

West London is also home to two American-style shopping malls. **Westfield** (www.westfield.com/london; Tube: Shepherd's Bush) takes up residence in Shepherd's Bush, and **Whiteleys** (www.whiteleys.com; Tube: Bayswater) sits in Bayswater. They're huge (the former especially), they have everything, and they're busy. If it's raining and you still want your high-street shops, then head here. Just don't expect to find anything special or out of the ordinary.

The City & East London

The financial district itself doesn't really offer much in the way of shopping—especially at the weekend, when everything tends to be shut. However, the **One New Change** shopping center (www.onenewchange.com; Tube: St. Paul's) is attracting a rich crowd for its luxury goods. It's opposite the eastern end of St. Paul's Cathedral. You'll also find a handful of tailors in the area, and there are high-end brands in the nearby **Royal Exchange** (www.theroyalexchange.com; Tube: Bank). However, unless you're often suited up for work, it's really not a shopping destination by itself.

Continue your adventure farther east on **Commercial Street** (Tube: Liverpool St./Train: Shoreditch High St.). Around here is where you'll find the best vintage shops in the city. They're on almost every corner and side street, and new ones seem to appear every day, alongside pop-up stores just here for the weekend. Make sure you hit **Absolute Vintage** and the smaller **Blondie** (p. 158) around the corner, on the way to the antiques market in **Spitalfields** (p. 154).

A short stroll north, **Columbia Road** (see below) is more than just a flower market; in many ways, the main attractions are the artist studios that line the street. Head up every single one of those staircases you see. If the door is open, you're allowed in. You'll find artists at work and shops like **J & B,** 158a Columbia Rd. (www.jessiechorley.com; ☏ **07708/921550;** Train: Shoreditch), selling handmade notebooks and jewelry. Once you're done with the studios and shops—**Ryan Town** sells fabulous papercuts—everything at the flower market will be going cheap come 3pm. **Westfield Stratford City** (www.westfield.com/stratfordcity; Tube: Stratford) brought mass mainstream shopping to East London in the form of this giant mall right next to London's 2012 Olympic Park.

Markets

London can't quite compete with the flea markets of Paris, but it does hold its own. London's markets are smaller, more niche, and perhaps slightly too expensive—but they are lots of fun. Take cash with you (and keep it safe), as most markets are a bit of a walk from any ATMs. Then do your best not to be tempted by all the wares on offer. Do haggle. Most items can be bought for cheaper than their price tag, if you're willing to negotiate. Round things down, ask for something for nothing, and get a bargain.

Borough Market ★★★ One of the largest outdoor food markets in the world, selling a mammoth variety of delectables from across the globe. Best buys are the more unusual items and British-reared meats, rather than standard food market fare, which is aimed at tourists with money to burn. The market is open Thursday 11am to 5pm, Friday noon to 6pm, and Saturday 9am to 5pm. Try to avoid a Saturday lunchtime, when everyone in London seems to descend. Southwark St., SE1. www.boroughmarket.org.uk. ℂ**020/7407-1002.** Tube: London Bridge.

Camden Market & the Stables ★ This market has had a revamp since a 2008 fire, but it hasn't lost any of its grungy charm. There's no doubting that Camden isn't the prettiest area in London, but it is cool in its dinginess. If you're looking for an alternative scene, head here for all the silver jewelry and PVC clubwear you'll ever need. Most stalls are open every day of the year except Christmas Day. A lot stay open well past 6pm, too. Camden High St., NW1. ℂ**020/7974-6767.** Tube: Camden Town.

Columbia Road Flower Market ★★ This East London flower market really is worth the trip (unless you suffer from hayfever). The flowers are beautiful, but it's the shops on either side of the road that deserve the most attention. Make sure you go up every open door—they're studios and usually full of lovely things. **Vintage Heaven,** 82 Columbia Rd. (www.vintageheaven.co.uk; ℂ **01277/215968**), has all sorts of tea sets and a little tea room out back. The market is open from 8am until 4pm every Sunday. Columbia Rd., E2. www.columbiaroad.info. ℂ**07708/921-550.** Tube: Old St./Train: Hoxton.

Covent Garden ★ Right in the middle of town, Covent Garden conveniently offers several markets, including the all-purpose Apple Market and hippy-style Jubilee Market, running Monday through Saturday from 10am to 6pm. The best way to tackle them is to just dive in and explore the area, stopping to watch the human statues and magicians along the way. Monday is antiques day. The Piazza, WC2. www.coventgardenlondonuk.com. ℂ**020/7836-9136.** Tube: Covent Garden.

Greenwich Indoor Market ★★ A haven for craft and vintage lovers, this market (open Wed–Sun) is great for gift buying. There are little boutiques around the outside (open daily), and a food market at weekends. There are smaller markets nearby as well: A farmers' market in Blackheath station parking lot (car park) (Sun 10am–2pm) and **Greenwich Clocktower Market** on Greenwich High Street. The outdoor area doesn't look anything special at first glance, but it's got some packed antiques stalls and is ever growing. Greenwich Market, SE10. www.greenwichmarket.net. ℂ**020/8269-5096.** DLR: Cutty Sark.

Portobello Market ★★ This is the market for West Londoners, spanning the whole of Portobello Road, and made world-famous by Richard Curtis' movie *Notting Hill.* It'll take you all day to walk down here properly on a Saturday. You'll pass through cheap tat, leather goods, antiques, and craft stalls. Take your time, enjoy, and haggle like you've never haggled before. It's open Monday to Wednesday and Friday from 8am to 6:30pm; Thursday 8am to 2pm; and Saturday 6am to 6:30pm. Portobello Rd., W10. www.portobellomarket.org. ℂ**020/8960-5599.** Tube: Notting Hill Gate.

Spitalfields Market & UpMarket ★ Spitalfields is one of the best all-rounders in London. A new area of "proper" shops leaves a little to be desired, and still feels out of place, but the old market is among the best for vintage clothing and antiques. The trendy **Sunday UpMarket** (www.sundayupmarket.co.uk; open Sun 10am–5pm) is a 5-minute walk away, at the Old Truman Brewery on Brick Lane, and if you're looking for more personal homemade items and unique clothes, this is the place for you. The food at both markets is tasty, so arrive hungry. Commercial St., E1. ℂ**020/7247-8556.** Tube: Liverpool St./Train: Shoreditch High St.

Shopping A to Z

ANTIQUES & COLLECTIBLES

Alfie's Antique Market This is the biggest (and one of the best-stocked) conglomerates of antiques dealers in London, crammed into the premises of a 19th-century store. It has more than 370 stalls, showrooms, and workshops in over 3,252 sq. m (35,004 sq. ft.) of floor space. You'll find the biggest **Susie Cooper** (a well-known designer of tableware and ceramics for Wedgwood) collection in Europe here. A whole antiques district has grown up around Alfie's along Church Street. 13–25 Church St., NW8. www.alfiesantiques.com.✆ **020/7723-6066.** Tube: Marylebone or Edgware Rd.

Grays Antiques & Grays Mews These markets have been converted into walk-in stands with independent dealers. There are two floors, two buildings, and more than 200 dealers selling everything you could imagine, from all over the world. If it's antique, you'll no doubt find it here. There's a cafe in each building too—shopping for priceless finds is thirsty work. 58 Davies St. and 1–7 Davies Mews, W1. www.grays antiques.com.✆ **020/7629-7034.** Tube: Bond St.

ART, CRAFTS & MUSEUM SHOPS

Blade Rubber Stamps This unique little shop has gained itself a bit of a following in crafty and stationery-loving camps. It sells all things stamp related (the rubber kind, not postage). Their selection is huge and if you're into handwriting letters and scrapbooking, head here after a trip to the nearby British Museum (p. 85). It's only been open since 1993, but it feels like it's been part of London for centuries. 12 Bury Place, WC1. www.custom.bladerubberstamps.co.uk.✆ **0845/873-7005.** Tube: Holborn.

Contemporary Applied Arts This association encourages traditional and progressive contemporary artwork. Many of Britain's established craftspeople, as well as promising talents, are represented within the space. The gallery houses a diverse display of glass, ceramics, textiles, wood, furniture, jewelry, and metalwork—all by contemporary artisans. 2 Percy St., W1. www.caa.org.uk.✆ **020/7436-2344.** Tube: Tottenham Court Rd.

Drink, Shop & Do ★★ The title of this shop sums up its ethos. Get yourself a drink, do some shopping, and then do some ... doing. This is the hippest crafty venue in the city, with a focus on the cafe and shopping—although they also run regular craft classes. 9 Caledonian Rd., N1. www.drinkshopdo.com. ✆ **020/3343-9138.** Tube: King's Cross.

Grosvenor Prints London's largest stock of antique prints, ranging from the 17th to the 20th centuries, is on sale here. Views of London are the biggest-selling items, which is perfect if you're looking for a reminder of your trip. Some prints depict significant moments in the city's history, including the Great Fire. The British are great animal lovers, so expect plenty of prints of dogs and horses as well. 19 Shelton St., WC2. www.grosvenorprints.com.✆ **020/7836-1979.** Tube: Covent Garden.

Tate Modern If you're an art lover, you should definitely swing by Tate Modern for a browse in the shop. It's a great store, full of prints and more art books than you'll ever be able to carry. Everything in their shop is inspired by the exhibitions, and if you see a piece of art you like when you're walking around, be sure to note the number so you can pick up a much more affordable postcard version to send home; it's easier than trying to sneak a Rothko into your handbag. Bankside, SE1. www.tate.org.uk/modern. ✆ **020/7887-8888.** Tube: Southwark.

V&A Shop ★★ The V&A has the best museum shop in London, perfect for design lovers. It stocks everything from exotic jewelry inspired by the exhibitions to its own line of toiletries and reclaimed prints. The museum takes design seriously, and it's celebrated in every single item in the shop. Cromwell Rd., SW7. www.vam.ac.uk. **020/7942-2000.** Tube: South Kensington.

BEAUTY & MAKE-UP

Angela Flanders ★★ This tiny Columbia Road shop sells bespoke perfumes and home scents. Try the English Rose perfume; it's basically the countryside in a bottle. As with the rest of Columbia Road, you can only rely on finding it open on weekends. 96 Columbia Rd., E2. www.angelaflanders-perfumer.com. **020/7739-7555.** Tube: Old St./Train: Hoxton.

Miller Harris ★★ Arguably the most famous perfumers in London. Their Nouvelle Edition is incredibly popular and hard to get hold of. Their scents make their way into candles and male products as well. The Miller Harris scent obsession even goes as far as tea—there's a perfumed tea room at the back of the Mayfair store. 21 Bruton St., W1. www.millerharris.com. **020/7629-7750.** Tube: Green Park.

CLOTHING & ACCESSORIES

Children

Amaia ☺ With descriptions like "easy-to-wear" and "elegant" you'd be forgiven for thinking that Amaia was a high-end designer boutique. And it is, but instead of being for adults, it's for the well-heeled children of London used to the finer things in life. 14 Cale St., SW3. **020/7590-0999.** Tube: South Kensington.

Elias & Grace ★★ ☺ Where do you go for the best dresses you can buy your little ones? Elias & Grace is (unsurprisingly) in the fancy "village" of Primrose Hill, and you'll find everything from designers Chloe and Marni, all perfectly sized for your mini-yous. 158 Regent's Park Rd., NW1. www.eliasandgrace.com. **020/7449-0574.** Tube: Chalk Farm.

Sasti ☺ If you're looking for something original, Sasti is an affordable children's boutique. It has one-off outfits for newborns and toddlers, so you can buy bright prints and cute outfits without spending hundreds. 281 Portobello Rd., W10. www.sasti. co.uk. **020/8960-1125.** Tube: Ladbroke Grove.

Jewelry

Comfort Station ★★ There is no jewelry brand that does quirky elegance quite like Comfort Station. From their barometer-inspired mood necklaces, to the earrings with the coordinates for Hope (a town in Devon) and Love (in Barbados), their pieces are all unique and special. Each one has a story to tell, yet few go over the £100 mark. 22 Cheshire St., E2. www.comfortstation.co.uk. **020/7033-9099.** Tube: Liverpool St./Train: Shoreditch High St.

Kabiri ★★★ At this high-end jewelry store that doesn't take itself too seriously, everything is colorful and playful. Little inside is cheap, although you will find a few pieces under £50. It's a fun place to shop, and very stylish indeed. 37 Marylebone High St., W1. www.kabiri.co.uk. **020/7224-1808.** Tube: Baker St.

Lazy Oaf ★ If you want something different (and well-priced), Lazy Oaf is it. Whether it's a brooch that announces that you're a lousy dancer, or a necklace with a slightly offensive slogan, Lazy Oaf will inspire you to buy something out of the ordinary and just a little bit cheeky. 19 Foubert's Place, W1. www.lazyoaf.co.uk. **020/7287-2060.** Tube: Oxford Circus.

Tatty Devine ★★ Tatty Devine started London's acrylic jewelry trend, and is still very good at it. Everything is handmade, everything is super cool, and everything is covetable. A dinosaur skeleton around your neck might not be subtle ... but that's a

There are several designer sample sales that are worth looking out for. They're often advertised in the local press, but you can find the best by signing up to e-mail alerts from the London edition of **Daily Candy** (www.dailycandy.com) or **Emerald Street** (www.emeraldstreet. com). Expect long queues, and fashionistas fighting over the best pieces—understandable given that most are discounted by 70%. Stock is often replenished daily, but that varies from sale to sale, so if you want the best stuff, try to arrive at least an hour before opening. You should also expect to pay to get in, usually around the £2 mark.

good thing, right? Cute, whimsical, and fun is what Tatty Devine does best. 236 Brick Lane, E1. www.tattydevine.com.✆ **020/7739-9191.** Tube: Liverpool St./Train: Shoreditch High St. Also at 44 Monmouth St., WC2 ✆ 020/7836-2685).

Lingerie

Bordello ★★   Scratchy lace is not desirable any time of the year, and Bordello has raised the bar when it comes to where the ladies of London buy their smalls. It's expensive here, but everything is sexy and screams luxury. If you're looking for very special lingerie, it should be the first place you visit—and it'll probably be the last place as well. 55 Great Eastern St., EC2. www.bordello-london.com.✆ **020/7503-3334.** Tube: Old St./Train: Shoreditch High St.

Myla ★★★   If you like your silk fine, your lace of the very best quality, and your wallet a little lighter, Myla is the store for you. The lingerie is simply beautiful. Sexy garments of the highest quality don't come cheap (expect to pay hundreds for a bra in some cases), so catch them while they've got a sale on. 77 Lonsdale Rd., W11. www. myla.com. ✆ **020/7792-8880.** Tube: Ladbroke Grove.

Men

Folk ★★   Folk is far too stylish for its own good, but that's the appeal. Trendy designers and a preppy look are the trademark style of this shop. It does a limited line in women's clothes too, but the focus is on the guys. 49 Lamb's Conduit St., WC1. www. folkclothing.com.✆ **020/7404-6458.** Tube: Holborn.

Ozwald Boateng ★★   If you're after swanky threads and a suit cut better than anywhere else, Savile Row should be your first stop—and Ozwald Boateng knows his way around a pattern. Expect a perfect fit, lush fabric, and a price tag to make your eyes water. 30 Savile Row, W1. www.ozwaldboateng.co.uk.✆ **020/7440-5231.** Tube: Piccadilly Circus.

Peckham Rye   Funky tailoring and accessories—all with a twist. If you can carry off the likes of yellow check, you'll have a blast. Skinny ties, woolen scarves, and a distinct Swinging Sixties vibe are all here for you to browse. 11 Newburgh St., W1. www. peckhamryelondon.com.✆ **020/7734-5181.** Tube: Oxford Circus.

Shoes & Accessories

Accessorize ★   This high-street chain store is possibly still the best on the high street for easy-to-wear and well-priced accessories and jewelry. You'll find one in most main train stations, and on almost every major shopping street—which is a good thing, because they have a fantastic range of items to complete an outfit. Hats, bags, and leather gloves are the best buys, and if you're in town make sure you hit their January sale, where most things are half price. 1 Piccadilly, W1. www.accessorize.com. ℂ**020/7494-0566.** Tube: Piccadilly Circus. Other locations throughout London.

James Smith & Sons ★★   This is an authentic London institution. Specializing in umbrellas, it's been open since 1830 and is still a family business. It makes its own brollies, and the shop is nothing short of spectacular to look at. It's also very handy if you get caught in the rain, which is quite likely. 53 New Oxford St., WC1. ℂ**020/7836-4731.** Tube: Tottenham Court Rd.

Kate Kanzier ★★ 🎁   Kate Kanzier might be the best-value shoe shop in the whole of London. The shop sells fashionable brogues in every color you could imagine, for around £30 a pair. The quality perhaps isn't first rank, but when you're paying so little for a favorite among London's most fashionable, you can't complain. 67–69 Leather Lane, EC1. www.katekanzier.com. ℂ**020/7242-7232.** Tube: Farringdon.

Lulu Guinness   This self-taught British handbag designer launched her business in 1989. Many of the world's greatest retail outlets, including Fortnum & Mason, sell her handbags. Her signature bags, such as the "Florist Basket" and the "House Bag," are immortalized in the fashion collection at the **V&A Museum** (p. 103)—and she's still popular with celebs like Madonna and Liz Hurley. 3 Ellis St., SW1. www.luluguinness.com. ℂ**020/7823-4828.** Tube: Sloane Sq.

Luna & Curious ★★★ 🎁   Have you ever thought to yourself, "I wish I could buy sexy designer tights and false paper eyelashes shaped like horses in the same shop?" Well, strange as it sounds, it works well at Luna & Curious. The only way to describe it is as an accessory shop, but it feels more special than that. It sells beautiful things that make you feel like you're shopping in Wonderland, and doesn't (always) charge you hundreds for the privilege. 24–26 Calvert Ave., E2. www.shoplunaandcurious.com. ℂ**020/7033-4411.** Tube: Liverpool St./Train: Shoreditch High St.

The Old Curiosity Shop ★ 🎁   Men are rarely well catered for in the shoe department, but this shop is one of the most special in the city. (It is the very "curiosity shop" that Charles Dickens based his novel on.) It sticks to traditional styles and the men's selection is better than the women's, but with such a beautiful building, steeped in so much history, it's worth popping in even if you aren't planning to buy. 13–14 Portsmouth St., WC2. www.curiosityuk.com. ℂ**020/7405-9891.** Tube: Holborn.

Vintage

Bang Bang ★★ 🎁   The flashy designer-clad mannequins in the window make this Goodge Street store stand out among the secondhand computer shops and lunchtime pitstops. It specializes in designer clothes and high-end high street, but all at bargain prices. You'll find cut-price Armani and cheap Topshop under the same roof, and stock changes regularly. Best bargains are accessories and tailored items, and prices are fair. 21 Goodge St., W1. ℂ**020/7631-4191.** Tube: Goodge St.

Blondie ★   This is the sister store to the larger **Absolute Vintage,** 15 Hanbury St. (ℂ 020/7247-3883). Don't let the small stature of the shop put you off—it has some real gems inside. Everything is arranged by color, so you can head straight to the red polka dots or little black dresses if you like. There's also an enormous shoe collection (mostly in smaller sizes, which is always the way with vintage) and a wide selection of Dior sunglasses. 114–118 Commercial St., E1. ℂ**020/7247-0050.** Tube: Liverpool St./Train: Shoreditch High St.

East End Thrift Store   Another vintage shop that's worth the trip to East London. This one is inside a large warehouse off the unattractive Stepney Green Road. Inside you'll find a massive array of vintage clothing, all well priced, but of varying quality and styles. Men do well here, thanks to an excellent selection of shirts, but vintage newbies might have to do a bit of hunting to find easier-to-wear items. Assembly Passage, E1.© **020/7423-9700.** Tube: Stepney Green or Whitechapel.

Emporium ★★   A quick trip over the river to Greenwich takes you to this classy vintage shop. Men fare slightly better for browsing (the best stuff for women is secreted in protective covers), but the accessories cabinet is an Aladdin's cave of treasures. 330–332 Creek Rd., SE10.© **020/8305-1670.** DLR: Cutty Sark.

Rokit   There are three locations for this small chain, but the most central and best stocked is in Covent Garden. The trick here is to browse at leisure, looking for that perfect item. That's when vintage shopping really becomes fun. You'll find the best buys in leather, denim, and '70s' fashions. 42 Sheldon St., WC2. www.rokit.co.uk.© **020/ 7836-6547.** Tube: Covent Garden. Other locations throughout London.

Women
Fever ★★★ 🛍️   Tucked just off Oxford Street, this is a shop for dress lovers. The designs are classic and reasonably priced. In its vintage section, you can buy the vintage originals so pretty that they inspired the mainstream range. 52 Eastcastle St., W1. www.feverdesigns.co.uk.© **020/636-6326.** Tube: Oxford Circus.

Joy ★★   If you have a thing for dresses, this is the shop for you. Day dresses, flirty dresses, little black dresses—this shop excels in them all. They're unique, but still well priced: Apart from the odd exception that creeps into three figures, everything is around the £50 mark. It does a great range of clothes (and a frankly tacky range of homewares and gifts), but the dresses will keep you occupied. The flagship branch in Greenwich is in a stunning old public baths building. 9 Nelson Rd., SE10. www.joythestore. com.© **020/8293-7979.** DLR: Cutty Sark. Other locations throughout London.

New Look   You can still get great London style even if you're on a tight budget. New Look is the place to start: It's one of the best-value chains on the British high street, and stocks items that will last more than three wears. Its range is not at the cutting edge, but dresses tend to stay under £30. 502–504 Oxford St., W1. www.newlook. com.© **020/7290-7860.** Tube: Marble Arch. Other locations throughout London.

Topshop ★   This shop is enormous (although surprisingly easy to navigate). Its versatile and ever-changing merchandise is aimed at younger shoppers, but that doesn't stop many fashionable women in their 30s and 40s from shopping here. The outlet was the first to release a range of designs from Kate Moss. The shop also has a men's floor, an entire floor of accessories, women's shoes, vintage clothing. Designer concessions are housed in the basement. 216 Oxford St., W1. www.topshop.co.uk. © **0844/848-7487.** Tube: Oxford Circus. Other locations throughout London.

DEPARTMENT STORES
Contrary to popular belief, **Harrods** is not the only department store in London. The British invented the department store, and have plenty of them. A lot are upscale, but you can usually still find a bargain in most. They're also getting better at catering for a younger shopper, and the concessions and food halls are usually the best sections.

Fenwick ★   Fenwick (with a silent "w") dates back to 1891. It's a stylish store that offers a large collection of (slightly conservative) designer womenswear. The perfume and toiletries are excellent if you're looking for something unique, although it comes

Between the high-street shops, the one-off boutiques, and the department stores, lies a strange retail beast known as the "collective shop." These are the stores that grab a selection of the very best of London fashion, and spread it out over several floors—meaning you're spoilt for choice whenever you visit. U.S. chain **Urban Outfitters**, 42–56 Earlham St., WC2 (www.urbanoutfitters.co.uk; 𝒞 **020/7759-6390;** Tube: Covent Garden), does this just right, and London has its own take on the format, with some stunning homemade shops doing the same. Over in southwest London, the **Shop at Bluebird,** 350 King's Rd., SW3 (www.theshopatbluebird.com; 𝒞 **020/7351-3873;** Tube: South Kensington) is chock-full of designers, and **Dover Street Market** ★, 17–18 Dover St., W1 (www.doverstreetmarket.com; 𝒞 **020/7518-0680;** Tube: Green Park), excels at eclectic fashion choices. It stocks apparently every fashionable designer that might take your fancy.

4

LONDON | Shopping

at a price. An extensive selection of lingerie in all price ranges is also sold. 63 New Bond St., W1. www.fenwick.co.uk. 𝒞020/7629-9161. Tube: Bond St. or Oxford Circus.

Fortnum & Mason ★★   Catering to well-heeled clients as a full-service department store since 1707, Fortnum & Mason has chilled out a bit and is better than ever. Offerings include one of the most exciting delicatessens in London, as well as stationery, gift items, porcelain, and crystal. The perfume section offers unique and rare items, all available for smelling. You'll find the items here traditional, elegant, and pricey. 181 Piccadilly, W1. www.fortnumandmason.com. 𝒞020/7734-8040. Tube: Piccadilly Circus.

Harrods ✋   Harrods remains a London institution, but it's not what you'd call cutting edge. For the latest trends, shop elsewhere; but it's as entrenched in history as Buckingham Palace and racing at Ascot, and is still an elaborate emporium. Buyers are trying to become more on trend, and they've added a pet emporium so you can purchase diamond collars for your pooch and gold food dishes for your kitty (there's even a few pets to cuddle). You'll also find a traditional barber, a jewelry department, and a section dedicated to younger customers. 87–135 Brompton Rd., SW1. www.harrods.com. 𝒞020/8479-5100. Tube: Knightsbridge.

John Lewis   This department store remains one of the most trusted outlets in London. Its motto is that it's never knowingly undersold, and they mean it. There are always great bargains here, and homewares are where it excels. Whatever you're looking for, ranging from Egyptian cotton bedding to clothing and jewelry, you'll find it. 278–306 Oxford St., W1. www.johnlewis.com. 𝒞020/7629-7711. Tube: Oxford Circus. Other locations throughout London.

Liberty ★★★   The glorious building and quirkiness of the stock makes Liberty our favorite destination in town. Not afraid to do something new, and always full of exciting designers, it's exclusive without being stuffy. The Tudor-style splendor that includes half-timbering and interior paneling houses six floors of fashion, china, and home furnishings. The famous Liberty Print fabrics cover everything—upholstery fabrics, scarves, ties, luggage, gifts, and much more. 210–220 Regent St., W1. www.liberty.co.uk. 𝒞020/7734-1234. Tube: Oxford Circus.

Selfridges ★   Those iconic yellow bags scream fashion, and Selfridges do it better than any other department store. You'll get lost in here (that's what they want, but there's a champagne bar so don't complain). Since it was founded in 1858, Selfridges has adapted to changing times and always been one to push trends. Wander the street-level "Wonder Room" for luxurious jewelry, and the shoe choice is one of the best in London. Don't leave without viewing the staggering food hall. 400 Oxford St., W1. www.selfridges.com.© **0800/123-400.** Tube: Bond St.

FOOD & DRINK

Camellia Tea House   This little cafe is the perfect pitstop if you're shopping in central London. In the top corner of Kingly Court, it's calm and quiet even on a busy Saturday. It's not just afternoon tea and cake, though; you'll also find a vast array of teas from around the world on sale. There's a tea for every mood and occasion, including teas to make you dream and to cure ailments. Pick up a pretty teapot or two as well; the china is beautiful. 212 Kingly Court, W1. www.camelliasteahouse.com.© **020/7734-9939.** Tube: Oxford Circus.

Gerry's   If you're a fan of interesting booze, you'll be like a kid in a tipsy candy store in Gerry's. It's a Soho institution, and houses every spirit you can think of. Some see it as just another bottle shop, but to locals it's beloved, and especially handy if you're trying to find a special gift for friends who sneer at duty-free bargains. 74 Old Compton St., W1. www.gerrys.uk.com.© **020/7734-2053.** Tube: Piccadilly Circus or Leicester Sq.

Hope and Greenwood ★★   Retro candy is trendy at the moment, and Hope and Greenwood make the sweet treats of yesteryear a pleasure to buy. The shop in Covent Garden is like a little timewarp, full of cola bottles, coconut ice, and traditional British fudge to take home. 1 Russell St., WC2. www.hopeandgreenwood.co.uk. © **020/7240-3314.** Tube: Covent Garden.

Laduree ★★   Who knew little squidgy discs of meringue would become so popular? This shop on the corner of Burlington Arcade is tiny, but what it lacks in size it makes up for in brash and gaudy interior. Don't be put off, the Aladdin's cave decor is why people love it here. That and the macaroons, which are famous across Europe. 71–72 Burlington Arcade, W1. www.laduree.fr/en/scene.© **020/7491-9155.** Tube: Green Park or Piccadilly.

La Fromagerie ★★   It's the cheese room that makes this shop special. Ignore the grocery displays when you enter and head straight to the good stuff. Remember to close the door behind you, because the temperature is set perfectly for the vast range of British and Continental cheeses. 30 Highbury Park, N5. www.lafromagerie.co.uk. © **020/7359-7440.** Tube: Arsenal. Also at 2–6 Moxon St., W1 (© **020/7935-0341).**

Melt ★★   This chocolate shop in Notting Hill is a West London favorite. It will tempt you with caramels and sweet treats, and if you're lucky, you'll even be able to peek into the kitchen where the chocolates are made. The proprietors run workshops (must be pre-booked), and their chili chocolate is something special. 59 Ledbury Rd., W11. www.meltchocolates.com.© **020/8962-0492.** Tube: Notting Hill Gate.

Neal's Yard Dairy ★   Specializing in British and Irish cheeses, this shop occupies the photogenic premises of what was once a warehouse for the food stalls at Covent Garden. Today you'll see a staggering selection of artisanal cheeses, including cloth-bound cheddars and a careful selection of ewe's and goat's milk cheeses, set in big display windows behind an antique, dark-blue Victorian facade. It also runs evening tutored cheese tastings (see p. 127). 17 Shorts Gardens, WC2. www.nealsyarddairy. co.uk.© **020/7240-5700.** Tube: Covent Garden. Also at 6 Park St., SE1 (© **020/7367-0799).**

Whole Foods The flagship Whole Foods shop in Kensington is a bit of a joy, if you have the money to enjoy it. Full of tasty (mostly organic) treats, this is a haven for foodies. It feels like an indoor market (without the haggling) and you'll find every type of food you could wish for. You won't be able to walk past the cakes without sampling something sweet, but avoid it at lunchtimes, when it draws a huge office crowd and gets too busy. 63–97 Kensington High St., W8. www.wholefoodsmarket.com. ℭ020/7368-4500. Tube: High St. Kensington.

GIFTS & SOUVENIRS

Ryan Town ★★★ There are iconic shops in the East End, and then there's Rob Ryan's. In the center of Columbia Road market (and as such, only open on weekends), this shop devoted to the paper-cut artist is famous across the design world. The whimsical and sentimental artworks adorn everything from greetings cards to cushions. Prices vary from £3 for a greetings card to £300 for an original print, but you'll find it hard to resist the romantic pieces. 126 Columbia Rd., E2. www.misterrob.co.uk. ℭ020/7613-1510. Train: Hoxton/Tube: Old St.

HOME DESIGN & HOUSEWARES

See also "Art, Crafts & Museum Shops," earlier in this section.

Snowden Flood ★★ Snowden Flood's striking ceramic designs, often featuring iconic London buildings, are becoming as recognizable as the landmarks themselves. Pick up a platter for £40, or a modestly-priced mug for little over £10. The range is hugely collectable. Don't visit on Mondays—that's Snowden's "design day." Unit 1.01 Oxo Tower Wharf, Bargehouse St., SE1. www.snowdenflood.com. ℭ 020/7401-8710. Tube: Southwark.

Twenty-Twentyone ★ This shop is all about the contemporary. If you're looking for an unusual cheese grater, this is where to come. If you don't want a standard footstool, head here. If you want a surprising interior gift, you'll find it on the shelves of this tiny Islington shop. 274–275 Upper St., N1. www.twentytwentyone.com. ℭ020/7288-1996. Tube: Highbury & Islington or Angel.

MUSIC

Collectors should browse **Notting Hill,** because the handful of record shops near Notting Hill Gate Tube station are excellent. Also browse **Soho** around Wardour Street and Berwick Street. Sometimes dealers show up at Covent Garden on weekends.

Dress Circle ★ This store is unique in London in that it's devoted to musical theatre and standard vocalists such as Frank Sinatra and Judy Garland. After half a century, recordings in the U.K. enter the public domain—hence the lower prices on re-released CDs of West End and Broadway musicals from the 1950s. New releases, of course, cost at least three times more. 57–59 Monmouth St., WC2. www.dresscircle.co.uk. ℭ020/7240-2227. Tube: Covent Garden.

Duke of Uke ★★ This fabulously named shop sells all things ukulele. It sells banjos and standard guitars as well, but really it's all about the uke. There's great events here as well, so keep your eyes (and ears) open. 22 Hanbury St., E1. www.dukeofuke. co.uk. ℭ020/7247-7924. Tube: Whitechapel or Aldgate East.

TECHNOLOGY

Camera Café ★ A cute little place just by the British Museum where they'll sell you a coffee, and let you play about with their secondhand cameras. There's free Wi-Fi, too. 44 Museum St., WC1. www.cameracafe.co.uk. ℭ07887/930826. Tube: Holborn.

Lomography ★★ Lomo photography is big in the U.K. Highly saturated color images and funky replica vintage cameras make this a cool and fairly simple hobby to pick up: You can buy a camera for £50 and start shooting right away. The Lomo shop has the biggest selection in London and some excellent examples of lomography to inspire you. 3 Newburgh St., W1. www.lomography.com. © **020/7434-1466.** Tube: Oxford Circus.

TOYS, COMICS & GAMES

Forbidden Planet ★ They're not strictly toys; they're collectables. However you phrase it, though, Forbidden Planet is the world's largest sci-fi and fantasy retailer, specializing in comics, graphic novels and, erm ... toys. If you want a comic book or model of a *Dr Who* Dalek, head here. 179 Shaftesbury Ave., WC2. http://forbiddenplanet. com.© **020/7420-3666.** Tube: Tottenham Court Rd.

Hamleys ☺ Possibly the finest toy shop in the world—more than 35,000 toys and games on seven floors of fun and magic. The huge selection includes soft, cuddly stuffed animals as well as dolls, radio-controlled cars, train sets, model kits, board games, outdoor toys, computer games, and more. Just don't ever think it's a good idea to visit when school's out. 188–196 Regent St., W1. www.hamleys.com.© **0844/855-2424.** Tube: Oxford Circus or Piccadilly Circus. Also at St. Pancras International Station, NW1 (© **020/ 7479-7366).**

Play Lounge ★ ☺ There's nothing dull about this toy shop aimed at young adults and big kids. If you like your Japanese figurines and interesting comics, you'll find something to keep you occupied. The shop is tiny but packed from floor to ceiling with goodies. It's pricey sometimes, but it stocks small toys and games on the counter that are perfect for pocket money. 19 Beak St., W1. www.playlounge.co.uk.© **020/7287-7073.** Tube: Oxford Circus.

Pollock's Toy Museum ★★ ☺ The key part to this traditional toy shop is that it's attached to its own museum, so you can buy cute presents and toys (including magic sets) and then have a wander around the exhibition, which costs £5. It's a lovely, old-fashioned store—and you won't find a single video game. 25 Scala St., W1. www.pollockstoymuseum.com.© **020/7636 3452.** Tube: Goodge St. Also at 44 The Market, WC2 (© **020/7379-7866).**

ENTERTAINMENT & NIGHTLIFE

Weekly publications such as *Time Out* carry full entertainment listings, including information on restaurants, nightclubs, and bars. You'll also find listings in all the daily newspapers, and *The Guide* distributed every Saturday inside the *Guardian* newspaper is an invaluable source of up-to-date information.

The Performing Arts

The theatrical capital of the world, London is home to some of the most famous companies on the planet, often housed in glorious buildings with rich and long histories. Few things here are as entertaining and rewarding as a visit to the theatre.

The number and variety of productions, and the standards of acting and directing, are unrivaled, and a London stage has also become the first port of call for many a Hollywood star looking to show off their thespian skills. The London stage accommodates both the traditional and the avant-garde and is, for the most part, accessible and reasonably affordable.

GETTING TICKETS

To see specific shows, especially hits, purchase your tickets in advance. Founded in 2000, **London Theatre Direct** (www.londontheatredirect.com; ℂ **0845/505-8500**) represents a majority of the major theatres in the city and tickets for all productions can be purchased in advance, either over the phone or via its website. Alternatively, try the **Society of London Theatre** (www.officiallondontheatre. co.uk; ℂ **020/7557-6700**), which has a ticket booth ("tkts") on the southwest corner of Leicester Square, open Monday to Saturday 10am to 7pm and Sunday 11am to 4pm. You can purchase all tickets here, although the booth specializes in half-price sales for shows that are undersold. These tickets must be purchased in person—not over the phone. A £2 service fee is charged. For phone orders, you should call **Ticketmaster** (www.ticketmaster.co.uk; ℂ **0870/060-2340**).

Visitors from North America can try **Keith Prowse,** 234 W. 44th St., Ste. 1000, New York, NY 10036 (www.keithprowse.com; ℂ **212/398-4175** in the U.S.), to arrange tickets and seek information before they leave home. Its London office is at 39 Moreland St., EC1 (ℂ **0844/209-0382;** Tube: Angel). Staff will mail your tickets, fax a confirmation, or leave your tickets at the appropriate production's box office. Instant confirmations are available for most shows. A booking and handling fee of up to 20% is added to the price of the ticket. **Applause Theatre and Entertainment Service,** 311 W. 43rd St., Ste. 601, New York, NY 10036 (www.applause-tickets.com; ℂ **800/451-9930** or 212/307-7050 in the U.S.), can sometimes get you tickets when Prowse can't. In business for some 2 decades, it is a reliable and efficient company.

Ticket prices vary greatly depending on the seat and venue—from £25 to £85 is typical. Occasionally gallery seats (the cheapest) are sold only on the day of the performance, so you'll have to head to the box office early in the day and return an hour before the performance to get in line, because they're not reserved seats.

Many of the major theatres, such as the **National** (see below), offer reduced-price tickets to students and those under 18 on a standby basis, but not to the general public. When available, these tickets are sold 30 minutes prior to curtain. Line up early for popular shows, as standby tickets go fast. You must show a valid student I.D.

TheatreFix (www.theatrefix.co.uk) is a website set up to help and encourage those aged 16 to 26 to attend London theatres. Sign up to the service and you can get cheap entry to many productions, as well as valuable advice if you are making your first trip to the city.

Finally, if you decide to check out the theatre on a whim—and you're not too fussy about what you see—**Lastminute.com** is a safe bet to pick up late tickets, often at discounted rates.

Warning: Beware of scalpers who hang out in front of theatres staging hit shows. Many report that scalpers sell forged tickets, and their prices can be outrageous.

MAJOR THEATRES

Donmar Warehouse ★★   Although its auditorium only seats 250 people, the Donmar Warehouse is still one of London's most important and acclaimed theatres. For the past 2 decades—first under the artistic directorship of Sam Mendes, then Michael Grandage, and now Josie Rourke—the Donmar has staged some of London's most memorable productions with several, such as *Frost/Nixon,* going on to tour internationally. It's renowned for an emphasis on performing new works and contemporary reworkings of the classics, so catching a performance here should be high on the priority list of any visiting theatre lover. 41 Earlham St., WC2. www.donmarwarehouse. com. ℂ**020/7240-4882.** Tube: Covent Garden.

National Theatre ★ Home to one of the world's greatest stage companies, the Royal National Theatre is not one but three theatres—the Olivier, reminiscent of a Greek amphitheatre with its open stage; the more traditional Lyttelton; and the Cottesloe, with its flexible stage and seating. The National presents the finest in world theatre, from classic drama to award-winning new plays, including comedies, musicals, and shows for young people. A choice of at least six plays is offered at any one time. Box-office hours are Monday to Saturday 10am to 8pm. South Bank, SE1. www. nationaltheatre.org.uk. ✆**020/7452-3000.** Tube: Waterloo, Embankment, or Charing Cross.

Old Vic ★★ The Old Vic has stood on its site near Waterloo Station for more than 190 years, and since 2004 has been under the stewardship of actor Kevin Spacey. His tenure and aim to "inject new life" into London theatre has generally been regarded as a success. Spacey's star power has enabled him to attract Hollywood names such as Richard Dreyfuss and Jeff Goldblum, alongside powerhouse directors of the caliber of Trevor Nunn. Productions range from modern classics through to Shakespearean tragedies and modern farces. In 2010 the Old Vic also opened a new performance space in tunnels that run beneath Waterloo Station, with productions and musical events staged specifically to make the most of the atmospheric subterranean space. 103 The Cut, SE1. www.oldvictheatre.co.uk. ✆**020/7928-2651.** Tube: Waterloo.

Shakespeare's Globe In May 1997, the new Globe Theatre—a replica of the Elizabethan original, thatched roof and all—staged its first slate of plays (*Henry V* and *A Winter's Tale*) yards away from the site of the 16th-century theatre where the Bard originally staged his works.

Productions vary in style and setting; not all are performed in Elizabethan costume. In keeping with the historic setting, no lighting is focused just on the stage, but floodlighting is used during evening performances to replicate daylight in the theatre (Elizabethan performances took place in the afternoon). Theatregoers sit on wooden benches of yore—in thatch-roofed galleries—but these days you can rent a cushion to make yourself more comfortable. About 500 "groundlings" can stand in the uncovered yard around the stage, just as they did when the Bard was here.

Due to the Globe's open-air nature there is a limited winter schedule, so check the website beforehand to see what's on; in any season the schedule can be affected by weather. New Globe Walk, Bankside, SE1. www.shakespeares-globe.org. ✆ **020/7902-1400.** Tube: Mansion House or Southwark.

Theatre Royal Drury Lane Drury Lane is one of London's oldest and most prestigious theatres, crammed with tradition—not all of it respectable. Nearly every star of London theatre has taken the stage here at some time. It has a wide-open repertoire but leans toward musicals, especially long-running hits. Guided tours (£11.50 adults, £9 children and seniors) of the backstage area and front of house are given Monday, Tuesday, Thursday, and Friday at 2:15 and 4:15pm, plus 10:15 and 11:45am Wednesday and Saturday. The box office is open Monday to Saturday from 10am to 8pm. Catherine St., WC2. www.reallyuseful.com. ✆**0844/412-2955.** Tickets £15–£45. Tube: Covent Garden.

FRINGE THEATRE

Some of the best theatre in London is performed on the "fringe"—at the dozens of venues devoted to alternative plays, revivals, contemporary drama, and musicals. These shows are usually more adventurous than established West End productions, and they're cheaper. Most offer discounted seats (often as much as 50% off) to students and seniors. Fringe theatres are scattered around London, so check listings in

Time Out or websites such as **Run-Riot.com** or **LeCool.com**, both of which cover leftfield theatre.

Almeida ★★ The Almeida is known for its adventurous stagings of new and classic plays. The theatre's legendary status is validated by consistently good productions at lower-than-average prices. Performances are usually held Monday to Saturday. The Almeida is also home to the **Festival of Contemporary Music** (also called the Almeida Opera) from mid-June to mid-July, which showcases everything from atonal jazz to 12-tone chamber orchestra pieces. The box office is open Monday through Saturday 10am to 6pm. Almeida St., N1. www.almeida.co.uk. © **020/7359-4404.** Tickets £6–£30. Tube: Angel or Highbury and Islington.

Young Vic ★★ Long known for presenting both classical and modern plays, the Young Vic tends to nurture younger talent than its sister theatre, the **Old Vic** (see above), and places a greater emphasis on working with young and emerging directors. Productions at the Young Vic could be almost anything, and are priced depending on the show—discounted tickets are available for students and anyone aged 26 or under. The box office is open Monday to Saturday 10am to 7pm. 66 The Cut, SE1. www.youngvic. org. © **020/7922-2922.** Tube: Waterloo or Southwark.

CLASSICAL MUSIC, OPERA & DANCE

Currently, London supports a sometimes unwieldy yet impressive five major orchestras—the **London Symphony,** the **Royal Philharmonic,** the **Philharmonia Orchestra,** the **BBC Symphony,** and the **BBC Philharmonic**—as well as several choirs, and many smaller chamber groups and historic instrument ensembles. Look for the **London Sinfonietta,** the **English Chamber Orchestra,** and the **Academy of St. Martin in the Fields.**

Barbican Centre ★★ Standing fortress-like on the fringe of the City of London, the Barbican is the largest art and exhibition complex in Western Europe. Roomy and comfortable, it's the perfect setting for enjoying music and theatre, and is the permanent home of the London Symphony Orchestra, as well as host to visiting orchestras and performers of all styles, from classical to jazz, folk, and world music.

In addition to its hall and two theatres, the Barbican Centre encompasses the Barbican Art Gallery, the Curve Gallery, and foyer exhibition spaces; Cinemas One and Two, which show recently released mainstream films and film series; the rooftop Conservatory, one of London's largest greenhouses; and restaurants, cafes, and bars. The box office is open Monday to Saturday from 9am to 8pm. Silk St., EC2. www. barbican.org.uk. © **020/7638-8891.** Tube: Barbican or Moorgate.

Royal Albert Hall ★ Opened in 1871 and dedicated to the memory of Queen Victoria's consort, Prince Albert, this circular building is one of the world's most famous auditoriums. With a seating capacity of 5,200, it's a popular place to hear music by major world-class performers from both the classical and the pop worlds.

Since 1941, the hall has hosted the **BBC Henry Wood Promenade Concerts,** known as "the Proms," an annual series that lasts for 8 weeks between mid-July and mid-September. The Proms incorporate a medley of mostly British orchestral music, and have been a national favorite since 1895. The final evening (the "Last Night of the Proms") is the most famous, when rousing favorites "Jerusalem" and "Land of Hope and Glory" echo through the hall. The Albert Hall allows tours both front of house (£8.50) and backstage (£12). The box office is open daily 9am to 9pm. Kensington Gore, SW7. www.royalalberthall.com. © **0845/401-5045.** Tube: South Kensington.

Royal Opera House ★★ The Royal Ballet and the Royal Opera are at home in this magnificently restored theatre. The entire northeast corner of one of London's most famous public squares was transformed, finally realizing Inigo Jones's original vision for his colonnaded Covent Garden.

Performances at the Royal Opera are usually sung in the original language, but surtitles are projected. The Royal Ballet, which ranks with top companies such as the Kirov and the Paris Opera Ballet, performs a repertory with a tilt toward the classics, including works by earlier choreographer-directors Sir Frederick Ashton and Sir Kenneth MacMillan. The box office is open Monday to Saturday from 10am to 8pm. Bow St., WC2. www.roh.org.uk. ✆**020/7304-4000.** Tube: Covent Garden.

Sadler's Wells ★ One of London's premier venues for dance and opera, Sadler's Wells occupies the site of a series of theatres, the first built in 1683. The original facade has been retained, but the interior was completely revamped in 1998 with a stylish, cutting-edge design. The new space offers classical ballet, modern dance of all degrees of "avant-garde-ness," and children's theatrical productions, usually including a Christmas ballet. Performances are generally at 7:30pm. The box office is open Monday to Saturday from 10am to 8pm. Rosebery Ave., EC1. www.sadlers-wells. com. ✆**0844/412-4300.** Tube: Angel.

Southbank Centre ★★ Its brutalist concrete exterior may not be to everyone's taste, but there's no denying that the Southbank Centre contains three of the most acoustically perfect concert halls in the world, the Royal Festival Hall, the Queen Elizabeth Hall, and the Purcell Room. Together, the halls present more than 1,200 performances a year, including classical music, ballet, jazz, popular music, and contemporary dance. Also here is the **Hayward Gallery** (p. 106). The box office opens daily 9am to 8pm.

The Centre itself usually opens daily at 10am, and offers an extensive array of things to eat, see, and do, including free exhibitions and musical performances in the foyers and a recently extended gift shop selling art and design items. South Bank, SE1. www.southbankcentre.co.uk. ✆**0844/875-0073.** Tube: Waterloo or Embankment.

Wigmore Hall An intimate auditorium, Wigmore Hall offers an excellent series of voice recitals, piano and chamber music, early and Baroque music, and jazz. With over 400 performances a year, plus workshops and community projects, Wigmore Hall is a vitally important venue, ensuring new generations are introduced to classical music. The box office is open Monday to Saturday 10am to 7pm and Sunday from 10:30am to 5pm. 36 Wigmore St., W1. www.wigmore-hall.org.uk. ✆**020/7935-2141.** Tickets £10–£35. Tube: Bond St. or Oxford Circus.

The Bar & Pub Scene
BARS & COCKTAIL LOUNGES
Alibi As Shoreditch has become ever more popular over the last decade, many of those originally drawn to that arty enclave of East London have been pushed out. Dalston and Bethnal Green have mopped up the overspill, and now hold the crown of London's hippest areas. The Alibi is the best among a number of bars to open in Dalston in 2010, and implements a policy of giving interesting record labels and promoters a small space in which to throw big parties. 91 Kingsland High St., E8. www. thealibilondon.co.uk. ✆**020/7249-2733**. Tube: Old St. then bus 243/Train: Dalston Kingsland or Dalston Junction.

Bourne & Hollingsworth Blink and you could easily miss this cupboard-sized space hidden under a Fitzrovia store. If you do manage to find the entrance, you could be forgiven for thinking you're the first to have managed the feat since the 1940s—you're greeted by a scene reminiscent of black-and-white movies. From the floral wallpaper to the china teacups for your cocktail, this is quite unlike any other bar in London. 28 Rathbone Place, W1. www.bourneandhollingsworth.com.✆ **020/7636-8228.** Tube: Tottenham Court Rd.

Callooh Calley A remarkably unpretentious cocktail bar hemmed in on all sides by Shoreditch's lively pubs and clubs. The drinks menu features everything that you would expect, but take the time to chat to any of the bar's friendly and knowledgeable staff and you'll soon find yourself going off-menu as they mix up a drink to suit your taste. Whilst the front bar is pleasant enough, for the full experience head through the concealed door (disguised as a wardrobe) to the atmospheric back room (officially a member's bar, so call ahead). 65 Rivington St., EC2. www.calloohcallaybar.com.✆ **020/7739-4781.** Tube: Old St.

Gordon's Wine Bar 👔 Gordon's can lay claim to being one of London's oldest and, in the eyes of those who have fallen for its charms, most unique wine bars. Descend the stairs into the bar's grotto-like basement and if you're lucky enough to find yourself a table, settle in for an evening of wine, sherry, and cheese. The service isn't always impeccable, but you can't fault the atmosphere, hence the eclectic mix of office workers, students, and artistic sorts who pack it out most nights. 47 Villiers St., WC2. www.gordonswinebar.com.✆ **020/7930-1408.** Tube: Charing Cross or Embankment.

Ice Bar A novelty, yes, but London's only bar constructed entirely from imported Swedish ice is still worth checking out. For obvious reasons the temperature is always kept at a chilly 5°F (15°C) year-round, so you'll want to make sure you wrap up tight in the silver cape and hood they provide. It's open Monday to Wednesday 3:30 to 11:45pm, Thursday 3:30pm to 12:30am, Friday 1:15pm to 1:15am, Saturday 11am to 1:15am, and Sunday 2 to 11:45pm. 31–33 Heddon St., W1. www.belowzerolondon.com. ✆ **020/7478-8910.** Admission Mon–Wed and Sun £12; Thurs–Sat £15. Tube: Oxford Circus.

Loungelover Expensive, garish, but also ever popular, Loungelover is adjacent to and run by the same people as the equally colorful restaurant **Les Trois Garçons** (p. 145). It's a warren of rooms, each with its own identity; the effect has been compared to a walk through a film set. The elegant cocktails are among the most original creations in London. Food is available on tapas-like platters. Even if you're only stopping in for a drink, make a reservation because space is limited. It's open Monday to Thursday and Sunday 6pm to midnight, Friday 5:30pm to 1am, and Saturday 6pm to 1am. 1 Whitby St., E1.✆ **020/7012-1234.** Tube: Old St./Train: Shoreditch High St.

Mark's Bar ★★ Attached to noted restaurant Hix, this dark and stylish bar offers up a slice of Manhattan deep in the heart of Soho. Its imaginative drinks menu, devised by Nick Strangeway, is packed full of historical curiosities that "hark back to another era before the Temperance Movement had reared its ugly head." Leave your mojitos at the door and try something a little different, such as the 19th-century inspired "Punch à la Regent." Open noon to 12:30am Monday through Saturday; 11am until 11pm Sunday. 66–70 Brewer St., W1. www.hixsoho.co.uk.✆ **020/7292-3518.** Tube: Piccadilly Circus.

Nightjar ★★ Hidden away a stone's throw from Old Street roundabout is this subterranean cocktail speakeasy. It might not be much to look at from the outside, but once you've found the place, you can settle into a dark corner and treat yourself to one (or several) of the drinks from their impressive menu of elegantly and inventively presented cocktails. 129 City Rd., EC1. www.barnightjar.com.✆ **020/7253-4101.** Tube: Old St.

Phoenix Artist Club   The favored watering hole of many a London actor, this basement bar has seen plenty of decadent sights over the years. This is where Laurence Olivier made his stage debut in 1930, although he couldn't stop giggling even though the play was a drama. Live music is occasionally featured, but it's the hearty welcome, good beer, and friendly patrons from ages 20 to 50 who make this theatre bar a worthwhile detour. It's "members only" after 8pm, but arrive early, find yourself a secluded spot, and you'll be able to drink long into the night. 1 Phoenix St., WC2. www.phoenixartistclub.com. ©**020/7836-1077.** Tube: Tottenham Court Rd.

69 Colebrooke Row ★★   Showing that size isn't everything, 69 Colebrooke Row is one of London's smallest bars, but also a must-visit for a cocktail aficionado. Serving up a range of exquisite bespoke beverages, Tony Conigliaro is widely regarded as one of the U.K.'s finest drinks creators, and applies a trademark sense of experimentation and scientific play to the bar. It's open 5pm until midnight Sunday to Wednesday, 5pm to 1am Thursday, and 5pm to 2am Friday and Saturday. 69 Colebrooke Row, N1. www.69colebrookerow.com. ©**07540/528593.** Tube: Angel.

The Social   While most bars in the West End exist solely to speed the separation of your money from your wallet, this curiously thin bar has much nobler aims. Founded by the team behind the Heavenly record label, the Social offers up great new bands, surprise big-name DJs, a decent selection of beers, and the guarantee that come 10pm on a Friday night the place will be jumping. Now entering its second decade, it shows no sign of slowing down, which is just how we like it. 5 Little Portland St., W1. www.thesocial.com. ©**020/7636-4992.** Tube: Oxford Circus.

Vertigo 42 ★ 📷   For a truly unique London experience head to Vertigo 42, the champagne bar at the top of Tower 42 (until 1990, the tallest building in London). At 183m (600 ft.), the bar offers panoramic views across all of London. Although the price of drinks may match the bar's own vertiginous heights, for special occasions few spots can match it. Tower 42, 25 Old Broad St., EC2. www.vertigo42.co.uk. ©**020/7877-7842.** Tube: Bank or Liverpool St.

Worship Street Whistling Shop ★★   Just as the likes of Heston Blumenthal have revolutionized British dining, combining ultra-modern cooking techniques with a rediscovery of past menus, we're increasingly seeing a more experimental and inventive approach to the "science" of mixology. Recreating forgotten drinks, and applying new techniques to create libations never before possible, the alchemists behind the bar here create liquid gold every time. 63 Worship St., EC2. www.whistlingshop.com. ©**020/7247-0015.** Tube: Old St.

PUBS

The quintessential British experience of dropping into the "local" for a pint of real ale is a great way to soak up the character of the different villages that form London. Note, websites such as **Beerintheevening.com** and **Fancyapint.com** host user reviews of nearly every London pub. Pub opening hours are flexible but fairly standard: In general you'll find them open from 11am or noon until at least 11pm daily (sometimes 10:30pm Sun). Many also open later on Friday and Saturday, and most can stay open if they like when things are still buzzing on any night of the week.

West End
French House   A remnant from Soho's louche past, the French House is a curious creature. No pint glasses and no cellphones are the rules of this house, and woe betide anyone who flouts either. A favorite of writers, poets, and actors over the years, the

French House makes few concessions to modernity—just the way its bohemian patrons like it. 49 Dean St., W1. www.frenchhousesoho.com.✆ 020/7437-2477. Tube: Leicester Sq.

Harp ★ Wedged between Covent Garden and Trafalgar Square, the Harp is a much loved traditional pub offering an authentic experience, and just as importantly, a refuge from the bustle outside. Break up the shopping trip with a leisurely pint (or two) from their interesting range of ales and lagers. 47 Chandos Place, WC2. www.harp coventgarden.com.✆ **020/7836-0291.** Tube: Leicester Sq. or Charing Cross.

Ye Olde Cheshire Cheese You could be forgiven for thinking the Cheshire Cheese was built for a BBC costume drama, but there has been a public house on this site for several centuries. The present building and its mazelike interior dates back to the 17th century, and for a living slice of olde London it's hard to beat—even if just for a quick drink. 145 Fleet St., EC4.✆ **020/7353-6170.** Tube: Chancery Lane or Temple.

The City & Clerkenwell

Counting House Located bang in the heart of the City, London's financial district, the Counting House is, suitably enough, housed in a former bank. As watering holes go this is a rather impressive one and its size, imposing architecture, and great glass domed ceiling offer a drinking experience unlike most other London pubs. 50 Cornhill, EC3.✆ **020/7283-7123.** Tube: Bank.

Craft Beer Co. One of the pioneers of craft beer in the city, the Craft Beer Co. opened its doors in 2006, and has since become one of the most highly-rated bars in Britain. With 16 cask ales on tap at any one time, not to mention bottled brews from around the world, this is the place to go in London if you're in search of something a little more interesting than a pint of fizzy lager. 82 Leather Lane, EC1. www.thecraftbeerco. com.✆ **020/7430-1123.** Tube: Farringdon.

Wilmington Arms Located just a short hop from bustling Exmouth Market, the Wilmington is a quality pub serving Clerkenwell locals a fine selection of seasonal ales, lagers, and decent, unfussy pub food in comfortable surroundings. Settle into the comfy sofas, and work your way through the day's newspapers, while the pub's well-stocked jukebox provides the soundtrack. If that all sounds a little too sedate then head out back where you can also catch up-and-coming indie bands and comedians on most nights. 69 Rosebery Ave., EC1. www.thewilmingtonarms.co.uk. ✆ **020/7837-1384.** Tube: Farringdon.

Ye Olde Mitre Tavern 👔 Ye Olde Mitre is the name of a working-class inn built here in 1547, when the Bishops of Ely controlled the district. Despite being slap bang in the heart of London, one of those historical anomalies that are so prevalent in Britain meant that until the 1930s it was considered part of Cambridgeshire. Hidden away and hard to find, it's a rough gem of a pub well worth searching out. 1 Ely Court, EC1.✆ **020/7405-4751.** Tube: Chancery Lane.

West London

Churchill Arms Stop here for a nod to the Empire's end. Loaded with Winston Churchill memorabilia, the pub hosts a week of celebration leading up to Churchill's birthday on November 30. Decorations and festivities are also featured for Halloween, Christmas, and St. Paddy's Day, helping to create the homiest village pub atmosphere you're likely to find in London. 119 Kensington Church St., W8.✆ **020/7727-4242.** Tube: Notting Hill Gate or High St. Kensington.

Ladbroke Arms Previously honored as London's "Dining Pub of the Year," the Ladbroke Arms is still highly regarded for its food. An ever-changing menu includes roast cod filet with lentils and salsa verde; and aged bone-in rib steak with mustard, peppercorn, and herb and garlic butter. With background jazz and rotating art prints, the place strays from the traditional pub environment. The excellent Eldridge Pope Royal is usually on tap. 54 Ladbroke Rd., W11. www.capitalpubcompany.com. **© 020/7727-6648.** Tube: Notting Hill Gate.

North London
BrewDog Camden Bar Recent years have seen an explosion of microbreweries and craft beer bars across the U.K. The Brewdog Brewery has been at the forefront of this wave, and their bar in Camden exemplifies the spirit of the company: It's loud, fun, and full of young people, but whilst it might appear a million miles away from the ale enthusiast stereotype, don't make the mistake of thinking they don't take their ale seriously here. There's a huge, ever-changing range of bottled and draught beers to work your way through. 113 Bayham St., NW1. www.brewdog.com/bars/camden. **© 020/7284-0453.** Tube: Camden Town.

Euston Tap ★ Pubs attached to rail stations are often dispiriting affairs, but the Euston Tap throws all that on its head. Occupying a small but curiously grand lodge in front of the station, it attracts not just those temporarily marooned by London's transport network, but also discerning ale drinkers from across the city. A stunning and ever-changing list of rare lagers and ales ensures that there's always something new on the menu. West Lodge, 190 Euston Rd., NW1. www.eustontap.com. **© 020/7387-2890.** Tube: Euston.

Holly Bush ★★ The Holly Bush is the real thing: authentic Edwardian gas lamps, open fires, private booths, and a tap selection of Fuller's London Pride, Adnams, and Harveys. Hidden away in a quiet area of Hampstead, the Holly Bush provides a warm welcome to those who can find it. After a hard day's shopping or walking on the Heath, settle into one of its snugs and revive yourself with a quality pint and traditional pub food from its well-regarded kitchen. 22 Holly Mount, NW3. www.hollybushpub.com. **© 020/7435-2892.** Tube: Hampstead.

East London
Mason & Taylor For a true taste of London, head to Mason & Taylor, a modern bar that focuses on the beers produced by a growing number of local craft brewers. Camden Town Brewery and the Kernel Brewery are particularly well stocked, but with 12 different beers on tap and a changing roster of bottled ales, whatever your tipple you'll be sure to find something that hits the spot. 51–55 Bethnal Green Rd., E1. www.masonandtaylor.co.uk. **© 020/7749-9670.** Tube: Bethnal Green.

Prospect of Whitby One of London's truly historic pubs, the Prospect was founded in the days of the Tudors, taking its name from a coal barge that made trips between Yorkshire and London. Come here for a tot, a noggin, or whatever it is you drink, and soak up the atmosphere. The pub has quite a pedigree: Dickens and diarist Samuel Pepys used to drop in, and painter Turner came here for weeks at a time studying views of the Thames. In the 17th century, the notorious Hanging Judge Jeffreys used to get drunk here while overseeing hangings at the adjoining Execution Dock. Courtyard tables overlook the river. 57 Wapping Wall, E1. **© 020/7481-1095.** DLR: Shadwell/Train: Wapping.

Southeast London
Florence★ A grand old pub with an impressive garden at the rear, the Florence is an oasis of calm and quality ales in Southeast London. With its own microbrewery on

site, you know they take their beer seriously here. Lazily passing a sunny afternoon in the garden with a pint of their own-brewed Weasel is one of life's true pleasures. 131–133 Dulwich Rd., SE24. www.capitalpubcompany.com/the-florence. ✆ **020/7326-4987.** Train: Herne Hill.

South Bank
George Inn   With its historic courtyard, wooden beams, and associated trappings, the George is many tourists' idea of an authentic English pub—indeed, it's even run by the National Trust. For that reason it's often busy, and many locals give it a clear steer. Worth popping in for one, but not the best for an evening's drinking. 77 Borough High St., SE1. ✆ **020/7407-2056.** Tube: Borough or London Bridge.

Royal Oak   A real ale fan's delight, the Royal Oak often stocks draught beers you won't find anywhere else in London—and for that reason is always busy. It's not exclusively for beer buffs though, and the pub itself is a remarkably pleasant inn with tasty, simple food and a friendly crowd. 44 Tabard St., SE1. ✆ **020/7357-7173.** Tube: Borough.

Southwest London
Cask & Glass   Tucked away just around the corner from Victoria rail station, the Cask and Glass is a popular spot with office staff requiring a post-work refresher before braving the journey home. Friendly and full of character, it's a touch on the small side, but there's plenty of space out front, and a healthy selection of Shepherd Neame ales to keep you entertained. 39–41 Palace St., SW1. ✆ **020/7834-7630.** Tube: Victoria.

Draft House Northcote ★★   For anyone serious about their ales, a visit to the Draft House is a must. Set up by the visionary Charlie McVeigh, it is an attempt to recapture all the best qualities of a British pub, and thereby create the perfect example. At any one time you'll find dozens of lagers, ales, and beers from all over the world on offer—and to help you in your quest to try them all, the Draft House is one of the few pubs in London to serve ⅓-pint measures. 94 Northcote Rd., SW11. www.draft house.co.uk. ✆ **020/7924-1814.** Train: Clapham Junction.

The Club & Music Scene
LIVE MUSIC
Every night in hundreds of venues across London, you'll find live music being played, from international superstars to those taking their first hesitant steps. Online guides such as **Spoonfed** (www.spoonfed.com) are often a good place to find leftfield events. Most small venues will allow you to purchase tickets on the night, but for larger and more popular events you may have to buy way in advance. Most venues have ticketing information on their own websites; failing that, check **SeeTickets. com, WeGotTickets.com,** or **Ticketweb.co.uk.**

Rock & Pop
Bush Music Hall ★★   One of London's most beautiful venues, this former Victorian music hall was renovated and reopened in 2001; despite its small capacity, bands and punters alike love its unique ambience. In recent years it's become a favored venue for large acts to perform one-off, often secret shows with the likes of Suede performing here in 2010 before their headline dates at the larger O2 Arena. 310 Uxbridge Rd., W12. www.bushhallmusic.co.uk. ✆ **020/8222-6955.** Tube: Shepherd's Bush.

CAMP   Set up by James Priestly, the man behind the legendary Secret Sundaze parties, the CAMP (City & Arts Music Project) lacks the niceties of other venues, but already in its short life a rough-and-ready basement has hosted some of the most anticipated gigs of recent times. Expect to hear all manner of edgy, underground music—from visiting American indie bands to homegrown dubstep and techno DJs. 70–74 City Rd., EC1. www.thecamplondon.com. ℭ020/7253-2443. Tube: Old St.

O2 Academy Brixton ★ For many indie and rock bands a night at Brixton Academy represents the measure of success. With a capacity of just under 5,000 it's one of London's most impressive venues, and that is reflected by the high caliber of artists that occupy its stage most nights. Voted best London venue by the readers of indie magazine *NME* 12 times, this former Art Deco cinema is now a rock institution. Shows at the Academy tend to sell out well in advance and ticket touts outside the venue can charge a hefty premium, but shows tend to be announced well ahead of time so look ahead and book through the venue's website if you'd like to experience one of London's premier live music venues. 211 Stockwell Rd., SW9. www.o2academy brixton.co.uk. ℭ020/7771-3000. Tube: Brixton.

Roundhouse ★★ Housed in a Victorian steam engine-repair shed, the Round-house in Camden is once again a cultural venue, presenting live music from emerging young talent, and even theatre and dance. Famous for all-night psychedelic raves in the 1960s, it reopened in 2006 and attracts a young crowd. In days of yore, Jimi Hendrix, Paul McCartney, and The Who performed here, and today it plays host to today's rising stars, urban festivals, and innovative acts. Chalk Farm Rd., NW1. www.round house.org.uk. ℭ0844/482-8008. Tube: Chalk Farm.

Union Chapel ★★★ 🖸 You'd be hard pressed to find a more beautiful setting for a concert than this 19th-century Islington church. Settle in on one of the venue's wooden pews and let yourself be awestruck by the surroundings. To suit the venue's natural ambience, music here tends toward the more reflective end of the spectrum, with folk, ambient electronica, and acoustic pop and rock particularly suited. Compton Ave., N1. www.unionchapel.org.uk. ℭ020/7359-4019. Tube: Highbury and Islington.

Wilton's Music Hall ★★ 🖸 London's oldest surviving music hall, Wilton's opened in the 1850s and was for many years one of East London's most vibrant venues, hosting all manner of bawdy entertainment. Years of neglect left the venue close to demolition, but recent efforts to secure its future has seen it become a vital part of the capital's entertainment scene. It hosts live gigs, theatre productions, and comedy events inside what is one of London's most atmospheric venues. Graces Alley, E1. www. wiltons.org.uk. ℭ020/7702-9555. Tube: Aldgate East.

Jazz & Blues

Blues Kitchen One of London's only dedicated blues bars, Camden's Blues Kitchen is the place to listen to stripped-down music from the Mississippi Delta while enjoying a plate loaded with Cajun food. Hosting DJ nights, real Blues legends from the States, and the occasional indie star looking to reconnect with their roots, a night at the Blues Kitchen is a lively alternative to the identikit indie nights that inhabit most Camden venues. 111–113 Camden High St., NW1. www.theblueskitchen.com. ℭ020/7387-5277. Admission from free to £3. Tube: Camden Town.

Café Oto 📖 Experimental is the watchword at Café Oto—on some nights the casual visitor might be forgiven for wondering if the sound coming out of the speakers is music at all, let alone jazz. For anyone open to some leftfield sonic experiences, however, Café Oto is a delight, and one of the few venues in London where acclaimed musicians can be sure to find an appreciative audience for even their most challenging works. 18–22 Ashwin St., E8. www.cafeoto.co.uk. © **020/7923-1231.** Admission £5–£10. Train: Dalston Kingsland or Dalston Junction.

Ronnie Scott's Jazz Club Inquire about jazz in London, and people immediately think of Ronnie Scott's, the European vanguard for modern jazz. Only the best English and American combos, often fronted by top-notch vocalists, are booked here. In the Main Room, you can watch the show from the bar or sit at a table, at which you can order dinner. The Downstairs Bar is more intimate. Reservations are recommended. 47 Frith St., W1. www.ronniescotts.co.uk.© **020/7439-0747.** Admission £10 £50. Tube: Leicester Sq. or Tottenham Court Rd.

Vortex ★ If Ronnie Scott's is the sanitized, tourist-friendly face of London's jazz scene, then Vortex in Dalston is the real deal, and the place where you're as likely to find yourself seated next to a jazz musician as watching them on stage. The club offers up an exciting mix of established players and up-and-coming talent, and caters for jazz fans of all persuasions, from the traditional to the more leftfield. Open 7 nights a week, the venue plays host to internationally acclaimed names, and purchasing advance tickets is always recommended. 11 Gillett Sq., N16. www.vortexjazz.co.uk. © **020/7254-4097.** Admission £8–£15. Train: Dalston Kingsland or Dalston Junction.

NIGHTCLUBS

Cable With its warren-like maze of tunnels and railway arches, the area around London Bridge has long been home to some of London's best underground clubs. This current "king of SE1" is also one of its newest arrivals: Launched in 2009 by the team who previously ran much-missed End, Cable has quickly become a byword for quality underground dance music, from house, disco, and techno through to dubstep and drum and bass. 33 Bermondsey St., SE1. www.cable-london.com. © **020/7403-7730.** Admission £5–£15. Tube: London Bridge.

Corsica Studios ★★ 🛍 Housed under the railway arches behind the Coronet, Corsica Studios harks back to the days before clubbing became corporate. While on first impressions the club may seem rather spartan, that's because those involved know that a good P.A., a dark space, and a few lights are all the best DJs need to work their magic. From techno and electronica, through to leftfield disco and experimental rock, Corsica Studios provides a haven for those seeking underground sounds. For this reason, it is regularly voted among the U.K.'s best small clubs. 5 Elephant Rd., SE17. www.corsicastudios.com.© **020/7703-4760.** Admission £5–£15. Tube: Elephant & Castle.

Fabric ★ While competitors have come and gone, Fabric continues to draw the crowds. Consistently ranked as one of the best clubs on the planet, every weekend Fabric plays host to the biggest DJs in town. On some crazed nights, at least 2,500 members of young London, plus a large percentage of international visitors, crowd into this mammoth place. It has a trio of dance floors, bars wherever you look, unisex toilets, and a sound system that you feel as much as hear. Friday nights tend to veer toward more live performances, dubstep, drum and bass, and electro music, while Saturday nights present the best techno and house DJs from around the world. Open Friday 9:30pm to 5am, Saturday 10pm to 7am. 77a Charterhouse St., EC1. www.fabric london.com.© **020/7336-8898.** Admission £15–£20. Tube: Farringdon.

The Nest ★ Dalston is a hotbed of pop-up parties in abandoned or appropriated spaces, and there are still relatively few proper venues to check out. Luckily one that is there, The Nest, is among the best around. Live events during the week usually feature bands at the cutting edge of whatever scene is current, and weekends are given over to respected techno, house, and disco DJs. With the kind of lineups you'd expect to see at Fabric (see above), not in the basement of a former furniture shop, the club is usually full by midnight. 36 Stoke Newington Rd., N16. www.ilovethenest.com. ©020/7354-9993. Admission £5–£10. Train: Dalston Kingsland or Dalston Junction.

Notting Hill Arts Club   West London has been left behind in the cool stakes in recent years, but this remains one of the hippest nighttime venues in London. Located close to the HQs of many big record labels, you can often find a music industry crowd here checking out the latest buzz bands, and Thursday night's YoYo party can see the likes of Mark Ronson take to the decks. The music is eclectic, varying from night to night—from jazz and world music through to electro, hip-hop, and indie. 21 Notting Hill Gate, W11. www.nottinghillartsclub.com. ©020/7460-4459. Admission £5–£15. Tube: Notting Hill Gate.

Plastic People ★★ 📷   For much of London's clubbing cognoscenti, a 200-capacity basement in Shoreditch is simply the best this city has to offer—and it's easy to see why. With probably the sharpest sound system in town, and a crowd who know their music, Plastic People manages to attract DJs more used to playing to parties numbered in the thousands. For dubstep, techno, or house, few other venues can compare to a night at Plastic People. 149 Curtain Rd., EC2. www.plasticpeople.co.uk. ©020/7739-6471. Admission £5–£15. Tube: Old St./Train: Shoreditch High St.

XOYO   XOYO (pronounced "X-O-Y-O") launched in 2010 to much fanfare and no little disaster, but despite an opening week that saw power cuts, closures, and general chaos, the venue has established itself as a valuable addition to London clubland. Thanks to the involvement of some top-rank promoters—such as Eat Your Own Ears and Bugged Out!—XOYO has become the place to check out exciting new bands from around the world and dance till the morning in the company of big-name DJs. 32–37 Cowper St., EC2. www.xoyo.co.uk. ©020/7490-1198. Admission £5–£15. Tube: Old St.

COMEDY CLUBS

Comedy Store   This is London's showcase for established and rising comic talent. Inspired by comedy clubs in the U.S., the venue has given many comics their start, and today a number of them are mainstream TV personalities. Visitors must be 18 and older; dress is casual. Reserve through **Ticketmaster** (© **0844/847-1637**); the club opens 1½ hours before each show. Tuesday to Sunday, doors open at 6:30pm and the show starts at 8pm; on Friday and Saturday, an extra show starts at midnight (doors open at 11pm). *Insider tip:* On Tuesday the humor is more cutting edge. 1a Oxendon St., off Piccadilly Circus, SW1. www.thecomedystore.co.uk. ©**0844/847-1728.** Admission £13–£20. Tube: Leicester Sq. or Piccadilly Circus.

99 Club   With shows running 7 nights a week, 52 weeks a year, you know the people behind the 99 Club are serious about their comedy. It's regularly voted one of the best places in London for alternative stand-up, and those on stage range from award-winning TV regulars to emerging talent. A safe bet. 28a Leicester Sq., WC2. www.99clubcomedy.com. ©**07760/488-119.** Admission £8–£16. Tube: Leicester Sq.

DANCE CLUBS & CABARET

Bathhouse 🎁   Unless you happen to work in the City, the Bathhouse isn't the easiest place to find—but trust us, it's worth the effort. This former Victorian opium den reopened in 2010 after an extensive renovation had brought it back to its decadent best. Now home to some of London's best cabaret nights—including wildly popular burlesque and rock 'n' roll sensation, the Boom Boom Club—you'll find a mixed crowd of openminded office workers and dressed-up burlesque scenesters taking in the live shows, or dancing through the night as DJs play from inside a golden birdcage. Nights change regularly at the Bathhouse, so check the website. 8 Bishopsgate Churchyard, EC2. www.thebathhousevenue.com. ✆ **020/7920-9207.** Admission £9–£45. Tube: Liverpool St.

Box Within weeks of opening Box had already generated its share of tall and scandalous stories, and seen everyone from the members of the Royal Family to popstars and models in attendance. Described as "Britain's seediest club" by the *Daily Mail,* it is fair to say that the entertainment is not for the priggish or fainthearted. Still, with some of the biggest names in cabaret gracing its stage, it's quite an experience— just expect to spend a few hundred per head for your table reservation to enjoy it to the full. 11 Walker's Court, W1. www.theboxsoho.com.✆ **020/7434-4374.** Tube: Leicester Sq.

The Gay & Lesbian Nightlife Scene

Admiral Duncan A popular, fun, and lively pub in the center of Soho, the Admiral Duncan has long been one of London's most popular gay bars, and most nights you'll find the pub packed with shot-downing regulars. Despite the fun within, the Admiral Duncan also occupies a sadder place in the history of Gay London, as the site of a bombing in 1999 that claimed the lives of three people. It's open daily from noon. 54 Old Compton St., W1.✆ **020/7437-5300.** Tube: Piccadilly Circus or Leicester Sq.

Candy Bar ★ This is the most popular lesbian bar-club in London at the moment. It has an extremely mixed clientele, ranging from butch to femme, and young to old. The design is simple, with bright colors and lots of mirrors upstairs and darker, more flirtatious decor downstairs. It's open Monday to Thursday 5 to 11:30pm, Friday and Saturday 5pm to 2am, and Sunday 5 to 11pm. Men are welcome as long as a woman escorts them. 4 Carlisle St., W1. www.candybarsoho.com.✆ **020/7494-4041**. Admission £5–£6. Tube: Tottenham Court Rd.

Dalston Superstore ★★ Cafe by day, disco bar by night, this Superstore is a welcome addition to trendy Dalston, providing a space for gays, lesbians, and their straight friends to party away from the mainstream scene. It's packed most nights with a friendly, arty, and openminded crowd, and the music is much the same as at any cutting-edge bar in this part of town, with disco, electro, and underground house normally on the playlist. 117 Kingsland High St., E8.✆ **020/7254-2273.** Train: Dalston Kingsland or Dalston Junction.

Fire One of the biggest gay clubs in London, Fire goes all night throughout the weekend, from Friday night right through to Monday morning, pumping out house and electro of various flavors to a devoted, full-on crowd. It's hot and sweaty, but not to worry … shirts soon come off at this hedonist's playground. The contrast between those staggering out of Fire on a Monday morning and commuters heading to work is one of the more surreal London sights. 34–41 Parry St., SW8. www.fireclub.co.uk.✆ **020/3242-0040.** Tube: Vauxhall.

George & Dragon A great deal of "Queer as Folk" life is shifting from Vauxhall and Soho to increasingly fashionable Shoreditch. Its epicenter is this pub where the late Alexander McQueen used to show up. London's *Evening Standard* raved, "it's possibly the best pub in the world ... ever." It's also been accused of "attracting flotsam," of being "grotty," and of looking "green and slimy." Regardless of the spin, the place is a subcultural phenomenon. Expect a kitsch decor of pink walls, a talking horse head on the wall, cowboy hats, and a sequined guitar worthy of Elvis. 2–4 Hackney Rd., E2.✆ **020/7012-1100.** Train: Shoreditch High St. or Hoxton.

Heaven This club, housed in the vaulted cellars of Charing Cross railway station, is a long-running London landmark, and one of the biggest and best-established gay venues in Britain. Reminiscent of an air-raid shelter, the club is divided into different areas, connected by a labyrinth of catwalk stairs and hallways. With the closing of the iconic Astoria, Heaven now hosts G-A-Y, on Thursdays, Fridays, and Saturdays. The biggest gay and lesbian party in the U.K. if not Europe, G-A-Y has featured performances by big name pop acts from Madonna to the Spice Girls. The Arches, Villiers St., WC2. www.heaven-london.com. *020/7930-2020.* Admission £12–£20. Tube: Charing Cross or Embankment.

Royal Vauxhall Tavern ★ The Royal Vauxhall Tavern was here long before Vauxhall became London's gay village, but even back in the late 1890s it was home to some of London's most colorful cabaret, so in some respects not too much has changed. London's oldest-surviving gay venue, the Royal Vauxhall is a much-loved institution and an essential stop-off before hitting one of the local clubs. Today it's open 7 nights a week, and you're likely to find all manner of fun inside from camp burlesque and cabaret to bingo, comedy nights, and plain old-fashioned discos. 372 Kennington Lane, SE11. www.theroyalvauxhalltavern.co.uk. *020/7820-1222.* Tube: Vauxhall.

Alternative Entertainment

ALT-CINEMA

Visiting the cinema—in central London at least—can be an expensive experience. Plus, given that mainstream Hollywood films are shown at most theatres, you could be in any city in the English-speaking world. Scratch beneath the surface, however, and you'll find alternative cinematic experiences. The **Curzon in Mayfair,** 38 Curzon St., W1 (www.curzoncinemas.com; *Ⓒ 0871/703-3989;* Tube: Green Park), caters for true cineastes with screenings of foreign and art-house films, Q&A sessions with directors, and one-off screenings of classics from the archive. Tickets usually cost around £10.

LITERARY EVENTS

A growing number of literary events have brought books out of silent libraries and into London's noisy nightclubs. The capital's premier regular event is **Book Slam** (www.bookslam.com), which takes place on the last Thursday of every month at the **Clapham Grand,** 21–25 St. John's Hill, SW11 (*Ⓒ 020/7223-6523;* Train: Clapham Junction); tickets are usually £10. Heavyweight authors such as Hanif Kureishi, Dave Eggers, and Nick Hornby have all guested alongside a variety of book-loving pop- and rockstars. Expect everything from poetry and book readings to live music and DJs.

Websites such as **Flavorpill** (www.flavorpill.com/london) and **Londonist** (www.londonist.com) carry information on forthcoming literary events.

COOL KARAOKE

There are plenty of places where enthusiastic amateurs can do terrible things to popular songs. Despite the British reputation for reserve, you'll find karaoke nights in pubs and bars all over the city, not to mention dedicated karaoke bars such as **Lucky Voice,** 52 Poland St., W1 (www.luckyvoice.co.uk; *Ⓒ 020/7439-3660;* Tube: Oxford Circus).

Alternatively, head east to **Hot Breath ★** (www.thehouseofhotbreath.com) at the Bethnal Green Working Men's Club, 44 Pollard Row, E2 (www.workersplaytime.net; *Ⓒ 020/7739-2727;* Tube: Bethnal Green), one of the funniest karaoke nights in town, running approximately monthly. Out-of-tune singing is just half the fun, so leave your inhibitions at the door and prepare to get involved in everything from synchronized dancing, through to hot dog eating competitions, while making liberal use of the dressing-up box. Tickets usually cost £5 to £10.

WHERE TO STAY

Recession? When it comes to hotel openings and revamps, the question appears to be, "What recession?" Barely a month goes by without a new boutique hotel or a multimillion-pound refurbishment being announced—London is a boomtown for accommodations.

At the cheapest and most expensive ends of the spectrum, the city's offering is hard to beat. The grand hotels of Mayfair offer the kind of gracious service and country-house ambience that are copied around the world. The more recent rise of the no-frills crashpad has been a welcome development in a city where rooms remain among the most expensive on the planet.

There are surprises in store for anyone not used to London's idiosyncratic ways, however: Air-conditioning is far from standard; the venerable age of many of London's best hotels means that rooms are smaller, and more variable, than in most modern cities; and hidden charges—especially for international phone calls and Wi-Fi access—are regrettably still common.

A recent boom in London hotel building, combined with the demands of an international clientele, means that the standard of rooms across the city is better than it has ever been. Unfortunately, it hasn't made prices any easier to swallow. An ever-increasing number of travelers coming to the city each year has found some hoteliers unembarrassed about over-charging and poor service.

London boasts some of the most famous hotels in the world—temples of luxury like **Claridge's** and the **Savoy**—but there's still a dearth of the kind of mid-range, family-run hotels that make staying in Paris or Rome such a pleasure. Even at the luxury level, you may be surprised at what you don't get. Many of the grand gems are so steeped in tradition that they lack conveniences standard in luxury hotels worldwide. The best have modernized with a vengeance, but others retain distinctly Edwardian amenities. While London has an increasing number of sleek, high-tech palaces—complete with high-end sound systems and gadget-filled marble bathrooms—these hotels frequently lack the personal service and spaciousness that characterize the grand old favorites.

The biggest change to the London hotel landscape this century has been the rise of the **boutique hotel.** The best of them offer the charm of a B&B with the facilities of much larger hotels, but sufficient numbers of very ordinary small hotels have rebranded themselves "boutique" as to make travelers wary. We've sorted the wheat from the chaff, concentrating on reasonably priced options with the best that category has to offer.

If you are on a tighter budget, there are options other than hotels. London has a tradition of families turning their homes into B&Bs, and the best of them offer a more friendly welcome than you'll find at a budget hotel. Just don't expect all of the hotelier's bells and whistles. If this appeals to you, your first stop should be the **London Bed and Breakfast Agency** (www.londonbb.com; ✆ **020/7586-2768**), a long-running agency for inexpensive accommodations in private homes costing around £30 to £100 per person per night, based on double occupancy (although some rooms cost a lot more). **London B&B** (www.londonbandb.com; © **800/872-2632** in the U.S.) offers B&B accommodations in private family residences or unhosted apartments. Homes are inspected for quality and comfort, amenities, and convenience.

Plenty of travelers have found apartments and rooms to rent through **Craigslist. org** over the last years, but an increasing number of scam artists have made it impossible to recommend. A much better bet is **AirBnB.com**, where owners rent out everything from single rooms to whole houses, but with a user-rating and verification system that discourages scammers. **Crashpadder.com** is more focused on the single-room booking, and has some real bargains. **Onefinestay.com** is another great bet for finding characterful homes to stay in—they offer space in private homes (or even whole houses) while the owners are away, but back it up with add-on hotel-style services like chefs and maids. **Housetrip.com** is a young company with excellent short-term rental properties around Europe. It's safe and reliable, and easy to use. **University Rooms** (www.londonuniversityrooms.co.uk), started by a young Cambridge University graduate, has rooms in university hostels in major university cities. Its London properties are central; all are vetted and it's very good value. Rooms are mainly available during vacations—that is, the peak traveling months of June through September. **9flats.com** has rooms in houses and apartments to rent in some of the trendiest parts of London like Shoreditch, Stratford, and Islington. Its rates are good and the information on what you are getting comprehensive. **Viveunique.com** offers more upscale lets, all personally vetted. It also offers a good bespoke service on airport transfers, theatre tickets, and more—and is great for business travel.

West End

BLOOMSBURY
Very Expensive
Chancery Court Hotel ★★   This opulent landmark 1914 building opened as a hotel in 2003, and it's retained some of the best architectural features of its Edwardian heyday while adopting cutting-edge comforts. The glamorous and exceedingly comfortable rooms are all furnished with fine linens and decorated in hues of cream, red, and blue. Some of the best are on the sixth floor, opening onto a cozy interior courtyard. The building has been used as a backdrop for such films as *Howard's End* and *The Saint* by filmmakers drawn to its soaring archways and classical courtyard.

252 High Holborn, London WC1V 7EN. www.chancerycourthotel.com. © **020/7829-9888.** Fax 020/7829-9889. 358 units. £169–£374 double. Rates include English breakfast. AE, DC, MC, V. Tube: Holborn. Parking £35. **Amenities:** 2 restaurants; 2 bars; health club & spa; concierge; room service; babysitting. *In room:* A/C, TV, minibar, hair dryer, Internet (£15 per day).

Expensive
Montague on the Gardens ★★   English country-house styling within sight of the British Museum makes the Montague a winning combination for traveling culture buffs. It's a little way back from the busy West End streets but still just a short walk from the theatres and the shopping of Oxford Street and Covent Garden. Guest rooms are individually sized and decorated; most aren't huge, but all are cozy and spotless. Some beds are four-posters, and most sport half-canopies. Bi-level deluxe king rooms feature pullout couches and would be classified as suites in many other hotels.

15 Montague St., London WC1B 5BJ. www.montaguehotel.com. ©**020/7637-1001** or 877/955-1515 in the U.S. and Canada. Fax 020/7637-2516. 100 units. £135–£175 double. AE, DC, MC, V. Tube: Russell Sq. **Amenities:** 2 restaurants; bar; fitness center; concierge; room service. *In room:* A/C, TV, fax (in some rooms), hair dryer, Wi-Fi (free).

Moderate

Arosfa ★ 👜 This tiny Georgian town house was once the home of pre-Raphaelite artist Sir John Everett Millais. Now a hotel, it's a cut above other Gower Street hotels, with fresh fruit in the rooms and black-and-white photographs on the walls. The location is prime, within walking distance of the British Museum and Theatreland, and small, neat, simple rooms have decent-sized marble bathrooms. The young staff is particularly welcoming; there's a garden at the back. An apartment sleeping six (ideal for a family) takes up the whole top floor.

83 Gower St., London WC1E 6HJ. www.arosfalondon.com. ℂ 020/7636-2115. Fax 020/7323-5141. 17 units. £70–£180 double. Rates include breakfast. MC, V. Tube: Goodge St. *In room:* TV, hair dryer, Wi-Fi (free).

Inexpensive

Thanet Hotel The family-owned Thanet no longer charges the same rates it did when it appeared in *England on $5 a Day*, but it's still an affordable option on a quiet Georgian terrace between Russell and Bloomsbury Squares. For the most part, rooms are small and adequately furnished, and some have original fireplaces. Ask for one of the refurbished rooms, and overlooking the back if you're a light sleeper. Wi-Fi is free but sometimes patchy.

8 Bedford Place, London WC1B 5JA. www.thanethotel.co.uk. ℂ 020/7636-2869. Fax 020/7323-6676. 16 units. £115 double. Rates include English breakfast. AE, MC, V. Tube: Holborn or Russell Sq. **Amenities:** Breakfast room. *In room:* TV, hair dryer, Wi-Fi (free).

KING'S CROSS
Very Expensive

St. Pancras Renaissance London Renaissance by name and a renaissance by nature, Gilbert Scott's iconic Gothic hotel stood unused for 76 years and narrowly escaped being torn down. It's been lovingly restored into an opulent reinterpretation of the golden age of railway hotels. The centerpiece is a sweeping double staircase that whisks you from the ornate vault of the lobby into luxuriously wide corridors and a maze of grand halls and intimate lounges. Attention to detail is so extraordinary— every surface gleams with Gothic ornamentation and period wallpaper—that the modern rooms, although large and perfectly serviceable, are a bit of a let-down. But this is as much spectacle as hotel; a place to sip martinis in style, explore at leisure, and plan a European adventure.

Euston Rd., London NW1 2AR. www.stpancrasrenaissance.com. ℂ 020/7841-3540. 245 units. £306–£834 double. AE, MC, V. Tube: King's Cross St. Pancras. **Amenities:** Restaurant; bar; concierge; pool; exercise room; spa; room service; valet parking (£50/day). *In room:* A/C, TV/DVD, minibar, CD player, Wi-Fi (£15/day).

Expensive

Rough Luxe ★ 👜 Just minutes from St. Pancras Station, this small boutique hotel was salvaged from the remains of one of the area's many nondescript guesthouses. Despite the setting in a row of Georgian town houses, the decor is almost industrial, resembling the interior of a warehouse art gallery. No two rooms are alike. Three units come with private bathroom, with glass-enclosed showers and "rainfall" shower heads. Decades of wallpaper and paint were peeled away, leaving distressed walls of hand-painted mosaic wallpaper and plaster. Many of the antiques found throughout were purchased at the auction of the Savoy Hotel's throwaways.

1 Birkenhead St., London WC1H 8BA. www.roughluxe.co.uk. ℂ 020/7837-5338. Fax: 020/7837-1615. 9 units (3 with bathroom). £189–£289 double. Rates include continental breakfast. AE, MC, V. Tube: King's Cross. **Amenities:** Breakfast room. *In room:* TV, hair dryer, Wi-Fi (free).

Inexpensive

Jesmond Dene Hotel   The King's Cross area is a bit of a curate's egg; unparalleled travel links—you can be in Paris or the Lake District within 3 hours—but at the cost of a scruffy, noisy district. So, hurray for the Jesmond Dene. This small but neat B&B is great value, surprisingly quiet, and renowned for friendly, helpful service. Not a place for a 2-week holiday but if you're looking for a base to explore London, that's also handy for day trips, you could do a lot worse.

27 Argyle St., London WC1H 8EP. www.jesmonddenehotel.co.uk. ℂ **020/7837-4654.** Fax 020/7833-1633. 20 rooms, some with private bathroom. £70 double without bathroom, £100 double with bathroom. AE, DC, MC, V. Tube: King's Cross. *In room:* TV, Wi-Fi (free).

COVENT GARDEN
Very Expensive

Covent Garden Hotel ★★★   The phrase we hear most often from guests who've stayed here is "expensive, but worth it." The former hospital building lay neglected for years until it was reconfigured in 1996 by hoteliers Tim and Kit Kemp—whose flair for interior design is legendary—into one of London's most charming boutique hotels. Upstairs, accessible via a dramatic stone staircase, soundproof bedrooms are furnished in English style with Asian fabrics, many adorned with hand-embroidered designs. The staff is among the friendliest and most knowledgeable in London—always useful in an area thronged with theatres, galleries, and rare bookstores.

10 Monmouth St., London WC2H 9HB. www.firmdale.com. ℂ **020/7806-1000** or 888/559-5508 in the U.S. and Canada. Fax 020/7806-1100. 58 units. £260–£365 double. AE, DC, MC, V. Tube: Covent Garden or Leicester Sq. **Amenities:** Restaurant; bar; exercise room; concierge; room service; babysitting. *In room:* A/C, TV/DVD, minibar, hair dryer, movie library, CD player, Wi-Fi (£20 per day).

One Aldwych ★★★   Hoteliers take note—One Aldwych is an object lesson in how to combine old-school London elegance with state-of-the-art facilities. Guests bask in an artfully simple layout that includes stylish minimalist furniture, bay windows, masses of flowers, and lashings of contemporary art. The bedrooms are sumptuous, decorated with elegant linens and rich colors, and accessorized with raw-silk curtains and deluxe furnishings. On Friday and Saturday evenings, and at Sunday brunch, movies play in the screening room. And, unusually for such a smart hotel, sustainability is taken seriously; the swimming pool is chlorine-free, toilets and showers use significantly less water than in most hotels, and the inhouse Axis restaurant uses local produce when possible.

1 Aldwych, London WC2B 4BZ. www.onealdwych.com. ℂ **020/7300-1000** or 800/745-8883 in the U.S. Fax 020/7300-1001. 105 units. £230–£470 double. AE, DC, MC, V. Parking £37. Tube: Temple or Covent Garden. **Amenities:** 2 restaurants; 3 bars; pool (indoor); health club; concierge; room service; babysitting. *In room:* A/C, TV/DVD, minibar, hair dryer, CD player, CD library, MP3 docking station, Wi-Fi (free).

The Savoy ★★   After a 3-year, £200 million restoration, the Savoy has settled into its role of providing glitzy, high-octane business. Updating such an iconic hotel—at various times home to Coco Chanel, Humphrey Bogart, Marlene Dietrich, Oscar Wilde, and Churchill's war cabinet—can be tricky, but here it has been a success. It's lost none of its turn-of-the-century appeal with rich fabrics and acres of gold leaf, but there's been a subtle updating to draw the 21st-century *belle monde* back to their spiritual home. The restoration has left no two rooms the same, despite their mix of Art Deco and Edwardian palettes, so ask to see your room before you move in. Us? We'll take one of the Edwardian rooms at the rear—the combination of Thames views and a real fireplace is London at its finest. The **Savoy Grill** (see p. 132) is as grand as ever.

Strand, London WC2R 0EU. www.fairmont.com/savoy. © **020/7836-4343.** Fax 020/7420-6040. 268 units. £350–£995 double. AE, DC, MC, V. Tube: Embankment or Charing Cross. **Amenities:** 3 restaurants, including Savoy Grill (see review, p. 132); 2 bars; exercise room; concierge; room service; babysitting. *In room:* A/C, TV/DVD, minibar, hair dryer, movie library, CD player, Wi-Fi (£10 per day).

Moderate
The Fielding ★ 🎁 If you remember the Fielding from the old days, you'll be delighted to hear that this favorite among theatregoers was bought four years ago and has had a much needed renovation. It is a little slice of Dickensian London in modern Covent Garden. Named after local novelist Henry Fielding, of *Tom Jones* fame, it lies on a pedestrian street still lined with 19th-century gas lamps. Rooms which differ in size are now prettily decorated in natural tones with splashes of bright color. There's no breakfast room, but no shortage of good cafes in the area.

4 Broad Court, Bow St., London WC2B 5QZ. www.thefieldinghotel.co.uk. © **020/7836-8305.** Fax 020/7497-0064. 25 units. £168–£192 double. AE, DC, MC, V. No children 12 and under. Tube: Covent Garden. *In room:* A/C, TV, hair dryer, Wi-Fi (free).

SOHO
Very Expensive
St. John Hotel ★★ 🎁 The rise of the "restaurant with rooms" continues, and this offering from much lauded caterers **St. John** (p. 145) epitomizes all that is best in this category. Right on Leicester Square, the former post-theatre eatery Manzi's has been converted into a shrine to Modern British cooking, with some cozy—and for the area, reasonably priced—rooms. Bedrooms are simple in white wood with turquoise floors, but this is a hotel for exploring—an elegant cocktail bar and great pre- and post-theatre dining should keep you from your room for a night or two at least.

1 Leicester St., London WC2H 7BL. www.stjohnhotellondon.com. © **020/3301-8020.** 15 units. £240–£330 double. AE, DC, MC, V. Tube: Leicester Sq. **Amenities:** Restaurant; bar; room service. *In room:* Wi-Fi (free).

The Soho Hotel ★★★ Entering The Soho always gets our hearts racing. The fans waiting for whichever Hollywood star is staying this week; the sleek lobby with its giant cat sculpture and hip staff; the buzz from the bar and the restaurant. *Tatler* called it "the most glamorous hotel in the world," which might be pushing it, but there's no denying it's a magnet for the glitterati. And behind the glitz it's a well-run, spacious hotel. Rooms are huge for Soho, and individually designed in granite and oak. All the famous Kemp touches can be found, from boldly striped furnishings to deep bathtubs for a late-night soak.

4 Richmond Mews, London W1D 3DH. www.firmdale.com. © **020/7559-3000** or 888/559-5508 in the U.S. and Canada. Fax 020/7559-3003. 91 units. £295–£380 double. AE, MC, V. Tube: Oxford Circus or Piccadilly Circus. **Amenities:** Restaurant; bar; exercise room; concierge; room service. *In room:* A/C, TV/DVD, hair dryer, CD player, Wi-Fi (£20 per day).

Expensive
Dean Street Townhouse ★★★ 🎁 Deep in the heart of town, this boutique hotel in a restored four-story Georgian town house is a fashionable base for exploring Theatreland and the nightlife of Soho. Formerly the home of the Gargoyle Club, its Georgian architecture has been more or less preserved. Atmosphere and location are the draw here—the price is that rooms are small even for central London, but have four-poster beds, hand-painted wallpaper, and other retro-chic touches. Amenities

from the trendy Cowshed range in the bathrooms include toothbrushes, toothpaste, and combs. Book your stay well in advance—this isn't the place for a last-minute bargain.

69–71 Dean St., London W1D 3SE. www.deanstreettownhouse.com. ✆ **020/7434-1775.** 39 units. £90–£410 double. AE, MC, V. Tube: Oxford Circus or Tottenham Court Rd. **Amenities:** Restaurant; bar. *In room:* TV/DVD, minibar, hair dryer, MP3 docking station, Wi-Fi (free).

Hazlitt's Hotel 1718 ★ ⛻ Character, character, character. Some hotels don't have it, however hard they try, but Hazlitt's has it in spades. You step from the heart of buzzing Soho into what feels like an untouched Georgian literary salon. Public areas are bookish and calm, decorated in a lived-in, 18th-century style, while the rooms mix up antiques, ancient portraits, free-standing baths, and fireplaces. Soho's a 24-hour kind of area, so unless you're a very heavy sleeper, opt for a room facing the back.

6 Frith St., London W1D 3JA. www.hazlittshotel.com. ✆ **020/7434-1771.** Fax 020/7439-1524. 30 units. £179–£255 (plus VAT) double. AE, DC, MC, V. Tube: Leicester Sq. or Tottenham Court Rd. **Amenities:** Concierge; room service. *In room:* A/C, TV, minibar, hair dryer, Wi-Fi (free).

Inexpensive
Z Hotel Soho ★ ⛻ The team behind Z Hotels, all with a hotel background, have got it absolutely right. What they offer is 5-star quality at 3-star prices, challenging the cheap chains. What is sacrificed is space: rooms are small, your suitcase goes under the bed, and clothes hang from hooks on the walls. Rooms are stylish, with triple-glazed windows, good bathrooms with frosted glass walls and top toiletries, goose feather pillows, top-quality bed linen, a chic wood and marble décor, and a 42-in. TV with satellite channels. And it's all bang in the middle of Soho.

17 Moor St., London W1D 5AP. www.thezhotels.com. ✆ **020/3551-3700.** 85 units. £102 double. AE, MC, V. Tube: Oxford Circus or Tottenham Court Rd. **Amenities:** 2 bars; cafe. *In room:* A/C, TV/DVD, hair dryer, MP3 docking station, Wi-Fi (free).

MAYFAIR
Very Expensive
Claridge's ★★★ No hotel epitomizes the rebirth of London's grand old hotels quite like Claridge's. Sure, it still boasts the Art Deco finery and a history stretching back to 1812, but Gordon Ramsay's flagship restaurant and two hip bars have made it a favorite with the fashion and media sets. Much of its '30s style remains, and the hotel's strong sense of tradition and old-fashioned "Britishness" are also intact; in spite of the gloss and the hip clientele, afternoon tea here remains a quintessentially English experience. The rooms are the most varied in London, ranging from the costly and stunning Brook Penthouse—complete with a personal butler—to the less expensive, so-called superior queen rooms with queen-sized beds.

Brook St., London W1A 2JQ. www.claridges.co.uk. ✆ **020/7629-8860.** Fax 020/7499-2210. 203 units. £339–£659 double. AE, DC, MC, V. Parking £50. Tube: Bond St. **Amenities:** 2 restaurants; 2 bars; health club & spa; concierge; room service; babysitting. *In room:* A/C, TV/DVD, minibar, hair dryer, Wi-Fi (free).

The Connaught ★★★ Built as a home-away-from-home for the denizens of Britain's toniest country houses, no hotel has updated the classic British style with quite as much élan as The Connaught. Leaded skylights, liveried doormen who seem to know every guest's name, and shady, masculine bars and restaurants are the picture of restrained 21st-century glamour, while the rooms are spacious Edwardian gems. Traditionalists opt for the Old Wing but we prefer the New Wing—it's where The Connaught's mix of the old and new is most successful.

Carlos Place, London W1K 2AL. www.the-connaught.co.uk. ℂ **020/7499-7070.** Fax 020/7495-3262. 122 units. £339–£369 double. AE, DC, MC, V. Parking £48. Tube: Green Park. **Amenities:** 2 restaurants; 2 bars; health club & spa; concierge; room service; babysitting. *In room:* A/C, TV/DVD, minibar, hair dryer, MP3 docking station, Wi-Fi (free).

The Dorchester ★★★   Few hotels have the time-honored experience of "the Dorch," which has maintained a tradition of fine comfort and cuisine since it opened in 1931. Breaking from the neoclassical tradition, the most ambitious architects of the era designed a building of reinforced concrete clothed in terrazzo slabs. The Dorchester boasts guest rooms outfitted with Irish linen sheets on comfortable beds, plus all the electronic gadgetry you'd expect, and double- and triple-glazed windows to keep out noise, along with plump armchairs, cherry wood furnishings, and, in many cases, four-poster beds piled high with pillows.

53 Park Lane, London W1A 2HJ. www.thedorchester.com. ℂ **020/7629-8888** or 800/727-9820 in the U.S. Fax 020/9629-8080. 250 units. £265–£695 double. AE, DC, MC, V. Parking £50. Tube: Hyde Park Corner or Marble Arch. **Amenities:** 5 restaurants, including Alain Ducasse (see review, p. 128); 3 bars; health club & spa; concierge; room service; babysitting. *In room:* A/C, TV/DVD, minibar, hair dryer, CD player, Internet (£20 per day).

45 Park Lane ★★★   The double-height entrance and restaurant beyond provide the first "wow" in the Dorchester Collection's 2011 opening. Public rooms are Art Deco-inspired with angular lights, marble floors, leather seating, and silk curtains. Bedrooms are equally sumptuous, large for London, and kitted out with bespoke desks, huge beds, and the crispest linen. Some of the upper floor rooms have balconies; all look over Hyde Park and beyond. And it's the extras that make 45 Park Lane outstanding, like the media room with 103-in. 3-D screen and surround sound for your latest film—or the family photo album. This is high-end London at its finest.

45 Park Lane, London W1K 1PN. www.45parklane.com. ℂ **020/7493-4545** or 800/727-9820 in the U.S. Fax 020/7319-7455. 45 units. From £395 (plus VAT) double. AE, DC, MC, V. Parking £50. Tube: Hyde Park Corner. **Amenities:** Restaurant; bar; fitness center; use of the Dorchester's spa (see below); concierge; room service. *In room:* A/C, TV/DVD, minibar, hair dryer, iPad, Wi-Fi (free).

Expensive

The Chesterfield Mayfair ★★   Only in super-expensive Mayfair could the Chesterfield be considered a bargain, but it serves up that ritzy grand hotel feeling at a better price than The Connaught or The Dorchester (see above). The hotel, once home to the Earl of Chesterfield, still sports venerable features that evoke an air of nobility, including richly decorated public rooms featuring woods, antiques, fabrics, and marble. The secluded Library Lounge is a great place to relax, and the glassed-in conservatory is a good spot for tea. The guest rooms are dramatically decorated and make excellent use of space—there's a ton of closet and counter space.

35 Charles St., London W1J 5EB. www.chesterfieldmayfair.com. ℂ **020/7491-2622** or 877/955-1515 in the U.S. and Canada. Fax 020/7491-4793. 107 units. £160–£375 double. AE, DC, MC, V. Tube: Green Park. **Amenities:** Restaurant; bar; use of nearby health club; concierge; room service; babysitting. *In room:* A/C, TV/DVD, minibar (suites only or on request), hair dryer, Wi-Fi (free).

ST. JAMES'S
Very Expensive
Haymarket Hotel ★★★   The understated Georgian entrance, right by the Haymarket Theatre, hides a surprisingly bold and colorful hotel. Public areas are a riot of turquoise, fuchsia, mango, and even acid green while rooms are classy in black and white. Although completely modernized and perhaps the most sophisticated small hotel in the city, many satisfying proportions of the original 19th-century John Nash

architecture remain. Bedrooms are sumptuously elegant with fine linens and the latest amenities. There's even an indoor pool lounge.

1 Suffolk Place, London SW1Y 4HX. www.firmdale.com. 📞 **020/7470-4000** or 888/559-5508 in the U.S. and Canada. Fax 020/7470-4004. 50 units. £265–£340 double. AE, DC, MC, V. Tube: Charing Cross or Piccadilly Circus. **Amenities:** Restaurant; bar; pool (indoor); exercise room; concierge; room service. *In room:* A/C, TV/DVD, hair dryer, CD player, Wi-Fi (£20).

The Stafford ★★★   Famous for its American Bar, its St. James's address, and the warmth of its Edwardian decor, the century-old Stafford attracts a tasteful, discerning clientele. All the guest rooms are individually decorated, reflecting the hotel's origins as a private home. Many singles contain queen-sized beds. Some of the deluxe units offer four-posters that will make you feel like Henry VIII. Much has been done to preserve the original style of these rooms, including preservation of the original A-beams on the upper floors, but you can bet that no 18th-century visitor ever slept with the stereo systems and quality furnishings that these rooms feature.

16–18 St. James's Place, London SW1A 1NJ. www.kempinski.com/london. 📞 **020/7493-0111.** Fax 020/7493-7121. 105 units. £290–£740 double. AE, DC, MC, V. No parking. Tube: Green Park. **Amenities:** Restaurant; bar; exercise room; concierge; room service; babysitting. *In room:* A/C, TV/DVD, hair dryer, CD player, Wi-Fi (free).

MARYLEBONE
Very Expensive
The Langham, London ★★★   Halfway between the high-end shopping of Bond Street and the calm and beauty of Regent's Park, The Langham is an opulent and practical choice in the West End. Guest rooms are attractively furnished and comfortable, featuring French provincial furniture and red oak trim. The bathrooms, and the English breakfast, are bigger and better than most. The hotel is within easy reach of Mayfair as well as Soho's restaurants and theatres. Sure, it's expensive; but we love The Langham for its beguiling mix of old and new: Any place that's home to the Art Deco elegance of afternoon tea's birthplace, the Palm Room, *and* a spa as sleek as the Chuan Spa water spa is always going to win hearts.

1C Portland Place, London W1B 1JA. http://london.langhamhotels.co.uk. 📞 **020/7636-1000** or 800/223-6800 in the U.S. Fax 020/7323-2340. 380 units. From £215 double. AE, DC, MC, V. Tube: Oxford Circus. **Amenities:** 2 restaurants; bar; health club & spa; pool (indoor); concierge; room service. *In room:* A/C, TV/DVD, minibar, hair dryer, Wi-Fi (free for checking e-mail, then £20 per day).

Expensive
Durrant's Hotel ★   For quintessential English charm in the "fairly sensible" price range, Durrant's is our choice. This historic hotel with its Georgian-detailed facade is snug, cozy, and traditional—you could invite the Queen here for tea. Over the 100 years that they have owned the hotel, the Miller family has incorporated several neighboring houses into the original structure. A walk through the pine-and-mahogany-paneled public rooms is like stepping back in time. Rooms have elaborate cove moldings and comfortable furnishings, including good beds. For a fresh, country chintz look, and more space, ask for a refurbished room.

26–32 George St., London W1H 5BJ. www.durrantshotel.co.uk. 📞 **020/7935-8131.** Fax 020/7487-3510. 92 units. £216–£326 double; £265 family room for 3. AE, MC, V. Tube: Bond St. or Baker St. **Amenities:** Restaurant; bar; concierge; room service; babysitting. *In room:* A/C (in most), TV, hair dryer, Wi-Fi (£10 per day).

Mandeville Hotel ★★   Marylebone Village is one of London's best-kept secrets—a charming warren of independent shops, neighborhood restaurants, and busy bars within walking distance of both high-end Bond Street shopping and the calm of Regent's Park. The once-staid Mandeville is now a hot address—one of London's leading interior designers, Stephen Ryan, was brought in to restyle the lobby, restaurant, and bar. Bedrooms too have had a makeover and are thankfully free of the chintz of some Marylebone hotels—rich autumnal tones and masculine furnishings are the order of the day here.

Mandeville Place, London W1U 2BE. www.mandeville.co.uk. © **020/7935-5599.** Fax 020/7935-9588. 142 units. £127–£339 double. AE, DC, MC, V. Tube: Bond St. **Amenities:** Restaurant; bar; exercise room; concierge; room service. *In room:* A/C, TV, minibar (in some), hair dryer, Wi-Fi (£13 per day).

The Sumner ★ 🎁 It's no wonder this Georgian town-house hotel is so popular—boutique hotels on quiet streets just minutes from Hyde Park and Oxford Street are as rare as hen's teeth. It retains much of its original architectural allure: The standard rooms are midsized and attractively furnished, but you can also choose deluxe rooms with artwork and better furnishings. All guest rooms are designer-decorated and luxuriously appointed, and there's an elegant sitting room with a working fireplace.

54 Upper Berkeley St., London W1H 7QR. www.thesumner.com. © **020/7723-2244.** Fax 087/0705-8767. 20 units. £210–£258 double. Rates include breakfast. AE, MC, V. Tube: Marble Arch. **Amenities:** *In room:* A/C, TV, fridge, minibar, hair dryer, Wi-Fi (free).

Moderate

Hart House Hotel ★ ☺ Hart House is a long-standing favorite of Frommer's readers. In the heart of the West End, this well-preserved Georgian mansion lies within walking distance of lots of shopping and dining. The rooms—furnished in a combination of styles, ranging from antique to modern—are spick-and-span, each one with its own character. Favorites include no. 7, a triple with a big bathroom and shower; no. 3 is large, sleeps four, and is at the back. For singles, no. 11 is a brightly lit aerie. Hart House has long been known as a good, safe place for traveling families, with many triple rooms and interconnecting units—and that remains true today.

51 Gloucester Place, London W1U 8JF. www.harthouse.co.uk. © **020/7935-2288.** Fax 020/7935-8516. 15 units. £145–£185 double; £150–£225 triple. Rates include English breakfast. MC, V. Tube: Marble Arch or Baker St. *In room:* TV, hair dryer, Wi-Fi (£5 per stay).

Inexpensive

Lincoln House Hotel ★ Some of the rooms may be small, but Lincoln House makes up for it with character and a central location that feels like a house rather than a hotel. Built in the late 18th century, it retains traditional charm and a delightful maritime theme—and is just a 5-minute walk from Marble Arch or Hyde Park. Midsize bedrooms are completely modernized, but decorated in a traditional fashion. All have showers; some have baths as well. The downstairs restaurant serves a good-value simple dinner as well as breakfast. Half of the hotel is air conditioned.

33 Gloucester Place, London W1U 8HY. www.lincoln-house-hotel.co.uk. © **020/7486-7630.** Fax 020/7486-0166. 24 units. £109–£129 double. AE, DC, MC, V. Tube: Marble Arch. **Amenities:** Restaurant. *In room:* TV, fridge, hair dryer, Wi-Fi (free).

South Bank

EXPENSIVE

London Bridge Hotel ★★ There's no doubt the London Bridge Hotel puts you right in the thick of things—the river, Borough Market, London's newest and tallest skyscraper, and the South Bank are all just seconds away, and efficient Tube and train links put the rest of London within easy reach too. A former telephone exchange building, this 1915 structure was successfully recycled into a bastion of comfort and charm. Bedrooms are completely up to date and offer homelike comfort and plenty of amenities. Rooms in the front have double-glazed windows to cut down on noise.

8–18 London Bridge St., London SE1 9SG. www.londonbridgehotel.com. ℂ **020/7855-2200.** Fax 020/7855-2233. 140 units. £143–£384 double. Children 11 and under stay free in parent's room. AE, DC, MC, V. Tube: London Bridge. **Amenities:** 2 restaurants; bar; access to nearby health club; babysitting. *In room:* A/C, TV/DVD, minibar, hair dryer, Wi-Fi (free).

West London
PADDINGTON & BAYSWATER
Moderate

Mornington Hotel ★   There's nothing flashy about the Mornington, but a 2010 refurbishment, easy access to London's parks or Oxford Street shopping, and staff who win plaudits from guests time and again, make it the best bet in the area. Just north of Hyde Park and Kensington Gardens, the hotel has a Victorian exterior and Scandinavian-inspired decor. Renovated guest rooms are tasteful and comfortable. Touches like a 24-hour reception and bar, a guest computer with printer (free access), and in-room iron and ironing board are typically thoughtful.

12 Lancaster Gate, London W2 3LG. www.morningtonhotel.co.uk. ℂ **020/7262-7361** or 800/633-6548 in the U.S. Fax 020/7706-1028. 70 units. £89–£199 double. AE, DC, MC, V. Tube: Lancaster Gate. **Amenities:** Bar; exercise room. *In room:* TV, hair dryer, Wi-Fi (free).

Inexpensive

Garden Court Hotel   We wish there were more hotels like this in London: It's been family run for more than 50 years, is meticulously managed, and is set on a tranquil Victorian garden. Most accommodations are spacious, with good lighting, generous shelf and closet space, and comfortable furnishings. If you're in a room without a bathroom, you'll generally have to share with the occupants of only one other room. There are many homelike touches throughout the hotel, including ancestral portraits and silk flowers. Rooms open onto the square in front or the gardens at the rear.

30–31 Kensington Gardens Sq., London W2 4BG. www.gardencourthotel.co.uk. ℂ **020/7229-2553.** Fax 020/7727-2749. 32 units, 24 with bathrooms. £85–£135 double. Rates include English breakfast. MC, V. Tube: Bayswater. *In room:* TV, hair dryer, Wi-Fi (£2.50 per day or £5 per stay).

St. David's Hotel   Another very reasonable garden square B&B, now completely renovated by the family that has been running it since 1980. Only a 2-minute walk from Paddington Station, the hotel was built when Norfolk Square knew a grander age. The bluebloods are long gone, but the area is still safe and recommended. The refurbished bedrooms are well maintained and furnished comfortably, a few with original features like fireplaces and wooden shutters. Some bathrooms are very small, but you can't beat the price. The cooked breakfast always wins plaudits.

14–20 Norfolk Sq., London W2 1RS. www.stdavidshotels.com. ℂ **020/7723-4963.** Fax 020/7402-9061. 70 units. £65 double without bathroom, £80 double with bathroom. Rates include English breakfast. AE, MC, V. Tube: Paddington. *In room:* TV, Wi-Fi (free).

Tudor Court Hotel   Originally built in the 1850s and much restored and altered, this Victorian structure is now a small hotel of tranquility and comfort, a 2-minute walk from Paddington Station. Bedrooms are compact to midsize, completely restored, and traditionally furnished, with single, double (or twin), triple, and family rooms available. Pod bathrooms with shower are well maintained and spotlessly clean. Family owned since 1989, the hotel really is concerned with guests' comfort, making this one a winner—and the breakfast, cooked by the owner to order, is a great draw.

10–12 Norfolk Sq., London W2 1RS. www.tudorcourtpaddington.co.uk. © **020/7723-6553/5157.** Fax 020/7723-0727. 38 units. £99–120 double. Rates include English breakfast. AE, DC, MC, V. Tube: Paddington. *In room:* TV, hair dryer, Wi-Fi (free).

NOTTING HILL
Moderate

The Main House ★★ *🍴*   The term "home-from-home" is bandied around all too frequently when hotels are discussed, but The Main House deserves the tag. Each guest gets a high-ceilinged floor of this Notting Hill town house to themselves, decorated in rare style from on-the-doorstep Portobello Road market—think gilded mirrors, watercolors of elegant 1930s' women, and antiques. Extra little touches make this place unique. A wonderfully cheap deal on the chauffeur service, cellphones to keep your call costs down, early morning tea or coffee in the room, and gleaming wood floors swathed in animal skins (reflecting owner Caroline Main's time as an explorer).

6 Colville Rd., London W11 2BP. www.themainhouse.co.uk. © **020/7221-9691.** 4 suites. £120–£150 suite. MC, V. Parking £2.50 per hour. Tube: Notting Hill Gate. **Amenities:** Bikes; access to health club & spa; room service; Internet (free). *In room:* TV, hair dryer.

Umi Hotel ★ ☺   Location, location, location. Given its proximity to Hyde Park, Portobello Road, and hip (plus very pricey) Notting Hill's browsing and dining, this charming little hotel is a true find. It's located in side-by-side row houses on a quiet square. Don't expect luxury—although the decor is modern and inviting, it's pretty basic. But that's just fine, given that the basics are done so well. Rooms are small but spotless and breakfast includes fresh and Fairtrade produce. Added bonus: The hotel offers both single and family rooms that can sleep four. Ask for one of the rooms at the front for the gorgeous view over the square's garden.

16 Leinster Sq., London W2 4PR. www.umihotellondon.co.uk. © **020/7221-9131.** Fax 020/7221-4073. 117 units. £160–£185 double. AE, DC, MC, V. Tube: Bayswater or Queensway. **Amenities:** Restaurant; bar; cafe; concierge. *In room:* TV, Wi-Fi (£3 per hour).

Inexpensive

Gate Hotel   This antiques-hunters' favorite is the only hotel along the length of Portobello Road—and because of rigid zoning restrictions, it will probably remain the only one for many years to come. It has seven cramped but cozy bedrooms over its four floors, and be prepared for some very steep stairs. Rooms are color coordinated, with a hint of style, and have such extras as full-length mirrors and built-in wardrobes. Especially intriguing are the wall paintings that show the original Portobello Market: Every character looks plucked straight from a Dickens novel.

6 Portobello Rd., London W11 3DG. www.gatehotel.co.uk. © **020/7221-0707.** Fax 020/7221-9128. 7 units. £85–£105 double. Rates include continental breakfast (served in room). AE, MC, V. Tube: Notting Hill Gate or Holland Park. **Amenities:** Room service. *In room:* TV/DVD, hair dryer, Wi-Fi (£10 per stay).

Southwest London
WESTMINSTER
Very Expensive

Corinthia Hotel London ★★★   Opened in 2011 as Corinthia Hotels' flagship property, the triangular-shaped building has retained the huge spaces, marble columns, and ceilings of its sumptuous past as the Metropole Hotel. Bedrooms are among the largest in London, decorated in natural colors; each has a media hub with international sockets and a Nespresso machine; bathrooms have TV screens wall-mounted by the tub. The Bassoon bar recalls the '30s Jazz Age, with a bar that ends in a grand piano. The flagship Espa Life on four floors aims to keep you young, beautiful, and fit in what must be London's most glamorous spa.

Whitehall Place, London SW1A 2BD. www.corinthia.com. © **020/7930-8181** or 877-842-6269 in the U.S. and Canada. Fax 020/7321-3001. 294 units. £339–£680 (plus VAT) double. AE, DC, MC, V. Tube: Embankment. **Amenities:** 2 restaurants; 2 bars; exercise room; spa; concierge; room service. *In room:* A/C, TV/DVD, minibar, hair dryer, Wi-Fi (free).

Royal Horseguards Hotel ★★ The Royal Horseguards is in a remarkable building. Once the National Liberal Club, built in the 1880s, it was also the headquarters of the Secret Service during World War I. All political ties have been severed, but the building still has some remarkable original architectural features like large spaces and high ceilings, a magnificent staircase, and glazed patterned tiling. Bedrooms are large and comfortable and the whole package still a little gentlemen's club-like in feel. The views are magnificent and the restaurant—a converted library—harks back to the hotel's illustrious past. A stay here adds up to a very special London experience.

2 Whitehall Court, London SW1A 2EJ. www.guoman.com/theroyalhorseguards. © **0871/376-9033** or 0845/305-8332. Fax 0871/376-9133 or 0845/305-8371. 282 units. £250–£480 double. AE, DC, MC, V. Tube: Embankment. **Amenities:** Restaurant; bar; exercise room; concierge; room service. *In room:* A/C, TV/DVD, minibar, hair dryer, Wi-Fi (free).

VICTORIA, BELGRAVIA & PIMLICO
Very Expensive

41 Hotel ★★★ 🛅 This is the very antidote to chain hotels—30 individually designed rooms, packed with romantic touches like open fireplaces and scented candles, all within walking distance of Hyde Park and Buckingham Palace. 41 Hotel is best suited to couples or those traveling alone—especially women. Public areas feature an abundance of mahogany, antiques, fresh flowers, and rich fabrics. Read, relax, or watch TV in the library-style lounge, where a complimentary continental breakfast and afternoon snacks are served each day. Guest rooms are individually sized, but all feature elegant black-and-white color schemes and beds with Egyptian-cotton linens.

41 Buckingham Palace Rd., London SW1W OPS. www.41hotel.com. © **020/7300-0041** or 877/955-1515 in the U.S. and Canada. Fax 020/7300-0141. 28 units. £275–£295 double. Rates include welcome drink, breakfast, afternoon snacks, and evening canapés. AE, DC, MC, V. Tube: Victoria. **Amenities:** Bar; access to nearby health club; concierge; room service; babysitting. *In room:* A/C, TV/DVD, hair dryer, CD player, MP3 docking station, Wi-Fi (free).

The Goring ★★★ This place is the very best of London's family-run hotels. In truth it has everything going for it; a location in the heart of royal London, close to Buckingham Palace, the royal parks, and Westminster Abbey; a staff that knows its stuff; and an air of splendor. Guest rooms offer all the comforts, including luxurious bathrooms with extra-long tubs and marble walls, and the beds are among the most comfortable in town. Queen Anne and Chippendale are the decor styles, and maintenance is of the highest order. Rooms overlooking the garden are best. Business travelers may baulk (though many of us will cheer) at a ban on cellphones and laptops in public areas, where you can take afternoon tea (see review, p. 149).

15 Beeston Place, London SW1W 0JW. www.thegoringhotel.com. © **020/7396-9000.** Fax 020/7834-4393. 69 units. £420–£850 double. AE, DC, MC, V. Parking £45. Tube: Victoria. **Amenities:** Restaurant; bar; access to nearby health club; concierge; babysitting. *In room:* A/C, TV/DVD, hair dryer, movie library, CD player, CD library, Wi-Fi (£5.25/hr. or £15.75 per day).

Moderate

B&B Belgravia ★ In its first year of operation (2005), this elegant town house won a Gold Award as "the best B&B in London." It richly deserved it. Design, service, quality, and comfort paid off. The prices are also reasonable, the atmosphere in this massively renovated building is stylish, and the location is grand: Just a 5-minute walk from Victoria Station. The good-size bedrooms are luxuriously furnished. Late risers may want to avoid Room 1—it's above the breakfast room and isn't the quietest.

64–66 Ebury St., London SW1W 9QD. www.bb-belgravia.com. © **020/7259-8570.** Fax 020/7259-8591. 17 units. £135–£145 double; £165–£175 family room. Rates include English breakfast. AE, MC, V. Tube: Victoria. *In room:* TV, movie library, Wi-Fi (free).

Inexpensive

Morgan House Hotel This Georgian house has a convenient address, and its rooms are often fully booked all summer. Guest rooms are individually decorated and have orthopedic mattresses. Many are small to midsize, while others are large enough to house up to four people. Hallway bathrooms are well maintained and adequate for guests who don't have their own private facilities. A hearty English breakfast is served in a bright, cheerful room, and there's a small courtyard open to guests.

120 Ebury St., London SW1W 9QQ. www.morganhouse.co.uk. © **020/7730-2384.** 11 units, 4 with private bathroom. £84 double without bathroom; £108 double with bathroom. Rates include breakfast. MC, V. Tube: Victoria. **Amenities:** Breakfast room. *In room:* TV, hair dryer, Wi-Fi (free).

KNIGHTSBRIDGE
Very Expensive

The Berkeley ★★★ The Berkeley's winning formula remains intact—a modern building decorated in grand Art Deco syle but with the kind of understated, helpful service that sets it apart from stuffier neighbors. Inside you'll find an environment inspired by French classical design, but with a contemporary edge. Each room offers high-end style, but most elegant of all are the suites, many of which have luxurious, marble-and-tile-trimmed baths. Request one of the refurbished rooms; some of the older units are looking a little tired.

Wilton Place, London SW1X 7RL. www.maybournehotelgroup.com or www.the-berkeley.co.uk. © **020/7235-6000** or 800/599-6991 in the U.S. and Canada. Fax 020/7235-4330. 214 units. £299–£329 double. AE, DC, MC, V. Tube: Knightsbridge or Hyde Park Corner. **Amenities:** 3 restaurants, including Marcus Wareing (see p. 140); 2 bars; health club & spa; concierge. *In room:* A/C, TV/DVD, hair dryer, CD player, CD library, iPad (free in suites), Wi-Fi (free).

The Capital ★★★ A luxury shopper's and gourmet's delight, The Capital manages, year after year, to combine boutique hotel charm with the amenities you'd expect in a far larger establishment. Only 45m (148 ft.) from Harrods department store, this family-run town-house hotel is also at the doorstep of London's "green lung," Hyde Park. Famed designer Nina Campbell furnished the spacious bedrooms with sumptuous fabrics, art, and antiques. David Linley, nephew of the Queen, assisted in the design. The liveried doorman standing outside has welcomed royalty, heads of state, and international celebrities.

22 Basil St., London SW3 1AT. www.capitalhotel.co.uk. © **020/7589-5171.** Fax 020/7225-0011. 49 units. £300–£400 double. AE, DC, MC, V. Parking £30. Tube: Knightsbridge. **Amenities:** Restaurant; bar; access to nearby health club; concierge; babysitting. *In room:* A/C, TV, minibar, hair dryer, Wi-Fi (free).

Expensive

30 Pavilion Road ★★ 🛍 A leafy rooftop restaurant, understated country-house ambience, and the most British of personal service—it's no surprise that many of the guests of this converted pumping station are repeat visitors. At this Knightsbridge oasis, you press a buzzer and are admitted to a freight elevator that carries you to the third floor. Upstairs, you'll encounter handsomely furnished rooms with antiques, tasteful fabrics, comfortable beds (some with canopies), and often a sitting alcove. Some of the tubs are placed right in your room.

30 Pavilion Rd., London SW1X 0HJ. www.searcys.com/30-pavilion-road. © **020/7584-4921.** Fax 020/7823-8694. 10 units. £229 double; £310 family room. Rates include breakfast. AE, DC, MC, V. Tube: Knightsbridge. **Amenities:** Room service. *In room:* A/C, TV, Wi-Fi (free).

KENSINGTON
Very Expensive
The Milestone ★★★ A firm favorite with Frommer's readers, The Milestone epitomizes everything good about the classic London hotel—understated elegance, service that regularly goes that extra mile, cozy public rooms awash with fresh flowers, dark woods, antique furnishings, and fabric wallcoverings, and a location close to some genuine London icons. Guest rooms and suites are spread over six floors and vary in size, decor, and shape (a few rooms are a bit small). For an iconic view, request a room overlooking Kensington Palace and Kensington Gardens.

1 Kensington Court, London W8 5DL. www.milestonehotel.com. © **020/7917-1000** or 877/955-1515 in the U.S. and Canada. Fax 020/7917-1010. 62 units. £250–£360 double. AE, DC, MC, V. Tube: High St. Kensington. **Amenities:** Restaurant; bar; health club; concierge; room service; babysitting. *In room:* A/C, TV/DVD, minibar, hair dryer, CD player, MP3 docking station, Wi-Fi (free).

Expensive
Parkcity Hotel ★★★ Entering the Parkcity is always a surprise—it's a modern, sleek-lined wolf in historical sheep's clothing. The staid Victorian frontage gives way to a thoroughly up-to-date hotel. Much better equipped than many of the hotels in the area (it has a business center and an exercise room), and boasting a staff that always seems to go the extra mile for guests, the hotel is building quite a repeat customer base. All rooms are bright and airy with a pleasingly modern sheen, but in the summer avoid the rooms overlooking the patio if you want peace and privacy.

18–30 Lexham Gardens, London W8 5JE. www.theparkcity.com. © **020/7341-7090.** Fax 020/7835-0189. 62 units. £149–£219 double. AE, MC, V. Tube: Gloucester Rd. **Amenities:** Bar; exercise room; concierge; room service. *In room:* AC, TV, minibar, CD player, Wi-Fi (in some rooms, free).

Inexpensive
Easyhotel ♦ This is the hotel that brought budget airline thinking to London's accommodation scene. Rooms are tiny (if spotlessly clean) at 6 to 7 sq. m (65–75 sq. ft.), with most of the space taken up by standard double beds. Ask for a room with a window to ease the claustrophobia. There are flatscreen TVs in every unit, but it costs an extra £5 fee to use the set. Still if all you're looking for in a hotel is somewhere to rest your head it's hard to argue with the price. Housekeeping service costs an optional £10 per day, there is no elevator, and checkout time is 10am. You must book by credit card through the hotel website.

14 Lexham Gardens, London W8 5JE. www.easyhotel.com. © **020/7706-9911.** 47 units. £39–£99 double. MC, V. Tube: High St. Kensington or Earl's Court. *In room:* A/C, TV, Wi-Fi (£10 per day).

CHELSEA
Very Expensive
Draycott Hotel ★★★ Everything about the Draycott reeks of British gentility, style, and charm. Guests are greeted like old friends when they enter by a staff that manages to be both hip and cordial. The hotel took its present-day form when a third brick-fronted town house was added to a pair of interconnected town houses that had

been functioning as a five-star hotel since the 1980s. That, coupled with tons of money spent on English antiques, rich draperies, and an upgrade of those expensive infrastructures you'll never see, including security, has transformed this place into a gem. Bedrooms are outfitted differently, each with haute English style and plenty of fashion chic. As a special feature, the hotel serves complimentary drinks—tea at 4pm daily, champagne at 6pm, and hot chocolate at 9:30pm.

26 Cadogan Gardens, London SW3 2RP. www.draycotthotel.com. ℂ **020/7730-6466** or 800/747-4942 in the U.S. and Canada. Fax 020/7730-0236. 35 units. £255–£345 (plus VAT) double. AE, DC, MC, V. Tube: Sloane Sq. **Amenities:** Bar; access to nearby health club & spa; room service. *In room:* A/C, TV/DVD, minibar, CD player, MP3 docking station, Wi-Fi (free).

San Domenico House ★★ Reclining in a four-poster bed, antiques scattered around the room, it's hard to believe that you're technically in a B&B. A redbrick Victorian town house that has been tastefully renovated in recent years, San Domenico House is in the heart of Chelsea near the shops of Sloane Square and the King's Road. Bedrooms range from small to spacious, but all are opulently furnished with flouncy draperies, tasteful fabrics, and sumptuous beds. Our favorite spot is the rooftop terrace; with views opening onto Chelsea, it's ideal for a relaxing breakfast or drink.

29 Draycott Place, London SW3 2SH. www.sandomenicohouse.com. ℂ **020/7581-5757** or 800/324-9960 in the U.S. and Canada. Fax 020/7584-1348. 16 units. £255–£335 double. AE, DC, MC, V. Tube: Sloane Sq. **Amenities:** Room service; babysitting. *In room:* A/C, TV/DVD, minibar, hair dryer, Wi-Fi (free).

SOUTH KENSINGTON & EARL'S COURT
Expensive
The Rockwell ★★ 🎁 Proof that London high style doesn't always come with a high price tag. This independently owned bastion of deluxe comfort occupies a converted Georgian manse in South Kensington. Its bedrooms are tricked out with oak furnishings and Neisha Crosland wallpaper, each crafted to combine traditional English aesthetics with modern design. The bedrooms are large and inviting and dressed with the finest Egyptian cotton, feather pillows, and merino wool blankets. All are bright and airy with large windows and simple lines, but we prefer the garden units with their own private patios.

181–183 Cromwell Rd., London SW5 OSF. www.therockwell.com. ℂ **020/7244-2000.** Fax 020/7244-2001. 40 units. £162–£210 double. AE, DC, MC, V. Tube: Earl's Court or Gloucester Rd. **Amenities:** Restaurant; bar; access to nearby exercise room; room service. *In room:* A/C, TV, minibar, Internet (free).

Moderate
Base2Stay 🍃 Visitors who value their independence, and bang for their buck, welcomed the opening of Base2Stay—no-frills apartment accommodation with no hidden extras. What you get are stylish, comfortably furnished rooms with small kitchenettes. The cheapest rooms contain bunkbeds for two, and suites can be made by way of interconnecting rooms. Living may be stripped to the basics, but this is no hostel, as there is a 24-hour reception as well as daily maid service. Its green credentials are impeccable too.

25 Courtfield Gardens, London SW5 OPG. www.base2stay.com. ℂ **020/7244-2255** or 800/511-9821 in the U.S. Fax: 020/7244-2256. 67 units. £122 bunk beds for 2; £97–£220 double. AE, MC, V. Tube: Earl's Court. **Amenities:** Wi-Fi (free). *In room:* A/C, TV, kitchenette.

Inexpensive
Henley House ★ 🍃 This B&B stands out from the pack around Earl's Court—and it's better value than most. The redbrick Victorian row house is on a communal

fenced-in garden that you can enter by borrowing a key from the reception desk. The decor is bright and contemporary; a typical room has warmly patterned wallpaper, chintz fabrics, and solid-brass lighting fixtures. The staff members take a keen interest in the welfare of their guests and are happy to take bewildered newcomers under their wing, so this is an ideal place for London first-timers.

30 Barkston Gardens, London SW5 0EN. www.henleyhousehotel.com. ✆ **020/7370-4111.** Fax 020/7370-0026. 21 units. £75–£159 double. Rates include breakfast. AE, DC, MC, V. Tube: Earl's Court. *In room:* TV, hair dryer, Wi-Fi (free).

The City, Shoreditch & Clerkenwell

VERY EXPENSIVE

Montcalm London City ★★   In the mid-18th century, the former brewery which houses the new Montcalm was London's largest beer producer. Today its huge vaulted ceilings and cast-iron columns take you back to the industrial past. Rooms have been cleverly converted; colors are browns and greens and, alongside all the tech you'd expect, each room has an aroma machine with different scents. The rooms in **London City Suites** opposite the main hotel have kitchenettes for longer stays. It may seem somewhat remote at weekends, but it's very near the Barbican (see p. 166) and a short walk from Spitalfields (p. 154).

52 Chiswell St., London EC1Y 4SD. www.themontcalmlondoncity.co.uk. ✆ **020/7614-0100.** Fax 020/7374-2577. 235 units. £99–£350 double. AE, DC, MC, V. Tube: Moorgate. **Amenities:** 2 restaurants; 2 bars; health club & spa; concierge; room service. *In room:* A/C, TV, minibar, hair dryer, MP3 docking station, Wi-Fi (free).

The Zetter ★★★   It was only a matter of time before a hotel blended the edgy Shoreditch scene with the creature comforts demanded by City types. Many of the features of an original Victorian warehouse were retained, as tradition was blended with a chic, urban modernity. Bedrooms, ranging from small to midsize, are spread across five floors, and open onto balconies that circle an atrium. The refurbishment was done with real concern for the environment—recycled timber and bricks in the construction, efficient heating and cooling systems, and "smart" rooms that turn off heating and lighting when not in use, all contribute to a low carbon footprint. Ask for a room at the rear—they back onto a quiet square.

St. John's Sq., 86–88 Clerkenwell Rd., London EC1M 5RJ. www.thezetter.com. ✆ **020/7324-4444.** Fax 020/7324-4445. 59 units. Mon–Thurs £222–£342 double; Fri–Sun £185–£342 double. AE, DC, MC, V. Tube: Farringdon. **Amenities:** Restaurant, Bistrot Bruno Loubet (see review, p. 144); bar; concierge; room service. *In room:* A/C, TV/DVD, CD player, MP3 docking station, Internet (free).

The Zetter Townhouse ★★★ 🏠   In sharp contrast to the contemporary Zetter (see above), the Zetter Townhouse occupies two 18th-century town houses in a large square. Behind the elegant facade there's a delightful, very chic, quirky, and slightly tongue-in-cheek hotel. You walk into a bar, crowded with a jumble of objects accumulated by an invented Great Aunt Wilhemina. It's relaxed, fun, comfortable, and inescapably cool in feel. Bedrooms are delightful with retro Roberts radios and antique furniture. Book no. 4 if you fancy a four-poster decorated with Union Jacks.

49–50 St. John's Sq., London EC1V 4JJ. www.thezettertownhouse.com. ✆ **020/7324-4567.** Fax 020/ 7324-4456. 13 units. £246–£294 double. AE, DC, MC, V. Tube: Farringdon. **Amenities:** Bar; room service. *In room:* A/C, TV/DVD, MP3 docking station, Internet (free).

EXPENSIVE

The Rookery ★ 🏠   Quirky, eccentric, and laden with a sense of the antique, The Rookery is a great choice for travelers who want a hotel with the atmosphere of

Dickens' or Dr. Johnson's London. Opened in the late 1990s, it salvaged three of the few remaining then-derelict antique houses in Clerkenwell. The result is an oasis of crooked floors, labyrinthine hallways, and antique accessories and furnishings that manage to mix the fun with the functional. Bedrooms are charming and quirky, furnished with carved 18th- and 19th-century bed frames, and lace or silk draperies.

Peter's Lane, Cowcross St., London EC1M 6DS. www.rookeryhotel.com. © **020/7336-0931.** Fax 020/7336-0932. 33 units. £179–£255 (plus VAT) double. AE, DC, MC, V. Tube: Farringdon. **Amenities:** Concierge; room service. *In room:* A/C, TV, minibar, Wi-Fi (free).

Shoreditch Rooms ★★ 🛅 Fitting perfectly into the once grungy, now thoroughly chic surroundings of Shoreditch, this venture is as young and hip as you'd expect. The industrial space, shared with Cowshed Pharmacy, is made to feel more like a club than a hotel. And in fact, most people use the hotel to gain access to adjoining members-only, ultra-fashionable Shoreditch House with its rooftop restaurants, swimming pool, and bars. But you're not shortchanged on the rooms: They're a decent size with kingsize beds, simply and sparsely furnished with a retro-style telephone, DAB radio, and open-drawer dresser. Colors are fresh; there's sisal matting on the floor and slatted wooden walls, rather New England in feel.

Ebor St., London E1 6AW. www.shoreditchhouse.com. © **020/739-5040.** 26 units. £60–£265 double. AE, MC, V. Tube: Liverpool St. or Old St. **Amenities:** 2 restaurants; bar; exercise room. *In room:* TV, minibar, hairdryer, Wi-Fi (free).

MODERATE
The Fox & Anchor ★ 🛅 The traditional English pub just got hip. Entering from the Smithfield meat market, you'd be forgiven for thinking this was just a great little inn—brass fittings, etched glass, and acres of mahogany—but upstairs are six classy rooms. Wood-floored and modern, and kitted out with high-end TVs, sound systems, and huge free-standing baths, they're more glamorous than your usual room above a pub. The meat market location has its pros and cons. Con: It can get a little noisy. Pro: Breakfast is a carnivore's dream.

115 Charterhouse St., London EC1M 6AA. www.foxandanchor.com. © **020/7550-1000.** Fax 020/7250-1300. 6 units. £115–£205 double. Rates include English breakfast. AE, DC, MC, V. Tube: Barbican or Farringdon. **Amenities:** Restaurant; bar. *In room:* TV, minibar, Wi-Fi (free).

INEXPENSIVE
The Hoxton ★ 🍴 The appeal of The Hoxton is straightforward—reasonable prices and quality service in a district best known for hotels with prices out of the range of those of us without an expense account. It's not just room rates that are competitive: 5p-a-minute calls to North America and supermarket prices for the minibar food are proof that budget airline tactics can work in a hotel. Of course there are downsides; the price means bedrooms are utilitarian and none too roomy, and booking in advance is vital. The Hoxton's popularity as a Shoreditch post-club crashpad also means it can be noisy at the weekends; but for a reasonably priced stay at the heart of the Shoreditch scene, there's no better option.

81 Great Eastern St., London EC2A 3HU. www.hoxtonhotels.com. ©**020/7550-1000.** Fax 020/7550-1090. 208 units. £69–£299 double. Rates include breakfast. AE, DC, MC, V. Tube: Old St. Amenities: Restaurant; bar; access to nearby exercise room (£7). In room: TV, fridge, hair dryer, Wi-Fi (free).

East London
EXPENSIVE
The Boundary ★ With Terence Conran, interior design supremo, at the helm you'd expect something rather special from this converted East End warehouse, and

you wouldn't be disappointed. The 17 rooms are a design junkie's dream, many boasting pieces specially created for the hotel, alongside chunky, reclaimed bathroom suites. And we were pleasantly surprised to see that, unlike in many new boutique hotels, rooms are spacious and airy. Plus there's enough going on downstairs (and up) to make this somewhere you won't want to leave. There's a rococo French restaurant in the basement, a roof terrace for barbecues in the summer, and a wonderful little bakery-cafe for lazy weekend breakfasts.

2–4 Boundary St., London E2 7DD. www.theboundary.co.uk. ✆ **020/7729-1051.** Fax 020/7729-3061. 17 units. £170–£260 (plus VAT) double. AE, DC, MC, V. Tube: Liverpool St. or Old St. **Amenities:** 3 restaurants, including Albion (see review, p. 146); bar; room service. *In room:* TV, minibar, iPad, Wi-Fi (free).

Town Hall Hotel ★★ There were sharp intakes of breath when this grand hotel opened in 2010 on an ordinary Bethnal Green side street. An imposing design hotel, with one of the hippest young chefs doing the food, this far east? The gamble has paid off, and London's East End finally has the luxury accommodations it needed. Rooms are somber and clean-lined, with beautiful mid-century design pieces. Viajante restaurant is the hottest ticket in town, but you can get a taste of the chef's superb cooking at the more casual, walk-in **Corner Room** restaurant. The smart pool and spa are a rare treat for London, too.

8 Patriot Sq., London E2 9NF. www.townhallhotel.com. ✆ **020/7871-0460.** Fax 020/7160-5214. 98 units. £162–£192 double. AE, DC, MC, V. Tube: Bethnal Green. **Amenities:** 2 restaurants, including Viajante (see review, p. 147); bar; indoor pool; exercise room; spa. In room: A/C, TV/DVD, hair dryer, Wi-Fi (free).

INEXPENSIVE

Avo ★ 👔 Nothing sums up the gentrification of East London like the story of the charming, small Avo boutique B&B hotel. It was a general shop and post office, until a supermarket opened next door. So the family turned their property into a stylish small hotel. Rooms' contemporary design with lots of wood, black tiles, and subtle lighting is tempered with fine Egyptian cotton sheets and luxurious fabrics sourced from India. Sparkly bathrooms are a cut above average and feature Elemis toiletries.

82 Dalston Lane, London E8 3AH. www.avohotel.com. ✆ **020/3490 5061.** 6 units. £79–£99 double. Rates include breakfast. MC, V. Train: Dalston Junction. *In room:* TV/DVD, MP3 docking station, Wi-Fi (free).

Tune Hotel 🗲 Tune's appeal lies in its great location in the middle of trendy Spitalfields, simple but spotlessly clean rooms (some without windows, so check when you book), power shower in the pod bathrooms, and a straightforward pricing policy. You pay for the room, then add on items like towels (£1.50), use of TV, and so on. It feels a little like a hostel, but a very friendly one. There's a coffee machine and snacks, and the wonderful bonus of a large garden. It's popular; there's another at 118–120 Westminster Bridge Rd., SE1 (✆ **020/7633-9317**), and more openings planned for 2013.

13–15 Folgate St., London E1 6BX. www.tunehotels.com/uk. ✆ **020/7456-0400.** Fax 020/7456-0409. 183 units. £35–£95 double. AE, MC, V. Tube: Old St. *In room:* A/C, TV (£3 per day, £10 per stay), hair dryer (£1), safe (£2), Wi-Fi (£1.50/hr. or £3/day).

THE THAMES VALLEY & THE CHILTERNS

by Stephen Keeling

The rich landscapes of the Chilterns and Thames Valley are rooted in 1,000 years of English tradition. Much of the tourist buzz comes from the region's connections with English high society: Royal castles, racecourses, rowing galas, and Britain's poshest university town. Yet it's also the home of innovative restaurants, dynamic local theatre, and a network of cycle paths and hiking trails rooted firmly in the 21st century.

5

SIGHTSEEING   **Windsor Castle** is still home to the Royal Family, a place to enjoy the pageantry of the daily Guard Mounting ceremony (or to even see the Queen herself). Upriver, the ancient university town of **Oxford** is dripping with history, elaborate medieval architecture, and a vibrant student population that gives it a surprisingly cosmopolitan atmosphere. Touring the nearby **Chilterns,** you can visit the cottage where John Milton composed poetry, or the village where Roald Dahl created his most beloved characters.

EATING & DRINKING   In a region with such a storied past, ancient pubs and fine English ales take center stage. Grab a pint at Oxford's **White Horse,** or sample craft beers in St. Albans, the home of the Campaign for Real Ale. The region's more creative, contemporary side is on show in a host of Michelin-starred institutions; dine on snail porridge at Heston Blumenthal's **Fat Duck,** or modern French cuisine at **Raymond Blanc's** exalted restaurants.

HISTORY   The area has a rich history. Travel back to Roman times at **St. Albans,** or take a peek into the lives of the English nobility at **Blenheim** and **Woburn.** You can meditate on the roots of freedom at **Runnymede,** where King John signed the Magna Carta, and wander the corridors of **Eton,** England's oldest school.

ARTS & CULTURE   Fuelled by its famous university, Oxford is also the cultural capital of the region, with a range of plays, performances, and concerts almost every night. Take in some Shakespeare at the **Oxford Playhouse,** or a high-quality classical recital at the **Sheldonian,** before

wandering over to the **Jericho Tavern** for a late-night folk concert. Art lovers can linger over the Old Masters at the **Christ Church Picture Gallery,** or head south to the thoughtful showcase for modern painter Stanley Spencer.

THE best TRAVEL EXPERIENCES IN THE THAMES VALLEY & THE CHILTERNS

- **Taking a ghostly tour in Oxford:** Oxford isn't just dreaming spires, old libraries, and colleges; it has ghosts too. Bill Spectre's Oxford Ghost Trails is an entertaining introduction to the creepy side of the city, a walking tour that takes in plenty of supernatural stories and sights. See p. 214.
- **Cruising on the Thames:** England's most-celebrated river is best experienced from the water. Jump on a boat trip at Windsor, Oxford, or Henley, or take the plunge and charter your own vessel; in a week you can cruise from the outskirts of London all the way to the City of Dreaming Spires. See p. 198.

- **Hiking the Ridgeway:** The Ridgeway National Trail runs for 87 miles from the Wiltshire Downs to the top of the Chilterns at Ivinghoe Beacon. The trail follows a prehistoric track through a bucolic landscape of rolling hills and beech forests, perfect for a day or more of easy hiking. See p. 230.
- **Punting the River Cherwell:** An hour or two of punting on a lazy summer's day in Oxford is as English as taking afternoon tea, though admittedly not as easy. Experts glide through the water like Venetian gondoliers, but be warned—it's lots of fun but harder than it looks. See p. 219.
- **Dining Tudor style at Hatfield House:** It is a touch touristy, but the Hatfield Banquets are tasty, entertaining, and a genuine attempt to open a window into the world of Elizabethan dining. See p. 238.

WINDSOR ★ & ETON

21 miles W of London

Windsor is a charming, largely Victorian town, with lots of brick buildings and a few remnants of Georgian architecture. All this is completely overshadowed of course by its great castle, which dominates the area like a giant crown of stone. **Windsor Castle** has been the home of the royal family since the reign of Henry I some 900 years ago, and despite the inevitable crowds this is a sight you should not miss; the State Apartments are especially lavish, adorned with some exceptional paintings from the royal collection.

Just across the Thames via the pedestrian-only Windsor Bridge, **Eton** is much smaller, essentially one narrow high street of mostly Georgian structures, exclusive shops, and pubs leading up to Britain's most exclusive private school.

Essentials

GETTING THERE Trains make the 35-minute trip from Paddington Station in London (First Great Western) to Windsor & Eton Central (opposite the castle entrance) every 20 to 30 minutes or so from around 5am to 11pm, with one change

---

Trips Along the Thames

Touring this historic waterway is still possible on foot or by boat. Stretching for 184 miles, the **Thames Path ★★** is a national trail that follows the river from its source, in the Cotswolds, through Oxford, Henley, and Windsor all the way to London's Docklands. It usually takes a minimum of 10 days (with plenty of pubs and B&Bs along the way), but you can also tackle smaller sections. For the less-energetic, boats glide along the river, offering a languid alternative to the road. **Salter's Steamers** (www.salterssteamers.co.uk; ℂ **01865/ 243421**) runs services in segments between Staines and Oxford, via Abingdon, Reading, Henley, Marlow, Windsor, and Maidenhead from late May to mid-September. Most segments cost around £6–10 one-way. If you fancy the role of captain yourself, contact **Kris Cruisers** in Datchet (www.kriscruisers.co.uk; ℂ **01753/543930**). The outfitter rents the largest fleet of fully equipped boats on the Thames, containing between two and eight berths. From Datchet, you can travel upstream to Windsor and Eton and on to Henley and Oxford. Prices range from £668 to £2125 per week.

at Slough. Trains run at similar intervals for the 1-hour trip from Waterloo Station direct to Windsor & Eton Riverside Station (a short walk from the castle). Standard one-way tickets are £9 from Paddington and £9.10 from Waterloo.

VISITOR INFORMATION   The **Royal Windsor Information Centre** is at the Old Booking Hall, Windsor Royal Shopping Centre on Thames Street, in the center of town (www.windsor.gov.uk; ✆ **01753/743900**). It is open Monday to Friday 9:30am to 5pm (to 5:30pm May–Aug), Saturday 9:30am to 5pm, and Sunday 10am to 4pm. It can also help with last-minute ticket offers for the Theatre Royal Windsor.

ORGANIZED TOURS   The tourist office can put you in touch with a **Blue Badge** guide (www.rendezvousguides.co.uk; ✆ **01628/823999**) to lead you on a **walking tour** of the town; in summer, tours usually depart every Saturday and Sunday at 11:30am. The cost depends on the number of people and the length of the tour, but is usually £6–7 per person. Advance booking is essential.

 City Sightseeing Open Top Bus Tours (www.city-sightseeing.com; ✆ **01708/866000**) makes 45-minute loops of Windsor and Eton with 11 hop-on, hop-off stops (mid-Mar–mid-Nov daily 10am–5pm; mid-Nov–mid-Mar Sat–Sun, public holidays only). Tickets, valid for 24 hours, are £10.50 for adults, £5 for children 5 to 15, and free for children 4 and under.

Exploring the Area

Eton College ★★ HISTORIC SITE   Eton is home to arguably the most famous public school in the world (non-Brits would call it a private school). The school was founded by Henry VI in 1440, and since then 20 prime ministers have been educated here, as have such literary figures as George Orwell, Aldous Huxley, Ian Fleming, and Percy Bysshe Shelley. Other notable students include Prince William, second in line to the throne, and David Cameron, elected prime minister in 2010. The real highlight inside is the Perpendicular Gothic **College Chapel,** completed in 1482, with its remarkable 15th-century wall paintings and reconstructed fan vaulting.

 The history of Eton College is depicted in the **Museum of Eton Life,** located in vaulted wine cellars under College Hall (originally used as a storehouse by the college's masters). The displays include a turn-of-the-20th-century boy's room, schoolbooks, and canes used by senior boys to apply punishment—the brutal flogging that characterized much of the school's history. Note that admission to the school and museum is by **guided tour only:** unless you have a group and reserve in advance, the only tours open to the public depart at 2pm and 3:15pm. If the school is closed you can take photos from the outside and make do with a visit to the **Eton College Gift Shop,** on the High Street, open daily 11am–4pm (closed late Dec–Jan).

Keats Lane, Eton. www.etoncollege.com. ✆ **01753/671000.** Admission £7 adults, £6 seniors and children 8–14, free for children 7 and under. Group tours: Mid-Mar–mid-Apr and early July–early Sept daily 10:30am–4:30pm; late Apr–June and early Sept–early Oct Wed and Fri–Sun 1:30–4:30pm. Public tours at 2pm and 3:15pm only (tickets at Eton College Gift Shop). Eton may close for special occasions; call ahead. Take a train from Paddington Station to Windsor (see "Getting There," above). If you go by train, you can walk from the station to the campus. By car, take the M4 to exit 5 to go straight to Eton. ***Insider tip:*** Parking is difficult, so we advise turning off the M4 at exit 6 to Windsor; you can park here and take an easy stroll past Windsor Castle and across the Thames footbridge. Follow Eton High Street to the college.

Windsor Castle ★★★   Looming high above the town, Windsor Castle is an awe-inspiring site, an enormous hulk of stone dating back to the days of William the Conqueror. The castle was originally constructed in wood in the 1080s; Henry II

Even if you don't see the Queen in Windsor, the **Changing of the Guard ★** here offers more pageantry than the London version. The guard marches through the town, stopping traffic as it wheels into the castle to the tunes of a full regimental band; when the Queen is not here, a drum-and-pipe band is mustered. From April to July, the ceremony takes place Monday to Saturday at 11am. The rest of the year, the guard is changed at 11am on alternate days. It's best to call (**℡ 020/7766-7304**) for a schedule.

started to rebuild it in stone in the 12th century and was the first monarch to live at Windsor. The history and art here are undeniably impressive, but what really draws the crowds is the association with the royal family; this is no ruin or museum, but one of the three homes of Queen Elizabeth II. Indeed, Windsor is the world's largest inhabited castle and the Queen is often in residence, especially at weekends (when the royal standard flies). Getting a glimpse is not that hard, as the town's hoteliers often have advance warning of when Her Majesty comes and goes.

Tours of the interior are self-guided, but we recommend that you take a free guided tour of the castle precincts (10:15am–2:15pm every 30 min.). Guides are very well informed and capture the rich historical background of the castle. You should also definitely grab one of the free **audioguides** at the entrance, as not much is labeled inside the castle.

Once you've entered the castle via St. George's Gate, the tour route leads along the battlements, past the iconic **Round Tower ★** (open Aug–Sept only, when you can climb the 200 steps to the top), and on to the **Queen Mary's Dolls' House ★ ☺**. A palace in perfect miniature, the Dolls' House was given to Queen Mary in 1923. It was a gift of members of the royal family, and designed by Sir Edwin Lutyens on a scale of 1 to 12. It is a miniature masterpiece; each room is exquisitely furnished, and every item is made exactly to scale. Working elevators stop on every floor, and there is running water in all five bathrooms.

Next door the **Drawings Gallery ★★** shows revolving exhibitions of material from the Royal Library, an exceptional collection that includes the world's finest ensemble of Leonardo Da Vinci drawings (over 600), and around 80 drawings by Hans Holbein (mostly of members of the Tudor court).

Beyond here lies the **State Apartments ★★★**, a series of lavish rooms (still used for ceremonial and state functions), loaded with rare artwork. The route begins at the aptly named Grand Staircase and Grand Vestibule, smothered with swords and suits of armor—look for the exotic items captured from Tipu Sultan in Mysore (India) in 1799. Art takes centerstage in the following series of rooms, with several works by Rubens and William Dobson—"the lost genius of British art"—adorning the King's Drawing Room. In the relatively modest King's Dressing Room is Rembrandt's self-portrait, as well as Breugel's *Massacre of the Innocents*. The Queen's Dressing Room boasts Van Dyck's lauded triple portrait of Charles I. The King's Dining Room, with its Gobelin tapestries, is the most spectacular space, while more Van Dyck portraits of Charles I adorn the Queen's Ballroom, along with the famous image of the young children of the soon-to-be executed king.

The elegant **Semi-State Rooms ★★** (open Oct–Mar only) were created by George IV in the 1820s for his personal use. Seriously damaged by fire in 1992, they were returned to their former glory five years later, with the immaculately restored **St. George's Hall** once again the setting for formal banquets. The **Crimson Drawing Room** is evocative of the George IV's flamboyant taste, with its crimson silk damask hangings and sumptuous art, while a suit of armor belonging to Henry VIII stands in the **Lantern Lobby** (where the fire started).

The final section of the castle before the exit is **St. George's Chapel** ★★★ (daily 10am–4pm; www.stgeorges-windsor.org; ✆ **01753/848885**), a perfect expression of the Medieval Perpendicular style and containing the tombs of 10 sovereigns. The present St. George's was founded in 1475 by Edward IV, on the site of the original Chapel of the Order of the Garter. You first enter the nave, which contains the tomb of George V (1936) and Queen Mary (1953). Just off the nave in the Urswick Chapel, the Princess Charlotte memorial provides an ironic touch; if she had survived childbirth in 1817, she, and not her cousin Victoria, would have ruled the British Empire. In the north nave aisle is the tomb of George VI (1952), the speech-impaired monarch featured in the movie *The King's Speech,* joined by Queen Elizabeth the Queen Mother and Princess Margaret in 2002. The nearby altar contains the remains of Edward IV (1483), while the Edward IV "Quire," with its imaginatively carved 15th-century choir stalls, evokes the pomp and pageantry of medieval days. Look up here to admire Henry VIII's lavish Tudor wooden oriel window. The vault beneath the choir contains the beheaded Charles I (1649), along with Henry VIII (1547) and his third wife, Jane Seymour (1537; the only one who provided him a son). On the way out you'll pass the tombs of Henry VI (reinterred here in 1484) and Edward VII (1910), Queen Victoria's son.

Castle Hill, Windsor. www.royalcollection.org.uk. ✆ **01753/831118** for recorded information. Admission £17 adults, £15.50 students and seniors, £10.20 children 5–17, free for children 4 and under, £44.75 family of 5 (2 adults and 3 children 16 and under); when State Apartments are closed: £9.30 adults, £8.25 students and seniors, £6.20 children 5–17, £25.25 family of 5. Mar–Oct daily 9:45am–5:15pm; Nov–Feb daily 9:45am–4:15pm.

Where to Eat

After a tour of the castle, plenty of visitors end up in the **Crooked House of Windsor,** 51 High St. (www.crooked-house.com; ✆ **01753/857534**), for afternoon tea. This classic tearoom occupies a creaky old house dating back to 1718 that really does lean to one side. Food can be hit-and-miss and prices (predictably) high, but the teas (sets £8.25–£38), Victoria sponge cake, and quirky historic atmosphere can make for an enjoyable visit. It's open daily 9:30am–5:30pm. For something more upscale, try

Windsor by Boat

The most appealing way to see the area around Windsor is from the water. **French Brothers, Ltd.,** Clewer Boathouse, Clewer Court Road, Windsor (www.boat-trips.co.uk; ✆ **01753/851900**) run a variety of informative **boat tours** up the Thames from Windsor Promenade, Barry Avenue, from 40-minute to 2-hour round-trips (£5.50–£8.80 for adults, £2.75–£4.40 for children 5 to 15). In addition, there's a 45-minute tour from Runnymede on board the *Lucy Fisher,* a replica of a Victorian paddle steamer. It passes Magna Carta Island, among other sights, and costs £5.50 for adults, £2.75 for children. The boats offer light refreshments and have a well-stocked bar; the decks are covered in case of an unexpected shower.

the **Tower Brasserie & Tea Room** (✆ 01753/863426) inside the Harte & Garter Hotel on the High Street. It also offers Sunday roast dinners (£15.50–£22.50), and a decent fish and chips for £13.

Cornucopia Bistro ★★ FRENCH   Justly regarded as the best deal in town, this French restaurant is usually full, so book ahead if you can. The dining room is simple and perennially under-staffed (though service is always friendly), but this is all about the exquisite food: Think perfectly steamed mussels, homemade venison and rosemary pâté, pan-fried partridge, buttery lamb shank, and top-notch wine. Set lunch menus (which change weekly) are a real bargain at £9.90 to £12.90 for two to three courses.

6 High St., Windsor. www.cornucopia-bistro.co.uk. ✆ **01753/833009.** Reservations recommended. Main courses £9.95–£22.95. AE, MC, V. Mon–Thurs noon–2.30pm and 6–9.30pm; Fri–Sat noon–2:30pm and 6–10pm; Sun noon–2:30pm.

Thames View CONTEMPORARY ENGLISH/CONTINENTAL   This pricey hotel restaurant, overlooking the river, is Windsor's most elegant, possessing garden terraces, a conservatory, and a dining room designed a bit like a greenhouse. For starters, try the tongue-tingling foie gras parfait or wild garlic soup. The main courses are all good, but stand-outs include the roasted sea trout, goat cheese and red onion tart, and crispy Gressingham duck. Take a walk by the river to feed the swans after your meal.

Sir Christopher Wren Hotel, Thames St., Windsor. www.sirchristopherwren.co.uk. ✆01753/442400. Main courses £15–27; lunch: 2 courses £25.50; 3 courses £31.50. AE, DC, MC, V. Daily 12:30–2:15pm and 6:30–9:45pm.

Watermans Arms PUB FARE   Just over the bridge in Eton, this Tudor pub, built in 1542, is a firm student favorite (next to the Eton College Boat House). In addition to the real ales from the local Windsor & Eton Brewery, there's classic pub food: traditional fish and chips; sausage, onion gravy, and mash; and traditional English ploughman's lunch. Best of all is the beef and Guinness pie.

Brocas St., Eton. www.watermans-eton.com. ✆ **01753/861001.** Main courses £6.50–£12.95. MC, V. Daily 11:30am–11:30pm.

Shopping

Windsor Royal Shopping, the shopping center at the main railway station (www.windsorroyalshopping.co.uk; ✆ **01753/797070**), has a concentration of shops, mostly the usual chains like Crabtree & Evelyn but also an arts and crafts section with locally owned **Simply Windsor Gifts** (www.simplywindsorgifts.co.uk; ✆**07799/622649**). Also here is **Hardy's Original Sweet Shop** (✆**01753/854242;** Mon–Sat 9am–6pm, Sun 11am–5pm), a Victorian-style confectionary, with big jars crammed with traditional sweets.

A colorful traditional English perfumery, **Woods of Windsor,** 50 High St. (www.woodsofwindsor.co.uk; ✆ **01753/868125**), dates from 1770. It offers soaps, shampoos, scented drawer liners, and hand and body lotions, all prettily packaged in pastel-floral and bright old-fashioned wraps.

At **Billings & Edmonds,** 132 High St., Eton (www.billingsandedmonds.co.uk; ✆ **01753/861348**), you may think you've blundered into a time warp. This distinctive clothing store supplies school wear, suits made to order, and a complete line of cufflinks, shirts, ties, and accessories.

The **Windsor Farm Shop ★** ▮ Datchet Rd. (B3021), Old Windsor (www.windsorfarmshop.co.uk; ✆ **01753/623800**) sells produce from the Queen's estates, including pheasants and partridges bagged at royal shoots. The meat counter is

Bray: Fat Ducks & Fine Dining

Just a couple of miles upstream from Windsor, **Bray,** population less than 5,000, is the unlikely home of two of only four restaurants in the U.K. to have been awarded three Michelin stars. For once the hype really is justified at **The Fat Duck ★★★**, High Street (www.thefatduck.co.uk; ✆ **01628/580333;** Tues–Sat noon–2pm and 7–9:30pm, Sun noon–2pm), home of culinary sorcerer Heston Blumenthal. Who said that ice cream can't be made of crab, or that mashed potatoes can't be mixed with lime jelly? The snail porridge is a tasty sensation, equaled by the salmon poached in licorice and powdered Anjou pigeon. Reservations months in advance are essential. Blumenthal also owns the **Hind's Head** pub ★ (www.hindshead bray.com; ✆ **01628/626151**) across the road, offering cheaper deals at lunchtime. The **Waterside Inn ★★★** (www.waterside-inn.co.uk; ✆ **01628/620691;** Wed–Sun noon–2pm and 7–10pm) on nearby Ferry Road is helmed by the indomitable Alain Roux, where the equally beautiful, crafted food will blow you away.

especially awesome, with its cooked hams and massive ribs of beef. It's open Monday to Saturday 9am to 5pm and Sunday 10am to 4pm.

Entertainment & Nightlife

Except for pub life, Windsor is fairly quiet at night. The chic **Browns Bar & Brasserie,** The Promenade, Barry Avenue (www.browns-restaurants.co.uk; ✆ **01753/831976**), on the river is packed with drinkers on Thursday and Friday nights thanks to its enticing outdoor areas, while the **Carpenters Arms,** 4 Market St., (✆ **01753/863739**), is a more traditional pub in the center of town, dating back to 1518.

The major cultural venue is **Theatre Royal,** Thames Street (www.theatreroyal windsor.co.uk; ✆ **01753/853888**), with a tradition of putting on plays that goes back 2 centuries. This is one of the finest regional theatres in England, often drawing first-rate actors from London's West End. The box office is open Monday to Saturday from 10am to 8pm (call the phone number above for bookings). Performances are Monday to Saturday at 8pm, with matinees on Thursday at 2:30pm and Saturday at 4:45pm. Most tickets cost between £11 and £30.

Where to Stay
EXPENSIVE
Macdonald Windsor Hotel ★★   Opened in 2010 in the heart of Windsor, the Macdonald is the top choice in town, with plush, comfy rooms, hearty breakfasts, and even under-floor heating in the bathrooms for those chilly English winters. The Georgian town house was given an artful makeover by award-winning interior designer Amanda Rosa, blending contemporary style with original Georgian fittings.

23 High St., Windsor, Berkshire SL4 1LH. www.macdonaldhotels.co.uk/windsor. ✆ **0844/879-9101.** 120 units. £145–£360 double. Breakfast £15. AE, DC, MC, V. Parking £25. Children 12 and under stay free in parent's room. **Amenities:** Restaurant; bar; room service. *In room:* A/C, TV, minibar, Wi-Fi (free).

The Oakley Court ★★   Built beside the Thames by a Victorian industrialist, the castle-like Oakley Court is hard to match for historic ambience and classical English country style. Today it's affiliated with the Principal Hayley hotel chain. The building's jutting Gothic gables and bristling turrets have appeared in several classic Hammer horror movies, as well as *The Rocky Horror Picture Show*. Although the grandest public areas are in the main house, most rooms are in a trio of well-accessorized modern wings that ramble through the estate's 37 acres of parks and gardens. Most suites offer four-poster beds and views of the River Thames.

Windsor Rd., Water Oakley, Windsor, Berkshire SL4 5UR. www.principal-hayley.com. ℂ **01753/609988.** Fax: 01628/637011. 118 units. £116–£275 double; £216–£375 suite. AE, DC, MC, V. Take the river road, A308, 3 miles from Windsor toward Maidenhead. Free parking. **Amenities:** Restaurant; bar; indoor heated pool; 2 outdoor tennis courts; health club; Jacuzzi; sauna; room service; babysitting. *In room:* A/C, TV, minibar, hair dryer, Wi-Fi (£4.99 per hr. or £9.99 per 24 hr.).

The Runnymede-On-Thames ★★ Because of the dearth of top-of-the-line hotels within Windsor itself, more and more guests are seeking out this hotel and spa on the shady banks of the Thames between Windsor and Staines. Rooms are smart, spacious, and stylish, with plenty of extras (free Wi-Fi, bathrobes, and so forth), and the on-site spa is one of the finest in the greater London area, offering exercise programs and healthful treatments, plus a splendid outdoor pool. The contemporary buffet-style **Leftbank** restaurant is perfect for drinks and dinner, opening onto a tranquil section of the Thames.

Windsor Rd., Egham, Surrey TW20 0AG. www.runnymedehotel.com. ℂ **01784/220960.** Fax: 01784/436340. 180 units. £155–£375 double. Rates include English breakfast. AE, MC, V. Take the A308 out of Windsor, a 15-min. drive. Free parking. **Amenities:** 2 restaurants; bar; outdoor pool (summer only); 3 outdoor tennis courts; exercise room; spa; room service; babysitting. *In room:* A/C, TV, hair dryer, Wi-Fi (free).

MODERATE

Park Farm B&B Located just a mile and half south of Windsor Castle (on the B3022), this family-owned B&B feels like a manor in the middle of the country. Hospitable hosts Caroline and Drew run the vast country house. Rooms are compact but modern and extremely cozy, with spotlessly clean bathrooms (showers only). The full English breakfasts won't disappoint (you can also order bacon sandwiches to go).

St. Leonards Rd., Windsor, Berkshire SL4 3EA. www.parkfarm.com. ℂ **01753/866823.** 5 units. £89 double. Rates include English breakfast. AE, MC, V. Free parking. **Amenities:** Common-use fridge and microwave. *In room:* TV, hair dryer, Wi-Fi (free).

Rainworth House ✦ This gem of a B&B is justly popular (advance bookings are essential), and only a short drive or taxi ride from central Windsor. The house is a handsome red-brick property set within 3 acres of gardens and fields, 2 miles from the town. Host Doreen Barclay maintains beautiful en suite rooms with four-poster beds and wood beams; some have views of the surrounding countryside. Doreen's sumptuous gut-busting English breakfasts are worthy of a Michelin star.

Oakley Green Rd., Oakley Green, Windsor, Berkshire SL4 5UL. www.rainworthhouse.com. ℂ **01753/856749.** 5 units. £78–£90 double. Rates include English breakfast. AE, MC, V. Free parking. Take the A308, 2½ miles from Windsor toward Maidenhead. *In room:* TV, Wi-Fi (free).

Side Trips from Windsor

Windsor Great Park ★ PARK Just to the south of Windsor sprawls this 5,000-acre park, once the private hunting ground of Windsor Castle but mostly open to the public today. You can pick up **Long Walk** just south of the castle on Park Street, then stroll 2.65 miles to the statue of King George III on Snow Hill for the best views of the area. The hill lies in the enclosed **Deer Park,** where red deer are often grazing in open view; look out also for several hundred green parakeets fluttering around, descendents of escaped pets living in the park since the late 1990s.

From Snow Hill you should also see **Frogmore House** ★, built in the 1680s and purchased by King George III as a country retreat for Queen Charlotte in 1792. On the grounds lies the **Royal Mausoleum,** the burial place of Queen Victoria and Prince Albert. The house and Royal Mausoleum are usually open to the public about six individual days each year, usually around Easter and the August public holiday. The mausoleum is also usually open on the Wednesday nearest Queen Victoria's birthday, May 24.

Just a 20-minute walk south of Snow Hill (1 hr. from Windsor on foot), the **Savill Garden** ★ forms part of the Royal Landscape section at the southern end of the park. Created in the 1930s, the 35-acre garden is one of the finest in England. The display starts in spring with rhododendrons, camellias, and daffodils beneath the trees; then, throughout the summer, spectacular displays of flowers and shrubs are presented in a natural and wild state. If driving, the garden is 4 miles from Windsor along the A30; turn off at Wick Road and follow the signs.

Adjoining Savill Garden are the **Valley Gardens,** full of shrubs and trees in a series of wooded natural valleys running to **Virginia Water,** an ornamental lake created in 1753. Both are open daily year-round. There is no admission charge to enter the Valley Gardens, but parking is a flat £6, or £1.50 for the first hour at Virginia Water.

Windsor Great Park. www.thecrownestate.co.uk. © **01753/860222.** Admission to park free; admission to Savill Garden (www.theroyallandscape.co.uk; © **01784/435544**) Mar–Oct £8.50 adults, £7.95 seniors, £3.75 children 6–16; Nov–Feb £6.25 adults, £5.75 seniors, £2.25 children; £15.50–£21 family ticket, children 5 and under free. Daily 10am–6pm (4:30pm in winter).

Legoland Windsor ☺ THEME PARK   Just outside Windsor, Legoland is a 150-acre children's theme park, based on the Lego toy system. Attractions, spread across several activity centers, include Duplo Land, offering a boat ride, puppet theatre, and waterworks, plus Miniland, showing European cities and villages recreated in minute detail from millions of Lego bricks.

Winkfield Rd. (B3022), 2 miles south of Windsor. www.legoland.co.uk. © **0870/504-0404.** Admission varies through the season, starting with cheaper online tickets from £26 for adults, £21 for seniors and children 3–15. Mid-Mar–mid-Nov daily 10am–5pm (until 7pm on school holidays). Closed late Nov–early Mar.

Runnymede HISTORIC SITE   Three miles southeast of Windsor lies Runnymede, a 188-acre water meadow ("mead") on the south side of the Thames, in Surrey. This is where it's believed that King John put his seal on the Great Charter in 1215, after intense pressure from his feudal barons and lords. The charter forced the king to accept a long list of individual liberties and is regarded as the founding document of English constitutional law, as well as inspiration for the U.S. Constitution (a copy of the Magna Carta is displayed in Washington D.C.'s National Archives). From the parking lot a signposted half-mile trail loops around the two main memorials here, while a longer 1.25-mile extension takes in the huge Commonwealth Air Forces Memorial on the hill.

First up, via a short hike up 50 granite steps, is the poignant **John F. Kennedy Memorial,** an acre of ground given to the United States by the people of Britain in 1965. The memorial itself is a 6.4-tonne (7-ton) block of Portland stone, engraved with lines from President Kennedy's inauguration speech in 1961. Further along the trail is the **Magna Carta Memorial,** a large pillar of English granite under a domed classical pavilion, erected by the American Bar Association in 1957.

Runnymede, ½ mile west of the hamlet of Old Windsor on the south side of the A308. www.national trust.org.uk. © **01784/432891.** Free admission. Daily dawn to dusk. Parking £1.50 per hr., to a maximum of £7 per day; parking lot open Apr–Sep 8:30am–7pm, Oct–Mar 8:30am–5pm. If you're driving on the M25, exit at junction 13. The nearest rail connection is at Egham, ½ mile away. The train ride from London's Waterloo Station takes about 25 minutes; taxis from Windsor or Egham will be around £6–£8; First Bus #71 from Windsor drops off at the Bells pub, a short walk away.

Ascot Racecourse RACECOURSE The first race meeting at Ascot, which is directly south of Windsor at the southern end of Windsor Great Park, was held way back in 1711. Ascot Racecourse has been a symbol of high society (and ludicrously extravagant hats), ever since, as pictures of the royal family enjoying the races there have been flashed around the world.

Ascot only hosts 27 days of racing yearly; the town itself isn't worth visiting otherwise. The highlight of the Ascot social season is the **Royal Meeting** (or **Royal Week**), just 5 days in June. To attend you must buy tickets for one of three distinctly different observation areas. These include the Royal Enclosure (members only); the Grandstand, largest of the three; and the Silver Ring, which does not enjoy direct access to the paddocks and has traditionally been the site of most of Ascot's budget seating. At other times you can buy cheaper tickets in all areas (when the Royal Enclosure is known simply as "Premier Admission"). Book online at www.ascot.co.uk from early November.

Ascot, 28 miles west of London. www.ascotkiosk.co.uk. © **0870/722-7227.** Admission £17–£25 for Silver Ring, £50–£66 for the Grandstand; free for children 15 and under). Car parking £18. Trains make the 50-minute trip between London's Waterloo and Ascot Station every 20–40 minutes during the day (£13.10 standard round-trip). Ascot Station is about 10 minutes from the racecourse.

Cliveden ★★ GARDEN Once the home of the formidable Astor family, the lavish Italianate mansion of Cliveden stands on a constructed terrace of mature gardens high above the Thames. Sir Charles Barry, the architect of the Houses of Parliament, built the current gracefully symmetrical structure in the 1850s. In 1893 the American billionaire William Waldorf Astor purchased the estate. After William's son Waldorf (the second Viscount Astor) and wife Nancy (who became the first female English MP) took over in 1906, the mansion became the center of an extravagant, if somewhat right-wing, social scene; in the 1930s the "Cliveden Set" were heavily criticized for supporting appeasement vis-à-vis Germany. The house remained part of the Astor legacy, a repository of a notable collection of paintings and antiques, until 1968, shortly after the Profumo affair had implicated the third Viscount Astor. The National Trust now owns Cliveden, but leases the property as a private hotel. Non-guests are permitted only limited access to the house.

The surrounding **gardens** are open to the public year-round, and are far more enjoyable for casual visitors. They feature a distinguished variety of plantings, ranging from Renaissance-style topiary to meandering forest paths, and vistas of statuary and flowering shrubs. Highlights include a glade garden, a magnificent parterre, and an amphitheatre where "Rule Britannia" was played for the first time.

Cliveden Rd., Taplow, 10 miles northwest of Windsor. www.nationaltrust.org.uk/cliveden. © **01628/668561.** Admission to grounds Feb–Oct £8.60 adults, £4.30 children 5–15, free for children 4 and under, family ticket £21.55; Nov–Dec £5.45 adults, £2.70 children, family ticket £13.60. Admission to house (extra £1.50 adults, 75p children) is limited and by timed ticket only from the information kiosk: Apr–Oct Thurs and Sun 3–5:30pm (3 rooms of the mansion are open to the public, as is the Octagon Temple, with its rich mosaic interior). Grounds mid-Feb–Oct daily 10am–5:30pm, Nov–Dec daily 10am–4pm. From Windsor, follow the M4 toward Reading to junction 7 (in the direction of Slough West). At the roundabout, turn left onto the A4, signposted

At the next roundabout, turn right, signposted Follow the road for 2½ miles to a T-junction with the B476. The main gates to Cliveden are directly opposite.

WHERE TO EAT & STAY

Cliveden House ★★★   The Astor's former estate is one of the most beautiful and luxurious hotels in England. Rooms—named after famous guests who've stayed here, including Lawrence of Arabia and Charlie Chaplin—are sumptuous, each furnished in impeccable taste. The bathrooms with deep marble tubs are among the country's finest. Less preferred rooms are those recently added in the Clutton Wing. Nothing (except perhaps renting Lady Astor's bedroom itself) is more elegant here than walking down to the river and boarding a hotel boat for a champagne cruise before dinner.

Cliveden, Taplow, Maidenhead, Berkshire SL6 0JF. www.clivedenhouse.co.uk. ℂ **01628/668561.** Fax: 01628/661837. 39 units. £185–£320 double; £550–£660 suite. There is a National Trust charge of £10.10 per person per stay. Rates include English breakfast. AE, DC, MC, V. Free parking. **Amenities:** 3 restaurants; bar; 2 pools (1 heated indoor, 1 outdoor); outdoor tennis court (lit); health club and spa; room service; babysitting. *In room:* A/C (in some), TV, hair dryer, Wi-Fi (free).

HENLEY-ON-THAMES

35 miles W of London

Henley-on-Thames, a small, affluent town on the Oxfordshire side of the river, is the location of the **Royal Regatta,** one of England's most vaunted high-society events held annually in early July. Lying on a stretch of the Thames that's known for its calm waters, unobstructed bottom, and predictable currents, Henley is a rower's dream. Women's and lightweight crews from Oxford and Cambridge University still compete here in March, and the regatta itself, which started in 1839, is the major annual competition among international oarsmen and oarswomen, who find it both

---

The Henley Royal Regatta ★★

The Henley Royal Regatta, held the first week in July (Wed–Sun), is the country's premier rowing event, with races held over a course of 1 mile, 550 yards. For a close-up view from the Stewards' Enclosure, you'll need a guest badge, obtainable only through a member—in other words, you have to know someone. Admission to the Regatta Enclosure, however, is open to all. Entry fees are £16 to £21 per day (children 13 and under free). Parking is £25–£30 per day. For information, call or visit the website (www.hrr.co.uk; ℂ **01491/572153**). During the annual 5-day event, up to 100 races are organized each day, with starts scheduled as frequently as every 5 minutes. This event is open only to all-male crews of up to nine at a time. In

late June, rowing events for women are held at the 3-day Henley Women's Regatta.

If you want to float on the waters of the Thames yourself, stop by the town's largest and oldest outfitter, **Hobbs & Sons, Ltd.,** Station Road Boathouse (www.hobbs-of-henley.com; ℂ **01491/572035**), established in 1870. Open April through October daily from 8:30am to 5:30pm, Hobbs has an armada of watercraft, including rowboats that rent for £15 to £20 per hour. Motorboats go for £28.50 to £60 per hour. Prices include fuel. An on-premises chandlery shop sells virtually anything a boat crew could need, as well as T-shirts and boaters' hats.

challenging and entertaining—though the real action takes place on the riverbanks, where the great and the good mix over Pimm's Cup and champagne.

If you visit at other times, Henley's Elizabethan buildings, tearooms, and inns can make for an appealing stopover en route to Oxford.

Essentials

GETTING THERE Trains depart from London's Paddington Station every hour during the day, but require a change at the junction in Twyford (some also require an additional change at Reading). The trip takes 40 minutes to 1 hour. Off-peak round-trip tickets are £19.70.

If you're driving from London, take the M4 toward Reading to junction 8/9, and then head northwest on the A404(M) and A4130. From Windsor you can take the A308 to the same M4 junction.

VISITOR INFORMATION The **Tourist Information Centre** is inside Henley Town Hall, Market Place (www.visitsouthoxfordshire.co.uk; ☎ **01491/578034**). Hours are Monday to Saturday 10am to 4pm (3pm in winter).

Exploring the Area

River & Rowing Museum MUSEUM This museum celebrates the Thames River and those who row upon it. The **Rowing Gallery** follows the history of rowing from the days of the Greeks. The **Thames Gallery** chronicles the saga of the river itself, while the **Henley Gallery** tells the story of the town. The showstoppers here include the Henley Hoard, an Iron Age treasure trove found in 2003, made up of 32 Celtic gold coins dating from around A.D. 50, and *Henley from the Wargrave Road,* painted in 1698 by Dutch master Jan Siberechts. Younger children will enjoy the **Wind in the Willows Gallery,** dedicated to Kenneth Grahame's whimsical creations largely inspired by his time at Cookham, a short paddle down the Thames (audioguides supply readings from the books). The gallery contains dioramas of Mr. Toad, Ratty, Badger, and Mole based on E.H. Shepard's famous illustrations.

Mill Meadows. ☎ www.rrm.co.uk. **01491/415600.** Admission £8 adults; £6 children 4–16; £24 family ticket for 4, £28 for 5, and £31 for 6. May–Aug daily 10am–5:30pm; Sept–Apr daily 10am–5pm. Free parking.

Where to Eat

Argyll 🍴 PUB FARE This is a traditional pub, with plenty of cozy nooks, wood fires in winter, and a beer garden for sunny days. Suffolk's Greene King cask ales dominate (IPA and Abbot Ale), but it's also a popular lunch spot with locals. The doorstep sandwiches (with fresh crusty bread and salad) are a good deal (from £5.75), and most of the main courses— Old English pork sausages with creamy mash, beer-battered haddock—range from £10 to £13.

15 Market Place. www.theargyllhenley.co.uk. ☎ **01491/573400.** Main courses and platters £9–£19.50. AE, MC, V. Sun–Thurs 11am–midnight; Fri–Sat 11am–1am.

Crooked Billet ★★ 🍴 GASTROPUB This venerable old pub, a few miles northwest of Henley, seemingly in the middle of nowhere, is well worth an excursion. Most people come to eat from the extensive menu of contemporary Italian, French provincial, and popular bistro dishes that changes seasonally. Expect delights such as smoked eel, slow roast Barbary duck, and spinach and ricotta filo strudel. Simple classics like the Welsh rarebit and a glass of stout, or warm treacle (sugar syrup) sponge with custard sauce are equally satisfying. The inn dates back to around 1642, and highwayman Dick Turpin supposedly hid out here in the 1730s, on account of his romantic attachment to the landlord's daughter.

Newlands Lane, Stoke Row. www.thecrookedbillet.co.uk. ℂ **01491/681048.** Reservations recommended. Main courses £13–£26.85. AE, MC, V. Mon–Fri noon–2:15pm and 7–midnight; Sat–Sun noon–midnight. Take the A1430 towards Wallingford, then B481 to Highmoor Cross, and look for signs to Stoke Row.

Hotel du Vin Bistro ★ BISTRO   Henley's top hotel also contains the best restaurant, a stylish bistro serving the best of modern British cooking, local ingredients fused with French techniques and a few outright French classics: The moules marinière makes a piquant starter. The core of the menu is all about fusion, though: think roast Yorkshire grouse with fondant potato, crisp ham, and orange jus; or pan-fried hake with herb risotto.

New St. www.hotelduvin.com. ℂ **01491/848400.** Main courses and platters £13.50–£22.95. AE, MC, V. Mon–Thurs noon–2:30pm and 6:30–10pm; Fri noon–2:30pm and 6–10:30pm; Sat 12:30–2:30pm and 6–10:30pm; Sun 12:30–2:30pm and 6:30–10pm.

Where to Stay

Falaise House ★   This is a first-class B&B in a Georgian town house built in 1755, with immaculate en-suite rooms (standard, deluxe, and superior); all are equally well equipped, with the main difference being that standard rooms are smaller. The owners, Jane and Richard, are gracious hosts, the location is perfect, and the finishing touch is the breakfasts: a vast choice of fresh fruit and cooked meals, including Scottish smoked salmon and scrambled eggs.

37 Market Place, Henley-on-Thames, Oxfordshire RG9 2AA. www.falaisehouse.com. ℂ **01491/573388.** 6 units. £85–£175 double. Rates include English breakfast. AE, MC, V. Public parking nearby (free overnight and Sun only). *In room:* TV, hair dryer, Wi-Fi (free).

Hotel du Vin ★★   The Hotel du Vin chain took the former Georgian Brakspears Brewery and imaginatively converted it into a fine example of industrial recycling. What has emerged is the poshest hotel in the area. Each of the beautifully furnished rooms, with solid oak pieces, is named after a vineyard. The decorator ordered that all walls be painted a "toast color," and installed thick wall-to-wall carpeting and "dreamboat beds." Fine Egyptian linens and spectacular power showers in the bathrooms are additional enticements.

New St., Henley-on-Thames, Oxfordshire RG9 2BP. www.hotelduvin.com. ℂ **01491/848400.** 43 units. £140–£315 double; £210–£515 suite. AE, DC, MC, V. Parking £15. **Amenities:** Restaurant; bar; room service. *In room:* TV, minibar, hair dryer, Wi-Fi (free).

Lenwade Bed & Breakfast 🗝   Built in the early 1900s, this welcoming Victorian guesthouse is owned and operated by Jacquie and John Williams. Entering from a small courtyard filled with flowering vines and lush foliage, you'll see a 1.5-m (6-ft.) stained-glass window thought to depict Joan of Arc. Another memorable detail is the winding staircase with its original handrails. The small to midsize bedrooms are individually decorated and comfortably furnished, while breakfast (a huge spread of juices and hot and cold dishes) is served at a congenial communal table.

3 Western Rd., Henley-on-Thames, Oxfordshire RG9 1JL. www.lenwade.com. ℂ **01491/573468.** 4 units. From £80 double (£60 single). Rates include English Breakfast. No credit cards. Free parking. *In room:* TV, hair dryer, Wi-Fi (free).

Side Trips from Henley

Mapledurham ★ HISTORIC SITE   The stately Blount family mansion lies beside the Thames in the unspoiled village of Mapledurham, just outside Reading. The aristocratic Blount family has lived here since 1490—the current mansion was completed in 1612 and is currently owned by John Eyston, a Blount descendant. Inside, you'll see Elizabethan ceilings and a great oak staircase, as well as portraits of the two beautiful sisters with whom the poet Alexander Pope, a frequent visitor here (1707–15), fell in love. The family chapel, built in 1789, is a fine example of modern Gothic architecture. On the grounds, the last working **water mill** on the Thames still produces flour.

The most romantic way to reach this gorgeous old house is to take the boat that leaves the promenade next to Caversham Bridge in Reading at 2pm on Saturday, Sunday, and public holidays, from Easter to September. The journey upstream takes between 30 and 80 minutes, and the boat leaves Mapledurham again at 5pm for the return trip to Caversham, giving you plenty of time to explore. The round-trip boat ride from Caversham costs £7 for adults and £5.50 for children 5 to 15. (An additional landing fee of £2 for adults and £1 for children is charged, but this is deducted from the cost of house entry.) You can get more details about the boat from **Thames Rivercruise Ltd.,** Pipers Island, Bridge Street, Caversham Bridge, Reading RG4 8AH (www.thamesrivercruise.co.uk; ✆ **0118/948-1088**).

Mapledurham, Reading. www.mapledurham.co.uk. ✆ **0118/972-3350.** Admission to house and mill £8.50 adults, £3.50 children 5–16, free for children 4 and under; house only £4.50 adults, £2 children; mill only £3.50 adults, £1.50 children. Sat–Sun and public holidays 2–5:30pm. Closed Oct–Easter. From Henley-on-Thames, head south along the A4155 to Reading; follow signs to the A329 through town. Mapledurham is signposted off this road, 3 miles west of the center. Or take the boat trip described above.

Stratfield Saye House & Estate ★ HISTORIC HOME   This combined house and country park provides tangible evidence of the fortune of one of England's greatest heroes, the Duke of Wellington. His descendants have lived here since he bought the estate in 1817 to celebrate trouncing Napoleon at the Battle of Waterloo (a grateful Parliament granted a large sum of money for its purchase). The park's centerpiece is Stratfield Saye House itself, built around 1630; the original red brick was covered in stucco in the 18th century. Many memories of the Iron Duke remain in the house, including his billiard table, battle spoils, and paintings. The funeral carriage that once rested in St. Paul's Cathedral crypt is also on display as part of the Wellington Exhibition in the old stables. In the gardens is the grave of Copenhagen, the charger ridden at Waterloo by the duke. There are also extensive landscaped grounds, together with a tearoom and a gift shop. Access to the house is by guided tour only.

Stratfield Saye, 6 miles south of Reading, off the A33 to Basingstoke. www.stratfield-saye.co.uk. ✆ **01256/882882.** Admission Mon–Fri £7 adults, £6 students and seniors, £4 children 3–15, free for children 2 and under; Sat–Sun £9.50 adults, £8.50 students, £5 children; garden only Mon–Fri £3, Sat–Sun £3.50 (all cash only). Easter weekend (Thurs–Mon) and mid-July–early Aug Mon–Fri 11:30am–3:30pm, Sat–Sun 10:30am–3:30pm; grounds close at 5pm. From Henley, head south along the A4155 to Reading, then the A33 toward Basingstoke.

MARLOW

This Thames-side town, 35 miles northwest of London and 8 miles east of Henley-on-Thames, is best known for its **fishing** associations, though many also prefer its more pastoral look to the larger Henley. Its most famous feature is the **suspension bridge** connecting the Buckinghamshire and Berkshire sides of the river, completed in 1832 according to the design of William Tierney Clark, who went on to build the far larger bridge linking Buda and Pest in Hungary. Local son and Olympic rowing hero **Sir Steve Redgrave**—born in Marlow in 1962—is honored with a statue in pleasant Higginson Park (between the river and the town center).

Along this middle stretch of the Thames is some of the most beautiful rural scenery in England. It was in these surroundings that **Izaak Walton** wrote his immortal work on fishing, *The Compleat Angler,* published in 1653. Walton pilgrims can visit the Compleat Angler Hotel for a drink (see below). The literary-minded should drop into the **Two Brewers** pub in St. Peter's Street (www.twobrewersmarlow.com; ✆ **01628/484140**), where Jerome K. Jerome wrote much of *Three Men in a Boat* in the 1880s, and visit 104 West Street, where a plaque commemorates former inhabitants Percy and Mary Shelley (the latter wrote *Frankenstein* here in 1817).

From the bridge, Marlow's pleasant High Street leads past some enticing shops and cafes, the **visitor information center** on Institute Road (✆ **01628/483597;** Mon–Fri 9am–5pm, Sat 9am–1pm), and **Beehive Treats,** 18 Spittal St. (www.beehivetreats.com; ✆ **01628/475154;** Mon–Thurs noon–5:30pm, Fri–Sat 10am–5:30pm, Sun 11am–5pm), a handsome old-fashioned candy shop specializing in traditional candies and real licorice.

To reach Marlow from Henley by car, take the A4155 and follow the signs. Trains from London Paddington take around 1 hour with a change in Maidenhead. Off-peak round-trip tickets are £13.70.

Stanley Spencer Gallery ★ GALLERY Just 3 miles downriver from Marlow (and some 11 miles from Henley), **Cookham** is another affluent river town notable chiefly as the former home of **Stanley Spencer** (1891–1959), one of Britain's greatest modern artists. If you've never heard of him, check out the Stanley Spencer Gallery, housed in a former Methodist chapel; the tiny gallery owns more than 100 of his early Modernist paintings and drawings, many of them a curious but powerful fusion of Biblical scenes and everyday life in Cookham from the 1920s to the 1950s. Perhaps the most intriguing exhibit is the battered old pram Spencer used to carry his easel and canvas while rambling around the village.

The Kings Hall, High St., Cookham. www.stanleyspencer.org.uk. ✆**01628/471885.** Admission £5 adults, £4 students and seniors, free for children under 16. Apr–Oct daily 10:30am–5:30pm; Nov–Mar Thurs–Sun 11am–4:30pm. From Marlow, continue southeast along the A4155. Park along High Street or at the train station (free for 2hr.).

Where to Eat & Stay

Hand & Flowers ★★ GASTROPUB Marlow's very own two-Michelin star winner (the only pub to win that accolade) is helmed by Tom and Beth Kerridge, who have crafted a menu of modern British as well as rustic French dishes. A mouth-watering example is the slow cooked duck breast, which Tom serves with Savoy cabbage, duck fat chips and a tasty, rich, gravy. Leave space for the desserts: The Hand & Flowers chocolate cake with salted caramel and muscovado ice cream is sensational.

126 West St. www.thehandandflowers.co.uk. ✆ **01628/482277.** Reservations recommended. Main courses £21–£32; Set-price lunch £15 (2 courses), £19.50 (3 courses). AE, MC, V. Mon–Sat noon–2:30pm and 6:30–10pm; Sun noon–3:30pm.

Macdonald Compleat Angler ★★ Marlow attracts many fishermen who like to stay at this posh hotel because of its associations with Izaak Walton (his book and other memorabilia are sold at reception). The hotel certainly has plenty of charm and character, though most of it was built long after the venerable Walton passed this way.

Nevertheless, it occupies an emerald swath of lawns stretching down to the banks of the Thames, and is a well-organized and impeccably polite center of English chintz, predictably elegant bars, and very fine dining thanks to the *Bowaters* and *Aubergine* restaurants. Each room is outfitted like a private country home, with antiques or reproductions and plush, comfortable beds. The more expensive rooms look out on the Thames. The finest accommodations are in a modern wing with balconies overlooking the rushing weir.

Marlow Bridge, Bisham Rd., Marlow, Buckinghamshire SL7 1RG. www.macdonaldhotels.co.uk/compleatangler. (C) **0844/879-9128.** Fax: 01628/486388. 64 units. £149–£210 double; £279–£340 suite. AE, DC, MC, V. Free parking. **Amenities:** 2 restaurants; bar; room service; babysitting; Wi-Fi in public areas (free). *In room:* A/C, TV, minibar, hair dryer.

OXFORD ★★★

54 miles NW of London

The city of Oxford, dominated by **Britain's oldest university,** is a bastion of English tradition, history, and eccentricity. Here students still get selected to join the archaic Bullingdon Club, rowing competitions attract a larger audience than soccer (football), and students still take exams dressed in black gowns (seriously). The creator of *Inspector Morse,* Colin Dexter, lives in town, and where else would you film the Harry Potter series?

Oxford certainly retains a special sort of magic. The hallowed halls and gardens of ancient colleges such as Magdalen and Christ Church are architectural gems, but not museums—students live and work here year-round. The High hasn't changed much since Oscar Wilde skipped along it, and the water meadows and spires that inspired John Donne, Christopher Wren, C. S. Lewis, Iris Murdoch, and J. R. R. Tolkien are still there.

When it comes to food, Oxford isn't stuck in the past. The city is the base of French-born celebrity chef Raymond Blanc, who masterminds a creative roster of dishes at **Brasserie Blanc** and the super exclusive **Le Manoir aux Quat' Saisons.** With a huge population of students there's also plenty of cheap eats in town, with the **Covered Market** a good place to start.

Pubs in Oxford have a fittingly rich heritage, and you'll be drinking in the same oak-paneled rooms once frequented by Samuel Johnson, Lawrence of Arabia, Graham Greene, Bill Clinton, and Margaret Thatcher; even *The Hobbit* was first read in the **Eagle and Child.** The city does have a life beyond the university: Radiohead played their first gig at Oxford's **Jericho Tavern** in 1986, an alternative venue that still hosts live bands.

Essentials

GETTING THERE Trains from London's Paddington Station reach Oxford in around 1 hour (direct trains run every 30 minutes). A standard round-trip ticket costs £31.50.

If you're driving, take the M40 west from London and follow the signs. **Parking** is a nightmare in Oxford; if you do find parking in town it will cost you around £30 per day (cars are banned from much of the center anyway). If you can find a spot, metered parking in St. Giles is £4 for a maximum 2 hours. However, there are five large **park-and-ride** lots (www.parkandride.net) around the city's ring road, all well signposted. After 9:30am Monday to Friday, and all day Saturday and Sunday, you pay £2.20 for a round-trip ticket for a bus ride into the city. The bus drops you off at St. Aldate's or Queen Street in the city center. The buses run every 8 to 10 minutes in

Oxford

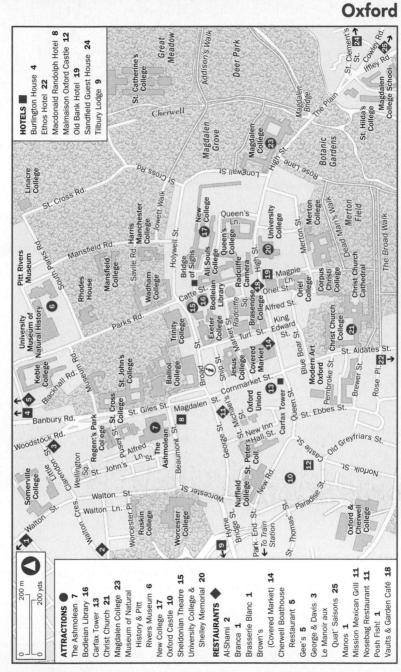

HOTELS ■

Burlington House **4**
Ethos Hotel **22**
Macdonald Randolph Hotel **8**
Malmaison Oxford Castle **12**
Old Bank Hotel **19**
Sandfield Guest House **24**
Tilbury Lodge **9**

ATTRACTIONS ●

The Ashmolean **7**
Bodleian Library **16**
Carfax Tower **13**
Christ Church **21**
Magdalen College **23**
Museum of Natural History & Pitt Rivers Museum **6**
New College **17**
Oxford Castle **10**
Sheldonian Theatre **15**
University College & Shelley Memorial **20**

RESTAURANTS ◆

Al-Shami **2**
Branca **1**
Brasserie Blanc **1**
Brown's (Covered Market) **14**
Cherwell Boathouse Restaurant **5**
Gee's **5**
George & Davis **3**
Le Manoir aux Quat' Saisons **25**
Manos **1**
Mission Mexican Grill **11**
Nosebag Restaurant **11**
Posh Fish! **1**
Vaults & Garden Café **18**

Oxford University has a complex history and a confusing structure, so it makes sense to take one of the many available **tours** to get a more detailed understanding.

For an easy orientation, take a 1-hour, open-top bus tour with **City Sightseeing Oxford** (www.citysightseeingoxford.com; ✆ **01865/790522**). Tours start from the railway station; other pickup points are the Sheldonian Theatre, Gloucester Green Bus Station, and Pembroke College. Buses leave daily at 9:30am and then every 10 to 15 minutes in the summer and every 30 minutes in winter. The last bus departs at 4pm November to February, at 5pm March and October, and at 6pm April to September. The cost is £13 for adults, £11 for students, £10 for seniors, and £6 for children 5 to 14 years old; a family ticket for two adults and three children is £33. Tickets can be purchased from the driver and are valid for 24 hours.

If you have more energy, take the entertaining 2-hour **walking tour** through the city and the major colleges from the Oxford Tourist Information Centre, 15–16 Broad St. (www.visitoxfordandoxfordshire.com; ✆ **01865/252200**), daily at 11am, 1, and 2pm. These cost £8 to £8.50 for adults and £4.50 to £5 for children 16 and under,

but they only include entry to colleges that don't charge admission fees. The Tourist Information Centre also offers a long list of excellent **theme tours,** everything from "Magic, Murder & Mayhem" and "Pottering in Harry's Footsteps" to "Jewish Heritage" and "Stained Glass." Our favorites include the 2-hour **"Inspector Morse Tour"** (Sat and Mon at 1:30pm, Mar–Sept; £8.50), where enthusiastic guides enliven a tour of all the locations associated with the city's celebrated TV detective (and his local pubs), created by Oxford author Colin Dexter.

For something spooky, try **Bill Spectre's Oxford Ghost Trails** (www.ghosttrail.org; ✆ **07941/041811**), on Friday and Saturday at 6:30pm from the Tourist Information Centre. Dressed as a Victorian undertaker, Bill illustrates his ghoulish walks with props and tricks, taking in all the most famous and gruesome Oxford ghost stories. He charges £7 for adults and £4 for children.

Finally, **Oxford River Cruises** (www.oxfordrivercruises.com; ✆ **0845/226-9396**) runs several boat tours along the River Thames, from the tranquil 1-hour "River Experience" (Apr–Oct; £9 adults, £6 children 15 and under) to a sunset picnic cruise (May–Sept) for £45 adults and £30 children.

each direction until 11:30pm Monday to Saturday and between 11am and 5pm on Sundays.

VISITOR INFORMATION The **Oxford Tourist Information Centre** is at 15–16 Broad St. (www.visitoxford.org; ✆ **01865/252200**). It sells a comprehensive range of maps, brochures, and souvenir items, as well as those Oxford University T-shirts that only tourists wear (students advertise their college, not the university). Hours are Monday to Saturday 9:30am to 5pm (5:30pm in summer), Sunday, and public holidays 10am to 3pm. **City Sightseeing** (see below) has a small but useful office inside the train station (daily 9:30am–5pm) that hands out free maps.

GETTING AROUND Central Oxford, which includes all the most interesting colleges and sights, is very compact and easily explored on foot, but there are plenty of local buses for those traveling farther afield. Local reliable taxi operators are ABC (© **01865/775577**) and Radio Taxis (© **01865/242424**).

Exploring the City

Most first-time visitors to Oxford have trouble determining exactly where the university is. Indeed, the quickest way to sound like a tourist in Oxford is to ask, "Where's the university?" This is because Oxford University is in fact made up of 39 autonomous, self-governing colleges sprinkled throughout the center of town; there is no campus as such and no central university building. Rarely will you see signs for "Oxford University." Students apply to specific colleges within the university umbrella, and apart from a handful of lectures (and final exams), it is the colleges that organize tuition and most activities; the majority of students experience sports, social events, and clubs at a college level and mixing between colleges is unusual.

Touring every college would be a formidable task, so it's best to focus on just a handful of the most intriguing and famous ones described below.

The Ashmolean ★★ MUSEUM   This oft-overlooked history museum contains some real gems, not least the **Alfred Jewel** ★★, a rare Anglo-Saxon gold ornament (on floor 2), dating from the late 9th century, adorned with the words "Alfred ordered me made" in Old English (thought to refer to Saxon ruler King Alfred).

You could easily spend half a day here. The museum is littered with exceptional pieces, but don't miss the following highlights. The lower floor ("Exploring the Past") contains the actual robe worn by Lawrence of Arabia, and more remarkably, the mantle of Powhatan, the Native American chief who confronted the Jamestown colony in Virginia, back in 1607. Here also is a mesmerizing cache of British treasures, including the Celtic Henley Hoard, and the Roman Chalgrove Hoard. Art on the second floor ("West meets East") includes exceptional paintings from Bassano, Constable, Gainsborough, Michelangelo, Renoir, Rubens, Titian, and Van Dyck. Silver coins from the Viking Cuerdale Hoard are also on display. European art from 1800 onwards holds court on the third floor: Pre-Raphaelite work from John Everett Millais (*Return of the Dove to the Ark*) and Ford Madox Brown (*The Seeds and Fruits of English Poetry*), and Monet's *Mill near Zaandam,* Van Gogh's *Restaurant de la Sirene,* and lots of stellar pieces from Pissarro and Renoir. The rooftop restaurant, the Ashmolean Dining Room (Tues, Wed, Sun 10am–6pm, Thurs–Sat 10am–10pm) is a great place for a bite after a visit.

Beaumont St. at St. Giles. www.ashmolean.org. © **01865/278002.** Free admission. Tues–Sun 10am–6pm. Closed Dec 24–26.

The Light of the World

The reproduction in St. Paul's Cathedral, London, is seen by more people, but William Holman Hunt's original masterpiece **The Light of the World** ★★ has been on display at red-brick **Keble College,** Parks Road (www.keble.ox.ac.uk; © **01865/272727**) since 1872. The famous Pre-Raphaelite painting, depicting Jesus preparing to knock on an overgrown and long-unopened door, hangs in the college chapel. Keble College is open to the public during the college vacations (July, August, and September; Christmas: mid-December to mid-January; and Easter: mid-March to mid-April) between 2pm and 5pm. Admission is free.

Bodleian Library ★★ LIBRARY   This famed university library was established in 1602 in the heart of Oxford. Over the years, it has expanded from the **Old Library** on Catte Street, and now includes the iconic **Radcliffe Camera** nearby. The Bodleian is home to an astonishing 50,000 manuscripts (including Mendelssohn's autographed *Hebrides Overture* and Jane Austen's unfinished novel, *The Watsons*), and more than 11 million books—like the British Library in London, it is entitled to a copy of every book published in the U.K. You can enter the **Exhibition Room** (which offers high-quality temporary exhibits on the library) and wander the quadrangles of these handsome structures for free, but to get a better understanding of their history take a tour of the interior. Standard tours (1 hr.) start with the University's oldest teaching and examination room, the **Divinity School** (completed in 1488), and include Duke Humfrey's medieval library. Purchase tickets in the lodge on the right-hand side of the Great Gate on Catte Street. The highly recommended extended tours also include the Old Library and Radcliffe Camera (90 min.). These tours normally run every Sunday at 11:15am and 1:15pm, most Saturdays at 10am, and most Wednesdays at 9:30am. Note that children under 11 are usually not permitted on these tours.

Catte St. www.bodleian.ox.ac.uk. ☏ **01865/277182.** Admission £1 Divinity School only (children 4 and under free); £6.50 (standard tour) or £4.50 for mini-tour (30 min.); £13 (extended tour). Exhibition Room Mon–Fri 9am–5pm; Sat 9am–4:30pm; Sun 11am–5pm. Closed Dec 24–Jan 3. Call to confirm specific tour times.

Carfax Tower ★ CHURCH   For a bird's-eye view of the city, climb the 99 steps up this 23-m (75-ft.) Gothic church tower in the center of town. Carfax Tower is all that remains of St. Martin's Church, which stood on this site from 1032 until 1896, when most of it was demolished to accommodate a wider road. Look for the church clock on the facade, adorned by two "quarter boys" who hit the bells at every quarter of the hour.

Carfax, Queen St., at the end of High St. www.citysightseeingoxford.com. ☏ **01865/790522.** Admission £2.30 adults, £1.20 children 15 and under. Children 4 and under are not admitted. Daily 10am–5:30pm (Nov–Mar closes 3:30pm). Closed Dec 24–Jan 1.

Christ Church ★★ CHURCH   Nothing quite matches the beauty and grandeur of Christ Church, one of the most prestigious and the largest of Oxford colleges. Established by Cardinal Wolsey in 1525, the college has a well-deserved reputation for exclusivity, wealth, and power: It has produced 13 British prime ministers, including William Gladstone, with other alumni including John Locke, John Wesley, William Penn, W. H. Auden, and Lewis Carroll. More recently, many scenes from the *Harry Potter* films have been shot here, with the cloisters, quads, and staircases standing in for Hogwarts.

Self-guided tours begin in the **cloister** and continue into the 1529 **Great Hall ★★**, the official college dining room, where there are portraits by Gainsborough and Reynolds, and Holbein's *Henry VIII* (a copy of the original). From here the route takes you through to **Tom Quad,** the largest quadrangle of any college in Oxford, with a small ornamental pond and a statue of Mercury in the center. Here also is the most distinctive main entrance in Oxford, Christopher Wren's **Tom Tower ★** completed in 1682. The tower houses Great Tom, an 8,182-kg (18,000-lb) bell. It rings at 9:05pm nightly, which used to be closing time for all colleges (no longer—students have keys). The 101 times it peals originally signified the number of students in residence when the college was founded. From the quad the tour continues into the 12th-century **Christ Church Cathedral,** once part of a

Often overlooked by the average visitor is an unheralded little gem known as **Christ Church Picture Gallery ★** (www.chch.ox.ac.uk; (℃) **01865/276172**), entered through the Canterbury Quad of Christ Church. (*Insider Tip:* To visit the gallery without paying for entrance to the rest of the college, enter through Canterbury Gate off Oriel Sq., from King Edward St.) Here you'll come across a small but stunning collection of Old Masters, mainly from the Dutch, Flemish, and especially the Italian schools, including works by Botticelli, Michelangelo, and Leonardo da Vinci. Look out especially for Filippino Lippi's *Wounded Centaur,* a precious *Virgin and Child* from Piero della Francesca, and the spectacular *Butcher's Shop* ★★ by Annibale Carracci. The gallery is open May through September, Monday to Saturday from 10:30am to 5pm, Sunday 2 to 5pm; October through April, Monday to Saturday from 10:30am to 1pm and daily 2 to 4:30pm. Admission is £3 for adults, £2 for students and seniors. If you've already paid to visit the college, you get a 50% discount.

medieval monastery and containing the shrine of St. Frideswide, patron saint of Oxford. The shrine was destroyed in the Reformation and rebuilt in 1889, while Edward Burne-Jones designed the spectacular St. Frideswide Window in 1858. Note that the Great Hall is sometimes closed to visitors during functions.

St. Aldate's. www.chch.ox.ac.uk. (℃) **01865/276150.** Admission £7 adults, £5.50 students, seniors and children 17 and under, free for children 5 and under. Mon–Sat 9am–5:30pm; Sun 2–5:30pm. Last admission 4:30pm. Closed Dec 25.

Magdalen College ★★ HISTORIC SITE Pronounced *Maud*-lin, this is the most beautiful college in Oxford, thanks to its bucolic location on the banks of the River Cherwell and some dazzling Gothic architecture, notably the elegant Magdalen Tower. There's even a deer park in the grounds and tranquil Addison's Walk, a picturesque footpath along the river.

The college was founded in 1458 by William of Waynflete, bishop of Winchester and later chancellor of England. It's another influential college with an alumni ranging from Thomas Wolsey to Oscar Wilde; prominent ex-students in the current Conservative Party include William Hague and George Osborne.

Soaring above the High Street, Magdalen Tower is the tallest building in Oxford (44m/144 ft.), completed in 1509 and where the choristers sing in Latin at dawn on May Day. You can also visit the 15th-century chapel, where the same choir sings Evensong Tuesday to Sunday at 6pm.

High St. www.magd.ox.ac.uk. (℃) **01865/276000.** Admission £4.50 adults, £3.50 children, seniors and students. July–Sept daily noon–7pm; Oct–June daily 1–6pm or dusk (whichever is earlier). Closed Dec 23–Jan 3.

Museum of Natural History & Pitt Rivers Museum ★ ☺ MUSEUM These two enlightening museums lie a short walk northeast of the center, well off the beaten path for most tourists but worthy diversions. The **Museum of Natural History** houses the university's extensive collections of zoological, entomological, and geological specimens in one grand Victorian, sun-lit hall—everything from stuffed crocodiles and a giant open-jaw of a sperm whale to the 16.5-cm (6.5-inch) fossil tooth of a prehistoric megalodon and tsetse fly collected by the explorer David Livingstone.

5

THE THAMES VALLEY & THE CHILTERNS Oxford

Highlights include superb sections on Darwin and his theory of evolution, the original Oxford dodo (now stuffed), and the 1912 Piltdown Man Hoax, once thought to be the "missing link."

At the far end you'll see the entrance to the dimly-lit **Pitt Rivers Museum,** a maze of Victorian curio cabinets containing over half a million archeological and ethnographic objects from all over the world. Objects are grouped according to how they were made or used, not by age or culture. Amongst them you'll find a precious Tahitian mourner's costume, collected by Captain Cook in 1773–74, ghostly Japanese Noh masks, and thick Inuit fur coats.

Parks Rd. and S Parks Rd. Museum of Natural History: www.oum.ox.ac.uk. (*) **01865/272950.** Free admission. Daily 10am–5pm. Pitt Rivers Museum: www.prm.ox.ac.uk. (*) **01865/270927.** Free admission. Mon noon–4:30pm; Tues–Sun 10am–4:30pm.

New College ★★ HISTORIC SITE   New College is another must-see, primarily for its exceptional architecture and spacious grounds. It's also a favorite *Harry Potter* location and has seen Kate Beckinsale, Hugh Grant, Naomi Wolf, and even Louisiana Governor Bobby Jindal pass through its pristine grounds. The college was founded in 1379 by William of Wykeham, Bishop of Winchester, but the real masterpiece here is the **chapel ★★**. Its handsome interior contains stained glass in the great West Window by Joshua Reynolds, Jacob Epstein's expressive modern sculpture of Lazarus, and El Greco's masterful painting of St. James. Don't miss the beautiful gardens, where you can stroll among the remains of the old city wall that now runs right through the college.

Holywell St. www.new.ox.ac.uk. (*) **01865/279500.** Admission £2 adults, £1.50 seniors and students, free for children 16 and under Easter–Oct; free Nov–Easter. Easter–Oct daily 11am–5pm; Nov–Easter daily 2–4pm.

Oxford Castle ☺ CASTLE   Offering an escape from all things academic, Oxford Castle is especially fun for youngsters, a shopping and heritage complex developed on the ruins of a fortress built by the Normans around 1071. Most of the castle was destroyed during the Civil War, and the site served as a prison until 1996, when part of it became the Malmaison hotel (see p. 225). Other than perusing the restaurants and shops, the highlight here is **Oxford Castle—Unlocked,** which allows access to the most historic parts of the site: St. George's Tower, the 900-year old crypt, the 11th-century motte and bailey castle mound, and the old prison cells. Costumed guides, playing characters such as Civil War radical John Lilburne and "sneaky thief" Gypsy Elizabeth Boswell, enliven the experience.

A Quiet Oasis

The oldest in Great Britain, the **Botanic Garden,** opposite Magdalen (www.botanic-garden.ox.ac.uk; (*) **01865/ 286690**), was first planted in 1621 on the site of a Jewish graveyard from the early Middle Ages. Bounded by a curve of the Cherwell, it still stands today and is the best place in Oxford to escape the tourist hordes. The Botanic Garden is open March through October, daily from 9am to 5pm (until 6pm May–Aug); November through February, daily from 9am to 4:30pm (last admission 45 min. before closing). Admission is £4 for adults, £3 for university students, and free for school-age children in full-time education.

Punting the River Cherwell

Punting on the River Cherwell is an essential, if slightly eccentric, Oxford pastime. At the **Cherwell Boathouse,** Bardwell Road (www.cherwellboathouse. co.uk; ℂ **01865/515978**), you can rent a punt (a flat-bottomed boat maneuvered by a long pole and a small oar) for the hourly rate of £14 (weekdays) or £16 (weekends), plus a £70 to £80 deposit. **Magdalen Bridge Boathouse,** the Old Horse Ford, High Street (www. oxfordpunting.co.uk; ℂ **01865/ 202643**), has an hourly charge of £16 (weekdays) or £20 (weekends). Punts are available from mid-March to mid-October, daily from 10am until dusk.

11 New Rd., at Castle St. www.oxfordcastle.com. ℂ **01865/201657.** Oxford Castle—Unlocked: www.oxfordcastleunlocked.co.uk. ℂ **01865/260666.** Oxford Castle—Unlocked admission £8.95 adults, £6.95 seniors and students, £5.95 children 5–15, free for children 4 and under. Daily 10am–5pm, last tour 4:20pm.

Sheldonian Theatre THEATRE   This exceptional piece of Palladian architecture stands next to the Bodleian, completed in 1668 according to a design by Sir Christopher Wren. As well as admiring the immaculate interior and ceiling frescos, you can climb up to the cupola and enjoy fine views over Oxford. University ceremonies (including graduation) are regularly held here, but it also hosts a varied program of classical recitals and concerts; contact the Oxford Playhouse (p. 223) for tickets.

Broad St. www.ox.ac.uk/sheldonian. ℂ **01865/277299.** Admission £2.50. Mar–Oct Mon–Sat 10am–12:30pm and 2–4:30pm; Nov–Feb Mon–Sat 10am–12:30pm and 2–3:30pm. Closed when used for events.

University College & Shelley Memorial ★ HISTORIC SITE   This modest and forward-looking college is one of the oldest in the university, founded in the 1240s by William of Durham. It's best known for the monument to Romantic poet Percy Bysshe Shelley, who came here in 1810 but was expelled the following year (for writing a pamphlet, *The Necessity of Atheism*). The memorial, solemnly displayed in a special hall since 1894, is an elegant white-marble sculpture of a drowned Shelley, as he washed up on the shore at Viareggio in Italy. Less romantic but equally influential alumni include Bill Clinton and Stephen Hawking.

High St. www.univ.ox.ac.uk. ℂ **01865/276602.** Free admission. Daily 9am–4pm; ask first at the porter's lodge at the entrance about visiting the Shelley Memorial (small groups only).

Where to Eat
VERY EXPENSIVE

Le Manoir aux Quat' Saisons ★★★ CONTEMPORARY FRENCH   This elegant showcase for celebrity Gallic chef Raymond Blanc offers the finest cuisine in the region. Some 12 miles southeast of Oxford, the gray-and-honey-colored stone manor house, originally built by a Norman nobleman in the early 1300s, provides a wonderful backdrop to Blanc's seasonal menu (he's known for using local and sustainable produce from his kitchen garden). Perennial favorites include the smoked haddock soup with sea bass tartare and caviar as a starter, as well as the slow-roasted wild woodcock for a main and the utterly irresistible raspberry soufflé.

Church Rd., Great Milton. www.manoir.com. ℂ **800/237-1236** in the U.S., or 01844/278881. Fax 01844/278847. Reservations required. Main courses £48 lunch or dinner; set lunch Mon–Fri £75 (5-courses), £120 (7-courses); 7-course lunch Sat–Sun £120; set dinner £130–£150. AE, DC, MC, V.

Daily 7am–10am, noon–2:30pm, and 7–10pm. Take exit 7 off M40 and head along the A329 toward Wallingford; after about 1 mile, look for signs for Great American Milton Manor.

EXPENSIVE

Cherwell Boathouse Restaurant ★ FRENCH/CONTEMPORARY ENGLISH

This Oxford landmark boasts an enchanting location overlooking the River Cherwell and an intriguing menu that changes every 2 weeks to take advantage of the freshest vegetables, fish, and meat. The success of the main dishes is founded on savory treats such as braised lamb shank with swede purée and roasted garlic creamed potatoes, crispy pork cutlets with a Provençal sauce, and wild mushroom risotto. Save room for the traditional English puddings, which are justly celebrated.

Bardwell Rd. www.cherwellboathouse.co.uk. (*) **01865/552746.** Reservations recommended. Fixed-price dinner from £21.25–£26.50; Mon–Fri set lunch £20–£24.50. AE, MC, V. Daily noon–2:30pm and 6–9:30pm. Closed Dec 24–30. Bus: Banbury Rd.

MODERATE

Branca ★ ITALIAN

This spacious, airy Italian bistro in the trendy enclave of Jericho, a short stroll north of the center, cooks up perfectly seasoned fish and al dente pasta, and a decent house Chianti is offered as well. The seafood risottos are a light and creamy delight, topped with just enough chopped parsley and lemon zest, but don't ignore the main dishes. Pork is masterfully done here: The pan-fried pork cutlet with Parmesan herb breadcrumbs and tomato-chili salsa is exceptional. Meat and vegetables are sourced locally. Lunch specials run Monday to Friday from £7.45.

111 Walton St. www.branca-restaurants.com. (*) **01865/556111.** Reservations recommended. Main courses £9.95–£16, pasta from £6.75, pizza from £9.75. MC, V. Daily noon–11pm.

Brasserie Blanc ★ BRASSERIE

Master restaurateur Raymond Blanc took a former piano shop and converted it into this stylish eatery. The informal brasserie, with its striking modern interior, offers a taste of this famous chef's creations without the high prices of the swanky Le Manoir aux Quat' Saisons (see above). Options are more straightforward here, with a menu based on food Blanc's mother once cooked him in Besançon, France. Highly praised dishes include his slow-cooked beef and onions with a parsnip purée, or Toulouse sausages with onion sauce and mash.

Oxford's Cheap Eats

Prices tend to be high at Oxford restaurants, but there are a few bargains to be had in the **Covered Market** (between the High Street and Cornmarket; www.oxford-covered-market.co.uk). Most places take cash only. An outpost of Bristol's gourmet pie company **Pieminister** (www.pieminister.co.uk; (*) **01865/241613;** Mon–Sat 10am–5pm, Sun 11am–4pm) sells savory meat pies from £5.30–£7. The original **Ben's Cookies** (www.benscookies.com; (*) **01865/247407;** Mon–Sat 8am–5:30pm, Sun 10am–4pm) bakes up delicious cookies for around £1.30, and **Fasta Pasta** ((*) **01865/241973;** daily 8am–6pm) is a great place to pick up sandwiches and bowls of pasta that start at £2.95. You can get fine British and European cheeses at the **Oxford Cheese Company** (www.oxfordfinefood.com; (*) **01865/721420**) or home-baked breads and cakes from **Nash's Oxford Bakery** (www.nashsbakery.co.uk; (*) **01865/242695**), which was established in nearby Bicester in 1930. And there's always **Brown's** (see below) for a hearty English fry-up.

71–72 Walton St. www.brasserieblanc.com. ✆ **01865/510999.** Reservations recommended. Main courses £9.50–£18.20. AE, MC, V. Mon–Fri noon–2:45pm and 5:30–10pm; Sat noon–10:30pm; Sun noon–9:30pm.

Gee's ★ CONTEMPORARY ENGLISH This restaurant, in a spacious Victorian glass conservatory dating from 1898, was converted from what was once the leading florist of Oxford. Its original features were retained by the owners, who have turned it into one of the most nostalgic and delightful establishments in the city. Classic English dishes are likely to include confit of pig cheeks with dandelion, exquisite local Bibury trout, and slow cooked Rofford beef. Finish with a traditional dessert: Steamed treacle (sugar syrup) sponge pudding. It's worth staying for the live jazz every Sunday evening (8–9:45pm), even if you're just having drinks.

61 Banbury Rd. www.gees-restaurant.co.uk. ✆ **01865/553540.** Reservations recommended. Main courses £15.75–£27; set lunch and pre-theatre menu £16.95–£20.95. AE, MC, V. Mon–Sat noon–2:30pm, Sun noon–3:30pm; daily 6–10:30pm. Bus: Banbury Rd.

INEXPENSIVE

Al-Shami LEBANESE Bearing the archaic name for the city of Damascus, it's worth the short walk to this enticing Lebanese restaurant that knocks out superb Middle Eastern cuisine. Many diners don't go beyond the appetizers, which include more than 40 delectable hot and cold mezze—everything from falafel and hummus to Armenian sausages and fried chicken livers. They may be described as "small dishes," but six-to-eight plates between two diners makes for a filling meal. Char-grilled chopped lamb, chicken, or fish constitute most of the main-dish selections. Desserts are chosen from the cart, and vegetarian meals are also available.

25 Walton Crescent at Richmond St., Jericho. www.al-shami.co.uk. ✆ **01865/310066.** Reservations recommended. Main courses £6.90–£12; mezze £2.50–£4.80. MC, V. Cover charge £1 per person, plus 10% service charge. Daily noon–midnight.

Brown's (Covered Market) ★★ TRADITIONAL ENGLISH Don't confuse this no-frills diner, deep inside the Covered Market, with the posh (and overrated) Browns on Woodstock Road. If you're curious about traditional Brit cafes, or just crave a "greasy spoon," you're in for a treat. Think sausage sandwiches, proper fish and chips, liver and bacon, steak and kidney pie, hearty fry-ups (fried bacon, mushrooms, eggs, and toast), apple pie and custard, and mugs of tea guaranteed to cure the deepest hangovers. Customers range from Oxford professors to locals on their lunch break.

Ave. 4, Covered Market (Market St. entrance). ✆ **01865/243436.** Main courses £3.50–£7.50. No credit cards. Mon–Sat 8am–5:30pm.

George & Davis DESSERT/CAFE This is Oxford's ice-cream headquarters, a brightly painted cafe serving artisanal homemade ice cream, as well as decent bagels, with plenty of *schmears* (cream cheese spreads), cookies, ethically sourced coffees and teas, and scrumptious cakes. Expect indulgent and traditional flavors such as dandelion and burdock, Greek yogurt and honey, vodka jelly, and golden secret (honeycomb and chocolate in a cream base), topped with gummy bears, M&Ms, nuts, or chocolate sprinkles.

55 Little Clarendon St. www.gdcafe.com. ✆ **01865/516652.** One ice-cream scoop £2.10, bagels from £2.75. No credit cards. Daily 8am–midnight.

Manos ★★ GREEK Even Greek expats end up at this cozy, no-frills taverna, a sunny place with great food enhanced by traditional Greek folk songs wafting through the air. Portions are big, and salads are heavy on the feta cheese, which is always a good sign; the indomitable Manos himself cooks up a wicked chicken *souvlaki* (flatbread filled with marinated grilled chicken or falafel, hummus, tzatziki, and salad), and a mouth-watering moussaka.

105 Walton St. www.manosfoodbar.com. ℂ **01865/311782.** Reservations recommended. Main courses £6.45–£8.60. MC, V. Mon–Wed 10:30am–9pm; Thurs–Fri 10:30am–10pm; Sat 9:30am–10pm; Sun 11:30am–8pm.

Mission Mexican Grill ★ MEXICAN   This place isn't quite on the level of the *taquerías* in San Francisco's Mission District (this is England after all), but it's a worthy tribute to Cal-Mex food nonetheless. The burritos here—a specialty—are some of the best in the U.K., with high-quality and flavorful meat, beans, sour cream, and flour tortillas. Each order involves selecting your dish, (taco, burrito etc), filling, extras, and salsa. The *carnitas* burrito (pork roasted slowly with herbs and orange zest) is spot on, and makes a tasty meal. The veggie options are also good (it's hard to beat grilled vegetables, guacamole, and black beans).

8 St. Michael's St. www.missionburritos.co.uk. ℂ **01865/202016.** Burritos £5.45–£5.95. MC, V. Sun–Wed 11am–10pm; Thurs–Sat 11am–11pm. There's another location at 2 King Edward St. ℂ **01865/722020.**

Nosebag Restaurant CAFE/HEALTH FOOD   Yes, it sometimes is mobbed with tourists and students, but there's a good reason this is a long-standing local favorite. It's the most conveniently located cafe in town and serves solid homemade quiches, baked potatoes, curries, casseroles, and lasagnas, all paired with a choice of three salads. Vegetarians are well catered for here (think sweet-pepper-and-lentil lasagna, and coconut root vegetable curry). The evening menu is a bit more expensive.

6–8 St. Michael's St. www.nosebagoxford.co.uk. ℂ **01865/721033.** Main courses £8.95–£12.50. MC, V. Mon–Thurs 9:30am–9:30pm; Fri–Sat 9:30am–10pm; Sun 9:30am–8:30pm.

Posh Fish! ★ FISH & CHIPS   Order this classic Brit treat to take-out or eat in (there's plenty of space). Huge portions of crispy battered haddock, cod, or plaice can be ordered with curry sauce, beans, mushy peas, and real, thick English chips. Aficionados can also enjoy battered sausage, kebabs, fish cakes, pies, and a full fry-up (any time of day). There are jacket potatoes for the (relatively) healthy.

109 Walton St., Jericho; also 150 London Rd., Headington. ℂ **01865/765894.** Main courses £4.50–£6.50. Sun–Mon 5–10:30pm; Tues–Thurs noon–2pm, 5–10:30pm; Fri–Sat noon–2pm, 5pm–midnight.

Vaults & Garden Café ★ CAFE/HEALTH FOOD   This cozy English cafe serves tasty soups in cups (try the leek and potato), artisan bread, and organic vegetables from nearby Worton Organic Garden. It's another of Oxford's good options for vegetarians, with dishes such as roast-vegetable Spanish tortilla, roasted butternut squash, coconut curry, and tofu-and-brown-rice vegetable stir-fry gracing the menu, and organic beef lasagna for meat-eaters. All main courses are served with salad, brown rice, or potatoes. The cafe occupies a gorgeous 14th-century hall on the grounds of the University Church of St. Mary the Virgin.

University Church of St. Mary the Virgin, Radcliffe Sq. www.vaultsandgarden.com. ℂ **01865/279112.** Main courses £6–£8.45. MC, V. Mon–Thurs 9:30am–9:30pm; Fri–Sat 9:30am–10pm; Sun 9:30am–8:30pm.

Shopping

Alice's Shop, 83 St. Aldate's (www.aliceinwonderlandshop.co.uk; ℂ**01865/723793**), is set within a 15th-century building that has housed some kind of shop since 1820, mostly a general store (selling brooms, hardware, and the like). Alice Liddell, thought to have been the model for *Alice in Wonderland,* used to buy her barley sugar sweets here when Lewis Carroll was a professor of mathematics at Christ Church. Today, the place is a favorite stopover of Lewis Carroll fans, who gobble up commemorative pencils, chess sets, bookmarks, and, in rare cases, original editions of some of Carroll's works. Open daily 10:30am to 5pm (July–Aug 9:30am–6:30pm).

The **Bodleian Library Shop,** Old School's Quadrangle, Radcliffe Square, Broad Street (www.shop.bodley.ox.ac.uk; ℂ **01865/277091**), specializes in Oxford souvenirs, from books and paperweights to Oxford banners and coffee mugs. It's open Monday to Friday 9am to 5pm, Saturday 9am to 4:30pm, and Sunday 11am to 5pm.

Castell & Son (The Varsity Shop), 13 Broad St. (www.varsityshop.co.uk; ℂ **01865/244000**), is the best outlet in Oxford for clothing emblazoned with the Oxford logo or heraldic symbol. Options include both whimsical and dead-on-serious neckties, hats, T-shirts, pens, beer and coffee mugs, and cufflinks. It's commercialized Oxford, but has got a sense of relative dignity and style. It's open Monday to Saturday 9am to 5:30pm, and Sunday 10am to 5pm. A second location is at 109–114 High Street (ℂ **01865/249491**).

The best bookstore in Oxford is venerable **Blackwells,** at 48–51 Broad St. (www.bookshop.blackwell.co.uk; ℂ **01865/333536**), open Monday to Saturday 9am to 6:30pm, Sunday 11am to 5pm.

Entertainment & Nightlife

Students tend to unwind in pubs, private college bars (which have "bops" or discos), and private student apartments in Oxford, so the nightlife can seem relatively tame to outsiders. There is, however, a steady supply of high-quality classical and choir music on offer, and a few places offer more energetic live music. In any case, the pubs are some of the most historic and atmospheric in the country (and London is only an hour away if you crave clubs).

THE PERFORMING ARTS

Highly acclaimed orchestras playing in truly lovely settings mark the **Music at Oxford** series (www.musicatoxford.com), based at the **Oxford Playhouse Theatre,** Beaumont Street (www.oxfordplayhouse.com; ℂ **01865/244806**). The season runs from October to early July. Tickets range from £10 to £42. Many performances are held in the Sheldonian Theatre and Christ Church Cathedral, particularly attractive locations (p. 219 and p. 216). The box office is open Monday to Saturday from 9:30am to 6pm (or until half an hour after the start of an evening performance) and on Sunday starting at least 2 hours before a performance.

New Theatre, George Street (www.newtheatreoxford.org.uk; ℂ **01865/320760;** or Ticketmaster www.ticketmaster.co.uk; ℂ **0844/847-1585** for tickets), is Oxford's primary theatre. Tickets range from £10 to £50. A continuous run of comedy, ballet, drama, opera, and even rock contributes to the variety. We highly recommend that you purchase tickets in advance. The box office is open Monday to Saturday from 10am to 8pm (to 6pm if there is no evening performance).

THE PUB SCENE

Pubs lie at the heart of Oxford social life. Almost every pub in the center has a long (and notorious) history, usually linked to the university or a specific college (see "Pubs with a Pedigree", below). Real ales are a staple, and plenty of places serve aromatic mulled wine in the winter. Aficionados should visit www.oxfordcamra.org.uk.

PUBS WITH A pedigree

Every college town the world over has a fair number of bars, but few can boast local watering holes with such atmosphere and history as Oxford.

A short block from the High, overlooking the north side of Christ Church, the **Bear Inn** ★, 6 Alfred St. (© **01865/728164**), is an Oxford institution dating back to 1242 (the current building was built in the early 17th century), and mentioned time and again in English literature. Alan Course, former owner of the Bear, developed an odd custom in the 1950s: Clipping neckties in exchange for a half pint of beer. Around the lounge bar you'll see the remains of thousands of ties, which have been labeled with their owners' names.

At the 17th-century **Eagle and Child,** 49 St. Giles St. (© **01865/302925**), literary history suffuses the dim, paneled alcoves. In the 1930s and 1940s it was frequented by the "Inklings," a writer's group that included the likes of C. S. Lewis and J. R. R. Tolkien. In fact, *The Chronicles of Narnia* and *The Hobbit* were first read aloud in this pub. It's a must-see for Tolkien fans; the "Rabbit Room" is adorned with extracts from his work (some original).

Another pub with roots in the 13th century, the **Turf Tavern** ★★, 7 Bath Place (off Holywell St.; www.theturf tavern.co.uk; © **01865/243235**), is reached via narrow St. Helen's Passage, which stretches between Holywell Street and New College Lane. (You'll probably get lost, but any student worth his or her beer can direct you.). It was "the local" of the future U.S. president Bill Clinton during his student days at Oxford. In warm weather, you can choose a table in any of the three separate gardens that radiate outward from the pub's central core. It's famed for its seasonal ales and warm mulled wine in the winter.

The tiny **White Horse** ★, 52 Broad St. (www.whitehorseoxford.co.uk; © **01865/204801**), squeezed between Blackwell's bookstores, is always a good place to soak up the collegiate atmosphere. It's one of Oxford's oldest pubs, dating from the 16th century, a popular feature in the *Inspector Morse* series and renowned for its real ales and fish and chips (£8.95).

Most Oxford pubs open from around 11am to midnight Monday to Saturday, and 11am to 10:30pm on Sunday. Pints of beer range £3.20–£3.50.

The **Head of the River,** Abingdon Road at Folly Bridge, near the Westgate Centre Mall (© **01865/721600**), is a lively place offering traditional ales and lagers, along with good sturdy bar food. In summer, guests can sit by the river and rent a punt or a boat with an engine. The congenial **King's Arms,** 40 Holywell St. (© **01865/242369**), hosts a mix of students, tourists, and professors. One of the best places in town to strike up a conversation, the pub, owned by Young's Brewery, features several of the company's ales on tap, along with visiting lagers and bitters that change periodically. The genial **Lamb & Flag** at 12 St. Giles (© **01865/515787**) has been around since 1695 and is owned by nearby St. John's College. Thomas Hardy used the pub as a setting in his novel *Jude the Obscure* (and may have written some of it here).

THE CLUB & MUSIC SCENE

In 1988, **Freud Café,** 119 Walton St. (www.freud.eu; © **01865/311171**), turned an 18th-century Greek Revival church, stained-glass windows and all, into a bar, jazz, and folk venue with an expansive array of cocktail options (the food is rather mediocre). There is no cover. Hours are Monday to Thursday 5pm to 11pm, Friday 5pm to 2am, Saturday 10am to 2am, and Sun 10am to 11pm.

O2 Academy Oxford, 190 Cowley Rd. (www.o2academyoxford.co.uk; ✆ **0844/ 477-2000**), is the best live indie-music venue in the city; tickets range from £5 to £25 (cash only on the door). Shows usually start at 6pm Tuesday to Saturday, and also at 2:30pm on Saturday.

The **Jericho Tavern,** 56 Walton St. (www.thejerichooxford.co.uk; ✆ **01865/ 311775;** tickets at www.wegottickets.com), comprises two levels. Downstairs, patrons consume the suds inside, or outside in the beer garden. Upstairs is another area for drinking. Live music (mostly alternative rock or folk) is featured Friday and Saturday, when a £5 to £9 cover is charged. Open Monday through Friday noon to midnight, Saturday and Sunday 10am to midnight.

Thirst, 7–8 Park End St. (www.thirstbar.com; ✆ **01865/242044**), is a popular student hangout with a cocktail bar and a small garden. Resident DJs rule the night. Open Sunday to Wednesday 7:30pm to 2am, Thursday to Saturday 7:30pm to 3:30am.

Where to Stay
EXPENSIVE
Macdonald Randolph Hotel ★   Open since 1864, the venerable Randolph is an Oxford landmark with elegant guest rooms furnished in a conservative English style. Fans of Inspector Morse should check out the Morse Bar (the fictional Morse often asserted that "they serve a decent pint" at the Randolph, and author Colin Dexter set several of the detective stories here), while the lounges, though modernized, are cavernous enough for dozens of separate and intimate conversational groupings. Some rooms are quite large and others a bit cramped. Overall the hotel is a little overpriced; you're paying primarily for the location and the rich history.

Beaumont St., Oxford OX1 2LN. www.macdonaldhotels.co.uk/Randolph. ✆ **0844/879-9132.** Fax: 01865/791678. 151 units. £230–£280 double; £528–£607 suite. AE, DC, MC, V. Limited parking £27 or public parking £30 for 24 hr. **Amenities:** Restaurant; 2 bars; spa; concierge; room service; baby-sitting. *In room:* TV, hair dryer, CD player, Wi-Fi (£9.99 per day).

Malmaison Oxford Castle ★★ 🛏   This place was formerly for inmates detained at Her Majesty's pleasure, and many aspects of prison life, including barred windows, have been retained. Guest rooms, in a converted Victorian building, are actually remodeled "cells" that flank two sides of a large central atrium, a space that rises three stories and is crisscrossed by narrow walkways. The former inmates never had it so good—great beds, mood lighting, power showers, satellite TV, and serious wines. In spite of its origins, this is a stylish and comfortable place to stay.

3 Oxford Castle, Oxford OXI 1AY. www.malmaison.com. ✆ **01865/268400.** 94 units. £185–£245 double; £275–£345 suite. AE, DC, MC, V. Parking (pre-booking required) £20. **Amenities:** Restaurant; bar; exercise room; room service. *In room:* TV/DVD, minibar, CD player, Wi-Fi (free).

Old Bank Hotel ★★   The first hotel created in the center of Oxford in 135 years, the Old Bank opened in 1999 and immediately surpassed the traditional favorite, the Randolph (see above), in both style and amenities. Located on Oxford's main street and surrounded by some of its oldest colleges and sights, the building dates back to the 18th century and was indeed once a bank. The hotel currently features a collection of 20th-century British art handpicked by the owners. Bedrooms are comfortably and elegantly appointed, many opening onto views. A combination of velvet and shantung silk-trimmed linen bedcovers gives the guest rooms added style.

92–94 High St., Oxford OX1 4BN. www.oldbank-hotel.co.uk. ℂ **01865/799599.** Fax 01865/799598.
42 units. £230–£350 double. AE, DC, MC, V. Free parking. **Amenities:** Restaurant; bar; room service; babysitting. *In room:* A/C, TV, hair dryer, CD player, Internet (free).

MODERATE

Burlington House ★★ ✦ This top choice on the edge of town makes up for the slightly inconvenient location with fabulous service, bargain prices, and immaculate, boutique-like rooms. Inside, old fittings and fireplaces blend with modern beds and flat-screen TVs; the power showers are especially welcome. Breakfasts are another highlight, with high-quality continental and hot items to try (marmalade omelet anyone?). The hotel sits on Banbury Road near a bus stop with frequent buses into the center (10- 20-min. walk), and there are plenty of bars and restaurants nearby, too.

374 Banbury Rd., Oxford OX2 7PP. www.burlington-hotel-oxford.co.uk. ℂ **01865/513513.** 12 units. £86–£160 double. AE, DC, MC, V. Rates include English breakfast. Free parking (weekends only). Bus: 2 or 7. **Amenities:** Lounge; dining room. *In room:* A/C, TV, hair dryer, Wi-Fi (free).

Ethos Hotel ★ ▮▮ Plush self-catering boutique hotel set within a Victorian terrace on the edge of the city center, close to the River Thames. A good choice if you don't mind the 15-minute walk into town, and want the option of cooking basic food in your room. Rooms feature designer wallpaper and furnishings, Italian marble shower-rooms with Raindance power-showers, iPod docks, toasters, kettles, microwave/grill/convection ovens, and tableware. A breakfast basket is delivered to the room each morning.

59 Western Rd., Grandpont. Oxford OX1 4LF. www.ethoshotels.co.uk. ℂ **01865/245800.** Fax 0800/007-3248. 12 units. £99–£135 double; £199–£215 suite. AE, DC, MC, V. Rates include breakfast. Free parking. **Amenities:** Reduced rates at Willows Leisure Club. *In room:* TV, DVD, minibar, hair-dryer, Wi-Fi (free).

INEXPENSIVE

Sandfield Guest House ★ Just off the main road to the M40 and London (A420) in the student suburb of Headington, friendly hosts Paul and Natália Anderson have created a welcoming B&B. It's 10 minutes by bus from central Oxford. Rooms are well equipped and very comfy—everything is new and spotlessly clean. (Room no. 3 has a slightly larger bathroom.) The full, cooked English breakfasts are high quality, very filling, and accompanied by yogurt, cereal, and fresh fruit. Headington is a pleasant neighborhood in its own right, with shops and a few restaurants within walking distance.

19 London Rd., Headington, Oxford OX3 7RE. www.sandfieldguesthouse.net76.net. ℂ **01865/767767.** 4 units. £80–£100 double; £45 single. Rates include English breakfast. MC, V. Free parking. Bus: U1. *In room:* TV, hair dryer, Wi-Fi (free).

Tilbury Lodge ★★ ▮▮ This unassuming red-brick home on the outskirts holds one of Oxford's secret gems, a B&B with fresh, modern decor, new bathrooms, and spacious rooms. It's the extras that make this special: Bathrobes, foot-massage machines, and a bevy of sweet treats baked by the affable owners, Stefan and Melanie. Expect homemade fudge, cookies, tea and coffee, and warm scones on arrival. The breakfasts are hard to beat, a wonderful spread of fresh fruits, yogurts, homemade breads, muffins, and tasty cooked plates. The city center is just 10 minutes by bus (the bus stop is on the corner).

5 Tilbury Lane, Oxford OX2 9NB. www.tilburylodge.com. ℂ **01865/862138.** 9 units. £88–£110 double. Rates include English breakfast. MC, V. Free parking. Bus: 4C, S1. **Amenities:** Conservatory

lounge. *In room:* TV, hair dryer, CD player, Wi-Fi (free). From Oxford, take the A420 then Westway to Botley, turn right onto Eynsham Rd. (B4044) and look for Tilbury Lane (first right). Closed Dec–Jan.

Side Trips from Oxford
WOODSTOCK

The small country town of **Woodstock,** 8 miles northwest of Oxford, was in 1330 the birthplace of the Black Prince, ill-fated son of King Edward III. Today it's a picturesque collection of 18th-century stone houses and the gateway to **Blenheim Palace** (see below). There's little of interest in the town itself, though the **Oxfordshire Museum,** Fletcher's House, Park Street (www.oxfordshire.gov.uk; ℂ **01993/ 811456**), is worth a quick look; it chronicles the history, culture, and crafts of Oxfordshire and has an attractive garden with a full-size replica of a megalosaurus that youngsters will love. The museum is open Tuesday to Saturday 10am to 5pm and Sunday 2 to 5pm; admission is free.

Bus S3, operated by **Stagecoach** (www.stagecoachbus.com; ℂ **01865/772250**), leaves Oxford about every 10 to 15 minutes during the day. The trip to Woodstock takes a little more than 30 minutes. If you're driving, take the A44 from Oxford. The **Tourist Information Centre,** located inside the Oxfordshire Museum (www. oxfordshirecotswolds.org; ℂ **01993/813276**) is open Monday to Saturday 10am to 5pm year-round.

Blenheim Palace ★★★ HISTORIC SITE   The extravagantly baroque Blenheim Palace is England's answer to Versailles. Blenheim is still the home of the Dukes of Marlborough, descendants of the first duke John Churchill, victor of the Battle of Blenheim (1704), a crushing defeat of Britain's archenemy Louis XIV. Blenheim was built for him as a gift from Queen Anne in the 1720s. The family, virtually bankrupt, hung on to the palace thanks to the brutally commercial marriage of Charles, 9th Duke of Marlborough (1871–1934) to Consuelo Vanderbilt, heiress to the wealthy American railroad dynasty. Blenheim was also the birthplace of the 9th duke's first cousin, Sir Winston Churchill. The room in which he was born in 1874 is included in the palace tour, as is the Churchill exhibition: four rooms of letters, books, photographs, and other relics.

The palace was designed by Sir John Vanbrugh, who was also the architect of Castle Howard; the landscaping was created by Capability Brown. The interior is loaded with riches: Antiques, porcelain, oil paintings, tapestries, and chinoiserie. The present owner is the 11th Duke of Marlborough (b. 1926), whom you may see wandering around. The duke had a small cameo in Kenneth Branagh's movie *Hamlet* (1996), which was filmed at Blenheim.

Churchill's Final Resting Place

The small village of Bladon, about 6½ miles northwest of Oxford and a short drive from Blenheim Palace, is the final resting place of Sir Winston Churchill. Following his state funeral in St. Paul's Cathedral, Churchill was buried in Bladon in January 1965. His relatively modest grave lies at the **Church of St.** **Martin,** a simple Gothic structure rebuilt in the 1890s. Churchill's white tomb also contains the remains of his wife, Clementine, who was buried here in 1977. To reach St. Martin's Church (ℂ **01993/ 880546**) from Oxford, take the A44 toward Woodstock, and then go on the A4095 toward Whitney.

Insider tip: **Marlborough Maze,** 540m (1,800 ft.) from the palace, is the largest symbolic hedge maze on earth, with an herb and lavender garden, a butterfly house, and inflatable castles for children. Also, be sure to look for the castle's gift shops, tucked away in an old palace dairy. Here you can purchase a wide range of souvenirs, handicrafts, and even locally made preserves.

Brighton Rd., Woodstock. www.blenheimpalace.com. © **01993/810530** or 0800/849-6500 for 24hr freephone information. Admission £20 adults (parks and gardens £11.50), £15.50 students and seniors (parks and gardens £8.50), £11 children 5–15 (parks and gardens £6), and £52 family ticket (parks and gardens £30); free for children 4 and under. Daily 10:30am–5:30pm. Last admission 4:45pm. Closed mid-Dec–mid-Feb (except for park).

THE CHILTERNS

North of the Thames Valley, the Chiltern Hills form a rolling green barrier between Oxford and the outer suburbs of London. While the hills are not dramatic or especially big (the highest point is just 267m/876 ft. at Haddington Hill, near Wendover), it is a protected area harboring **pretty villages,** ancient **beech woodlands,** handsome **stately homes,** and **intriguing museums.** The hills are actually part of a chalk escarpment stretching some 50 miles from Goring-on-Thames in Oxfordshire, through Buckinghamshire, to Bedfordshire and the edge of East Anglia, but everything is an easy drive or bus ride from London or Oxford.

Essentials

GETTING THERE To make the most out of this region, you'll need a car, though all the main towns are connected to London by frequent buses and trains. The Chilterns' largest towns are Aylesbury in the north and High Wycombe in the south. **Aylesbury** is 1 hour by train from London's Marylebone Station (£14.40 one-way), or 25 minutes off the M25 via the A41. Trains to High Wycombe (£11.90 one-way) from London Marylebone take 25 to 40 minutes.

VISITOR INFORMATION The **Aylesbury Tourist Information Centre,** Kings Head Passage, off Market Square (www.visitbuckinghamshire.org; © **01296/ 330559**), is open April through October, Monday to Saturday 9:30am to 5pm, and November through March, Monday to Saturday 10am to 4:30pm. The High Wycombe **Tourist Information Centre** (www.visitbuckinghamshire.org; © **01494/ 421892**) is located inside High Wycombe Library at the Eden Shopping Centre, 5 Eden Place (near the bus station). It's open Tuesday to Friday 9:30am to 5:30pm, Saturday 9:30am to 4pm. You should also check out www.chilternsaonb.org and www.chilternsociety.org.uk for more information.

Exploring the Area
AYLESBURY

The county town of Buckinghamshire, Aylesbury has retained much of its 18th-century provincial charm and character, despite rapid expansion in recent years, and plenty of celebrity connections. The town features extensively in British cult TV series *Midsomer Murders,* and **Chequers**—the official country residence of British prime ministers since 1921—lies just 5 miles to the south (it's strictly off-limits).

The most historic streets surround **St. Mary's Church,** in the center, which dates from the 13th century and features an unusual spire from the reign of Charles II. The 15th-century **King's Head Public House** (©**01296/381501;** daily 11:30am–11pm), one of the few working pubs owned by the National Trust, at King's Head Passage, Market Square, has seen many famous faces in its time, including Henry VIII, who was a frequent guest while he was courting Anne Boleyn. The thriving town **market** is definitely worth a look, held on Wednesday, Friday, and Saturday (with a flea market on Tuesday). Aylesbury also hosts the **Roald Dahl Festival,** a procession of giant puppets based on the author's characters, every July (see www.aylesburyvaledc.gov.uk). Dahl was a long-time resident of the Chiltern area (see "Great Missenden," below).

Buckinghamshire County Museum ☺ MUSEUM   This museum focuses on the cultural heritage of Buckinghamshire, through interactive exhibits and displays of Celtic gold coins, Roman artifacts, paintings, and British studio ceramics. The complex also includes the **Roald Dahl Children's Gallery,** where the author's children's books, especially *Charlie and the Chocolate Factory* and *James and the Giant Peach,* come to life as visitors ride in the Great Glass Elevator and crawl inside the Giant Peach. Entry to the Children's Gallery is through a timed ticket system; visits last an hour and entry is on the hour, but there are a limited number of tickets so booking ahead is advised.

Church St. www.buckscc.gov.uk/museum. ✆ **01296/331441.** Free admission to main museum. Children's Gallery £6 adults, £4 children 3–18, free for children 2 and under, family ticket £17.50. Tues–Sat 10am–4pm; call ahead to confirm times to Children's Gallery.

Tiggywinkles ★★ ☺ SANCTUARY   This earnest animal hospital and hedgehog center is guaranteed to get children and animal lovers swooning with excitement. Tiggywinkles treats over 10,000 animal casualties every year (mostly from road accidents); be prepared to get weepy as baby deer limp around on crutches and tiny hedgehogs shuffle mournfully along trails of leaves. The visitor center uses interpretation boards and videos to describe the history of the hospital, the type of animals treated, and some of the techniques employed; in the spring and summer visitors can also see the nursery areas where the animals are treated.

Aston Rd., Haddenham. www.sttiggywinkles.org.uk. ✆ **01844/292292.** Admission £4.90 adults, £3.20 children 5–18, free for seniors, children 4 and under, £13.50 family ticket. Easter–Sept daily 10am–4pm; Oct–Easter Mon–Fri 10am–4pm. Haddenham is 5 miles southwest of Aylesbury via the A418. Trains run about every half-hour to Haddenham from London Marylebone. Arriva bus no. 110 from Aylesbury gets you within walking distance.

Waddesdon Manor ★★ HISTORIC HOME   Built in the 1870s by Baron Ferdinand de Rothschild (a member of the Rothschild banking dynasty), this château-like monument to the Gilded Age features whimsical French neo-Renaissance architecture and a priceless collection of elegant French furniture, carpets, and Sèvres porcelain. The place is so ornate it doubled for Buckingham Palace in the movie *The Queen* (2006). Eighteenth-century artwork by several famous English painters (Gainsborough and Reynolds among them) is exhibited, and you can also view a writing desk owned by Marie-Antoinette. Don't miss the wine cellar, crammed with the finest bottles from Château Lafite Rothschild dating back to 1868. On the premises are a restaurant and a gift shop, both featuring a vast assortment of Rothschild wines.

High St. (A41), Waddesdon. www.waddesdon.org.uk. ✆ **01296/653226.** Admission to house and grounds £13.60–£15.40 adults, £10–£11.80 children 5–16, free for children 4 and under; grounds only £5.90–£7.20 adults, £3.10–£4 children 5–16, £15–£18.63 family ticket, free for children 4 and younger. House Apr–Oct Wed–Fri noon–4pm, Sat–Sun 11am–4pm; closed Nov–Mar; grounds and aviary Jan–mid-Mar Sat–Sun 10am–5pm, mid-Mar–Dec Wed–Sun 10am–5pm. Waddesdon is 12 miles from Aylesbury via the A41. Take Arriva bus no. 16 or 17.

The **Ridgeway National Trail** (www.nationaltrail.co.uk) links the downs of Wiltshire with the Chilterns via a well-marked and wonderfully scenic 87-mile path from Overton Hill, near Avebury (p. 334) to Ivinghoe Beacon in Buckinghamshire. The path follows an ancient track used since prehistoric times, and is by far the most enticing way to experience the woods and lanes of the Chilterns. You'll probably take 6 full days to walk the whole thing, an average of 14 miles a day. The trail website has lodging and transport details, as well as specialist tour companies that can arrange the whole trip. There's also the **Chiltern Way,** a circular trail of around 125 miles; see www.chilternsociety.org.uk for more information.

The **Chilterns Cycleway** is a 170-mile cycle loop through the Chilterns, taking in the best of its scenery and villages. The route is mainly on-road and is signposted throughout. You'll find several bike-rental shops along the way, including Dees Cycles at 39 Hill Ave., Amersham (www.deescycles.com; ☎ **01494/727165**), and Henley Cycles at 69 Reading Rd., Henley-on-Thames (www.henleycycles.co.uk; ☎ **01491/578984**).

CHALFONT ST. GILES

Just 25 miles from London, perched on the eastern edge of the Chilterns, Chalfont St. Giles has been relatively successful in preserving its traditional center despite the rapid urbanization all around, with local shops, pubs, and cafes clustered around the rustic green and village pond. It's best known as the place where poet **John Milton** took refuge whilst the Great Plague ravaged London in 1665. To reach the village, take the A355 north from the M40 (junction 2), until you come to the signposted turn for Chalfont St. Giles to the east. Carousel bus A30 runs to the village from Heathrow Airport and from Amersham (London Tube station).

Chiltern Open Air Museum ★ MUSEUM   This absorbing 45-acre museum has been restoring aging Chiltern buildings and relocating them here since the 1970s, and now more than 30 are on view (you can go inside most of them). Among the rustic wooden barns and farm buildings are a reconstruction of an Iron Age round-house, a Victorian prefab chapel, an 1860 forge, and an 18th-century thatched barn converted into two simple cottages. In between is parkland grazed by sheep and rolling woods.

Newland Park, Gorelands Lane. www.coam.org.uk. ☎ **01494/872163.** Admission £8 adults, £5 children 5–16, £23 family ticket. Apr–Oct daily 10am–5pm (last admission 3:30pm). The museum is signposted from the A413 at Chalfont St. Giles. Walking from the village should take around 30 min.

John Milton's Cottage ★ HISTORIC HOME   John Milton finished off his epic poem *Paradise Lost* in this humble 16th-century cottage in 1665. It's the only one of his homes still standing, evocative of his generally frugal, hardworking life. The great poet had been working on the poem for 7 years and was already blind by the time he lived here. Its four rooms contain many relics and exhibits devoted to Milton, including a precious collection of 17th-century first editions.

21 Deanway, at School Lane. www.miltonscottage.org. ☎ **01494/872313.** Admission £5 adults, £3 children 14 and under. Mar–Oct Tues–Sun 10am–1pm and 2–6pm.

GREAT MISSENDEN

Tucked away in the heart of the Chilterns, the large village of Great Missenden is best known for the former **home of Roald Dahl,** the internationally famous children's author. His home, **Gipsy House** (on Whitefield Lane, just outside the village), is still privately owned by his widow, Felicity, but you can visit the garden on select open days throughout the year (entry £4). See www.ngs.org.uk for details. You can also view Dahl's simple tomb (often strewn with toys and flowers) at St. Peter & St. Paul's Church, Church Lane (www.missendenchurch.org.uk).

Roald Dahl Museum & Story Centre ★★ ☺ MUSEUM   This fabulous tribute to Roald Dahl chronicles the life of the beloved author and includes a replica of the hut where he created his most popular characters. Youngsters will love the hands-on **Story Centre,** which allows fans to dress up as Dahl characters, make up stories and poems, or get creative in the craft room. The on-site **Café Twit** serves Puro fair-trade coffee, organic juices, Bogtrotter chocolate cake, giant cookies, and sweet chili jam.

81–83 High St. www.roalddahlmuseum.org. ℰ **01494/8921922.** Admission £6 adults, £4 children 5–18, £19 family tickets. Tues–Fri 10am–5pm; Sat and Sun 11am–5pm. Closed Dec 24–25. Great Missenden is 40 min. by train from London Marylebone; the museum is a 5-min. walk from the station. Driving from London, take the A413; from High Wycombe it's a short ride along the A4128.

HIGH WYCOMBE

High Wycombe, 30 miles west of London, mostly serves as a commuter suburb of the capital today, and there's little to see in the center. Focus instead on the far more appealing village of West Wycombe, and the great stately home on the outskirts, Hughenden. **Turville,** 5 miles west of High Wycombe, is as gorgeous a traditional English village as you're likely to find, serving as a backdrop for the British hit TV series *The Vicar of Dibley.*

Hughenden ★★ HISTORIC HOME   This handsome red-brick Victorian mansion gives insight into the remarkable Benjamin Disraeli, the only prime minister of Britain to hail from a Jewish family. His fame rests on his stewardship as Conservative prime minister from 1874 to 1880. He fashioned a close working relationship with Queen Victoria (who made him Earl of Beaconsfield in 1876), and engineered the British purchase of shares in the Suez Canal. He died in 1881 and was buried in the graveyard of Hughenden Church.

Disraeli acquired Hughenden in 1848, a country house that befitted his fast-rising political and social position. Today the manor has been restored to its appearance in the 1860s, containing Disraeli's own furnishings and an odd assortment of memorabilia, including a lock of Disraeli's hair and letters from Victoria. The World War II room in the cellars recalls the manor's unlikely role as secret wartime base, code-named "Hillside."

Hughenden Rd. (A4128), north of High Wycombe. www.nationaltrust.org.uk. ℰ **01494/755565.** Admission £7.70 adults, £3.85 children 5–15, free for children 4 and under, £19 family ticket; garden only £3.05 adults, £2.05 children. Mar–Oct daily noon–5pm; Nov, Dec, and Feb daily 11am–3pm. The manor is 1½ miles north of High Wycombe on the A4128. From High Wycombe, take Arriva bus 300 (High Wycombe–Aylesbury).

WEST WYCOMBE ★

The ravishing village of West Wycombe is one of the most atmospheric in the Chilterns, with rows of neat Georgian and Victorian cottages enhanced by the **Church of St. Lawrence,** perched on West Wycombe Hill and topped by a huge golden ball. Parts of the church date from the 13th century; its interior was copied from a 3rd-century Syrian sun temple. The view from the hill is worth the trek up alone. Near the church stands the **Dashwood Mausoleum,** built in 1765 in a style derived from Constantine's Arch in Rome, but the main attraction here is **West Wycombe Park** (see below for admission information), seat of the Dashwood family. Now owned by the National Trust, the mansion is one of the best examples of Palladian-style architecture in England thanks to infamous libertine Sir Francis Dashwood, who began to overhaul the property in exuberant Italianate style in the 1740s. The interior is lavishly decorated with paintings and antiques from the 18th century, with ceiling frescos copied from Italian *palazzi*. The rococo-style gardens are also well worth exploring, littered with ornamental buildings and statuary.

Sir Francis also commissioned the excavation of the **Hell-Fire Caves** (see below for admission information) on the estate in the 1750s to give employment to local villagers. Later the caves served as a meeting place for the notorious **Hellfire Club,** which spent its time partying and drinking. The cave is about a half-mile long, filled with stalactites, stalagmites, and man-made chambers such as the slightly creepy Banqueting Hall, Inner Temple, and Franklin's Cave, named after Dashwood's American pal and frequent guest, Benjamin Franklin.

West Wycombe Park: High St. www.nationaltrust.org.uk. © **01494/755571.** Admission £7.70 adults, £3.85 children 5–15, free for children 4 and under, £19 family ticket; grounds only £3.70 adults, £2.15 children. June–Aug Sun–Thurs 2–6pm; grounds only Apr–May Sun–Thurs 2–6pm. Located 2 miles west of High Wycombe at the west end of West Wycombe, south of A40; take Arriva bus 40 (from High Wycombe to Thame). Hell-Fire Caves: Church Lane, West Wycombe. www.hellfirecaves.co.uk. © **01494/533739.** Admission £5 adults, £4 seniors and children 3–16, £15 family ticket. Apr–Oct daily 11am–5:30pm; Nov–Mar 11am–dusk.

WOBURN

On the southern border of Bedfordshire, at the very northern edge of the Chilterns (some 44 miles north of London), lies the village of Woburn and its justly celebrated abbey (actually a mansion). The great 18th-century Georgian home has been the traditional seat of the dukes of Bedford for more than 3 centuries.

Woburn Abbey ★★★ ABBEY   You'll need the best part of a day to do this spectacular Georgian country house justice. The history of the abbey dates back to 1145, when it really was a religious house for Cistercian monks, but it did not become the family home of the Russell family until 1619 (William Russell became the first Duke of Bedford in 1694). Most of what you see today dates from construction in the 1740s and 1802.

Its three floors are crammed with 18th-century French and English furniture, lavish silver and gold collections, and a wide range of porcelain. Paintings by Gainsborough, Reynolds, Van Dyck, and Canaletto are on display (including the latter's 21 views of Venice, in the dining room), while the Blue Drawing Room is supposedly where the tradition of afternoon tea was "invented" in 1840. Look out also for George Gower's *Armada Portrait* of Elizabeth I. Her hand rests on the globe, as Philip's invincible armada perishes in the background.

Today, Woburn Abbey is surrounded by a 3,000-acre deer park, home to 10 species of deer, including native Red Deer and Fallow Deer, and the largest herd of Pere David Deer in the U.K.

Woburn Safari Park (£19.99 adults, £17.99, £14.99 children 3–15, £59.96 family ticket) was added to the grounds in 1970, and today is a thriving business with a separate entrance. It boasts lions, tigers, giraffes, camels, monkeys, and other animals. Children will enjoy this and it can be fun, but it's a little incongruous considering the surroundings; skip it unless you crave the novelty of seeing exotic animals in the English countryside.

Woburn Park, Bedfordshire, a half-mile southeast of the village of Woburn, 13 miles southwest of Bedford. www.woburn.co.uk/abbey. © **01525/290333.** Admission £13.50 adults, £11.50 seniors, £6.50 children 3–15; park only £4.50 adults, £3.50 seniors, £1.75 children. House mid-Apr–Oct daily

11am–5pm (last entry 4pm); park daily 10am–4pm. If driving from London, take the M1 north to junction 12 or 13, where directions are signposted. House closed Nov–early Apr. There is no public transportation directly to Woburn Abbey, but the house is only a 15-minute taxi ride from Flitwick train station.

Where to Eat & Stay

The Black Horse ★ GASTROPUB   Our favorite pub in Woburn opened in 1824 as a coaching inn, and it retains a dark, woodsy interior evocative of that era. It sits behind a stucco-sheathed Georgian facade on the town's main street. Accompanying the ales and a simple but selective wine list are cold cuts and cheese, with main courses ranging from chargrilled steaks and sweet potato and roast vegetable croquettes, to Woburn venison hotpot and a hearty sausage and mash. Most ingredients are seasonal, and locally and ethically produced. Afternoon tea comes with fruit scones, clotted cream, and homemade jam. Suffolk's Greene King IPA and Abbot Ale are served on tap.

1 Bedford St., Woburn. www.blackhorsewoburn.co.uk. ℂ **01525/290210.** Main courses £10.75–£18.50. AE, MC, V. Daily 11am–midnight.

Bugle Horn PUB FARE   This traditional country pub serves great homemade food at reasonable prices. The Bugle began as a Georgian farmhouse, but became a wine store for Hartwell House (see below) in the early 1800s and a pub soon afterward. The menu features all the classics: Lancashire hotpot; chicken, leek, and ham pie; scampi and chips; and beer-battered fish and chips. Seasonal and organic ingredients are used where possible. It has an enticing garden for those warm summer afternoons, and superb cask ales—Charles Wells Bombardier and Wadworth 6X among them.

Oxford Rd., Hartwell, Aylesbury. www.vintageinn.co.uk/thebuglehornhartwell. ℂ **01296/747594.** Main courses £9.75–£16.95. Fixed-price menu £8 (2 courses), £10 (3 courses). AE, MC, V. Daily 11am–midnight.

Hartwell House ★★   This is one of England's great showcase country estates, just 2 miles southwest of Aylesbury on the A418. The mansion was built in landscaped parkland in the 17th century for the Hampden and Lee families, ancestors of Robert E. Lee, the Confederate general in the U.S. Civil War. Wander from the morning room to the oak-paneled bar, pausing in the library where a former tenant, the exiled Louis XVIII, signed the document returning him to the throne of France. Bedrooms are as regal as the prices. The stellar guest rooms ooze with comfort, charm, and character, and the **dining room,** which is equally pricey, features seasonal local farm produce and exceptional traditional and contemporary English cuisine (main courses £19–£33).

Oxford Rd., Aylesbury, Buckinghamshire HP17 8NR. www.hartwell-house.com. ℂ **01296/747444.** 33 units. £205–£390 double; £370–£700 suite. AE, MC, V. Free parking. **Amenities:** 2 restaurants; bar; indoor heated pool; 2 outdoor tennis courts; exercise room; spa; room service; laptop rental £20 for 24 hr. *In room:* A/C, TV, hair dryer, Wi-Fi (free).

Inn at Woburn   After visiting Woburn Abbey (see above), head to this Georgian coaching inn for food and accommodation at the gates of the estate. Guests are housed in one of several well-furnished and beautifully maintained rooms, while a more modern block provides "executive bedrooms," which don't have the charm of the older units but are more up to date and comfortable. If you fancy a break from pub fare, **Olivier's Restaurant** serves imaginative contemporary English and continental cuisine such as baby monkfish tail with a crab ravioli (main courses £14.50–£18.85), while afternoon tea is served in the bar.

1 George St., Woburn, Bedfordshire MK17 9PX. www.woburn.co.uk/inn. ℂ **01525/290441.** 55 units. £77–£138 double. Children 15 and under stay free in parent's room. AE, DC, MC, V. **Amenities:** Restaurant; bar; concierge; room service. *In room:* TV, minibar, hair dryer.

Nag's Head Inn ★ GASTROPUB   Roald Dahl was a regular in this lovely old English pub (it's a short walk from the Roald Dahl Museum; p. 231), which also provides comfortable guest rooms. The food blends traditional English dishes with French flair—think puff pastry topped with mushrooms in a calvados sauce, lamb with butternut squash purée and red onion jus, and seafood gratin in a Chardonnay cream.

The five **double bedrooms** come with flat-screen TVs (Wi-Fi in public areas), and are a good deal at £95 to £115.

London Rd., Great Missenden. www.nagsheadbucks.com. ℂ **01494/862200.** Main courses £14.95–£24.95. AE, MC, V. Daily noon–midnight (Sun noon–10:30pm).

West Lodge Hotel ★ 🍴   Close to Aylesbury, this Victorian hotel (once a gardener's lodge on the adjacent Rothschild estate) outdoes all others in the area with its facilities and value for money. The comfortable bedrooms are furnished with nice extras (tea- and coffee-making facilities, trouser press, and so forth), and private shower-only bathrooms. The **restaurant** serves a huge breakfast (included) and dinner, and the village also has Thai and Indian restaurants.

45 London Rd. (A41), Aston Clinton, Aylesbury, Buckinghamshire HP22 5HL. www.westlodge.co.uk. ℂ **01296/630362.** 9 units. £74–£94 double. AE, MC, V. Free parking. **Amenities:** Restaurant; bar; Jacuzzi; sauna; room service. *In room:* TV/DVD, hair dryer, Wi-Fi (free).

5

ST. ALBANS ★

27 miles NW of London; 41 miles SW of Cambridge

Founded as the Roman town of Verulamium in the 1st century, the city of St. Albans grew up on the hill above the Roman site 500 years later. It's still home to some of the best **Roman ruins** in the country, and an awe-inspiring **cathedral.** The city was named after a Roman soldier who became the first Christian martyr in England, around A.D. 250. A great **abbey** grew up to protect his shrine, becoming a major pilgrimage site in the Middle Ages, a role it has started to regain in recent decades. St. Albans flourished in later years as the first major stop on the coaching route north from London, which explains the large number of **historic pubs** in the center today.

Essentials

GETTING THERE   Trains whisk you from London's St. Pancras Station to St. Albans in just 20 to 35 minutes (£10.60 one-way). If you're driving, take the M25 junction 21A or 22; M1 junctions 6, 7, or 9; and finally the A1(M) junction 3. Parking at several multi-storey garages is signposted in the center of town—the Maltings shopping mall (entrances in Victoria St. and Marlborough Rd. off of London Rd.) charges £1.30 for the first hour, and £5 for up to 6 hours.

VISITOR INFORMATION   The **Tourist Information Centre** is at the Georgian Town Hall, Market Place (www.stalbans.gov.uk; ℂ **01727/864511**). Hours are Monday to Friday 10am to 4:30pm, and Saturday 10am to 5pm. Check also www.allaboutstalbans.com.

ORGANIZED TOURS   The Tourist Information Centre (see above) provides entertaining themed **guided walks** (www.stalbanstourguides.co.uk) that generally cost £3 for adults and £1.50 for children 5 to 15 (children 4 and under are free).

These include "The Ghost Walk" (£4 adults, £2 children), "The Wars of the Roses," "Monks, Mysteries & Mischief," and "Crime and Punishment."

Exploring the Area

The heart of modern St. Albans is a thriving shopping area of Victorian, Georgian, and modern buildings, but there are plenty of medieval remnants around the cathedral, especially along George Street and Market Place. Climb the 93 steps to the top of the **Clock Tower** on the High Street (completed in 1412), for a birds-eye view of the town (© **01727/751815;** Easter–Sep Sat–Sun 10:30am–5pm; adults 80p, children 40p).

Cathedral of St. Albans ★ CATHEDRAL   This majestic cathedral is the oldest site of continuous Christian worship in Britain. It contains the shrine of St. Alban, the first British martyr, who was buried here after being executed by the Roman authorities around A.D. 304. Construction of the cathedral began in 1077; it is one of England's earliest Norman churches, but displays a variety of architectural styles from Romanesque to Gothic. The flint and red-brick walls are especially unusual; the bricks, especially visible in the Norman tower, came from Verulamium, the old Roman city located at the foot of the hill.

Inside the nave, exposed 13th-century frescoes hint at the color and imagery that would have covered the walls before the Dissolution of the Monasteries. Behind the altar—adorned by an elaborate, remarkable altarpiece known as the Wallingford Screen (1480), destroyed by Henry VIII and restored in the 1880s—lies the shrine of St. Alban itself, reconstructed in the 1890s (the original was also destroyed by Henry VIII).

The modern **Chapter House** contains an information desk, gift shop (Mon–Sat 10am–5pm Sun 1–5pm), and the Abbot's Kitchen restaurant (Mon–Sat 10am–4:30pm, Sun 1–4:30pm).

Sumpter Yard, Holywell Hill (on the High St.). www.stalbanscathedral.org. © **01727/860780.** Free admission. Daily 8:30am–5:45pm.

Museum of St. Albans MUSEUM   This small but enlightening museum chronicles the history of St. Albans from the departure of the Romans to the present day; the life and subsequent cult of St. Alban is explained, and there are especially detailed sections on the Benedictine monastery (dissolved by Henry VIII) and Victorian St. Albans. Look out for the startlingly well-preserved 15th-century leather shoe. Located on the edge of the city center, the museum is a 5-minute walk from St. Albans City Station and 15 minutes from the cathedral.

Hatfield Rd. www.stalbansmuseums.org.uk. © **01727/819340.** Free admission. Mon–Sat 10am–5pm; Sun 2–5pm. Closed Dec 25–Jan 2. Free parking on site.

Roman Theatre HISTORIC SITE   Built around A.D. 140, this is the only example of a Roman theatre in Britain, an evocative sight just a short distance from Verulamium (see below). Not much remains, of course, but the stage and banked stone seating are clearly visible, and a stage column has been re-erected to give some sense of its former grandeur.

Hemel Hempstead Rd., Bluehouse Hill. www.romantheatre.co.uk. © **01727/835035.** Admission £2.50 adults, £2 students and seniors, £1.50 children 5–16, free for children 4 and under. Daily 10am–5pm. Located on the western outskirts of St. Albans, just off the A4147, in an area known as Bluehouse Hill.

Verulamium Museum ★★ MUSEUM   Roman Britain is brilliantly evoked at this enlightening museum, located on the site of the ancient Roman city of the same name. Here you'll view some of the finest Roman mosaics in Britain as well as recreated Roman rooms, rare bronze statues (including the "Verulamium Venus"), and Celtic coins. Part of the Roman town hall and the outline of houses and shops are still visible in the park that surrounds the museum.

Check out also the 1,800-year-old **Hypocaust** (under-floor heating system) and ornate mosaic floor in the park. The site has been left *in situ,* and is now protected by a modern shell. Opening times are April to September Monday to Saturday 10am to 4:30pm and Sunday 2 to 4:30pm; October to March the site closes at 3:45pm. Admission is free.

St. Michael's St. (15 min. walk from the cathedral). www.stalbansmuseums.org.uk. © **01727/751810.** Admission £3.80 adults, £2 seniors and children 5–16, free for children 4 and under, £10.20 family ticket. Mon–Sat 10am–5:30pm; Sun 2–5.30pm. Closed Dec 24 Jan 2. By car, Verulamium is 15–20 min. from junction 21A on the M25; it is also accessible from junction 9 or 6 on the M1; follow the signs for St. Albans and the Roman Verulamium. St. Albans City Station is 2 miles from the museum.

Where to Eat

Freddie's ★ CONTINENTAL   This elegant, modern restaurant attracts a loyal clientele of locals and visitors. The menu is fun, eclectic, and sure to please everyone in your group. The seared monkfish fillet is always good, but there are also solid meat dishes to savor: Slow cooked belly of pork with rosemary jus, rosti potato, and vegetables; and duck breast with banana chutney. Save room for the delectable dark rum crème brulée or baked-apple-and-blackberry crumble with hot custard.

52–56 Adelaide St. www.stalbansmuseums.org.uk. © **01727/811889.** www.stalbansmuseums.org. uk. Reservations highly recommended. Main courses £11.95–£22.25; set lunch (2 courses) £12.95; set dinner (3 courses) £19.95. AE, DC, MC, V. Daily noon–2:30pm and 6–10pm.

Secret Garden ★ CAFE   This delightful coffee shop is tucked away off historic George Street. The garden is open in summer, and at other times the cozy interior serves cakes, teas, coffees, and light lunches such as lamb shank tangine and a decent classic burger.

9a George St. www.secretgardencafe.org. © **01727/857035.** Main courses £4.45–£8.50. AE, DC, MC, V. Tues–Fri 10am–4pm; Sat 10am–5pm; Sun 11am–4pm.

Shopping

The twice-weekly **street market,** held every Wednesday and Saturday along St. Peters Street, features over 170 stalls, a mixture of discounted factory merchandise, fruit and vegetable sellers, and upmarket purveyors of everything from merino-wool blankets to artisan cheese. The excellent **Farmers' Market** runs on the second Sunday of each month, from 8am to 2pm, in tandem with a flea market inside the Old Town Hall (admission 20p). A better bet for genuine arts and crafts is the **St. Albans Artisans, Arts & Crafts Market,** held the second Saturday of every month (10am–4pm), also in the Old Town Hall.

You'll find a selection of intriguing shops amid the quieter streets and lanes clustered around the cathedral. For antiques and local crafts, visit **By George Craft Arcade,** 23 George St. (© **01727/853032**), St. Albans's largest antiques and craft center. The building also houses a tearoom and crafts arcade. It's open Monday to Saturday 9:30am to 5pm and Sunday 1 to 5pm.

Fans of the graphic novel should check out **Chaos City Comics** (www.chaoscity comics.com; © **01727/838719**), at 20 Heritage Close. It's open Monday to Friday 11am to 5:30pm, Saturday 10am to 5:30pm, and Sunday noon to 4pm. See www. shopstalbans.co.uk for more shopping ideas.

Entertainment & Nightlife

St. Albans's nightlife centers on a thriving pub scene and a small but healthy roster of provincial theatre. The Company of Ten, with its base at the **Abbey Theatre,** Westminster Lodge, Holywell Hill (www.abbeytheatre2.org.uk; ℭ **01727/857861**), is one of the leading amateur dramatic companies in Britain. The troupe presents 10 productions each season in either the well-equipped main auditorium or a smaller studio. Performances begin at 8pm; most tickets cost from £9 to £12. The box office is open Monday to Saturday 10:30am to 7pm.

Maltings Arts Theatre, in the Maltings Shopping Centre (www.maltingsarts theatre.co.uk; ℭ **07807/521436**), presents performances ranging from Shakespeare plays to movies and live concerts. Performances are generally presented at 2 or 8pm Saturdays, with most tickets ranging from £5 to £12.50. Tickets can be purchased by telephone, in person when the theatre is open for performances, or at www.ticket source.co.uk/ovo.

Bigger touring shows and concerts use the **Alban Arena,** Civic Centre (www. alban-arena.co.uk; ℭ **01727/844488**).

THE PUB & BAR SCENE

As befits an ancient town (and the home of the Campaign for Real Ale, or CAMRA), St. Albans boasts some classic old pubs, notably **Ye Old Fighting Cocks,** 16 Abbey Mill Lane (www.stufish.wordpress.com; ℭ **01727/869152**), one of the oldest watering holes in England (it's between the cathedral and Roman site). Named after the cockfights that once took place here, the pub allegedly dates back to A.D. 793, though the current site probably dates to the 11th century. The dark, timber-smothered interior is the perfect place to enjoy traditional cask ales.

Another atmospheric spot for a pint is **The Goat,** 37 Sopwell Lane (www.goatinn. co.uk; ℭ **01727/833934**), with at least five real ales on tap such as St. Austell's Tribute and Spitfire. This Tudor inn has been serving drinks since the 1580s. **The Boot,** centrally located at 4 Market Place (ℭ **01727/857533**), rounds out a history-laden pub crawl; this alehouse has been open since at least 1719 in a creaky timber building that dates back to the medieval period. It's also a decent venue for live bands, as is the **Farmer's Boy,** 134 London Rd. (ℭ **01727/860535;** www.farmersboy. co.uk), which serves beers from the town's only microbrewer, the Verulam Brewery.

Where to Stay

Black Lion Inn 🖋   This is the most inviting pub-hotel in the area, as well as one of the best bargains. A former bakery, built in 1837, it lies in the most colorful part of town, St. Michael's Village, where bustling coaches from London once arrived. Bedrooms are simple and plain and, although a bit cramped, they're well maintained; some have original exposed brick and timber features.

198 Fishpool St., St. Albans, Hertfordshire AL3 4SB. www.theblacklioninn.com. ℭ **01727/848644.** Fax: 01727/891041. 16 units, 14 with bathroom. £65–£75 double; £90 family room. Breakfast £4.95–£9.95 extra. AE, MC, V. Free parking. **Amenities:** Bar; babysitting; Wi-Fi (free, in public areas). *In room:* TV, hair dryer, Wi-Fi (free, in some).

St. Michael's Manor ★★   Set in 5 acres of beautifully maintained lakeside gardens, this handsome property dates from 1586. Rooms are individually decorated with fine antique pieces and come stocked with everything from mineral water to a teddy bear to sleep with. The manor also has a superb restaurant, the **Terrace Room,** with an ornate Victorian conservatory overlooking the floodlit lawns.

Fishpool St., St. Albans, Hertfordshire AL3 4RY. www.stmichaelsmanor.com. ☎ **01727/864444.** 30 units. £115–£275 double. Rates include English breakfast. AE, MC, V. Free parking. **Amenities:** Restaurant; bar; room service. *In room:* A/C, TV/DVD, hair dryer.

Side Trips from St. Albans

Hatfield House ★★ HISTORIC SITE   This stately Jacobean mansion and its beautifully manicured gardens make for an alluring day trip from London or St. Albans. Built in 1611 by Robert Cecil, 1st Earl of Salisbury and Chief Minister to King James I, it has been the home of the Cecil family ever since (the current owner is the 7th Marquess of Salisbury). Yet Hatfield is more famous for the royal palace that previously occupied this spot, the childhood home of Elizabeth I. In 1558, Elizabeth learned of her succession to the throne of England while at Hatfield; the site of this famous moment is marked by the Queen Elizabeth Oak.

Indeed, though only the banqueting hall of the first palace remains, it is the Elizabeth association that gives the house much of its appeal.

The **Hatfield Banquets** are staged with much gaiety and music in the banqueting hall of the Old Palace on Fridays from 7 to 11:30pm. Guests share long tables for a four-course feast with continuous entertainment from a group of players, minstrels, and jesters. Wine is included in the cost of the meal, but pre-dinner drinks are not. The menu isn't particularly medieval, and you're granted the (modern-day) luxury of knives and forks. The banquets are very touristy, but they are lots of fun and packed every night. The cost of the banquet starts at £55.50. Call ☎ **01707/262055** for details.

6 miles east of St. Albans on the A414. www.hatfield-house.co.uk. ☎ **01707/287010** for information. Admission house and park £10 adults, £9 seniors, £5.50 children 5–15; park only £3 adults and seniors, £2 children 5–15. House Easter–Sept Wed–Sun and public holidays noon–5pm (last admission 4pm); park and gardens 11am–5:30pm. Closed Oct–Good Friday. From St. Albans, take the A414 east and follow the brown signs that lead directly to the estate. Bus: Take the university bus from St. Albans City Station. Hatfield House is directly across from Hatfield Station.

Shaw's Corner ★ 🏛 HISTORIC HOME   The great Irish playwright George Bernard Shaw lived in this peaceful ivy-smothered house from 1906 to 1950, knocking out all his best work in the small revolving shed in the garden (including *Pygmalion*, on which the musical *My Fair Lady* was based and for which he received an Oscar in 1938, which is on display).

Off Hill Farm Lane, in the village of Ayot St. Lawrence. www.nationaltrust.org.uk/shaws-corner. ☎ **01438/829221.** Admission £6 adults, £3 children 5–15, free for children 4 and under. Mar–Oct Wed–Sun and public holidays 1–5pm. Closed Nov–Feb. From St. Albans, take the B651 to Wheathampstead. Pass through the village, go right at the roundabout, and then take the 1st left turn; 1 mile up on the left is Brides Hall Lane, which leads to the house.

Behind the Magic of Harry Potter

Guests at the **"Warner Bros. Studio Tour London The Making of Harry Potter"** can see firsthand the sheer scale and detail of the actual sets, costumes, animatronics, special effects, and props used in all eight of the *Harry Potter* films. Tickets are priced at £28 for adults and £21 for children (5–15), and must be booked in advance via a dedicated website (www.wbstudiotour.co.uk).

KENT, SURREY & SUSSEX

by Nick Dalton & Deborah Stone

At first glance, the Southeast might seem to be lacking the grandeur of other parts of the country. No mountains, just a green and pleasant land. Yet look closer and you find a place that's full of beauty, from the Surrey Hills to the White Cliffs of Dover. There are picturesque towns and lovely beaches, the bright lights of Brighton, and the meandering Thames. And, from London, it's all a lot easier to get to than more rugged outposts.

CITIES & TOWNS This is not the region for big, industrial cities, but there are smaller, individual places that provide a contrast to the rest of England. **Canterbury,** in Kent, with its glorious cathedral is the seat of the Church of England. **Rochester,** nearby, is full of history. Charles Dickens lived locally and wrote some of his classic novels here. **Brighton,** the Sussex seaside resort, is an unlikely city, a vibrant mix of arts and bawdy coastal fun. Handsome **Chichester** has the air of a country town, while in Guildford, **Surrey,** the 20th-century red-brick cathedral stands high on a hilltop, and presides over a city barely outside London.

COUNTRYSIDE Kent is called the **Garden of England,** a lush county dotted with stately homes and gardens (such as Winston Churchill's Chartwell). Move into Sussex and there are the **South Downs,** a chain of hills (the heart of Britain's newest National Park) that stretch for 100 miles and provide walks with views of country and coast. The ancient landscape, where forests mix with wild heathland, continues into the **Surrey Hills** with **Leith Hill** (294m/965 ft.), the highest spot in the Southeast.

EATING & DRINKING The bounty of the sea is here. Sampling the oysters of **Whitstable** from quayside stalls or fresh fish at Brighton's unpretentious Regency seafront restaurant are experiences second to none—although there are also Michelin-starred restaurants for a real treat. Produce from Kent's market gardens adds a delectable garnish, and the county's copious amounts of hops are turned into real ales.

COAST This is a land that sent Nelson off to sea (from Chatham dockyards), where J. M. W. Turner painted his evocative seascapes (on show at Margate's new **Turner Contemporary** museum), and where the mighty **White Cliffs** delineate Dover and beyond. But more than anything, this is a region of beaches, resort towns, and coastal strolls, much of it possible to enjoy on day-long jaunts from London.

THE best TRAVEL EXPERIENCES IN KENT, SURREY & SUSSEX

o **Walking the Thames:** Only a few miles from London the river turns into a rural delight, with grassy footpaths along the banks, the sound of oars breaking the water, little boats putt-putting by, and relaxed riverside pubs to pop into. See p. 286.

o **Hiking the South Downs:** Stand on these chalk hills, gazing at the sea and undulating countryside; the hills follow the south coast and are an inspiring walk with almost constant sea views. Go for an afternoon's stroll, or throw yourself into a week-long hike. See p. 277.

o **Eating seafood at Whitstable:** This fishing town's quay on a warm Sunday afternoon is the place to be, snacking on a single oyster or sitting down to a full seafood lunch after browsing stalls selling everything from fish to antiques. See p. 251.

o **Experiencing Leeds Castle:** Britain's most gorgeous castle sits in the middle of a lake surrounded by landscaped parkland. Picnic, walk, and marvel at the serene sight that has survived for centuries. See p. 259.

o **Seeing the sea as Turner did:** The new seafront Turner Contemporary art museum in Margate not only has a collection of the artist's wonderful seascapes, but also sits on the site of the boarding house he used to stay in and has windows recreating the view and the light that so entranced him. See p. 250.

CANTERBURY ★★

56 miles SE of London

This medieval city appears in *The Canterbury Tales,* Chaucer's story of pilgrims telling tales as they journeyed from London to the shrine of Thomas Becket, Archbishop of Canterbury, who was murdered by four knights of Henry II in 1170. The shrine was finally torn down in 1538 by Henry VIII, as part of the Reformation, but Canterbury was already a tourist attraction.

The city, on the River Stour, is the **ecclesiastical capital of England** and gives its name to the Archbishop of Canterbury, leader of the Church of England. The slaying of Thomas Becket was its most famous incident, but it witnessed other major events, too. Richard the Lionheart popped in on his way back from the Crusades, Henry VIII's Catholic daughter Bloody Mary ordered 41 Protestants to be burned at the stake between 1555 and 1558, and Charles II passed through on the way to claim his crown in 1642. There are still plenty of traces of old city walls, but Canterbury suffered in the World War II Blitz of 1941, when much of its medieval feel was destroyed. Today it's a very busy mix of day-trippers and students from the University of Kent. There's still plenty to see, not least the **cathedral:** one of Europe's great religious monuments. The city is also good as a base for exploring the coast and countryside.

Essentials

GETTING THERE There are trains to Canterbury from London's Victoria, St. Pancras, and Charing Cross stations (calling at Waterloo East and London Bridge). All take about 1½ hours and cost about £30 one-way. The National Express bus from

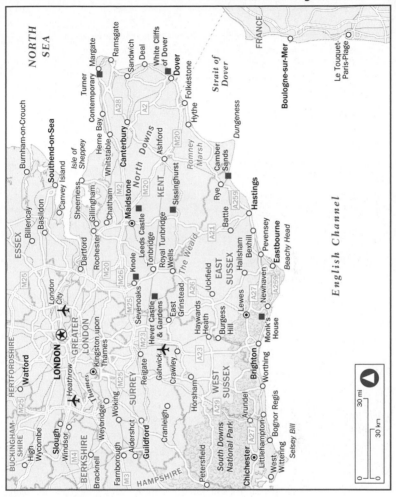

London's Victoria Coach Station takes 1½ to 2 hours and leaves every hour, costing from about £10.

If you're driving from London, take the A2, and then the M2. Canterbury is sign-posted all the way. The heart of the city is traffic-free, but it's only a short walk from several parking areas to the cathedral.

VISITOR INFORMATION Near St. Margaret's Church, **Canterbury Tourist Information Centre,** 12–13 Sun St. (www.canterbury.co.uk; ☏ **01227/378100**), is open Monday to Saturday 9:30am to 5pm (4pm off-season). Only from here can you buy the **Canterbury Attractions Passport** (£26.50 adults; £23 seniors; £13 children 5–15), which gives entrance to the cathedral, St. Augustine's Abbey, The Canterbury Tales, and museums, and money off tours and boat rides).

GETTING AROUND   You may want to bicycle around Canterbury. **Downland Cycles,** St. Stephens Road (www.downlandcycles.co.uk; ✆ **01227/479643**), rents out bikes for £15 a day (tandems £35, to be paid for in advance). A credit card is needed as deposit.

An interesting and easy family ride is the Crab & Winkle route to the coast at Whitstable. It follows the route of the world's first passenger railway line of the same name, built by George Stephenson in 1830 and torn up in 1953. It's 8 miles one way, mostly traffic-free. For more information, see www.sustrans.org.uk.

ORGANIZED TOURS   Canterbury Tourist Guides (www.canterbury-walks. co.uk; ✆ **01227/459779**) has daily walking tours, £6 for adults, £5.50 for students and seniors, £4.25 for children 11 and under, and £16 for a family ticket. Meet at the Tourist Information Centre (see above). Tours tend to leave year-round daily at 11am, with an additional 2pm tour July to September and public holidays.

Canterbury Historic River Tours (www.canterburyrivertours.co.uk; ✆ **07790/ 534744**) operates 40-minute boat trips with commentary that let you see Canterbury from a different perspective. Prices are £8 for adults, £7 for seniors and students, £5.50 for children 12 to 16, and £4.50 for children 11 and under. March to early November, tours leave daily every 15 to 20 minutes between 10am and 5pm. Tours begin just below the Weavers House restaurant, at 3 St. Peters St.

Exploring the Area

Canterbury Cathedral ★★★ CATHEDRAL   This is one of the most visited sites in Britain, and still one of the leading places of pilgrimage in Europe. St. Augustine, sent by Pope Gregory the Great, arrived in A.D. 597 as a missionary and became the first archbishop, establishing his seat ("Cathedra"). It was here, in 1170, that Thomas Becket was murdered on a dark December evening in the northwest transept. The quire (which housed Becket's shrine until it was demolished during the Reformation) is one of England's earliest examples of Gothic architectural style.

The cathedral, along with St. Augustine's Abbey and St. Martin's Church, forms a World Heritage Site. Its foundations date from the time of Augustine, but the earliest part of the building is the great Romanesque crypt from around A.D. 1100, which still contains traces of wall painting.

The 72-m (235-ft.) **Bell Harry Tower ★★**, completed in 1505, is the cathedral's most distinctive feature. You enter through **Christ Church Gate ★** (from the early 16th century). The fan-vaulted colonnades of the **Great Cloister ★** on the northern flank of the building never fail to impress. From the cloister you enter the **Chapter House,** with its web of intricate tracery from the 1300s. This architectural ensemble supports the roof and a wall of stained glass, depicting scenes from Becket's life.

There are medieval tombs of the likes of King Henry IV and Edward the Black Prince. The later Middle Ages are represented by the great 14th-century nave as well as by the Bell Harry Tower. Sitting amid walled precincts, the cathedral is surrounded by medieval buildings and ruins. The wonderful Romanesque water tower once supplied the bakery and brewery. Becket's tomb is in Trinity Chapel, near the high altar. The saint is said to have worked miracles, and the cathedral has some rare stained glass depicting those feats. The glass, regarded as the country's finest, was removed at the start of World War II and therefore survived Hitler's bombs.

The Precincts. www.canterbury-cathedral.org. ✆ **01227/762862.** Admission £9.50 adults, £8.50 seniors, £6.50 children 17 and under. Easter–Sept Mon–Sat 9am–5:30pm; Oct–Easter Mon–Sat 9am–5pm (crypt from 10am); year-round Sun 12:30–2:30pm. Guided tours (daily except Sun) £5 adults, £4 students and children.

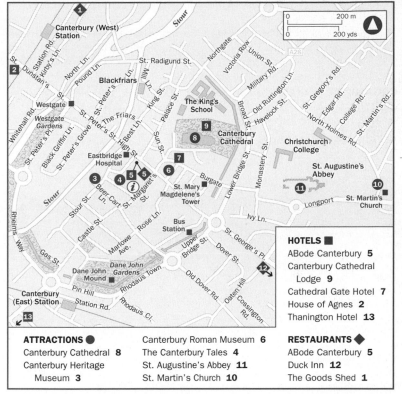

HOTELS ■
ABode Canterbury **5**
Canterbury Cathedral
  Lodge **9**
Cathedral Gate Hotel **7**
House of Agnes **2**
Thanington Hotel **13**

ATTRACTIONS ●		RESTAURANTS ◆
Canterbury Cathedral **8**	Canterbury Roman Museum **6**	ABode Canterbury **5**
Canterbury Heritage	The Canterbury Tales **4**	Duck Inn **12**
Museum **3**	St. Augustine's Abbey **11**	The Goods Shed **1**
	St. Martin's Church **10**	

Canterbury Roman Museum MUSEUM   This is a subterranean experience—it's built around archeological excavations of a house site containing mosaics unearthed by a wartime bomb. Interactive exhibits and Roman artifacts that can be handled bring the past to life. The Roman town of Durovernum Cantiacorum (Canterbury) was established after Emperor Claudius's invasion in A.D. 43, and flourished for nearly 400 years. Other exhibits include the reconstruction of a Roman market.

Butchery Lane. www.canterbury.co.uk. ℂ **01227/785575.** Admission £6 adults, £5 students and seniors, up to 4 children 5–16 free per family. Daily 10am–5pm; last admission 4pm.

The Canterbury Tales ☺ MUSEUM   Ah, classic Middle Ages literature turned into a sideshow! But it does it in such a fun way that it's hard to object. Indeed, Chaucer was a populist author of his day. Here, inside the ancient setting of St. Margaret's Church, which gets a splendid makeover as a scene from 14th-century England, Chaucer's stories (and the murder of Thomas Becket) come to life for all the family. Headsets, tableaux, and life-size figures enhance the experience.

23 St. Margaret's St. (off High St., near the cathedral). www.canterburytales.org.uk. ℂ **01227/479227.** Admission £7.95 adults, £6.95 students and seniors, £5.90 children 5–15, free for children under 5. Mar–June and Sept–Oct daily 10am–5pm; July–Aug daily 9:30am–5pm; Nov–Feb daily 10am–4:30pm.

Canterbury Heritage Museum ★ ☺ MUSEUM   Here you'll find the city's history, from the Romans to Nazi bombs, Viking raids to religion, told with an impressive array of interactive, family-friendly video, computer, and hologram effects. Also celebrated are the children's animated TV series *Bagpuss* and *The Clangers,* which were created nearby, and author Joseph Conrad—he lived locally and his study is here. The setting is the ancient Poor Priests' Hospital with its medieval interiors and soaring oak roofs. Within it is the Rupert Bear Museum, a homage to the oh-so-English cartoon bear, which is as appealing to grandparents who remember the pioneering cartoon strips in the *Daily Express* as to youngsters who can play with giant toys.

Stour St. www.canterbury.gov.uk. 𝒞 **01227/475202.** Admission £8 adults, £6 students and seniors, up to 4 children 5–16 free per family. Daily 10am–5pm (last admission 4pm).

St. Augustine's Abbey ★★ ABBEY   This is where the cathedral's founder was buried; only ruins remain, but it is still a major religious site. After Augustine was sent by Pope Gregory to convert the Saxons, Ethelbert, the Saxon king, allowed Augustine and his followers to build a church outside the city walls, and it endured until Henry VIII tore it down. The abbey church rivaled the cathedral in size, and the ruins are still cathedral-like in their proportions. Nearby are the abbey buildings that were converted into a royal palace by Henry VIII and used briefly by several monarchs, including Elizabeth I and Charles I. Entry includes an audio tour and the small museum.

Monastery St. www.english-heritage.org.uk. 𝒞 **01227/767345.** Admission £4.80 adults, £4.30 students and seniors, £2.90 children 5–15. Apr 1–June 30 Wed–Sun 10am–5pm; July–Aug daily 10am–6pm; Sept–Mar 31 Sat–Sun 11am–5pm.

St. Martin's Church CHURCH   The oldest church in the English-speaking world still used for worship, this was Augustine's first project when he arrived in A.D. 597. However, it was built on the site of a Roman building, and it's possible that some of the walls are actually from the Roman period. The place is a jigsaw of time: The nave is mostly masonry but with occasional courses of Roman brick; the chancel is similar, but its east wall is flint, although one end, and part of the south wall, are wholly of Roman brick. As a whole, the church is distinctly of the 7th century.

North Holmes Rd. www.martinpaul.org. 𝒞 **01227/768072.** Free admission. Daily during daylight hours.

Where to Eat

ABode Canterbury ★★★ ENGLISH/CONTINENTAL   The beautifully designed restaurant, part of Michelin-starred chef Michael Caines empire, is in the ABode, the town's top hotel (see below). Local ingredients from Kent, the "garden of England," are used, and the cooking is simple and effective. One of the signature dishes is roast sirloin of Kentish beef with wild mushroom purée, roasted salsify, and Madeira jus. You might also find local rabbit, and seafood from Whitstable.

ABode Canterbury hotel, High St. www.abodehotels.co.uk or www.michaelcaines.com. 𝒞 **01227/766266.** Reservations required. Main courses £22.50–£25.50. AE, DC, MC, V. Mon–Sat noon–2:30pm and 6–10pm; Sun noon–2:30pm.

Deeson's ★★★ 🍴 MODERN BRITISH   Near the cathedral in this most English of cities, Deeson's offers the most British of menus. Sam Deeson's dream, on two floors, has expanded into an adjoining building, the historic timelessness designed discreetly by his artist wife Cath (whose prints line the walls). A smallholding supplies Berkshire rare breed pork and vegetables for the ever-changing menu that might feature pan-fried fillet of sea trout on crayfishtail crushed new potatoes, with samphire, cockle and dill butter sauce, alongside Romney Marsh duck, Sussex beef and saltmarsh lamb. Desserts are neat takes on classics such as rhubarb crumble and treacle tart.

25 Sun St. ℂ **01227/767854.** www.deesonsrestaurant.co.uk. Reservations recommended. Main courses £15–£19. AE, MC, V. Mon–Sat noon–3pm and 5–10pm; Sun noon–3pm.

The Goods Shed ★★ ENGLISH   Everything that's good about well-sourced food you'll find at The Goods Shed, a barn of a market near the station (the restaurant is on a platform overlooking the action). Meat arrives as whole carcasses in the butchery, there's rustic bread from the bakery, and the daily menu reflects the other produce on offer. That might mean braised ox cheeks, creamed shallots, and bay leaf, or Kentish Ranger chicken, prunes, and cobnuts (a local hazelnut). Breakfast, lunch, and dinner all adhere to the same high standard.

Station Rd. West. http://thegoodsshed.co.uk/. ℂ **01227/459153.** Main courses £11–£20. AE, MC, V. Tues–Fri 8–10:30am, noon–2:30pm, and 6–9:30pm; Sat 8–10:30am, noon–3pm, and 6–9:30pm; Sun 9–10:30am, noon–3pm.

Shopping

The Goods Shed, Station Road West (www.thegoodsshed.co.uk; ℂ 01227/459153), is a massive, ethically sound food market, and while you might not be able to take the delectable fresh produce home from your holiday, you'll also find lots of other souvenirs such as chutneys and mustards. See review above, under "Where to Eat."

The **Chaucer Bookshop,** 6–7 Beer Cart Lane (www.chaucer-bookshop.co.uk; ℂ 01227/453912), sells first editions (both old and modern), out-of-print books, leather-bound editions, and a large selection of local history books.

Entertainment & Nightlife

The **Old Brewery Tavern,** part of the ABode hotel complex (www.alberrys.co.uk; ℂ 0871/402-3262), is an attraction in its own right, with an entrance on Stour Street. It's a modern take on a pub, all pale wood and white walls, and serves a gastropub innovative-but-casual menu (two courses £10.95). It turns into a club with DJs (10pm–2am; free entry). The ABode's **Michael Caines Champagne and Cocktail Bar** (www.michaelcaines.com; ℂ 01227/766266) is sleek and modern, the city's most stylish bar, the place where you can get a simple glass of fizz or treat yourself to a magnum of the best. A favorite local pub, **Alberry's Wine Bar,** 38 St. Margaret's St. (www.alberrys.co.uk; ℂ 01227/452378), offers a clubby atmosphere every night with a DJ spinning hip-hop, drum and bass, or chart music. There's a cover of several pounds after 9pm Tuesday to Thursday, and after 10pm on Friday and Saturday.

The **Cherry Tree,** 10 White Horse Lane (ℂ 01227/451266), has a wide selection of beers, including Cherry Tree ale.

The **Gulbenkian Theatre,** University of Kent, Giles Lane (www.kent.ac.uk/gulbenkian; ℂ 01227/769075), features touring drama, comedy, and music, as well as regular movies. Modern but pushing toward the artier side of things, it's on the edge of town, so you'll need to drive or get a cab. The **Marlowe Theatre,** The Friars (www.marlowetheatre.com; ℂ 01227/787787), is a purpose-built, modern landmark theatre for drama, jazz, and classical concerts plus dance and ballet. Tickets cost £10 to £40. The box office is open Monday to Saturday 9am to 5:30pm with telephone bookings until 6pm or 7pm on performance nights. Most shows begin at 7:30pm.

Where to Stay

EXPENSIVE

ABode Canterbury ★★   This is the place to stay, a hotel with a history dating back to 1588, but now part of the luxurious ABode chain, closely associated with chef Michael Caines (described by *The Sunday Times* as Britain's number 1 restaurateur). The location is perfect (inside the ancient city walls and within minutes of the cathedral), and the rooms are even more so, with hand-crafted beds, minimalist chic, and stylish wet rooms. The **Michael Caines Restaurant** is Canterbury's best (p. 244).

High St., Canterbury, Kent CT1 2RX. www.abodehotels.co.uk.ⓒ **01227/766266.** Fax 01227/451512. 72 units. £155–£195 double; from £265 suite. AE, DC, MC, V. Parking £5. **Amenities:** Restaurant; bar; exercise room; room service; babysitting. *In room:* TV/DVD, hair dryer, Wi-Fi (free).

MODERATE

Canterbury Cathedral Lodge   Within the cathedral precincts, this modernistic building with castle-like walls and turrets is a luxury hotel and conference center. Most of the simple-but-elegant rooms have cathedral views, which can also be enjoyed from the private Campanile Garden; there is also the Library to relax in. Guests get breakfast (in the **Refectory restaurant,** with terrace seating in the summer) and cathedral entry.

The Precincts, Canterbury, Kent CT1 2EH. www.canterburycathedrallodge.org.ⓒ **01227/865350.** Fax 01227/8653885. 29 units. £89–£129 double. Rates include English breakfast. AE, DC, MC, V. Free parking (booking required). **Amenities:** Restaurant (breakfast only, except for groups). *In room:* TV, hair dryer, Wi-Fi (free). (No frills option in separate building: £60 double, per room).

House of Agnes ★★★ 🏠   This quirky, luxurious B&B in a timbered building was an inn back in the 14th century. It's so named because it was the fictional home of Agnes Wickfield in Charles Dickens's *David Copperfield*. The house has eight rooms themed on world cities, from the flamboyantly medieval Canterbury to the pale New England feel of the Boston. The Stables Rooms are an additional eight rooms opening onto their own terrace. Some can be linked for families, one has a spa bath and shower, and the others have smart shower cubicles. Then there's the walled garden: huge, with a centuries-old ash and yews that date back to the spot's time as a Roman cemetery.

71 St. Dunstans St., Canterbury, Kent CT2 8BN. www.houseofagnes.co.uk.ⓒ **01227/472185.** Fax 01227/470478. 16 units. £75–£130 double. Rates include English breakfast. AE, MC, V. Free parking. **Amenities:** Lounge. *In room:* TV/DVD, hair dryer, MP3 docking station, Wi-Fi (free).

INEXPENSIVE

Cathedral Gate Hotel   The name says it all: This is right next to the Christchurch Gate and overlooks the Buttermarket. Built in 1438, it's packed with original details, such as twisting corridors and beams in the odd-shaped rooms in the roof. It's impossible to give some of them en suite facilities, so the hotel remains a good-value option at the city's heart. The restaurant offers cheap tourist fare (fish and chips, chili, lasagna). There's also a small reception bar, and you can take your drink to the lounge with its cathedral view, or to the roof terrace.

36 Burgate, Canterbury, Kent CT1 2HA. www.cathgate.co.uk.ⓒ **01227/464381.** Fax 01227/462800. 25 units, 12 with bathroom (shower only). £62–£75 double without bathroom, £105 with bathroom. Rates include continental breakfast; English breakfast for £7.50. AE, DC, MC, V. Parking nearby £5. **Amenities:** Restaurant; bar; room service. *In room:* TV, hair dryer.

Thanington Hotel ★ 🏊   This small, luxury, family-run hotel in a late 18th-century building is a stone's throw from the cathedral. It may have only 15 rooms, but it has a decent pool in an outbuilding with glass doors opening onto the pretty garden with a fish pond, and a private bar (with an impressive collection of malt whiskies). The rooms are understated, and superior rooms have four-poster beds.

140 Wincheap, Canterbury, Kent CT1 3RY. www.thanington-hotel.co.uk. © **01227/453227.** 15 units. £65–£140 double. Rates include English breakfast. AE, MC, V. Free parking. **Amenities:** Bar; 2 breakfast rooms; indoor pool; TV lounge. *In room:* TV, hair dryer, Wi-Fi (free).

ROCHESTER ★ & CHATHAM ★

30 miles SE of London

The north Kent coast is an area that pays tribute to a pair of historic figures: Charles Dickens and Admiral Nelson. The twin towns of Rochester and Chatham are less than a mile apart, on either side of the meandering River Medway. The river proved such a safe, deep spot that it was where England's warships were built for hundreds of years, from wooden galleons to submarines. And it was the dockyards that, curiously, were responsible for much that we remember of Dickens's work. He came here as a youngster when his father started work at the Navy yard, fell in love with the area, and featured its locales in his novels. Nowadays it's a place where history rules, and you get a feel for the past in its museums and festivals.

Essentials

GETTING THERE   Southeastern trains (about £20 one-way) run from London's St. Pancras to Chatham every half an hour (40-min. trip), and hourly from Victoria (1-hr. trip, and the cheapest tickets) and from Cannon Street (1hr. 15 min.) at rush hours; they call at Rochester several minutes earlier.

If you're driving from London, once you're on the M25 heading east, you simply follow the M20, then turn left at junction 4 onto the A228 for Rochester, or junction 6 onto the A229 for Chatham.

VISITOR INFORMATION   The Medway **Visitor Information Centre** is at 95 High St., Rochester (www.visitmedway.org; © **01634/843666**). Open hours vary but are mostly Monday to Saturday 10am to 5pm; closed Sundays October to March.

Exploring the Area

ROCHESTER   Charles Dickens, having found literary fame, bought Gad's Hill Place in Higham, just outside Rochester, in 1856 and lived there until his death in 1870. The author was regularly seen wandering around this and other Kent towns (such as Gravesend). The house (where Hans Christian Anderson came to visit and stayed 5 weeks) is now Gad's Hill School and not open to the public. The Rochester area was the inspiration for many of Dickens's greatest works. Restoration House in Rochester was the fictional Satis House, Miss Havisham's home in *Great Expectations*. In *The Pickwick Papers* Mr. Pickwick stays in the Bull Hotel (now the Royal Victoria and Bull), and walks on the now-gone Rochester Bridge. Rochester, renamed Cloisterham, is also the setting for his unfinished novel *The Mystery of Edwin Drood*, which was filmed by the BBC in 2012. The town loves its famous son: **The Dickens Festival** (www.rochesterdickensfestival.org.uk) in early June has been running for more than 30 years and is a boisterous mix of music, dance, drama, and street theatre celebrating Victorian times. There's also a **Dickensian Christmas** with a parade in December, and a Christmas market at Rochester Castle. Rochester's Sweeps Festival celebrates the traditional May Day annual holiday of chimney sweeps with a parade, top folk musicians, and Morris dancers.

Rochester has England's second oldest **cathedral,** founded in A.D. 604, although the present building is from 1080. Admire one of the country's finest Romanesque facades, the nave's Norman architecture, some superb Gothic styling, and an inspiring 14th-century Chapter Library door. The cathedral is open daily from 7:30am to 6pm (Sat to 5pm). Admission is free; audioguides £3. **Rochester Castle** (www.english-heritage.org.uk) is one of the best preserved examples of Norman architecture in England. See website for details of Overseas Visitor Passes or ask at the castle.

Restoration House, 17 Crow Lane (www.restorationhouse.co.uk; ✆ **01634/848520**), is an exquisite Elizabethan city-mansion and inspiration for part of Dickens's novel *Great Expectations.* In 1668 it was used as a stopover for soon-to-be King Charles II as he returned from exile following Oliver Cromwell's death, hence the name Restoration House. Much original decor has been exposed in continuing renovation. It has a large walled garden, part formal, part productive. The house is open only Thursdays and Fridays, June to September (£6.50 for adults, £5.50 for seniors, and £3 for children 6–16; garden only £3).

CHATHAM   Charles Dickens, born in Portsmouth, came to Chatham as a child in 1817 when his father took a job at the dockyard. The family lived here until 1822 when they moved to London, but Dickens never lost his affection for the area. In 1856 he bought Gad's Hill Place, near Rochester (see above). Given his imagination, it's likely he would have appreciated **Dickens World** on Leviathan Way (www.dickensworld.co.uk; ✆ **01634/890421**). It's an indoor theme park where you can take a Great Expectations boat ride, visit Scrooge's haunted house, see a 4-D cinema show at Peggotty's Boathouse or an animatronic version of Dickens's life, and come face to face with the author's literary creations in a Victorian setting. It's open Monday to Friday 10am to 4:30pm, weekends and holidays until 5:30pm. Closed Mondays from September to Easter. (£13 adults, £11 seniors, and £8 children 5–15).

Upnor Castle (www.english-heritage.org.uk; ✆ **01634/718742**), off the A228 in the village of Upnor, is an Elizabethan fortification built to protect warships moored at Chatham (although it failed to do so in 1667, when the Dutch sailed past it to attack the English fleet). Open daily April to October, 10am to 6pm; closed November to March (£5.50 adults, £3.50 seniors and children 5–15).

Historic Dockyard Chatham ★★★ ☺ HISTORIC SITE   From the Spanish Armada to the Falklands Crisis, ships were built and repaired here. Records date back to 1547 and by the mid-18th century it was the largest industrial set-up in the world, with thousands of skilled workers. Most of the English fleet wintered on the Medway and Nelson's flagship, HMS *Victory,* was built here and launched in 1765. Today it exudes history, and has featured in movies such as *Sherlock Holmes,* with Robert Downey Jr., and *The Golden Compass.*

You can visit the Victorian Navy sloop HMS *Gannet,* the submarine HMS *Ocelot,* which served until 1991, and the World War II destroyer HMS *Cavalier.* There's also a covered slipway from 1838 with a midget sub, tank, and other vehicles; an exhibition of Nelson and the Battle of Trafalgar, and the Royal Navy Lifeboat Institute's national lifeboat collection. Even the restaurant, Wheelwrights, is part of history, housed in a 1738 building forged from old warship timbers. Its menus are full of Kent produce.

Nearby is **Fort Amherst** (www.fortamherst.com; ✆ **01634/847747**), a fort from the times of the Napoleonic wars with a large network of tunnels. It was part of original fortifications that extended 4 miles and enclosed the Royal Dockyard. Entry varies, but the grounds are open Monday to Friday 10am to 3:30pm.

The Historic Dockyard. www.thedockyard.co.uk. ℂ **01634/823800.** Admission £16.50 adults, £14 seniors and ex-service members, £11 children 5–16, £45 family ticket. Daily March–Oct 10am–6pm; Nov–Feb 10am-4pm; closed Dec–Jan. From junction 1 of the M2, follow the brown tourist signs.

Where to Eat & Stay

Ship and Trades This 1875 quayside engineering shop, overlooking one of the yacht basins at the dockyard, has been converted into a smart pub-cum-hotel by local brewer Shepherd Neame. The result is excellent beer (try the Spitfire) in a relaxed, modern setting with ropes, maps, and other nautical memorabilia on the walls. Waterfront seating looks across the Medway. The bar has decent pub fare while the upstairs restaurant serves modern and traditional meals. Main courses (£7.95–£15.95) range from chicken Caesar salad to a 10-oz. sirloin steak. Ship and Trades has 11 B&B rooms, smartly modern (one especially designed for disabled access).

Maritime Way, Chatham Maritime, Kent ME4 3ER. www.shipandtradeschatham.co.uk. ℂ **01634/895200.** 11 units. £75 double. Rates include English breakfast. AE, MC, V. **Amenities:** Breakfast room. *In room:* TV, hair dryer. Wi-Fi (about £10 per 24 hr., access from www.btopenzone.com).

WHITSTABLE ★ & MARGATE ★★

Whitstable 50 miles SE of London; Margate 65 miles SE of London

This is one of Britain's few areas of north-facing coast, and has a very different light to other regions—which is why the painter J. M. W. Turner was attracted to it. It is an area devoted to the pleasures of the sea, whether the charms of seafood (**Whitstable**) or the fun of the seaside (**Margate**). But it is also a place to get away from it all on the **old-fashioned beaches** between the towns of Herne Bay and Margate. Across the headland (the Isle of Thanet) looking out to the east, you'll find **Broadstairs** (with the seafront Charles Dickens pub, housed in the old assembly rooms where Dickens himself was a visitor) and **Ramsgate,** which sits on Pegwell Bay, a sandy beach protected by cliffs, and a National Nature Reserve.

Essentials

GETTING THERE Trains (Southeastern) run from London's St. Pancras Station twice an hour (with a change at Rochester), and hourly from Victoria, each taking about 90 minutes to Whitstable, a little longer to Margate. A one-way journey costs about £25. There are two trains an hour from Canterbury West to Margate (30 min. trip, **about £5 one-way**), and two trains an hour from Canterbury East to Whitstable, changing at Ramsgate or Faversham and taking up to 1 hour (**about £7 one-way**). There are two trains an hour between Whitstable and Margate, taking around 20 minutes (**about £6.50 one-way**), more at peak times.

By car from London head south on the M25 east, then the M20. At junction 7 head east on the A249 and then join the M2, also east. When the motorway ends, take the A299.

VISITOR INFORMATION Whitstable has a touch-screen **Tourist Information Point** at the harbor office (www.canterbury.co.uk; ℂ **01227/378100**). Margate's **Tourist Information Centre,** The Droit House, Stone Pier (www.visitthanet.co.uk; ℂ **01843/577577**), is open Easter to September, daily 10am to 5pm; the rest of the year, Tuesday to Saturday 10am to 5pm, Sunday 11am to 4pm.

WHITSTABLE Whitstable is an oyster-fishing port that has reinvented itself as the home of oyster feasts and seafood cuisine. It started quietly in the late 1970s with the **Whitstable Oyster Company,** a pleasingly informal restaurant. Others followed and now the quayside is awash with stalls selling, crab, cooked fish, and lots of chips. At weekends you'll also find a market with stalls selling all manner of crafts and bric-a-brac. There are seafront pubs, notably the **Old Neptune** (✆ 01227/272262), right on the beach and in town there's the famous **Wheelers Oyster Bar.** It has a simple menu and you can take your own wine. It's tiny though, and fills up fast.

As befits a reborn seaside town, there are galleries, coffee bars, and individual shops. But this is a place to wander. Lots of tiny alleys connect the streets to the sea, and there's a seafront path that's busy with families, jolly groups, and couples holding hands. Turn left on the path and you pass wonderful little cottages (including one with a blue plaque proclaiming it to be the former home of horror film actor Peter Cushing), then beach huts and, as the seafront curls around, the village of Seasalter. Go the other way and you find the quayside and its black-painted wooden sheds, which includes delights such as the **Fish Market,** selling the day's catch (whitebait, for instance), as well as cooking it for you to eat on paper plates outside or upstairs in the **Crab and Winkle** restaurant, with its range of fish products for souvenirs. Walk around the quay to East Quay, where you can find a quieter stretch of pebble beach, just before the **Hotel Continental,** to sit and eat your chips. Round the headland and you come to the village of Tankerton. There's plenty of parking available near the seafront.

MARGATE This was one of England's earliest seaside resorts, where 18th-century gentry came to enjoy the newly fashionable, health-giving properties of sea bathing. Margate has been through some hard times more recently but, located on sandy beaches at one of England's easternmost tips, it was always going to re-emerge. Its renaissance is led by **Turner Contemporary ★★**, an art gallery (www.turner contemporary.org; ✆ 01843/233000), which opened in April 2011, to celebrate the artist J. M. W. Turner. He first came here to go to school at age 11, returned to sketch here at age 21, and from the 1820s until his death in 1851 he was a regular visitor. He told writer and art critic John Ruskin that "… the skies over Thanet are the loveliest in all Europe," and more than 100 of his works, including his famous seascapes, were inspired by the East Kent coast.

The modernist building is on the site of the Cold Harbour guesthouse, where Turner regularly stayed. It recreates the sea and quayside views that the artist saw. The gallery, the biggest exhibition space in the Southeast outside London, features changing exhibitions of Turner's work, along with that of other artists.

Alongside the gallery, the **Harbour Arm,** a concrete pier that protects the seafront, has been revamped into a happening place. There's also the **Lighthouse Bar** (✆ 07980/727668), smart and modern with a wood-burning stove; **BeBeached** (www.bebeached.co.uk; ✆ 07961/402612), a "real food cafe" with veggie tendencies; a gallery used by local artists; and **Caitlin's Beach Cruisers** (www.caitlins beachcruisers.com; ✆ 07956/395896), which rents out restored and retro bicycles.

The seafront **Dreamland** amusement park (www.dreamlandmargate.com) is being reborn as a "heritage" amusement park in a multimillion-pound project; its Scenic Railway wooden rollercoaster (which was here when the park opened in 1921) is being refurbished and joined by historic rides rescued from around the U.K. The listed Art Deco cinema is being restored, too, and will open as a concert venue, the grounds are being restored to their former glory, and the place will be full of the sights, sounds, and smells of a classic amusement park. Stage one is hoped to open in 2013.

All these are within a few yards of each other, and facing the sea. In one direction are **Margate Main Sands,** a long stretch of golden sand that still has traditional donkey rides and deckchairs. On the promenade (The Parade), you can gorge on fish and chips, candy floss (cotton candy), and cockles and whelks, but you'll also come across trendy cafes, such as the **Harbour Cafe Bar** (✆ 01843/290110). On the other side of the Harbour Arm a narrower, but far longer, beach stretches up to the grander Cliftonville area. Dip into Margate's old town and you'll find the Creative Quarter, with a growing number of individual shops and galleries.

One other quirky attraction is the **Shell Grotto** (www.shellgrotto.co.uk; ✆ **01843/ 220008**). Below ground, 4.6 million sea shells cover 20m (70 ft.) of tunnels leading to an oblong chamber. The result is enchanting and Roman-like (cockles, whelks, and oysters create trees of life, gods, and even an altar), but mysterious. It was discovered when the ground fell while a farmer dug a duck pond in 1835, and no one has any idea who built it. There's some suggestion that it was a sun temple, with rays entering through a hole in a small dome at summer solstice. Whatever the answer, it really is somewhere that will leave you speechless. There's also a small museum, Eighth Wonder Cafe, and of course a shop. It's open daily from Good Friday to Halloween, 10am to 5pm; in winter, it's open weekends only, 11am to 4pm. Admission for adults is £3, £1.50 children 4 to 16.

Where to Eat

The Sportsman ★★ ENGLISH At this gastropub *par excellence,* chef/owner Stephen Harris has a Michelin star for his modern take on country food. Here they even make their own salt from buckets of seawater (the pub is just off the beach at Seasalter, a coastal stroll from Whitstable). There's a daily menu on the chalkboard, with dishes such as seared thornback ray with brown butter, cockles, and sherry vinegar dressing, and the famed Monkshill Farm pork belly and apple sauce, slow cooked with the world's best crackling. There's also a tasting menu, available Tuesday to Friday, pre-ordered and for a maximum of six people.

Faversham Rd., Seasalter, Whitstable. www.thesportsmanseasalter.co.uk. ✆ **01227/273370.** Reservations recommended. Main courses £18–£23; tasting menu (Tues–Fri) £65. AE, DC, MC, V. Tues–Sat noon–2pm and 7–9pm; Sun noon–2:30pm. Bar open daily.

Tartar Frigate ★★ SEAFOOD One of Kent's leading fish restaurants, the Frigate is in an 18th-century flint building looking over Viking Bay. The restaurant is upstairs, with glorious views; the pub below. The ultimate dish is the Grand Seafood platter (£55 for two), heaped with two crabs, half a lobster, cockles, mussels, shrimp, oysters, and more. The friendly bar has live music and is a focal point of Broadstairs Folk Week each August; you can also take your beer onto the beach.

37 Harbour St., Broadstairs. www.tartarfrigate.co.uk. ✆ **01843/862013.** Reservations recommended. Main courses £15–£18; AE, MC, V. Pub 11am–11pm (closes 10:30pm Sun). Restaurant: Mon–Sat noon–2:30, 6pm–9pm; Sunday lunch, sittings at 12:30pm and 3:30pm.

Whitstable Oyster Company ★★ SEAFOOD This still leads the pack in the converted seafront Royal Native Oyster Stores warehouse, with piles of oyster shells outside and oyster beds off the beach. A half-dozen oysters start at £9, and dishes include whole local lobster served simply with potato salad. The place opened in 1978 when the oyster company was near closing; the family-run business now includes the Whitstable Brewery, with ales such as Harbour Light, Hotel Continental, Whitstable Brewery Bar, and the East Quay bar and Lobster Shack restaurant.

The Horsebridge, Whitstable. www.whitstableoystercompany.com. ℂ **01227/276856.** Reservations recommended. Main courses £13–£28. AE, MC, V. Mon–Thurs noon–2:30pm and 6:30–9pm; Fri noon–2:30pm and 6:30–9:30pm; Sat noon–9:45pm; Sun noon–8:30pm.

Entertainment & Nightlife

Whitstable is an unlikely place for nightlife, but the **Whitstable Brewery Bar** (ℂ **01227/772157**) is bringing the clubbing scene to this little town. It's on East Quay, on the far side of the quay from most of the seafront attractions, and looks like a shed from the outside, but is smart and modern with a big DJ booth, lighting rig, and sound system inside. It's open every Friday and Saturday night from 10pm until 3am for soul, funk, drum 'n' bass, and house, often featuring well-known DJs. The bar is also open daily in the summer, from noon to 9pm for a more laid-back experience, and has tables out on the pebble beach. The nearby sister **East Quay Venue** (ℂ **01227/262003**) is open for special events, including live music of the caliber of Dr Feelgood and The Beat.

Margate has **Rokka** (www.rokka.com; ℂ **01843/230183**), at the bottom of the High Street, facing the sea. By day it's a swish coffee bar, by night the chic red-and-white decor is enveloped in a rosy glow and it becomes a hip bar with guest DJs, even bongo players. It's open Friday and Saturday evenings until 2am (no cover). There's also a branch in Ramsgate. In Margate on a summer's night the **Harbour Arm** is a good place to hang out, having a drink outside **The Lighthouse Bar,** maybe a bite to eat in **BeBeached** (see above for all these); it all turns into a bit of a party atmosphere.

Where to Stay

Hotel Continental This neat, rather French-style hotel is part of the growing Oyster Company empire and sits alone on the seafront. There are 23 rooms, some with iron balconies overlooking the sea. There are also eight converted fishermen's huts on the beach; they are on two floors, finished in dark wood with green painted shutters. The Anderson Shed is perfect for families, sleeping four adults and two children. The airy bistro serves a decent menu, and the bar is big and sunny.

29 Beach Walk, Whitstable, Kent CT5 2BP. www.hotelcontinental.co.uk. ℂ **01227/280280.** Fax 01227/284114. 31 units. £70–£145 double; £100–£175 huts. Rates include English breakfast. MC, V. Free parking. **Amenities:** Restaurant; bar. *In room:* TV, hair dryer, Wi-Fi (free).

The Reading Rooms This Georgian town house is divided into three large rooms, each occupying an entire floor and overlooking a tree-lined square. The feel is airy, fairytale luxury with oak floors, candelabra, hand-carved super-king beds, and lots of white, from original plasterwork to linens. It's a B&B, although breakfast arrives as room service. The sea is a stroll away.

31 Hawley Sq., Margate, Kent CT9 1PH. www.thereadingroomsmargate.co.uk. ℂ **01843/225166.** Fax 01304/206705. 3 units. £135–£180 double. Rates include English breakfast. AE, MC, V. Free overnight parking; £2 daily. **Amenities:** Room service. *In room:* TV/DVD, hair dryer, Wi-Fi (free).

Walpole Bay Hotel This Margate institution was opened in 1914, extended in 1927, and is now being brought back to its old grandeur. The hotel is a living museum; it was owned by the same family until 1995 when the present owners took over. It sits above the sea in the Cliftonville area. There's a flower-bedecked covered veranda, a snooker room, a 1920s' ballroom with its original sprung maple dance floor … and the original Otis elevators. The restaurant (with terrace) has local plaice and sea bass (main courses £11.95–£17) as well as Sunday lunch, accompanied by a pianist on a 1908 pianola. There are also cream teas. Oh, and the rooms are neatly Edwardian in feel.

Fifth Ave., Cliftonville, Margate, Kent CT9 2JJ. www.walpolebayhotel.co.uk. ℂ **01843/221703.** Fax 01843/297399. 3 units. £75–£125 double. Rates include English breakfast. AE, MC, V. Free parking. **Amenities:** Restaurant; 2 bars; snooker room. *In room:* TV/DVD, hair dryer, Wi-Fi (free).

DOVER'S WHITE CLIFFS & MORE

76 miles SE of London; 84 miles NE of Brighton

The White Cliffs of Dover, captured in the World War II song by Dame Vera Lynn, are truly one of Britain's iconic images. Unfortunately, you have to be at sea (probably on a ferry coming from France) to appreciate them. Dover was a seaside resort back in Victorian times but today is mostly known as a port. It's on (and in) the cliffs that you'll find the town's main attraction, **Dover Castle.** Beneath its medieval might is a warren of wartime tunnels. Five miles to the north is the fishing port of Deal, and 8 miles south is Folkestone, another port but also a traditional beach resort.

Essentials

GETTING THERE Trains run about every 30 minutes from London's St. Pancras Station (Southeastern, costing about £37 one-way), and there are two trains an hour from Canterbury East (Southeastern, about £8). Because of its importance as a ferry port, there are regular National Express buses from London's Victoria Coach Station until late (from about £10). If you're driving from London, once you're on the M25 heading east, you simply follow the M20.

VISITOR INFORMATION Dover's **Tourist Information Centre** on Old Town Gaol Street (www.whitecliffscountry.org.uk; ℂ **01304/205108**) is open June to August, daily 9am to 5:30pm; the rest of the year, Monday to Friday 9am to 5:30pm, Saturday and Sunday 10am to 4pm. **Discover Folkestone** (www.discoverfolkestone. co.uk; ℂ **01303/258594**), in Folkstone's Bouverie Place shopping center, is open Monday to Friday 9am to 5pm.

Exploring the Area

The best view of the **white cliffs** ★★★ is on board a boat. If you can't do that, walk to the end of the Prince of Wales pier, the largest of the town's western docks. From here, the cliffs loom above you. Another option is Samphire Hoe, just off the A20 leaving town, and through the cliffs in a single-lane tunnel (www.samphirehoe.co.uk; daily 7am to dusk, free admission but pay parking). It's a man-made nature reserve of grassy hills and ponds at the foot of the cliffs, constructed from the Channel Tunnel spoils. There are paths, access to a little beach, a concrete seawall for sunbathing, and a little tea bar with free maps as well as guided walks, second-hand books, and even home-grown plants.

Although you go to Dover for specific sights, **Folkestone** is a much more attractive prospect as a town. It features winding streets (including arty shops in the Creative

Quarter), a grassy, cliff-top promenade, and a pretty little quayside (with views of the white cliffs). The beach, a short walk down the hill, stretches away into the distance. Just south of Folkestone is Hythe, from where the **Romney, Hythe & Dymchurch railway** (www.rhdr.org.uk; *C* **01797/362353**) runs along the coast to wild and windy Dungeness. The fishermen's cottages made from old railway carriages provide stark contrast to the modern power station. Here you'll find an **RSPB reserve** (www.rspb.org.uk; *C* **01797/320588**), a flat expanse of pebble beach and marsh that is home to seabirds and a stop-off for migrant birds. It is open daily 9am to 9pm (or to sunset if that's earlier), and has a visitor center (10am–5pm; until 4pm Nov–Mar); admission is £3 adults, £1 children 15 and under. Allow time for the locally caught fish and chips at the station's **Light Railway Cafe** on the way back.

Deal Castle ★ CASTLE This is one of the finest surviving Tudor artillery castles and can be explored from top to bottom, including its dank passages. The seafront fort, built around 1540, is the most spectacular example of the low, squat forts constructed by Henry VIII; its 119 gun positions also made it the most powerful. The circular keep was protected by an outer moat, the entrance approached by a drawbridge with an iron gate. The admission price includes an audio tour.

On the seafront. www.english-heritage.co.uk.*C* **01304/372762.** Admission £4.80 adults, £4.30 seniors, £2.90 children 5–16. Daily Apr–Sept 10am–6pm; Oct–March weekends 10am–6pm.

Dover Castle ★★★ CASTLE Rising more than 100m (340 ft.) above the port is one of the oldest castles in England. Its keep was built by Henry II, in the 12th century, but the castle was returned to active duty as late as World War II. Over the past several years it has been undergoing a multimillion-pound makeover. Plenty has gone into the Great Tower, the interior of which is a multimedia experience of the royal court of Henry II. It is considered the most ambitious attempt to recreate a medieval palace in more than a century, with hangings, furnishings, and other objects created by craftsmen. You can walk the battlements, laze on the lawns, and see the Pharos, one of Europe's best-preserved Roman lighthouses. The castle also houses the **Secret Wartime Tunnels,** 60m (200 ft.) below ground, which actually date back to medieval times. They were first adapted during the Napoleonic Wars to house cannons in case the French invaded. They were turned into a secret World War II bolthole, the headquarters of Operation Dynamo, when 300,000 troops were evacuated from Dunkirk. Touring them (including an operating theatre and hospital), you can feel the weight of the white cliffs above you, and can hardly imagine what it must have been like during the war's darkest days. Don't miss the hidden cliff-top balcony, where Churchill stood during the Battle of Britain. This can be a full day out for the entire family.

Castle Hill. www.english-heritage.co.uk.*C* **01304/211067.** Admission £16 adults, £14.90 students and seniors, £9.90 children 5–15. Price includes castle audio tour and tunnels tour. Daily Apr–Sept 10am–6pm (Aug 9:30am); Oct 10am–5pm; weekends Nov–March 10–4pm.

Roman Painted House ★★ HISTORIC SITE Britain's "buried Pompeii," a Roman building 1,800 years old, has exceptionally well-preserved walls and an underfloor heating system. It's famous for its unique Bacchic murals. Brass-rubbing is also offered. You'll find it in the town center near Market Square.

New St. www.theromanpaintedhouse.co.uk.*C* **01304/203279.** Admission £3 adults, £2 seniors and children 16 and under. 10am–5pm, variable dates but generally late Apr–May Tues and Sat only; Easter and June–mid-Sept Tues–Sun; Oct–Mar by prior arrangement.

Where to Eat

The Allotment ★★ ENGLISH   The name says it all: The owner/chef is an allotment holder and most of the produce used comes from his and friends' vegetable patches. The result is an urban bistro at Dover's culinary forefront. The food is straightforward but inventive (maybe roasted Dungeness mackerel followed by slow-roasted "crying" shoulder of Canterbury lamb). Breakfast (sourdough pancakes, eggs Benedict, and the like), lunch, and tea are also served.

9 High St., Dover. www.theallotmentdover.co.uk. 🕐 **01304/214467.** Reservations recommended. Main courses £8–£16. AE, DC, MC, V. Tues–Sat 8:30am–11pm.

Wallett's Court ★ MODERN ENGLISH   This restaurant is at a country-house hotel, with refreshing seasonal English cuisine, a rich, traditional setting, and a countryside backdrop. As for the menu, the Kentish venison three ways (roast loin, pan-fried liver, and suet pudding) with celeriac fondue, red-onion marmalade, and truffled pomme purée sets the standard. Or you might find goose breast, guinea fowl, or turbot. There is also a good-value 2-course set lunch (£15).

Wallett's Court Hotel, Westcliffe, St. Margaret's-at-Cliffe, Dover. www.wallettscourthotelspa.com. 🕐 **01304/852424.** Reservations recommended. 3-course dinner menu £40, set menu lunch £17 for 2 courses. AE, DC, MC, V. Daily 7:30–9:30am, noon–2pm, and 7–9pm.

Where to Stay

East Lee Guest House   This former home of local artist William Henry East is smartly furnished to maintain its Victorian atmosphere. Run by the same couple for more than 30 years, it's a welcoming B&B, an easy stroll from the heart of town. Bedrooms have the feel of a bygone age (although with all modern conveniences), and breakfast is served in the elegant dining room.

108 Maison Dieu Rd., Dover, Kent CT16 1RT. www.eastlee.co.uk. 🕐 **01304/210176.** Fax 01304/206705. 4 units. £65–£70 double. Rates include English breakfast. Free parking in street. MC, V. *In room:* TV, hair dryer. Wi-Fi (£3 unlimited).

The Relish   A pastel-hued Victorian mansion in the heart of Folkestone, The Relish combines boutique flair and personal care. There's a complimentary glass of wine or beer each day, as well as unlimited coffee, tea, and homemade cakes. Rooms are richly modern, and have rainforest showers and organic toiletries. A terrace looks over Augusta Gardens, a park accessible only to residents of The Relish and to the spiffy Radnor Estate, which backs on to it.

4 Augusta Gardens, Folkestone, Kent CT20 2RR. www.hotelrelish.co.uk. 🕐 **01303/850952.** Fax 01303/850958. 10 units. £95–£145 double. Rates include English breakfast. MC, V. Unrestricted street parking. **Amenities:** Breakfast room. *In room:* TV/DVD, CD player, hair dryer, Wi-Fi (free).

Wallett's Court ★ 🎁   A Norman conquest-era manor house (mentioned in The Domesday Book), Wallett's Court is set in an open landscape not far from the clifftops. It was rebuilt in Tudor style in the 1400s, and boasts a Jacobean staircase that takes you up to three bedrooms with four-posters. The other rooms are in converted Kentish hay barns, stables, and cow sheds. All are individually decorated with Edwardian country-house chic. There's a bar with a fire for winter, a terrace for summer. The spa has a splendid pool, and the restaurant is terrific (see "Where to Eat"). There are cliff walks, and a path leads to St. Margaret's Bay with its beach and white cliffs.

Westcliffe, St. Margaret's-at-Cliffe, Dover, Kent CT15 6EW. www.wallettscourthotelspa.com. 🕐 **01304/852424.** Fax 01304/853430. 17 units. £140–£210 double; £210–£250 suite. Rates include

English breakfast. AE, DC, MC, V. Closed Dec 24–27. Off the A258 just east of Dover. **Amenities:** Restaurant; bar; indoor heated pool; health club and spa; room service; babysitting. *In room:* TV/ DVD, hair dryer, CD player, Wi-Fi (free).

KENT'S CASTLES & GARDENS

Kent is home to a wealth of country houses, castles, and gardens, many of them the finest in England. **Leeds Castle** claims to be the loveliest castle in the world, but there's so much more to see. Names like Anne Boleyn, Winston Churchill, Charles Darwin, and William Waldorf Astor crop up as you tour the area. If you're going to choose, go for **Knole, Hever, Leeds, Penshurst,** and **Chartwell.** You'll need a car to get around as most are, in the way of country houses, in the country. From London, it's an easy drive (many routes head southeast which all reach the M25 ring road, Kent's unofficial northern boundary) with many places do-able as a day trip. You could also head for Canterbury (see "Essentials," in the "Canterbury" section, p. 240). Guided tours are often on offer, but even the most ardent history buffs can suffer information overload, so often it's best to simply wander around and soak up the atmosphere.

Exploring the Area

Chartwell ★ HISTORIC HOME   This was the home of Sir Winston Churchill, from 1922 until his death in 1965. It's not as grand as his birthplace (Blenheim Palace; p. 227), but it has wonderful views over the Weald of Kent. The rooms are as if the former prime minister had just stepped into the garden: maps, documents, paintings, photos, mementos, and so forth are all on show. There are displays of his trademark suits and hats, as well as gifts from people around the world in thanks for leading the Allies to wartime victory. Churchill was an accomplished artist, and many of his works are displayed in a garden studio. The walls that he built with his own hands are still standing strong, and the kitchen gardens they contain are undergoing restoration to be more in keeping with how he tended them (produce is used in the restaurant). *Insider tip:* The house can get busy, and entry is on a timed ticket so it pays to get there early.

Mapleton Rd., Westerham. www.nationaltrust.org.uk. ℭ **01732/868381.** Admission to house, garden, and studio £12.90 adults, £6.50 children 5–16, £32.20 family ticket (garden only £6.50/£3.20/£16.10). In winter garden only £4.90/£2.20)/£12. House mid-Mar–early July and late Aug–Oct Wed–Sun 11am–5pm; early July–mid-Aug Tues–Sun 11am–5pm; closed Nov–mid-Mar. Garden, exhibition, and restaurant also open Nov–mid-Dec Tues–Sun 11am–4pm, mid-end Dec daily 11am–4pm. M25 junction 5, then follow signs.

Down House HISTORIC HOME   Naturalist Charles Darwin lived here for 40 years until his death in 1882. When he moved in he wrote "House ugly, looks neither old nor new." Nevertheless, he lived here "in happy contentment" for 4 decades. The drawing room, dining room, billiard room, and old study have been restored to the way they were when Darwin was working on his famous, and still controversial, book *On the Origin of Species,* published in 1859. The original landscaping remains, along with the Sand Walk, the "Thinking Path," where Darwin took his daily solitary walk.

Luxted Rd., Downe. www.english-heritage.org.uk. ℭ **01689/859119.** Admission £9.90 adults, £8.90 students and seniors, £5.90 children 5–16, £25.70 family ticket. Apr–June and Sept–Oct Wed–Sun 11am–5pm; Nov–Dec 20, Feb and Mar Wed–Sun 11am–4pm; July–Aug daily 11am–5pm. Closed Dec 21–Jan 31. From Westerham, take the A233 several miles north and follow signs for Downe.

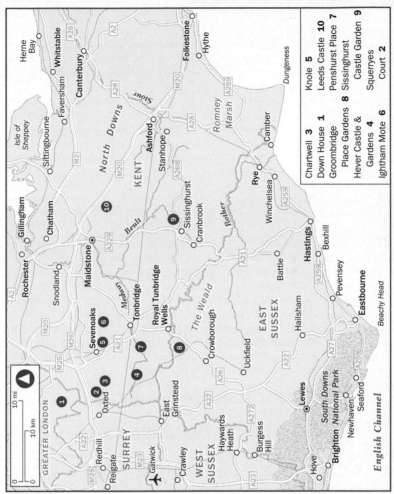

Chartwell **3**	Knole **5**
Down House **1**	Leeds Castle **10**
Groombridge	Penshurst Place **7**
Place Gardens **8**	Sissinghurst
Hever Castle &	Castle Garden **9**
Gardens **4**	Squerryes
Ightham Mote **6**	Court **2**

Groombridge Place Gardens ☺ GARDEN   These formal gardens, dating from the 17th century but with modern additions, are divided into walks, gardens, and other experiences. The White Rose Garden is compared to that at fabled Sissinghurst, the English Knot Garden is based on panels in the drawing room of an English country house, and Fern Valley is a forest of huge tree ferns. Children are well catered for with the Enchanted Forest, full of playgrounds, flowers, swings, and deer, Crusoe's World, and Dinosaur and Dragon Valley. At the heart is a beautiful 17th-century moated manor house. Sir Christopher Wren is believed to have been involved in its design. Sir Arthur Conan Doyle was a regular visitor to take part in séances, and the manor was the setting for the Sherlock Holmes mystery *The Valley of Fear*.

Groombridge. www.groombridge.co.uk.℃ **08192/861444.** Admission £9.95 adults, £8.45 seniors and children 3–12, £33.95 family ticket. (Extra £1 mid-July–early Sept and some peak days.) Mid-March–Oct 10am–5:30pm.

Hever Castle & Gardens ★★ CASTLE   Hever Castle dates from 1270, when the massive gatehouse, outer walls, and moat were built. Some 200 years later, the Bullen (or Boleyn) family added a Tudor house. Hever was the childhood home of Anne Boleyn, second wife of Henry VIII and mother of Queen Elizabeth I. In 1903 William Waldorf Astor bought the estate and restored the castle, building the Tudor Village and creating the gardens and lakes. The Astor family's contribution to Hever's rich history can be appreciated through the castle's collections of furniture, paintings, and art, as well as the woodcarving and plasterwork. The gardens are ablaze with vibrant shades throughout most of the year. The Italian Garden contains statuary and sculpture dating from Roman to Renaissance times. There's also a large lake, a maze, and many streams, cascades, and fountains.

Hever, near Edenbridge. www.hevercastle.co.uk. ℃ **01732/865224.** Admission to castle and gardens £14.50 adults, £12.50 students and seniors, £8.30 children 5–15, £37.30 family ticket. Audio tour £3.25. Daily mid-Feb–Christmas (Wed–Sun March, Nov, early Dec): Gardens 10:30am–5pm; castle noon–5pm (closes at 4pm Feb, Mar, Nov, Dec). Follow the signs northwest of Royal Tunbridge Wells; it's 3 miles southeast of Edenbridge, and 30 min. from junction 6 of the M25.

Ightham Mote ★ HISTORIC SITE   Ightham Mote, dating from 1320, is a gorgeous moated manor house with Tudor touches such as the chapel with painted ceiling, timbered outer wall, and ornate chimneys. You'll cross a stone bridge over a moat to its central courtyard. From the Great Hall, with its magnificent windows, a Jacobean staircase leads to the chapel on the first floor. Other highlights include the crypt and a dog kennel that is a Grade I listed building. Ightham Mote passed from one medieval knight to another, to Henry VIII's courtiers. and to high-society Victorians. Each left his mark: When the last owner died (an American responsible for much of the restoration) he left the house to the National Trust, which chose to keep the Robinson Library laid out as it was in a 1960 edition of *Homes & Gardens*.

Mote Rd., Ivy Hatch. www.nationaltrust.org.uk.℃ **01732/810378.** Admission £11.50 adults, £5.75 children 5–15, £29 family ticket. Mar–Oct Thurs–Mon; June–Aug Wed–Mon 11am–5pm; Nov–mid-Dec Thurs–Sun 11am–3pm. Garden also Feb weekends. Drive 6 miles east of Sevenoaks on the A25 to the village of Ivy Hatch; the estate is 2½ miles south of Ightham, signposted from the A227.

Knole ★★ ARCHITECTURE   Built in the mid-15th century by Thomas Bourchier, Archbishop of Canterbury, and set in a 1,000-acre deer park, Knole is one of the largest private houses in England and one of the finest examples of pure English Tudor-style architecture. Henry VIII liberated the former archbishop's palace from the Church in 1537. He spent considerable sums of money on Knole, but history records only one visit (in 1541) rom the reluctant Archbishop Cranmer. It was a royal palace until Queen Elizabeth I granted it to Thomas Sackville, 1st Earl of Dorset, whose descendants have lived here ever since. (Virginia Woolf, often a guest of the Sackvilles, used Knole as the setting for her novel *Orlando*.) The house has 365 rooms, 52 staircases, and 7 courts. The elaborate paneling and plasterwork provide a background for the 17th- and 18th-century tapestries and rugs, Elizabethan and Jacobean furniture, and family portraits. If you want to see a bed to die for, check out the state bed of James II in the King's Bedroom.

5 miles north of Tunbridge, at the Tunbridge end of the town of Sevenoaks. www.nationaltrust.org. uk.℃ **01732/462100.** Admission to house £11.50 adults, £5.75 children 5–15, £28.75 family ticket;

gardens £5 adults, £2.50 children. House mid-Mar–Oct Wed–Sun noon–4pm; gardens every Wed of the month late Mar–late Oct 11am–4pm (last admission 3:30pm); park daily to pedestrians and to cars only during house hours. To reach Knole from Chartwell, drive to Westerham, head east on the A25 for 8 miles. Frequent train service is available from London (about every 30 min.) to Sevenoaks; then take the connecting hourly bus service or a taxi, or walk the remaining 1½ miles to Knole.

Leeds Castle ★★★ CASTLE   Once described by Lord Conway as the loveliest castle in the world, Leeds Castle dates from A.D. 857. First constructed of wood, it was rebuilt in 1119 in stone on two small islands in the lake, making it an almost impregnable fortress. Henry VIII took to it and converted it into a royal palace.

There are strong ties to America through the 6th Lord Fairfax who, as well as owning the castle, owned a large area of Virginia and was a close friend and mentor of the young George Washington. The last private owner, the Hon. Lady Baillie, who restored the castle with a superb collection of fine art, furniture, and tapestries, bequeathed it to the Leeds Castle Foundation. Since then the royal apartments, known as Les Chambres de la Reine (the Queen's Chambers), in the Gloriette, the oldest part of the castle, have been open to the public. The Gloriette, the last stronghold against attack, dates from Norman and Plantagenet times with later additions by Henry VIII.

Within the surrounding parkland, a lovely place to walk, is a wildwood garden and a collection of rare swans, geese, and ducks. The **Aviary** collection includes parakeets and cockatoos, the **Culpepper Garden** is an English-country flower garden, while the **Dog Collar Museum** speaks for itself, with a collection dating back to the Middle Ages. Beyond are greenhouses, a maze, underground grotto, and a vineyard that was recorded in The Domesday Book (1086) and is once again producing white wine. There is also a 9-hole **golf course,** which is open to the public. You won't go hungry: There are various cafes including **Fairfax Hall,** a restored 17th-century tithe barn.

7 miles east of Maidstone, off junction 8 of the M20. www.leeds-castle.com. © **01622/765400.** £18.50 adults, £11 children 4–15. Daily Apr–Sept 10am–6pm (last admission 4:30pm); Oct–Mar until 5pm (last admission 3pm). Trains on the London Victoria–Maidstone/Ashford International line call at Bearsted, from where there are bus transfers (see castle website).

Penshurst Place ★★ ☺ HISTORIC SITE   Penshurst is one of Britain's outstanding country houses, as well as one of England's greatest defended manor houses, standing in a peaceful rural setting that has changed little over the centuries. In 1338, Sir John de Pulteney, four times lord mayor of London, built the manor house whose Great Hall still forms the heart of Penshurst. Henry VIII's son, the boy king Edward VI, presented the house to Sir William Sidney and it has remained in that family ever since. The Nether Gallery, below the Long Gallery with its ebony-and-ivory furniture from Goa, houses the Sidney family collection of armor. In the Stable Wing is a toy museum, with playthings from past generations. On the grounds are nature and farm trails plus an adventure playground for children.

6 miles west of Royal Tunbridge Wells. www.penshurstplace.co.uk. © **01892/870307.** Admission to house and grounds £9.80 adults, £6.20 children 5–16, £26 family ticket; grounds only £7.80 adults, £5.80 children 5–16, £23 family ticket. Daily Apr–Oct, house noon–4pm, grounds 10:30am–6pm (weekends only in late Feb and Mar). From M25 junction follow the A21 to Tunbridge, leaving at the Tunbridge (north) exit; then follow the brown tourist signs.

Sissinghurst Castle Garden ★★ GARDEN   In 1930 Bloomsbury set writer and noted gardener Vita Sackville-West and her diplomat husband Harold Nicolson moved into the property. The grounds had fallen into sorry disrepair but in the years that followed Vita turned them around, using the ruins of an Elizabethan manor to which they belong as a focal point. Today they are truly spectacular. In spring the gardens are awash with flowering bulbs and daffodils fill the orchard. The white garden reaches its peak in June. The large herb garden, a skillful montage that reflects Sackville-West's profound plant knowledge, has something to show all summer long. The cottage garden, with its flowering bulbs, is at its finest as summer fades, while an on-site restaurant uses fruit and vegetables from the gardens and meat from the tenant farmer.

Sissinghurst, Biddenden Rd., near Cranbrook. www.nationaltrust.org.uk.© **01580/710700.** Admission £11.50 adults, £5.50 children 5–15, £29 family ticket. Mid-Mar–Oct Fri–Tues 10:30am–5pm. Estate daily dawn–dusk, free. 53 miles southeast of London. It's often approached from Leeds Castle, which is 4 miles east of Maidstone at the junction of the A20 and M20. From this junction, head south on the B2163 and A274 through Headcorn. Follow the signposts to Sissinghurst.

Squerryes Court HISTORIC SITE   This manor house, built in 1861, was the home of British General James Wolfe, who commanded forces in the bombardment of Quebec. There are still pictures and relics of his family on display. The formal gardens have been restored using an 18th-century plan, with avenues, parterres, and hedges, as well as adding borders, spring bulbs, and old roses for year-round tones. There is a fine collection of Old Master paintings from the Italian, 17th-century Dutch, and 18th-century English schools, along with antiques, porcelain, and tapestries, but if time is limited the gardens are what you should see. General Wolfe received his commission on the grounds—the spot is marked by a cenotaph.

A half-mile west of Westerham (10 min. from M25 junction 5 or 6). www.squerryes.co.uk.© **01959/562345.** Admission to house and garden £7.50 adults, £7 students and seniors, £4 children 15 and under, £16 family ticket; garden only £5 adults, £4.50 seniors, £2.50 children 15 and under, £9.50 family ticket. Apr 1–Sept 30 Wed, Sun, and public holidays, house 12:30–5pm, grounds 11:30am–5pm. House and grounds closed Oct–Mar. Take the A25 just west of Westerham and follow the signs.

HASTINGS, EASTBOURNE & RYE

Hastings: 63 miles SE of London; Eastbourne 64 miles; Rye: 62 miles;

Hastings gives its name to the Battle of Hastings in 1066 where King Harold was defeated by the invading troops of William, Duke of Normandy. From this point England's history became entwined with that of France and nothing was the same again. The battle actually occurred at what is now **Battle Abbey** (8 miles away), but William used Hastings as his base. The main stretch of Hastings' seafront is disappointing but the old town portion, The Stade, is undergoing a major revamp, and there are quaint streets and nice hotels in the old town itself. **Rye** was once one of England's major ports, one of the places that filled and fed Navy ships as they kept the French and Spanish at bay, until storms filled in the harbor. The pretty town, now a quaint river port, is full of antiques shops and historic inns. **Eastbourne** is a classic Regency seaside town, with somewhat fading grand hotels. Sister resort Brighton went on to be hip and happening, and now Eastbourne is determined to do the same.

Essentials

GETTING THERE   Southeastern trains leave London Victoria for Hastings 5 times an hour with a change at Brighton. The trip takes just over 2 hours and costs about

£28 one-way. There are three trains from Victoria to Eastbourne every hour, taking 1½ hours, some with a change at Brighton, for about £28 one-way, and two trains from Victoria to Rye every hour, changing at Ashford International. These take nearly 2½ hours and cost about £30. Two trains an hour leave London Charing Cross and London Bridge for Hastings. Both routes take just over 1½ hours and cost about £30. The trip from London Bridge to Eastbourne takes 1½ hours with a change at East Croydon and costs about £28 (although a planned fast service could cut this by 30 min.). There are also two trains an hour from London St. Pancras to Rye, with a change at Ashford, which cost about £35, and four trains an hour from London Bridge to Rye, also changing at Ashford, for about £30. For Battle there are trains from London Charing Cross and London Bridge:; both routes cost about £26 and take just over an hour.

If you're driving, the A21 runs all the way to Hastings from junction 5 of the M25. From here the coastal A259 runs east to Rye and west to Eastbourne. The A22 runs all the way to Eastbourne from Croydon in south London, via junction 6 of the M25. There are various pretty routes to Battle from the coast. Hastings and Eastbourne are linked by the 99 bus (www.stagecoachbus.com/eastsussex) every 20 minutes. Frequent buses run to Battle from Rye and Hastings in summer.

VISITOR INFORMATION **Hastings Tourist Information Centre,** Queen's Square, Priory Meadow (www.visit1066country.com; ✆ **01424/451111**), is open Monday to Friday 8:30am to 6:15pm, Saturday 9am to 5pm, and Sunday 10:30am to 4pm. **Battle Tourist Information Centre,** at Battle Abbey Gatehouse (www.visit 1066country.com; ✆ **01424/776789**), is open daily April to September 10am to 6pm, October to March 10am to 4pm. **Rye Tourist Information Centre** is at 4–5 Lion St. (www.visitrye.co.uk; ✆ **01797/226696**), open daily April to September 10am to 5pm, October to March 10am to 4pm. **Eastbourne Tourist Information Centre,** Cornfield Road (www.visiteastbourne.com; ✆ **0871/633-0031**), is open May to September Monday to Friday 9:15am to 5:30pm, Saturday to 5pm, Sundays 10am to 1pm; March, April and October Monday to Friday 9:15am to 5:30pm, Saturday to 4pm, closed Sundays; November to February Monday to Friday 9:15am to 4:30pm, Saturday 9:15am to 5pm, closed Sundays.

Exploring the Area

Battle Abbey ★★★ ☺ RUINS See how England's history turned on a grassy field. It was on Senlac Hill where King Harold, last of the Saxon kings, fought to the death against the Norman invaders on October 14, 1066. Harold, as legend has it, was killed by an arrow through the eye, and it was the end of Anglo-Saxon England. History hangs heavy over the spot, but this is a lively, modern attraction. Battle Abbey (much of what's left is now a private school) was built by William the Conqueror to celebrate his victory, but it is the slope behind it that holds sway. Take the battlefield walk, listen to the audio tour, and immerse yourself in a turning point in civilization. The modern visitor center features a film, while interactive displays portray England at the time of the conquest. There's also a museum in the gatehouse. This is a great place for children, with a themed play area, activity sheet, and places to run around with a sword (available in the shop). The medieval town of Battle, which sprung up around the abbey, is worth a stroll.

Battle High St., Battle. www.english-heritage.org.uk.✆ **01424/773792.** £7.30 adults, £6.60 students and seniors, £4.40 children 5–15, £18 family ticket. Apr–Sept daily 10am–6pm; Oct–Mar daily 10am–4pm.

A DROP OF rye

Rye was once an important port and a smugglers' haunt, but a huge storm in the 13th century changed the coastline and it was left high and dry 2 miles inland. It was occupied by the French after the Norman invasion of 1066, but reclaimed for England in 1247 by Henry III. It was all but leveled in 1377, only to be rebuilt in Elizabethan style. The old town entrance is Land Gate, where traffic passes between 12-m-high (40 ft.) stone towers. The top of the gate has holes through which boiling oil used to be poured on unwelcome visitors (mostly the French). **Rye Castle Museum,** 3 East St., actually in an old brewery, tells the tale (Apr–Oct Sat–Sun and holidays 10:30am–5pm). The castle is the **Ypres Tower** (Apr–Oct daily 10:30am–5pm, Nov–Mar 10:30am–3:30pm), a coastal fortification built around 1250 by Henry III. It contains various exhibitions and has views across land that used to be sea (www.ryemuseum.co.uk; ✆ **01797/ 226728;** joint ticket £4 adults, under-16s free).

These days tourists invade to wander narrow, twisting cobblestone streets (full of stores selling antiques) and admire the ancient buildings, which prop each other up like a house of cards. The 12th-century **St. Mary's Church** (www.rye parishchurch.org.uk; ✆ **01797/224935**) was called the "Cathedral of East Sussex" due to its size; for £1 (under-17s free) you can climb the tower for splendid views.

Rye's pottery, white glazed and hand-painted, has been made for centuries. **Rye Pottery,** Wishward Street (www.rye pottery.co.uk; ✆ **01797/223038**), keeps the tradition going with statues depicting characters from *The Canterbury Tales* and the Bayeaux Tapestry.

Rye Heritage Centre, Strand Quay (www.ryeheritage.co.uk; ✆ **01797/ 226696**), has a sound-and-light show of 700 years of history (£3.50 adults, £1.50 children 15 and under; daily Apr–Oct 10am–5pm, Nov–Mar 4pm).

Beachy Head ATTRACTION   You feel that you could be blown all the way to France from this grassy expanse atop white cliffs with their equally white lighthouse. There are walks along the cliffs (called the Seven Sisters), and others away on to the South Downs and to the village of East Dean with its Tiger Inn pub and Hiker's Rest cafe. It's a great stroll up from the seafront at Eastbourne, or there are various pay parking lots. The beach below is accessible at Birling Gap.

Beachy Head Rd., (off A259). www.beachyhead.org.uk. ✆ **01323/423878.**

Eastbourne's public face is its Georgian promenade with classic pier, ornate bandstand, and still-grand Grand Hotel, yet behind the genteel smile the push is on to introduce a trendy edge, Brighton but calmer. In spring 2012 a market selling antiques, vintage clothing, and local food started in Terminus Road, just off the seafront. Here **Central Eating** (✆ **07980/339864**) is at the forefront of the changes, a bright, lively cafe-coffee bar with a retro heart where you can have a Jack Daniel's or a cappuccino with your scampi and chips, and treat yourself from the jars of boiled sweets on the counter. It's generally open until around teatime, but there are forays into evening opening. Just along the short street it's been joined by **Neate's Cakery** (www.neatescakery.co.uk; ✆ **01323/729001**), full of icing-topped treats.

Hastings Castle CASTLE   This was the first Norman castle in England, built immediately after the Norman conquest. Now only ruins remain on the hilltop site overlooking the sea. The fortress was unfortified by King John in 1216, and was later used as a church. There is an audiovisual presentation of the castle's history, as well as the battle of 1066. It's a nice walk, or you can take the West Hill Lift, one of England's earliest and steepest funiculars, with its entrance in George Street.

Castle Hill Rd., West Hill, Hastings. www.discoverhastings.co.uk.(℗ **01424/444412.** Admission £4.25 adults, £3.95 seniors and students, £3.50 children 5–15, £13.25 family ticket. Easter–Sept daily 10am–5pm. West Hill Cliff Railway from George St. to the castle £1.60 adults, £1 children.

Hastings Stade ★★ HISTORIC AREA   This is the eastern end of the town's seafront on pretty Rock-a-Nore Road, the shingle where the country's biggest fleet of beach-launched fishing boats comes ashore. Here there are fish sheds, tall wooden net sheds, a fish market, and the charming **Fisherman's Museum** in an old church (www.hastingsfish.co.uk; ℗ **01424/461446;** free, open daily, hours vary), which has one of the last sail-powered fishing boats. The Stade is undergoing arty redevelopment, replacing a parking lot with a festival space and adding a hotel in traditional wood-faced style. The first change is the **Jerwood Gallery** (www.jerwoodgallery.org; ℗ **01424/425809**), which opened in spring 2012, to display the collection of late philanthropist John Jerwood. This includes modern British art alongside romantic works by the likes of Sir Walter Sickert and Augustus John. (Open daily July–Sept and school holidays 11am–6pm; March, April, May, Oct–Dec Tues–Sun 11am–4pm; £7 adults, £3.50 children 5–16, family ticket £17.) There is also the **Blue Reef Aquarium** (www.bluereefaquarium.co.uk; ℗ **01424/718776**). You can also take the East Hill Lift, a steep funicular, up the cliff to Hastings Country Park for great views.

Lamb House HISTORIC HOME   American-born author Henry James lived here from 1898 to 1916. His belongings are scattered throughout the big brick house, which is set in a large walled garden with lawns and mature trees. Some of his best-known works, including *The Ambassadors*, were written here. James picked up the house cheaply after its owner joined the American gold rush and died in the Klondike.

West St., Rye. www.nationaltrust.org.uk.(℗ **01580/762334.** Admission £4 adults, £2.10 children 5–15. Mid-Mar–mid-Oct Tues and Sat 2–6pm. Closed late Oct–early Mar.

Smallhythe Place 📷 HISTORIC HOME   This was the country house of Dame Ellen Terry, the actress acclaimed for her Shakespearean roles. She died here, on the outskirts of Winchelsea, in 1928. The early 16th-century house is filled with memorabilia—playbills, props, makeup, and many costumes.

Smallhythe (on the B2082 near Tenterden). www.nationaltrust.org.uk.(℗ **01580/762334.** Admission £5.80 adults, £3.15 children 5–15, £15 family ticket. Late Feb–Oct Sat–Wed 11am–5pm; Dec Sat–Sun noon–3pm. Closed Nov and Jan–mid-Feb. Take bus no. 312 from Tenterden or Rye.

Where to Eat & Stay

Black Rock House ★   Look behind the seafront and things are happening in Hastings. A string of stylish new guesthouses (the Swan House, the Cloudsley, and in the old town, the Laindons) are changing people's perceptions of what the place is about. Black Rock is a great example, a B&B with a boutique hotel feel. The Victorian town house is a sea of dreamy white with deft contrasting touches, there are champagne afternoon teas on offer, and you can sit on the terrace with evening drinks.

10 Stanley Rd., Hastings, East Sussex TN34 1UE. www.hastingsaccommadation.com. ⓒ **01424 438448.** 5 units. £110–£130 double. Rates include English breakfast. MC, V. Free parking. **Amenities:** Sitting room; honesty bar; terrace. *In room:* TV/DVD, hair dryer, Wi-Fi (free).

Fisherman's Cottage ★★ ☺ In a quiet street, 50 yards from the seafront, this isn't so much a cottage as a three-bedroom house decked out in luxury seaside style, from the stripy blue sofas to the yacht motifs on the main bedroom wallpaper. It's great for families, sleeping five. If you like self-catering, the kitchen (oven, microwave, dishwasher, washing machine) is splendid, with a sizeable dining area and the chance to eat in the courtyard garden. It is one of 16 mostly historic properties with a coastal feel, (generally with gardens or balconies) in a group in the town, sleeping 2–6.

11 Desmond Rd., Eastbourne, East Sussex BN22 7LF. www.eastbourneholidaycottages.co.uk. ⓒ **01323/639309.** £460–£720 per week (3-night breaks available Oct–March). AE, MC, V. Free parking on street. **Amenities:** TV/DVD; hair dryer; kitchen; Wi-Fi (free).

The Gallivant ★★★ ☺ 🏨 A divine modern coastal-style hotel opposite towering dunes and 3-mile Camber Sands. The big rooms have chunky driftwood furniture made by a local reclamation project. Family rooms are huge, with a super-king bed for parents. There's also a comfy lounge and TV room. The Beach Bistro has weathered wood table tops, lobster prints, and driftwood art. Food is exceptional; try the rich fish soup followed by roast whole Rye Bay lemon sole with brown butter, capers, and baby potatoes, but there's also local flounder, Dungeness cod, and salt marsh lamb. Mains are £12.50–£19.50. Over the road there's a path through the dunes, and a stirring walk all the way to Rye harbor.

New Lydd Rd., Camber, East Sussex TN31 7RB. www.thegallivanthotel.com. ⓒ**01797/225057.** 18 units. £115–£135 double; £135–£215 family room (plus £20 per child). Rates include English breakfast. AE, MC, V. Free parking. **Amenities:** Restaurant; bar. *In room:* TV/DVD, hair dryer, Wi-Fi (free).

The George ★ Rye has several excellent, historic hotels, two of them former smugglers' haunts: The **Hope Anchor,** on a cobbled street at the high point of town, and the **Mermaid Inn,** where the cutthroat Hawkhurst Gang made their base. But this boutique hotel tops the list. It's a timbered coaching inn from 1575 and some of the beams may be from a wrecked English ship broken up at Rye after the defeat of the Spanish Armada. Rooms are pale and inviting: rich linens, marble-top baths, and in some a four-poster bed. The **restaurant** (with courtyard tables) has a local, seasonal menu (main courses £14–£18), featuring Mediterranean-inspired dishes. The bar, **George's Tap,** promises to stay open until the last guest has given in.

High St., Rye, East Sussex TN31 7JT. www.thegeorgeinrye.com. ⓒ **01797/222114.** Fax 01797/224065. 24 units. £135–£195 double; £245 suite. Rates include English breakfast. AE, DC, MC, V. Free overnight parking on street; parking lot nearby, £2 per 24 hr. **Amenities:** Restaurant; bar; room service; babysitting. *In room:* TV/DVD, hair dryer, Wi-Fi (free).

Entertainment & Nightlife

Eastbourne has plenty of entertainment: its **Congress Theatre,** on Carlisle Road, is a large, modern building with a sleek 1950s feel that features lots of ballet, classical music, and opera, as well as populist theatre and music. The neighboring **Winter Garden,** on Compton Street, dating from 1875, has everything from bands to comedy clubs to tea dances. The **Devonshire Park Theatre,** also on Compton Street, is one of the country's best small Victorian theatres, and a place for big-name touring drama. All share a box office: www.eastbournetheatres.co.uk; ⓒ **01323/412000.**

BRIGHTON

52 miles S of London

Brighton is a party place. It's where Londoners flee for a day out or a fun weekend. It's now officially a city and is packed with bars, clubs, restaurants, and hotels. It was one of England's first great seaside resorts, and then went through a bad time as its clientele started holidaying abroad. Now it's back, bigger and brighter than ever. It has taken on the ambience of London, which is only an hour away, with boutique lodgings, hip nightspots, and trendy shops. It's not for everyone, though: Once you're here, you'll find little respite from the crowds, and the beaches are pebble. Yet many visitors can't help falling in love with Brighton.

It was the fun-loving Prince of Wales (later George IV) who put Brighton on the 18th-century tourist map when he arrived in 1783. The town blossomed, with attractive town houses and smart squares and crescents—many still here today. From the Prince Regent's title came the word *Regency,* which sums up an era, but more specifically refers to the period between 1811 and 1820. George IV's successor, Queen Victoria, found the place a bit too racy. The **Prince Regent's Royal Pavilion** summer home is still here and a must-see. Despite the emphasis on old-time fun—the beachfront is lined with bars, fish and chip shops, cheap souvenir stalls, and then there's the pier with its amusements—Brighton is indeed fashionable once again.

Essentials

GETTING THERE   Fast trains leave London Victoria (Southern) and London Bridge (First Capital Connect) stations roughly every 15 minutes; the journey is less than an hour. A ticket starts at about £15 one-way. National Express buses from London's Victoria Coach Station take around 2 hours; tickets are about £12.

If you're driving, the M23 (signposted from central London) leads to the A23, which takes you straight into Brighton.

VISITOR INFORMATION   The **Tourist Information Centre,** 4–5 Pavilion Buildings (www.visitbrighton.com; ℰ **01273/290337**), is next to the Royal Pavilion shop and open Monday to Saturday 10am to 5pm (Sunday 4pm in summer and public holidays).

GETTING AROUND   You really don't want to drive around Brighton—parking is difficult and expensive and the seafront gets clogged with traffic. There are plenty of buses (www.buses.co.uk; ℰ **01273/886200**), and a Saver ticket (£3.50 for 1 day, £17.50 for a week) gives unlimited daytime travel. It's available in shops and newsstands (newsagents), but it's cheaper online. Free route maps are available at the Tourist Information Centre (see above).

SPECIAL EVENTS   In May, the **Brighton Festival** (www.brightonfestival.org; ℰ **01273/709709**) is the largest arts festival in England. It features drama, literature, visual art, dance, and concerts ranging from classical to rock.

Exploring the Area

Brighton Marina   MARINA   A mile or so east of the city, tucked beneath the chalky cliffs, is the modern marina. It's Britain's biggest, with 1,600 moorings, and there are plenty of sea-view houses and flats too. It's also a massive entertainment complex with 20-plus restaurants (mostly chains, including Marco Pierre White's diner Frankie & Benny's), bars, a modest outlet mall, a bowling alley, a cinema, a health club, playgrounds, and bicycle rental. You can stay at the **Hotel Seattle** (www. hotelseattlebrighton.com; ✆ **01273/679799**) or rent a luxury pad. There's also the **Walk of Fame** (www.walkoffame.co.uk), a Hollywood-style tribute set up by record producer and musician David Courtney (behind hits for Roger Daltrey, Leo Sayer, and Adam Faith) to those with Brighton connections: From The Who (their mod movie *Quadrophenia* was set here) to *Brighton Rock* author Graham Greene. It's an easy seafront walk from town, there's a 24-hour bus, plenty of free parking, or you can take the **Volks Electric Railway** (www.volkselectricrailway.co.uk; ✆ **01273/292718**), Britain's first electric train, which started running in 1873.

Brighton Marina, Waterfront. www.brightonmarina.co.uk. ✆ **01273/628627.** Bus: no. 7.

Brighton Museum & Art Gallery ★★ MUSEUM   Once the Royal Pavilion's magnificent stable block, this is now a treasure-trove of beautiful and curious things. The museum is in the park adjoining the Pavilion (see below), and a £10 million redevelopment has created a bright, white environment to showcase one of the most important collections of decorative arts in England outside London. And it's free. The first thing you come to is Salvador Dalí's Marilyn Monroe Lips sofa, which rubs shoulders, as it were, with some exquisite pieces by Charles Rennie Mackintosh. There are modernistic bentwood chairs and the original ornate copper elevator interior from London's Selfridge's department store. Farther on you find the history of Brighton, from its discovery by the bright young things to the dark days of World War II bombings, plus exhibitions of stage costumes and fashion, while upstairs are modernist paintings including works by Walter Sickert, as well as special exhibitions and a cafe.

Royal Pavilion Gardens. www.brighton-hove-rpml.org.uk. ✆ **03000/290900.** Free admission. Tues–Sun and public holidays 10am–5pm.

The Royal Pavilion at Brighton ★★★ HISTORIC SITE   From the outside, the Pavilion appears a bit seaside-resort garish, a melee of vaguely eastern-looking domes, painted an unattractive beige, that you suspect might house an entertainment complex. Yet the place is a pleasure palace of another kind. This was the royals' idea of a seaside hideaway. It's a phantasmagoric collection of Oriental architecture, furniture, and fittings; a playful place that fitted in with the resort's somewhat wild reputation even when it was built. Everywhere you look, mythical creatures roar and

HITTING THE heights

Brighton seafront is the setting for two new lofty attractions. The first is the **Brighton Wheel** (www.brightonwheel.com; ✆ **01273/722822**), a ferris wheel opposite the Palace Pier. At 45m (147 ft.) it's a third of the height of the London Eye (p. 108), the big wheel by the Thames in London, but is tall enough to give fabulous views along the seafront and over to the South Downs. Daily 10am–11pm. Adults £8, children 4–16 £6.50, 1–3 £2, family ticket £25. The

360 Tower, along the seafront, opposite the Hilton Metropole, is due to open sometime in 2013. It's on the site of the entrance to the now-derelict West Pier. The slim tower's circular, spaceship-like viewing deck is also its elevator, carrying crowds up to the 150-m (492-ft.) summit. It will be Britain's highest viewing tower, and is by the same team that created the London Eye. Check www.westpier.co.uk for latest information.

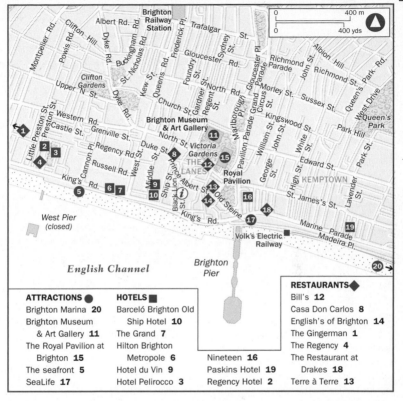

Brighton Railway Station · Albert Rd. · Montpelier Rd. · Clifton Hill · Powis Rd. · Clifton Rd. · Dyke Rd. · Buckingham Rd. · St. Nicholas Rd. · Frederick Pl. · Trafalgar St. · Sydney St. · Gloucester Rd. · Richmond Parade · John St. · Richmond St. · Albion Hill · Queen's Park Rd. · Foundry St. · Gloucester Pl. · Grand Parade · Morley St. · Sussex St. · West Drive · Queen's Park · North Rd. · Kingswood St. · John St. · White St. · Park Hill · Park St. · Clifton Gardens · Upper N St. · Kew St. · Queens Rd. · Regent St. · Gardner St. · Church St. · Marlborough Pl. · William St. · George St. · Edward St. · High St. · KEMPTOWN · Lavender St. · Little Preston St. · Preston St. · Western Rd. · Castle St. · Grenville St. · Regency Rd. · Duke St. · West St. · North St. · Victoria Gardens · THE LANES · Royal Pavilion · St. James's St. · Cannon Pl. · Russell Rd. · Middle St. · Ship St. · Prince Albert St. · Old Steine · Marine Parade · King's Rd. · Madeira Pl. · West Pier (closed) · Volk's Electric Railway · English Channel · Brighton Pier

Brighton Museum & Art Gallery **11** · **8** · **15** · **12** · **13** · **14** · **16** · **18** · **17** · **19** · **20** · **1** · **2** · **3** · **4** · **5** · **6** · **7** · **9** · **10**

0 — 400 m
0 — 400 yds

ATTRACTIONS ●
Brighton Marina **20**
Brighton Museum
& Art Gallery **11**
The Royal Pavilion at
Brighton **15**
The seafront **5**
SeaLife **17**

HOTELS ■
Barceló Brighton Old
Ship Hotel **10**
The Grand **7**
Hilton Brighton
Metropole **6**
Hotel du Vin **9**
Hotel Pelirocco **3**

Nineteen **16**
Paskins Hotel **19**
Regency Hotel **2**

RESTAURANTS ◆
Bill's **12**
Casa Don Carlos **8**
English's of Brighton **14**
The Gingerman **1**
The Regency **4**
The Restaurant at
Drakes **18**
Terre à Terre **13**

writhe on ceilings, walls, and artwork. It was created for the Prince Regent, later King George IV, between 1787 and 1823. Queen Victoria later stayed here, but both it and Brighton were a little too much for her prim and proper tastes.

The dining room is superb, a 24-seat table under a domed roof (painted to resemble a palm canopy) from which hangs the most amazing chandelier you'll ever see: a huge dragon breathing fire over floral lights and mirror shards. The music room is hardly less dramatic: eight chandeliers, and a fireplace from which another dragon emerges.

The Pavilion is also showcases the Industrial Revolution that was sweeping Britain at the time; the original wooden farmhouse construction was surrounded by an innovative iron framework on which the rest was built. The Pavilion was a hospital for Indian soldiers after World War I (there's a fascinating exhibition), and just escaped being demolished after World War II. A cafe allows you to rest amid Regency wonders. The gardens feature a skating rink at Christmas. Entry includes an audioguide.

Victoria Gardens. www.royalpavilion.org.uk. ⓒ **01273/290900.** Admission £9.80 adults, £7.80 students and seniors, £5.60 children 5–15, £25.20 family ticket, free for children 4 and under. Apr–Sept daily 9:30am–5:45pm (last entrance 5pm); Oct–Mar daily 10am–5:15pm (last entrance 4:30pm).

LITERARY lights: **KIPLING & WOOLF**

This part of the country has been home to many artistic and literary figures. **Charleston ★★★** (www.charleston.org.uk; ☎ **01323/811626**), on the A27 at Charleston, was the residence of artists Vanessa Bell and Duncan Grant, the glittering faces of the artistically influential Bloomsbury Group early in the 20th century. The house is a work of art in itself, with the group's decorative style covering walls, doors, and furniture. There are other Bloomsbury works, plus pieces by Picasso, Renoir, and more. It was also sometime home to economist Maynard Keynes, while Virginia and Leonard Woolf, novelist E. M. Forster, and biographer Lytton Strachey visited often. Virginia was Vanessa's sister. The walled garden has a Mediterranean theme, with some enigmatic sculptures. It is open April until October, Wednesday to Saturday 1–6pm (July–Aug from noon) and Sunday 1–5:30pm. Admission is £9.50 for adults, £8.50 for seniors, £5.50 for children 6 to 16, and £24.50 for a family ticket. You can see the house only with a tour, included in the price, except Sundays when it is open access. The annual literary and arts festival (late May) is a regular sell-out.

Just east of Brighton, near Lewes, is Rodmell, where Virginia Woolf lived until her death in 1941. **Monk's House** (www.nationaltrust.org.uk; ☎ **01273/474760**) was bought by Virginia and Leonard Woolf in 1919, and Leonard remained there until his death in 1969. Much of it was furnished and decorated by Vanessa Bell and Duncan Grant. The house, where Woolf did much of her writing, has a tenant, so visiting hours are limited: April to October, Wednesday and Saturday, 2 to 5:30pm (£4.85 adults, £2.45 children 5–15, £12.10 family ticket).

In the village of Burwash, on the A265, 27 miles northeast of Brighton, is **Bateman's ★** (www.nationaltrust.org.uk; ☎ **01435/882302**), the 17th-century house in which author Rudyard Kipling lived from 1902 until his death in 1936. "Heaven looked after it in the dissolute times of mid-Victorian restoration and caused the vicar to send his bailiff to live in it for 40 years, and he lived in peaceful filth and left everything as he found it," wrote the creator of *The Jungle Book* about the place. Bombay-born Kipling loved Sussex, a love expressed in *Puck of Pook's Hill*, written in 1906. The following year he won the Nobel Prize for literature. Kipling lived in the U.S. after his marriage to Caroline Balestier in 1892. They moved to England in 1896, to a house at Rottingdean on the Sussex Downs, where he wrote the line: "What should they know of England who only England know?" The couple set out to explore Sussex in a steam-driven car, and one day spotted Bateman's. "It is a good and peaceable place standing in terraced lawns nigh to a walled garden of old red brick, and two fat-headed oasthouses with redbrick stomachs, and an aged silver-gray dovecot on top," Kipling wrote.

A World War I memorial, unveiled by Kipling, is in Burwash church. The church and an inn opposite appear in *Puck of Pook's Hill* under "Hal o' the Draft." Bateman's is filled with rugs, bronzes, and other mementos from India and elsewhere. The house and gardens are open mid-March to October, Saturday to Wednesday 10am to 5pm. Admission is £9 for adults, £4.50 for children 5 to 15, and £22.50 for a family ticket. Gardens only are open November to Christmas, 11am to 4pm, free admission.

The Seafront ★★ WALKWAY Brighton's promenade exists on two levels: There's the path and cycleway that runs along King's Road, above the beach; and there's the beachfront path, down some steps, awash with candy sellers and carousels, bars, and shellfish stalls. It runs from Brighton Pier (a Victorian structure now featuring a fun fair with roller coaster and other hair-raising, over-water rides, bars, and restaurants) to the entrance of the old West Pier, with businesses occupying arches under the road. Star attractions are **Brighton Smokehouse,** where fish are smoked in a beach hut, and you can buy a hot kipper sandwich for £2.80; the free **Brighton Fishing Museum** (www.brightonfishingmuseum.org.uk; ℰ **01273/ 723064**), with fishing boats and lots of memorabilia and old photos; the **Fortune of War** (ℰ **01273/205065**), is the oldest seafront pub, seedy but atmospheric, with live music and DJ nights; and the **Ohso Social** (www.ohsosocial.co.uk; ℰ **01273/ 746067**), a cafe/bar/restaurant with a terrace that has a driftwood feel and views over the pier (great in the evening as all the lights go on). You'll find music pouring out of bars, bands playing on the beach, rollerbladers whizzing by, and people just out for a stroll.

SeaLife ★★ AQUARIUM This was the world's first aquarium, opening as the Royal Aquarium in 1872. It retains a *Twenty Thousand Leagues Under The Seas* feel, thanks to its subterranean setting. Many of the tanks are under low, vaulted ceilings, but the days of dolphin tanks are long gone, and it's now part of a major set-up. There is plenty to see here: Rays, crabs, and other local sealife as well as exotic fish. That's just the opener before you walk into a darkened Amazonia Jungle zone and eventually emerge into a glass tunnel snaking through a massive tank alive with fish, sharks, and a pair of magnificent turtles. (Lulu is 70-plus years old and weighs 152 kg/335 lb.) You can then pop upstairs to see it all from above in a glass-bottom boat.

Marine Parade. www.visitsealife.com/Brighton. ℰ **0871/423-2110.** Admission £16.20 adults, £11.40 children 3–14, £48 family ticket. Discounts of about 25% for online booking. Daily 10am–5pm.

Where to Eat
EXPENSIVE

The Gingerman ★ MODERN BRITISH This is the original, a discreet place just off the seafront that's a celebration of rich local fare (Sussex beef, Rye Bay scallops), but there are also three Ginger pubs: The Ginger Dog, in Brighton's Kempstown area, the Ginger Pig, on the seafront to the west of town, and the Ginger Fox, 15 minutes north of Brighton. All three offer gastropub food (mains £13–£20) such as hare and trotter pie or pan-fried filet of sea bream with smoked potato veloute, buttered spinach, leek croquettes, and truffle oil.

21a Norfolk Sq. www.gingermanrestaurant.com.ℰ **01273/326688.** Reservations recommended. Set dinner menu £30 for 2 courses; £35 for 3 courses. AE, MC, V. Tues–Sun 12:30–2pm and 7–10pm.

The Restaurant at Drakes ★ MODERN BRITISH/FRENCH This is the smartest restaurant in Brighton, combining contemporary British style with French twists. The atmosphere in this basement is intimate and soothing. Food is inventive (a starter of local scallops and black pudding purée with roasted apples and beurre blanc, perhaps, followed by poached and roasted breast of Sussex White chicken with pithivier of braised leg meat, cep mushroom purée, thyme croquettes, and truffle sauce). Drakes may be best, but if you want true Brighton, go to the Regency (see below).

A Delight in the Garden

Twenty minutes north of Brighton, Borde Hill Gardens are charming in themselves, but inside is **Jeremy's** (www.jeremysrestaurant.co.uk; ✆ **01444/441102**), a restaurant that does more that simply feed the visitors. It's also open when the gardens have closed, tucked away in the Victorian walled garden. Proprietor Jeremy Ashpool comes up with an a la carte menu (main courses £15–£21, with dishes such as assiette of Southdown lamb, pumpkin gratin, spinach, and roasted garlic sauce), the "Amazingly-good-value menu of the day," £18 for three courses, and a six-course tasting menu on the first Tuesday of the month (£35, £60 with wine), and weekends by request. It's open for dinner Mon–Sat 7–10pm, plus lunch Mon–Sun 12:30–2:30pm. Jeremy's adjoining, conservatory-style Café Elvira is open daily, 9:30am–5pm, for cakes and snacks. Make a day of it with a visit to the gardens (www.bordehill.co.uk) with their views across the Sussex High Weald.

Drakes Hotel, 44 Marine Parade. www.therestaurantatdrakes.co.uk. ✆ **01273/696934.** Reservations recommended. Set menu £30 for 2 courses; £40 for 3 courses. AE, MC, V. Daily 12:30–2pm and 7–9:45pm.

MODERATE

Casa Don Carlos ★★ SPANISH   This bustling, atmospheric tapas restaurant in a cobblestone alley in the narrow, trendy Lanes has been a Brighton institution for a quarter of a century. Lots of small dishes to choose from, some obvious (patatas bravas, paella), some less so, with kidney and rabbit, all topped by the trays of flaming chorizo that waiters manage to carry between the snug tables. Most costing under £5, and staff will help you make a good selection. The place can be frenetic but there are tables outside.

5 Union Street. ✆ **01273/327177.** Meals £20–£25. Reservations recommended. AE, MC, V. Daily noon–11pm.

English's of Brighton SEAFOOD   Charlie Chaplin and Laurence Olivier are among those who have eaten at this cosy Edwardian-style seafood restaurant, run by the same family for 60 years. You can drop in for a glass of champers and snack at the marble-topped oyster bar, or enjoy a full meal in the plush Red Room (in summer the terrace is pleasant). It's good English fare with starters such as potted shrimp or dressed crab. The likes of Dover sole and lobster dominate the main courses, although you'll also find tuna, and local steak. There are good-value set menus.

29 East St. www.englishs.co.uk. ✆ **01273/327980.** Reservations recommended. Main courses £12–£29.95. AE, DC, MC, V. Mon–Sat noon–10pm; Sun 12:30–9:30pm. See website for special deals.

INEXPENSIVE

Bill's ★ 🎁 MODERN BRITISH   Once the maverick Bill's Produce Store, selling and serving local produce in a fresh, cheery way, it's now Bill's with the concept expanded into a chain (even in London's Covent Garden). The original is in Lewes, six miles away down the A27, but the Brighton version is in an old bus depot in the heart of town, and excellent. There are big breakfasts (plenty of bubble and squeak: Mashed potato fried with cooked cabbage), lunch, snacky things, and early dinner: Hummus, Thai green prawn curry, burgers and steaks and the like.

The Depot, 100 North St. www.billsproducestore.co.uk.℃ **01273/692894.** Main courses £7.95–£16. AE, MC, V. Mon–Sat 8am–8pm; Sun 10am–4pm.

The Regency ★★★ ENGLISH If you're only going to eat in one Brighton restaurant, it should be this one. A fish restaurant that starts at the cod and chips end and effortlessly takes in fabulous Dover sole (grilled or meunière), vast crab salads, and delectable sardines, right up to the Shellfish Extravaganza (£40), and yet doesn't glorify the product or the prices. It's a happy family place with views over the sea, and some outside tables. And if you need history, it's been serving since the 1930s, and was previously the seaside getaway of Harriott Mellon, widow of banker Thomas Coutts, wife of the 9th Duke of St. Albans and the richest woman in Europe.

131 King's Rd. www.theregencyrestaurant.co.uk.℃ **01273/325014.** Main courses £6.75–£17. AE, MC, V. Daily 8am–10:30pm.

Terre à Terre ★★ 📖 VEGETARIAN/VEGAN This is a vegetarian restaurant, sure, but it's also a place for people who like eating dishes made out of vegetables rather than wanting something coyly pretending to be meat. Dishes come from around the continents (curries, stir-fries, rosti, souffles) and are embellished with a touch of Brighton charm. The restaurant is a jolly brasserie and does a sort of global tapas (a selection menu is £21 for two), and serves organic wines.

71 East St. www.terreaterre.co.uk.℃ **01273/729051.** Reservations recommended. Main courses all around £14–£15. AE, DC, MC, V. Tues–Fri noon–10:30pm; Sat noon–11pm; Sun noon–10pm.

Shopping

For shopping, head to the **Lanes,** a collection of alleyways and small streets behind North Street and its big-name shops. The area is full of boutiques, cafes, and arty stores. Those in the know hit **North Laine**—between the Lanes and the station—which is seen as the area for up-and-coming talent. Innumerable shops in the Lanes carry old books and jewelry, and many boutiques are found in converted backyards on Duke Lane just off Ship Street. At the heart of the Lanes is Brighton Square, ideal for relaxing or people-watching near the fountain on one of the benches or from a cafe-bar.

Regent Arcade, which is between East Street, Bartholomew Square, and Market Street, sells artwork, jewelry, and gifts, as well as high-fashion clothing. Bargain hunters head for the **Flea Market in bohemian Kemptown's** (also known as Kemp Town) Upper James Street, held Monday to Saturday 9:30am to 5:30pm and Sunday 10:30am to 5pm. The Sunday **flea market** in the train station's parking lot has moved to Brighton Marina. Open from 7am to noon.

Brighton has plenty of big-name stores and designer clothes shops, too. Try **Churchill Square,** which is home to major chain stores.

Entertainment & Nightlife

Offering drama year-round is the **Theatre Royal,** New Road (www.atgtickets.com; ℂ **0844/871-7650**), with pre-London shows. Bigger concerts are held at **Brighton Centre,** King's Road (www.brightoncentre.co.uk; ℂ **01273/290131**), a 5,000-seat facility featuring mainly pop-music shows.

Komedia, 44 Gardner St. (www.komedia.co.uk; ℂ **0845/293-8480**), hosts everything from top indie bands (British Sea Power) to the Banff Film Festival tour, and from top comedy to Brighton Jazz Club. **The Latest Music Bar,** 14 Manchester St. (www.thelatest.co.uk; ℂ **01273/687171**), combines the latest in live music with party-style club nights. Pubs all over the city regularly have live music, often free.

There are plenty of nightclubs in Brighton; some have been around for a while, others come and go. Check www.visitbrighton or www.brightonlife.com for up-to-date info. There's often free admission early on or midweek, rising to £10, but times and prices often vary from week to week or season to season.

Honeyclub (www.thehoneyclub.co.uk; © 01273/202807), 214 King's Rd. Arches, is a bar by day and a lively club at night, with a downstairs dance floor. **Audio,** 10 Marine Parade (www.audiobrighton.com; © 01273/606906), is another of the places that continues to buzz, with a clutch of different, hard-hitting club nights. **Casablanca,** 3 Middle St. (www.casablancajazzclub.com; © 01273/321817), is still clubbing but with a funk-latin-jazz feel.

Oceana, West Street (www.oceanaclubs.com; © 0845/296-8590), is a massive place, with five themed bars (e.g. Aspen ski lodge, Tahiti), and two nightclubs. The main one has Europe's largest illuminated dance floor, and the retro New York disco.

Pubs are a good place to kick off an evening, especially the **Colonnade Bar,** 10 New Rd. (© 01273/328728), serving drinks for more than 100 years. It gets a lot of theatre business because of its proximity to the Theatre Royal. **Cricketers,** Black Lion Street (© 01273/329472), is worth a stop as it's Brighton's oldest pub, parts of which date from 1549. Or just walk along the beach and see what takes your fancy.

Where to Stay
EXPENSIVE
The Grand ★★   Brighton's leading hotel opened in 1864 and entertained some of the most eminent Victorians and Edwardians; today it still lords it over the sea-front. Inside is as grand as out, with a plush lobby and sweeping staircase. Rooms are big and airy, with huge windows—many overlooking the sea. The **King's restaurant**

BRIGHTON'S GAY scene

Brighton has long been regarded as Britain's gay capital. It has the country's biggest gay festival (Pride, in early Aug), and a thriving scene of bars, clubs, and hotels. Most of the action is in the Gay Quarter in Kemp Town, a compact strip just off the seafront. **Dr Brighton,** 16 King's Rd. (www.doctorbrightons.co.uk; © 01273/208113), opposite the pier is one of the mainstays, and has a street party during Pride. **Legends,** 31 Marine Parade (www.legendsbrighton.com; © 01273/624462), is one of the country's leading gay hotels and has two venues, **Legends** cafe-bar and **The Basement** nightclub. **The Marlborough,** 4 Princes St. (© 01273/570028), is a richly traditional pub opposite the Royal Pavilion with a cabaret theatre. Of the clubs, **Revenge,** 32–34 Old Steine (www. revenge.co.uk; © 01273/606064), is the biggest, with lots of gay-friendly live acts from reality TV shows such as *X Factor.* **The Charles Street Bar & Club,** 8 Marine Parade (www.charles-street.com; © 01273/624091), combines a downstairs bar, which spills onto the street, with a popular club above. Of the hotels, **Colson House,** 17 Upper Rock Gardens (www.colsonhouse.co.uk; © 01273/694922), features eight rooms themed after stars such as Marilyn Monroe; while the **Amsterdam,** 11 Marine Parade (www.amsterdam.uk.com; © 01273/68825), combines a men-only sauna, chill-out bar with sun terrace, and decent restaurant. The official tourist office site, www.visitbrighton.com, has a sizable gay section while www.gscene.com is a local site devoted to gay and lesbian matters.

is suitably grandiose and serves English classics with a modern edge, while the Victoria lounge and bar opens into a huge seaview conservatory and is the place for everything from morning coffee to a classy cream tea to a relaxing evening cocktail.

97–99 King's Rd., Brighton, East Sussex BN1 2FW. www.devere.co.uk. © **01273/224300.** Fax 01273/224321. 201 units. £115–£175 double; from £295 suite. Rates include English breakfast. AE, DC, MC, V. Parking £26–£30. **Amenities:** Restaurant; bar; indoor heated pool; exercise room; spa; concierge; room service; babysitting. *In room:* TV, minibar, hair dryer, Internet (free).

Hilton Brighton Metropole ★★   Sitting alongside The Grand, this is the other big hotel on the seafront, a giant (Brighton's biggest hotel) of red brick and iron balconies. The lobby is unassuming, but the rooms are big and high-ceilinged, so much so that even the king-size beds in many are dwarfed by their surroundings. The decor is simple and modern. There's a decent pool, along with a spa. Breakfast is a joy in the lofty, white, Windsor restaurant (like a cross between an orangerie and a ballroom) with its huge sea-view windows, ornate plasterwork, and giant chandeliers. The room, which is part of the hotel's Victorian heritage is, by evening, a rather nice **restaurant** with a set menu (£25 for 3 courses).

106 King's Rd., Brighton, East Sussex BN1 2FU. www.hilton.co.uk/brightonmet.© **01273/775432.** Fax 01273/207764. 334 units. £115–£215 double; £265–£340 suite room only. English breakfast £11–16. AE, DC, MC, V. Parking £16. **Amenities:** Restaurant; 2 bars; indoor heated pool; exercise room; spa; concierge; room service; babysitting. *In room:* TV, hair dryer, Internet (£14.99 for 24 hr.).

Hotel du Vin   Down a little street just off the seafront, this member of a small, upmarket chain looks delicious in a jumble of Gothic and Tudor-revival buildings. Its entrance is beneath a stone arch, and neat window frames are a pale green. Inside it's dark and cool in a mod-ish sort of way, with a double-height lounge and bar beneath a high-beamed ceiling. There's also a discreet, woody **bistro** and trendy **Pub du Vin.** Rooms are light and modern. Top choice is the One-of-a-kind room, massive with wooden floors, four-poster bed, and two free-standing baths in the middle of the room.

Ship St., Brighton, East Sussex BN1 1AD. www.hotelduvin.com. © **01273/718588.** 49 units. £125–£400 double. AE, DC, MC, V. Parking £19 (£24 weekends). **Amenities:** Restaurant; bar; room service. *In room:* TV/DVD, hair dryer, Internet (free).

MODERATE

Barceló Brighton Old Ship Hotel ★   An inn in 1559, this seafront hotel has its place in history: It hosted the Prince Regent's Ball in 1819, a Paganini violin recital in 1831, and the banquet celebrating the opening of the London to Brighton Railway in 1841. The largely Victorian rebuild is now a boutique affair and the rooms are pleasing in a contemporary-traditional way. A limited number have sea views. The **Location 3 restaurant,** with its continental feel, attracts far more than hotel guests, while the woody bar spills out onto a promenade seating area.

31 King's Rd., Brighton, East Sussex BN1 1NR. www.barcelo-hotels.co.uk.© **01273/329001.** Fax 01273/820718. 154 units. £99–£165 double. Children under 12 stay free with parents in premium rooms. AE, DC, MC, V. Parking £23. **Amenities:** Restaurant; bar; concierge; room service. *In room:* TV, hair dryer, Wi-Fi (free).

Hotel Pelirocco ★★★ 📖   Take your sunglasses with you when you check into this seafront town house, the arty rock 'n' roll face of Brighton. The Pelirocco is a riot of color, with rooms all themed around pop culture or personalities: Soul Supreme (Motown), Ali (Muhammad Ali), Pretty Vacant (Sex Pistols). The **PlayStation bar,** open until 1am Sunday to Thursday, and until 4am at weekends, has snazzy cocktails and a clientele to match. The food is just as fun, all cupcakes and samosa-style nibbles (continental breakfast is an extra charge). It's the ultimate kitsch weekend break.

10 Regency Sq., Brighton, East Sussex BN1 2FG. www.hotelpelirocco.co.uk. ℂ **01273/327055.** 19 units. £109–135 double. Rates include English breakfast. AE, DC, MC, V. Parking £12.50. **Amenities:** Bar, Wi-Fi (free). *In room:* TV/DVD, hair dryer.

Nineteen ★ ▮▮   One road back from the beach, near the pier, Nineteen is an oasis of white, punctuated by works from local artists. King rooms have glass-brick platform beds illuminated by subtle blue lighting. The Courtyard room has a private courtyard that's a fern jungle with a chemical-free hot tub. The classy continental breakfast (with champagne, buck's fizz, or bloody Mary at weekends) is served in-room, and there's a kitchen where you can find coffee and cakes.

19 Broad St., Brighton, East Sussex BN2 1TJ. www.hotelnineteen.co.uk. ℂ **01273/675529.** Fax 01273/675531. 7 units. £85–£250 double. Rates include continental breakfast. 2-night minimum Sat–Sun. AE, DC, MC, V. Parking £8. **Amenities:** Bar; concierge; room service. *In room:* TV/DVD, hair dryer, CD player, Wi-Fi (free).

Paskins Hotel   This has been an eco-friendly hotel since before that was trendy, with organic breakfasts, washing towels with soap nut shells, and such. The Paskins is a Victorian town house, a couple of streets back from the seafront near the pier. Inside, Edwardian, Art Nouveau, and Art Deco touches create a rich, arty feel. The rooms are individually furnished (you can get a four-poster). The full English breakfast is a treat, with locally cured bacon and small-batch sausages (they try up to 50 varieties a year), and veggie sausages homemade from sun-dried tomatoes and tarragon.

18 Charlotte St., Brighton, East Sussex BN2 1AG. www.paskins.co.uk. ℂ **01273/601203.** Fax 01273/621973. 19 units. £90–£150 double. Rates include English breakfast. AE, MC, V. Parking £5. **Amenities:** Room service. *In room:* TV, hair dryer, Wi-Fi (free).

INEXPENSIVE

Regency Hotel   Just back from the sea, this Regency town house, once the home of Jane, dowager duchess of Marlborough and great-grandmother of Sir Winston Churchill, is a skillfully converted family-managed hotel with a bar and modern comforts. Most rooms enjoy views across the square and out to the sea. Some have a historic feel (with four-posters); others (including several family rooms) are simple and modern. The Regency Suite has antique furniture, and a balcony facing the sea.

28 Regency Sq., Brighton, East Sussex BN1 2FH. www.regencyhotelbrighton.com. ℂ **01273/202690.** Fax 01273/220438. 14 units (shower only). £60–£155 double. Rates include English breakfast. AE, DC, MC, V. Parking £13. **Amenities:** Breakfast room; bar; room service. *In room:* TV, hair dryer, Wi-Fi (free).

CHICHESTER & ARUNDEL

Chichester: 31 miles W of Brighton; 69 miles SW of London. Arundel: 21 miles W of Brighton; 58 miles SW of London

Chichester has it all. On one side there's the sea, a natural harbor with 48 miles of coastline, where you'll see plenty of yachts. On the other side are the **South Downs,** Britain's newest National Park. And Chichester itself? It has all the charms of a smart market town yet is actually a city, courtesy of its **cathedral.** It can also boast being the former Roman city of Noviomagus. The streets are neat and historic, no more so than at the Tudor Market Cross, a stone structure where East, West, North, and South streets cross. And there are many upmarket shops (there aren't many places in

England where you'll find an Orvis store). It's an arty place and home to the **Chichester Festival,** one of the country's leading arts festivals, which takes place each July in the 1950s-era Festival Theatre in Oaklands Park. At other times of the year the building also hosts everything from orchestras to the likes of folk-rock veterans Fairport Convention.

Arundel is a small town a short drive from Chichester. It is dominated by the might of **Arundel Castle,** and is filled with antiques shops and pretty boutiques: The River Arun crosses it, serene and regal (this was once a river port), then meanders, like a scene from the Middle Ages, through water meadows that make for lovely walks.

Essentials

GETTING THERE   Trains depart from London's Victoria Station every 30 minutes during the day. The trip takes 1½ hours to Arundel, another few minutes to Chichester. The Southern service costs about £25 one-way to either. However, if you visit Chichester for the theatre, you'll need to stay over—the last train back is mid-evening.

If you're driving, take the A3 from London, turning onto the A286 for Chichester. From Chichester take the A27 east to Arundel.

VISITOR INFORMATION   **Chichester Tourist Information Centre,** 29A South St. (www.visitchichester.org; ✆ **01243/775888**), is open October to March, Monday 10:15am to 5:15pm and Tuesday to Friday 9:45am to 5:15pm, Saturday 9:15am to 5:15pm; April to September it's open Monday 10:15am to 5:15pm, Tuesday to Friday 9:45am to 5:15pm, Saturday 9:15am to 5:15pm, and Sunday 10:30am to 3:30pm. **Arundel Tourist Information Centre,** 1–3 Crown Yard Mews, River Road (www.sussexbythesea.com; ✆ **01903/882268**), a self-serve information point, is available at Arundel Museum, open daily 10am to 3pm but not always as volunteer-run.

Exploring the Area

Arundel Castle ★★   CASTLE   The ancestral home of the dukes of Norfolk, Arundel Castle is a much-restored mansion of considerable importance. It received fame as the backdrop for the movie *The Madness of King George* (it doubled as Windsor Castle). Arundel Castle suffered during the Civil War when it was stormed by Cromwell's troops, in likely retaliation for the sizable contribution to Charles I made by the 14th Earl of Arundel. In the early 18th century the castle had to be virtually rebuilt, and in late Victorian times it was remodeled and extensively restored again. Today it's filled with works by Old Masters such as Van Dyck and Gainsborough, and with antiques. It sits amid sizeable grounds, including a walled kitchen and formal gardens. It is all circled by a vast park containing Swanbourne Lake.

Mill Rd., Arundel. www.arundelcastle.org.✆ **01903/882173.** Admission £8–£17 adults, £8–£14.50 students and seniors, £8 children 5–16, £39–£41 family ticket, free for children 4 and under. April–Oct Tues–Sun, grounds 10am–5pm, castle keep 10am–4:30pm, castle rooms noon–5pm (last admission 4pm). Closed Nov–Mar.

Arundel Cathedral CATHEDRAL   The Roman Catholic Cathedral of Our Lady and St. Philip Howard stands at the highest point in Arundel. A. J. Hansom, inventor of the Hansom cab, built it for the 15th Duke of Norfolk. However, it was not consecrated as a cathedral until 1965. The interior includes the shrine of St. Philip Howard, featuring Sussex wrought-iron work.

London Rd., Arundel. www.arundelcathedral.org. ☏ **01903/882297.** Free admission; donations appreciated. Daily 9:30am–dusk. From the middle of town, continue west from High St.

Chichester Cathedral CATHEDRAL   Completed in 1123, the cathedral is light and airy and topped by a sharp, narrow spire. This spire was completed in 1867 after the earlier one fell in 1860. The cathedral is accumulating a collection of modern art. Look for the abstract stained-glass window by Marc Chagall; the painting, *Noli Me Tangere*, of Christ appearing to Mary at Easter by Graham Sutherland; and the mural, *The Baptism of Christ*, by German artist Hans Feibusch. There is also a 3m-high (10 ft.) stainless-steel hand of Christ floating high in the Nave, the work of Jaume Plensa, the renowned sculptor whose Crown Fountain graces Chicago's Millennium Park.

Cathedral Cloisters, South St., Chichester. www.chichestercathedral.org.uk. ☏ **01243/782595.** Free admission. Daily 7am–6pm (from 7:15am in winter). Guided tours Mon–Sat 11:15am and 2:30pm.

Fishbourne Roman Palace HISTORIC SITE   This is what remains of the largest Roman residence discovered in Britain. Built around A.D. 75, it has many mosaic-floored rooms and an under-floor heating system. The gardens have been restored to their 1st-century plan. There is also a computer reconstruction of the palace. Roman artifacts are on display in the Discovery Centre. There are guided tours twice a day.

North of the A259, off Salthill Rd. (signposted from Fishbourne; 1½ miles from Chichester). www.sussexpast.co.uk. ☏ **01243/785859.** Admission £8.20 adults, £7.30 students and seniors, £4.20 children 5–15, £21.50 family ticket. Jan Sat–Sun 10am–4pm; Feb daily 10am–4pm; Mar–Oct daily 10am–5pm; Nov–mid-Dec 10am–4pm (rest of Dec weekends only).

Goodwood RACECOURSE   This stately home, in the hills of the South Downs, is best known as one of the world's most famous motor-racing circuits. It's been restored to how it looked 50 years ago to host historic car events such as the Festival of Speed (July) and Goodwood Revival (Sept). Goodwood House is a Jacobean mansion that was extended into a palace over the centuries. It has a superlative art collection (Van Dyck, Canaletto, Stubbs, Reynolds) and Regency furniture. The 12,000-acre estate also features the Goodwood horse-racing circuit, notable for the Glorious Goodwood event (end of July), two golf courses, and clay and game shooting.

www.goodwood.co.uk. ☏ **01243/755000.** Admission £9.50 adults, £4 children 12–18, free children 11 and under. House mid-March–late Sept Sun–Mon 1–5pm; Aug Sun–Thurs 1–5pm. Take the A3 to Milford, the A283 to Petworth, then the A285 to Halnaker, and follow the signposts to Goodwood.

Pallant House Art Gallery GALLERY   This is a gallery of modern art, set up in 1982 following the gift of a collection featuring Henry Moore and Graham Sutherland; it has since attracted many bequests. There's *The Beatles 1962* by Peter Blake, which preceded his design of the Sgt. Pepper album; the studio of German artist Hans Feibusch (who fled the Nazis and has a mural in Chichester Cathedral), plus works by Picasso, Duncan Grant and more. Its Field & Fork restaurant serves food such as game pie, truffled Savoy cabbage, and peppered jus in the evening (£20 for two courses).

9 North Pallant, Chichester. www.pallant.org.uk. ☏ **01243/774557.** Admission £9 adults, £3.50 children 6–16, £21.50 family ticket. Tues adults half-price, Thurs adults £4.50 from 5pm. Tues-Sat 10am–5pm (Thurs 8pm); Sun 11am–5pm. Closed Mon.

Weald & Downland Open Air Museum MUSEUM   In the beautiful Sussex countryside, historic buildings saved from destruction are reconstructed on a large

The South Downs Way runs for 100 miles, from the promenade at Eastbourne, all the way to Winchester in Hampshire. It climbs the chalk cliffs of Beachy Head, passes by the giant chalk figure of the Long Man of Wilmington, skirts Charleston Farmhouse (where the Bloomsbury set of artists lived), takes an undulating, breathtaking path to the north of Brighton, and forges onward. It follows chalk ridges, dips into river valleys, and crosses bare hillsides feeling as remote as anything you'll find in more far-flung parts of the country. It would take an average walker 8 days to complete (and there are plenty of pubs and hotels on or near the route), but it's as easy to enjoy an afternoon stroll on any section. Stop at one of the parking lots at Beachy Head (see p. 262), for instance, and start walking. Visit www.nationaltrail.co.uk for information and maps.

downland site. They show the development of local traditional building, from medieval times to the 19th century. Exhibits include a Tudor market hall, a water mill producing stone-ground flour, a blacksmith's forge, plumbers' and carpenters' workshops, a toll cottage, and a charcoal burner's camp. Shops are in Longport House, and there's a 16th-century building rescued from the site of the Channel Tunnel.

At Singleton, 6 miles north of Chichester on the A286 (the London Rd.). www.wealddown.co.uk. ℰ **01243/811363.** Admission £10 adults, £9 seniors, £5.40 students and children 5–15, £28 family ticket. Apr–Oct daily 10:30am–6pm; Nov–Dec 22 daily 10:30am–4pm; Jan 3–mid-Feb Wed and Sat–Sun 10:30am–4pm. Bus no. 60 from Chichester.

West Wittering Beach ★★ BEACH   West Wittering, a short drive from Chichester, is one of southern England's best beaches; a natural, unspoiled south-facing sweep of sand a mile or more long and backed by dunes. It's on private land, the West Wittering Estate, hidden away down a narrow lane, so you have to pay to park, but it's free for pedestrians. The parking lot is next to a big field behind the dunes, a place for kicking a ball about and barbecues when the sea breeze is too strong for the beach. There's also a cafe, a bucket and spade shop, and toilets. At one end is the National Trust's East Head, a sand dune spit where you can take salt-splashed strolls for free.

Off the A27 (from the middle of Chichester, follow signs to Wittering). www.westwitteringbeach. co.uk. ℰ **01243/514143.** Parking lot Nov–March £1 weekdays, £2 weekends; April–May and Oct £3.50 weekday, £5.50 weekend; June–Sept £5.50 weekday, £7.50 weekend. Summer time (late Mar–late Oct) 6:30am–8:30pm; rest of year 7am–6pm.

Where to Eat

Comme Ça ★ FRENCH   This restaurant celebrated its 25th anniversary in 2011, and it's easy to see why, with its French dishes combined with local ingredients. The decor is more English country than faux French, although the beautiful patio, draped in greenery with wrought ironwork and canopy, does make you feel as if you should be in Provence. There are two set menus, available for lunch or dinner, which include dishes such as slow cooked rabbit leg in whole grain mustard and Madeira sauce, or grilled lemon sole with chive oil. The bar, with log fire, has its own hearty menu, which includes a tartelette of Selsey crab scented with saffron and sweet sun-dried tomatoes.

67 Broyle Rd., Chichester (a 10-min. walk from the middle of town). www.commeca.co.uk. ℰ **01243/788724.** Reservations required. Fixed-price menu 2 courses lunch/dinner £22/£30, 3

courses £25/£35. Bar menu main courses £16–£17. AE, DC, MC, V. Wed–Sun 11:30am–2pm; Tues–Sat 6–10pm.

Queen's Room Restaurant ★★★ ENGLISH   This restaurant is in an upstairs hall in Amberley Castle. You sit among armor, medieval weapons, paintings, an open fire and candles, under a barrel-vaulted 12th-century ceiling. Two cannons are outside the door, and there really is a feeling of being part of history. And the food is as good as you'd hope: Roast loin of rabbit, polenta, black pudding, spinach, and root vegetable purée, for instance; or roast partridge, confit leg, sweet corn purée, and partridge reduction. And starters include fois gras and Jerusalem artichoke risotto. There are wines from around £30, or you can treat yourself to a Chateau Petrus 2002 for £4,450. It's a fabulous experience. The fairytale Mistletoe Lodge treehouse in the grounds is also available as a private dining room for two, and the chef will create a personal menu.

Amberley Castle hotel (see below), Amberley, near Arundel. www.amberleycastle.co.uk. ✆ **01798/ 831992.** Reservations required. Set lunch £28 for 2 courses, £33 for 3 courses; set dinner £35/£55 for 2 courses, £40/£65 for 3 courses. Tasting menu £87.50. AE, DC, MC, V. Daily noon–2pm and 7–9pm.

Entertainment & Nightlife

Chichester Festival Theatre ★★   This 1,400-seat theatre on the edge of Oaklands Park is a five-minute walk from the cathedral. It opened in 1962, and its first director was Laurence (later Lord) Olivier. It features plays and musicals with top names, plus orchestras, opera, theatre, and ballet. Minerva Studio Theatre, from the 1980s, features more experimental performances. The famed Chichester Festival is actually a season of performances from April to September, with plays both classic and contemporary, along with musicals and other events. (www.cft.org.uk; ✆ **01243/ 781312**).

Where to Stay

Amberley Castle ★★★ 📖   Yes, it is a real castle. And, yes, it is everything you might expect. Suits of armor, muskets, and swords everywhere, a library full of interesting old books, and even a working portcullis, which is dropped each evening from the tower over the gateway arch. The Amberley goes back 900 years and has seen its share of celebs—Elizabeth I stayed awhile, and Oliver Cromwell did his best to stop anyone from leaving during a siege when it was a royal stronghold. Now you'll find dark, warm, medieval-tinged rooms mostly with four-poster beds, all with spa baths and flat-screen TVs, and some with signs asking you to shut the door to keep the peacocks out. Two rooms even have private access to a tower leading to the battlements and views across the South Downs. The gardens are full of yew topiary, the grounds are dotted with ponds, and there's a professional 18-hole putting course. **The Queen's Room** restaurant (see "Where to Eat") is a destination in itself.

Amberley, nr. Arundel, West Sussex BN18 9LT. www.amberleycastle.co.uk. ✆ **01798/831992.** Fax 01798/831998. 19 units. £240–£745 double. Rates include English breakfast. AE, DC, MC, V. Free parking. Take the B2139 north of Arundel; the hotel is 1½ miles southwest of Amberley. **Amenities:** Restaurant; putting course; outdoor tennis court; room service. *In room:* TV, minibar, hair dryer, Wi-Fi (patchy but free).

Norfolk Arms ☺   This is an old coaching inn, right on the main street. The two bars and Arun restaurant are in the typical English country-inn style. Bedrooms are simple but classic, some of them in a separate modern wing overlooking the courtyard. Four bedrooms are large enough for families.

22 High St., Arundel, West Sussex BN18 9AD. www.norfolkarmshotel.com. ✆ **01903/882101.** Fax 01903/884275. 34 units. £70–£90 double. Children 13 and under stay free in parent's room. Rates include English breakfast. AE, DC, MC, V. Free parking. **Amenities:** Restaurant; 2 bars; room service. *In room:* TV, hair dryer, Wi-Fi (£10 per 24 hr.).

Ship Hotel A classic Georgian building, the Ship is only a few minutes' walk from Chichester Cathedral. Built as a private house in 1790 for Admiral Sir George Murray, it retains an air of elegance and comfort but with a modern touch. A grand staircase leads from the entrance to the bedrooms, which are named after historic ships. Some have four-poster beds; others are specially for families (£135 plus £25 per child). The revamped restaurant is a brasserie affair, all white walls and wooden floors and tables, serving smart fish, burgers, pasta, and such (main courses £11.50–£17.95).

57 North St., Chichester, West Sussex PO19 1NH. www.theshiphotel.net. ✆ **01243/778000.** Fax 01243/788000. 36 units. £110–£185 double. Rates include English breakfast. AE, DC, MC, V. Free parking. **Amenities:** Restaurant; bar; room service. *In room:* TV, hair dryer, Wi-Fi (free).

GUILDFORD

30 miles S of London; 45 miles NE of Brighton

This is Surrey's picturesque county town (actually city); quaint streets, timbered buildings, the River Wey running through it, and lots of history, including a castle. Charles Dickens claimed that the High Street, which slopes to the river, was one of the most beautiful in England. And the Guildhall has a clock dating from 1683. It is a lovely place to stay and wander, but it is also an excellent base for exploring farther afield, such as the Surrey Hills (p. 282) or the banks of the river.

Essentials

GETTING THERE Trains depart London's Waterloo Station and take 35 minutes; the South West Trains cost about £12 one-way. Guildford is an easy drive from London, on the A3, several miles outside the M25.

VISITOR INFORMATION **Guildford Tourist Information Centre** is at Guildford House, High Street (www.visitguildford.com; www.visitsurrey.com; ✆ **01483/444333**). It's open Monday to Saturday 9am to 5pm and (May to Sept) Sunday 11am to 4pm.

Exploring the Area

The streets and the river walk are all there to be enjoyed. Guildford Castle dates from shortly after the Norman Conquest of 1066 and, although only the tower remains, atop its man-made mound, it has been well renovated this century and contains exhibits on its history. It's open May to September, daily 10am to 5pm; October, March/April 11am to 4pm. Adults £2.80, children 5 to 15 £1.40. The grounds (free entry, daily 8am–dusk) were turned into gardens to celebrate Queen Victoria's Golden Jubilee in 1888. The ornamental bedding displays are renowned; you'll also find places to stop and relax, as well as an open-air theatre. Guildford Museum in Castle Arch, Castle Hill, just off the High Street (www.guildford.gov.uk/heritage; ✆ **01483/444751;** Mon–Sat 11am–5pm; free admission), dates back to 1898 and features a collection of old Surrey items donated by famed garden designer Gertrude Jekyll in 1907.

    Stoke Park is a huge area comprising woodland and formal gardens, plus a boating pond, paddling pool, children's play area, tennis courts, putting green, all-weather sports pitches, indoor and outdoor bowls, a trim trail, and a skateboard park. It's also where the Surrey County Show and GuilFest are held (see "Entertainment & Nightlife," below).

Dapdune Wharf ★ HISTORIC SITE   The Wey was one of Britain's first waterways to be made navigable, opening to barge traffic in 1653 and linking with the Thames. The Godalming Navigations, opened in 1764, allowed barges to go an extra 4 miles upstream. Interactive exhibits and displays tell the story of the work, and of those who sailed the barges, there's the site where huge Wey barges were built, and you can climb aboard the *Reliance,* one of three surviving barges. There are also short boat trips on an electric boat. The 19-mile towpath is open to walkers.

Wharf Rd. (just off the A322 in Guildford). www.nationaltrust.org.uk. *C* **01483/561389.** Admission to wharf £3 adults, £2 children 5–15. Boat rides £3.50 adults, £2 children 5–15. Late Mar–Oct Thurs–Mon 11am–5pm. Closed Nov–Mar.

Guildford Cathedral ★ CATHEDRAL   This modern, red-brick affair sits on an open hilltop and is visible from much of the city and far beyond. Work was started in 1936 and, after a halt during World War II, was consecrated in the presence of the Queen in 1961. It's still a work in progress, with statues at the West Front completed in 2005, and work now focusing on landscaping of the grounds. The result is a stirring 1930s' architectural masterpiece, with an interior of grand simplicity.

Stag Hill. www.guildford-cathedral.org. *C* **01483/547860.** Free admission daily; guided tours £3.

Loseley House ★ HISTORIC SITE   The Loseley estate has been in the same family since the early 16th century, and they had this gorgeous Elizabethan mansion built in the 1560s. It's been visited by Queen Elizabeth I, James I (the Drawing Room has a gilded ceiling created especially for his visit), and Queen Mary. It's full of works of art that include paneling from Henry VIII's Nonsuch Palace and a unique carved chalk chimney piece. There is a superb walled garden, divided into flowers, herbs, and roses, the latter featuring more than 1,000 historic bushes. The Courtyard Tearoom, in the old kitchen and scullery, serves cakes from its own bakery, as well as lunches.

Loseley Park (2½ miles southwest of Guildford). www.loseley-park.com. *C* **01483/304440.** Admission to house and gardens £8.50 adults, £7.50 students and seniors, £4 children 5–15; gardens only £5 adults, £4 students and seniors, £2.25 children. House May–Aug Tues–Thurs and Sun 1–5pm; gardens May–Sept Tues–Sun 11am–5pm.

RHS Garden Wisley ★★★ GARDEN   Possibly Britain's most important garden and the home of the Royal Horticulture Society. It's actually a whole world of gardens, from the herbaceous borders that line Battleston Hill to the wild, rhododendron woods at the summit; from the clipped show gardens to the wildflower heaven, which rolls down to the little stream. This isn't just a pretty garden, it's a scientific project, where seeds and plants are grown in trials so at the right time you might find a profusion of runner beans or chrysanthemums down in the trial beds. It's a good place to spend the day—not just for garden-lovers—and great for a stroll while tots run around the landscaped grassland and through the trees. The huge Glasshouse, on a manmade lake, opened in 2007 and displays delicate plants from several climatic zones in a theme park-like faux rock setting. In the early part of each year it's also turned into a butterfly house. Wherever you walk, and no matter what season, you'll find something different. There's also the Conservatory cafe and restaurant, and various coffee bars, but it's a joy to bring a picnic and sit under the towering trees outside the gate. Large plant and gift shops mean there's no shortage of souvenirs.

Wisley (just off the M25, junction 10, on the A3 London–Portsmouth Rd.). www.rhs.org.uk. ☎ **01483/224234.** Admission £11.55 adults, £4.95 children 6–16, free for children 5 and under. Mar–Oct Mon–Fri 10am–6pm, Sat–Sun 9am–6pm; Nov–Feb Mon–Fri 10am–4:30pm, Sat–Sun 9am–4:30pm (last admission 1 hr. before closing).

Entertainment & Nightlife

The **White House,** 8 High St. (www.fullers.co.uk; ☎ **01483/302006**), a riverside pub with a conservatory overlooking a lovely waterside garden, is a great spot to wind down on a summer evening. **The Electric Theatre,** Onslow Street (www.visit guildford.com; ☎ **01483/444789**), is a modern riverside venue that features music, drama, film, and other shows. **The Boiler Room,** 13 Stokefields (www.theboile room.net; ☎ **01483/440022**), is a hip live music venue featuring emerging acts (Sun–Thurs 7pm–midnight, Fri–Sat to 7pm–1am; tickets £4–£12). The new **G Live** venue (www.glive.co.uk; ☎ **0844/770-1797**) at the end of the High Street can accommodate 1,700 people for concerts and shows, from classical to rock.

In mid-July Guildford's Stoke Park is home to **Guilfest** (www.guilfest.co.uk; ☎ **0871/230-1106**), one of the country's most relaxed music festivals. From Friday evening to Sunday a vast collection of acts, from modern-day stars such as Olly Murs to Roger Daltrey (who, in 2011, played The Who's rock opera *Tommy* in its entirety), appear on seven stages in an atmosphere that is more garden party than rock-fest; it's regularly voted one of Britain's top family festivals. It's an easy walk from the station, and there's plenty of free parking, accessible for day visitors. A weekend pass in advance is £130 (children 12–15 £ 65) but, unlike many festivals, it's generally possible to buy a day ticket at the gate.

Guildford Lido, also in Stoke Park, is a classic 1930s outdoor swimming pool. The 50-m (164-ft.) heated pool is surrounded by gardens. It is open May to mid-September daily 10:30am to 6:30pm, with several early-morning sessions from 6:30am. The lawns are perfect for picnics, and there is a cafe. Also in the park is **Guildford Spectrum** (☎ **01483/443355**) one of Britain's leading leisure complexes, including a pool with slides, a 25-m (82-ft.) swimming pool, teaching pool, diving pool, bowling, ice-skating, and other sports. Times and prices vary. **Surrey Sports Park** (www.surreysportspark.co.uk; ☎ **01483/689112**), at the University of Surrey, is open to the public and has a 25-m (82-ft.) swimming pool, 12-m (39-ft.) climbing wall, tennis, squash, and other sports. It is home to Guildford Heat basketball team. Times and prices vary.

Where to Eat & Stay

Asperion   This boutique guesthouse, which aims to be socially responsible, is within walking distance of town. There are sustainable practices and green energy. Organic breakfasts are sourced from local suppliers, and there are Fairtrade tea and coffee, organic chocolate and toiletries in the rooms, and organic wine from the bar. The rooms are crisp and white, with Egyptian cotton sheets and down duvets.

73 Farnham Rd., Guildford, Surrey GU2 7PF. www.asperion.co.uk. ☎ **01483/579299.** Fax 01483/457977. 15 units. £85–£105 double. Rates include English breakfast. AE, MC, V. Amenities: Lounge, honesty bar. Free parking. *In room:* TV, hair dryer, Internet (free).

Mandolay ★   Mandolay is four 19th-century town houses converted into a luxury hotel that sits at the end of the High Street. There's been plenty of expansion and grooming over the past decade, and the place now has a seriously swish atmosphere with a sleek modern touch. The **m.Brasserie and Grill** serves locally sourced lunches and dinners with imaginative pairings such as roast cod and cider poached chorizo with smoked bacon bubble and squeak, fennel beurre blanc, and prosciutto crisp (mains £11–£17). The m.Bar is also one of Guildford's most stylish.

36–40 London Rd., Guildford, Surrey GU1 2AE. www.guildford.com. ✆ **01483/303030.** Fax 01483/534669. 72 units. £120–£175 double. AE, DC, MC, V. Free parking. **Amenities:** Restaurant; bar. *In room:* TV, hair dryer, Wi-Fi (free).

Radisson Edwardian   The glass and stone of this new, modern hotel stands out from the crowd on Guildford's ancient High Street while the huge chandelier and lots of art brings the cavernous entrance hall to life. Rooms are big and crisply smart, the spa has a gorgeous pool, and there are two restaurants, the modern British brasserie, Relish, and the cocktail bar feel of MKB.

3 Alexandra Terrace, High Street, Guildford, Surrey GU1 3DA. www.radissonedwardian.com. ✆ **01483/792300.** Fax 01483/792301. 183 units. £99–£215 double. AE, DC, MC, V. Parking £10/24 hr. **Amenities:** 2 restaurants; bar; indoor pool; exercise room; spa; room service. *In room:* TV, hair dryer, Wi-Fi (free).

THE SURREY HILLS

30 miles from London

The Surrey Hills were designated an Area of Outstanding Natural Beauty in 1958, and offer some of the Southeast's most beautiful and accessible countryside. The highest point is **Leith Hill,** while the commons and heathland are remarkably dramatic, with yews and pines in natural formation and studded with gorse bushes (their bright yellow flowers are extravagant in spring). The ancient woodlands (home to many deciduous trees) are also full of rhododendrons, adding powerful shade in late spring (although these foreign invaders, introduced by the Victorians, strangle other undergrowth and are being eradicated). Among the hills and trees is a web of paths as well as narrow, winding lanes often cut between chalky embankments. The hills stretch across the chalk North Downs from Farnham in the west—above Guildford, Dorking, and Reigate—to Oxted in the east. To the south you'll find the Greensand Hills, which take in the Devil's Punch Bowl (see below). In between are the river valleys of the Wey, Tillingbourne, and Mole, and heaths of Frensham, Thursley, and Blackheath.

Essentials

GETTING THERE   There are regular South West trains to Dorking (45 min. from London Victoria or Waterloo, about £10.60 one-way) and Guildford (35 min. from Waterloo, about £12 one-way). However, you really need a car to explore the byroads among the hills. The A3 from London is the main artery, with many small routes running south, just south of the M25.

VISITOR INFORMATION   The **Surrey Hills Partnership,** Warren Farm Barns, Headley Lane, Mickleham, Dorking (www.surreyhills.org; ✆ **01372/220653**), has information on its website that features a downloadable information pack with maps. The office is not for personal callers, but does take phone calls during office hours. Also see the "Guildford" section, above.

Exploring the Area

Box Hill ★ ☺ NATURE RESERVE   This is an iconic destination for walking, for children to run free, and for appreciating the countryside safely south of London (but not too far away). It's an area of woodland and open chalk downland, with views across the edge of the South Downs. There are walks in the woods and on open paths, a hilltop Discovery Zone for youngsters to play in, and a cafe that's usually busy with red-cheeked hikers.

Box Hill Rd., Tadworth (just off the A24, a half-mile north of Dorking). www.nationaltrust.org.uk. ✆ **01306/885502.** Free access, but National Trust pay parking lot.

Devil's Punch Bowl ★★ NATURE RESERVE   This is a remarkable piece of countryside, like something one might expect to find in America's northwest: A natural basin, heavily forested and with a real wilderness feel, particularly since the A3 London–Portsmouth road that skirted it was replaced by a modern road through a tunnel in July 2011. It's thought to get its name from the way mist gathers and pours over the rim. The fact that it's surrounded by lowland heath and Hindhead Commons makes it even more fascinating. The Punchbowl is Europe's largest spring-eroded valley, and its beauty can be appreciated from the viewpoint 50 yards from the cafe at the parking lot, although a circular walk deep inside is recommended.

Just off the A3, 10 miles southwest of Guildford. www.nationaltrust.org.uk. ✆ **01494/755565** or **755573.** Free access, but National Trust pay parking lot.

Leith Hill ★ NATURE RESERVE   This is the highest point in southeast England, topping 300m (1,000 ft.). You can walk up and find all manner of woodland paths (full of rhododendrons in early summer) marked on a free map. It is topped by an 18th-century Gothic tower with a spiral staircase, and 360-degree views (try the telescope) to London in one direction and across countryside almost to the English Channel in the other. There's the chance of a cup of tea from the cafe and, in late spring, you can cross the road at the bottom and delve into the bluebell woods for a magical circular walk.

Leith Hill, near Coldharbour village (4 miles southwest of Dorking); A25 Guildford–Dorking Rd. runs nearby. www.nationaltrust.org.uk. ✆ **01306/712711.** Hill has free access. Admission to Tower £1.30 adults, 70p children 5–15.

Hill has free access dawn to dusk. Tower: Fri–Sun April–Oct, 10am–5pm; weekends Nov–March 10am–3:30pm, plus bank holidays and some school holidays. Free parking on roads, and National Trust pay parking lot.

Polesden Lacey GARDEN   This Regency villa is set among the hills, with gardens dropping down to (with views over) a farming valley. The house is full of antiques, paintings, and tapestries. But many people come here simply to enjoy the countryside. There are marked walks in the gardens, the wooded grounds, and around the 1,400-acre estate. The 18th-century gardens, with sweeping lawn, and other areas divided into rooms with roses and herbaceous borders, are a treat.

Signposted from Great Bookham, off the A246 Leatherhead–Guildford Rd. www.nationaltrust.org.uk. ✆ **01372/452048.** Admission to grounds £7.40 adults, £3.70 children 5–15, £18.50 family ticket; house and grounds £12 adults, £6 children, £30 family ticket. Grounds daily Feb–Oct 10am–5pm, Nov–Jan 10am–4pm; house Mar–Oct Wed–Sun and public holidays 11am–5pm, weekends 11am–4pm rest of the year (closed some weekends and Jan, Feb, Nov by guided tour only).

Where to Eat & Stay

Devil's Punch Bowl Hotel   Alongside the Punchbowl and Hindhead Commons, this is a warm and pleasing place that's good for a drink (in the traditional bar with lots of real ales), a decent dinner, or a night's rest. Some of the rooms are simple, others are sizable with four-poster beds. The **restaurant** offers few surprises but covers the bases (wild boar sausages, steak, lamb shank) with mostly local ingredients at a good price (main courses £7.95–£14.95), and there is also a bar menu and Sunday carvery.

52 London Rd., Hindhead, Surrey GU26 6AG. www.devilspunchbowlhotel.co.uk. ℂ **01428/606565.** Fax 01428/605713. 32 units. £55–£80 double. Rates include English breakfast. AE, MC, V. Free parking. On the A3, just north of Hindhead. **Amenities:** Restaurant; bar, Wi-Fi. *In room:* TV, hair dryer.

Mercure Burford Bridge Hotel ★   At the foot of beautiful Box Hill, and near the Mole River, this is a four-star place with many historical associations. Keats, Wordsworth, and Robert Louis Stevenson all stayed here. Some rooms are in the original buildings, some in more modern (but still reasonably old) additions, and all are classically furnished. Breakfast is not included. The gardens have lovely views, and the **Emlyn restaurant** is elegantly modern.

Box Hill, Dorking, Surrey RH5 6BX. www.mercure.com. ℂ **01306/884561.** Fax 01306/887821. 57 units. £110–£160 double. AE, DC, MC, V. Free parking. Take the A24 1½ miles north of Dorking. **Amenities:** Restaurant; bar; outdoor pool; concierge; room service. *In room:* TV, hair dryer, Wi-Fi (£4 per hr., £12 for 10 hr.).

Mercure White Horse Hotel   Charles Dickens is known to have popped into the bar here, the fictional home of the Marquis of Granby in *The Pickwick Papers.* This timbered inn, in the upmarket town of Dorking, has four-poster beds in some rooms, which are smart and comfortable. The **Coach House restaurant** offers a moderately priced set menu, as well as a la carte dishes. The bar, with log fire, fills with locals.

High St., Dorking, Surrey RH4 1BE. www.mercure.com. ℂ **01306/881138.** Fax 01306/887241. 78 units. £62–£132 double. AE, DC, MC, V. Free parking. **Amenities:** Restaurant; bar; room service. *In room:* TV, hair dryer, Wi-Fi (£4 per hr., £9 for 3 hr.).

THE THAMES NEAR LONDON

You don't have to go far from London to find the beauty of the countryside and the attractions of the River Thames. **Richmond-upon-Thames** is actually so close it's even on the Tube. And **Kingston-upon-Thames** is only a swift train ride. Both are attractive towns that make the most of their riverside, but they're also bustling places with plenty of shops, as well as good restaurants.

Essentials

GETTING THERE   Richmond is at the end of one of the branches of the Tube's District Line; a journey from the Earls Court interchange takes around 20 minutes. It is also on a fast South West train line from London Waterloo, a journey of around 15 minutes, costing about £4.50 one-way. Slower local trains make a loop from Waterloo, via Richmond and Kingston, in both directions, before arriving back at Waterloo.

VISITOR INFORMATION   There are self-serve information stands at Richmond Reference Library in the Old Town Hall, Whittaker Avenue (www.visitrichmond. co.uk; ℂ **020/8734-3308**), open Monday to Saturday 9am to 5pm. For Kingston, see www.kingston.gov.uk.

Exploring the Area

Kingston ★ is an ancient market town, and now a major shopping destination, with **Bentalls** department store the hub of the three-floor indoor Bentall Centre. There's a large branch of Britain's leading department store, John Lewis, across the street while the **market** is a mass of vegetable, fruit, fish, and meat stalls. It sells good coffee and snacks and operates in the Market Place Monday to Saturday, 9am to 5pm. Each Monday (8am–2pm) in the Cattle Market parking lot there's a market selling everything from fashions to tools to plants.

The Rotunda entertainment complex has a 14-screen Odeon cinema, plus seven restaurants including a branch of Marco Pierre White's Frankie & Benny's American/ Italian chain. **Kingston Museum** in Wheatfield Way (www.kingston.gov.uk; ✆ 020/ 8547-5006; Tues–Sat & Thurs, 10am–5pm; free admission) has a gallery devoted to pioneer photographer and movie-maker Eadweard Muybridge, who was born here. There are also good history displays. The coronation of several Anglo-Saxon kings took place in Kingston, and an ancient **Coronation Stone** is outside the Guildhall near historic Clattern Bridge, and the excellent Rose Theatre.

While Kingston is the shopping and entertainment hub, **Richmond** ★ is its arty cousin with more individual shops and restaurants. It's somehow summed up by the river's lazy curve through the town, rather than its straight rush through in Kingston. There are cafes and restaurants dotted along the riverside walk, and more cafes plus lovely antiques shops, galleries, and clothes boutiques up Richmond Hill. At the top of the hill is a breathtaking view of the river, the only view in England to be protected by an Act of Parliament. From here you can see down to **Ham House and Garden,** (www.nationaltrust.org.uk; ✆ 020/8940-1950), a 17th-century Thames-side palace, close to Petersham Meadows, which has cows grazing in summer and was painted by J. M. W. Turner, among others. Here you'll find the glorious **Petersham Nurseries** (www.petershamnurseries.co.uk; ✆ 020/8940-5230), which, in addition to selling plants and unusual gardening kit, has a bohemian cafe/restaurant (for a time it held a Michelin star) where you'll often spot showbiz types.

Chessington World of Adventures ★★★ THEME PARK One of Britain's leading theme parks (which celebrated its 25th anniversary in 2012), Chessington offers a full-blown mix of white-knuckle rides (the revolving, head-dunking Ramases Revenge; the feet-swinging roller-coaster Vampire; and the spinning coaster Dragon's Fury) alongside family fun such as the new Madagascar Live, a stage romp based on the movie. And then there's the zoo on which the park was based with tigers, lions, gorillas, and penguins, plus SeaLife. It's exceptional for families and the young-at-heart. The Holiday Inn Chessington, a safari-themed hotel outside the park, has views from the bedrooms, restaurant, and terrace over the Wanyama Reserve's zebras. There are park/hotel packages, and the hotel is also a good place from which to explore the area. Nearby, trains to London Waterloo take 35 minutes.

On the A243, 3 miles south of Kingston. www.chessington.com. ✆ **0871-663-4477.** Admission £39.60 adults, £28.80 children 11 and under (free for children under 1m/3 ft., 4 in. tall), £108 family ticket. Zoo days: £14.40 adult £10.80 children 12 and over, £7.80 children 11 and under (free for children under 1m/3 ft., 4 in tall), £36 family ticket. Around 15–30% discount for online purchases. Parking £2. Theme park daily mid-Mar–Oct from 10am, mostly to 6pm; otherwise 5pm (10pm at Halloween). Zoo only Jan–Mar weekends 10am–3pm.

Hampton Court Palace ★ HISTORIC SITE Henry VIII's Lord Chancellor, Cardinal Wolsey, began building this magnificent palace with its glorious gardens in 1515, but the king liked it so much he claimed it for himself and made it even grander. Highlights include the Tudor Great Hall with its richly ornamented ceiling, and the Chapel Royal with a fan-vaulted wooden ceiling. The 16th-century kitchens are fantastic—the largest to survive from Tudor times—and you can still visit the courts Henry had built for real tennis. *Insider tip:* Hampton Court Palace is featured on the London Pass (see "A Money-Saving Pass," p. 111), which gives entry to many attractions in the city but also features a number of places in the surrounding areas.

Hampton Court. www.hrp.org.uk. © **0844/482-7777.** Admission £16.95 adults, £14.30 seniors and students, £8.50 children 5–15, £43.36 family ticket (discounts for online booking). Apr–Sept daily 10am–6pm; Oct–Mar daily 10am–4:30pm. Closed Dec 24–26. Short walk from Hampton Court rail station (around 35 min. from London Waterloo, but 35–50 min. from Kingston or Richmond as it sits at the end of a branch line) or a 1-mile walk from Kingston, slightly farther along the Thames Path.

Richmond Park ★ PARK   This is the king of royal parks: 12,500 acres of hills, woods, and grassland with views as far as St. Paul's Cathedral in one direction and Windsor Castle in the other. The circular road is a wonderful drive, past herds of red and fallow deer. Attractions include the Isabella Plantation, beautiful in late spring with its azaleas and rhododendrons. The park is home to tawny owls and sparrow hawks, plus swans and waterfowl on Pen Ponds. In summer the gardens are pretty at historic Pembroke Lodge, where there's a cafe with outdoor seating.

Richmond Park is between Richmond and Kingston and has gates at Richmond, Petersham (pedestrian), Ham, and Kingston as well as at Sheen and Roehampton. www.royalparks.org.uk. © **020/8948-3209.** Free admission. Daily 7am to dusk (opens at 7:30am mid-Sept–Feb). There are several free parking lots, Pembroke Lodge restaurant, a cafe, and various official refreshment vans plus children's play areas.

River cruises ★ CRUISE   **Turk Launches,** Town End Pier, 68 High St., Kingston (www.turks.co.uk; © **020/8546-2434**), a family company with a 300-year history of boat building and operating, runs a Richmond–Kingston–Hampton Court

THE thames PATH

The Thames Path runs 184 miles from the sea to the river's source in the Cotswolds. Having passed through London, and skirted Kew Gardens and the huge Old Deer Park, it instantly takes on a more rural feel, like something out of a 19th-century canvas once you get to Richmond. From Richmond you pass through Petersham Meadows, where you still expect to see someone cutting hay, past Marble Hill House and Marble Hill Park (on the other side, but here you'll find a foot ferry plying the placid waters between tree-lined banks), and arrive at the grandeur that is Ham House—well worth a visit (see above). Continuing on, you walk alongside fields and a nature reserve, with views across to Eel Pie Island and the town of Twickenham behind. Soon you come to Teddington Lock and Weir. It's here that the first Thames lock was built in 1810. Barge Lock, the river's largest, is here.

This is the point at which the Thames is no longer tidal. It's a good place for a break: Cross the Victorian footbridge and drop in at **The Anglers** (www.the anglersteddington.co.uk; © **020/8977-7475**), a pub/restaurant with a riverside garden that can hold 600 people in summer. The modern British food is good anytime, but weekend barbecues and hog roasts are exceptional, washed down with Fuller's beer, brewed by the river in Chiswick. From Teddington it's a swift walk to Kingston, where you cross Kingston Bridge to continue along the edge of Hampton Court Park to Hampton Court Palace itself. For official information, visit www.nationaltrail.co.uk/ThamesPath, but www.thames-path.org.uk gives an enthusiastic section-by-section commentary.

RIVER rocks

The area of southwest London and Surrey was at the forefront of British rock music, where London's response to the Beatles was fermenting in the early 1960s. The Rolling Stones, The Yardbirds, Downliners Sect, and other cult names played here regularly. The old clubs have gone but newer places fly the flag. The **Eel Pie Club** (www.eelpieclub. com) is a successor to the place that existed on Eel Pie Island; it's at the Cabbage Patch pub, 67 London Rd., Twickenham, across from the station, and has shows by the Downliners, Pretty Things, and other survivors. The **Boom Boom Club** (www.feenstra.co.uk; ✆ 020/8761-9078), a short drive from Kingston, in Sutton, attracts the likes of the Zombies, Yardbirds, and even Jefferson Starship, to its small, friendly home at Sutton United Football Club, Gander Green Lane.

service from April to October. The stretch of river includes Twickenham, little Eel Pie Island, and Teddington Lock. The latter, between Richmond and Kingston, dates back more than a century, and is the point where the tidal Thames ends. It is spanned by a Victorian footbridge. There are also Sunday jazz, dinner and dance, and disco cruises. The fleet of five boats ranges from a Mississippi-style sternwheeler to the elegant 1892 side-wheeler Yarmouth Belle to little Jeff, which was one of the Dunkirk ships, rescuing troops during the war. **Parr Boats,** Queen's Promenade, Portsmouth Road, Kingston (www.parrboats.co.uk; ✆ 020/8546-2434), operates during the same season, with Kingston to Hampton Court trips, and a circular trip from Richmond to Teddington. Fares from £3.50 for a Kingston–Hampton Court trip.

Thorpe Park THEME PARK   The sister park to Chessington World of Adventures; or maybe its big brother as the feel here is somewhat more mature. A bevy of big rides include The Swarm (new in 2012), a dark sci-fi rollercoaster (and Europe's tallest) with seats on a wing that does a 39-m (127-ft.) headfirst, inverted drop, Saw—The Ride with its rotating blades, based on the slasher movies, and X:\No Way Out, an indoor, pitch-black ride in reverse. And then there's SAW Alive, a live action horror maze. Get the picture? There are, however, opportunities for younger visitors to get dizzy and wet too, following it up with burgers and fries.

Staines Rd., Chertsey, Surrey (near jcts 11 and 13 of M25). www.thorpepark.com. ✆ 0871/663-1673. Admission £42 adults, £33.60 children 11 and under (free for children under 1m/3 ft., 4 in. tall), £136.80 family ticket. Around 25% discount for online purchases. Parking £2. Mid-Mar–Oct, mostly 10am–6pm, 9:30am–7pm school holidays, with variable closing times.

Entertainment & Nightlife

Kingston's riverfront options are rather limited. The brash **Bishop out of Residence** pub (✆ 020/8546-4965) is a possibility on a summer's evening, with good Young's beer, and there are bars and restaurants with outdoor seating overlooking the river at Charter Quay near the Rose Theatre. In Richmond the **White Cross** (✆ 020/8940-6844) at the end of Water Lane is a classy old pub, where drinkers perch outside by the slipway. The chain bar/restaurant **Pitcher & Piano,** 11 Bridge St. (www.pitcher andpiano.com; ✆ 020/8940-1362), has cast-iron balconies overlooking the river, while the **Cricketers** (✆ 020/8940-4372) and **Prince's Head** (✆ 020/8940-1572) are classic British pubs on Richmond Green. The **Roebuck** (✆ 020/8948-2329) on Richmond Hill is a neat, dark, pub where you can stand outside and enjoy sunsets over the river below, and the **Marlborough** (☏ 020/8940-8513), around the corner at 46 Friars Stile Rd., is a decent gastropub that looks unassuming from its small entrance but spreads out into a parklike garden.

Where to Eat & Stay

The Bingham ★   A delicious, heady combination of restaurant and hotel in two Georgian town houses by the river. The former, a vision in opulent white, is the work of chef Shay Cooper. It features delights such as Scottish halibut, smoked eel carbonara, compressed cucumber, parsley purée, cockle butter sauce (set menu £45 for three courses; six-course tasting menu £60); set lunches (£19.50 for three courses); breakfasts; and afternoon tea with cucumber sandwiches (£25). Individually decorated rooms, some with river views, are cool and modern yet with a hint of the 1930s. The terrace and landscaped gardens add a finishing touch of discreet luxury.

61–63 Petersham Rd., Richmond, Surrey TW10 6UT. www.thebingham.co.uk. ☏ **020/8940-0902.** 15 units. £190–£285 double. AE, DC, MC, V. Free parking (limited); otherwise £10. **Amenities:** Restaurant; bar. *In room:* TV/DVD, hair dryer, Wi-Fi (free).

Richmond Hill Hotel   This is a boutique hotel, albeit with loads of rooms, with views down across the meadows and the Thames winding away into the distance, in one direction, and Richmond Park in the other. Rooms are in both a Georgian building and a modern wing (the former tend to be slightly larger), but all have a modern touch. Suites have a mix of king-sized bed, balconies, and dressing rooms. The Cedars health club is in the grounds and free for guests. The **Pembroke restaurant** (main courses £11–£18.90) serves staples such as grilled sea bass and slow cooked lamb.

144 Richmond Hill, Richmond, Surrey TW10 6RW. www.richmondhill-hotel.co.uk. ☏ **020/8940-2247.** Fax 020/8940-5424. 149 units. £109–£179 double. AE, DC, MC, V. Parking £5. **Amenities:** Restaurant; bar; health club; room service. *In room:* TV, hair dryer, Wi-Fi (1 hr. free in restaurant or (£12.95 for 24 hr.).

White Hart   A striking timbered building just across Kingston Bridge, and an easy walk from Hampton Court Palace, the White Hart is part of the brewer Fuller's chain. It has a lively public outdoor area at the front, and a private one at the back. Rooms are smartly furnished in comfy country style, and one has a four-poster. Food is posh pub fare (mains £8.50–£16) such as Fuller's beer-battered hake with hand-cut chips.

1 High St., Hampton Wick, Surrey KT1 4DA. www.fullershotels.com. ☏ **020/8977-1786.** 37 units. £120–£170 double. AE, DC, MC, V. Free parking. **Amenities:** Restaurant; bar; access to nearby Virgin Active health club. *In room:* TV, hair dryer, Wi-Fi (free).

HAMPSHIRE & DORSET

by Donald Strachan

Hampshire and Dorset are where England began. They formed the core of Alfred's 10th-century kingdom of Wessex, which was ruled from Winchester. They became Wessex once again—this time fictional—in the 19th-century Dorchester tales of writer Thomas Hardy. A tour of these two southern English counties leads you gently from London's coattails to the rural peace of tiny villages, coastal walks, and serene, idyllic isolation.

SIGHTSEEING   Jane Austen wrote about the middle-class inhabitants of Hampshire in her six novels, including *Pride and Prejudice* and *Sense and Sensibility*. Fans can visit her memorial in **Winchester Cathedral** and her home, now the **Jane Austen's House Museum,** in nearby Chawton. The Gothic fan vaults at **Sherborne Abbey** showcase medieval architectural ingenuity, and the nearby **Jurassic Coast** is home to geological wonders formed over millions of years.

EATING & DRINKING   Both Hampshire and Dorset look seaward for culinary inspiration—seafood here is much more than fish and chips wrapped in yesterday's newspaper. Restaurants including Weymouth's **Crab House Café** and Portsmouth's **Restaurant 27** offer contrasting visions of contemporary coastal dining. The country pubs of the **New Forest** are places to eat gastropub food and drink local ales.

OUTDOOR ACTIVITIES   Away from the twin (and rival) cities of **Southampton** and **Portsmouth,** these are largely rural counties. Keen walkers will find empty tracts, out of season, on the **Isle of Wight** and in the **New Forest National Park.** For livelier sands and surfing, make for the Victorian resort of **Bournemouth** or its trendy neighbor, **Boscombe.**

HISTORY   Like the food, the history of these coastal counties is closely tied to the English Channel. Portsmouth has long been England's naval capital, and the **Historic Dockyard** is where Nelson's HMS *Victory* and the remains of Henry VIII's flagship, the *Mary Rose,* are berthed. Across the Solent, on the Isle of Wight, **Osborne House,** where Queen Victoria lived and died, is a preserved time capsule. The pretty harbor at **Lyme Regis** seems like a fishing port plucked straight from the history books.

THE best TRAVEL EXPERIENCES IN HAMPSHIRE & DORSET

○ **Cycling or hiking to a New Forest pub (or two):** The National Park is crisscrossed by a network of bike and walking trails, and dotted with some of southern England's best country pubs. Arm yourself with a good map, and work up an appetite for hearty Hampshire produce washed down with a Ringwood ale. See p. 303.

○ **Exploring below-decks on Nelson's flagship:** HMS *Victory* is the centerpiece of Portsmouth's Historic Dockyard. A 45-minute guided tour, which takes you above and below decks, is packed with enough living history and grizzly anecdotes to please everyone. See p. 297.

○ **Admiring Lyme Regis from the tip of the Cobb:** This 18th-century sea defense snakes out to sea from Lyme's sandy beach, wrapping the pretty little harbor in a protective embrace. Afterward, browse a quirky resort high street that's almost unchanged since Jane Austen visited in the early 1800s. See p. 318.

○ **Enjoying fresh air and fine food in the West Wight:** The tiny yachtie port of Yarmouth makes a quaint jumping-off point for the best of the Isle of Wight. A brisk half-day walk takes in the Needles and Freshwater Bay, and leaves time for refined dining in a formal restaurant or gastropub. See p. 308 and 309.

○ **Acquainting yourself with architectural genius in Sherborne:** The fan vault was the peculiarly English Gothic solution to supporting a huge ceiling with grace and elegance. Sherborne Abbey showcases one of Britain's most impressive examples—pack your binoculars to view it up close. See p. 322.

WINCHESTER ★★

72 miles SW of London; 12 miles N of Southampton

Hampshire's history hotspot, once the capital of the ancient kingdom of Wessex, **Winchester** has long been linked with King Alfred, who is honored today by a statue on the High Street. Alfred the Great, born in 849, was crowned king in 871, ruling until his death in 899. He is remembered as "the Great" because he defended Anglo-Saxon England against Viking raids, formulated a code of laws, and fostered a rebirth of religious and scholarly activity.

Its past glory but a memory, Winchester is today a well-kept market town on the water meadows along the Itchen River, with a well curated (and free) **City Museum,** a **Cathedral** that dates to the 11th century, and an intriguing array of **independent shops.** Hampshire is also a draw for Jane Austen fans. You can visit her grave in the cathedral, as well as the **Jane Austen's House Museum** in Chawton, where she lived during her most productive years.

Essentials

GETTING THERE   Frequent daily trains run from London's Waterloo Station to Winchester. The journey takes around 1 hour and costs from around £29 for a round-trip. Arrivals are at Winchester Station, Station Hill, a 10-minute walk northwest of the center.

If you're driving from Southampton, head north on the A335 until it joins the northbound M3; from London, take the M3 motorway southwest.

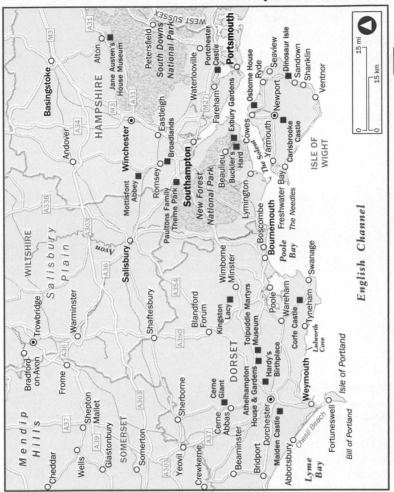

VISITOR INFORMATION   The **Tourist Information Centre,** Broadway (www. visitwinchester.co.uk; © **01962/840500**), is open Monday to Saturday 10am to 5pm (May–Sept also Sun 11am–4pm). It offers a free "greeter" service to help visitors get oriented: Email tourism@winchester.gov.uk around 10 days ahead of your arrival and staff will try to arrange a local to come and meet you, answer questions, and generally point you in the right direction. Keep up with the latest local happenings at twitter.com/King_Alf.

TOURS   The Tourist Information Centre (see above) has a number of helpful free pamphlets, including one that details a self-guided Keats circuit round the town and environs—Keats' 1819 ode *To Autumn* was inspired by a visit here. Guided **walking tours,** which depart from the tourist office and last 1½ hours, cost £4.50 per adult (children go free). Departure times vary by season; check once you're in town or at www.winchestertouristguides.com.

Exploring Winchester

The interactive, hands-on displays at the historic **City Mill,** Bridge Street (www. nationaltrust.org.uk/winchestercitymill; © **01962/870057**), are well suited to school-age children. Visitors can access the bowels of a working corn mill, and view displays on the history and processes involved in flour-making. Admission costs £4 adults, £2 children. Hours are 10am to 5pm daily between mid-February and Christmas (10:30am opening during December), and 11am to 4pm Friday through Monday otherwise. The excellent little **City Museum ★**, The Square (© **01962/863064**), traces the history of Winchester from its establishment as Roman Venta Belgarum in A.D. 70 to the present day. Admission is free. It's open April to October Monday to Saturday 10am to 5pm, Sunday noon to 5pm; off-season it closes an hour earlier and all day Monday.

Castle Great Hall ★ HISTORIC SITE   This is the only remaining part of the castle first erected in Winchester by William the Conqueror and rebuilt by Henry III. Dating from the 1200s, it is one of the finest examples of a medieval hall in England, with its timber roof supported by Gothic arches resting on columns of Purbeck marble. The English Parliament met here for the first time in 1246; a Victorian mural lists every Hampshire Member of Parliament between 1283 and 1868. The castle also hosted the trial of Sir Walter Raleigh, who was condemned to death in 1603 for conspiring against James I. The giant (5.5m/18 ft. diameter) painted Round Table hanging on the west wall doesn't in fact stretch back to the time of King Arthur—its 1,220kg (2,690 lb.) of English oak has been carbon dated to around 1280, and it was probably the property of Edward I.

Castle Ave. www.hants.gov.uk/greathall. © **01962/846476.** Free admission. Daily 10am–5pm (Nov–Feb closes 4pm).

Hospital of St. Cross ★★ RELIGIOUS SITE   Founded in 1132, the Hospital (for hospitality, not medicine) is the oldest charitable institution in England, and still houses 25 robed Brethren in its almshouses. It was established by Henri de Blois, grandson of William the Conqueror, as a link for social care and to supply life's necessities to the local poor and famished travelers. It continues the tradition of providing refreshments to visitors today: Stop in at the Porter's Lodge for the Wayfarer's Dole, some bread and ale. Arranged around the inner courtyard are the Brethren's houses that date from 1450, a 16th-century ambulatory, and the Norman church, begun in 1135 and completed around 1250; check out the graffiti on the choir stalls, etched by churchgoers as long ago as 1572.

St. Cross Rd. www.stcrosshospital.co.uk. © **01962/851375.** Admission £4 adults, £3.50 students and seniors, £2 children under 13. Apr–Oct Mon–Sat 9:30am–5pm, Sun 1–5pm; Nov–Mar Mon–Sat 10:30am–3:30pm.

Winchester Cathedral ★★★ CATHEDRAL   The longest medieval cathedral in Britain dates from 1079, and its Norman heritage is still in evidence. When a Saxon church stood on this spot, Swithun, Bishop of Winchester and tutor to young King Alfred, suggested modestly that he be buried outside. Following his subsequent indoor burial, it rained for 40 days. The legend lives on: If it rains on St. Swithun's Day, July 15, you'll get a prediction of rain for the next 40 days.

Winchester

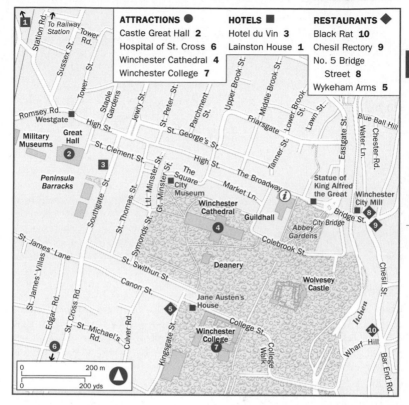

ATTRACTIONS ●	HOTELS ■	RESTAURANTS ◆
Castle Great Hall **2**	Hotel du Vin **3**	Black Rat **10**
Hospital of St. Cross **6**	Lainston House **1**	Chesil Rectory **9**
Winchester Cathedral **4**		No. 5 Bridge
Winchester College **7**		Street **8**
		Wykeham Arms **5**

The **Perpendicular Gothic nave,** with its two aisles, is the architectural high-light. The elaborately carved choir stalls from 1308 are England's oldest, as is the retrochoir's medieval tiled floor. The astonishing Great Screen was carved between 1470 and 1490, although the original statues fell victim to the iconoclasm of the Reformation years. Those in place today are Victorian replacements.

Jane Austen is buried in the north aisle; note how her original gravestone makes no mention of her writing. The son of William the Conqueror, William Rufus (who reigned as William II), is also buried at the cathedral, as are the bones of Danish King of England, Cnut (985–1035).

The Close. www.winchester-cathedral.org.uk. ✆ **01962/857275.** Admission £6.50 adults, £5 seniors, £3.75 students, free for children 15 and under. Mon–Sat 9am–5pm; Sun 12:30–3pm; free guided tours hourly 10am–3pm.

Winchester College ★ CULTURAL INSTITUTION   Winchester College was founded by William of Wykeham, Bishop of Winchester and chancellor to Richard II, who also founded New College, Oxford. Its buildings have been in use since 1393, making it the oldest continuously open school in England. Exploration is possible only by guided tour, lasting an hour and covering the Chamber Court, the 14th-century

Gothic chapel, and the College Hall, among other sights. *Insider tip:* During term time, you can attend Evensong for free on a Tuesday. Arrive at the Porter's Lodge by 5:30pm.

73 Kingsgate St. www.winchestercollege.org/guided-tours. © **01962/621209.** Admission £6 adults, £5 students and seniors. Guided tours Tues and Thurs 10:45am and noon; Mon, Wed, and Fri–Sat 10:45am, noon, 2:15, and 3:30pm; Sun 2:15 and 3:30pm.

BEYOND THE CITY

Jane Austen's House Museum ★ HISTORIC HOME This cottage in the village of Chawton is where Jane Austen spent most of the last 7½ years of her life, her most productive period. In unpretentious but pleasant surroundings, she penned new versions of three of her books and wrote three more, including *Emma*. You can also see examples of Austen's needlework and jewelry, the rector's George III mahogany bookcase, and a silhouette likeness of the Reverend Austen presenting his son to the Knights. Jane Austen became ill here in 1816 with what was diagnosed as Addison's disease—though crime author Lindsay Ashford's 2011 *The Mysterious Death of Miss Austen* suggests arsenic poisoning as a possibility. She died in College Street, Winchester, in July 1817.

Chawton (1 mile southwest of Alton off the A31, 15 miles east of Winchester). www.jane-austens-house-museum.org.uk. © **01420/83262.** Admission £7 adults, £6 students and seniors, £2 children 6–16. June–Aug daily 10am–5pm; Sept–Dec and Mar–May daily 10:30am–4:30pm; Jan–Feb Sat–Sun 10:30am–4:30pm.

Where to Eat

Black Rat ★★ MODERN ENGLISH If you like your food with an adventurous edge, this fine-dining spinoff from the Black Boy pub (see below) is the best choice in town. The dining room is decked with mighty tables, the oak floors are dressed with worn Persian rugs, and the decor is simple—although the kitchen is anything but, having first been awarded a Michelin star in 2011. Dishes always use ingredients from reputable local suppliers; main courses might include cider-braised pig cheeks with chorizo and truffled butter beans, or saddle of venison with haunch suet pudding and parsley root purée.

88 Chesil St. www.theblackrat.co.uk. © **01962/844465.** Reservations recommended. Main courses £18–£22. MC, V. Mon–Sun 7–9:30pm; Sat–Sun noon–2:30pm.

Chesil Rectory ★★ MODERN ENGLISH There's a buzz again about this eatery housed in Winchester's oldest building, thanks largely to a revamped menu and some exceptional fixed-price meal deals. The half-timbered interior, hunting-lodge decor, and woodburning stove ooze tradition, and seasonal dishes are full of brawny British flavors and burst with heady perfumes. Expect the likes of roast Hampshire partridge with creamed cabbage and bacon, or pan-fried bream with a casserole of Dorset mussels and saffron.

1 Chesil St. www.chesilrectory.co.uk. © **01962/851555.** Reservations recommended. Main courses £15–£21.50; Mon–Sat lunch and 6–7pm fixed-price 2 courses £16, 3 courses £20. DC, MC, V. Mon–Sun noon–2:20pm; Mon–Thurs 6–9:30pm; Fri–Sat 6–10pm.

No. 5 Bridge Street ★ CONTEMPORARY ENGLISH There are regular mains at this 2011-opened "bar-kitchen," but the reason to stop in is for a tasty lunch of British "small plates" in stone-and-brick, vaguely industrial surrounds. Excellent local charcuterie includes venison "bresaola" and smoked lamb "prosciutto." There are also cheese platters, sandwiches, and salads alongside creative, bitesize dishes like rabbit "Wellington" served with a shot glass of mustard foam. Prices are perhaps a touch high for the portion sizes, but there's no doubting the quality of ingredients and flavors.

5 Bridge St. www.no5bridgestreet.co.uk. ℂ **01962/863838.** Reservations recommended. Small plates £3–£7.50; main courses £10–£18. MC, V. Mon–Fri noon–3pm and 6–9:30pm; Sat noon–10pm; Sun noon–9pm.

Wykeham Arms GASTROPUB   A long-time favorite in central Winchester, the Wykeham lies behind a 200-year-old brick facade opposite the school. The inn-style dining room is furnished in a period style, with antiques or reproductions, a roaring log fire, chunky furniture, and a parquet floor. Food ranges from simple, hearty dishes like Wyk Pie (minced beef topped with potato and cheese) to contemporary flourishes such as seared scallops served with cauliflower purée and fried seaweed. No children 13 and under.

75 Kingsgate St. www.fullershotels.com. ℂ **01962/853834.** Reservations recommended on weekends. Main courses £9–£16. MC, V. Daily noon–3pm and 6–9pm.

Shopping

Winchester is crammed with excellent shops. The artisan stores along **Parchment Street** and **Great Minster Street** provide plenty of window browsing. Fill up your suitcases at **Cadogan,** 30–31 The Square (www.cadoganandcompany.co.uk; ℂ **01962/ 877399**), which carries traditional woolens, shirts, and accessories for men and women. For a unique piece of jewelry, silver tableware, or a handmade hat, stop by designer Carol Darby's **Free Spirit ★,** 6 Little Minster St. (ℂ **01962/867671**). The oldest book dealer in town is **P&G Wells,** 11 College St. (www.bookwells.co.uk; ℂ **01962/852016**), offering both new releases and local interest titles. At **World of Beads,** 1 Stonemasons Court, Parchment St. (www.worldofbeads.co.uk; ℂ **01962/ 861255**), you can buy all you need to create your own piece of jewelry from glass and semiprecious stones—or design it and have them make it for you (£12 extra).

The city's farmers' market, on the second and final Sunday mornings of every month, is among the best in England. See www.hampshirefarmersmarkets.co.uk.

Entertainment & Nightlife

Your best spots for a decent pint are the tiny, traditional bar at the **Eclipse,** 25 The Square (ℂ **01962/865676**); or, if you don't mind a gentle 10-minute walk from the center, the **Black Boy ★,** 1 Wharf Hill (www.theblackboypub.com; ℂ **01962/ 861754**). The latter is a freehouse specializing in local ales. In 2011, the same owners opened the **Black Bottle,** 4 Bridge St. (www.theblackbottle.co.uk; ℂ **01962/ 621563**), where you can perch on rustic benches under a low-slung ceiling to enjoy an interesting range of wines by the glass or bottle.

For a dose of culture, the eclectic program at the **Theatre Royal Winchester,** Jewry Street (www.theatreroyalwinchester.co.uk; ℂ **01962/840440**), might include anything from mainstream comedy to touring opera or a children's show.

Where to Stay

Hotel du Vin ★★   Everything's cozy at this wine-themed boutique inn built into a town house that dates from 1715. It brings a touch of urban chic to Winchester, with rooms that are intimate and contemporary without being aggressively overdesigned; 2012 saw a major refurbishment of 21 out of 24 units. Superior rooms are

📎 DAY-TRIPPING IN THE test VALLEY

Join the dots in the gentle countryside around **Romsey,** along the banks of the River Test, to create a day trip with something for the entire family. **Mottisfont Abbey** ★, near Romsey (www.nationaltrust.org.uk/mottisfont; ✆ **01794/340757**), began as a 13th-century Augustinian priory before being transformed (thanks to the Reformation) into a grand, riverside private home. The gardens are radiant in the height of summer, especially the **walled rose garden** ★★, home to Britain's national collection of old-fashioned roses. Perfumes and colors are in full effect during June, when the garden gets very busy on weekends. Admission costs £8 adults, £4 children 5 to 16. Hours are 10am to 5pm daily from late February through October; a winter garden was inaugurated in 2011, and that's open November through January Friday to Monday 10am to 5pm. Nearby **Broadlands** (www.broadlandsestates.co.uk; ✆ **01794/505010**), one of the most stately examples of Palladian architecture in southern England,

was landscaped by Capability Brown in the 18th century. It was the family home of Earl Mountbatten until he was assassinated by the Provisional IRA in 1979. The estate is open to visitors in summer only, Monday to Friday from 1 to 5:30pm. Admission costs £8 for adults, £4 for children aged 5 to 16, which includes a guided tour of the interior. The excellent 2011 addition to **Paultons Family Theme Park,** Ower, near Romsey (www.paultonspark.co.uk; ✆ **023/8081-4455**), is Peppa Pig World, aimed at under-5s, which joins fairly gentle roller coasters, a fun log ride, and other theme-park favorites ideal for children 7 to 12. Admission costs £24 per person (seniors pay £21.50), with children under 1m (3 ft., 4 in.) entering free. You can save £3 each by pre-booking tickets online. Paultons is open daily between April and September (and during off-season school breaks), Thursday to Monday in October, Friday to Monday in March, and weekends only in November and December.

larger, with handsprung, king-size beds and views over the walled rear garden; garden rooms were entirely remodeled. The modern English take on French fare in the on-site **Bistro** is good value. Stay-and-eat packages tend to be priced the best on Sunday nights.

14 Southgate St., Winchester, Hampshire SO23 9EF. www.hotelduvin.com. ✆ **01962/841414.** Fax 01962/843285. 24 units. £140–£250 double. AE, MC, V. Free parking. **Amenities:** Restaurant; bar. *In room:* A/C, TV, hair dryer, MP3 docking station, Wi-Fi (free).

Lainston House ★★   The beauty of this restored William and Mary redbrick manor-house hotel strikes visitors as they approach via a curving, tree-lined drive. It's situated on 63 acres of rolling land and linked with the name Lainston in The Domesday Book. Elegance is key inside the stately main house, where panoramic, large suites are located. Double rooms are less spacious, but are also comfortably fitted and furnished in rich, traditional tones—and every room comes with a choice of pillows from a menu of options.

Woodman Lane, Sparsholt, Winchester, Hampshire SO21 2LT. www.lainstonhouse.com. ✆ **01962/776088.** Fax 01962/776672. 50 units. £245–£365 double; £485–£525 suite. AE, DC, MC, V. Free parking. Off the B3420, 1½ miles northwest of Winchester. **Amenities:** Restaurant; bar; 2 outdoor tennis courts; exercise room; room service. *In room:* TV/DVD, Jacuzzi (in some), hair dryer, MP3 docking station (in some), Wi-Fi (free).

PORTSMOUTH ★ & SOUTHSEA ★

75 miles SW of London; 19 miles SE of Southampton

There are at least 10 places in the world called **Portsmouth,** but the original is this old port city on the Hampshire coast, seat of the British Navy for 500 years. The seaport was rebuilt after World War II devastation, and its **Historic Dockyard** is an essential stop for visitors interested in the nautical history of England. From Sally Port, in **Old Portsmouth,** countless naval heroes have embarked to fight England's battles, including on June 6, 1944, when Allied troops set sail to invade occupied France.

Genteel **Southsea,** adjoining Portsmouth, is a traditional seaside resort with a pebble beach, two fine restaurants, and a small **D-Day Museum** displaying the Overlord Embroidery, England's postwar answer to the Bayeux Tapestry. It's also the better accommodation base. Ascend Portsmouth's harborfront **Spinnaker Tower** to see this "twin city" laid out below you.

Essentials

GETTING THERE   Trains from London's Waterloo Station stop at both local stations, Portsmouth & Southsea (for the center) and Portsmouth Harbour (for the Historic Dockyard). There's a frequent service throughout the day, and the trip takes between 1½ and 2 hours, costing around £36 for a round-trip. To reach Southsea from Portsmouth Harbour, take bus no. 5, 6, or 700 from the interchange outside the rail station.

By car from London and points north, head south on the M3 then turn east on the M27 and follow signs.

VISITOR INFORMATION   The **Visitor Information Service** is inside the D-Day Museum (see below; www.visitportsmouth.co.uk; ✆ 023/9282-6722). It is open the same hours as the museum, and sells discounted tickets for a handful of local attractions. You can pick up event news and also the odd deal by following them at twitter.com/visitportsmouth.

TOURS   Most weekends of the year (usually Sun 2:30pm), you can join a guided walk on such themes as "Authors of Southsea," "Henry VIII," or the popular evening ghost walk. Buy tickets (£3 adults, free for children) at the Visitor Information Service.

Exploring Portsmouth Harbour

You can buy a combination ticket that includes admission to several attractions on the **Portsmouth Historic Dockyard,** the highlight of any visit to the city: HMS *Victory,* Victorian fighting ship HMS *Warrior 1860,* the Mary Rose Museum, and the National Museum of the Royal Navy are linked on a single admission that costs £21.50 for adults, £18.35 for seniors, £16 for children 5 to 15 and students, and £62 for a family. The ticket also includes a boat trip around the harbor (summer months only). Stop by the visitor center at the **Historic Dockyard,** The Hard (✆ 023/9272-8060), or buy tickets online at www.historicdockyard.co.uk. The center is open daily 10am to 5:30pm (Apr–Oct 6pm). Last ticket sales are 1½ hours before closing. There's also plenty going on at twitter.com/PompeyDockyard.

HMS Victory ★★★ ☺ ICON   The highlight of any visit to the Historic Dockyard is an engaging 45-minute guided tour of Admiral Lord Nelson's flagship, a 104-gun, first-rate ship that is the oldest commissioned warship in the world, built from over 3,000 trees and launched May 7, 1765. It earned its fame on October 21, 1805, in the Battle of Trafalgar, when the English scored a victory over the combined Spanish and French fleets. The spot on the upper deck where Nelson was shot by a French sniper is marked with a plaque, as is the area below-decks where he lived the final minutes of his illustrious life. His flagship, after being taken to Gibraltar for repairs, returned to Portsmouth with Nelson's body pickled in one of the ship's brandy barrels. Tall visitors should be prepared for lots of ducking while below-decks.

The Hard. www.historicdockyard.co.uk. ✆ **023/9272-8060.** See above for combined admission prices. Apr–Oct daily 10am–4:30pm; Nov–Mar daily 10am–3:45pm. Closed Dec 24–26.

Mary Rose & Museum ★★ HISTORIC SITE/MUSEUM The *Mary Rose*, flagship of the fleet of King Henry VIII's wooden men-of-war, sank in the Solent in 1545 in full view of the king. In 1982, the *Mary Rose* once again broke the water's surface after more than 4 centuries on the ocean floor, not exactly in shipshape condition, but surprisingly well preserved. It is now showcased by a £35-million museum constructed over the remains of the vessel and opened in 2012. The hull and more than 20,000 items brought up by divers constitute England's most significant aquatic archeological discovery. On display are the equipment of the ship's barber-surgeon, with cabin saws, knives, ointments, and plaster all ready for use; longbows and arrows, some still in shooting order; carpenters' tools; leather jackets; and some fine lace and silk.

The Hard. www.historicdockyard.co.uk. ✆ **023/9272-8060.** See above for combined admission prices. Apr–Oct daily 10am–5:30pm; Nov–Mar daily 10am–4:45pm. Closed Dec 24–26.

Millennium Promenade Walk ★ WALKING TRAIL This marked waterfront walk links The Hard, by Portsmouth Harbour, with atmospheric **Old Portsmouth ★**, where you can explore abandoned sea defenses and the few remaining streets of the original maritime city—the rest took severe punishment during World War II. Pass occasional clapboard houses and walk a winding cobblestoned lane to finish with a pint of ale at the **Still & West ★**, Bath Square (✆ **023/9282-1567**), Portsmouth's best quayside pub. Its terrace enjoys harbor views. The walk should take under 45 minutes at a leisurely pace.

Start from Spinnaker Tower (see below) and follow pavement markers. No phone. Open 24 hr.

National Museum of the Royal Navy MUSEUM This is the only museum in Britain devoted exclusively to the history of the Royal Navy. The best of the multimedia displays focuses on the "real" Horatio Nelson, the revered Admiral and naval hero who lost an eye at the Siege of Calvi in 1794, lost an arm at the Battle of Tenerife in 1797, and was killed aboard HMS *Victory* at Trafalgar in 1805. Additionally, there are unique collections of ship models, naval ceramics, figureheads, medals, uniforms, weapons, and other naval memorabilia. Opening may be occasionally disrupted between 2012 and 2014, as a major expansion of the museum is undertaken.

The Hard. www.royalnavalmuseum.org. ✆ **023/9272-8060.** See above for combined admission prices. Apr–Oct daily 10am–5pm; Nov–Mar daily 10am–4:15pm. Closed Dec 24–26.

Royal Navy Submarine Museum ☺ MUSEUM Across Portsmouth Harbour in Gosport lies sub HMS *Alliance*, now part of the Submarine Museum, which traces the history of underwater warfare and life from the earliest days to the present. Alongside the refurbished historical galleries, the highlight is the 45-minute tour of HMS

Portsmouth & Southsea

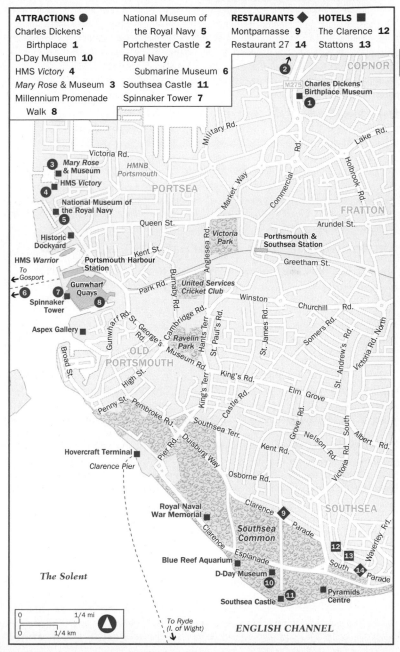

ATTRACTIONS ●
Charles Dickens' Birthplace **1**
D-Day Museum **10**
HMS *Victory* **4**
Mary Rose & Museum **3**
Millennium Promenade Walk **8**

National Museum of the Royal Navy **5**
Portchester Castle **2**
Royal Navy Submarine Museum **6**
Southsea Castle **11**
Spinnaker Tower **7**

RESTAURANTS ◆
Montparnasse **9**
Restaurant 27 **14**

HOTELS ■
The Clarence **12**
Stattons **13**

COPNOR

M275
Charles Dickens' Birthplace Museum **1**

Military Rd.
Lake Rd.
Victoria Rd.
Mary Rose & Museum **3**
HMNB Portsmouth
HMS *Victory* **4**
National Museum of the Royal Navy **5**
Historic Dockyard
HMS *Warrior*
To Gosport
Spinnaker Tower **7**
Gunwharf Quays **8**
Aspex Gallery

Rd.
Holbrook Rd.
FRATTON
PORTSEA
Queen St.
Market Way
Commercial
Arundel St.
Anglesea Rd.
Victoria Park
Porthsmouth & Southsea Station
Kent St.
Greetham St.
Portsmouth Harbour Station
Park Rd.
Burnaby Rd.
United Services Cricket Club
Winston
Churchill Rd.
Somers Rd.
St. Andrew's Rd.
Victoria Rd. North

Gunwharf Rd.
St. George's Rd.
Cambridge Rd.
Hants Terr.
Ravelin Park
Museum Rd.
St. Paul's Rd.
St. James Rd.
Broad St.
OLD PORTSMOUTH
High St.
King's Terr.
King's Rd.
Castle Rd.
Elm Grove
St. Andrew's Rd.
Grove Rd.
Nelson Rd.
Victoria Rd. South
Albert Rd.
Penny St.
Pembroke Rd.
Southsea Terr.
Kent Rd.

Hovercraft Terminal
Clarence Pier
Pier Rd.
Duisburg Way
Osborne Rd.

Royal Naval War Memorial
Clarence Parade
Montparnasse **9**
SOUTHSEA
Waverley Rd.
Southsea Common
The Clarence **12**
Stattons **13**
Esplanade
Blue Reef Aquarium
D-Day Museum **10**
Restaurant 27 **14**
South Parade
Southsea Castle **11**
Pyramids Centre

The Solent

0   1/4 mi
0   1/4 km

To Ryde (I. of Wight)

ENGLISH CHANNEL

Alliance itself; after a brief audiovisual presentation, visitors are guided through the boat by ex-submariners.

To reach Gosport, take one of the ferries that depart from behind Portsmouth Harbour rail station; between four and eight depart every hour, taking 10 minutes, with a round-trip price of £2.50. In summer, combo tickets with the Portsmouth Harbour Waterbus are available; see www.portsmouth-boat-trips.co.uk.

Haslar Jetty Rd., Gosport. www.submarine-museum.co.uk. ℭ **023/9251-0354.** Admission £10 adults, £7 children 5–15 and students, £8 seniors, £28 family ticket. Apr–Oct daily 10am–5:30pm; Nov–Mar Wed–Sun 10am–4:30pm. Last tour 1 hr. before closing. Closed Dec 24–27 and Dec 31–Jan 3.

Spinnaker Tower ★ ☺ OBSERVATION POINT Towering over Portsmouth Harbour, this 170-m (558-ft.) sail-shaped structure has become (literally) one of the biggest attractions along the south coast. On a clear day, you can see for 23 miles in all directions—including across the Solent to the Isle of Wight. From up there, you can also experience the thrill of "walking on air," by daring to traverse the largest glass floor in Europe.

Gunwharf Quays. www.spinnakertower.co.uk. ℭ **023/9285-7520.** Admission £8.25 adults, £7.40 students and seniors, £5 children 3–15, free for children 2 and under. Children 15 and under must be accompanied by an adult. Daily 10am–6pm (Aug also Sun–Thurs until 7:30pm).

Exploring the Rest of Portsmouth & Southsea

Charles Dickens' Birthplace HISTORIC HOME This 1804 small terrace house, in which the Victorian novelist was born in 1812, has been restored and furnished to illustrate the middle-class tastes of the early 19th century. Each first Sunday of the month sees a reading of the author's work at 3pm.

393 Old Commercial Rd. (off Mile End Rd./M275 and off Kingston Rd.), Portsmouth. www.charles dickensbirthplace.co.uk. ℭ **023/9282-7261.** Admission £4 adults, £3.50 seniors, £3 children 6–17, free for accompanied children 17 and under. Apr–Sept daily 10am–5pm.

D-Day Museum ★ MUSEUM The highlight of this museum, devoted to the Normandy landings, is the Overlord Embroidery, a modern-day Bayeux Tapestry that creatively illustrates the background to and story of Operation Overlord, the D-Day landings of June 6, 1944. The giant appliquéd embroidery, believed to be the largest of its kind (82m/272 ft. long and 1m/3 ft. high), was commissioned in 1968, designed by Sandra Lawrence, and took 20 women of the Royal School of Needlework 5 years to complete. An audiovisual program includes displays such as reconstructions of various stages of the mission, and there's a comprehensive collection of memorabilia about the landings.

Clarence Esplanade, Southsea. www.ddaymuseum.co.uk. ℭ **023/9282-7261.** Admission £6.50 adults, £5.50 seniors, £4.50 students and children 6–17, free for accompanied children 17 and under. Apr–Sept daily 10am–5:30pm; Oct–Mar daily 10am–5pm. Closed Dec 24–26.

Portchester Castle ★ CASTLE On a spit of land on the northern edge of the Solent are the remains of this castle, plus a Norman church. Built in the late 12th century by King Henry II, the castle is set inside the Roman walls of a 3rd-century fort first built as a defense against Saxon pirates, when this was the northwestern frontier of the declining Roman Empire. Though the original castle itself is long gone, the keep remains (and was used as a prison during the Napoleonic Wars), and from it you can take in a panoramic view of the harbor and coast. The free historical audioguide is excellent.

Portsmouth's twin, Southsea, makes the better base if you're staying here overnight. As well as two of the most stylish urban hotels in Hampshire (see below), this former seaside resort has fine dining worth traveling miles for. For indie shopping, browse the eclectic boutiques along **Marmion Road,** between Richmond Place and Victoria Road South.

Church Rd., Portchester (off the A27 btw. Portsmouth and Southampton, near Fareham). www. english-heritage.org.uk. ✆ **023/9237-8291.** Admission £4.80 adults, £4.30 seniors, £3 children 5–15, free for children 4 and under. Apr–Sept daily 10am–6pm; Oct–Mar Sat–Sun 10am–4pm.

Southsea Castle CASTLE   A fortress built of stones from Beaulieu Abbey in 1544 as part of King Henry VIII's coastal defense plan, the castle has been much altered since. It now houses exhibits that trace the development of Portsmouth as a military stronghold, as well as the naval history and the archeology of the area. It was from here that Henry VIII watched his flagship, the *Mary Rose,* sink in the Solent.

Clarence Esplanade, Southsea. www.southseacastle.co.uk. ✆ **023/9282-7261.** Free admission. Mar–Oct Tues–Sun 10am–5pm.

Where to Eat

Finding great food close to the Historic Dockyard isn't easy. Outlet retail mecca **Gunwarf Quays,** Portsmouth Harbour (www.gunwharf-quays.com; ✆ 023/9283-6700), is home to a number of quality, if unadventurous, chain restaurants such as Japanese-style Wagamama, Loch Fyne Seafood Bar, and eclectic, family-friendly joint, Giraffe. Alternatively, the **Old Customs House,** Gunwharf Quays (www.the oldcustomshouse.com; ✆ 023/9283-2333), serves hearty pies and a menu of pub classics in the atmospheric former revenue-men's headquarters, built in 1811. Main courses range between £8 and £12. There's Fuller's ales on tap—it's a good place for a pint even if you don't want to dine.

Montparnasse ★ ENGLISH/FRENCH   With a long established reputation for cooking the best food in the city, Montparnasse serves up a welcoming, intimate atmosphere in bijou bistro surrounds. The cooking is a now-familiar but superbly executed fusion of English and French flavors, with an emphasis on locally sourced meat and fish. Expect to be bowled over by such dishes as maple-roasted breast of pheasant with caramel walnuts, or filet of gilthead bream with prawn bon bon.

103 Palmerston Rd., Southsea. www.bistromontparnasse.co.uk. ✆ **023/9281-6754.** Reservations recommended. Main courses £14–£20; fixed-price 2-course dinner £32; fixed-price 3-course dinner £37. AE, MC, V. Tues–Sat noon–2pm and 7–9:30pm.

Restaurant 27 ★★ 🍴 CONTEMPORARY BRITISH   An unassuming side street off Southsea's fading esplanade is the unlikely home of one of Hampshire's genuine destination restaurants. Behind a whitewashed exterior, the contemporary dining room offers exciting, modern cooking to match. Menus change with the seasons, but you can expect the likes of 30-hour belly of pork with chervil root, prune, and licorice, or loin of lamb with hickory onions and bubble and squeak.

27a South Parade, Southsea. www.restaurant27.com. ✆ **023/9287-6272.** Reservations recommended. Fixed-price 3-course dinner £40; fixed-price lunch (Sun) £27. AE, MC, V. Wed–Sat 7–9:30pm; Sun noon–2:30pm.

The south coast's principal city, historic merchant port, and now passenger terminus isn't really a place for an extended stay. Its supremacy dated from Saxon times, when the Danish conqueror Cnut was proclaimed king here in 1017. Southampton was especially important to the Normans and helped them keep in touch with their French homeland. During World War II, some 31 million men set out from here (in World War I, more than twice that number), and Southampton was repeatedly bombed, destroying much of its old character. On the Western Esplanade is a memorial to the Pilgrims, who set out on their voyage to the New World from Southampton on August 15, 1620.

Opened in 2012, the city's main cultural draw is the **SeaCity Museum,** Civic Centre, Commercial Road (www.seacity museum.co.uk; ✆ 023/8083-3007). Its exhibits trace the history and importance of Southampton's relationship with the sea—immigration and emigration are major themes. Also here is "Titanic Story": RMS *Titanic* was partly built in Southampton and sailed from here on its fateful, fatal voyage. Admission costs £8.50 for adults, £6 for seniors, students, and children ages 5 to 16. It's open daily 10am to 5pm.

Next door, the modest but interesting **Southampton City Art Gallery,** Civic Centre (✆ 023/8083-3007), houses an eclectic collection that includes everything from altarpieces to abstracts, and spans almost 700 years of painting. Among mostly minor works, one highlight is Pre-Raphaelite Edward Burne-Jones's series of 10 gouache studies for the *Perseus Story* (1878). Admission is free, and it's also open daily 10am to 5pm.

The **Tudor House and Garden,** Bugle St. (www.tudorhouseandgarden.com; ✆ 023/8083-4242), is a restored, medieval timbered merchant's house stuffed with muiltimedia exhibits. Aimed squarely at family groups, displays tell the story of the house from the Middle Ages through the Georgian and Victorian periods. It's educational fun. Admission costs £4.75 for adults, £3.75 for seniors, and £3 for children ages 7 to 16. It's open daily from 10am to 5pm.

If you have an early ferry to catch or arrive late, the best place both to eat and to overnight is the **White Star ★,** 28 Oxford St. (www.whitestartavern. co.uk; ✆ 023/8082-1990). Stripped wood floors and bookish decor in the bar-style dining room complement a gently fashionable atmosphere and clientele. Full meals on the changing menu might include such classics-with-a-twist as haunch of local venison with celeriac vanilla mash and red cabbage, and there's a selection of creative lunchtime "small plates" (£4 each) such as devilled whitebait with garlic saffron mayo. Main courses range from £11 to £18 at dinner. Upstairs, midsize rooms are decorated in muted, modern tones with walk-in showers and Egyptian cotton fabrics. As you climb the price grades, rooms get bigger and add a roll-top tub. Doubles cost £99 to £149.

The city's **Visitor Information Centre,** inside Central Library, Civic Centre (www. visit-southampton.co.uk; ✆ 023/8083-3333), is open Monday to Friday 9:30am to 5pm, Saturday 9:30am to 4pm.

Where to Stay

IN SOUTHSEA

The Clarence ★★ This large Edwardian residence has been given a makeover in a 1920s style, and is the ideal choice for a romantic weekend. Rooms are decorated with dazzling feature walls, and all include king-size beds and sharp, contemporary embellishments. Executive rooms are worth the £10 to £20 extra, for much more space: Our favorites are room no. 1, which has a sunken bath, and cherry-toned no. 5, with more traditional decor, a super-king-size bed, and a double hydromassage tub. All that's missing from an almost perfect boutique package is a good view. Children 17 and under are not accepted.

Clarence Rd., Southsea, Hampshire PO5 2LQ. www.theclarencehotel.co.uk. © **023/9287-6348.** Fax 023/9229-6346. 8 units. £95–£225 double. Rates include English breakfast. AE, MC, V. Free parking. **Amenities:** Bar; room service. *In room:* A/C, TV, hair dryer, movie library, Jacuzzi (in some), Wi-Fi (free).

Stattons ★★ 🏠 On the outside, it's a three-story, red-brick corner villa in a handsome Southsea side street. Inside, it's a boutique hotel where a creative mix of oriental and Victorian decor combine with verve and elegance. High ceilings are hung with glass chandeliers, walls are decked in bold-print or textured wallpaper, and rooms are dressed with solid-wood furniture and period mirrored dressing tables sourced from local emporium, Victoriana. It's showy, certainly, but also warm and friendly.

6 Florence Rd., Southsea, Hampshire PO5 2NE. www.stattonshotel.co.uk. © **023/9282-3409.** Fax 023/9200-3965. 9 units. £99–£179 double. Rates include English breakfast. AE, MC, V. Free parking. **Amenities:** Bar. *In room:* TV, hair dryer, Wi-Fi (free).

THE NEW FOREST ★

95 miles SW of London; 10 miles W of Southampton

Covering 140,000 acres, the **New Forest National Park** is a tract of serene, rolling—and not entirely wooded—terrain largely demarcated by William the Conqueror as an 11th-century private hunting preserve. Henry VIII loved to hunt deer here, but he also used it to build up the British naval fleet by supplying oak and other hard timbers to the boatyards at **Buckler's Hard** on the Beaulieu River, the remains of which survive. It was Henry, too, who oversaw the 16th-century Dissolution of **Beaulieu Abbey,** the grounds of which are now home to the **National Motor Museum.**

Away from the main roads, where signs warn drivers of wild New Forest dwarf ponies and deer, you'll find a private world of pasture, heath, and mixed woodland. The smallest National Park in the U.K. is a haven of peace and quiet, ideal for walking, foraging, and **cycling**—and for sampling some of southern England's best country **pubs.** Autumn is the best time to visit, when summer crowds have thinned, the winding roads have emptied, and the full spectrum of woodland colors is in full effect.

Essentials

GETTING THERE   Direct trains leave London Waterloo half-hourly during the day for Brockenhurst, the main station in the heart of the New Forest. Journey time is around 1½ hours and costs from £40 for a round-trip. Minor New Forest stops like Sway, New Milton, and Ashurst are mostly served by local trains. Either change at Brockenhurst or connect from Southampton or Bournemouth.

If you're driving from Southampton, head west on the A35. From farther east and north, enter the New Forest from junction 1 or 2 of the M27 and, if possible, avoid the traffic bottleneck at Lyndhurst. Traffic queues in high season and on good-weather weekends can be alarmingly long.

GETTING AROUND   The relatively gentle contours of the New Forest are ideal for **cycle** touring. Either bring your own in the car—Lyndhurst is a natural start-point for a pedal-powered adventure—or rent. If you're arriving by train, try ideally located **New Forest Cycle Hire,** Brockenhurst Train Station (www.newforestcyclehire. co.uk; ℂ **01590/623407**). Mountain bikes cost £14 per day, children's bikes £6 to £7. Their website suggests excellent cycle routes for first-timers.

VISITOR INFORMATION   The **New Forest Visitor Information Centre,** Main Parking Lot, Lyndhurst (www.thenewforest.co.uk; ℂ **023/8028-2269**), is open daily from 10am to 5pm. The Centre is the best place to pick up maps and advice on walking trails suited to your group.

Exploring the New Forest

Cocoa lovers should stop at **Beaulieu Chocolate Studio** ★, High Street, Beaulieu (www.beaulieuchocolatestudio.co.uk; ℂ **01590/612279**). The shop's selection includes bars of artisan chocolate and individual chocolates with fillings ranging from the adventurous (chili and lime) to the everyday (runny orange and strawberry creams). It's all handmade on the tiny premises. Nearby **Exbury Gardens** ★, Exbury (www.exbury.co.uk; ℂ **023/8089-1203**), is known for its Rothschild Collection of rhododendrons, azaleas, and camellias. The magical 200-acre site is at its blooming best in spring. Admission costs £9.50 for adults, £9 seniors, and free for children 15 and under. The gardens open mid-March through October daily from 10am to 5pm. The attractive Georgian High Street at **Lymington** ★ is the best spot for window browsing—and also a staging post for a ferry to the **Isle of Wight** (p. 306).

Beaulieu ★ HISTORIC HOME/MUSEUM   This is a huge and varied family attraction that mixes authentic history with fun and fast cars. The **Palace House,** surrounded by gardens, was the gatehouse of an abbey before it was converted into a private residence in 1538—and it has remained in the family of resident Lord Montagu ever since. Cistercian **Beaulieu Abbey** ★ was founded here in 1204, and although much was destroyed during the Reformation overseen by Henry VIII, you can still enjoy the tranquil cloisters and herb garden, and see the lay brothers' refectory.

The 2011-renovated **National Motor Museum** ★★, one of the most comprehensive automotive museums in the world, displays more than 250 vehicles. Famous autos include four land-speed record holders, among them Donald Campbell's *Bluebird*. Some of the vehicles used in James Bond movies are on display, as well as those once used by everybody from Eric Clapton to Marlene Dietrich. Themed tours of the collection run daily at noon and 2:30pm.

Beaulieu (5 miles southeast of Lyndhurst and 14 miles southwest of Southampton). www.beaulieu. co.uk. ℂ **01590/612345.** Admission £19 adults, £17.50 seniors and students, £11.25 children 13–17, £9.50 children 5–12, £50 family ticket. June–Sept daily 10am–6pm; Oct–May daily 10am– 5pm. Closed Dec 25. Bus: 112 from Lymington or Hythe (Mon–Sat only).

Buckler's Hard ★ HISTORIC SITE   Two unassuming rows of 18th-century shipwrights' cottages, tumbling down to the banks of the tidal River Beaulieu, are all that's left of one of the most significant shipyards in British history. It was here that much of Nelson's fleet was built, including the admiral's favorite ship, *Agamemnon,* as well as *Euryalus* and *Swiftsure.* The Maritime Museum exhibits focus on the village's shipbuilding history and on Henry Adams, master shipbuilder, who lived in the cottage closest to the dock (now the Master Builder's House Hotel; see below).

Drinking & Dining Pubs in the New Forest

The New Forest is blessed with an array of great country pubs—often dining destinations in themselves, as well as places to just enjoy a pint of local ale. The bar at the **Master Builder's House Hotel** (see below) also serves tasty, affordable fare to nonguests.

Mill at Gordleton ★★ This tranquil, refined take on a riverside inn comes complete with babbling brook and weeping willows in the garden. The management has a firm commitment to locally sourced, organic produce, which is prepared with skill in such dishes as English wild duck with thyme braised potatoes, and red cabbage. There's also a bar menu with simpler, cheaper lunches and snacks. Silver St., Hordle, nr. Lymington. www.themillatgordleton.co.uk. ℭ **01590/682219.** Reservations recommended. Main courses £17–£27. Lunch and dinner daily.

Oak Inn The main menu of pub staples is a little uninspiring, but plenty of locally-landed fish dishes star on a blockbuster specials board. Dive into the likes of a cassolette of flounder, perch, and mussels. Sit inside under a low-slung beamed ceiling or out in a covered garden. Portions are large.

Pinckney Lane, Bank, nr. Lyndhurst. www.fullers.co.uk. ℭ **023/8028-2350.** Reservations recommended. Main courses £10–£17. Lunch and dinner daily. No children 10 and under in the evening.

Red Lion ★ This cozy, mazelike inn seems still to have one foot in the 15th century. The menu is in the "traditional pub grub" mold, but dishes like ham and chips with a free-range egg, or slow roasted Hampshire pork belly are well executed. In summer, the garden is one of the best spots in the New Forest for sitting in the sun with a pint of ale from nearby Ringwood brewery. Rope Hill, Boldre, nr. Lymington. www.theredlionboldre.co.uk. ℭ **01590/673177.** Reservations recommended on weekends. Main courses £9–£17. Lunch and dinner daily.

Ship in Distress ★ An unremarkable exterior hides a fine place for not only liquid sustenance but also some of the best seafood in the county. Dishes change with the catch: Expect the likes of roast filet of cod with black pudding and celeriac mille feuille or splash out on the mixed local shellfish platter. 66 Stanpit, Christchurch. www.theshipindistress.com

---

The walk back to Beaulieu, 2½ miles through the woodland along the riverbank, is well marked.

Buckler's Hard. www.bucklershard.co.uk. ℭ **01590/616203.** Admission £6.20 adults, £5.80 seniors, £4.40 children 5–17, £18 family ticket. River cruise (Easter–Oct only) £4.50 adults, £4 seniors, £2.50 children, £11 family ticket. Nov–Feb daily 10am–4:30pm; Mar–June and Sept–Oct daily 10am–5pm; July–Aug daily 10am–5:30pm.

Christchurch Priory ★ 📷 CHURCH   The founding stones of this imposing, yet intimate sacred space were laid in the first decades after the Norman conquest of England. The rounded arches of the nave arcades are typical of an Augustinian priory church dating to the 1090s, but the Great Quire and Lady Chapel, separated by a magnificent stone **Quire Screen ★** dating to 1320, are products of the later Gothic style. Protruding from the wall above the ambulatory is the priory's so-called "Miraculous Beam," placed there by a mysterious carpenter said to be the resurrected Jesus Christ himself—hence the church's (and town's) re-christening in the 12th century.

Quay Rd., Christchurch. www.christchurchpriory.org. ℭ **01202/485804.** Free admission (£3 donation appreciated). Mon–Sat 9:30am–5pm; Sun 2:15–5:30pm; often closes 1 hr. earlier in winter.

Where to Eat & Stay

Master Builder's House Hotel ★   The phrase "snug and secluded" could have been invented for the remote former house of Admiral Nelson's "master builder," Henry Adams (1744–1805). The decor throughout is appropriately nautical, and brought alive with flashes of contemporary color and decorative bric-a-brac. Superior rooms (all in the wonderfully labyrinthine original building) have an estuary and garden view, and are well worth the extra money over standard rooms in the new wing. Opened in 2011, the **Cottage** provides luxurious accommodation over two floors inside one of the original row houses at Buckler's Hard (see above).

The **cozy, wood-beamed Yachtsman's Bar** serves tasty dishes like dressed Lymington crab or a daily pie served with mash and seasonal vegetables, with main courses ranging between £9.50 and £20. There's also a formal **restaurant.**

Buckler's Hard, Hampshire SO42 7XB. www.themasterbuilders.co.uk. ✆ **01590/616253.** 26 units, 8 in historic building. £130–£205 double; £220–£275 Cottage. Rates include English breakfast. MC, V. Free parking. Min. 2-night stay in Cottage. **Amenities:** 2 restaurants; bar; bike rental (1 wk. notice required); room service; Wi-Fi (free). *In room:* TV, DVD (on request), hair dryer.

Montagu Arms Hotel ★   The gnarled old ivy clinging to the brick walls of this inn in the heart of Beaulieu village tells you what to expect inside. A baronial ground floor oozes Olde England (garden walls were built with stones salvaged from Beaulieu Abbey after it was demolished by Henry VIII). Bedrooms are decorated in the English-country-house tradition, with lavish use of chintz fabrics, and come in a range of shapes and sizes. Those overlooking the ornamental garden are the most tranquil. The Terrace **restaurant** (closed Mon) serves up French-inspired fine dining using New Forest produce. A 2-course set lunch costs £19; a la carte dinner is £65.

Palace Lane, Beaulieu, Hampshire SO42 7ZL. www.montaguarmshotel.co.uk. ✆ **01590/624467.** Fax 01590/612188. 22 units. £148–£238 double Sun–Thurs; £198–£348 double Fri–Sat. Rates include English breakfast. AE, MC, V. Free parking. **Amenities:** 2 restaurants; 2 bars; use of nearby health club & spa; bike rental; room service. *In room:* TV, hair dryer, Wi-Fi (free).

The Pig ★★★ 🍴   This woodland "restaurant with rooms" is the sort of informal, utterly relaxing hideaway you just sink into. Throughout the updated manor house, floorboards are stripped, antiques are stylishly scattered, and a Georgian palette of greens and creams reigns. Three grades of hotel room (Snug, Comfy, and Spacious) vary in little besides size—all are a delight. There's a distinctive food philosophy in the **kitchen,** based on New Forest produce, vegetables from their own gardens, home-cured meats, and foraged ingredients when available—it's largely sourced from within 25 miles, and is served in a lively, shabby-chic orangery. Main courses such as roast Hampshire lamb rump with broad bean hummus range from £14 to £21.

Beaulieu Rd., Brockenhurst, Hampshire SO42 7QL. www.thepighotel.co.uk. ✆ **01590/622354.** 26 units. £125–£175 double Mon–Thurs; £155–£195 double Fri–Sun. Breakfast £10–£15. AE, DC, MC, V. Free parking. **Amenities:** Bar; restaurant; outdoor tennis courts; bike rental (£16/day); room service; babysitting. *In room:* TV/DVD, hair dryer, Wi-Fi (free).

THE ISLE OF WIGHT ★

91 miles SW of London; 4 miles S of Southampton

A trip to the Isle of Wight is like stepping back in time. This diamond-shaped island at the mouth of the Solent measures just 13 miles from Cowes in the north to St. Catherine's Point in the south, and 23 miles from Alum Bay in the west to the easternmost point, near Bembridge. It is known for its family-friendly, sandy **beaches,** its 67-mile **Coastal Path,** and its ports, long favored by the yachting set.

The island has attracted such literary figures as Alfred, Lord Tennyson, and Charles Dickens. Tennyson wrote his poem "Crossing the Bar" en route across the Solent from Lymington to **Yarmouth.** Queen Victoria lived (and died) on the island, making her home at **Osborne House.** More recently, Jimi Hendrix headlined the iconic 1970 Isle of Wight Festival, just 3 weeks before his death.

GETTING THERE   Efficient car and passenger ferries link the Isle of Wight with Portsmouth, Southampton, and Lymington, on the edge of the New Forest.

Red Funnel (www.redfunnel.co.uk; ✆ 0844/844-9988) operates between 12 and 18 daily vehicle ferry services from Southampton to East Cowes; the trip takes around 1 hour. Car fares include up to six passengers, and are priced according to season and demand. Off season, look for deals that might go as low as £37 for the round-trip; in summer, fares of £150 aren't unusual. A quicker option is the **Red Jet,** a high-speed, passenger-only catamaran operating from Southampton's Town Quay and going to West Cowes; the trip takes 25 minutes. Fares vary slightly by season, but expect a round-trip fare to cost around £25 for adults, £17 for seniors, and £12 for children 5 to 15. Off-peak fares are a little lower.

Wightlink (www.wightlink.co.uk; ✆ 0871/376-1000) operates three routes. A passenger-only catamaran connects Portsmouth Harbour and Ryde, taking 20 minutes and costing £22 for adults, £17 seniors, and £12 for children, standard round-trip. Daytime departures are every 30 minutes in summer and every hour in winter. Ferries also connect Portsmouth with Fishbourne (40 min.), and Lymington with Yarmouth (35 min.), in West Wight. The latter two routes can accommodate cars, too. You might be able to secure a winter Super Saver fare for under £40 for a car and four passengers; in high summer, fares can cost quadruple that or more.

Hovertravel (www.hovertravel.co.uk; ✆ 08434/878887) provides the quickest route across the Solent, connecting Southsea with Ryde by hovercraft (for foot passengers only) in around 10 minutes. Standard adult round-trip tickets cost £23, £17 for seniors, and £12 for children 5 to 15. "Flights" generally depart hourly.

VISITOR INFORMATION   The island closed all its official walk-in tourist services in 2011, but information is available during business hours on ✆ 01983/813813 or at www.islandbreaks.co.uk. There are also private visitor information points at bus stations in Ryde, Newport, and Yarmouth. For events and festivals, also consult www.gowight.com or twitter.com/myisleofwight.

GETTING AROUND   A Rover ticket allows you unlimited travel on the island's bus network. A 24-hour Rover costs £10 for adults, £5 for children 5 to 18, and £20 for a family; 48-hour Rover tickets cost an extra 50%. A 1-week Freedom ticket costs £24, or £12 for children. For information, contact **Southern Vectis** (www.island buses.info; ✆ 0871/200-2233).

Roads are winding and scenic, so if you don't have a car, consider renting a bike or moped. Rentals are available at **Top Gear,** 1 Terminus Rd., Cowes (www.islecycle. co.uk; ✆ 01983/299056), and cost £15 per day for a bike (£10 if you pre-book). In Ryde, try **TAV Cycles,** 140 High St. (www.tavcycles.co.uk; ✆ 01983/812989), where cycles rent for £12 a day.

SPECIAL EVENTS   **Cowes Week** (www.cowesweek.co.uk) is the world's oldest sailing regatta, filling a week in early August each year with nautical high-jinks. The final Friday sees a major firework display. Set up in 2004 as "boutique" alternative to

Glastonbury, **Bestival** ★ (www.bestival.net) occupies Robin Hill Country Park for a long weekend in September. Expect the very best in electronica, indie rock, folk, and urban music. Book tickets well ahead of your arrival.

Exploring the Isle of Wight

Cowes is probably the island's most famous town, and the premier port for yachting in Britain. Henry VIII ordered the castle built here, now the headquarters of the Royal Yacht Squadron. In West Wight, **Yarmouth** ★ is prettier, a tiny port frequented all summer by yachties from the mainland. Yarmouth is also the jumping-off point for walking the most scenic stretch of the Isle of Wight's Coastal Path (see below).

The best island sands for children are at **Sandown,** but nearby **Shanklin** also has a decent beach and a more characterful, if slightly faded, Victorian esplanade. The preserved thatched cottages of **Shanklin Old Village** ★ provide a glimpse of how Victorian holidaymakers would have experienced Wight. Farther along the coast, **Ventnor** ★ is sometimes called the "Madeira of England" because it rises dramatically from the sea in a series of steep hills. It's resolutely Victorian in feel, packed with smart villas that are visibly influenced by the Gothic Revival architectural style, and our favorite Wight base. Inland, **Godshill** is another pretty roadside village.

Carisbrooke Castle ★ CASTLE   The chief claim to fame of this medieval castle is the fact that King Charles I was imprisoned (and tried to escape from) here prior to his execution in London in 1649. Within a largely intact ring of walls (climb up for classic Wight countryside views), you'll also find the 16th-century Well House, where, during periods of siege, donkeys took turns treading a large wheel connected to a rope that hauled up water from a well. Also inside the courtyard is a museum with exhibits on the social history of the Isle of Wight, the re-created bedroom used by Charles I, and displays on the later, tragic death here of Charles's daughter, Elizabeth.

Castle Hill, Newport (1¼ miles southwest of center). www.english-heritage.org.uk/iow. © **01983/ 522107.** Admission £7.30 adults, £6.60 seniors and students, £4.40 children 5–15. Apr–Sept daily 10am–5pm; Oct–Mar Sat–Sun 10am–4pm. Bus: 7 or 12.

Dinosaur Isle ☺ MUSEUM   This "interactive museum" is aimed squarely at dino-lovers in the 7 to 12 age range, and there's also an educational bent to the

 The Wight Stuff: Island Produce

The Isle of Wight is home to a small but reputable wine industry. At the island's biggest producer, **Rosemary Vineyard,** Smallbrook Lane, Ryde (www.rosemary vineyard.co.uk; © **01983/811084**), you can taste a range of regular and fruit wines. Whites are generally made from flowery German varietals; there's also a range of twice-fermented liqueurs (£9) made from local fruit such as elderberries and raspberries. Tasting is free and 30-minute winery tours run Saturday to Tuesday. The island is also famous for the quality of its garlic, and you'll find all things for alliophiles at the **Garlic Farm,** Mersley Lane, Newchurch (www. thegarlicfarm.co.uk; © **01983/867333**). On sale are pickles, garlic grappes grown on the farm, cookbooks, and more—even garlic beer. Isle of Wight seafood is excellent, and you'll find a fresh supply at **Ventnor Haven Fishery** (see below). Beer lovers should look out for ales made by island brewers **Yates** and **Goddards.**

exhibits. The collection mixes the serious (fossils, geology exhibits, and dinosaur skeletons) with the outright fun, including menacing dinosaur growls and a giant model of the largest former Wight inhabitant so far unearthed, the Iguanodon. The museum also runs **fossil walks ★** on local fossil-rich beaches, for which you should book ahead, or just take your finds to the desk and an inhouse expert will assess them for you.

Culver Parade, Sandown. www.dinosaurisle.com. ℂ **01983/404344.** Admission £5 adults, £4 seniors and students, £3.70 children 3–15. Fossil walks £4.80 adults, £3.20 children. Apr–Aug daily 10am–6pm; Sept–Oct daily 10am–5pm; Nov–Mar daily 10am–4pm (closures common in Jan; call ahead). Bus: 2, 3, or 8.

Isle of Wight Coastal Path ★ WALKING TRAIL Sixty-seven miles of gentle coastal path circumnavigate the island. For the best stretch, strike west from Yarmouth's main parking lot toward the sand cliffs of **Alum Bay** and the three chalk pinnacles known as the **Needles,** at the island's westernmost point. Once you've conquered the lighthouse, head east as far as **Freshwater Bay,** along a stretch well known to poet Tennyson, who lived for 40 years at nearby Faringford House (now a hotel). The sheltered pebble cove here is popular with families. Return to Yarmouth via a gladed cycleway that follows the Yar Estuary north. The whole circuit should take around 6 hours at a comfortable pace.

No phone. Open 24 hr.

Osborne House ★★ HISTORIC HOME Queen Victoria's most cherished residence owes much to the characteristic thoroughness of her beloved husband, Prince Albert, who contributed to the design of their honey-colored Italianate mansion. The rooms remain as Victoria knew them, down to the French piano she used to play and the cozy clutter of her sitting room. Grief-stricken at the death of Albert in 1861, she asked that Osborne House be kept as it was, and so it has been. The house is surrounded by lush, tranquil gardens, with a panoramic terrace that looks right across the Solent to Portsmouth's 21st-century Spinnaker Tower (p. 300). Victoria died on January 22, 1901, in her bedroom at Osborne House.

The Avenue, East Cowes (1 mile southeast of center). www.english-heritage.org.uk/iow. ℂ **01983/ 200022.** House and grounds £11.50 adults, £10.40 seniors and students, £6.90 children 5–15, £30 family ticket. Apr–Sept daily 10am–5pm; Oct and Mar Sat–Sun 10am–4pm; Nov–Feb (often grounds only) Sat–Sun 10am–4pm. Bus: 4 or 5.

Where to Eat

The best fish and chips on the island come from the fryer at **Ventnor Haven Fishery,** Esplanade, Ventnor (ℂ **01983/852176**), where a meal to go costs around £7 to £8. It's closed Sunday evening and all-day Monday.

El Toro Contento ★ TAPAS Taste authentic flavors from beyond these shores, and wash them down with a glass of Tempranillo. The glass-fronted main bar reeks of old Castile, with rustic wooden furniture and walls decorated with haphazardly hung maps of Spain. A long menu of authentic small platters includes the likes of shrimp cooked with garlic and sherry, and piquillo peppers stuffed with hake and crab.

2 Pier St., Ventnor. www.eltorocontento.co.uk. ℂ **01983/857600.** Reservations recommended. Tapas £3–£9. MC, V. Daily 5–10pm. Bus: 3 or 6.

New Inn ★ GASTROPUB This dining pub has earned its reputation over more than a decade. Fish is a specialty here, and the menu features favorites as well as sustainable alternatives like hake and megrim sole, alongside shellfish platters loaded with local crab and lobster. Meat eaters are catered for with the likes of breast of local pheasant with wild mushrooms, redcurrants, and rosemary sauce. If you prefer pub classics, try a doorstep sandwich, the ploughman's platter, or the fish pie. The wine list is way above the pub average and includes local bottles.

Mill Rd., Shalfleet. www.thenew-inn.co.uk. (©01983/531314. Reservations recommended. Main courses £10–£15. AE, MC, V. Daily noon–2:30pm and 6–9:30pm. Bus: 7.

Robert Thompson at the Hambrough ★★★ CONTEMPORARY EURO-PEAN   Inside a stylish boutique hotel (see below), this Michelin-starred restaurant is the finest on the island—and, in fact, among the best in Britain. Trained in some of the leading kitchens in England, chef Robert Thompson makes clever use of the island's bounty from sea and land. His best dishes have a seafood accent: Specifics depend on the catch, but expect the likes of pan-fried filet of red mullet with zucchini (courgette) tagliatelle and purple basil pesto.

Hambrough Rd., Ventnor. www.robert-thompson.com. (©**01983/856333.** Reservations required. 3-course lunch £32; 3-course dinner £60. DC, MC, V. Tues–Sat noon–1:30pm and 7–9:30pm. Bus: 3 or 6.

Where to Stay

For self-catering cottages or apartment rentals, consult local specialists **Wight Locations** (www.wightlocations.co.uk; © **01983/811418**) or **Island Cottage Holidays** (www.islandcottageholidays.com; © **01929/481555**). Prices on most Wight accommodations are highly seasonal: Expect a big discount midweek in winter, but your negotiating potential will be minimal in midsummer. If there's a festival on—particularly a major one like Cowes Week or Bestival—book well ahead of arrival.

Insider tip: Ask your hotel about special prices on ferry crossings; they may be able to save you up to £50 per car if you're coming in peak season.

The George ★   The island's best traditional hotel is at this former governor's residence dating from the 17th century. Between the quay and the castle, overlooking the Solent, this is a tranquil, wood-paneled oasis in the port beloved by yachties. The good-size bedrooms are individually decorated, the best retaining heavy wood paneling in keeping with the building's heritage. Restaurant **The Brasserie** ★ has a rep for the creative use of local produce, the best view of Yarmouth pier through floor-to-ceiling glass windows, and an exceptional English cheese board. Main courses at dinner range £16 to £23. *Insider tip:* The hotel website often advertises low-season, midweek doubles at £99.

Quay St., Yarmouth, Isle of Wight PO41 0PE. www.thegeorge.co.uk. (©**01983/760331.** Fax 01983/760425. 20 units. £190–£308 double. Rates include English breakfast. 2-night minimum Sat. AE, MC, V. Parking £6. **Amenities:** Restaurant; bar; room service. *In room:* A/C, TV, hair dryer. Bus: 7.

The Hambrough ★★   Not just a weekend bolthole, but a gateway to another world—from the moment you step through the door of this clifftop villa-turned-hotel. Piped classical music and sisal carpets are the warm-up for individually-decorated guest rooms that capture the essence of the contemporary English seaside. Decor is sophisticated and understated, mixing soft, muted colors and natural textures. The best rooms (nos. 1 and 2) are large, with panoramic balconies where you can relax, dine, and eat breakfast if you wish.

Hambrough Rd., Ventnor, Isle of Wight PO38 1SQ. www.robert-thompson.com. (©**01983/856333.** 7 units. £170–£300 double. Rates include English breakfast. MC, V. Free street parking. **Amenities:** Restaurant (Robert Thompson; see review, above); bar; bike rental; room service; babysitting. *In room:* TV/DVD, minibar, MP3 docking station, Wi-Fi (free). Bus: 3 or 6.

Seaview Hotel ★   Old-fashioned seaside charm is what the Isle of Wight is all about, and few places capture the mood as well as the Seaview. There's been a hotel here, within earshot of waves lapping the shore, since 1898. Rooms in the original building retain a traditional feel: Gold rooms at the front have handsome bay windows and Solent views. The annex is like a different hotel altogether: "Modern" rooms are much larger, decorated in pleasing, contemporary greys and taupes, and even have TVs in the bathroom. Take your pick. Both the restaurant and bars are popular with islanders.

High St., Seaview, Isle of Wight PO34 5EX. www.seaviewhotel.co.uk. Ⓕ **01983/612711.** Fax 01983/613729. 28 units. £100–£255 double. Rates include English breakfast. MC, V. Free street parking. **Amenities:** Restaurant; 2 bars. *In room:* TV/DVD, CD player, Wi-Fi (free). Bus: 8.

BOURNEMOUTH

104 miles SW of London; 31 miles SW of Southampton

This south-coast resort at the doorstep of the New Forest didn't just happen: **Bournemouth** was carefully planned and executed. The resort was developed back in Queen Victoria's day, when sea bathing became an institution, and the beach hut was "invented" here in 1908. It has Dorset's best **sandy beach** and is filled with an abundance of Victorian and Edwardian architecture.

Bournemouth's most distinguished feature is its chines—narrow, shrub-filled, steep-sided ravines scattered along the coastline. For the best view of them, walk along the waterfront promenade, appropriately called the **Undercliff.** These days, the artificial reef off adjacent **Boscombe** attracts a surfing crowd, who pack the sands alongside the traditional bucket-and-spade family visitors.

Essentials

GETTING THERE   A train from London's Waterloo Station to Bournemouth takes just under 2 hours, with frequent service throughout the day and round-trips from around £53. Bournemouth also has direct rail links with local stations in the New Forest, Birmingham, and Manchester.

If you're driving, take the M3 southwest from London then the M27 westbound, followed by the A31, and then the A338 south to Bournemouth. *Insider tip:* In summer months, the A31 and A338 can get very busy. Leave early, or bring plenty of patience.

VISITOR INFORMATION   The **Tourist Information Centre** is at Westover Road (www.bournemouth.co.uk; Ⓕ **0845/051-1700**). In July and August, it's open Monday to Saturday from 9:30am to 5pm, Sunday from 11am to 3pm. Between April and June, and during September and October, it's open Monday to Saturday 10am to 4:30pm. From November to March, hours are Monday to Saturday 10:30am to 4pm, except during December and January when it's closed Saturday. For more on local beaches and watersports, see www.coastwiththemost.com.

Exploring Bournemouth

Bournemouth & Boscombe Beach ★ ☺ BEACH   It's probably only worth a special journey here if you (or the children) enjoy passing time on the sands. This seaside resort serves 7 miles of uninterrupted beach stretching from Hengistbury Head to Alum Chine, 1½ miles of it sandwiched between the twin piers at Bournemouth and **Boscombe** ★. However, you should choose your spot carefully. Sands are quieter away from the piers, and families will enjoy the stretches around Westbourne or Southbourne, beyond Boscombe. Surfers, on the other hand, should make right for the artificial **Urban Reef,** 200m (656 ft.) offshore and just east of Boscombe Pier. Arrange lessons or hire equipment through **Sorted Surf Shop,** 42 Sea Rd., Boscombe (www.sortedsurfshop.co.uk; © 01202/399099).

If you want to do Boscombe in style, rent a designer **beach pod,** complete with kitchenette, at the contemporary Overstrand development (www.bournemouth beachhuts.co.uk © 0845/055-0968). A pod costs between £90 and £300 per week, depending on season.

www.coastwiththemost.com. No phone. Free admission. Open 24 hr.

Russell-Cotes Art Gallery & Museum ★ MUSEUM Museum fans will find an intriguing, slightly bizarre collection of exuberant Victoriana in the time-capsule that is this former home of the Russell-Cotes family. The owners were avid traveler-collectors and eclectic hoarders: Inside are stuffed faux marble busts, minor Victorian canvases—some in the pre-Raphaelite mold—Japanese, Moorish, Spanish, and Italian *objets,* and lashings of Gothic Revival design elements.

East Cliff Promenade. www.russell-cotes.bournemouth.gov.uk. © **01202/451858.** Free admission. Tues–Sun 10am–5pm.

Where to Eat

The **Green Room,** inside The Green House (see "Where to Stay," below) is another place to consider for fans of creative British cooking.

The Crab at Bournemouth ★★ SEAFOOD This glass-fronted restaurant almost opposite Bournemouth Pier is the best place in town to enjoy seafood in a contemporary, refined setting. (Not surprisingly, it's packed most weekends.) Dishes take their culinary influences from near and far, so expect to see the likes of local seared cod with brown shrimp and mussel broth alongside tagine of local monkfish with couscous, or tandoori whole sea bream. There are good options for meat lovers and vegetarians, too, but the seafood is the reason to come.

Exeter Rd. www.crabatbournemouth.com. © **01202/203601.** Reservations recommended. Main courses £16–£24; fixed-price lunch 2 courses £16, 3 courses £20. AE, DC, MC, V. Mon–Sat noon–2:30pm and 5:30–10pm; Sun noon–3pm and 5:30–9:30pm.

Urban Beach Café ★ INTERNATIONAL This laid-back two-floor boardwalk bar-restaurant brings a slice of Pacific styling to beachfront Boscombe. The cafe menu is informal, mixing local classics, like a sustainable fish pie, with the likes of Cornish mussels in garlic and white wine. At night, the dining moves upstairs, and adds more formal dishes like slow-braised Purbeck lamb with dauphinoise potatoes. You can also eat English breakfast until 11:30am daily, or just stop by for a beachfront coffee.

Overstrand, Undercliff Dr., Boscombe. www.urbanreef.com. © **01202/443960.** Reservations recommended. Main courses £9–£18. MC, V. Daily 9am–11pm (cafe menu until 5pm, dinner menu 6–10:30pm); closes 5pm Sun–Mon Nov–Mar.

Entertainment & Nightlife
THE ARTS & MUSIC
Bournemouth is an essential stop for most shows touring the U.K.—the **Bournemouth International Centre** ("the BIC") and **Pavilion** dominate the center of town, and both have a program that includes everything from children's spectaculars,

to bands, comedians, and musicals. Look for performances by the world-famous **Bournemouth Symphony Orchestra ★**, which offers regular local concerts. The venues have joined forces: Ticket information for either is available by calling ✆ **0844/576-3000,** or see www.bic.co.uk. If niche indie-rock is more your thing, check what's on at the **O2 Academy,** 576 Christchurch Rd. (www.o2academy bournemouth.co.uk; ✆ **0844/477-2000** for tickets).

THE PUB & BAR SCENE

You'll find Bournemouth's alt-fashionable bar crowd keeping much later hours on the squashy sofas and stripped-wood floors inside **Sixty Million Postcards ★**, 19–21 Exeter St. (www.sixtymillionpostcards.com; ✆ **01202/292697**). It's lively till late every night. Ale fans are in for a treat at the **Goat and Tricycle ★**, 27–29 West Hill Rd. (www.goatandtricycle.co.uk; ✆ **01202/314220**). This traditional pub has an ever-changing range of 11 or so cask ales on tap. Hours are noon to 11pm daily; it's in West Cliff, a 10-minute walk from the center. Downstairs, the **Urban Beach Café** (see above) is all about the bar after 6pm.

Where to Stay

Cottonwood Boutique Hotel   The mad, mod-rococo, shocking-pink and turquoise bar is trying to tell you something: This isn't the traditional seafront hotel you were expecting when you walked up. Spacious rooms are decorated in a vaguely Indian-inspired style, with bold feature walls and scattered secondhand furniture. The 2011 "boutique" makeover isn't perfect—and in areas, looks like it isn't quite finished—but it has certainly injected some 21st-century personality into one of Bournemouth's old stagers.

East Overcliff Dr., Bournemouth, Dorset BH1 3AP. www.quantumhotelgroup.co.uk. ✆ **01202/553183.** 32 units. £70–£210 double. AE, MC, V. Free parking. **Amenities:** Restaurant; bar; use of nearby pool (outdoor). *In room:* TV/DVD, hair dryer, Wi-Fi (free).

The Green House ★★   Eco-chic has arrived in Bournemouth in the shape of this quietly luxurious hotel in East Cliff. Opened in 2010, The Green House has good-sized, crisply designed rooms: All units in the Large and Master categories add roll-top baths (tubs) to a spec that includes designer decor and walk-in rainfall showers throughout. Sustainability is more than just a marketing gimmick here: The wallpaper was all printed with vegetable ink, flat-screen TVs are low-energy certified, and even the pillows are stuffed with organic down. Check the website for low-season deals.

The on-site **Green Room** restaurant is rapidly establishing a reputation for outstanding creative British cuisine using local, ethically reared ingredients. A 3-course set menu is good value at £25.

4 Grove Rd., Bournemouth, Dorset BH1 3AX. www.thegreenhousehotel.co.uk. ✆ **01202/498900.** Fax 01202/551559. £140–£240 double. Rates include English breakfast. AE, MC, V. Free parking. **Amenities:** Restaurant; bar; bike rental. *In room:* TV, hair dryer, MP3 docking station, Wi-Fi (free).

Langtry Manor   The Red House, as this hotel was originally called, was built in 1877 for Lillie Langtry, a gift from Edward VII to his favorite mistress. The house has all sorts of reminders of its illustrious inhabitants, including initials scratched on a windowpane. Bedrooms vary a great deal, from ordinary twins to the romantic Lillie Langtry Suite, Lillie's own room, with a four-poster bed and a double heart-shaped bathtub. If you really want to splurge, rent the Edward VII Suite, furnished as it was when His Royal Highness lodged here, complete with an impressive fireplace.

26 Derby Rd. (north of Christchurch Rd., A35), East Cliff, Bournemouth, Dorset BH1 3QB. www.
langtrymanor.co.uk. ✆ **01202/553887.** Fax 01202/290115. 27 units. £95–£225 double. Rates
include English breakfast. Closed 2 weeks in Jan. AE, MC, V. Free parking. **Amenities:** Restaurant;
bar; access to nearby health club; room service. *In room:* TV, minibar, hair dryer, Jacuzzi (in some),
Wi-Fi (free).

7 En Route to Dorchester: A 17th-Century Mansion

Kingston Lacy ★ HISTORIC HOME   An imposing 17th-century mansion set
on 250 acres of gentle wooded parkland, Kingston Lacy was the family home of the
Bankes family for more than 300 years. They entertained such distinguished guests
as King Edward VII, Kaiser Wilhelm, Thomas Hardy, and George V. The house has
one of England's finest provincial art collections, including works by Rubens, Titian,
and Van Dyck, as well as an important collection of Egyptian artifacts. Allow at least
1½ hours to see it.

The present structure replaced **Corfe Castle** (see "The Island That Isn't: Purbeck,"
below), the Bankes' family home that was destroyed in the English Civil Wars. During
her husband's absence, while performing duties as chief justice to King Charles I,
Lady Bankes led the defense of the castle, withstanding two sieges before being forced
to surrender to Cromwell's forces in 1646, because of the actions of a treacherous
follower. The keys to Corfe Castle still hang in the library at Kingston Lacy.

Wimborne Minster (on the B3082 Wimborne–Blandford Rd., 1½ miles west of Wimborne). www.
nationaltrust.org.uk/kingston-lacy. ✆ **01202/883402.** Admission to house and garden,£11.70
adults, £6 children 5–16, £30 family ticket; garden only £6.30 adults, £3 children, £16 family ticket.
House mid-Mar to Oct Wed–Sun 11am–5pm; garden mid-Mar to Oct daily 10:30am–6pm, Nov to
mid-Mar daily 10:30am–4pm.

DORCHESTER ★

120 miles SW of London; 27 miles W of Bournemouth

In his 1886 novel, *The Mayor of Casterbridge,* Thomas Hardy bestowed upon
Dorchester literary immortality. Differences between his fictional Casterbridge and
the town of Dorchester were thinly veiled, on purpose, and visits to **Hardy's Cottage**
are as popular as ever. Actually, Dorchester was notable even in Roman times, when
nearby Maumbury Rings was filled with the sound of 12,000 spectators screaming for
the blood of the gladiators. You can get a sense of how wealthy locals lived at England's best-preserved **Roman Townhouse.**

Dorchester remained important enough to warrant a 1669 visit from Cosimo III,
Grand Duke of Tuscany, but was soon notorious for the Bloody Assizes of "Hanging
Judge" Jeffreys—over 300 local men were executed or transported for involvement in
the Duke of Monmouth's unsuccessful 1685 rebellion against King James II. Today
Dorchester is a thriving market town with an excellent **County Museum,** but it also
seems to go to bed right after dinner. It's a good base for exploring the countryside
and coast of southern and western Dorset.

Essentials

GETTING THERE   Direct trains run from London's Waterloo Station to Dorchester South at least hourly during the day, stopping en route at Winchester, Southampton, and Bournemouth. The trip takes around 2½ hours, costing around £60 for a
round-trip.

THE island THAT ISN'T: PURBECK

The so-called "Isle" of Purbeck is a peninsula dangling off the Dorset coast south of Poole Harbour. It's best reached by taking the A351 from Poole to Wareham and beyond, or catching the 5-minute **Sandbanks Chain Ferry** (www.sandbanksferry.co.uk; ✆ 01929/450203) that connects the millionaires' mansions of Sandbanks with Shell Bay, in the National Trust's Studland Nature Reserve. Foot passengers pay £1; it's £3.50 for a car and its occupants (cash only).

The man-made highlight of Purbeck is the romantic ruin of **Corfe Castle ★** (www.nationaltrust.org.uk/corfecastle; ✆ 01929/481294), silhouetted on the hill above the quaint but well-touristed village of the same name. The castle was the ancestral home of the Bankes family (see Kingston Lacy, above), and was sacked and destroyed by Parliamentary forces in 1646 during the English Civil Wars. It's open daily all year, and admission costs £8 for adults, £4 for children 5 to 16. If you want to arrive at Corfe in style, ride the **Swanage Railway** (www.swanagerailway.co.uk; ✆ 01929/425800), where traditional steam trains with old-fashioned carriages ply a 6-mile track. The timetable is complex (see the

website), but there's a good service most days between April and October. A standard round-trip costs £10.50 for adults, £7 for children.

The natural highlights of Purbeck lie along its English Channel coast (an extension of the **Jurassic Coast;** see p. 317). **Durdle Door ★**, a mighty rock arch formed by millennia of sea erosion, is linked by coastal path with **Lulworth Cove ★★**, a photogenic, horseshoe-shaped bay half a mile to the east. Six miles west of Corfe Castle, off the B3070, the "ghost village" of **Tyneham ★** was requisitioned in 1943 by the War Office for use as a tank range—with a promise it would be returned to its occupants after World War II. It never was. You can look inside the tiny, preserved Victorian schoolhouse and parish church, both frozen in the 1940s. From Tyneham, a 20-minute walk brings you to **Worbarrow Bay,** where there's a small pebble beach and fewer crowds than at nearby Lulworth. The tank range is still live, but is now open most weekends and all summer; see www.tynehamopc.org.uk for opening times.

For more on Purbeck, see www.visitswanageandpurbeck.co.uk.

If you're driving from London, take the M3 then M27 southwest to its end, and continue westward on the A31, following signs to Dorchester. Expect the journey to take around 3 hours, more during peak holiday periods.

VISITOR INFORMATION The **Tourist Information Centre** is on Antelope Walk (www.westdorset.com; ✆ 01305/267992). It's open April through October, Monday to Saturday 9am to 5pm, and November through March, Monday to Saturday 9am to 4pm.

Exploring Dorchester & Around

About 2 miles southwest of central Dorchester are the remains of the vast Iron Age fort known as **Maiden Castle ★**. The site was occupied for around 4,000 years, and its dramatic hillside concentric fortifications date to the period just before the Romans arrived. The site is well signposted and open to walk round.

Ten miles northeast of Dorchester, the one-room **Tolpuddle Martyrs Museum,** Memorial Cottages, Tolpuddle (www.tolpuddlemartyrs.org.uk; ✆ 01305/848237), tells the story of six local farm workers who in 1834 successfully fought brutal odds, a rigged trial, and a sentence of 7 years exile to Australia to form a labor union. Admission is free, and April through October hours are Tuesday to Saturday 10am to 5pm, Sunday 11am to 5pm; November to March hours are Thursday to Saturday 10am to 4pm, Sunday 11am to 4pm.

Athelhampton House & Gardens ★ HISTORIC HOME   This is one of southern England's great medieval houses, a manor whose earliest rooms date from the reign of King Edward IV, and whose site matches one of King Athelstan's 10th-century palaces. The wood-paneled Great Hall is resonant of Athelhampton's Tudor roots. The rest is packed with furniture from just about every period since: It feels like a lived-in film set, and indeed served that role for the 2009 movie *From Time to Time*. Thomas Hardy was a frequent visitor, and set his short story "The Waiting Supper" here.

The gardens are even more inspiring. Laid out in 1891, they are full of vistas, and their beauty is enhanced by the River Piddle flowing alongside. You'll see tulips and magnolias, roses, and lilies, the famous topiary pyramids, and a 15th-century dovecote.

Athelhampton, nr. Puddletown. www.athelhampton.co.uk. ✆ **01305/848363.** Admission £7 adults, £1 children 15 and under. Mar–Oct Sun–Thurs 10:30am–4:30pm; Nov–Feb Sun 11am–dusk. Take the Dorchester–Bournemouth Rd. (A35) east of Dorchester for 5 miles then follow signs.

Dorset County Museum ★ MUSEUM   Dorchester's skillfully curated museum is the place to acquaint yourself with Dorset history, lore, and archeology, as well as the lives and works of notable local writers like J. Meade Falkner, author of smuggling tale *Moonfleet* (1898), and poet William Barnes (1801–86). There's also a gallery devoted to memorabilia from Thomas Hardy's life, including a re-creation of the study at his Dorchester home, and an archeological gallery with displays and finds from Maiden Castle (see above). The latest major arrival is a fossilized giant pliosaur skull, found in Weymouth Bay.

High West St. (next to St. Peter's Church). www.dorsetcountymuseum.org. ✆ **01305/262735.** Admission £6.50 adults; free for 2 accompanied children 5–15, additional children £2; free for children 4 and under. Apr–Oct Mon–Sat 10am–5pm; Nov–Mar Mon–Sat 10am–4pm.

Hardy's Birthplace ✋ HISTORIC HOME   Thomas Hardy was born in this thatched cottage on the fringe of Thorncombe Wood, Higher Bockhampton, in 1840. The home where he later wrote *Far from the Madding Crowd* (1874), and its lovely cottage garden, are a National Trust property and open to the public. Unless you're a real Hardy geek there's not a great deal to see, but the pleasant setting and adjacent woodland offer a chance to take a stroll and perhaps spot badgers and deer. Approach the cottage on foot—it's a 5-minute walk after parking your vehicle in the space provided in the woods. Alternatively, ask at Dorchester's tourist office (see above) for a free **self-guided 3-mile walk** from the town to Hardy's Cottage, via water meadows and ancient woodland.

Higher Bockhampton (3 miles northeast of Dorchester and ½ mile south of Blandford Rd./A35). www.nationaltrust.org.uk/hardy-country. ✆ **01305/262366.** Admission £4. Mid-Mar to Oct Wed–Sun 11am–5pm.

Roman Townhouse RUINS   Dorchester's Roman Townhouse is the best preserved of its kind in Britain—though is still very much a ruin, dating from the 4th century A.D. However, many of the original intricate mosaics from this once grand residence in Roman "Durnovaria" have been left in situ.

Colliton Park (entrance in Northernhay). www.romantownhouse.org. ✆ **01305/221000.** Free admission. Open 24 hr.

Where to Eat

The best spot in the town itself for afternoon tea, a lunchtime light bite, or a selection of changing daily hot specials is the **Horse with the Red Umbrella,** 10 High West St. (✆ 01305/262019). For a good pint of Dorset ale, stop in at the **Blue Raddle,** 9 Church St. (✆ 01305/267762). Children 13 and under are not admitted. **Yalbury Cottage** (see "Where to Stay," below) is an alternative, outstanding local restaurant.

Sienna ★★ MODERN EUROPEAN   This tiny, intimate dining room at what seems like the wrong end of Dorchester's main street is the unlikely home of Michelin-starred chef Russell Brown. Decor is simple and modern, with plain wooden furniture and red banquette seating. The menu features classic combinations of top-class ingredients sourced from across the Southwest: Start, perhaps, with a poached filet of Cornish hake with crab, before tackling roast saddle of venison with spiced quince paste, and finishing with a regional cheese platter.

36 High West St. www.siennarestaurant.co.uk. ✆ **01305/250022.** Reservations required. 2- or 3-course a la carte lunch £26/£29; 2- or 3-course a la carte dinner £37/£43. MC, V. No children aged 12 and under. Wed–Sat 12:30–2:30pm; Tues–Sat 7–9pm.

Where to Stay

Yalbury Cottage ★★ 🛏   This thatched-roofed cottage with chimney corners and beamed ceilings is in a small country village within walking distance of Hardy's birthplace. The cottage is some 350 years old and was once home to the keeper of the water meadows. Midsize rooms are simply decorated with new beds and cream walls, plus individual design touches like elm headboards crafted by local woodcarvers. Room no. 4 has the best aspect, looking over empty pastures and right at the sunrise.

The excellent **restaurant ★★**—also open to nonguests Tuesday to Saturday evening and Sunday for lunch—serves French-influenced cuisine that pushes the local/seasonal mantra to the limit: All meat on the menu is sourced from within a few miles, for example. Dinner costs £31 for 2 courses, £36 for 3 courses. Tapas lunches are served on a pretty terrace all summer.

Lower Bockhampton, Dorchester, Dorset DT2 8PZ. www.yalburycottage.com. ✆ **01305/262382.** Fax 01305/266412. 8 units. £115 double. Rates include English breakfast. MC, V. Free parking. Head 2 miles east of Dorchester on the A35 and follow signs to Lower Bockhampton. **Amenities:** Restaurant; bar. *In room:* TV/DVD, hair dryer, CD player, movie library, Wi-Fi (free).

DORSET'S JURASSIC COAST: WEYMOUTH TO LYME REGIS ★★

Weymouth: 137 miles SW of London, 8 miles S of Dorchester; Lyme Regis: 155 miles SW of London, 63 miles S of Bristol

Stretching from Swanage, in Purbeck, to Exmouth, in East Devon, the 95-mile **Jurassic Coast** is a UNESCO World Heritage site named after the rock strata laid down between 135 and 190 million years ago along its length. (The beaches they shelter have been a favorite haunt of fossil hunters for 2 centuries.) The most appealing base here is **Lyme Regis,** a quirky resort with steep and winding streets that are barely changed since Jane Austen visited between 1803 and 1804.

At **Weymouth,** you'll find a sandy strand, one of Dorset's best seafood **restaurants,** and lots of traditional English seaside fun. The town also claims a tragic place in English history: It was at Weymouth that the Black Death first arrived on English soil in 1348, on its way to killing half the country's population.

Essentials

GETTING THERE The easiest train connection for this stretch of coastline is Weymouth, served via an approximately half-hourly direct train from London's Waterloo Station, calling at Southampton and Bournemouth en route. Journey time is just under 3 hours, costing around £64 for a round-trip.

To get to Lyme Regis direct from London Waterloo, take the hourly London–Exeter train and disembark at Axminster (2¾ hr. away). From there, catch bus no. 31 from Axminster Station to Lyme Regis (20 min.; hourly service during the day). The X53 Jurassic Coast bus serves stops along the coast, between Exeter in the west and Poole in the east, including Lyme Regis and Weymouth. See www.firstgroup.com for timetables.

If you're driving to the Jurassic Coast from the east, head west along the A35 as far as Dorchester. To get to Lyme Regis, continue farther along the A35 beyond Bridport, cutting south to the coast at the junction with the A3070. For Weymouth, head immediately south from Dorchester for 9 miles on the A354.

VISITOR INFORMATION In Lyme Regis, the **Tourist Information Centre,** Guildhall Cottage, Church Street (www.westdorset.com; ℂ **01297/442138**), is open November through March, Monday to Saturday 10am to 3pm, and April through October, Monday to Saturday 10am to 5pm and Sunday 10am to 4pm. Another useful resource is www.lymeregis.org. The **Weymouth Tourist Information Centre,** The Pavilion, The Esplanade (www.visitweymouth.co.uk; ℂ **01305/785747**), is open daily 9:30am to 5pm between April and October, closing an hour earlier the rest of the year. For more on this World Heritage Coast, see www. jurassiccoast.com.

TOURS The coast surrounding Lyme is made largely from blue Lias, a sedimentary rock well suited to the formation of fossils (especially ammonites). Landslips from cliffs weakened by 19th-century quarrying are common, and each reveals new finds—winter is the best season for **fossil hunting ★**. Lyme's tourist office has a list of guides offering local fossil hunting trips. Most last around 2 hours and cost between £5 and £10 for adults, £5 or less for children. If you're striking out unsupervised, then **only hunt on a falling tide** and **stay away from the cliffs.**

Exploring the Jurassic Coast

The highlight of the Jurassic Coast is wandering the steep, winding streets and unique harbor at **Lyme Regis ★** (see "Shopping in Lyme Regis," below). Completed in its current form in 1756 as a breakwater, the handsome **Cobb ★** has protected Lyme's thriving little seaport for 2½ centuries. Along with providing the iconic image from 1981 movie *The French Lieutenant's Woman* (written by local John Fowles), the Cobb is the place to head if you fancy trying scenic **mackerel fishing.** In good weather, boats depart the harbor regularly on trips lasting 1 hour and costing £8. There's also a small, sandy **beach** adjacent to the harbor. In 1810, Mary Anning (at the age of 11) discovered one of the first articulated ichthyosaur skeletons nearby. She went on to become one of the world's first professional fossilists (a fascinating tale told in *The Dinosaur Hunters,* by Deborah Cadbury). She is buried in the churchyard of Lyme's Parish Church, **St. Michael Archangel,** on Church Street.

Just east of Lyme, the seaside village of **Charmouth** is the best jumping-off point for beachfront walks at the foot of **Golden Cap.** At 191m (627 ft.), they're the tallest seacliffs along the southern coast and in times past they served as a fine brandy smugglers' lookout. The best spot here for a coastal pint is the **Anchor Inn,** Seatown, Chideock (✆ **01297/489215**). Suitably refreshed in this former smugglers' tavern, you can strike out for a clifftop walk or stroll along the adjacent pebble beach.

Dorset's best produce fills the shelves at **Washingpool Farm Shop ★**, North Allington, Bridport (www.washingpool.co.uk; ✆ **01308/459549**). The offerings change with the seasons but always include local organic meats and vegetables, chutneys, cakes baked in the farm kitchen, and even Dorset wines.

Starting just east of Bridport, at West Bay, the pebble bank known as **Chesil Beach ★** begins its 18-mile sweep to Portland. It's said that an experienced Dorset seaman can tell exactly where he is along the beach just from the size of the pebbles underfoot—an anecdote that plays a role in J. Meade Falkner's fictional children's smuggling tale, *Moonfleet.* Drive parallel to the Chesil, along the B3157, for spectacular coastal views, especially around the village of **Abbotsbury.** *Warning:* Don't be tempted to swim off the Chesil: Currents here are extremely dangerous, and at least 50 major shipwrecks have occurred just offshore, with many thousands of souls drowned.

Adjacent to the Chesil's eastern end lies **Weymouth,** a busy resort first popularized by King George III and home to this coast's best sandy beach, with a shallow shelf ideal for young bathers. Besides playing host to the Olympic sailing events, the major news in summer 2012 was the opening of the **Weymouth Sea Life Tower** (www.weymouth-tower.com; ✆ **0871/282-9242**), which stands 53m (174 ft.) over Festival Pier. The rotating gondola offers spectacular 360 degree views inland and along the Jurassic Coast. A ride to the top costs £8.

Where to Eat

The best place in central Lyme Regis for fish and chips is **Lyme Fish Bar,** 34 Combe St. (✆ **01297/442375**).

NEAR LYME REGIS

For a nearby pub lunch, stop in at the thatched, roadside **George Inn ★**, Chideock (www.georgeinnchideock.co.uk; ✆ **01297/489419**). There's a roaring fire, outdoor tables, and a menu of pub classics—but also a sprinkling of refined dishes like pan-fried pigeon breast on garlic bruschetta. Main courses range £7 to £17.

The Wild Garlic ★★   Exposed brick, chunky wooden tables, and a daily menu on the chalkboard give this restaurant owned by TV *Masterchef* winner Mat Follas a studied "refined rustic" look. Food is heavily influenced by the tastes and aromas of West Dorset, by Follas's love of foraging, and by the proximity to the sea—there's a fish of the day on every menu. Dishes are generally simple, and rely on the finest, freshest ingredients producing big flavors—think brill ceviche for starters, followed by Barnsley (lamb) chops served with coarse pesto and crushed new potatoes, and rounded off with a chocolate fondant.

4 The Square, Beaminster. www.thewildgarlic.co.uk. ✆ **01308/861446.** Reservations recommended. Main courses £15–£24; light lunch set menu 2 courses £14, 3 courses £17. MC, V. Wed–Sat 9:30am–3pm and 7–11pm.

Shopping in Lyme Regis

Lyme's tumbledown Broad Street is little changed since Jane Austen set *Persuasion* here in 1816. (The book was posthumously published.) You'll doubtless find a thumbed copy at **The Sanctuary,** 65 Broad St. (✆ **01297/445815**), an eccentric but superb secondhand bookstore with a warrenlike basement and stock that ranges from 1931 *Kelly's Directory of Dorsetshire* to used pulp fiction, and everything in-between. Almost opposite, **Lucy Ann** ★, 4a Broad St. (www.lucyann.co.uk; ✆ **01297/443968**), sells funky,

handmade jewelry at reasonable prices, made on-site using semiprecious stones. Lyme's former mill now hosts interesting independent shops, among them the **Town Mill Brewery,** Mill Lane (www.townmillbrewery.com; ✆ **01297/444354**), a modern microbrewery that brews and sells on the premises. The **Town Mill Cheesemonger** ★, Mill Lane (www.townmillcheese.co.uk; ✆ **01297/442626**), one of the Southwest's best cheese vendors, is the place to pick up the local specialty, Dorset Blue Vinny.

NEAR WEYMOUTH

Crab House Café ★★ 🍴   Seafood shacks don't come any tastier, any fresher, or any more ethical than this oyster farm turned eatery on the eastern edge of Chesil Beach. The menu makes extensive use of their own shellfish, and bought-in fish is sourced from three fleets within 40 miles of the restaurant. House specialties include whole crab however you like it—brought to the table with tools and a bucket—and whatever's landed today, which may include unusual (and sustainable) species like gurnard or flounder. Sides and garnishes are organic or biodynamically farmed, and from the property's own garden where possible.

Ferrymans Way, Portland Rd., Wyke Regis. www.crabhousecafe.co.uk. ✆01305/788867. Reservations highly recommended. Main courses £13–£26. MC, V. Wed–Thurs noon–2pm and 6–8:30pm; Fri noon–2:30pm and 6–9pm; Sat noon–2:30pm and 6–9:30pm; Sun noon–3:30pm. Closed mid-Dec to early Feb. From Weymouth, follow signs toward Portland; restaurant is on the right before the causeway.

Where to Stay
IN LYME REGIS

Alexandra Hotel ★★   A major 2008 revamp gave this comfortable hotel, built in 1753, a chic, contemporary edge to complement its classy, traditional styling. Perched on a hill about 5 minutes from both the center and the harbor, it has the best bedrooms in town. Most rooms command sea views over Lyme Bay, but paying a little extra for one of two Gould Rooms guarantees the best full-length bay window panorama in Dorset. Even if you're not staying here, stop in for **afternoon tea** (£12.50) in the elegant drawing room or on the panoramic lawn.

Pound St., Lyme Regis, Dorset DT7 3HZ. www.hotelalexandra.co.uk. ✆ **01297/442010.** Fax 01297/443229. 26 units. £177–£295 double. Rates include English breakfast. MC, V. Free parking. **Amenities:** 2 restaurants; bar; room service; babysitting; Wi-Fi (free). *In room:* TV, hair dryer, MP3 docking station (in some).

1 Lyme Townhouse ★ 🍴   Behind the facade of a handsome, polished seaside town house is a temple to designer ultra-modernity. The Georgian architecture remains intact, but midsize, sparsely furnished rooms scream 21st-century chic, with liberal use of cool whites and outrageous splashes of color. Our favorite room with a view, no. 5, has a double panorama of Lyme's high street and the Golden Cap cliffs in the distance. Hamper breakfasts (optional) are served in your room.

1 Pound St., Lyme Regis, Dorset DT7 3HZ. www.1lymetownhouse.co.uk. © **01297/442499.** 7 units. £105–£125 double. Rates include breakfast. MC, V. **Amenities:** Bike rental. *In room:* TV/DVD, hair dryer, MP3 docking station, Wi-Fi (free) no phone.

IN WEYMOUTH

B+B Weymouth 🎁   Simple, Scandinavian-inspired lodgings right opposite Weymouth's sandy arc of beach. Rooms are plain, and slightly spartan, but high ceilings and uncluttered modern furnishings give them a pleasant, spacious feel. The communal sitting room has snacks and drinks available all day. You're right at the heart of the action in seafront Weymouth, so rooms at the front can be noisy.

68 The Esplanade, Weymouth, Dorset DT4 7AA. www.bb-weymouth.com. © **01305/761190.** Fax 01305/839609. 24 units. £75–£105 double. Rates include breakfast. AE, MC, V. Limited free street parking. **Amenities:** Bar; bike rental. *In room:* TV, Wi-Fi (free).

SHERBORNE ★ & NORTH DORSET

128 miles SW of London; 19 miles NW of Dorchester

A little town with preserved medieval, Tudor, Stuart, and Georgian buildings, Sherborne is surrounded by the gentle hills, wooded glades, and chalk downs of rural North Dorset. It was here that Sir Walter Raleigh lived before his fall from fortune, in **Sherborne Castle.** There are also 13 centuries of local Christian history, much of it is encapsulated in the stones of Gothic **Sherborne Abbey.**

Essentials

GETTING THERE   Frequent direct trains depart from London's Waterloo Station through the day, stopping at Salisbury en route. The trip takes 2¼ hours and costs around £55 for a round-trip.

If you're driving from London, take the M3 west, continuing southwest on the A303 and then joining the southbound B3145 beyond Wincanton. Plan for a journey time of around 3 hours.

VISITOR INFORMATION   The **Tourist Information Centre,** Digby Road (www.westdorset.com; © **01935/815341**), is open April through September Monday to Saturday 9am to 5pm; October and November Monday to Saturday 9:30am to 4pm; and December through March Monday to Saturday 10am to 3pm.

Exploring Sherborne & North Dorset

Provincial Sherborne's compact center is a delightful place to stroll for an hour, and the tiny cluster of surviving medieval buildings around the abbey (see below) are especially atmospheric. **Church Lane,** leading from the Conduit (a hexagonal building where the monks washed their clothes), seems transplanted from another era. **St. Johns' Almshouses,** Half Moon Street, were built in 1438 to house 12 poor men and 4 women, although the cloister is a later neo-Gothic addition. You can see inside from May through September, Tuesday, Friday, and Saturday between 2 and 4pm. Admission costs £2. Lovers of small, independent stores should spend some time window-browsing along **Cheap Street ★.**

Cerne Giant HISTORIC SITE   Nobody is quite sure when a 60-m (180-ft.), naked—and somewhat explicit—outline of a giant was originally carved into the rolling chalk hills of North Dorset. It may be an ancient fertility symbol. It might be a representation of Hercules. Or it might be a lewd, mocking caricature of Oliver Cromwell, the victorious Parliamentarian leader during the English Civil Wars. You can view and photograph from the roadside, or walk right up to (but not onto) the giant.

Cerne Abbas (viewing area by A352, 11 miles south of Sherborne). www.nationaltrust.org.uk/cernegiant. © **01297/489481.** Free admission. Daily dawn to dusk.

Sherborne Abbey ★★CHURCH   This monumental abbey church, founded in A.D. 705 as the Cathedral of the Saxon Bishops of Wessex, dominates the 21st-century town. In the late 10th century, it became a Benedictine monastery, and since the Dissolution it has been Sherborne's rather grand parish church. Look immediately up to see the soaring, intricate **fan-vaulted ceiling ★★** stretching the full length of the nave. Fan vaults were a particularly graceful—and peculiarly English—solution to spreading the weight of a large ceiling, originating in the West Country in the early 15th century. In addition to being staggeringly beautiful, it's notable for the intricate carved bosses and corbels that were so high up that they escaped the destructive iconoclasts of the English Reformation. Pack binoculars to appreciate them fully.

Abbey Close. www.sherborneabbey.com. © **01935/812452.** Free admission (£2 donation welcomed). Apr–Sept daily 8am–6pm; Oct–Mar daily 8am–4pm. Guided tours Tues 10:30am and Fri 12:30pm.

Sherborne Castle ★HISTORIC HOME   "Castle" is in fact a misnomer for this Elizabethan residence, built for Sir Walter Raleigh after he decided that it wouldn't be feasible to restore the Old Castle (see below) to suit his stately needs. The original 1594 residence was a square mansion; later owners added four Jacobean wings to make it more palatial. After King James I had Raleigh imprisoned in the Tower of London, the monarch gave the castle to a favorite Scot, Robert Carr, banishing the Raleighs from their home. In 1617, it was bought by Sir John Digby, and has been the Digby family home ever since. The mansion was enlarged by Sir John in 1625, and in the 1750s, the formal Elizabethan gardens and fountains of the Raleighs were altered by Capability Brown, who created a serpentine lake between Sherborne's two castles. Highlights of the house's interior include paintings by Gainsborough, Lely, and Kneller; an intact basement kitchen dating from 1595; and a portrait of Raleigh said to be an accurate likeness.

Off New Rd. (1 mile east of center). www.sherbornecastle.com. © **01935/812072.** Castle and gardens £10 adults, £9.50 seniors, free for children 15 and under; £5 grounds only. Apr–Oct Tues–Thurs, Sun, and public holidays Mon 11am–4:30pm; Sat 2–4:30pm (grounds from 11am).

Sherborne Old Castle ★ ☺RUINS   The town's original castle was built by the powerful Bishop Roger de Caen in the early 12th century, but was seized by the crown at about the time of King Henry I's death in 1135 and Stephen's troubled accession to the throne. The buildings were mostly destroyed in the aftermath of the English Civil Wars, when it was besieged twice, but three gatehouses, some graceful arcades, and a barrel-vaulted undercroft remain.

Castleton Rd. (½ mile east of center). www.english-heritage.org.uk/sherborne. © **01935/812730.** Admission £3.40 adults, £3.10 seniors and students, £2 children 5–16. Apr–June and Sept daily 10am–5pm; July–Aug daily 10am–6pm; Oct daily 10am–4pm.

Cottage Rental in Sherborne

Local agency **Sherborne Cottages ★** (www.sherbornecottages.com; ℂ **01935/ 810815**) has a small, high-quality portfolio of apartments and cottages in and around central Sherborne, sleeping up to six people. All are simply decorated in a clean, modern style, maintained to a high standard, and available for 3 nights or more. Weekly rates range from £350 to £700.

Where to Eat & Stay

For a late breakfast, light lunch, or the best mug of coffee in town, head to **Oliver's,** 19 Cheap St. (ℂ **01935/815005**). The **Digby Tap ★**, Cooks Lane (www.digbytap. co.uk; ℂ **01935/813148**), is a friendly, genuinely local pub serving great beer and hearty, cheap food (lunch only Mon–Sat). Large portions of simple dishes such as ham, egg, and chips generally cost under £5.

If you've visiting the Cerne Giant (see above), the handsome brick pub in the nearby village, the **New Inn ★** (www.thenewinncerneabbas.co.uk; ℂ 01300/341274), 14 Long St., Cerne Abbas, serves seasonal gastropub food worth driving miles for. Mains such as a homemade burger or stuffed rabbit leg with cavolo nero range from £10 to £15. Totally remodeled in 2012, it also has 12 rooms that stay true to the inn's deep historical roots, but with modern amenities.

Eastbury Hotel ★　Built in 1740, this town-house hotel has a traditional ambience, with its own library of antiquarian books and a tranquil walled garden. Bedrooms, named after flowers, are all handsomely maintained, with superior rooms decorated in a contemporary style with imaginative, bold-print walls. Restaurant **The Conservatory ★★**, refurbished in 2012, offers some of Dorset's best fine dining, with a fusion of French techniques and local ingredients. Expect the likes of West Bay cod with fennel bahjee and purée on a 7-course tasting menu that costs £45. There's also a bistro menu, at lunch and dinner, with mains such as whole smoked partridge with roasted squash costing from £14 to £19 (a 2-course set lunch costs £17).

Long St., Sherborne, Dorset DT9 3BY. www.theeastburyhotel.co.uk. ℂ **01935/813131.** Fax 01935/817296. 23 units. £139–£189 double. Rates include English breakfast. AE, MC, V. Free parking. **Amenities:** Restaurant; bar; access to nearby health club; bike rental; room service; babysitting. *In room:* TV, hair dryer, Wi-Fi (free).

Queens Arms ★★ 🛏️　A modern take on a Georgian country inn, complete with roaring fireplace, flagstone floors, relaxing beer garden, and food and drink menus that employ the rural bounty on the doorstep. Cozy, traditionally decorated guest rooms are upstairs: Room no. 2 is the standout, with an antique French bed and vast cast-iron tub. Downstairs you can **dine** on classic, affordable dishes such as boiled ham served with parsley sauce and bubble and squeak; or take a refined route via the likes of baked lemon sole with mussel and saffron butter.

Corton Denham, Sherborne, Dorset DT9 4LR. www.thequeensarms.com. ℂ **01963/220317.** 8 units. £80–£120 double. Rates include breakfast. AE, MC, V. Free street parking. Off B3145, 6 miles north of Sherborne. **Amenities:** Restaurant; bar; babysitting. *In room:* TV/DVD, MP3 docking station, Wi-Fi (free).

WILTSHIRE & SOMERSET

by Stephen Keeling & Donald Strachan

The Regency charms of Bath, the prehistoric mysteries of Stonehenge and Avebury, and the monumental architecture of New Sarum: Wiltshire and Somerset, two of England's ancient counties, practically define the best of the West Country.

Wiltshire, the closer of the two to London, is a largely rural idyll that's home to the compact, medieval city of Salisbury. In Somerset, you'll discover everything from the regenerated harborfront in Victorian Bristol to the Gothic glory of Wells Cathedral.

SIGHTSEEING   Regal Bath achieved fame and fortune twice in its history, first as a spa in Roman times, then thanks to the Georgian builders of the elegant **Royal Crescent. Salisbury** and **Wells** have retained the architecture and atmosphere of small cities that reached their peak in medieval times. The counties also contain some of the finest stately homes in southern England, notably at **Wilton House,** near Salisbury, and **Montacute,** in south Somerset.

EATING & DRINKING   Somerset and Wiltshire are also known for their produce. **Cheddar** cheese, named after a Somerset village, is still aged in limestone caves there. The heady local cider known as **Scrumpy** hails from Somerset. Wiltshire is hunting country, and the county's best gastropubs usually feature game on the menu. That most English of traditions, **afternoon tea** has been big in Bath for centuries, and is paired here with a Sally Lunn or Bath bun.

HISTORY   The history of Britain is written in the buildings of Wiltshire and Somerset. Avebury and Stonehenge date back to prehistoric times, way before the Romans first popularized their spa at Bath. Cathedrals in the small cities of Salisbury and Wells are as close to the ideal Gothic as you'll find in England. Regency architecture is rarely as beautiful as it is at Bath's Royal Crescent, and **Bristol,** a powerhouse port of the Industrial Revolution, is forever linked with Victorian genius Isambard Kingdom Brunel.

NATURE   The west Somerset coast is hiking country, with the wilderness of the **Exmoor National Park** home to some fine long-distance trails—the Two Moors Way and the Southwest Coast Path—that can be tackled in bits or all at once. The **Mendips** offer serene, rolling vistas above ground, but they're much more spectacular below ground, with limestone caves shaped over millennia at Cheddar and **Wookey Hole.** In the magnificent, year-round garden at **Stourhead,** nature had a helping hand from the 18th-century's most skilled landscapers.

THE best TRAVEL EXPERIENCES IN WILTSHIRE & SOMERSET

○ **Getting up close and personal with Avebury's ancient stone circle:** In medieval times, a remote farm village grew up among giant sarsen stones that had been standing for millennia. Only fragments of that village remain, but you're free to roam among the stones and skirt the massive ditch that, in its Neolithic prime, would have been 7m (23 ft.) deep. See p. 334.

○ **Soaking in the Thermae Bath Spa:** Nothing beats watching the sunset over the enchanting rooftops of Georgian Bath, as you slowly simmer in the outdoor hot-spring pool at Thermae. The waters are the same as those enjoyed by the Romans, but the facilities are resolutely 21st-century England. See p. 340.

○ **Ballooning over Bristol:** Float over southwest England's largest city, taking in the historic docks, River Avon, and Brunel's Clifton Suspension Bridge. Bristol is a lot more scintillating by air—and the experience is surprisingly affordable. See p. 346.

○ **Meeting the English Gothic at Salisbury:** Britain isn't short of pointed arches and flying buttresses, but rarely has Gothic been expressed so harmoniously as at Salisbury Cathedral. It was built in under 40 years, leaving it unpolluted by later styles. Climb the bell tower for views that stretch far beyond the water meadows loved by painter John Constable. See p. 327.

○ **Sampling the scrumpy in rural Somerset:** West Country apples and a brewing tradition stretching back longer than anyone can record make Somerset the home of the traditional, alcoholic cider known as scrumpy. Tour the county's best niche producers, then visit one of the oldest Christian sites in Britain, Glastonbury Abbey, to taste their award-winning version. See p. 362 and 359.

SALISBURY ★★, STONEHENGE ★★ & SOUTH WILTSHIRE

90 miles SW of London; 53 miles SE of Bristol

Long before you enter the city, the spire of **Salisbury Cathedral** comes into view—just as great English painters John Constable and J. M. W. Turner captured it on canvas. The 121-m (404-ft.) pinnacle of the Early English Gothic cathedral is the tallest in England, but is just one among many historical points of interest in Wiltshire's most visited city.

Salisbury, once known as "New Sarum," lies in the valley of southern Wiltshire's River Avon. Filled with Tudor inns and tearooms, it is an excellent base for visitors keen to explore nearby **Stonehenge.** The old market city also has a lively arts scene, and is an interesting destination on its own. If you choose to linger, you find an added bonus: Salisbury's pub-to-citizen ratio is among the highest in England.

Essentials

GETTING THERE Trains for Salisbury depart half-hourly from Waterloo Station in London; the trip takes under 1½ hours and costs around £36 for a round-trip. The city also has fast, regular connections with Portsmouth, Bristol, Cardiff, and Southampton.

If you're driving from London, head west on the M3 and then M27 to junction 2, continuing the rest of the way on the A36.

VISITOR INFORMATION Salisbury's friendly **Tourist Information Centre** is on Fish Row (www.visitsalisbury.com; © **01722/334956**). Budgets have been squeezed, but the office is generally open Monday to Saturday at least between 10am and 4pm. For information on the wider south Wiltshire area, you should also consult www.visitwiltshire.co.uk.

SPECIAL EVENTS During the annual **Salisbury International Arts Festival** (www.salisburyfestival.co.uk) the city drapes itself in banners, and street theatre, concerts, children's events, and more are staged everywhere. It takes place from mid-May to the beginning of June.

TOURS You can easily see Salisbury on foot, either on your own or by taking a guided daytime or evening walk with **Salisbury City Guides** (www.salisburycityguides.co.uk; © **07873/212941**). Tickets are £4 for adults and £2 for children 4 to 15. They also run themed walks, including a popular ghost one, and walks for children. For the more energetic, **Heritage Cycle Tours** (www.heritagecycletours.com; © **01980/862099**) runs weekly, 1-day guided tours in the saddle from Salisbury, that take in Stonehenge and New Sarum (see below). They cost £45 per person, including equipment rental.

Exploring Salisbury

Church of St. Thomas & St. Edmund ★ CHURCH This medieval church is notable for a 1475 **Doom painting** ★★, above the chancel arch. Once common in English holy buildings, such depictions of the Last Judgment were largely whitewashed or erased during the Reformation. Salisbury's survived—by chance. Spot the clothed female figure among the naked souls being dispatched to Hell: She was reputedly a local brothel keeper who later repented and gave all her "ill-gotten gains" to charity—still damned, but allowed to retain her modesty.

St. Thomas's Sq. www.stthomassalisbury.co.uk. © 01722/322537. Free admission. Daily 8:30am–6pm.

Mompesson House HISTORIC HOME Built in 1701 by Charles Mompesson, while he was a Member of Parliament for Old Sarum (see below), Mompesson House is an archetypal example of the Queen Anne style, and is known for its plasterwork ceilings and paneling. Also used as a location for the 1995 Oscar-winning movie *Sense and Sensibility,* it houses an important collection of 18th-century drinking glasses. In summer, there's a garden tearoom.

The Close. www.nationaltrust.org.uk/mompessonhouse. © 01722/420980. Admission £5.20 adults, £2.60 children 17 and under, £13 family ticket. Mid-Mar–Oct Sat–Wed 11am–5pm.

Salisbury & South Wiltshire Museum ★ MUSEUM This slightly haphazard museum includes displays that place nearby Stonehenge and Wiltshire's other prehistoric sites in their local historic context. The "History of Salisbury" gallery houses a small collection of Turner's Salisbury watercolors.

King's House, 65 The Close. www.salisburymuseum.org.uk. © 01722/332151. Admission £5.45 adults, £2 children 15 and under. Mon–Sat 10am–5pm (Jun–Sept also Sun noon–5pm).

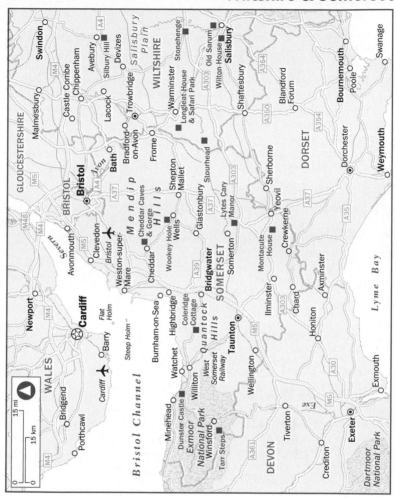

Salisbury Cathedral ★★★ CATHEDRAL You'll find no better example of the Early English Gothic architectural style. Construction on the building began in 1220 and took only 38 years to complete. (By contrast, many of Europe's grandest cathedrals took up to 300 years to build.) As a result, Salisbury Cathedral is one of the most homogenous and harmonious of all the great cathedrals—approached in the fading light of a winter's eve, it's an unforgettable sight. The best vantage point for fully appreciating its internal architecture is behind the **choir stalls** (Britain's oldest), looking directly down the nave.

The cathedral's 13th-century octagonal Chapter House possesses one of the four surviving original texts of **Magna Carta**—one of the founding documents of democracy and justice, signed by King John in 1215. Britain's largest cloisters and adjacent Cathedral Close further enhance the cathedral's beauty.

Insider tip: The 123-m (404-ft.) spire is the tallest in Britain, and was one of the world's tallest structures when completed in 1315. In 1668, Sir Christopher Wren expressed alarm at its tilt (notice how internal columns have bowed under the weight), but no further shift has since been measured. If you trust towering architecture from 700 years ago, you can explore the heights on a 1½-hour **Tower Tour ★★** costing £8.50 for adults, £6.50 for seniors and children 5 to 17, £25 for a family of five (fee includes cathedral donation). Between April and September, there are five tours a day Monday to Saturday (hourly from 11:15am), and two on Sunday (1 and 2:30pm). From October to March, there are usually one or two daily, depending on weather, but no tour on Sunday. Children must be 7 and over, and everyone will need a head for heights.

The Close. www.salisburycathedral.org.uk. (© **01722/555156.** Suggested donation £5.50 adults, £4.50 students and seniors, £3 children 5–17, £13 family ticket. Cathedral Mon–Sat 9am–5pm, Sun noon–4pm; Chapter House Mon–Sat 10am–4:30pm, Sun 12:45–3:45pm. Closed Dec 25.

Exploring Stonehenge & South Wiltshire

Old Sarum ★ RUINS   Believed to have been an Iron Age fortification, Old Sarum was used again by the Saxons and flourished as a walled town into the Middle Ages. The Normans built a cathedral and a castle here; parts of this old cathedral were taken down to build the city of "New Sarum," later known as Salisbury, leaving behind the dramatic remains you see today. In the early 19th century Old Sarum was one of the English Parliament's most notorious "Rotten Boroughs," constituencies that were allowed to send a Member of Parliament to Westminster despite having few—in Old Sarum's case, no—residents. The Rotten Boroughs were finally disbanded in 1832.

2 miles north of Salisbury off the A345 Castle Rd. www.english-heritage.org.uk/oldsarum. (© **01722/335398.** Admission £3.70 adults, £3.30 seniors, £1.20 children 5–15. Apr–June and Sept daily 10am–5pm; July–Aug daily 9am–6pm; Mar and Oct daily 10am–4pm; Nov–Jan daily 11am–3pm; Feb daily 11am–4pm. Bus: 5, 6, 7, 8, or 9 (approx. every 30 min.).

Stonehenge ★★ 📷 ICON   This circle of lintels and megalithic pillars is the most important prehistoric monument in Britain. The concentric rings of standing stones represent an amazing feat of late Neolithic engineering because many of the boulders were moved many miles to this site: the bluestones from southwest Wales—a 2011 scientific study pinpointed the exact spot, Pont Saeson, north of the Preseli Hills—the massive sarsens just 20 miles from the Marlborough Downs. If you're a romantic, come see the ruins in the early glow of dawn or else when shadows fall at sunset. The light is most dramatic at these times, the shadows longer, and the effect is often more mesmerizing than in the glaring light of midday. The mystical experience is marred only slightly by an ugly (but necessary) perimeter fence protecting the stones from vandals and souvenir hunters. Your admission ticket gets you inside the fence, but no longer all the way up to the stones.

The widely held view of 18th- and 19th-century Romantics, who believed Stonehenge was the work of the Druids, is without foundation. The boulders, many weighing several tons, are believed to have pre-dated the arrival in Britain of the Celtic culture, and may be a Neolithic "computing machine" capable of predicting eclipses. In truth, its ultimate purpose will remain a mystery. However, it appears from the beginning to have been a monument to the dead, as revealed by radiocarbon dating from human cremation burials around the brooding stones. The site was used as a

Salisbury

ATTRACTIONS ●

Church of St. Thomas
  & St. Edmund **5**
Mompesson House **6**
Salisbury & South
  Wiltshire Museum **7**
Salisbury Cathedral **8**

RESTAURANTS ◆

Anokaa **2**
Côte **4**

HOTELS ■

Lazy Cow **9**
Legacy Rose &
  Crown Hotel **11**
Peartree Serviced
  Apartments **1**
St. Ann's House **10**
Wyndham Park Lodge **3**

cemetery from 3000 B.C. until after the first of the giant stones was erected around 2500 B.C. It was used for about 1,500 years then abandoned.

Archeologists have also uncovered hearths, timbers, and other remains of what was probably the village of workers who erected these monoliths on Salisbury Plain. These ancient ruins appear to form the largest Neolithic village ever found in Britain. The trenches of this discovery, **Durrington Walls,** lie 2 miles northeast of Stonehenge.

Insider tip: From the road, if you don't mind the noise from traffic, you can get a good view of Stonehenge without paying the admission charge for a close-up encounter. Alternatively, climb **Amesbury Hill,** visible 1½ miles up the A303. From here, you'll get a free panoramic view.

At the junction of the A303 and A344 (2 miles west of Amesbury). www.english-heritage.org.uk/stonehenge. *℃***0870/333-1181.** Admission £7.50 adults, £6.80 students and seniors, £4.50 children 5–15, £19.50 family ticket. June–Aug daily 9am–7pm; Mar 16–May and Sept–Oct 15 daily 9:30am–6pm; Oct 16–Mar 15 daily 9:30am–4pm.

Wilton House ★ ☺ HISTORIC HOME   This grand Palladian home of the earls of Pembroke dates from 1551 but has undergone successive alterations after fires,

Wilts & Dorset (www.wdbus.co.uk; ℰ **01983/827005**) runs around four buses per hour between Salisbury bus station and Amesbury (30 min. away), which is as close as you can get by public transportation. It's a half-hour walk to Stonehenge from there. There is also the hop-on, hop-off **Stonehenge Tour** (www.thestonehengetour.info; ℰ **01983/ 827005**), which runs approximately hourly from Salisbury railway and bus stations, passing via Old Sarum (see above) on the way to the stones, taking 35 minutes each way. A round-trip ticket costs £11 for adults, £5 for children; including entrance to Stonehenge and Old Sarum, prices are £18 adults, £15 students, and £9 children. If you're **driving** from Salisbury, head north from the center on Castle Road. At the first roundabout (traffic circle), take the exit toward Amesbury (A345). Continue along this road for 8 miles, and then turn left onto the A303 in the direction of Exeter. You'll see signs for Stonehenge, leading you up the A344 to the right.

most recently in the early 19th century. It is noted for its exquisite 17th-century staterooms, designed by architect Inigo Jones (1573–1652). Shakespeare's troupe supposedly entertained at Wilton—although this is as yet unproven—and Eisenhower and his advisers prepared here for the D-Day Normandy landings, with only the Van Dyck paintings as silent witnesses. The house is stocked with beautifully maintained furnishings by the likes of Chippendale and world-class art, including paintings by Rubens, Brueghel, Rembrandt, and Reynolds. You can also visit a reconstructed Tudor kitchen and Victorian laundry.

On the 21-acre estate are giant cedars from Lebanon, the oldest of which were planted in 1630, as well as rose and water gardens, riverside and woodland walks, and an adventure playground for children.

Wilton, 3 miles west of Salisbury on the A36. www.wiltonhouse.com. ℰ **01722/746714.** Admission to house and grounds £14 adults, £11.25 seniors, £7.50 children 5–15, £34 family; grounds only £5.50 adults, £5 seniors, £4 children 5–15, £16.50 family. Easter plus May–Aug Sun–Thurs 11:30am– 4:30pm (last entry 3:45pm); grounds also open part of Apr and Sept. Bus: Red 3 (15 min.).

Where to Eat

Meat lovers should reserve a table at the downstairs steakhouse of recommended hotel, the **Lazy Cow** (see "Where to Stay," below). For an informal Thai meal, the flavors are spot on at recommended pub **Rai d'Or** (see "The Pub Scene," below). Mains such as stir-fried squid with hot basil range from £7 to £10.50.

IN SALISBURY

Anokaa ★ MODERN INDIAN Through the length and breadth of the country, creative chefs continue to give the traditional Indian-British "curry" a 21st-century makeover. This relaxed dining room serves up contemporary cuisine from a number of Indian regions, from Punjab in the north to Kerala in the south. *Anokaa* means "different," and when you taste the chicken lababdar, flavored with coconut, ginger, and sweet chili, or the twice-cooked goan pork curry, you'll understand why the name fits. At lunchtime, there's also a buffet service set menu: Although the choice is limited, the cooking is well executed and at £9 offers excellent value.

60 Fisherton St., Salisbury. www.anokaa.com. ✆ **01722/414142.** Reservations recommended. Main courses £11–£18. MC, V. Daily noon–2pm and 5:30–11pm.

Côte FRENCH There is, certainly, a whiff of the chain about this brasserie installed in a twee, historic square opposite St. Thomas's Church. However, the Salisbury outpost of Côte is also a dependable place to head for good food at a fair price. Inside, decor is true to its French aspirations, and the menu is a pleasing *mélange* of hearty classics such as half a chargrilled Breton chicken served with *frites,* confit duck leg, or sirloin steak with Roquefort butter.

8 St. Thomas's Sq., Salisbury. www.cote-restaurants.co.uk. ✆**01722/335164.** Reservations recommended. Main courses £10–£18; 2-course lunch menu £10. MC, V. Mon–Fri 8am–11pm; Sat 9am–11pm; Sun 9am–10:30pm.

ELSEWHERE IN SOUTH WILTSHIRE

Compasses Inn ★★ GASTROPUB Behind the whitewashed walls and latched wooden door of this remote thatched inn lies one of the finest pub kitchens in Wiltshire. The chalkboard menu covers country gastro classics like pork and leek sausages with mash, or local game pie, but also lets fly with some creative combinations served in hearty portions. Expect the likes of slow-cooked veal brisket with parsley mash and a wild mushroom sauce. Real ales on tap include local brews.

Lower Chicksgrove, Tisbury, nr. Salisbury. www.thecompassesinn.com. ✆**01722/714318.** Reservations recommended. Main courses £9–£16. MC, V. Daily midday–2pm and 6:30–9pm (closed Mon lunch in winter). Take the westbound A30 from Salisbury to Shaftesbury, turning off 1½ miles west of Fovant toward Chicksgrove, from where you should follow signs down a single-track road.

Shopping

You'll find the usual chains along the **High Street** and in the adjacent **Old George Mall** (www.oldgeorgemall.co.uk). Salisbury's best indie shopping spot is **Fisherton Mill** ★, 108 Fisherton St. (www.fishertonmill.co.uk; ✆ **01722/415121;** closed Sun–Mon), where a converted Victorian grain mill hosts open artisans' studios selling contemporary crafts, as well as a cafe.

Entertainment & Nightlife
THE PERFORMING ARTS

The city's arts scene is thriving and varied. The **Salisbury Playhouse** ★, Malthouse Lane (www.salisburyplayhouse.com; ✆ 01722/320333), stages some of the finest theatre in southwest England—the program could feature anything from an Austen adaptation to a touring contemporary drama, and includes productions aimed at youngsters. At the **City Hall,** Malthouse Lane (www.cityhallsalisbury.co.uk; ✆ 01722/434434), next door, you're more likely to encounter a big-name comedian or tribute band. The **Salisbury Arts Centre,** Bedwin Street (www.salisburyarts centre.co.uk; ✆ 01722/321744), housed within the former St. Edmund's Church, offers a broad, occasionally edgy mix of music, contemporary and classic theatre, and dance performances, plus cabaret, comedy, and family shows.

THE PUB SCENE

Hopback is the local brewer to look out for, and the best of Salisbury's many pubs usually have at least one of its beers on tap. Real ale geeks can make the pilgrimage to the pub where the brewery began, the **Wyndham Arms,** 27 Estcourt Rd. (✆ 01722/331026). Also standing just outside the center, freehouse **Deacons** ★, 118 Fisherton St. (✆ 01722/504723), has a local reputation for serving ale the way it should be. The tiny, characterful bar is worth the short walk. Even in a city full of ancient, half-timbered inns, there's nowhere quite like the **Haunch of Venison ★**, 1 Minster St. (www.haunchofvenison.uk.com; ✆ **01722/411313**). The haphazard interior layout and wood-paneled rooms of this former chophouse ooze medieval charm—and are reputedly haunted. **Rai d'Or,** 69 Brown St. (www.raidor.co.uk; ✆ **01722/327137**), may look nondescript in comparison, but the bar sells a range of interesting local microbrews.

Where to Stay
IN SALISBURY

Lazy Cow   Part crazy-bovine, part traditional Salisbury, the Lazy Cow opened in 2011 inside an ancient city inn—its layout is delightfully haphazard. The grandest units, no. 5 with regal black-and-gold decor, and wood-paneled, baronial no. 6, are at the front, overlooking a noisy road: For a quiet night, pick a room in the annex. Downstairs in the **steakhouse restaurant,** it's (nearly) all about the cow. Decor is ranchlike, banquettes are covered in cowhide, and beef is the star ingredient. Main courses range £10 to £30, with succulent steaks occupying the top of that range.

9–13 St. John St., Salisbury SP1 2SB. www.thelazycowsalisbury.co.uk. ✆ **01722/412028.** 17 units. £90–£145 double. Rates include breakfast. AE, MC, V. **Amenities:** Restaurant; bar; room service. *In room:* TV, hair dryer, MP3 docking station, Wi-Fi (free).

Legacy Rose & Crown Hotel ★   This half-timbered 13th-century inn stands with its feet almost in the River Avon, in a tranquil location that's an easy 10-minute walk over a stone bridge to the center of Salisbury. The hotel has both new and old wings: Room nos. 1 through 5 have original beamed ceilings and antique decor, but look out over a (generally quiet) road. Newer units are bigger with less character, but they have a view over the water meadows to Salisbury Cathedral. Take your pick.

Harnham Rd., Salisbury SP2 8JQ. www.legacy-hotels.co.uk. ✆ **0844/411-9046.** Fax 0844/411-9047. 29 units. £95–£160 double. Rates include breakfast. Free parking. AE, DC, MC, V. Take the A3094 1½ miles south from the center. **Amenities:** Restaurant; 2 bars; room service. *In room:* TV, hair dryer; Wi-Fi (free).

Peartree Serviced Apartments ★ 🎁   Opened in 2010, these modern apartments inside a whitewashed former station hotel offer the convenience of kitchen facilities on top of all the basic hotel amenities. Units are well designed, simply decorated, and come in a range of sizes from compact studios to 2-bedroom apartments suited to families, or even adults traveling together—both bedrooms are en suite. It's worth the extra £15 or so to upgrade to a more spacious executive unit. The apartments overlook a busy road, but soundproofing is excellent.

Mill Rd., Salisbury SP2 7RT. www.peartreeapartments.co.uk. ✆ **01722/322055.** Fax 01722/327677. 11 units. £85–£150 apartment. Free parking. AE, MC, V. *In apartment:* TV, kitchen, hair dryer, no phone, MP3 docking station (on request), Wi-Fi (free).

St. Ann's House ★★ 🍴   This refined town-house B&B is a delightful mix of the contemporary and the traditional: A typical room might see fresh colors partnering a restored walnut armoire and antique writing desk. Mattresses are luxurious, linens of the highest quality, and a spritz of lavender water on your pillow sends you gently off to sleep. No unit is large, in keeping with the original Georgian floorplan, so spend an extra £5 to upgrade to a bigger Premium Room. Breakfast is an event, indulging the food passions of the owner, a former chef. Expect a daily fresh frittata or *asheray,* a Turkish dish made with fruits, nuts, and cinnamon.

32–34 St. Ann's St., Salisbury SP1 2DP. www.stannshouse.co.uk. ☏ **01722/335657.** 8 units. £64–£89 double. Rates include breakfast. AE, MC, V. *In room:* TV, hair dryer, no phone, Wi-Fi (free).

Wyndham Park Lodge   This appealing corner villa in a residential neighborhood offers great value B&B and a friendly welcome just 10 minutes' walk from the center of Salisbury. The small to midsize rooms in the main house are dripping in Victoriana and comfortably furnished with Edwardian antiques. The annex "garden room" has more space, less period character, plus a private patio.

51 Wyndham Rd., Salisbury SP1 3AB. www.wyndhamparklodge.co.uk. ☏ **01722/416517.** Fax 01722/328851. 3 units. £65–£75 double; £70–£85 family room for 3. Rates include English breakfast. Free parking. No children 7 and under. MC, V. *In room:* TV/DVD, hair dryer, Wi-Fi (free).

ELSEWHERE IN SOUTH WILTSHIRE

Howard's House ★ 📷   This converted 17th-century dower house is the most appealing small hotel and restaurant in the idyllic countryside west of Salisbury; its comfortable seclusion and country-house decor are popular with shooting and fishing enthusiasts. As well as a snug area added in 2010, the hotel has attractive gardens, and on chilly evenings, log fires burn. Rooms are spacious, with one large enough for a family and another with a four-poster bed. The **restaurant** menu is designed to showcase its ingredients in classic English dishes. Two courses, which might include the likes of loin of roe deer with beetroot gratin and shallot puree, cost £36.

Teffont Evias, near Salisbury, Wiltshire SP3 5RJ. www.howardshousehotel.co.uk. ☏ **01722/716392.** Fax 01722/716820. 9 units. £190–£210 double. Rates include English breakfast. Free parking. AE, MC, V. On the A30 out of Salisbury, continue for 3 miles to the B3089 for Barford Saint-Martin. Continue for 4 miles to the village of Teffont Evias. **Amenities:** Restaurant; bar. *In room:* TV, hair dryer, Wi-Fi (free).

Newton Farmhouse ★ ☺   This restored 16th-century farm-guesthouse makes a perfect touring base for visiting Salisbury, the New Forest, and the best of Hampshire (see chapter 7). Rooms conform to the charming, haphazard layout of the original buildings, and are comfortable and full of character, with all bathrooms renovated in 2010. Interconnecting units are adapted to families, as is the garden. The only downside is the adjacent road, but glazing is efficient, so only the lightest of sleepers should be deterred.

Southampton Rd., near Salisbury, Wiltshire SP5 2QL. www.newtonfarmhouse.com. ☏ **01794/884416.** 9 units. £70–£150 double. Rates include English breakfast. Free parking. MC, V. On the A36, 7 miles southeast of Salisbury. **Amenities:** Pool (outdoor). *In room:* TV, hair dryer, Wi-Fi (free).

NORTH & WEST WILTSHIRE ★

Longleat: 108 miles SW of London, 28 miles SE of Bristol; Stourhead: 6 miles SW of Longleat.

Two very different ideas about what a country house and gardens should be in the 21st century grace the rural southwestern corner of Wiltshire, adjoining the Somerset and Dorset borders. The **Stourhead** estate is home to a magical "English garden," a landscape crafted during the 18th century where architecture and nature combine with exquisite beauty and harmony. Rather than surrender his inheritance, the 6th Marquess of Bath took the unusual decision in the 1940s to open his country seat, **Longleat,** to visitors. The range of attractions surrounding this grandiose Elizabethan mansion has been expanding ever since; it's all aimed squarely at the family day-tripper market. Stately it isn't, perhaps, but it's lots of fun with little ones in tow.

Northern Wiltshire's most intriguing spot is the ancient stone circle at **Avebury.**

Essentials

If you're **driving,** you can visit both Longleat and Stourhead in one busy day. From Bath, take the A36 south to Warminster; then follow the signs. From Salisbury, take the A36 northwest to Warminster, following signs to Longleat. To reach Stourhead from Longleat, drive 6 miles down the B3092 to Stourton, 3 miles northwest of Mere. **Avebury** is on the A4361, between Swindon and Devizes, 1 mile off the A4.

By **public transportation,** for Longleat, take the train to Warminster; then hop in a taxi to Longleat (about 10 min.). Getting to Stourhead by public transportation is difficult; you can take the train from Bath to Frome, or from Salisbury to Gillingham (both 30-min. trips). From the former it's a 10-mile taxi ride, from the latter 7 miles. Avebury has no convenient public transport links. The closest rail station is at Swindon, 11 miles away, which is served by quarter- or half-hourly trains from London Paddington Station (55 min.). An hourly bus service (no. 49) runs from Swindon Station to Avebury, taking 40 minutes. **Heritage Cycle Tours** (www.heritagecycle tours.com; ✆ **01980/862099**) offers a 1-day itinerary that leads you from Marlborough to Avebury and back. Pickup from Salisbury is also possible. The tour costs £49 including cycle rental.

Exploring North & West Wiltshire

Avebury ★★ HISTORIC SITE   A visit to one of Europe's most expansive prehistoric sites is a more organic experience than a trip to Stonehenge—you can walk right up to and around this "henge" (earthwork and stone circle). Avebury village is spread over a 28-acre site, winding in and out of the circle of more than 100 stones. The stones are made of sarsen, a sandstone local to Wiltshire, and some weigh up to 45 tonnes (50 tons). Native Neolithic tribes are believed to have built the circles as part of a sacred complex that encompasses nearby **Silbury Hill** ★, a 31-m (102-ft.) mound of chalk and rubble that protrudes from the Wiltshire grassland like an overgrown Egyptian pyramid. It's Europe's tallest manmade mound.

Also at Avebury is the **Alexander Keiller Museum and Barn,** which houses a small but important archeological collection, including material from excavations here, which Keiller oversaw in the 1930s. Keiller even re-erected some of Avebury's fallen stones to their upright positions.

Avebury, Wiltshire. www.nationaltrust.org.uk/avebury. ✆ **01672/539250.** Stone circle: free admission; Museum: £4.40 adults, £2.20 children, £12 family ticket. Stone circle daily dawn to dusk; museum: Nov–Mar daily 10am–4pm, Apr–Oct daily 10am–6pm.

Longleat House & Safari Park ☺ HISTORIC HOME/ZOO   On first glimpse, this magnificent Elizabethan stately home built in the early Renaissance style is romantic enough, and once you're inside, it's hard not to be dazzled by the lofty rooms and their exquisite paintings (including a Titian) and furnishings. From the surviving Elizabethan Great Hall, which Elizabeth I visited in 1574, to the State Rooms and late Georgian Grand Staircase, Longleat is filled with all manner of gorgeous things.

Surrounding the house, the number of attractions aimed squarely at children continues to expand. Around Longleat House is **Longleat Safari Park,** which opened in 1966 as Britain's first drive-through animal park. It hosts several species of endangered wild animal, including white rhinos and Rothschilds giraffes, that are free to roam the Capability Brown-landscaped parkland. You can also see a pack of Canadian timber wolves, two separate prides of lion, and endangered Siberian tigers, all from the comfort and safety of your car. Alternatively, see the animals by train, for a railway

EN ROUTE TO BATH: TWO glorious
WILTSHIRE VILLAGES

Tiny **Lacock** ★ is one of the best-pre-served villages in England. Turned over to the National Trust in 1944, it's crammed with enchanting medieval and 16th-century homes, gardens, and churches. **Lacock Abbey,** High Street (www.nationaltrust.org.uk/lacock; (℗ **01249/730459**), is actually a whimsi-cal country house, built upon the foun-dations of a nunnery dating from 1232. The first-floor rooms and the Great Hall are open to visitors. While on the grounds, stop by the medieval barn, home to the **Fox Talbot Museum** (℗ **01249/730459**). This is where Wil-liam Henry Fox Talbot carried out his early experiments with photography, making the first known photographic prints in 1833. The galleries here tell the story of the pioneer and display tempo-rary photography exhibitions.

The Abbey grounds, cloisters, and museum are open November through February daily 11am to 4pm, and March to October daily 10:30am to 5:30pm. The Abbey rooms are open November

to February Saturday and Sunday noon to 4pm, and March to October Wednes-day to Monday 11am to 5pm. Admission is £10.40 for adults and £5.10 for chil-dren ages 5 to 13; a family ticket costs £26.50. Admission to the grounds and museum only is £7.70 for adults, £3.80 for children, and £19.50 for a family ticket.

Located 12 miles northeast of Bath, the village of **Castle Combe** ★★ is another gorgeous old Wiltshire village, comprising one street lined with aging stone cottages and easily explored dur-ing a morning or afternoon. It's espe-cially popular with filmmakers: *Dr. Doolittle* was filmed here in 1966, and the 15th-century Dower House, used as Rex Harrison's residence in the movie, is one of Castle Combe's most attractive buildings. In 2009 the village provided the creepy backdrop for Benicio del Toro and Anthony Hopkins in *Wolfman*, while Steven Spielberg shot most of *War Horse* here in 2010.

adventure, or ride on a safari boat around the park's lake to view hippos and feed sea lions. The park provides some low-key theme-park amusements as well, including an Adventure Castle and a Hedge Maze. *Insider tip:* Beware summer weekends, which can get very busy.

Warminster, Wiltshire. www.longleat.co.uk. (℗**01985/844400.** Admission to House: £13.50 adults, £11.50 seniors, £8.50 children 3–14; All-in-One ticket: £27.50 adults, £22 seniors, £19.50 children 3–14. Feb 11–Feb 18 and Apr–Oct Mon–Fri 10am–5pm, Sat–Sun 10am–5:30pm; Mar weekends only 10am–5pm.

Stourhead ★★ PARK/GARDEN   In a county (and country) of superlative green spaces, Stourhead stands out as the most celebrated example of 18th-century English landscape gardening. More than that, it's a delightful place to wander—among its trees, flowers, and colorful shrubs are tucked bridges, grottoes, follies, and temples. This is nature carefully crafted into a work of art.

The **Temple of Flora** was the first building in the garden, designed by the archi-tect Henry Flitcroft in 1744. The **Grotto,** constructed in 1748, is lined with tufa, a water-worn limestone deposit. The springs of the Stour flow through the cold bath, where a lead copy of a sleeping Ariadne lies. The **Pantheon** was built in 1753 to house Rysbrack's statues of Hercules and Flora and other classical figures. Every corner you roam brings a new angle on this magical creation—pack a camera. Although Stourhead is a garden for all seasons, it is at its most idyllic in summer, when the rhododendrons bloom.

The stately home at Stourhead is less spectacular. Designed by Colen Campbell, a leader in the Georgian neoclassical revival, it was built for Henry Hoare I between 1721 and 1725. The Hoare banking family subsequently oversaw the creation of the 100 acres of landscaped gardens to complement it, notably during the time of Henry Hoare II (1705–85), known immodestly as "Henry the Magnificent."

Stourton, nr. Mere. www.nationaltrust.org.uk/stourhead. © **01747/841152.** Admission to house and gardens £12.10 adults, £6 children 5–16, £29 family ticket; gardens only £7.30 adults, £4 children, £17.40 family ticket. House mid-Mar–mid-July and Sept–mid-Oct Fri–Tues 11am–5pm; mid-July–Aug and mid-Oct–Nov 6 daily 11am–5pm; Dec Fri–Sun 11am–3pm (when also decorated for Christmas). Garden daily 9am–6pm.

BATH ★★★

115 miles W of London; 13 miles SE of Bristol

Few cities in England are as elegant as Bath. Set in the leafy Avon Valley, the town boomed in the 18th century, when England's high society flocked here to "take the waters." The spa town's ravishing Georgian architecture, Palladian mansions, and aged pubs have been virtually untouched by modern development, making this one of the most enticing destinations in the country; it's also one of the most popular.

Bath's historical roots are commemorated at the **Roman Baths and Pump Room,** sensitively restored and now an illuminating window into the lives of Roman Britons. **Bath Abbey** is the other major historic draw, but the city's **Georgian splendor** is best absorbed by wandering down handsome terraces such as the Royal Crescent.

Bath was established by the Romans as a hot-spring spa in A.D. 43—the curative waters were thought to ease rheumatism. Today those same waters provide the best cure for a hard day of sightseeing, with **Thermae Bath Spa** providing modern, sophisticated facilities and an open-air pool in which to soak.

Bath also boasts a surprisingly eclectic dining scene, but afternoon tea is a particular art form here, taken in wonderfully atmospheric rooms with Sally Lunn's famous buns, sweet "Bath buns" at the Pump Rooms, or "with Mr. Darcy" at the Jane Austen Centre—the beloved author set much of *Persuasion* and *Northanger Abbey* in the city.

Nightlife in Bath revolves around its collection of venerable pubs, fine Georgian watering holes such as the Raven of Bath, and the Bell Inn in the artsy Walcot district. Expect real ales, meaty pies, and inviting log fires in the winter.

Essentials

GETTING THERE Trains leave London's Paddington Station bound for Bath once every half-hour during the day; the trip takes about 1½ hours (£39–£84 one-way). The train ride from Bristol to Bath takes 11 to 15 minutes (£6.80); if you're arriving at Bristol Airport, catch the airport bus to Bristol's Temple Meads Station, where you can get the train to Bath.

If you're driving from London, head west on the M4 to junctions 17 (A350) or 18 (A46) and continue south to Bath.

VISITOR INFORMATION The **Bath Tourist Information Centre** is at Abbey Chambers, Abbey Church Yard (www.visitbath.co.uk; © **09067/112000**), next to

Bath

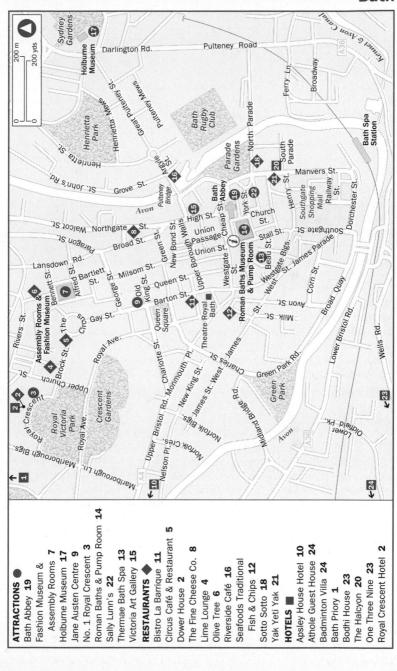

ATTRACTIONS ●
Bath Abbey **19**
Fashion Museum &
    Assembly Rooms **7**
Holburne Museum **17**
Jane Austen Centre **9**
No. 1 Royal Crescent **3**
Roman Baths & Pump Room **14**
Sally Lunn's **22**
Thermae Bath Spa **13**
Victoria Art Gallery **15**

RESTAURANTS ◆
Bistro La Barrique **11**
Circus Café & Restaurant **5**
Dower House **2**
The Fine Cheese Co. **8**
Lime Lounge **4**
Olive Tree **6**
Riverside Café **16**
Seafoods Traditional
    Fish & Chips **12**
Sotto Sotto **18**
Yak Yeti Yak **21**

HOTELS ■
Apsley House Hotel **10**
Athole Guest House **24**
Badminton Villa **24**
Bath Priory **1**
Bodhi House **23**
The Halcyon **20**
One Three Nine **23**
Royal Crescent Hotel **2**

8

WILTSHIRE & SOMERSET | Bath

Bath Abbey. It's open June through September, Monday to Saturday 9:30am to 6pm and Sunday 10am to 4pm; October to May, Monday to Saturday 9:30am to 5pm and Sunday 10am to 4pm. Closed December 25 and January 1.

TOURS To get a unique perspective on Bath, take the **Bizarre Bath Walking Tour** (www.bizarrebath.co.uk; ✆ **01225/335124**), a 1½-hour tour of Bath's lesser-known sights during which the guides pull pranks and tell jokes. It runs nightly at 8pm from Easter to October (no reservations necessary; just show up at the Huntsman Inn at North Parade Passage). Cost is £8 for adults, £5 for students and children. Conventional **open-top bus tours** (50 min.) are operated by **Bath Bus Company** (www.bathbuscompany.com; ✆ **01225/330444**) and cost £12.50 for adults, £10.50 for seniors and students, £7 for children 5 to 15. **Free walking tours** are provided by Mayor of Bath Honorary Guides (✆ **01225/477411;** 2hr.; Sun–Fri 10:30am, 2pm; Sat 10:30am) from outside the Abbey Churchyard entrance to the Pump Room (May–Sept additional tours Tues, Fri at 7pm).

SPECIAL EVENTS The **Jane Austen Festival** (www.janeausten.co.uk/jane-austen-festival; ✆ **01225/443000**) celebrates the life of the famous author every September, with concerts, walking tours, food events, talks, and dancing held all over the city. The **Bath Christmas Market** (www.bathchristmasmarket.com) is held from late November to mid-December, with around 130 small German-style wood chalets set up around the abbey selling everything from Christmas cards and gifts to bratwurst.

Exploring Bath

Bath is easy to explore on foot, with everything a short walk from the Roman Baths and Bath Abbey. John Wood the Elder (1704–54) designed much of Georgian Bath; his masterpiece is the elegant **Circus ★★★** of 1768, a series of three Palladian crescents arranged in a circle, at the northern end of Gay Street. Be sure to cross the River Avon via the shop-lined **Pulteney Bridge,** designed by Robert Adam in 1778 and often compared to the Ponte Vecchio in Florence.

Bath Abbey ★★ ABBEY   Bath Abbey is the last of the great medieval churches of England, a fine example of the late Perpendicular style. The stupendous West Front is the sculptural embodiment of a dream that inspired the Abbey's founder, Bishop Oliver King, to pull down an older Norman cathedral on this site in 1499 and build the one you see today. When you go inside and see its many ornate windows, you'll understand why the abbey is called the "Lantern of the West." For a bird's-eye view of the city, take the Abbey Tower Tour (45–50 min.), climbing 212 steps to the top of the abbey's vaulted ceiling, the clock face, and belfry (tours usually run Apr–Oct Mon–Sat 10am–4pm on the hour; Nov–Mar at 11am, noon, and 2pm). Every year, from mid-February through October, the abbey nave is adorned with Sue Symon's *One Man's Journey to Heaven,* better known as the **Bath Abbey Diptychs ★**. This extraordinary work depicts the life of Christ in 35 pairs of vividly decorated panels.

Abbey Churchyard. www.bathabbey.org. ✆ **01225/422462.** Free admission (suggested donation £2.50). Tower tours £6 adults, £3 children 5–15. Abbey Apr–Oct Mon 9:30am–6pm, Tues–Sat 9am–6pm; Nov–Mar Mon 9:30am–4:30pm, Tues–Sat 9am–4:30pm; year-round Sun 1–2:30pm and 4:30–5:30pm.

Fashion Museum & Assembly Rooms ★ MUSEUM   The grand Assembly Rooms, designed by the younger John Wood and completed in 1771, once played host to dances, recitals, and tea parties. Damaged in World War II, the elegant rooms have been gloriously restored and look much as they did when Jane Austen and

Thomas Gainsborough attended society events here. If there are no events taking place, you can wander the Ball Room, Tea Room, and Octagon and Card Room with their nine magnificent chandeliers, and view Gainsborough's portrait of *Captain William Wade* (1769).

Housed in the same building, the **Fashion Museum** offers displays enhanced by audioguides charting the history of fashion from the 16th century to the present day. Highlights include an extremely rare "silver tissue" dress made in 1660, a whalebone corset from the 1780s, and an extensive range of women's fashion through the 19th century right up to contemporary haute couture. There's also a special "Corsets and Crinolines" display, where enthusiastic visitors can try on reproduction period garments.

Bennett St. www.fashionmuseum.co.uk. © **01225/477789.** Admission (includes audio tour and Assembly Rooms) £7.50 adults, £6.75 students and seniors, £5.50 children 6–16, £21 family ticket, free for children 5 and younger. Admission to the Assembly Rooms only £2, free for children 16 and under. Nov–Feb daily 10:30am–4pm; Mar–Oct daily 10:30am–5pm. Last admission 1 hr. before closing. Closed Dec 25–26.

Holburne Museum ★★ MUSEUM   This once stuffy art museum was utterly transformed by a stunning redevelopment by top Brit architect Eric Parry in 2011. The original classical facade, built in 1796, has been enhanced by a ceramic and glass extension and restaurant, with an interior of bright stylish galleries. Highlights on the first floor include a fascinating selection of curios put together by museum founder Sir William Holburne in the 19th century: a tiny Venus made in Italy in 1550, 120 antique silver spoons, and a display of worthy fakes, like a huge carved ivory horn purporting to be from the time of George I. Holburne's Flemish and Dutch paintings are also worth lingering over, especially Breugel's lively *Visit of the Godfather*. On the mezzanine level a cleverly curated exhibition of everyday items throws light on culture in Georgian Britain and especially booming Bath, with porcelain from Wedgewood's shop (which opened here in 1772), and oriental luxuries collected by the wealthy. On the second floor you'll find the museum's fine British artwork (1700–1840), with paintings from Constable, Reynolds, Stubbs, and Turner's *Pembroke Castle*. There's also plenty from Gainsborough, including the famous *Byam Family*, and the humorous *Sylvester Daggerwood* by Samuel De Wilde, once owned by writer Somerset Maugham.

Great Pulteney St., at Sydney Place. www.holburne.org. © **01225/428126.** Free admission. Mon–Sat 10am–5pm; Sun 11am–5pm.

Jane Austen Centre MUSEUM   This small homage to Britain's favorite 19th-century writer occupies a graceful Georgian town house on a street where Ms. Austen once lived (at no. 25). Visits start with a talk from enthusiastic volunteers (who will reveal that Jane was fairly unhappy here, despite setting two books in the city), and a special room dedicated to the two *Persuasion* movies (1995 and 2007). Well-presented exhibits and a 15-minute video downstairs convey a sense of what life was like when Austen lived in Bath, between 1801 and 1806. Ladies can also learn the esoteric skill of using a fan to attract an admirer. The upstairs tearoom is manned by staff in period costume (p. 341).

40 Gay St. www.janeausten.co.uk. © **01225/443000.** Admission £7.45 adults, £5.95 students and seniors, £4.25 children 6–15, £19.50 family ticket. Apr–Oct daily 9:45am–5:30pm; Nov–Mar Sun–Fri 11am–4:30pm, Sat 9:45am–5:30pm. Closed Dec 24–26 and Jan 1.

No. 1 Royal Crescent MUSEUM   This small but edifying museum provides a glimpse of what it was like to live at Bath's most sought-after address. The younger John Wood (1727–81) designed the landmark **Royal Crescent ★★★**, a gorgeous half-moon row of town houses completed in 1774. The Georgian interior of no. 1 has been redecorated and furnished in late 18th-century style, replete with period Chippendale furniture and authentic flowery wallpaper. Guides in each room provide context. A major expansion into the property next door should be complete by 2013, allowing an increased focus on servants and the kitchens dubbed "The Whole Story."

1 Royal Crescent. www.bath-preservation-trust.org.uk. ℂ **01225/428126.** Admission £6.50 adults, £5 students and seniors, £2.50 children 5–16, £13 family ticket. Mid-Feb–Oct Tues–Sun 10:30am–5pm; Nov–mid-Dec Tues–Sun 10:30am–4pm (last admission 30 min. before closing).

Roman Baths ★★★ & Pump Room ★★ MUSEUM   Blending Roman ingenuity and Georgian style, one of England's top historic attractions reopened after a magnificent renovation in 2010. Free audioguides (with additional commentary by Bill Bryson), high-tech displays, and costumed actors help interpret the site, a complex of buildings built over hot springs in Roman times but much altered over the centuries. Most of what you see above ground was actually designed by the ubiquitous John Wood, and later Victorian architects in the 1890s, and only the stonework below the pillars is original Roman—much of the appeal comes from the way the museum has been able to expose and present what remains of these ancient Roman foundations dating back to the 1st century. The **Great Bath** is the most evocative part of the museum, with its steaming emerald waters and vast network of surrounding sweat baths and pools providing a real sense of its Roman heyday.

Coffee, lunch, and tea, usually with classical music from the Pump Room Trio, can be enjoyed in the adjacent 18th-century **Pump Room** (ℂ **01225/444477;** daily 9:30am–5pm), overlooking the King's Bath. Even if you're not eating or drinking here, pop in to sample the famed spa waters, pumped up from the original spring, filtered and served lukewarm from the King's Fountain for 50p a cup (free for diners). Charles Dickens famously (and accurately) described the water as tasting of "warm flat irons."

Bath Abbey Church Yard, Stall St. www.romanbaths.co.uk. ℂ **01225/477785.** Admission £12.25 adults (£12.50 July–Aug), £10.75 seniors, £8 children 6–16, £35 family ticket. Nov–Feb daily 9:30am–4:30pm; Mar–June and Sept–Oct daily 9am–5pm; July–Aug daily 9am–9pm.

Sally Lunn's MUSEUM/CAFE   This creaky, timber-framed medieval gem, tea-room and restaurant, is an unashamedly touristy but fun monument to the Sally Lunn Bun (a light, semisweet bread, like a big brioche). Sally Lunn—the erstwhile creator of the bun—was a French Huguenot refugee who came to Bath in 1680. The tasty bun she created (best eaten with cheese) is eagerly wolfed down by hordes of tourists in the antique-laden dining rooms here, which also serves more formal dinners. The tiny museum in the basement preserves Sally's original kitchen and "Faggot Oven," which was first built by monks in the 1150s. Roman foundations have been found here, though most of the house you see today dates from the 1620s (the oft quoted date of 1482 refers to the first written mention of a house on this site).

4 North Parade Passage. www.sallylunns.co.uk. ℂ **01225/461634.** Museum admission 50p adults; free for children, seniors, and cafe customers. Sally Lunn Bun £3.38–6.18. Cafe Mon–Thurs 10am–9:30pm; Fri–Sat 10am–10pm; Sun 11am–9:30pm. Museum Mon–Sat 10am–6pm; Sun 11am–6pm.

Thermae Bath Spa ★★ BATHS   The waters at the old Roman baths are unfit for bathing, so if you want to sample the city's celebrated hot springs make for this plush, modern spa—the water might be 10,000 years old but the facilities are pure 21st-century. Regular admission gives you access to the indoor Minerva Pool, the stylish steam baths (four scented all-glass steam rooms), and the Open-Air Rooftop Pool, where you can watch the sun setting over the Abbey while you soak. The historic Cross Bath complex, site of a Roman well and where James II's wife once bathed, is also available for private rental (£160 per hr.). Book ahead for treatments, and aim to visit on a weekday to avoid the busiest times.

Hot Bath St. www.thermaebathspa.com.✆ **0844/888-0844.** Admission £26 for 2 hr., £36 for 4 hr. Towel hire £3, robe hire £4. Daily 9am–10pm, last entry 7:30pm. Closed Dec 24–25 and Jan 1–7. Children under 16 not permitted (children of 12 and over can use the Cross Bath accompanied by an adult).

Victoria Art Gallery GALLERY   This less visited gallery showcases a fine collection of British and European art, including paintings by artists who lived and worked in the Bath area such as Gainsborough. The main Upper Gallery is a wonderfully bright, Victorian space dating from 1900, with some real gems on display from the permanent collection. In addition to portraits from Gainsborough such as *Sir Thomas Rumbold,* highlights include David Hardy's poignant *Boys Playing Marbles* (1855) and the twisted humor of Rex Whistler's *The Foreign Bloke* (1933). Special exhibitions are shown in the two large modern galleries downstairs; these change every 6 to 8 weeks and are likely to feature anything from cartoons to boat sculpture.

Bridge St. www.victoriagal.org.uk.✆ **01225/477233.** Free admission. Tues–Sat 10am–5pm; Sun 1:30–5pm.

Where to Eat
VERY EXPENSIVE
Dower House ★ ENGLISH   This is one of the West Country's finest dining choices, and the best place to splurge on a classic high-class English eating experience. The setting is romantic, with hand-painted wall coverings and alfresco dining on the sunny terrace in the summer. The contemporary British menu is seasonal, featuring everything from roasted rump of salt marsh lamb, to a summery wild sea bass with a smoked eel tortellini. You might finish with one of the lush desserts, such as a hazelnut chocolate teardrop autumn truffle ice cream with Marsala syrup.

Royal Crescent Hotel (see below), 16 Royal Crescent. www.royalcrescent.co.uk.✆ **01225/823333.** Reservations required. Fixed-price lunch £35 for 2 courses, £42 for 3 courses; fixed-price dinner £53 for 3 courses. AE, DC, MC, V. Daily noon–2pm and 7–9:30pm (until 10:30pm Sat).

Taking Tea in Bath

Bath is the ideal place to indulge in that quintessentially English tradition of afternoon tea, served with jam, clotted cream, and scones. Try the **Pump Room** ★★ at the **Roman Baths** (p. 340), which serves "Bath buns" (sweet buns sprinkled with sugar; £6.75), cream teas for £9.25, and a lavish afternoon tea for £17.50 (champagne tea £24.50). At **Sally Lunn's** ★ (p. 340) you can get a range of traditional Sally Lunn cream teas for £6.18 to £11.88, which include toasted and buttered Sally Lunn buns served with strawberry jam and clotted cream. The **Regency Tea Rooms** ★, at the Jane Austen Centre (p. 339), even offer "Tea with Mr. Darcy" sets for £12.50 to £23.50 for two (£25 for champagne), basic cream tea sets from £5.50, and just tea from £2.50.

Olive Tree ★★ MODERN ENGLISH/MEDITERRANEAN A highly rated alternative to the Dower House (above), the Olive Tree offers a posh English dining experience. It's also another restaurant that emphasizes fresh, local produce and a seasonal menu, though the dishes have a more playful, creative quality here; think pressing of Somerset game and roasted duck foie gras to start, and tempting main courses such as pavé of wild Cornish turbot, potato crisp tiger prawns, zucchini (courgette) ribbons, and champagne cream.

Queensberry hotel, Russell St. www.olivetreebath.co.uk. © **01225/447928.** Reservations highly recommended. Main courses £17.50–£31. AE, MC, V. Mon–Sat noon–2pm and 7–10pm; Sun noon–2pm and 7–9:30pm.

EXPENSIVE

Circus Café & Restaurant ★★ ENGLISH Not quite as posh as the Dower House or the Olive Tree, this still ends up being one of the finest eating experiences in Bath at half the price, located in a Georgian beauty right on the famous Circus itself. Head chef Alison Golden works with a seasonal, locally sourced menu with a British bias; offerings might include fresh squid from Lyme Bay; oxtail, potted in its own jelly with allspice and star anise; or frizzled pork belly, black pudding, glazed apples, and black cabbage. Finish off with a Yorkshire rhubarb fool, or a bitter chocolate tart with parsnip ice cream—it really works.

34 Brock St. www.thecircuscafeandrestaurant.co.uk. © **01225/466020.** Reservations recommended. Main courses £14–16. AE, DC, MC, V. Mon–Sat 10am–midnight.

Sotto Sotto ★★ ITALIAN Opening to rave reviews in 2011, this hip Italian restaurant with a Pugliese slant (the chef hails from Puglia) is set into artfully restored medieval stone vaults beneath the surface of Bath, a truly atmospheric place to end the day over a glass of Chianti. The food is exceptionally good and great value: start with a chicken liver bruschetta then opt for a fabulous home-cooked osso bucco, chicken stuffed with speck and cheese, or fresh sea bass. Finish with "Tuscan tea and biscuits" (aka *biscotti* dunked in *vin santo* or Italian dessert wine).

10 North Parade. www.sottosotto.co.uk. © **01225/330236.** Reservations highly recommended. Main courses £12–£18. AE, MC, V. Tues–Sat 6–10pm.

MODERATE

Bistro La Barrique ★★ FRENCH Renowned chef Michel Lemoine created quite a buzz when he opened this branch of his popular Bristol-based restaurant in Bath, with his justly lauded *petits plats* (French tapas) concept. Order several dishes to share with some crusty French bread; wild mushroom flan, the sea bass, creamed salted cod, and roast pork with parsnips and honey are solid choices, but the bourguignon-style braised ox cheek with mash is truly exquisite. The relaxed atmosphere makes this a great place to just grab a glass of wine and small snack if you're not in the mood for a full meal.

31 Barton St. www.bistrolabarrique.co.uk. © **01225/463861.** Small plates £5.95–£8.95. MC, V. Mon–Fri noon–2:30pm and 5:30–10:30pm; Sat noon–10:30pm.

Lime Lounge ★★ MODERN ENGLISH/CONTINENTAL Some of the best and friendliest service in the region separates this cozy bistro from the competition, though the food is also top-quality. The daytime menu features homemade soups and cakes, salads, burgers, and a range of sandwiches on specialty breads. Evenings are characterized by more substantial dishes such as pork with creamed apple and a cider and stilton sauce. But there are also riffs on old Brit classics: Think "posh" fish and chips (monkfish with Cajun and lime-dusted fat chips) and smoked kippers (herring) for breakfast. Hot chocolate fans are also in for a treat.

11 Margarets Buildings, off Brock St. www.limeloungebath.co.uk. © **01225/421251.** Reservations recommended. Lunch from £7.95; dinner main courses £10.95–£21.95. MC, V. Mon–Sat 8am–late; Sun 10am–10pm.

INEXPENSIVE
The Fine Cheese Co. ★ ⚡ DELI/CAFE   One of the country's finest artisan cheesemongers has a tiny cafe next door serving cheese sandwiches, savory tarts, and cakes (think flaky pastry sausage rolls and chewy pistachio macaroons). They also knock out superb bowls of soups such as celery, new potato, and scallions, served with rye sourdough bread, and plates of cheese with fruit and crackers (try locally produced Bath Soft Cheese, or the Wyfe of Bath). Outdoor seating is available in the summer.

29 & 31 Walcot St. www.finecheese.co.uk. © **01225/483407.** Main courses from £6.95, sandwiches from £4.60. MC, V. Mon–Fri 9:30am–5:30pm; Sat 9am–5:30pm.

Riverside Café ★ ⚡ CAFE   This place is all about the fabulous location, offering a rare chance to snack overlooking the River Avon, right under the Pulteney Bridge. Riverside serves some of the best coffee in Bath, decent cakes, and plenty of good food; the full breakfasts are especially tasty, but the fish and chips, (all their fish comes fresh from St. Mawes, Cornwall), Cornish mussels, and sandwiches are all solid bets for lunch or dinner.

17 Argyle St. www.riversidecafebath.co.uk. © **01225/480532.** Main courses £8.75–£9.95. MC, V. Mon–Sat 9am–9pm; Sun 9am–5pm.

Seafoods Traditional Fish & Chips ★ FISH & CHIPS   This family-owned shop has been serving this English fast-food staple for over 50 years, with cod, haddock, and plaice fried in a traditional, crispy batter and served with real thick-cut chips. It also does battered sausages, pies, mushy peas, fishcakes (cod, potatoes, and parsley), scampi, and even an extremely rich "posh" fish and chips (salmon). Take-out or grab a small table inside.

38 Kingsmead St. www.fishandchipsbath.co.uk. © **01225/465190.** Posh fish & chips £8.95; Main courses £6.25–£8.95. MC, V. Mon–Wed 11:30am–9pm; Thu–Sat 11:30am–10pm.

Yak Yeti Yak ★ ⚡ NEPALESE   At this enticing Nepali basement restaurant you can eat exceedingly well for under £12, from a menu that includes subtly spiced dishes such as lamb slow-cooked with bamboo shoots, black-eyed peas, and potato, or marinated chicken stir-fried with peppers and fresh chili. It's especially rewarding for vegetarians, with superb Aloo Channa (potato and chickpeas stir-fried with cumin) and some of the best black dhal in the region.

12 Pierrepont St. www.yakyetiyak.co.uk. © **01225/442299.** Main meat courses £7.30–£8.90, main vegetable dishes £5.50–£6.10. MC, V. Mon–Sat noon–2:30pm and 5–10:30pm; Sun noon–2:30pm and 5–10pm.

Shopping
SouthGate pedestrian mall (www.southgatebath.com) is fast becoming the primary outdoor shopping area in Bath, just north of the train station. Trendy **Milsom Place** (www.milsomplace.co.uk) has more fashionable designers, while the old-fashioned department store **Jolly's** is at 13 Milsom St. (www.houseoffraser.co.uk; © **0844/800-3704;** Mon–Thurs 9:30am–5:30pm; Fri 9:30am–6pm; Sat 9am–6pm; Sun 10:30am–5pm), founded in 1831 and now part of the House of Fraser chain. **Walcot Street** is the home of arty, independent stores, including **Bath Aqua Glass,** 107 Walcot St.

(www.bathaquaglass.com; ☎ **01225/428146**), a high quality glass studio open Monday to Saturday 9:30 to 5pm (demo times 11:15am and 2:15pm; £4). Royal fans should visit the **Highgrove Shop,** 38 Milsom St. (www.highgroveshop.com; ☎ **01225/445125;** Mon–Fri 9:30am–5:30pm, Sat 9:30am–6pm, Sun 10:30am–5pm), which sells fresh produce from the estate of Prince Charles.

Entertainment & Nightlife

As befits one of Britain's oldest cities, there are plenty of characterful pubs in Bath (for nightclubs, Bristol is much better). Look for beers from local microbreweries **Abbey Ales, Bath Ales,** and **Box Steam Brewery.** You'll find them among nine cask ales served at the **Bell ★**, 103 Walcot St. (www.walcotstreet.com; ☎ **01225/460426**), which also features live music ranging from jazz and country to reggae and blues on Monday and Wednesday nights and Sundays. **The Raven of Bath,** 6–7 Queen St. (www.theravenofbath.co.uk; ☎ **01225/425045**), also offers a range of excellent ales and wines, but is best known for its tasty meat pies. For live sports on big screens and a heated beer garden try the **Pig & Fiddle,** 2 Saracen St. (www.thepigandfiddle.co.uk; ☎ **01225/460868**). Pubs tend to open Monday to Saturday 11:30am to 11pm, and Sunday noon to 10:30pm.

Vegetarians and students love the **Porter,** 15 George St. (www.theporter.co.uk; ☎ **01225/424104**), a grungier option specializing in vegetarian food (£5–7) and live music, open-mic nights, ambient DJs, and comedy. Next door at 14 George St. is **Moles,** (www.moles.co.uk; ☎ **01225/404445**), Bath's premier dance club and live music venue. For something a bit more sophisticated, the **Circo Bar & Lounge** occupies the atmospheric cellars below the Halcyon hotel (see below), with luxurious Chesterfield sofas and plenty of cocktails (from £7.50).

Where to Stay
VERY EXPENSIVE

Bath Priory ★★ Bath's most historic and luxurious hotel is surrounded by award-winning gardens with manicured lawns and flower beds. The rooms are furnished with lavish antiques; our favorites are Heather and Lilac, on the top floor, with wonderful balconies overlooking the gardens (all rooms are named after flowers or shrubs). Rooms range from medium in size to spacious deluxe units, the latter with views, sitting areas, and generous dressing areas. Each has a lovely antique bed (two have four-posters).

Weston Rd., Bath, Somerset BA1 2XT. www.thebathpriory.co.uk. ☎ **01225/331922.** Fax 01225/448276. 27 units. £195–£400 double. Rates include English breakfast. AE, DC, MC, V. Free parking. **Amenities:** Restaurant; bar; 2 pools (1 heated indoor, 1 outdoor); exercise room; spa room service; babysitting. *In room:* A/C, TV, minibar, hair dryer, Wi-Fi (free).

Royal Crescent Hotel ★ Rates at this venerable hotel reflect the stunning location, in the center of the famed Royal Crescent. Guest rooms, including the Jane Austen Suite (a converted coach house), are luxuriously furnished with four-poster beds and marble tubs. Generally quite spacious, the bedrooms are also decked out with thick wool carpeting, silk wall coverings, and antiques. Each room is individually designed and offers such comforts as bottled mineral water and fruit plates.

16 Royal Crescent, Bath, Somerset BA1 2LS. www.royalcrescent.co.uk. ☎ **01225/823333.** Fax 01225/339401. 45 units. £199–£445 double; £449–£935 suite. Rates include English breakfast. AE, DC, MC, V. Free parking. **Amenities:** Restaurant (Dower House, p. 341); bar; indoor heated pool; exercise room; sauna babysitting; room service. *In room:* TV/DVD, minibar (in some), hair dryer, Wi-Fi (free).

EXPENSIVE

Apsley House Hotel ★★   This charming hotel, only about a mile west of the center of Bath, is one of the best deals in the city. The house dates from 1830 and was built for the Duke of Wellington (you can stay in his room). Style and comfort are the keynotes here, and all the relatively spacious bedrooms are invitingly appointed with plush beds (some four-posters), country-house chintzes, antiques, and oil paintings.

141 Newbridge Hill, Bath, Somerset BA1 3PT. www.apsley-house.co.uk. 🕐 **01225/336966.** Fax 01225/425462. 12 units. £70–£185 double. Rates include English breakfast. AE, MC, V. Free parking. Take the A4 to Upper Bristol Rd., fork right at the traffic signals into Newbridge Hill, and turn left at Apsley Rd. **Amenities:** Bar; room service. *In room:* TV, hair dryer; Wi-Fi (free).

MODERATE

Athole Guest House ★★ 🍴   Spacious, luxurious rooms, and friendly owners make this one of the best deals in the city. The key is value for money; rooms cost less than £100 most of the year, yet you get the amenities associated with a four-star hotel, as well as free transfers from the train station (taxis to the center are around £5). The house is Victorian, but the rooms are bright and contemporary. And the breakfasts are magical; from full English (with everything) to kippers, Welsh rarebit, and pancakes.

33 Upper Oldfield Park, Bath, Somerset BA2 3JX. www.atholehouse.co.uk. 🕐 **01225/320000.** 4 units. £60–£130 double. Rates include English breakfast. 2-night minimum stay Sat–Sun. AE, MC, V. Free parking. *In room:* A/C, TV, fridge, hair dryer, Wi-Fi (free).

The Halcyon ★   This is a true boutique hotel amid all the Georgian chintz, with a crisp contemporary theme. The property is a 1743 Georgian town house, but the compact rooms feature large, springy beds, bright colors (yellow, scarlet, or mauve), big plasma TVs, and Philippe Starck fittings in the bathroom. Fun extras in the rooms include jars filled with colored candy and gummy bears (though you have to pay for these). Rooms on the first floor are biggest, and the ones at the front have the best views.

2/3 South Parade, Bath, Somerset BA2 4AA. www.thehalcyon.com. 🕐 **01225/444100.** Fax: 01225/331200. 21 units. £99–£125 double. Breakfast extra £6.99. AE, MC, V. Public parking nearby £12. **Amenities:** Bar. *In room:* A/C, TV, Wi-Fi (free).

One Three Nine 🍴   This is another inviting alternative to Bath's numerous Georgian-theme hotels, a stylish contemporary B&B with nary an antique in sight. The house is a Victorian residence from the 1870s, but rooms feature modern English design, power showers, flat-screen TVs, and Molton Brown products. It's on the southern side of the city, on the A367 road to Exeter, just a 10-minute walk from the center of Bath, with minibuses passing by frequently.

139 Wells Rd., Bath, Somerset BA2 3AL. www.139bath.co.uk. 🕐 **01225/314769.** Fax 01225/443079. 8 units. £59–£185 double. Rates include English breakfast. 2-night minimum stay Sat–Sun. AE, MC, V. Free parking. *In room:* A/C, TV/DVD, CD player, hair dryer, Wi-Fi (free).

INEXPENSIVE

Badminton Villa 🍴   Located about a half-mile south of the city center, this is an atmospheric B&B that dates not from the Georgian era but the Victorian, constructed in 1883. Built of honey-colored blocks of Bath stone, it lies on a hillside with sweeping views over the city. Rooms are relatively free of the antiques that grace most historic hotels, but the wood and rattan furniture is tasteful nonetheless, and the breakfast and free Internet make this good value.

10 Upper Oldfield Park, Bath, Somerset BA2 3JZ. www.badmintonvilla.co.uk. ☏**01225/426347.** Fax 01225/420393. 4 units. £75–£85 double; £110 family room. No children 7 and under. Rates include English breakfast. MC, V. Free parking. Bus: 14. *In room:* TV, DVD, hair dryer, Wi-Fi (free).

Bodhi House ★ Stylish, modern B&B just outside the center (but within walking distance), hosted by the friendly and knowledgeable Taylor family (they'll usually give you a lift into town). Rooms come with comfy beds, flat-screen TVs, and tea- and coffee-making facilities (room 1 has the best views of Bath). Eco-friendly touches include hot water provided by solar power (rainwater is harvested and used wherever possible), rooms cleaned without the use of harsh chemicals, and breakfasts containing mostly locally-sourced and organic produce.

31A Englishcombe Lane, Bath, Somerset BA2 2EE. www.bodhihouse.co.uk. ☏**01225/461990.** 3 units. £70–£98 double; £70–140 family room. Rates include English breakfast. AE, DC, MC, V. Free parking. Bus: 17. *In room:* TV, DVD, hair dryer; Wi-Fi (free).

BRISTOL ★★

120 miles W of London; 13 miles NW of Bath

Bristol, the West Country's largest city (pop. 441,000), is a medieval port that has reinvented itself as a dynamic cultural center in the last few decades, home not just to a reinvigorated downtown but a host of pop icons, from 1990s "trip-hop" bands such as Tricky, Massive Attack, and Portishead, to irreverent graffiti artist Banksy and the risqué teenage U.K. TV series *Skins*.

Linked to the sea by 7 miles of the navigable River Avon, Bristol has long been rich in seafaring traditions. In 1497, Venetian John Cabot sailed from Bristol and was the first European to "discover" North America (at Newfoundland) since the Vikings. The city's most celebrated sights were built by Isambard Kingdom Brunel in the Victorian era: the Clifton Suspension Bridge and the SS *Great Britain*.

Essentials

GETTING THERE **Bristol Airport** (www.bristolairport.co.uk; ☏ **0871/334-4444**) is conveniently situated beside the A38, a little more than 7 miles from the city center. The **Bristol Airport Flyer** bus (flyer.bristolairport.co.uk; ☏ **0117/955-8211;** £6 adults, £5 children 15 and under) runs to the city bus station, Clifton, and the Temple Meads station (30 min.) every 10 minutes.

Frequent **train** services from London's Paddington Station run to Temple Meads, in the center of Bristol, and to Parkway, on the city's northern outskirts. The trip takes 1¾ hours and costs £39 to £89.50 one-way. The train ride from Bath to Bristol takes

---

Boats & Balloons

Soak up Bristol's seafaring roots by jumping on board a **Bristol Ferry Boat Company** ferry ★★ (www.bristolferry.com; ☏ **0117/927-3416**). Boats run throughout the day along the River Avon, enabling you to hop-on and hop-off for £1.90 per trip or £4.90 for a circular tour of the entire route. For a more exhilarating view of the city, take to the skies with **Bristol Balloons** ★★ (www.bristolballoons.co.uk; ☏ **0117/947-1050**), which runs a variety of thrilling "flights" from just £90.

Bristol

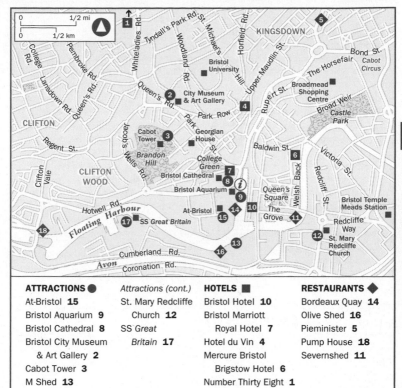

ATTRACTIONS ●	Attractions (cont.)	HOTELS ■	RESTAURANTS ◆
At-Bristol **15**	St. Mary Redcliffe	Bristol Hotel **10**	Bordeaux Quay **14**
Bristol Aquarium **9**	Church **12**	Bristol Marriott	Olive Shed **16**
Bristol Cathedral **8**	SS *Great*	Royal Hotel **7**	Pieminister **5**
Bristol City Museum	*Britain* **17**	Hotel du Vin **4**	Pump House **18**
& Art Gallery **2**		Mercure Bristol	Severnshed **11**
Cabot Tower **3**		Brigstow Hotel **6**	
M Shed **13**		Number Thirty Eight **1**	

11 to 15 minutes (£6.80). **Megabus** (uk.megabus.com) runs cheap buses between London and Bristol for as low as £7 (2 hr. 30 min.).

If you're driving, head west from London on the M4. The Park and Ride scheme is the hassle-free way to visit for the day; parking is free (follow the signs from the motorway) and buses into the center cost £2.50 to £3.50 round-trip.

VISITOR INFORMATION   Bristol's **Tourist Information Centre** is at E Shed, 1 Canon's Rd. (www.visitbristol.co.uk; ✆ **0906/711-2191**). Hours are daily from 10am to 5pm (10am–6pm Apr–Sept).

ORGANIZED TOURS   Guided 2-hour **walking tours** are conducted on Saturdays at 11am from April to September (www.bristolwalks.co.uk; ✆ **0117/968-4638**). They cost £5 per person (children 11 and under free) and depart from the Tourist Information Centre. Or you can don an eye patch and join a 2-hour walking tour led by **Pirate Pete** (www.piratewalks.co.uk; ✆ **07950/566483;** £7.50 adults, £3.50 children), Saturday and Sunday at 2pm starting at the Beetle sculpture in Anchor Square; Pete will tell you all about notorious Bristol residents like Blackbeard. **City Sightseeing** (www.citysight seeingbristol.co.uk; ✆ **0906/711-2191**) runs open-top bus tours of the city mid-March to October (£10 adults plus one free child; £5 children 5–15).

Georgian Bristol

Often overshadowed by Bath, its elegant neighbor, Bristol, is nevertheless studded with handsome Georgian relics. **Queen's Square** is Bristol at its most refined, a wide, leafy space completed in 1727 and sporting an equestrian statue of William III in the center. **Georgian House,** Great George St. (✆ **0117/921-1362;** May–Oct Wed–Sun 10:30am–4pm, July–Aug open Tues also; free), was built in 1790 for John Pinney, a wealthy slave plantation owner and sugar merchant. It has been restored to its 18th-century appearance, providing an insight into life for the upper and lower classes at the time. The humble **New Room,** 36 The Horsefair (✆ **0117/926-4740;** www.newroombristol.org.uk; Mon–Sat 10am–4pm; free), dates from

1739, when it was built as the meeting and preaching base of John and Charles Wesley, founders of Methodism—as such, it's considered the oldest Methodist chapel in the world. Today you can view the chapel as it was in the 18th century, wander the gallery, and visit the enlightening museum on the top floor, which highlights the lives of the Wesley brothers and early Methodism with portraits, rare mementos (such as a lock of John's hair), and personal effects. The **Red Lodge Museum** on Park Row (✆ **0117/921-1360;** May–Oct Wed–Sun 10:30am–4pm; free) was added to in Georgian times, but actually dates back to 1580, with rooms restored in both Georgian and Tudor styles.

SPECIAL EVENTS The **Bristol International Balloon Fiesta** (www.bristol balloonfiesta.co.uk; ✆ **0906/711-2191**) is a mesmerizing spectacle held every August, Europe's largest annual hot air balloon event (free). The **Bristol Harbour Festival** (www.bristolharbourfestival.co.uk; ✆ 0117/922-3287) is Bristol's biggest cultural event, with live music and street performances held on the waterside in late July or early August.

Exploring Bristol

Exploring central Bristol is relatively easy on foot, with the rough-and-ready 19th-century docks now the heart of the modern city, converted into hotels, enticing restaurants, shops, and art centers. The Floating Harbour—a watery ribbon that shadows the River Avon—rounds the old city with most sights within walking distance of Centre Promenade and the visitor center, or close to a Bristol Ferry stop.

At-Bristol ☺ PLANETARIUM   This entertaining, interactive science center is targeted primarily at children and families, with special exhibits on animation, flight, human inventions, and a stunning planetarium. Youngsters will love the "walk-in tornado," "leaning lounge," and "play TV," where they get to direct or present their own shows.

Anchor Rd. www.at-bristol.org.uk. ✆**0845/345-1235.** Admission £11.35 adults, £7.25 children 3–15, £32.25 family ticket. Mon–Fri 10am–5pm; Sat–Sun and school holidays 10am–6pm. Bus: 8 or 9.

Bristol Aquarium ★ ☺ AQUARIUM   This beautifully landscaped aquarium contains a diverse array of marine life, beginning with creatures found off the shores of Britain; tanks of moon jellyfish, mullet, whiting, and the bizarre snake pipefish. The "Bay of Rays" (feeding time 1pm) contains a selection of frisky blonde, painted, and thornback rays, while it's not often you can view a Giant Pacific octopus up close. Other tanks display the almost unreal looking big-bellied seahorses, and special sections cover the Amazon (including red-bellied piranhas) and coral reefs, with sharks, tropical fish, a whole tank of "Nemo" fish (aka clownfish) and the oddest looking creature here, the two-pronged cowfish.

Anchor Rd. www.bristolaquarium.co.uk. ℭ **0117/929-8929.** Admission £12.50 adults, £11.50 seniors and students, £8.75 children 3–14, £38.50 family ticket. Daily 10am–5pm (to 6pm Sat–Sun and holidays). Closed Christmas Day. Bus: 8 or 9.

Bristol Cathedral CATHEDRAL This fine example of monumental Gothic architecture was originally an Augustinian abbey founded in 1140, though most of the current structure dates from the 14th and 15th centuries and a 19th-century restoration. The eastern end of the cathedral, especially the choir, is one of Britain's most brilliant examples of early Decorated Gothic style, while the Elder Lady Chapel (1220) contains unusual carvings. The oldest part of the structure can be found off the south transept, where the simple but beautiful Romanesque lines of the Chapter House date back to 1185.

College Green, West End. www.bristol-cathedral.co.uk. ℭ **0117/926-4879.** Free admission; £2 donation requested. Mon–Sat 8am–6pm; Sun 7:20am–5pm. Bus: 8 or 9.

Bristol City Museum & Art Gallery MUSEUM Bristol's biggest museum is stuffed with an eclectic range of exhibits, from Egyptian mummies and Chinese art, to dinosaur skeletons and exquisite silverware. Highlights include the Bristol Boxkite (a biplane), the "Bristol dinosaur" (Britain's oldest), and paintings by Bellini, Renoir, Pissarro, and Jan Griffier, whose *Noah's Ark* is a museum favorite.

Queen's Rd., West End. www.bristol.gov.uk/museums.ℭ **0117/922-3571.** Free admission. Mon–Fri 10am–5pm.

Cabot Tower ★ OBSERVATION POINT This 32-m (105-ft.) sandstone tower was built in 1897 on Brandon Hill to commemorate John Cabot's voyage from Bristol to Newfoundland 400 years earlier. Today clambering up the narrow spiral staircase to the top provides the best views of the city.

Brandon Hill Park, just off Park St., West End.ℭ **0117/922-3719.** Free admission. Daily 8am to 30 min. before dusk.

M Shed ★★ ☺ MUSEUM Housed in an old warehouse, this absorbing museum takes a fresh, modern approach to charting the history and culture of Bristol. The "Bristol Places" gallery tackles the city's history from Saxon "Brycgstow," with a special section on the Bristol Blitz in World War II (in which much of the city was destroyed), and samples from the Welsh Back Coin Hoard, dating from the 16th century. "Bristol People" commemorates worthy Bristol citizens, but also tackles the thorny issue of

---

Banksy's Bristol ★★

Who is **Banksy?** Officially, it's a secret, although the now world-famous graffiti artist is certainly a Bristol native. You can see plenty of his iconic work around the city: His Frogmore Street *Love Triangle"* (a man hangs from an open window to escape his lover's husband) adorns the side of a sexual health clinic (get the best views from the small bridge on Park Street), while *Mild Mild West* (riot police versus a teddy bear) is located on Stokes Croft, next to the Canteen Bristol. Banksy also stenciled the Grim Reaper on the side of the Thekla (p. 354), a boat moored in the harbor (best viewed from the opposite bank). See also www.banksy.co.uk.

slavery with a thought-provoking exhibit (Bristol merchants were heavily involved in the slave trade in the 18th century), as well as the theme of protest and boycotts, from the 1831 Bristol riots to the St. Pauls riots of 1980. "Bristol Life" focuses on the multi-cultural identity of Bristol, with some rare items on display, including the fur suit of one of three Inuit abducted by English explorer Martin Frobisher in 1577 (all three died in Bristol within a month), and a piece on Hollywood heart-throb Carry Grant, who was actually born in Bristol in 1904 and became an American citizen in 1942 (there's a statue of the star in Millennium Square, on the other side of the Floating Harbour).

Wapping Rd., Princes Wharf. www.mshed.org. © **0117/925-1470.** Free admission. Tues–Fri 10am–5pm; Sat–Sun and public holidays 10am–6pm.

SS Great Britain ★★★ HISTORIC SITE   Bristol's pride and joy, the SS *Great Britain* was the world's first iron steamship when it was launched here in 1843. Two years later it crossed the Atlantic in 14 days—a record at the time. Damaged in a ferocious storm off Cape Horn in 1886, it served out its days as a floating warehouse in the Falkland Islands, and was abandoned in the 1930s. Thanks to a remarkable salvage project in 1970 and subsequent restoration, you can now appreciate the skill and vision of designer Isambard Kingdom Brunel. The revolutionary dry dock takes you below the water line into a climate-controlled chamber where the awe-inspiring outer hull is preserved, while the adjacent Dockyard Museum provides detailed background and history on the ship. Finally, you get to explore the ship itself, magnificently restored to evoke the 1850s—even smells (coal fires, cooking food) are re-created, and free audioguides add context to the first class and steerage quarters, the engine room, and the bowels of the ship.

When it's in port, a replica of John Cabot's ship, **The Matthew** (check www.matthew.co.uk for cruise times; © **0117/927-6868**), is usually moored just outside the Great Britain site. You can usually look around for free during office hours (11am–5pm; donation suggested).

Great Western Dockyard, Gas Ferry Rd. (off Cumberland Rd). www.ssgreatbritain.org. ©**0117/926-0680.** Admission £12.50 adults, £9.95 seniors, £6.25 children 5–16, £33.50 family ticket. Apr–Oct daily 10am–5:30pm; Nov–Mar daily 10am–4:30pm. Last admission 1 hr. before closing. Bus: 500 (from city center).

St. Mary Redcliffe Church CHURCH   Queen Elizabeth I, on her visit in 1574, is said to have described this church as "the fairest, goodliest, and most famous parish church in England." St. John's Chapel (aka the "American Chapel") contains a whale rib bone brought back from North America by John Cabot in 1497, while the South Transept contains the tomb of Sir William Penn, father of Pennsylvania's founder; his armor and memorial are displayed high above the West End of the church (in contrast to his Quaker son, Sir William was a very successful soldier).

12 Colston Parade. www.stmaryredcliffe.co.uk. © **0117/929-1487.** Free admission; donations welcome. Mon–Sat 8:30am–5pm; Sun 8am–8pm.

CLIFTON ★★

Two miles west of central Bristol lies the leafy Georgian neighborhood of **Clifton,** best known for the graceful **Clifton Suspension Bridge,** spanning the precipitous Avon Gorge. The architect, Isambard Kingdom Brunel, died 5 years before its final completion in 1864. Today you can walk across the soaring structure (free; cars £0.50) to the small **visitor center** (daily 10am–5pm; free) on the other side, which contains a display area and DVD explaining the history of the bridge. **Clifton Village** itself is worth exploring, a gorgeous collection of Georgian homes and streets dating back to the 18th century; wander along the Mall or Clifton Down Road for the best of the shops and restaurants.

Where to Eat
EXPENSIVE
Bordeaux Quay CONTINENTAL/BRASSERIE   This solid harborside choice is convenient for the center of town and offers a range of dining options under the same roof. The **first-floor restaurant** offers fine dining—think Cornish sea bass with coco beans, butternut squash, curry spices, and spinach—while the street-level **brasserie** (✆ 0117/943-1200) offers cheaper fare in the form of burgers, goat cheese tart, and mussels. For hefty sandwiches and take-out there's the **Deli** (✆ 0117/906-5563) next door, or you can just grab a drink at the wine bar.

V-Shed building, Canon's Rd. www.bordeaux-quay.co.uk.✆ **0117/943-1200.** Reservations recommended for restaurant/brasserie. Main courses £14–£22 in the restaurant; £9.50–£13 in the brasserie. AE, MC, V. Restaurant Tues–Sat 6–10pm; Sun noon–3pm. Brasserie Mon–Fri 8–11pm; Sat 9–11pm; Sun 9–4pm. Deli Mon–Sat 8am–6pm; Sun 9am–4pm.

Pump House ★★ GASTROPUB   Inventive contemporary English cuisine, housed in an historic 1880s pumping station just off the Floating Harbour (close to the last Bristol Ferry stop). This really is a great pub that also offers extraordinary food, not a posh restaurant. Order dishes such as jugged hare; steamed Cornish hake; or delectable beetroot ravioli of horseradish, Colston Basset stilton, and dehydrated pears, in a bar of exposed beams and stone that also serves pints of locally produced Butcombe and Bath ales. Eat on the terrace in the summer.

Merchants Rd., Hotwells. www.the-pumphouse.com. ✆ **0117/927-2229.** Reservations recommended. Main courses £14–£20; fixed-price menu £20 for 3 courses. AE, MC, V. Bar Sun–Wed 11am–11pm; Thurs–Sat 11am–midnight. Restaurant Tues–Sat 7–9:30pm; Sun noon–3pm.

MODERATE
**Olive Shed ★ ** SPANISH/MODERN ENGLISH   This restaurant, with a riverside location in the heart of the city, uses fair-trade and organic produce for most food and drink items, including, unusually, all its wine. Menus are seasonal and change weekly, but expect vibrant combinations: Moroccan shoulder of lamb with date and

---

Eating in Clifton

Clifton is a prime target for foodies. The area around The Mall is littered with top restaurants such as modern British specialist **Clifton Sausage ★★**, 7–9 Portland St. (www.cliftonsausage.co.uk/clifton; ✆ **0117/973-1192;** Mon–Thurs 11am–3pm, 6:30–10pm, Fri 11am–3pm, 6:30–11pm, Sat 11am–4pm, 6:30–11pm, Sun 11am–4pm, 6:30–9pm). Try the relaxed **Mall Deli Café ★**, 14 The Mall (www.themalldeli.co.uk; ✆ **0117/973-4440;** Mon–Fri noon–2:30pm, Sat noon–3pm), for salads, pies, and different flavors of scotch egg, or Italian superstar **Prosecco ★★**, 25 The Mall (www.proseccoclifton.com; ✆ **0117/973-4499;** Tues–Thurs 6–11pm, Fri–Sat noon–2:30pm, 6–11:30pm). **Clifton Village Fish Bar ★**, 4 Princess Victoria St. (✆ **0117/974-1894**), does cod and chips for £4, while popular chain **Boston Tea Party** across the road at 4 Princess Victoria St. (www.bostonteaparty.co.uk; ✆ **0117/973-4790;** Mon–Fri 7:30am–6:30pm, Sat 7:30am–7pm, Sun 9am–7pm) does coffee and snacks.

Bristol's Cheap Eats

For inventive but cheap food in central Bristol, head to **St. Nicholas Market** (www.stnicholasmarketbristol.co.uk; Mon–Sat 9:30am–5pm) on Corn Street, where the **Exchange Café** is a classic "greasy spoon" serving an all-day breakfast (sausage, bacon, egg, beans and toast, tea) for just £3.90, as well as traditional faggots, and cod and chips. Trawl the nearby Glass Arcade for the **Bristol Sausage Shop** (www.bristol sausageshop.co.uk; ☎ 07817/478302; Mon–Sat 10am–4:30pm), which does sausage sandwiches and mash from £3–4, and **Caribbean Wrap** (☎ 07989/745944), which adds some Jamaican flavor with ackee and salt-fish, callaloo, and spiced chicken. Lauded **Al Bab Mansour** ★ (☎ 07979/976113; main dishes £5.95–£6.95; Mon–Sat noon–4pm) brings a tiny piece of North Africa to Bristol, with mouth-watering couscous, lamb tagine, and falafel. You can eat at tables in the covered arcade or inside the textiles-draped dining room.

cumin stuffing, or beetroot and chickpea fritters with peach and orange salsa. The tapas menu is just as inspiring, with feta-stuffed mini peppers complementing classics such as anchovies, Spanish tortilla, and squid.

Princes Wharf. www.theoliveshed.com. ☎ **0117/929-1960.** Reservations recommended. Main courses £10.50–£18.95; tapas £2.95–£8.95. AE, MC, V. Daily noon–3pm and 6–11pm (winter hours Thurs–Sat noon–10pm, Sun 11am–4pm). Closed Dec–Jan.

Severnshed ENGLISH/MEDITERRANEAN   The best choice for reasonably priced waterfront dining in the heart of the city, this restaurant is said to be the former boathouse of Isambard Kingdom Brunel. The decor is contemporary, however, with a menu that combines fresh, seasonal British produce with the flair of the Portuguese chef. The lobster risotto is superb, but all the main courses are excellent—from the beer-battered cod and chips to the pan-seared tuna with crab and lime butter and green beans. The tapas-like small plates (think whitebait and garlic lemon mayonnaise) are perfect for a lighter meal.

The Grove. www.severnshedrestaurant.co.uk. ☎ **0117/925-1212.** Main courses £10.95–£15.95; small plates £3.95; lunch set menus (Mon–Fri) £6.95 1 course, £10.95 3 courses. AE, MC, V. Sun–Thurs 10am–11pm; Fri–Sat 10am–midnight.

INEXPENSIVE

Pieminister ★★ TRADITIONAL ENGLISH   Bristol's very own pie shop sells scrumptious savory pies to eat in or take out. The menu offers nine pies, including minty lamb (lamb, carrot, swede, mint, and rose wine), the moo & blue (British beef steak with red-wine gravy and stilton), and the veggie Heidi pie (goat's cheese, sweet potato, spinach, red onion, and roast garlic). All are made from fresh produce and free-range meat, and crammed inside a thick crust of butter-rich pastry. There's a smaller branch in St. Nicholas Market, in the center of the city (Mon–Sat 10am–5pm).

24 Stokes Croft. www.pieminister.co.uk. ☎**0117/942-9372.** Pies from £3.75; pie, mash, and gravy from £5.75. AE, MC, V. Mon–Sat 11am–7pm; Sun 11am–5pm.

Shopping

The biggest shopping area in Bristol is known as **Broadmead** (www.bristolbroad mead.co.uk), centered on the pedestrianized strip of Broadmead itself with branches of all the usual high-street stores. Just off Broadmead, the **Galleries Shopping Centre** (www.galleriesbristol.co.uk) is a fully enclosed mall, while **Cabot Circus** (www.cabotcircus.com) to the east is another huge shopping zone (some of it covered), with a similar range of tenants. Dividing the Galleries and Cabot Circus is the **Quakers Friars** open-air piazza, where you'll find smaller and more exclusive designers anchored by the Brasserie Blanc restaurant. **Park Street** is best for trendy clothes, record shops, and quirky independent shops.

In the old center is **St. Nicholas Market** (www.stnicholasmarketbristol.co.uk; Mon–Sat 9:30am–5pm), which opened in 1745. It's still going strong, crammed with independent sellers of antiques, memorabilia, handcrafted gifts, jewelry, and second-hand clothes.

In **Clifton** you'll find a wide array of shops selling antiques, arts and crafts, and designer clothing. The Victorian **Clifton Arcade,** Boyces Avenue (www.clifton arcade.co.uk; Mon–Fri 10am–5:30pm, Sat 9:30am–5:30pm, Sun 11am–4pm), houses 14 shops, a pub, and a cafe, while The Mall and Princess Victoria Street are lined with posh boutiques and restaurants.

Entertainment & Nightlife
THE PERFORMING ARTS
The **Bristol Old Vic,** King Street (www.bristololdvic.org.uk; ✆ 0117/987-7877), is the oldest working theatre company in the country, known for its musicals, traveling shows, and plays. The largest concert venue in Bristol is **Colston Hall,** Colston Street (www.colstonhall.org; ✆ 0117/922-3686), which hosts everything from touring rock bands to alternative comedy and classical music.

Smaller venues include the atmospheric **St. George's Bristol** (www.stgeorges bristol.co.uk; ✆ 0845/402-4001), a converted Greek Revival church built in the 1820s, now known for its classical, jazz, folk, world music, and opera concerts, and the **Tobacco Factory** ★ Raleigh Road, Southville (www.tobaccofactory.com; ✆ 0117/902-0060), a dynamic studio theatre. Tickets are cheaper than at the Old Vic, typically less than £10.

Circomedia ★ (www.circomedia.com; ✆ 0117/924-7615) is an internationally-respected school for circus and physical performance training, but it also stages an exciting range of shows at St. Paul's Church, Portland Square. Tickets usually run £12–£15.

On the harborside, **Arnolfini** ★★, 16 Narrow Quay (www.arnolfini.org.uk; ✆ 0117/917-2300), is one of Europe's leading centers for the contemporary arts, with temporary art exhibitions (Tue–Sun 11am–6pm) and film screenings, in addition to live performance, dance, and talks.

For a lively program of independent film, digital media, and other live events, check out the **Watershed** arts cinema, 1 Canons Rd. (www.watershed.co.uk; ✆ **0117/927-6444;** box office Mon–Fri from 9am, Sat and Sun from 10pm, till 15 min. after last performance).

THE PUB & BAR SCENE
Bristol has a buzzing nightlife, with most of the action in the city center, along the harborside, and along Park Street. One of Bristol's oldest and most atmospheric pubs is the **Llandoger Trow,** King Street (✆ **0117/926-0783;** Mon–Sat 11am–midnight, Sun noon–11pm), all timber beams and tiny nooks, built as a terrace in 1664 and turned into a pub in subsequent years. Legend has it that this is where Daniel Defoe met Alexander Selkirk, Defoe's inspiration for *Robinson Crusoe* and also the

man behind the Benn Gunn character in Robert Louis Stevenson's *Treasure Island.* The Regency period is on show at the **Commercial Rooms,** 43–45 Corn St. (✆ **0117/927-9681;** Sun–Thurs 8am–midnight, Fri–Sat 8am–1am), with a stunning bar created out of a merchant's club built in 1811, while champagne and cocktails are the focus at **Goldbrick House,** 69 Park St. (www.goldbrickhouse.co.uk; ✆ **0117/945-1950**).

For waterside drinking aim for **Mud Dock Café,** 40 The Grove (www.mud-dock. co.uk; ✆ **0117/934-9734;** Sun–Mon 10am–5pm, Tues–Thurs 10am–11pm, Fri 10am–11pm, Sat 9am–11pm), an old boat house on the harborside in the center of town. In addition to serving fine set meals (£18.95–£25.95), you can enjoy the first floor deck with a coffee or beer.

Another good option is the **Grain Barge** ★, Mardyke Wharf, Hotwells Road (www.grainbarge.com; ✆ **0117/929-9347;** Tues–Thurs noon–11pm, Fri–Sat noon–11:30pm, Sun noon–11pm), a converted barge on the water, within sight of SS *Great Britain.*

If you prefer cider (the alcoholic kind, not the North American juice version), the **Apple,** Welsh Back (www.applecider.co.uk; ✆ **0117/925-3500;** Mon–Fri 4pm–midnight, Sat noon–midnight, Sun noon–10:30pm), occupies a smaller barge and quayside terrace farther along the river, with a fine selection of ciders and beers. Real aficionados make for the **Bristol Cider House** ★, 8–9 Surrey St. (www.bristolcider-house.co.uk; ✆ **0117/942-8196;** daily noon–midnight), where more than 20 types of strong ciders and perries (from pears) are served.

Bristol isn't just famous for cider. Wine merchant John Harvey & Sons opened here in 1796, and in the 19th century developed the world's first cream sherry, now known as Harvey's Bristol Cream. Celebrate this legacy at **Harvey's Cellars** ★, 12 Denmark St. (www.harveyscellars.co.uk; ✆ **0117/929-4812**), a tapas bar in the former Harvey's wine cellars. Enjoy a glass with Spanish tapas and delights like sherry trifle.

In Clifton it's worth having at least one pricey drink at the **White Lion Bar** in the Avon Gorge Hotel, Sion Hill (www.theavongorge.com; ✆ **0117/973-8955**), which has a gasp-inducing terrace overlooking the famous suspension bridge.

THE CLUB & MUSIC SCENE

Weekly club nights, acid jazz, and other types of live music rain down in **Thekla,** East Mud Dock, The Grove (www.theklabristol.co.uk; ✆ **0117/929-3301**), a converted freight steamer. The **Old Duke,** 45 King St. (www.theoldduke.co.uk; ✆ **0117/927-7137;** Sun–Thurs noon–midnight, Fri, Sat noon–1am), is popular for blues and traditional jazz (and must have the only U.K. pub sign featuring Duke Ellington).

Bristol's club scene is constantly evolving, but current major clubs include **Panache,** All Saints Street (www.panachebars.com; ✆ **0845/241-7185**), which hosts the biggest student nights in the city (Phat Nights on Fri, cover £5; and Paparazzi on Sat £6); and **The Syndicate,** 15 Nelson St. (bristol.thesyndicate.com; ✆ **0117/945-0325;** cover £2–£5), the biggest arena-like "superclub" in town. **Oceana,** South Building, Canons Road (www.oceanaclubs.com/bristol; ✆ **0845/293-2860;** cover £4.50–£8), rounds out the top three with a little more glamour, housing five glitzy themed bars and two club floors (one for R&B, the other for 1980s' music). Clubs tend to open Thursday to Saturday from 9pm to 3am. Check Bristol-nightlife.com for the latest.

Where to Stay

EXPENSIVE

Bristol Hotel ★ Luxury in a top location right on the harbor sets this place apart. Although rooms are small, they are beautifully decked out with sleek, modern lines, soothing colors, and stylish, contemporary furniture. The views over the city are a bonus, and the power showers, iPod docks, and Nespresso coffee machines are thoughtful extras.

Prince St., Bristol BS1 4QF. www.doylecollection.com.✆ **0117/923-0333.** Fax 0117/923-0300. 187 units. £99–£130 double. AE, DC, MC, V. Free parking 5:30pm–9:30am. **Amenities:** 2 restaurants; bar; gym; concierge; 24-hr. room service; Wi-Fi (free). *In room:* A/C, TV, Internet (free).

Bristol Marriott Royal Hotel ★★ This plush Victorian hotel, all polished marble, mahogany, and brass, dates from the 1860s, offering top-notch accommodation and service in the heart of the city (next to the cathedral and a short walk from the harbor). Rooms are stylish and contemporary, equipped with all the usual Marriott amenities and plenty of desk space for business travelers. On the downside, the Internet is very expensive. Check the website for last-minute deals.

College Green, Bristol BS1 5TA. www.marriott.co.uk.✆ **0117/925-5100.** Fax 0117/925-1515. 242 units. £139–£159 double. AE, DC, MC, V. Parking £12.50. **Amenities:** 2 restaurants; bar; indoor heated pool; exercise room; spa; concierge; room service; babysitting. *In room:* A/C, TV, minibar, hair dryer, Wi-Fi (£6 per hr; £15 per day).

Hotel du Vin ★ This stylish boutique hotel is one of Bristol's best examples of recycling. Six 18th-century sugar-refining warehouses, lying in the vicinity of the docklands, were taken over and sensitively restored. Today, you'll find a series of "loft-style" bedrooms with the original industrial features of the warehouses retained for dramatic effect. Even if you're not a guest, you may want to stop for a drink in the **Sugar House Bar** or a first-class meal in the contemporary **French restaurant.**

Narrow Lewins Mead, Bristol BS1 2NU. www.hotelduvin.com.✆ **0117/925-5577.** Fax 0117/925-1199. 40 units. £115–£245 double; £165–£355 suite. AE, DC, MC, V. Parking £19. **Amenities:** Restaurant; 2 bars; room service. *In room:* A/C, TV, DVD, minibar, hair dryer, Wi-Fi (free).

Mercure Bristol Brigstow Hotel ★ In a prime position on the water, this modern hotel opens onto panoramic riverside frontage in the heart of the city. The bedrooms are spacious and stylish, with muted colors and contemporary design; most rooms have ceiling-to-floor windows with views of the river or the city. Breakfast is an additional £17. **Ellipse,** the on-site restaurant, serves fresh and well-prepared food in light and airy surroundings, with views of the river.

5–7 Welsh Back, Bristol BS1 4SF. www.mercure.com.✆ **0117/929-1030.** Fax 0117/929-2030. 116 units. £67–£140 double. AE, DC, MC, V. Public parking nearby £15. **Amenities:** Restaurant; bar; use of nearby gym; room service. *In room:* A/C, TV, minibar, hair dryer, Internet (£10.99 per day).

Number Thirty Eight ★ 🏷 Stylish B&B that's more like a boutique hotel, with its Georgian interior cleverly remodeled with a blend of contemporary furnishings and colored paneling, modern art, and original antiques—the suites feature panoramic city views and old-fashioned brass tubs. Breakfast is fresh and locally sourced. The terrace is a great place for a coffee in the summer, adorned with rattan chairs and plants from the Isles of Scilly (the home of the owners).

38 Upper Belgrave Rd., Clifton, Bristol BS8 2XN. www.number38clifton.com.✆ **0117/946-6905.** 10 units. £95–£115 double; suites £155–£175. Rates include English breakfast. AE, MC, V. Free parking. *In room:* TV, hair-dryer, Wi-Fi (free).

WELLS ★★ & THE MENDIP CAVES ★

123 miles SW of London; 21 miles SW of Bath

The tiny cathedral city of **Wells** is a little slice of medieval England sitting under the southern lip of the Mendip Hills, which divide southern Somerset from the more visited north of the county. Wells was a vital link in the Saxon kingdom of Wessex—important long before the arrival of William the Conqueror. Once the seat of a bishopric, it was eventually toppled from its perch by the rival city of Bath. But the subsequent loss of prestige has paid off handsomely for 21st-century Wells: After the pinnacle of prestige, it fell into a slumber—and much of the center's old look has been preserved, nowhere better than at **Wells Cathedral.**

At the point where the limestone Mendips dive into the flatter terrain known as the Somerset Levels, millions of years of erosion have created a vast underground network of caves. There's no need to be a serious spelunker to enjoy the family-oriented fun at either **Wookey Hole** or **Cheddar Caves and Gorge.**

Essentials

GETTING THERE   Wells has no railway station, but does have good bus connections. One option is to take the train to Bath (see "Bath," earlier in this chapter) and continue the rest of the way via bus no. 173 (1¼ hr.). Departures are generally every hour Monday through Saturday, and every 1½ hours on Sunday. An alternative is to take the train to Bristol and then bus no. 376 (1 hr.), which runs half-hourly, hourly on Sundays. See www.firstgroup.com/ukbus for timetables.

If you're driving from London, take the M4 west, cutting south on the A4 toward Bath and continuing along the A39 into Wells.

VISITOR INFORMATION   The **Visitor Information Service** is inside the **Wells & Mendip Museum,** 8 Cathedral Green (✆ **01749/671770**). It's open October through March daily 11am to 4pm, and April through September Monday to Saturday 11am to 5pm and Sunday 11am to 4pm.

Exploring Wells

Besides the famous cathedral, the center's other highlight is the moat-surrounded **Bishop's Palace and Gardens** (www.bishopspalace.org.uk; ✆ **01749/988111**). The Great Hall, built in the 13th century, is in ruins, and the tranquil grounds house the well springs which gave the city its name. The palace is still used by the Bishop of Bath and Wells. Admission costs £6.35 adults, £2.70 children 5 to 18, which includes a guided tour at 11:30am daily. The palace is open late April through October daily 10:30am to 6pm. The cobbled lane known as the **Vicars' Close ★**, north of the cathedral, has some of the best preserved ecclesiastical terrace dwellings in Britain.

A Unique (& Portable) Souvenir from Wells

The showroom at **Black Dog of Wells ★**, Tor St. (www.blackdogofwells.com; ✆ 01749/672548), sells decorative terracotta tiles made in its own workshops. Single decorative tiles in over 100 designs cost £11, or you can have one created just for you and mailed worldwide for £35.

Wells Cathedral ★★★ CATHEDRAL   Begun in the 12th century, this magnificent church is among England's best-preserved examples of early Gothic architecture. The medieval sculpture (six tiers of statues) of its West Front is without equal in a country where so much religious statuary was destroyed by zealots during the Reformation. This western facade was completed around 1230, the central tower coming later in the 14th century, with the internal fan vaulting erected later still. The most striking feature of the cathedral interior is the **Scissor Arches** ★★ at the crossing, an amazing feat of engineering; they were built between 1338 and 1348, when the west piers of the crossing tower began to sink. The inverted arches strengthened the top-heavy structure and prevented the tower from collapsing. It was the master mason, William Joy, who devised this ingenious solution, which has done the job nicely for 6½ centuries.

Much of the cathedral's stained glass dates from the 14th century, as does the **Lady Chapel,** constructed in the Decorated style. Up steps to the north of the crossing is the octagonal, fan-vaulted **Chapter House,** completed in 1306 but since restored. Young visitors might be more enchanted by the **Wells Clock,** which dates from 1390. Every quarter-hour, it chimes, and jousting knights gallop around a platform above its face.

Chain Gate, Cathedral Green. www.wellscathedral.org.uk. © **01749/674483.** Free admission, but donations appreciated: £6 adults, £4 seniors, £3 students and children. Apr–Sept daily 7am–7pm; Oct–Mar daily 7am–6pm. Guided tours usually hourly 10am–3pm Mon–Sat.

Where to Eat

For a casual pint or a meal that's a notch above regular pub grub, walk behind the cathedral to the **Fountain Inn,** 1 St. Thomas St. (www.fountaininn.com.uk; © 01749/672317). Main courses such as lamb shank with fresh mint and Port wine jus range from £9 to £16.

Goodfellows FRENCH/SEAFOOD   Take your pick between fine fish dining or an eclectic lunchtime cafe menu at this central restaurant that's always busy with locals. The short, French-influenced seafood menu is the better choice; it changes according to the catch, but might include the likes of gray mullet with cucumber spaghetti or filet of sea trout with black pudding and asparagus, and always offers meat options such as confit duck with roasted vegetables. The decor isn't noteworthy, but details like attentive service and a bread basket baked in-house each morning ensure a consistently excellent dining experience.

5 Sadler St. www.goodfellowswells.co.uk. © **01749/673866.** Reservations recommended. Main courses £13–£24; cafe set-menus £10 and £17 including a glass of wine. MC, V. Mon–Sat noon–2pm (cafe menu only Mon); Wed–Sat 6:30–10pm.

Where to Stay

The Crown at Wells ★   This landmark building lies right on the Market Place in the heart of Wells, and has been used for overnighting since medieval times. The building retains most of its 15th-century character, although the bedrooms are up to date—in fact, many are furnished in a Nordic style with chunky light-oak furniture. For a more traditional mood, ask for one of a quartet of "suites" graced with four-posters. Rooms at the front overlook the atmospheric, but occasionally noisy, Market Place.

Market Place, Wells, Somerset BA5 2RP. www.crownatwells.co.uk. © **01749/673457.** Fax 01749/679792. 15 units. £95 double; £115 suite. Rates include English breakfast. AE, MC, V. **Amenities:** Restaurant; bar. *In room:* TV, hair dryer, Wi-Fi (free).

Swan Hotel ★   Set behind a mustard-colored facade, this place was originally built in the 1400s as a coaching inn. Rooms vary in style and size, and have been undergoing a rolling process of conversion from traditional to contemporary-edged decor; the luxurious Cathedral Suite with its panoramic windows facing Wells Cathedral might just be the best hotel room in Somerset. The spacious and elegant public areas have blazing baronial fireplaces, and 2011 saw the addition of modern self-contained mews apartments sleeping up to 4. *Insider tip:* The front terrace smack in front of the cathedral is the best-located place in town for a mid-morning coffee.

11 Sadler St., Wells, Somerset BA5 2RX. www.swanhotelwells.co.uk. ℂ **01749/836300.** Fax 01749/836301. 54 units. £144–£194 double; £300–£500 Cathedral Suite; £115–£150 apt. (min stay 2 nights). Rates include English breakfast (rooms only). AE, DC, MC, V. Free parking. **Amenities:** Restaurant; bar; room service. *In room:* TV, hair dryer, Wi-Fi (free).

Side Trips to the Mendip Caves

Cheddar Caves & Gorge ★ ☺ NATURAL ATTRACTION   The town that gave its name to a cheese, Cheddar lies at the foot of Cheddar Gorge, under which lie the Cheddar Caves, underground caverns with impressive formations and plenty of fun, educational commentary. The caves were inhabited by Stone Age tribes, but the miles of tunnels lay undiscovered until the workmen of George Cox found them in 1837. The most spectacular, **Gough's Cave,** is named after Cox's nephew (who discovered it in 1890), and has walls that shimmer with colors reflected from iron oxide, copper carbonate, and lead deposits in the limestone. The outstanding feature is the calcite waterfall in the chamber that Gough christened King Solomon's Temple. Adjacent **Cox's Cave** is also famed for its brilliant colors. You can climb Jacob's Ladder for Gorge-top walks, and the Lookout Tower for views beyond the 137-m (450-ft.) cliffs of the Gorge and across Somerset.

Cheddar. www.cheddarcaves.co.uk. ℂ **01934/742343.** Admission £18.50 adults, £12 children 5–15; tickets 10% cheaper if booked online. July–Aug daily 10am–5:30pm; Sept–June daily 10:30am–5pm. Closed Dec 24–25. From the A38 or M5, cut onto the A371 to Cheddar.

Wookey Hole ★ ☺ NATURAL ATTRACTION   Legend has it that in the first chamber of these slightly cheesy but fun caves, the Witch of Wookey was turned to stone by a Saxon abbot—along with her cat. The rest of the labyrinthine complex consists of chambers hewn by groundwater and the subterranean River Axe over millennia into creepy caverns and deep, crystal-clear lakes. Parts of the complex were probably inhabited by prehistoric people at least 60,000 years ago, and in 1935 Wookey was the site of the world's first ever cave dive. The caves are still used to age Cheddar cheese in the traditional way.

Paper has been made here since the 17th century. The preserved **mill** hosts regular demonstrations of the ancient art as well as hands-on vats, where visitors can try making a sheet.

Wookey Hole, Wells. www.wookey.co.uk. ℂ **01749/672243.** Tours (allow 2 hr.) £16 adults; £11 seniors, students, and children 3–14; £49 family ticket. Apr–Oct daily 10am–5pm; Nov–Mar daily 10am–4pm. Closed Dec 25–26 and weekdays in Dec and Jan. Follow the signs from the center of Wells for 2 miles. Bus: 172 from Wells.

GLASTONBURY & SOUTH SOMERSET ★

136 miles SW of London; 26 miles S of Bristol; 6 miles SW of Wells

Raised over the flattish terrain between the Mendip and the Quantock hills known as the Somerset Levels, mystical **Glastonbury** may be one of the oldest inhabited sites in Britain. Excavations have revealed Iron Age lakeside villages on its periphery. It's an ancient Christian center too: Joseph of Arimathea, a biblical (and perhaps mythical) figure, is said to have journeyed to what was then the "Isle of Avalon" with the Holy Grail in his possession. According to one tradition, he buried the chalice at the foot of **Glastonbury Tor** (a conical hill visible for miles around), and a stream of blood burst forth, close to what's now the **Chalice Well.** Scale the Tor today for stunning views across the Levels.

Later in history, Arthurian myth held sway, and Glastonbury now harbors a subculture of mystics and hippies. It is England's New Age center, where Christian spirituality blends with druidic beliefs. It's also a good jumping-off point for Elizabethan **Montacute House,** in rural south Somerset.

Essentials

GETTING THERE   Connections to Glastonbury are awkward using public transportation. No train service runs to Glastonbury. You can, however, take a train to Bristol Temple Meads (trip time is 1¾ hr. from London Paddington, costing around £65 for a round-trip), from where you can catch bus no. 376 to Glastonbury. Buses run twice an hour from this station, half of them direct and half requiring a change in Wells; journey time to Glastonbury is around 1¼ hours. See www.firstgroup.com/ukbus for timetables.

If you're driving from London, take the M4 west, and then cut south on the A4, via Bath, to Glastonbury.

VISITOR INFORMATION   The **Tourist Information Centre** is at the Tribunal, 9 High St. (www.glastonburytic.co.uk; ✆ **01458/832954**). It's open October through March, Monday to Saturday 10am to 3:15pm; and April through September, Sunday to Thursday 10am to 5pm, Friday and Saturday till 5:30pm.

SPECIAL EVENTS   Every June the area really comes alive for Europe's most feted outdoor music event, the **Glastonbury Festival ★★★**. It's been running since 1970, and always attracts the leading names from the rock and indie music scene, with occasional surprise guests. If you want tickets, you'll need to plan early: Register for information at www.glastonburyregistration.co.uk about a year ahead of time.

Exploring Glastonbury

In recent decades, this ancient Christian town has had its spirituality spiced up with some New Age ingredients: The handsome hamstone buildings of the High Street are peppered with psychic readers, hippie bookstores, street flautists, tarot parlors, and all things hemp. In the same building as the Tourist Information Centre (see above) is the **Lake Village Museum** (✆ **01458/832954**). A small collection attempts to recreate the life of the Iron Age settlers in the surrounding Somerset Levels, which at the time were marshy flatlands. Admission is £2.50 adults, £2 seniors, and £1 children. The museum opens the same hours as the tourist office (see above).

Glastonbury Abbey ★ RUINS   Though now just a handsome ruined sanctuary, Glastonbury Abbey was once one of the wealthiest and most prestigious monasteries in England. It provides Glastonbury's claim to historical greatness, an assertion augmented by legendary links to such figures as Joseph of Arimathea, King Arthur, and Queen Guinevere. It's also the reason there's a town here at all: Glastonbury grew up to service its abbey.

Joseph, so it goes, erected a church of wattle and daub in Glastonbury. (The town, in fact, may have had the oldest Christian church in England, as excavations have shown.) A large Benedictine Abbey of St. Mary grew out of that early wattle church. St. Dunstan, who was born in nearby Baltonsborough, was the abbot in the 10th century and later became Archbishop of Canterbury. Edmund, Edgar, and Edmund "Ironside," three early English kings, were buried here.

Another famous chapter in the story, popularized by Victorian poet Tennyson, holds that Arthur and Guinevere were buried in the grounds. In 1191, monks supposedly dug up the skeletons of two bodies on the south side of the Lady Chapel, said to be those of the king and queen. In 1278, in the presence of Edward I, the bodies were transferred to a black marble tomb in the choir. Both the burial spot and the shrine are marked.

In 1184, a fire destroyed most of the abbey and its vast treasures. It was eventually rebuilt, after much difficulty, only to be dissolved by Henry VIII in 1539. The best-preserved building on the 36-acre grounds is a 14th-century octagonal **Abbot's Kitchen,** where oxen were once roasted whole to feed the wealthier pilgrims.

The on-site shop sells award-winning **Glastonbury Abbey Cider** ★, made using apples from the abbey's orchards.

Magdalene St., Glastonbury. www.glastonburyabbey.com. (℃ **01458/832267.** Admission £6 adults, £5 students and seniors, £4 children 5–15, £16 family ticket. Dec–Feb daily 9am–4pm; Mar–May daily 9am–6pm; June–Aug daily 9am–9pm; Sept–Nov daily 9am–5pm. Closed Dec 25.

Glastonbury Tor ★★ ICON   Views for miles across the Somerset Levels are to be had after a short, sharp climb 155-m (509-ft.) above the town. The Tor (meaning "hill") has long been a place of pilgrimage, both pagan and Christian, and is topped by the 15th-century **St. Michael's Tower.** (English Christian sites built over pagan sacred places were often dedicated to St. Michael, to invoke his power to purify them.) The last abbot of Glastonbury Abbey, Richard Whiting, was hanged at Glastonbury Tor in the year of the Abbey's dissolution, 1539. It's a 20- to 30-minute walk to the top of the Tor from the Somerset Rural Life Museum (see below).

Nr. Glastonbury. www.nationaltrust.org.uk/glastonbury-tor. (℃ **01643/962452.** Free admission. Open 24 hr.

Where to Eat

The best place in Glastonbury itself for pub grub is the **Who'd A Thought It Inn,** 17 Northload St. (www.whodathoughtit.co.uk; (℃ **01458/834460**). Classic dishes such as honey-roast ham, egg, and chips, or steak-and-ale pie are well executed in pleasant, traditional surroundings. Main courses range from £8 to £16. The ales are supplied by Palmer's, a traditional brewer based on the Dorset coast.

Hundred Monkeys ★ INTERNATIONAL/VEGETARIAN   This friendly, vaguely hippie cafe-restaurant with a strict food ethics policy serves up everything from organic brunch to soup with homebaked bread to North African-flavored dinners. The daily chalkboard menu is especially suited to vegetarians, and always includes meat dishes alongside a range of meal-sized salads. Expect the likes of winter vegetable ragout with goat cheese and polenta, or pork Valentine with cider sauce and mustard mash. Outside of mealtimes, the range of specialty teas and homebaked cakes is superb, and the understated jazz soundtrack, stripped floorboards, and chunky furniture gives the place an unintrusive, slightly funky feel.

52 High St., Glastonbury. (℃ **01458/833386.** Reservations recommended at weekend evenings and Sun lunch. Main courses £9–£12. MC, V. Mon–Tues 10am–8pm; Wed–Thurs 10am–4pm; Fri–Sat 10am–9pm; Sun 11am–4pm.

Shopping

If New Age is your thing, there's no shortage of well-stocked indie stores in town. **Glastonbury Galleries,** 10a High St. (www.glastonburygalleries.com; ✆ **01458/837888;** closed Mon), sells prints, oils, photography, and watercolors by local artists. At **Little Imps,** 8b Market Place (www.littleimps.co.uk; ✆ **01458/830099**), children can browse a charmingly old-fashioned selection of toys, games, craft kits, and the like. Bargain-hunters should head 2 miles south of town to **Clark's Village,** Farm Road, Street (www.clarksvillage.co.uk; ✆ **01458/840064**). Over 90 familiar high-street and luxury-brand outlets, including Barbour and Whistles, offer genuine discounts on their end-of-line ranges. Cider lovers should also make the short journey from there to stock up on scrumpy at nearby **Hecks** (see p. 362).

Where to Stay

Middlewick Holiday Cottages, Wick Lane, Glastonbury BA6 8JW (www.middlewickholidaycottages.co.uk; ✆ **01458/832351**), offers self-catering accommodations on a pretty converted farm complex just outside the town. There's an indoor swimming pool and family-friendly activities on the doorstep. The cottages began a rolling scheme of renovations in 2011; ask for a modernized unit, as they are brighter. Units sleep from 3 to 6 guests, and are bookable by the night.

Chalice Hill House ★   Glastonbury's lack of quality hotels is compensated for by a plethora of B&Bs—and this is the most seductive of the lot. The elegant Georgian interior has been decorated with a fusion of traditional 1830s' heritage and design influences (and colors) from Glastonbury's New Age present. The Sun and Moon Room offers the best combination of space and aspect, but Phoenix has a super-king-sized bed and faces the sunset. Tucked away in private grounds above a quiet cul-de-sac, the guest house is also just a short walk from the center.

Dod Lane, Glastonbury, Somerset BA6 8BZ. www.chalicehill.co.uk. ✆ **01458/830828.** Fax 01458/835233. 3 units. £100–£120 double. Rates include English breakfast. AE, MC, V. Free parking. *In room:* TV, hair dryer, Wi-Fi (free).

WEST SOMERSET & EXMOOR ★★

West Somerset stretches from the low-lying Quantock Hills to Exmoor on the Devon border, a captivating region of moorland and rolling hills that plunge into the Bristol Channel. The most precious sections are protected within **Exmoor National Park,** best explored on foot or by car, but there are several enticing targets on the fringes.

 Somerset Steam

The **West Somerset Railway** ★★ (www.west-somerset-railway.co.uk; ✆ **01643/704996**) is one of Britain's longest and most alluring heritage railways, where vintage steam trains puff through the lush Somerset countryside between Bishop's Lydeard (4 miles west of Taunton on the A358) and Minehead on the coast. Trains run daily May to October (4–8 trains in each direction), and to limited schedules the rest of the year (check the website for details). Day Rover tickets give unlimited travel for the day (£17 adults, £8.50 children 5–15, £45 family ticket), but you can also buy one-way tickets: Bishop's Lydeard to Minehead is £11.40 one-way or £17 round-trip for adults.

Scrumpy Country

The West Country, and especially Somerset, is celebrated for its **strong apple ciders,** known locally as "scrumpy," best sampled at smaller producers that use traditional methods. Note that unlike North American ciders, British cider is alcoholic (scrumpy tends to be 7–8% alcohol).

- **Hecks,** 9–11 Middle Leigh, Street (www.hecksfarmhousecider.co.uk; *℃* **01458/442367**), has been making cider since 1840, and sells scrumpy straight from the cask, alongside perry (made from pears), jams, and chutneys. In summer it's open Monday to Saturday 9am to 5:30pm and Sunday 10am to 12:30pm, closing a half-hour earlier in winter.

- **Perry's Cider** (www.perryscider.co.uk; *℃* **01460/55195**), Dowlish Wake, south of Ilminster (see website for directions), is a rustic farm and cider shop dating from 1920. It's open Monday to Friday 9am to 5:30pm,

Saturday 9:30am to 4:30pm, and Sunday 10am to 1pm.

- **Sheppy's Cider** (www.sheppyscider. com; *℃* **01823/461848**), just off the A38, 3 miles south of Taunton at Three Bridges, Bradford-on-Tone (M5 junction 26), has been making fine cider here since 1917. In addition to its farm shop, you'll find a small **rural life museum** (£3 adults, £1.50 children). It's open Monday to Saturday 8:30am to 6pm (tearoom 10am–4pm); also Sunday 11am to 4pm in July and August.

- **Somerset Cider Brandy Co.,** Pass Vale Farm, Burrow Hill, Kingsbury Episcopi (www.ciderbrandy.co.uk; *℃* **01460/240782**), is a 150-year-old family cider farm specializing in **cider brandy.** It's open Monday to Saturday 9am to 5:30pm.

- **Glastonbury Abbey** also makes cider (p. 359).

Essentials

GETTING THERE The main train station in the region is Taunton, easily reached from London's Paddington Station every 30 minutes (trip time is around 2 hr; £39–£105 one-way). From Bristol, Bridgwater (trip time 1 hr; £8.50–£15.70) is more convenient.

At Taunton, you can take a bus to Minehead via Dunster operated by **First Somerset** (www.firstgroup.com; *℃* **0845/6064446**), leaving hourly. Trip time is around 90 minutes.

If you're driving from London, head west along the M4, cutting south at junction 20 with the M5 until you reach junction 23 with the A39, going west to Minehead. The A39 passes Coleridge Cottage and Dunster before reaching Minehead and Exmoor.

VISITOR INFORMATION The **Exmoor National Park Centre** is at Dunster Steep (www.exmoor-nationalpark.gov.uk; *℃* **01643/821835**), 2 miles east of Minehead. It's open from Easter to October, daily 10am to 5pm, plus limited hours the rest of the year (call ahead). **Taunton Tourist Information Centre,** Paul Street (www. visitsomerset.co.uk; *℃* **01823/336344**), is open Monday to Saturday 9:30am to 4:30pm year-round and can help with transport and lodging.

GETTING AROUND The best way to see the region is by car—public transport is very limited, other than between Taunton and Minehead.

8

WILTSHIRE & SOMERSET   West Somerset & Exmoor

Exploring the Area

Coleridge Cottage HISTORIC HOME   The great Romantic poet Samuel Taylor Coleridge lived in this humble 17th-century cottage from 1797 to 1798, an incredibly productive period during which he penned *The Rime of the Ancient Mariner, Kubla Khan,* and *Christabel.* Today the parlor, reading room, and bed chambers above have been restored to look much as they were when Coleridge and his friends William and Dorothy Wordsworth (who lived nearby) explored the Quantock Hills together.

35 Lime St., Nether Stowey (just off the A39, 8 miles west of Bridgwater). www.nationaltrust.org.uk. **① 01278/732662.** Admission £5 adults, £2.50 children. Mid-Mar–Oct Thurs–Mon 11am–5pm. Closed Nov–early Mar. From Minehead, follow the A39 east about 30 miles, following signs to Bridgwater.

Dunster Castle ★★ CASTLE   Dunster Castle is one of the most picturesque stately homes in the West Country, located on a high, craggy hill overlooking the Bristol Channel. All that remains of the original Norman castle is the 13th-century gateway, and what you see today dates mainly from the faux-Gothic renovation of 1868–72. The Luttrell family owned the castle between 1376 and 1976, when it was given to the National Trust together with 30 acres of surrounding parkland. The wonderfully preserved rooms inside blend Jacobean and Victorian features, including elaborate plasterwork ceilings, wood paneling, and paintings in the entrance halls. The King Charles Bedroom is said to be the most haunted room in the castle (future Charles II slept here in 1645). Save time for the gardens and their lemon trees and unusual "strawberry trees."

The village of **Dunster** itself has an ancient priory church and dovecote, a 17th-century gabled yarn market, water mill, and little cobbled streets dotted with white-washed cottages.

Dunster, on the A396 (just off the A39). www.nationaltrust.org.uk. **①01643/823-0004.** Admission to castle and grounds £8.80 adults, £4.20 children 5–13, £21 family ticket; grounds only £4.80 adults, £2.20 children, £11.90 family ticket. Castle Mar–Oct Fri–Wed 11am–5pm; closed Nov–Feb. Grounds Jan–early Mar and Nov–Dec daily 11am–4pm; mid-Mar–Oct daily 10am–5pm; closed Jan–Feb. Bus: 398 Minehead to Tiverton.

 Hiking Exmoor

Hiking is the best way to soak up the subtle charms of Exmoor. Serious walkers should tackle the **South West Coast Path ★** that begins in the resort of Minehead in the east and goes along the coast all the way to Poole Harbour in Dorset (630 miles). Few visitors have time to walk the entire trail, but if you leave Minehead in the morning, you will have seen the path's most beautiful scenery and reach Porlock (10 miles) or even Lynmouth (21 miles) by nightfall. For more information, contact the **South West Coast Path Association** (www.

southwestcoastpath.com; **① 01752/896237**). Another enticing option is the 102-mile **Two Moors' Way ★★** (www.devon.gov.uk/walking/two_moors_way.html), linking Lynmouth and Exmoor with Dartmoor in Devon (p. 377). The trail is hard to follow in parts, but crosses some mesmerizing country.

At the **Dulverton National Park Centre,** 7–9 Fore St., Dulverton (**① 01398/323841**), you can pick up a brochure that lists events, guided walks, and visitor information.

EXMOOR NATIONAL PARK ★★

Some of the most romantic landscapes in western England lie within **Exmoor National Park** (www.exmoor-nationalpark.gov.uk; 𝄐 **01398/323665**), an unspoiled plateau of misty moors, wild ponies, and herds of red deer on the Somerset and Devon borders. One of the smallest but most cherished National Parks in Britain, it includes the wooded valleys of the rivers Exe and Barle, the Brendon Hills, a sweeping stretch of rocky coastline, and such sleepy but charming villages as **Culbone, Selworthy, Parracombe,** and **Allerford.** The moors reach their highest point at Dunkery Beacon, 512m (1,707 ft.) above sea level.

The best way to see Exmoor is on foot (see "Hiking Exmoor," below), but there is a handful of enticing sights to seek out by car if you don't have time to hike. In the Exe Valley lies **Winsford ★★** (just off the A396), one of the prettiest villages on the moor, a jumble of thatched cottages on a green surrounded by streams and seven tiny bridges. The **Tarr Steps ★**, 4 miles northwest of Dulverton via the B3223, is an astonishing prehistoric clapper bridge across the River Barle. The bridge is 55-m (180-ft.) long and was built of stone around 1000 B.C. The main parking lot is around 400m (1,312 ft.) from the bridge via a footpath, but there are plenty of longer walking options in the area. At the eastern Devon end of Exmoor lie the gorgeous waterside twins of **Lynton** and **Lynmouth** (p. 366).

Where to Eat & Stay

Luttrell Arms ★★   The best choice in Dunster, this modern hotel is the outgrowth of a guesthouse from the 14th century. Bedrooms range in size and are attractively decorated in keeping with the hotel's long history; five units have four-poster beds. Rooms in a section called the "Latches" are cottage-like in style, with tight stairways and narrow corridors. It's also the best eating option, with a **formal restaurant** serving modern British food and a **traditional pub** with log fires and garden in the summer.

32–36 High St., Dunster, Somerset TA24 6SG. www.luttrellarms.co.uk. 𝄐 **01643/821555.** Fax 01643/821567. 28 units. £100–£150 double. Rates include English breakfast. AE, MC, V. Free parking. **Amenities:** Restaurant; bar; room service; babysitting. *In room:* TV, hair dryer.

Three Acres Country House ★★   This enchanting country house on the edge of Exmoor offers luxury and scintillating views over the moors. With only six rooms, it retains a tranquil, exclusive feel; the three superior rooms are larger and face south. All rooms are furnished in a warm, modern style, with cozy armchairs. Breakfast includes seasonal fruit salads, organic yogurt, and daily specials that might include Exe Valley cold smoked trout.

Brushford, Dulverton, Somerset TA22 9AR. www.threeacrescountryhouse.co.uk. 𝄐 **01398/323730.** 6 units. £45–£60 double. Rates include English breakfast. AE, MC, V. Free parking. **Amenities:** Restaurant; bar. *In room:* TV, hair dryer, Wi-Fi (free).

DEVON

by Christi Daugherty

With its spectacular coast, pastoral scenery, and dramatic red cliffs, Devon is endlessly rewarding to explore. You can get lost on foreboding Dartmoor, spend whole days exploring historic hillside villages like Clovelly, or lounge on the (sometimes) sunny beaches around Torquay. Whether you're into surfing, hiking, or sipping tea, Devon will have something that appeals to you.

CITIES Devon is largely rural, but **Exeter** is a bustling, workaday city that still retains bits and pieces of its historic past in the form of a gorgeous cathedral and ancient guildhall. There's even a Norman gatehouse that once opened the way to William the Conqueror's castle. **Plymouth** was the last bit of England the Pilgrims visited before setting off for the New World, and tiny fragments of its largely lost history can be found in its medieval **Barbican.**

COUNTRYSIDE From green **pastures** to dark, gloomy **moors** to breathtaking **cliffs** plunging down to the blue sea, Devon changes constantly as you move through it. Dartmoor's brooding hills, topped with rugged, bare stones worn down by centuries of wind and rain, are surrounded by fields of soft pink heather—the scent of it is everywhere in the summer. Thatch-roofed cottages and ancient pubs complete the picture of a rural idyll.

EATING & DRINKING Devon is famed for its **scones** and **clotted cream,** and for the afternoon tea at which those are traditionally consumed. But there's much more to the local cuisine than tea and cake. In fishing villages along the coast, restaurants serve **seafood** fresh off the boats, and use only the lightest of sauces so that the briny taste comes to the fore. In Dartmoor and Exmoor, **venison** and local **lamb** predominate, along with **pheasant** in season.

COAST With towering red cliffs overlooking ivory crescent beaches and the midnight-blue sea, Devon's coastline is dramatic. Historic villages like **Clovelly** in the south and **Lynmouth** and **Lynton** in the north, cling to the edges of land, the sea held just at bay. By contrast, **Torquay** is a modern resort town, packed with beach lovers, surfers, and snorkelers.

THE best TRAVEL EXPERIENCES IN DEVON

○ **Getting lost on Dartmoor:** The narrow, winding roads traversing this vast and hilly wilderness are notoriously un-numbered and unmarked. To find your way around, you follow signs indicating the names of villages ahead. Inevitably you lose your way, which is when you'll discover all the most beautiful places. See p. 377.

○ **Spending a day at the beach near Torquay:** With 20 sandy beaches within a few miles of one another, Torquay is perfect for sun-worshippers. Surfers can catch a wave here although, even on the hottest summer day, the water is bracingly cold. Whether you prefer busy beaches with paddling pools or private sandy spots surrounded by cliffs, you'll find your space here. See p. 383.

○ **Climbing the streets of Clovelly:** This protected, historic town has cobbled streets so steep and narrow that donkeys still haul goods from the top of the hill to the bottom. For walkers, the precipitous stroll down to the seafront is simply beautiful, as the streets are lined with flower-bedecked cottages. See p. 370.

○ **Taking the cliff train from Lynmouth:** This century-old, water-powered train climbs 183m (600 ft.) from the fishing village of Lynmouth at the foot of the cliff to the little town of Lynton at the top. The views along the way are sweeping. The entire experience is both exhilarating and, frankly, terrifying. See p. 368.

○ **Traveling by boat from Dartmouth to Totnes:** A winding journey through Devon's green and peaceful countryside, this river-boat journey is a relaxing way to spend an afternoon. The fields and pastures pass by, dotted with sheep and ponies, and you'll see jagged hills off in the distance. On a sunny day, it's heavenly. See p. 389.

LYNTON-LYNMOUTH & THE NORTH DEVON COAST ★★

206 miles W of London; 59 miles NW of Exeter

For centuries, Lynton and Lynmouth have attracted artists drawn by the twin **Victorian villages'** beauty and picturesque setting at the edge of Exmoor National Park. The harbor town is Lynmouth, while Lynton is on the cliff 183m (600 ft.) above it; the two are linked by a cliff railway. Thomas Gainsborough called Lynmouth "the most delightful place for a landscape painter this country can boast." Another notable visitor was poet Percy Bysshe Shelley, who honeymooned here with his 16-year-old bride, Harriet Westbrook, and on a later visit wrote *Queen Mab*. From the clifftop, you can look across the Bristol Channel to the Welsh coast.

Exmoor National Park (See Chapter 8) straddles the border between Devon and Somerset. Less distinctive than its gloomier sibling, Dartmoor, it nonetheless provides miles of captivating countryside to hike across, and is home to an astonishingly beautiful stretch of coastline.

Essentials

GETTING THERE   These villages are rather remote, and we recommend that you rent a car to get here. Another option is to take one of the First Great Western trains from Exeter to Barnstaple (£9 one-way); buses travel from there to Lynton about once an hour. Call ℰ **01392/427711** for bus schedules.

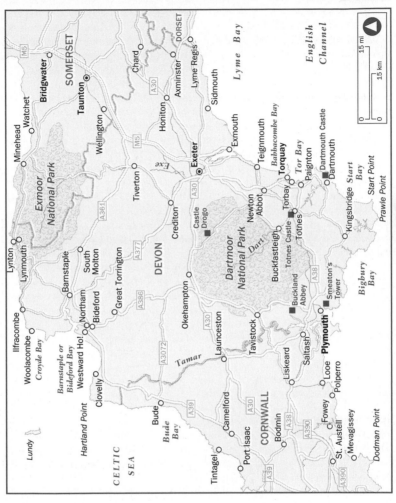

If you're driving, take the A39 to the Lynton-Lynmouth exit and follow the signs.

VISITOR INFORMATION   The **Tourist Information Centre** is at the Town Hall, Lee Road, Lynton (www.lynton-lynmouth-tourism.co.uk; ✆ **0845/458-3775**). It's open Easter to October, Monday to Saturday 9:30am to 5pm and Sunday 10am to 4pm; and November to Easter, Monday to Saturday 10am to 4pm and Sunday 10am to 2pm.

Exploring the Area

The main attractions of Lynton and Lynmouth are the towns themselves. Seemingly hewn from the cliffside in stone and slate, they have, over time, become part of the topography. On rainy days, Lynmouth, at the top of the cliff, seems to disappear in mist. The two are linked by an extraordinary water-powered train system, the **Lynton & Lynmouth Cliff Railway** (www.cliffrailwaylynton.co.uk; © **01598/ 753486**). The century-old train uses no electricity. Instead, the railway employs a complicated network of cables and pulleys, and the water tanks pull the train cars up approximately 150m (500 ft.). The train carries about 40 passengers at a time for £3 adults, £1.85 children 4–13. Trains depart daily from March to October, at 2- to 5-minute intervals.

If you'd prefer, you can hike between the two towns, although be aware the climb is steep.

This area is popular with hikers—or "ramblers"—drawn by the numerous trails and the striking countryside. A popular short walk is known as the North Walk, a 1-mile trail leading to the **Valley of the Rocks ★**. This grouping of rugged rock formations rises from a grass-covered valley to peaks of bare sandstone and shale, believed to have been carved during the Ice Age. The centerpiece of the formation is Castle Rock, known for its resident herd of wild goats.

To learn more about the best hikes in the area, go to the tourist office (see above), where you can pick up maps, guides, and other information. You might want to pick up a copy of the book *Walking in North Devon,* which has maps of tried and tested walks in the region.

From Lynton it's a 12-mile drive north on the A39 to another historic coastal town—the village of **Porlock**—composed of a tiny cluster of thatched cottages in a peaceful estuary that seems straight out of Middle Earth. The poet Coleridge lived here while writing *Kubla Khan.*

About a 20-minute drive south of Lynton is the faded Edwardian town of **Ilfracombe,** a traditional English seaside village that's virtually preserved in aspic. Its rock candy shops, seaside promenade, and fish and chip eateries are straight out of a film. Sea-battered but not uncharming, Ilfracombe is well located for walks around the headland and for days spent at its beaches, which are reached through tunnels carved through the rock (follow signs).

A 10-minute drive south down the coast from Ilfracombe brings you to the small village of **Croyde,** and the surfing mecca of **Croyde's Bay.** This isolated area of rugged coastline has miles of sandy beach, much of it pounded by thunderous surf—perfect for surfers, but not so great for swimmers. However, about a mile away, around the rocky headland of **Baggy Point,** are the beaches of **Saunton Sands** and **Braunton Burrows,** which provide expansive stretches of sand dunes to explore, and quieter water can be found in sheltered coves on either side of Croyde.

South of Croyde is the quixotically named **Westward Ho!,** named after the book by the author Charles Kingsley, who lived in nearby Bideford. When Kingsley's novel became a huge hit in 1855, a local developer smelled opportunity and came up with the idea of building a planned holiday village with the same name. The town is charming enough, but the main draw is its **Blue Flag Beach,** which stretches for miles of flat, soft sand and rolling surf.

Where to Eat & Stay

Bonnicott House ★   Spacious and welcoming, Bonnicott House sits on the crest of the cliff with sweeping views of the town and surrounding countryside. Bedrooms are done in shades of light blue, cream, or pale green, and most have a mix of well-chosen antiques and more modern furniture. Beds are comfortable and big, while

Life's a Beach

Devon is famed for its beaches, and for good reason: Golden crescents of sand or stone beneath soaring red cliffs—beaches here are dramatic settings for an afternoon of sunbathing or surfing. Here's a list of some of the best:

- **Blackpool Sands** (signposted from Dartmouth on the A379): This peaceful cove lies at the foot of a steep, forested cliff. Nearly a mile long and almost perfectly crescent shaped, it's popular for windsurfing, sailing, and sunbathing.
- **Croyde Bay** (10 miles south of Ilfracombe on the coastal road): Said to have the best surfing in Devon, with hollow barrel waves at low tide, Croyde Bay has miles of beaches, long stretches of sand dunes, and sheltered bays.
- **Ilfracombe Tunnels** (follow signs for Ilfracombe, and then tourist signs in town for seafront and tunnels): These secluded beaches are accessed by four tunnels from the town of Ilfracombe. The beaches have wonderful views of Lundy Island and South Wales. A tidal swimming pool is popular with children.
- **Oddicombe Beach** (at the edge of Torquay, accessed by a steep footpath): A small, isolated sandy beach at the foot of enormous cliffs, Oddicombe is popular but not overcrowded.
- **Westward Ho!** (from Clovelly, take the B3236, follow signs): With 2 miles of flat, golden sand and plenty of space for sunbathing, Westward Ho! is handy for those staying in Clovelly, and popular with surfers drawn by its low-tide waves.

bathrooms are small but have all the necessities. The gardens here are beautifully cultivated and pleasant to wander through. The guest lounge has a fireplace crackling on cold days; when the sun is out, the light pours in. Breakfasts are good and hearty, and the owners know everything about the area.

10 Watersmeet Rd., Lynmouth, Devon EX35 6EP. www.bonnicott.com. ©/fax **01598/753346.** 8 units. £65–£110 double. Rates include English breakfast. MC, V. Free street parking. **Amenities:** Lounge; bar. In room: TV, hair dryer.

Hewitt's at the Hoe ★ This exquisite mansion hotel, surrounded by lush gardens and thick forests, clings to the edge of the cliff near Lynmouth. Once the home of the man who built the cliff railway, the building has been sympathetically restored over the years—the polished oak paneling gleams—and filled with quality antiques. Most rooms have sweeping views of the sea, and all have big, comfortable beds and sizable bathrooms. The owners cultivate a country-house atmosphere, so you feel like a welcome guest in a gracious home. Breakfasts are pleasingly ample, tea and scones are served each afternoon in the lounge, and the dinners (£35 per person; hotel guests only), served in the elegant dining hall, are worth staying in for.

The Hoe, North Walk, Lynton, Devon EX35 6HJ. www.hewittshotel.co.uk. ©**01598/752293.** Fax 01598/752489. 5 units. £140–£160 double; from £490 self-catering apt (per week). AE, MC, V. Free parking. **Amenities:** Restaurant; bar; room service. In room: TV, hair dryer, Wi-Fi (free).

St. Vincent House ★ This charming house was built by a master mariner in 1834 and has since been sensitively converted. Guest rooms are small but sunny, with tiny bathrooms and comfortable beds. The house itself is lovely. Many of the original features of the seaman's home, including a beautiful Regency spiral staircase, have been retained. The Belgian owner, Jean-Paul Saltpetier, is a gourmet chef, and breakfasts are wonderfully varied (for England) with options like Belgian waffles, vegetarian cooked breakfast, and smoked salmon, alongside the inevitable English breakfast. New guests are welcomed with a glass of sherry to help them settle in.

Castle Hill, Lynton, Devon EX35 6JA. www.st-vincent-hotel.co.uk. ✆ **01598/752244.** Fax 01598/752244. 7 units. £70–£80 double. MC, V. Free parking. Closed Nov–Easter. **Amenities:** Restaurant; lounge. *In room:* TV, hair dryer, Wi-Fi (free).

Vanilla Pod BRITISH   This relaxed and friendly eatery is a great option in Lynton. During the day it's a coffee bar, where you can linger over a pastry or a sandwich and latte. At night it's a candle-lit restaurant with a simple menu that emphasizes fresh local meats, fish, and produce. The menu changes regularly but can include dressed crab, caught that morning, grilled Cornish sardines, or Exmoor venison. There are plenty of options for vegetarians as well—and vegans can call ahead for a special menu. The desserts are irresistible.

10–12 Queen St. ✆ **01598/753706.** Sandwiches and light lunches £3.50–£5; main courses (dinner) £8–£15. MC, V. Daily 10am–9pm (often later in summer).

CLOVELLY ★★

240 miles SW of London; 11 miles SW of Bideford

The lovely village of Clovelly, a short drive south along the coastal road from Westward Ho!, spreads across one side of a steep hill in a way that all but forbids you to pass without stopping. This is a **no-car zone,** as the precipitous and narrow cobblestone High Street makes driving virtually impossible. Instead, you park at the top and make the trip down on foot; everybody does the same—even supplies for the village stores are still carried down on sleds pulled by donkeys. It's worth the effort because every step provides views of tiny cottages, with their terraces of flowers lining the main street.

Somewhat controversially, you have to pay an admission charge just to enter the village. It's not particularly expensive, and certainly worth the price considering it also covers parking and entry to two (tiny) **museums** (see below), but there is some dispute about the legality of charging visitors this fee. Still, given that the money goes toward the upkeep of this historic village, few people object.

Once you've paid the toll, you won't find many sights within town, but that's really not the point: The major attraction of Clovelly, you might say, is Clovelly itself. Victorian author Charles Kingsley (who lived here) once said, "It is as if the place had stood still while all the world had been rushing and rumbling past it."

After you've worked your way all the way down to the quayside, the climb back to the top can look intimidating. If it's too much for you, do what many other visitors do and, behind the Red Lion Inn, catch a Land Rover. For £2 per person, it will take you up via a back road. In summer, the wait for the ride can get rather long, though.

Insider tip: To avoid the tourist crowds in the summer, stay out of Clovelly from around 11am until 4pm. When the midday crowds are filling the town, visit nearby villages such as Bucks Mills (3 miles to the east) and Hartland Quay (4 miles to the west).

Essentials

GETTING THERE It's not easy to get to Clovelly by public transportation. From London's Paddington Station, you have to catch a train to Exeter (around £69 for a round-trip), and then from there you take a local train to Barnstaple. Travel time from Exeter to Barnstaple is 1¼ hours on First Great Western trains. From Barnstaple there are relatively frequent buses to Clovelly (though sometimes you need to change at Bideford). Check at the station for details. The entire journey essentially takes all day.

If you're driving from London, head west on the M4, cutting south at the junction with the M5. At the junction near Bridgwater, continue west along the A39 toward Lynton. The A39 runs all the way to the signposted turnoff for Clovelly.

VISITOR INFORMATION To gain entry to the village, you're required to buy a ticket from the **Clovelly Visitor Centre** (www.clovelly.co.uk; ✆ **01237/431781**). The cost is £6 for adults, £3.65 for children 7–16, and £16 for a family ticket. This also covers parking for the day; a tour of a fisherman's cottage; and admission to the Kingsley Exhibition, a tiny museum devoted to (former resident) Charles Kingsley, author of *The Water Babies*. The center is open July through September, daily 10am to 4pm; April through June and October, Monday to Saturday 9am to 5:30pm; and November through March, daily 9am to 4:30pm. If you arrive outside of these times, you don't have to pay the entrance fee, nor do you pay if you're staying overnight in the village (in which case the Land Rover service is also free).

Where to Eat & Stay

East Dyke Farmhouse ★ Set above Clovelly village, with gorgeous views over field and sea, this working farmhouse is a lovely place to stay. Named after the Iron Age hill fort that backs onto the garden, the house has three comfortable and reasonably sized bedrooms done in shades of blue and cream. One room is a twin; the others are doubles. Room 3 has stunning sea views. With homemade bread and jam, as well as local honey, breakfasts here are slightly more varied than just the usual B&B fare. The helpful owners try to make you feel at home.

Higher Clovelly, Devon EX39 5RU. www.bedbreakfastclovelly.co.uk. ✆ **01237/431216**. 3 units. £60–£70. Rates include breakfast. No credit cards. **Amenities:** Restaurant; bar. *In room:* TV, hair dryer, Wi-Fi (free).

New Inn Hotel About halfway down High Street from the top of the hill, this small historic inn is a charming option, with beamed ceilings, fireplaces, and sea views. At night, when most tourists have gone, the traffic-free street is quiet and peaceful and you feel as if you have the town to yourself. The inn's pub and restaurant are as popular with locals as they are with guests. The guest rooms, in two buildings on opposite sides of the steep street, are relatively small but comfortable, although the decor could use a facelift in places. Two rooms are large enough for families. Note: If you're driving, you should park in the lot at the entrance to the town and walk down. If you need help with your luggage, the hotel will arrange for it to be brought down by sledge.

High St., Clovelly, Devon EX39 5TQ. www.clovelly.co.uk/new_inn_acc.php. ✆**01237/431303**. Fax 01237/431636. 19 units. £82–£119. Rates include English breakfast. MC, V. **Amenities:** Restaurant; bar. *In room:* TV, Wi-Fi (free).

EXETER

201 miles SW of London; 46 miles NE of Plymouth

Exeter was a Roman city founded in the 1st century A.D. on the banks of the River Exe. Two centuries later it was encircled by a mighty **stone wall,** traces of which remain today. Over the subsequent centuries, numerous invaders—including Saxons, Vikings, and Normans—stormed the fortress. None was more thorough than William the Conqueror, who brought Exeter to its knees in 1067.

As time passed, the city grew and prospered. By the 17th century, it was an economic powerhouse and a leading trading place for wool. But in the 19th century, as wool became less profitable and industrialization powered other cities forward, its importance waned.

In the 20th century, the city became a favorite target of the German Luftwaffe, which flew 18 raids over Exeter between 1940 and 1942, flattening much of the city's historic architecture and killing many of its inhabitants. In May 1942, in response to the British bombing of Lubeck, 40 acres of the city were leveled in a devastating attack. The town was rebuilt in the 1950s, but its grand Georgian crescents and priceless timbered Tudor buildings were replaced by utilitarian, modern shops and office towers. Fortunately, some of the city's historic structures were spared, and Exeter still has a **Gothic cathedral,** a renowned university, and several **historic houses.**

Its location makes Exeter a good base for exploring Dartmoor and Exmoor National Parks (see "Dartmoor National Park," later in this chapter).

Essentials

GETTING THERE   First Great Western trains travel from London's Paddington Station to Exeter St. David Station every hour; the trip takes 2½ hours. One-way fares cost £40 to £55. Trains also run every 20 minutes between Exeter and Plymouth; that trip takes 1 hour.

A **National Express** bus departs from London's Victoria Coach Station every 2 hours during the day; the trip takes 4½ hours. One-way fares cost £29. For information and schedules, visit www.nationalexpress.com or call ✆ **0871/781-8181.** You can also take **Stagecoach** bus no. X38 or X39 between Plymouth and Exeter. During the day, two buses depart per hour for the 1-hour trip.

If you're driving from London, take the M4 west, cutting south to Exeter on the M5.

VISITOR INFORMATION   The **Tourist Information Centre** is at the Civic Centre, Paris Street (✆ **01392/665700**). It's open from September to June, Monday to Saturday 9am to 5pm; and in July and August, Monday to Saturday 9am to 5pm and Sunday 10am to 4pm.

SPECIAL EVENTS   The **Exeter Summer Festival,** held over 2 weeks in June or July, includes more than 150 classical music performances and events—from concerts and operas to lectures. The schedule varies from year to year. Information about this year's event is posted on the town's website by April or May (www.exeter.gov.uk; ✆ **01392/265200**).

Exploring Exeter

Exeter Cathedral ★★ CATHEDRAL   The Anglican cathedral at Exeter can trace its history to 1050, when the Bishop of Devon and Cornwall was transferred

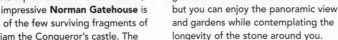

A Relic from William the Conqueror

At the top of Castle Street in Exeter, the impressive **Norman Gatehouse** is one of the few surviving fragments of William the Conqueror's castle. The gatehouse and walls are all that survive, but you can enjoy the panoramic view and gardens while contemplating the longevity of the stone around you.

here to escape Viking sea raids. Only temporary church buildings stood on the site until 1112, when William Warelwast, a nephew of William the Conqueror, was given the district and began building a church in the Norman style. The twin Norman towers he designed still stand, but the building was not completed until 1400, when styles had changed, so most of the building is a spectacular concoction of Gothic architecture, with a remarkable vaulted ceiling 20m (66 ft.) tall and 90m (300 ft.) long. The structure is no longer complete—sadly, the cloisters were destroyed by Oliver Cromwell's forces, and a German bomb finished off the twin chapels of St. James and St. Thomas in 1942. Its sheer size is moving, and the early carving work is delightful. Its famous choir sings Evensong Monday to Friday at 5:30pm and again at 3pm on Saturday and Sunday.

1 The Cloisters. www.exeter-cathedral.org.uk. ☏ **01392/285983.** Admission £5 adults, £3 children 15 and under. Mon–Sat 9am–4:45pm.

Exeter Guildhall ARCHITECTURE   This grand old building on Exeter's main shopping street has been at the center of life here for more than 800 years. The building was renovated in the 16th century; the architecture is a mishmash of Tudor and faux Tudor. The elaborate frontage was added in the 1590s (and was described by a wit at the time as "just as picturesque as it is barbarous"). The interior was similarly "restored" by the Victorians. But much did survive their well-intended meddling, including the medieval oak-paneled hall and the original beamed ceilings.

High St. ☏ **01392/665500.** Free admission. Tues–Sat 10:30am–1pm. Opening hours and days change frequently; call before visiting.

Powderham Castle ★ CASTLE   Originally built in the late 14th century (but much altered in the 19th century), this is a grand, Gothic-influenced structure with sprawling grounds. Today it's still in the hands of the descendants of its original owners, the Countess and Earl of Devon. Inside, the decor is traditional, with family portraits and fine furniture, some 17th-century tapestries, and a chair used by William III for his first council of state at Newton Abbot. The chapel dates from the 15th century, with hand-hewn roof timbers and carved pew ends.

Powderham, Kenton. www.powderham.co.uk. ☏ **01626/890243.** Admission £10 adults, £9 seniors, £8 children 5–14, £29 family ticket, free for children 4 and under. Sun–Fri 11am–4:30pm (July, Aug till 5:30pm). Closed Nov–Mar. Take the A379 Dawlish Rd. 8 miles south of Exeter; the castle is signposted.

Where to Eat

Harry's ★ ENGLISH   This popular restaurant and bar packs the locals in, night after night. They're drawn to its relaxed atmosphere, reasonably priced menu, and warm ambience. In an elegant, colonnaded building smack dab in the town center, the restaurant upstairs serves straightforward, homestyle cooking: Steaks, burgers, pizzas, and fajitas as well as big sandwiches and salads. The downstairs grill bar takes a more formal approach and offers French-influenced dishes such as warm mushrooms on brioche, River Exe mussels in Somerset cider, and roasted loin of venison in blackberry sauce, as well as perfectly cooked steaks.

6 Northernhay Place, Baily St. www.harrys-exeter.co.uk. © **01392/438545.** Reservations recommended. Main courses £10–£15. MC, V. Mon–Sat noon–2:30pm and 6–10:30pm.

Michael Caines Restaurant at ABode Exeter ★★ FRENCH   This swanky restaurant in the ABode Hotel (see below), at the edge of Cathedral Green, is where Exeter goes for important business lunches, celebratory family dinners, and critical first dates. Executive Chef Michael Caines is double Michelin starred, and one meal will explain why—he uses the freshest local produce, and he has a fine touch with French cuisine. The dining room is comfortably stylish with white table linens and cream walls. The menu changes constantly, but starters could include pan-fried Brixham scallops with truffle soy vinaigrette or cannelloni of Brixham crab. Main courses might feature filet of Brixham halibut with oxtail tortellini, poached and roasted pheasant with pumpkin purée, or loin of local venison. Desserts are decadent, and service is outstanding. This place is popular, so make reservations at least a day in advance.

In the ABode Exeter at the Royal Clarence Hotel, Cathedral Yard. www.michaelcaines.com. © **01392/223638.** Reservations required. Main courses £22–£25; fixed-price 2-course lunch £17, 3-course lunch £24; 7-course table d'hôte menu £72. AE, DC, MC, V. Mon–Sat noon–2pm and 7–10pm.

Ship Inn ★ 🍴 ENGLISH   In a lovely historic building that dates back to the 16th century, this inn was, in its day, visited by Sir Francis Drake, Sir Walter Raleigh, and Sir John Hawkins. Today it's a busy pub restaurant where you can have a drink or two, or stay for a full meal. A selection of snacks is available in the bar; full meals are served in the restaurant upstairs. The menu offers fairly good pub options, including steak, fried and grilled fish, and sandwiches and hamburgers at lunchtime. Prices are reasonable.

St. Martin's Lane. © **01392/272040.** Reservations recommended. Restaurant main courses £6–£13. MC, V. Daily noon–9pm.

Treasury Restaurant ★ CONTINENTAL   A small but classy eatery in St. Olaves Hotel in the center of town, the Treasury is a good option for those who like the personal touch. The dining room is beautifully decorated with white linens and dark, polished wood floors—the tables are gathered loosely around a fireplace. The menu reflects the sophisticated palate of the congenial owners with French-influenced local cuisine. Starters could include mushroom risotto, or goat cheese salad with pickled cauliflower. Main courses include roasted local lamb with pomme purée and red onion confit, or sea bream with stir-fried vegetables. The cheese plate is worth trying for its rich local creations.

In the St. Olaves Hotel, Mary Arches St. www.stolaves.co.uk. © **01392/217736.** Reservations recommended. Set menu: 2 courses £20; 3 courses £25. MC, V. Daily noon–2pm and 7–9:30pm.

Shopping

If you're looking for arts and crafts or antiques, head to the historic Quay off Western Way. The **Quay Gallery Antiques Emporium** (www.exeterquayantiques.co.uk; © 01392/213283) houses 10 dealers who sell furniture, porcelain, metalware, and other collectibles. The **Antique Centre,** on the Quay (© 01392/493501), has 20 dealers, each with its own specialty era. The **South Gate Gallery,** 64 South St. (www.southgategallery.co.uk; ✆ **01392/435-8000**), sells original local art and prints.

The High Street, which runs through the town's center, is the primary shopping street in Exeter for clothing, books, food, and other day-to-day goods. The modern **Princesshay** shopping center (on Princesshay Street, signposted off the High Street; ✆ **01392/459838**) also has plenty of useful shops and restaurants including Accessorize (for inexpensive jewelry), an Apple Store, Dorothy Perkins, Topshop, and Debenhams (for clothing).

Entertainment & Nightlife

Exeter is a lively university town offering an abundance of classical music concerts and theatre productions, as well as clubs and pubs.

Concerts, opera, dance, and film can be found year-round at the **Exeter Phoenix,** Bradninch Place, Gandy Street (www.exeterphoenix.org.uk; ✆ **01392/667080**), and Exeter University's **Northcott Theatre,** Stocker Road (www.exeternorthcott.co.uk; ✆ **01392/493493**), which is also home to a professional theatre company.

The **Well House Tavern,** Cathedral Close (✆ **01392/223611**), is a friendly, historic place to stop for a pint. The lunch menu of pub food, overseen by Chef Michael Caines, is outstanding. The building dates to the 14th century, and the atmosphere is laid-back and welcoming.

Perched at the edge of the canal, **Double Locks,** Canal Banks (www.doublelocks. co.uk; ✆ **01392/256947**), welcomes a lively crowd. It features live music (jazz, rock, and blues) with no cover charge, and you can get traditional pub grub to go with your pint. In the summer, you can sit outside and watch the boats go by.

Where to Stay
EXPENSIVE
ABode Exeter at the Royal Clarence Hotel ★★ A short walk from the rail station and just steps from the cathedral, the ABode Exeter is one of the city's most talked about hotels, with a cutting-edge restaurant, a gorgeous tavern, and coolly modern rooms. The hotel building dates to the 18th century, but inside, clever design has combined history with modernity and comfort. Rooms have a contemporary feel, with handmade, luxurious beds, monsoon showers, and personal DVD players. Michelin-starred chef **Michael Caines** runs the hotel's acclaimed restaurant (p. 374), and the Well House Tavern, a historic pub, offers more casual dining.

Cathedral Yard, Exeter, Devon EX1 1HD. www.abodehotels.co.uk/exeter. ✆ **01392/319955.** Fax 01392/439423. 53 units. £120–£175 double; £230–£330 suite. AE, DC, MC, V. Parking £9. **Amenities:** Restaurant (Michael Caines, p. 374); cafe; 2 bars (including Well House Tavern; see above); exercise room; spa; room service; babysitting. *In room:* A/C, TV, hair dryer, Wi-Fi (free).

Buckerell Lodge Hotel ★ Resembling a gracious country manor house, this picture-perfect hotel, set amid sprawling grounds and gardens, is a popular wedding location. The building may be Victorian, but bedrooms are contemporary and spacious, done up in neutral tones of taupe with splashes of bright color. The best (most-expensive) rooms are in the main house; the others, though cheaper, are in a more sterile modern addition. The hotel restaurant, Veitch's, is formal and a little old-fashioned, serving French-influenced cuisine. There's also a more relaxed bar where you can order light meals.

Topsham Rd., Exeter, Devon EX2 4SQ. www.akkeronhotels.com. © **0844/855-9112.** Fax 01392/424333. 54 units. £85–£130 double. AE, DC, MC, V. Free parking. Take the B3182 1 mile southeast, off junction 30 of the M5. **Amenities:** Restaurant; bar; room service. *In room:* TV, hair dryer, Wi-Fi (free).

MODERATE

Gipsy Hill Hotel   This late-Victorian country estate surrounded by gorgeous gardens is on the eastern fringe of the city—just far enough away to feel bucolic. Rooms are comfortable, although not at all fancy. One has a (slightly creaky) four-poster bed squeezed into a space so small you can barely get around it, which is odd given that some other rooms are much larger. Like the rooms, the restaurant is a bit old-fashioned, but it's handy if you don't feel like going into town, and in the summer you can dine outside. Generally, the place could use some updating (carpets are thin, curtains are fussy, walls are oddly unadorned), but the grounds are delightful, the staff is helpful, and the price is reasonable. They'll even let you bring your dog.

Gipsy Hill Lane (via Pinn Lane), Monkerton, Exeter, Devon EX1 3RN. www.gipsyhillhotel.co.uk. © **01392/465252.** Fax 01392/464302. 37 units. £60–£100 double. AE, DC, MC, V. Free parking. **Amenities:** Restaurant; bar; room service; babysitting. *In room:* TV, hair dryer, Wi-Fi (free).

St. Olaves Hotel ★   In a creamy white Georgian town house with a secluded walled garden, St. Olaves is a special place to stay. The location is ideal, within a short walk of Exeter's sights, especially the cathedral, which is so close that you can hear its bells. Outside, it's pristine, while inside it's been tastefully furnished with a mix of antiques and modern furniture. Guest rooms are spacious and comfortable, done in tones of ivory and blue. Bathrooms are not huge, but they have power showers. The **Treasury Restaurant** has an interesting, French-influenced menu and a refined ambience.

Mary Arches St. (off High St.), Exeter, Devon EX4 3AZ. www.olaves.co.uk. © **01392/217736;** 800/544-9993 in the U.S. Fax 01392/413054. 14 units. £110–£125 double; £165 family room; £155 suite. Rates include English breakfast. MC, V. Free parking. **Amenities:** Restaurant (Treasury Restaurant, p. 374); bar; room service. *In room:* TV, hair dryer.

INEXPENSIVE

Park View Hotel   This hotel, near the heart of town and the train station, offers cheap and cheerful rooms with no frills. The tall Georgian town house has comfortable but plainly furnished rooms in varying sizes (the layout of the old house means that some are bigger than others). Some have teeny tiny private bathrooms, but cheaper rooms use shared bathrooms. The usual fried English breakfast is served in a slightly crowded dining room that looks out over the hotel's pleasant garden.

8 Howell Rd., Exeter, Devon EX4 4LG. www.parkviewexeter.co.uk. © **01392/271772.** Fax 01392/253047. 13 units, 10 with bathroom. £60 double without bathroom; £72 double with bathroom. Rates include English breakfast. MC, V. Free parking. **Amenities:** TV lounge. *In room:* TV.

Woodbine Guesthouse   This centrally located B&B has sunny and basic small rooms at a reasonable price. In a Victorian house near the town's landmark clock tower and park (some guest rooms look out over the park's green fields), the Woodbine is certainly convenient. Its rooms are small (there will be no swinging of cats here), but they have all you need, including Lilliputian en suite bathrooms. Fried English breakfast is served in the cozy dining room.

1 Woodbine Terrace, Exeter, Devon EX4 4LJ. www.woodbineguesthouse.co.uk. © **01392/203302.** Fax 01392/254162. 5 units. £52–£66 double. Rates include English breakfast. MC, V. Free parking. *In room:* TV, free Wi-Fi (free).

DARTMOOR NATIONAL PARK ★★★

213 miles SW of London; 13 miles W of Exeter

Ominous and brooding, this vast, sprawling moorland park undulates and curves for miles, stretching across the county from Exeter in the east to Tavistock and Okehampton in the west. As you travel across it, the landscape constantly changes, rising to steep hills (as high as 621m/2,037 ft.), and then plunging into deep gorges with rushing water. It is distinguished by its flora of spiny **moor shrubs,** and the **scented heather** that rouges the hillsides in the summer and turns black in the winter. Famously, Dartmoor is home to herds of **wild ponies** that nibble peacefully on the heather and occasionally block traffic on the tiny, winding roads. The area's wild look led Arthur Conan Doyle to set his spookiest tale, *The Hound of the Baskervilles,* here.

> ### Inspiring Sherlock Holmes
>
> The High Moorland Visitors Centre sits inside an impressive 19th-century building. Two centuries ago, the building was The Old Duchy Hotel. Arthur Conan Doyle stayed there while researching *The Hound of the Baskervilles.* So the view from the center, down the windswept hill, is the view that inspired his descriptions of the desolate moor.

Essentials

GETTING THERE   You really need a car to get around the moors, particularly in the winter. In the summer, the **Transmoor Link** bus service runs between the villages on the moor and surrounding towns. For timetables, contact **Travel Line** (www.traveline.info; ℂ **0871/200-2233**).

If you're driving from Exeter, head west on the B3212 to such centers as Dartmoor, Chagford, Moretonhampstead, and North Bovey. From these smaller towns, tiny roads—often not really big enough for two cars—cut deeper into the moor. Old signposts list the names of towns on these roads, which are too small to be numbered. Prepare to pull over if traffic comes the other way.

VISITOR INFORMATION   The **Tourist Information Centre,** Town Hall, Bedford Square, Tavistock (ℂ **01822/612938**), is in the bustling town of Tavistock just outside the park. It has brochures and information about nearby towns. From April to October, it's open daily from 9:30am to 5pm. From November to March, it's open on Monday, Tuesday, Friday, and Saturday from 10am to 4:30pm. The **High Moorland Visitors Centre** (Old Duchy Hotel, Princetown; ℂ **01822/890414**) is an essential stopping point for a thorough exploration of the park. It stocks maps for hiking and biking across the moors, as well as guides and brochures. Its staff can answer any questions you might have. It's open daily 10am to 5pm in the summer, and 10am to 4pm the rest of the year.

CHAGFORD

218 miles SW of London; 13 miles W of Exeter; 20 miles NW of Torquay

Chagford is a charming ancient village in north Dartmoor overlooking the River Teign and surrounded by high granite tors (rocky hilltop outcrops). Its High Street and

The Real Lorna Doone

In Chagford, the Church of St. Michael was the scene of a famous tragedy in which a beautiful local girl was killed on her wedding day. According to legend, on October 11, 1641, young Mary Whiddon was married in the church. As her guests gathered in front of the building to cheer the new bride and groom, she was gunned down when she walked out the door. The killer was a jealous suitor whose proposals she had refused. The event was fictionalized in R. D. Blackmore's classic *Lorna Doone*. Poor Mary is buried in the church's graveyard. The inscription on her gravestone reads BEHOLD A MATRON, YET A MAID. By tradition, every bride married in the church leaves a flower from her bouquet on the tombstone.

picturesque town square still have some original store fronts, giving it a lovely lost-in-time look, and its plentiful pubs and tea shops make it a good place to stop for lunch.

Historic buildings to look out for include the 16th-century **Endecott House** in the town square, named after John Endecott, a Pilgrim and governor of the Massachusetts Bay colony, who lived in Chagford before striking out for America. The house is now used as the town's meeting hall.

The village hall (**Jubilee Hall**) near the public parking lot is another local gathering place, which holds Friday markets and the local library.

The rambling, 13th-century **Three Crowns Hotel** is worth exploring for its sheer longevity. Not far away, the **Church of St. Michael** dates to the 15th century and retains many of its original features. It was the scene of an infamous murder hundreds of years ago (see "The Real Lorna Doone," below).

To get here, catch Stagecoach bus no. 173. If you're driving from Exeter, drive west on the A30, and then south on the A382 following signs to Chagford.

Exploring the Area

Buckland Abbey ABBEY   Less an abbey anymore than a grand house, Buckland was built in the 13th century by Cistercian monks who created a vast estate around it. Centuries later, it was converted into a home by Sir Richard Grenville, which was then purchased by Sir Francis Drake. Over the years, the shape of the building was changed, but it's still an extraordinary structure, and the grounds are lovely and peaceful, with orchards and, in the spring, bluebell forests. The house has a mixture of rooms furnished in period style and interactive galleries telling the tale of the building and of the men who lived there.

Buckland Abbey, Yelverton. www.nationaltrust.org.uk. © **01822/853607.** Admission £9 adults, £5 children 16 and under, £23 family ticket. Mid-Mar–Oct daily 10:30am–5:30pm; Nov Fri–Sun 11am–4:30pm; Dec–early Mar 11am–4:30pm. Last admission 45 min. before closing. The house is 3 miles west of Yelverton off the A386; follow signs.

Castle Drogo ☺ CASTLE   This massive granite castle, in the hamlet of Drewsteignton, 17 miles west of Exeter, might look medieval, but it was really a flight of fancy, designed and built between 1910 and 1930. Constructed of granite, and castellated and turreted like a fortress, the castle occupies a bleak but dramatic position high above the River Teign, with views sweeping out over the gloomy moors.

The castle has always been—and is still a family home, but it's open to guided tours, which include a series of formal rooms done up in Edwardian style. In many

ways, the secluded gardens are more strikingly beautiful than the house. They include a sunken lawn enclosed by raised walkways, a circular croquet lawn (you can rent a croquet set to play here), shaped yew hedges, and a children's playroom.

Drewsteignton, 4 miles northeast of Chagford and 6 miles south of the Exeter-Okehampton Rd. (A30). www.nationaltrust.org.uk. © **01647/433306.** Admission to castle and grounds £8.90 adults, £4.10 children 16 and under, £24 families; grounds only £5 adults, £3 children. House Mar–Oct daily 11am–5pm; Nov Sat–Sun 11am–4:30pm; Dec daily 11am–4pm; closed Dec 24–Feb 28. Grounds Mar–Oct daily 9am–5:30pm; Nov–Dec 23 daily 11am–5pm; Jan–Feb daily 11am–4pm; closed Dec 24–31. Take the A30 and follow the signs.

Where to Eat & Stay

VERY EXPENSIVE

Bovey Castle ★★★ ☺   More country manor house than castle, Bovey is a grand old pile. Built in 1907, it sprawls across 400 acres of rolling fields, waterland, and pasture. Guests can amuse themselves with trout fishing and archery, as well as the usual golf (there's an 18-hole, championship course). You can learn to be a country lord here (they offer classes in the making of cider and sloe gin) or lady of leisure (there's an elegant spa). There is even a falconry display after breakfast. The spacious bedrooms are tastefully decorated with country prints, traditional furniture, and comfortable beds. There are 14 self-catering lodges on the grounds, which offer more space and privacy. You can choose from three restaurants and a bar, which is just as well as the town of North Bovey is a 20-minute walk away, through meadows and across streams.

North Bovey, Devon TQ13 8RE. www.boveycastle.com. © **01647/445000.** Fax 01647/445020. 63 units. £230–£350 double; £515–£615 suite. AE, MC, V. Rates include English breakfast. **Amenities:** Restaurant; bar; 2 pools (1 indoor, 1 outdoor); 18-hole golf course; 2 outdoor tennis courts; exercise room; spa; room service; archery center; children's farm; equestrian center; falconry; fly-fishing; movie theatre. *In room:* A/C, TV, minibar, hair dryer, Wi-Fi (free).

Gidleigh Park Hotel ★★★ This gorgeous hotel, surrounded by impeccable gardens and run with grace and style, has been lavished with awards over the years, and for good reason—it's simply extraordinary. Amid 54 acres of private forest and flowers, the sprawling Arts and Crafts mansion has panoramic vistas of the surrounding hills. Guest rooms are spacious and tastefully decorated in tones of cream and ivory; much of the furniture was handmade. Bathrooms are big, modern, and elegant; beds are orthopedic and comfortable. The hotel restaurant—headed by double-Michelin-starred chef Michael Caines—is revered by food critics throughout the nation. In fact, many people stay here primarily for the food. The spa treatments, the tennis courts, and the miles of grounds on which to wander make this a perfect country retreat.

Gidleigh Park (2 miles outside town), Chagford, Devon TQ13 8HH. www.gidleigh.com. © **01647/432367.** Fax 01647/432574. 24 units, 1 cottage. £310–£500 double; £1,175 suite. Rates include English breakfast, morning tea, and dinner. AE, MC, V. **Amenities:** Restaurant; bar; golf course; putting green; tennis court; spa treatments; babysitting; bowling green; croquet lawn. *In room:* TV, hair dryer, Wi-Fi (free).

INEXPENSIVE

Easton Court Bed & Breakfast ★ Just outside Chagford, this pleasant guesthouse amid lush gardens and paddocks is a favorite of the literati and theatre folk. Evelyn Waugh lived here while writing *Brideshead Revisited,* and the atmosphere is still that of a relaxed English country cottage. Guest rooms are snug and comfortable, decorated in subtle shades of cream and white; many have brass beds and William Morris prints. All have peaceful countryside views. The owners are friendly, and breakfast is hearty.

Easton Cross, Chagford, Devon TQ13 8JL. www.easton.co.uk. © **01647/433469.** 5 units. £75–£80 double. Rates include English breakfast. MC, V. No children 10 and under. Take the A382 1½ miles northeast of Chagford. **Amenities:** Guest lounge. *In room:* TV, CD player, hair dryer.

Globe Inn This friendly pub restaurant on Chagford's main street has looked out for wayfarers since the 16th century. The pub is traditional, with dark wood paneling and floors and big fireplaces. Locals and visitors meet here for drinks and hearty pub food. The guest rooms upstairs are not posh, but they're comfortable and modern, with plenty of space and peaceful views.

High Street, Chagford, Devon TQ13 8AJ. www.theglobeinnchagford.co.uk. © **01647/433485.** 7 units. £80–£95 double. Rates include English breakfast. MC, V. **Amenities:** Pub/restaurant. *In room:* TV, hair dryer, Wi-Fi (free).

Whiddons ENGLISH TEA At teatime, drop in at Whiddons, a tea shop in a 16th-century thatched cottage. You can sip your Earl Grey or English Breakfast tea while nibbling freshly baked scones and delicate cucumber sandwiches. It makes a great break from sightseeing.

On the High St., Chagford. ☎ **01647/433406.** Sandwiches/scones £4–£8. MC. V. Mon–Sat 9am–4pm.

OTHER TOWNS IN DARTMOOR

Most travelers enter the moors through **Okehampton,** a pleasant enough workaday town right at the edge of Dartmoor. It has a handful of restaurants and a gas/petrol station (these are rare in the moors, so it's a good idea to fuel up first), so you're likely to run into other visitors if you stop in.

A few miles inside the moor on the A382, the peaceful market town of **Moreton-hampstead** is perched on a hillside, surrounded by moorland. Along with little tea shops and pubs, it contains rare 17th-century colonnaded almshouses and an old Market Cross, which for hundreds of years has marked the site of the local market, still held here on Fridays and Saturdays.

From Moretonhampstead, you can head 6 miles down the winding narrow B3212 to the little village of **Postbridge,** which has a rare, ancient "clapper" bridge. Clapper bridges were made by supporting large flat slabs of granite (some weighing several tons) on sturdy stone piers. (The word "clapper" is believed to be a corruption of the Anglo-Saxon word *cleaca,* which meant "stepping stones.") Historians believe this particular bridge was built in early medieval times to speed the movement of tin across the moor by pack horse.

The much-visited Dartmoor village of **Widecombe-in-the-Moor,** 7 miles north-east of Moretonhampstead, is worth seeing for both its overall prettiness and its 14th-century church (the church of St. Pancras). You can have a drink in one of its tea shops. On a sunny day, it's a good spot for a picnic.

The highest town in all the moors is **Princetown** (435m/1,427 ft.; it's on the B3212). It's a favorite starting point for hill walkers striking out across the moors, but

"My Dear Mother"

Down a winding country road near Widecombe-in-the-Moor, the tiny village of Buckland-in-the-Moor, with its chocolate-box thatched-roof cottages and fluffy Dartmoor ponies, has a unique church. Built in the 13th century of locally quarried stone, **St. Peter's Church** has a distinctive clock on its tower, which denotes the hours with letters instead of numbers. The letters, which may at first seem to be in no particular order, actually spell out MY DEAR MOTHER. The clock was donated in 1931 by a parishioner whose mother had recently died, and he had it made to memorialize her.

Inside, the ancient church has wonderfully preserved carving work and an extraordinarily rare medieval rood screen with much of its original painting. The screen shows a variety of religious figures believed to include the Archangel Gabriel, the Virgin Mary, and St. Anne, among others. Most such screens were destroyed when the Catholic Church was suppressed in England, and some of the paintings here have been defaced. But what survives gives you a wonderful view of how medieval English churches might have once looked.

it's a gloomy old place. The looming form of Dartmoor Prison dominates it, and the weather seems always to be gray. The prison was built in 1809 to house American and French prisoners of war. For the curious, there's a **prison museum** (www.dartmoor. prison.co.uk) that tells the tale of the place and sells crafts made by the inmates.

Exploring the Moors on Foot & Horseback

Dartmoor is notoriously wild and challenging for hikers and cyclists, but thousands of hardy folk traverse it every year. It is crisscrossed with about 500 miles of trails covering sometimes rough terrain. Its bogs pose a challenge for those who off-road, and the weather here can be downright dangerous, with sudden thick fogs and high winds. In short, feel free to explore, but be prepared with good hiking boots, a compass, plenty of water, and proper maps. Or, in the interest of safety, take a guided walk.

The **Dartmoor National Park Authority (DNPA)** runs **guided walks** of varying difficulty, ranging from 1½ to 6 hours and treks of some 9 to 12 miles. Details are available from the **High Moorland Visitor Centre,** Tavistock Road, Princetown (www.dartmoor-npa.gov.uk; ✆ **01822/890414**). Costs for guided tours range from £3 to £8. Local stables offer treks on horseback across the moors at the cost of around £18 per hour with an experienced guide. Try **Skaigh Stables,** at Belstone (www. skaighstables.co.uk; ✆ **01837/840917**), just off the A30 Exeter–Okehampton road. Their treks traverse dramatic moorland and take in amazing views. Morning and afternoon rides are offered from mid-April until the end of September, with 2-hour rides from £36 per person.

Where to Eat & Stay

Castle Inn   A good stopover on the road between Okehampton and Tavistock, this inn dates from the 12th century. With its pink facade and row of rose trellises, it is the hub of the village. The owners have maintained the character of the roomy old rustic lounge. The menu is stocked with quality pub food—grilled fish, sausages and mash, meat pies, and steaks—and it's well priced; only the steak costs more than a tenner. Bedrooms are a bit old-fashioned but pleasantly furnished, some with mahogany and Victorian pieces. It's a friendly, peaceful place to spend the night or just stop for dinner.

Lydford, near Okehampton (1 mile off the A386), Devon EX20 4BH. www.castleinndartmoor.co.uk. ✆ **01822/820241.** Fax 01822/820454. 8 units. £65–£90 double. MC, V. **Amenities:** Restaurant; bar. *In room:* TV, Wi-Fi (free).

Cherrybrook Hotel   This family-run guesthouse in the center of the Dartmoor National Park sits inside a rugged 200-year-old farmhouse perched high on a hill overlooking the moors. The guest lounge and bar, with their beamed ceilings and slate floors, are meeting places where travelers share their adventures. The rooms are pleasantly done up in neutral tones with pine furniture and colorful throw pillows. The hotel's perch on a high moor makes it popular with hikers and cyclists … and their pets. This is a dog-friendly hotel so it's a good idea to stay here only if you're dog-friendly too.

On the B3212, between Postbridge and Two Bridges, Yelverton, Devon PL20 6SP. www.thecherry brook.co.uk. ✆/fax **01822/880260.** 7 units. £85–£100 double. Rates include English breakfast. MC, V. Closed Dec 22–Jan 2. **Amenities:** Restaurant; bar; lounge. *In room:* TV, hair dryer, Wi-Fi (free).

Horn of Plenty Hotel ★   In a gracious, vine-covered Regency house set amid acres of lush gardens, this elegant hotel and restaurant is popular with travelers and food critics alike. The decor is tasteful and romantic, with chenille-covered sofas and peaceful views of green heather-covered hills. Guest rooms, which have luxurious beds, are done up in soothing tones of cream or mauve, with polished wood floors, and thick curtains. Lunch and dinner in the sunny dining room are events: The cooking is inventive, with an emphasis on fresh, local meats and produce. Later, you can have a drink on the terrace before wandering up to your welcoming room.

Gulworthy, Tavistock, Devon PL19 8JD. www.thehornofplenty.co.uk. ✆ **01822/832528.** 10 units. £125–£225 double. Rates include English breakfast. Fixed-price 3-course lunch £25; fixed-price 3-course dinner £50. AE, MC, V. **Amenities:** Restaurant; bar. In room: TV/DVD, hair dryer.

Lewtrenchard Manor   This 17th-century Jacobean house on the northwest edge of Dartmoor sits almost completely alone in a valley. The craggy stone building is lovely with original oak paneling, leaded windows, and beamed ceilings. Its extensive grounds wander through gardens, and across streams and ponds. The walled garden was recently restored, and the hotel's vegetables are grown there. The rooms in the oldest part of the building are the most interesting, with paneled walls and antiques. Those in the newer parts of the building are just as pleasant, though they're more contemporary in feel.

Lewdown, Devon EX20 4PN. www.lewtrenchard.co.uk. ✆ **01566/783222.** Fax 01566/783332. 14 units. £155–£355 double; £295–£375 suite. Rates include English breakfast. 2-night minimum stay on weekends. AE, DC, MC, V. **Amenities:** Restaurant; bar; room service. In room: TV, hair dryer.

TORQUAY & PAIGNTON ★

223 miles SW of London; 23 miles S of Exeter

Hugely popular with British families escaping to the seaside during school breaks, the town of **Torquay** is a rambling **Victorian relic,** with its tall, 19th-century villas perched regally at the edge of the sea. The area around Torquay is known as Torbay, and includes the charming seaside community of **Paignton** and the small fishing port of **Brixham.** Their location smack dab in the middle of 22 miles of dramatic coastline with miles of good **beaches** within easy reach makes this a handy place to base yourself while you're exploring coastal Devon. Surfers bob on the waves at all times of the year, and the restaurants, bars, and pubs are packed with the young, sand-covered set. In some ways, it's a traditional seaside town with game arcades, fish and chip stands, and candy stalls, but its increasing wealth also means there's a hip undercurrent as well, bringing in better restaurants and shops.

Essentials

GETTING THERE   First Great Western trains run throughout the day from London's Paddington Station to Torquay's station in the town center on the seafront, costing around £78 for a round-trip. The trip takes 2½ hours. For rail information, visit www.nationalrail.co.uk or call ✆ **0845/748-4950.**

Buses from London's Victoria Coach Station leave every 2 hours during the day for the 5-hour trip to Torquay.

If you're driving from Exeter, head west on the A38, veering south at the junction with the A380.

The **Tourist Information Centre** is at Vaughan Parade (www.englishriviera.co.uk; © 0844/474-2233). It's open June through September, Monday to Saturday 9:30am to 5:30pm and Sunday 10am to 4pm, and October through May, Monday to Saturday 9:30am to 5pm.

Exploring the Area

For most visitors, Torquay's main draw can be summed up in one word: Beaches. Within a few miles of the town center there are 20 beaches upon which you can lounge. Inspired by this, the local tourism board dubbed the area the "English Riviera" and you'll see those optimistic words everywhere you go. "Riviera" is certainly a stretch, but some of the beaches are very good: Some are sandy while others are pebble-covered, and many are at the base of dramatic cliffs.

Babbacombe Beach BEACH   Arguably the locals' favorite beach, Babbacombe stretches out toward the sea beneath red cliffs that soar 75m (240 ft.) above it. You can rent a beach lounger or just stretch out on the sand, taking in the view. A funicular chugs up the steep cliffs—the view from the top is endless.

Seafront, Babbacombe, Torquay. Free admission.

Babbacombe Model Village ☺ OFFBEAT SITE   This knee-high world recreates much of England in miniature—towns, countryside, farms, parts of London, and the rail system are all recreated across 4 acres of charming weirdness. Children adore it, the lights work (the mini-Piccadilly Circus is particularly amazing), the trains chug by, and frankly it is all just rather strange.

Hampton Ave., Babbacombe, Torquay. www.babbacombemodelvillage.co.uk. © **01803/315315.** Admission £8 adults; £5.50 children 3–14. Year-round daily 10am–dusk.

Kents Cavern ☺ HISTORIC SITE   A fun place to take youngsters and an archeological site of genuine scientific interest, this cave system was created around 2 million years ago and was occupied for hundreds of years by early species. In 2009, teeth and bones from Ice Age animals including hyenas, wooly rhinos, and deer were discovered during a dig in the cave. Tours wander through caverns and caves where the early creatures lived; guides are great with children.

89 Ilsham Rd., Torquay. www.kentscavern.co.uk. © **01803/215136.** Admission £9 adults; £8 children 3–15. Tours hourly in the summer 11am–4:30pm, 4 times daily in the winter.

Oldway Mansion ARCHITECTURE   This lavish, Palladian mansion offers a window into the glory of England's Gilded Age. Built in 1874 by Isaac Merritt Singer, founder of the sewing-machine empire, the building is a symphony of excess. The grand staircase is made of marble, and the balusters are made of bronze. The ceiling is covered in an ornate painting based on a design from the Palace of Versailles. An upstairs gallery, a reproduction of the Hall of Mirrors in Versailles, leads into a gilded ballroom. The house is surrounded by 17 acres of Italian gardens. Singer's son, Paris, famously had a love affair with the dancer Isadora Duncan, who used Oldway as both rehearsal space and performance venue.

Torbay Rd., Preston, near Paignton. © **01803/207933.** Free admission. Mon–Fri 9am–5:30pm.

Where to Eat

The Boathouse Bar & Grill STEAKS & SEAFOOD   It's worth coming to this seafront restaurant in the Paignton area of Torquay for the view alone. From your

ATTRACTIONS ●
Babbacombe Beach **3**
Babbacombe
Model Village **2**
Kents Cavern **5**
Oldway Mansion **12**

HOTELS ■
Barceló Torquay
Imperial Hotel **8**
Colindale **13**
Elmdene Hotel **13**
Meadfoot Bay Hotel **6**
Orestone Manor **1**
Palace Hotel **4**

RESTAURANTS ◆
The Boathouse
Bar & Grill **11**
The Elephant **9**
Number 7 **10**
Orange Tree
Restaurant **7**

table on the terrace you can see clearly across the bay to the neighboring town of Brixham. This is a relaxed place, popular with surfers and locals, and the menu has a something-for-everyone approach with pizzas, burgers, steaks, and fresh local fish. You can feast on the Boathouse surf 'n' turf (steak and shrimp), or try a local rib-eye steak with grilled tomatoes, mushrooms, and French fries. Start with nachos or dough balls while you sip a cocktail from the busy bar and enjoy the view.

Marine Drive, Paignton. www.boathousebar.co.uk. © **01803/665066.** Reservations recommended. Main courses £8–£12. MC, V. Mon–Thurs 5–10pm; Fri–Sun 10am–midnight.

The Elephant ★★ MODERN BRITISH   With a perfect location on Torquay's seafront, this Michelin-starred restaurant is considered by many foodies to be Torquay's best gourmet eatery. The restaurant is essentially divided into two: Upstairs is a formal fine-dining option dubbed The Room (open only in the summer), while downstairs is a more laid-back (cheaper) brasserie, which is open year-round. Both specialize in using local seafood, fresh off the docks, along with local meats and produce grown in the area, and both have a French-influenced cooking style. In the brasserie, dishes include options like Paignton crab with spaghetti and chili, or whole

English lobster with skinny fries. In The Room, you could start with beet and curds, then move on to ham hock tortellini, and halibut with parsnips and golden sultanas.

3–4 Beacon Terrace, Torquay. www.elephantrestaurant.co.uk. ☎ **01803/200044.** Reservations required. Brasserie main courses £14–£19. The Room set menu £55. AE, MC, V. Brasserie Tues–Sat noon–2pm and 6:30–9pm. The Room Tues–Sat 7–9:30pm.

Number 7 SEAFOOD   This bustling seafood bistro in the harbor is packed every night, and the main draw is the kitchen's talent for cooking fresh local fish. In a small, crowded dining room you can try fish fresh off the boat, including tender lemon and dover sole, and scallops simmered with mushrooms, vermouth, and lemon. Eating here can be a bit hectic, but the food makes it worth it—and the prices are reasonable.

Beacon Terrace, Torquay. www.no7-fish.com. ☎ **01803/295055.** Reservations necessary. Main courses £11–£20. MC, V. Lunch Wed–Sat noon–2pm, dinner daily 6:30–11pm.

Orange Tree Restaurant ★ MODERN BRITISH   Set back from the seafront near Torquay Harbour, this restaurant has character, atmosphere, and good food. The chefs create innovative, French-influenced dishes and change the menus seasonally. Starters can include options like baked goat cheese with cranberry and quince chutney and Brixham crab bisque. Main courses might feature pan-seared sea bass with toasted almonds and capers, or pheasant with pancetta and white wine jus. The atmosphere here is friendly and relaxed, and the food can be exceptional.

14–16 Parkhill Rd., Torquay. www.orangetreerestaurant.co.uk. ☎ **01803/213936.** Reservations required. Main courses £15–£24. MC, V. Mon–Sat 7–9:30pm.

Entertainment & Nightlife

Torquay's nightlife is geared rather strongly toward the young and pretty, and many of the bars and clubs are clustered around Babbacombe Road near the seafront. Among these are **Barcode,** Palk Street, Torquay (☎ **01803/200110**), a trendy place with big, comfortable chairs and even bigger cocktails. The food isn't bad either—the music is turned up later in the evening, but early on you can just about hold a conversation. **Bohemia,** 39–41 Torwood St., Torquay (www.bohemianightclub.com; ☎ **01803/292079**), packs out with 20-somethings for Thursday-to-Sunday house music. The cover varies from £3 to £20. If you prefer a relaxing pub, try **Hole in the Wall,** 6 Park Lane, Torquay (☎ **01803/200755**), an ancient inn, with beamed ceilings and cobbled floors, that claims to be the oldest in town. They pour a mean pint.

Torquay is very popular with young people on holiday, so after about 10:30pm in the summer, and on weekend nights the rest of the year, the town can seem overrun by drunken 20-somethings. It can be genuinely unpleasant to walk down Babbacombe Road at that time, and can even feel threatening. At that time of day, you may want to avoid the areas where most bars are located, or take a taxi.

Where to Stay
EXPENSIVE
Barceló Torquay Imperial Hotel ☺   A faded local grande dame, this big Victorian hotel was all the rage in 1866 when it first opened. It's still one of the city's best-known hotels, sitting amid acres of flourishing gardens and looking out over rocky cliffs to the Channel. The lobby area is extraordinary, with soaring ceilings and marble floors. The swimming pools and "kids club" mean it's good for families traveling with children. Guest rooms are hit or miss, though. Standard rooms are plain and

a bit disappointing, with cream walls and cheap-looking furniture, while deluxe rooms have an old-fashioned elegance, with flowered curtains and bedspreads. Some rooms have balconies and sweeping sea views. Many rooms have been renovated, and are somewhat more contemporary, while others haven't been so fortunate. The Regatta restaurant has views of the waterfront, and makes a great spot for lunch.

Park Hill Rd., Torquay, Devon TQ1 2DG. www.barcelo-hotels.co.uk. © **01803/294301.** Fax 01803/294301. 169 units. £223–£273 double. Rates include English breakfast. AE, MC, V. Parking £15. **Amenities:** Restaurant; bar; 2 heated pools (indoor, outdoor); tennis courts; squash courts; health club; spa; sauna; room service; solarium; steam room. *In room:* TV, minibar, hair dryer, Wi-Fi (£14 per day).

Orestone Manor ★   A few miles outside Torquay in the village of Maidencombe, Orestone Manor is in a gabled Victorian house surrounded by colorful gardens. The lounge exudes old-fashioned grandeur, but many of the guest rooms have been decorated in contemporary style. The best are spacious and sunny with waxed wood floors and sitting areas with sofas and chairs. Rooms in the gables are quite small and a bit of a climb but have the best views. The restaurant is highly rated for its use of fresh local produce and seafood; on sunny days you can breakfast on the terrace. The only drawback is that prices are rather high for what's on offer.

Rockhouse Lane, Maidencombe, Torquay, Devon TQ1 4SX. www.orestonemanor.com. © **01803/328098.** Fax 01803/328336. 12 units. £150–£225 double. Rates include English breakfast. AE, MC, V. Free parking. Closed 2 weeks in Jan. Drive 3½ miles north of Torquay on the A379. **Amenities:** Restaurant; bar; outdoor pool; room service; babysitting. *In room:* TV, hair dryer, Wi-Fi (free).

Palace Hotel   From the outside, this elegant hotel (built in the 1920s) is wedding cake pretty in creamy white and sky blue. It stands poised amid glorious terraced gardens, and looks for all the world as if F. Scott Fitzgerald were going to walk by at any moment in search of a cocktail. Unfortunately, the illusion ends when you walk in the door. Like so many of these grand old hotels, this one feels tattered around the edges. Guest rooms are old fashioned, with dark wood furniture and tired carpets. Mattresses can be lumpy and tabletops water-marked. The lounges and restaurants are better maintained, but staff seem hapless, and you may wait some time for that cup of tea. Unless you get a steep discount or somebody else is paying, it's not really worth the high price charged.

Babbacombe Rd., Babbacombe, Torquay, Devon TQ1 3TG. www.palacetorquay.com. © **01803/200200.** Fax 01803/299899. 141 units. £140–£230 double; £270–£310 suite. Rates include English breakfast. AE, DC, MC, V. Free parking. Bus: 32. Driving from the town center, take the B3199 east. **Amenities:** Restaurant; 2 bars; 2 pools (1 indoor, 1 outdoor); 9-hole golf course & putting green; 6 tennis courts; 2 squash courts; exercise room; sauna; room service; babysitting; croquet. *In room:* TV, minibar, hair dryer.

MODERATE

Meadfoot Bay Hotel   This immaculate guesthouse was created from a Victorian family residence, just 5 minutes' walk uphill from the seafront. Guest rooms are decorated in contemporary style, with off-white walls and white comforters, and beds are wrapped in Frette linens. Bright throws, cushions, and art provide splashes of color. Bathrooms are small but modern. Some rooms have direct access to the sunny garden, while others have a balcony. When they arrive, guests are welcomed with a drink from the bar, or a cup of tea, but prices are still a little high for what's offered here.

Meadfoot Sea Rd., Torquay, Devon TQ1 2LQ. www.meadfoot.com. ⓒ **01803/294722.** 19 units. £90–£150 double. Rates include breakfast. MC, V. No children under 14. **Amenities:** Bar. *In room:* TV/DVD, hair dryer, Wi-Fi (free).

INEXPENSIVE

Colindale ★ ✴ This rambling Victorian guesthouse has a welcoming, lived-in look—the lounge has soft sofas you can sink into, and a fire crackles comfortingly in the old stone fireplace on cold days. Its location is handy: It's a 5-minute walk from Corbyn Beach and even closer to the railway station. Rooms are attractive, with good fabrics, comfortable beds, and cheerful decor—colors vary from room to room. In a lovely touch, guests can borrow "honesty books" from the hotel's well-stocked shelves. Breakfasts—hot or continental—are excellent. Colindale offers good value for the price.

20 Rathmore Rd., Chelston, Torquay, Devon TQ2 6NY. www.colindalehotel.co.uk. ⓒ**01803/293947.** 8 units. £60–£75 double. Rates include English breakfast. MC, V. Free parking. No children 10 and under. **Amenities:** Bar; breakfast room; TV lounge. *In room:* TV, hair dryer, Wi-Fi (free).

Elmdene Hotel ★ ▥ This well-run B&B near the seafront has legions of fans who visit it over and over for the good service, quiet, attractive guest rooms, and friendly vibe. A short walk from shops, sights, and the train station, it sits on a leafy street just far enough away from the hustle and bustle to ensure peace. Rooms are spacious and decorated with a masculine touch, in tones of maroon and white or cream and taupe. Bathrooms are tiny but have all you need. There's a small bar downstairs where you can have an evening cocktail—in the summer you can drink it in the garden. If you don't feel like going out to eat, light meals are also available. Breakfasts include healthful yogurts and cereals as well as eggs and bacon. The owners know everything about the town and will happily point you in the right direction.

Rathmore Rd., Torquay, Devon TQ2 6NZ. www.elmdenehotel.co.uk. ⓒ/fax **01803/294940.** 8 units. £62–£85 double. Rates include breakfast. MC, V. Free parking. **Amenities:** Bar. *In room:* TV, hair dryer, Wi-Fi (free).

TOTNES ★

224 miles SW of London; 12 miles NW of Dartmouth

A hilly castle town on the banks of the River Dart, Totnes rests quietly in the past. This is a charming place where you always seem to be walking either up or down a steep hill. Its cobbled streets are lined with **Elizabethan** and **Tudor buildings,** as well as one of the original city gates through which visitors have passed since the Middle Ages. The town centers on the dramatic ruins of a **Norman castle,** an ancient guildhall, and the 15th-century **Church of St. Mary.**

Essentials

GETTING THERE First Great Western trains travel hourly to Totnes from London's Paddington Station; the trip takes 2¾ hours, costing around £76 for a round-trip.

If you're driving from Torquay, head west on the A385.

Between Easter and October, you can travel between Totnes and Dartmouth by boat. Contact **Dartmouth River Boats,** 5 Lower St., Dartmouth (www.dartmouth railriver.co.uk; © **01803/555872**). Round-trip tickets cost £14.

VISITOR INFORMATION The **Tourist Information Centre** is at the Town Mill, Coronation Road (www.totnesinformation.co.uk; © **01803/863168**). It's open April through October, Monday to Friday 9:30am to 5pm, Saturday 10am to 4pm; November through March it's open Monday to Friday 10am to 4pm and Saturday 10am to 1pm.

Exploring the Area

Elizabethan House Museum MUSEUM   In a 16th-century house so authentic it's a wee bit crooked, this museum demonstrates what the life of a wealthy merchant was like in those times. There's a display of furniture, costumes, documents, and farm implements.

70 Fore St. www.devonmuseums.net. © **01803/863821.** Admission £2.50 adults, £1.50 seniors, £1 children 3–13. Mon–Fri 10:30am–5pm. Closed Nov–mid-Mar.

Totnes Castle CASTLE   Crowning the hilltop at the northern end of High Street, this well-preserved castle keep is all that's left of a castle built by the Normans shortly after the conquest of England in 1066. The castle was used to subdue and dominate what was, until then, a Saxon town. All that's left are some walls and the handsome, crenellated keep. It's a fine example of motte-and-bailey construction (in which the central castle was built on a steep, man-made hill surrounded by a high stone wall). Climb to the top of the castle's hill for sweeping views of the town and surrounding countryside.

Castle St. www.englishheritage.org.uk. © **01803/864406.** Admission £3.40 adults, £3.10 students and seniors, £2 children 5–15. Apr–June and Sept daily 10am–5pm; July–Aug daily 10am–6pm; Oct daily 10am–4pm. Closed Nov–Mar.

Totnes Guildhall MUSEUM   In many ways the symbol of Totnes, this admirable old building was originally constructed as a priory (monastery) in 1553. Today it's a museum with an old gaol (jail) and the table Oliver Cromwell used to sign documents during his visit to Totnes in 1646.

Ramparts Walk. www.totnestowncouncil.gov.uk. © **01803/862147.** Admission £1.35 adults, 30p children 3–13. Mon–Fri 10:30am–4pm.

Where to Eat & Stay

Greys Dining Room ★★ BRITISH/ENGLISH TEA   A Devon institution, Greys is beloved for its reverence for teatime, and rightly so. It serves fine breakfasts and lunches as well, but each afternoon it comes into its own, setting out the silver and china to welcome you into another era, where dining rooms are paneled in oak and filled with antiques. You can choose from 40 different teas, as well as from a dazzling selection of freshly made cakes and scones with decadent clotted cream.

96 High St., Totnes. © **01803/866369.** Main courses £5–£10. MC, V. Wed–Sat 10am–5pm.

Orchard House ★ 🐾   This B&B in an old stone farmhouse a few miles outside Totnes is a real find for those who want to spend some time in the peaceful countryside. Set amid an apple cider orchard, it's a relaxing place and the owners do all they can to ensure that you feel at home. Guest rooms have brass or pine beds, creamy walls, and dark wood wardrobes, and each unit has a sweeping view of green lawns,

Butterflies, exotic birds, and adorable otters all frolic happily in the Disney-like environment of the **Buckfast Butterflies & Dartmoor Otter Sanctuary** at the edge of Dartmoor. The sanctuary not only provides safe haven for all its creatures, but also nurses wounded otters back to health. Human guests are welcome but dogs are forbidden (otters hate them). Feeding times at 11:30am and 2pm are the best times to see the otters. The sanctuary is in the town of Buckfastleigh (www.ottersandbutterflies. co.uk; © **01364/642916**), and is open from April to October daily 10am to 5:30pm. Admission is £5 for adults, £3 for children 3 to 15.

pastures, and gardens. The well-equipped rooms include little refrigerators stocked with fresh milk and water. Breakfasts are made with local eggs and meats.

Horner, Halwell (near Totnes), Devon TQ9 7LB. www.orchard-house-halwell.co.uk. © **01548/ 821448.** 3 units. £55–£60 double. Rates include English breakfast. No credit cards. Closed Nov–Feb. *In room:* TV/DVD, hair dryer, MP3 docking station, Wi-Fi (free), no phone.

Royal Seven Stars Hotel   A former coaching inn in the center of Totnes, this hotel dates from 1660 and overlooks a square in the town center, near the banks of the River Dart. The interior courtyard, once used for horses and carriages, is now enclosed in glass and decorated with antiques and paintings, making an inviting entrance to the inn. Guest rooms are modern and spacious, nicely decorated with white walls and red accents (throws, cushions, splashes of wallpaper). Downstairs, the handy restaurant and pub mean you don't have to go out if you don't want to; this is a good place for dinner whether or not you're spending the night here.

The Plains, Totnes, Devon TQ9 5DD. www.royalsevenstars.co.uk. © **01803/862125.** Fax 01803/ 867925. 16 units. £119–£159 double. Rates include English breakfast. AE, MC, V. **Amenities:** Restaurant; bar; room service. *In room:* TV, hair dryer, Wi-Fi (free).

DARTMOUTH ★

236 miles SW of London; 35 miles S of Exeter

With its houses stacked on the side of a steep hill like toy pieces in some bizarre game of balance, Dartmouth is an alluring, historic seaside town. This ancient seaport at the mouth of the River Dart has an esteemed maritime history. This was where knights set out for the Crusades in the 12th century, and it was the home of the Royal Navy for so long that Warfleet Creek at the edge of town is believed to have been so named in honor of the many fleets that gathered in the harbor nearby before setting off for battle. Given that military history, it's no surprise that the river is flanked by two once-heavily fortified castles—**Dartmouth Castle** and **Kingswear Castle.** Wonderfully, much survives of this town's long history—streets are lined with houses dating to Tudor and Elizabethan times, and even more from the 18th and 19th centuries.

Essentials

GETTING THERE   Dartmouth is not easily reached by public transportation. CrossCountry trains run to Totnes and Paignton where you can catch buses that run about once an hour to Dartmouth. Visit www.stagecoachbus.com or call ☎ **0870/608-2608** for schedules.

If you're driving, at Totnes turn onto the A381 and follow signs for Dartmouth. There's only one parking lot in town, and it can get full in the summer. If that happens, park at the edge of town by the leisure center, in the park-and-ride lot on the A3122—signs will direct you there.

You can also travel between Totnes and Dartmouth by boat from Easter to October on **Dartmouth River Boats,** 5 Lower St., Dartmouth (www.dartmouthrailriver.co.uk; ☎ **01803/555872**). A round-trip journey costs £14.

VISITOR INFORMATION The **Tourist Information Centre** is at the Engine House, Mayors Avenue (www.discoverdartmouth.com; ☎ **01803/834224**). It's open April through October, Monday to Saturday 9:30am to 5:30pm and Sunday 10am to 2pm; in the off season, hours are Monday to Saturday 9:30am to 4:30pm.

Exploring the Area

Dartmouth is a gorgeous town just to wander in. It does have sights worth seeing, but the main attraction is the town itself, with its watercolor Victorian houses stacked above one another on the steep hill. While you're wandering, pop into the local church, **St. Petrox,** on Castle Road, a 17th-century stone structure with an ivy-draped graveyard where the tombstones evoke the sorrows of Dartmouth's maritime past. The church is open daily from 7am to dusk.

It's also worth walking along the waterfront to **Bayard's Cove,** near the end of Lower Street. One of Dartmouth's oldest surviving neighborhoods, its cobbled streets and half-timbered buildings are wonderfully complete. It prospered in the 1600s thanks to its ship-repair services. In 1620, this is where the Pilgrims' historic ships, the *Speedwell* and the *Mayflower,* were repaired.

You can explore the area by boat as well. **Dartmouth River Boats,** 5 Lower St., Dartmouth (www.dartmouthrailriver.co.uk; ☎ **01803/555872**), ply the waters around the town. Schedules vary according to the season. For tickets and information, go to the kiosk at the Dartmouth Embankment, or check the website. Prices range from £12 to £23 for adults.

Dartmouth Castle CASTLE Standing ruggedly on the shore at the edge of Dartmouth, this castle looks no worse for wear after 600 years. Originally built during the 15th century as fortified defense against French invasion, it was later outfitted with artillery and employed by the Victorians as a coastal defense station. A tour of its bulky ramparts and somber interiors provides insight into the changing nature of warfare through the centuries, and offers sweeping views of the surrounding coast and flatlands.

Castle Rd. (½ mile south of the town center). www.english-heritage.org.uk. ☎ **01803/833588.** Admission £4.70 adults, £4.20 seniors, £2.80 children 5–15. Apr–June and Sept daily 10am–5pm; July–Aug daily 10am–6pm; Oct daily 10am–4pm; Nov–Mar Sat-Sun 10am–4pm.

Dartmouth Museum MUSEUM This small, quirky museum is located in a marvelous historic building—a merchant's house built between 1635 and 1640, and set amid an interconnected row of 17th-century buildings known as the Butter Walk. The overhanging, stilt-supported facade was originally designed to provide shade for the butter, milk, and cream sold there. The museum's displays are quite limited—some old photographs, rather a lot of ships in bottles, and so forth. Some of the rooms are quite charming, however.

The Butterwalk. © **01803/832923.** Admission £2 adults, £1.50 seniors, 50p children 5–15. Apr–Oct Mon–Sat 10am–4pm. Closed Nov–Mar.

Where to Eat

Angelique ★★ CONTINENTAL   This inventive restaurant with a Michelin-starred chef strives to offer something for everyone. The street-level restaurant is lively and casual, with an open kitchen where you can watch the staff work. The upstairs dining room is more elegant and romantic, perfect for a quiet meal. The top floor is a cocktail bar, ideal for a drink before or after dinner. The menu changes daily but always uses fresh local ingredients. Dishes could include slow-cooked beef with crispy panceto and Cavelo Nero, roast lamb with kofte and couscous, or fried Pollock with chorizo and smoked paprika mash.

If you like the place, you can spend the night. There are six attractive, **comfortable bedrooms** (£85–£95 double).

2 South Embankment. www.thenewangel.co.uk. © **01803/839425.** Reservations required. Main courses £19–£31; fixed-price 2-course menu £22, 3-course menu £26. AE, MC, V. Wed–Sun noon–2:30pm; Tues–Sat 6:30–9:30pm.

The Cherub Inn PUB FARE   First built in 1380 as the harbormaster's house, this historic pub still retains many of its early features, including leaded windows and timbered walls. With its fireplaces and drinking nooks, this is a fine place to stop for a pint or a steak and kidney pie. Drinking and casual dining takes place downstairs in the beamed main pub; upstairs there's a more formal restaurant.

13 Higher St., Dartmouth. www.the-cherub.co.uk. © **01803/832571.** Main courses £6–£11. MC, V. daily noon–11pm.

Where to Stay

Browns ★★ 🎒   This small, town-house hotel in the center of Dartmouth is a real find. Guest rooms are not big, but they're artfully appointed in neutral shades with bright splashes of color. The hotel has an arty vibe, with pieces by local artists throughout the building. Beds are comfortable and piled with feather pillows and down duvets (non-feather options are available for the allergic). Breakfast is a high point, with fresh-squeezed juices, homemade jams and marmalades, and local eggs and meats. It's taken in a sunny room, with deep leather chairs, perfect for lingering over the morning papers. The hotel restaurant is popular with locals, drawn by its modern take on classic British food.

27–29 Victoria Rd., Dartmouth, Devon TQ6 9RT. www.brownshoteldartmouth.co.uk. © **01803/832572.** 10 units. £95–£185 double. Rates include English breakfast. MC, V. Free Parking permits provided. *In room:* TV, hair dryer, Wi-Fi (free).

Hill View House ★   This B&B in a typical Dartmouth five-story Victorian house is perched—as the name implies—up the hill from the harbor, with sweeping views of the town and the sea. Its five guest rooms are tastefully furnished in shades of cream and white, and they range in size from pretty spacious to rather tiny. Bathrooms are very small but have all that you need. The owners are welcoming and helpful, and the price is reasonable.

76 Victoria Rd., Dartmouth, Devon TQ6 9DZ. www.hillviewdartmouth.co.uk. © **01803/839372.** 5 units. £70 double. Rates include English breakfast. DC, MC, V. *In room:* TV, hair dryer, Wi-Fi (free).

Royal Castle Hotel ★   A sympathetically restored, grand old inn on the waterfront, the Royal Castle has been welcoming guests—including Queen Victoria,

Charles II, and Edward VII—for hundreds of years. The glassed-in courtyard, with its winding wooden staircase, displays the service bells once connected to the guest rooms. Rooms are spacious and decorated in pale, soothing colors, with big comfortable beds—many units have sweeping views of the marina, though these cost more. Breakfasts are so filling you may not need to eat again until dinner, and staff are consistently polite. The hotel pub—with its thick wood beams—is in the oldest part of the building, and is a great place for an evening drink.

11 The Quay, Dartmouth, Devon TQ6 9PS. www.royalcastle.co.uk. © **01803/833033.** Fax 01803/835445. 25 units. £126–£166 double. Rates include English breakfast. AE, MC, V. Free parking. **Amenities:** Restaurant; 2 bars; room service; babysitting. *In room:* A/C (in some), TV, hair dryer, Wi-Fi (surcharge).

Soar Mill Cove ★★★ Just off a pristine beach between the towns of Dartmouth and Plymouth, this lovely and welcoming hotel is worth the drive. Soar Mill is a low-slung, family-friendly hotel with everything you wouldn't expect to find at the end of a country lane—modern and elegant rooms, French-influenced cuisine, a Bollinger bar, a spring-fed heated pool, and a dreamy spa. The owners set out to make the kind of hotel they'd want to stay in themselves and it's a very appealing place. Rooms are big and many have sea views—all have private patios with tables and chairs. The restaurant overlooks the dramatic surrounding countryside, and you can walk to gorgeous Soar Mill Cove beach.

Soar Mill Cove, Near Salcombe, Devon TQ7 3DS. www.soarmillcove.co.uk. © **01548/561566.** 23 units. £150–£280 double; suites £200–£330. Rates include English breakfast. AE, MC, V. Free parking. **Amenities:** Restaurant; bar; pool; spa; room service. *In room:* TV, DVD, hair dryer, Wi-Fi (free).

PLYMOUTH

242 miles SW of London; 161 miles SW of Southampton

"It's seen better days"—if ever a town fit that cliché, it's Plymouth. Historic and once-beautiful, Plymouth was founded in the 11th century and grew to become the principal seaport of Tudor England. All the known world sailed here and walked its narrow medieval streets. Few places in the south of England are as rich in romantic lore.

Sadly, most of that old Plymouth has gone. German bombing raids during World War II devastated the city; as many as 75,000 buildings were destroyed. Whatever the Nazis didn't destroy, spectacularly bad development in the 1950s and '60s did. Huge swathes were replaced with oppressive, brutalist concrete buildings. Today, Plymouth is the kind of city that one passes through and winces at the thought of how good it must once have looked.

However, not everything in the old town was lost. The tiny Elizabethan section, known as the **Barbican,** contains some original buildings, and a few good sights relating to the first Pilgrim Fathers who colonized America. The *Mayflower* and *Speedwell,* which sailed from Southampton in August 1620, docked into Plymouth after suffering storm damage. The *Speedwell* was abandoned; the *Mayflower* made the trip alone. The next stop from here was the New World.

In Britain, Plymouth is more associated with its most famous son, Sir Francis Drake—the swashbuckling admiral and one-time favorite of Queen Elizabeth I, who fought off the Spanish Armada in 1588. Legend has it that he was playing bowls up on Plymouth Hoe (a stretch of cliff overlooking the bay) when a messenger galloped over to tell him of the impending invasion. "There is plenty of time," he is said to have replied, "to finish this game and beat the Spaniards."

Unless you're a Tudor history buff, there is little to detain you in this workaday town. The Barbican is interesting, and its historic sights impressive—but not impressive or plentiful enough to warrant more than an afternoon's detour.

Essentials

GETTING THERE   First Great Western trains run frequently throughout the day from London's Paddington Station to Plymouth; the trip takes 3¼ to 4 hours, costing around £75 for a round-trip. For rail information, visit www.firstgreatwestern.co.uk or call ☏ **0845/748-4950** or 0845/700-0125. In Plymouth, the rail station is on North Road, north of the center. Several buses run from the rail station to the heart of Plymouth.

Buses run daily from London's Victoria Coach Station to Plymouth. The trip takes about 5½ hours. Fares cost around £33.

If you're driving from London, take the M4 west to the junction with the M5 going south to Exeter. From Exeter, head southwest on the A38 to Plymouth.

VISITOR INFORMATION   The **Tourist Information Centre** is at the Mayflower, in the Barbican (www.visitplymouth.co.uk; ☏ **01752/306330**). It's open April through October, Monday to Saturday 9am to 5pm and Sunday 10am to 4pm; November to March, Monday to Friday 9am to 5pm and Saturday 10am to 4pm.

Exploring the Area

To commemorate the spot from which the *Mayflower* sailed for the New World, a white archway, erected in 1934 and capped with the flags of Britain and the United States, stands at the base of Plymouth's West Pier, on the Barbican. Incorporating a granite monument that was erected in 1891, the site is referred to as both the ***Mayflower* Steps** and the **Memorial Gateway.**

The **Barbican** is a mass of narrow streets, old houses, and quayside shops selling antiques, brass work, old prints, and books. Fishing boats still unload their catch at the wharves, and passenger-carrying ferryboats run short harbor cruises.

Merchant's House MUSEUM   Arguably the most complete Tudor building in Plymouth, Merchant's House now contains a museum of local history. Its higgledy-piggledy collection includes an old ducking stool, once used to punish women for crimes and minor infractions. Women believed to have gossiped or been too critical were strapped onto the stool and then plunged into the icy waters of the river. Less excitingly, there's also a replica Victorian schoolroom.

33 St. Andrew's St. ☏ **01752/304774.** Admission £2 adults, £1 children 5–16, £5 families. Apr–Oct Tues–Sat 10am–5pm. Closed Nov–Mar. Any city center bus.

Plymouth Gin Distillery DISTILLERY   One of Plymouth's oldest-surviving buildings, this is where the Pilgrims spent their last night before sailing for the New World. It wasn't a distillery then, of course, but a meeting place for "Non-Conformists," and a refuge for oppressed Huguenots. This historic site dates back to 1425, when a Dominican monastery was built here. After the monastery was closed in the 16th century, the building changed hands many times. Plymouth Gin has been produced here for the last 200 years. You can tour the historic site and enjoy a tipple.

Black Friars Distillery, 60 Southside St. www.plymouthgin.com. ☏ **01752/665292.** Admission £6 adults, children free (with adult only). Daily 10:30am–4:30pm; Sun 11:30am–3:30pm. Bus: 54.

Smeaton's Tower OBSERVATION POINT   Built in 1759, this picturesque, candy-striped lighthouse was moved to its current location atop Plymouth Hoe in the late 1800s, when it was found to be in danger of collapsing the cliff on which it once stood. Today it's no longer in use, but has been fully restored to its original condition. At a little over 21m (70 ft.) tall, the views of Plymouth and the English Channel from the top are spectacular.

The Hoe. ℂ **01752/304774.** Admission £2.50 adults, £1 children 5–16, £6 families. Apr–Oct Tues–Sat 10am–3pm. Closed Nov–Mar. Any city center bus.

Where to Eat

Tanners Restaurant ★★ INTERNATIONAL   Popular with local diners, this restaurant is certainly one of the most handsome places to eat around here; the converted 15th-century house has mullioned windows, exposed stone, antique tapestries, and even an illuminated water well. Locally caught seafood is a specialty, although meat lovers are equally well catered for. Typical dishes include filet of brill with buttered leeks and cockles, and Devon sirloin with marrowbone gratin. For dessert you may find warm pear and cinnamon cake with almond ice cream, or chestnut parfait with toasted white chocolate marshmallow. Unusually, the restaurant requires a £10 deposit for all weekend dinner bookings.

Prysten House, Finewell St. www.tannersrestaurant.com. ℂ **01752/252001.** Reservations required. Main courses £16–£28. AE, DC, MC, V. Tues–Fri noon–2:30pm; Sat noon–2pm; Tues–Sat 7–9:30pm.

Tudor Rose Tea Rooms BRITISH   This ultra-traditional restaurant in an old Tudor pub dates from 1640—when, according to a sign on the wall, "New Street was new." The menu is neither innovative nor particularly varied, but it's reliably good, no-nonsense fare. Lunch dishes include sandwiches, fish and chips, steak and kidney pudding, and sausage and mash; or you could just come for a traditional afternoon tea, complete with dainty sandwiches and cakes. Best of all, prices are very reasonable.

36 New St. www.tudorrosetearoom.co.uk. ℂ **01752/255502.** Sandwiches and light lunches £3.50–£5; lunch main courses £4–£11; afternoon tea £5–£7. MC, V. Daily 10am–5pm (often later in summer).

Where to Stay

Athenaeum Lodge   This bijou guesthouse is about 10 minutes' walk from the Barbican district. Owners Jane and David Kewell really seem to enjoy what they do, and their knowledge of the local area is second to none. The decor may be a little traditional for some tastes (striped red-and-white wallpaper and red curtains in the dining room), but bedrooms are comfortable and spotlessly clean. Breakfasts are well done (though don't expect much variety).

4 Athenaeum St., The Hoe, Plymouth, Devon PL1 2RQ. www.athenaeumlodge.com. ℂ **01752/665005.** 8 units. £50–£60 double; £55–£70 family room. Rates include English breakfast. DC, MC, V. Limited free parking overnight; £2 permit parking nearby. **Amenities:** Guest computer. In room: TV, Wi-Fi (free).

CORNWALL

by Nick Dalton and Deborah Stone

Cornwall is far-flung England, as far as you can go, a jagged peninsula that culminates in Land's End, 265 miles from London (more than 300 by road). Waves crash against giant cliffs and roll onto exquisite beaches in huge bays.

It is a leading place for family trips—thanks in no small part to its balmy southern climate—and it is also a destination for adventurers, offering some of the best surfing in Europe. You're never far from the sea here, a coast dotted with picturesque fishing ports, yet there is also a strong creative feel. It's possible to view striking modern art at Tate St. Ives, explore the legacy of author Daphne du Maurier, and then eat some of the nation's finest food at the restaurants of famed chefs Jamie Oliver and Rick Stein.

10

COAST   You can't get away from it; the farther you drive, the closer it gets. In Cornwall you're rarely more than 20 miles from the sea, and you're generally much closer, or have a sea view from a lofty moor. Whether the arty sophistication of St. Ives, the surf sensation of Newquay, or a quiet spot on the Isles of Scilly, the climate's balmy and there's fun to be had. And there's a walk that follows the length of the coast.

SIGHTSEEING   Visit the **Eden Project,** with its rainforest under futuristic domes, and the lovely **Lost Gardens of Heligan;** there are many other exquisite gardens too. The **National Maritime Museum** in **Falmouth** is a family-friendly delight. Village sea ports such as **Looe** cry out for a walk around the tiny streets. And you can go deep in a **tin mine**—Cornwall's mining landscape is a UNESCO World Heritage site.

EATING & DRINKING   This is a place for seafood, with fish arriving daily on tiny boats at tiny quaysides. And the restaurants are there to use it, whether celebrity chef Rick Stein's empire in **Padstow,** Jamie Oliver's **Fifteen** on Watergate Bay, or newcomer **Nathan Outlaw,** also in Padstow—or just enjoy fish and chips eaten beside the sea. And there's always pasties (meat pies), and clotted cream teas.

OUTDOOR ACTIVITIES   It's the coast again, with surfing and sailing being huge. Walking along the sea is big—the South West Coast walk takes in the whole of the county's coast. There are plenty of inland strolls too, around Bodmin Moor, along rivers, and over hills. Old railway lines have been turned into **cycle** routes, such as the **Camel Trail** that runs for 18 miles along the tranquil Camel estuary.

THE best TRAVEL EXPERIENCES IN CORNWALL

o **Splashing in Watergate Bay:** This expanse of west-facing beach (p. 418) is what Cornwall is all about, wild, grand, and otherworldly, yet on the edge of Newquay and home to the delights of The Hotel and Jamie Oliver's Fifteen restaurant.

o **Finding the Lost Gardens of Heligan:** Palm trees and delicate flowers abound in these hidden, historic gardens that only a few years ago were completely overgrown. The sub-tropical climate means it's like being lost on a desert island.

o **Having your photo taken at Land's End:** OK, the attraction that's grown up in this beauty spot might not be perfect, but who could resist posing in front of the signpost (p. 409) that can tell you how far it is to home, whether New York or Newcastle.

o **Seeing the light in St. Ives:** It only takes a moment to understand why artists flocked to this pretty fishing village (p. 415) at the end of the 19th century. And why people still do, with the Tate St. Ives gallery and the studio of sculptor Barbara Hepworth.

o **Visiting the Isles of Scilly:** So near and yet so far, these unspoiled islands 28 miles off the coast are a timeless world of beautiful beaches, sparkling seas, rich birdlife, and history. Take a helicopter across for the ultimate adventure. See p. 412.

THE SOUTHEAST COAST ★

Looe: 264 miles SW of London, 20 miles W of Plymouth; Polperro: 271 miles SW of London, 26 miles W of Plymouth, 6 miles SW of Looe

This is the Cornwall that has most in common with the rest of southern England, a gentle place just over the River Tamar from Devon. It's often passed by as visitors head straight down the A30 toward the county's more distinctive spots, but take a detour and there's much to appreciate here. No sooner are you across the Tamar than Whitsand Bay is the first of many idyllic beaches that stretch along the coast.

The coast is dotted with fishing villages and little ports: Looe, its two halves divided by the River Looe; Polperro, with fishermen's cottages dating back to the 16th century and a quayside to match; and Fowey, with steep, narrow streets falling away to the pretty waterfront. Novelist Daphne du Maurier lived nearby, and her tales of shipwrecks and smuggling come to life in and around the tight bays and jagged coast.

Essentials

GETTING THERE   The nearest mainline station is at Liskeard, almost 4 hours, about £50 by **First Great Western** train (www.firstgreatwestern.co.uk; ✆ **0845/700-0125**) from London's Paddington Station, with the delightful Looe Valley Line branch to Looe (another 30 minutes) costing from £4 per person one-way.

If you're **driving** to Looe, take the A38 west once you've crossed the Tamar from Plymouth into Cornwall, and then the B3253. To get to Polperro, follow the A387 southwest from Looe. For Lostwithiel, take the A38 west, then the A390. Continue on this southwest to branch off for Fowey.

VISITOR INFORMATION   **Looe Tourist Information Centre,** Guildhall, Fore Street (www.visit-southeastcornwall.co.uk; ✆ **01503/262072**), is open Easter to September, daily 10am to 5pm; October, daily 10am to 2pm; and November to

Easter, Monday to Friday 10am to 1pm. **Fowey Tourist Information Centre,** 5 South St. (www.fowey.co.uk; ✆ **01726/833616**), is open daily 10am to 4:30pm. **Lostwithiel Tourist Information** is at Lostwithiel Community Centre on Liddicoat Road just off the A390 (www.lostwithieltouristinformation.webs.com; ✆ **01208/872207**). It's open Easter to November Monday to Friday 10am to 5pm, Saturday 10am to 1pm; November to Easter Monday to Friday 10am to 1pm.

Exploring the Area

Looe is charming. It's a real fishing port with one of the largest fleets in Cornwall. It's also a place of stone cottages and a stone bridge across the River Fowey connecting the two halves of town, which are backed by green hills. The tourist area is East Looe, where there's a sandy beach. In West Looe the beach is littered with rocks and dotted with pools. The **Old Guildhall Museum & Gaol** (Higher Market St.; ✆ **01503/262070;** admission £1.80; March–mid-Oct daily 11am–4pm), in the 16th century former courthouse and jail, charts the town's history, from French and Spanish invasions, to the evacuees who fled here from bombed Plymouth in World War II.

Go east and you find the dramatic expanse of **Whitsand Bay,** cliffs backing a gorgeous unspoilt beach that stretches all the way to Rame Head which sticks out into the English Channel and is topped by a 14th-century chapel. There's parking, sometimes along the road, at various points where steep paths go down to the beach, such as Tregonhawke (where there's a cafe) and Sharrow Point.

Just west of Looe is **Polperro,** another place where quayside and beach exist close together. A little farther and there is **Fowey** (pronounced *Foy*), pretty with streets rolling down the hill to the quayside. Novelist Daphne du Maurier lived close by, and an annual literary festival celebrates her work. A small ferry crosses the River Fowey to the village of **Polruan** with its waterfront pubs. It's nice walking along the River Fowey; take the ferry then stroll up to **Bodinnick** where another ferry gets you back.

Upriver is the market town of **Lostwithiel,** the Cornish capital until the river silted up in medieval times. The Stannary Parliament, which regulated the sale of local tin, sat here from the 14th to 17th centuries in the **Duchy Palace,** built in 1292 by Edmund, King John's grandson. The Duchy of Cornwall was created to provide the heir to the throne with an income. Prince Charles has turned it into a brand with Duchy Originals products (www.duchyoriginals.com), from biscuits to organic beer, in shops nationwide. The Duchy Palace, foreboding and ancient, isn't open to the public but is being restored by the Prince's Regeneration Trust (www.princes-regeneration.org).

When the river silted up, Fowey became the area port and set off on a lively history. It was raided by a Spanish fleet in 1380, then Henry VIII had **St. Catherine's Castle** (www.english-heritage.org.uk; free admission; daily) built. The footpath from Ready Money Cove has great views of town. A ship sailed from here to fight with Drake against the Spanish Armada, and others joined the D-Day landings of World War II.

Looe Island NATURE RESERVE   This small island offers lovely, lofty walks through trees and wildflower meadows up to the highest point, where there is a 12th century Benedictine chapel. There are seabirds, including the great black-backed gull, and plenty of seals. The Islander boat runs a frequent but irregular service from Buller's Quay in East Looe.

www.cornwallwildlifetrust.org.uk. ✆ **01873/273939.** Return trips £6 adults, £4 children, landing fee £2.50 adults, £1 children. Trips run Easter–Sept are tide dependent, and last around 2 hours.

Cornwall

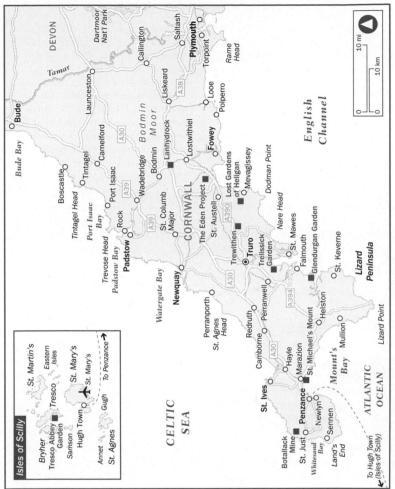

Lanhydrock HISTORIC SITE   This mansion has 50 rooms to explore, as well as beautiful grounds that roll down to the banks of the River Fowey. The house combines grand Victorian style with William Morris Arts and Crafts, as well as much older touches including a 400-year-old painted ceiling

Between Lostwithiel and Bodmin, off the A390. www.nationaltrust.org.uk. (C) **01208/265950.** Admission: House and garden £10.40 adults, £5.10 children, £26 family ticket; garden only £6.10 adults, £3.30 children. House March–late Oct Tues–Sun 11am–5pm (closed 5:30pm Apr–Sept); gardens Year-round daily 10am–6pm.

Restormel Castle CASTLE   Sitting above the River Fowey, this striking, circular castle ruin has great views and the walls give you a good idea of the shape of the

The Charms of Looe

For a little place, Looe has a goodly share of great seafood restaurants. **The Old Sail Loft,** Quay Street (www.theoldsailloft restaurant.com; ℭ **01503/262131**), in a 16th-century smugglers' bolthole is awash with maritime relics. Maybe start with a seafood chowder then go for filet of Looe sea bass with cauliflower cheese purée, sautéed potatoes, and samphire. Main courses £11–£20. **Squid Ink** (www.squid-ink.biz; ℭ **01503/262674**), off the quayside in Lower Chapel Street, has a modern feel and combines local fare with Mediterranean (tagliatelle nero with filet

of Cornish sea bream) and Asian (local squid in tempura batter with wasabi mayo) influences. Main courses £17–£21. **Trawlers on the Quay** (www.trawlers-restaurant.co.uk; ℭ **01503/263593**) on Quay Street looks over East Looe waterfront where day boats provide crab, cuttlefish, brill, and other joys. The food is simple, occasionally with a dash of wasabi, or Creole spicing. It's part of the food and rooms group headed by the Barclay House hotel (see p. 401). Main courses £11–£16.

rooms inside. It was built in the 13th century and last saw action in the English Civil War in the mid-1600s. It is a popular place for picnics, particularly at bluebell time in spring.

Nr. Restormel Rd. (just north of Lostwithiel off the A390). www.english-heritage.org.uk. Admission £3.40 adults, £2 children 5–15. Apr–late June and Sept 10am–5pm; July–late Aug 10am–6pm; Oct 10am–4pm.

Where to Eat

Food for Thought BRITISH   An ever-popular restaurant on the Fowey waterfront, in a 14th-century Grade II listed building with exposed beams and shale walls. Starters include River Fowey mussels and potted Fowey crab, and main courses such as "posh" fish and goose fat chips (cod, lemon sole, sea bass, and king prawn, with mushy peas). The lunch menu includes crab salad and sandwiches.

4 Town Quay. www.foodforthought.fowey.com. ℭ **01726/832221.** Main courses £14–£25. AE MC, V. Daily 11am–2:30pm and 7–9:30pm, but closed Sun evenings Mar–Apr. Closed Nov–mid-Mar.

Trewithen BRITISH   Near the Duchy Palace in Lostwithiel, the white tablecloths contrast wonderfully with the 18th-century building and the modern cuisine. Dishes veer from hot and spicy halibut stew, to venison streak marinated in red wine and thyme, with red cabbage, sultanas, pine nuts, and Manchego shavings. The daily brunch menu features rosti and steak in ciabatta. Eating in the courtyard is pleasant.

Fore St., Lostwithiel. www.trewithenrestaurant.com. ℭ **01208/872373.** Main courses £14.50–£21.50. MC, V. Tues–Sat 11am–2pm and 6:30–9pm.

The View SEAFOOD   The name says it all: Stirring views from a Whitsand Bay clifftop. Pine and white linen give an airy feel to what is mostly a seafood restaurant in summer, with more meat in winter. Dishes might include Whitsand plaice with razor clams, lemon, and garlic, but wood pigeon or venison steak in colder months. Chef/proprietor Matt Corner is fast being mentioned alongside Rick Stein as a Cornwall star.

Treninnow Cliff Rd., Millbrook, Cornwall, PL40 1JY. www.the-view-restaurant.co.uk. ℭ **0871/272366.** Reservations recommended. Main courses £13.50–£18.50. AE, MC, V. April–Oct Wed–Sun noon–1:45pm and 7–8:45pm; Nov–Mar Thurs–Sun noon–1:45pm, Thurs–Sat 7–8:45pm.

Shopping

The **Polperro Gallery** (www.polperrogallery.co.uk; ℭ **01503/272577**) is good for Cornish art, while in East Looe **Purely Cornish,** Fore Street (www.purelycornish.co.uk; ℭ **01503/262680**) has local food and drink, including splendid Camel Valley wines, and the **Pasty Shop,** Buller Street, makes its own pasties. **Cornish Orchards** (www.cornishorchards.co.uk; ℭ **01503/269007**), at Westnorth Manor Farm, Duloe, near Looe, sells its own cider and apple juice.

Entertainment & Nightlife

This is an area for pubs. Perhaps the most relaxed of Fowey's is the riverside **Galleon Inn,** 12 Fore St. (www.galleon-inn.com; ℭ **01726/833014**), in a 400-year-old warehouse. There's pub food and outside tables. In West Looe, the **Harbour Moon,** Quayside (www.harbourmoonlooe.co.uk; ℭ **01503/262873**), is a family-friendly place with a waterfront garden. In East Looe there are plenty of old pubs; the **Jolly Sailor** (ℭ **01503/263387**) just away from the water's edge dates back to the 1500s and has weekly folk and shanty evenings. Polperro's **Blue Peter Inn,** Quay Road (www.thebluepeter.co.uk; ℭ **01503/272743**), is quaint with local ales and live music.

Port Eliot Festival, on a waterfront site at St. Germans, west of Plymouth, in July, is one of Britain's most innovative arts events. It's a literary festival run as a music festival.; authors and poets are encouraged to perform in outrageous or spontaneous ways. Those who have range from artist Grayson Perry to Bob Dylan's son Jakob, novelist Hanif Kureishi to Brit-pop veteran Jarvis Cocker. There's also music, food from the likes of Jamie Oliver's Fifteen in Newquay, and boutique camping—you can hire an Airstream, gypsy caravan, or yurt (www.porteliotfestival.com; ℭ **01503/232783**).

Where to Stay

Barclay House ★★   The view over the Looe River from this family-run hotel is lovely, and the wooded hillside behind it is equally special. Rooms are light and modern, and there's a terrace for breakfast or drinks. There are also self-catering cottages.

Daphne, *Rebecca,* & *The Birds*

Author Daphne du Maurier did much to promote the wild, windswept image of Cornwall in novels such as *Rebecca* and *Jamaica Inn* (named after the pub on Bodmin Moor, see p. 423), tales of love, storms, and shipwrecks, that became two of Alfred Hitchcock's earliest films, the former a 1940 Academy Award winner. It was her 1952 short story, *The Birds,* that was adapted into one of Hitchcock's most famous films. Du Maurier lived from 1943 to 1969 in Menabilly, a secluded house, near Fowey, and latterly at nearby Kilmarth; both are in private hands. The Daphne du Maurier Festival (www.dumaurierfestival.co.uk), a mix of talks, readings, and musical performances, takes place each May in Fowey.

The **restaurant** has a set menu (chargrilled Looe mackerel or slow-roasted Cornish pork belly) at £25 for 2 courses, while the 6-course tasting menu is £39.

St. Martins Rd. (the B3253 Plymouth-Looe Rd.), East Looe, Cornwall, PL13 1LP. www.barclayhouse. co.uk. © **01503/262929.** Fax: 01503/262632. 20 units, including 8 cottages. £125–£165 double with breakfast, £299–£1,499 cottage per week. AE, MC, V. **Amenities:** Restaurant; bar; outdoor heated pool; exercise room; sauna; Wi-Fi (free) in public areas. *In room:* TV, hair dryer.

Fowey Hall Hotel ★★ ☺ A member of the Luxury Family Hotels group, this Victorian, hillside fantasy (believed to have been the inspiration for Toad Hall in *The Wind in the Willows*) is certainly that. Aside from the registered crèche, there's a playroom for tots and a games room with Xbox for the older ones. Food is excellent; there's a choice of high tea for youngsters, so you can dine alone later, or an early family dinner sitting, all with excellent, intelligent children's menus. There is a 12-m (40-ft.) indoor pool and a spa. And it's all only a short walk from town.

Hanson Dr., Fowey, Cornwall PL23 1ET. www.foweyhallhotel.co.uk. © **01726/833866.** Fax 01726/834100. 36 units. £170–245 double; £260–£420 large suite. Dinner, B&B option also available. MC, V. **Amenities:** Restaurant; indoor pool; spa; babysitting; billiard room; crèche. *In room:* TV/DVD, hair dryer.

Old Quay House ★ This 150-year-old waterside property on the Fowey Estuary is full of boutique chic. The rooms, all calm in white and cream in a New England sort of way, are discreetly luxurious. Some have small balconies, and the penthouse features a claw-foot bath. The terrace is a spot for lunch, tea, and drinks. The Q restaurant, cool and calm as the rooms, is heavy on local seafood (Fowey river oysters, Cornish scallops) but there are other delights such as slow-roasted West Country duck.

28 Fore St., Fowey, Cornwall PL23 1AQ. www.theoldquayhouse.com. © **01726/833302.** Fax 01726/833668. 11 units. £180–£270 double; £320 penthouse suite. Rates include breakfast; add £37.50pp for dinner. AE, MC, V. Free parking. No children under 12. **Amenities:** Restaurant; bar. *In room:* TV, hair dryer, Internet (free).

ST. AUSTELL TO THE LIZARD ★★★

St. Mawes: 290 miles SW of London, 2 miles E of Falmouth, 18 miles S of Truro

After the discreet charm of the south coast, Cornwall here starts to get wilder and more mysterious. Take a quick look at a map and it seems as if Cornwall simply ends at a point but, in fact, there are two of them. Follow the intricately beveled coast (it's easy to believe this was smuggling country) and you get to the Lizard, the most southerly point of mainland U.K. At first it seems that the coast (St. Austell, Mevagissey, Falmouth, the Roseland Peninsula) is everything. But look inland and, cosseted by the sub-tropical climate, you'll find gorgeous gardens, from the futuristic Eden Project to the glorious Lost Gardens of Heligan, as well as Truro, Cornwall's county town.

Essentials

GETTING THERE **Trains** leave London's Paddington Station for St. Austell and Truro roughly every two hours. The trip takes 4½–5 hours and costs about £55 one-way. At Truro you connect with trains for the 25-minute journey to Falmouth. Buses run from Truro to St. Mawes and Falmouth or you can take a taxi from Truro or St. Austell.

National Express buses (www.nationalexpress.com; ✆ **0871/781-8181**) leave London's Victoria Coach Station four times a day for Truro. The trip takes 7–8 hours. If you're **driving**, the A391 branches off the A30 to St. Austell; farther along the A30 the A39 branches off for Truro and then Falmouth.

VISITOR INFORMATION   Truro's **Tourist Information Centre,** Municipal Buildings, Boscawen Street (www.tourism.truro.gov.uk; ✆ **01872/274555**), is open Easter to late October, Monday to Friday 9am to 5:30pm, Saturday 9am to 4pm; rest of year Monday to Friday 9am to 5pm.

Exploring the Area

St. Austell is a lovely market town with hills (including white peaks of debris from the china clay mines) on several sides and a slope down to the sea a couple of miles away on the other. It's a good base for almost a dozen beaches. Carlyon Bay has three—Crinnis, Shorthorn, and Polgaver—that have formed over the last century as debris (including quartz) from tin and clay mining was swept down Sandy River. It has long been under threat from development, and locals continue to fight even after permission was given in 2011 for 500 holiday homes. Other options are pretty little Polkerris, and quaint Charlestown with caves in the cliffs and a port. There are unusual walks to be had into the clay mountains—www.claytrails.co.uk has maps of walks and bike paths.

The **St. Austell Brewery,** 63 Trevarthian Rd. (www.staustellbrewery.co.uk; ✆ **01726/68965**), operates in a Victorian brewhouse, making beers such as the cask-conditioned Tribute, and the pale, bottled Clouded Yellow with its yeasty trail. Brewery tours (£8 adults) include the interactive museum and sampling.

Go southwest and you find the sleepy **Roseland Peninsula ★★**, which points south between the sea and the River Fal. Near its tip is St. Mawes, perfectly positioned for sailing and with a ferry to Falmouth (a 20-minute journey, every half hour in summer). **St. Mawes Castle** (www.english-heritage.org.uk) was built by Henry VIII as protection against French and Spanish attack. Its three round towers are elaborately decorated. The castle is open April to June and September Sunday to Friday 10am to 5pm; July to August daily 10am to 6pm; October daily 10am to 4pm; and November to March weekends 10am to 4pm. Admission is £4.30 adults, £2.60 children 5–15.

The village of St. Just features **St. Just in Roseland,** a 13th-century church on a tidal creek, with gardens containing many sub-tropical plants. It was built on the site of a 6th-century Celtic church. Nearby, the **King Harry Floating Bridge,** a chain-link car ferry, crosses the river, saving a 27-mile drive to Falmouth. It runs every 20 minutes all year (waits in summer can be long).

Falmouth, full of seafaring tradition, is home to the **National Maritime Museum.** It has the world's third-deepest harbor, was a Royal Mail pack station in 1688 (a stepping stone to the empire), and was the landing point for news that Admiral Nelson had died at Trafalgar. It is protected by Pendennis Castle, sister to St. Mawes Castle and a full-on attraction with exhibitions and subterranean Victorian and World War II defenses. Admission is £6.30 adults, £3.80 children 5–15. Other details are at St. Mawes Castle. Castle Beach stretches toward town, rock pools at one end, sand at the other.

Insider tip: Pause for a Cornish pasty and coffee at the family-run Castle Beach Café (www.castlebeachcafe.co.uk; ✆ **01326/313881**). There's inside seating, a deck, or you can hire a deck chair and sit on the sands.

The **Lizard Peninsula** is awash with villages (Mawnan, Manaccan, Maenporth) and the neat town of Helston. There are plenty of beaches, mostly hidden below cliffs and surrounded by rocks. **Kynance Cove,** with its strange rock formations, has been an attraction since Victorian times and is now looked after by the National Trust (www.nationaltrust.org.uk), which has a pay parking lot. Kennack Sands is bigger, with bigger waves, up to 1.5m (5 ft.), which attract surfers. There is excellent information at www.visitlizardcornwall.co.uk on two dozen beaches in the area.

Lizard Point—the mainland's southernmost spot—is a place to stand and stare with the wind in your hair. Here is a twin-towered lighthouse that has stood since 1751, yet was only automated in 1998. The old engine room features an exhibition, with the chance to sound a foghorn and climb the tower. The lighthouse (www.lizard lighthouse.co.uk; *✆* **01326/290202**) is open April to October Monday to Friday 11am to 5pm, plus some winter days (times vary). Admission is £6 adults, £3 children under 17.

Truro is a small, lively city, with Georgian and Victorian buildings built by wealthy mine owners and merchants. **Truro Cathedral,** St. Mary's Street (www.truro cathedral.org.uk; *✆* **01872/276782;** Mon–Sat 7:30am–6pm, Sun 9am–7pm; free admission), is a Victorian masterwork in Gothic style, the first new cathedral to be built since the 13th century. There are frequently choral concerts and organ recitals. The **Royal Cornwall Museum,** River Street (www.royalcornwallmuseum.org.uk; *✆* **01872/272205;** Mon–Sat 10am–4:45pm; free admission), is also worth a visit with its Cornish art (Newlyn copperwork, works from the St. Ives and Newlyn schools) and drawings by J. M. W. Turner and John Constable, as well as archeology and geology.

National Maritime Museum ★★ ☺ MUSEUM   One of Britain's great museums, and a modern one at that. The striking contemporary building on the quayside, with a lighthouse-like viewing tower looking over the town, is full of boats. They hang from the ceiling (in the huge atrium), sit on the floors, and bob outside on the little dock (including visiting celebrity boats). There are classic yachts, Thames cruisers, fishing boats, and dinghies, plus exhibitions, an underwater viewing area from where you can watch the tide rise and fall, and a toy boat tank. Oh, and Antarctic explorer Sir Ernest Shackleton's string vest. Great fun for everyone.

Discovery Quay. www.nmmc.co.uk. *✆* **01326/313388.** Admission £9.50 adults, £7.75 seniors, £6.50 full-time students and children 6–15, £27 family ticket. Daily 10am–5pm.

The Eden Project ★★★ ☺ GARDEN   Not just a garden but a sci-fi garden, rather like a scene from Dr. Who, a rainforest inside what could be a spaceship. In fact the setting is a jumble of giant geodesic domes (futuristic greenhouses) sitting in a former china clay quarry. The contents allow you to wander the world, from the tropics to the Mediterranean, with all their native plants. There's plenty about conservation, too, plus outdoor gardens, picnic spots, walks, and play areas. It's fun for all the family.

Bodelva, St. Austell. www.edenproject.com. *✆* **01726/811911.** Admission £23 adults, £9.50 children 5–16 (reductions for online sales, or arriving by public transport). Late Mar–late Oct daily 9:30am–6pm (last entry 4:30pm); Nov–mid-Mar daily 9:30am–4:30pm (last entry 3pm). Winter hours can vary, so check first. The site is 6 miles from St. Austell rail station, a half-hour bus journey.

Lost Gardens of Heligan ★★★ ☺ GARDEN   These gardens date back to the 1700s, and were being developed until the beginning of the 20th century, an extravagant vision of exotic, sub-tropical planting. World War II came and they fell into

Cornwall's Garden Heritage

The Eden Project and Heligan are the ones that get all the publicity, yet this region has around 20 other gardens that, were they not up against two of the greats, would have made more of a name for themselves. A couple that stand out are **Glendurgan** (www.national trust.org.uk; *©* **01736/363148**), a subtropical paradise near Falmouth, that's set in three valleys and pours down to the Helford River. It's a family-friendly place (who could resist the twists and turns of the 175-year-old cherry laurel maze, or lovely Durgan Beach) packed with exotic plants and hillside strolls. It's open Tuesday to Saturday from mid-Feb to October, 10:30am to 5pm. Admission £6.30 adult, £3.20 children 5–15. **Trelissick** (www.nationaltrust.org.uk;

© **01872/862090**) is at Feock on the River Fal near Truro and was planted 200 years ago. There are riverside walks and you can arrive by ferry from Falmouth, Truro, and St. Mawes. Palm trees mingle with giant wisteria and other plants that have grown mighty in the warm, moist climate. It's open daily, mid-Feb to October 10:30am to 5:30pm, Nov to Feb 11am to 4pm. Admission £7 adult, £3.50 children 5–15. The area's gardens, and many more around the county, come under **Gardens of Cornwall** (www.gardensof cornwall.com; *©* **01872/322900**) which publishes a good, free map and guide, available to order or pick up from tourist offices.

neglect, only to be rediscovered in 1990. But while they were overgrown, Cornwall's mild climate had created a sub-tropical jungle, which has been undergoing restoration ever since. The effect is entrancing, with palms and ancient trees rubbing shoulders with restored Victorian kitchen gardens and pleasure grounds.

Pentewan, St. Austell. www.heligan.com. *©* **01726/845100.** Admission £10 adults, £6 children 5–16, £27 family ticket. Daily Apr–Sept 10am–6pm (last admission 4:30pm) and Oct–Mar 10am–5pm (last admission 3:30pm). From St. Austell, take the B3273 to Mevagissey, then follow signs to Heligan.

Wheal Martyn China Clay Country Park ★ ☺ MUSEUM   Much more interesting than it might sound. This place combines a Victorian china clay works, with all its chunky machinery, with views over the working pit where men still mine with even bigger machines. There's a museum, a working water wheel, and a cafe in the remains of a clay settling tank, and it's all in wooded parkland crisscrossed by nature trails and walking and cycling paths.

Wheal Martyn, Carthew, 2 miles north of St. Austell. www.wheal-martyn.com. *©* **01726/850362.** Admission £8.50 adults, £4.75 children 6–16, £22 family ticket. Summer daily 10am–5pm; winter Tues–Sun 10am–4pm.

Where to Eat

The Greenhouse ★ BRITISH   Rustic dishes prepared from Newlyn-landed fish, meat from local farms, and mostly organic produce, served in a smart, understated setting. The husband and wife team are as likely to take your order as cook it. The daily-changing menu might include a starter of fried sprats or molasses home-cured salmon, with a main of baked whole plaice with brown shrimp and parsley butter.

6, High St., St. Keverne, Helston. www.tgor.co.uk. *©* **01326/280800.** Main courses £9.50–£19. AE, MC, V. June–Oct Tues–Sat (plus Sun in Aug) 6:30–9:30pm; Nov–May Wed–Sat.

Gylly Beach ★ BRITISH   Although notionally a cafe, this is really a smart restaurant that lets the sandy children run about. It's right on one of Cornwall's best beaches, overlooking Falmouth Bay, with a divine terrace. There are breakfasts (bacon and egg baps) and light lunches (posh burgers and sandwiches) while by night it becomes more of a restaurant, although still featuring seaside classics such as fish and chips (albeit battered in St. Austell Tribute ale).

Gyllyngvase Beach, Cliff Rd., Falmouth. www.gyllybeach.com. © **01326/312884.** Main courses £12–£17. MC, V. Daily 9am–9pm (closing time varies).

Oliver's ★ BRITISH   Take an inventive chef who's come home after working at London's Dorchester and for Gordon Ramsay, give him local ingredients, and you wind up with dishes such as venison (steak, faggot, sausage) with celeriac rosti, carrots, poached lettuce, and cacao butter sauce in this discreet place just off the waterfront.

33 High St., Falmouth. www.oliverstheeatery.com. ©**01326/218138.** Main courses £11–£20. MC, V. Tues–Sat noon–2:30pm and 7–9pm; Sun 6–9pm (closed Sun–Mon Oct–April).

Smugglers ★ ■▌BRITISH   An old inn down a windy lane right on the Fal estuary that has had a 21st century makeover beneath its newly thatched roof. Lunch is basically paninis and salads, while evenings have a short menu of the upmarket steak/chicken/burger variety. Outside is the Tea Bar, selling a perfect English cuppa—Smugglers is owned by the Tregothnan estate, the only place in Britain to grow tea.

Tolverne, Philleigh. www.tregothnan.com. ©**01872/520000.** Main courses £9–£16. MC, V. Mon–Sat noon–9pm; Sun until 4pm. From the A3078 follow signs to King Harry Ferry, then for Tolverne.

Shopping

St. Austell has a local produce market each Saturday outside the old market hall. Truro is Cornwall's shopping hub, with everything from M&S to surfwear chains. **Lemon Street Market** (www.lemonstreetmarket.co.uk) is an attractive indoor spot with lots of small shops and the Lander gallery, which sells Newlyn School works by artists such as Stanhope Forbes. In St. Mawes the **Waterside Gallery,** Marine Parade (www.watersidegallery.co.uk; © 01326/270136), stocks works by Cornish artists. Falmouth has clothes shops, galleries, food stores, and souvenir shops. As well as the High Street area, there are also shops at Discovery Quay, by the Maritime Museum.

Entertainment & Nightlife

Like much of Cornwall, this is a place for pubs, as the waters lap against the many quaysides. The 300-year-old **Ferry Boat Inn** in Helford is a classic with views across Helford Passage; sit outside, wander onto the beach, or snack on local oysters. **Restormel Arts** (www.restormelarts.co.uk; © 07865/072744) is the focal point for arts in the St. Austell Bay area, from touring shows at the Keay Theatre (www.cornwall.ac.uk/thekeay) to jazz at the brewery. Truro has a lively nightlife, with clubs such as the L2 (l2nightclub.co.uk), which gets Radio 1 DJs, while Bar 200 has live music, film, and comedy.

Where to Stay

The Hen House ★★ ■▌   One room of this tiny B&B really was a hen house, the other was a pig shed, while a stone barn is now self-catering with a wood-burning stove. Hidden amongst wildflower meadows in the Helston Peninsula, this charming place is very green, using solar panel for electricity and harvesting rainwater for its vegetables. Breakfasts (English, cold meats and cheeses, or smoked fish) are huge, including eggs from chickens who still live here. There's complimentary tai-chi, too.

Manaccan, Helston, Cornwall TR12 6EW. www.thehenhouse-cornwall.co.uk. ℂ **01326/280236.** 3 units (1 self-catering). £90 double (rates include breakfast); self-catering barn £200–£500 per week. MC, V. No children under 12. **Amenities:** Patio and Gardens. *In room:* TV/DVD, hair dryer, Wi-Fi (free).

Hotel Tresanton ★★★ ☺ TV hotel guru Olga Polizzi lets her imagination run wild here, a breathtaking mix of country-house style, modern chic, and seaside airs. The rooms, big, with luxurious bathrooms, all have sea views and some have a terrace. A new master suite has a wood burning stove and crow's nest terrace; it and other rooms are in two cottages, which can be booked separately or as a whole for grand family gatherings. A playroom, cinema, and garden make this ideal for children. The **restaurant,** with a terrace, has a daily changing menu, rich with oysters and lobster.

St. Mawes, Cornwall TR2 5DR. www.tresanton.com. ℂ **01326/270055.** Fax 01326/270053. 31 units. £190–£340 double; £320–£500 suite. 2-night minimum stay Sat–Sun. AE, MC, V. Free parking. **Amenities:** Restaurant; bar; room service; babysitting; playroom. *In room:* TV, hair dryer.

Lizard Youth Hostel ★★ 🏠 Youth Hostels have been given a makeover in recent years and are no longer places where grizzled hikers stop for a night in a dorm. This one, open year-round, is a former Victorian hotel in an enviable position on Lizard Point, just about England's most southerly building. The rooms sleep three to six, perfect for families. There's a kitchen, shop, lounge, and inspiring sea views.

Lizard Point, Cornwall TR12 7NT. www.yha.org.uk. ℂ **0845/371-9550.** Fax 0870/770-6121. 7 units. £10–£22.40 per person, sharing (YHA members; £3 supplement for non-members); under-18s half price. MC, V. **Amenities:** Lounge; kitchen.

St. Michael's Hotel & Spa Sitting amid palm trees in a sub-tropical garden above the lovely Gyllyngvase Beach, and with views right down to the Lizard. There's a definite New England coastal feel to the pale, airy rooms with stripy fabrics and the modern, nautical theme of the **Flying Fish** restaurant with its roof terrace. The smart spa has a large indoor pool, sauna, Jacuzzi, steam room, fitness suite, and a sun deck.

Gyllyngvase Beach, Falmouth, Cornwall TR11 4NB. www.stmichaelshotel.co.uk. ℂ **01326/312707.** Fax 01326/211772. 61 units. £118–£298 double. Rates include English breakfast. AE, MC, V. **Amenities:** Restaurant; bar; indoor swimming pool; spa. *In room:* TV, hair dryer, Wi-Fi (free).

WEST TO LAND'S END

Penzance 307 miles SW of London; 77 miles SW of Plymouth

This is the heart of Celtic Cornwall, and somewhere that still feels a place apart from the rest of England. And with the peninsula's waist only 7 miles across, the final stretch has the air of an island. Yet for all its history and beauty, the spot we're all truly heading for is Land's End, the end of the road. It's not quite the cerebral experience one might hope, being a tourist attraction of shops and snack bars. But you need to have done it (and the views are stupendous) before you can relax into the true Cornish experience: the astonishing island abbey of **St. Michael's Mount,** the seaside resort town of **Penzance,** the wild, dreamy beaches, and the little arty fishing ports.

Penzance is Cornwall's largest town and became popular when the train rolled in during Victorian days. It's still a good base for exploring the area, which also includes the villages of **Mousehole** and **Newlyn,** and lots of twisting country lanes with views over megalithic burial sites and Bronze Age stone circles.

Essentials

GETTING THERE   Trains to Penzance leave London's Paddington Station every hour or two and take at least 5 hours (costing around £55 one-way). National Express buses, leave Victoria Coach Station half a dozen times a day (including overnight journeys), taking 8½–10 hours, costing from £15 one-way. The A30 runs through the heart of Cornwall to Penzance.

VISITOR INFORMATION   **Penzance Tourist Office,** Station Approach (www. purelypenzance.co.uk; ℂ 01736/362207), is open Easter to September Monday to Friday 9am to 5pm, plus Saturday 10am to 4pm.

Exploring the Area

This part of the country is about beaches. Heading west from Helston the first you come to is **Praa Sands,** a mile-plus stretch popular with families and surfers on Mount's Bay, Cornwall's biggest bay. A little farther on is **Perranuthnoe,** with its rocks to climb, while Penzance has its own, a crescent of sand and pebbles, overlooking St. Michael's Mount. On the other side of Land's End is **Porthcurno,** a big sandy cove backed by cliffs. **Whitsand Bay** at Sennen Cove is perhaps best of all, vast and open. You have to pay to park and it can be a crush in high season.

   Penzance, with its Regency and Georgian buildings, is a nice place to stroll, out to the beach, around the quayside (where ferries leave for the Isles of Scilly), and among the maze of little streets. The striking 1935 Art Deco **Jubilee Pool** (www. jubileepool.co.uk; ℂ 01736/369224), Britain's largest open-air lido (100-m/300-ft. long), juts into Mount's Bay. It is open late May until September. **Morrab Gardens** (free entry) still keeps its Victorian design with a cast-iron bandstand amid subtropical plants. **The Exchange,** on Princess Street (www.newlynartgallery.co.uk; ℂ 01736/363715), is a free-entry modern art space that features leading experimental works.

   The **Penlee House Gallery and Museum** (www.penleehouse.org.uk; ℂ 01736/ 363625), in Penlee Park, features paintings from the Newlyn School, the artists' colony that existed in **Newlyn** largely from the 1890s until the 1920s. Newlyn is a fishing village that's a seafront stroll from Penzance. **Newlyn Art Gallery** (www. newlynartgallery.co.uk; ℂ 01736/363715) holds exhibitions largely of contemporary artists. Newlyn is also Cornwall's busiest fishing port and its history can be seen in the **Pilchard Works** (www.pilchardworks.co.uk; ℂ 07809/609545) award-winning free museum in a former fish cannery.

   Another must-see village is **Mousehole** (pronounced "mou-zel"), with walled harbor and hillside houses. Author Dylan Thomas called it "the loveliest village in England." There are art galleries and a small beach but you'll have to park on the outskirts and walk in as it can't cope with tourist traffic. A sign pays tribute to Dolly Pentreath who, in 1777, was said to be the last person to speak only the Cornish language.

Botallack Mine ★★ HISTORIC SITE   The sight of the engine houses of this Victorian complex hanging on to the cliffs above the waves says everything that you

The Golden Age of Tin & Copper

Botallack Mine is 1 of 10 areas featuring 18 sites around the county that make up the **Cornwall Mining World Heritage Site** (www.cornish-mining.org.uk). It's a rich history: Metal (largely tin and copper) has been mined in Cornwall since Roman times. But it's a story that's not over yet. South Crofty, at Pool near Redruth, the last working tin mine in Europe, closed in 1998, but now, amid the soaring price of minerals, has been drastically rebuilt and was set to start mining for tin, copper, and zinc in 2012. Places not to miss include **Levant** (www. nationaltrust.org.uk; ℂ **01736/786156**) and **Geevor** (www.geevor.com;

ℂ **01736/788662**) mines, near Botallack, which have the most undersea workings of any mines in the world. Levant reached 540m (1,770 ft.) beneath the waves; visits include an underground tour and cliff walks. **East Pool Mine** (www.national trust.org.uk; ℂ **01209/315027**) near Redruth has one of the biggest Cornish-made steampowered beam engines, while there's a great tour of the tunnels at **Poldark Mine,** Wendron, near Helston (www. poldark-mine.co.uk; ℂ **01326/573173**). Opening times vary widely and many sites aren't open in winter.

need to know about the harsh romance of this part of the country. The tin and copper mine had tunnels under the sea and deep into the rock. The National Trust is renovating some buildings but visitors can only wander the ruins. A free online walking trail (www.landsendarea.com/trails/botallack.htm) gives full details of the mine.

Near St. Just-in-Penwith. ℂ**01736/788588.** Free admission. Daily 10am–4pm.

Godolphin ★ HOUSE An abandoned 17th-century family house in divine grounds, this is Cornwall at its most romantic. The garden, with its medieval layout, all but unchanged since the 16th century, is seen as one of Europe's most important. There are also the remains of the Godolphin family mine and six miles of walks.

Godolphin Cross, Helston. www.nationaltrust.org.uk. ℂ **01736/763194.** Admission house and garden £7 adults, £3.50 children 15 and under; garden only £4/£2. Estate daily dawn to dusk; garden daily Feb–mid-Dec 10am–4pm; house occasional dates 10am–4pm

Land's End ★ ATTRACTION The land at Land's End, England's farthest, most westerly point is privately owned and has been turned into this carnival-like attraction. You might feel you should avoid it, but you mustn't. It's £3 to park, then you can enjoy the great clifftop, sea-crashing views and have your photo taken in front of the signpost that points to world destinations. Whether you go near the souvenir and craft shops, and the 4-D film experience and petting zoo (both chargeable), is up to you, but the Land's End Hotel and restaurant (see p. 411) has been nicely done up.

Sennen, at end of the A30. www.landsend-landmark.co.uk. ℂ **0871/720-0044.** Free admission. Attractions variable hours Easter–late Oct; shops daily 10:30am–3:30pm.

Minack Theatre ★★ THEATRE Perhaps Britain's most unusual theatre, a carved-out cliffside performance space above the sea. It looks centuries old but was only created 80 years ago. The summer season of shows ranges from Shakespeare to singer-songwriter Suzanne Vega's opera, to *Titanic–the Musical*. The 750 seats are on the grass or rocky ledges. It's also open for daytime visits, when you can enjoy the lofty cafe and the sub-tropical gardens. *Insider tip:* Bring a raincoat … and a cushion.

Porthcurno. www.minack.com. ✆ **01736/810181.** Ticket prices vary; day visits £4 adults, £3 seniors, £2 children 12–15, free children 11 and under. Day visits daily Apr–Sept 9:30am–5pm; Oct 10am–4:30pm; Nov–Mar 10am–3:30pm. Performances Apr–Sept. From Penzance, take the A30 heading toward Land's End and follow the signs to Porthcurno.

Penrose Estate ★ GARDEN   Cornwall's largest lake, Loe Pool, is cut off from the sea only by a shingle spit. The setting is splendid and there are walks around the placid waters, which often have a backdrop of the crashing Atlantic. Either side of the headland are sandy coves, and the Gunwalloe reedbed is a haven for birdlife.

2 miles SW of Helston on the B3304. www.nationaltrust.org.uk. ✆**01326/561407.** Free admission. Daily dawn to dusk.

St. Michael's Mount ★★ CASTLE   If one spot is the overriding image of Cornwall it's this island castle and monastery poking into the sky like something from a fairytale. You can walk across the causeway at low tide, or get a boat from the village of Marazion at other times. There was a Benedictine monastery here in the 12th century, but the site became of military importance and in 1588 the first beacon was lit here to warn of the coming Spanish Armada. Today it's still a working island, the castle home to the St. Aubyn family who have been here since the 17th century, with workers living in the waterfront cottages. For your money you get to see ornate medieval rooms and terraced sub-tropical gardens clinging to the cliffs. The Sail Loft restaurant serves local seafood.

St. Michael's Mount, Mount's Bay. www.stmichaelsmount.co.uk. ✆ **01736/710507.** Admission castle £7 adults, £3.50 children 5–15, £17.50 family ticket; admission gardens £3.50 adults, £1.50 children 5–15, free children 4 and under; combined tickets £8.75 adults, £4.25 children 5–15, free children 4 and under, £21.75 family ticket. Castle late Mar–Oct Sun–Fri 10:30am–5pm; Nov–late Mar guided tours Tues/Fri 11am/2pm. Gardens mid-Apr–late Jun Mon–Fri 10:30am–5pm; July–Aug Thurs–Fri 10:30am–5:30pm; Sept Thurs–Fri 10:30am–5pm; closed Oct–mid-Apr.

Trengwainton Garden ★ GARDEN   The glades of giant tree ferns make you (or at least the children) feel that you're lost in the jungle, yet the next moment you're on a grassy sward with hilltop views over the sea. Trengwainton is a treasure trove from the days of the Victorian plant hunters, with exotic specimens from around the world as well as a walled kitchen garden and woodland walks.

West of Heamoor, off the Penzance-Morvah Rd. www.nationaltrust.org.uk. ✆ **01736/363148.** Admission £6.10 adults, £3 children 5–15, £15.10 family ticket. Mid-Feb–Oct Sun–Thurs 10:30am–5pm.

Shopping

This area is good for arts and crafts, with galleries in Penzance, Mousehole, Newlyn, and St. Just-in-Penwith selling paintings, drawings, prints, and crafts. **Lamorna Pottery** (www.lamornapottery.co.uk; ✆ **01736/810330**), operating since 1948 in the village of Lamorna, near Penzance, has good glazed ceramic ware.

Entertainment & Nightlife

Penzance has two dance clubs (the Barn Club and Club 2K) but you probably came here for the local ambiance. The main performance venue is the **Minack Theatre** (see above), but the **Bash Street Theatre**, Belgravia Street (www.bashstreet.co.uk; ✆ **01736/360795**), has a nice line is slapstick, silent movie-style comedies. The **Turks Head,** Chapel Street (www.turksheadpenzance.co.uk; ✆ **01736/363093**), is one of Cornwall's oldest pubs, reputed to date from 1233, the time of the Crusades. You can still see the smugglers' tunnel connecting what is now the dining room with the waterfront. Mousehole's **Ship Inn,** South Cliff (www.shipmousehole.co.uk; ✆ **01736/731234**), is a great place to watch the sunset; there's also food (Cornish fish pie, seafood chowder) and half a dozen neat bedrooms.

Where to Eat & Stay

Camilla House ★ This is a charming seafront Georgian town house turned guesthouse. Rooms have an historic charm along with a modern touch. There's a lovely dining room for breakfast and a simple supper menu (fish of the day, grilled, line-caught mackerel, and a handful of other offerings). Picnic hampers are available for days out or a Minack Theatre evening, and there's a lounge and small bar.

12 Regent Terrace, Penzance, TR18 4DW. www.camillahouse.co.uk. ✆ **01736/363771.** 8 units. £77–£89 double. Rates include breakfast. MC, V. Free parking. **Amenities:** Restaurant, bar. *In room:* TV, hair dryer, Wi-Fi (free).

Cornish Range ★ SEAFOOD This is a former pilchard factory that used to salt and process the catch from Mousehole's boats. Now it turns the catch into altogether more delicate delights (crab chowder, tempura monkfish) and serves them in a pale, relaxing environment. There are also three equally smart **bedrooms** (£65–£110 double with TV), with king- or super-king-size beds.

6 Chapel St., Mousehole, TR19 6SB. www.cornishrange.co.uk. ✆ **01736/731488.** Reservations recommended for dinner in summer. Main courses £11.50–£21.50. MC, V. Easter–Sept daily 10:30am–2:30pm and 5:30–9pm; winter 5:30–9pm.

Dolphin Tavern A solid pub with views over Penzance waterfront and St. Michael's Mount. There's a seafaring history (in 1585 it was where Cornishmen were recruited to fight the Spanish Armada, and Sir Walter Raleigh is said to have smoked his first pipe of tobacco here), which is reflected in the trappings on the granite walls. There are only two bedrooms, one with a sofa bed that's good for families. The restaurant sticks to straightforward local fare, a grilled Cornish rump steak, grilled sole, cod, or mackerel (the latter dusted with sea salt and served with salad and crusty bread). Mains are £8–£14. Beer is from the historic St. Austell Brewery.

Quay Street, Penzance, Cornwall TR18 4BD. www.dolphintavern.co.uk. ✆ **01736/364106.** 2 units. £70–£85 double. Rates include full English breakfast. MC, V. Free parking. **Amenities:** Restaurant; bar. *In room:* TV, hair dryer, Wi-Fi (free).

Ennys ★ 🛏 Run by the amiable and welcoming Gill Charlton, Ennys is a luxury guesthouse set in peaceful surroundings a mile from any road down a private drive. This historic Georgian estate boasts landscaped gardens in a bucolic setting and has well-appointed rooms with original works of art on the walls, and furnishings from local craftspeople. For a birthday, honeymoon, or special occasion it is ideal, but what really marks it apart is its concierge service that means your every whim (be it theatre tickets and restaurant reservations or yoga, surfing, or wild swimming) is taken care of.

St. Hilary, Penzance, Cornwall TR20 9BZ. www.ennys.co.uk. ✆ **01736/740262.** Fax 01736/740055. 6 units £105–£165 double; £155–£195 family suite. Rates include breakfast and afternoon tea. MC, V. Free parking. No children 16 and under. **Amenities:** Dining room; outdoor heated pool; tennis court. *In room:* TV/DVD, hair dryer, MP3 docking station, Wi-Fi (free).

The Land's End Hotel ★ The name says it all. There are views from the cliffs to rocks, the sea, Longships Lighthouse, and, on a clear day, the Isles of Scilly. The hotel combines Edwardian style with a contemporary feel. The restaurant (given a major makeover in 2011 by designers who had worked on Jamie Oliver's Fifteen in Newquay) makes the most of the panorama, while chef Paul Brennan (who has worked under Marco Pierre White) uses local fare including Sennan Cove lobster (a whole one in a salad is £38) and St. Austell Bay mussels. Mains are £12.50–£20.

Lands End, Cornwall TR19 7AA. www.landsendhotel.co.uk. © **01736/871844.** Fax 01736/871599. 30 units. £120–£150 double. Rates include English breakfast. MC, V. Free parking. *In room:* TV, hair dryer, Wi-Fi (free).

THE ISLES OF SCILLY ★

27 miles SW of Land's End

Just off the radar of most people who visit Cornwall, this cluster of islands is a world unto itself. Balmy (with Britain's mildest weather), laid-back, and timeless, the islands are a destination that is increasingly coming to terms with its boutique charm. There are five inhabited islands (and 140 that aren't inhabited) and all have their own feel. **St. Mary's** is the biggest, with Hugh Town the nearest you'll find to a regular town with its port and shops. **Tresco** is an idyllic place of beaches and the glorious Abbey Garden. **St. Martin's** combines some rugged coast with lovely beaches, **St. Agnes** is the most southerly and loved by bird watchers, while **Bryher,** the smallest of the five, combines placid beaches, the wild waves of Hell Bay, and great views across uninhabited islands from Samson Hill. You come to the islands for peace and quiet; visitors aren't allowed to drive, so you walk, cycle, or island-hop on small boats. For an island overview on St. Mary's look in the **Isles of Scilly Museum** (www. iosmuseum.org; © **01720/422337;** hours vary).

Essentials

GETTING THERE   Isles of Scilly Skybus (www.ios-travel.co.uk; © **0845/710-5555**) has 2 to 12 flights a day (Mon–Sat) between Land's End and St. Mary's. Flight time is 15 minutes. There are 1 to 4 flights a day (Mon–Sat) from Newquay year-round and daily flights (Apr–Oct, but exact dates vary, Mon–Sat) from Exeter, Southampton, and Bristol. A round-trip from Land's End starts at £75, a one-way flight from £60.

The same operator runs a daily ferry from Penzance (Quay Street) to St. Mary's (Apr–mid-Oct, Mon–Fri). There are additional sailings on some high season dates, and some sailings in late October and March. Sailing time is 2 hr. 40 min. A round-trip is £35, a one-way ticket from £42.50.

British International (www.islesofscillyhelicopter.com; © **01736/363871**) has been operating up to 9 helicopter flights a day (Mon–Sat) between Penzance and St. Mary's and Tresco. However Penzance heliport was due to close in late 2012, with services switching to Land's End.

VISITOR INFORMATION   The **Tourist Information Centre,** Hugh Street, St. Mary's (www.simplyscilly.co.uk; © **01720/424031**), is open summer (usually Apr–Oct) Monday to Saturday 8:30am to 5:30pm, Sunday 9am to 2pm; winter (usually Nov–Mar) Monday to Friday 9am to 5pm, Saturday 9am to noon. Its website is an indispensible source of information. Visitors aren't allowed to drive on the islands, but there are taxis (in some cases tractor and trailer) to get you to your hotel. There are regular boats between the islands (see "Outdoor Activities in the Isles of Scilly" below).

Exploring the Area

St. Mary's is, relatively, the bright lights, where you'll find the most accommodations, from hotels to B&Bs to camp sites. But the fact that there are 9 miles of roads yet 30 miles of coastal paths says it all. What action there is, is in **Hugh Town,** which also has some shops, galleries, and bicycle hire. One of the best walks takes in the hilltop remains of Bant's Carn megalithic village, where you can crawl inside a burial chamber (free access), and the **Telegraph Tower** at the island's highest point. The Civil War fortifications at the **Garrison,** including Star Castle (now a hotel, see below), are also worth exploring. Of the beaches, try Pelistry, a deserted bay (apart from the nearby cafe) from where you can swim to tiny Toll's island, and the busier Porthcressa, although there's also little Town Beach right by the quayside.

Tresco has a handful of shops, a heliport, a posh hotel, a good pub, and some splendid beaches, all of it run as one by the descendants of Augustus Smith, who leased the island from the Duchy of Cornwall in 1834. Its leading attraction is **Tresco Abbey Garden ★★**, a sub-tropical dream created by Smith and featuring 20,000 exotic plants from 80 countries, many in bloom year round. The setting is a ruined priory said to be founded by Benedictine monks possibly as early as A.D. 964. There's also the Valhalla Museum, a collection of figureheads from local shipwrecks (www.tresco.co.uk; ✆ **01720/424108;** admission £12 adults, free for under-16s; daily 10am–4pm). Near the Gardens are the fine white sands of gently curving **Appletree Bay,** one of the islands' loveliest spots while the almost mile-long sands of **Pendle Bay** are great for shell collectors and backed by dunes and sub-tropical vegetation.

St. Martin's is only 2 miles long yet is a place of huge contrasts, its sheltered south coast all flat sand drifting down to the sea past the rock pools, the north side a place of cliffs, although there are beaches at their feet. This is the place for family beaches, with Lawrence's Bay and Par Beach, the former with its shallows and dunes, the latter where you can picnic amongst the long grass. Both touch Higher Town, where the boats dock and where you'll find a handful of shops. Its hotel, **St. Martin's On The Isle** (www.stmartinshotel.co.uk; ✆ **01720/422090**) is designed to look like fishermen's cottages, and its Tean restaurant had a Michelin star for a couple of years.

St. Agnes is home to the Bar, an unusual beach that's a spit of sand connecting St. Agnes with uninhabited Gugh. Periglis is the far point of the U.K., all rock pools

OUTDOOR activities IN THE ISLES OF SCILLY

You can rent bikes from **St. Mary's Bicycle Hire,** The Strand (✆ **07796/638506**). **Book A Bike On Scilly** (www.bookabikeonscilly.co.uk; ✆ **01720/422786**) has hire with free delivery on St. Mary's (and, by arrangement, to other islands). A variety of boat trips, including bird-watching specials, are available from the **St. Mary's Boatmen Association,** The Strand (www.scillyboating.co.uk; ✆ **01720/423999**). **Bryher Boat Services** (www.bryherboats.co.uk;

✆ **01720/422886**) runs ferries from Bryher and Tresco, as well as charters, fishing, and wildlife trips, and jetboat joyrides. **St. Agnes Boating** (www.st-agnes-boating.com; ✆ **01720/422704**) offers similar services.

Scilly Diving (www.scillydiving.com; ✆ **01720/422848**) offers dives, lessons, and courses from St. Mary's and St. Martin's. There are also trips that take you snorkeling amongst the seals.

and shell-strewn sands, with views over Western rocks and the Bishop Rock lighthouse. The island doesn't have a hotel but there is a camp site.

Bryher, like St. Martin's, is a place of extremes. Rushy Bay in the south of the island is so gentle that you wouldn't believe it was on the same tiny island as Hell Bay, where the waves crash amongst the rocks. The latter beauty spot is home to one of Britain's top-rated hotels, the Hell Bay, while the island also features Britain's most westerly pub, the Fraggle Rock Bar.

Shopping

St. Mary's has some good arts-and-crafts shops, including **Phoenix Stained Glass,** Portmellon Industrial Estate (www.phoenixstainedglass.co.uk; ✆ **01720/422900**), where you can watch stained-glass items being made. St. Mary's also has a market each Thursday in summer, with lots of local produce on sale.

Where to Eat & Stay

Hell Bay Part of the Tresco company (see New Inn below), this is more luxury coastal chic, but perhaps chic-er and edgier. The Empress suite is a large shed-like building, with white-painted floorboards and its own garden, while even simpler options are in an old boat house. They call it New England and the Caribbean meet Cornwall, and it's hard to disagree. The restaurant uses local and seasonal ingredients for dishes such as roast fillet of Cornish cod, puy lentil, new potato, and crayfish broth.

Bryher, Isles of Scilly TR23 0PR. www.tresco.co.uk. ✆**01720/422947.** Fax 01720/423004. 25 units. £270–£600 double. Rates include dinner and breakfast. AE, MC, V. **Amenities:** Restaurant; bar. *In room:* TV, hair dryer, Wi-Fi (free).

New Inn A row of waterfront, white-painted fishermen's cottages now turned into a comfy hotel and pub. The bedrooms, some with sea views, are creamy pale with blue stripes, while the Driftwood Bar (where you can sup St. Agnes-brewed Ales of Scilly beer) is dark and filled with nautical memorabilia. The restaurant is somewhere in between, with outside tables, and a reasonably-priced menu that features seafood (sea bream, scallops) as well as steak. Sister properties include the **Sea Garden Cottages,** 25 cottages sleeping up to 10, opened in spring 2012. They share the facilities of the **Flying Boat Club,** another dozen luxury seafront properties, which includes a spa with indoor and outdoor pool, sauna, Jacuzzi, and tennis, as well as the **Ruin** restaurant/bar.

Tresco, Isles of Scilly TR24 0QQ. www.tresco.co.uk. ✆**01720/422844.** Fax 01720/423200. 15 units. £110–£240 double. AE, MC, V. **Amenities:** Restaurant; 2 bars; heated outdoor pool; beer garden; Wi-Fi (free in bar). *In room:* TV, hair dryer.

Star Castle Hotel ★ ☺ This is a real castle, built in 1593 to defend against Spanish attacks, and it really is star shaped. There are rooms both within the castle (which are the most traditional) and in an annex (which are more modern and open onto gardens). Either way, the setting is excellent with the sort of commanding views you'd expect of a coastal watchtower. There are two restaurants, the Conservatory (summer only) and the Castle, both featuring plenty of local seafood. The **Dungeon** bar has rugged rock walls adorned with muskets and other historical artifacts.

The Garrison, St. Mary's, Isles of Scilly TR21 0TA. www.star-castle.co.uk. ✆**01720/422317.** Fax 01720/422343. 38 units. £176–£334 double. Rates include breakfast and dinner. AE, MC, V. Closed Jan. **Amenities:** 2 restaurants; bar; indoor pool; room service; Wi-Fi (free). *In room:* TV, hair dryer.

ST. IVES ★★

305 miles SW of London; 21 miles NE of Land's End; 10 miles NE of Penzance

A fishing village turned artists' retreat, St. Ives has radiated a discreet style since the 19th century. It's not just about art, though; the sunlight here in the far west (although the village faces north) exquisitely lights up the sandy beaches and the pale cottages and sends shadows cascading down the narrow streets. The St. Ives School of Art was around as early as 1925 when avant-garde artists saw the light, but took form when sculptor Barbara Hepworth moved here, and continued into the early 1960s. Today the town revels in art, with courses at the St. Ives Art School, galleries everywhere, and Tate St. Ives, a modernistic building that is part of London's Tate Gallery and which recognizes the importance of the area in British art history.

There are several beaches, the most stunning perhaps being the open expanse of sand and surf that is **Porthmeor Beach,** although **Porthminster,** calmer and half a mile long, has its own fans. The latter has a path to Carbis Bay, just around the headland, an enchanting beach with a hilly backdrop. St. Ives gets busy in summer but does have more than its fair share of mostly smart restaurants and cafes, so it can cope. And you can take the South West Coast path to get away from the crowds.

Essentials

GETTING THERE   There are no direct trains, so change at St. Erth, on the line from London Paddington, which is a short—and very scenic—ride to St. Ives. The journey is about 5 hr. 30 min. and costs from £55 one-way. **National Express** (www. nationalexpress.com; ✆ **0871/781-8181**) runs several buses a day from London Victoria, with prices from about £35 and taking up to nine hours.

During the summer, many streets are closed, and it's a good idea to leave your car just outside the town at the park-and-ride, with a bus taking you the final mile or so. From May to September, there is a train park-and-ride service from Lelant Saltings, allowing you to ride the picturesque St. Erth line into the resort.

Exploring the Area

Barbara Hepworth Museum & Sculpture Garden ★ MUSEUM   Hepworth was one of Britain's most important sculptors; she lived and worked at Trewyn Studio, now the museum, from 1949 until her death in 1975. Now looked after by London's Tate Gallery, this is a monument to her life and work. The house and workshop are full of sculptures, drawings, and unfinished work, while the garden that she laid out is the setting for bigger pieces in bronze and stone.

Barnoon Hill. www.tate.org.uk/stives/hepworth. ✆ **01736/796226.** Admission £5.50 adults, under-19s free. Mar–Oct daily 10am–5:20pm; Nov–Feb Tues–Sun 10am–4:20pm.

Tate St. Ives ★★★ ☺ GALLERY   An elegant modern building is the seafront outpost of London's Tate. It focuses on the St. Ives school of art, with changing exhibitions from its central collection. You might see works by Barbara Hepworth (her studio, above, is under Tate control) and her husband, Ben Nicholson, but there are plenty of paintings and sculpture to choose from. Children are well catered for with an interactive room, art trails, and activities. The gallery (and its cafe) gets very busy (an extension is planned), and it has to close 6 weeks a year for exhibition changeovers.

Porthmeor Beach. www.tate.org.uk. ℂ **01736/796226.** Admission £6.50 adults, under-19s free; £10 joint ticket with Hepworth Museum. Mar–Oct daily 10am–5:20pm; Nov–Feb Tues–Sun 10am–4:20pm.

Where to Eat

Alba Restaurant ★★ ☺BRITISH   Now *this* is a seafront restaurant, not only with views across St. Ives Bay, but actually in the former lifeboat house. A second view, downstairs, takes in the chefs and the seafront streets. It's artily modern British, as befits a restaurant in this town. Its signature dish (seen on one of those TV mastercheffy shows) is filet of lightly smoked Cornish wild sea bass, steak pudding, braised leek, chantrelle mushrooms, and poached oyster jus.

Old Lifeboat House, The Wharf. www.thealbarestaurant.com. ℂ**01736/797222.** AE, MC, V. Main courses £13.50–£23.50. Daily noon–2:30pm and 5:30–9:30pm.

Porthminster Café ★ SEAFOOD   This is what the Southwest is all about, something that has the air of a beach cafe but is actually much more. And happily, there are a number of these kind of places around. Right on the beach with the hillside of Porthminster Point behind, this iss a stunning location, and has food to match. There's a daily menu that uses local produce such as nettles and samphire. Tasters might include white anchovy fritters with vanilla salt and mayo, followed by monkfish curry.

Porthminster Beach. www.porthminstercafe.co.uk. ℂ **01736/795352.** Reservations recommended. Main courses £16–£19. MC, V. Daily from 9am for coffee, food served noon–4pm and 6–9:30pm.

Shopping

St. Ives has some decent beach and outdoor wear stores as well as galleries and shops for local arts, gifts, and food. The main shopping street is cobblestoned Fore Street, with quaint shops hiding at the bottom of the hill. On The Wharf the **Fishermen's Co-operative** store (www.fishermensco-op.co.uk; ℂ 01736/796276), sells outdoor and waterproof clothing. A **Farmers' Market** is held every Thursday on The Stennack.

Entertainment & Nightlife

St. Ives has pubs and bars, even a club, the **Isobar** (www.theisobar.co.uk; ℂ 01736/796042), combining laid-back bar and loud dancefloor. Pubs include the **Sloop Inn** (www.sloop-inn.co.uk; ℂ 01736/796584), a quayside inn dating back to the early 14th century. Out of town, the **Gurnard's Head,** a short drive west of St. Ives (www.gurnardshead.co.uk; ℂ 01736/796928), is a classic country gastropub with rooms (sister to the equally delicious Felin Fach Griffin in the Brecon Beacons); the **Tinners Arms** in Zennor (www.tinnersarms.co.uk; ℂ 01736/796927) does a similar job from its oceanview perch. **St. Ives September Festival** (www.stivesseptemberfestival.co.uk; ℂ 01736/366077) is an arty mix of music and literature.

Where to Stay

Boskerris Hotel ★★   A super-stylish boutique hotel above Carbis Bay, on the edge of St. Ives; it has been welcoming guests since 1931 but only recently assumed its white, hip Mediterranean-influenced persona. A terrace has panoramic views. The individually decorated rooms mostly gaze over the sea, and have smart bathrooms.

Boskerris Road, Carbis Bay, St. Ives, Cornwall TR26 2NQ. www.boskerrishotel.co.uk. (C) **01736/ 795295.** 15 units. £115–£240 double. Rates include full English breakfast. AE, MC, V. Free parking. **Amenities:** Breakfast room; terrace. *In room:* TV/DVD, hair dryer, Wi-Fi (free).

Primrose Valley Hotel ★ 🛏 Just off Porthminster Beach, this Edwardian villa is a stylish retreat, all soft Italian leather chairs and oak tables. There's a "non-hotel" feel as you arrive in a room that's somewhere between lounge and cafe. The rooms are individually furnished, in a shiny, modern way, and there's a beauty therapy room.

Porthminster Beach, St. Ives, Cornwall TR26 2ED. www.primroseonline.co.uk. (C) **01736/794939.** 9 units. £105–£170 double; £199–£240 suite. Rates include breakfast. AE, MC, V. Limited free parking. No children under 9. **Amenities:** Bar; beauty room. *In room:* TV/DVD, hair dryer, Wi-Fi (free).

Queen's Hotel ★★ 🛏 An old pub just off the seafront, elegantly reborn as a gastropub with rooms in 2011. The main area is a wealth of wood and muted tones with antiques and old pictures while the five bedrooms are light and pale with quirky vintage furniture. Two rooms have an extra single bed for families, and a fold-up bed can be added. The high-quality but reasonably priced food (mains £8–12) might include a starter of River Exe mussels in garlic and white wine followed by braised lamb faggot, crispy pork belly, carrot purée, cabbage and bacon, and onion gravy.

High St., St. Ives, Cornwall TR26 1RR. www.queenshotelstives.com. (C) **01736/796468.** 5 units. £60–£130 double; £70–£140 family room. Rates include full Cornish breakfast. MC, V. Limited free street parking. **Amenities:** Bar; restaurant. *In room:* TV, hair dryer, Wi-Fi (free).

NEWQUAY ★ & PADSTOW ★

Newquay: 280 miles SW of London, 45 miles NE of Lands End; Padstow: 275 miles SW of London, 59 miles NE of Lands End

This really is the chic part of Cornwall, two resorts that have smart restaurants and hotels to match, but where the money-rich meet the idealistic young. This is where Michelin-starred chefs mix it up with surf bums and the golden glow of the sun on the gorgeous west-facing beaches makes everyone happy. Newquay is a bustling seaside resort that lords it over the magnificence of Watergate Bay, while Padstow is a fishing village where the catch is almost worth its weight in gold to the illustrious restaurants. Both can get packed yet it is still possible to get away from it all on the Cornwall Coast Path, or the Camel Trail, which follows the Camel Estuary inland.

Essentials

GETTING THERE Trains from London Paddington pass through on their way to Penzance. Newquay (changing at Par, near St. Austell) is around 5 hours and costs about £50 one-way. The nearest station to Padstow is Bodmin Parkway, a 4-hour journey from London with another hour on a connecting bus; cheapest ticket is £75 one-way.

If you're driving, turn off the A30 at Bodmin onto the A389 for Padstow; for Newquay, the A30 goes to within 10 miles, where you turn off at the beautifully named Indian Queens onto the A392.

Newquay airport (www.newquaycornwallairport.com; (C) **01637/860600**) is 3 miles from Newquay, and receives flights from London Gatwick and Manchester year-round, and seasonal flights from the East Midlands, Norwich, Glasgow, and Dusseldorf. Flights also go year-round to the Isles of Scilly. Car rental is available.

VISITOR INFORMATION Newquay Tourist Information Office, Marcus Hill (www.visitnewquay.org; (C) **01637/854020**), is open April to September Monday to

Friday 9:15am to 5:30pm, weekends 10am to 4pm. From September to March it's open Monday to Friday 10am to 4pm, weekends 10am to 3pm. **Padstow Tourist Information Office,** North Quay (www.padstowlive.com; © **01841/533449**), is open summer Monday to Friday 9am to 5pm, weekends 10am to 4pm. Winter hours are Monday to Friday 10am to 4pm, Saturday 10am to 2pm.

Exploring the Area

Newquay is Cornwall's biggest and liveliest seaside resort. It's also Britain's surfing capital. Put those two facts together and you could be put off by the prospect of crowds of partying youngsters. The pace can be frenetic, yet there's a laid-back, away-from-it-all feel that comes from the town's setting on the cliffs gazing west. The town looks over four beaches (Great Western, Tolcarne, Harbour, and Towan). To the west is the sweep of Fistral beach and a little farther is Crantock, while round a headland to the east (a 45-min. walk) is Watergate Bay, a 2-mile stretch of cliff-backed sand and surf.

Just north are the **Bedruthan Steps,** huge rocks set in the sand of a cliff-backed beach. Legend says that a giant, Bedruthan, put them there to help him climb out of the sea. There's a National Trust pay parking lot (off the B3276). The beach is magical but the 140-plus steep steps are hard work, and most of it is cut off at high tide.

Should you want more, the **Blue Reef Aquarium** (www.bluereefaquarium.co.uk; © **01637/787134**) at Towan beach, has displays from Cornwall to the Caribbean, and a glass tunnel beneath its vast tank, and **Newquay Zoo** (www.newquayzoo.org. uk; © **0844/474-2244**) is more than just about the animals (lions, wildebeests, and so on) with its setting in sub-tropical lakeside Trenance Gardens.

Padstow, in contrast to Newquay, is a fishing village on the Camel estuary with a small working fleet and lots of history; Sir Walter Raleigh lived here when he was Warden of Cornwall. It's now nicknamed "Padstein" due to all the restaurants and hotels of celebrity chef Rick Stein. Sit by the quay and enjoy fish and chips or an ice cream, and pop into the **London Inn,** 6/8 Lanadawell St. (www.staustellbrewery. co.uk; © **01841/532554**) for a drink. Padstow is the end of the **Camel Trail,** a cycle/walking route that runs 18 miles on an old railway line by the River Camel from Wenfordbridge. Bike rental is available from **Trail Bike Hire,** South Quay, Padstow (www.trailbikehire.co.uk; © **01841/532594**). Across the Camel, beyond the beach at **Polzeath,** is the **Church of St. Enodoc,** where poet Sir John Betjeman is buried.

Prideaux Place ☺ HISTORIC SITE   With gorgeous views over Padstow, this Elizabethan house has for centuries been the home of the Prideaux family and contains fine plasterwork, paintings, and furniture. The gardens are being restored, while the deer park is thought to be the oldest in the country.

Padstow. www.prideauxplace.co.uk. © **01841/532411.** Admission £8 adults, £2 children 6–16. House Easter and mid-May–early Oct Sun–Thurs 1:30–4pm; grounds and tearoom 12:30–5pm.

St. Agnes Beacon ★ VIEWPOINT   Fires were once lit on this hill to warn of the coming Spanish Armada. The National Trust parking lot is the starting point for walks. The village is a jumble of cottages, galleries, and shops while sandy **Trevaunance Cove** is popular with families and surfers. Nearby, in a steep-sided valley, is **Blue Hill Tin Streams** (www.bluehillstin.com; © **01872/553341**), the last place in Cornwall where tin is produced. There are tours from April to October Monday to Saturday 10am to 2pm, July and August 10am to 4pm; £6 adults, £3 children.

CELEBRITY kitchens: STEIN & OLIVER

Cornwall might be famous for beaches and mines, but it's also won acclaim for two of Britain's best-known TV chefs. **Jamie Oliver,** chirpy champion of good food on both sides of the Atlantic, opened **Fifteen Cornwall ★★** at Watergate Bay in Newquay. It's part of his foundation that helps underprivileged youngsters create a life and has become a hip destination combining Italian-influenced fine dining establishment (boasting that more than 80% of its produce is from Cornwall) with a beach bar feel. There's breakfast 8:30–10am, a set three-course lunch (£28), plus a la carte options, noon to 4:30pm, and a £60 five-course Cornish tasting menu (dishes such as chargrilled monkfish, Newlina's waxy beans, taggiasche olives, and peperonata) 6:15pm to midnight (last orders 9:15). It's not just a summer haunt; in winter the food takes on a richer air, with pheasant, partridge, and the like. The Beach, Watergate Bay. www.fifteen cornwall.co.uk. ℂ **01637/861000.** Reservations recommended. AE, MC, V. All children welcome at breakfast and lunch, for smaller portions of menu dishes, but those aged 7–12 can only eat dinner, the tasting menu, at 6:15pm and 6:45pm seatings.

Rick Stein has gone from being a seafood champion to an all-round culinary hero. His Padstow hometown is nicknamed "Padstein" due to his empire; four restaurants and six places to stay. Top of the pile is **The Seafood Restaurant ★★**; it's not cheap, and some view it as unnecessarily overpriced (fish, chips, and mushy peas at £18), but it can be special, whether a chargrilled Dover sole with sea salt and lime (£35), monkfish vindaloo, or local lobster—for £50. The airy, pale restaurant isn't stuffy, but it can be noisy and rushed. Excellent children's food (steak, goujons of lemon sole), at a price. Riverside, Padstow. Reservations recommended, but free seating at the seafood bar.

St. Petroc's Bistro ★, an old, white-painted building with courtyard and garden seating, reflects Stein's interest in French comfort food (with a Cornish touch): Steaks, terrines, duck confit. New Street, Padstow. Main courses £15–25. Daily noon–2pm and 6:30–10pm.

Rick Stein's Café ★★ is, for many, the most popular choice, combining flair with reasonable prices (mains £12–17). There's an international feel, with Italian influences, Cornish ribeye with chips, or grilled sea bass with lemongrass, spiced paste, kachumber salad, and steamed rice. There's also breakfast, whether a full English or huevos rancheros, and coffee and cakes. Middle Street, Padstow. Breakfast Mon–Fri 8–10:30am (Sat–Sun 11:30am); lunch daily noon–2:30pm; dinner Sun–Thurs 6:30–8:30pm, Fri–Sat 9:30pm.

Stein's Fish & Chips is a stylish take on a chip shop, where you spend £8.50 for battered cod and chips to take away, £10 to eat in. More than you might expect to pay elsewhere but not frighteningly so. In the mornings there's coffee, pastries, and bacon baps. South Quay, Padstow. Daily 10–11:30am, noon–2:30pm (Sun 4pm), 5–8pm (not Sun).

The Stein empire's **40 rooms** to rent vary from the balcony sea views of those above the Seafood Restaurant, to the Georgian **St. Petroc's Hotel,** to the pretty, stylish backstreet offerings at the Café, and take in the chic minimalism of **St. Edmund's House** and the estuary views of neat, one-bedroom **Bryn Cottage.** Doubles, £97–£310, include full English or continental breakfast taken at one of the restaurants. *All Stein enquiries: www.rickstein.com. ℂ **01841/532700.** AE, MC, V.

Where to Eat

Nathan Outlaw ★★ MODERN BRITISH   He might not have the celeb clout of Stein and Oliver, but Outlaw is catching up fast. He runs two restaurants at Rock's St. Enodoc Hotel, across the bay from Stein's Padstow fortress. **Restaurant Nathan Outlaw** won two Michelin stars in 2011 and serves a seven-course tasting menu with the likes of bream with brown shrimps, squid, and saffron sauce for £85 in a city-style setting. **Seafood & Grill** is more relaxed, like a place that you might find on the east coast of the US. A choice of fish (lemon sole, mackerel, lobster) is paired with a sauce (oyster cream, potted shrimp butter, citron mayonnaise); mains £14–£46.

St. Enodoc Hotel, Rock. www.nathan-outlaw.com. ✆ **01208/862737.** Seafood & Grill main courses £14–£42 (without veg). AE, MC, V. Seafood & Grill daily noon–3pm and 6–9:30pm (cream teas and snacks 3–6pm). Restaurant Nathan Outlaw Tues–Sat 7–9pm.

Pescadou SEAFOOD   A Padstow quayside restaurant (in the chic Old Custom House hotel) that doesn't have a celeb chef in sight, but manages splendidly. The catch determines the menu, which might feature grilled day boat half-shell scallops with lemongrass and lime, then grilled hake with roast langoustine bisque sauce.

South Quay, Padstow. www.oldcustomhousepadstow.co.uk. ✆ **01841/532354.** Main courses £13–£35. AE, MC, Visa. Daily breakfast 8–9:30am, lunch noon–3pm, and dinner 7–9pm.

Surf City Here We Come

Newquay is regarded as Britain's California: Great waves, great atmosphere, great nightlife. It's a lifestyle that is embraced by the group that runs the **Reef Surf Lodge** and **Reef Island Lodge** (hip, happening accommodations and nightlife, retro in a 1970s–meets-the-1990s sort of way) and the **Reef Surf School** in the heart of town. The Surf Lodge (10 Berry Rd.) is like a hostel for the clubbing generation, welcoming student groups, party weekenders, and individuals alike with beds from £10 in shared rooms with widescreen TVs, CD players, and fluorescent bathrooms, and public areas that have huge TVs showing surf films, a lively bar, restaurant, live reggae and rock bands, and a sun deck. The Island Lodge (30 Island Crescent), a few steps away on Great Western Beach, has the same feel but in a more exclusive way, all its 27 rooms (including a penthouse sleeping six) having sea views. A bed starts at £15 December to March and £30 June to August. A double room, en suite, with breakfast can be had for £45. Both offer packages with the almost-adjoining Surf School; a 3-night midweek learn-to-surf package with equipment can be had for £60. Information: www.reefsurflodge. com; ✆ **01637/879058.** Much of the surf action is on Watergate Bay, just outside town. There's the highly-rated **O'Neill Surf Academy** (www.oneillsurf academy.co.uk; **01841/520052**), which has children's sessions (ages 6–13) in the summer, and **Extreme Academy** (www. watergatebay.co.uk; ✆ **01637/860543**), which also gives lessons in kite-surfing and other sports, and is linked to **The Hotel** (see below). Just west of the town is Holywell Bay where the **Surf Academy** (www.cornwallsurfacademy. com; ✆ **0870/240-6693**) offers surf lessons and courses lasting 1 to 5 days. The schools have equipment for hire, but if you want the trendiest clothes and gear, head for **The Shop on the Beach** at Watergate Bay (www.shop thebeach.com; ✆ **01637/860051**).

The **South West Coast Path** (www. southwestcoastpath.com) runs 630 miles, from Minehead in Somerset to Poole in Dorset, and takes in the length of the Cornish coast. There are challenging stretches but it also offers easier walks. The **Saints' Way** runs 30 miles from coast to coast, from Padstow in the north to Fowey in the south. Route cards are available from Boscastle Visitor Centre (✆ **01840/250010**). A circular walk, the **Copper Trail** (www.ldwa. org.uk), runs for 60 miles along footpaths and tracks around Bodmin Moor, past many ancient sites. The enthusiastic website www.walkingincornwall.info has details and web links to hundreds of walks across the county, starting from 1 mile long.

Viners ★★ ▮BRITISH   This bar/restaurant in a 17th-century stone farmhouse, is run by Kevin Viner, who won Cornwall's first Michelin star (when at Pennypots, in Falmouth). The food is straightforward (starters of Fowey mussels or Cornish crab, with Cornish lamb or chicken stuffed with Cornish brie to follow) but imposing. There's a good Sunday lunch (with fish and vegetarian choices), which is popular with families as the place is relaxed with gardens and play area.

Carvynic, Summerscourt (inland, off the A3058). www.vinersrestaurant.co.uk. ✆**01872/510544.** Main courses £9.95–£23. AE, MC, V. Tues–Sat 6:30–9pm, Sun noon–mid-afternoon.

Where to Stay

The Hotel ★★   This sprawling Victorian hotel on the sands in Watergate Bay has been given a beach-chic makeover, all white walls, wood flooring, and splashes of cheery color. Each room is different, a standalone bath here, a chaise longue there, and there are family suites for six. Diners are spoilt for choice. There's the sleek, city-style **Brasserie** with its set dinner menu (2 courses £28), with the likes of filet of sea bass, Jerusalem artichoke risotto, and crispy pancetta; the **Living Space,** a modern bar/restaurant with steaks, Caesars, sandwiches (£6–20); and the super-cool **Beach Hut,** anything but a hut, all wood and wicker chairs, ceiling-high windows thrown open to the sunset. It serves breakfasts, moving on to burgers, ribs, and such daily, with dinner service Fridays and Saturdays (mains £10–20). There's also the Venus Cafe (10am to 5pm) for breakfasts, paninis, and burgers. Add to that **Fifteen Cornwall** (see "Celebrity kitchens: Stein & Oliver", p. 419), which shares the site, and the **Extreme Academy** surf school (see "Surf city here we come" above) and you may never want to leave.

On The Beach, Watergate Bay, Cornwall TR8 4AA. www.watergatebay.co.uk. ✆**01637/860543.** Fax 01637/860333. 69 units. £105–£355 double; £170–415 suite. Rates include breakfast. AE, MC, V. **Amenities:** 5 restaurants; 2 bars; water sports. *In room:* TV/DVD, hair dryer, Internet (free).

St. Enodoc Hotel ★   In the village of Rock, with lofty views over the Camel Estuary, this is a classic reinvention of a seaside hotel, with bright, airy, rooms, lots of floorboards and flagstones in the public areas, and original art throughout. The two restaurants are by Nathan Outlaw (see p. 420), there's an outdoor pool, and it's a stroll to the beaches and foot ferry to Padstow. Family suites have microwave and fridge.

Rock, Cornwall PL27 6LA. www.enodoc-hotel.co.uk. ✆**01208/863394.** 20 units. £130–£235; family suites £155–£340, plus £50 per child. Rates include breakfast. AE, MC, V. **Amenities:** 2 restaurants; bar; heated outdoor pool; library; billiard room; playroom. *In room:* TV, hair dryer, Wi-Fi (free).

10

CORNWALL

Newquay & Padstow

BODMIN, TINTAGEL & BUDE

Bodmin 264 miles SW of London; 33 miles W of Plymouth; Bude 190 miles SW of London; 40 miles NW of Plymouth

Bodmin Moor is one of those places that sticks in the memory from childhood trips, a bleak place that nevertheless said that you were now in Cornwall as you crossed it on the A30 and looked out for the stone edifice of the Jamaica Inn. It is, however, a place worth stopping at, for walks up **Rough Tor** (pronounced row-ter) and **Brown Willy,** Cornwall's highest points (the latter 419m/1,375 ft.), and to gaze into Dozmary Pool where King Arthur's sword, Excalibur, is said to have risen from the waters. Other sights include Trethevy Quoit, a Neolithic burial chamber, the remains of copper mines, and wild ponies. **Bodmin** itself is a sturdy stone town which, despite its position, is only 30 minutes from beaches on both north and south coast. The main attraction is **Bodmin Jail** (www.bodminjail.org; © **01208/76292**), a prison on six floors dating from 1779. It's all quite gruesome, and has a working execution pit, where prisoners were hanged. It's open daily, 10am to dusk, £6.50 adults, £4.50 children 5 to 15.

Tintagel, 20 miles away on the wild north coast, is where you'll find **Tintagel Castle,** the legendary birthplace of King Arthur. Thirty miles farther is Bude, the largest town in this area, and a beach resort—**Widemouth Bay** is where surfers congregate.

Essentials

GETTING THERE   By **train,** Bodmin Parkway is on the London Paddington line to Penzance; the journey of 4 hours from London is about £55 one-way. By **car,** Bodmin is on the A30 route into Cornwall, at the junction of the A38. Tintagel is about a 30-minute drive away.

VISITOR INFORMATION   Bodmin **Tourist Information Office,** Shire Hall, Mount Folly Square (www.bodminlive.com; © **01208/76616**), is open Easter to late October Monday to Saturday 10am to 5pm; October to Easter Monday to Friday 10am to 5pm, not open Saturday.

Exploring the Area

Bodmin is a good base for exploring. The **Bodmin and Wenford Railway** (www. bodminandwenfordrailway.co.uk; © **0845/125-9678**) runs steam trains on a 13-mile round-trip, February to December. The Camel Trail, an 18-mile track for walkers and cyclists, follows the River Camel to Padstow in one direction from Bodmin, and in the other heads to the moor. Hire cycles from **Bodmin Bikes,** Dennison Road, Bodmin (www.bodminbikes.co.uk; © **01208/73192**, adults £13/day, children £7/day). **Camel Valley Vineyards,** Nanstallon, (www.camelvalley.com; © **01208/77959**), boasts a sparkling rosé that in 2011 was named world's best for the second year at the Bollicine del Mondo awards in Verona. There are tours with tastings (Apr–Sept Mon–Fri 2:30pm, £7.50), plus two converted barns for holiday lets.

Tintagel Castle ★★★ CASTLE   Whether or not this was the home to King Arthur, it is a place that is so powerful as to inspire legends. The remains of a 13th-century castle sit on windblown cliffs (at the top of 100 steep, stone steps) with the wild Atlantic crashing at their base. The Romans were here, and the Celts, while the castle was built by Richard, Earl of Cornwall. At low tide you can also pop into Merlin's Cave.

Bossiney Rd. www.english-heritage.org.uk. © **01840/770328.** Admission £5.50 adults, £3.30 children 5–15. Daily Apr–Sept 10am–6pm; Oct 10am–5pm; Nov–Mar weekends 10am–4pm.

Where to Eat & Stay

Bay View Inn ★   A family-run place that blurs the distinction between pub, hotel, and restaurant. Rooms, pale and coastal-smart, have rural views over the Atlantic; a couple have roll-top baths and there are two family options. The restaurant shares the views and serves local produce such as smoked trout, fish pie, and mussels in a cider, smoked bacon, and wholegrain mustard sauce (mains £10–£17). There's a long children's menu (all £4.95) with a decent burger and Cornish sausages. The bar, serving Cornish beers, has a sea view terrace. The South West Path passes the door.

Widemouth Bay, Bude, Cornwall EX23 0AW. www.bayviewinn.ndo.co.uk. ©**01288/361273.** 6 units. £80–£120 double; family rooms for 4–5, £80–£90 plus £15 children 1–14. Rates include English breakfast. Free parking. **Amenities:** Restaurant; bar. *In room:* TV, hair dryer, Wi-Fi (free).

Camelot Castle Hotel ★★   Not King Arthur's abode but a clifftop Victorian affair overlooking it and the Atlantic. In its long history it has welcomed the likes of Ava Gardner, Noel Coward, and Winston Churchill, but a turn of the millennium revamp created a place where Hollywood country-house glitz meets new age mysticism. There are carved four-posters in some rooms yet simpler options still have movie star magic. There's a private beach, and a gallery filled with the works of co-owner Ted Stourton. Irina's Restaurant is a mix of modern Italian and classic British (2 courses £21.95).

Tintagel, Cornwall PL34 0DQ. www.camelotcastle.com. ©**01840/770202.** Fax: 01840/770978. 64 units. £78–£270 double. East Tower suite £400–£500. Breakfast £10. **Amenities:** Restaurant; bar; private beach. *In room:* TV, hair dryer, Wi-Fi (free).

Jamaica Inn   A stark, stone coaching inn on Bodmin Moor that looks much as it did in the 1770s when it was central to the smuggling trade, and when, in 1930, Daphne du Maurier spent a night here and was inspired to name her novel after it. It has its own (free) smuggling museum, with a Du Maurier room complete with her writing desk. The place is dark, snug, and solid, the spot to hunker down in a storm. Some rooms are simple, others have four-posters and beams. The two bars are low and warm, one with a log fire. The inn, on the main A30 into Cornwall, is a popular journey breaker; even if you can't stay, pop in for coffee and breakfast (from 9am), or pub food (noon–9pm).

Bolventor, Launceston, Cornwall PL15 7TS. www.jamaicainn.co.uk. © **01566/86250.** Fax 01566/86177. 16 units. £85–£115 double. Rates include English breakfast. **Amenities:** Restaurant; 2 bars. *In room:* TV, Wi-Fi (free).

THE COTSWOLDS

by Stephen Keeling

Between Oxford and the River Severn, the pastoral Cotswolds comprise a stretch of rolling limestone hills, steep escarpments, and meandering streams. Some of England's most ravishing villages dot this bucolic region, made rich from the medieval wool trade and distinctively built of honey-brown Cotswold stone.

SIGHTSEEING Enchanting villages such as **Bibury, Painswick, Broadway,** and **Chipping Campden** are likely to be your most endearing memories of the region. Eating at medieval inns, soaking up the picture-perfect scenery, and wandering the narrow lanes—before the crowds arrive—is at the heart of the Cotswold experience. There are plenty of traditional sights, of course: **Gloucester** is home to a handsome cathedral; Cheltenham is a sophisticated spa town; and **Sudeley Castle** provides some historical glamour.

EATING & DRINKING When it comes to food, the Cotswolds is all about fresh, locally grown produce. You'll find **farmers' markets** and organic farm shops, like the one near **Cirencester,** throughout the region, and organic meat and vegetables are served at numerous restaurants. You can buy **fresh fish** at trout farms, like those at Bibury and Donnington. **Cheltenham** is the gastronomic capital of the region, with a host of stylish and acclaimed restaurants led by **Le Champignon Sauvage.**

OUTDOOR ACTIVITIES The lesser-traveled roads of the Cotswolds make tempting targets for **cyclists,** and there are plenty of rental shops and specialist cycle tour companies to help. Another enticing outlet for healthy activity is the **Cotswold Way,** a 100-mile trail that cuts across the most seductive of the region's landscapes, towns, and mercifully, historic pubs.

ARTS & CULTURE Cheltenham is also the region's art and culture hub, celebrated for its roster of **festivals** that cover everything from folk, jazz, and classical music to literature. Elsewhere, the 19th-century Arts and Crafts Movement has a shrine in the form of **Kelmscott Manor,** the home of William Morris, while the **New Brewery Arts center** in Cirencester harbors 12 contemporary artists who craft all manner of goods for sale.

On Your Bike

Biking the country roads of the Cotswolds is one of the best ways to experience the quiet beauty of the area. For a self-guided tour (but with a lot of help), you can hook up with **Cotswold Country Cycles** (www.cotswoldcountrycycles.com; ⓒ **01386/438706**), whose tours are designed to take you off the beaten track. Lodging is arranged in advance, often at manor houses or historic homes. A typical offering is the 3-day, 2-night adventure called "Simply Cotswolds," based in Chipping Campden (p. 449) and starting at £245 per person. A simpler option is offered by **Hartwells Cycle-Hire** (www.hartwells.supanet.com; ⓒ **01451/820405**), which rents bikes (£14 a day, £9 children 15 and under) from its base on Bourton-on-the-Water (p. 439).

THE best TRAVEL EXPERIENCES IN THE COTSWOLDS

o **Hiking the Cotswold Way:** This rustic hiking trail is one of the most popular in England, for good reason—it winds its way through 100 miles of lush Cotswold countryside, taking in some of the region's most awe-inspiring towns and villages: Chipping Camden, Painswick, and Bath. See p. 428.

o **Shopping for English antiques:** The Cotswolds is a major center for high-quality antiques, and you could spend several weeks digging around for bargains in its numerous antique stores; expect anything from Georgian furniture to Victorian dolls. Stow-on-the-Wold is the best place to begin. See p. 444.

o **Climbing Broadway Tower:** Make your way up this 17-m (55-ft.) folly designed by Capability Brown—the second highest point in the Cotswolds—for gasp-inducing views across the entire region. See p. 446.

o **Going to the races:** Every year in March, Cheltenham hosts the Gold Cup, the most prestigious horse-jump race in the U.K. Races are often dramatic, raucous affairs, and a unique slice of English life. See p. 433.

o **Sleeping in a four-poster bed:** The Cotswolds are littered with old country houses, pubs, and inns that have been converted into plush hotels, unashamedly cashing in on the region's historic appeal with a liberal sprinkling of four-poster beds—the Swan Hotel in Bibury is a good example. See p. 432.

BURFORD ★

73 miles NW of London; 20 miles W of Oxford

Built of classic honey-gold Cotswold stone, the unspoiled medieval town of **Burford** serves as the best gateway to the region coming from London or Oxford. The town was one of the last of the great wool centers, the industry bleating out its last breath during Queen Victoria's reign. Today it's best known for its Norman church and its long, steep High Street lined with old coaching inns and antique shops.

The River Windrush, which toward Burford is flanked by willows and meadows, passes beneath a packhorse bridge and goes around the church and away through more meadows toward **Widford.** Strolling along its banks is a delightful experience and a fitting introduction to the Cotswolds.

Essentials

GETTING THERE   If you're driving, Burford is easy to reach from Oxford via the A40. Otherwise, you'll have to take the bus; the best option is the **Swanbrook** (www. swanbrook.co.uk; ⓒ **01452/712386**) Oxford to Gloucester service that passes through Burford (the Oxford stop is at the Taylorian Institute on St. Giles Street). Three buses per day (just one on Sun) make the 45-minute run to Burford (£3.40 one-way; £5.40 round-trip). Burford has no railway station: the nearest is at Shipton, five miles north, but this is only served by two trains daily from London (Mon-Sat; off-peak £26–£28 one-way). From Shipton **Stagecoach** (www.stagecoachbus.com) runs six to 11 buses (Mon–Sat only) to Burford (20min). National Express runs eight buses direct to Cirencester from London daily (off-peak £8.50 one-way), taking between 2 and 2.5 hrs.

VISITOR INFORMATION   The **Tourist Information Centre** is at 33a High Street (www.oxfordshirecotswolds.org; ⓒ **01993/823558**). It's open Monday to Saturday 9:30am to 5pm, and Sunday 10am to 4pm.

Exploring the Area

Though the wool trade has long since vanished, most of Burford remains unchanged in appearance, with medieval stone houses in the High Street, which sweeps down to the River Windrush, covered with roofs of Stonesfield slate. Burford's magnificent **Church of St. John the Baptist** (www.burfordchurch.org), dating from 1175, is almost cathedral-like in size, while the **Tolsey,** 126 High St., is where, from the 12th century, wool merchants paid their tolls and taxes. On the upper floor is the tiny **Tolsey Museum** (ⓒ **01993/823236;** Apr–Oct Tues–Sun 2–5pm; free), where you can see a medieval seal bearing Burford's insignia, the "rampant cat."

Cotswold Wildlife Park ☺ZOO   Two miles south of Burford on the A361 lies the incongruous but entertaining Cotswold Wildlife Park, a guaranteed hit with children. The 160 acres of gardens and forests around the 1804 Bradwell Grove manor house have been transformed into a jungle of sorts, with a Noah's Ark consortium of animals ranging from voracious ants to rare Asiatic lions, rhinos, and a Madagascar exhibit for fans of the animated movie. Children can also romp around the farmyard and the adventure playground. A narrow-gauge railway runs from April to October, and there are extensive picnic areas as well as a cafeteria.

A361, south of Burford. www.cotswoldwildlifepark.co.uk. ⓒ **01993/823006.** Admission £13 adults, £9 seniors and children 3–16, free for children 2 and under. Apr–Oct daily 10am–6pm (last entry 4:30pm); Nov–Mar daily 10am–5pm (last entry 3:30pm).

Kelmscott Manor ★★ HISTORIC HOME   This handsome Elizabethan mansion was the home of William Morris (1834–96), artist, craftsman, socialist, and founder of the influential Arts and Crafts movement. The manor was built around 1600 and leased by Morris and the Pre-Raphaelite painter Dante Gabriel Rossetti in 1871. Inside you'll find a fine collection of Morris's work and personal possessions, from handcrafted furniture to original textiles, paintings, carpets, ceramics, and metalwork. Morris is buried in the grounds of nearby St. George's Church. Admission to the house is by timed ticket (last entry 4:30pm).

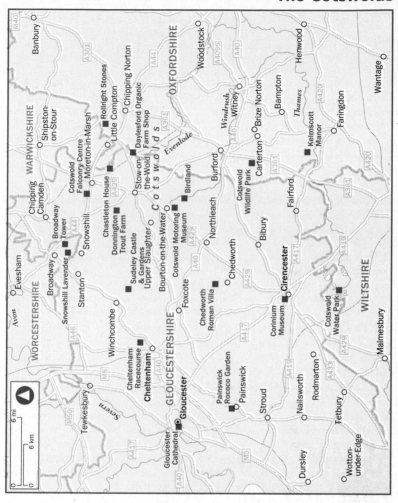

Kelmscott, Lechlade, Gloucestershire (off the A417), 10 miles south of Burford. www.kelmscott manor.org.uk. ☏**01993/823006.** Admission £9 adults, £4.50 students and children 8–16, free for children 7 and under; garden only £2.50. Apr–Oct Wed and Sat 11am–5pm. Closed Nov–Mar.

Where to Eat & Stay

Huffkins ★★, 98 High St. (www.huffkins.com; ☏ **01993/822126**), has been baking cakes and serving fine teas in Burford since 1890. The tearoom is open Monday to Friday 9am to 5pm, Saturday 9am to 5:30pm, and Sunday 10am to 5pm.

Bay Tree Hotel ★ This atmospheric old inn was built for Sir Lawrence Tanfield, the unpopular lord chief baron of the exchequer to Elizabeth I. Modern comforts

The **Cotswold Way** (www.nationaltrail. co.uk/cotswold) meanders for just over 100 miles from Chipping Campden to Bath (p. 336), taking in the best of the area's landscapes and traditional villages. You can hike the trail easily in a week or so, staying in country pubs or cozy B&Bs along the way. Several companies can arrange all the details. **Cotswold Walking Holidays** (www. cotswoldwalks.com; ℂ **01242/518888**) is a dependable choice, offering 7-night self-guided tours (including B&B, route instructions/map, and luggage transportation) for £425 per person. Alternatively, the **Sherpa Van Project** (www. sherpavan.com; ℂ **0871/520-0124**) will just transfer your luggage between accommodations from £8 per bag per day. Check also www.cotswold-way. co.uk.

have been discreetly installed in the English country-style accommodations, some of which have four-poster beds. Try to get a room overlooking the terraced gardens at the rear of the house. The house has oak-paneled rooms with stone fireplaces throughout, and a high-beamed hall with a minstrel's gallery. The elegant **Bay Tree Restaurant** is open daily for modern English food, while lighter meals and drinks can be enjoyed in the Woolsack Bar.

12–14 Sheep St., Burford, Oxfordshire OX18 4LW. www.cotswold-inns-hotels.co.uk. ℂ **01993/ 822791.** Fax 01993/823008. 21 units. £170–£210 double; £220–£260 suite. Rates include English breakfast. AE, DC, MC, V. Free parking. **Amenities:** Restaurant; bar; room service; babysitting. *In room:* TV, hair dryer, Wi-Fi (£10 for 24 hr.).

The Bull ★★   A meal in this top-class restaurant and hotel is the perfect way to cap off a visit to Burford. The restaurant is a sort of posh gastropub, knocking out exquisite modern British cuisine such as pan-seared filet of beef with an oxtail ravioli, bone marrow boudin and glazed carrots; and steak and Guinness pie served with wild mushrooms, savoy cabbage, and mustard mash (mains £13.90–£23.50). Built in 1475 and littered with fine antique furnishings, the Bull is also an enticing place to spend the night, with bedrooms blending modern comforts with original fittings and four-poster beds; the Trafalgar Suite is named after the visit of Lord Nelson and Lady Hamilton in 1802.

105 High St., Burford, Oxfordshire OX18 4RG. www.bullatburford.co.uk. ℂ **01993/822220.** 9 units. £70–£140 double. Rates include English breakfast. MC, V. Free parking (limited). **Amenities:** Restaurant; bar; room service. *In room:* TV, hair dryer, Wi-Fi (free).

Burford House ★★★   Just eight immaculate and beautifully furnished rooms occupy this gorgeous 17th-century inn. Each comes adorned with antiques, spacious bathrooms, and huge tubs. Fresh cookies, water, tea, and coffee are supplied daily. Even if you don't stay here, come to eat. **Lunch** (Mon–Sat) and **dinner** (Thurs–Sat) feature the best of contemporary English cooking, with fresh organic vegetables, meats, and poultry sourced as locally as possible. Failing that, stop by for morning coffee with toasted crumpets (savory griddle cakes made from flour and yeast, a bit like a thick pancake), or the decadent afternoon teas with homemade scones, cakes, and pastries.

99 High St., Burford, Oxfordshire OX18 4QA. www.burford-house.co.uk. ℂ **01993/823151.** Fax 01993/823240. 8 units. £179–£199 double; £279 suite. Rates include English breakfast. Free street parking available nearby. AE, DC, MC, V. **Amenities:** Restaurant; bar. *In room:* TV, DVD, hair dryer, CD player, Wi-Fi (free).

CIRENCESTER ★

20 miles SW of Burford; 89 miles W of London; 16 miles S of Cheltenham; 36 miles W of Oxford

Cirencester is the unofficial "capital of the Cotswolds." Founded by the Romans as Corinium and then destroyed by the Saxons 300 years later, it boomed again in the Middle Ages thanks to the great Cotswold wool trade. Little remains from the medieval period, but plenty of well-preserved stone houses from the 17th and 18th centuries are still intact.

Today, Cirencester is chiefly a market town that makes a good base for touring. Visit the **Market Place** in the center on Monday or Friday 9am to 3pm, when it's packed with local traders.

Essentials

GETTING THERE   Cirencester has no railway station, but Cheltenham-bound Great Western trains depart every hour from London's Paddington Station for the 80-minute trip to Kemble (off-peak £18–£20 one-way), which is 4 miles southwest of Cirencester. You may have to transfer trains at Swindon. From Kemble station, buses travel to Cirencester (20–25 min.) but don't always meet the trains; **Stagecoach** (www.stagecoachbus.com) has seven departures (Mon–Sat only).

If you're driving from London, take the M4 west to junction 15, then the A419 north to Cirencester.

VISITOR INFORMATION   The **Cirencester Visitor Information Centre** is located in the Corinium Museum, Park Street (www.cirencester.gov.uk; ✆ **01285/654180**). Hours are Monday to Saturday from 10am to 5pm, Sunday from 2 to 5pm (Nov–Mar closes at 4pm).

Exploring the Area

Church of St. John the Baptist CHURCH   A church may have stood here in Saxon times, but the present building overlooking the Market Place in the town center dates from the 15th and 16th centuries. In size, it appears more like a cathedral than a mere parish church, with a variety of styles, largely Perpendicular, as in the early 15th-century tower (49m/162 ft.). Among the treasures inside are a 15th-century "wineglass" pulpit and a silver-gilt cup given to Anne Boleyn 2 years before her execution.

Market Place. www.cirenparish.co.uk. ✆ **01285/659317.** Free admission; donations welcomed. Mon–Sat 9:30am–5pm; Sun 2:15–5pm.

Corinium Museum ★★ MUSEUM   The Roman town of Corinium was the second largest in Roman Britain, and this museum houses a fine collection of archeological remains from that period, found locally in and around Cirencester. Highlights include intricate mosaic pavements, excavated on Dyer Street in 1849, and rare provincial Roman sculpture, including such figures as Minerva and Mercury. The museum has been completely modernized to include full-scale reconstructions and special exhibitions on local history from the Iron Age through the English Civil War.

Park St. www.cotswold.gov.uk. ✆ **01285/655611.** Admission £4.95 adults, £4.10 seniors, £3.30 students, £2.45 children 5–16. Mon–Sat 10am–5pm; Sun 2–5pm (closes at 4pm Nov–Mar).

Cotswold Water Park ★ WATER PARK   For fresh air and easy walks, head south from the Market Place for 3 miles on the A419 to this 40-sq.-mile reserve of parkland and woodland trails. Britain's largest water park contains more than 140

lakes surrounded by picnic tables, barbecue sites, and a network of footpaths. Concessions here will hook you up for sailing, fishing, canoeing, cycling, kayaking, horseback riding, and water-skiing (but no jet-skiing and no waterslides). All equipment needed is available for rent on-site. Swimming is possible June through September at Lake 32 (www.ukwatersports.co.uk) and Lake 16 (www.southcerneyoutdoor.co.uk).

Gateway Centre, Spine Rd., South Cerney (B4696). www.waterpark.org. *℗* **01285/861459.** Basic admission free, otherwise varies according to activity and location; see website for details. Gateway Information Centre daily 9am–5pm.

New Brewery Arts ARTS & CRAFTS   The heart of this arts complex is the workshop area of 12 resident crafts workers who produce everything from baskets to chandeliers. Other components of the center (built in 1820 as a brewery) include three galleries, featuring crafts and fine-art exhibitions alike, a theatre, education classes, a shop selling the best in British crafts, and a coffeehouse.

Brewery Court. www.newbreweryarts.org.uk. *℗* **01285/657181.** Free admission. Mon–Sat 9am–5pm; Sun 10am–4pm (closed Sun Jan–Mar).

Shopping

The **Organic Farm Shop** ★★ just 2 miles outside Cirencester at Abbey Home Farm, Burford Road (the B4425; www.theorganicfarmshop.co.uk; *℗***01285/640441**), sells over 100 varieties of fresh, home-produced organic vegetables and herbs. It's open Tuesday to Saturday 9am to 5pm, and Sunday 11am to 4pm. Even if you're not buying it's a great place to visit, and also has a cafe that serves up the produce.

Entertainment & Nightlife

For a pint, head for the **Crown** ★, 17 W. Market Place (www.crownciren.com; *℗* **01285/653206**), a friendly pub enjoyed by locals and students alike. The place boasts a 400-year-old tradition of serving ale and victuals on this site, and it has the most convivial nightlife in town. The **Waggon & Horses** ★★, 11 London Rd. (www.thewaggonandhorses.co.uk; *℗* **01285/652022**), is an 18th-century coaching inn that not only serves at least six real ales on tap, but also surprisingly good Thai food (cooked up by a Thai chef).

Where to Eat & Stay

Barnsley House ★★   The Cotswolds is studded with expensive country-house resorts, but few are as chic, glamorous, and trendy as the former home of garden designer Rosemary Verey. The 17th-century mansion is surrounded by the best-landscaped gardens in the Cotswolds, and the soothing Garden Spa is spell-binding. The rooms blend stone fireplaces, wooden floors, and beams with contemporary furnishings and the latest technology—you can even take a bath while watching a DVD. The on-site **Potager Restaurant** uses local and fresh produce from the gardens to conjure up English dishes with an Italian influence, such as pumpkin cappelletti, and smoked haddock and pea risotto (main courses £12–£27).

Barnsley (4 miles NE of Cirencester), B4425, Gloucestershire GL7 5EE. www.barnsleyhouse.com. *℗***01285/740000.** Fax 01285/740925. 11 units. £250–£325 double; £250–£475 suite. Rates include continental breakfast. AE, MC, V. Free parking. **Amenities:** Restaurant; bar; spa; room service; private cinema. *In room:* TV/DVD, minibar, hair dryer, CD player, CD & DVD library, MP3 docking station, Wi-Fi (free).

Best Western Stratton House Hotel ★   Now part of the Best Western stable, this inviting country house is especially well priced, despite looking a bit tired and old-fashioned in places. Built in several stages throughout the 18th century, with a modern wing added in the 1990s, it has large, well-furnished rooms (the "cozy" rooms being the smallest of the lot); some have four-poster beds. It's 1¼ miles (20-min. walk) northwest of Cirencester town center.

Gloucester Rd. (A417), Cirencester, Gloucestershire GL7 2LE. www.strattonhousehotel.co.uk. ©01285/651761. Fax 01285/640024. 40 units. £69–£115 double. Rates include English breakfast. AE, DC, MC, V. Free parking. **Amenities:** Restaurant; bar; room service. *In room:* TV, hair dryer, Wi-Fi (free).

The Fleece at Cirencester ★   For a historic choice in the center of town, it's hard to beat this half-timbered Elizabethan coaching inn. Charles II hid out on this site, posing as a servant to the house mistress, Jane Lane, in 1651, with Cromwell's troops in hot pursuit. The inn was enlarged in the Georgian period and renovated in 2011, offering comfortable, small-to-midsize rooms decorated in a classic English country style. Two rooms are large enough for families, and two have four-poster beds. The on-site **1651 restaurant and bar** serves Thwaites cask ales and excellent English and French cuisine (specials include beef bourguignon on Wednesdays and Brittany fish stew on Fridays).

Market Place, Cirencester, Gloucestershire GL7 2NZ. www.thefleececirencester.co.uk. ©01285/658507. Fax 01285/651017. 28 units. £85–£125 double. Rates include English breakfast. AE, MC, V. Free parking. **Amenities:** Restaurant; bar; room service. *In room:* TV, hair dryer, Wi-Fi (free).

Ivy House ★★   Just 3 minutes' walk from the town center, this congenial B&B gets high marks for location and comfy, no-nonsense rooms. The attractive ivy-smothered Victorian building was built in 1870, and features compact but spotless rooms supplied with bottled water, tea, coffee, hot chocolate, and cookies. Breakfast is a real treat—try the home-baked granola.

2 Victoria Rd., Cirencester, Gloucestershire GL7 1EN. www.ivyhousecotswolds.com. ©01285/656626. 4 units. £70–£90 double. Rates include English breakfast. MC, V. Free parking. *In room:* TV, hair dryer, Wi-Fi (free).

Made by Bob ★★ ITALIAN/MODERN BRITISH   Chef Bob Parkinson has created quite a buzz with his contemporary trattoria-style restaurant and deli in the heart of town, combining fresh local ingredients with Italian, French, and even North African flavors. The menu might include a classic fish soup, calves liver with fondant potato and beetroot, or brochette of lamb with pickled chilis and a cooling cucumber yogurt. Save space for the bread and butter pudding. Be prepared to wait for a table.

Unit 6, The Cornhall, 26 Market Place. www.foodmadebybob.com. ©01285/641818. No reservations. Main courses £8–£22. AE, DC, MC, V. Mon–Sat 7:30–10am and noon–3pm (afternoon tea 3–6:30pm).

Old Bungalow Guest House ★   If you like cozy, friendly B&Bs you'll love this unassuming place, but book well ahead—it has a loyal clientele of regulars. The rooms are simple but homey and feature all the usual amenities; three rooms come with a double and single bed, while the rest just have double beds. Gary and Hannah are gracious and informative hosts, and their breakfasts are always beautifully prepared. They also have a modern self-catering one-bedroom bungalow in the gardens (full kitchen) from £78.

93 Victoria Rd., Cirencester, Gloucestershire GL7 1ES. www.bandbcirencester.co.uk. ©01285/654179. 6 units. £68–£78 double. Rates include English breakfast. AE, DC, MC, V. Free parking. No children 9 and under. **Amenities:** Bar. *In room:* TV, hair dryer, Wi-Fi (free).

Side Trips from Cirencester
BIBURY ★★

Bibury is one of the loveliest spots in the Cotswolds. In fact, William Morris called it England's most beautiful village. In more recent times it's become especially popular with Japanese tourists thanks to artists such as Ryutaro Ikeda (Emperor Hirohito also came here as a prince in 1921).

On the banks of the tiny River Coln, 7 miles northeast of Cirencester on the B4425, Bibury is especially noted for **Arlington Row.** Built in 1380 as a monastic wool store, it was converted into a row of weavers' cottages in the 17th century. Today these houses are Bibury's biggest and most photographed attraction (go early to avoid the tour bus crowd), but it's rude to peer into the windows, as many do, because people still live here.

To get a view of something a bit out of the ordinary for the Cotswolds, check out **St. Mary's Parish Church,** at the end of Cemetery Lane. Much of its original Romanesque architecture has been left intact, as well as the 14th-century Decorated-style windows. The so-called "Decorated" style was the second period of English Gothic architecture, mainly from the late 13th to the mid-14th centuries, when adornments became more elaborate and stone construction lighter and more spacious.

It's also worth visiting the **Bibury Trout Farm** (www.biburytroutfarm.co.uk; ✆ **01285/740215**), in the heart of the village, where visitors can stroll around the fish ponds as rainbow trout are fed. You can buy fresh or smoked trout at the farm shop. Admission is £3.95 for adults, £3.50 for seniors, and £2.95 for children 5 to 15 (free for children 4 and under). The farm is open daily 8am to 6pm (it closes at 5pm Mar and Oct, and 4pm Nov–Feb).

The **Swan Hotel** ★★ (www.cotswold-inns-hotels.co.uk; ✆ **01285/740695;** £170–£290 double; £290–£420 suite) offers the finest accommodations, tearoom, and restaurant in the village. It originated as a riverside cottage in the 1300s, but most of what you see today dates from the 17th century. Rooms are outfitted in a traditional, warm-toned design evocative of a discreetly upscale stately home, with tartan and flowered fabrics and autumn-inspired colors. A three-course dinner in the **Gallery Restaurant** is normally £35 per person; full afternoon tea set in the bar is £17.95.

With no connecting buses into Bibury, you'll need to drive or take a taxi from Cirencester. For more information visit www.bibury.com.

Chedworth Roman Villa ★ HISTORIC SITE   Reopening after a major renovation, the remains of one of the largest Roman villas in the country provides a fascinating insight into 4th-century Roman Britain. The real highlights here are the stunning mosaics, in situ.

Yanworth (off the A429), 9 miles north of Cirencester. www.chedworthromanvilla.com. ✆ **01242/890256.** Admission £6.30 adults, £3.60 children 5–15, £16.20 family ticket. Mar & Nov daily 10am–4pm, Apr–Oct 10am–5pm.

CHELTENHAM ★

99 miles NW of London; 43 miles W of Oxford; 9 miles NE of Gloucester

Once the spa capital of England, Cheltenham boasts some of the nation's best examples of Regency architecture, excellent restaurants, and extensive 19th-century gardens. Cheltenham owes its size and position to the discovery of a mineral spring

Going to the Races

Organized horse racing came to Cheltenham in 1815, with the location of **Cheltenham Racecourse** (www.cheltenham.co.uk; *©* **0844/579-3003**), in the nearby village of Prestbury (just a few minutes from the town center), dating from 1831. Since 1898 it's been the home of National Hunt (steeplechase) horse-racing in the U.K. Meetings are hosted from October to April, but the highlight of the season is the **Cheltenham Gold Cup,** which is normally held in the middle of March, during what's dubbed the "Cheltenham Festival." The cheapest tickets ("Best Mate Enclosure") range from £20 to £25 (£35–£40 for the actual Gold Cup). Race day buses link Cheltenham railway station to the racecourse. See the website for more details.

in 1716. King George III arrived in 1788 to take the waters (thought to have curative powers), launching a boom that lasted well into the 1800s. The spa is still here, but these days more people visit for the **Gold Cup,** the premier meet of British steeplechase horse-racing.

Cheltenham is also a major cultural center, with a decent roster of museums, live music venues, and numerous festivals in addition to its lauded architecture. Indeed, the main street, the Promenade, is one of the most beautiful thoroughfares in the Cotswolds.

Essentials

GETTING THERE   Great Western trains depart twice an hour from London's Paddington Station for the 2½-hour trip (off-peak £22.50–£39 one-way). You may have to change trains at Swindon. Trains between Cheltenham and Bristol (£8–£10.40) take 40 minutes to an hour, with continuing service to Bath. Cheltenham station is inconveniently located 1 mile west of the center—plenty of metered taxis meet trains, though, with trips to most hotels around £6.

If you're driving from London, head northwest on the M40 to Oxford, and continue along the A40 to Cheltenham.

VISITOR INFORMATION   The **Tourist Information Centre,** 77 Promenade (www.visitcheltenham.com; *©* **01242/522878**), is open Monday to Saturday from 9:30am to 5:15pm. On Wednesday mornings, it opens at 10am.

Exploring the Town

Cheltenham Art Gallery & Museum ★ MUSEUM   This absorbing museum chronicles the town's rise to fame in the Regency period; it also houses one of the foremost collections of the Arts and Crafts Movement, notably the fine furniture of William Morris and his followers. Another gallery is devoted to Edward Wilson, Cheltenham's native son, who died with Captain Scott in the Antarctic in 1912. Note that the museum will be closed for an ambitious redesign until the first half of 2013.

Clarence St. www.cheltenhammuseum.org.uk. *©* **01242/237431.** Free admission. Daily 10am–5pm (Nov–Mar 4pm). Closed public holidays.

Holst Birthplace Museum MUSEUM   This is a small but enlightening tribute to Gustav Holst, composer of *The Planets,* who was born in this Regency terrace

Cheltenham has a well-deserved reputation as a cultural center, with an especially rich line-up of annual festivals. The **Folk Festival** (tickets from £25) kicks things off in February, while the **Jazz Festival** (end Apr–early May) features a roster of international artists and the **Science Festival** (June) boasts lectures from a who's who of British and international science. Also in June, the alternative **Wychwood Music Festival** (www.wychwoodfestival.com) at Cheltenham Racecourse offers 3 days of music, comedy, cabaret, workshops, and film from £115. The **Music Festival** (July) showcases classical music, while the **Literature Festival** (Oct) offers an eclectic schedule of events, talks, and readings. See www.cheltenhamfestivals.com for more details. For something a bit more offbeat, try the annual **Cheese Rolling Festival** (www.cheese-rolling.co.uk), at Cooper's Hill, 6 miles south of town on the A46. Usually held at the end of May or early June, huge rounds of Double Gloucester cheese are rolled down the hill to wild (and boozy) applause. Note that the term "Cheltenham Festival" actually refers to horse-racing (p. 433).

house in 1874. The rooms inside have been faithfully restored in Regency and Victorian style, with William Morris-inspired wallpaper, portraits, and personal items, telling the story of Holst and his music. An expressive life-size **statue** of the great composer stands in Imperial Gardens, at the southern end of the Promenade.

4 Clarence Rd. www.holstmuseum.org.uk. (℗ **01242/524846.** Admission £4.50 adults, £4 seniors and children 5–16, £10 family ticket. Mid-Feb–mid-Dec Tues–Sat 10am–4pm. Closed late Dec–mid-Feb.

Pittville Pump Room HISTORIC SITE   Cheltenham spring water is the only natural, consumable alkaline water in Great Britain and can still be drunk at one of the town's finest Regency buildings, built in the 1820s. The Greek Revival Pittville Pump Room looks like a grand country mansion at the top of Pittville Park, though it's now used primarily as a concert and private function venue. Visitors can still sample the pungent spring water from the original 1830 pump (free), tucked away inside the Main Hall, and climb up to the Gallery for a closer look at the elegant interior and cupola.

East Approach Dr., Pittville Park (2 miles north of the center). www.cheltenhamtownhall.org.uk. (℗ **0844/576-2210.** Free admission. Wed–Sun 10am–4pm. From the town center, take Portland St. and Evesham Rd.

Where to Eat

For a cheap but classic **afternoon tea** in Cheltenham aim for the charming **Well Walk Tea Room** ★★, 5–6 Well Walk (www.wellwalktearoom.co.uk; (℗ **01242/ 574546**), open Monday to Saturday 10am to 5pm. Burford baker and tearoom **Huffkins** ★ also has a branch at 25 Promenade (www.huffkins.com; (℗ **01242/ 539372**). It's open Monday to Friday 9am to 5pm, Saturday 9am to 5:30pm, and Sunday 10am to 5pm.

Brasserie Blanc ★ FRENCH/CONTEMPORARY ENGLISH   Already a bit of a dining legend in Oxford, Master Chef Raymond Blanc's *brasserie de luxe* has decor inspired by turn-of-the-20th-century Paris, a row of unusual sculptures that runs up the middle, and a hip and knowledgeable staff. Cuisine is beautifully presented and prepared with the freshest available ingredients. Mouth-watering examples include Raymond's hot smoked salmon and haddock fishcake; Loch Fyne mussels in white wine and cream; and pork and leek sausages, with chive and mustard butter sauce and mash.

Queen's Hotel, the Promenade. www.brasserieblanc.com. © **01242/266801.** Reservations recommended. Main courses £9.50–£18.20 dinner; fixed-price 2-course lunch £12.50, 3-course lunch £14.95; fixed-price 2-course dinner £16, 3-course dinner £18.45. AE, DC, MC, V. Daily noon–2:45pm and 5:30–10:30pm.

Daffodil ★ CONTEMPORARY ENGLISH It's hard to top this magnificent setting in the auditorium of a former 1920s' Art Deco cinema, where the old movie screen has been replaced with the kitchen. The food is top-notch—check out the homemade salmon fishcakes or roast wood pigeon—and the service is usually friendly and attentive, but it can be hit and miss when it gets busy. It is best to avoid the restaurant altogether during the Christmas office-party season.

18–20 Suffolk Parade. www.thedaffodil.com. © **01242/700055.** Reservations recommended. Main courses £12.95–£23.95. Fixed-price lunch £13.50 for 2 courses, £15.50 for 3 courses. AE, DC, MC, V. Mon–Fri noon–2pm and 6:30–10pm; Sat noon–2pm and 6–10:30pm.

Le Champignon Sauvage ★★ FRENCH This Michelin-star winner is among the culinary highlights of the Cotswolds, with superb French cuisine and especially scrumptious desserts. Main courses can include such artfully crafted dishes as wood pigeon with a carrot tagine; lamb with pea purée, pistachio, and wilted lettuce; and hake poached with artichokes. Dessert options include a sensational bitter chocolate and olive tart with fennel ice cream, and a tongue-tingling salted chicory iced mousse. The downside? It's expensive (of course), and the decor is a bit dull considering the quality of the food.

24–26 Suffolk Rd. www.lechampignonsauvage.co.uk. © **01242/573449.** Reservations required. Set lunch £26 2 course, £32 3 courses; set dinner £48 2 courses, £59 3 courses. AE, DC, MC, V. Tues–Sat 12:30–2:30pm and 7:30–8:45pm. Closed 2 weeks in June, 1 week in Dec.

Shopping

Trawl the **Montpellier quarter** for individual boutiques, crafts, and specialty shops. The **Courtyard,** on Montpellier Street in the heart of the quarter, is an award-winning shopping mall that offers a blend of shops specializing in fashion, furniture, and gift items. From Montpellier, continue to the nearby **Suffolk quarter** (around Suffolk Parade) to find most of Cheltenham's antiques stores, as well as a growing number of artisan jewelers, clothes and accessories, rugs, and prints shops.

An enjoyable short stroll along the **Promenade** takes you by stores featuring clothing and shoes, as well as several bookstores. **Cavendish House,** on the Promenade (© **01242/521300**), has been a department store since 1823, and is now part of the House of Fraser group.

The Promenade ends at the **High Street,** which is mostly pedestrian-only, and you'll find several brand-name department stores in the nearby **Beechwood Shopping Centre.**

The **weekly market** is in the Henrietta Street parking lot on Thursday (9am–2pm), while a **Farmers' Market** is held on the second and last Friday of the month on the Promenade (9am–3pm).

Entertainment & Nightlife

The major venue for entertainment is the **Everyman Theatre,** Regent Street (www.everymantheatre.org.uk; ☎ **01242/572573**). Designed in the 1890s, the theatre attracts some of England's top dramatic companies with a program of Shakespeare, musicals, comedies, and other genres. Most tickets range from £12 to £55, depending on the event.

You'll find more theatre at the **Playhouse,** Bath Road (www.playhousecheltenham.org; ☎ **01242/522852**), which often presents new local, amateur productions of drama, comedy, dance, and opera staged every 2 weeks. Tickets usually run from £12 to £35.

THE PUB & BAR SCENE

The Beehive, 1–3 Montpellier Villas (www.thebeehivemontpellier.com; ☎ **01242/702270**), is an award-winning pub known for its fine local ales (including Battledown Brewery), Thatchers ciders, board games, a superb upstairs restaurant, and courtyard garden. The pub is open daily noon to midnight. The **Royal Well Tavern,** 5 Royal Well Place (www.theroyalwelltavern.com; ☎ **01242/221212**), is more of a gastropub serving fine food, but it's also great for wine.

For something a little more sophisticated, the **Montpellier Wine Bar,** Bayshill Lodge, Montpellier Street (www.montpellierwinebar.com; ☎ **01242/527774**), offers alfresco dining and a decent selection of wines by the glass (open daily 10am–11pm).

Subtone, 117 Promenade (www.subtone.co.uk; ☎ **01242/575925**), is Cheltenham's most popular nightclub and live music venue, with a host of visiting DJs and bands from around the globe (open Thurs–Sat 9pm–3 or 5am; cover £2–£7). Cocktails, jazz-funk DJs and sushi rule at super-cool **D'Fly,** 1a Crescent Place (www.dflycheltenham.co.uk; ☎ **01242/246060**).

Where to Stay

Beaumont House   One of the best-rated guesthouses in the area, this house is set in a lovely garden a short walk from the town center. Its luxurious bedrooms are among the best in Cheltenham—indeed, they've won awards. No two guest rooms are alike, ranging from small singles to spacious rooms suitable for families. Comfort and style combine with a warm welcome to make this a desirable choice—and the price is right, too.

56 Shurdington Rd., Cheltenham, Gloucestershire GL53 0JE. www.bhhotel.co.uk. ☎ **01242/223311**. Fax 01242/520044. 16 units. £89–£175 double; £249 suite. AE, MC, V. Free parking. **Amenities:** Bar. *In room:* TV, hair dryer, Wi-Fi (free).

George Hotel ★   This elegant hotel, set in a Regency-period building from the 1840s, is the top choice in town, perfectly located 2 minutes from the Promenade. The interior is chic and contemporary; small and standard doubles are modern and comfy but nothing special, with the superior and deluxe doubles considerably more stylish.

St George's Rd., Cheltenham, Gloucestershire GL50 3DZ. www.stayatthegeorge.co.uk. ☎ **01242/235751**. Fax 01242/224359. 21 units. £125–£165 double; £185 suite. AE, DC, MC, V. Free parking. **Amenities:** Restaurant; bar; room service; free membership at CLC Sports Centre. *In room:* TV, hair dryer, Internet (free).

Lypiatt House ★ 🎇   Offering the best-value accommodations in town, this beautifully restored Victorian home stands in the Montpellier area, the most fashionable part of Cheltenham. Bedrooms are spacious and beautifully furnished with a mix of modern and original Victorian fittings, the friendly owners are incredibly helpful, and there's an elegant drawing room with a colonial-style conservatory and "honesty bar."

Lypiatt Rd., Cheltenham, Gloucestershire GL50 2QW. www.lypiatt.co.uk. © **01242/224994.** Fax 01242/224996. 10 units. £95–£130 double. Rates include English breakfast. AE, MC, V. Free parking. **Amenities:** Bar. *In room:* TV, Wi-Fi (free).

Portland Apartments ★★   These luxurious serviced apartments on the edge of the town center are an especially good choice for families or longer stays. You get a fully equipped kitchen (with Dulce Gusto coffee machines for espresso snobs), washing machine, spacious lounge, and separate bedroom, though the six apartments do feature different decor; we like the African-themed Battledown suite (with the zebra painting), but the Montpellier suite is the best choice if you're looking to re-live the opulent heyday of Regency Cheltenham.

43 Portland St., Cheltenham, Gloucestershire GL52 2NX. www.pachcltenham.com. © **01242/ 525547.** 6 units. £99–£129 apartments. Rates include breakfast. AE, DC, MC, V. Free parking. *In room:* TV, DVD, kitchen, washer/dryer, hair dryer, Wi-Fi (free).

Strozzi Palace ★★   For something a bit different, try these stunning Italian-themed boutique luxury suites (there's a key code system, no reception or staff, but suites are serviced every day), just 5 minutes walk from the center. The building dates from 1894, and the facade really was based on the Palazzo Strozzi in Florence. Each suite has a kitchen, flat-screen TV, and rainshower—the smallest, cheapest, but coolest is the Roma studio, which features a sky-view atrium with retractable roof. No children under 12.

55 St. George's Place, Cheltenham, Gloucestershire GL50 3LA. www.strozzipalace.co.uk.© **01242/ 650028.** 6 units. £89–£129 suites. Rates include breakfast. AE, MC, V. Free parking if booked on-line (otherwise £6.75 per day). *In room:* TV, DVD, kitchen, hair dryer, Wi-Fi (free).

Side Trips from Cheltenham

Sudeley Castle & Gardens ★ CASTLE   This 15th-century mansion is one of England's finer stately homes. It has a rich history that began in 1442, when it was built by Baron Ralph Boteler, passing to the royal family just 25 years later. In 1548, Catherine Parr, the sixth wife of Henry VIII, lived and died here. Her marble tomb is in St. Mary's chapel on the grounds.

After the English Civil War the castle was virtually abandoned, and only restored in the Victorian period. For the past 40 years, Lady Ashcombe, an American by birth, has owned the castle with her children, often struggling to keep it open. The castle houses many works of art by Constable, Turner, Rubens, and Van Dyck, among others, and has several permanent exhibitions of magnificent furniture and glass, and many artifacts from the castle's past. To tour the private apartments, there is an additional cost of £13 per person. These highly recommended "connoisseur tours" are available Tuesday to Thursday at 11am, 1, and 3pm and include the stone-built drawing room, the library, and the billiard room.

Winchcombe, 6 miles northeast of Cheltenham. www.sudeleycastle.co.uk. © **01242/602308.** Admission £11 adults, £10 seniors, £6.50 children 5–15, £33 family ticket. Castle Apr–Oct daily 10:30am–5pm (last admission 4:30pm); closed Nov–Mar. From Cheltenham, take the regular bus to Winchcombe and get off at Abbey Terrace. Then walk the short distance along the road to the castle. If you're driving, take the B4632 north out of Cheltenham, through Prestbury, and up Cleve Hill to Abbey Terrace, where you can drive right up to the castle.

GLOUCESTER

Just 10 miles west of Cheltenham, the medieval city of **Gloucester** gets far fewer visitors, despite being the county town of Gloucestershire. Though it remains a bit rough around the edges, much has been done to improve the center in recent years, with pleasant, pedestrianized thoroughfares and a host of medieval and Tudor relics.

The main attraction is **Gloucester Cathedral** ★★ (daily 8am–6pm; www.gloucester cathedral.org.uk; free) off Westgate Street, the greatest example of grandiose Perpendicular style in the country. Note in particular the spectacular **East Window** ★, completed in the 1350s and the largest medieval window in Britain; and the graceful **Cloisters,** completed in 1367 with the first fan vaulting in the country (you might recognize this area from the *Harry Potter* movies). The cathedral also contains the tombs and effigies of some of the most illustrious failures of medieval England, notably the pinnacle-smothered Gothic marble shrine to **Edward II** (murdered in 1327), and an effigy of **Robert Curthose,** eldest son of William the Conqueror but destined never to rule England. Look out for the small memorial to John Stafford Smith, born here in 1750 and later the writer of the U.S. national anthem. You can also clamber up the 269 steps of the 69-m (225-ft.) **Tower** ★ for mesmerizing views of the surrounding countryside (Apr–Oct Wed–Sat afternoons only; £3 adults, £1 children). Admission to the cathedral is free, but adults are asked for a donation of £5.

Near the cathedral on narrow College Court, Beatrix Potter fans should visit the **House of the Tailor of Gloucester** (✆ 01452/422856; Mon–Sat 10am–5pm, Sun noon–4pm; free), home of one of her fictional characters and now a small shrine (and store) dedicated to the author.

If you have more time, stroll over to the revitalized Gloucester Docks area and the illuminating **Gloucester Waterways Museum** (www.gloucesterwaterwaysmuseum. org.uk; ✆ 01452/318200), which covers just about everything associated with Britain's extensive canal network through historic boats, hands-on displays, and archive films. The museum opens daily 11am to 4pm (July–Aug 10:30am–5pm). Admission is £4.95 for adults, £3.95 for over-60s, £3.50 for children 4 to 16, and free for children 3 and under.

Trains regularly connect Gloucester and Cheltenham (round-trip £4.20); Gloucester station is a short walk from the center. The **information center** is at 28 Southgate St. (www.thecityofgloucester.co.uk; ✆ 01452/396572), open Monday 10am–5pm and Tuesday to Saturday 9:30am–5pm.

Where to Eat

Take lunch or afternoon tea at the delightful **Lily's Restaurant & Tea Room,** 5A College Court, near the cathedral (www.lilysrestaurant.co.uk; ✆ 01452/307060), or grab a pint at the **New Inn** (www.newinngloucester.com; ✆ 01452/522177) at 16 Northgate St., one of the few galleried coaching inns dating from the Middle Ages.

PAINSWICK ★

This sleepy stone-built Cotswold wool town, 10 miles southwest of Cheltenham, vies with Bibury for the title of the most beautiful in the region. Its mellow gray stone houses and inns date from as early as the 14th century. It's best admired by strolling down ironically named **New Street** in the center of the village, which dates from 1450.

St. Mary's Church, the centerpiece of the village, was originally built between 1377 and 1399, and was reconstructed into its present form in 1480. Its churchyard contains 99 massive yew trees, each of which is at least 200 years old. Local legend states that no matter how hard well-meaning gardeners have tried, they've never been able to grow more than 99 of them.

Painswick Rococo Garden ★, on the B4073, a half-mile north of Painswick (www.rococogarden.co.uk; ✆ **01452/813204**), is a rare English garden from the flamboyant rococo period, which dominated art and design in England from 1720 to 1760. Today, the garden is best known for its spectacular display of snowdrops that appear in the early spring, sometimes when snow is still on the ground. Admission is £6.50 for adults, £5.50 for seniors, £3 for children 5 to 16, and £17 for a family ticket (two adults, two children); visits are possible from mid-January to October, daily 11am to 5pm.

Bus no. 46 links Cheltenham Promenade and Painswick every hour (reduced service Sun), taking around 30 minutes.

Where to Eat & Stay

By far the hippest place to stay around here is **Cotswold 88 ★★**, Kemps Lane (www.cotswolds88hotel.com; ✆ **01452/813688**), a former vicarage turned stylish boutique with rooms decorated with works by photo artists David Hiscock and Leigh Bowery. Its similarly fashionable restaurant and bar serve afternoon tea, modern English cuisine, and snappy cocktails with a view.

If you're looking for something simpler (and cheaper), opt for the **Royal Oak ★**, St. Mary's St. (www.theroyaloakpainswick.co.uk; ✆ **01452/813129**), which serves excellent pub food, real ales (including local organic ale from Stroud Brewery), and Thatcher's Heritage and Black Rat farmhouse ciders.

BOURTON-ON-THE-WATER ★

85 miles NW of London; 36 miles NW of Oxford

The quintessential Cotswold village, Bourton-on-the-Water tends to be overrun with tourists and bus tours all year, especially in summer. Get up early enough though and you'll still experience the magic that attracted them in the first place; a dream-like collection of 15th- and 16th-century stone cottages, willow trees, and five romantic stone bridges over the River Windrush. Perhaps, like radio DJ and part-time travel writer Stuart Maconie, you'll be "zombified by the sheer pleasantness" of it all.

Essentials

Hereford-bound First Great Western trains run hourly from London's Paddington Station to nearby Moreton-in-Marsh, a trip of 1½ hours (£32 one-way). From here, bus no. 801, operated by **Pulham's Bus Company** (www.pulhamscoaches.com; ✆ **01451/820369**), travels the 6 miles to Bourton-on-the-Water (40 min.) around nine times daily. The same bus stops at Stow-on-the-Wold and terminates at Cheltenham Royal Wells Bus Station (35 min. from Bourton).

If you're driving from Oxford, head west on the A40 to the junction with the A429 (Fosse Way). Take it northeast to Bourton-on-the-Water. Parking is notoriously difficult—try to arrive early.

Exploring the Area

Once you've soaked up the bucolic charms of the village (preferably at the crack of dawn), make time for attractions in the surrounding area, best explored by car. Within

THE GREAT COTSWOLD ramble

One of southern England's most inspiring walks, the well-worn footpath known as **Warden's Way** meanders for 13 miles beside the edge of the swift-moving River Eye, between Winchcombe and Bourton-on-the-Water. If you're short of time, try the section between the villages of Upper and Lower Slaughter (1 mile each way), with an optional extension to Bourton-on-the-Water (2½ miles). From its well-marked beginning in Upper Slaughter's central parking lot, the path passes sheep grazing in meadows, elegantly weathered houses crafted from local honey-colored stone, stately trees arching over ancient millponds, and footbridges that have endured centuries of pedestrian traffic and rain.

the town itself is a handful of mildly interesting museums, each of which was established from idiosyncratic collections amassed over the years by local residents. Children might enjoy the **Bourton Model Railway Exhibition & Toy Shop,** High Street (www.bourtonmodelrailway.co.uk; ✆ **01451/820686;** £2.75 adults, £2.25 seniors and children 5–15; June–Aug daily 11am–5pm, Sept–May Sat–Sun 11am–5pm; closed Jan), and the **Model Village at the Old New Inn,** High Street (www.theoldnewinn.co.uk/village.htm; ✆ **01451/820467**), a scale model (1:9) of Bourton-on-the-Water completed in 1937. Though it's realistic and big enough that you can walk through it, the models haven't been touched up in years and it's rather pricey considering you'll be finished in 15 minutes. Admission is £3.60 adults, £3.20 for seniors, £2.80 for children 4 to 13, and free for children 3 and under. It's open daily 10am to 5:45pm (winter daily 10am–3:45pm).

Birdland ☺ ZOO   This handsomely designed attraction sits on 8½ acres of field and forests on the banks of the River Windrush, about 1 mile east of Bourton-on-the-Water. It houses about 500 birds, including three species of penguins, guaranteed to amuse even the most jaded of children. Other feathered friends include pelicans, storks, flamingos, cranes, parrots, toucans, kookaburras, and pheasants. Birdland also has a picnic area and a children's playground.

Rissington Rd. www.birdland.co.uk. ✆ **01451/820480.** Admission £8.25 adults, £7.25 seniors, £5.25 children 3–15, £25 family ticket, free for children 2 and under. Apr–Oct daily 10am–6pm; Nov–Mar daily 10am–4pm (last admission 1 hr. before closing).

Cotswold Motoring Museum & Toy Collection ☺ MUSEUM   Children and adults will love this collection of vintage cars, motorcycles, caravans, and associated bric-a-brac. The exhibits include everything from London taxis and Morris Minors to Brough Superior bikes and a plush Jaguar XK140. Some youngsters might especially enjoy seeing the little car from the BBC TV show *Brum,* which was filmed here.

Sherborne St. www.csmaclubretreats.co.uk. ✆ **01451/821255.** Admission £4.50 adults, £3.20 children 4–16, £13.99 family ticket, free for children 3 and under. Mid-Feb–mid-Dec daily 10am–6pm. Closed late Dec–early Feb.

Cotswold Perfumery ★ FACTORY TOUR   This perfume maker has been in business since 1965, one of only a handful in Europe that make and sell their products on site. Perfumes are sold in the shop, ranging from £2 to £35 each, depending on their size. To get a greater understanding of what goes into them, take the

45-minute factory tour, which also chronicles the history of the perfume industry and its production (tours must be pre-booked).

Victoria St. www.cotswold-perfumery.co.uk. ℂ **01451/820698.** Factory tours £5 adults, £3.50 children 4–16. Mon–Sat 9:30am–5pm; Sun 10:30am–5pm. Closed Dec 25–26.

Cotswold Pottery ★ ARTS & CRAFTS   Tucked away at the back of the village, this delightful ceramics workshop is the home and studio of artists John and Jude Jelfs (John is a wheel-thrown pot specialist, while Jude focuses on hand-built sculpture). You'll often be able to see them working inside, where examples of their exceptional pieces are on sale, from mugs and teapots to larger ornamental pots and sculpture.

Clapton Row. www.cotswoldpottery.co.uk. ℂ **01451/820173.** Free admission. Mon–Sat 9:30am–5pm; Sun 10:30am–5pm.

Where to Eat & Stay

Chester House Hotel ★   This Victorian house, built on the banks of the Windrush River, offers immaculate rooms that mix a fresh contemporary style with antique beds and fittings (some with four-posters). The **Chester House bar and lounge** is a great place to eat, open from 9am for morning coffee and serving contemporary French and English food and snacks until 5pm. The bar is open for drinks until 11pm.

Victoria St., Bourton-on-the-Water, Cheltenham, Gloucestershire GL54 2BU. www.chesterhouse hotel.com. ℂ **01451/820286.** Fax 01451/820471. 22 units. £90–£125 double; £125–£155 family room. Rates include English breakfast. AE, MC, V. Closed Jan. Free parking. **Amenities:** Restaurant; bar; babysitting. *In room:* TV, hair dryer, Wi-Fi (free).

Cranbourne House ★★   This is the best B&B in town, a short walk from the center. Rooms are richly equipped and decorated, mainly with adorable French period furnishings dating from the 1890s. Breakfasts here are particularly good and worth lingering over; expect locally sourced full English fry-ups, oatmeal, fresh fruit, jams, smoked trout, and black pudding (blood sausage). Homemade cakes, tea, coffee, and hot chocolate are laid on in the afternoon.

Moore Rd., Bourton-on-the-Water, Cheltenham, Gloucestershire GL54 2AZ. www.cranbourne housebandb.co.uk. ℂ **01451/821883.** Fax 01451/821883. 6 units. £78–£130 double. Rate includes English breakfast. MC, V. Free parking. **Amenities:** Wi-Fi in public areas (free). *In room:* TV, hair dryer.

Dial House Hotel ★   The top hotel in town is also the oldest structure and the best place to eat. The house dates back to 1698 and is set in 1½ acres of manicured gardens, overlooking the River Windrush. Each room has individual character, and some boast four-poster beds. Two of the rooms, as charming as those in the main building, are in a converted coach house. Log fires burn on chilly nights, and there are two small dining rooms, one with an inglenook fireplace. The **restaurant** features artfully crafted seasonal dinner menus, playful twists on English, French, and continental classics.

The Chestnuts, High St., Bourton-on-the-Water, Gloucestershire GL54 2AN. www.dialhousehotel. com. ℂ **01451/822244.** Fax 01451/810126. 14 units. £155–£255 double. Rates include English breakfast. MC, V. Free parking. **Amenities:** Restaurant; bar; room service. *In room:* TV, hair dryer, Wi-Fi (free).

Old Manse Hotel ★ 📖   An architectural gem, the Old Manse sits in the center of town by the river. Built of Cotswold stone in 1748, with chimneys, dormers, and small-paned windows, it has been frequently modernized. Rooms are midsize and cozy, much like something you'd find in the home of your favorite great-aunt.

Victoria St., Bourton-on-the-Water, Cheltenham, Gloucestershire GL54 2BX. www.oldenglishinns. co.uk/bourton-water. © **01451/820082.** Fax 01451/810381. 15 units. £70–£109 double. Rates include English breakfast. AE, DC, MC, V. Free parking. **Amenities:** Restaurant; bar. *In room:* TV, hair dryer, Wi-Fi (free).

Side Trips from Bourton-on-the-Water
UPPER & LOWER SLAUGHTER ★★

Nestled between Bourton-on-the-Water (2 miles) and Stow-on-the-Wold (4 miles) are two of the prettiest villages in the Cotswolds: Upper and Lower Slaughter. Don't be put off by the name—"Slaughter" is actually a corruption of *de Sclotre,* the name of the original Norman landowner. Houses here are constructed of the usual honey-colored Cotswold stone, and a stream meanders right through the center of Lower Slaughter, providing a home for free-wandering ducks, which beg scraps from kindly passersby.

The only conventional "sight" here is the **Old Mill** in Lower Slaughter (www. oldmill-lowerslaughter.com; © **01451/820052**), a sturdy 19th-century stone structure built on the River Eye with the sole purpose of grinding out flour. Entrance to the mill costs £1.25 for adults, and 50p for children 5 to 15, which also includes an ice-cream parlor and tearoom (daily 10am–6pm).

To reach Lower Slaughter from Bourton-on-the-Water, head west along Lansdowne Road, turning right (north) onto the A436; after a short distance, you'll see a signpost pointing left into Lower Slaughter along an unmarked road. The walk along the river to Upper Slaughter takes around 1 hour (see "The Great Cotswold ramble," above).

Where to Eat & Stay

Lords of the Manor Hotel ★★★   A 17th-century manor house set on several acres of rolling fields, the Lords of the Manor successfully maintains the quiet country-house atmosphere of 300 years ago. Set within gardens with a stream featuring brown trout, it offers luxurious, modern rooms and exceptional service. Half the rooms are in a converted old barn and granary, and many have heart-melting views.

Upper Slaughter, Gloucestershire GL54 2JD. www.lordsofthemanor.com. © **01451/820243.** Fax 01451/820696. 27 units. £199–£390 double; £495 suite. Rates include English breakfast. AE, DC, MC, V. **Amenities:** Restaurant; bar; room service. *In room:* TV/DVD, minibar, hair dryer, MP3 docking station.

Lower Slaughter Manor ★★   This is another atmospheric country inn with spacious and sumptuously furnished rooms, some with four-poster beds. Bedrooms in the main building have more old English character, although those in the annex are equally comfortable and include the same luxuries. The hotel dates from 1658, when it was owned by Sir George Whitmore, high sheriff of Gloucestershire.

Lower Slaughter, Gloucestershire GL54 2HP. www.lowerslaughter.co.uk. © **01451/820456.** Fax 01451/822150. 19 units. £150–£272 double; £295–£425 suite. Rates include English breakfast. AE, DC, MC, V. No children 11 and under. **Amenities:** Restaurant; lounge; tennis court; room service. *In room:* TV, hair dryer, Internet (free).

STOW-ON-THE-WOLD ★

21 miles S of Stratford-upon-Avon; 9 miles SE of Broadway; 10 miles S of Chipping Campden; 4 miles S of Moreton-in-Marsh

Straggling along the top of a 240-m (800-ft.) escarpment, the old wool town of Stow-on-the-Wold makes an enticing base for exploring the northern Cotswolds.

The town grew to prominence as a major sheep market, with alleyways known as "tures" running between the buildings once used to herd flocks into the square to be sold. The handsome market square is still there, but the sheep have gone, replaced by cafes, pubs, and antique shops. These days the town's market roots are maintained by the **Stow Fair,** a traditional bi-annual horse market attended by Romani people (or "Travelers") from all over the country. It's a colorful but controversial event, with thousands descending on the area (many in traditional horse-drawn caravans), on the nearest Thursdays to May 12 and October 24. Locals are divided about the disruption it often causes, but the market can be fun to visit, with horse trading enlivened by young Romani woman parading the town in their finest (and brightest) threads.

Essentials

GETTING THERE   Several First Great Western trains run daily from London's Paddington Station to Moreton-in-Marsh, a trip of 1½ hours (£29 one-way). From Moreton-in-Marsh, **Pulham's** (www.pulhamscoaches.com; ✆ **01451/820369**) runs frequent buses to Stow-on-the-Wold (20 min.) and on to Bourton-on-the-Water (10 min.) and Cheltenham (50 min.).

If you're driving from Oxford, take the A40 west to the junction with the A424, near Burford. Head northwest along the A424 to Stow-on-the-Wold.

VISITOR INFORMATION   The privately run **Tourist Information Centre** (Go-Stow) is at 12 Talbot Court and Sheep Street (www.go-stow.co.uk; ✆ **01451/870150**). It's usually open Monday to Saturday 10am to 5pm, and Sunday 11am to 4pm, with reduced hours in winter (Nov–Easter; it tends to opens at 11am and closes between 3 and 5pm most days, but call ahead to confirm).

Exploring the Area

Other than browsing the shops and pubs, there's not a lot to see in the town itself beyond the 15th-century **Market Cross** in the Market Square, the old wooden **stocks** on the green (where offenders would be pelted with eggs), and the stately **Church of St. Edward,** built between the 11th and the 15th centuries. The **Royalist Hotel,** at the end of Digbeth Street, is said to be the oldest inn in England, with parts of it dating back to the first incarnation of A.D. 947.

Chastleton House ★★ HISTORIC SITE   Make time for this captivating Jacobean country house, built between 1607 and 1612 by a prosperous Welsh wool merchant. What makes this place different is the state of the interior; the Jones family owned the property, little-changed, until 1991. The National Trust has since preserved the time-warped flavor of the rooms, with no ropes or barriers, and the kitchen ceiling is still blackened by soot—it's like stepping back into the 17th century. The extensive gardens also include England's first ever croquet lawn (the laws of the game were codified here in 1865).

Chastleton, Oxfordshire, 5 miles east of Stow-on-the-Wold via the A436. www.nationaltrust.org.uk/main/w-chastleton. ✆ **01494/755560.** Admission £8.25 adults, £3.85 children 5–15, free for children 4 and under, £20.25 family ticket. Apr–Sept Wed–Sat 1–5pm; Mar and Oct Wed–Sat 1–4pm. Admission by timed ticket (180 available each day). Last admission 1 hr. before closing.

Cotswold Falconry Centre ☺ ZOO   For a fascinating lesson on birds of prey, stop by this family-friendly bird center, housing between 80 to 100 eagles, hawks, and falcons. You'll also see over 40 owls, mean-looking vultures, and rare caracara, many of which are bred at the center.

Don't be fooled by the village's sleepy, country setting: Stow-on-the-Wold has developed over the last 20 years into the antiques buyer's highlight of Britain, boasting at least 60 merchandisers scattered throughout the village and its environs.

Set within four showrooms inside an 18th-century building on the town's main square, **Antony Preston Antiques Ltd.** (www.antonypreston.com; ✆ **01451/ 831586**) specializes in English and French furniture, including some large pieces such as bookcases, and decorative objects that include paperweights, lamps, and paintings on silk.

Baggott Church Street Ltd., Church Street (www.baggottantiques.com; ✆ **01451/830370**), is the smaller, and perhaps more intricately decorated, of two shops founded and maintained by a local antiques merchant, Duncan ("Jack") Baggott, a frequent denizen at estate sales of country houses throughout Britain. The shop contains four showrooms loaded with furniture and paintings from the 17th to the 19th centuries.

Covering about half a block in the heart of town, **Huntington's Antiques Ltd.,** Sheep Street (www.huntington-antiques.com; ✆ **01451/830842**), contains one of the largest stocks of quality antiques in England. Wander at will through 10 street-level rooms, and then climb to the next floor where a long gallery and a quartet of additional showrooms bulge with refectory tables, unusual cupboards, and all kinds of finds. Shops tend to open Monday to Saturday 10am to 5pm, with limited hours in winter and on Sundays.

Batsford Park (just north of Moreton-in-Marsh, off the A429). www.cotswold-falconry.co.uk. ✆ **01386/701043.** Admission £8 adults, £6 seniors and students, £4 children 4–14, free for children 3 and under, £20 family ticket. Mid-Feb–mid-Nov daily 10:30am–5:30pm. Flying displays daily at 11:30am, 1:30, and 3pm.

Daylesford Organic Farm Shop ★ SHOP   The "poshest shop in England" sells incredibly fresh organic produce from the farm, garden, creamery, and bakery owned by Sir Anthony and Lady Bamford. It's worth a visit just to sample the goods at the adjacent cafe. Explore the farm by following signposted footpaths across the property.

Daylesford, near Kingham (from Stow-on-the-Wold, take the A356 east). www.daylesfordorganic. com. ✆ **01608/731700.** Free admission. Mon–Wed 9am–5pm; Thurs–Sat 9am–6pm; Sun 10am–4pm.

Donnington Trout Farm FARM   This small family farm raises both brown and rainbow trout in spring-fed tanks and ponds. The shop sells smoked trout, eel, and salmon from the on-site smokery, as well as their justly celebrated smoked trout pâté. They also offer fly-fishing on the farm (call for more details).

Upper Swell, Gloucestershire (from Stow-on-the-Wold, take the B4077 1 mile west to Upper Swell). www.donningtontrout.co.uk. ✆ **01451/830873.** Free admission. Tues–Sat 10am–5:30pm.

Rollright Stones ★ HISTORIC SITE   Some 6 miles east of Stow-on-the-Wold, these enigmatic Stone Age monuments date back an astounding 4,000 years, though their purpose remains a mystery. Not as dramatic as Stonehenge, the weathered circle of 77 megalithic oolitic limestone blocks known as the King's Men is just as intriguing. The complex also includes the Bronze Age King Stone, and the much older

Whispering Knights, four standing stones thought to be part of a Neolithic tomb. Souvenirs and a booklet about the site can be purchased at Wyatts Farm Shop, 1 mile east of the Stones (across the crossroads on the way to Great Rollright), where there is also a cafe and restrooms.

Little Rollright, Oxfordshire. www.rollrightstones.co.uk. No phone. Admission £1 adults, 50p children 7–16. Daily sunrise to sunset. From Stow-on-the-Wold, take the A436 toward Chipping Norton, then the road to Little Rollright at the junction with the A44.

Where to Eat & Stay

EXPENSIVE

Fosse Manor Hotel ★ Fosse Manor offers great value for an English country-house experience. Built in a neo-Gothic style in 1901 by the Lord of Maugersbury Manor, it's been a hotel since the 1950s. Inside, the interior is conservatively modern, with compact but homey principal and superior bedrooms, and far more luxurious deluxe rooms. All rooms include DVD players or a Sony PlayStation (which can also play DVDs). The **restaurant** is top-notch, featuring modern British cooking with a rich array of locally sourced produce.

Fosseway, Stow-on-the-Wold, Cheltenham, Gloucestershire GL54 1JX. www.fossemanor.co.uk. ✆ **01451/830354.** Fax 01451/832486. 22 units. £80–£200 double. Rates include English breakfast. Children 9 and under stay free in parent's room. AE, DC, MC, V. Free parking. Take the A429 1¼ miles south of Stow-on-the-Wold. **Amenities:** Restaurant; bar; lounge; room service; DVD library; Wi-Fi in public areas (free). *In room:* TV/DVD, hair dryer.

Kings Arms ★★ The Kings Arms is a fine choice for real ale and pub food (think tankers of prawns and warm salt beef sandwiches), right in the center of town, but it's also an excellent B&B. Rooms are decorated in a contemporary Cotswold country style, with exposed stone walls and roof beams contrasting with the modern beds, drapes, and furnishings. The upscale **Chop House ★** restaurant cooks up some of the finest steaks, fish, and game in the region (Mon–Sat 6–9:30pm).

Market Sq., Stow-on-the-Wold, Gloucestershire GL54 1AF. www.kingsarmsstow.co.uk. ✆ **01451/830364.** 11 units. £100 double. Rates include English breakfast. AE, DC, MC, V. Free parking. **Amenities:** Restaurant; bar. *In room:* TV, Wi-Fi (free).

Number Four at Stow ★★★ Stow's best hotel is a stylish boutique that also operates one of the best restaurants in town, showcasing a seasonal menu of locally sourced produce. **Cutler's Restaurant ★★** offers the finest of modern British cooking, from its cream-of-parsnip soup to roast Cotswold partridge; Sunday lunches are a real treat. The hotel rooms are chic and contemporary with king-size beds and flat-screen TVs—no period decor and no antiques.

Fosseway, Stow-on-the-Wold, Cheltenham, Gloucestershire GL54 1JX. www.hotelnumberfour.co.uk. ✆ **01451/830297.** Fax 01451/831768. 18 units. £110–£120 double. AE, DC, MC, V. Free parking. **Amenities:** Restaurant; bar; lounge; room service. *In room:* A/C, TV, hair dryer, Wi-Fi (free).

Stow Lodge Hotel Venerable Stow Lodge was built as a Rectory in the mid-1700s, and is ideally located on the market square. Rooms are ample and well furnished in classic English country style, with plenty of flowery bedspreads and curtains, red carpets, and cozy armchairs; one has a four-poster bed. Rooms 17 and 18—the smallest in the hotel—share a private bathroom.

The Square, Stow-on-the-Wold, Cheltenham, Gloucestershire GL54 1AB. www.stowlodge.co.uk. ✆ **01451/830485.** Fax 01451/831671. 20 units. £88–£139 double. Rates include English breakfast. MC, V. Free parking. Closed mid-Dec–late Jan. No children 4 and under. **Amenities:** Restaurant; bar; room service, Wi-Fi (free in lounge). *In room:* TV, hair dryer.

MODERATE

Mole End ★★   This is consistently rated Stow's top B&B, with spacious, luxurious rooms decked out like a Victorian dolls house. Owners Trevor and Jane are incredibly thoughtful hosts, and the breakfasts will have you feeling warm and happy the entire day. Mole End is about a 10-minute walk from the market square on the edge of town, with open views of the surrounding country.

Moreton Rd., Stow-on-the-Wold, Gloucestershire GL54 1EG. www.moleendstow.co.uk. © **01451/870348.** 3 units. £85–£110 double. Rates include English breakfast. MC, V. Free parking. *In room:* TV, hair dryer, Wi-Fi (free).

BROADWAY ★

15 miles SW of Stratford-upon-Avon; 93 miles NW of London; 15 miles NE of Cheltenham

The Cotswolds is blessed with many beautiful villages, but Broadway is especially charming. Flanked by stone cottages and chestnut trees overlooking the Vale of Evesham, its **High Street** is a real gem, remarkable for its harmonious style and design. It tends to get swamped by coach tours in the summer, of course, and once you've walked up and down the main street, you've done Broadway. Yet most of the tourists are gone by evening and many prime attractions of the Cotswolds, and Shakespeare Country (p. 452), are nearby, making this an appealing alternative to Stow as a base for exploring the region.

Essentials

GETTING THERE   The nearest train stations are at Moreton-in-Marsh (7 miles away) or at Evesham (5 miles away). Buses to Broadway are infrequent, however, so it's best to take a taxi from either place (try Cotswold Horizons; © **01386/858599**).

If you're driving from Oxford, head west on the A40, and then take the A44 to Woodstock, Chipping Norton, and Moreton-in-Marsh.

VISITOR INFORMATION   The **Tourist Information Centre** is at Unit 14, Russell Square (www.beautifulbroadway.com; © **01386/852937**). The office is open year-round Monday to Friday 10am to 5pm, and Sunday 2 to 5pm.

Exploring the Area

Broadway's **High Street** ★★ is one of the most beautiful in England. Many of its striking facades date from 1620 or a century or two later. The most famous is that of the **Lygon Arms** (see below), a venerable inn that has been serving wayfarers since 1532. Even if you're not staying here, you may want to visit for a meal or a drink.

Broadway Tower OBSERVATION POINT   On the outskirts of Broadway stands this whimsical folly, created by Capability Brown for the 6th Earl of Coventry in 1798. You can climb the 17-m (55-ft.) tower on a clear day for a panoramic vista of 12 shires. It's the second highest point (312m/1,024 ft.), and the most awe-inspiring view in the Cotswolds. You can also bring a picnic here and eat lunch in the surrounding grounds.

Middle Hill, A44 (1 mile SE of Broadway). www.broadwaytower.co.uk. © **01386/852390.** Admission £4.50 adults, £2.50 children 4–14, £12 family ticket. Daily 10:30am–5pm.

Cotswold Lavender ★ FARM   Visit this fragrant lavender farm in high summer, when an ocean of lilacs, purples, and blues seems to stretch to the horizon. You can stroll into the middle of the fields, breathing in the aromas, buy the product in the

Broadway became the unlikely location of an **American artist colony** in the 1880s, where its two most notable members—writer Henry James and painter John Singer Sargent—came to soak up the Cotswolds landscape. Indeed, Sargent's first major success at the Royal Academy came in 1887, with his much-loved *Carnation, Lily, Lily, Rose*, an image of two young girls lighting lanterns in a Broadway garden. It's now owned by the Tate Gallery (p. 102). Today the 14th-century monastic ruin known as **Abbot's Grange,** which the artists restored and converted into a studio, is a gorgeous B&B (see www.abbotsgrange.com). Sadly, the town has no connection with New York's theatre district.

shop, or munch lavender scones, cakes, and shortbread in the Lavender Tea Room. Lavender planting started here in 2000, and today there are some 53 acres of lavender under cultivation.

Hill Barn Farm, Snowshill. www.cotswoldlavender.co.uk. ℭ **01386/854821.** Admission to shop free; admission to lavender fields during flowering £2.50 adults, £1.50 children 15 and under. Apr–May and Sept–Oct Wed–Sun 10am–5pm; June–Aug daily 10am–5pm.

Snowshill Manor OFFBEAT SITE   This pleasant Cotswold manor house owes its appeal to the bizarre collection of curios that lies within its honey-stone walls. Parts of the house date from around 1500, but most of what you see today was built in the 17th century. In 1919, the then-dilapidated house was purchased by Charles Paget Wade, a craftsman and eccentric who collected over 22,000 unusual handicrafts up to his death in 1951. You'll find a little bit of everything here: Flemish tapestries, toys, lacquer cabinets, narwhal tusks, mousetraps, and cuckoo clocks—a glorious mess, like a giant attic of the 20th century. The highlight is the collection of 26 suits of Samurai armor in the Green Room.

Snowshill, 3 miles south of Broadway. www.nationaltrust.org.uk/snowshill-manor. ℭ **01386/852410.** Admission £8.80 adults, £4.40 children 5–15, free for children 4 and under, £22.50 family ticket. Apr–June and Sept–Oct Wed–Sun noon–5pm; July–Aug Mon and Wed–Sun 11:30am–4:30pm. Admission by timed ticket. Last admission 4pm. Closed Nov–Mar.

Where to Eat & Stay

The best place in Broadway for a cup of tea is **Tisanes Tea Rooms,** 21 The Green (www.tisanes-tearooms.co.uk; ℭ **01386/853296**), offering perfectly blended teas with a variety of sandwiches and salads (daily 10am–5pm).

VERY EXPENSIVE

Dormy House Hotel ★★   Dormy House is pricey but exceptional, featuring rooms that blend the core of this 17th-century farmhouse with lavish, contemporary furnishings. The owners have also brought glamour to an old adjoining timbered barn, converted into two executive suites and eight deluxe doubles, a real step up in comfort from the standard doubles. The **Dining Room** ★★ and **Barn Owl Brasserie** ★ are both charming and well-managed restaurants; the former is open for dinner and a popular Sunday lunch (£23.50), turning out high-quality classics such as Warwickshire pork, local partridge, and Hereford beef, while the brasserie offers slightly cheaper but just as creative fare for lunch and dinner.

Willersey Hill, Broadway, Worcestershire WR12 7LF (take the A44 2 miles southeast of Broadway). www.dormyhouse.co.uk. © **01386/852711.** Fax 01386/858636. 48 units. £180–£200 double; £200 four-poster room; £210–£220 suite. Rates include English breakfast. AE, DC, MC, V. Free parking. Closed Dec 24–29. **Amenities:** Restaurant; bar; exercise room; room service; babysitting. *In room:* TV, hair dryer, Internet (free).

The Lygon Arms ★   It's not as good as it once was, but this many-gabled structure still basks in its reputation as one of the great old English inns. The oldest rooms date from 1532 or earlier, and the timber and flagstone floors, wood paneling, doors, and stone mullions have been retained. Standard doubles are comfy enough, with modern amenities, but the premium and deluxe doubles are worth the extra; you get a choice of swish, contemporary rooms with Bang & Olufsen sound system and flat-screen TV, or traditional rooms in the main house with beamed ceilings, antiques, and open fires.

High St., Broadway, Worcestershire WR12 7DU. www.barcelo-hotels.co.uk. © **01386/852255.** Fax 01386/854470. 78 units. £105–£223 double. AE, DC, MC, V. Free parking. **Amenities:** 2 restaurants; cafe; bar; pool (indoor); health club; spa; room service. *In room:* TV, hair dryer, Internet (£12 for 24 hr.).

EXPENSIVE

Russell's ★★   This chic boutique hotel is also one of the best places to eat in the region. If you've had enough of heritage hotels look no further; everything about the rooms is modern and stylish, from the art on the walls to the fixtures and flat-screen TVs. The food in the **restaurant** is high-quality bistro; bread is made here each morning while the menu features filo-baked goat cheese, fresh fish, sticky toffee pudding, and British cheeses. Expect sexy main courses (£14–£28) like Russell's crab cocktail, curried scallops, and Kalamata olive and rosemary gnocchi.

20 High St., Broadway, Worcestershire WR12 7DT. www.russellsofbroadway.co.uk. © **01386/ 853555.** 7 units. £98–£185 double. Rates include English breakfast. AE, DC, MC, V. Free parking. **Amenities:** Restaurant; bar. *In room:* TV, hair dryer, Internet (free).

MODERATE

The Olive Branch ★ 🍃   In the heart of an expensive village, this is a terrific bargain. The old coaching house, dating from 1592, retains its traditional Cotswold architectural features, as well as a walled English garden. Most rooms are decked out in white and light pinks, a simple but less chintzy interpretation of the usual country-house theme. One family room can accommodate up to four people, and one room has a four-poster bed.

78 High St., Broadway, Worcestershire WR12 7AJ. www.theolivebranch-broadway.com. © **01386/ 853440.** Fax 01386/859070. 8 units. £82–£110 double. Rates include English breakfast. AE, DC, MC, V. Free parking. **Amenities:** Lounge; Wi-Fi (free). *In room:* TV, minibar, hair dryer.

Windrush House ★★ 🍃   In high-priced Broadway, Evan and Judith Anderson run a congenial and affordable B&B. It's not your average guesthouse; bedrooms have been refurbished in a chic contemporary style more akin to a boutique, with individual color schemes, opulent fabrics, and flat-screen TVs. All rooms toy with traditional English design, but our favorite is the Bourton Room, which sports a hip Victorian neo-Gothic vibe. Breakfasts feature local produce and eggs laid by the owner's chickens.

Station Rd., Broadway, Worcestershire WR12 7DE. www.broadway-windrush.co.uk. © **01386/ 853577.** Fax 01386/852850. 4 units. £90 double. Rates include breakfast. AE, DC, MC, V. Free parking. *In room:* TV, hair dryer, Wi-Fi (free).

A Side Trip from Broadway: Chipping Campden ★★

Chipping Campden epitomizes the dreamy English village that you've seen depicted in a thousand postcards. Except for the heavy traffic, especially in summer, the long **High Street** still looks as it did centuries ago and it's lined with stone houses dating from the 16th century. One of the most arresting buildings along here is the arched **Market Hall,** erected in 1627 to provide shelter for the local produce market.

The village landmark is the soaring tower of the **Church of St. James** (www. stjameschurchcampden.co.uk; ✆ **01386/841927;** free admission, suggested donation £1), which dates back to 1260. It's open March to October Monday to Saturday 10am to 5pm, and Sundays 2 to 6pm (Nov and Feb Mon–Sat 11am–4pm, Sun 2–4pm; Dec–Jan Mon–Sat 11am–3pm, Sun 2–3pm).

The **Court Barn Museum** (www.courtbarn.org.uk; ✆ **01386/841951**), next to the church, celebrates the rich Arts and Crafts heritage of the area. C. R. Ashbee brought the Guild of Handicraft to Chipping Campden in 1902, and though it closed 6 years later, a tradition of craftsmanship remained in the village. The museum opens April to September Tuesday to Sunday 10am to 5pm (Oct–Mar 10am–4pm). Admission is £4 for adults and £3.25 for students and seniors (free for children 15 and under).

The **Old Silk Mill,** Sheep Street (Mon–Fri 9am–5pm, Sat 9am–noon), is where the Guild of Handicraft was actually established in 1902. Today it has been revived with a series of craft workshops. One of them is **Hart Gold & Silversmiths** (www. hartsilversmiths.co.uk; ✆ **01386/841100**), where silver and gold is expertly smithed by descendants of George Hart, an original member of the Guild of Handicraft.

Elsewhere, the **Robert Welch Studio Shop,** Lower High Street (www.welch. co.uk; ✆ **01386/840522**), is where the Welch family has been crafting silverware, stainless steel, and cutlery for more than 50 years. The shop is open Monday to Saturday 9:30am to 5:30pm and Sunday 10am to 4pm.

The **Tourist Information Centre** is at the Old Police Station, High Street (www. chippingcampdenonline.org; ✆ **01386/841206**). It's open daily 10am to 5:30pm in summer, and 10am to 1pm in the off season.

WHERE TO EAT & STAY

The Cotswold House Hotel ★★   This stately, formal Regency house, dating from 1800 and situated opposite the old wool market, is the best place to stay in the village. The four cottage bedrooms tucked away in the garden are more secluded and beautifully furnished; the Montrose Rooms include trendy touches such as color-changing shower lights, and sand and light sculptures. The inn-house **restaurant ★** and the garden terrace is the most romantic place to take **afternoon tea** in the village.

The Square, Chipping Campden, Gloucestershire GL55 6AN. www.cotswoldhouse.com. ✆ **01386/840330.** Fax 01386/840310. 30 units. £120–£220 double; £170–£320 cottage or suite. Rates include English breakfast. AE, MC, V. Free parking. **Amenities:** 2 restaurants; 2 bars; indoor pool; spa; room service; babysitting. In room: A/C (in suites), TV/DVD, minibar, hair dryer, Internet (free).

Ebrington Arms ★★ GASTROPUB   One of the best pubs in the Cotswolds, Ebrington Arms is 2 miles from Chipping Campden and best known for exceptional English food. The menu includes twists on traditional classics—ploughman's platter and a fine fish and chips—but also Cotswold lamb, pan-fried John Dory, and rabbit with pistachio mousse. Save room for the glazed rice pudding, or addictive marmalade bread and butter pudding. They also offer three cozy rooms (£100–£130) upstairs, including breakfast.

Ebrington, Chipping Campden. www.theebringtonarms.co.uk. © **01386/593223.** Reservations recommended. Main courses £11.50–£18. AE, MC, V. Free parking. Restaurant daily noon–2:30pm and 6:30–9pm (8:30pm Sun). Pub daily noon–midnight.

The Kings Hotel ★   The Kings is a solid 18th-century pub and restaurant choice in the heart of Chipping Campden. It's also another pub that doubles as a wonderfully atmospheric hotel, with 14 stylish rooms in the main house, and five cottage rooms that offer a little more space and luxury. When it comes to eating, the Kings boasts the best bar snacks in town, as well as real ales including local Hook Norton. Artfully prepared modern British food features at the main **restaurant** and the more informal **brasserie.** Expect dishes such as organic salmon filet with seafood bisque, wild rabbit dumplings, and homemade fudge.

The Square, Chipping Campden, Gloucestershire GL55 6AW. www.kingscampden.co.uk. © **01386/840256.** Fax 01386/841598. 19 units. £90–£195 double. Rates include English breakfast. AE, MC, V. Free parking. **Amenities:** 2 restaurants; bar. *In room:* TV, minibar, hair dryer, Wi-Fi (free).

Kissing Gate Bed & Breakfast ★★★ ✦   Fans of B&Bs will adore this mellow place in the quaint village of Ebrington, just 2 miles east of Chipping Campden. Welcoming hosts Anne and Dougal Bulger run an informal, friendly home with just three bright and airy rooms for a bargain price. You'll be treated to homemade cookies, fresh milk, and plenty of tea or coffee on arrival, and there's a common-use fridge, books, and board games to enjoy. Bacon, eggs, sausages, and fresh produce are all locally sourced.

Coldicott Leys, Ebrington, Chipping Campden, Gloucestershire GL55 6NZ. www.kissinggate.net. © **01386/593934.** 3 units. £80 double; £140 family room. Rates include English breakfast. AE, MC, V. Free parking. *In room:* TV, hair dryer, Wi-Fi (free).

THE HEART OF ENGLAND

by Stephen Keeling

The West Midlands occupies the heart of England, an incredibly dynamic region that contains the finest Shakespearean theatre in the world, the grandest medieval castle in the country, and is the birthplace of the Industrial Revolution. The clubs, pubs, and galleries of England's second city provide the contemporary allure, while the Welsh border country offers a pastoral and far less touristy contrast of small market towns and hiking trails.

SIGHTSEEING   Everyone makes a pilgrimage to Shakespeare's **Stratford,** of course, but don't skip **Warwick Castle,** an awe-inspiring example of medieval craftsmanship and power. Nearby **Coventry Cathedral** is a poignant reminder of the destructiveness of war, while cathedrals at Worcester and Hereford provide more conventional but equally jaw-dropping architecture. Even choco-skeptics should visit the spiritual home of British chocolate, **Cadbury World,** on the edge of Birmingham, where the aromas of melting cacao will have you converted before you can say "Fruit and Nut."

EATING & DRINKING   **Birmingham** is the culinary heart of the region, with all three of its top-rated restaurants—Purnell's, Simpsons, and Turners—more than a match for anything in London. Make time, though, for the real star of the city, the Pakistani-inspired Balti curry houses. South Asian food is especially good throughout the West Midlands, but you'll also find Michelin-rated gems in the most unlikely of places; many people journey to the small town of **Ludlow** just to eat.

HISTORY   **Stratford** is the most obvious historical target in the heart of England, but not just because of Shakespeare; its wonderfully preserved halls and houses offer an unusually authentic window into life in Tudor England. Georgian elegance is on full display in nearby **Leamington Spa,** while the grit, grime, and boundless invention that characterized the Industrial Revolution are commemorated at the enlightening museums of **Ironbridge** and the **Potteries.**

ARTS & CULTURE   Unsurprisingly, Birmingham is also the cultural capital of the West Midlands, with a rich spread of world-class performance spaces for theatre, ballet, and popular music. The **National**

Exhibition Centre is based here, and the city has also developed an exciting contemporary arts scene. Established venues such as the **Ikon Gallery** complement spaces for emerging artists in the Digbeth and Eastside areas.

THE best TRAVEL EXPERIENCES IN THE HEART OF ENGLAND

- **Seeing the Royal Shakespeare Company perform in Stratford:** The Royal Shakespeare Company is the world's premier ensemble when it comes to performing the Bard's full repertoire, and few experiences match seeing them perform in Stratford on a warm summer evening. The RSC Theatre by the river was recently given a gorgeous renovation. See p. 454.
- **Dining on a Balti:** If you like South Asian food you're in for a treat. Birmingham's Balti Triangle is crammed with cheap Indian and Pakistani restaurants touting a dish concocted by Kashmiri chefs right here. Seasoned and spicy meats are cooked fresh over a hot flame, and served in the pan with vegetables. See p. 474.
- **Cruising the canals of Birmingham:** It's not Venice, but Birmingham is laced with canals that offer a unique perspective on the city—its grim industrial past and its brighter present of renovated wharves, cafes, and shopping malls. Rides by barge are affordable and fun, and you can even rent your own boat. See p. 469.
- **Hiking the Malvern Hills:** Fine views and fresh walks are rarely so easily accessible, but the wonderfully rustic Malvern Hills lie just a short walk from Great Malvern station. Stroll the paths that inspired Edward Elgar, and rehydrate with the Queen's favorite spring water. See p. 480.
- **Crossing the Ironbridge:** Visit the cradle of the Industrial Revolution, stroll across the River Severn on the world's first iron bridge, and dip into the area's illuminating museums. See p. 488.

STRATFORD-UPON-AVON ★★

91 miles NW of London; 40 miles NW of Oxford; 8 miles S of Warwick

The birthplace of **William Shakespeare,** England's greatest playwright, Stratford commemorates the Bard with a spread of beautifully maintained historic sights from the Tudor period. The other major draw for visitors is the **Royal Shakespeare Theatre,** where Britain's foremost actors perform during a long season that lasts from April to November.

Shakespeare was born here in 1564, and though he spent most of his career in London, this otherwise plain-looking town has been cashing in on the connection ever since. Crowds, bus tours, and unashamed tourism now dominate the center, but visiting the sights themselves, and especially taking in a play or two, transports you right back to the 16th century.

Essentials

GETTING THERE Trains from London Marylebone to Stratford-upon-Avon take about 2¼ hours, with one-way tickets ranging from £15 to £46. Trains link Stratford with Birmingham Snow Hill station (55 min.) every hour, for £6.80, and less frequently, with Warwick (25 min.) for £5.

The Heart of England

452

Warwickshire: Shakespeare Country

The Royal Shakespeare Theatre

In Shakespeare's day, Stratford didn't have a theatre—all the Bard's plays were performed in London. The current red-brick **Royal Shakespeare Theatre** (www.rsc.org.uk; ✆ **01789/403444**) was completed in 1932 on the banks of the Avon, and reopened in 2010 after an ambitious renovation. It remains a major showcase for the acclaimed **Royal Shakespeare Company (RSC),** with a season that runs from April to November and typically features five Shakespearean plays. The RSC also stages productions in the smaller **Swan Theatre,** an intimate 430-seat space next to the Royal Shakespeare Theatre.

For **ticket reservations** book online or call ✆ **0844/800-1110.** A small number of tickets is always held for sale on the day of a performance, but it may be too late to get a good seat if you wait until you arrive in Stratford. The box office is open Monday to Saturday 9am to 8pm, although it closes at 6pm on days when there are no performances. Seats range in price from £14 to £58.

Even if you're not seeing a performance, you can take a guided **Theatre Tour,** which lasts an hour and runs every 2 hours from 9:15am (Mon–Sat) and from 10:15am (Sun and public holidays). Tickets cost £6.50 for adults and £3 for children 17 and under. Advance booking is recommended.

You can also take an elevator up the newly constructed 36-m (118-ft.) **Tower** (daily 10am–5pm) for a unique bird's-eye view of the town. Tickets cost £2.50 for adults and £1.25 for children 17 and under.

If you're driving from London, take the M40 to junction 15 and continue to Stratford-upon-Avon on the A46/A439.

VISITOR INFORMATION The **Tourist Information Centre,** Bridgefoot, on the A3400 (www.discover-stratford.com; ✆ **01789/264293**), provides any details you may wish to know about the Shakespeare houses and properties; it will also assist in booking rooms (see "Where to Stay," below). The center is open daily 10am to 5pm (10am–4pm Nov–Feb).

ORGANIZED TOURS **City Sightseeing** (www.citysightseeing-stratford.com; ✆ **01789/412680**) runs 1-hour guided bus tours, taking in the town's five Shakespeare properties, on a constant loop. The most logical starting point is the sidewalk in front of the Pen & Parchment Pub, at the bottom of Bridge Street. Tour tickets are valid all day, so you can hop on and off the buses as many times as you want. The tours cost £11.75 for adults, £9.75 for seniors and students, and £6 for children 5 to 15 (children 4 and under ride free). A family ticket goes for £25.50. April to September buses depart daily every 15 minutes from 9:30am to 6pm; October to March buses run Monday to Friday 10am to 3pm every hour, and Saturday and Sunday 9:30am to 3:30pm every 30 minutes.

Exploring the Area

Most of Stratford's historic attractions are administrated by the **Shakespeare Birthplace Trust** (www.shakespeare.org.uk; ✆ **01789/204016**). One combination ticket (£21 for adults, £19 for seniors and students, and £13.50 for children 5–15 and 16–17 in full-time education) lets you visit the five most important sights, described below. You can also buy a family ticket, £55.50 for two adults and three children—a

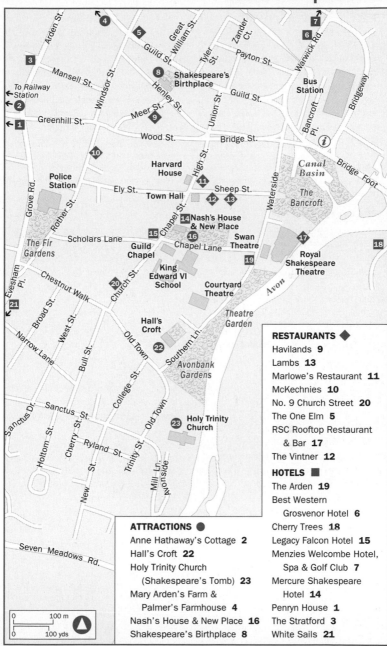

RESTAURANTS ◆

Havilands **9**
Lambs **13**
Marlowe's Restaurant **11**
McKechnies **10**
No. 9 Church Street **20**
The One Elm **5**
RSC Rooftop Restaurant
  & Bar **17**
The Vintner **12**

HOTELS ■

The Arden **19**
Best Western
  Grosvenor Hotel **6**
Cherry Trees **18**
Legacy Falcon Hotel **15**
Menzies Welcombe Hotel,
  Spa & Golf Club **7**
Mercure Shakespeare
  Hotel **14**
Penryn House **1**
The Stratford **3**
White Sails **21**

ATTRACTIONS ●

Anne Hathaway's Cottage **2**
Hall's Croft **22**
Holy Trinity Church
  (Shakespeare's Tomb) **23**
Mary Arden's Farm &
  Palmer's Farmhouse **4**
Nash's House & New Place **16**
Shakespeare's Birthplace **8**

good deal. Buy the ticket at your first stop at any one of the Trust properties. Free admission for children 4 and under.

Anne Hathaway's Cottage ★ HISTORIC HOME   The childhood home of Anne Hathaway, Shakespeare's long-suffering wife, is the Trust property most evocative of the Tudor period—a gorgeous thatched wattle-and-daub cottage going back to the 1480s, located in the hamlet of Shottery, 1 mile from the center of Stratford. The Hathaways were yeoman sheep farmers, and their descendants lived in this cottage until 1911. Many original furnishings, including various kitchen utensils and the courting settle (the bench on which Shakespeare is said to have wooed Anne), are preserved inside the house. Will was only 18 when he married Anne Hathaway in 1582 (she was 8 years older), and a special exhibit chronicles the marriage.

Cottage Lane, Shottery (take the City Sightseeing bus, p. 454, from Bridge St., or walk via a marked pathway from Evesham Place in Stratford across the meadow to Shottery). www.shakespeare.org. uk. ℂ **01789/292100.** Admission £8.50 adults, £7.50 seniors and students, £5 children 5–15 and 16–17 in full-time education, £22 family ticket. Combination tickets available (see above). Apr–Oct daily 9am–5pm; Nov–Mar 10am–4pm. Closed Dec 25–26.

Hall's Croft HISTORIC HOME   Hall's Croft is an outstanding Tudor house with a walled garden, furnished in the style of a middle-class home of the time. It was here that Shakespeare's eldest daughter Susanna probably lived with her husband, Dr. John Hall, who was widely respected and built up a large medical practice in the area. Fascinating exhibits illustrate the theory and practice of medicine in Dr. Hall's time.

Old Town St. (near Holy Trinity Church). www.shakespeare.org.uk. ℂ **01789/292107.** Admission includes Shakespeare's Birthplace and Nash's House & New Place; £13.50 adults, £12.50 seniors and students, £9 children 5–15 and 16–17 in full-time education, £36 family ticket. Apr–Oct daily 10am–5pm; Nov–Mar 11am–4pm. Closed Dec 25–26.

Holy Trinity Church (Shakespeare's Tomb) CHURCH   In a bucolic setting near the River Avon is the Norman parish church where Shakespeare is buried ("and curst be he who moves my bones"). The Parish Register records his baptism in 1564 and burial in 1616; copies of the original documents are on display. Shakespeare's tomb lies in the chancel. Alongside his grave are those of his widow, Anne, and other members of his family. Nearby on the north wall is a bust of Shakespeare that was erected approximately 7 years after his death.

Old Town St. (walk 4 min. past the Royal Shakespeare Theatre, with the river on your left). www. stratford-upon-avon.org. ℂ **01789/290128.** Free admission to church; Shakespeare's tomb £2 adults, £1 students. Apr–Sept Mon–Sat 8:30am–6pm, Sun 12:30–5pm; Mar and Oct Mon–Sat 9am–5pm, Sun 12:30–5pm; Nov–Feb Mon–Sat 9am–4pm, Sun 12:30–5pm. Closed to visitors Good Friday, Christmas Day, Boxing Day (St. Stephen's Day), and New Year's Day.

Mary Arden's Farm & Palmer's Farmhouse ★ FARM   The childhood home of Mary Shakespeare, née Mary Arden (1537–1608), the mother of Will Shakespeare, still operates as a working farm in Wilmcote, three miles from Stratford. Visitors can tour the property and see firsthand how a farming household functioned in the 1570s—cows to be milked, bread to be baked, and vegetables cultivated in an authentic 16th-century manner. In the barns, stable, cowshed, and farmyard is an extensive collection of farming implements illustrating life and work in the local countryside from Shakespeare's time to the present. Until 2000 the Arden's red-brick farmhouse was known as Glebe Farm—the far more romantic, timber-framed house next door was thought to be the Arden home. Thanks to research by local historian

Dr. Nat Alcock, Glebe Farm was properly renamed, and what was known for years as "Mary Arden's House" was dubbed Palmer's Farmhouse.

Station Rd., Wilmcote (take the A3400 towards Birmingham for 3½ miles). www.shakespeare.org. uk. © **01789/293455.** Admission £9.50 adults, £8.50 seniors and students, £6.50 children 5–15 and 16–17 in full-time education, £25.50 family ticket. Combination tickets available (see above). Apr–Oct daily 10am–5pm. Closed Nov–Mar.

Nash's House & New Place HISTORIC HOME   Shakespeare retired to New Place in 1610 (a prosperous man by the standards of his day) and died here 6 years later. Regrettably, the house was torn down, so only the garden remains. A mulberry tree planted by the Bard was so popular with latter-day visitors to Stratford that the garden's owner chopped it down. It is said that the mulberry tree that grows here today was planted from a cutting of the original tree. You enter the gardens through Nash's House, which contains 17th-century period rooms and an exhibition illustrating the history of Stratford. Thomas Nash married Elizabeth Hall, a granddaughter of the poet.

Chapel St. www.shakespeare.org.uk. © **01789/292325.** Admission includes Shakespeare's Birthplace and Hall's Croft; £13.50 adults, £12.50 seniors and students, £9 children 5–15 and 16–17 in full-time education, £36 family ticket. Nov–Mar daily 11am–4pm; Apr–Oct daily 10am–5pm. Closed Dec 25–26.

Shakespeare's Birthplace ★★ MUSEUM   The son of a glover and whittawer (leather worker), Will Shakespeare was born in this half-timbered structure in 1564. Bought by public donors in 1847, it has been preserved as a national shrine ever since and is filled with Shakespeare memorabilia. You can visit the living room, the bedroom where Shakespeare was probably born, a fully equipped kitchen of the period (look for the "babyminder"), and a Shakespeare museum, illustrating his life and times.

Built next door to commemorate the 400th anniversary of the Bard's birth, the modern **Shakespeare Centre** serves both as the administrative headquarters of the Birthplace Trust and as a library and study center. An extension houses the **Birthplace Visitor Centre**.

Henley St. www.shakespeare.org.uk. © **01789/204016.** Admission includes entry to Hall's Croft and Nash's House & New Place; £13.50 adults, £12.50 seniors and students, £9 children 5–15 and 16–17 in full-time education, £36 family ticket. Nov–Mar daily 10am–4pm; Apr–May and Sept–Oct daily 10am–5pm; June–Aug daily 9am–6pm. Closed Dec 23–26.

Where to Eat
MODERATE

Lambs ★ CONTEMPORARY ENGLISH   Near the Royal Shakespeare Theatre, this stylish cafe/bistro is housed in a building dating from 1547. It's ideal for a light meal or pre-theatre dinner. The menu changes monthly, but expect finely executed English classics such as slow-roasted lamb shank with creamed potato and glazed carrots, as well as more exotic creations such Goan-style fish curry (salmon, halibut, prawn, and mussels). It's hard to beat the addictive sticky toffee pudding for dessert.

12 Sheep St. www.lambsrestaurant.co.uk. © **01789/292554.** Reservations required for dinner Fri–Sat. Main courses £10.25–£18.75. MC, V. Mon and Tues 5–9pm; Wed–Sat noon–2pm and 5–9pm; Sun noon–2pm and 6–9pm.

Marlowe's Restaurant CONTEMPORARY ENGLISH   The place to come for olde Elizabethan atmosphere—the large bar, with a fireplace blazing with logs in winter, opens onto a splendid oak-paneled room, and in summer there is a spacious courtyard for alfresco dining. The food is also pretty good; start with seared scallops or chicken livers flambéed in masala cream, and continue with one of the chargrilled steaks or homemade pie of the day. Drunken duck has been a long-time specialty here: It's marinated in gin, red wine, and juniper berries before it's roasted in the oven.

18 High St. www.marlowes.biz. ℂ **01789/204999.** Reservations recommended. Main courses £7.95–£20.15. AE, MC, V. Mon–Thurs noon–2:15pm and 5:30–10pm; Fri noon–2:15pm and 5:30–10:30pm; Sat noon–2:15pm and 5:30–11pm; Sun noon–2:15pm.

No 9 Church Street ★★ CONTEMPORARY ENGLISH   This is one of Stratford's finest and most stylish restaurants, with a creative seasonal menu by talented chefs Wayne Thomson and Dan Robinson. Starters might include piquant delights such as Warwickshire rarebit, marinated mushrooms, artichokes, and crispy pancetta, with main courses such as winter squash and black truffle ravioli, prime cuts of venison, and Cornish ling (fish) with seared scallops. Leave room for the Bramley apple and sultana tipsy cake with cinnamon palmiers.

9 Church St. www.no9churchst.com. ℂ **01789/415522.** Reservations recommended. Main courses £11–£18. MC, V. Tues–Sat noon–2:30pm and 5–9:30pm; Sun noon–3:30pm.

The One Elm ENGLISH   Convenient thanks to its long hours of food service, with a pub section, street-level restaurant, and a tranquil courtyard for dining and drinking (try the real ale from Warwickshire brewery Purity). Dishes utilize fresh produce, including ethically sourced Guatemalan coffee, and free-range pork, chicken, eggs, and high-quality beef from Leamington Spa butcher Aubrey Allen. Grab a sandwich; a classic bar meal such as ham, egg, and chips; or the Deli Board, featuring all sorts of antipasti and charcuterie such as mustard sausages and marinated anchovies. Among the most enticing main dishes are the smoked pollock, leek, and wholegrain mustard fishcakes.

1 Guild St. www.oneelmstratford.co.uk. ℂ **01789/404919.** Main courses £10.75–£17.50; Deli Board £11.50; sandwiches from £6.50. MC, V. Mon–Sat 11am–10pm; Sun noon–3pm and 6:30–9:30pm.

RSC Rooftop Restaurant & Bar ENGLISH/CONTINENTAL   This restaurant enjoys the best location in town—it's wrapped around the top of the Royal Shakespeare Theatre itself—with floor-to-ceiling windows providing an unobstructed view of the swans on the Avon. Consider the cafe a venue for lunch, pre-show dining, or a supper of freshly prepared and simply cooked modern English food. Main courses might include John Dory with braised gem, cauliflower, and oyster fritter, or lip-smacking roast lamb with potatoes, olives, and beans.

Royal Shakespeare Theatre, Waterside. www.rsc.org.uk. ℂ **01789/403449.** Reservations recommended. Main courses £13.95–£19.95; fixed-price menu (before 6:15pm) £11.50 for 1 course, £15.50 for 2 courses, or £18.50 for 3 courses. AE, MC, V. Mon–Sat 11:30am–11pm; Sun noon–6pm.

The Vintner ENGLISH/CONTINENTAL   In a timber-framed structure little altered since its construction in the late 15th century, the Vintner may very well be the place where William Shakespeare went to purchase his wine. The Vintner is both a cafe/bar and a restaurant owned by the same family for 5 centuries; its location makes it ideal for a pre-theatre lunch or supper. Good-tasting main courses include salmon fishcakes with wilted spinach and sorrel sauce, and well-priced steaks. For dessert, try that British favorite, sticky toffee pudding with vanilla ice cream.

4–5 Sheep St. www.the-vintner.co.uk. ℂ **01789/297259.** Main courses £11.25–£22.50. DC, MC, V. Mon–Sat 9:30am–10pm; Sun 9:30am–9pm.

INEXPENSIVE

Havilands ENGLISH TEA/CAFE   This well-respected caterer opened a charming tearoom and take-out in 2009, serving fresh, locally sourced food. Grab a stilton and grape sandwich; turkey, cranberry, and stuffing quiche; or spicy teacake, and relax on the sunny terrace. It also serves high-quality pies, soups, and salads.

4–5 Meer St. www.havilandscatering.com. ℂ **01789/415477.** Cakes from £1.35, sandwiches from £2.25. MC, V. Mon–Sat 9am–5pm; Sun 10:30am–5pm.

McKechnies CAFE/COFFEEHOUSE   This cozy cafe serves the best coffee in Stratford. It's another independent place that sources its food and milk from local suppliers; tasty all-day Warwickshire breakfasts (dry cured bacon, Hatton sausage, field mushrooms, fresh beef, tomatoes, and free-range eggs), toasted ciabattas, chunky farmhouse sandwiches, zesty soups, and cupcakes from locally based Tea Cake Company. The cappuccino is justly celebrated (beans sourced from James' Gourmet Coffee Company), and they also serve 17 types of tea.

37 Rother St. www.mckechniescafe.talktalk.net. ℂ **01789/299575.** Soups/sandwiches from £3.75. MC, V. Mon–Sat 8am–5:30pm; Sun 9:30am–4:30pm.

Shopping

The **Shakespeare Bookshop,** 39 Henley St. (www.shakespeare.org.uk; ℂ **01789/ 292176;** Wed–Sat 9:30am–5:30pm, Sun noon–5pm), across from the Shakespeare Birthplace Centre, is the region's premier source for books on the Bard and his works, from picture books for junior-high students to weighty tomes geared to those pursuing a Ph.D. in literature.

Entertainment & Nightlife
THE PUB & BAR SCENE

Despite the millions of tourists passing through, Stratford is essentially a small town where nightlife revolves around the RSC Theatre and local pubs. Everyone who visits Stratford grabs at least one drink at the **Dirty Duck ★★** (www.dirtyduck-pub-stratford-upon-avon.co.uk; ℂ **01789/297312;** restaurant daily noon–10pm, bar daily 11am–11pm), close to the RSC Theatre on Waterside. This creaky old watering hole has been a popular hangout for Stratford players since the 18th century, its walls lined with autographed photos of its many famous patrons.

Part of the Greene King stable, the **Garrick Inn ★**, at 25 High St. (www.garrick-inn-stratford-upon-avon.co.uk; ℂ **01789/292186;** daily 11am–11pm), is the oldest pub in Stratford, a handsome black-and-white timbered structure that dates back to the 14th century.

Stratford's oldest structure (not its oldest pub) is reputed to be the **White Swan** on Rother Street (www.fullershotels.com; ℂ **01789/297022;** daily noon–11pm). Dating back to 1450, it's a plush hotel today, but the pub section is an atmospheric place for a drink, with cushioned leather armchairs, oak paneling, and fireplaces.

Where to Stay
EXPENSIVE

The Arden ★★★   Stratford's best hotel and the most convenient for the RSC Theatre reopened in 2010 after a comprehensive refurbishment. All the rooms have been decked out in an elegant, contemporary English style with the latest amenities, some with views of the river; the main difference between the Deluxe, Superior, and Classic rooms is size. The excellent location and on-site dining choices—the **Waterside Brasserie** and **Champagne Bar**—means you won't need to stray far from the hotel.

Waterside, Stratford-upon-Avon, Warwickshire CV37 6BA. www.theardenhotelstratford.com. © **01789/298682.** Fax 01789/206989. 45 units. £99–£235. Basic package rates include English breakfast. AE, MC, V. Free parking. **Amenities:** 3 restaurants; 2 bars; room service. *In room:* TV/DVD, hair dryer, Wi-Fi (free).

Best Western Grosvenor Hotel A pair of Georgian town houses, built in 1832 and 1843, join to form this hotel, one of the top choices in Stratford. In the center of town, with lawns and gardens to the rear, it's a short stroll from the Avon River, Bancroft Gardens, and the Royal Shakespeare Theatre. Bedrooms are midsize to spacious, each personally designed with a high standard of tasteful modern furnishings, a cut above usual chain-hotel fare.

12–14 Warwick Rd., Stratford-upon-Avon, Warwickshire CV37 6YT. www.bwgh.co.uk. © **01789/269213.** Fax 01789/266087. 73 units. £82–£144 double. Breakfast £10 extra. AE, MC, V. Free parking. **Amenities:** Restaurant; bar; room service; babysitting. *In room:* TV, hair dryer, Wi-Fi (free).

Menzies Welcombe Hotel, Spa & Golf Club ★★ Built in 1866 in a grand Jacobean style, this historic country house is a 10-minute ride from the heart of town. Its key feature is an 18-hole golf course, but the spa is equally appealing and it makes for a romantic stay whatever you aim to do in Stratford. Bedrooms are luxuriously outfitted in traditional Jacobean style, with fine antiques and elegant fabrics. Most rooms are seemingly big enough for tennis matches, but those in the garden wing, although comfortable, are small.

Warwick Rd., Stratford-upon-Avon, Warwickshire CV37 0NR. www.menzies-hotels.co.uk. © **01789/295252.** Fax 01789/414666. 78 units. £150–£210 double. AE, DC, MC, V. Free parking. Take the A439 1¼ miles northeast of the town center. **Amenities:** 2 restaurants; bar; indoor pool; golf course; tennis court; exercise rooms; spa; room service. *In room:* TV, hair dryer, Wi-Fi (free).

MODERATE
Cherry Trees ★★ 🎁 This small B&B has a fabulous location, a short walk across the bridge to the RSC Theatre and the center of Stratford. The Garden Room features a king-size four-poster, there's a modern leather king-size bed in the Terrace Room (both have large conservatories and access to the garden), and the gorgeous Tiffany Suite offers a king-size bed and separate sitting room. Whichever room you choose, you'll be welcomed with tea and scones on arrival, get a huge cooked breakfast, and have access to a well-stocked fridge and selection of teas.

Swans Nest Lane, Stratford-upon-Avon, Warwickshire CV37 7LS. www.cherrytrees-stratford.co.uk. © **01789/292989.** 3 units. £105–£125 double. Rates include breakfast. MC, V. Free parking. *In room:* TV, hair dryer, Wi-Fi (free).

Legacy Falcon Hotel The Falcon blends the very old and the very new, with parts of the hotel dating back to the 16th century; connected to its rear by a glass passageway is a more sterile extension added in 1970. The rooms in the older section have oak beams, diamond leaded-glass windows, antiques, and good reproductions. In the inn's intimate **Merlin Lounge,** you'll find an open copper-hooded fireplace where fires are stoked under beams salvaged from old ships.

Chapel St., Stratford-upon-Avon, Warwickshire CV37 6HA. www.legacy-hotels.co.uk. © **0844/411-9005.** Fax 0844/411-9006. 83 units. £60–£143 double. AE, DC, MC, V. Free parking. **Amenities:** 2 restaurants; 2 bars; room service. *In room:* TV, hair dryer, Wi-Fi (free).

Mercure Shakespeare Hotel ★   Filled with historical associations, the original core of this hotel dates from the 1400s. Quieter and plusher than the Falcon (see above), it is equaled in the center of Stratford only by the Arden (see above). Bedrooms are named in honor of noteworthy actors, Shakespeare's plays, or Shakespearean characters. The oldest are capped with hewn timbers, and all have modern comforts. Even the newer accommodations are at least 40 to 50 years old and have rose-and-thistle patterns carved into many of their exposed timbers.

Chapel St., Stratford-upon-Avon, Warwickshire CV37 6ER. www.mercure.com. © **01789/294997.** Fax 01789/415411. 74 units. £56–£96 double. Children 12 and under stay free in parent's room. AE, DC, MC, V. Breakfast £15.50. Parking £10. **Amenities:** Restaurant; bar; room service. *In room:* A/C, TV, minibar (in some), hair dryer, Wi-Fi (first hour free, then £9 per 24hr.).

The Stratford ★   This is definitely not one of the historic inns of Stratford-upon-Avon, but a plush, modern hotel with up-to-date conveniences. A member of the QHotels group, its location is only a short walk from the banks of the River Avon. The bedrooms are spaciously and elegantly appointed, some with four-poster beds and Tudor-style, but others are more geared to commercial travelers seeking streamlined conveniences—not romance. Deftly prepared market-fresh dishes change with the seasons in the on-site **Quills Restaurant.**

Arden St., Stratford-upon-Avon, Warwickshire CV37 6QQ. www.qhotels.co.uk. ©/fax **01789/271000.** 102 units. £112.50–£175 double. AE, DC, MC, V. Parking £5. **Amenities:** Restaurant; bar; small exercise room; room service. *In room:* TV, hair dryer, Internet (free).

White Sails ★★   This luxurious B&B is just a 15-minute walk from the town center. The four spacious rooms sport a crisp, contemporary design, enhanced with modern art, sculptures, and huge beds (the Warwick room has a four-poster). Thoughtful extras include chocolates by the bed and a tea tray stocked with treats. There's a huge choice at breakfast, from full English to cinnamon toast, cereals, and fruit, and the hosts are a mine of local information.

85 Evesham Rd., Stratford-upon-Avon, Warwickshire CV37 9BE. www.white-sails.co.uk. © **01789/264326.** 5 units. £100–£132 double. Rates include English breakfast. AE, DC, MC, V (1.5% surcharge). Free parking. **Amenities:** Guest lounge with complimentary sherry. *In room:* TV, fridge, minibar, hair dryer, Wi-Fi (free).

INEXPENSIVE

Penryn House ★ 🖋   The location is convenient and the price is right at this B&B, where hosts Anne and Robert Dawkes are among the most welcoming in town. They justifiably take special pride in their breakfasts, right down to their superb "Harvest of Arden" English apple juice. Free-range Worcestershire eggs are served along with fresh seasonal fruit and locally produced bacon and sausage. They even prepare a vegetarian breakfast if requested. The bedrooms are a bit small, but well furnished and comfortable. The location is close to the train station, Anne Hathaway's Cottage, and the heart of town.

126 Alcester Rd., Stratford-upon-Avon, Warwickshire CV37 9DP. www.penrynguesthouse.co.uk. © **01789/293718.** Fax 01789/266077. 7 units. £60–£70 double. Rates include English breakfast. MC, V. Free parking. *In room:* TV, hair dryer, Wi-Fi (free).

Ice Cream Kings

The **Henley Ice Cream Company** has been dreaming up some of the most addictive ice cream in the country since 1934. Make a pilgrimage to their tea-rooms and ice cream parlor at 152 High St., Henley in Arden (www.henleyice cream.co.uk; ✆ **01564/795172;** Apr–Sep Mon–Fri 9am–6pm, Sat 9:30am–6:30pm, Sun 10am–7pm; Oct–Mar Mon–Fri 10am–4:30pm, Sat 9:30am–5:30pm, Sun 10am–5:30pm), 8 miles north of Stratford via the A3400. Frequent trains take 14 minutes and cost £3.40 return from Stratford.

WARWICK

94 miles NW of London; 9 miles NE of Stratford-upon-Avon

This small Midlands town is best known for **Warwick Castle,** one of the finest medieval fortresses in England. The castle reflects the town's importance in the Middle Ages, when it was the base of the **earls of Warwick,** initially of the Norman Beauchamp family. The Great Fire of 1694 destroyed most of the medieval town, and though it was rebuilt, Warwick declined in influence thereafter, despite remaining the county town of Warwickshire.

Today the historic center is charming but easily explored on a day trip from Stratford or Birmingham. Nearby lie the romantic ruins of Kenilworth Castle, the elegant town of Leamington Spa, and Coventry, a much larger industrial city celebrated for its modern cathedral.

Essentials

GETTING THERE   Trains run every 2 hours between Stratford-upon-Avon and Warwick (25–30 min.). A one-way ticket costs around £5. Hourly trains run to Warwick from Birmingham Snow Hill station (30 min.) for £6.80.

Stagecoach bus no. 16 departs Stratford-upon-Avon every hour during the day. The trip takes roughly half an hour. Go to www.stagecoachbus.com for schedules.

Take the A46 if you're driving from Stratford-upon-Avon.

VISITOR INFORMATION   The **Tourist Information Centre** is at the Court House, Jury Street (www.visitwarwick.co.uk; ✆ **01926/492212**), and is open Monday to Saturday from 9:30am to 4:30pm, and Sunday 10am to 4pm (closed Dec 24–26 and Jan 1).

Exploring the Area

Lord Leycester Hospital HISTORIC SITE   This attractive group of 14th-century timber-framed buildings was never a hospital in the modern sense, but rather a charitable institution "for the housing and maintenance of the needy, infirm or aged." The structures originally housed medieval guilds, but the hospital was founded in 1571 by Robert Dudley, Earl of Leicester, as a home for old soldiers. It's still used by ex-service personnel or "brethren," some of whom act as enthusiastic guides. On top of the West Gate is the attractive little **Chapel of St. James,** dating from the 12th century but renovated many times since; all hospital residents are still required to attend the daily service at 9:30am, and the chapel is lit (and warmed) by candlelight only. Look out for the William Morris designed hangings around the altar, and his stained glass *Annunciation* over the door (1866). The 15th-century Guildhall is home to the **Museum of the Queen's Own Hussars,** tracing the regiment's history from 1685 through to the modern tank era.

60 High St. www.lordleycester.com. © **01926/491422.** Admission £4.90 adults, £4.40 seniors, £3.90 children 5–15, free for children 4 and under. Easter–Oct Tues–Sun 10am–5pm; Nov–Easter Tues–Sun 10am–4pm (museum closed on Sundays).

St. Mary's Church CHURCH   Though destroyed in part by the fire of 1694, St. Mary's contains some exceptional works of art and architecture. The Perpendicular Gothic choir dates from the 14th century; the Norman crypt and chapterhouse are from the 11th century; and the Gothic tomb of Thomas Beauchamp (1313–1369), 11th Earl of Warwick, stands in front of the high altar (the tiny figures around its base provide a unique depiction of 14th-century English fashion). The magnificent **Beauchamp Chapel** encases the marble tomb of Richard Beauchamp (1382–1439), the 13th Earl of Warwick, commemorated by a gilded bronze effigy. Beauchamp was even more powerful than King Henry V, and his tomb is one of the finest examples of the Perpendicular Gothic. In the same chapel are the ornate tombs of Robert Dudley (1533–1588), Earl of Leicester, a favorite of Elizabeth I, his brother Ambrose Dudley (1530–1590), another Earl of Warwick, and Robert's son, the "Noble Impe," who died as an infant in 1584. Climb the 160 steps to the top of the church tower (53m/174ft.), for scintillating views of the town and surrounding countryside.

21 Church St. www.saintmaryschurch.co.uk. © **01926/403940.** Free admission (£2 donation recommended); tower £2.50 adults, £1 children 5–15. Apr–Oct daily 10am–6pm; Nov–Mar daily 10am–4:30pm.

Warwick Castle ★★★ CASTLE   Perched on a rocky cliff above the River Avon, this magnificent 14th-century fortress looms over Warwick like a giant fist. It's the definitive medieval castle, with chunky towers, crenellated battlements, and a moat surrounded by gardens, lawns, and woodland where peacocks roam freely. You'll need the best part of a day to do it justice.

Though it has roots in the Anglo-Saxon period, the Beauchamp family, which controlled the medieval earldom of Warwick during its most illustrious period, is responsible for the appearance of the castle today; much of the external structure remains unchanged from the mid-14th century. When the castle was granted to Sir Fulke Greville by James I in 1604, he spent £20,000 (an enormous sum in those days) converting the existing castle buildings into a luxurious mansion. The Grevilles have held the Earl of Warwick title since 1759, but sold the castle to Tussaud's in 1978. As a result, the ornate interiors have been embellished with exhibitions and waxwork displays to create a vivid picture of the castle's turbulent past and its important role in the history of England. The new **Merlin: The Dragon Tower** attraction (inspired by the hit BBC drama), and trips to the ghoulish **Castle Dungeon** (unsuitable for young children) cost extra.

Warwick. www.warwick-castle.co.uk. © **0870/442-2000.** Admission £21.60 adults, £15.60 children 4–11, £16.80 seniors, £69 family ticket, free for children 3 and under; with castle dungeon £28.20 adults, £22.80 children 4–11, £24 seniors, £97.20 family ticket; with dungeon and Merlin: The Dragon Tower £30.60 adults, £25.80 children 4–11, £27 seniors, £107.40 family ticket; 15% discount for tickets purchased online. Daily 10am–5pm. Closed Dec 25.

Where to Eat

Brethren's Kitchen ENGLISH TEA   For a break from sightseeing, it's hard to beat the Tudor ambience at this tearoom, part of the historic Lord Leycester Hospital

(p. 462), with stone floors and wonderful exposed oak beams. Order the full cream tea with scones and fresh cream, or a variety of tempting homemade cakes. They also do cheap but tasty lunches of home-cooked soup or sandwiches—try the Warwickshire pork sausages.

Lord Leycester Hospital, 60 High St. www.brethrenskitchen.co.uk. © **07733/550497.** Main courses £6–£12. AE, MC, V. Feb–Dec Tues–Sat 10am–5pm, Sun 11am–5pm, and public holiday Mon. Closed Jan.

Catalan ★ 🍴 MEDITERRANEAN   It's the castle, not the cuisine, that draws most tourists to Warwick, but this bistro is notable for serving affordable food that tastes good and is prepared with fresh ingredients. If you come for lunch, you'll be greeted with a Spanish tapas menu that is experimental and tasty, with plenty of jamón Serrano, seasoned fava beans, and patatas bravas. There's also lighter fare such as sandwiches, panini, and salads. Dinner is more elaborate, with dishes such as Mediterranean fish stew or grilled lamb cutlets with garlic mash.

6 Jury St. www.cafecatalan.com. © **01926/498930.** Reservations recommended. Tapas £1.95–£7.95; main courses £17.25–£22.95; Mon–Fri 2-course fixed-price lunch £11.85. AE, MC, V. Mon–Sat noon–3pm and 6–9:30pm.

Tailors ★★★ 🍴 CONTEMPORARY ENGLISH   Tailors serves incredibly creative food from two of the regions up and coming young chefs. The seasonal menus are a masterpiece; expect exquisite combinations such as braised shoulder and filet of Lincolnshire pork with black pudding (blood sausage), white beans, smoked almonds, and caramelized sprouts; or Hereford beef with cepe mushrooms, swede, cheddar cheese, and purple potatoes. Everything is artfully presented and tastes sensational.

22 Market Place. www.tailorsrestaurant.co.uk. © **01926/410590.** Reservations recommended. Lunch £12.95 for 2 courses; dinner £29.50 for 2 courses, £34.50 for 3 courses. AE, MC, V. Tues–Sat noon–2pm and 6:30–9:30pm.

Entertainment & Nightlife

Real ale drinkers should make for the **Old Fourpenny Shop Hotel** (www.4pennyhotel. com; © **01926/491360**), 27–29 Crompton St., which offers a changing selection of traditional cask beers from all over the country and a selection of quality wines (they also offer rooms, see below). The **Rose & Crown,** at 30 Market Place (www.roseandcrownwarwick.co.uk; © **01926/411117**), is another inn and restaurant that's a great place for a drink, with beers such as Black Sheep, Warwickshire Purity Gold, and a weekly guest ale on tap.

Where to Stay

Old Fourpenny Shop Hotel ★★ 🍴 🏨   This charming pub is an atmospheric place to stay, with cozy rooms and a hearty breakfast thrown in, all for an incredibly low price (single travelers save even more). You won't hear much noise from the pub in the older rooms upstairs, and especially in the motel-style rooms converted from the stables at the back. Free parking in central Warwick is a real bonus, but it's only a 10 to 15 minute walk to the train station. The building dates back to around 1800; the pub was originally the Warwick Tavern, but got the new name after charging four pennies for a cup of coffee and a tot of rum.

27–29 Crompton St., Warwick, Warwickshire CV34 6HJ. www.4pennyhotel.co.uk. © **01926/491360.** Fax 01926/411892. 11 units. £80 double. Rates include English breakfast. AE, DC, MC, V. Free parking. **Amenities:** Restaurant; bar. In room: TV, hair dryer, Wi-Fi (free).

Park Cottage ★★   This gorgeous B&B set in a 15th-century timber-frame cottage was once owned by the earls of Warwick. It's justly popular in large part thanks to thoughtful hosts Janet and Stuart Baldry and their exceptional rooms. All feature wood or parquet floors, oak beams, and antique furniture; the Elizabeth Room has a beautifully carved four-poster. The cottage is literally opposite the castle entrance, and is adorned with hanging baskets overflowing with blossoms.

113 West St., Warwick, Warwickshire CV34 6AH. www.parkcottagewarwick.co.uk. ℭ**01926/410319.** Fax 01926/497994. 7 units. £70–£85 double. Rates include English breakfast. DC, MC, V. Free parking. **Amenities:** Bar. *In room:* TV, hair dryer, Wi-Fi (free).

Premier Inn Warwick ★   Though it's outside of town in a business park (just off junction 15 of the M40), the spanking new Premier is the best choice if you're using Warwick as a base to explore the area. Rooms are a cut above standard chain fare, and come with flat-screen TVs and all the usual amenities, while the restaurant offers Costa Coffee, evening meals, and a bar in addition to breakfast (extra). Lying at the junction of a network of highways, tourists find that its comfort and easy-to-find location make it perfect for road-trips and overnight stops.

Opus 40, Haywood Rd., Warwick CV34 5AH. www.premierinn.com. ℭ **0871/527-9320.** Fax 0871/527-9321. 124 units. £65–£75 double. AE, DC, MC, V. Free parking. **Amenities:** Restaurant; cafe; bar. *In room:* A/C, TV, hair dryer, Wi-Fi (free for 30min; £3 for 24hr.).

Side Trips from Warwick
ROYAL LEAMINGTON SPA★

Like other English spa towns, Leamington Spa boomed in the 18th century when taking spring water was popularized for its medicinal qualities. In 1814 the handsome **Royal Pump Rooms & Baths** were opened on The Parade, close to the River Leam, and a plethora of fine Georgian buildings followed in subsequent years (the "royal" prefix was added after queen-to-be Victoria came here in 1831). Today the town makes an inviting day trip, with its faded Georgian grandeur and the pump rooms now containing the absorbing **Leamington Spa Art Gallery & Museum** (www.warwickdc.gov.uk; Tues, Wed, Fri, and Sat 10:30am–5pm, Thurs 1:30–8pm, Sun 11am–4pm; free), a visitor information center (ℭ **01926/742762;** Mon–Fri 10am–4:30pm, Sat 10am–3pm, Sun 10am–2pm), and a cafe where you can take afternoon tea (Mon–Fri 9:30am–5pm, Sat 9:30am–5:30pm, Sun 10:30am–5pm). The museum chronicles the history of the town from the 1780s, and displays a handful of choice paintings, such as Stanley Spencer's *Cookham Rise* (1938).

You can also stop by **Aubrey Allen** ★★ at 108 Warwick St. (www.aubreyallen. co.uk; ℭ **01926/311208**), one of Britain's most respected butchers. The shop's deli section is a great place to load up for a picnic (cheeses, quiches, cured meats) or take-out meals (think curries or breakfast sausage baps). It's open Monday to Saturday 8:30am to 6pm.

Stagecoach (www.stagecoachbus.com) runs regular bus services between Leamington and Warwick, just 3 miles west.

Kenilworth Castle ★ CASTLE   The big attraction in Kenilworth, an otherwise ordinary English market town 5 miles north of Warwick, is its enigmatic castle, founded in the 1120s by Geoffrey de Clinton, a lieutenant of Henry I. At one time, its walls enclosed an area of 7 acres, but it is now in majestic ruins. Caesar's Tower, with its 5-m (16-ft.) thick walls, is all that remains of the original structure. Entry includes the excellent audioguides.

Castle Green, Castle Rd., Kenilworth. www.english-heritage.org.uk. © **01926/852078.** Admission £8.20 adults, £7.40 seniors, £4.90 children 5–16, free for children 4 and under; family ticket £21.30. Apr–Aug daily 10am–6pm; Sept–Oct daily 10am–5pm; Nov–Mar Sat–Sun 10am–4pm. Closed Jan 1, Dec 24–26. Stagecoach buses X17 and 16 connect Kenilworth with Warwick, Leamington Spa, and Coventry.

Coventry Cathedral ★ CATHEDRAL   Thirteen miles northeast of Warwick is Coventry, the second largest city in the Midlands, and an industrial center with few tourist attractions save one—its remarkable cathedral. Coventry's fine medieval center was totally destroyed by German bombers during the Coventry Blitz in 1940, and postwar planners replaced it with brutalist shopping malls and concrete buildings. Coventry's 14th-century St. Michael's Cathedral was also destroyed by the bombs; only the tower, spire, outer wall, and the bronze effigy and tomb of its first bishop survived. In 1962, Sir Basil Spence's controversial replacement was consecrated. Today Coventry Cathedral is considered one of the most poignant and religiously evocative modern churches in the world.

Outside is Sir Jacob Epstein's bronze masterpiece, *St. Michael Slaying the Devil.* Inside, the outstanding feature is the 21-m (70-ft.) high altar tapestry by Graham Sutherland, said to be the largest in the world. The floor-to-ceiling abstract stained-glass windows are the work of the Royal College of Art. The West Screen (an entire wall of stained glass) depicts rows of saints and prophets with angels flying among them.

In the undercroft of the cathedral is the Walkway of Holograms, where the walls are accented with 3-D images of the Stations of the Cross, created with reflective light. One of the most evocative objects here is a charred cross wired together by local workmen from burning timbers that crashed to the cathedral's floor during the Nazi bombing. Located in the ruins next door, the **Blitz Experience Museum** contains five 1940s' room reconstructions commemorating the destruction of the city (additional £2.50).

Stagecoach buses X17 and 16 connect Warwick, Leamington Spa, and Coventry. Trains runs every 15 minutes from London's Euston Station to Coventry (trip time: 1hr–1½ hr.). One-way tickets range £6 to £20. Trains from Birmingham run every 10 minutes or so (20–30 min.) and cost £3.10 to £4.10. From Stratford-upon-Avon, four **National Express** buses, with a trip time of 45 minutes, travel to Pool Meadow bus station, at Fairfax Street in Coventry.

Priory Row, Coventry. www.coventrycathedral.org.uk. © **024/7652-1200.** Admission £7 adults, £5 students, seniors, children 12 to 18; free for children 11 and under; £20 family ticket. Tower admission £2.50 adults, £1 children. Mon–Sat 9am–5pm, Sun noon–3:45pm; tower during summer months when staff availability permits.

BIRMINGHAM ★★

120 miles NW of London; 25 miles N of Stratford-upon-Avon

England's second-largest city, **Birmingham** has undergone something of a renaissance in recent decades, transforming itself from a dreary industrial conurbation to a vibrant cultural and education center. While it still bears some of the scars of industrial excess, an energetic building boom, revitalized canals, new areas of green space, and the cultivation of a first-rate symphony and ballet company, as well as art galleries and museums, have all made Birmingham far more appealing.

Birmingham city center is a rich trove of grand Victorian buildings, including the **Museum and Art Gallery** and its precious collection of pre-Raphaelite paintings.

ATTRACTIONS ●

Aston Hall **17**
Back to Backs **10**
Barber Institute of Fine Arts **10**
Birmingham Museum &
   Art Gallery **11**
Ikon Gallery **5**
Museum of the Jewellery Quarter **16**
National Sea Life Centre **2**
Sherborne Wharf Heritage
   Narrow Boats **1**
Thinktank at Millennium Point **14**

RESTAURANTS ◆

Asha's **12**
Bank **3**
Canalside Café **8**
Purnell's **15**
Simpsons **7**

HOTELS ■

Hilton Garden Inn **4**
Nite Nite **9**
Novotel Birmingham
   Centre **6**
Premier Inn Birmingham
   Central (East) **18**
Staying Cool at
   the Rotunda **13**

12

THE HEART OF ENGLAND | Birmingham

[Map of Birmingham with labeled streets and numbered locations: Charlotte St., Old Snow Hill, Fazeley Canal, Birmingham & Fazeley Canal, Newhall St., Lionel St., Gt. Charles St. Queensway, Cornwall St., Edmund St., Livery St., Snow Hill Station, University of Aston, Sandpits Parade, George St., Clement St., Cambridge St., Repertory Theatre, Birmingham Museum & Art Gallery, Paradise Circus, Council House, Library of Birmingham (under construction), Colmore Row, St. Philips Cathedral, Victoria Square, New Street, Town Hall, Great Western Arcade, Corporation St., Moor St. Station, Nat'l Sea Life Centre, Int'l Convention Centre, Brindleyplace, Ikon Gallery, Gas Street Basin, Berkley St., Gas St., Holliday St., Mailbox Shopping Centre, Suffolk St. Queensway, Navigation St., New Street Station, Station St., Bullring Shopping Centre, Selfridges, Bus Station, Sheepcote St., Broad St., Granville St., St. Commercial St., Gough St. Scale: 300 m / 300 yds]

The city's other showstoppers lie on the outskirts: The **Black Country Living Museum** commemorates the region's industrial heritage while **Cadbury World** celebrates Britain's favorite chocolate.

Shopping in Birmingham doesn't quite match London, but there are some real highlights. The iconic **Selfridges** building is worth visiting as much for the architecture as for the plush department store inside, while the **Jewellery Quarter** is home to numerous artisan jewelry makers.

Birmingham's **culinary scene** is led by a trio of acclaimed restaurants famous throughout the country—at Purnell's, Simpsons, and Turners expect the very best of English contemporary cuisine. In stark contrast, the **Balti Triangle** is one of the top places in the country to try Indian and Pakistani food.

As befits the home of Ozzy Osbourne, UB40, '80s' pop idols Duran Duran, and, more recently, The Streets (aka local boy Mike Skinner) and the Editors, Birmingham nightlife is eclectic and extremely lively. Choose from ancient pubs like the **Old Crown,** hip bars such as **Revolution,** live music venues such as **02 Academy,** megaclubs like **Gatecrasher Birmingham,** and stand-up comedy joints like **Glee Club.**

Essentials

GETTING THERE Major international carriers operate transatlantic flights with direct service to **Birmingham International Airport** (BHX; www.birmingham airport.co.uk; ℂ **0844/576-6000**). Birmingham's airport lies about 8 miles southeast of the city center and is easily accessible by public transportation. The AirRail Link monorail (free) connects the terminals with the Birmingham International Rail Station and National Exhibition Centre (NEC) every 10 minutes (daily 5:15am–2am). Rail services operate regularly from Birmingham International to Birmingham city center (New Street) every 10 minutes (the journey takes 10 min. and costs £3.30 one-way).

Trains connect London Euston and Birmingham New Street every 15 to 30 minutes and take 1 hour 25 minutes (tickets £13–£33.50). Trains leave Manchester's Piccadilly Station nearly every hour for Birmingham New Street. The trip takes 1½ hours (tickets from £16). Trains from Stratford-upon-Avon arrive at Birmingham Snow Hill every hour (£6.80).

From London, the best route driving is via the M40, which leads onto the M42, the motorway that circles south and east of Birmingham. Once on the M42, any of the roads from junctions 4 to 6 will lead into the center of Birmingham. The drive takes about 2 to 2½ hours, depending on traffic conditions. Parking is available at locations throughout Birmingham.

VISITOR INFORMATION The most central **Birmingham Visitor Centre** is a glass cube near the Rotunda, at the junction of New Street and Corporation Street (www.visitbirmingham.com). It opens Monday to Saturday 9am to 5pm, and Sunday 10am to 4pm. The center at **Birmingham Central Library** (ℂ **0844/888-3883**; Mon–Fri 10am–6pm, Sat 9am–5pm), Chamberlain Square, can assist travelers in arranging accommodations, obtaining theatre or concert tickets, and planning itineraries. The visitor center at the **airport** is usually open daily 7am to 8pm.

GETTING AROUND Birmingham's city center hosts a number of attractions within easy walking distance, but to see the outskirts you'll need to drive or use public transport. By far the most enticing way to travel around is by **canal boat** (see box p. 469). **Centro** (www.centro.org.uk; ℂ **0121/200-2787**) provides information on all local bus and rail services within Birmingham and the West Midlands area. Day-Saver bus tickets are £3.80, while single journeys are £1.70–£1.90 (no change given). Midland Metro is a 13-mile tram system connecting Birmingham Snow Hill train station with Wolverhampton (£3.50), but the line is being extended into the city center and New Street Station.

Taxis line up at various spots in the city center, at rail stations, and at the National Exhibition Centre, and are a safer way to travel at night. Travelers can also ring up a radio-cab operator such as **TOA Taxis** (www.toataxis.net; ℂ **0121/427-8888**).

SPECIAL EVENTS Victoria Square hosts the U.K.'s largest Frankfurt Christmas Market & Craft Fair (www.birmingham.gov.uk/frankfurtmarket; ℂ **0121/303-3008**) from mid-November to December 23 each year. The **International Jazz & Blues Festival** runs each July (www.birminghamjazzfestival.com), while **Birmingham Pride,** the city's gay festival (www.birminghampride.com), takes place in the Gay Village over the spring public holiday weekend (late May).

Exploring the City

Stephenson Place, at the intersection of New and Corporation streets, is a good starting point for touring the city center, close to the **visitor center.** Pedestrianized

Birmingham by Boat

One of the more intriguing ways to see Birmingham is by boat, as the city is laced with canals created as the "motorways" of their day during the Industrial Revolution. Many of these canals have been cleaned and restored, and sightseeing boats depart from the International Convention Centre Quayside (at Brindleyplace), taking you on 1-hour tours of Birmingham from the water. It's the best way to appreciate the renaissance of the city, as swathes of abandoned wharves and warehouses are gradually converted to offices, shops,

and cafes. **Sherborne Wharf Heritage Narrow Boats** ★★ (www.sherborne wharf.co.uk; ✆ **0121/455-6163**) runs tours Easter to October (and weekends in the winter) at 11:30am, 1pm, 2:30pm, and 4pm. Tickets are £6.50 adults, £5.50 seniors, £5 children 5–16. he firm also runs the **Waterbus** service between Brindleyplace and the Mailbox (every half hour; daily 10:30am–5pm; £3.50 or 75p per stop), and the **Floating Coffee Boat** at the quayside, normally open daily 9am–5pm.

streets link all the premier shopping areas from here; a short walk east along New Street leads to the new **Bull Ring shopping center,** where the real star is the distinctive bubble-wrap exterior of **Selfridges.** Opened in 2003 and designed by architects Future Systems, the famous department store is smothered in 15,000 aluminum discs. It's open 10am to 8pm Monday to Saturday and 11am to 5:30pm on Sundays.

A 5-minute stroll from the visitor center in the other direction along New Street leads to Birmingham's grand civic heart, **Victoria Square,** where **Council House** (www.birmingham.gov.uk; ✆ **0121/303-2438**), the city's most impressive Victorian building, anchors the piazza. Completed in 1879, it is still the meeting place for the Birmingham City Council and a handsome example of the Italian Renaissance style. Note also the restored **Birmingham Town Hall,** built in 1834 and looking like a grand Roman temple (now a concert venue). On adjacent Chamberlain Square lies the equally grand Birmingham Museum and Art Gallery (see p. 470).

Continuing west along Broad Street you pass the new library and the vast ICC building before reaching Birmingham's revitalized canal district. **Brindleyplace** (www.brindleyplace.com) is an upmarket development of offices, restaurants, and attractions, while south of Broad Street the canal leads to **Gas Street Basin,** dotted with canal boats and waterside pubs. From here the towpath continues south to the **Mailbox** (www.mailboxlife.com; ✆ **0121/632-1000**) on Wharfside Street, a fashionable shopping and entertainment center complemented by the **Cube,** Birmingham's latest piece of mind-bending contemporary architecture.

Aston Hall ★★ MUSEUM   This stunning Jacobean mansion was built for the land-owning Holte family in the 1630s, a few miles north of the city center. American novelist Washington Irving visited the house while living in Birmingham with his sister, and used it as the model for *Bracebridge Hall* (1822). Inside, display rooms chronicle the history of the mansion, including its role in the English Civil War (Charles I spent an uneasy night here before the Battle of Edgehill in 1642). The artfully renovated interior is the real highlight, however, especially the magnificent Long Gallery. Taxis from the city center should be around £8.

Trinity Rd., Aston (10- to 15-min. walk from Aston or Witton train stations). www.bmag.org.uk/
aston-hall. 𝄞 **0121/675-4722.** Admission £4 adults, £3 students, children 15 and under free.
Apr–Oct Tues–Sun noon–4pm. Bus: 65, 104, and 105 stop nearby in Lichfield Rd.

Back to Backs ★ MUSEUM

Offering a fascinating glimpse into the lives of
ordinary Birmingham workers, these 19th-century terraced homes (houses built literally back-to-back around a communal courtyard), have been developed as a museum
highlighting four different periods between 1840 and 1977. Visits are by timed ticket
and guided tours only, enhanced by enthusiastic docents—call ahead to book a spot.
Make sure you pop into **Candies ★**, the old-fashioned sweet shop just outside at 55
Hurst St. (www.traditional-sweets.co.uk; 𝄞 **0121/622-5951;** Tues–Sat 11am–
5pm), in business since the 1930s.

55–63 Hurst St./50–54 Inge St. www.nationaltrust.org.uk/birmingham-back-to-backs. 𝄞**0121/666-
7671.** Admission £6.30 adults, £3.20 children 5–15, family £14.80. Daily 10am–5pm (during term
time property closed Tues–Thurs 10am–1pm for schools).

Barber Institute of Fine Arts ★★ MUSEUM

This is one of the best kept
secrets in central England, a free art gallery with a cache of spectacular Old Masters.
Everything in the Barber—arranged chronologically—is worth lingering over, but
there are several showstoppers. From Renaissance Italy there's a rare youthful *St.
John the Evangelist* (1320) by Simone Martini, Bellini's masterful *St. Jerome in the
Wilderness* (1460), and a gloriously rich *Adoration of the Magi* (1560s) from Bassano,
as well as a *Madonna & Child* (1490s) from the studio of Botticelli. Work from the
Flemish school includes the heart-breaking *Ecce Homo* (1626) by Anthony Van Dyck
(rotated with the National Gallery every five years), Frans Hals' mysterious *Man
Holding a Skull* (1614), and a rare landscape from Rubens. Gainsborough's iconic
Harvest Wagon (1767) is here, as is the incredibly candid, mesmerizing *Portrait of
Countess Golovine* (1800) by Elisabeth Vigée-Lebrun. The sumptuous *Blue Bower*
(1865) by Rossetti, and Whistler's two girls in *Symphony in White, No. III* (1867), are
perhaps the most memorable images in the collection, but there is also a decent trove
of Impressionist work from Degas, Manet, and Monet, and Van Gogh's dignified *Peas-
ant Woman Digging* (1885).

The gallery lies within the campus of the **University of Birmingham,** mostly a
1960s creation, but with a core of magnificent Edwardian Byzantine-style buildings—try and peek inside the Aston Webb Building, and admire the soaring Joseph
Chamberlain Memorial Clock Tower, a grand campanile completed in 1908.

University of Birmingham (just off Edgbaston Park Rd., near the University's East Gate, 2½ miles
south of the city center). www.barber.org.uk. 𝄞**0121/414-7333.** Free admission. Mon–Sat 10am–
5pm; Sun 11am–5pm. Train from New Street to University Station (10 min.; £1.60), then a 10 min.
walk. Bus: 61, 62, or 63 from the city center.

Birmingham Museum & Art Gallery ★★ MUSEUM

Opened back in 1885,
this elegant Victorian edifice is instantly recognized by its "Big Brum" clock tower. It's
much bigger than it looks, and with a new section—"A City in the Making," covering
the history of Birmingham—opening in early 2013, you'll need at least two hours
here. The art galleries on the second floor contain plenty of European gems, from
Degas and Pissarro to Rubens and Bellini, but the core collection is British, especially
the work of pre-Raphaelite painters. Gallery 14 is devoted entirely to Birmingham-
born Edward Burne-Jones; his vast *The Star of Bethlehem* was commissioned by the
gallery in 1887. Holman Hunt is the star of gallery 18, where his symbolic *The Finding of the Saviour in the Temple* and *Valentine Rescuing Sylvia from Proteus* hold court,

along with Rossetti's *La Donna Della Finestra*. Rossetti's second famous painting of *Beata Beatrix* (finished by Ford Madox Brown) is in gallery 17, along with the allegorical *Blind Girl* by John Everett Millais. Make time also for the wonderfully restored Industrial Gallery, with a vast selection of ceramics, glass and stained glass, and the Staffordshire Hoard, a stunning cache of Anglo-Saxon treasure comprising 5kg (11 lbs) of gold and 1kg (2.2 lbs) of silver, found just north of Birmingham in 2009.

Chamberlain Sq. www.bmag.org.uk. © **0121/303-1966.** Free admission; varying charges for special exhibitions. Mon–Thurs and Sat 10am–5pm; Fri 10:30am–5pm; Sun 12:30–5pm.

Black Country Living Museum ★ MUSEUM   Much of the area immediately
surrounding Birmingham is called the Black Country (after the black smoke that billowed over the area during the iron-working era). That period is commemorated at this open-air museum in Dudley, a suburban town about 10 miles northwest of central Birmingham. The museum occupies a sprawling landscape in the South Staffordshire coal fields, and recreates what it was like to work and live in the Black Country of the 1850s. An electric tramway takes visitors to a thick underground coal seam, and trolleys move through a reconstructed industrial village with a schoolhouse, anchor forge, working replica of a 1712 steam engine, and trade shops.

Tipton Rd., Dudley (3 miles north of junction 2 exit on the M5; parking £2). Tipton train station, on the Birmingham to Wolverhampton line, is 1 mile from the museum. www.bclm.co.uk.© **0121/557-9643.** Admission £14.95 adults, £11.95 seniors, £7.95 children 5–16, £39.95 family ticket. Mar–Oct daily 10am–5pm; Nov–Feb daily 10am–4pm.

Cadbury World ★ FACTORY TOUR   Chocoholics beware—this is the British
home of all things cocoa. It's not quite Willie Wonka's Chocolate Factory, but it comes pretty close. The exhibition inside contains 14 themed zones, starting with the origins of chocolate in Aztec Mexico, and ending, unsurprisingly, with a vast store so crammed with rare and special-edition chocolate you'll be tempted to take out a small loan (you'll get some free tasters along the way). The only part of the actual factory you get to see is the packaging plant, where chocolate is wrapped and put into boxes for distribution.

Linden Rd., Bournville (follow the signs from M5 junctions 2 and 4, or M42 junction 2). www.cadbury world.co.uk. © **0844/880-7667.** Tickets £14.75 adults, £11.10 seniors and students, £10.75 children 4–15, £45 family ticket. Feb–Dec Mon–Fri 10am–3pm; Sat–Sun 10am–4pm. Closed Jan; call ahead to confirm seasonal changes. 15-min. walk from Bournville train station (10 min. from Birmingham New Street station).

Ikon Gallery ★ GALLERY   This contemporary art gallery occupies an old schoolhouse in up-and-coming Brindleyplace, near the canals. The well-curated, high-quality temporary exhibitions here cover a variety of forms, including sound, film, mixed media, photography, painting, sculpture, and installation. The musical elevator adds a touch of humor.

1 Oozells Sq., Brindleyplace. www.ikon-gallery.co.uk. © **0121/248-0708.** Free admission. Tues–Sun 11am–6pm.

Museum of the Jewellery Quarter MUSEUM   Just a 10-minute walk from
the city center is the Jewellery Quarter (www.jewelleryquarter.net) encompassing more than 100 jewelry shops. A unique time capsule of the ancient craft of jewelry, the quarter also offers bargain hunters the opportunity to arrange repairs, design a custom piece, or just browse. The museum itself occupies the old Smith and Pepper factory, where guided tours include a demonstration of jewelry-making techniques at a jeweler's bench.

75–80 Vyse St. www.bmag.org.uk/museum-of-the-jewellery-quarter. (C) **0121/554-3598.** Admission £4 adults, free for children 15 and under. Tues–Sat 10:30am–4pm.

National Sea Life Centre ★ AQUARIUM   This is one of England's best aquariums, and a must-see if you're traveling with children. Best known for its sea-horse breeding program, its one-million-liter ocean tank also houses two giant green sea turtles, hammerhead sharks, and thousands of tropical reef fish, with a fully transparent underwater tunnel you can walk through. Special sections are dedicated to "Nemo" (aka clownfish), spectacular lionfish, and giant catfish from the Amazon. Half way through the complex you can catch a show at the Sensorama 4-D Cinema, where 3-D glasses are enhanced by sensations such as wind, salt spray, and real smells depending on the film.

The Waters Edge, Brindleyplace. www.visitsealife.com. (C) **0121/643-6777.** Admission £18 adults, £17 seniors and students, £14.40 children 3–14. Mon–Fri 10am–5pm; Sat–Sun 10am–6pm.

Thinktank at Millennium Point ★★ ☺ MUSEUM   Ever wanted to know why polar bears don't slip on ice, or how microwaves work? This spectacular high-tech science museum is aimed squarely at youngsters, with a vast range of fun, hands-on exhibits covering everything from how the body functions and the latest surgical techniques (a real human brain is displayed), to steam engines and recycling. The lower floors chronicle the development of Birmingham from its humble beginnings in 1086 through to the boom years of the 1960s. A fabulous display of old machines and steam engines highlights the Victorian golden years of manufacturing, though the grimness of working life is also remembered with exhibits on child labor. The Planetarium (entry included) on level 3 screens movies throughout the day (check times at the entrance). The same building also houses the **Giant Screen at Millennium Point** IMAX movie theatre.

Millennium Point, Curzon St. www.thinktank.ac. (C) **0121/202-2222.** Admission £12.25 adults, £8.40 seniors, students, and children 3–15, family £39; with IMAX £20.50 adults, £14.50 seniors, students, and children 3–15, family £65. Daily 10am–5pm. Call for IMAX schedule.

Where to Eat
EXPENSIVE
Purnell's ★★ CONTEMPORARY ENGLISH   The cooking of Glyn Purnell is bold and innovative, but despite the Michelin star, his two-course lunch menu is Birmingham's best bargain. You dine in a room with arched floor-to-ceiling windows, a chic, contemporary setting with a bar and lounge area for diners only.

Dishes might include pork belly with a truffle pear purée, or wreck fish with coconut milk and Indian lentils. The salad of Devonshire crab—with apple and celeriac mayonnaise and smoked paprika honeycomb—is a real delight, and the desserts are just as playful. Think burnt English custard egg surprise with a warm autumn fruit crumble, hazelnuts, and quince sorbet.

55 Cornwall St. www.purnellsrestaurant.com. (C) **0121/212-9799.** Reservations required. 2-course lunch £22; 3-course lunch £27; 2-course dinner £40; 3-course dinner £50; 8-course tasting menu £80. AE, MC, V. Tues–Fri noon–4:30pm and 7pm–1am (last food orders 9:30pm); Sat 7pm–1am (last food orders 9:30pm). Closed 1 week at Easter, last week in July, 1st week in Aug, and 1 week at Christmas.

Simpsons ★★★ CONTEMPORARY ENGLISH/FRENCH   The grandest and best dining in Birmingham, set in an impressive Georgian mansion with an outdoor terrace and brightly lit dining room with windows into the kitchen. Michelin-starred

Harborne: Chips, Markets, & Michelin Stars

Harborne lies just three miles southwest from Birmingham city center, a leafy, affluent Victorian suburb that was the childhood home of W. H. Auden. Today it's the home of some culinary gems, well worth the bus or taxi fare. Legendary **George and Helen's Chip Shop** ★★ at 72 Court Oak Rd. (✆ **0121/427-2684**) is the best place to sample this British classic, while the **Farmer's Market,** held on the High Street on the second Saturday in every month (9am–2pm), features such treasures as the **Handmade Scotch Egg**

Co ★ (www.handmadescotcheggs. co.uk), which sells 40 varieties of luscious scotch eggs. Then there's **Turners of Harborne** ★★, 69 High St. (www. turnersofharborne.com; ✆ **0121/426-4440**), Birmingham's third Michelin-starred restaurant—Chef Richard Turner conjures up a menu that is contemporary and cutting-edge but inspired by classical French cooking. It's open Tues–Fri noon–2pm and 6:45–9:30pm; Sat 6:45–9:30pm. From the city center, take bus 11A, 11C, 22, 23, 24, or 29.

chef Andreas Antona uses only the finest of seasonal produce. Specialties are forever changing, but main courses might include a magnificent home-salted cod, with crispy-fried whitebait; or a more elaborate loin of rabbit, with macaroni gratin and roasted artichokes. Presentation is spectacular and service is exceptional; expect to be regaled with the odd amuse-bouche.

20 Highfield Rd., Edgbaston. www.simpsonsrestaurant.co.uk. ✆ **0121/454-3434.** Fax 0121/454-3399. Reservations recommended (required Fri–Sat). Main courses £23–£24.95; 3-course lunch £38. AE, DC, MC, V. Daily noon–2pm (to 2:30pm Sat–Sun); Mon–Thurs 7–9:30pm; Fri–Sat 7–10pm. Closed Dec 24–27 and Dec 31–Jan 1.

MODERATE

Asha's ★★ INDIAN   High-quality meals and low prices make this one of the best Indian restaurants in the city. It's named after singing legend Asha Bhosle, who came up with the concept and remains associated with the chain. The menu features all the usual Indian regional classics, but with a contemporary twist: The peppered garlic prawns come with salad drizzled in raspberry citrus dressing, and the sensitively spiced curries are served with mounds of white rice and thick sour cream. The house specialty is Tandoori kebabs, perfect for sharing—try the fiery Jaipur chicken tikka.

Edmund House, 12–22 Newhall St. www.ashasuk.co.uk. ✆ **0121/200-2767.** Reservations recommended. Main courses £7.25–£15.95. AE, DC, MC, V. Mon–Wed noon–2:30pm and 5:30–10:30pm; Thurs–Fri noon–2:30pm and 5:30–11pm; Sat 5–11pm; Sun 5–10pm.

Bank ★ BRASSERIE   The Birmingham outpost of this chic brasserie consistently delivers, with chefs working feverishly in the open-plan kitchen. For a main dish, you can sample superb options such as tandoori-baked sea bass, smoked Severn salmon, slow-cooked lamb shank, or the smoked haddock and leek risotto with poached egg. Desserts include a classics such as English chocolate fudge pudding with vanilla ice cream. Get a seat overlooking the canal, or on the terrace in summer.

4 Brindleyplace. www.bankrestaurants.com. ✆ **0121/633-4466.** Reservations recommended. Main courses £9.50–£31.95. AE, DC, MC, V. Mon–Fri noon–11pm; Sat 11:30am–11:30pm; Sun 11:30am–10pm.

"Bucket Dining" in the Balti Triangle

Birmingham's best-known culinary experience was actually created by Pakistani Kashmiri chefs in the Sparkhill area of the city in the late 1970s. *Balti* literally means bucket, but it refers to a Kashmiri style of cooking meat and vegetables very fast over a hot flame. A good balti-style curry should be flavorful but not necessarily spicy, and is traditionally served with naan bread, not rice. With the city's large Pakistani Kashmiri population, there are now over 50 balti houses in Birmingham's Balti Triangle (roughly within Ladypool Road, Stoney Lane, and Stratford Road, south of the city center), most of which

are bare-bones, Bring your own Beer (BYOB) affairs. One of the better ones is **Adil,** 353–355 Ladypool Rd. (www.adilbalti.co.uk; ✆ **0121/449-0335**), which claims to be the original Birmingham balti house; open Sunday to Thursday noon to midnight, Friday 4pm to midnight, and Saturday noon to 1am. The connoisseurs choice is **Al Frash** ★★ (www.alfrash.com; ✆ **0121/753-3120**), 186 Ladypool Rd., open daily 5pm to midnight. Take bus no. 37 from Navigation Street, near New Street Station, to Stratford Road, opposite Ladypool Road (5 min.). Taxis should be £5–6.

INEXPENSIVE

Canalside Café CAFE/COFFEEHOUSE   This old waterside lock-keeper's cottage is a laid-back cafe during the day and a decent pub by night, with a range of real ales on tap. The food is solid, home-cooked stuff: Vegetable soups, sandwiches, and a selection of organic and vegan options. Sit outside in sunny weather and watch the barges glide past, or enjoy the cluttered, antique-strewn interior.

Canalside Cottage, 35 Worcester Bar, Gas St. (at the Gas St. Basin). ✆ **0121/248-7979.** Main courses from £3.95. MC, V. Daily 11am–11pm.

Shopping

There are hundreds of retail stores in Birmingham, and many people in the Midlands come here just to shop, especially along **New Street** and in the shiny new **Bullring** (www.bullring.co.uk; ✆ **0121/632-1500**), which has been developed into Europe's largest city-center retail area. Here also is the iconic **Selfridges** building (see above). A short walk from the Bullring is the **Custard Factory** (www.custardfactory.co.uk; ✆ **0121/224-7777**), built 100 years ago and now home to galleries, artists, independent shops, and restaurants. From here art lovers should head farther into the **Eastside** district, where galleries such as **VIVID,** 140 Heath Mill Lane (www.vivid.org.uk; ✆ **0121/766-7876;** Thurs–Sat noon–5pm), and **Eastside Projects,** 86 Heath Mill Lane (www.eastsideprojects.org; ✆ **0121/771-1778;** usually Thurs noon–6:30pm, Fri–Sat noon–5pm), organize a variety of mixed-media contemporary art exhibitions

The city's **Mailbox** complex, at Wharfside Street (www.mailboxlife.com; ✆ **0121/632-1000**), is a gargantuan shopping center, with such stores as Harvey Nichols, Emporio Armani, Fat Face, Hugo Boss, Jaeger, and Crabtree & Evelyn, along with restaurants and a spa. For a touch of Victorian elegance, head to the **Great Western Arcade** (www.greatwesternarcade.co.uk), just opposite Snow Hill railway station, which houses smaller, independent stores like Mr Simms Olde Sweet Shop.

If you're here on a Tuesday, Thursday, Friday, or Saturday (9am–5pm), visit the **Rag Market** on Edgbaston Street (www.ragmarket.com; ✆ **0121/464-8349**), a lively collection of 350 stalls selling vintage clothing, hats, and jewelry.

Entertainment & Nightlife
THE PERFORMING ARTS

The vast **International Convention Centre** (ICC) on Broad Street holds numerous events but is best known as the home of **Symphony Hall** (www.thsh.co.uk; ✆ 0121/780-3333), hailed as an acoustical gem since its completion in 1990. Base of the **City of Birmingham Symphony Orchestra,** it also hosts special classical music events.

Just across the canal, the **National Indoor Arena (NIA),** King Edward's Road (✆ 0844/338-8000; www.thenia.co.uk), seats 13,000 and is a favorite site for jazz, pop, and rock concerts, as well as sporting events and conventions. The same group manages the **LG Arena** (www.lgarena.co.uk; ✆ 0121/780-4141) at the National Exhibition Centre, the venue for the biggest concerts and events.

Adjacent to the ICC along Broad Street, the **Birmingham Repertory Theatre,** at Centenary Square (www.birmingham-rep.co.uk; ✆ 0121/236-4455), houses one of the top companies in England. Note that the theatre will reopen sometime in 2013 after a major renovation.

The restored **Birmingham Hippodrome,** Hurst Street (www.birminghamhippodrome.com; ✆ 0844/338-5000), is home to the **Birmingham Royal Ballet** and visiting companies from around the world. It hosts a variety of events, from the Welsh National Opera to musicals to dance. The box office is open Monday to Saturday 9:30am to 8:30pm.

The **Midlands Arts Centre,** in Cannon Hill Park (www.macarts.co.uk; ✆ 0121/446-3200), is close to the Edgbaston Cricket Ground and reached by bus numbers 1, 45, or 47. The MAC houses three performance areas and stages a lively range of drama, dance, and musical performances, as well as films. The box office is open daily from 9am to 8:45pm.

The **New Alexandra Theatre,** Station Street (www.alexandratheatre.org.uk; ✆ 0121/643-5536), hosts national touring companies, including productions from London's West End. Contact the box office for show details.

Note: Tickets for all Birmingham theatres are available through Birmingham visitor offices, or www.theticketfactory.com.

THE PUB & BAR SCENE

As befits England's second city, Birmingham boasts a varied and energy-charged nightlife with clusters of bars and venues in a wide range of neighborhoods. Most visitors are content with the traditional nightlife hub concentrated along Broad Street and Brindleyplace in the city center, but you should also check out the clubs and bars in the flourishing Eastside and Digbeth districts. It's here you'll find Birmingham's oldest pub, the **Old Crown,** 188 High St., Deritend (www.theoldcrown.com; ✆ 0121/248-1368), a half mile walk from the Bullring. The pub has roots back in 1368, and is open daily noon to 11pm. Back in the center, facing the cathedral, the **Old Joint Stock,** 4 Temple Row (www.oldjointstocktheatre.co.uk; ✆ 0121/200-1892), was a bank built in 1864, now a large pub and theatre venue open daily from noon for a range of homemade pies, bangers and mash, and a full-range of Fuller's ales. At **Jekyll & Hyde** (www.thejekyllandhyde.co.uk; ✆ 0121/236-0345), 28 Steelhouse Lane, the Victorian-inspired upstairs Gin Parlour has the Midlands' largest selection of gins.

The Jewellery Quarter is also home to some atmospheric pubs, notably **The Lord Clifden** ★, 34 Great Hampton St., Hockley (www.thelordclifden.com;

© 0121/523-7515), celebrated for its collection of street art, including pieces by Banksy. It's open daily 10am to 2am. If pubs are not your thing, **Revolution,** back on Broad Street (www.revolution-bars.co.uk; © 0121/665-6508), is a vodka bar drawing a hip under-40 crowd (Mon–Wed 11:30am–midnight, Thurs–Sat 11:30am–3am, Sun noon–2am). Cocktail lovers should check out **Island Bar ★,** 14–16 Suffolk St., (www.bar-island.co.uk; © 0121/632-5296), with live music and club nights at the weekend, and a Tiki Bar every Friday.

THE CLUB & MUSIC SCENE

The live music scene is especially strong in Birmingham. The **02 Academy,** 16–18 Horsefair, Bristol Street (www.o2academybirmingham.co.uk; © 0121/622-8247), hosts a wide range of live acts as well as club nights like **Propaganda** every Friday, the U.K.'s biggest indie dance night. The **Hare and Hounds** pub, 106 High St. (www.hareandhoundskingsheath.co.uk; © 0121/444-2081), in Kings Heath features a healthy roster of everything from hip-hop DJs to protest folk rock and poetry nights. The **hmv Institute** (venues.meanfiddler.com/hmv-institute/home; © 0121/643-0428), 78 Digbeth High St., runs alternative indie club nights every month, as well as a variety of live bands and performers.

Live music and especially stand-up **comedy** dominates at the **Glee Club** in the Arcadian on Hurst Street. (www.glee.co.uk/birmingham; © 0871/472-0400). The **Jam House,** 3–5 St. Paul's Sq. (www.thejamhouse.com; © 0121/200-3030), is a popular live music bar directed by Jools Holland with an emphasis on blues, soul, and boogie-woogie. Jazz also has a following in the city; visit www.birmingham jazz.co.uk to see what's going on.

Digbeth also contains some of the city's best nightclubs, including the hangar-like **Air Nightclub** in the Custard Factory complex on Heath Mill Lane (www.airbirmingham.com), the current home of dance institution **Godskitchen** (www.godskitchen. com; © 01789/739989) on Saturday nights (monthly). Megaclub **Gatecrasher Birmingham,** which got started here in the 1990s, is now at 182 Broad St. (www.gatecrasher.co.uk; © 0121/633-1520), while **Vudu** (www.vuduclub.com; © 0121/643-0859), 51 Smallbrook Queensway, is Birmingham's biggest alternative

> ### The Gay Scene
>
> Birmingham has a thriving gay and lesbian community, with more than a dozen gay venues in the "gay village" in and around **Hurst Street,** just south of the city center. One of the most popular venues is **Nightingale,** 18 Kent St. (www.nightingaleclub.co.uk; © 0121/6226-1718), with five bars and two frenzied dance floors. The cover varies but is often around £5. Open Monday and Thursday to Saturday 9pm to 4am. Good resources include www.visitgay brum.com.

music club. Elegant **Bambu** (www.bambubar.co.uk; © 0121/622-4124), Kottwall House, Wrottesley Street, is the place to spot celebs (if you can get in), and **Reflex** (www.reflexbirminghambroadstreet.co.uk; © 0121/643-0444), 36–37 Broad St., is the place for music from the 1980s.

Where to Stay

EXPENSIVE

Hilton Garden Inn ★★ 🍴 Right in the heart of the revitalized canal district and Brindleyplace, the former *Mint Hotel* is a stylish option featuring sleek, compact rooms with contemporary fittings, a whole roster of high-tech amenities, floor-to-ceiling windows, and rainforest showers. Each room comes with an iMac that can access cable TV, skype, and free Internet, and play radio, CDs, your iPod, or DVDs (the hotel keeps a selection). Deals online can make this the best bargain in the city.

1 Brunswick Sq., Brindleyplace, Birmingham B1 2HW. hiltongardeninn.hilton.com. © **0121/643-1003.** Fax 0121/643-1005. 238 units. £79–£119 double. AE, DC, MC, V. Parking £12.50. **Amenities:** Restaurant; bar; exercise room; 24-hr. room service. *In room:* A/C, TV, hair dryer, iMac multimedia entertainment system, Wi-Fi (free).

MODERATE

Novotel Birmingham Centre   In Brindleyplace next to the *Hilton,* this is a well-run chain hotel that offers good, comfortable rooms that have a bit of character. Bedrooms, midsize for the most part, are in the motel style. The on-site brasserie serves affordable food made with fresh ingredients, and the bar is a popular rendez-vous. All in all, especially considering the reasonable prices, this isn't a bad choice.

70 Broad St., Birmingham B1 2HT. www.novotel.com. © **0121/643-2000.** Fax 0121/643-9786. 148 units. £79–£94 double. Children stay free in parent's room. AE, MC, V. Parking £13. **Amenities:** Restaurant; bar; exercise room; Jacuzzi; sauna; room service. *In room:* A/C, TV, minibar, hair dryer, Wi-Fi (£10 per day).

Staying Cool at the Rotunda ★★★   Certainly the coolest hotel in Birmingham, these chic serviced apartments occupy the restored and iconic 1960s' Rotunda in the city center, with suitably awe-inspiring views from the top three floors it occupies. Each apartment has huge floor-to-ceiling windows, washing machines, Mac computers, an iPod player, and a full kitchen. Oranges and an electric juicer are supplied, along with top-of-the-range espresso machines. The apartments combine contemporary design with a cool Brit 1960s' style, and come in four sizes—small, medium, large, and extra large (amenities are the same in all guest rooms).

150 New St., Birmingham B2 4PA. www.stayingcool.com. © **0121/285-1290.** 26 units. £109.50–£349 double. AE, MC, V. Parking £8.50, at the Bullring. *In room:* A/C, TV, kitchen, hair dryer, Wi-Fi (free).

INEXPENSIVE

Nite Nite ★   This novel hotel certainly wins the prize for most original accommodations, perfect for short stays and for guests who spend most of their time out on the town. Rooms are tiny cubes, a bit like a luxury cabin on a yacht, dominated by a huge TV and a bed that takes up most of the space. There are no windows; this is a Japanese-style "capsule hotel" experience, though the bathrooms are great and everything is spotlessly clean.

18 Holliday St., Birmingham B1 1TB. www.nitenite.com. © **0845/890-9099.** Fax 0121/634-3236. 104 units. £38–£55.95 double. AE, DC, MC, V. Parking £14. **Amenities:** Restaurant; bar; ironing rooms located on each floor. *In room:* A/C, TV, hair dryer, Wi-Fi (free).

Premier Inn Birmingham Central (East)   Lying between the M6 motorway and the city center, this is a modern, well-kept, and well-run chain hotel. It offers substantially comfortable, though rather standard, bedrooms. For the motorist just passing through Birmingham or spending only a night, it should be ideal. The hotel also has an affordable on-site restaurant, so you don't have to drive into the center of Birmingham at night.

Richard St., Aston, Waterlinks, Birmingham B7 4AA. www.premierinn.com. © **0871/527-8080.** Fax 0871/527-8081. 60 units. £37–£52 double. AE, MC, V. Free parking. **Amenities:** Restaurant; bar. *In room:* A/C, TV, hair dryer, Wi-Fi (free).

Olde Worlde at New Hall

Tudor four-posters and afternoon tea in Birmingham? One of the Midlands' most enticing and exclusive historic hotels lies in Sutton Coldfield, 8 miles from central Birmingham and easily accessible by road (or £6.50 from Sutton Coldfield train station by taxi). The **New Hall Hotel ★★** (www.handpickedhotels. co.uk/newhall; *C* **0845/0727-577**), Walmley Road, Sutton Coldfield, offers country chic accommodations in a 12th-century manor house once owned by the Earls of Warwick (it's even surrounded by a moat). Guests are treated to a spa, 26 acres of tranquil gardens, and various historic rooms, some of which go back to the Tudor period. The best suite preserves the bedstead used by a young Elizabeth I. If you just want to check out the premises, go for **afternoon tea ★★★** (£7.50–£29.50), one of the best in England—the food is exquisite, served in a comfy lounge of sofas (with wood fire in winter).

WORCESTER & THE MALVERNS

Worcester 112 miles NW of London; Great Malvern 117 miles NW of London

The ancient town of **Worcester** has been an important trading center since Neolithic times thanks to its strategic location on the River Severn. Royal Worcester Porcelain was established here in 1751, while the town's most celebrated product, Lea & Perrins Worcestershire Sauce, goes back to 1838. Royal Worcester closed in 2009, but the sauce factory is still there, and just as secretive as ever. The great cathedral provides the obvious focus for most visitors, surrounded by a hodgepodge of Tudor, Georgian, and modern streets.

The beautiful and historic Malvern hills lie just west of Worcester, rising suddenly from the Severn Valley and stretching for 9 miles. The genteel Victorian spa town of **Great Malvern** itself is still the home of legendary Morgan Cars, though the town's other icon, Malvern Water, closed in 2010 (the local spring water has been a royal favorite for more than 400 years, and is still bottled by Holywell Spring Water). Hiking the hills is the main pastime here, with an abundance of refreshing air and country vistas that inspired England's greatest composer, Sir Edward Elgar.

Essentials

GETTING THERE   From London's Paddington Station, trains leave every 2 hours to Worcester (from £28.60 one-way) and Great Malvern (from £29 one-way). Trains run between Worcester and Great Malvern every 15 minutes or so (and take around 15 min.). Tickets are £4.60 one-way. Fairly frequent trains from Birmingham take around 1 hour to both towns (£7–9 one-way).

VISITOR INFORMATION   The **Worcester Tourist Information Centre** is located in the old Guildhall on the High Street (www.visitworcester.com; *C* **01905/ 726311**). It's open Monday to Saturday 9:30am to 5pm. The **Malvern Tourist Information Centre,** 21 Church St., Great Malvern (www.visitthemalverns.org; *C* **01684/892289**), is open daily 10am to 5pm. On Sundays from December to March, it closes at 4pm.

TOURS   Guided walks (90 min.; £5 per person; www.discover-history.co.uk) dubbed **"the Worcester Story"** run daily at 6pm from the Guildhall in the High

Street— make reservations at © **07949/222137.** One of the best ways to see Worcester is from the river aboard one of the 45-minute cruise trips (£5.50) offered by **Worcester River Cruises,** 22 Britannia Rd., (www.worcesterrivercruises.co.uk; © **01905/611060**). A cream tea cruise costs £13.50. Cruises operate daily April to October.

Exploring the Area

The Commandery ★★ MUSEUM   Originally the 11th-century Hospital of St. Wulstan, the Commandery serves as an absorbing museum today, a labyrinth of 35 creaky, wood-paneled rooms and timber-beamed halls dating from the 15th century. Most rooms are empty or sparsely furnished, but the hand-held audioguides (included) provide some color. Each room tackles a different theme, from games and clothing, to sickness and death, and you can choose commentary for each based on one of six key periods: The monastic hospital from around 1480; the house of Robert Wylde, a wealthy merchant, in 1607; the house as the headquarters of King Charles II during the Battle of Worcester in 1651; the Georgian house in 1767; the College of the Blind in 1880; and the building's last role, as a printworks after World War II. The most memorable rooms include the kitchen (room 22), where the "Commandery skeletons" were found, buried just before the medieval hospital closed, and the **Painted Chamber ★★** (room 29), where rare 15th-century frescoes were uncovered, with vivid images of martyred saints and the Holy Trinity.

109 Sidbury St., Worcester. www.worcestercitymuseums.org.uk. © **01905/361821.** Admission £5.50 adults, £4.25 seniors, £2.50 children 5–16, free for children 4 and under. Mon–Sat 10am–5pm; Sun 1:30–5pm. The Commandery is a 3-min. walk from Worcester Cathedral.

Malvern Museum MUSEUM   This small but enlightening museum is just a 5-minute walk from Malvern Priory and the Tourist Information Centre in Great Malvern. Seven themed rooms tell the story of the town, from local prehistoric sites and the Benedictine monastery established in 1085, to Malvern's famous mineral water and the creation of the Morgan Motor Works in the 1890s.

Abbey Rd., Great Malvern. www.malvernmuseum.co.uk. © **01684/567811.** Admission £2 adults, 50p children 5–16, free for children 4 and under. Apr–Oct 10:30am–5pm. Closed Wed.

Sir Edward Elgar's Birthplace Museum ★★ HISTORIC HOME   This charming red-brick country cottage is where one of England's greatest composers was born in 1857. Serving as a memorial to Elgar, the cottage houses a unique collection of manuscripts and musical scores, photographs, and other personal memorabilia. Just yards from the cottage, a visitor center introduces you to the man and his music, even showing film clips of the composer with his beloved dogs. Sir Elgar wrote, among other pieces, *The Enigma Variations* and the *Dream of Gerontius.*

  St. Wulstan's Church, 2 miles west of Great Malvern on the Ledbury Road, is where Elgar is buried with his wife and daughter.

Crown E. Lane, Lower Broadheath. www.elgarfoundation.org. © **01905/333224.** Admission £7.50 adults, £6.50 seniors, £4.50 students, £3.50 children 16 and under, £15 family ticket. Daily 11am–5pm. Closed Dec 24–Jan 31. Drive out of Worcester on the A44 toward Leominster. After 2 miles, turn off to the right at the sign. The house is a half-mile ahead on the right.

Worcester Cathedral ★★ CATHEDRAL   Set majestically on the banks of the River Severn, Worcester Cathedral and its handsomely carved central tower is one of the most striking in England. St. Wulfstan started the current building in 1084, with

Hiking in the Malverns

The **Malvern Hills** ★★ run north–south for about 9 miles between Great Malvern and the village of Colwall, offering fine views across the Severn Valley and some relatively easy and rewarding hikes; legend has it they were Tolkien's inspiration for the White Hills of Gondor. The entire length of the hills is open to the public and is crisscrossed with bridleways and footpaths. The quickest access point is **St. Ann's Well Café** ★ (www.stannswell.co.uk; ℂ **01684/560285;** Fri 11:30am–3:30pm, Sat–Sun 10am–4pm), St. Ann's Road, a popular pit-stop where Malvern spring water seeps from the ground, around 0.8 miles from Great Malvern train station. From here you can make a 3.5 miles (2-hr.) loop up to the highest point in the Malverns, Worcestershire Beacon at 425m (1,394 ft.), or an equally bracing stroll around North Hill and North Quarry (2¾ miles). At the southern end of the hills, a hike up the Herefordshire Beacon (338m/1,109 ft.) and the British Camp Iron Age site is made more enticing by **Just Rachel** ★★, Rachel Hick's ice cream kiosk (www.justrachel.com; ℂ **01684/540262**)—try the gooseberry and elderflower flavor. Visit www.malvern hillsaonb.org.uk or www.malvernhills.org. uk for more information.

most of the soaring Gothic interior completed in the 12th and 13th centuries. Inside, in front of the altar, lies the tomb of infamous King John, who died in 1216 just one year after signing the Magna Carta. Nearby is the tomb of Prince Arthur, the popular elder brother of Henry VIII, who died at just 15 years of age. Take a peek at the Norman crypt with its cushion capitals dating from 1084, then walk through the cloisters to the 12th-century octagonal chapterhouse, one of the finest in England. Climb the tower for stupendous views of the city.

College Yard, at High St. www.worcestercathedral.co.uk. ℂ **01905/732900.** Free admission; adults asked for a £5 donation. Tower £3 adults, £1 children 15 and under; tours £3 adults, free for children. Daily 7:30am–6pm; tower Easter–Sept Sat and school holidays 11am–5pm. Tours: Dec–Mar Sat 11am and 2:30pm; Apr–Nov Mon–Sat 11am and 2:30pm.

Worcester Porcelain Museum ★ MUSEUM   Just south of the cathedral in what was once the red-brick industrial quarter of the city, the world's largest collection of Worcester porcelain features some real beauties, with lavish tea sets, vases, and bowls engraved with multi-colored flowers, temples, portraits, and peacocks. The Georgian galleries contain some rare 18th-century pieces such as the "Wigornia Creamboat," a delicately crafted jug, and opulent tea and dining sets created for George III in 1807. Upstairs, the Victorian galleries begin with the ornate "Nelson Teapot," commissioned for the Lord Admiral himself in 1802, and contain some incredibly opulent pieces created for the Chicago Expo in 1893. The 20th-century galleries also include information on kilns and the manufacturing process. Portmeirion Pottery now owns the Royal Worcester brand—the latter went bankrupt in 2009 after 258 years of trade.

Severn St., Worcester. www.worcesterporcelainmuseum.org.uk. ℂ **01905/746000.** Admission £6 adults; £5 seniors, students, and children under 18; £12 family ticket. Behind-the-scenes tours £6 for all visitors and includes museum entry. Easter–Oct Mon–Sat 10am–5pm; Nov–Easter Tues–Sat 10:30am–4pm.

Where to Eat

The Fig Tree ★★ MEDITERRANEAN   This stylish contemporary restaurant is the best place to eat in Malvern, just a short walk from the train station. The menu takes inspiration from all over the Mediterranean. Feast on a sumptuous chargrilled lamb souvlaki, with minted yogurt, saffron rice, and salad, or some exquisite seafood ranging from chargrilled sea bass and swordfish to squid served Spanish style with chorizo and seared salmon scallops. All meats are locally sourced.

99b Church St., Great Malvern. www.thefigtreemalvern.co.uk. ℂ **01684/569909.** Reservations recommended. Main courses £11.95–£16.95. AE, MC, V. Tues–Sat 12:30–2:30pm and 6–10pm.

Little Ginger Pig ★ ENGLISH/CONTINENTAL   This bright, healthful cafe and bistro strives to serve fresh ingredients, sourced as locally, seasonally, and as "free range" as possible. Grab a coffee and cake or a light lunch of salads and baguette sandwiches during the day, or enjoy the cozy candle-lit ambience at night. The same crew runs the Balcony Café in the City Art Gallery & Museum on Foregate Street, a good choice for a take-out sandwich.

9 Copenhagen St., Worcester. www.littlegingerpig.co.uk. ℂ **01905/338913.** Main courses £3.50–£6.60. AE, MC, V. Cafe Mon–Sat 9:30am–4:30pm. Bistro Mon–Thurs 9:30am–4pm; Fri 9:30am–5pm; Sat 8:30am–5pm; Sun 10am–2:30pm.

Mac & Jac Café Deli DELI/CAFE   This bright, modern deli and cafe on Worcester's most attractive historic street is perfect for a coffee, a take-out sandwich, home-made flatbreads with a variety of fillings, or a light lunch—traditional dishes might include warm pheasant pudding or grilled black pudding. There are also plenty of vegetarian options, such as a tasty leek, tarragon, and goat cheese risotto. Peruse the deli for zesty fishcakes, Scotch eggs, and irresistible cakes. Mostly local produce is used here.

44 Friar St., Worcester. ℂ **01905/731331.** Sandwiches from £4.20; Main courses £9–£10.95. AE, MC, V. Tues–Thurs 10am–4pm; Fri 9am–5pm; Sat 9–6pm.

Pub at Ye Old Talbot Hotel PUB FARE   This venerable hotel, pub, and bistro contains heaps of Victorian nostalgia and old-fashioned wood paneling that has been darkened by generations of cigarette smoke and spilled beer. It offers traditional pub grub—haddock and chips, beef and Ruddles ale pie—that's better than expected, especially when it's accompanied with a pint of the house's half-dozen ales on tap. The fine Sunday roast is £8.99.

Friar St., at College St., Worcester. www.oldenglishinns.co.uk/worcester. ℂ **01905/235730.** Main courses £7.69–£9.29, steaks from £16.99. AE, MC, V. Bar daily 11am–11pm. Bistro Mon–Sat 7am–10pm; Sun 8am–10pm.

Where to Stay
VERY EXPENSIVE

The Elms Hotel ★ ☺   This is one of the most impressive hotels in the region, a Queen Anne mansion built in 1710 by Gilbert White, a disciple of Sir Christopher Wren. Like Bant's (see below), it lies on the outskirts of Worcester, is easy to get to, and offers a sort of fantasy version of olde England. The Elms, however, is far more upscale, complete with mahogany or walnut 18th- and 19th-century antiques, a lavish modern spa, and log-burning fireplaces. Bedrooms come in various shapes and sizes, and feature twin or double beds. ***Insider tip:*** If you notify the staff in advance, a member will round up all your baby needs in advance, from food to nappies (diapers).

On A443 (2 miles west of Abberley, near Worcester), Worcester WR6 6AT. www.theelmshotel.com. © **01299/896666.** Fax 01299/896804. 23 units. £150–£260 double. Basic package rates include English breakfast. AE, DC, MC, V. Free parking. Take the A443 for 6 miles west of Worcester, following the signs to Tenbury Wells. **Amenities:** Restaurant; bar; tennis court; spa; room service; babysitting; croquet lawn. *In room:* TV, hair dryer, Wi-Fi (free, in some).

EXPENSIVE

The Abbey ★ This is Great Malvern's most romantic hotel, an ivy-smothered pile, dating back to the town's Victorian heyday, right next to the Benedictine priory. Standard rooms are simply but comfortably decorated in a classical English style, while superiors are a notch up in style and space, many with views of the Malvern Hills.

Abbey Rd., Great Malvern, Worcestershire WR14 3ET. www.sarova.com/abbey. © **01684/892332.** Fax 01684/892662. 103 units. £70–£155 double. Rates include English breakfast. AE, DC, MC, V. Free parking. **Amenities:** 2 restaurants; bar; room service. *In room:* TV, hair dryer, Internet (free).

Bant's Pub ★ This gorgeous 16th-century country inn lies a 10-minute drive outside Worcester in rolling countryside. It's not so convenient for exploring the center of the city, but perfect for driving around the area. The oak-beamed rooms are warmly decorated and extremely cozy. It's been owned and managed by the Bant family since 1985, and the pub downstairs serves local cider, beer, and solid bar food sourced from local suppliers.

Worcester Rd. (A422), Upton Snodsbury, Worcester WR7 4NN. www.bants.co.uk. © **01905/381282.** Fax 01905/381173. 9 units. £65–£150 double. AE, DC, MC, V. Free parking. **Amenities:** Restaurant; bar. *In room:* TV/DVD, hair dryer, Wi-Fi (free).

Cottage in the Wood ★ There is indeed a cottage in the woods associated with this hotel—it contains four cozy bedrooms and dates from the 17th century. But most of the inn occupies a nearby Georgian house from the late 1700s. Originally built for the semi-retired mother of the lord of a neighboring estate, it's referred to as the "Dower House" and is appropriately outfitted in an attractive Laura Ashley style. The bedrooms are small, but this place is so charming and offers such panoramic views that most visitors don't mind.

Holywell Rd., Malvern Wells, Worcestershire WR14 4LG. www.cottageinthewood.co.uk. © **01684/588860.** Fax 01684/560662. 31 units. £84–£182 double. AE, MC, V. Free parking. After leaving Great Malvern on the A449, turn right just before the B4209 turnoff on the opposite side of the road. The inn is on the right. **Amenities:** Restaurant; bar; room service; babysitting. *In room:* TV/DVD/video player, hair dryer, Wi-Fi (free).

INEXPENSIVE

Manor Coach House ★★ This is the Worcester's best B&B, a series of modern red-brick apartments converted from the outbuildings adjacent to the main house. The simple but elegant and spotless rooms are well equipped and include a two-floor suite with kitchenette (ideal for families). Apartment no. 4 has access to an outdoor deck, perfect for lounging in the sun. Add in a huge home-cooked breakfast to start the day, and you have an excellent deal.

Hindlip Lane, Hindlip, Worcester WR3 8SJ (just off the A449). www.manorcoachhouse.co.uk. © **01905/456457.** Fax 01905/767772. 5 units. £80 double. AE, DC, MC, V. Rates include breakfast. Free parking. *In room:* TV/DVD, hair dryer, Wi-Fi (free).

THE WELSH MARCHES

The borderlands between England and Wales became known as the **Welsh Marches** in the Middle Ages, an alluring area of rolling hills and market towns encompassing the modern counties of Herefordshire and Shropshire.

Situated on the Wye River, 16 miles east of the Welsh border, the city of **Hereford** is a bustling market town today, known for its fine cathedral and world-famous cattle industry. Heading north, **Ludlow** is an essential stop; a mellow town on the tranquil Teme River lined with Georgian and Jacobean timbered buildings, and a handful of world-class restaurants and pubs.

One of the finest Tudor towns in England, **Shrewsbury** is noted for its black-and-white buildings of timber and plaster, built by the powerful and prosperous wool traders, or drapers, in the shadow of the town's once great castle. Charles Darwin was born in Shrewsbury in 1809—although he spent most of his life elsewhere, he continued to visit the town until his father's death in 1848. A statue commemorates the great man outside the library on Castle Street.

With more time (and a car), you can explore the Wye Valley, with **Hay-on-Wye**, right on the Welsh border, the nucleus of Britain's secondhand book trade, and **Ross-on-Wye** downriver, a good base for the sylvan charms of the lower Wye valley.

Essentials

GETTING THERE   By train from London's Paddington Station, Hereford is a 3-hour trip, and involves changing at Newport in South Wales (£36 one-way). Trains run every hour from Birmingham (1½ hr.) for £14.20 and from Worcester (45 min.) for £8.20 (both one-way). Shrewsbury is 2½ to 3 hours from London Euston with one change at Birmingham or Crewe (one-way from £26.50). Trains run between Birmingham and Shrewsbury every 30 min (around 1 hr.) and cost £12.60 (again, one-way).

VISITOR INFORMATION   Hereford's **Tourist Information Centre** (www.visit herefordshire.co.uk; ✆ 01432/268430) is located at 1 King St. and is open April to September daily 9:30am to 4:30pm, and October to March Monday to Friday 10am to 4:30pm.

The **Shrewsbury Tourist Information Centre,** in Rowley's House Museum on Barker Street (www.visitshrewsbury.com; ✆ 01743/281200), is open May to September Monday to Saturday from 10am to 5pm, Sunday 10am to 4pm. From October to April, its hours are Monday to Saturday from 10am to 5pm.

Exploring the Area
HEREFORDSHIRE

Hereford's most prized possession is the Mappa Mundi (see below), but make time for the impressive **Cider Museum,** 21 Ryelands St., (www.cidermuseum.co.uk; ✆ 01432/354207), to learn about the history of local cider-making. The museum is open Tuesday to Saturday 10am to 5pm (Nov–Mar 11am–3pm). Admission is £5.50 for adults and £3 for children 16 and under.

Around 13 miles to the east, **Ledbury** is a pretty market town studded with timber-framed buildings, including the raised Market House, built in the 17th century. The **Ledbury Heritage Centre** (✆ 01531/635680) on Church Lane chronicles

WYE river VALLEY ★★

The **River Wye** snakes its way south from the Welsh mountains through some of the most scenic landscapes in the region, emptying into the Severn estuary at Chepstow on the Welsh border. The most enticing sections are the upper reaches around Hay-on-Wye, and the lower river, where it cuts through the magical woods of the **Forest of Dean.** You'll need a car to make the most of the area.

A good place to base yourself is **Ross-on-Wye,** a small town 16 miles southeast of Hereford. Perched above a loop on the river, Ross is a relaxed, arty place, with a handful of 17th-century buildings and plenty of cafes and B&Bs. It's just 7 miles south along the river from Ross to **Symonds Yat Rock,** a stupendous viewpoint over the entire valley.

Some 20 miles west of Hereford, **Hay-on-Wye** straddles the Welsh–English border, a tiny but attractive riverside town celebrated the world over thanks to **books.** Hay's first secondhand bookstore opened in 1961, and now virtually the whole place is given over to the trade. The **Hay Festival** (www.hay festival.com) takes place over 10 days in May and attracts major names in the world of literature and the arts. See p. 695 for more on Hay.

the history of the town and its famous residents, poets John Masefield and Elizabeth Barrett-Browning among them. It's open April to October daily 10:30am to 4:30pm. Admission is free. Ask here about visiting the extraordinary **Painted Room** nearby, discovered in the town council offices in 1989, and one of the best examples of Elizabethan wall painting anywhere.

Hereford Cathedral & Mappa Mundi ★★ CATHEDRAL   This is one of the oldest and most beguiling cathedrals in England (its cornerstone was laid in 1080). The cathedral is primarily Norman and includes a 13th-century Lady Chapel, as well as a majestic "Father" Willis organ, one of the finest in the world. Exhibited together in the new library building at the west end of the cathedral are two priceless historical treasures: The **Mappa Mundi** of 1300, which portrays the world oriented around Jerusalem, and a 229-book **Chained Library** of medieval manuscripts, with some dating from the 8th century. In the summer you can also climb the 218 steps to the top of the Tower for bird's-eye views of the town.

Cathedral Close, Hereford. www.herefordcathedral.org. ℂ **01432/374200.** Free admission and tours, donation of £5 suggested. Admission to Mappa Mundi and Chained Library £6 adults, £5 seniors and children 5–18, £14 family ticket, free for children 4 and under. Cathedral Mon–Sat 9:15am–5:30pm, Sun 9:15am–3:30pm; Mappa Mundi and Chained Library Mon–Sat 10am–4pm, Sun 11am–3:30pm (closed Sun Nov–Mar).

SHREWSBURY

Shrewsbury is Shropshire's ancient county town, almost completely hemmed in by a meandering loop of the River Severn. Fictional setting of the *Brother Cadfael* novels by Ellis Peters, **Shrewsbury Abbey** (www.shrewsburyabbey.com; ℂ **01743/232723**) was founded back in 1083 by Norman earl, Roger de Montgomery. This small but handsome abbey church is the only surviving portion of a once great Benedictine monastery. It's open daily April to October 10am to 4pm, and November to March 10:30am to 3pm. Located at Wroxeter, 5 miles east of Shrewsbury on the B4380,

Wroxeter Roman City ★ (www.english-heritage.org.uk; ⓒ **01743/761330**) preserves the remains of the fourth largest city in Roman Britain. In 2012 a Roman town house was reconstructed on the site for a Channel 4 TV show, and is now open to the public. The site is open March to October daily 9am to 5pm. Admission is £5 for adults, and £3 for children 15 and under.

Shrewsbury Castle CASTLE   Founded between 1066 and 1074, during the reign of William the Conqueror, Thomas Telford remodeled the interior of this red sandstone castle as a private house in the late 18th century. Today, it houses the Shropshire Regimental Museum, which includes a rather dry collection of pictures, uniforms, medals, and weapons associated with various Shropshire regiments; it's enlivened by a lock of Napoleon's hair and an American flag captured during the seizure and burning of the White House during the War of 1812.

Castle St., Shrewsbury. www.shrewsburymuseums.com/castle. ⓒ**01743/361196.** Admission £2.50 adults, £1.50 seniors, free for students and children 18 and under. Jun–Aug Mon–Wed and Fri–Sat 10:30am–5pm, Sunday 10:30am–4pm; Mid-Feb–May and Sept–Dec Mon–Wed and Fri–Sat 10:30am–4pm. Closed Thurs all year, and Dec 23–Feb 12. Call ahead, as hours may change.

SHROPSHIRE HILLS

South of Shrewsbury lie the "blue remembered hills" that poet A.E. Housman wrote about in *A Shropshire Lad* (1896), a rolling country of farms, small towns, and walking trails.

The most accessible hills are within the **Long Mynd** (516m/1,693ft.) plateau, near **Church Stretton,** the "Little Switzerland" of the region and a thriving antiques center. The National Trust runs a tearoom and shop in the Carding Mill Valley, 1 mile from Church Stretton. Another beautiful area to check out is **Wenlock Edge,** a 15-mile limestone escarpment running between Craven Arms and Much Wenlock at around 330m (1082 ft.) above sea level. Get your bearings in the small town of **Craven Arms,** home to the **Shropshire Hills Discovery Centre,** School Road (www.shropshire.gov.uk/shropshirehills.nsf; ⓒ **0345/678-9024**), which explains the complex geology, ecology, history, and culture of Shropshire. Admission is £3.50 adults, £3.25 students and seniors, £3 children 5–16 (£10 family ticket), and free for children 4 and under. The center opens Thursday to Tuesday 10am to 5pm (Nov–Mar to 4:30pm) and Wednesday 10am to 7pm all year. See also www.shropshirewalking.co.uk.

Ludlow is one of the most attractive towns in the Midlands, and a great place to eat. Learn about its history at **Ludlow Museum,** at Castle Square (www.shropshire. gov.uk; ⓒ **01694/781306**). It's open April to October only, Monday to Saturday 10am to 5pm (June–Aug also Sun 10am–5pm). Admission is free.

Ludlow Castle ★ CASTLE   This spell-binding Norman castle was built around 1094 as a frontier outpost to keep out the as-yet-unconquered Welsh. The original castle, or the inner bailey, was encircled in the early 14th century by a very large outer bailey and transformed into a medieval palace by Roger Mortimer, the most powerful man in England at the time. Since 1811 the castle has been owned by the earls of Powis. Many of the original buildings still stand, including the Chapel of St. Mary Magdalene, with one of England's last remaining circular naves.

Castle Sq., Ludlow. www.ludlowcastle.com. ⓒ**01584/873355.** Admission £5 adults, £4.50 seniors, £2.50 children 6–16, £13.50 family ticket, free for children 5 and under. Dec–Jan Sat–Sun 10am–4pm; Feb–Mar and Oct–Nov daily 10am–4pm; Apr–July and Sept daily 10am–5pm; Aug daily 10am–7pm. Last admission 30 min. before closing time.

Where to Eat

Church Inn PUB FARE Ludlow's most atmospheric and evocative pub, the Church is everybody's favorite source of beer, gossip, and good cheer. Drinks have flowed here since at least 1446—even earlier, according to some historians. Whether you eat informally in the bar or head for the more formal restaurant, the food and prices are exactly the same: Straightforward, British, and rib-sticking, with traditional pub grub such as beef pie, breaded scampi, and chicken breasts with Shropshire blue cheese and mushroom sauce. The owners only use fresh local produce.

Church St., Buttercross, Ludlow. www.thechurchinn.com. ℭ **01584/872174.** Main courses £6.95–£15. MC, V. Mon–Sat 11am–11pm; Sun noon–10:30pm. Meals served daily noon–3:30pm and 6:30–9pm.

Golden Cross ★★ CONTEMPORARY ENGLISH This handsome medieval hotel is reputed to be the oldest inn and watering hole in Shrewsbury, dating from 1428. Today it's also a mouth-watering restaurant specializing in seasonal, local produce and twists on classic English and continental cuisine. Expect creations such as oxtail ravioli with horseradish cream, parsley salad, and Parmesan; or an exceptional potato gnocchi served with roasted sweet English onions and goat cheese fondue. The local cheese, Shropshire Blue, always features somewhere, along with utterly addictive puddings.

14 Princess St., Shrewsbury. www.goldencrosshotel.co.uk. ℭ **01743/362507.** Reservations recommended. Main courses £11.50–£18.50. MC, V. Daily noon–2:30pm and 6–10pm.

Mr. Underhill's ★★★ CONTEMPORARY ENGLISH/MEDITERRANEAN Serious foodies think nothing of journeying here from Oxford or Birmingham for dinner. Chris Bradley, the chef and owner, turned this threadbare inn into a charming Michelin-starred restaurant beneath the ruins of an 11th-century castle. The menu changes every night; you might start with duck liver custard on sweetcorn cream with lemongrass glaze, and follow with hake on fondant tomato with chorizo and orange. For dessert, think Yorkshire rhubarb sponge with custard ice cream.

Many diners choose to overnight here, and we recommend you follow their example. The **B&B** rate is £220 to £300 for a double.

Dinham Weir, Ludlow. www.mr-underhills.co.uk. ℭ **01584/874431.** Reservations required. Fixed-price 8-course dinner plus coffee and petits fours £59.50–£67.50. MC, V. Wed–Sun 7–11pm.

The Peach Tree ★ 🍴 ENGLISH/CONTINENTAL Parts of this oak-beamed restaurant and cafe, a solid choice for a cheap lunch, date from the 15th century. The food is based on solid, time-tested recipes made with fresh ingredients and loads of European savoir-faire. Dishes range from a satisfying Shropshire steak burger on ciabatta with fat chips to a more complex risotto of slow roasted tomatoes, spinach, sage, and melted goat cheese.

21 Abbey Foregate, Shrewsbury. www.thepeachtree.co.uk. ℭ **01743/355055.** Reservations recommended Sat–Sun. Main courses £8.20–£19.95. AE, DC, MC, V. Daily 8am–10pm (last order).

Where to Stay

De Grey's Townhouse ★★ Ludlow is blessed with an abundance of attractive accommodation options, but it's hard to beat this "tea shop with rooms" for atmosphere, comfort, and historic charm. Framed with oak beams and white-washed walls, the cozy rooms are enhanced with elegant period furniture and wonderfully spacious, modern bathrooms. Breakfast is served in the celebrated tearooms downstairs, accompanied by fresh bread and warm pastries cooked in the on-site bakery—you'll be spellbound by the aromas long before you see them.

Broad St., Ludlow, Shropshire SY8 1NG. www.degreys.co.uk. ℂ **01584/872764.** 9 units. £110–£145 double. Rates include English breakfast. AE, DC, MC, V. Free parking. **Amenities:** Tearoom. *In room:* TV/DVD, hair dryer, Wi-Fi (free).

Grove Farm House ★ Shrewsbury's best B&B is a ravishing Georgian farmhouse just 6 miles south of the town, ideally located for touring by car. Rooms are furnished in a bright, contemporary style, with thoughtful extras such as bathrobes and a hospitality tray loaded with homemade biscuits. In the morning, you'll have a veritable feast, beginning with a cold buffet and including a cooked full English breakfast. Afternoon tea with homemade cake is available by arrangement.

Condover, Shrewsbury, Shropshire SY5 7BH (drive south on the A49 and look for the left turn to Condover). www.grovefarmhouse.com. ℂ**01743/718544.** 6 units. £85–£90 double. Rates include English breakfast. AE, DC, MC, V. Free parking. *In room:* TV/DVD, CD player, hair dryer, Wi-Fi (free).

The Old House Suites ★★★ Always wanted to spend the night in a romantic 500-year-old house, but crave five-star luxury at the same time? This enchanting timber-framed B&B seamlessly blends the two, set in the oldest residential property in the heart of Shrewsbury (dating from the 1490s). The most luxurious rooms are in the Catherine of Aragon suite, set in its own lavishly decorated wing of the house with living room, bathroom, and wood-paneled bedroom with two double beds. The breakfast is outstanding and Tony and Mary Walters are superb hosts.

The Old House, 20 Dogpole, Shrewsbury, Shropshire SY1 1ES. www.theoldhousesuites.com. ℂ **01743/271092.** Fax 01743/465006. 3 units. £85–£135 double. Rates include English breakfast. AE, DC, MC, V. Free Parking. *In room:* TV, hair dryer, Internet (free).

IRONBRIDGE

135 miles NW of London; 36 miles NW of Birmingham; 18 miles SE of Shrewsbury

Some 200 years ago, the small village of **Ironbridge** was humming with industrial activity. Today the factories and smelters are long gone, and tourists and tour buses come to soak up a heavy dose of Britain's industrial heritage. This stretch of the Severn Valley has been an important industrial area since the Middle Ages because of its iron and limestone deposits. But the event that clinched the area's importance came in 1709, when a Quaker ironmaster, Abraham Darby I, discovered a method for smelting iron by using coke as a fuel, rather than charcoal. This paved the way for the first iron rails, boats, wheels, aqueducts, and the first iron bridge itself, cast here by Darby's grandson in 1779. The village of Ironbridge grew up around the bridge in subsequent years, and since the late 1960s most of the gorge, including the adjacent settlement of Coalbrookdale, has formed a giant historical park, home to 10 absorbing museums.

Essentials

GETTING THERE The nearest train and long-distance bus station is in **Telford,** 5 miles north of Ironbridge and well connected to London and Birmingham. The Gorge Connect bus service links Telford Central Station to Ironbridge, a 20-minute ride. Fares are 50p per ride or £2.50 for an unlimited Day-Rover pass, useful as the bus also connects all the major sights in Ironbridge. The catch is that the bus only runs on weekends and public holiday Mondays April to October; buses run every 30 minutes or so between 9:30am and 3:54pm from Telford. Alternatively, Arriva runs regular buses Monday to Friday to Ironbridge from Telford and Shrewsbury. See www.arrivabus.co.uk for timetables.

VISITOR INFORMATION   The **Ironbridge Tourist Information Centre,** the Tollhouse (www.visitironbridge.co.uk; ✆ **01952/884391**), is open Monday to Friday 9am to 5pm, Saturday and Sunday 10am to 5pm.

Exploring the Area

The Ironbridge Valley plays host to several illuminating museums, collectively called the **Ironbridge Gorge Museums ★★** (www.ironbridge.org.uk; ✆ **01952/433522** Mon–Fri, or 01952/432166 Sat–Sun). These include the **Coalbrookdale Museum of Iron** with its Darby Furnace (£7.95 adults; £7.25 over-60s; £6.45 full-time students and children 5–18); **Darby Houses,** the restored 19th-century homes of the Quaker ironmasters (£4.95 adults; £3.95 over-60s; £3.45 full-time students and children 5–18); the remarkable **Iron Bridge ★★**, with its original tollhouse (free); the **Museum of the Gorge** (£3.95 adults; £3.25 over-60s; £2.75 full-time students and children 5–18) with a scale model of the gorge in 1796; the **Jackfield Tile Museum** (£7.95 adults; £7.25 over-60s; £5.25 full-time students and children 5–18), where you can see demonstrations of tile pressing, decorating, and firing; **Blists Hill Victorian Town ★★**, with its illuminating open-air recreation of a 19th-century village (£15.45 adults; £12.35 over-60s; £10.25 full-time students and children 5–18); the absorbing **Coalport China Museum and Tar Tunnel ★★**, with ceramics displays (£7.95 adults; £7.25 over-60s; £5.25 full-time students and children 5–18) and a tour of an underground mine (£2.75 adults; £2.50 over-60s; £2.25 full-time students and children 5–18); **Broseley Pipeworks,** a 50-year-old abandoned tobacco pipe-making factory (£4.95 adults; £3.95 over-60s; £3.45 full-time students and children 5–18); and **Enginuity,** an interactive exhibit that allows children to become engineers for a day (£8.25 adults; £6.95 over-60s, full-time students, and children 5–18). *Insider tip:* If time is short, we recommend that you at least visit the Iron Bridge, Blists Hill Victorian Town, and the Coalport China Museum.

A passport ticket to all museums in Ironbridge Gorge is £23.25 for adults, £18.75 for seniors, £15.25 for students and children 5 to 18, £64 for families of two adults and up to three children, and free for children 4 and under. Between April and October the sites are open daily from 10am to 5pm with the exception of Tar Tunnel, open 10:30am to 4pm, and Broseley Pipeworks, which is open daily from the end of May to the end of September from 1 to 5pm. The Tar Tunnel, Darby Houses, and Broseley Pipeworks are closed from November to March, with the other sites open 10am to 5pm (Blists closes at 4pm).

Where to Eat & Stay

Best Western Valley Hotel   This riverside inn blends modern amenities and historic ambience—it was originally built as a private home around 1750, and was enlarged over the years into the sprawling, brick building you see today. Fifteen of the hotel's rooms lie within the original stable and are accessible via a glass-roofed courtyard. Although rooms in the main house usually have more panoramic views, many visitors prefer the coziness of the former stables. All units are well maintained and modern; some have four-poster beds.

Outfitted with crisp napery, Windsor-style chairs, and a high ceiling, the hotel's highly rated restaurant, **Chez Maw** (www.chezmawrestaurant.co.uk; ✆ **01952/ 432247**), serves contemporary British food. Try the free-range Staffordshire chicken breast, with house smoked sausage, cannellini bean and root vegetable cassoulet, or the roasted filet of Loch Duarte salmon, with parsnip and potato mash, purple sprouting broccoli, and red wine and pancetta sauce.

Buildwas Rd., Ironbridge, Telford, Shropshire TF8 7DW. www.thevalleyhotel.co.uk. ✆ **01952/ 432247.** Fax 01952/432308. 44 units. £88–£110 double. Rates include breakfast. AE, DC, MC, V. Free parking. **Amenities:** Restaurant; 2 bars; room service. *In room:* TV, hair dryer, Wi-Fi (free).

Library House ★★ 🛍 This restored landmark, parts of which date from 1752, has been used for many purposes, including a doctor's surgery clinic and even the village library, from which the B&B takes its name. Today it's one of the finest hotels in the area, with a dazzling breakfast and delightful bedrooms, named after English writers George Eliot, Hardy, Milton, and Chaucer. Each one is individually designed and decorated, from Georgian to contemporary to Oriental styles. There is also a pretty terraced garden.

11 Severn Bank, Ironbridge, near Telford, Shropshire TF8 7AN. www.libraryhouse.com. ✆ **01952/ 432299.** Fax 01952/433967. 4 units. £80–£100 double. Rates include English breakfast. No credit cards. Free parking. *In room:* TV/DVD, hair dryer, Wi-Fi (free).

THE POTTERIES

162 miles NW of London; 59 miles NW of Leicester; 46 miles N of Birmingham; 41 miles S of Manchester

Anyone with an interest in pottery should make a pilgrimage to **Stoke-on-Trent,** one of author Arnold Bennett's famous *Five Towns.* Kilns were busy here in the 14th century, long before Josiah Wedgwood (1730–95), England's most distinguished potter, arrived. Most of the great kilns have disappeared, but shops such as Wedgwood, Royal Doulton, Portmeirion, Moorcroft, and Aynsley are among the 30 pottery attractions still based in the city.

Today Stoke-on-Trent is a loose confederation of six towns (Tunstall, Burslem, Stoke, Fenton, Longton, and Hanley, the most important) with little else to detain you, though it's also famous for being one of the original 1960s' centers of what's dubbed **northern soul** (the focus being on lesser-known Motown-style soul groups). Northern soul has made a comeback in recent years; venues like King's Hall on Glebe Street (www.goldsoul.co.uk) host "all-nighters" (9pm–7am) four times a year, though the dancers are likely to be in their 40s these days.

Essentials

GETTING THERE From London's Euston Station, half-hourly trains take 1½ to 2½ hours to Stoke-on-Trent (one-way from £11.50–£29).

By car from London, drive along the M1 and then the M6 to the A500 at junction 15. It will take you 2 to 3 hours. Trains from Birmingham also run every 30 minutes or so (around 1 hr.) and returns cost £15.50.

Exploring the Area

The history of Stoke's oldest-surviving family potter is chronicled inside the cavernous bottle oven at the **Dudson Museum,** Hope St., Hanley (www.dudson.com; ℭ **01782/285286**), open Monday to Friday 10am to 3pm (free admission). **The Gladstone Pottery Museum** ★ (www.stokemuseums.org.uk/gpm; ℭ **01782/ 237777**), Uttoxeter Road, Longton, preserves a Victorian pottery factory with craftspeople providing daily demonstrations in the original workshops. Admission is £6.95 adults, £5.50 seniors and students, £4.75 children 4 to 16, and £20 for a family ticket. It's open daily 10am to 5pm. **The Moorcroft Museum & Factory Tour** (www. moorcroft.com; ℭ **01782/820500**), Sandbach Road, Burslem, commemorates the company founded in 1898 by William Moorcroft, who produced his own special brand of pottery and was his own exclusive designer until his death in 1945. The factory tour (Mon and Wed–Thurs 11am and 2pm, Fri 11am only; all tours must be booked 2 weeks in advance), is a bit like going back in time; things have changed little on the factory floor since Moorcroft's day. You'll observe all the handmade processes of mold-making, slip casting, hand turning, tube lining, hand painting, kiln firing, and finally glazing. The museum is open Monday to Friday 10am to 5pm, and Saturday 9:30am to 4:30pm. Factory tours are £4.50 for adults, £3.50 seniors, and £2.50 for children 11 to 16.

The **Potteries Museum & Art Gallery,** Bethesda Street, City Centre (www. stoke.gov.uk/museum; ℭ **01782/232323**), is the best place to learn about the history of the Potteries, with the world's greatest collection of Staffordshire ceramics and even a World War II Spitfire on show. The star attraction is the Staffordshire Hoard, the most precious collection of Anglo-Saxon treasure and gold ever found. It's open Monday to Saturday 10am to 5pm and Sunday 2 to 5pm. Admission is free. The

---

The Great Potteries Outlet Tour

With around 25 high-quality factory shops and outlets spread around the Stoke area, your biggest headache is likely to be shipping all your purchases back home. **Wedgwood** (see below) is an obvious target, but there are plenty of other worthy choices (see www.visit stoke.co.uk for a complete list):

Aynsley China, Sutherland Road, Longton, Stoke-on-Trent (ℭ **01782/ 339420**), has a wide selection of the U.K.'s favorite best-quality fine bone china. Mon–Thurs 10am–5pm, Fri 10am–4pm, Sun 11am–4pm.

Dudson Factory Outlet, Nile Street,

Burslem, Stoke-on-Trent (ℭ **01782/ 821075**). Mon–Fri 9am–5pm, Sat 10am–4pm.

Moorcroft Factory Shop, Phoenix Works, Nile Street, Cobridge, Stoke-on-Trent (ℭ **01782/820505**). Mon–Fri 10am–5pm, Sat 9:30am–4:30pm.

Portmeirion Factory Shop, 473 King St., Longton, Stoke-on-Trent (ℭ **01782/ 326661**), has tons of choices, with seconds (pieces that have minor flaws), and Spode and Royal Worcester ware, at least 30% off retail prices. Mon–Sat 9am–5:15pm, Sun 10am–4pm.

excellent **Wedgwood Museum & Visitor Centre** ★★ (www.wedgwoodmuseum.org.uk; ✆ **01782/371919**) in Barlaston pays tribute to the most celebrated pottery brand in England, though at the time of writing it was facing closure to help pay off Wedgwood debts. Call ahead for the latest. The museum is otherwise open Monday to Friday 9am to 5pm and Saturday and Sunday 10am to 4pm. Museum admission is £6 adults, and £5 seniors, students, and children 5–16; Visitor Centre and Museum entry is £10 adults, £8 seniors, students, and children 5–16, and £32 family ticket.

Where to Eat

The Old Plough ★ PUB FARE   This atmospheric old-fashioned pub is the best place to eat in Stoke, with a menu anchored by a choice of perfectly chargrilled, hearty steaks and homemade sauces. The dining room is decorated with all sorts of vintage bric-a-brac, old posters, pub signs, and the like, and the real ales, and friendly and attentive staff, round out the experience.

147 Etruria Rd., Etruria, Stoke-on-Trent. ✆ **01782/269445.** Reservations recommended. Main courses £15–£38. MC, V. Daily 11:30am–11pm.

CAMBRIDGE & EAST ANGLIA

by Nick Dalton & Deborah Stone

13

East Anglia—Essex, Cambridgeshire, Suffolk, and Norfolk—was a kingdom in itself in Anglo-Saxon times, and, as you head east from London, it's easy to see why. The low, flat land has open fields, crisscrossed by dykes and ditches, forest and heathland, while the watery haven of the Norfolk Broads is like America's bayous but with cream teas.

The coast is equally low and striking. And yet at the heart of all this is that seat of university learning, Cambridge, with its ornate colleges and chapels.

CITIES & TOWNS   Here are some of England's oldest cities. **Colchester** was England's Roman capital, **Norwich** is one of Britain's most perfect medieval cities, and **Ipswich** is a picturesque river port. **Bury St. Edmunds** is an ancient religious settlement, while the spire of **Ely's** cathedral rises starkly from the pancake-flat fens. And exquisite **Cambridge** has college buildings dating back to the 14th century, the grassy Backs dividing them from the River Cam where students still punt by pushing along flat-bottomed boats with long poles.

COUNTRYSIDE   In some places you can see for miles across **fens, heath,** and **marshes,** but there are gentle **hills** too and acres of **farmland** punctuated by small villages of pastel-painted cottages. This is a landscape (captured in oils by John Constable) perfect for walking and cycling. And the **Norfolk Broads,** an expanse of waterways where you can sail and potter about in a cabin cruiser, offer scenery like nowhere else in the country.

EATING & DRINKING   **Crabs** from Cromer, **fish** from smokehouses, **pork** from pigs that have grown up smelling the sea air, and famed **sea salt** from Maldon in Essex: This is a place of good food, which can be found everywhere from traditional butcher's shops to fine restaurants. The region is also home to two of the country's most celebrated brewers, Greene King (Bury St. Edmunds) and Adnams (Southwold), whose beer dominates the many charming pubs. And renowned chef/proprietor Marco Pierre White has recently bought a string of inns in Norfolk and Suffolk.

COAST   Whether it's the boisterous, traditional resort towns such as **Clacton** and **Southend** in Essex or **Great Yarmouth** in Norfolk, or somewhere more refined, such as **Southwold** and **Aldeburgh** in Suffolk, or a remote boutique hotel on the north Norfolk coast, there's something here for all tastes. There are charming estuaries, long stretches of beach, bird sanctuaries in brackish, windblown spots, and even the option of a seal-spotting boat trip.

THE best TRAVEL EXPERIENCES IN CAMBRIDGE & EAST ANGLIA

- **Punting on the Cam:** Perched precariously on the back of a little boat and trying to propel (and steer) with a big pole is great fun as you pass by Cambridge's iconic colleges. Take a picnic and relax under a willow on a grassy bank, before heading back. See p. 498.

- **Spending a day in Southwold:** Walking across the common with views over the sea, strolling through the chain store-free streets, then heading down the steps onto the beach, and finishing with a walk along the river quayside, for some fish and chips. See p. 523.

- **Walking in north Norfolk:** The beaches are big and windswept, often backed by bird reserves and ponds. There's a real feel of being out on the edge and, indeed, this is as far as you can go east before you hit the mainland Europe. See p. 531.

- **Seeing Ely Cathedral:** This medieval masterpiece rises from the pancake-flat Fens, and can be seen from miles around; it's just as impressive when you actually get close up. See p. 507.

- **Exploring the Blackwater Estuary:** This is a hidden Essex delight, a waterway of times gone by, where Thames sailing barges still tie up at Maldon's Hythe Quay. It's the place to sit with a beer at sunset. See p. 520.

CAMBRIDGE

55 miles N of London; 80 miles NE of Oxford

The university city of Cambridge is a place of contrasts: Its historic college buildings with their magnificent chapels, turrets, and spires provide a romantic backdrop to delight any tourist, while its high-tech industries—dubbed "Silicon Fen"—lead the way in global technology. Of course these two aspects of Cambridge are connected—brilliant minds with brilliant ideas.

Visit Cambridge and it feels like a little of that fairy dust rubs off on you too, as you discover the **Bridge of Sighs** while punting on the River Cam; walk along **The Backs** of the colleges as the spring bulbs produce a carpet of flowers; and explore the narrow streets in the footsteps of Sir Isaac Newton, John Milton, Charles Darwin, Virginia Woolf, and many more. But Cambridge is not just a collection of old colleges (as inspiring as they are); it is a living, working town.

At its heart is the market place, a cobbled square with daily stalls, and running through the city is the **River Cam,** which drifts past magical open spaces such as Midsummer Common, Jesus Green, The Backs, and Sheeps Green. Everyone should try punting, floating past riverside pubs, or punting up to Grantchester Meadows (many people will know that name from the song on the Pink Floyd's *Ummagumma* album; band members Roger Waters, Syd Barrett, and Dave Gilmour grew up in the city) for afternoon tea. Afterward you can relax in one of those pubs—there are more than 100 in the city. The Mill and Fort St. George are two of the best riverside taverns.

The Flying Bus

The Busway, opened in autumn 2011, is a strange sight; a concrete track cuts across the flat countryside and you can be walking on the Great Ouse riverbank in the middle of nowhere when there's a whirring that grows until a double-decker bus roars past at 55 mph. Conventional buses are fitted with guide wheels that keep them on track (following a disused rail line), but allow them to move onto normal roads. The off-road stretch of 16 miles, most of it between Cambridge and the town of St. Ives (with Park and Rides at St. Ives and Longstanton), is the longest guided bus-way in the world. Buses continue from St. Ives to Huntingdon in one direction and across Cambridge, to Trumpington Park and Ride, in the other. It's worth taking simply for the ride. There is a stop at the free RSPB nature reserve of flooded gravel pits at Fen Drayton, and a concrete cycle path runs alongside the track. Single tickets cost £3 to £5, with information at www.thebusway.info.

Essentials

GETTING THERE   First Capital Connect trains from London's King's Cross take 45 minutes to an hour. A one-way ticket costs from £21.20. Trains from London's Liverpool Street with NXEA take 80 minutes and cost from £18.60 one-way.

If you're driving from London, head north on the M11. If you're driving from the northeast, use the A1 and from the Midlands take the M6 onto the A14.

VISITOR INFORMATION   For free information on attractions and public transport visit the **Cambridge Tourist Information Centre,** Peas Hill (www.visit cambridge.org; ✆ **0871/226-8006,** or 0044/122-346-4732 from overseas). Staff can also book tours and lodging. The center is open year-round, Monday to Saturday 10am to 5pm (Apr–Oct also Sun and public holidays 11am–3pm).

GETTING AROUND   City parking is expensive and the traffic can be unbearable. There are five Park and Ride sites, at Trumpington, Madingley Road, Milton, Newmarket Road, and Babraham Road. Park and Ride round-trip bus tickets cost £2.40 from machines (£2.70 from bus drivers); accompanied children ride free. Buses leave every 10 minutes (every 15 min. on Sun and public holidays) and call at a number of stops around the city.

Cambridge is best seen on foot, or you can join the locals and cycle. **Station Cycles** (www.stationcycles.co.uk; ✆ **01223/307125**) has rentals, £7 for up to 4 hours, £10 for a day, or £25 for a week (£60 deposit). There's a shop outside the railway station and at Grand Arcade in Corn Exchange Street near the market. Both open Monday to Friday 8am to 6pm (7pm on Wed), Saturday 9am to 5pm, and Sunday 10am to 4pm (5pm Apr–Sept), and have left-luggage facilities. Park your bike for free at Park Street or Grand Arcade parking lots. There's free pushchair loan for parents who arrive with children on bicycle seats, from Park Street and Station Cycles' shop at the station. **City Cycle Hire** in Newnham Road (www.citycyclehire. com; ✆ **01223/365629**) has bikes for £6 per half-day, £9 per day, or £17 per week.

Stagecoach (www.stagecoachbus.com; ✆ **01223/423578**) serves the area with a network of buses. A day pass costs from £3.50, or £6 for a family day pass. The tourist office has bus schedules.

SPECIAL EVENTS   **Cambridge Folk Festival** (www.cambridgefolkfestival.co. uk) in the last weekend of July features international roots artists from Richard Thompson to Robert Cray, but sells out quickly. Weekend tickets are about £120. **Strawberry Fair** (www.strawberry-fair.org.uk) on Midsummer Common (June) has bands, cabaret, and family fun. **Cambridge Shakespeare Festival** (www.cambridge shakespeare.com; ✆ **07955/218824**) in July and August has open-air Shakespeare performances in the grounds of several colleges.

ORGANIZED TOURS   The **Cambridge Tourist Information Centre** (see "Visitor Information," above) has several 2-hour walking tours of the city, £15 for adults, and £7.50 for children under 12. Book tours by visiting www.visitcambridge.org or calling ✆ **01223/457574**.

City Sightseeing (www.city-sightseeing.com; ✆ **01223/423578**) uses open-top, double-decker buses and has 20 hop-on hop-off stops including the railway station. Daily tours with recorded commentary depart every 20 minutes from Silver Street near The Backs, 9:30am to 4pm in summer and 10:20am to 3pm in winter. Tickets are valid for 24 hours, and the tour is a good way to get to out-of-town attractions such as the American Cemetery, and those on the outskirts (Cambridge Folk Museum and Cambridge University Botanic Gardens). Tickets are £13 adults, £9 seniors and students, £7 children 6 to 15, and free for children 5 and under. City walking tours with **Cambridge Tailor-made Tours** (www.cambridgetmtours.co.uk; ✆ **01223/207378**) are available for small or large groups. Prices depend on the size of the group.

Exploring Cambridge University

Scholars have been studying at Cambridge since the early 13th century, with Henry III granting the students his protection in 1231. At this stage they were a loose group, but during medieval times the university was arranged in a similar style to Oxford, with a foundation course leading to graduation and degrees. It wasn't until the late 14th century that the university began acquiring premises, beginning with the site now known as Senate House Hill. Land and buildings were sometimes donated by wealthy people on condition that students, mostly studying to become clergymen, prayed for them. The university grew even more quickly in the 16th century, with Henry VIII founding Trinity College. Already-established colleges, such as Emmanuel and Magdalene, took over larger premises, and the study of Greek, Latin, and classics (as well as divinity) indicated a move away from simply educating clerics. During the late 1600s and 1700s mathematics and science began to dominate the university. This was thanks largely to Sir Isaac Newton, who formulated the principles of gravity. During this period, the University Press, the Botanic Garden, and the University Library were established. Reforms during the 19th century rearranged the university into something like the institution we know today, and two colleges for women were established: Girton in 1869 and Newnham in 1872. However, women could not become full members of the university until 1947, and it wasn't until the 1960s that some of the older colleges began to admit female students. Cambridge University now consists of 31 colleges, all co-educational except three still female-only: Newnham, Murray Edwards, and Lucy Cavendish. The colleges are all open to the public at certain times, but each has its own opening times and admission prices. The following are some of the most interesting colleges, and if you have time you could also visit **Magdalene College,** on Magdalene Street, founded in 1542; **Pembroke College,** on Trumpington Street, founded in 1347; **Christ's College,** on St. Andrew's Street, founded in 1505; and **Corpus Christi College,** on Trumpington Street, which dates from 1352.

 Caution: Students at Work

The colleges can be closed at times during May and June when students are taking exams. Check with the Cambridge Tourist Information Centre (see above) for opening times, or with each individual college. They are also closed during graduation ceremonies, at Easter, public holidays, and other times without notice.

Cambridge

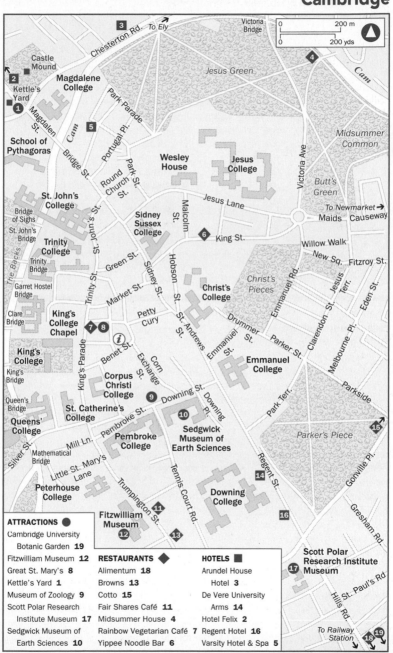

Victoria Bridge

Chesterton Rd. To Ely

Castle Mound

Magdalene College

Kettle's Yard

Jesus Green

Cam

200 m
200 yds

Midsummer Common

School of Pythagoras

Magdalen St.

Cam

Bridge St.

Portugal Pl.

Park Parade

Round Church St.

Park St.

Wesley House

Jesus College

Victoria Ave

Butt's Green

St. John's College

Bridge of Sighs

St. John's Bridge

Trinity College

Trinity Bridge

The Backs

Garret Hostel Bridge

Clare Bridge

King's College Chapel

King's College

King's Bridge

Queen's Bridge

Queens' College

Mathematical Bridge

Silver St.

Mill Ln.

Peterhouse College

Sidney Sussex College

St. John's St.

Trinity St.

Green St.

Market St.

King's Parade

Benet St.

Corn Exchange St.

Corpus Christi College

St. Catherine's College

Pembroke St.

Pembroke College

Malcolm St.

Jesus Lane

King St.

Christ's College

Hobson St.

St. Andrews St.

Petty Cury

Emmanuel St.

Emmanuel Rd.

Maids Causeway

To Newmarket

Willow Walk

New Sq.

Fitzroy St.

Jesus Terr.

Eden St.

Christ's Pieces

Drummer St.

Parker St.

Clarendon St.

Melbourne Pl.

Emmanuel College

Downing St.

Downing Pl.

Sedgwick Museum of Earth Sciences

Tennis Court Rd.

Little St. Mary's Lane

Trumpington St.

Fitzwilliam Museum

Downing College

Park Terr.

Regent St.

Parker's Piece

Parkside

Gonville Pl.

Gresham Rd.

Scott Polar Research Institute Museum

St. Paul's Rd.

Hills Rd.

To Railway Station

ATTRACTIONS ●

Cambridge University
    Botanic Garden **19**
Fitzwilliam Museum **12**
Great St. Mary's **8**
Kettle's Yard **1**
Museum of Zoology **9**
Scott Polar Research
    Institute Museum **17**
Sedgwick Museum of
    Earth Sciences **10**

RESTAURANTS ◆

Alimentum **18**
Browns **13**
Cotto **15**
Fair Shares Café **11**
Midsummer House **4**
Rainbow Vegetarian Café **7**
Yippee Noodle Bar **6**

HOTELS ■

Arundel House
    Hotel **3**
De Vere University
    Arms **14**
Hotel Felix **2**
Regent Hotel **16**
Varsity Hotel & Spa **5**

📷 punting ON THE CAM

You haven't really experienced Cambridge if you haven't been punting on the **River Cam.** There's nothing more enjoyable on a sunny day than sitting back in one of the flat-bottomed wooden boats and gliding past the ivy-covered colleges and their gardens along the mirror-like river. All you have to do is put the long pole, about 5m (16 ft.), straight down into the shallow water until it finds the riverbed, then gently push and retrieve the pole in one deft, simple movement. Actually, it's easy once you know how, but watching inexperienced enthusiasts lose their pole or steer into the bank is traditional entertainment. Rent a punt from **Scudamore's Punting Company** any time of year to punt past The Backs from its Magdalene Bridge or Mill Lane stations, or you can punt up to Grantchester from its Mill Lane Boatyard in Granta Place, Mill Lane (www.scudamores.com; ✆ **01223/ 359750**). Punts cost £18 per hour (maximum of six people per punt). A credit card imprint is required as deposit.

Grantchester is 2 miles upriver, and was immortalized by World War I poet Rupert Brooke in *The Soldier:* "Stands the Church clock at ten to three? And is there honey still for tea?" it asks. If you walk the 1 mile from the river at **Grantchester Meadows** to the village you can see for yourself, and have tea at the **Orchard Tea Garden** (www.orchard-grantchester.com; ✆ **01223/551125**) or have a drink at the 400-year-old **Green Man,** in the High Street (www.thegreen mangrantchester.co.uk; ✆ **01223/ 844669**).

Emmanuel College HISTORIC SITE Emmanuel, on St. Andrew's Street, was founded in 1584 by Sir Walter Mildmay, Elizabeth I's chancellor of the exchequer. Mildmay was a Puritan and of the 100 Cambridge graduates who emigrated to New England before 1646, 35 were from Emmanuel. The college's gardens, designed by Sir Christopher Wren, are attractive, as are the cloister and chapel, consecrated in 1677.

Insider tip: John Harvard, of the eponymous American university in Cambridge, Massachusetts, was among the Emmanuel graduates who emigrated to New England. There's a memorial to him in the chapel.

St. Andrew's St. www.emma.cam.ac.uk. ✆ **01223/334200.** Free admission to grounds and chapel.

King's College ★★ HISTORIC SITE Henry VI founded King's College in 1441, and although most buildings date from the 18th century or later, the famous **King's College Chapel** ★★★ was started in the Middle Ages and is regarded as one of Europe's finest Gothic buildings. Rubens's *Adoration of the Magi* (1634) is a highlight, as are the stained-glass windows (most paid for by Henry VIII). Carols are broadcast worldwide from the chapel on Christmas Eve, and there are concerts and organ recitals throughout the year, with tickets available from the Shop at King's, on King's Parade.

Insider tip: See the chapel at its best by attending a service. Evensong on a summer's evening is an uplifting experience. And while the chapel is beautiful inside, it is best viewed from The Backs, where you can take a picnic and have a break from sightseeing. E. M. Forster came here to contemplate scenes for his novel *Maurice.*

King's Parade. www.kings.cam.ac.uk. ✆ **01223/331100.** Admission £6.50 adults; £4.50 children 12–16, students, and seniors; free for children 11 and under.

Peterhouse College HISTORIC SITE   This is the oldest Cambridge college, founded in 1284 by Bishop of Ely Hugh de Balsham. The dining hall, built in 1286, is the only surviving 13th century building, and it was rebuilt in the 1860s in Gothic Revival style by Sir George Gilbert Scott, who was responsible for London's Parliament buildings. The stained-glass windows were designed by Arts and Crafts founder William Morris and pre-Raphaelite artists Ford Madox Brown and Edward Burne-Jones. Other buildings from down the centuries include the chapel, from 1632, which was renovated in 1754. Ask to enter at the porter's lodge at the gate.

Insider tip: Little St. Mary's, the church next door, was the college chapel until 1632 and has a memorial to Godfrey Washington, who died in 1729. The Washington family's coat of arms contains an eagle on top of stars and stripes, and is believed to be the inspiration for the United States flag.

Trumpington St. www.pet.cam.ac.uk. ✆ **01223/338200.** Free admission to grounds.

Queens' College ★★ HISTORIC SITE   Founded by English queens Margaret of Anjou, the wife of Henry VI, and Elizabeth Woodville, the wife of Edward IV, the college dates from 1448 and is regarded as the most beautiful of Cambridge's colleges. Entry and exit is by the old porter's lodge in Queens' Lane. Its second cloister is the most interesting, flanked by the 16th-century half-timbered President's Lodge. The old hall and chapel are usually open to the public when not in use. The Mathematical Bridge, an arched, wooden, self-supporting bridge connects the college's two parts, and is best viewed from the Silver Street Bridge, dating from 1902.

Silver St. www.quns.cam.ac.uk. ✆ **01223/335511.** Late June–early Oct 10am–4:30pm admission £2.50 adults, free for children 11 and under (free admission other times). Oct daily 2–4pm (weekends 10am–4:30pm); Nov–late May daily 2–4pm (sometimes 4:30pm; also closed late May–late June and some other dates).

St. John's College ★★ HISTORIC SITE   St. John's was founded in 1511 by Lady Margaret Beaufort, mother of Henry VII, who established Christ's College a few years earlier. The impressive gateway has the Tudor coat of arms, and the Second Court is a fine example of late Tudor brickwork. The college's best-known feature is the Bridge of Sighs crossing the River Cam. It was built in the 19th century, inspired by the covered bridge at the Doge's Palace in Venice. It connects the older part of the college with New Court, a Gothic Revival folly with a main cupola and pinnacles that students nicknamed the wedding cake. The bridge is closed to visitors but can be seen from Kitchen Bridge. Wordsworth was an alumnus of this college, and visitors can attend choral services in the chapel.

St. John's Street. www.joh.cam.ac.uk. ✆ **01223/338600.** Admission £3.20 adults, £2 seniors and children 12–17, free for children 11 and under. Mar–Oct 10am–5:30pm; Nov–Feb Sat 10am–3:30pm.

Trinity College ★★ HISTORIC SITE   This is Cambridge's largest college, not to be confused with Trinity Hall. It was founded in 1546 when Henry VIII consolidated a number of smaller colleges on the site. The courtyard is the most spacious in Cambridge, built when Thomas Neville was master. The Wren Library, from 1695, was designed by Sir Christopher Wren. It contains manuscripts and books that were in the college library by 1820, together with various special collections including 1,250 medieval manuscripts, early Shakespeare editions, many books from Sir Isaac Newton's own library, and A.A. Milne's Winnie-the-Pooh manuscripts.

Insider tip: Sir Isaac Newton calculated the speed of sound here, at Neville's Court, and Lord Byron used to bathe naked in the Great Court's fountain with his pet bear. The university forbade students from having dogs, but there was no rule against bears. Years later, Vladimir Nabokov walked through that same courtyard dreaming of the young lady he would later write about as *Lolita*.

Trinity St. www.trin.cam.ac.uk. ☏ **01223/338400.** Free admission. The Wren Library Mon–Fri noon–2pm, Sat 10:30am–12:30pm. Various other areas are open at different times; ask at the porter's lodge.

Exploring the Rest of Cambridge

Cambridge University Botanic Garden ★★ GARDEN   The winter garden is noted for the extravagance of stems and bark while the woodland garden bursts into life with flowering spring bulbs. The garden opened in 1846 and the magnificent avenue of trees along Main Walk includes giant redwoods grown from seeds collected in California in 1851, the first ever brought to England.

1 Brookside, Bateman St. www.botanic.cam.ac.uk. ☏ **01223/336265.** Admission £4 adults, £3.50 students and seniors, children 15 and under free. Mar–Oct and all weekends and public holidays. Daily Apr–Sept 10am–6pm; Feb, Mar, and Oct 10am–5pm; Jan, Nov, and Dec 10am–4pm.

Fitzwilliam Museum ★★ MUSEUM   Suits of armor, Greek and Roman pottery, Chinese jades, Japanese ceramics, and an art collection that includes Rubens, Van Dyck, Canaletto, Hogarth, Gainsborough, Constable, and the Impressionist painters: You'll find them all here in a first-class museum that isn't so large that fatigue sets in. There's also a good cafe and gift shop and regular lectures of a standard you would expect from this Cambridge University-owned institution.

Trumpington St., near Peterhouse. www.fitzmuseum.cam.ac.uk. ☏ **01223/332900.** Free admission; donations appreciated. Tues–Sat 10am–5pm, Sun and Mon public holidays noon–5pm. Closed Mon, Good Friday, Dec 24–26 and 31, and Jan 1. Sat guided tours at 2:30pm (£5).

Great St. Mary's CHURCH   Closely associated with events of the Reformation because the leaders of the movement (Erasmus, Cranmer, Latimer, and Ridley) preached here, this university church was built mostly in 1478 on the site of an 11th-century church. The cloth that covered the hearse of King Henry VII is on display and there is a fine view of Cambridge from the top of the tower.

Senate House Hill. www.gsm.cam.ac.uk. ☏ **01223/462914.** Guided tours £10 adults, £5 children; tower only £3.50 adults, £1.70 children 5–16. Tower summer daily 10am–4:30pm, winter 10am–3:30pm; Sun year-round 12:30–4pm. Church daily 9am–6pm.

Kettle's Yard ★★ HISTORIC HOME   This oasis of calm and good taste was the home of Jim and Helen Ede during the 1950s to early 1970s. As curator of London's Tate Gallery in the 1920s and 1930s, Jim built up an enviable collection of paintings and sculptures, including work by Joan Miró, Henry Moore, and Barbara Hepworth, which are still on display more or less where the Edes left them. Around the corner is Kettle's Yard Gallery, with a respected collection of 20th-century and contemporary art, and ever-changing exhibitions.

Castle St. www.kettlesyard.co.uk. ☏ **01223/748100.** Free admission; donations appreciated. Tues–Sun and Mon public holidays 1:30–4:30pm (late Sept–early Apr 2–4pm). Closed Mon, Good Friday, Dec 24–28, and Jan 1.

Museum of Zoology ★★ MUSEUM   Specimens collected by Cambridge graduate Charles Darwin during his voyage on the *Beagle* in the 1830s are on display here, as well as rare examples of the dodo and great auk. Other historic collections gathered during the great expeditions of the 19th century are also here.

Downing St. www.museum.zoo.cam.ac.uk.☏ **01223/336650.** Free admission; donations appreciated. Mon–Fri 10am–4:45pm; Sat 11am–4pm. Closed over Christmas and New Year period.

Scott Polar Research Institute Museum ★★ MUSEUM After a £1.75 million redesign and reopening in 2010, the only word to describe this unique museum is cool. Very cool. The history of polar exploration is here and includes the last letters of Captain Scott, the expedition diaries of Sir Ernest Shackleton, and artifacts from the British search for the Northwest Passage.

Lensfield Rd. www.spri.cam.ac.uk.☏ **01223/336540.** Free admission; donations appreciated. Tues–Sat 10am–4pm. Closed Sun, Mon, and public holidays including Christmas and New Year.

Sedgwick Museum of Earth Sciences ★★ MUSEUM You have to get past the skeleton of an Iguanodon dinosaur to see the rest of this fabulous collection, which includes the remains of a 125,000-year-old hippopotamus found in Cambridgeshire. You'll see a treasure-trove of fossils, rocks, and minerals from around the world as you explore 550 million years of history.

Downing St. www.sedgwickmuseum.org.☏ **01223/333456.** Free admission; donations appreciated. Mon–Fri 10am–1pm and 2–5pm; Sat 10am–4pm. Closed Sun and public holidays.

Where to Eat
EXPENSIVE
Midsummer House ★★ FRENCH This has been the best dining in town for many years, and it's the only two-star Michelin restaurant in East Anglia. Its lovely riverside setting on Midsummer Common gives it an extra-special atmosphere.

Midsummer Common. www.midsummerhouse.co.uk.☏ **01223/369299.** Reservations essential. Set menu £40 for 3 courses, £50 for 4 courses, £60 for 5 courses. AE, MC, V. Wed–Sat noon–2pm; Tues–Thur 6:30–9:30pm (set menu lunch Wed–Sat and dinner Tues–Thur; tasting menu lunch Wed–Sat and dinner Tues–Sat ; NOTE: tasting menu only dinner Fri–Sat).

MODERATE
ALIMENTUM ★ MODERN BRITISH Chef/patron Mark Poynton is the former head chef at Midsummer House (see above) and is now bringing a growing reputation to his own discreet place. Slow cooking is the thing, dishes such as a starter of quail ballotine, sweetcorn, popcorn, and truffle followed by venison loin with potato terrine, sprout leaves, and juniper.

152–154 Hills Rd. www.restaurantalimentum.co.uk.☏ **01223/413000.** Fixed-price menu £45 three courses, £32.50 two courses; lunch £22.50/£16.50; tasting menu £65. AE, MC, V. Mon–Sat noon–2:30pm and 6pm–10pm; Sun noon–3:30pm.

Cotto ★ BRITISH/CONTINENTAL Cotto offers quality food on the pricey side of moderate, but the £40 three-course fixed-price dinners have seasonal menus and locally sourced ingredients. Main courses such as salt marsh lamb shank can't be hurried. Lunch dishes, individually priced, include the delightful grilled vegetable salad with Wobbly Bottom goat cheese for £8.50. Cakes and pastries are also available.

183 East Rd. www.cottocambridge.co.uk.☏ **01223/302010.** Reservations recommended for dinner. Fixed-price dinner £40; lunch main courses £7.50–£17. AE, MC, V. Tues–Fri 9am–3pm; Thurs–Sat 7–10pm.

INEXPENSIVE
Browns ★ 🍴 BRITISH/CONTINENTAL Browns, part of a posh burger/steak/pasta chain, has wicker chairs, high ceilings, fans, and conservatory-style airiness that

create a genteel atmosphere. It's also a good place for breakfast, brunch, and afternoon tea. Outdoor seating is available.

23 Trumpington St. (opposite the Fitzwilliam Museum). www.browns-restaurants.co.uk. © **01223/ 461655.** Reservations accepted. Main courses £9–£20. AE, MC, V. Mon–Thurs 10am–10:30pm; Fri–Sat 10am–11pm; Sun 10am–10pm.

Fair Shares Café 🍴 BRITISH   This cafe is highly recommended by locals for its wholesome homemade lunches. Fair trade products are used wherever possible, and the cafe is run in a non-profit partnership with the church (where it's located) and Mencap volunteers.

Emmanuel United Reformed Church, Trumpington St. © **01223/351174.** Main courses £4.50–£8. AE, MC, V. Tues–Fri 10:30am–3pm.

Rainbow Vegetarian Café VEGETARIAN/VEGAN   This long-established pioneer of vegetarian eating also offers vegan and gluten-free food and organic wine and cider. Spinach lasagna is the signature dish, but super specials include artichoke parcels and Jamaican patties. There is a children's menu and free organic baby food. This award-winning cafe also serves fair trade coffee and homemade cakes in its basement setting.

9A King's Parade (across from King's College). www.rainbowcafe.co.uk. © **01223/321551.** Reservations not accepted. Main courses £8–£10. MC, V. Tues–Sat 10am–10pm; Sun 10am–4pm. Closed Mondays.

Yippee Noodle Bar CHINESE   You'll find informal canteen dining here, but there's a sense of style, too. The food is fast and fresh, with a choice of noodles or rice dishes. It is very popular with local young people, and good for vegetarians.

7–9 King St. www.yippeenoodlebar.co.uk. © **01223/518111.** Main courses £8–£12. MC, V. Mon–Fri noon–3pm and 5–10:30pm; Sat–Sun noon–10:30pm.

Shopping

There's great shopping, starting in the central Market Square. Monday to Saturday is the **General Market** with fruit and vegetables, clothes, books, and jewelry, while Sunday is **Arts and Crafts and Local Produce** with crafts plus homemade cakes, bread, and organic food. **All Saints Garden Art and Craft Market** off Trinity Street is good for gifts and mementoes on Saturdays, and there are gift shops galore in **King's Parade,** which runs into Trinity Street and then St. John's Street. There's been a bookstore since 1581 on the site of the **Cambridge University Press bookshop,** 1–2 Trinity St. (www.cambridge.org; © **01223/333333**), while bookstore **Heffers,** 20 Trinity St. (www.heffers.co.uk; © **01223/568568**), is a Cambridge institution.

Rose Crescent, near the market, offers smart clothes and cosmetics, while the **Benet Street Area,** or Arts Quarter, off King's Parade, has fashion, ceramics, and jewelry. The newest destination is **Grand Arcade,** in St. Andrews Street (www.grand arcade.co.uk; © **01223/302601**), with big name shops. If you're looking for bohemian shops, try **Mill Road,** off Parker's Piece, for secondhand shops including **Cambridge Antiques Centre,** at Gwydir Street off Mill Road (www.cambs antiques.com; © **01223/356391**).

Entertainment & Nightlife

Cambridge Corn Exchange, 3 Parsons Court (www.cornex.co.uk; ©**01223/357851**), is your best bet for mainstream shows, bands, and comedians, and **Cambridge Arts**

Theatre, 6 St. Edward's Passage (www.cambridgeartstheatre.com; © **01223/503333**), has some wonderful stage productions. It used to be the venue for **Cambridge Footlights,** the university theatre group that produced some of Britain's best-known actors, comedians, and satirists, such as John Cleese of Monty Python, and *House* star Hugh Laurie. The Footlights Spring Revue now takes place at the **Amateur Dramatic Club,** in Park Street near Jesus Lane (www.adctheatre.com; © **01223/300085**), and it's the place to see other university or local drama productions. **The Junction,** Clifton Way (www.junction.co.uk; © **01223/511511**), has bands, comedians, stage and dance shows, and club nights.

Cambridge also has some wonderful old pubs. The oldest is **The Pickerel Inn,** Magdalene Street (© **01223/355068**), dating from 1432. It has ceiling beams and little alcoves and is near the river. **The Eagle,** Benet Street, off King's Parade (© **01223/505020**), is where Nobel Laureates Watson and Crick first announced their discovery of the DNA double helix. It was also loved by American airmen during World War II. **The Anchor,** Silver Street (© **01223/353554**), and **The Mill (Tap & Spile),** 14 Mill Lane, off Silver Street Bridge (© **01223/357026**), are good for sitting out near the river. Alternately, escape other tourists at **The Free Press,** Prospect Row (www.freepresspub.com; © **01223/368337**), with its cozy bars and courtyard, or try **The Cambridge Blue,** 85–87 Gwydir St. (www.the-cambridgeblue. co.uk; © **01223/471680**), which serves good food and has a great beer garden.

Where to Stay

EXPENSIVE

De Vere University Arms ★   This 19th-century hotel looks as though it belongs to one of the colleges, particularly with its picturesque position on Parker's Piece a few minutes' walk from the heart of the city. Despite a modern extension you'll find many original architectural features, an elegant bar that serves afternoon tea, and the highly regarded **Restaurant 17.** There are classic and executive rooms plus two suites, some with four-poster beds, some with Sony PlayStations. Family rooms are also available.

Regent St., Cambridge CB2 1AD. www.devere-hotels.co.uk.© **01223/273000.** Fax 01223/315256. 119 units. £84–£150 double; £250 suite. Rates include English breakfast. AE, MC, V. Parking £16. **Amenities:** Restaurant; bar; room service; babysitting. *In room:* TV, hair dryer, Wi-Fi (free).

Hotel Felix ★★   This boutique hotel is a 15-minute walk from town in landscaped gardens. Stylish and luxurious, the Victorian mansion is a blend of old and new with specially commissioned modern art and unfussy decor. It has an exceptional restaurant, **Graffiti** (mains £16–£21), with dishes such as game and local ale pie, horseradish mash, and chantenay carrots. There's a terrace for drinks, dining, and tea.

Whitehouse Lane, Huntingdon Rd., Cambridge CB3 0LX. www.hotelfelix.co.uk.© **01223/277977.** Fax 01223/277973. 52 units. £110–£250 double; from £295 suite. Rates include continental breakfast. AE, MC, V. Free parking. **Amenities:** Restaurant; bar; access to health club; room service. *In room:* TV, hair dryer, CD player, Wi-Fi (free).

Varsity Hotel & Spa   A boutique property in a striking modern building on the banks of the Cam with views over the colleges from the 7th floor roof terrace (where you can sip a sunset drink from a sofa). Rooms have floor–to-ceiling windows, oak floors, the occasional roll-top bath and four-poster, and combine up-to-the-minute style with tradition. There's free entry to the extravagant Glassworks health club next door where you can watch punts going past from the Jacuzzi. The River Bar

Steakhouse & Grill, stripped brick walls contrasting with shiny fittings, flame grills steaks (a 22oz porterhouse), burgers, and fish (swordfish, salmon).

Thompson's Lane (off Bridge St.), Cambridge CB5 8AQ. www.thevarsityhotel.co.uk. © **01223/ 306030.** Fax 01223/305070. 48 units. £155–295 double; £255–£500 suite. Rates include full English breakfast. AE, MC, V. Parking £7/day. **Amenities:** Restaurant; bar; health club. *In room:* A/C, TV, hair dryer, iPod dock, Wi-Fi (free).

MODERATE

Arundel House Hotel Overlooking the River Cam and Jesus Green, this is one of the loveliest sites in Cambridge. The hotel consists of six connected Victorian houses—all fronted with dark-yellow local bricks. There's a good restaurant (2 courses £18.95) plus light lunches and dinners in the conservatory. Rooms overlooking the river and green cost more, as do those on lower floors (there's no elevator).

53 Chesterton Rd., Cambridge CB4 3AN. www.arundelhousehotels.co.uk. © **01223/367701.** Fax 01223/367721. 103 units. £95–£140 double; £145–£165 family room. Rates include continental breakfast. AE, MC, V. Free parking. **Amenities:** Restaurant; bar. *In room:* A/C, TV, hair dryer, Wi-Fi (free).

Regent Hotel This is another hotel overlooking Parker's Piece, and very convenient for the sights. It's one of the best of Cambridge's reasonably priced small hotels. The building, a lovely Regency mansion, dates from the 1840s and was Newnham College until it outgrew the site. Rooms are pale and comfortable, and there is a small bar.

41 Regent St., Cambridge CB2 1AB. www.regenthotel.co.uk. © **01223/351470.** Fax 01223/464937. 22 units. £103–£156 double. Rates include continental breakfast. AE, MC, V. **Amenities:** Bar. *In room:* A/C, TV, hair dryer, Wi-Fi (free).

NEAR CAMBRIDGE: SAFFRON WALDEN & NEWMARKET

Newmarket: 62 miles NE of London; 13 miles NE of Cambridge; Saffron Walden: 40 miles NE of London; 14 miles SE of Cambridge

There are several small, lovely market towns within a half-hour drive of Cambridge. Newmarket is known as the headquarters of British horse-racing, and that's why most people visit. Medieval Saffron Waldon, full of half-timbered buildings, is home to the largest parish church in Essex. St. Mary the Virgin was built in 1430 under the eye of John Wastell, who designed the Chapel at King's College, Cambridge, while the award-winning Saffron Walden Museum next door is charmingly traditional and you can picnic in the grounds beside the ruins of the 12th century castle. Many of Saffron Walden's old buildings have fine examples of pargetting, a decorative plasterwork unique to East Anglia. You'll see more at nearby **Thaxted,** where **St. John the Baptist Church** is one of the most impressive in Essex. Composer Gustav Holst lived in the village from 1914 to 1925 and worked on *The Planets* here. He also started a music festival that was resurrected in 1980 and takes place in June and July. **Finchingfield** is another pretty Essex village worth calling at for a stroll around the antiques shops or to feed the ducks on the pond at the classic village green.

Essentials

GETTING THERE Regular trains to Newmarket from London's Liverpool Street Station (change at Cambridge), cost from about £28 one-way and take about 2 hours.

If you're driving from Cambridge, head east on the A133. NXEA Trains to Saffron Walden take about an hour from Liverpool Street to Audley End (about £18 one-way), 2 miles away. If you're driving from London, it's just off the M11 at junction 8.

VISITOR INFORMATION Newmarket **Tourist Information Centre** (www.visit eastofengland.com; ☎ **01638/719749**) is at the Guineas Shopping Centre. A self-guided walking leaflet, Newmarket Horseshoe Trail, is available there. Saffron Walden **Tourist Information Centre,** 1 Market Place (www.visitsaffronwalden.gov. uk; ☎ **01799/524002**), has free copies of the Saffron Walden Town Trail.

Exploring the Area

National Horseracing Museum MUSEUM Discover 300 years of horse-racing in this museum housed in the old subscription rooms (early 19th-century betting room). See paintings, statues, silverware, and royal memorabilia including the preserved head of Persimmon, the best horse bred by the royal family. Book an Equine Tour (by phone) to take you into the stable yards and training grounds; there are various tours and prices start at about £25, including museum entrance. **Palace House** was built for Charles II for his visits to the races—tours are sometimes available; call for details.

99 High St. www.nhrm.co.uk. ☎ **01638/667333.** Admission £6.50 adults, £5.50 seniors, £3.50 children 15 and under, £15 family ticket. Mar–Dec daily 10am–5pm.

National Stud WORKING FARM See behind the scenes at the home to some of the world's finest horses and a renowned breeding stud operation. During the 75-minute tour you'll see mares, foals, and stallions. Booking is recommended.

Next to the July Course (see below) on the A1303. www.nationalstud.co.uk. ☎ **01638/663464.** Admission £7 adults, £5 seniors and children 5–15, £20 family ticket, free for children under 6. Feb–Sept daily 11:15am and 2pm; Oct daily 11:15am. Closed Nov–Jan.

Newmarket Racecourses RACECOURSE The **July Course** is known for its beech trees and thatched-roof buildings; it is one of the loveliest racecourses in the world and part of the English social calendar. Races take place from June to October, highlighted by the July Cup. The **Rowley Mile,** the "Course of Champions," is the focus for some of the highest-class races in the world. Prestige events include the Guineas Races and the Champion Stakes, while evening meetings are often followed by concerts featuring stars such as Van Morrison and Tom Jones.

Newmarket Racecourses, Westfield House, The Links, Newmarket. www.newmarketracecourses. co.uk. ☎ **0844/579-3010.** Open only for races and special events. Ticket prices vary, but are around £13 to £40; online bookings receive a 20% discount. Free for children 17 and under.

Audley End HISTORIC SITE Charles II is one of the former owners of this house, originally built in 1538 on the grounds of Walden Abbey after the Reformation. Architects Sir Christopher Wren and Robert Adam were involved in redesigns, and landscape guru Capability Brown remodeled the grounds. The highlights these days are the kitchen, dairy, larder, and laundry as well as the gardens and parkland.

Insider tip: Entrance is free to English Heritage members; 1-week or 2-week Overseas Visitors Passes are available from £21.50. Buy online for collection at any English Heritage property.

Audley End, Saffron Walden. www.english-heritage.org.uk. ☎ **01638/667333.** Admission £12.50 adults, £7.50 children 5–15, £32.50 family ticket. Apr–Sept Wed–Sun and public holidays 11am–5pm (grounds 10am–6pm), Oct until 4pm (grounds 5pm); house closed Nov–Mar. Grounds only weekends Nov–Christmas and early Feb, then Wed–Sun until end Mar mostly 10am–4pm. House sometimes open only for guided tours; see website for details.

Imperial War Museum Duxford MUSEUM   This is Britain's leading air museum, vast hangars at a real airfield (it was a World War I airfield and one of the earliest Air Force stations). Arrive early because there's lots to see. Duxford Airfield played its part in both World Wars, as you'll see in the 1940s' Operations Room and the permanent Battle of Britain exhibition, which has a Spitfire and Hurricane on display. There are more than 30 historic aircraft in the AirSpace hangar, including a Concorde which you can tour, while the American Air Museum houses a huge collection of U.S. warplanes. It also has some of the best air shows in Britain and other regular events.

Duxford Airfield, Duxford. www.iwm.org.uk. ©**01223/835000.** Admission £17 adults, £14 seniors, children 15 and under free. Mid-Mar–Oct daily 10am–6pm; Nov–Mar daily 10am–4pm (last admission 5pm in summer, 3pm in winter).

Where to Eat & Stay

The Cricketers ★   There are no hotels in Saffron Walden, although the Tourist Information Centre (see above) can help with B&Bs. But try the Cricketers in Clavering, which has a mix of contemporary and four-poster bedrooms in a 16th-century inn. It's been owned and run by TV chef Jamie Oliver's parents since the 1970s. The food is award winning and was well regarded when Jamie worked there as a lad before becoming a catering superstar; he now supplies veg and salad from his organic garden. Pasta (homemade) starts at £11 with dishes such as braised shank of Little Braxted lamb with a root vegetable and redcurrant sauce £15–£22.

Wicken Rd., Clavering, Essex CB11 4QT. www.thecricketers.co.uk. ©**01799/550442.** Fax 01799/550882. 14 units. £95–£115 double. AE, MC, V. Free parking. **Amenities:** Restaurant; bar. *In room:* TV, hair dryer, Wi-Fi (free).

Rutland Arms Hotel   This old Georgian building, once a coaching inn and built around a cobbled courtyard, retains a lot of character and is in the heart of Newmarket. It has elegant en suite bedrooms, the reasonably priced **Carriages** restaurant, and the Nell Gwynn lounge bar with open fires in winter.

33 High St., Newmarket, Suffolk CB8 8NB. www.oxfordhotelsandinns.com. ©**01638/664251.** Fax 01638/666298. 46 units. £65–£168 double. Rates include English breakfast. MC, V. Free parking. **Amenities:** Restaurant; bar; room service. *In room:* TV, hair dryer, Wi-Fi (£3 per hr.).

Swynford Paddocks ★   A beautiful 17th-century country house where Lord Byron once lived and worked with grounds overlooking a stud farm. The luxury hotel has individually designed rooms, each named after a racing great and some with four-poster beds and claw-foot baths. The Byron Room offers intimate fine dining while **Silks Brasserie,** a conservatory with a wooden floor and a colonial touch, serves lunch and lighter fare. Children's meals are available. There is also afternoon tea.

London Rd., Six Mile Bottom, Newmarket, Suffolk CB8 0UE. www.swynfordpaddocks.com. ©**01638/570234.** Fax 01638/570283. 15 units. £135–£175 double; prices rise during race meetings. Rates include English breakfast. AE, DC, MC, V. Free parking. **Amenities:** 2 restaurants; bar; room service. *In room:* TV, hair dryer, Wi-Fi (free).

Shopping

Newmarket is small with a mix of chain stores and independent shops. **Powters the Pork Shop,** Wellington Street (www.powters.co.uk; © **01638/662418**), sells

Newmarket sausages. The originals, made by Musks Ltd., are available online (www.musks.com). Many of Saffron Walden's ancient buildings are now antiques shops. A **Country Market** takes place on Friday mornings at the back of the town hall, and there are stalls on Tuesdays and Saturdays in the Market Place.

ELY & THE FENS

70 miles NE of London; 16 miles N of Cambridge

You can see Ely's magnificent cathedral miles before you reach England's second smallest city. The ship of the Fens, as it is known, was built in the 11th century when Ely was an island surrounded by freshwater marshes. Pilgrims came to Ely for centuries to visit the shrine of Saint Etheldreda, until it was destroyed in the Reformation in the mid-1500s. Follow the **Eel Trail** from **Oliver Cromwell's House,** which now doubles as a tourist office, through town to the River Ouse, where **The Maltings** has a restaurant and bar overlooking the water. The circular walk then heads through delightful **Cherry Hill** Park, up past **Ely Cathedral** to tourist attractions, independent shops, pubs, cafes, and restaurants.

Essentials

GETTING THERE   There are First Capital Connect trains from London's King's Cross (some direct, some involve a change at Cambridge onto an INEA service), costing about £25 one-way and taking a little over an hour. If you're driving from Cambridge, take the A10 north.

VISITOR INFORMATION   The **Tourist Information Centre** is at Oliver Cromwell's House, 29 St. Mary's St. (www.visitely.org.uk; ☎ **01353/662062**). It's open April to October, daily 10am to 5pm, and November to March, Monday, Friday, and Sunday 11am to 4pm, Saturday 10am to 5pm.

Exploring the Area

Ely Cathedral ★★ CATHEDRAL   The original cathedral was built by a monastic community founded in the 7th century. Pilgrims visited the shrine of Saint Etheldreda, who died in 680, daughter of the king of East Anglia and estranged wife of King Egfrith of Northumbria. The present 11th-century cathedral is regarded as one of England's most beautiful ecclesiastic buildings. Start at the Galilee Porch in the West Tower, where a 19th-century labyrinth is laid out on the floor. Ely is the fourth longest cathedral in England, and the massive Norman nave with its string of impressive columns leads to the Octagon Tower and its distinctive lantern roof, which was built in the 14th century when the Norman tower collapsed. The Octagon is in the Gothic style, but incorporates medieval carvings that tell the story of Etheldreda. Guided tours are included in the entrance fee from Monday to Saturday. For an extra charge there are guided tours of the Octagon and West towers, which have magnificent views. The Refectory Café, accessed through the West Tower or Cathedral Bookshop, is open daily (afternoons only on Sunday). There is a Stained Glass Museum in the South Triforium. The **Almonry Tea Rooms,** in a vaulted undercroft, has a garden seating.

www.elycathedral.org. ☎ **01353/667735.** Admission £7 adults, £6 students and seniors, free for children 11 and under. Apr–Oct daily 7am–6:30pm; Nov–Mar Mon–Sat 7am–6:30pm, Sun 7am–5:30pm.

Ely Museum MUSEUM   Just a few minutes from the cathedral and set in the city's former jail, you can find out about the Iceni rebellion against the Romans led by Queen Boudicca, the effect of the Norman invasion of 1066, and life among the waterways of the Fens from medieval times onward.

Old Gaol, Market St. www.elymuseum.org.uk. 🕿 **01353/666655.** Admission £3.50 adults, £2.50 students and seniors, free for children 16 and under. Summer Mon–Sat 10:30am–5pm, Sun 1–5pm; winter Mon–Sat 10:30am–4pm, Sun 1–4pm (closed Tues in winter). Check for Christmas opening.

Oliver Cromwell's House HISTORIC HOME   Oliver Cromwell was the Lord Protector of the Commonwealth, after the Civil Wars between 1642 and 1651 left England a short-lived republic for the only time in its history. Charles I was executed and Cromwell became "king in all but name"—an extraordinary feat for a gentleman farmer and MP for Cambridge. He lived in Ely for 10 years, and this restored family home not only gives an insight into the man—a Puritan who "banned Christmas"—but also into 17th-century domestic life. The tourist information office is in the building.

29 St. Mary's St. (next to St. Mary's Church). www.visitely.eastcambs.gov.uk. 🕿 **01353/662062.** Admission £4.50 adults, £4 seniors and students, £3.10 children 6–16, £13 family ticket, free for children 5 and under. Apr–Oct daily 10am–5pm; Nov–Mar Sun–Fri 11am–4pm, Sat 10am–5pm.

Where to Eat

Escape the crowds at **The Almonry Restaurant & Tea Rooms,** in The College, Ely Cathedral, High Street (www.elycathedral.org; 🕿 **01353/666360**). Not only is the setting peaceful (a 12th-century undercroft with a garden for summer dining) but the home-cooked lunches and afternoon teas are excellent. Lunch starts at around £11. It's open Monday to Saturday 9am to 5pm and Sunday 11am to 5pm.

Boathouse ★ BRITISH/CONTINENTAL   This is the best gastropub-cum-restaurant in town, housed in a converted boathouse that opens onto the Great Ouse, a 10-minute walk from the city's heart. The menu is seasonal and ingredients are locally sourced; for instance, co-owner Richard Bradley's home-produced sausages are made from Gloucestershire Old Spot pork. There's a set lunch on weekdays with starters including pigeon and black-pudding salad, and main courses such as steamed steak and kidney pudding. Evening meals and Sunday lunches are a la carte.

5 Annesdale. www.theboathouseely.co.uk. 🕿 **01353/664388.** Reservations recommended. 2-course lunch £15; dinner main courses £10–£24.50. AE, MC, V. Daily noon–2:30pm (Sun noon–2:45pm) and Mon–Thurs 6:30–9pm; Fri–Sat 6:30–9:30pm; Sun 6:30–8:30pm.

Old Fire Engine House ★ 🍴 BRITISH   This converted fire station with a walled garden and art gallery is near Oliver Cromwell's House. The menu is British farmhouse, with dishes such as rabbit with prunes and bacon, while afternoon tea (£17.50) is finger sandwiches, scones with clotted cream, and homemade jam followed by homemade cakes and pastries. In summer you can dine in the garden.

25 St. Mary's St. (opposite St. Mary's Church). www.theoldfireenginehouse.co.uk. 🕿**01353/662582.** Main courses £15–£18. MC, V. Daily 12:15–2pm, 3:30–5:15pm, and 7:15–9pm.

Where to Stay

Lamb Hotel   This coaching inn was known as The Holy Lambe in the 1400s by pilgrims visiting the cathedral, across the street. Today the Lamb is beautifully decorated (rich-hued walls and wooden floors), with traditionally furnished rooms with modern comforts and big polished wood beds. The **restaurant** (main courses

£8–£17) has a variety of steaks, and there's lots of use of Colman's mustard, which is made in the region. The bar is warm and comfy.

2 Lynn Rd., Ely, Cambridgeshire CB7 4EJ. www.thelamb-ely.com. © **01353/663574.** Fax 01353/ 662023. 31 units. £90–£110 double. Rates include English breakfast. AE, MC, V. Free parking. **Amenities:** Restaurant; bar; room service. *In room:* TV, hair dryer, Wi-Fi (free).

CONSTABLE COUNTRY

63 miles NE of London; 8 miles NE of Colchester

Dedham Vale was already known as Constable Country when the artist John Constable was alive. Nearly 200 years later, this Area of Outstanding Natural Beauty on the Essex–Suffolk border is still a magnet for art lovers. They are drawn to **East Bergholt,** the pretty village where Constable was born; to **Dedham,** the small market town where he went to school; and to **Flatford Mill,** which he made immortal in his paintings. There's a display dedicated to Constable at **Bridge Cottage** near Flatford Mill. Constable Country takes in three long-distance footpaths: the **Essex Way,** the **Stour Valley Path,** and the **Suffolk Coast and Heaths Path,** and is an easy hour's countryside walk from **Manningtree** railway station.

The **Sir Alfred Munnings Art Museum** is also in Dedham, created in the artist's own home after his death in 1959. It is filled with his work and possessions. Not far away, at **Sudbury,** is the home of 18th-century artist Thomas Gainsborough. As founder of the English school of painting, he was much admired by Constable, who once said: "I fancy I see a Gainsborough in every hedge and hollow tree." Gainsborough's house contains more of his paintings, drawings, and prints than can be seen anywhere else. But the greatest glory of Constable Country is still, as in Constable's time, a lazy river meandering through green fields past ancient trees and hedgerows under the huge East Anglian skies.

Essentials

GETTING THERE   Trains (NXEA) leave hourly from London's Liverpool Street Station to Sudbury, an 80-minute journey (changing at Marks Tey), or several times an hour to Manningtree, an hour's ride; both cost about £27 one-way. It's also possible to take the train to Colchester, 5 miles from Dedham. There are taxis at the station, and buses at the bus station on **Queen Street** (www.firstgroup.com; © **01206/ 282645**).

If you're driving from London, take the A12 past Colchester and turn off at East Bergholt, following signs for Dedham.

Exploring the Area

The focal point of Dedham is the Georgian High Street with its independent shops and cafes and the Dedham Grammar School on Royal Square, where Constable was a pupil. At Dedham's heart is St. Mary's Church, which featured in much of Constable's work and where his painting *The Ascension* is on permanent display. Many people from this part of Essex were among the Pilgrims to America, and there are carvings in the church pews to commemorate *The Mayflower* and other U.S. connections.

Flatford Mill & Bridge Cottage HISTORIC SITE   There is no public access to Flatford Mill, which now runs art courses, but you can walk around the mill pond and along the river, providing ample opportunity to follow in Constable's footsteps, or just have a picnic. Signposts direct drivers to the Flatford Mill parking lot, and there's a small Tourist Information Centre on the road down to the mill. On the road is Bridge Cottage, where there's an exhibition about Constable and a cafe. **River Stour Trust** boat trips leave from nearby (weekends and public holidays; www.riverstour trust.org; $\textcircled{C}$ **01787/313199**), or you can walk along the riverbank.

Flatford Lane, East Begholt. www.nationaltrust.org.uk. $\textcircled{C}$ **01206/298260.** Free admission. Bridge Cottage, Visitor Centre, tea room and shop May–Sept 10:30am–3:30pm, April, Oct 11am–5pm, Nov–Christmas 11am–3:30pm, closed Christmas–March, but do check as dates can vary. Opening times vary according to season.

Sir Alfred Munnings Art Museum MUSEUM   Munnings was born in 1878, and his early work captured the disappearing country people and scenes of East Anglia, but he is best known for his equestrian paintings; he was the official war artist to the Canadian Cavalry Brigade during World War I. His most famous paintings are of racehorses and courses, and many of these are displayed here in what was his home. Munnings left his paintings to the nation, and his widow set up the trust that now runs the museum, which includes two galleries, beautiful gardens, and a cafe.

Castle House, East Lane, Dedham. www.siralfredmunnings.co.uk. $\textcircled{C}$ **01206/322127.** Admission £5 adults, £1 children 5–15. Apr–Oct Wed, Thurs, Sat, Sun and public holidays 2–5pm.

Where to Eat & Stay

Maison Talbooth ★★★   This Victorian country house, which overlooks the Stour Valley, is now an award-winning designer hotel with 12 luxury suites, a day spa, outdoor pool with sun-lounge area and hot tub, and a tennis court. Lunch and tea are available, and its sister hotel, **Milsoms,** on the same road ($\textcircled{C}$ **01206/322795**), has an all-day bistro and rooms. The company also owns **Le Talbooth** restaurant ($\textcircled{C}$ **01206/322367**), a short drive away in Gun Hill, over the other side of the A12.

Stratford Rd., Dedham, Colchester CO7 6HN. www.milsomhotels.co.uk. $\textcircled{C}$ **01206/322367.** Fax 01206/322752. 12 units. £195–£405 double. Rates include continental breakfast. AE, MC, V. Take the Stratford Road ½ mile west of the town. **Amenities:** Bar; outdoor heated pool; tennis court; spa; room service; babysitting. *In room:* TV, hair dryer, Wi-Fi (free).

The Sun Inn ★   This old coaching inn has beautiful boutique hotel bedrooms, two with four-poster beds, a cozy bar with real ale and Suffolk cider, and a highly respected restaurant serving local produce with an Italian twist. There's a lunchtime bar menu and children's menu.

High St., Dedham, Colchester C07 6DF. www.thesuninndedham.com. $\textcircled{C}$ **01206/323351.** 5 units. £105–£160 double. Rates include English breakfast. AE, MC, V. Free parking. **Amenities:** Restaurant; bar. *In room:* TV, hair dryer, iPod dock, Wi-Fi (free).

SUDBURY

This busy market town, at the heart of the pre-Industrial Revolution weaving industry, was one of the "wool towns" that created wealth in East Anglia, as you can see with a glance at impressive **St. Peter's Church,** which dominates the market place where there are stalls on Thursdays and Saturdays. No longer used as a church, it features regular concerts and exhibitions. Outside is a statue of artist Thomas Gainsborough, who was born in a house down the hill. **Gainsborough's House** is the main attraction, but there are lovely walks across the commons and meadows around the River Stour, which encloses the town on three sides. **Sudbury Heritage Centre &**

Museum traces the town's history from before its mention in the 1086 Domesday Book through its woolen-cloth prosperity in the Middle Ages to the 19th-century silk mills. Here is also the Tourist Information Office (www.sudburysuffolk.co.uk), with leaflets for the Talbot Trail, which guides you to places of interest.

Exploring the Area

Gainsborough's House HISTORIC HOME Thomas Gainsborough was born here in 1727, and by the time he died in 1788 he had become one of Britain's greatest painters. The biggest collection of his paintings, drawings, and prints are exhibited here in this house, built in 1500, with its Georgian facade and later additions. The museum also holds exhibitions of other artists' work and runs art courses.

46 Gainsborough St. www.gainsborough.org. © **01787/372958.** Admission £4.50 adults, £2 students and children 5–18. Mon–Sat 10am–5pm. Closed Sun, Dec 24–Jan 2, and Good Friday.

Where to Eat & Stay

The Mill ★★★ You can still see the working mill wheel behind a glass screen in the oak beamed restaurant of this old world hotel. You can also see the mummified cat behind another glass screen, which the medieval builders bricked into the mill floor for good luck. This isn't a boutique hotel but it's relaxing with views over the commons to the river from the restaurant and bar, the latter of which has an outdoor terrace.

Walnut Tree Lane, Sudbury, Suffolk CO10 1BD. www.themillhotelsudbury.co.uk.© **01787/375544.** Fax 01787/373027. 56 units. £90–£115 double; suite £200–245. Rates include English breakfast. AE, MC, V. **Amenities:** Bar; restaurant; room service; Wi-Fi (free, in public areas). *In room:* TV, hair dryer.

BURY ST. EDMUNDS & THETFORD FOREST

70 miles NE of London; 25 miles E of Cambridge; 9 miles N of Lavenham

The cathedral city of Bury St. Edmunds is still "a handsome little town, of thriving and cleanly appearance," as Charles Dickens described it in *The Pickwick Papers*. The classic market town is only a few miles from the start of the heathland and forest which culminates in Thetford Forest Park, 11 miles north along the A134. It is Britain's largest lowland pine forest covering 50,000 acres straddling the Suffolk–Norfolk border and has been an area of human settlement since Neolithic times (about 2500 B.C.). The prehistoric **Icknield Way,** which runs close to Thetford, is the oldest road in Britain. Bury St. Edmunds was founded thanks to its **Benedictine abbey** in 1020, and named after King Edmund of the East Angles, who was buried here in 903. According to legend, England's reformer barons met in the abbey in 1214 and agreed to force King John to sign the Charter of Liberties, which led to the Magna Carta of 1215—the most significant document in English history, introducing the right of law. The city has many modern buildings, such as the **Arc shopping center,** but there are lovely old corners with echoes of a medieval past. It was also prosperous during the 17th and 18th centuries due to the textiles industry, as seen from fine buildings, such as the **Theatre Royal,** the only surviving Regency theatre in the U.K., and the **Athenaeum,** once the Assembly Rooms, where balls were held in Georgian times. Town tours can be booked at the Tourist Information Centre. Markets, Wednesdays and Saturdays, are overlooked by **Moyse's Hall Museum,** one of the last

Norman-built houses in the U.K. There's a reconstructed Anglo-Saxon settlement at West Stow Country Park six miles away.

Essentials

GETTING THERE Trains to Bury St. Edmunds leave London's Liverpool Street (change at Ipswich), or King's Cross (change at Cambridge), and take between 90 minutes and 2 hours, costing about £37 one-way. Trains from Cambridge (£8.90 one-way) take 40 minutes and **Stagecoach** buses (www.stagecoachbus.com; © **01223/423578**) leave the city's Drummer Street Station for Bury St. Edmunds almost hourly and take 1 hour 20 minutes, costing £4.40.. By car from London take the M25 to the M11, and the A45 near Cambridge. It takes about 1½ hours. It's a 45-minute drive from Cambridge on the A45.

Trains (NXEA) from Cambridge to Thetford take about 40 minutes costing about £11, and from Norwich to Thetford (NXEA) it's about 30 minutes (about £8).. Trains also go to Thetford via Ely from London King's Cross, and take 1¼ hours costing about £37. For onward buses contact **Brecks Bus Service** (www.brecks.org; © **01638/608080**), a service that you have to book in advance and that takes up to five passengers. If you're driving from London, take the M25 to the M11, then the A11 and B1107.

VISITOR INFORMATION The **Bury St. Edmunds Tourist Information Centre,** 6 Angel Hill (www.stedmundsbury.gov.uk; © **01284/764667**), is open Easter to October (Mon–Sat 9:30am to 5pm). May to September it also opens Sunday 10am to 3pm. From November to Easter it's open Monday to Friday 10am to 4pm, Saturday 10am to 1pm, and public holidays 10am to 3pm. **Thetford Tourist Information Centre** is at 20 King St. (www.explorethetford.co.uk; © **01842/751975;** Mon–Fri 9am–5pm, Sat 9am–4pm).

SPECIAL EVENTS The 17-day **Bury St. Edmunds Festival** (www.buryfestival.co.uk; © **01284/758000**) is held every May and includes everything from classical to contemporary music, exhibitions, talks, walks, films, plays, and a fireworks display.

Exploring the Area

Ancient House Museum MUSEUM Discover the truth behind the Thetford Treasure—silver spoons, gold rings, pendants, and necklaces hidden in Roman times—dug up in 1979, and find out about Thetford residents such as Thomas Paine, who had a hand in American independence and the French Revolution, when you visit this beautiful medieval merchant's house museum.

White Hart St., Thetford. www.museums.norfolk.gov.uk. © **01842/752599.** Admission £3.70 adults, £2 children 4–16. Tues–Sat 10am–5pm (closes 4pm Oct–Mar, when admission is free).

Abbey of Bury St. Edmunds ★★ ABBEY This was among the largest Norman buildings in Europe and there are still signs of its greatness, particularly the lofty **Abbey Gate** on Crown Street. The abbey fell into disrepair after Henry VIII's Dissolution of the monasteries, but the gate tower survived and is now the entrance to gardens in the grounds. Up the street is **St. Mary's Church,** part of the original complex, third largest parish church in the country and burial place of Henry VIII's sister Mary, mother of Lady Jane Grey who briefly succeeded Henry VIII's son Edward VI. Next door is the Norman tower, gateway to the abbey precincts, which houses the bells of the cathedral. **St. Edmundsbury Cathedral** was the parish church of St. James when it was built in the 12th century. A 16th-century nave was added, followed by a 19th-century chancel (by architect Sir Gilbert Scott, designer of London's Albert Memorial), and it was declared a cathedral in 1914. It remained unfinished until 2005, when a tower was built, and 2010 saw the inauguration of a grandiose organ and the unveiling of an arched, painted wooden ceiling in the tower. A nice refectory serves lunch and snacks Monday to Saturday, and a shop sells souvenirs such as CDs of the choir. You can still see a few abbey ruins, including Samson Tower, in the gardens. Laid out as botanic gardens in 1831, these now feature bedding displays, the Sensory Garden, and the Pilgrim's Herb Garden.

Angel Hill. www.stedscathedral.co.uk. ℂ **01284/748720.** Free, but donations welcomed. Daily 8am–6pm. St. Mary's www.stmarystpeter.net. ℂ **01284/754680.** Donations welcomed. Abbey Gardens and ruins year-round Mon–Sat 7:30am to dusk; Sun 9am to dusk.

Dad's Army Museum MUSEUM   The much-loved BBC comedy series was filmed in Thetford and its forest, and after you've seen the TV memorabilia you can have your photo taken next to the Captain Mainwaring statue. Then take a self-guided Dad's Army Trail, which you can download from www.explorethetford.co.uk.

Cage Lane, Thetford. www.dadsarmythetford.org.uk. ℂ **01842/751975.** Free admission. Easter to Christmas Sat 10am–2pm, also Tues in Aug, and other days during school holidays.

Greene King Brewery Visitor Centre BREWERY   Real ale fans will enjoy a pilgrimage to the home of Abbot Ale and Old Speckled Hen. A museum tells how the Greene and King families founded the present company in 1887, although there has been a brewery on the site since 1700. Tours through the historic brewery include tastings at the Brewery Tap.

Westgate Street. www.greeneking.co.uk. ℂ **01284/714297.** Tours daily, varied times, £8, (£10 evenings). No children under 12.

Grimes Graves HISTORIC SITE   These are the largest and best-preserved Neolithic flint mines in Britain, and the only ones open to the public. There are 400 pits, which produced heads for spears, arrows, and knives for prehistoric tribes, but nobody knew what this unnaturally undulating scrubland was until 1870, when they were excavated. One mine is accessible, involving a child-thrilling 9-m (30-ft.) ladder descent (children 4 and under are not allowed down). There's also an excellent display explaining the site's history, a shop, and the moon-like surface for walks.

Lyndford, Thetford (on the B1107, 2¾ miles northeast of Brandon). www.english-heritage.org.uk. ℂ **01842/810656.** Admission £3.30 adults, £3 students and seniors, £2 children 5–15, £8.60 family ticket. Mar and Oct Thurs–Mon 10am–5pm; Apr–Sept daily 10am–5pm (6pm in July and Aug).

High Lodge SPORTING ACTIVITY   A Forestry Commission-run spot with an adventure playground, sculpture trail, cafe, and even barbecue rentals, where you can also stop for a picnic, go cycling, or take a walk.

Brandon. www.forestry.gov.uk/highlodge. ℂ **01842/815434.** Free, but parking £1.90 an hour (£10 maximum). Daily Nov–Mar 9am–5pm; Apr, Sept and Oct 9am–6pm; May–Aug 9am–7pm.

Ickworth House HISTORIC SITE   The extraordinary home of the eccentric Hervey family is a central rotunda with two wings running east and west, set in formal gardens within a superb country estate. It's a fabulous place for walking, cycling, or just exploring. The house was built for the 4th Earl of Bristol, and the central rotunda contains many of the family's personal possessions, including an impressive collection of silver. One wing is now a lovely cafe and restaurant while the other is an extremely comfortable hotel, with a fine restaurant open to non-guests.

The Rotunda, Horringer. www.nationaltrust.org. © **01284/735270.** House, park, and gardens £9.55 adults, £4.15 children 5–15, £22.70 family ticket; park and gardens only £3.60 adults, £1 children, £8.15 family ticket. House Mar–Oct daily 11am–5pm; closed Nov–Feb. Gardens Mar–Oct daily 10am–5pm; Nov–Apr daily 11am–4pm. Park daily 8am–8pm.

Suffolk Regiment Museum MUSEUM   One of the finest regimental collections in the U.K., housed in the former officers' mess. The rhino-horn powder flask of Tippoo Sultan of Mysore is among the medals, badges, uniforms, flags, and more.

The Keep, Gibraltar Barracks, Newmarket Rd. www.suffolkregiment.org. ©**01284/769505.** Free admission. 1st and 3rd Wed of each month and 1st Sun of each month 9:30am–3:30pm.

Theatre Royal THEATRE   The best way to experience the intimacy of the only surviving Regency theatre in the U.K. is to see a show, but you can also tour the building, which opened for business in 1819 and has recently been restored. Contact the theatre for details of the new tours schedule.

5 Westgate St. www.theatreroyal.org. ©**01284/769505.** Ticket prices vary.

Entertainment & Nightlife

The **Theatre Royal** (see above) has been entertaining people for several centuries, but now there's also **The Apex,** Charter Square (www.theapex.co.uk; © **01284/758000**), for concerts and live bands, in the new Arc shopping center a few minutes from the heart of town. There are plenty of traditional pubs, but start at the **Nutshell,** Traverse and Abbeygate Street (© **01284/764867**), the smallest pub in England. If that's looking full, try the 17th-century **Dog & Partridge,** 29 Crown St. (© **01284/764792**), where bar scenes from the BBC detective series *Lovejoy* were filmed. The **Masons Arms,** 14 Whiting St. (© **01284/753955**), has a family atmosphere and welcomes children, with home-cooked food and a patio garden. The award-winning **One Bull,** Angel Hill (www.theonebull.co.uk; © **01284/848220**), serves superior pub grub in a relaxed contemporary atmosphere, while its sister pub, the **Beerhouse,** 1 Tayfen Rd. (www.burybeerhouse.co.uk; © **01284/766415**), sells real ales and has its own microbrewery, Brewshed, which supplies its pubs and sports clubs.

Where to Eat & Stay

Angel Hotel ★   Ivy covers the grand Georgian facade of what was originally a smaller 15th-century coaching inn overlooking Abbey Gardens and the cathedral. It aims for an upmarket, home-away-from-home atmosphere with contemporary casual bedrooms, and the **Eaterie** offers a good-value set-price lunch menu of 2 courses £13.95) and a la carte dinner menu (mains £16–£28).

3 Angel Hill, Bury St. Edmunds, Suffolk P33 1LT. www.theangel.co.uk. © **01284/714000.** Fax 01284/714001. 75 units. £120–£160 double; £220–£270 suite. Rates include English breakfast. AE, DC, MC, V. Free parking. **Amenities:** 2 restaurants; bar; room service; babysitting. *In room:* A/C (in some), TV, hair dryer, Wi-Fi (free).

The Cadogan ★   This pub with rooms is a calm, modern haven, whether you want a decent pint, gastropub food, or to relax in one of the seven smart rooms. The Cadogan manages to be both stylish and family-friendly, with children's portions of adult meals, a big garden, and a play area. In the bar there are "grazing boards"

(£13.50) for sharing cheese, fish, charcuterie, and even puddings. The restaurant does things like steak, burgers, and shepherd's pie in an up-to-date way (mains £11–£15) and you can eat on the heated deck. It's owned by the people behind The Beerhouse and One Bull pubs.

The Street, Ingham, Bury St. Edmunds, Suffolk IP31 1NG. www.thecadogan.co.uk. © **01284/728443.** 7 units £70 single; £100 double/twin. Rates include breakfast. AE, MC, V. Free parking. **Amenities:** Restaurant; bar. *In room:* TV, hair dryer, Wi-Fi (free).

Ickworth Hotel ★★★ ☺   Wellies (boots) at the grand front door of this stately home-turned-grand-family-hotel speak volumes. Borrow them for walks in the surrounding parkland, then just put them back. It's English country-house hospitality and part of the Luxury Family Hotels group. Half of this Palladian palace is National Trust (guests have free entry), but hotel guests get to stay in the high-ceilinged rooms and walk the echoing corridors. Rooms are big and comfy, with the personal feel of a house, and children can run free; there are also one- and two-bedroom apartments in the Dower House, in the grounds near the church, and the three-bedroom Butler's Lodge in a walled garden. There's a big swimming pool in a barn, a cellar games room with table tennis and PlayStation, a tennis court and trampoline outside, and bikes for hire; adults get the spa. There are two excellent restaurants, **Frederick's** (adults only) and the **Conservatory,** the original orangery, for family meals and huge breakfasts.

Horringer, Bury St. Edmunds, Suffolk IP29 5QE. www.ickworthhotel.co.uk. © **01284/735350.** 38 units (inc. 11 apartments in Dower House, and Butler's Lodge). £205–£440 double; £295–£465 apartments. Rates include English breakfast. AE, DC, MC, V. Free parking. **Amenities:** 2 restaurants; bar; indoor pool; spa; bikes; room service. *In room:* TV/DVD, hair dryer, Wi-Fi (free).

SUFFOLK WOOL TOWNS: LONG MELFORD & LAVENHAM ★

Lavenham: 66 miles N of London; 35 miles S of Cambridge; 9 miles S of Bury St. Edmunds

East Anglia was a wealthy region during the medieval period thanks to England's lucrative wool trade, when raw wool was exported to Flemish weavers. In the 14th and 15th centuries it became even richer thanks to cloth manufacturing; East Anglia's wool-based worsted was the best in the world. Landowners built massive churches to impress their rivals, and splendid guildhalls were created. That all ended with the mass production of cloth in northern England in the industrial revolution of the late 1700s. By the mid-1800s many Suffolk villages were in poverty and their buildings left to go to rack and ruin. Fast forward a few centuries to the growth of tourism, and Suffolk became known for its medieval wool towns. **Lavenham** is the most famous, with its half-timbered shops and pubs, but the jewel in the crown is the **Guildhall** on the main square. The town's huge **Church of St. Peter and St. Paul** has wonderful carvings on the misericords and the chancel screen, as well as ornate tombs. Nearby is **Long Melford,** full of antiques shops, many featured in the TV detective series *Lovejoy.* Its beautiful "wool church" and **Melford Hall,** where Beatrix Potter was a regular visitor, are also worth seeing. Other wool towns include **Clare,** dominated by the Church of St. Peter and St. Paul, **Cavendish,** with its thatched cottages and village green, and **Kersey,** where there's still a ford in the main street.

Essentials

GETTING THERE Trains go from London's Liverpool Street Station to Colchester with connections to Sudbury. For connecting buses, contact **Chambers & Son** (www.chamberscoaches.co.uk; ✆ **01787/227233**). Trip time to Lavenham is up to 2½ hours. If you're driving from London take the A12, it goes from just outside the City all the way there, from Bury St. Edmunds, take the A134 south then follow signs to Lavenham on the A1141.

VISITOR INFORMATION The **Lavenham Tourist Information Centre,** Lady Street (www.southandheartofsuffolk.org; ✆ **01787/248207**), is open from mid-March to October, daily 10am to 4:45pm and 11am to 3pm from November to Christmas, then weekends from January to mid-March.

ORGANIZED TOURS The Tourist Information Centre (see above) offers guided walking tours of the village from Easter to October (Sat 2:30pm, Sun, and holiday Mon 11am). Cost is £3, age 13 and under free. Booking recommended.

Exploring the Area

Lavenham has plenty of antiques shops and lovely cafes. **Timbers,** High Street (✆ **01787/247218**), houses numerous antiques and collectibles stalls, selling books, toys, military artifacts, glass, porcelain, and more. It's open daily. One of the most interesting cafes is **Tickled Pink Tearooms,** 17 High St. (✆ **01787/249517**), in a timber-framed house built in 1530.

Church of St. Peter and St. Paul CHURCH This cathedral-sized church was finished just before the Reformation. Work started in the late 1400s, and among the architects was John Wastell, who was involved with King's College Chapel and Great St. Mary's in Cambridge. Some of the carvings inside depict creatures that are half-human, half-animal, and the main porch is also richly decorated.

Church St. (A1141, the Hadleigh–Bury St. Edmunds Rd.) Free admission. Open daylight hours.

Lavenham Guildhall HISTORIC SITE The exhibitions inside this marvelously creaky old building explain the rise and fall of East Anglia's textile industry. The Guildhall's walled garden still houses the tiny village jail. There's also a half-timbered tearoom with outside seating in fine weather, and a shop.

Market Place. www.nationaltrust.org. ✆ **01787/247646**. Admission £4.30 adults, £1.80 children 5–15, £10.40 family ticket. Guildhall, shop, and tearoom late Mar–Oct daily 11am–5pm; early Mar Wed–Sun 11am–5pm; Nov Sat–Sun 11am–4pm. Shop also Nov–Dec Thurs–Sun and Jan–Feb Sat–Sun. Tearoom also Dec Sat–Sun.

Where to Eat & Stay

Great House Hotel ★ An exquisite novelty: a boutique hotel in a timbered building in a tiny country town with an award-winning French restaurant. Although there are oak beams and an inglenook fireplace, its Georgian facade distinguishes it from other buildings in the market place, and four of its five rooms are suites with separate lounges, all stylishly decorated, one with a king-size Jacobean four-poster. The **restaurant** uses local produce with Gallic flair, for instance belly of Suffolk pork confit. A two-course lunch is £17.50; a three-course dinner is £32, or a la carte.

Market Place, Lavenham, Suffolk CO10 9QZ. www.greathouse.co.uk. ✆ **01787/247431**. Fax 01787/248007. 5 units. £95–£195. Breakfast £10–£15. AE, MC, V. Free street parking. **Amenities:** Restaurant. *In room:* TV, Wi-Fi (free).

Swan Hotel ★★★ Just over the road from the Guildhall is this distinctive, half-timbered 15th century hotel. It's one of the oldest and best-preserved buildings in the village and has been refurbished recently. The rooms are all charmingly unique, with a mix of contemporary and antique furniture. Some have four-poster beds, some have timbered ceilings, some look out onto the cloistered courtyard and gardens. You can eat in the historic **Airmens Bar** (U.S. Air Force men were stationed at Lavenham Airfield during World War II), in the gardens, or in the **Swan Brasserie.** More formal meals are served in the **Gallery Restaurant,** where a two-course lunch costs £15.

High St., Lavenham, Suffolk CO10 9QA. www.swanatlavenham.co.uk. ℭ **01787/247477.** Fax 01787/248286. 45 units. £200–£280 double; £300 suite. Rates include English breakfast. AE, MC, V. Free parking. **Amenities:** Restaurant; bar; lounge; room service. *In room:* TV, hair dryer, Wi-Fi (free).

COLCHESTER & THE ESSEX COAST

62 miles NE of London; 48 miles E of Cambridge; 59 miles S of Norwich

Colchester is the U.K.'s oldest recorded town and was the Roman capital of Britain. It still has the remains of Roman walls, gates, and a temple but, unlike other cities steeped in history, it has never made much of its cultural heritage. It was at Camulodnum, now Colchester, that the British kings of Gosbecks surrendered to Emperor Claudius in A.D. 43. The Romans took over the settlement, but 17 years later it was razed to the ground and every Roman executed by Queen Boudicca and the Iceni tribe of Suffolk and Norfolk.

The Norman invaders of 1066 built **Colchester Castle** over the Roman Temple of Claudius, and you can still spot the Roman tiles and bricks they used. During the English Civil War in 1648, the town was besieged by the Parliamentary army for nearly 3 months, which is when the Roman walls were breached (stretches of the wall are visible). Over the centuries, Colchester has thrived as a market town, but it is only now that its hidden delights are finding the limelight. This includes the varied coastline 16 miles away, which has bucket-and-spade seaside resorts such as **Walton-on-the-Naze** and **Clacton** plus Walton's upmarket relative **Frinton-on-Sea.** The sand is good and you pass through some lovely villages to reach the sea. Southend is further south and a classic day-trip destination. More unique is the **Blackwater Estuary,** where you'll find **Mersea Island** and **Maldon,** home of Maldon sea salt.

Essentials

GETTING THERE There several Colchester-bound trains (NXEA) leaving London's Liverpool Street every hour. Most take less than 60 minutes and cost about £25.50 one-way. If you're driving from London, take the A12; from Cambridge take the A120 and join the A12 north.

VISITOR INFORMATION The **Tourist Information Centre** is opposite Castle Park at 1 Queen St. (www.visitcolchester.com; ℭ **01206/282920**). April to June, it's open Monday to Saturday 9:30am to 5pm (Wed 10am–5pm); July and August, Monday to Saturday 9:30am to 5:30pm and Sunday 11am to 4pm; and October to March Monday to Saturday 10am to 5pm.

Exploring the Area

Beth Chatto Gardens ★ GARDEN Essex has the least rainfall in Britain, and these famous gardens pioneered the concept of drought-tolerant planting in the U.K. when they opened in 1960, before ecology was trendy. The result is a gravel garden that's at its best in spring and early summer, in an area where the soil is sandy, and a stream-fed water garden where the soil is a heavy clay, which is every shade of green from early summer to autumn. A little cafe sells locally-made cakes and ice creams.

Elmstead Market. www.bethchatto.co.uk. © **01206/331292.** Admission £6, free for children 13 and under. Summer Mon–Sat 9am–4pm, Sun 10am–4pm; winter 9am–4pm, Sun 11am–4pm.

Colchester Castle ☺ CASTLE Just off the main shopping area and within the delightful Victorian Castle Park you'll find Colchester's most important historical building. The Norman keep is said to be the biggest and best preserved in Europe, and inside you'll find hands-on displays that recount Britain's history over 2,000 years. There are plenty of child-friendly activities, regular exhibitions, and a good cafe. The park has riverside walks, a cafe, children's play area, and boating lake.

Castle Park. www.cimuseums.org.uk © **01206/282939.** Admission £6.25 adults, £4 children, £16.75 family ticket. Mon–Sat 10am–5pm; Sun 11am–5pm. Closed Christmas period and January 1.

Colchester Zoo ☺ ZOO You can spend a full day at this award-winning zoo, which has one of the largest collection of animals in Europe. Highlights include seeing the elephants and giraffes, and walking through the underwater viewing tunnel to watch the sea lions. This is a big site, with some fairly steep paths in places.

Maldon Rd., Stanway. www.colchester-zoo.com. © **01206/331292.** Admission £13.50 adults, £8.50 children 3–14. Daily 9:30am to 4:30–6:30pm depending on season.

Firstsite GALLERY This increasingly popular contemporary visual arts gallery has moved to a new purpose-built center in the garden of East Hill House, Colchester. The only permanent exhibition is the Berryfield Mosaic, a Roman floor discovered on the site in 1923. As well as exhibitions there is a shop and cafe.

Lewis Gardens, High St. www.firstsite.uk.net. © **01206/577067.** Free admission unless otherwise stated. Tue–Wed and Fri–Sun 9am–5pm; Sun 11am–5pm.

Natural History Museum MUSEUM The decommissioned All Saints Church is the unusual setting for this museum, with country, coast, and urban exhibitions.

High St. www.cimuseums.org.uk. © **01206/282941.** Admission free. Mon–Sat 10am–5pm; Sun 11am–5pm.

RHS Garden Hyde Hall ★ GARDEN A garden that's growing. Hyde Hall was a working farm and small, pretty garden until the land was gifted to the Royal Horticultural Society (RHS). Now it's turning into a very relevant attraction, sweeps of dry hillside planted with plants that need little water. There's also a cafe with outdoor seating, and a shop.

Creephedge Lane, Rettendon. www.rhs.org.uk. © **0845/265-8071.** Admission £7 adults, £3.50 children 5–16. Daily March–Oct 10am–6pm; Nov–Feb 10am–4pm.

Entertainment & Nightlife

The **Mercury Theatre,** Balkerne Gate (www.mercurytheatre.co.uk; ©**01206/573948**), produces serious drama but also features touring shows, bands, and comedians. Big name shows can be seen at **Charter Hall,** Cowdray Avenue (www.charter-hall.co.uk;

THE joys OF SOUTHEND

As the nearest seaside resort to London's East End, Southend has always been a day-trip destination with the emphasis on fun. It has the world's longest pier, stretching 1.34 miles, with its own narrow-gauge railway. The sands have been smartened up thanks to a recent £25 million City Beach Project. They are now backed by a landscaped promenade that includes fun fountains and cycle paths. A bag of chips or tub of winkles are all part of the traditional experience here, but Leigh-on-Sea is the place to go for local seafood. Head west along the coast road and you'll reach the suburb which just about retains its fishing village feel, especially if you wander past the seafront cockle sheds where you can buy the best cockles in England, doused in vinegar and seasoned with pepper. For something more substantial try **Simply Seafood** (www.simplyseafood.co.uk; ✆ **01702/712645**) on Leigh High Street.

The area's good time image also transferred to rock 'n' roll with a host of bands, such as country pop rockers the **Kursaal Flyers,** named after the town's amusement parks (one of the world's oldest). It's now sadly gone but an ornate seafront main building operates as the **Kursaal** (www.kursaalfunctions.com; ✆ **01702/468830**), which has a bowling alley and regular events such as band reunions. Other names such as Dr Feelgood and Eddie and the Hot Rods have emerged from the area and the outlying oil refinery hub of Canvey Island. Southend's **Cliffs Pavilion** (www.thecliffspavilion.co.uk; ✆ **01702/351135**) hosts regular concerts, from 1960s folkies Fairport Convention to modern rockers the Kaiser Chiefs. The **Railway Hotel,** Clifftown Road (www.railwayhotelsos.co.uk; ✆ **01702/343194**), is the place for live music, including local R'n'B hero Steve Hooker. The spirit of U.S.-infused Southend music lives on in the **Ugly Guys** (www.myspace.com/theuglyguys), a band featuring a couple of ex-Kursaal Flyers playing the music of Gram Parsons with a fiery British edge.

✆ **01206/282020**). **Colchester Arts Centre,** Church Street (www.colchesterartscentre.com; ✆ **01206/500900**), is good for bands and comedy, while **Essex University,** Wivenhoe Park, has Comedy Central Live nights, plus music and films, at its **Lakeside Theatre** (www.essex.ac.uk; ✆ **01206/573948**).

There are many traditional pubs in Colchester, and one of the oldest is **The Marquis,** 24–25 North Hill (✆ **01206/577630**), which has real ale and pub food, plus bands, karaoke, quiz nights, and TV sport. It's popular with students so expect it to be lively. More upmarket is **The King's Arms,** 63 Crouch St. (www.gkpubs.co.uk; ✆ **01206/572886**), a stripped-wood contemporary-style pub that has a wine menu as well as local Greene King beers and food. Just along is **The Bull,** 2–4 Crouch St. (www.thebullcolchester.co.uk; ✆ **01206/366647**), regarded as the city's top music venue.

Where to Eat & Stay

Camelia Hotel ★ The new face of jolly Southend, a family-run boutique property on the seafront, with a terrace where you can sip a drink while watching the sunset over the Thames Estuary before slipping into the cool, white restaurant for fish caught from those very waters hours earlier. There are 34 rooms and six suites, many with sea views, and some with four-posters amongst the chic furnishings.

MALDON & THE blackwater ESTUARY

This is Essex at its most traditional and best. The picturesque little town of Maldon is at the southern end of the Blackwater Estuary which empties into the North Sea. The River Blackwater is one of the eerily beautiful waterways that riddle the Essex countryside, creating tiny islands among the mudflats and oyster beds. Native oysters have been enjoyed here since Roman times, and there are oyster festivals in Colchester and Maldon every September at the start of the oyster season. Maldon is a good base for exploring the area, with its red-sailed Thames barges moored at Hythe Quay at the bottom of the town's winding high street. Here you'll find riverside pubs like the **Jolly Sailor** (www.jollysailor.com; ⊘ **01621/853463**), which offers meals and lodging, and the **Queens Head** (www.thequeensheadmalson; ⊘ **01621/854112**), which has impressive real ales and a good menu. Next door is **Promenade Park,** with a riverside walk, great children's play areas, and good parking facilities. Maldon is the second oldest town in Essex after Colchester, with a rich history of Saxon, Danish, and Viking conflicts. Now it's just a lovely place from where to explore the mudflats and marshes, where the world-famous Maldon Salt is still produced.

Head for nearby **Heybridge Basin** (where you'll find a couple of pubs and a cafe) and walk along the sea wall with cornfields on one side and migrating seabirds on the other, or take the road to **Bradwell-on-Sea,** possibly the most remote corner of Essex, where you can walk to the remarkable, barn-like chapel of **St. Peter-on-the-Wall** (www.bradwell chapel.org; ⊘ **01621/776203**), built by St. Cedd in A.D. 645.

There are three islands in the estuary, all accessed by causeways flooded twice a day by the tide. **Northey Island** is nearest to Maldon, and a haven for birdwatchers and walkers. Although it has been given to the National Trust, access is by appointment only (www.national trust.org.uk; ⊘ **01621/853142**). **Osea Island** is also privately owned (Osea Island Resort; www.oseaisland.co.uk; ⊘ **07810/753226**), but is an upmarket retreat with a 10-bedroom manor house, 14 cottages, and 7 apartments for rent, with outdoor heated pool, gym, TV room, and the private Chapel restaurant. **Mersea Island** has fine walks in unspoiled countryside and one of the most popular fish restaurants in Essex. **The Company Shed,** 129 Coast Rd., West Mersea (www.west-mersea.co.uk; ⊘ **01206/382700**), is the place to eat. Once just a fish shack, it is now a fishmonger's where you can choose what you want from the catch of the day, and they'll cook it for you to eat at retro Formica tables (bring your own drink and bread). In summer the place is packed and parking difficult. Walk off lunch at **Cudmore Grove Country Park,** East Mersea (www.visitparks.co.uk; ⊘ **01206/383868**), where there's a beach and paths for walkers and cyclists.

There are also many picturesque villages and small towns in this part of Essex. **Burnham on Crouch,** south of Maldon, is a lovely little yachting town, with traditional Essex clapboard buildings and half-timbered cottages. **Tiptree,** north of Maldon, is the home of Wilkins & Sons' famous Tiptree Jam, and has a free museum and visitor center. You can also get a splendid afternoon tea on-site at the Tiptree Tea Room (www.trooms.com; ⊘ **01621/814524**). A few miles west, over the A12, is **Coggeshall** with the stunning 16th-century half-timbered merchant's house, Paycocke's (www.nationaltrust.org.uk; ⊘ **01376/561305**).

176 Eastern Esplanade, Southend SS1 3AA. www.cameliahotel.com. © **01702/587917.** 40 units. £70–£100; suites £100–£130. Rates include English breakfast. AE, MC, V. Parking free. **Amenities:** Restaurant; bar. *In room:* TV, hair dryer, Wi-Fi (free).

North Hill Hotel ★ 👔 A historic building with contemporary style is a winning combination in this simple but splendid hotel. The **Green Room** restaurant uses local produce such as Mersea Island fish and oysters and Blythburgh pork for its seasonal menus. The lunch menu starts at £6.25 for tempura soft shell crab, bean sprout, carrot and rocket salad, crème fraîche and smoked chili jam while dinner might include chargrilled Essex-reared 28-day-aged 10oz rump steak, Montpellier butter, fries, and seasonal salad (main courses £10–£17).

North Hill, Colchester CB2 1AD. www.northhillhotel.com. © **01206/574001.** 13 units. £65–£118 double. Rates include English breakfast. AE, MC, V. Parking £5. **Amenities:** Restaurant; bar; room service. *In room:* TV, hair dryer, Wi-Fi (free).

IPSWICH

70 miles NE of London; 44 miles E of Cambridge; 39 miles south of Norwich

Ipswich is Suffolk's county town and it not only has a rich medieval history but a thriving arts scene. Just minutes off the A12 it's a good base for exploring East Anglia's pretty wool towns and villages. Ipswich Waterfront on the River Orwell is a lively area with hotels, bars, and restaurants in old flour mills and maltings, plus a marina. The river is key to the town's prosperity: Ipswich won trading privileges as a King's Port in the 16th century because of its proximity to the North Sea. Many pioneers set out from here to the New World in the 17th century including Bartholomew Gosnold, who sailed from Ipswich and arrived in New England in 1602, where he named Cape Cod after its plentiful fish and Martha's Vineyard after his daughter. He also helped to found Jamestown, Virginia, in 1607 with other adventurers from this area. The town's soccer (football) team, Ipswich Town, was the training ground for two England national team managers: Sir Alf Ramsey (who led England to World Cup glory in 1966) and Sir Bobby Robson (who came close in 1990).

Essentials

GETTING THERE From London's Liverpool Street Station, take a train (NXEA) to Ipswich. It takes an hour and costs nearly £35 one-way. **Ipswich Buses** (www.ipswichbuses.co.uk; © **0800/919390**) serve the town and **First Eastern Counties Buses** (www.firstgroup.com; © **0845/602-0121**) go farther afield. If you're driving from London take the A12 and follow signs for Ipswich.

VISITOR INFORMATION The **Tourist Information Centre** is at St. Stephen's Church, St. Stephen's Lane (www.visitipswich.com; © **01473/258070**).

SPECIAL EVENTS The **Ip-art** (www.ip-art.com; © **01473/433100**) takes place in June and July with Shakespeare, films, opera, dance, music, and art in venues from the Council Chamber to parks. Ipswich Music Day is a free family-friendly festival of rock, folk, and classical. New Wolsey Theatre's Pulse Festival (May/June) showcases up-and-coming music (www.pulsefringe.com; © **01473/295900**). The Suffolk Show (www.suffolkshow.co.uk; © **01473/707110**) is a celebration of Suffolk's country life, with livestock competitions, a garden show, food stalls, and more in May/June.

Exploring the Area

Start by visiting the Tourist Information Centre, if only because it is housed in one of the town's 12 medieval churches. You can book a guided walk (℗ **01473/258070**) or a ticket for the hop-on hop-off City Sightseeing tourist bus (city-sightseeing.com; ℗ **01473/232600**). Boat trips down the River Orwell start from the waterfront area and some go as far as the coast, passing the **Pin Mill,** where children's author Arthur Ransome lived; the seventh of his *Swallows and Amazons* books, *We Didn't Mean To Go To Sea,* is set on the Orwell. An unusual attraction is **Clifford Road Air Raid Shelter Museum** (cliffordroadshelter.org.uk; ℗ **01473/251605**), a World War II air raid shelter found under a school playground in 1989. Opening times are limited.

Christchurch Mansion MUSEUM   There is the biggest collection of John Constable paintings outside London and many Thomas Gainsborough pictures at this 500-year-old Tudor mansion in beautiful Christchurch Park. Period rooms include a Tudor kitchen and Victorian wing, an excellent collection of toys, and a very good cafe. The park is a 10-minute walk from town, and has no car parking.

Soan St. www.cimuseums.org.uk. ℗ **01473/433554.** Admission free. Tues–Sun 10am–5pm. Closed Mon.

Ipswich Museum MUSEUM   The highlight for many will be the glorious wooden cabinets of the Victorian Natural History Gallery, although some of its collection may upset animal lovers, not least the stuffed giraffe. There are also historic collections including an Egyptian Gallery and Anglo-Saxon artifacts found in Suffolk.

High St. www.cimuseums.org.uk. ℗ **01473/433551.** Admission free. Tues–Sat 10am–5pm. Closed Sun & Mon.

Jimmy's Farm ATTRACTION   Home of TV celebrity farmer Jimmy Doherty who has championed rare breeds. This is a working farm (home of the Essex pig, a stripy descendant of the Anglo-Saxon and Norman pigs that foraged the great East Anglian forests, plus unusual cows, goats, and sheep) with gardens, restaurant, and, of course, a shop selling Jimmy's sausages. Entry is free but there is a charge for the nature trail, with its animal paddocks, butterfly house, and woodland walks. There are also regular events such as comedy nights in the restaurant, live music, and a sausage and beer festival.

Pannington Hall Lane. www.jimmysfarm.com. ℗ **01473/604206.** Admission free, but nature trail £4.50 adults, £3.50 children 2–16. Daily 9:30am–5:30pm.

Town Hall Galleries ART   There are different exhibitions of contemporary art and photography all the time in this lovely old building in the center of town, and the chance to buy contemporary crafts from local artists.

Cornhill. www.cimuseums.org.uk. ℗ **01473/432863.** Admission free. Tues–Sat 10am–5pm.

Entertainment & Nightlife

Ipswich Regent, St. Helen's Street (www.ipswich.gov.uk; ℗ **01473/433100**), is East Anglia's biggest theatre and has seen some of Britain's greatest entertainers, including The Beatles. It attracts touring shows from national stage groups, bands, and comedy. There's a similar line-up at the **Corn Exchange,** King Street (www. ipswich.gov.uk; ℗ **01473/433100**). The **Sir John Mills Theatre,** Gatacre Road (www.easternangles.co.uk; ✆ 01473/211498), is a studio used by several stage companies including Eastern Angles, which tours East Anglia, while **DanceEast,** based at **Jerwood DanceHouse,** Foundry Lane (www.danceeast.co.uk; ✆ 01473/295230), on the waterfront, stages productions and holds classes. Ipswich's biggest nightclub is **Liquid Envy,** West Leisure Terrace, Cardinal Park (www.liquidenvy.com; ✆ 01473/218850). There's live music at **The Swan,** King Street (✆ 01473/252485); real ale, a beer garden, and food at **The Cock and Pye,** Upper Brook Street (www.gkpubs.co.uk; ✆ 01473/254213); and all things Irish plus live music and sports coverage at **McGinty's,** Northgate Street (www.pjmi.co.uk; ✆ 07767/626860). The pubs at the Waterfront include **Isaacs,** Wherry Quay (www.isaaclord.org; ✆ 01473/259952), a spectacular refurbishment of quayside buildings.

Shopping

The main shopping areas are **Tower Ramparts,** Tavern Street (www.towerramparts.com; ✆ 01473/226386), and **Buttermarket,** St. Stephens Lane (www.buttermarketipswich.com; ✆ 01473/281580). St. Nicholas Street, St. Peters Street, and The Walk have non-chain, independentshops.

Where to Eat & Stay

Quayside   A restaurant, cafe, and bar on the Waterfront with a loft-style feel and contemporary menus, plus views across the marina. The evening set menu isn't extravagant but might include the likes of Procters' tumblehome sausages, mash, roasted red onion, and red wine sauce. There's free Wi-Fi too.

Regatta Quay, Key St., IP4 1FF. www.quayside-ipswich.co.uk. ✆ **01473/218811.** Set lunch £10 for 2 courses; set dinner £14 for 2 courses, Fri and Sat dinner menu from £9 for main courses. AE, MC, V.

Salthouse Harbour Hotel ★   This award-winning luxury hotel fills old quayside buildings with the rich, esoteric style of a distant port. There's original modern art, exposed brickwork, and individually-styled bedrooms, some with freestanding copper baths and worn-in leather armchairs. Local produce is a feature of the waterfront Eaterie restaurant (main courses £14–£28).

Neptune Quay, IP4 1AX. www.salthouseharbour.co.uk. ✆ **01473/226789.** Fax 01473/226927. 70 units. £165–£295. Rates include breakfast. AE, MC, V. **Amenities:** Restaurant. *In room:* TV, hairdryer, Wi-Fi (free).

SOUTHWOLD & ALDEBURGH

Southwold: 94 miles NE of London, 26 miles S of Norwich; Aldeburgh: 97 miles NE of London, 41 miles SE of Norwich.

Southwold is a breath of fresh air on Suffolk's North Sea coast, with a sandy beach perfect for family holidays and a stylish twist to a functional but pretty town that attracts weekend Londoners. Southwold has wonderful pubs, thanks to the town's Adnams brewery; a landmark lighthouse; an award-winning pier; lovely boutiques; outrageously expensive beach huts; and a happy, holiday atmosphere. The town's famous Greens, created after the great fire of 1659, give it a leisurely feeling of space, as do the commons and marshes down to the river quayside. From here (where there are fish stalls, fish and chip restaurants, and a pub), you can walk over a footbridge and back up the river to **Walberswick,** home of the British Open Crabbing Championships in August and a sandy beach, which is fast becoming a kitesurfing hotspot. Walk along the beach and you'll get to **Dunwich,** now little more than a few cottages since the town fell into the sea several centuries ago. Here the beach is more pebbles than sand and you can walk the 19 miles to **Aldeburgh** along the coastal path (partly just the beach), passing Maggi Hambling's 4-m-high (13 ft.) Scallop sculpture.

Essentials

GETTING THERE   From London's Liverpool Street Station, take a train (NXEA) to Ipswich, then the Lowestoft line and get off at Saxmundham for Aldeburgh (6 miles away) or at Halesworth for Southwold 9 miles away. Both take around 2 hours and cost about £40 one-way. **Anglian Buses** (www.anglianbus.co.uk; ✆ **01502/711109**) run from Halesworth to Southwold (about 35 minutes, £3.40 one-way), and **First Eastern Counties Buses** (www.firstgroup.com; ✆ **0871/200-2233**) run from Saxmundham to Aldeburgh, about 30 minutes, around £3 one-way.

The Lowestoft train also stops at Woodbridge.

If you're driving from London take the M25 to the A12 and follow signs to any of the towns mentioned above, which are just off the A12.

VISITOR INFORMATION   There are **Tourist Information Centres** at 152 High St., Aldeburgh (✆ **01728/453637**), at 69 High St., Southwold (✆ **01502/724729**), and at Station Buildings, Woodbridge (✆ **01394/382240**). For more information on all these towns go to www.visit-suffolk.co.uk.

SPECIAL EVENTS   Aldeburgh was the home of composer Benjamin Britten (1913–76), best known for the opera *Peter Grimes*. Many of his compositions were first performed at the **Aldeburgh Festival** (www.aldeburgh.co.uk; ✆ **01728/687110**), which he founded in 1948 with Peter Pears. The 2-week festival every June features internationally known performers.

Exploring the Area

Lovely little **Southwold Museum,** on Victoria Street (www.southwoldmuseum.org; ✆ **01502/726097**), charts the town's history. After that, walk along the High Street, past the Crown and Swan hotels, and past the Lord Nelson, an Adnams pub (although you might be tempted to join the throng outside for a drink). Here you're on a little clifftop with views along the coast, over the pier to the left, and down to Walberswick on the right. The **Sailor's Reading Room** has fascinating photographs and seafaring memorabilia. The seafront is a place for beach fun and for walking along the seafront path. The town has never succumbed to chain stores, so is full of individual shops, cafes, boutiques, and the Adnams Cellar & Kitchen Store (4 Drayman Sq.), which has a cafe with seating on a courtyard that hosts Friday farmers' markets. Mark's Fish & Chips (32 High St.) has seating but you'll probably want to buy and then head for the common or a viewpoint over the beach; beware, it keeps early hours (generally 5:30pm–8:30pm), and always has a queue.

You might also want to check out the **Dunwich Museum** (www.dunwich museum.org.uk; ✆ **01728/648796**) to learn about Dunwich's history.

Aldeburgh is a yachtie town, famous for its festival and a magnet for Londoners. It's a nice place to walk, whether along the single street with its collection of individual shops, or back along the seafront where you'll find huts selling oysters and fish, but not many people actually walk on the pebbly beach. The town is bracing and enchanting without being a conventional seaside resort. Shops include the preppy, yachtie chic of Jack Wills while the **Lighthouse** (www.lighthouserestaurant.co.uk; ✆ **01728/453377**) is the place to eat. The food (main courses £11–£19) is simple but special, such as local dover sole with spinach, new potatoes, and lemon oil. Benjamin Britten, who established the Aldeburgh Festival, is buried at St. Peter and St. Paul Church here. **Aldeburgh Museum** (www.aldeburghmuseum.org.uk; © **01728/ 454666**) in timber-framed Moot Hall features old maps, prints, and Anglo-Saxon burial urns.

This coastline, from Felixstowe to north of Southwold, is an Area of Outstanding Natural Beauty, but there's plenty to explore inland. Dunwich Heath is a place for walks amongst the gorse and scrub; there are various free parking lots, as well as a National Trust one (with cafe) where it hits the coast. **Woodbridge,** a market town on the River Deben, has riverside walks, antiques, and local produce shops.

Framlingham Castle CASTLE   Unusually attractive, this is one of the few 12th-century castles still standing in East Anglia. Henry VIII's eldest daughter, Mary Tudor, took refuge here before succeeding her brother to the throne in 1553. The historic town is also worth exploring, and has interesting shops and cafes plus a Saturday market.

9 Church St., Framlingham. www.english-heritage.org.uk. © **01728/724033.** Admission £6.30 adults, £3.80 children 5–15, £16.40 family. Apr–Oct daily 10:30am–5pm; Nov–Mar Sat–Sun 11am–4pm.

RSPB Minsmere NATURE RESERVE   Avocets, marsh harriers, and booming bitterns are regularly spotted on this bird reserve, along with visiting geese, ducks, swans, and wading birds. The reserve starts among the trees and visitor center, and comes all the way down to the beach. There are lovely walks, any time of the year.

Westleton (on the coast several miles south of Southwold). www.rspb.org.uk. © **01728/648281.** Admission £5 adults, £1.50 children 5–15. Daily 9am–5pm (Nov–Jan to 4pm).

Snape Maltings ENTERTAINMENT COMPLEX   This is where the acclaimed **Aldeburgh Festival** is held, in a concert hall among historic buildings, many of which have been converted into upmarket (if somewhat twee) shops, along with a cafe, tea shop, and pub. There's a farmers' market on the first Saturday of every month and the Aldeburgh Food and Drink Festival every September. But on any day it's good to park (for free), have a picnic, and take a long walk along rush-lined paths with sailing boats appearing to be gliding amid the fields as waterways meander down to the sea.

Snape Maltings (on the B1069). www.snapemaltings.co.uk. © **01728/688303.** Free admission. Shops mostly Easter–Nov 10:30am–5:30pm (Aug 6pm).

Southwold Lighthouse HISTORIC SITE   This working lighthouse is in the middle of town and has been used since 1890. It's not often that a lighthouse is so easily accessible, and the views are splendid. It also houses other items of historical interest.

Stradbrook Rd. www.trinityhouse.co.uk. © **01502/724629.** Admission £3.50 adults, £2.50 children up to 16, £10 family. June–Aug daily noon–5pm; Apr–May and Sept–Oct daily 2:30–5pm.

Sutton Hoo ★★ ☺ MUSEUM   The most stunning Viking treasures ever found in England were dug up here in the 1930s from a burial mound, which even housed a longboat. The originals are now safe in the British Museum but the copies here in an award-winning exhibition are excellent. The grounds are extraordinary, with a path that takes you past several burial mounds, and you can visit Tranmer House, home of

Edith Pretty who owned the land when the treasures were discovered. There's also a cafe, picnic tables, and an adventure playground—good for families.

Tranmer House, Sutton Hoo, Woodbridge. www.nationaltrust.org.uk. © **01394/389700.** Admission £6.20 adults, £3.55 children 5–15, £17 family ticket. Mar Wed–Sun 10:30am–5pm; Apr–Oct daily 10:30am–5pm; Nov–Feb Sat–Sun 11am–4pm. Additional opening during winter/spring school holidays.

Where to Eat & Stay

Brudenell Hotel   Right on the famous beach at the southern end of Aldeburgh, the Brudenell was totally refurbished in 2010 and its rooms are decorated in cool, calm seaside shades. Many of the bedrooms face the sea and the **restaurant** is relaxed with fabulous sea views and a locally sourced, seasonal menu.

The Parade, Aldeburgh, Suffolk IP15 5BU. www.brudenellhotel.co.uk. © **01728/452071.** Fax 01728/454082. 44 units. £147–£314 double. Rates include English breakfast. AE, MC, V. Free parking. **Amenities:** Restaurant; bar; room service. *In room:* TV, hair dryer, Wi-Fi (free).

The Crown ★★★   This is a lovely old hotel with contemporary style: The bedrooms range from attic rooms to suites big enough for families. The hotel is at the heart of the quiet seaside town of Southwold, and its two **restaurants** are renowned for excellent, modern British food. If the Crown is full try its sister hotel, The Swan, a few doors up the High Street overlooking the tiny market place. It's a little more genteel and therefore more expensive, but with a perfect lounge for afternoon tea. See the Adnams website, below, for other stylish hotels in Suffolk and Norfolk.

90 High St., Southwold, Suffolk IP18 6DP. www.adnams.co.uk. © **01502/722186.** 14 units. £154–£184 double; £216 suite. Rates include English breakfast. AE, MC, V. Free parking. **Amenities:** 2 restaurants; bar; room service, Wi-Fi in lounge and bar (free). *In room:* TV, hair dryer.

House in the Clouds   This folly from 1923 is six floors high and appears to be a cottage floating above the trees. In fact it's a converted water tower. The "cottage" is where the tank was, sitting on a clapboard-covered tower. The tower, with 68 steps, has five double bedrooms and three bathrooms; there's a double sofa bed in the drawing room. The cottage has an airy games room with snooker table and superb views. In the private grounds there is a tennis court. It's in Thorpeness, just north of Aldeburgh.

Thorpeness, Suffolk. www.houseintheclouds.co.uk. © **020/7224-3615.** 1 unit. £520–£750 per night (two nights min); £2,130–£3,200 per week (weekly bookings only high summer and Christmas). AE, MC, V. Free parking. **Amenities:** Kitchen; dining room; games room; garden.

NORWICH ★★

109 miles NE of London; 20 miles W of the North Sea

Norwich is the very essence of East Anglia. Until the Industrial Revolution it was England's second city and, like much of the region, hugely wealthy. As a result its **Norman cathedral** is one of the finest examples of Romanesque architecture in Europe: it has the largest cloisters in England and second tallest spire. However, when East Anglia's textile trade collapsed and the city and the river port silted up it became little more than a backwater. Happily, during the 19th and 20th centuries, this meant it retained many medieval streets—with 31 medieval churches—and it is now regarded as one of the most complete medieval cities in England.

Essentials

GETTING THERE   Trains from London's Liverpool Street take just under 2 hours (NXEA; from £45 one-way). If you're driving from London, take the M25, M11, and A11.

VISITOR INFORMATION   The **Norwich Tourist Information Centre** is in The Forum, 2 Millennium Plain, Bethel Street, NR2 1TF (www.visitnorwich.co.uk; ℂ **01603/213999;** open April–Oct Mon–Sat 9:30am to 6pm, Nov–March 9:30am–5:30pm, closed Sundays).

GETTING AROUND   For buses, contact **Norwich Bus Station,** Surrey Street (ℂ **0344/800-8020**). The city is compact but the bus saves walking out to some of the farther points. Buses are operated by First (www.firstgroup.com; ℂ **0871/200-2233**).

ORGANIZED TOURS   Walking tours of the city can be booked at the Tourist Information Centre in The Forum (see above), or try the hop-on hop-off **City Sightseeing** bus (www.city-sightseeing.com; ℂ **01708/866000**).

Exploring the Area

Norwich's history and relaxed atmosphere have attracted tourists for decades, and as the only city for miles it has excellent shopping—particularly its huge market, which is open Monday to Saturday. **Royal Arcade** is one of the city's most picturesque shopping areas, where you'll find the **Colman's Mustard Shop** (www.colmans mustardshop.com; ℂ **01603/627889**). Colman's Mustard is one of Norwich's most famous names and you can buy mustard products and see fascinating memorabilia here. Another famous spot is **Norwich City Football Club,** which boasts the best food of any soccer (football) club in England thanks to its patron, TV cook Delia Smith. **Delia's Restaurant & Bar** is open Friday and Saturday nights at the stadium in Carrow Road (www.deliascanarycatering.com; ℂ **01603/218705**).

Take the time to walk along the **River Wenson** to see the ancient **Norwich Bishop Bridge** and the 15th-century arch at **Pulls Ferry.** And don't miss **Tombland,** the Anglo-Saxon market square where there are now plenty of restaurants and bars, plus **Tombland Antiques Centre,** 14 Tombland (ℂ **01603/619129**), opposite the cathedral with 60-plus dealers. Nearby is cobbled **Elm Hill** with more Tudor houses than the whole of the city of London, many now attractive little shops and restaurants.

Blickling Hall ★★ HISTORIC HOME   This was the home of the Boleyn family—Anne Boleyn was Henry VIII's second wife and their marriage was the trigger for the Reformation of the Catholic Church in England. This version of the house was built in the early 17th century and is one of the best examples of such architecture in the country. The long gallery has an elaborate 17th-century ceiling, and the Peter the Great Room has a fine tapestry. The house is set in ornamental parkland with a formal garden and orangery.

Blickling (off the A140 Norwich–Cromer Rd., near Aylsham). www.nationaltrust.org.uk. ℂ **01263/738030.** House and gardens £9.75 adults, £4.75 children 5–15, £26 family ticket; gardens only £6.50 adults, £3.30 children, £13.30 family ticket. House late Feb to mid-July Wed–Sun 11am–5pm; mid-July to early-Sept Wed–Mon 11am–5pm; early Sept to late-Oct Wed–Sun 11am–5pm; closed Nov to late-Feb. Garden Jan to late-Feb, Nov and Dec Thurs–Sun 11am–4pm; late-Feb to Oct daily 10:15am–5:15pm.

Norwich Castle ★★ CASTLE   This handsome Norman keep was once part of a larger castle. It was used as a jail in the 14th century and was turned into a museum in 1894. It now has a fascinating collection of paintings from the Norwich School of Artists as well as other fine art, natural history, and archeological exhibits.

Castle Meadow. www.norwich12.co.uk.© **01603/493625.** Admission £6.60 adults, £4.80 children 4–16. Late June–Oct Mon–Sat 10am–5pm, Sun 1–5pm; closes 4:30pm rest of year.

Norwich Cathedral ★★ CATHEDRAL   Dating from 1096, the Norman-designed cathedral is noted for its long nave and high columns and took more than 200 years to build. The impressive choir stalls have handsome 15th-century misericords, and the 13th-century quadrangular cloisters are the largest monastic cloisters in England.

62 The Close. www.cathedral.org.uk.© **01603/218300.** Free admission; £4 suggested donation. Daily 7:30am–6:30pm.

Sainsbury Centre for Visual Arts GALLERY   The private art collection of Sir Robert and Lady Sainsbury is on display at the University of East Anglia, 3 miles west of Norwich on Earlham Road. The award-winning 1978 exhibition hall was designed by Sir Norman Foster and has large areas of glass, providing superb light to view the modern, ancient, classical, and ethnographic art, including works by Francis Bacon, Alberto Giacometti, and Henry Moore.

Earlham Rd. www.scva.org.uk.© **01603/593199.** Free but special exhibitions cost from £2. Tues–Sun 10am–5pm. Bus: 22, 25, or 35.

Second Air Division Memorial Library LIBRARY   The 7,000 members of the Second Air Division of the 8th U.S. Army Air Force who lost their lives in the Second World War are remembered in the Millennium Library. There's a 4,000 book lending library covering all aspects of American life and culture, and a specialist collection devoted to the history of the 2nd Air Division while it was based in East Anglia.

The Forum, Millennium Plain. www.2ndair.org.uk.© **01603/774747.** Free admission and Internet access. Mon–Sat 9am–5pm. Closed Sundays and public holidays.

Where to Eat

The Britons Arms 🍴 BRITISH   This wonderful coffeehouse and restaurant is in a medieval thatched building that's the only surviving béguinage (a religious refuge for women) in England from the Middle Ages. It's never been a pub, and it is now a friendly daytime spot run by two sisters producing home-cooked hearty meals, puddings, and cakes. There's an open fire in winter and small terraced garden with views over the rooftops of historic Elm Hill.

9 Elm Hill.© **01603/623367.** Main courses £10–£14. AE, MC, V. Mon–Sat 9:30am–5pm.

Roger Hickman's Restaurant ★ BRITISH   This talented chef presents market-fresh and imaginative cuisine in a stylish dining room with top-notch service. Starters include venison with beets or roast scallops with crispy pork belly. Choose from main courses such as braised beef cheek or roasted globe artichoke.

79 Upper St. Giles St. www.rogerhickmansrestaurant.com.© **01603/633522.** Reservations recommended. Fixed-price lunch £17 for 2 courses, £20 for 3 courses; fixed-price dinner £30 for 2 courses, £39 for 3 courses. AE, MC, V. Tues–Sat noon–2:30pm and 7–10pm.

St. Benedict's Restaurant ENGLISH/FRENCH   There's a warm welcome, along with well-prepared food, at this modern brasserie with a simple setting. The chef, Nigel Raffles, shops for some of the freshest market produce available. Expect menus that include suckling pig, slow cooked crispy duck and swordfish "sous vide."

9 St. Benedict's St. www.stbenedictsrestaurant.co.uk. © **01603/765377.** Reservations recommended. Fixed-price lunch £8.95 for 2 courses; dinner £19 for 2 courses, £24 for 3 courses. AE, DC, MC, V. Tues–Sat noon–2pm and 7–10:30pm.

Entertainment & Nightlife

You'll find touring companies performing drama, opera, and ballet at **Theatre Royal,** Theatre Street (www.theatreroyalnorwich.co.uk; © **01603/630000**). **Norwich Playhouse,** 42–58 St. George's St. (www.norwichplayhouse.org.uk; © **01603/ 598598**), has well-known names from music, comedy, and drama. The box office is open Monday to Saturday 9:30am to 6pm. **Maddermarket Theatre,** 1 St. John's Alley (www.maddermarket.co.uk; © **01603/620917**), a half-timbered playhouse, presents touring plays and entertainers. **Norwich Puppet Theatre,** St. James, Whitefriars (www.puppettheatre.co.uk; © **01603/629921**), has shows in converted medieval St. James church and **Norwich Arts Centre,** 51 St. Benedict's St. (www. norwichartscentre.co.uk; © **01603/660352**), another converted church (St. Swithins), features bands, ballet, comedy, and exhibitions.

Norwich's oldest pub is the **Adam & Eve,** 17 Bishopgate (© **01603/667423**), serving since at least 1249 when it was owned by monks. It's small but there is outside seating and well-kept real ale. The **Fat Cat ★★**, 49 West End St. (www.fatcat pub.co.uk; © **01603/624364**), has been *The Good Pub Guide*'s "Beer Pub of the Year" several times and has a wide range of real ales including its own Fat Cat beer.

Where to Stay

De Vere Dunston Hall ★★   It has all the style of an Elizabethan mansion with tall brick chimneys and red-brick gables, but this 19th-century mansion-turned-hotel is a 21st-century dream of elegant comfort. It even has its own golf course. There are wonderful four-poster bedrooms, large family rooms, and attic hideaways plus a spa with a nice pool and three restaurants.

Ipswich Rd., Norwich, Norfolk NR14 8PQ. www.devere.co.uk. ©**01508/470444.** Fax 01508/470689. 169 units. From £109 double. AE, MC, V. Free parking. **Amenities:** 3 restaurants; bar; indoor pool; 18-hole golf course; bikes; gym spa; sauna; hot tub; steam room. *In room:* TV, hair dryer, Wi-Fi (free).

Maids Head Hotel   In business since 1272, the Maids Head may well be the oldest continuously operated hotel in the U.K.; certainly Elizabeth I is said to have stayed here, and the four-poster Queen Elizabeth I Suite is very popular. The hotel is a mix of Elizabethan and Georgian architectural styles, and many bedrooms have oak beams, but there's nothing old-fashioned about the decor. You'll find the hotel opposite the cathedral, and you don't have to stay the night to use the **Maids Head Bar,** where Norfolk hero Horatio Nelson once drank.

Tombland, Norwich, Norfolk NR3 1LB. www.maidsheadhotel.co.uk. © **01603/209955.** Fax 01603/613688. 84 units. From £89 double. AE, MC, V. Free parking. **Amenities:** Restaurant; bar; room service. *In room:* TV, hair dryer, Wi-Fi (free).

THE NORFOLK BROADS ★★

Wroxham: 7 miles NE of Norwich

The Broads were created by locals cutting peat for fuel between the 12th and 14th centuries. Whether you're messing about with boats, walking past reedbeds, or just sitting at a waterside pub, they are a unique holiday destination. The **Broads National Park** (www.broads-authority.gov.uk; ✆ **01603/610734**) created in 1989, is Britain's largest protected wetlands and third largest inland waterway. The lake-like waterways linked by the rivers Bure, Waveney, and Yare are between Norwich and the coast, with some winding down to Suffolk. You can use your own boat or hire one for a day or more to explore the 124 miles of navigable waterways. Day trips are also available. As you meander through the waterways you'll spot alder, willow, and birch trees along the riverbanks and marshes, which are home to rare plants and animals. **Wroxham,** on the River Bure, is the center of the Broads and a good base for exploring the area.

Essentials

GETTING THERE Trains (NXEA) from London's Liverpool Street Station go to Norwich; trains from Norwich to Hoveton and Wroxham station take 15 minutes; the full journey takes 2½ hours and costs about £46 one-way. **Traveline** buses (www.travelineeastanglia.org.uk; ✆ **0871/200-2233**) cover all of Norfolk. If you're driving from Norwich take the A1151 to Wroxham.

VISITOR INFORMATION **Broads Information Centre** Hoveton/Wroxham, Station Road (✆ **01603/7560970**), April to October, daily 9am to 1pm, 1:30 to 5pm.

Exploring the Area

Barnes Brinkcraft, Riverside Road, Wroxham (www.barnesbrinkcraft.co.uk; ✆ **01603/782625**), has day boats from £15 an hour to £850 a week. Alternatively, book a tour with **Broads Tours,** near Wroxham Bridge (www.broads.co.uk; ✆ **01603/782207**). Trips start at £7 for 1-hour trips.

Bewilderwood ★★ ☺ AMUSEMENT PARK This is less a theme park than a magical forest, with family adventures in tree houses, along rope bridges, and zip wires, and with boat trips and walks in the marshes.

Horning Rd., Hoveton. www.bewilderwood.co.uk.✆ **01603/783900.** Admission £10.50–£12.50 depending on height (free for children under 1m/3 ft.); £8.50 seniors. Feb school holidays plus every weekend until Apr–Nov daily 10am–5:30pm or dusk.

Fairhaven Woodland & Water Garden ★★ GARDEN These wonderful gardens are hidden away and crisscrossed by little streams. They have an amazing collection of spring-flowering candelabra primulas in late May and early June, plus rhododendrons, azaleas, bluebells, and summer wildflowers, with lovely autumn foliage.

School Rd., South Walsham. www.fairhavengarden.co.uk. ✆ **01603/270449.** Admission £5.50 adults, £5 seniors, £3 children 5–15. Daily Mar–Nov 10am–5pm; Dec–Feb 10am–4pm.

The Museum of the Broads MUSEUM Find out how the Broads have shaped Norfolk's landscape and affected the lives of locals at this award-winning museum, which has an exhibition of boats from the last 200 years, and boat trips on the Victorian steam launch *Falcon* on Tuesdays, Wednesdays, and Thursdays from 11am to 3pm.

The Staithe, Stalham. www.museumofthebroads.org.uk.✆ **01692/581681.** Admission £4 adults, £3.50 children 5–15, £11 family ticket. Boat trips £3.50 adults, £2.50 children. Daily Easter–Oct 10:30am–5pm. Closed in winter.

NORTH NORFOLK COAST ★★

Hunstanton: 105 miles NE of London; 53 miles N of Cambridge

This low, beautiful stretch of beach, dunes, and marshes, interspersed with the odd tourist town, is a world of its own. It's a place for walking and thinking, bird-watching (whether you're an expert or not), and relaxing any time of year—on the vast stretches of sands or in front of a log fire in one of the region's exceptional small hotels. It can be entrancingly bleak in winter here (the wind whipping across the north-facing sands), but there's a friendliness that goes with being in a far-flung outpost of the country.

Essentials

GETTING THERE   Trains leave London's Liverpool Street Station for Norwich, where you can take Greater Anglia's Bittern Line to Cromer (45 minutes) and Sheringham (1 hour), both about £7 one-way. Trains leave London's King's Cross for Kings Lynn (hourly), take 1 hour and 35 minutes and cost about £31 one-way. The **Coasthopper bus** (www.coasthopper.co.uk; ✆ **01553/776980**) runs between Cromer and Hunstanton (and onto Kings Lynn) daily, half-hourly in summer, roughly hourly in winter. There are one-way and round-trip tickets plus a variety of passes including other buses and trains, and 1, 3, or 5-day Coasthopper Rover tickets.

If you're driving from Norwich, take the A140 to Cromer, then the A149 coast road to Sheringham, Blakeney, Wells-next-the-Sea, Holkham, or Hunstanton.

VISITOR INFORMATION   There are **Tourist Information Centres** at Sheringham, Station Approach (www.sheringhamtown.co.uk; ✆ **0871/200-3071**), Wells-next-the-Sea, Staithe Street (www.wellsnextthesea.co.uk; ✆ **01328/710885**), and Hunstanton, The Town Hall, The Green (www.visitwestnorfolk.com; ✆ **01485/532610**).

Exploring the Area

The seaside town of **Cromer** (with its century-old wooden pier and end-of-the-pier Pavilion Theatre featuring British variety acts) is a good starting point. It's a few miles from **Sheringham,** another old-fashioned seaside town where you can enjoy a short walk along the front and maybe a swift lunch such as local fish at the Caribbean-hued

---

 halting **IN HOLT**

The small town of Holt comes as a surprise. A few miles from the coast, it's a discreet, upmarket place that seems to have dropped in from the Cotswolds. The idiosyncratic department store Bakers & Larners rambles through a line of high-street shop fronts, with a food hall like a mini Harrods, as well as an enviable selection of Barbours, posh wellies (boots), and the like. The galleries go for big names—Doric Arts regularly has a selling exhibition of David Hockney prints, and Baron Art is full of Clarice Cliff. You can get here on the Poppy Line steam train from Sheringham (it's a mile walk or a bus ride from the station; see "Exploring the Area"), and there are plenty of places to rest; Bakers & Larners coffee shop, the Horatio Mugs tearoom (named after local boy Lord Nelson), and the Feathers hotel, established 1650, with its pleasing Plume restaurant.

Funky Mackerel Cafe with its seafront terrace, or a lobster sandwich at Joyful West's Shellfish Bar on the high street. The **North Norfolk Steam Railway** (the Poppy Line), leaves Sheringham Station (www.nnrailway.co.uk; ℂ **01263/820800**), for a 30-minute run with sea, field, and woodland views to the outskirts of Holt.

The A149 road then passes through **Salthouse** (a bird reserve of lagoons and marsh protected from the sea by a shingle bank), and on to **Cley-next-the-Sea** (pronounced Clee), noted for Cley Smokehouse (www.cleysmokehouse.com; ℂ **01263/740282**), which produces home-cured seafood and meat, and **Cley Marshes Norfolk Wildlife Trust** viewing hall (www.norfolkwildlifetrust.org.uk; ℂ **01263/740008**), a free site with interactive displays, as well as a shop, cafe, and parking. Access to the reserve, which runs down to the sea is £5, children free.

Wells-next-the-Sea is a pleasing little town, with its busy quayside. Parking at the beach offers a walk along the water (and view of the odd seal) into town. The beach, backed by pine forest and dunes, stretches to **Holkham** beach, near **Holkham Hall.** The unspoiled coast ends at the bucket-and-spade seaside resort of **Hunstanton** (the only coastal town in Norfolk to face west). Despite top-quality sands and famous striped cliffs, many head south to **Sandringham,** the Queen's holiday retreat (see review, below), and a little farther for **Castle Rising** (www.castlerising.co.uk; ℂ **01553/631330**), a fine example of a 12th-century stone keep.

Blakeney National Nature Reserve ★★ NATURE RESERVE West from Cley Marshes Norfolk Wildlife Trust, take a right-hand turn to Cley lifeboat station where there's a cafe and walks to Blakeney Point. You can see common and gray seals and birds at this National Trust reserve. Morston Quay is the base for boat trips.

Cley Rd., Blakeney. www.nationaltrust.org.uk. ℂ **01263/740241.** Free access daily, but National Trust pay parking lot.

Holkham Hall ★★ HISTORIC SITE This is the magnificent family home of the earls of Leicester. You can visit the Palladian-style house, walk around the deer park, and visit the Bygones Museum in the stables to see vintage cars, steam engines, and displays on life here over the centuries. Over the road (A149) is Holkham beach, wild and unspoiled and part of an Area of Outstanding Natural Beauty. There's a boardwalk along the beach, dunes, and a huge expanse of sand when the tide goes out (and out).

Holkham (on the A149). www.holkham.co.uk. ℂ **01328/710227.** Hall and museum admission £12 adults, £6 children 5–15, £30 family ticket. Museum only admission £4 adults, £2 children. Hall Apr–Oct Sun–Mon and Thurs noon–4pm. Museum Apr–Oct daily 10am–5pm. Closed Nov–Mar, but the park, with cafe and shop, is open year-round, free, to walkers.

Sandringham House & Gardens ★★ HISTORIC SITE One of the Queen's preferred residences with some rooms open to the public, a separate museum, and extensive woodland gardens with flowering bulbs and rhododendrons in spring and stunning autumn displays. The house retains its Edwardian style with gifts from Russian and German royal relatives on show, while the museum is a collection of personal items and gifts from state visits abroad. The house is usually closed for a week in July.

Sandringham (off the A149). www.sandringhamestate.co.uk. ℂ **01485/545400.** House, museum, and gardens admission £11.50 adults, £6 children 5–15, £29 family ticket. Late Apr–late Oct daily 11am–5pm (from 9:30am for visitor center, cafe, and shop; 10:30am for gardens). Closed rest of year.

Titchwell Marsh RSPB Reserve ★★ NATURE RESERVE One of the first places many geese, ducks, and wading birds land as they head south from the Arctic is this reserve with its salt and freshwater ponds, which you can see from the new

📷 NORFOLK coast PATH

You can walk from Cromer to Hunstanton on the Norfolk Coast Path. It leaves the coast for a short stretch across the hills to Sheringham, but hugs the beach and sea all the way to Cley then takes a straight line to Wells (to the rear of marshland but keeping to the sea-side of the A149), then through the beachfront pines at Holkham. It's 46 miles, but passes by or near many excellent hotels to make a comfortable multiday trip. Or you can just go for as long as you fancy, getting the Coasthopper bus back (the trail heads inland, the same distance again, as the Roman Peddar's Way to Thetford Forest.) Visit www.nationaltrail. co.uk for maps and more information.

Parrinder Hide, a striking architectural retreat from the wind. A raised walkway takes you to the beach, where you'll see more birds, possibly seals, and rusting World War II tanks.

Titchwell (on the A149). www.rspb.org.uk. ✆ **01485/210779.** Free admission; parking £4. Shop daily 9:30am–5pm; cafe daily 9:30am–4:30pm.

Where to Eat & Stay

Montague House ★★ 🎁   In the quiet backstreets of Sheringham, this boutique B&B occupies a smart Edwardian house, packed with the owners' collection of art and antiques (including many large oils, old and modern), with the steam engines of the Poppy Line passing by the bottom of the pretty garden. The three bedrooms are all furnished individually, right down to the varied organic toiletries and truffles from local producers. The Gold Suite has a four-poster bed and all have flat-screen TVs. The country-house-style breakfast room spills out onto a terrace, and doubles as a lounge and games room. Breakfasts cooked on the Aga are sensational, ranging from organic bacon to locally smoked kippers and haddock to blueberry pancakes and French toast. Picnic baskets and packed lunches are made to order.

3 Montague Rd., Sheringham, Norfolk NR26 8LN. www.montague-house.co.uk. ✆ **01263/822510.** 3 units. £80–£100 double; £100–£130 suite. Rates include English breakfast. MC, V. Free parking. **Amenities:** Lounge; breakfast room; garden. *In room:* TV/DVD, hair dryer, Wi-Fi (free).

Titchwell Manor ★★   This farmhouse has expanded into outbuildings and is now one of the region's leading small hotels, with views across RSPB Titchwell Marsh bird sanctuary to the sea. Rooms are all unique, from sumptuous hotel rooms to the flagstones and modish decor of the timbered Herb Garden lodges, or the Victorian fittings and wood-burning stove in The Lounge, a cottage-like original room. All have lavish bathrooms, and foldaway beds for children are £15. The **Conservatory,** over-looking the walled garden, features a modern menu with local produce such as veni-son from the Houghton estate and Brancaster oysters. The informal **Eating Rooms,** with seaview terrace, has a brasserie menu. There's also a good, friendly bar.

Titchwell, Kings Lynn, Norfolk PE31 8BB (on the A149). www.titchwellmanor.com. ✆ **01485/210221.** 31 units. £110–£250 double. Rates include English breakfast. AE, MC, V. Free parking. **Amenities:** 2 restaurants; bar; lounge. *In room:* TV, hair dryer, Wi-Fi (free).

EAST MIDLANDS

by Rhonda Carrier

With walking, cycling, fell-running, rock-climbing, caving, horse-riding, watersports, and fishing in abundance, the upland but not mountainous Peak District in northern Derbyshire is this region's big draw. Most of it falls within the Peak District National Park, designated Britain's first national park in 1951. However, green spaces and rich historical sites abound in neighboring Nottinghamshire and Leicestershire—alongside thoroughly modern British cities.

14

CITIES & TOWNS **Nottingham** has reinvented itself for the 21st century as a shopping and nightlife destination, yet historical gems, including a honeycomb of man-made caves that served, over time, as medieval tanneries, factories, and air-raid shelters, underpin its flashy facade. Similarly, **Leicester's** Roman past still reasserts itself within the context of a many-layered multicultural city studded with modern attractions such as the National Space Centre.

COUNTRYSIDE Plunging waterfalls, swooningly gorgeous moors and dales, rolling hills, and verdant valleys bring walkers and cyclists from far afield to the lovely **Peak District;** less well known are the lush country and forest parks within Nottinghamshire's **Sherwood Forest,** remnants of former royal hunting terrain, and craggy **Charnwood Forest** in Leicestershire, dotted with volcanic rocks and home to a medieval deer park concealing the ruined dwelling of a beheaded queen.

EATING & DRINKING Cheese is big and bold in the East Midlands—the world-renowned blue-veined Stilton can only be produced in Derbyshire, Nottinghamshire, and Leicestershire, while the latter county is also known for its crumbly, nutty, orange-hued Red Leicester. Sample and buy them, and other local produce and specialties, including Melton Mowbray **pork pies,** at farm shops and **farmers' markets** all over the region, not least the famous **Chatsworth Farm Shop,** or enjoy them at a cozy country pub. Make sure to sample one of Leicester's famed **Indian restaurants,** too.

NATIONAL PARKS Quirky **Matlock Bath,** on the edge of the Peak District, was once described as "Little Switzerland" by Daniel Defoe for its riverside cliffs. It has something for everyone, from cable-car rides up to a hilltop park with walking trails, tours of an old mine, and a fossil museum, to the aptly named Giddy Edge walk, canoeing on the river, and a museum of photography. It's also the start of the UNESCO-listed Derwent Valley Mills World Heritage Site, a stunning array of early cotton mills.

THE best TRAVEL EXPERIENCES IN THE EAST MIDLANDS

○ **Exploring the Peak District:** Britain's original National Park is a walkers' and cyclists' paradise, especially the Monsal Trail past the stunning Monsal Falls, while Chatsworth House is the region's unmissable "jewel in the crown." See p. 538.

○ **Following in the footsteps of Robin Hood:** The legendary outlaw, who left his mark all over Sherwood Forest, lives on in lively local pageants and festivals, as well as special trails and footpaths. See p. 546.

○ **Marveling at Lincoln Cathedral:** Rising majestically from the heart of a walkable city of medieval streets lined by Tudor houses, Lincoln's fine Gothic cathedral was described by critic John Ruskin as no less than "the most precious piece of architecture in the British Isles." See p. 554.

○ **Charting the growth of the National Forest:** Though not yet a true forest, this area of southern Derbyshire and northern Leicestershire is packed with attractions, from a woodland adventure park and wildlife aplenty to some of Britain's best off-road cycling. See p. 557.

○ **Getting outdoorsy at Rutland Water:** The biggest man-made reservoir in all Europe offers up activities from watersports and walking to wildlife encounters, plus a unique museum within a half-submerged church. See p. 559.

DERBYSHIRE & THE PEAK DISTRICT

Derby: 130 miles N of London; 41 miles NE of Birmingham

Most of the county of Derbyshire falls within the Peak District National Park, designated Britain's first National Park in 1951 and attracting about 10 million visitors a year for its gritstone edges, waterfalls, and moorlands (Dark Peak to the north), and its limestone dales, rolling hills, and green valleys divided by dry-stone walls (White Peak to the south). Its popularity is explained by the 555 sq. miles of public paths and 202 sq. miles of open-access land all within easy reach of several major British cities, including **Manchester** (p. 566). South and east Derbyshire are certainly less scenically dramatic but have plenty of diversions in the form of historic houses and buildings, industrial heritage, and family attractions.

Essentials

GETTING THERE   Direct trains to Derby from London St. Pancras or Euston take between 1½ hours to 2 hours, costing around £58–£81 for an off-peak round-trip. To reach Buxton by train from London, you have to go first to Stockport and then change to a train from Manchester (p. 566), taking about 1 hour. If you're flying into Manchester, bus no. 199 runs directly from the airport to Buxton. Also handy for the Peak District are **East Midlands Airport** (www.eastmidlandsairport.com) near Derby, with international flights, and Doncaster–Sheffield Airport and Leeds–Bradford Airport in Yorkshire.

Derby is minutes from the M1 running north from London, just over 124 miles away. Mainly direct **National Express** buses (www.nationalexpress.com; ✆ 0871/781-8178) from London to Derby take about 3¾ hours. Buses from London to Buxton (most requiring a change at Derby) take about 6 hours.

Buxton is a 25-mile drive southeast of Manchester, but the most scenic routes take longer. **Transpeak** (www.trentbarton.co.uk/services/transpeak; ✆ 01773/712265) runs regular Manchester–Nottingham buses stopping at points in Derbyshire, including Buxton, Bakewell, Haddon Hall, Matlock Bath, and Derby.

VISITOR INFORMATION   Note that some Derbyshire attractions and tourist information and visitor centers have restricted opening times or close altogether for all or most of the winter. Call ahead to confirm opening times of the visitor centers below. An invaluable resource for any visitor to the area is www.peakdistrict.gov.uk.

Bakewell Visitor Centre, Old Market Hall, Bridge Street (✆ 01629/816558).

Buxton Tourist Information Centre, inside Pavilion Gardens gift boutique (www.visitbuxton.co.uk; ✆ 01298/25106).

Castleton Visitor Centre, Buxton Road (✆ 01629/816572).

Derby Tourist Information Centre, Market Place (www.visitderby.co.uk; ✆ 01332/255802).

Matlock Tourist Information Centre, Crown Square (www.visitpeakdistrict. com; ✆ 01629/583388).

Upper Derwent Visitor Centre, Fairholmes, Bamford (✆ 01433/650953).

GETTING AROUND   Getting around the National Park is for many people the point of visiting (see "Best Peak District Trails," below). The official **bike-rental** centers are at Ashbourne, Derwent, and Parsley Hay (see www.peakdistrict.gov.uk/cycle). If you're not so hearty, use **local buses** (more frequent on Sunday, especially in summer); timetables are available at tourist information centers or from www.nationalparks.gov.uk.

SPECIAL EVENTS   The **Buxton Festival** (www.buxtonfestival.co.uk; ✆ 01298/70395), a world-renowned feast of opera, music, and literature, is held during around 2 weeks each July. **Chatsworth House's** (p. 539) large-scale seasonal events include an **International Horse Trials** in May and a **Country Fair** in September. Derby, England's real ale capital, hosts the **CAMRA Summer Beer Festival** each July.

Well-dressing (www.welldressing.com) involves decorating Derbyshire's freshwater springs with a mosaic of petals, berries, bark, leaves, and moss, with ceremonies held in different villages and towns May to September. In the autumn, Matlock Bath hosts its Victorian-origin **Illuminations and Venetian Nights** event, with neon-lit boats on the river and fireworks over the floodlit cliffs.

Exploring Derbyshire

BUXTON: GATEWAY TO THE NATIONAL PARK ★★

This picturesque spa town, nestled between two areas of the National Park, merits exploration in its own right. It can make a good base for discovering Derbyshire, though its setting in a valley means it's often swathed in cloud for weeks at a time. Its thermal waters were known to the Romans, whose settlement here was called Aquae Arnemetiae, but afterward was largely forgotten until the reign of Elizabeth I, when the baths were reactivated. Mary, Queen of Scots took the waters here while being held captive by the Earl of Shrewsbury and his wife, Bess of Hardwick, at nearby

Chatsworth House (p. 539). Bess's descendant, the 5th Duke of Devonshire, had plans to turn Buxton into another Bath; he failed, but what you see today is largely the legacy of his 18th-century development, including **The Crescent,** modeled on Bath's Royal Crescent and at the time of writing scheduled to undergo transformation into a five-star hotel, thermal spa, and natural mineral-water spa, with completion due in 2014 (the previous thermal baths closed in the 1970s).

Pavilion Gardens ★★ ☺ Restored between 1998 and 2004 to its Victorian splendor, this lovely spot has lakes, a bandstand, a minitrain, a cafe, and an ice-cream parlor. Events across the year include farmers' markets, fine-food fairs, books and antiques fairs, and the Great Peak District Fair each October, which includes the Buxton Beer Festival, family activities, and music.

St. John's Rd. www.paviliongardens.co.uk. © **01298/23114.** Free admission. Daily 9:30am–5pm.

Poole's Cavern ★★ ☺ This limestone cave on the outskirts of Buxton, inhabited by Stone Age people, Romans, and finally medieval outlaws, has chambers studded with stalactites and stalagmites, accessible via guided tour. It's within Buxton Country Park, home to the leaning Victorian folly Solomon's Temple on Grin Low

Best Peak District Trails

Of the countless wonderful walking and cycling routes in the Peak District, the most evocative is the **Monsal Trail**, running for about 8 miles (about half can be cycled) along the old Midland Railway Line and passing the gorgeous Monsal Falls. It starts at Blackwell Mill Junction at Wyedale, about 3 miles east of Buxton, and ends at Coombs Viaduct just over a mile south of Bakewell. Then there's the linking **High Peak and Tissington trails,** which combined offer about 30 miles of walking, cycling, and horse-riding tracks along former train lines studded with relics of the railway's past and interpretation panels. For more on these and other Peak District routes, including downloadable maps, and details of bike-rental centers and refreshment stops en route, see www.peakdistrict.gov.uk.

The Peak District National Park is also the southern starting point for the **Pennine Way** (www.nationaltrail.co.uk), Britain's oldest long-distance national walking trail, which begins at Edale and takes you 268 miles up to the Cheviot Hills in Northumberland (p. 671), via the Yorkshire Dales National Park (p. 650).

Hill, with views across High Peak, and **Go Ape!** forest adventure course (www.goape.co.uk; ✆ **0845/643-9215**), with admission prices from £20; call for hours.

Green Lane. www.poolescavern.co.uk. ✆**01298/26978.** Admission £8 for adults, £4.75 children 5–16. Call for tour times.

THE NATIONAL PARK ★★★

Dark Peak (or **High Peak**) is the highest, wildest section of the National Park, and though it's dramatically scenic, it's bleak in bad weather (an impression reinforced by the military aircraft wrecks). In summer, staff at the **Upper Derwent Visitor Centre** (p. 536) near the dam will advise you on getting the most of its moorlands, forests, and reservoirs (Howden, Derwent, and Ladybower).

At the base of **Mam Tor** ("Heights of the Mother"), pretty **Castleton** attracts visitors with its imposing Norman ruins and four underground show caves. To the east, scenic **Hathersage** plays up its possible links with the Robin Hood legend but has a firmer claim to fame as the place where Charlotte Brontë wrote part of *Jane Eyre,* while staying at the vicarage to visit a friend. Walkers and rock-climbers flock here for its surrounding moorland, gritstone edges, and tors (high rocky hills). It's also home to the David Mellor museum (p. 543).

About 12 miles southeast of Buxton, **Bakewell** is another good base and indeed the only town within the National Park itself. (For the Monsal Trail between Buxton and Bakewell, see "Best Peak District Trails," p. 538.) This pleasant market town is best known as home to the eponymous pudding (though not the Bakewell tart, which hails from elsewhere). It's available all over but best sampled at **The Old Original Bakewell Pudding Shop** (www.bakewellpuddingshop.co.uk; ✆ **01629/812193**). Most visitors time their trip to coincide with the traditional market each Monday. Bakewell is just minutes from one of the greatest of English country houses, Chatsworth House, which you may recognize from the 2005 movie adaptation of *Pride and Prejudice,* and from nearby **Haddon Hall,** another location for the movie.

The southern section of the National Park has no large attractions, but **Dovedale** ★★★—National Trust-owned farmland—is good walking territory:

Highlights are the famous stepping stones across the River Dove, the Lion's Head Rock, and the Dove Holes caves. The village of **Hartington** to the north is home to a Stilton cheese factory and a famous little cheese shop, a real ale brewery, the tiny Beresford Tea Rooms (also comprising the village post office and shop), and one of Derbyshire's most famous youth hostels (p. 545). It's popular with walkers using local trails, including the Tissington.

Blue John Cavern ★ ☺   Along with nearby **Treak Cliff Cavern**, this is the only place in the world where the blue-and-yellow semiprecious mineral Blue John—discovered by the Romans—is found. Tours let you see clearly how the caverns are formed in limestone strata, themselves formed by the deposits of once-great oceans—as the fossilized remains of marine animals demonstrate.

Buxton Rd., Castleton. www.bluejohn-cavern.co.uk. ℂ **01433/620638.** Admission £9, £4.50 children up to 15. Daily 9:30am–5:30pm (10am–dusk in winter).

Caudwell's Mill ★   This 19th-century flour mill offers you the chance to watch the machinery in action; learn about the flour-making process; buy flour, oat products, and recipe books; and enjoy fresh breads, cakes, cream teas, and other home-cooked fare in the cafe. There are also crafts galleries in the yard.

Rowsley. www.caudwellsmill.co.uk. ℂ **01629/734374.** Admission £3.50 adults, £1.25 children 5–15. Daily 10am–5:30pm.

Chatsworth House ★★★ ☺ HISTORIC SITE   The "jewel of the Peak District" is currently home to the 12th Duke of Devonshire, Peregrine Cavendish, but it was his mother, Deborah Mitford (of the famous sisters), who was the driving force behind transforming this once-ailing estate into the impressive visitor attraction and charitable trust it is today (she now lives on the edge of the estate). In addition to the lavish interiors and art treasures, visitors can explore its superb grounds with their fountains, modern sculptures, maze, excellent adventure playground, and a farmyard. From horse trials to Christmas markets, there are reasons to visit year-round. You can even stay on the vast estate (see "Manifold Farm" review, p. 543), and there are eateries at the house and around the estate plus the famed Chatsworth Farm Shop at nearby Pilsley and the new Chatworth Butchers & Delicatessen in Bakewell.

Chatsworth, 4 miles east of Bakewell. www.chatsworth.org. ℂ **01246/565300.** "Discovery" tickets to entire site £17.50–£19.50 adults, £10.50–£11.50 children 4–16, but tickets to separate attractions available. House: Feb school break and mid-Mar–late Dec daily 11am–5:30pm. Garden, farmyard, and playground have slightly different hours.

Haddon Hall ★   Home to the Manners family since the 16th century, this atmospheric, fortified medieval manor near Chatsworth House is best visited at Christmas for its traditional decorations, Tudor music, carols, and candlelight tours. A tour highlight is the late-14th-century Banqueting Hall complete with Minstrel's Gallery and manacle and lock for any guest "who did not drink fayre." For a review of Lord Manners' hotel, The Peacock at Rowsley, see p. 544.

Bakewell. www.haddonhall.co.uk. ℂ **01629/812855.** Admission £9.50 for adults, £5.50 children aged 5–16. Apr and Oct Sat–Mon, May–Sept and 2 weeks before Christmas daily noon–5pm.

Peveril Castle ★ ☺   These imposing Norman ruins high above Castleton, affording wonderful Peak District views, boast a keep built by Henry II in 1176, where you can still see the medieval lavatory. There's also a visitor center with displays on Peveril as the administrative focus of the hunting preserve of the Royal Forest of the Peak.

Market Place, Castleton. www.english-heritage.org.uk. © **0870/333-1181.** Admission £4.30 adults, £2.60 children aged 5–16. Daily 10am–4/5pm.

EASTERN DERBYSHIRE

The Chatsworth estate came into the hands of the Cavendish family when it was bought by royal courtier Sir William Cavendish, forebear of the current duke. You can see more of the family's legacy a few miles east, at **Hardwick Hall.** A couple more historic buildings north of that also warrant a visit.

Bolsover Castle ★ This hilltop 17th-century has restored interiors, one of the U.K.'s finest surviving indoor riding schools, a Discovery Centre, and events such as Ghost Tours and Knights & Princesses days for children. Bring a picnic and enjoy the views over the Vale of Scarsdale.

Castle St., Bolsover. www.english-heritage.org.uk. © **0870/333-1181.** Admission £7.80, £4.70 children 5–16. Daily 10am–4/5pm.

Hardwick Hall ★★ Built by Sir William Cavendish's third wife, Elizabeth Talbot ("Bess of Hardwick") in the 1590s, this splendid house boasts six towers, an evocative Long Gallery, a wonderful collection of tapestries and embroideries, herb gardens, orchards and lawns, and a newly restored historic stableyard. You can also rent two cottages on the estate, accommodating 6 and 12 respectively.

Doe Lea. www.nationaltrust.org.uk. ©**01246/850430.** Admission £11, £5.50 children 5–16; less for just the garden; see website for days and times.

SOUTHERN DERBYSHIRE ★★

Just outside the National Park, south of Chatsworth, lies Matlock, Derbyshire's county town. But what will detain you is the former spa-resort of **Matlock Bath ★**, south of Matlock and nicknamed (a touch hyperbolically) "Little Switzerland" by Daniel Defoe for the cliffs rising on either side of the River Derwent. Though its thermal baths are gone, there are attractions aplenty, including the **Heights of Abraham** (see below), **Mining Museum** (www.peakmines.co.uk; © 01629/583834), a **Museum of Photography & Old Times** (www.lifeinalens.com; ©01629/583325) complete with Victorian teashop, a **theme park** (www.gulliversfun.co.uk; © 01925/444888), and an **aquarium** (www.matlockbathaquarium.co.uk; ©01629/583624) that also has a petrifying well, hologram gallery, and gemstone and fossil exhibition. The Derwent is popular for canoeing, and Matlock Bath is also the start of the UNESCO-listed Derwent Valley Mills World Heritage Site and a short hop from Crich Tramway Village & the National Tramway Museum (for both, see below).

Southwest of Matlock Bath lies **Carsington Water ★** (www.moretoexperience.co.uk; © 0870/179-1111), a reservoir with watersports and bike rentals, a visitor center, and playgrounds. Then due south lies **Derby** itself, which—though hardly the most scenic or culturally compelling of British cities—has a fine Cathedral Quarter (www.derbycathedralquarter.co.uk) with Victorian arcades, Georgian and Renaissance buildings, and independent shops and galleries, and close by, the **Silk Mill Museum of Industry and History** (see below).

Around Derby are three National Trust (www.nationaltrust.org.uk) properties. Just north, near Quarndon, is **Kedleston Hall,** while south of the city, at Ticknall, is **Calke Abbey,** and providing a worthy finale to Derbyshire 16 miles west of Derby is **Sudbury Hall and the National Trust Museum of Childhood.** For all, see below.

Note that some attractions in southern Derbyshire are within the **National Forest** (p. 557), while just over the border in Staffordshire, **Alton Towers** (www.altontowers.com; © 0871/222-3330) is one of the U.K.'s best theme parks.

Calke Abbey ★ HISTORIC SITE   This country house fallen into disrepair is a charming place to ramble around, with its overgrown courtyards, faded walled gardens, and peeling paintwork. As you do, consider that the same fate almost befell Chatsworth House (p. 539). Take advantage of fine weather to explore the vast parkland, a national nature reserve with red and fallow deer and a deer shelter, and a restored wetland area that's a haven for wildlife. Four on-site rental cottages (sleeping 3–14) include two former gatehouse lodges.

Ticknall, 14 miles south of Derby. www.nationaltrust.org.uk. ℂ **01332/863822.** Admission house and garden £8.80 adults, £4.50 children 5–16; less for park and stables, or garden only. Park daily 7:30am–7:30pm; see website for house, gardens, and stables.

Crich Tramway Village & the National Tramway Museum ★★ ☺ MUSEUM/PARK   This restored period village with its cobblestones and collection of original facades from buildings around the U.K. displays trams, both horse-drawn and modern (some offering rides), and also has a viewing gallery from which you can watch trams being restored. Other attractions include a woodland walk, an adventure playground, a family-friendly pub that was saved from demolition in Stoke and rebuilt here, a tearoom, an ice-cream parlor, and an old-fashioned candy shop.

Crich, 6 miles southeast of Matlock Bath. www.tramway.co.uk. ℂ **01773/854321.** Admission £12 adults, £7 children 4–15. Feb school break and Mar weekends 10:30am–4:30pm; Apr–Oct daily 10am–5:30pm; usually also some weekends in Dec 10:30am–6:30pm.

Derwent Valley Mills World Heritage Site ★★   This unparalleled collection of early cotton mills dotted along 15 miles of the river valley leading south from Matlock to Derby includes some of the world's first "modern" factories. The highlight is Cromford Mills, where the eponymous Sir Richard pioneered the water frame spinning machine that revolutionized textile manufacture. There are separate or combined tours of the mill and workers' village, plus various high-quality shops, a wholefood cafe, and a canalside bookstore and restaurant.

www.derwentvalleymills.org. ℂ **01629/823256** (Cromford Mills). Free admission; tours £5, or £4 for village or mill only. Cromford Mills complex daily 9am–5pm.

Heights of Abraham ★★ ☺ PARK   This wooded hilltop park is an excellent bet for a family day out, with walking paths, tours of a former mine, a fossil museum, and play areas. Best of all, you get here by cable-car from the base of the opposite cliff, High Tor. Fit visitors can also climb High Tor itself, along a narrow winding path dubbed Giddy Edge.

Matlock Baths. www.heightsofabraham.com. ℂ **01629/582365.** Admission £12.50 adults, £8.80 children 5–16. Feb school break and late Mar–Oct daily 10am–4:30pm (later at peak times), plus weekends early–mid-Mar.

Sudbury Hall & the National Trust Museum of Childhood ★★ ☺ HISTORIC SITE/MUSEUM   The 17th-century country home of the Lords Vernon boasts gorgeous plasterwork, wood carvings, and classical story-based murals, with the Great Staircase and Long Gallery particularly worthy of admiration. But it's also worth visiting for its museum on childhood in days gone by, with eight themed galleries including the Outdoor Adventure Gallery complete with a Victorian street with traditional games to play.

Sudbury, 14 miles west of Derby. www.nationaltrust.org.uk. ℂ**01283/585305.** Admission hall and museum £14.50 adults, £7.80 children 5–18; separate admission available. Hall mid-Feb–Oct Wed–Sun 1–5pm. Museum mid-Feb–March Wed–Sun 11am–5pm; April–Oct daily 11am–5pm; Nov–mid-Dec Sat and Sun 11am–4pm.

Where to Eat

Café@The Green Pavilion ★★ 👔 INTERNATIONAL Buxton's best cafe, adjunct to a florist's shop and winner of a regional "Food Heroes" award for its commitment to using top local produce, is a welcoming spot for English breakfast; morning coffee and cakes; light lunches including sandwiches, salads, Derbyshire oatcakes, homity (open vegetable) pie, falafel, and New York style meatballs; and afternoon tea. The outdoor tables are great for people-watching in warmer weather. The cafe is tiny, so you may have to wait for a table, but all food can be ordered to take out—perhaps to make up a picnic in the nearby Pavilion Gardens (p. 537). Both the cafe and the flower shop sell homemade jams, preserves, and chutneys.

4 Terrace Rd., Buxton. www.greenpavilion.co.uk. ✆ **01298/77480.** Reservations not accepted. Main courses £4–£6.50. MC, V. Mon–Sat 7:30am–5:30pm; Sun 9am–5pm.

The Dining Room at Ashbourne ★★ 👔 This award-winning six-table restaurant, within an early-17th-century building in a market town that bills itself as the "gateway to Dovedale," is run by a couple passionate about local produce; who garner ingredients from producers, suppliers, and foragers within a 35-mile radius where possible; and who also do all their own baking, butchery, curing, smoking, preserving, and air-drying. Unsurprisingly, the resulting cuisine is true food for foodies—the likes of cauliflower soup with hempseed, Lincolnshire Poacher cheese, and golden raisins; chicken with Douglas fir pine, lemon, and grains of paradise; and Wakefield rhubarb and crema catalana with almond, orange, and rose. And there's no choice—diners eat from a 6/7- (weekdays) or 9-course (Saturdays) weekly-changing menu. This and the fact that there is just one chef in the kitchen means you must book ahead, and that there is a set arrival time of 7pm. Guests can stay over in an adjoining apartment for two, costing £120 per night.

33 St. John St., Ashbourne. www.thediningroomashbourne.co.uk. ✆**01335/300666.** Reservations required. Weekday menu £40 for 6 courses, £48 for 9 courses. MC, V.Thurs–Sat from 7pm; Tues and Weds by appointment for 8 guests or more.

The George ★★ 👔 The epitome of the cosy country pub, with a log fire, farmhouse furniture, and lime-washed walls, this village local close to Ashbourne is a deceptively simple setting for serious pub food, served amidst candlelight and fresh flowers and accompanied by real ales or well-chosen wines. Locally sourced ingredients (some from as close at hand as the pub's only pesticide-free garden) go into simply cooked and hearty yet ambitious dishes such as game and pistachio terrine with Waldorf dressing, and market-catch fish of the day with crayfish and potato dumpling cassoulet. At lunch there are sandwiches too, while Sundays see traditional roasts as well as good burgers, sausages, fish and chips, and other options.

Alstonefield. www.thegeorgeatalstonefield.com. ✆ **01335/310205.** Main courses £12–£25. MC, V. Mon–Sat noon–2:30pm and 6:30–9pm; Sun noon–2:30pm and 6:30–8pm.

PeliDeli ☺ BREAKFAST/SNACKS/LUNCH This award-winning and genuinely local shop and cafe in the center of Matlock offers seasonal produce hand-selected by the owners from local providers. Breakfast might consist of crumpets (savory griddle cakes) or an onion bagel with cream cheese, and a hot or cold smoothie; later in the day choose from paninis or other sandwiches (perhaps Derbyshire ham and Derby cheese with real-ale chutney), and daily-changing soups and salad platters. If it's winter, warm up with one of the incredible hot chocolates with hazelnut syrup or Cointreau. There's a second branch in Wirksworth, 5 miles south of Matlock.

Derbyshire & the Peak District

EAST MIDLANDS

1 Jubilee Buildings, Crown Sq., Matlock. www.pelideli.com. © **07980/694841.** Main courses £2.75–£5.50. MC, V. Mon–Fri 8am–5pm; Sat 8:45am–4pm.

Royal Oak at Hurdlow ★ 🍷 ☺ TRADITIONAL BRITISH   This pub in the midst of countryside just off the Tissington Trail (p. 538) attracts weary walkers and cyclists with its open fires, cosy nooks, beer garden, cask-conditioned ales, and hearty pub food based on produce sourced within a small distance. Relaxed and friendly, it's a good place for families, especially at Sunday lunch, when there are traditional roasts but also sandwiches and other main courses such as haddock and chips, or butternut squash, spinach, and walnut lasagna. Children get their own menu all week (£4.95 for a main course). For those who'd like to linger or are walking in the area, there's a bunk-barn with **rooms** to accommodate four, six, or eight guests and a communal kitchen, plus a family-friendly campsite. The Bunk Barn is £13–£15 and the campsite is £14–£16 per night for camper vans and £7–£24 for tents (minimum stay of 2 nights weekends from Apr to Sept).

Hurdlow. www.peakpub.co.uk. © **01298/83288.** Reservations recommended (dinner). Main courses £5.75–£20.95. MC, V. Daily noon–9pm.

Entertainment & Nightlife

Derbyshire won't ever set the world alight with its nightlife, but there is no end of cosy pubs around the county for enjoying its famed real ales. In Derby, sample produce from the city's microbreweries at the **Greyhound** (© **01332/344155**) on Friar Gate, dating back to 1734; the characterful (and allegedly haunted) **Ye Olde Dolphin Inn** (© **01332/267711**) near the cathedral, which runs its own beer festivals; or the Victorian **Brunswick** (© **01332/290677**) near the station.

The city's culture complex, Quad (www.derbyquad.co.uk), includes exhibition space, an arthouse cinema, and a British Film Institute movie archive.

Shopping

Local produce is one of the great assets of Derbyshire, so farmers' markets and farm shops—of which the Chatsworth Farm Shop (p. 539) is the most famous—are in abundance here. Look out for Hartington Stilton and other handmade cheeses, gingerbread, and local honey. The main markets are listed below (check with local tourist boards if you are making a special trip).

> **Bakewell**   Agricultural Centre, last Saturday of month, starts 9am
> **Buxton**   Market Place, first Thursday of month, 8:30am to 4:30pm
> **Castleton**   Village Hall, first Sunday of month, 10am to 3pm
> **Derby**   Market Place, third Thursday of month, 9am to 3pm
> **Hartington**   Hartington Moor, Sundays June to mid-September, 10am to 5pm

In the northern Peak District, the walkers' paradise of Hathersage is home to the **David Mellor Cutlery Factory, Design Museum,** and **Country Shop** (www. davidmellordesign.com; © **01433/650220**) showcasing (and selling) the work of the iconic designer and his son Corin, plus other local crafts. Inside the Round Building, an award-winning factory, you can watch some of Mellor's cutlery being made, and there's a stunning on-site cafe serving local produce.

Where to Stay

For the bunk rooms and campsite at the **Royal Oak at Hurdlow,** see p. 543.

Manifold Farm ★★ ☺ 🏠   If Chatsworth House is the "jewel in the crown" of the Peak District, where better to holiday in the region than a traditional holiday cottage on one of its estates? All cottages are comfortable and cosy rather than luxurious—exactly right for walkers, dog-owners, and families. Of a total of 19 cottages, Manifold, a former dairy farm south of Matlock, accounts for five. An attractive complex of stone buildings set around a courtyard, they sleep 2 to 10 guests. All but one has a log-burning stove, and each has its own garden. There's also a shared games room. For those who wish to explore, there's a network of footpaths on the doorstep, Carsington Water only 4 miles away and Chatsworth House within a 20-minute drive (weekly guests get free tickets). A fresh-baked farmhouse Victoria spongecake and tea-tray greet your arrival at your cottage.

Other options on Chatsworth's estates include **Swiss Cottage,** on a hill behind Chatsworth House, overlooking its own lake (it sleeps up to six); the 16th-century **Hunting Tower,** on an escarpment also just above the House, sleeping four plus two in a stone annex; and the newly available Russian Cottage for up to four, so-named because it was a gift to the 6th Duke of Devonshire from Tzar Nicholas in 1844. There are also four **hotels/pubs with rooms** on the estate.

Shottle, Derbyshire DE56 2DX. www.chatsworth.org. ✆**01246/565379.** 5 units. £405–£586/week cottage for 2; £600–£876/week cottage for 4 (3/4-night bookings sometimes available). MC, V. Free parking. **Amenities:** Games room. *In room:* TV/DVD, kitchen (w/dishwasher and washer/dryer), CD player.

The Peacock at Rowsley ★★ 🏠   This haven of cosy country-house chic has been refurbished by Lord Manners of Haddon Hall, and its 16 rooms unite antiques and original fireplaces with chic contemporary furnishings, fine fabrics, crisp white sheets, and large beds (king-size in standard rooms, super-king in large doubles, and four-poster in one plum room). The Peacock is a romantic rather than a family retreat, as the rule concerning children over-10 being allowed Sun–Thurs only denotes. Lord Manners lured the head chef back from working with Tom Aikens in London to oversee the smart, award-winning restaurant with its focus of Modern European dishes based on local produce. The evening fine-dining menu includes the likes of belly pork with celeriac baked in rosemary, onions, and apple; and red-legged partridge with black trompette mushrooms, cabbage, spätzli, and quince—pricey but worth it. The bar menu (available lunch daily, plus dinner Mon–Fri) has more accessible comfort-food dishes.

Rowsley. www.thepeacockatrowsley.com. ✆**01629/733518.** 16 units. £155–£258 double. MC, V. Rates include continental breakfast. **Amenities:** Restaurant and bar; DVD library; fishing (equipment sold at reception). *In room:* TV/DVD, hairdryer; iPod docking stations (by request), free Wi-Fi.

Rivendale Leisure Park ★ 🗡 ☺   In a disused quarry amid stunning countryside with easy access to the "Trails Triangle" formed by the Tissington Trail (p. 538), High Peak Trail, and the cycleway around Carsington Water, this is a good budget and eco-friendly base for cyclists and walkers, who can relieve muscle strain in the wood-fired hot tub (or rent a tub for their own pitch). Plans are also afoot for a sauna and steam room. Bring your own caravan, motor home, or tent, or there are timber or canvas yurts with a stove (accommodating 3–8), camping pods (insulated wooden mountain huts for up to 5, with electricity), static caravans, and B&B rooms. Some pitches are in a wildflower meadow or on an isolated hillside, and all guests have access to much of the surrounding meadows and woodland with its dragonflies, woodpeckers, owls, falcons, and more. Bring flashlights—there's little lighting so that guests can view the night sky in all its glory. There's a play area, plus a restaurant/pub with a family room.

The campsite is now part of Electrical Bicycle Network (www.electricbicyclenetwork. com), meaning you can hire and/or recharge electric cycles here.

Buxton Rd., Alsop-en-le-Dale, Derbyshire DE6 1QU. www.rivendalecaravanpark.co.uk. © **01335/310441.** £15–£23 campsite pitch; £38 timber yurt for 4, £38–48 camping pod. MC, V. Free parking. **Amenities:** Restaurant/pub and cafe with Internet access; shop; shower and toilet building; electrical hook-up (exc in meadow); electric bike hire; play area. *In room:* TV and CD player (static caravan), hot-tub rental, fire pit loan, BBQ equipment (some), kitchen (some).

YHA National Forest ☺ There are several youth hostels in Derbyshire so appealing that even those who aren't on a tight budget will be tempted to stay. This fairly new hostel in the Derbyshire section of the National Forest is an especially good (and very eco-friendly) base for families, handy for Conkers, Rosliston Forestry Centre, and Snibston (p. 557), and for walking and cycling routes for all ages and abilities. All rooms are en suite (accommodating two to five guests), and some have double beds and even wetrooms. The well-priced restaurant offers local produce, ales, and organic wines, though you can cut costs by using the well-equipped communal kitchen (including at breakfast, which costs £4.95 (£2.95 for children) in the restaurant).

Other good hostels in the area are **Hartington Hall,** a 17th-century manor near Buxton, and **Ilam Hall,** a National Trust-owned Victorian Gothic manor in Dovedale.

8 Bath Lane, Moira, Derbyshire DE12 6BD. www.yha.org.uk. © **0845/371-9672.** 23 units. 2-bed room £32–£53, plus £3pppn for non-YHA members. MC, V. Free parking. **Amenities:** Restaurant; kitchen; lounge; games room; Wi-Fi (£1 per 20 min.).

NOTTINGHAMSHIRE

Nottingham: 127 miles N of London; 81 miles SE of Manchester; 280 miles S of Edinburgh

Derbyshire's neighbor is largely taken up (in terms of historic boundaries if not tree coverage) by **Sherwood Forest,** remnant of a former royal hunting forest and legendary stamping ground of Robin Hood, but it also lures visitors with a city and a few towns rich in both folklore and shopping opportunities, whether your tastes run to designer clothes or antiques. Nottinghamshire is also a good base for exploring the cathedral city of **Lincoln** over in Lincolnshire.

Essentials

GETTING THERE Direct trains from London's St. Pancras or King's Cross Stations to Nottingham take just under 2 hours, costing around £84 for a round-trip off-peak. Direct buses (www.nationalexpress.com; © **0871/781-8181**) take 3¼ hours and cost. By car from London, it's a 127-mile journey of at least 2½ hours, almost all of it on the M1 motorway, which runs a few miles west of Nottingham. For If you're heading from the north, Transpeak buses run from Manchester to Nottingham via the Peak District, see p. 536.

For those coming from farther afield, Nottingham is 15 miles northeast of **East Midlands Airport** (p. 535). **Robin Hood Airport Doncaster–Sheffield** is just outside the county border, in South Yorkshire, while **Birmingham International Airport** (p. 468) is also within easy reach.

VISITOR INFORMATION **Nottingham Tourism Centre,** 1–4 Smithy Row (www.experiencenottinghamshire.com; © **0844/477-5678**), is open Monday to Saturday 9:30am to 5:30pm, plus some Sundays and public holidays.

References to Robin Hood, the archer and swordsman who "robbed from the rich to feed the poor," go back as far as the 13th century, but nobody knows whether the heroic outlaw is invention or was based on real people. Regardless, Robin and his Merry Men continue to exert a powerful hold on the public imagination—as the popularity of the 2006–09 BBC series and 2010 Russell Crowe movie attest.

Locations pertaining to the legend, including spots where Robin Hood lived, fought, hunted, or preyed on the wealthy, include Nottingham Castle, Thieves Wood, Rufford Abbey Country Park, Sherwood Forest Country Park, King John's Palace, Edwinstowe, and Clumber Park. Buy an "In the footsteps of Robin Hood" CD and interactive map/guide (£1.99) from the Sherwood Forest Visitor Centre to follow a route linking many of them by bike or car. Alternatively, follow the **Robin Hood Way** (www.robinhoodway.com), a 107-mile footpath from Nottingham to Southwell via Edwinstowe, also taking in areas linked with the outlaw.

For those exploring the area with children, there is plenty of scope to make like Robin and learn archery together. Center Parcs Sherwood Forest (p. 552) offers Little Outlaws fun sessions for ages 3+, Robin Hoods and Little Johns sessions for ages 6–9 and parents, plus field archery through the forest for ages 10+, plus target archery for ages 10+ in a purpose-built center. Alternatively, the new-in-2012 Sherwood Forest Cabins (p. 553) offer archery for ages 8 and up, or you can try it out at the Sherwood Forest Country Park (p. 548) or the Robin Hood Pageant (below).

The **Sherwood Forest Visitor Centre**, Edwinstowe (www.newark-sherwooddc. gov.uk; ✆ **01623/823202**), is seasonal so call ahead.

SPECIAL EVENTS The Sherwood Forest Visitor Centre is the focus for the week-long **Robin Hood Festival** (www.nottinghamshire.gov.uk/robinhoodfestival) in July or August, celebrating the outlaw with medieval crafts, children's theatre and food stalls, and jugglers, jesters, and other costumed characters. Alternatively, October sees the **Robin Hood Pageant** at **Nottingham Castle** (p. 549), with the castle green alive with historical reconstructions between the outlaws and the sheriffs' men, some of them on horseback, artisan displays, performances by jesters, wandering minstrels and storytellers, and archery sessions. Nottingham is also known for its **Goose Fair,** a huge 5-day fun fair dating back more than 700 years. Held each October, it was named after the thousands of geese that used to be driven to Nottingham from Lincolnshire to be sold.

To the east of the country, Newark hosts the **International Antiques and Collectors Fair** (www.iacf.co.uk/newark), Europe's largest such event, held every other month and attracting dealers and buyers from around the globe.

Exploring the Area

SHERWOOD FOREST NATIONAL NATURE RESERVE

Not all of Sherwood Forest is actually wooded, and although most exploration of the area will be inevitably focused on its wealth of marvelous green spaces, there are several sites of literary and general historic interest worth seeking out.

Clumber Park ★★★ ☺   Set in the northernmost part of the forest and offering spectacular scenery within the grounds of the long-lost country house of Clumber Hall, destroyed by fire in the 1930s, this idyllic spot is best discovered on more than 22 miles of cycle routes, one of them around the lake. But you can also roam the walled kitchen garden (which provides many ingredients for the restaurant), seek out a few moments of peace in the Victorian chapel, or stroll the elegant paths of the 18th-century pleasure ground, designed to give the dukes of Newcastle who lived here secluded walks. A state-of-the-art Discovery & Visitor Centre opened in the former stableyard in late 2011, and there's now also a campsite on the premises.

Worksop. www.nationaltrust.org.uk. ☏ **01909/544917.** Free admission. Daily 7am–dusk (see website for opening times of facilities, restaurant, and kitchen garden).

Cresswell Crags Museum & Heritage Centre ★★ ☺ MUSEUM   The U.K.'s only known Ice Age rock art was discovered on this site near Clumber Park in 2003, and you can also view stone tools and animal remains that were found within this limestone gorge honeycombed with caves and smaller fissures. At weekends and in local school vacations you take a Rock Art or an Ice Age tour; at other times you can learn more about the site—one of the most northerly on Earth to have been inhabited by ancient peoples—in the museum and visitor center. Walking trails take in the surrounding country park and wildlife reserve.

Crags Rd., Welbeck. www.creswell-crags.org.uk. ☏ **01909/720378.** Admission £3 adults, £1.50 children 5–16; for tour prices, see website. Exhibition daily Feb and Oct 10am–4:30pm; Mar–Sept daily 10am–5:30pm; Nov–Jan Sat–Sun 10am–4:30pm; for cave tours see website.

DH Lawrence Birthplace Museum ★ HISTORIC HOME   This unassuming terraced miner's cottage has been restored to the way it would have looked when the writer most famous for the scandal-raising *Lady Chatterley's Lover* spent part of his childhood here. The timed tours (which you are advised to book ahead) give the background to Lawrence's working-class mining heritage; at weekends and in school vacations they're given a family-friendly spin. The tour charge also gives access to the **DH Lawrence Heritage Centre** a short walk away, with additional displays on the town's famous son, who was born in 1885 and attended Nottingham University, and on mining.

8a Victoria St., Eastwood. www.broxtowe.gov.uk. ☏ **01773/717353.** Admission £5 adults, £3.50 children 5–16. Tours daily 11:15am, 12:15pm, 1:45pm, and 2:45pm.

Newstead Abbey ★ ☺ HISTORIC SITE   This partly ruined Augustinian priory was once home to Romantic poet Lord Byron, and on Sundays in summertime visitors can take a tour of his private apartments and see some of his possessions, in addition to exploring various Victorian rooms plus the medieval cloisters and chapterhouse, now a chapel. A wildlife trail through the gardens and parkland with their lakes, ponds, and cascades keeps youngsters engaged.

Ravenshead, 12 miles north of Nottingham. www.newsteadabbey.org.uk. ☏ **01623/455900.** Admission gardens only £4 adults, £3 children 2–16; house and gardens £10 and £8. Grounds daily 9am–6pm (or dusk if earlier); house Sundays Apr–Sept by guided tours at 1pm and 2pm (subject to demand).

Rufford Abbey Country Park ★ ☺   This swath of historic parkland and gardens includes woodland and lakeside walks, a play village with a maze and a children's garden, a modern sculpture trail, and a contemporary craft center. They are also the ruins of a medieval monastery, with an exhibition on the life of Rufford's monks, and a camera obscura.

Ollerton, 32 miles north of Nottingham. www.nottinghamshire.gov.uk. ✆ **01623/821338.** Free admission, parking £3 at peak times. Daily 9:30am–5:30pm (for individual attractions, see website).

Sherwood Forest Country Park ★★ ☺

Most famous as home to the 800-year-old Major Oak, in the trunk of which Robin Hood hid (at least according to local lore), this park also offers marked walks and footpaths through the woods, starting from its visitor center (see p. 546; with a restaurant). You can also buy self-guided family trails maps or sign up for guided walks and activities, from archery and birds-of-prey sessions to costumed re-enactments, woodland crafts, and puppetry.

Edwinstowe, 18 miles north of Nottingham. www.nottinghamshire.gov.uk. ✆**01623/823202.** Free admission. Parking free, or £3 at peak times. Daily 8am–5pm; visitor center closed most of winter, although restaurant, shops, and toilets remain open.

Sherwood Pines Forest Park ★★★ ☺

Run by the Forestry Commission, this park has another visitor center running activities and events, plus another Go Ape! treetop adventure course (p. 557), woodland play areas, bike-rental for the popular mountain-bike trails, Segways, and a Forest Holidays site with wooden lodges (p. 553).

Edwinstowe. www.forestry.gov.uk. ✆**01623/822447.** Free admission; parking £4. Daily 8am–dusk.

NOTTINGHAM ★

Nottinghamshire's county town founded its wealth on lace-making as well as coal-mining, and although these days it's the shops and nightlife that draw most visitors, especially since the 2006 redevelopment of the Old Market Square, there's an interesting mix of historical attractions to detain you a while.

Attenborough Nature Centre ★ ☺

This award-winning modern visitor facility is a worthy addition to the Attenborough Nature Reserve on the city's western fringes, which was opened by Sir David himself on former gravel pits in 1966. Its ecologically friendly buildings house interactive displays, a nature shop, and an organic/fair-trade cafe, while outside are a sensory nature trail, guided walks, wildlife-viewing activities, and a bird hide.

Barton Lane. www.attenboroughnaturecentre.co.uk. ✆**0115/972-1777.** Free admission. Mon–Fri 10am–4pm; Sat–Sun 9am–4pm (reserve daily 7am–dusk).

City of Caves ★ ☺ HISTORIC SITE

Nottingham's famed caves, carved out of the soft Sherwood limestone underlying the city, were probably inhabited as early as the 11th century, and some remained so until 1845. Over time they were used as store rooms, factories, pub cellars, medieval tanneries, and air-raid shelters. These slightly schlocky but informative tours (audio tours during the week and performance tours with costumed actors at weekends) take you on a journey through Nottingham's history and include a recreation of the Slums of Drury Hill. Joint tickets are available with the Galleries of Justice Museum (see below).

Upper Level, Broadmarsh Shopping Centre. www.cityofcaves.com. ✆**0115/988-1955.** Admission £5.95 adults, £4.50 children. Mon–Fri 11:30am–5pm; Sat–Sun 10:30am–5pm.

National Water Sports Centre ★ ☺

Just east of the city, this is the place to come if you want to try out whitewater rafting, sailing, canoeing and kayaking, water-skiing, or powerboating. You can make a day or even longer of it—the Centre is surrounded by a country park with lakes, lagoons, and nature trails, an assault (obstacle) course, and a hostel-style hotel and a campsite.

Holme Pierrepont. www.nwscnotts.com. ℂ **0115/982-1212.** Free admission (to country park); activities vary by cost. Regatta lake Mon, Wed, and Fri 7am–4pm; Tues 7am–6pm; Thurs 7am–6:30pm; Sat 7am–4:30pm; Sun 7am–12:30pm.

Nottingham Castle ★★ ☺ MUSEUM   Not a castle at all but a ducal mansion erected on the site of the city's medieval castle, this is now a cutting-edge museum and art gallery with collections of silver, glass, decorative items, and visual arts (much of it contemporary and global in scope), as well as local archeology and history. If that makes it sound a bit heavy-going, know that there's also an interactive gallery aimed at under-5s, a medieval-style playground, and a picnic area.

Off Friar Lane. www.nottinghamcity.gov.uk. ℂ **0115/915-3700.** Admission £5.50 adults, £4 children 15 and under. Tues–Sun 10am–5pm (4pm in winter).

Wollaton Hall ★ ☺   This well-preserved Elizabethan mansion on a hill outside the city center offers up gardens and deer-filled parkland, plus a natural history museum and Nottingham's Industrial Museum. The latter is open solely on the last Sunday of each month for "Sunday Steamings," with the chance to see old engines and machinery (including a miniature fairground) in action, to watch a blacksmith at work, and to look around the transport gallery.

About 3 miles west of city center. www.wollatonhall.org.uk. ℂ **0115/915-3900.** Free admission; Sunday Steamings £1 for adults, free to children; car parking £2–4. Hall and museum daily 11am–5pm (4pm in winter); park 8/9am–dusk.

EASTERN NOTTINGHAMSHIRE ★

Beyond Sherwood Forest and the city of Nottingham, the county is low-key, but there are a few gems. The town of Southwell, 15 miles northeast of Nottingham, has an interesting array of historic buildings, plus a literary claim to fame as the place where Lord Byron stayed (in his mother's rented house) during holidays from school and then Cambridge University—though he had by then inherited Newstead Abbey (p. 547), he couldn't afford to make it habitable. Earlier, during the English Civil War, King Charles I spent his last night as a free man in the King's Head (now the Saracen's Head pub), before capitulating to the Scottish army at nearby Kelham. Cromwell may also have stayed in the King's Arms; his troops sequestered the archbishop's palace as stables, contributing to its ruin, and ransacked much of the town.

The market town of **Newark-on-Trent** ★ is also good for a wander, with historic buildings lining its main square, a local-history museum, and a ruined castle holding scenic sway over the River Trent; a heritage center on the grounds of the latter traces this town's role in the English Civil War, when, a major supporter of the Royalist cause, it was besieged three times. But Newark's main draw is its antiques emporia and shops and famous bi-monthly antiques fairs (see "Shopping," below).

All Saint's Church ★   Described as one of the most exciting buildings in all Britain by art and architecture scholar Nikolaus Pevsner, by virtue of the carvings on its Easter Sepulchre and on its sedilia, this medieval church not far from Southwell is worth a detour for fans of ecclesiastical architecture. To date, no one has solved the mystery of why a small village church was endowed with such incredible carvings.

Hawton, south of Newark-on-Trent near border with Lincolnshire. www.farndon-hawton.org.uk. ℂ **01636/704811.** Free admission. By arrangement only.

Southwell Minster ★ This splendid example of Norman and Early English architecture has pyramidal spires of lead unique in Britain. In addition to its stunning interior, you can admire part of a Roman mural from the remains of a large and opulent villa excavated beneath the minster and churchyard in the 1950s.

Church St., Southwell. www.southwellminster.org. ℰ **01636/812649.** Free admission. Daily 7am–7pm.

The Workhouse ★ The most complete workhouse in existence, giving a powerful overview of what life was for the 19th-century poor through its segregated work yards, day rooms, dorms, master's quarters, cellars, and recreated 19th-century garden, which produces fruit and vegetables for the shop. Living History events bring the venue most vividly to life.

Upton Rd., Southwell. www.nationaltrust.org.uk. ℰ **01636/817260.** Admission £6.75 for adults, £3.40 children 5–16. Mar–Oct Wed–Sun noon–5pm.

Where to Eat

VERY EXPENSIVE

Restaurant Sat Bains ★★ MODERN EUROPEAN Nottingham's only Michelin-starred restaurant is named after its TV celebrity chef, born in Derby and with experience of working with Raymond Blanc and at L'Escargot in London. The location—southwest of the center, near an industrial estate and motorway flyover—is uninspiring, but once inside the low-slung building by the River Trent, with its dining room, conservatory, and eight guest rooms set around a courtyard, you'll forget all that as you embark on a journey of culinary revelation. Dinners are tasting menus of 7 or 10 courses, or you can go for broke with a bespoke version. You can also book the Chef's Table to watch Bains at work, including at lunchtime. Locally foraged wild foods are used in abundance here; the menu changes seasonally but might include wild hare with cauliflower, quince, and chocolate; and sea buckthorn tart with marshmallow and pine. **Rooms and suites** start at £129 for a double B&B; packages including a room, a tasting menu, and breakfast start at £135.

Lenton Lane, Nottingham. www.restaurantsatbains.com. ℰ **0115/986-6566.** Reservations required. Fixed-price dinner £75–£95pp. AE, DC, MC, V. Tues–Sat 7–8:30pm, lunch by arrangement.

MODERATE–EXPENSIVE

Launay's ★★★ ☺ 🎁 MODERN EUROPEAN/INTERNATIONAL A few minutes' walk from the Sherwood Forest Visitor Centre (p. 546) and also handy for Center Parcs and Sherwood Forest Cabins (p. 553), this much-lauded restaurant and bar in a 16th-century building overlooks the church where Robin Hood is said to have married Maid Marian. It comes into its own in summer, when you can sit out on the terrace and play boules, allowing you to avoid the somewhat garish interior decor. Seasonal local ingredients go into the English and French dishes tinged with modern global influences—think pan-fried cod cheeks with pickled slaw, sesame oil, pork belly teriyaki, and prawn cracker; or lemon and thyme chicken ravioli. If you have a sweet tooth, leave room for the fun Retro Sweet Shop dessert, including a white chocolate mousse, candy floss (cotton candy), a brownie, a cola cube, and a marshmallow. Dinner takes the form of mix-and-match set menus; lunch is more down-to-earth, with sandwiches, pasta, fish and chips, and the like, plus good children's dishes (£4–£4.95).

Church St., Edwinstowe. www.launaysrestaurant.co.uk. ℰ **01623/822266.** Reservations recommended. Main courses £4.50–£20.95. MC, V. Mon–Sat noon–3pm and 6:30–10pm; Sun noon–4pm.

MODERATE

Nottingham is an excellent place for Indian food; a standout is **The Cumin** at 62–64 Maid Marian Way (www.thecumin.co.uk; ℭ **0115/941-9941**), where the dishes are often inflected by the Punjabi family's background in Kenya.

Ibérico World Tapas ★★ SPANISH/INTERNATIONAL   In a historic building in the heart of Nottingham's history-drenched Lace Market, this runner-up in the prestigious *Observer Food Monthly* Awards 2011 for Best U.K. Restaurant takes you to another world with its Moorish tiles, frescoes, and wrought ironwork. As with all tapas joints, this is the place to share lots of little platters of enticing goodies, both Spanish and more exotic, including the incredible black cod with spicy miso, and the likes of lime, salt, and pepper squid; rabbit saddle; chorizo cooked in cider; or crispy zucchini flowers. You can also get charcuterie and cheese platters. Express lunch deals (Mon–Fri) give you two tapas dishes, Catalan bread, and a dessert for a bargain (£11.95). There are also plenty of bar stools for anyone who just wants to graze while sampling from the interesting list of sherries, or enjoy a churro and hot chocolate or some Spanish ices.

The Shire Hall, High Pavement, Nottingham. www.ibericotapas.com. ℭ**0115/941-0410.** Reservations recommended (dinner). Tapas dishes £3.50–£9.50. MC, V. Mon–Fri noon–2pm and 6–10pm; Sat noon–2pm and 6–10:30pm.

The Wollaton Pub & Kitchen ★ ☺ TRADITIONAL BRITISH   A runner-up in the *Observer Food Monthly's* list of the best Sunday lunches in the U.K. in 2010, this London-style gastropub in west Nottingham continues to hit the spot with its largely traditional cuisine plus the odd surprise dish based on mainly local produce, served from brunch through lunch to afternoon tea and dinner. The famous Sunday lunches, served to 5pm for those who like to take it slow, include traditional roasts but also the likes of pan-fried red bream with sun-blushed tomato mash and spinach. There's also a very good children's menu, available all week, featuring everything from baked beans and cheese on toast to roast chicken with chips and pod vegetables. Service suffers at busy times.

Lambourne Dr., Wollaton, Nottingham. www.thewollaton.co.uk. ℭ**0115/928-8610.** Reservations recommended. Main courses £5–£20.95. MC, V. Mon–Thurs 11am–9pm; Fri 11am–10pm; Sat 10am–10pm; Sun 10am–9pm.

Shopping ★★

Nottingham's long-standing popularity as a shopping destination has been enhanced by the multimillion-pound redevelopment of the vast **Old Market Square**—it's from this huge social space that most of the city's prime shopping streets branch off. Fashion is a specialty—this *is* the hometown of Brit designer par excellence **Paul Smith,** whose original shop remains at 10 Byard Lane (www.paulsmith.co.uk; ℭ **0115/950-6712**). Those who love designer threads and shoes will lose endless hours browsing the area of historic cobbled streets around **Low Pavement** and **Bridlesmith Gate.** For more bohemian fashions, head east from the Square into **Hockley,** where you'll also find everything from contemporary furniture to hip dance-music stores in the shadow of Nottingham's grand former lace mills. There are more quirky independent stores on **Derby Road** and **Maid Marian Way,** also not far from the Square.

For foodie visitors, the **Nottingham Regional & Speciality Food Market** brings the cream of local produce to Old Market Square on the third Friday and Saturday of the month. **Farmers' markets** take place across the county, including Mansfield (third Tues of month), Southwell (third Thurs), and Newark (first Weds). Mansfield also has a 5-day-a-week (Mon and Wed–Sat) open market dating back 700 years, while Newark holds a traditional street market (Wed, Fri, Sat) and antiques, craft, and bric-a-brac markets (Mon and Thurs), in addition to the famous **International Antiques and Collectors Fair** (p. 546).

In the heart of Sherwood Forest near Clumber Park, Welbeck Abbey, home to the Duke and Duchess of Portland, is the site of the **Harley Gallery** (www.harleygallery. co.uk; ✆ **01909/501700**) of crafts workshops in a former kitchen garden, plus the **Notcutts Dukeries Garden Centre** (www.dukeries.co.uk; ✆ **01909/476506**) in the original glasshouses, **Welbeck Farm Shop** (www.thewelbeckfarmshop.co.uk; ✆ **01909/478725**), and the **School of Artisan Food** (www.schoolofartisanfood. org; ✆ **01909/532171**) in the former estate gasworks. The Farm Shop sells Stichelton, the first organic raw-milk blue cheese produced in Britain since the late 1960s (Stilton is now required to be pasteurized).

Entertainment & Nightlife ★

Don't miss a real ale in Nottingham's famed **Ye Olde Trip to Jerusalem** in Brewhouse Yard (www.triptojerusalem.com; ✆ **0115/947-3171**), built into the rockface and dating from 1189—which is said to make it the oldest inn in all England.

Otherwise, Nottingham's large student population keeps it buzzing, with the Old Market Square the meeting place for revelers setting out to discover the city's famous nightlife, especially the hip **Lace Market and Hockley** neighborhood, where late-night bars line cobbled streets. The recently developed canalside **Castle Wharf** houses a Jongleurs comedy club as well as lots of bars and restaurants in its former warehouses. Gay residents and visitors are well catered for with lots of gay and gay-friendly bars and clubs and other venues. For events listings, pick up a free copy of **Left Lion** magazine from selected venues, or see www.leftlion.co.uk.

Where to Stay

For rooms at **Restaurant Sat Bains** in Nottingham, see p. 550. There's a modern, purpose-built **Sherwood Forest Youth Hostel** (www.yha.org.uk; **0845/371-9139**) at Edwinstowe, or for camping there's no better spot than the new **campsite at Clumber Park** (p. 547), with camping pods and wigwams for up to five, a yurt for up to four, plus spaces for those with their own tents. With children, try **Readyfields Farm** (part of the Feather Down Farm group that also includes Dolphinholme in Lancashire; p. 594); this mixed farm allows guests staying in its upmarket tents to play with the bloodhound puppies, help bottlefeed the calves, and watch sheep-shearing in summertime.

Center Parcs Sherwood Forest ★★ ☺ Primarily of interest to families, this holiday village is one of four such in the U.K. (others are in Suffolk, Wiltshire, and the Lake District; a fifth is in the pipeline in Bedfordshire), all of them offering an indoor waterpark, a superb spa, and indoor and outdoor activities galore. This one in the home of Robin is a particularly apt place to learn archery, with sessions starting for youngsters as young as 3 (see p. 546), but it also distinguishes itself by offering accommodation in two-story, four-bedroom treehouses, which come complete with an infrared physiotherm sauna room, a balcony hot tub, a games den with a pool table, and daily maid service. Otherwise, there's a wide range of self-catering accommodation on-site to suit various budgets, all with open fires (logs can be bought in the shop), plus a good choice of eateries, from a Dutch pancake house to an Indian restaurant.

Rufford, NG22 9DN. www.centerparcs.co.uk. ✆ **0844/826-7723.** 786 units. 1-bedroom Comfort Villas from £289, 4–bedroom treehouses from £2199 for 3-night weekend stay according to time of year. MC, V. Free parking. **Amenities:** Restaurants, cafes, and bars; shops; bike hire including children's bikes and trailers; indoor and outdoor activities (extra charge for some); children's club (extra charge). *In room:* TV, DVD/CD player (some), kitchen (some with dishwasher), hairdryer, outdoor hot tub (some), sauna (some), steam room (some), games room (some), iPod docking stations (some), Wi-Fi (some).

Sherwood Forest Cabins ★★ 🎁

Set within Sherwood Pines Forest Park (p. 548), this latest Forest Holidays site (there are others in Cornwall, Gloucestershire, Yorkshire, and Scotland) offers several grades of luxurious wooden cabins with 1–5 bedrooms, with the largest featuring a bedroom within a treehouse extension for added "back to nature" cachet. These latter and certain other cabins also have their own outdoor hot tub, and some also have a wood-burning stove for extra cosiness. But it's really all about the surrounding forest with its cycle trails, woodland walks, and children's play areas; there are also a variety of ranger-led activities and walks plus the chance to try out archery (where better than the legendary home of Robin Hood himself?). Breaks can be 3 nights (weekends), 4 nights (weekdays), or whole weeks.

Edwinstowe, NG21 9JL. www.forestholidays.co.uk. ✆ **0845/130-8223.** 65 units. 1-bedroom cabin £251–801, 5-bedroom treehouse cabin £571–1849, for a 3-night weekend stay, according to time of year. MC, V. Free parking. **Amenities:** Grocery and coffee shop; launderette; mountainbike hire including children's trailers; organized walks and activities. *In room:* TV (with films, music, Wi-Fi and Internet at extra charge), DVD player (some), kitchen, Wii games console (some), outdoor hot tub (some), wood-burning stove (some).

Willoughby House ★★ 🍴

By virtue of its antiques market (p. 546), Newark and its surroundings are chockfull of delightful B&Bs of a standard you'd be hard pressed to find elsewhere. This lovingly run little spot in a handsome Georgian village house 4 miles north of the town mixes a certain modern boutique chic with quirky antique touches to give it a wholly individual feel; unlike many B&Bs, it's also child-friendly, with a family suite. The wonderful breakfast of local fare is served on beautiful china in a cosy dining room with a roaring fire on chilly mornings. Little treats such as homemade flapjacks, bathrobes, and a complimentary DVD selection also set the place apart, although other excellent options in the vicinity include **Bridge House B&B** (www.arnoldsbandb.co.uk; ✆ **01636/674663**) and **The Hollies** (www.theholliesnewark.co.uk; ✆ **01636/676533**).

Main St., Norwell, NG23 6JN. www.willoughbyhousebandb.co.uk. ✆ **01636/636266.** 4 units. £85–£95 double. AE, MC, V. Free parking. **Amenities:** Lounge; evening meals by arrangement. *In room:* TV, hair dryer, Wi-Fi (free).

LEICESTERSHIRE & RUTLAND

Leicester: 100 miles N of London

In the south of the East Midlands region, industrialized **Leicester** (pronounced *Lester*) combines a vibrant multiethnic cultural scene and modern museums with a rich history, while surrounding **Leicestershire** harbors more historic sites, including one

This ancient city 20 miles northeast of Newark was the site of a Bronze Age settlement, then, in the 3rd century, one of four provincial capitals of Roman Britain. In the Middle Ages, it was the center of Lindsey, a famous Anglo-Saxon kingdom. After the Norman conquest, it grew increasingly important, its merchants becoming rich by shipping wool directly to Flanders.

Much of the past lives on here, in the form of medieval streets, half-timbered Tudor houses, the Norman **castle** (www.lincolnshire.gov.uk; ℂ **01522/511068**), and, best of all, magnificent **Lincoln Cathedral ★★★** (www.lincolncathedral.com; ℂ **01522/561600**), which dominates its surroundings like no other English minster, with a central tower 81-m (271-ft.) high and visible from up to 30 miles away. Construction on the original Norman cathedral began in 1072, but the present cathedral is Gothic in style, particularly the Early English and Decorated periods. Virtually in its shadow, the ruined **Lincoln Medieval Bishops' Palace,** Minster Yard (www.english-heritage.org.uk; ℂ **01522/527468**), was the site of the biggest diocese in England in the Middle Ages.

Also worth a wander are the **Museum of Lincolnshire Life,** Burton Road (www.lincolnshire.gov.uk; ℂ **01522/528448**) and **The Collection and Usher Gallery,** Danes Terrace (www.thecollectionlincoln.org; ℂ **01522/550990**), with paintings, antique clocks, ceramics, literary mementos—including portraits of Lincolnshire-born Alfred Lord Tennyson—and a new play activity center for youngsters.

The best place to stop-over in Lincoln is The Castle Hotel on Westgate (www.castlehotel.net; ℂ **01522/538801**), with doubles from £120 B&B. For eating out, try brunch or lunch at **The Cheese Society,** 1 St. Martin's Lane (www.thecheesesociety.co.uk; ℂ **01522/511003;** no bookings or children under 10), serving breakfasts from 10 to 11:30am and lunch until 3:30pm, and featuring the likes of Lincolnshire Poacher cheese and spring onion and chive pâté. In the evening, **The Jews House Restaurant,** 15 The Strait (www.jewshouserestaurant.co.uk; ℂ **01522/524851**), set in one of the city's most historic buildings, is popular for its inventive Modern European cuisine (sample dish: truffle potato and egg yolk ravioli, artichoke, and pea shoots). The **Wig and Mitre pub,** 30–32 Steep Hill (www.wigandmitre.com; ℂ **01522/535190**), is an atmospheric spot for eating and drinking, including with children.

On the coast 35 miles southeast of Lincoln, **Boston** has a Pilgrim Fathers Memorial dedicated to those who emigrated from here, often to found other settlements of the same name, most notably in Massachusetts.

of England's most important battlefields. At its north, Leicestershire links with Derbyshire and Staffordshire by means of the **National Forest,** which, though only a "forest in the making," conceals many attractions. Leicestershire once included adjoining **Rutland,** a great place for outdoors activities focused around its reservoir. A jaunt to the south, into Northamptonshire, takes you to **Althorp,** resting place of Princess Diana.

Essentials

GETTING THERE Frequent trains from London's St. Pancras to Leicester take just over 1 hour, costing around £78 for a round-trip off-peak; there you can change to a train to Melton Mowbray (15 min.). From St. Pancras or King's Cross to Oakham takes a little under 2 hours, with a change at Leicester or Peterborough in Cambridgeshire.

Leicester is just off the M1, 100 miles (2 hr.) north of London, with Melton Mowbray 17 miles farther northeast on the A607. Oakham is 25 miles (45 min.) east of Leicester off the main A47. **National Express** buses (www.nationalexpress.com; ✆ **0871/781-8181**) from London's Victoria Coach Station to Leicester take from 2¼ hours.

The M1 between junctions 21 and 23 crosses the eastern edge of the National Forest near Leicester. Train stations useful to access the National Forest are Leicester and Loughborough in Leicestershire; Derby and Willington in Derbyshire; and Tamworth, Burton on Trent, Lichfield, and Tutbury & Hatton in Staffordshire. For local buses, see www.traveline.org.uk.

VISITOR INFORMATION   **Leicester Tourist Information Centre:** 7–9 Every St., Town Hall Square (www.goleicestershire.com; ✆ **0844/888-5181**).

Rutland Water Tourist Information Centre: Sykes Lane, Empingham (www.discover-rutland.co.uk; ✆ **01780 686800**).

SPECIAL EVENTS   The globally acclaimed **Leicester Early Music Festival** (www.earlymusicleicester.co.uk) is now an all-year event, but music devotees should come in September, when the city also hosts the **Leicester International Music Festival** (www.leicesterinternationalmusicfestival.org.uk) featuring some big names in classical music.

There's south Asian music, plus dance, food, and more at the **Leicester Belgrave Mela** (www.leicester-mela.co.uk) each July, while Diwali celebrations in the city are among the largest outside India itself.

October sees food-lovers converge on Melton Mowbray for the **East Midlands Food & Drink Festival** (www.eastmidlandsfoodfestival.co.uk).

Exploring the Area

LEICESTER & LEICESTERSHIRE ★

Leicester may be off the tourist trail but it lays claim to being one of England's 10 biggest cities, one of its most ethnically diverse, and also one of its oldest, founded by the Romans as Ratae Coritanorum in A.D. 50. Roman ruins are now among its main draws, although there are various other compelling historical remnants plus some superb modern attractions to be enjoyed. Similarly, Leicestershire as a whole may not be a visitor hotspot but is dotted with low-key but interesting sights that make it well worth exploration—many of them in the nascent National Forest (see p. 557)—and also offers up the foodie hub of **Melton Mowbray** (also home to the small theme-park **Twin Lakes** (www.twinlakespark.co.uk; ✆ **01664/567777**).

Abbey Park ★ ☺   A 15-minute walk north of the center, this park holds the evocative remains of the richest Augustinian monastery in England, built in 1132. It was at this abbey that, in 1530, Cardinal Wolsey died, demoralized and broken after his conflicts with Henry VIII. The park also has a mini-railway, pets' corner, boating lake, lavender maze, and a state-of-the-art playground that was opened by local hero, soccer player Gary Lineker.

Abbey Park Rd., Leicester. www.leicester.gov.uk. ✆ **0116/252-7003.** Free admission. Daily dawn–dusk.

STAY, play & EXPLORE ★

Those discovering Leicestershire with children can take advantage of an ongoing short break offering that gives admission to three of the country's top family attractions and overnight accommodations starting at a superb-value £109 for four people. Choose from the National Space Centre, Snibston, Bosworth Battlefield Heritage Centre and Country Park, Conkers, and Twycross Zoo (for all, see below); accommodations options are the Marriott Leicester, the Hilton Leicester, the Barcéló Hinckley Island, and the Holiday Inn Leicester City, all of them with swimming pools. See www.gole icestershire.com/short-breaks/Stayplay explore.aspx for more details. Family Adventure breaks are also available.

Abbey Pumping Station, Leicester's Museum of Science & Technology

★ ☺ Continuing the scientific theme of the neighboring National Space Centre (see below), this imposing red-brick Victorian building, originally a sewage pumping station of all things, now harbors displays on light and optics, historic transport, and public health, plus restored pump engines that can be seen in action on Steam Days.

Corporation Rd., Leicester. www.leicester.gov.uk. ✆ **0116/299-5111.** Free admission exc special events/activities. Feb–Oct daily 11am–4:30pm.

Belvoir Castle ★★ ☺ CASTLE On Leicestershire's border with Lincolnshire, this seat of the dukes of Rutland since the time of Henry VII, rebuilt by Wyatt in 1816, contains paintings by Holbein, Reynolds, and Gainsborough, as well as tapestries in its staterooms. The location for the movies *Little Lord Fauntleroy* and *Young Sherlock Holmes*, it hosts medieval jousting tournaments in summer, plus, on selected weekends, "historical cameos" performed by its costumed guides about local events such as the trial of the Belvoir Witches. For children there's a quiz and treasure trail, an Old Nursery and School Room where they can play as youngsters did in Regency times, plus gardens and woodlands.

Belvoir, 36 miles northeast of Leicester. www.belvoircastle.com. ✆ **01476/871002.** Admission castle and gardens £15, £8 children 5–16. May–Aug Mon and Sun; gardens 11am–5pm; castle by guided tour at 11:15am, 1:15pm, and 3:15pm.

Bosworth Battlefield Heritage Centre & Country Park ★★ HISTORIC

SITE This site in West Leicestershire commemorates the 1485 battle that ended one of England's most important conflicts, the War of the Roses between the houses of York and Lancaster. When the fighting subsided, King Richard III, last of the Yorkists, lay dead, and Henry Tudor, a Welsh nobleman banished to France to thwart his royal ambition, was proclaimed victor. Henry became King Henry VII, and the Tudor dynasty was born. The site has been improved in recent years by the addition of a gallery about how archeologists discovered the true location of the battle, with displays including bullets fired by early handguns, and an outdoor interpretation trail. Events include guided walks, falconry displays, ferret racing, re-enactments, and a medieval camp.

Sutton Cheney, 13 miles west of Leicester. www.bosworthbattlefield.com. ✆ **01455/290429.** Admission £7 adults, £4 children 3–16. Heritage center daily Apr–Oct 10am–5pm; Nov–Dec and Feb–Mar to 4pm. Country park daily Apr–Sept 8:30am–5:30pm; Oct–Mar to 4:40pm.

Great Central Railway ★★ ☺ This is the U.K.'s only double-track mainline heritage railway and the only place in the world where full-size steam engines can be seen passing each other. It's worth timing your visit to coincide with one of the special

The National Forest ★★

This "forest in the making" (www.nationalforest.org) was established in 1990 to convert a 200-sq.-mile area of Leicestershire, Derbyshire, and Staffordshire into woodland, and in doing so create forestry and tourism jobs. Linking the ancient forests of Needwood in Staffordshire and Charnwood in Leicestershire, it stretches west from the outskirts of Leicester to Burton upon Trent and beyond.

Though it's still far from a true forest, the 20 million trees slated to be planted over the next 30 to 40 years will cover a third of the area, with the rest given over to farmland, villages, and open land. But it's already a great place to visit, especially with youngsters. The focal point is **Conkers ★** (near Swadlincote in south Derbyshire; www.visitconkers.com; ℂ 01283/216633), where indoor and outdoor zones and activities include an adventure playground, woodland discovery center, and Enchanted Forest with a simulated treetop walk and rope walkways. It's open daily 10am to 6pm (5pm in winter), and admission is £8.50 for adults, £6.95 for children 3 to 15. Also near Swadlincote, the **Rosliston Forestry Centre ★★** (www.roslistonforestrycentre.co.uk; ℂ 01283/563483) is another hive of activity, including off-road cycling trails (the National Forest Cycling Centre, opened here in 2011, offers rental), birds-of-prey sessions, archery, laser games, astronomy walks, and woodland playgrounds. The site is free to enter; activities vary in price. You can stay in lodges on-site or camp nearby at **Beehive Woodland Lakes** (www.beehive farm-woodlandlakes.co.uk; ℂ 01283/763981). (For the YHA National Forest youth hostel, see p. 545.)

To the east, in Coalville in Leicestershire, **Snibston Discovery Museum ★** (www.leics.gov.uk/snibston_museum; ℂ 01530/278444) is a former mine with an interactive museum in the former colliery buildings, a historic mining railway, and a country park and nature reserve with trails and play areas (museum open Apr–Oct daily 10am–5pm; Nov–Mar Mon–Fri 10am–3pm, Sat, Sun, and school holidays 10am–5pm, with some variations over Christmas and New Year and in the first half of Jan). Admission is £6.95, £4.75 children 3 to 15; colliery tours and train rides are extra.

The National Forest embraces the western part of **Charnwood Forest,** with its craggy landscape dotted with volcanic rocks. A popular walk is to the summit of **Bardon Hill**—at 278m (918 ft.) Leicestershire's highest point. But Charnwood's highlight is **Bradgate Park & Swithland Wood Country Park ★**, Newton Linford (ℂ 0116/236-2713), a medieval deer park with the ruins of Bradgate House, home to Lady Jane Grey, queen for 9 days before being beheaded in 1554, and an 18th-century hilltop folly, Old John Tower. The park is free to enter, dawn to dusk.

Other attractions within or on the fringes of the Forest include **Twycross Zoo** (www.twycrosszoo.com; ℂ 0844/474-1777), **Ashby de la Zouch Castle** (www.english-heritage.org.uk; ℂ 01530/413343), the **National Forest Adventure Farm** with its summer Maize Maze (www.adventurefarm.co.uk; ℂ 01283/533933), and even **llama-trekking** at Burton-on-Trent in Staffordshire (www.nationalforestllamatreks.co.uk; ℂ 01283/711702).

If you're in the East Midlands in high summer, you might make a foray into Northamptonshire, specifically **Althorp** (www.althorp.com; ℰ **01604/770107**), 32 miles south of Leicester. After her death in 1997, Princess Diana was brought to this, her childhood home, to be buried on an island in an artificial lake, which visitors can glimpse but not access. What you can do is tour an exhibition, in former stables, celebrating Diana's life through displays including her bridal gown and items relating to her charity work, and also look around the house, with paintings by Van Dyck, Reynolds, Gainsborough, and Rubens. You'll also see rare French and English furniture and porcelain by Sèvres and others. Admission is £15.50 (£6 children 5–17). It's open only from July 1 (Diana's birthday) to August 30, daily from 11am to 5pm.

events, which include a Drive a Train Experience for children and Santa trains. You can also dine aboard (in First Class).

Great Central Rd., Loughborough, 12 miles north of Leicester. www.gcrailway.co.uk. ℰ **01509/230726.** Prices vary by event; All Line Day Runabout on non-event days £14 for adults, £9 children 5–15. Trains run weekends and public holidays, and daily in summer (see website for timetable).

Jewry Wall Museum ★★ ☺ MUSEUM   Set beside an excavated Roman baths with a wall that, at 12m (40 ft.), is higher than any other piece of ancient Roman architecture in Britain, this museum about a 10-minute walk from the city center offers up some fine Roman mosaics and rare wall plaster, intricately painted. Also tracing the city's history from prehistoric times to the Middle Ages, it has plenty of hands-on displays for younger visitors.

St. Nicholas Circle, Leicester. www.leicester.gov.uk. ℰ **0116/225-4971.** Free admission exc certain activities on event days. Daily Feb–Oct 11am–4:30pm.

Leicester Cathedral   Unusual oak vaulting beneath the north porch is a highlight of this building, which began life as a Norman church and became a cathedral in 1927. Look out too for the memorial slab for King Richard III and the fine bishop's throne carved with an image of St. Martin on horseback.

7 Peacock Lane, Leicester. www.cathedral.leicester.anglican.org. ℰ **0116/261-5200.** Free admission. Mon–Sat 8am–6pm; Sun 7am–5pm.

National Space Centre ★★ ☺ ENTERTAINMENT COMPLEX   Rising incongruously out of the Midlands townscape 2 miles north of the city center (take First Bus 54), the futuristic rocket tower that comprises part of this modern attraction showcases a number of satellites, capsules, and so on, and also has several mezzanine galleries with displays, interactive and otherwise. The rest of the building includes a domed Space Theatre with changing surround-sound shows. Look out too for occasional Live Stargazing nights hosted by the local astronomical society. You save money on entry if you visit as part of a Stay Play Explore (www.stayplayexplore.co.uk) package (p. 556).

Exploration Drive, Leicester. www.spacecentre.co.uk. ℰ **0116/261-0261.** Admission £13 adults, £11 children 5–16. Tues–Fri 10am–4pm; Sat–Sun 10am–5pm (see website for closed dates).

New Walk Museum & Art Gallery ★ MUSEUM   Displays on archeology, natural history, geology, and space coexist here with a collection of 18th–20th-century paintings by British and European artists including Gainsborough, Hogarth, and Francis Bacon. Highlights are the Egyptian mummies and artifacts brought back to the Midlands by Thomas Cook, the 19th-century travel mogul, and *Charnia masonia*, discovered in Charnwood Forest (p. 557) and, at about 560 million years of age, the U.K.'s oldest fossil.

53 New Walk, Leicester. www.leicester.gov.uk. ✆ **0116/225-4900.** Free admission exc certain activities on event days. Mon–Sat 10am–5pm; Sun 11am–5pm.

RUTLAND ★★

Due south of Belvoir lies the U.K.'s smallest historic county (briefly absorbed by Leicestershire from 1974 to 1994). Home to just two towns, the county town of Oakham (known for its antiques shops) and market town of Uppingham, it finds its focus at western Europe's largest man-made reservoir, Rutland Water.

Oakham Castle This structure survives solely in the form of its splendid great hall of 1180–90, which contains a collection of ceremonial horseshoes, some of them outsize, that had to be left as forfeits, according to an old custom, by royalty and peers passing through. They're hung upside-down—in Rutland, this is said to stop the devil from sitting in the shoe's hollow (the motif also appears in the local coat of arms).

Castle Lane, Oakham. www.rutland.gov.uk/castle. ✆ **01572/722577.** Free admission. Mon and Wed–Sat 10am–4pm.

Rutland Country Museum & Visitor Centre ☺ This small local museum houses thought-provoking displays on local history, archeology, and rural life plus a family corner and regular family activities, a program of live performances and film screenings, and a visitor information area.

Catmos St., Oakham. www.rutland.gov.uk/museum. ✆ **01572 758440.** Free admission. Mon, Wed, Fri, and Sat 10am–4pm.

Rutland Falconry & Owl Centre This idyllic spot is the place to come to witness birds of prey in flight, but bring binoculars and you might also catch a glimpse of fallow deer, muntjac, foxes, badgers, and other mammals.

Burley Bushes, Exton. www.rutland-falconry.com. ✆ **07778/152814.** Admission £5, £3.50 children 5–16. Daily 10am–late (to 4pm in winter).

Rutland Water Park ★★★ As well as being a prime spot for watersports and cruising on the man-made reservoir itself, this vast area of open countryside also offers the opportunity for biking (rentals available), walking, climbing, fishing, outdoor adventure (wall-climbing and high ropes), and getting up close and personal with wildlife on the nature reserve. There's a museum within the half-submerged **Normanton Church** (✆ **01780/686800**) on the south shore, with prehistoric remains and an Anglo-Saxon skeleton as well as an exhibition on the development of the reservoir.

For visitor center, see p. 555. Free admission (charges for some sites and activities); 4 main car parks, charging £2/3/day. Daily, but most attractions and activities Easter–October only.

Where to Eat

VERY EXPENSIVE

For Stapleford Park and Hambleton Hall, see "Where to Stay," below.

The Grey Lady ★ MODERN EUROPEAN Not everyone is won over by the modern decor at this restaurant in a beautiful setting overlooking Bradgate Park

(p. 557). Prices can be on the high side, too, though lunch is a good deal Monday through Saturday (£12.50 for two courses, £16.50 for three), and might include pea, asparagus, and broad bean risotto with Parmesan tuile. You can also get nibbles and finger-food including flatbreads. Dinner is a little more elaborate. Sunday lunches (with children's portions and pricing) are popular with families enjoying the great outdoors nearby.

If it's full, the nearby **The Village** (www.thevillagerestaurantnewtownlinford. co.uk; © **01530/245801**) was started by the same family.

Sharpley Hill, Newtown Linford. www.the-grey-lady.co.uk. © **01530/243558.** Reservations recommended. Main courses £12–£24. MC, V. Daily noon–3pm (3:30pm Sun) and 5:30–9:30pm.

EXPENSIVE

Maiyango ★★ INTERNATIONAL   Leicester's only boutique hotel is best visited for its restaurant, which will whisk you away with its exotic decor, soundtrack of world beats, "gastronomic" cocktails (Black Forest Gateau cocktail, for example!), and dishes influenced by the chef's travels (though most of the produce comes from community allotments, farms, and other ultralocal suppliers). Many dishes lean firmly toward the East: green tea and pickled ginger cured organically reared salmon with pickled fennel, wasabi crème fraîche, and chargrilled focaccia, for instance. Lunch features a slightly reduced version of the same menu at about £10 less per head. Book one of the booths for a romantic experience. Alternatively, 2011 saw the opening of the **Maiyango Kitchen Deli** just around the corner on Highcross Street, where you can eat in (breakfast, lunch, or afternoon cake and treats) or grab some restaurant-standard prepared meals and gifts to take home with you (or have delivered). Cookery and cocktail-making lessons are also available.

The 13 **guest rooms** and one suite (from £99, including breakfast) have Asian inflected decor and some have super-king beds.

13–21 St. Nicholas Place, Leicester. www.maiyango.com. © **0116/251-8898.** Reservations recommended. Dinner £29 for 3 courses. MC, V. Mon–Tues 6–11pm; Wed 12:30–11:30pm; Thurs 12:30–midnight; Fri 12:30pm–1am; Sat 12:30pm–1:30am; and Sun 6:30–10:30pm.

MODERATE

Boboli ★★ ☺ ITALIAN   Though somewhat off the beaten track as far as any tourist attractions are concerned, this casual all-day eatery in a large village in south Leicestershire is worth the detour for convivial family meals done Italian style—especially a Sunday lunch, when traditional English roasts feature alongside tempting Tuscan fare such as pea and proscuitto risotto. Children 11 and under get Sunday lunch for half price, or they can choose from the Boboli Bambini menu (£7.50 for two courses, until 8pm) or even get smaller portions from the main menu. Outside of main mealtimes, there's a snack menu of *piadine* (flat pizza sandwiches), veal burgers, and pastries. The same owners run the more formal and pricier (and more adult) **Firenze** (http://firenze.co.uk; © **0116/279-6260**) in the same village.

88 Main St., Kibworth. www.bobolirestaurant.co.uk. © **0116/279-3303.** Reservations recommended (dinner). Main courses £4.50–£19.75. MC, V. Tues–Sat 10am–10pm; Sun 10am–4pm.

Olive Branch ★★ ☺ PUB FOOD/MODERN BRITISH   Rustic charm abounds at this traditional inn in a pretty Rutland village, renovated to its former glory with the aid of local restorers and cabinet makers. In winter you can sit around open fires (scented with roasting chestnuts) and drink sloe gin, damson vodka, and mulled wine made with berries from surrounding hedgerows, perhaps accompanied by a tapas board for two. In summer, enjoy barbecues in the garden accompanied by homemade lemonade, Pimms, and strawberry vodka. Despite the informal vibe, it has held a Michelin star for the last decade. Local ingredients including game and orchard fruits star in salads, sandwiches, and soups, pub classics, and more formal dishes—everything from fish and chips to seared scallops with quince purée and roast salsify. Even at dinner, the menu is set up so that those dining together can eat as their appetite, mood, and budget dictates; children get a well-priced menu, too (£6.95 for two courses).

You can stay over in one of six gorgeous **guest rooms and suites** (from £115 double, including breakfast) in **Beech House,** on the opposite side of the street; one room is set up for families. The same folks run the equally charming **Red Lion Inn** at Stathern near Belvoir Castle (see p. 305).

Main St., Clipsham. www.theolivebranchpub.com. ✆ **01780/410355.** Reservations recommended. Main courses £5.50–£25. MC, V. Mon–Fri noon–2pm and 7–9:30pm; Sat noon–2pm, 2:30–5pm, and 7–9:30pm; Sun noon–3pm and 7–9pm.

INEXPENSIVE

Leicester's hub for Indian restaurants is Belgrave Road; try longstanding vegetarian **Bobby's,** 154–156 Belgrave Rd. (www.eatatbobbys.com; ✆ **0116/266-0106**), or the award-winning **Curry Fever,** 139 Belgrave Rd., (www.thecurryfever.co.uk; ✆ **0116/266-2941**).

Shivalli ★ 🍴 INDIAN   The "Village Vegetarian" is actually on a busy main road in the center of Leicester; the village in question is in Karnataka in southern India, famous for its *idli* (savory cakes), *vada* (savory donuts), *dosa* (crispy pancakes), and *upma* (a semolina dish), served on plantain leaves and eaten by hand. Like most Indian restaurants, Shivalli has its occasional detractor, but most diners are more than satisfied by the likes of *rasam* (spicy tomato) soup, *rava masala dosa* (with chilis, coconut, cumin, potato, onions, and peas), and fluffy, fried *bathura* breads, all served at prices that seem almost obscenely low, especially for the lunchtime buffets.

21 Welford Rd., Leicester. www.shivallirestaurant.com. ✆ **0116/255-0137.** Reservations recommended. Main courses with rice £5.75–£9.50. MC, V. Mon–Fri noon–3pm and 6–11pm; Sat noon–11pm; Sun noon–10pm.

Shopping

If not exactly a shopping mecca, Leicester has a respectable array of big-name department stores, mostly within **Highcross** (www.highcrossleicester.com), formerly known as The Shires. **St. Martins Square** (www.martinssquare.com) is a pleasant enclave of restored buildings housing interesting smaller shops including **Just… Fairtrade,** 36 Silver St. (www.justfairtrade.com; ✆ 0116/253-8032). **Belgrave Road,** running north out of the center, is home to the **Golden Mile,** named for its jewelry shops but also rich in stores offering fine Indian fabrics and saris.

In Melton Mowbray, **Ye Olde Pork Pie Shoppe,** 10 Nottingham St. (www.porkpie.co.uk; ✆ **01664/482068**), sells the town's famous pork pies as well as local meats, cheeses, chutneys, and preserves, and Melton Hunt (fruit) cake. Nearby, at 8 Windsor St., **The Melton Cheeseboard** (www.meltoncheeseboard.co.uk; ✆ **01664/562257**) can't be beat for its local Stilton (produced by only six dairies in Leicestershire, Nottinghamshire, and Derbyshire) and Red Leicester. At nearby

Eastwell, **Crossroads Farm Shop** (✆ 01949/860242), housed in a 17th-century building with a museum of farm memorabilia, offers home-produced vegetables, meat, eggs, and cakes, and local jams and cordials.

In Rutland, Oakham is a hotspot for antiques; try **Swans,** 17 Mill St. (www. antiquefrenchbeds.co.uk; ✆ 01572/724364), and **Chedwich Antiques,** 31a Pillings Rd. (www.chedwichantiquebeds.co.uk; ✆ 01572/722952). On Wednesdays and Saturdays, Oakham also holds an open-air **market** in its main square. Its farmers' market takes place the 3rd Saturday of the month; in Uppingham, it's the 2nd Friday of the month.

Entertainment & Nightlife

Leicester's new **Cultural Quarter** (http://cqart.leicester.gov.uk) includes **Phoenix Square,** Midland Street (www.phoenix.org.uk; ✆ 0116/242-2800), showcasing film and digital media, and the **Curve Theatre,** Rutland Street (www.curveonline. co.uk; ✆ 0116/242-3595), for plays, comedy, and family shows. Otherwise, Leicester is a lively enough city for nightlife, partly by virtue of its large student population. For events, see http://whatson.oneleicester.com, or pick up flyers in record stores and boutiques.

Where to Stay

For **Beech House** (part of the Olive Branch restaurants) in Rutland, see p. 560. For **Maiyango** in Leicester, see p. 560. For the **YHA National Forest,** just inside Derbyshire, see p. 545. And for hotels involved in the Stay, Play, Explore family short-break package, see p. 556.

The Dandelion Hideaway ★★ 🎁 ☺   Since spring 2011, lovely Osbaston House Farm (mainly dairy goats) on the fringes of the National Forest less than 3 miles from Bosworth Battlefield (bang on the Leicestershire border with Warwickshire) offers family fun with a vintage country-chic twist in five canvas "cottages," all with fabulous countryside views. Included in a break here are child-oriented tours of the premises by the farmer and youngsters get the chance to milk goats and to groom ponies. Some guest families are also designated as keepers of the hen coop for their stay (everyone can help themselves to freshly laid eggs). The electricity-free, tent-like structures have wood-burning stoves (wood is included in the price for this and for campfire), old-fashioned "slipper" baths, and for entertainment an explorer's trunk with binoculars for spotting rabbits, hares, buzzards, badgers, and perhaps even barn owls (there's an on-site nature hide), I-spy books to help you identify insects, birds, and trees, a magnifying glass, and classic card and board games. Each sleeps up to six in two regular bedrooms and a secret wooden cabin within the cottage, much loved by children. For couples, the opulent Bluebell has been added in a more secluded part of the farm, complete with sleigh bed, a tandem to explore the countryside, and a breakfast basket and bottle of sparkling wine.

Lount Rd., Osbaston, Nuneaton, Warwickshire CV13 0HR. www.thedandelionhideaway.co.uk. ✆ 01455/291291. 5 units. £296–£589 3-night weekend stay, £241–£539 4-night midweek stay, £436–£846 1-week stay. MC, V. **Amenities:** Honesty shop and library area; farm tours. *In room:* kitchen, BBQ, games and activities chest, baby equipment.

Hambleton Hall ★★   A member of the prestigious French Relais & Châteaux group, this is one of the finest country-house hotels in England, with spectacular views over Rutland Water and an intimate vibe, with the emphasis on comfort and good food. Some rooms may be a little chintzy for the modern-hotel lover's taste, so study the website. For families, the Croquet Pavilion suite has a double and a twin on two levels, and sitting and breakfast rooms. The fine-dining **restaurant** offers the likes of wild garlic panacotta with radish, parmesan, and hazelnuts; and simply roast guinea fowl with Israeli couscous flavored with nettles, (about £35 for a main course; set menus at lunch and dinner make things considerably more affordable).

Hambleton, Rutland LE15 8TH. www.hambletonhall.com. © **01572/756991.** 16 units. £245–£415 double. Rates include full English breakfast. AE, DC, MC, V. Free parking. Minimum 2-night stay at weekends. **Amenities:** Restaurant; lounge; heated outdoor pool; croquet; room service, Wi-Fi (free). *In room:* TV, hair dryer.

THE NORTHWEST

by Rhonda Carrier

World-class cities within easy reach of wonderful, unspoiled countryside make the often-neglected northwest of England a must-see for those who really want to get to know modern Britain. The star turns are Manchester and Liverpool, reasserting themselves after decades in the doldrums while remaining firmly rooted in their industrial heritage; but there's rich history elsewhere too, including Chester with its Roman amphitheatre, Lancaster with its witchhunter's castle, and even tacky Blackpool. There's also wildlife in the open spaces of Cheshire and Lancashire, plus seaside fun, unexpectedly good beaches, and traditional resorts.

15

CITIES & TOWNS   It may not be Britain's prettiest landscape, but the 21st-century revival of **Manchester's Salford Quays,** new home to much of the BBC, makes for a fascinating case study in urban regeneration—especially when contrasted with historical depictions of the area in the world-famous paintings of L. S. Lowry, many of them displayed in the state-of-the-art cultural center named after him.

COUNTRYSIDE   The narrow, steep-sided valley of the **Trough of Bowland** remains a bit of a hidden gem for walkers and cyclists—compared with the more touristy Lake District and Yorkshire Dales—with winding paths, blissful picnic spots, and a wild boar park, where children can enjoy animal encounters and woodland walks.

EATING & DRINKING   Eating out is a serious business all over the northwest, but **Lancashire's Ribble Valley Food Trail** showcases the region's finest local produce within an Area of Outstanding Natural Beauty.

COAST   Antony Gormley's *Another Place* raises the status of **Crosby,** north of Liverpool, from unremarkable seaside town to globally significant art site, with its beach studded with 100 cast-iron statues of the sculptor's own body, faces turned to the horizon in silent expectation.

THE best TRAVEL EXPERIENCES IN THE NORTHWEST

- **Discovering Manchester's industrial heritage:** In England's second most popular city, explore the outstanding Museum of Science and Industry but also the buildings and the artifacts of industry embedded in the very fabric of the city. See p. 566.
- **Witnessing the lightning-paced transformation of Liverpool:** See how this once-great maritime city is rapidly shaking off the effects of its late 20th-century decline, not least in the new-in-2011 Museum of Liverpool. See p. 583.
- **Walking Chester Walls:** A tour of Britain's most complete city walls can be combined with a gander at the remains of its largest Roman amphitheatre and the world-famous collection of Roman tombstones in the Grosvenor Museum. See p. 578.

- **Experiencing surreal Formby:** Cross the otherworldly sand dunes and pine woods with their rare red squirrel and natterjack toad populations to reach the beach with its Neolithic/early Bronze Age footprints of humans and animals. See p. 590.
- **Stepping into the Forest of Bowland:** Tour one of Britain's wildest landscapes, perhaps via the Pendle Witch Trail following in the footsteps of the local ladies taken for trial at Lancaster Castle. See p. 596.

MANCHESTER ★★

202 miles NW of London; 86 miles N of Birmingham; 35 miles E of Liverpool

Said by many to be Britain's "second city" in terms of its economic and cultural importance, **Manchester** has re-emerged, phoenix-like, from post-industrial neglect and the effects of an IRA bombing to become a major shopping and leisure destination. Old red-brick warehouses and factories housing boutique hotels, loft apartments, and nightclubs, and sleek new architecture juxtaposed with impressive Victorian remnants, make for one of the U.K.'s most compelling cityscapes. Meanwhile, large student, gay, and ethnic populations (many descended from immigrant factory laborers, including Britain's biggest Chinese population outside London), and a continuing influence on the global music scene, ensure that Manchester remains at the forefront of modern British culture, even if it's still best known worldwide for football (soccer).

Manchester also is a great jumping-off point for exploring the Peak District (p. 535) as well as for discovering Chester and surrounding Cheshire.

Essentials

GETTING THERE Frequent direct trains from London Euston to Manchester Piccadilly take just over 2 hours, costing around £75 for an off-peak round-trip. There are also direct trains from Birmingham (about 1½ hr.), Leeds (just under 1 hr.), York (about 1¼ hr.), and Edinburgh (about 3¼ hr.). Direct **National Express** (www. nationalexpress.com; ℂ 0871/781-8181) buses from London to Manchester take about 5 hours. There are also direct buses from Birmingham (2–3 hr.), Leeds (about 1 hr.), and Edinburgh (about 6½ hr.).

Manchester is about 3½ hours from London by road, although traffic can be heavy on the M1 and M6 (the Midland Expressway will allow you to move more quickly past Birmingham, at a cost of £3.80–£8.60 depending on time of day). **National Express** (www.nationalexpress.com; ℂ 0871/781-8181) buses also serve **Manchester International Airport** (www.manchesterairport.co.uk; ℂ 0871/271-0711), 15 miles south of the center, which links with London and other U.K. cities, plus many European and global destinations. The airport's own station has frequent direct rail links with the city (about 20 min. away) and other destinations including Liverpool (about 1¼ hr.) and Leeds (about 1¼ hr.).

VISITOR INFORMATION Manchester Visitor Information Centre, Piccadilly Plaza, Portland Street (www.visitmanchester.com; ℂ 0871/222-8223), is open Monday to Saturday 9:30am to 5:30pm, Sunday 10:30am to 4:30pm.

SPECIAL EVENTS Manchester is busy all year, but events worth timing your visit to coincide with are the biennial **Manchester International Festival** (www.mif. co.uk; next in summer 2013), which specializes in world premieres, and, in October, the **Manchester Science Festival** (www.manchestersciencefestival.com) and the

ATTRACTIONS ●

Chetham's Library **1**
Imperial War
  Museum North **22**
John Rylands Library **6**
Manchester Art Gallery **11**
Manchester Museum **17**
Manchester Town Hall **10**
Manchester United Museum
  & Tour Centre **22**
Museum of Science
  & Industry **21**
National Football
  Museum **2**
People's History
  Museum **4**
Whitworth Art Gallery **17**

HOTELS ■

ABode Hotel **12**
Hilton Manchester
  Deansgate **19**
Lowry Hotel **3**
Malmaison
  Manchester **13**
Novotel Manchester
  Centre **16**
Radisson Edwardian **18**
Roomzzz Manchester
  City **15**
YHA Manchester **20**

RESTAURANTS ◆

Australasia **7**
Cicchetti **5**
Croma **9**
Michael Caines **12**
Mr Thomas's
  Chop House **8**
Red Chilli **14**

Manchester Literature Festival (www.manchesterliteraturefestival.co.uk). Also in October, look out for the Manchester Weekender (www.creativetourist.com), combining offerings from separate festivals with other special events for a two-day cultural blast.

Other great events in the city are **Chinese New Year** (late Jan/mid-Feb); the **Manchester Mega Mela** (July), with Asian music, dance, food, and more; **Diwali,** the Hindu festival of lights (late Oct/early Nov); and **Christmas,** with markets, a snow-slide, an ice rink, and illuminations.

Exploring Manchester

Manchester's central sights are walkable, but there's a good bus, tram, and local train network: www.gmpte.com is your resource for planning all journeys.

CENTRAL MANCHESTER

Having begun life as the Roman settlement Mamucium ("camp by the breast-like hill"!), Manchester was catapulted to the forefront of the industrial movement by both its textile industry and its role as a hub in the development of the railway. So it's apt that its excellent **Museum of Science & Industry** (see below), which brings the city's industrial heritage stunningly to life, occupies the site of the world's first passenger railway station and offers visitors the chance to ride on a replica steam train. This museum lies in the Castlefield district about a 10-minute walk from the city center, where Roman Mamucium took seed and also where canals were built to transport supplies during the city's late-19th-century heyday. A stroll in the **Castlefield Urban Heritage Park** (Britain's first) will take you along the canals to the remains of the Roman fort; boat trips are also available, and there are some good picnic spots.

Chetham's Library ★ An incredible slice of local history, this library within the renowned Chetham's School of Music is not only Britain's oldest free public reference library (in continuous use since 1653), but also the meeting place of Marx and Engels when the former visited Manchester, and you can see displays of books that they consulted.

Long Millgate. www.chethams.org.uk. ✆**0161/834-7961.** Free admission. Mon–Fri 9am–12:30pm and 1:30–4:30pm.

John Rylands Library ★★★ This library, built in the 1890s and one of the world's loveliest, holds collections of international significance. But it's not just a place for academic study—a lively and imaginative program of exhibitions, tours, events, and readings for all the family make it a must-see while in Manchester. These include special tours for photographers, who get access to viewpoints not usually accessible to the public, technical tours looking at the building from an engineering and architectural point of view, and children's tours taking in the array of fantastical creatures bedecking the library's walls and ceiling. There's also a great cafe hosting regular tasting events drawing inspiration from the Library's historic cookery books.

150 Deansgate. www.library.manchester.ac.uk. ✆ **0161/306-0555.** Free admission; extra charge for some events. Tues–Sat 10am–5pm; Mon–Sun noon–5pm.

Manchester Art Gallery ★★★ ☺ GALLERY Home to one of the best art collections in the north of England, this central venue with its airy modern glass and steel atrium is best known for its Pre-Raphaelite paintings and its works by L. S. Lowry. But it also houses British and European art from the 17th century to the

Manchester Mini Explorers ★

Manchester is crammed with things to do with children, most of them free. But to really get to know this city with youngsters, invest in a Manchester Mini Explorer pack (www.creativetourist.com; £8 from the Visitor Information Centre or from some museums, galleries, and hotels). As well as four playful self-guided 2-hour trails (one of them of Roman Castlefield; see p. 568) suitable for ages 5–10, it includes an activity book, stickers, fun cards, and discount vouchers.

present day, and a strong craft and design collection, from ceramics and dolls houses to contemporary furniture and lighting. Temporary exhibitions give you a reason to keep coming back for more, while youngsters get their own gallery (Clore Interactive), free activity backpacks or explorer tool belts, and more.

Mosley St. www.manchestergalleries.org. ✆ **0161/235-8888.** Free admission (entry fee for some temporary exhibitions). Tues–Sun 10am–5pm, plus public holiday Mondays.

Manchester Museum ★★★ ☺ MUSEUM   This university-owned venue is both modern, with a focus on the interactive visitor experience, and old-fashioned, in that it's all-embracing: Within its walls you'll find everything from mummies, dinosaur skeletons, and stuffed animals to live amphibians and reptiles. A stunning revamped Living Worlds gallery was opened by celebrity naturalist Steve Backshall in April 2011; at the time of writing, new Ancient Worlds galleries were set to follow in late 2012. Children's amenities and activities include a Play+Learn (and picnic) area, free family backpacks and tails, and a monthly Big Saturday themed event.

Oxford Rd., near Booth St. www.museum.manchester.ac.uk. ✆ **0161/275-2634.** Free admission. Tues–Sat 10am–5pm; Sun–Mon 11am–4pm.

Manchester Town Hall ★★   This impressive Victorian Gothic Revival building is home to several government departments, but during office hours visitors can tour its wonderful Sculpture Hall with its famous figures involved in the city's history, including Gnaeus Julius Agricola, founder of Mamucium. You'll have to sign up for one of the regular tours (booking essential) to see the Great Hall with its 12 imposing murals by Ford Madox Brown on events central to Manchester's history and themes dear to Victorian Mancunians: Christianity, commerce, and the textile industry.

Albert Sq. www.visitmanchester.com. ✆ **0871/222-8223.** Free admission; tours £6. Mon–Fri 10am–5pm (Sculpture Hall and cafe); for tours see website.

Museum of Science & Industry ★★★ ☺ MUSEUM   A wonderful example of an interactive and ultra-family-friendly modern museum, MOSI has a Victorian sewer to crawl through (with authentic smells and sounds), a planetarium, a 4-D theatre, a motion simulator ride, and steam train rides—all alongside one of the world's largest collections of working steam engines, plus fascinating displays on printing, electricity, textile manufacture, flight, and aerospace exploration. The Revolution Manchester Gallery has sections on the city's role in developments in transport, computer technology, energy, and more.

Liverpool Rd. www.mosi.org.uk. ✆ **0161/832-2244.** Free admission (small charges for some attractions). Daily 10am–5pm.

National Football Museum ☺ Housed within Urbis, a shimmering glass structure that was originally built to house a now defunct museum about urban cultures, the National Football Museum was scheduled to open as this guide went to press. Its offerings include a national football hall of fame, various temporary and permanent exhibitions on everything footie-related, from stadiums to toys and games, and an under-5s Discovery Zone. There's a charge for the Football Plus experience allowing you to challenge yourself, virtually, against the professionals.

Cathedral Gardens. www.nationalfootballmuseum.com. ℂ **0161/870-9275.** Free admission. Mon–Sat 10am–5pm; Sun 11am–5pm.

People's History Museum ★ Telling the story of democracy and of the working class in the U.K, this is a must-see for those interested in the role played by northwest England in the Industrial Revolution, and in Manchester's importance in the political arena. Temporary exhibitions plus tours, talks, and family events and explorer packs keep things lively.

Left Bank. www.phm.org.uk. ℂ**0161/838-9190.** Free admission. Daily 10am–5pm.

Whitworth Art Gallery ★★★ ☺ GALLERY Rounding off Manchester's fine array of free museums and galleries, the Whitworth, about 10 minutes south of the center, holds some of the U.K.'s finest art and design collections, including modern and historic fine art, prints, textiles, and rare wallpapers. There's also a busy program of activities, many for families, and an award-winning cafe. An upcoming £12-million redevelopment and expansion will double the exhibition space as well as adding an art garden.

Whitworth Park. www.whitworth.manchester.ac.uk. ℂ**0161/275-7450.** Free admission. Mon–Sat 10am–5pm; Sun noon–4pm.

TRAFFORD & SALFORD QUAYS

A short hop west of the center, the metropolitan borough of Trafford—part of Greater Manchester—will be familiar to most visitors as home to the "Theatre of Dreams," Manchester United's home stadium of Old Trafford. But you'll also find here the northern outpost of the Imperial War Museum (p. 571), while the Lowry (or Millennium) Bridge over the canal takes you to the regenerated docklands area of **Salford Quays,** now home to The Lowry cultural center (p. 574) and to MediaCityUK, the new site for several departments of the BBC and for ITV production, including sets of the famous and long-running TV soap *Coronation Street.*

Trafford is also home to the affluent market town of **Altrincham,** historically a part of Chester (p. 578), about 8 miles southwest of the center of Manchester. Home to many professional footballers (including Manchester United and Manchester City players), *Coronation Street* and other TV actors, and music-industry celebrities, it's centered on its Old Market Place with part timber-framed buildings.

Dunham Massey Hall ★★ ☺ HISTORIC SITE Located within a vast deer park on the outskirts of Altrincham, this early Georgian house was home to the 7th Earl of Stamford, who caused a scandal by marrying a former bareback circus rider. Visitors get to learn about him and other inhabitants, explore the interiors (including the Gallery, where you can play the piano and Edwardian games), and stroll in Britain's biggest winter garden and around the estate. Children get free quizzes and trails and family activities, and in summer you can play croquet on the lawn.

Altrincham. www.nationaltrust.org.uk. ℂ**0161/942-3989.** Admission £10 adults, £5 children. Park daily 9am–5pm; garden 11am–5:30pm (4pm in winter); house Mar–Oct Sat–Wed 11am–5pm.

Imperial War Museum North ★★ ☺ MUSEUM   Like its counterpart in London (p. 108), the museum aims to show in a vivid fashion "how war shapes lives." Open since 2002 in an award-winning—and symbolic—building by Daniel Libeskind, it has both permanent displays and temporary exhibitions, some of them aimed at children, plus hourly audiovisual presentations projected onto the very walls of the galleries, to evoke in visitors the dread and panic experienced by those who lived through the Blitz. The museum (including its excellent child-friendly cafe) overlooks an area of Manchester that was heavily bombed in 1940—the Manchester Ship Canal, then a key industrial zone.

The Quays, Trafford Wharf Rd. www.iwm.org.uk/visits/iwm-north. ☏ **0161/836-4000.** Free admission. Daily 10am–5pm.

Manchester United Museum & Tour Centre ★★ ☺   Tickets to see the world's biggest team are notoriously scarce and expensive, but the museum at Manchester United's homeground offers displays on 130 years of football (soccer), plus the option to see the stadium through the eyes of its players on a tour.

Sir Matt Busby Way, Old Trafford. www.manutd.com. ☏ **0161/868-8000.** Adults £14 for museum and tour, children 5–15 £10. Center daily (except match days) 9am–5pm, with tours up to every 10 min (9:40am–6:30pm).

Trafford Centre   Far more than just a shopping mall, the Trafford Centre offers ample scope for retail therapy and eating out but is also home the **Legoland Discovery Centre** ★★ (www.legolanddiscoverycentre.co.uk; ☏ **0871/222-2662**) for ages 3 to 12, including Miniland (with Lego models of northern English attractions such as the Peak District and the Blackpool Illuminations), a high-ropes adventure course (www.aerialextreme.co.uk; ☏ **0845/652-1736**), a tropical themed adventure golf course (www.paradiseislandgolf.com; ☏ **0161/202-9544**), a multi-screen cinema, and various other family attractions that make it a leisure destination in its own right.

Right by the mall you'll also find **Chill Factore** (www.chillfactore.com; ☏ **0161/749-2222**), a year-round indoor real snow center.

Trafford. www.traffordcentre.co.uk. ☏ **0161/749-1717.** Free admission; prices vary for different attractions. Mon–Thurs 10am–midnight; Fri 10am–midnight or later; Sat 9am–midnight or later; Sun 11am–midnight; see website for individual shops and attractions.

Where to Eat
VERY EXPENSIVE

For the **River Restaurant at The Lowry Hotel,** see p. 575. The **Second Floor at Harvey Nichols** (www.harveynichols.com; ☏ **0161/828-8898**) is very highly regarded for its Modern European cookery; there's also a cheaper but still very good brasserie.

Michael Caines ★★ MODERN BRITISH/EUROPEAN   Refurbished in 2012, this stylish, award-winning venue in the basement of the **ABode Hotel** near Piccadilly Station is named after one of Britain's most acclaimed chefs, who has other dining rooms in the same hotels in nearby Chester (p. 578), Glasgow, and, to the south, Exeter and Canterbury. Accessible fine dining, with the emphasis on regional produce, is the order of the day: Characteristic dishes are parsnip soup with pickled apples and vanilla oil; and assiette of Yorkshire rabbit with braised haricot beans, kohlrabi, and rabbit jelly. If you're not ravenously hungry or just wary of inflicting too much damage on your wallet, you can eat from the Grazing Menu (also available in the Champagne Bar). Lunchtimes see a great-value "Amazing Graze" menu of 3–5 courses, with or without wine to accompany each dish, or there's a similarly well-priced early dining menu (6–7pm; 2/3 courses). Under-5s eat free at Michael Caines, but those with children are likely to feel most comfortable eating in the daytime.

The **MC Café Bar & Grill** at street level of the hotel offers more casual eating and drinking from breakfast to late evening (including Sunday brunches and roasts). Standard rates for **doubles at the hotel** start at £160, without breakfast

107 Piccadilly. www.michaelcaines.com. *☎* **0161/200-5678.** Reservations recommended. Main courses £19.50–£25.50. AE, DC, MC, V. Mon–Sat noon–2:30pm and 6–10pm.

EXPENSIVE

Australasia ★ PAN-ASIAN   One of the best spots in town for a dose of Manchester bling, this relative newcomer to the city's eating scene has a tremendously buzzy atmosphere to match its quite daring food, which consists mainly of Japanese dishes with an Australian twist, such as sushi, sashimi, oysters, and tempura, but also includes steaks and other meat, fish, and tofu dishes. The fact that drinks lists are on iPads will seem gimmicky to some (you can't actually order using the devices), but most diners rate the innovative cocktails and food, with recurrent highlights being the rose and lychee martinis, the salt and pepper tofu, and the mango soufflés. Starters and mains are available, but you're encouraged to choose a handful of smaller dishes to share, tapas-style. Set in a basement in the modern Spinningfields district, Australasia is accessed via a glass triangular structure and then a fittingly see-and-be-seen staircase.

1 The Ave. www.australasia.uk.com. *☎* **0161/831-0288.** AC, MC, DC, V. Main courses £13.50–£60. Sun–Wed noon–midnight; Thurs noon–1am; Fri–Sat noon–3am.

MODERATE

Central Manchester has the usual family-friendly chains, including **Carluccio's** and **Wagamama;** some of them also have branches in the Trafford Centre mall (p. 571).

Cicchetti ★★ 🍴 ITALIAN   Noisy, brash, and heaps of fun, Cicchetti is named for the tapas-style sharing dishes that are a specialty of Venice. In the rather incongruous setting at street level of the House of Fraser department store, with views into the shop, it's perpetually crowded by Italian couples, families, and groups of friends, and also attracts its fair share of famous northern footballers. Food could be an afterthought, but most dishes— the likes lobster ravioli, wild asparagus with garlic and chili, or risotto with peas and scallops—are spot on, if not specifically Venetian. We've often been charmed by the staff here, but some diners have complained of brusque service. Cicchetti—which is also a good place for (non-Italian) breakfast or for afternoon teas—is an offshoot of the long-established San Carlo on the same street.

King St. West. www.sancarlocicchetti.co.uk. *☎* **0161/839-2233.** Main courses £4–£14. AE, DC, MC, V. Mon–Fri 8am–11pm; Sat and Sun 9am–11pm.

Mr Thomas's Chop House ★ TRADITIONAL ENGLISH   Probably Manchester's best-preserved Victorian pub, "Tom's"—together with its nearby sister eatery, **Sam's Chop House**—offers a slice of vogueish tradition in the heart of the city. Named after 16th-century chophouses, where businessmen came to do their deals over hearty cuisine and fine wines or local ales, Tom's places the same emphasis on comforting, seasonal fare served in a convivial, informal atmosphere. Expect the likes of brown onion soup, lovingly cooked for 36 hours and served with a large Cheddar crouton, or homemade steak and kidney pie with chips, mushy peas, and a jug of

Unsurprisingly, given that its name was shortened from "Ramson's Bottom," meaning "wild garlic valley," the market town of Ramsbottom, on the western slopes of the Pennines (14 miles north of Manchester), has become a bit of a pilgrimage site for foodies. In addition to a farmers' market (second Sunday of each month), it hosts a 2-day **Chocolate Festival** (http://chocfest.wordpress.com/) in March/April, with family-friendly activities as well as chocolate, cocktail, wine, and beer sampling in venues such as **The Lounge** (www.theloungeramsbottom.co.uk; ℂ **01706/828392**) and **The First Chop** (www.thefirstchop.co.uk;

ℂ **01706/827722**). But year-round, the town is worth visiting for its **Chocolate Café** (www.chocolate-cafe.co.uk; ℂ **01706/822828**), **Cultured Bean** (www.theculturedbean.com; ℂ **01706/825232**) coffee bar and chocolate shop (try the prize-winning chocolate torte), and **Ramsbottom Sweet Shop** (www.ramsbottomsweetshop.com; ℂ **01706/822166**). As if that weren't enough, it also has an award-winning Italian restaurant, **Ramsons** (ℂ **01706/825070**; www.ramsons-restaurant.com), a superb South Indian eatery, **Sanmini's** (www.sanminis.com; ℂ **01706/821831**), and other good restaurants and pubs.

gravy. The interior is almost unchanged since 1901, but do look closely at the "period" photos—they're actually of present-day regulars!

52 Cross St. www.tomschophouse.com. ℂ**0161/832-2245.** Main courses £10.99–£28.50. AE, MC, V. Mon–Sat 11:30am–11pm; Sun noon–9pm.

Red Chilli ★★ CHINESE Reassuringly packed with Chinese diners, this is where those in the know come for serious Beijing and Sichuan cuisine. Concessions are made to western palates and notions about Chinese food, but look beyond the usual favorites on the menu for more authentic dishes (if in doubt, peek at what your Chinese neighbors are eating and ask for some of the same). We recommend the stir-fried sliced eel with chili sauce, and the spicy-hot poached mutton; or investigate the "Home Style" section of the menu with its frog's legs and whelk specialties. Despite a recent attempt to inject glamour into the decor, prices remain fair, and portions are huge, so don't over order. There's a second branch in student territory, at 403–419 Oxford Rd. (ℂ **0161/273-1288**).

70–72 Portland St. www.redchillirestaurant.co.uk. ℂ**0161/236-2888.** Reservations recommended for dinner. Main courses £4.50–£18. MC, V. Mon–Fri noon–11pm; Sat–Sun noon–midnight.

INEXPENSIVE

Like Bradford, Manchester is famous for its Indian restaurants, but even on the **"Curry Mile"** (Rusholme, south of the center), it's difficult to find one that is consistently good enough to recommend. On the other hand, there are some great Middle Eastern canteens here; try **Jazera,** 22 Wilmslow Rd. (ℂ **0161/257-3337**) or **Sadaf,** 167 Wilmslow Rd. (ℂ **0161/257-3557**).

Croma ★★ ☺ ITALIAN/PIZZA Injecting a dose of minimalist chic into the budget Italian scene, Croma offers a winning formula with its gourmet salads, pizzas, and oven-baked pastas, all at very reasonable prices. Salads include the likes of tandoori chicken, or smoked haddock and potato; for pizzas, think everything from margarita to Thai chicken. For parents, the excellent cocktails are also well priced, while the children's menu is a bargain at £4.95 for a drink, pizza, or pasta dish, small salad, ice cream, and baby-ccino (frothy milk). Young diners also get drawing materials. There are branches in the trendy suburb of Chorlton in south Manchester (500 Wilbraham Rd.; ℭ 0161/881-1117) and Prestwich in north Manchester (30 Longfield Centre, ℭ 0161/798-7666).

1–3 Clarence St. www.cromapizza.co.uk. ℭ **0161/237-9799.** Reservations accepted only for parties of 6 or more (none on Sat night). Main courses £5.10–£7.95. MC, V. Mon–Sat 11am–11pm; Sun 11am–10:30pm.

Shopping

Manchester is a shopping mecca, rivaling London in scope if not in size. Much of the center is made up of pedestrian-only shopping areas or streets full of designer shops, boutiques, and high-street stores, including **King Street** and **St. Ann's Square, Market Street, The Avenue,** and the **Arndale Centre,** rebuilt as part of the remodeling of the center after the 1996 IRA bomb. Relative newcomers are chic department stores **Selfridges,** 1 Exchange Sq. (www.selfridges.com; ℭ **0800/123400**), and **Harvey Nichols,** 21 New Cathedral St. (ℭ **0161/828-8888**). Off Piccadilly Gardens, Oldham Street leads you into the hip **Northern Quarter,** best known for its indie fashion emporium **Afflecks** ★, 52 Church St. (www.afflecks.com; ℭ **0161/839-0718**), but home to plenty more retro boutiques, record stores, and so on, including kitsch gift store **Oklahoma,** 74–76 High St. (ℭ **0161/834-1136**). Also here is the excellent **Manchester Craft Centre,** 17 Oak St. (www.craftanddesign.com; ℭ **0161/832-4274**), within an atmospheric Victorian market building.

You'll find lots more shops—plus amenities, entertainment, and eateries galore—west of the center in the **Trafford Centre** (p. 571), including a smaller branch of Selfridges.

Manchester's **Real Food Market** (ℭ **0161/234-7357**) takes place on the second and fourth weekend (Fri–Sat 10am–6pm) of the month in Piccadilly Gardens, offering products from local farms and producers, from Lake District reared meats and Lancashire cheeses to curries, plus handcrafted ethical gifts and jewelry. For other Manchester markets, see www.manchestermarkets.com.

Entertainment & Nightlife

Manchester is rich in the performing arts. Among the major venues is the **Lowry Theatre** ★★ (www.thelowry.com; ℭ **0843/208-6000**) at Salford Quays, with two main theatres, a studio space, and exhibition galleries with an emphasis on the work of L. S. Lowry (1887–1976), who documented England's bleak industrial north. In the city center, the **Royal Exchange** ★★ (www.royalexchangetheatre.org.uk; ℭ **0161/833-9833**), Britain's largest theatre-in-the-round, stunningly housed in a glass-walled capsule suspended within the Great Hall of the Exchange on St. Ann's Square, offers a reliably exciting program. And **The Bridgewater Hall,** Lower Mosley Street (www.bridgewater-hall.co.uk; ℭ **0161/907-9000**), a state-of-the-art, 2,400-seat concert hall, is home to the renowned Hallé Orchestra, BBC Philharmonic, and Manchester Camerata, as well as hosting some pop and comedy. There are countless smaller venues, too; keep your finger on the pulse by consulting www.creativetourist.com.

The same website, as well as www.manchesterconfidential.co.uk, will help you when it comes to the exciting, ever-evolving **live music, nightlife,** and **bar scene** of the city that gave birth to The Smiths, New Order, Oasis, and The Stone Roses. If in doubt, head to the **Northern Quarter** for a reliably good night out, or even to the southern suburbs, to the fashionable student enclave **West Didsbury** with its good bars, cafes, and restaurants. Manchester's loud, proud, and straight-friendly **Gay Village** spreads across Canal Street in a once-seedy factory district of the center.

Where to Stay

Manchester's **Malmaison**, set in a handsome former warehouse, has two football-themed suites (Manchester United and Manchester City); doubles here are about £129–£149 without breakfast. The city's **Hilton**, in a landmark modern tower, is best known for its **Cloud 23** bar offering stunning views from floor-to-ceiling windows; doubles cost from about £169 without breakfast. The city's **ABode Hotel**, home to **Michael Caines** (p. 571), has doubles from about £160 without breakfast.

Lowry Hotel ★★ ☺ Manchester's most expensive and best hotel is on the banks of the Irwell, with views over Santiago Calavatra's ultra-modern Trinity Bridge. Though this makes it feel slightly apart and aloof, it means that it's quiet while being only a 5-minute walk from the center. *The* place to stay for just about every visiting celeb, it differs from most hotels in the global Rocco Forte group in that it's very modern, inside and out. But despite the minimalist esthetic, the level of comfort is the same, with all rooms and suites boasting marble bathrooms and walk-in wardrobes. The best have river views. Like most hotels in the group, it welcomes families, with complimentary connecting/adjoining rooms, a prize trail, a chest of games, toys, and DVDs, and free "mocktails." Children 9 and under eat free in the waterside **River Restaurant,** and there's an affordable menu for children 15 and under, plus children's afternoon teas including a gingerbread matchstick man (L. S. Lowry style) to decorate. Slow-ish service is made up for by excellent food including, for adults, the likes of roast rack of venison with blueberry and venison sausage and juniper sauce; and pan-seared Scottish salmon with artichoke ragout, cockles, and clams.

50 Dearmans Place, Chapel Wharf, Manchester M3 5LH. www.thelowryhotel.com. ☎ **0161/827-4000.** 165 units. £423–£453 double; from £970 suite. AE, DC, MC, V. Parking £12. **Amenities:** Restaurant; bar; exercise room; spa; room service; Wi-Fi. *In room:* TV, minibar, hair dryer, CD player (upon request), iPod docking station.

Roomzzz Manchester City ★★ 🖋 ☺ Claiming to combine the best features of boutique hotels and serviced apartments, this "apart-hotel" offers good facilities and high standards at an enticing price—especially for advanced purchase (rates rise as occupancy increases). Centrally located a few minutes' walk from Piccadilly Gardens, with subtle decorative nods to surrounding Chinatown, Roomzzz offers cleverly designed Smart and larger Grande studios and Liberty Suites sleeping two, or one- or two-bedroom suites for four, all with compact "kitchen pods" including dishwashers and washer-driers. Furniture is multifunctional—in some units, desks become dining tables, for example—and all rooms have mini Apple Macs and free Wi-Fi. Rates include a "Grab & Go" breakfast of fruit, fruit juice, pastries, and tea/coffee.

36 Princess St., Manchester M1 4JY. www.roomzzz.co.uk. ☎ **0844/499-4888.** 48 units. Standard midweek rate £88–£98 studio for 2; £106 1-bedroom suite; £118 2-bedroom suite. Rates include continental breakfast. AE, MC, V. Parking (nearby) £15. *In room:* Kitchen (w/dishwasher and washer-drier), Apple iMac or minicomputer/TV, hair dryer, Wi-Fi (free).

YHA Manchester A good example of a modern youth hostel, this building is well located by the barge-filled canals of trendy Castlefield. It's a 10-minute walk from the bustle and chaos of the city center, right by the Museum of Science and Industry. The decor is bright, fresh, and fun, with an almost Pop Arty feel, and the staff is friendly. Rooms range from en suite private rooms for two to six-bed family rooms, and there's a dining room for cheap but decent meals, including optional breakfast costing £4.95 (£2.95 for children).

Potato Wharf, Manchester M3 4NB. www.yha.org.uk. ✆ **0845/371-9647.** 35 units. From £15.50 per person, £11 children 17 and under. MC, V. Free parking. **Amenities:** Restaurant; games room; TV lounge; shop; communal kitchen; launderette; discounted access to fitness center; Wi-Fi (free).

CHESHIRE ★★

Chester: 194 miles NW of London; 80 miles NW of Birmingham; 45 miles SW of Manchester; 28 miles S of Liverpool

With its magnificent country-house estates and other fine historic buildings set amidst pretty landscapes, Cheshire offers a green respite for those exploring the cities of the northwest. Of its cities and towns, **Chester,** full of Roman remnants, half-timbered houses and shops (some Tudor but others Georgian and Victorian), and good attractions for families, is particularly worthy of a day or two's exploration.

Essentials

GETTING THERE Frequent direct trains from London's Euston Station to Chester take 2 hours, costing around £75 for an off-peak round-trip. There are also direct trains from Manchester (1½ hr.) and Liverpool (40 min.). Manchester and Liverpool airports (p. 566 and p. 584) are the handiest for Chester but you'll have to travel into those cities themselves for public transport links. For those exploring Cheshire, the train stations of Manchester (p. 566), Stockport, Macclesfield, Wilmslow, Crewe, and also Stoke on Trent (in Staffordshire) can all be handy.

There are a few direct **National Express** (www.nationalexpress.com; ✆ **0871/781-8181**) buses between London and Chester, taking just over 6 hours, but most services require a change at Birmingham. There are also direct buses from Manchester (about 1 hr.) and Liverpool (50 min.).

If you are exploring the area without a car, consult www.traveline-northwest.co.uk.

Chester is about 3½ hours northwest of London by road, mainly via the M1 and M6. From Birmingham it's about 80 miles (1½ hr.), from Manchester about 45 miles (just under 1 hr.), and from Liverpool about 28 miles (40 min.).

VISITOR INFORMATION **Chester Visitor Information Centre,** Town Hall Square (www.visitchester.com; ✆ **0845/647-7868**), is open Monday to Saturday 9am–5:30pm, Sundays and public holidays 10am–5pm.

SPECIAL EVENTS Each April, the **Chester Food, Drink & Lifestyle Festival** (www.visitchester.com), held at the Racecourse, includes the Cheese Rolling Championships waged between Cheshire, Lancashire, and Stilton teams; Camperfest allows you to camp on-site (campervans, caravans, and tents). It's followed by the classical **Summer Music Festival,** held over 2 weeks in July, and by the October **Chester Literature Festival** (both www.chesterfestivals.co.uk; ✆ **0845/241-7868**). Summer also sees the **Midsummer Watch Parades** (www.midsummer watch.co.uk), one of Britain's oldest festivals, featuring medieval giants, devil and angel puppets, and flocks of geese, while Chester is particularly atmospheric at Christmas.

Chester

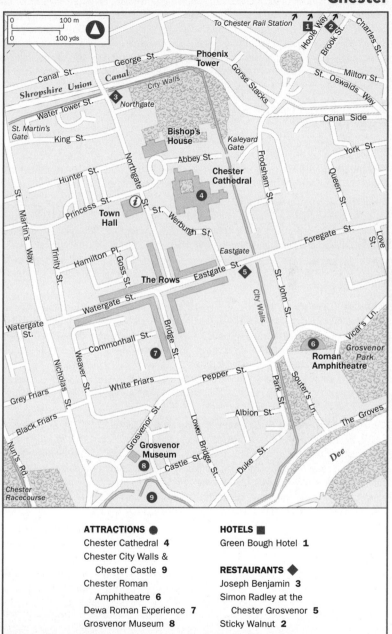

ATTRACTIONS ●
Chester Cathedral 4
Chester City Walls &
  Chester Castle 9
Chester Roman
  Amphitheatre 6
Dewa Roman Experience 7
Grosvenor Museum 8

HOTELS ■
Green Bough Hotel 1

RESTAURANTS ◆
Joseph Benjamin 3
Simon Radley at the
  Chester Grosvenor 5
Sticky Walnut 2

The season at **Chester Racecourse** (www.chester-races.co.uk; ✆**01244/304610**; May–Sept) includes a May Festival; a Roman day with races, displays, and family entertainment; and an Autumn Festival. Also known as the Roodee, the early 16th-century course is the oldest still in use in Britain.

From May to August, Chester's costumed **town-crier** appears at the City Cross at noon (Tues–Sat) to shout news about exhibitions, attractions, and the like. Cheshire's great country houses run packed programs of events year-round; see individual reviews (below) and websites.

Exploring the Area

CHESTER ★★

The traditional county town of mainly rural Cheshire, Chester was founded by a Roman legion on the River Dee in the 1st century A.D. and reached its pinnacle as a bustling port in the 13th and 14th centuries. Though it declined as the river gradually silted up, its largely intact fortified **city walls** are Britain's most complete.

Blue Planet Aquarium ★ ☺AQUARIUM   Europe's biggest collection of sharks (and the opportunity to dive with some of them) and a Coral Cave with state-of-the-art lighting effects are among the draws at this large aquarium, but try to avoid school holidays, when the place gets uncomfortably crowded despite the high entry fee.

Junction 10 off the M53, Ellesmere Port. www.blueplanetaquarium.com. ✆ **0151/357-8804.** Admission £15.50 adults, £11.25 for children 13 and under (taller than 95cm/3 ft. 2 in.). Mon–Fri 10am–5pm, until 6pm Sat–Sun.

Chester Cathedral ★   Founded in 1092 as a Benedictine abbey and made an Anglican cathedral church in 1541, Chester's cathedral boasts a fine range of monastic buildings, particularly the cloisters and refectory, plus chapterhouse and superb medieval woodcarving in the choir stalls. The admission fee includes a 45-minute audio tour (children's version available).

Abbey Sq. www.chestercathedral.com. ✆**01244/324756.** Admission £6 adults, up to 3 children free with paying adult, then £2.50 per child under 16. Mon–Sat 9am–5pm; Sun 1–4pm, but call ahead if making special trip in case of services or events.

Chester City Walls & Chester Castle ★★   Chester's largely intact Roman wall is walkable for almost all of its 2 miles. Climbing the steps close to the much-photographed **Eastgate Clock** in the center of Chester, you can walk along the top of the wall, past various 18th-century buildings and some Roman ruins you can explore for free. At the wall's southwestern corner lie fragments of medieval Chester Castle, and in old barracks within the castle confines the **Cheshire Military Museum** (www.cheshiremilitarymuseum.co.uk; ✆ **01244/327617;** daily 10am–5pm, admission £3 adults, £2 children).

Castle: Grosvenor St. www.english-heritage.org.uk. ✆**01829/260464.** Free admission. Open only for guided tours, late Apr–late Oct, call for times

Chester Roman Amphitheatre ★★   Britain's largest Roman amphitheatre was used for military training and entertainment (cock-fighting, bull-baiting, classical boxing, gladiatorial combat, and more) by the 20th Legion. Half-exposed (the other half is covered by listed buildings), it only came to light in 1929 and further excavation took place in 2007–9, with a *trompe l'oeil* mural added shortly afterwards to give visitors at least the illusion of being surrounded by the entire structure. The

Cheshire

THE NORTHWEST

amphitheatre is a good starting point for a stroll along Chester's 18th-century riverside promenade, **The Groves,** newly refurbished in 2011

Vicars Lane. www.english-heritage.org.uk. ℂ **0870/333-1181.** Free access 24 hr.

Chester Zoo ★ ☺ ZOO   One of the very best British zoos, Chester's has a strong reputation for its conservation work, plus well-sized enclosures. The quirky 1970s-style monorail lets you peer down into some of the enclosures as you travel across the park, which is noted for its gardens replicating many of the animals' native environments; there's also a waterbus along the zoo's canal system (weekends only outside school holidays). There are also play areas, and golf and minigolf courses.

Upton-by-Chester. www.chesterzoo.org. ℂ **01244/380280.** Admission varies by season; in school holidays £18adults, £14 children 3–15, with the monorail and waterbus extra. Daily 10am–4/6pm according to season.

Dewa Roman Experience ★ ☺ HISTORIC SITE   This schlocky but educational attraction goes down very well with children aged about 8 and up, who like the recreated Roman streets, the Roman galley, and the studio where they can handle archeological remains, sit in a chariot, fire a catapult, try on armor, build a Roman central heating system, and even smell Roman smells. In school holidays it also runs tours of Chester led by Roman soldier patrols.

Pierpoint Lane. www.dewaromanexperience.co.uk. ℂ **01244/343407.** Admission £4.95 adults, £3.25 children 5–15. Feb–Nov Mon–Sat 9am–5pm, Sun 10am–5pm; Dec–Jan daily 10am–4pm.

Grosvenor Museum ★ MUSEUM   This modest but fascinating museum is home to a world-famous collection of Roman tombstones, plus art, silver, and social and natural history displays. If you're visiting with children, join in with a rich program of family events.

27 Grosvenor St. www.cheshirewestandchester.gov.uk. ℂ **01244/402033.** Free admission. Mon–Sat 10:30am–5pm; Sun 1–4pm.

CHESHIRE COUNTRY HOUSES & GARDENS ★★

Though there is little to tempt visitors to the other major towns in Cheshire (including Warrington, Crewe, Widnes, and Macclesfield), this affluent county beloved by footballers and their wives and by soap-opera stars, and said to have more millionaires per square mile than anywhere else in the country (at least in the Alderley Edge area), has plenty of other attractions, whether you like myth-soaked landscapes, country houses, or science and industry.

Alderley Edge ★★★   Located just outside the town of the same name—once home to the Beckhams and still Cheshire's "capital of bling"—this dramatic redsandstone escarpment dotted with ancient copper-mining relics offers woodland walks and lovely views over the Cheshire countryside, especially from Stormy Point, Castle Rock, and The Beacon, where fires were lit to warn of the imminent invasion by Spain in 1588. From the escarpment, there's a pathway to **Hare Hill** (ℂ **01625/584412;** mid-March–Oct Tues–Sun 10am–5pm; admission £4 adults, £2 children 5–15), a woodland garden with wire sculptures and exotic plants. Refuel at the **Wizard Tearoom** (ℂ **07742/333463**) or **Wizard Pub** (www.ainscoughs.co.uk; ℂ **01625/584000**), both on Macclesfield Road and named after the magician Merlin (King Arthur and his men are said to sleep beneath the sandstone cliffs here).

Alderley Edge. www.nationaltrust.org.uk. ℂ **01625/584412.** Free, open access (parking lot daily 8am to 5–6pm; £5).

Jodrell Bank Centre for Astrophysics ★★ ☺ The iconic Lovell Telescope, one of the world's most powerful radio telescopes, is the star of Jodrell Bank when it comes to visitors; a pathway around the base allows you an up-close view. Otherwise, the Centre's new-in-2011 Discovery Centre has a Space Pavilion hosting exhibitions and events about the Universe, plus a glass-walled cafe with spectacular views of the telescope. Frequent Ask the Expert sessions are popular with youngsters, and there's also a new playground, picnic area, and space-themed Galaxy Garden. There are hopes to replace the old planetarium, demolished in 2003.

Just off A535 between Holmes Chapel and Alderley Edge. www.jb.man.ac.uk. ©**01477/571339.** Admission £5.50–£6.50 adults, £4–£4.50 children 4-16, depending on season. Daily 10am–5pm.

Lyme Park ★★ ☺PARK Set in gardens and its own huge deer park, this country house on the threshold of the Peak District (p. 535) will be recognizable to many as Mr. Darcy's Pemberley in the BBC's 1995 *Pride and Prejudice*. For adults, a highlight is the liturgical Lyme Caxton Missal in the library, with a touch-screen facility so you can "turn" its pages and hear chants sung as they would have been 500 years ago; for children, the Crow Wood Playscape, opened in 2011, is an innovative playground with a treehouse, rope, and timber walkways, tree-trunk climbing, and giant badger sets. There's a cottage for hire on the grounds, sleeping four.

Disley. www.nationaltrust.org.uk. ©**01663/762023.** Admission £5 per vehicle, then house and garden £11 adults, £5.50 children 5–16 (separate tickets also available). Park daily 8am–6pm; garden Mar–Oct daily 11am–5pm; house Mar–Oct Fri–Tues 11am–5pm.

Quarry Bank Mill & Styal Estate ★★ ☺ One of the best industrial heritage sites in the U.K., based around a complete working Georgian cotton mill, Quarry Bank is the place to come to find out all about the Industrial Revolution in this area. Hand-spinning demonstrations, working machinery, steam engines, a waterwheel, tours of the Apprentice House, which housed the pauper children who worked in the mill, and entry to the mill owners' gorgeous valley garden bring it all alive, and there are also family trails and a play area. Styal village, built to house the mill workers, remains a vibrant community.

Styal. www.nationaltrust.org.uk. ©**01625/445896.** Admission mill, Apprentice House, and garden £14.50 adults, children 5–15 £7.25 (separate tickets available). Garden daily 10:30am–5pm; mill and apprentice house Mar–Oct daily 11am–5pm, rest of year Wed–Sun 11am–3:30pm.

Tatton Park ★★★ ☺PARK Surrounded by a magnificent deer park, this superb mansion and estate is Cheshire's big-hitter, host to legions of prominent events throughout the year, including antique fairs, classic car shows, flower shows, outdoor concerts and theatre, and Christmas events. As well as the mansion itself, visitors can access the lovely gardens and working rare-breeds farm, while children love the (free) adventure playground and the seasonal fun-fair rides, and there's bike rental. Two holiday cottages allow you the chance to stay on-site.

Knutsford. www.tattonpark.org.uk. ©**01625/374400.** Admission £5 per vehicle, then £10 adults, £5 children 5–15 (or £5.50/£3.50 per individual attraction). Park Apr–Oct daily 10am–7pm; Nov–Mar Tues–Sun and public holiday Mon 11am–5pm. Gardens Apr–Oct daily 10am–6pm; Nov–Mar Tues–Sun and public holiday Mon 11am–4pm; for mansion and farm (closed Mon exc public holidays in high season) see website.

Where to Eat

As in Manchester, there's a **Michael Caines** restaurant at the ABode hotel (p. 582).

Dun Cow ★★ 🍴 MODERN BRITISH   This award-winning dining pub not far from Tatton Park is a hotspot for creative, beautifully executed cuisine based on top local produce. Menus change seasonally, but you might enjoy Cheshire guinea fowl and partridge with wild mushrooms, truffle, baby leeks, and crab apple jelly; followed by a selection of local artisan cheeses or a to-die-for dessert such as iced ginger and meringue parfait, with brandy snap shards, coffee cream, and frappe. The bar, with its old beams and log fires, is a cozy spot for real ales.

Chelford Rd., Ollerton. www.duncowknutsford.co.uk. ⓒ **01565/633093.** Reservations recommended. Main courses £16–£25. MC, V. Mon noon–3pm; Tues–Fri noon–3pm and 5–11pm; Sat noon–11pm; Sun noon–5pm.

Joseph Benjamin ★★★ 🍴 MODERN BRITISH/EUROPEAN   This award-winning restaurant, deli, and cookshop by Chester's city walls is a handy all-day spot for breakfast, lunch, and afternoon tea, plus a candlelit dinner and/or drinks in the latter part of the week. The compact menu of seasonal dishes based on local ingredients changes completely every few weeks but may include black pudding and smoked haddock salad with Shropshire blue cheese mayonnaise; or 7-hour braised Cumbrian ox cheek with saffron risotto, globe artichoke, and gremolata. It's invariably packed, but on a fine day a good alternative is to arm yourself with a gourmet picnic from the deli counter—with champagne or wine if you wish—and picnic in the cathedral gardens.

134–140 North Gate St., Chester. www.josephbenjamin.co.uk. ⓒ **01244/344295.** Reservations recommended. Main courses £12.50–£17.50. MC, V. Tues–Wed 9am–5pm; Thurs–Sat 9am–midnight; Sun 10am–5pm.

Simon Radley at the Chester Grosvenor ★★ MODERN FRENCH   Holder of a Michelin star, this fine-dining restaurant within the city's swankiest hotel was revamped and renamed in 2008 (it used to be The Arkle). Resolutely formal (smart attire; no children 11 and under; cellphones must be silenced), it may be a little stiff and rarefied for some. And dishes such as breast of Gressingham duck with cocoa nib granola, fondant liver, and liquid cherries will be too far out for many non-foodies. For the latter, however, the eight-course tasting menu will be a slice of gourmet heaven. There's a similar vibe (and no under-11s rule) in the hotel's chic **Ark Bar and Lounge,** where you can enjoy morning coffee, light lunches, and afternoon tea—the latter with champagne if you desire, or in a "Gentleman's Indulgent" version accompanied by a gin and tonic. A more casual option within the hotel is the Parisian-style **La Brasserie,** open daily for breakfast, lunch, and dinner, which features lots of traditional English and Continental favorites with a twist, from braised ox cheek with caramelized carrots and horseradish dumpling, to garlic snails with red wine egg, baguette, and potato puree. There's also a great children's menu.

   The Chester Grosvenor & Spa itself—which belongs to the Duke of Westminster's family—is the *grande dame* of the city's hotel scene, though its rooms are lightened by boutique-hotel-style touches, and there's a modern spa with a steam room, herb sauna, ice fountain, themed shower, and salt grotto. The various packages include spa rituals and retreats, plus several family offers, some including tickets to local attractions such as Chester Zoo and one including a ghost tour of Chester. Doubles start at £220, suites at £425.

Eastgate, Chester. www.chestergrosvenor.co.uk. ⓒ **01244/895618.** Reservations required. A la carte menu £69; 8-course tasting menu £90. AE, DC, MC, V. Tues–Sat 6:30–9pm (last order), plus Sun preceding a public holiday Mon (but closed Tues after that holiday).

Afternoon Tea, Cheshire-Style

Cheshire's many lovely tearooms are great for a decadent afternoon tea and usually also morning coffee and cakes, hot and cold lunches, and children's meals, making them great all-day options for family eating that won't cost the earth. Most also focus on local produce—Cheshire cheeses, local venison, and in the case of Tatton Park, meat and produce grown on the estate itself.

These are some of our favorite venues:
Restaurant at **Lyme Park** (p. 580).
Stables Restaurant, Tatton Park (p. 580).
Wizard Tearoom, Alderley Edge (p. 579).
Züger's Tea Rooms, St. John's Street, Chester (www.zugerstearooms.co.uk; ✆ **01244/348041**).

Sticky Walnut ★★★ ✦ MODERN EUROPEAN   Offering upscale, creative modern cooking at very good prices, this cozy restaurant is well worth the slight schlepp from central Chester (it's a 10-min. walk outside the walls)—but do reserve ahead, as word has spread. This is hearty rather than fine dining, with a fashionable, rustic edge to it: According to the season, expect oven-roast beets with fresh ricotta, sticky walnuts, and spicy pumpkin seeds; and breast of grouse, venison sausage, braised red cabbage, and cocotte potatoes.

11 Charles St., Hoole, Chester. www.stickywalnut.com/menu.html. ✆ **01244/400400.** Reservations recommended. Main courses £8–£25. MC, V. Tues–Sat noon–10pm; Sun noon–6pm.

Shopping ★★

Chester is a prime shopping destination, with the highlight being the unique **Rows,** with one tier of shops at street level, the others stacked on top along a sort of galleried balcony. Offerings on the Rows include both high-street stalwarts and quirkier one-offs, including tobacco shops, china shops, jewelers, and antiques dealers. Several Chester stores, including wine and spirits merchant **Corks Out,** 21 Watergate St. (✆ **01244/310455**), are in atmospheric medieval crypts.

North of Chester, at Ellesmere Port, the **Cheshire Oaks (McArthur Glen) Designer Outlet** (www.cheshireoaksdesigneroutlet.com; ✆ **0151/348-5600**) has 145 designer and high-street stores offering reductions of up to 60%.

Where to Stay

For the **Chester Grosvenor and Spa,** see Simon Radley at the Chester Grosvenor, above, under "Where to Eat." You'll find self-catering holiday cottages on the grounds of both **Tatton Park** (p. 580) and **Lyme Park** (p. 580).

ABode ★★★ This flagship hotel of the small chain co-founded by chef Michael Caines occupies an unexciting modern building on a roundabout just outside the center of Chester, but once inside you'll be wowed by its light-flooded rooms with their clean, contemporary palette and airy layout using glass and Perspex instead of solid walls. For families, Enviable Plus rooms have extra space and a sofabed in the lounge area. Some overlook the city's famous racecourse, others have private balconies, and some have freestanding rolltop baths and walk-in monsoon showers. All have super-comfy beds. Upper categories of room and suites come with a complimentary tuck-box of regional treats, but don't overindulge if you want to try Caines' acclaimed cooking in the top-floor restaurant (see p. 571 for a review of the **Michael Caines** restaurant at the Manchester Abode). The top-floor also has an excellent champagne bar, while at street level there's a lounge bar and the MC Café Bar & Grill. Treatment rooms were added in early 2012.

Grosvenor Rd., Chester, Cheshire CH1 2DJ. www.abodehotels.co.uk. ⓒ**01244/347000.** Units 85. £195–£250 double, suite from £430, without breakfast. AE, DC, MC, V. Parking £10 for 24 hr. (limited amount). **Amenities:** 2 restaurants; 2 bars; room service; treatment rooms; exercise room. *In-room* TV/DVD, drinks maker, entertainment center (suites), Wi-Fi (free).

Mickle Trafford Manor ★★ 🏅 🎁 This 16-century Tudor manor just northeast of Chester has great facilities for its price range: An outdoor hot tub, a sauna, and a small gym. The Master Bedroom boasts a vaulted beamed ceiling, vast bed, and double-ended bath, but all three guest rooms are very pleasant, and there's a sunny lounge with a conservatory plus a cosy hall with an open fire. Packed lunches can be ordered for days out. The hotel also now offers two cottages for rental.

Mickle Trafford, Cheshire CH2 4EA. www.mickletraffordmanor.co.uk. ⓒ **01244/300555.** 3 units. Free parking. Double £80–£95. Rates include English breakfast. MC, V. **Amenities:** Lounge and honesty bar; exercise room; sauna; hot tub. *In room:* TV.

Wizard's Thatch ★★ 🎁 Eccentric and not to everyone's taste, this cute-as-a-button ivy-covered thatched cottage, with small-paned windows and beamed ceilings, houses three suites (one sleeping four) filled with antique knick-knacks and prints and four-poster beds draped with gold and red tapestries. Named after the legendary magician of Alderley Edge (p. 579) and another good spot for a romantic break, it offers packages including champagne and chocolates on arrival, and boasts a pond where you can sit out by candlelight. Quirky decorative details include shelves lined by old ginger-beer bottles and framed *Punch* cartoons and ancient newspapers on the walls; the building's age means you have to contend with uneven floors, narrow stairs, and very low beams and doorways.

Summerhill Cottages, Macclesfield Rd., Alderley Edge, Cheshire SK9 7BG. www.wizardsthatch. co.uk. ⓒ**01625/599909.** 3 units. £185–£265 suite for 2. MC, V. Free parking. **Amenities:** DVD and CD library; books and games. *In room:* TV/DVD, kitchen facilities (fridge, toaster, and microwave), hair dryer, CD player, MP3 docking station (in 1 suite), Wi-Fi (free).

LIVERPOOL ★★★ & MERSEYSIDE ★★★

Liverpool: 219 miles NW of London; 103 miles NW of Birmingham; 35 miles W of Manchester

Like Manchester, **Liverpool** has re-emerged from decline to become a world-class city, enjoying an unprecedented cultural and economic reawakening and proudly asserting its extraordinary maritime heritage. But the rest of heavily urbanized **Merseyside** also bears some, notably **Crosby** beach with its eerie Anthony Gormley art installation, **Formby** with its nature reserve and sand dunes studded with ancient footprints, and the thoroughly English traditional seaside resort of **Southport.**

Essentials

GETTING THERE Frequent trains from London's Euston Station to Liverpool take just over 2 hours direct but more usually 2½ hours, with a change at Crewe in Cheshire, costing about £75 for an off-peak round-trip. There are also direct trains to

Liverpool from Birmingham (about 1¾ hr.), Manchester (about 1 hr.), Chester (about 45 min.), Leeds (about 1¾ hr.), and York (about 2¼ hr.).

Direct Liverpool–Southport trains take about 45 minutes, and National Express buses cover the same route (26 miles) in about 55 minutes.

Direct **National Express** (www.nationalexpress.com; ✆ **0871/781-8181**) buses to Liverpool from London's Victoria Coach Station take about 5¼ hours; there are also buses from Manchester (about 1¼ hr.) and Leeds (about 2¼ hr.).

Liverpool is about 3¾ hours northwest of London by road, mainly on the M1 and M6, about 1¼ hours northwest of Birmingham, and about 45 minutes west of Manchester.

Liverpool **John Lennon Airport** (www.liverpoolairport.com; ✆ **0871/521-8484**), serving mainly European and a few U.K. destinations, is linked by bus to central Liverpool and Manchester. There are also direct buses from **Manchester International Airport** to central Liverpool.

VISITOR INFORMATION **Albert Dock (Liverpool) Visitor Centre,** Anchor Courtyard (www.visitliverpool.com; ✆ **0151/233-2008**), is open daily 10am to 5/5:30pm. There's also an information desk at the airport.

Southport Visitor Information Centre, 112 Lord St. (www.visitsouthport.com; ✆ **01704/533333**), is open March to October Monday to Saturday 9am to 5:30pm (Nov–Feb Mon–Sat 10am–4pm).

SPECIAL EVENTS The Grand National at Sefton's **Aintree Racecourse** (www.aintree.co.uk; ✆ **0151/523-2600**) in April is said to be the world's greatest steeplechase. Liverpool's **International Beatles Week** (www.beatlesfestival.co.uk) attracts about 100,000 fans and bands from more than 20 countries for a 7-day celebration in various venues each August.

Southport's highlights are its August **Flower Show** (www.southportflowershow.co.uk) and seafront **Air Show** (www.visitsouthport.com), usually in September.

Exploring the Area
LIVERPOOL
The last decade or so has seen a significant transformation of this once-great merchant port, partly by virtue of its being awarded UNESCO World Heritage site status in 2004. Though generally best known for producing The Beatles, this 18th- and 19th- century industrial, maritime, and mercantile hothouse was a leader in both the expansion of the British Empire and the development of modern dock technology and maritime transport. The UNESCO listing applies to six areas—buildings at Pier Head, the Albert Dock and Stanley Dock Conservation Area, the Castle Street commercial center, the William Brown Conservation Area, and Duke Street ("Ropewalks"). But despite money being pumped into regeneration projects—the most obvious being Albert Dock and the new Liverpool One shopping center—much of Liverpool's appeal comes from its continued edginess, seediness, and dereliction coexisting with sparkling new shops, hotels, and attractions.

It's strange to think that Liverpool began as a 12th-century fishing village. Granted a charter as early as 1207 by King John, it grew to prominence in the 18th century through its sugar, spice, and tobacco trade with the Americas. Under Queen Victoria, it became Britain's biggest commercial seaport. Despite population hemorrhages over the past couple of decades, it retains a compelling ethnic mix, including Britain's oldest black community (descendants of 18th-century seamen, slaves, and traders'

Liverpool

HOTELS ■
Base2Stay 11

RESTAURANTS ◆
Host 13
Lunya 10

300 m
300 yds
0
0

Catharine St.

Dansie St.

Brownlow Hill

Villars St.

London Rd.

The Walker Art Gallery

World Museum Liverpool

St. John's Garden

Roe St.

Lime St. Station

Lime St.

Coppersas Hill

Warren St.

Elliot St.

Church St.

Renshaw St.

Metropolitan Cathedral of Christ the King

Mt. Pleasant

Maryland St.

Hope St.

Leece St.

Rodney St.

Pilgrim St.

Hardman St.

Roscoe St.

Berry St.

Upper Duke St.

Liverpool Art Institute

Canning St.

Cathedral Church of Christ

Huskinsson St.

Rathbone St.
Great George St.

Central Station

Bold St.

Wood St.

Seel St.

Fleet St.

Parr St.

Duke St.

Henry St.

Seel St.

School Ln.

Hanover St.

Paradise St.

Sailor's Home

Argyle St.

Lydia Ann St.

Gilbert St.

Upper Pitt St.

Kent St.

Nelson St.

Cornwallis St.

Hardy St.

St. James St.

Jamaica St.

Parliament St.

Park Lane

Nile St.

Corn St.

Tabley St.

Sparling St.

Blundell St.

Kitchen St.

Bridgewater St.

Wakinson St.

Norfolk

Brick St.

Wapping

Chaloner St.

Wapping Dock

Queen's Dock

Wapping Basin

Jury's Inn

King's Parade

Queen's Wharf

Victoria St.

Whitechapel

North St.

Johnson St.

Halton Garden

Cheapside

Smithfield St.

Vernon St.

Tithebarn St.

Batchelor St.

Stock Exchange

Chapel St.

Moorfields Station

Derby House

Old Hall St.

Earl St.

Cotton St.

Exchange Station

Langelots Hey

New Quay

King Edward St.

Bath Street

Princes Dock

Royal Liver Building

Cunard Building

Port of Liverpool Building

Cook St.

Fenwick St.

Lord St.

S. John St.

Liverpool One

Strand St.

James St. Station

Thomas Steers Way

Canning Dock

Museum of Liverpool

Merseyside Maritime Museum

Salthouse Dock

Albert Dock

Tate Liverpool

Mersey

Tunnel

Queensway

BIRKENHEAD

ATTRACTIONS ●
Anfield 1
Anglican Cathedral
  Church of Christ 14
Ferry 'Cross
  the Mersey 4
Manchester Ship
  Canal Cruise 5
Merseyside Maritime
  Museum 8
Metropolitan Cathedral
  of Christ the King 12
Museum of Liverpool 7
Sefton Park 15
Tate Liverpool 6
Walker Art Gallery 2
World Museum
  Liverpool 3
Yellow Duckmarine 9

children) and Europe's oldest Chinese community (with 19th-century seamen fore-bears), plus many Welsh and Irish, the latter due to migration from the Great Famine.

It also continues its transformation into a major world city. In 2011 the **Museum of Liverpool** (p. 588) opened in a fabulous new landmark building on the Mann Island site at Pier Head, at the core of the waterfront World Heritage site. Pier Head is also home to the listed **Royal Liver Building ★**, one of the city's "Three Graces," along with the neighboring Cunard Building and Port of Liverpool Building. Home to the Royal Liver Assurance friendly society, the landmark Royal Liver Building stands out for the famous pair of metal-sculpture Liver Birds sitting on top of it—Liverpool's symbols, these mysterious cormorant-like birds are said to protect the city's people as well as sailors coming into its port, and if one were to fly away, the city would cease to be. It's from Pier Head that you can catch a famous Ferry "Cross the Mersey" (below) or alternatively sail up the Manchester Ship Canal to Salford Quays (p. 570).

Due south of Pier Head lies another hive of activity, the handsomely regenerated red-brick **Albert Dock complex** (www.albertdock.com), now home to shops, restaurants, hotels, and several attractions, including the **Merseyside Maritime Museum** (p. 588), the **Tate Liverpool** (p. 589), and one of The Beatles Story sites (see below). The Dock is also the starting-point for tours of the city in the **Yellow Duckmarine** (p. 589).

Anfield ★ ☺ Home to Liverpool Football Club, this stadium north of the center offers tours, some led by club "legends" and some for families, or you can just look round the museum and refuel in the Boot Room Sports Café with its children's menu.

Anfield Rd. www.liverpoolfc.tv. ℭ **0151/260-6677.** Stadium tour and museum £15, £9 under-16s (£11/8 off peak); museum only £5/3. Museum daily 10am–5pm; tours daily except match days—see website for times.

Anglican Cathedral Church of Christ (Liverpool Cathedral) ★★ South and uphill of the center, the first of Liverpool's two cathedrals was built between 1904 and 1978, making it the world's newest Gothic-style cathedral. It's also England's largest church, with the world's highest vaulting under its tower, at 53m (175 ft.), and one of the world's longest cathedrals, at 186m (619 ft.). Its organ has nearly 10,000 pipes, the most found in any church, and its tower's bells are the highest (66m/219 ft.) and heaviest (28 tonnes/31 tons) in the world! "Attractions" tickets get you an audio tour (children's versions available) and admission to the tower (two consecutive elevators, then 108 stairs) with its views as far as North Wales, as well as to the hidden gem of the Elizabeth Hoare Gallery with its ecclesiastical embroideries.

St. James's Mount. www.liverpoolcathedral.org.uk. ℭ **0151/709-6271.** Free admission; attractions ticket (£5 adults, £3.50 children 5–16. Daily 8am–6pm, but may vary at short notice due to services, concerts, and award ceremonies. Recommended viewing times on Sundays noon–2:30pm. Tower Mon–Wed and Fri–Sat 10am–4:30pm; Sun about 11:45am–3:30pm.

Ferry 'Cross the Mersey ★★ Serving as both a locals' shuttle service and a tour boat offering the best views of Liverpool's awesome skyline with its mixture of the historic and the ultra-modern, the Mersey ferry also lets you take in attractions at terminals across the water (with joint tickets available): **Spaceport,** Seacombe Terminal (www.spaceport.org.uk; ℭ **0151/330-1566**), with themed galleries and temporary exhibitions, and **U-Boat Story,** Woodside Terminal (www.u-boatstory.co.uk; ℭ **0151/330-1000**), a real German submarine housing interactive displays and archive film footage. Seacombe Terminal is also home to a soft-play area and cafe.

In the new-in-2011 **Museum of Liverpool** (p. 588), you can learn much about The Beatles, a local band that, hugely influenced by its place of birth, changed popular music and wider culture on a global scale. The Wondrous Place gallery displays unique band-related objects, including the original stage on which John Lennon's band The Quarrymen played in 1957 when he met Paul McCartney, and also shows a Beatles film (for which you need to pick up a free timed ticket at the reception desk).

But the city also has plenty more Liverpool sights and attractions for Beatles aficionados. Pier Head and Albert Dock are each home to a **Beatles Story "experience"** ★, (www.beatlesstory.com; ✆ **0151/709-1963**). The one at the Dock has band memorabilia including George Harrison's first guitar, a children's discovery zone, a replica **Cavern Club** (where the band played in the early '60s), and even a Beatles-themed Starbucks; the smaller Pier Head site has special exhibitions and the Fab4-D "multisensory" journey. They're open daily April to October, 9am to 7pm, 10am to 6pm the rest of the year (last admission 5pm year-round); tickets (£15.95, £13 children 5–16) give access to both locations and all exhibitions.

Of the many Beatles tours on offer, the best are **Cavern City Tours** ★ (www.cavernclub.org/beatles-tours; ✆ **0151/236-9091**), which end at and include a look around the legendary Cavern Club. Tickets for the 2-hour bus-and-club tour cost £15.95. For truly ardent fans, **Pool of Life** ★ (www.poologlifetours.com; ✆ **07762/769296**) offers both full-day Beatles Extravaganza Tours (£98 per person) or custom tours lasting from 2 hours to 2 days. Alternatively, you can just drop into the **Cavern Club,** 10 Mathew St. (www.cavernclub.org; ✆ **0151/236-9091**), still an active bar and club hosting new and tribute bands, open daily from 10am to midnight (1:30am Thurs), with free admission Monday to Wednesday (and until 8pm Thurs, Fri, and Sun, and until 2pm Sun).

To tour both **Mendips** ★ and **20 Forthlin Road,** Lennon and McCartney's childhood homes, restored to how they would have looked in the 1950s, you need to book a place on a minibus from the city center (www.nationaltrust.org.uk/beatles; ✆ **0151/427-7231**); there's no independent access. Tickets cost £20 (£3.40 children 5–16). Tours run February to November Wednesday to Sunday and public holidays, and book up well in advance.

Finally, diehard fans may want to check into the **Hard Days Night Hotel,** North John Street (www.harddaysnighthotel.com; ✆ **0151/236-1964**), combining Beatles memorabilia with boutique chic. Themed offers include a "Magical Mystery" package at £384 for 2 people for 2 nights in a luxury room, with breakfast, Beatles Story entry, a Magical Mystery Tour, Cavern Club membership, and hotel T-shirts.

Pier Head. www.merseyferries.co.uk. ✆ **0151/639-0609.** Round-trip River Explorer tickets £6.70 adults, £4 children 5 to 15. Departures daily on the hour Mon–Fri 10am–3pm, Sat, Sun, and public holidays 10am–5pm; see website for return sailings from each terminal.

Knowsley Safari Park ★ ☺ A drive-through zoo and more, Knowsley offers up exotic animals from African wild dogs to wildebeest, plus amusement rides, a woodland walk, a new-in-2012 bird-of-prey center, and a treetop adventure course (www.aerialextreme.co.uk).

About 10 minutes east of center, along A57 (in Merseyside). www.knowsleysafariexperience.co.uk. ✆ **0151/430-9009.** Admission adults £16, children 3–15 £12; amusement rides and treetop adventure course extra. Mar–Oct daily 10am–4pm (last entry); Nov–Feb Sat and Sun 10:30am–3pm (last entry). Amusement rides mid-Feb–Oct Sat, Sun, and school holidays, from noon.

Manchester Ship Canal Cruise ★★　Running from the Mersey along the 35-mile waterway to Salford Quays (p. 570), these fascinating live-commentary cruises give you the chance to learn about the canal itself, which helped shape the history of Manchester and the northwest as a whole, as well as taking in sights such as the U-Boat Story (p. 586) or Manchester's Imperial War Museum North (p. 571). The journey takes 6 hr.; a 1-hr. bus ride brings you back to Liverpool. The 2-hour optional stopoff is available on most cruises. Refreshments are available on-board.

Seacombe or Woodside Terminal. www.merseyferries.co.uk. ✆ **0151/639-0609**. Tickets adults £37, children 2–15 £35, with return bus transfer. See website for dates.

Merseyside Maritime Museum ★ MUSEUM　Mass emigration via Liverpool, shipbuilding on Merseyside, Liverpool-linked sea tragedies including the *Titanic,* the Battle of the Atlantic, and transatlantic slavery are all examined at this museum, with the permanent displays backed up by floating exhibits, crafts demonstrations, and working displays, plus tours of the nearby Old Dock and a former pilot boat (the latter in summer only). Some of the museum's themes are reprised in the **International Slavery Museum** within the same building. There's a themed play area for children aged 8 and under.

Albert Dock. www.liverpoolmuseums.org.uk. ✆ **0151/478-4499**. Free admission. Daily 10am–5pm.

Metropolitan Cathedral of Christ the King　Visible from the tower of Liverpool's original cathedral about a half-mile northeast, along Hope Street, this circular Roman Catholic cathedral was started in 1930 to a design by Sir Edward Lutyens but ultimately scaled down and completed in 1967 to a Space Agey Modernist design by Sir Frederick Gibbert. The highlight, the crypt and its treasury, is the only part that remains of Lutyens' design.

Mount Pleasant. www.liverpoolmetrocathedral.org.uk. ✆ **0151/709-9222**. Free admission; crypt £3. Daily 7:30am–6pm; crypt Mon–Sat 10am–4pm.

Museum of Liverpool ★★ ☺ MUSEUM　New to the city in 2011, this impressive waterfront venue is best visited for its Wondrous Place gallery, which looks at how Liverpool has produced such an amazing roll call of creative folk, from musicians to footballers, as well as examining the development of the Liverpudlian dialect, Scouse. Global City, meanwhile, is focused around a 180-seat theatre where work by local filmmakers, writers, and artists tells the story of how Liverpool came to be the commercial and mercantile equal of London and New York. Children under 6 get their own hands-on Little Liverpool gallery, for which you need to pick up a free timed ticket from reception on arrival.

Pier Head. www.liverpoolmuseums.org.uk. ✆ **0151/207-0001**. Free admission. Daily 10am–5pm.

Sefton Park　About 15 minutes' walk southeast of Liverpool Cathedral, this park is English Heritage listed for its historic design and landscaping. Its magnificent three-tier palm house bears sculptures of Cook, Columbus, Darwin, Linnaeus, and other explorers, navigators, botanists, and so on, while in its grounds is a statue of Peter Pan that was unveiled in the presence of J. M. Barrie himself. The park's **Palm House** (www.palmhouse.org.uk; ✆ **0151/726-2415**) hosts concerts, tea dances, and other events, while its Victorian bandstand is claimed to be the inspiration for The Beatles' *Sgt Pepper's Lonely Hearts Club Band.*

Queen's Dr. http://liverpool.gov.uk. ☏**0151/233-2008.** Free admission. Park open 24 hr.; for Palm House, see website.

Speke Hall, Garden & Estate ★ ☺ This rare surviving Tudor manor to the south of Liverpool, down by the airport, boasts restored Victorian interiors with William Morris wallpaper, encircled by lovely gardens and woodland affording views of the Welsh hills and including a new hedge maze. Events include Victorian-costumed guided tours and outdoor theatre and concerts, and the Home Farm Visitor Centre on the grounds has a play area and picnic tables.

Speke, 14 miles south of Liverpool. www.nationaltrust.org.uk. ☏ **0151/427-7231.** Admission to house, garden, and grounds £8.90 adults, £4.40 children 5–16; separate tickets available. Mid-Mar–Oct Wed–Sun 11am–5pm, plus weekends late Feb–mid-Mar and Nov–mid-Dec 11am–4pm.

Tate Liverpool ★★★ ☺ GALLERY A little sister to the Tate Britain and Tate Modern in London (p. 110), this bright and funky modern gallery is home to international modern and contemporary art collections and major changing exhibitions, some on artists as eminent as Picasso and Magritte. Like other Tates, it's strong on family activities and events, and has a great cafe (p. 591).

Albert Dock. www.tate.org.uk/liverpool. ☏ **0151/702-7400.** Free admission exc special exhibitions. Daily 10am–5pm.

Walker Art Gallery ★★ ☺ This central venue has an outstanding collection of European art from the 1300s but is especially rich in European Old Masters and Victorian, pre-Raphaelite, and contemporary British works, and also has an award-winning sculpture gallery, a craft and design gallery, and a children's gallery.

William Brown St. www.liverpoolmuseums.org.uk. ☏ **0151/478-4199.** Free admission. Daily 10am–5pm.

World Museum Liverpool ★ ☺ MUSEUM Since doubling in size in 2005, close to the Walker Art Gallery this museum has galleries devoted to dinosaurs, geology, "Space and Time" (with a planetarium), the natural world (including live bugs and an aquarium), world cultures, and the ancient world. Family activities and events are a forte, and the emphasis is very much on hands-on experiences, but try to avoid school holidays when the place gets uncomfortably busy.

William Brown St. www.liverpoolmuseums.org.uk. ☏ **0151/478-4393.** Free admission. Daily 10am–5pm.

Yellow Duckmarine ★ ☺ These converted World War II DUKW amphibious landing craft offer hour-long tours of Liverpool and its major sights, from the Chinese Arch to the two cathedrals, before splash-landing in the Salthouse Dock. An alternative is the same firm's Yellow Boat Cruise, a water-based heritage tour.

Albert Dock. www.theyellowduckmarine.co.uk. ☏ **0151/708-7799.** Tickets £9.95–12.95 adults, £7.95–£9.95 children (off peak/peak, with peak being Feb–Oct public holidays and preceding weekends, plus school holidays). Tours daily from 10:30am or 11am and running every 15–30 min (75 min at very quiet times).

THE REST OF MERSEYSIDE

Merseyside is highly urbanized even outside the confines of Liverpool, though the borough of Sefton north of Liverpool boasts some gems on its coast. The first stop north of the city is **Crosby,** where globally renowned sculptor Antony Gormley—also behind the Angel of the North (p. 667)—has sited his art installation *Another Place* ★★★ (www.sefton.gov.uk). Along 2 miles of Crosby's beach and about a half-mile out to sea stand 100 cast-iron casts of Gormley's own body, sunk to various depths in the sand and appearing to stare out to the horizon in silent expectation. The work is generally read as a response to the ambivalence of emigration—sadness at leaving tempered by hope for a better future. The artwork is within the Crosby Coastal Park, which is also home to the **Crosby Lakeside Adventure Centre** (www.crosbylakeside.co.uk; ✆ **0151/966-6868**) offering watersports and other activities.

Next up as you follow the coast north is **Formby,** an affluent town on the Irish Sea. In summer, its population—which includes (or has included) several famous local footballers—swells considerably as visitors flock to its beach (see below). This stretch of coast as a whole is popular with kite-surfers and golfers alike; its several links golf courses include **Royal Birkdale** (www.royalbirkdale.com; ✆ **01704/552020**), sometimes host to The Open.

Birkdale is on the outskirts of **Southport ★★**, a gloriously old-fashioned seaside resort in the proper English manner and yet also surprisingly elegant, with fine examples of Victorian architecture and town planning. Indeed, it's been suggested that the years that Louis-Napoléon Bonaparte spent in exile on broad, tree-lined Lord Street, now famous for its shopping (see below), inspired his redevelopment of much of the medieval center of Paris when he eventually became emperor.

Southport is the starting point for the 215-mile **Trans Pennine Trail** (www.transpenninetrail.org.uk), linking the Irish Sea with the North Sea for walkers, cyclists, and horse-riders, via the Peak District (p. 535) and Yorkshire (p. 632).

Formby ★★ ☺ Formby's beach is backed by sand dunes and pine woods that constitute a National Trust reserve, home to some of Britain's dwindling red squirrel population. This is also a rare breeding spot for natterjack toads, who can be heard "singing" in the late evening. On some parts of the beach, sand erosion has revealed Neolithic/early Bronze Age footprints of humans and animals, including red deer, while the sand dunes are famous for their asparagus, which used to be served on luxury liners setting out from Liverpool (there have been recent efforts to revive the crop and set up an "asparagus trail").

Freshfield, Formby. www.nationaltrust.org.uk. ✆ **01704/878591.** Free admission; car parking £3/3.50. Beach accessible daily 6.05am–6.05pm; for woodland see website.

Model Railway Village ★ ☺ Next to Southport's Marine Lake Bridge, this quaint attraction has miniature trains running through rural, village, and town scenes typical of Lancashire (of which Southport used to be a part). Combine a visit with nearby **New Pleasureland** (www.southportfunfair.co.uk; ✆ **01704/532717**), a recent (and lesser) reincarnation of the town's long-standing fun fair, or the indoor **Dunes Splash World** (www.splashworldsouthport.com; ✆ **01704/537160**).

Kings Gardens. www.southportmodelrailwayvillage.co.uk. ✆ **01704/538001.** Admission £3.50 adults, £3 ages 1–15. Apr–Oct Sat–Thurs 10am–5pm, plus Fri in school holidays.

Southport Pier ★★★ ☺ Britain's second longest pleasure pier, at more than half a mile, has been restored to its Victorian glory in the last decade and boasts an array of traditional seaside amusements, from fun-fair rides at one end to a pavilion at the other housing restored "penny in the slot" machines to play on and an exhibition on this coastline and its wildlife. The views across the vast sand-flats are also utterly stunning. Disconcertingly, the pier actually begins a long way inland, and you can catch either a tram or a minitrain along its length. Before reaching the sea, the pier crosses Marine Lake, where you can take out a mini-motorboat or pedal-boat or ride the Mississippi-style paddlesteamer the **Southport Belle** (✆ **01704/539701**).

Promenade, Southport. ©**01704/539701.** Free admission; charge for tram, minitrain, and penny slot machines. Daily 11am–5pm (10am–6pm summer school holidays).

Where to Eat

There are several quality chains in **Liverpool One** (p. 592), many of them good for children, including **Wagamama,** a lively and open Asian fusion experience.

The Dolphin ★ ☺ FISH & CHIPS   A Southport institution just back from the Promenade, this traditional "chippy" may lack glamour and a alcoholic drinks license but can always be counted on for a warm welcome and great fish and chips, plus a huge selection of other fare including roasts, pies, sandwiches, beans on toast, and the like, afternoon tea, and that seaside favorite the knickerbocker glory (ice-cream sundae). Children's dishes—fish fingers or fishcakes with chips and beans—will set you back a paltry £3 or so, while food to carry out is available if you fancy combining lunch or dinner with a stroll along the pier.

30–34 Scarisbrick Ave., Southport. http://dolphinsouthport.com. ©**01704/538251.** Main courses £4.95–£7.25. MC, V. Daily 11am–6pm.

Host ★ ASIAN FUSION   This 1950s-inspired dining room near Liverpool Cathedral offers Thai-, Chinese-, and Japanese-style nibbles and dishes, plus cocktails, making it a great place for a convivial meal with friends (the bench seating and some long communal tables militate against romance). Standout dishes include corn fritters with tamarind caramel, and sweet chili chicken with nasi goreng and asian slaw. The highly original desserts are almost scandalously good: Think chocolate and chili brownie, or peanut butter brûlée with strawberry-jam spring rolls.

31 Hope St., Liverpool. www.ho-st.co.uk. © **0151/708-5831.** Reservations recommended. Main courses £8.50–£11.95. MC, V. Daily 11am–11pm.

Lunya ★★ 🍴☺ SPANISH   This Catalan fusion restaurant and deli in an 18th-century warehouse on the edge of the Liverpool One mall (p. 592) brings recipes, ideas, and ingredients from Spain and the U.K. together in exciting tapas dishes. It's hard to narrow down the field from the vast menu, but we can vouch for the slow-cooked ox cheeks in red wine with celeriac purée, and the hot smoked baby mackerel. You can also get paella. Children get an excellent menu of child-friendly tapas including homemade meatballs, *patatas bravas* (fried potatoes), *croquetas* (croquettes), Spanish omelet, and, to round it off, homemade *churros* (long thin donuts) to dunk into thick hot chocolate; on Sunday mornings, they can get a Spanish lesson while you browse the papers over breakfast. Lunya's unusual breakfasts include baked eggs "flamenco," with a tomato and onion sauce, seasonal vegetables, Serrano ham, and chorizo. There are also regular Gourmet Nights offering a seven-course menu paired

---

Eating in Liverpool's Museums & Galleries

Some of Liverpool's best eateries are set in its cultural venues: The World Museum's cafe is awful, but we do recommend the **Maritime Dining Rooms** (www.liverpoolmuseums.org.uk; © **0151/478-4056**) at the **Merseyside** **Maritime Museum,** the **Tate Liverpool Café** (www.tate.org.uk; © **0151/702-7400**), and the **Upstairs Bistro** (www.thebluecoat.org.uk; © **0151/702-5324**) at The Bluecoat. All have children's menus.

with top-notch wines, featuring the likes of pig's trotter escudella with lavender-syrup-coated Southport brown shrimp.

18 College Lane, Liverpool. www.lunya.co.uk. ✆ **0151/706-9770.** Reservations recommended. Tapas dishes £3.75–£16.95. MC, V. Mon–Sat 9am–late; Sun 10am–11pm.

Shopping

Liverpool's rebirth has included the creation of the vast, retail-led **Liverpool One complex** ★★ (www.liverpool-one.com), which opened to widespread acclaim in 2008–9 on underused land near the Albert Dock. Home to about 170 shops and services and divided into six districts, it's the U.K.'s 11th-largest shopping center, with its own terraced park. Forward-thinking in design, it's been criticized for drawing retailers away from the center proper (around Lime St. Station), but that area in turn is being transformed into Central Village, with completion scheduled for 2013.

Where Liverpool One has mainly familiar high-street names such as John Lewis and Topshop, the nearby **Metquarter** (www.metquarter.com), opened on Whitechapel in 2006 and dubbed the "Bond Street of Liverpool," has mainly upmarket boutiques. For more bohemian shopping (and eating), head south to villagey **Lark Lane** (www.larklane.com) off Sefton Park.

In Southport, **Lord Street** attracts shoppers with its Victorian covered arcades full of high-street names as well as one-off boutiques.

Entertainment & Nightlife

European Capital of Culture in 2008, Liverpool is positively bursting with creative energies, whether it's in established venues or more underground spots. Among the former are the **Liverpool Philharmonic Hall** ★, Hope Street (www.liverpoolphil.com; ✆ **0151/210-2895**), home to one of the best orchestras outside London and also hosting concerts by touring musicians.

The Liverpool rock, pop, and dance music scenes also continue to thrive, particularly in the Ropewalks district. **Nation,** Wolstenholme Square (✆ **0151/707-1309**), hosts the long-standing, world-famous **Cream** ★★ (www.cream.co.uk) dance night, typically held four times a year and attracting superstar DJs. For listings at Nation and elsewhere, see www.anightinliverpool.com, or pick up flyers in shops and cafes.

Liverpool is also very gay friendly, as evidenced by plans announced in 2011 to revamp the newly pedestrianized Gay Quarter (focused on Stanley, Cumberland, Victoria, and Eberle streets) to make it one of the U.K.'s gay hubs. The area also received official recognition by the City Council in August 2011, and in November of the same year Stanley Street became the first U.K. city to bear the Gay Pride flag on its street signage. There's also a month-long festival of gay culture, **Homotopia** (www.homotopia.net) in October/November.

Where to Stay
EXPENSIVE

There's a **Malmaison** in Liverpool, at William Jessop Way (www.malmaison.com; ✆ **0151/229-5000**), with views of the Mersey and Royal Liver Building from some rooms (£129–£186 doubles). Of its two suites themed for local football teams Liverpool and Everton, Kop has its own games room. For the Beatles-themed **Hard Days Night Hotel,** see p. 587.

MODERATE–EXPENSIVE

Ramada Plaza Southport ★ ✦ ☺ The best located of Southport's hotels for those who like to be reminded they're at the Great British seaside, this ocean-liner-like building has views over Marine Lake, the pier, and the sea. It's surprisingly stylish for a chain, with fresh contemporary decor in its light-flooded rooms (the eight Marine Lake Executive rooms have 180-degree views of the coastline through picture windows) and a waterside **brasserie** with a pleasant terrace. Packages include theatre breaks (the hotel adjoins Southport Theatre), golf breaks, and tickets for local attractions such as WWT Martin Mere (p. 598). Families are comfortably accommodated in rooms with two double beds. Guests get free access to the leisure center opposite, with an adults-only pool, family pool, learner pool, gym, sauna, and steam room.

Marine Lake, Southport PR9 0DZ. www.ramadaplazasouthport.co.uk. ℂ**01704/516220.** 133 units. £69–£180 double; £169–£210 suite including English breakfast (room-only rates available). MC, V. Free parking. **Amenities:** Restaurant; bar; free access to leisure club with indoor pools. *In room:* TV, fridge, Wi-Fi (free).

INEXPENSIVE

There's a very good new **Novotel** just by Liverpool One (40 Hanover St., ℂ **0151/702-5100**), with a great basement pool and rooms for up to four guests from about £75 without breakfast.

The Crosby Lakeside Adventure Centre (p. 590) has 14 bedrooms, some specially for families, with bunkbeds.

Base2Stay ★★★ ✦ ☺ The second incarnation of a concept that has found great favor in London (p. 192), this innovative budget-meets-boutique hotel in the UNESCO-listed Ropewalks area offers visitors great value for money, as well as flexibility and a funky vibe (although note that, at certain times, some rooms would fall into our "Expensive" category). Opened in 2010 in a converted 1850s' engineering works, it offers in-room mini-kitchens instead of a restaurant or bar, the freedom to order in meals from local providers (some at a discount), and free coffee. The decor is muted, modern, and quite chic, but original architectural features in many rooms, including the original roof timbers, believed to have come from 18-century ships, bring dashes of character. Rooms include duplex Gallery Studios and the unique Secret Garden Suite with its own courtyard to sit out in. The latter, sleeping five, is

---

Liverpool: Charm & Character on a Shoestring

Those visiting Liverpool on a budget are in luck: Its Albert Dock redevelopment, home to some outstanding cultural venues, houses two budget hotels that transcend the limits of their respective chains with guest rooms featuring some of the original warehouses' cast iron and red brick. **Express by Holiday Inn ★** (www.exliverpool.com; ℂ **0844/875-7575**) offers doubles and family rooms with views over the Mersey or the dock itself

from just £59 (or less with nonrefundable early booking). **Premier Inn** (www.premierinn.com; ℂ **0871/527-8622**), a similarly sympathetic conversion, has doubles and family rooms from around £73. Less characterful but even easier on the wallet, the purpose-built modern **youth hostel** nearby (25 Tabley St; www.yha.org.uk; ℂ **0845/371-9527**) has rooms sleeping 2–8, with en suite 2-bed rooms going for as little as £30 per night.

the best option for families, although many rooms can sleep three or four, and some rooms can interconnect. The singles are very comfortable for solo travelers.

29 Seel St., Liverpool L1 4AU. www.base2stayliverpool.com. © **0151/705-2626.** 106 units. £59–£155 double; £129–£225 suite. MC, V. **Amenities:** Lounge with free coffee machine; breakfast-box service (extra charge). *In room:* TV with free Internet, kitchenette, games, Wi-Fi (free).

Carleton House ★ 🍴 This charming, lovingly run little B&B within a handsome Victorian property a short walk east of Southport's Promenade offers singles, doubles/twins, and family rooms stylishly decorated in creams and beiges, with flat-screen TVs. There's also a self-catering apartment in the garden. Breakfasts (including full English if desired) are excellent—the extremely friendly owners have a farming background and are passionate about local produce.

17 Alexandra Rd., Southport PR9 0NB. www.thecarletonhouse.co.uk. © **01704/538035.** 12 units. £75–£95 double. Rates include English breakfast. MC, V. **Amenities:** Lounge. *In room:* TV, hair dryer, Wi-Fi (free).

LANCASHIRE ★★★

Blackpool: 246 miles NW of London; 51 miles NW of Manchester; 56 miles N of Liverpool; 88 miles W of Leeds

Often overlooked in favor of the more spectacular Lake District, Lancashire is best known as home to one of Britain's biggest tourist attractions, **Blackpool's** Pleasure Beach. But while kitsch Blackpool, like Las Vegas, which it resembles in some respects, is an acquired taste, there are large swaths of this county with glorious wild landscapes perfect for lovers of the great outdoors, especially the scorchingly beautiful Forest of Bowland. And Lancashire is also one of Britain's great foodie destinations, with many top-ranking chefs settling here to make the best of the superb local produce in their creative cuisine.

Essentials

GETTING THERE Trains to Blackpool from London Euston require at least one change, at Preston (also in Lancashire) or Manchester, and take a little over 2¾ hours or more; tickets are around £80 for an off-peak round-trip). From Manchester, it's about a 1¼-hour trip. Direct trains from Liverpool take just under 1½ hours; from Leeds it's 2¼ hours. Direct **National Express** buses (www.nationalexpress.com; © **0871/781-8181**) from London take 7 hours or more, with some requiring a change at Manchester, about 1½ hours away. There are also direct buses from Leeds, taking about 3¼ hours.

Blackpool is just over 4 hours northwest of London by road, mainly via the M1 and M6, about 1 hour northwest of Manchester, 1¼ hours north of Liverpool, and about 1½ hours west of Leeds. **Blackpool International Airport** (www.blackpool international.com), just south of the town, has links with a dozen or so other European destinations.

Trains from London Euston to Lancaster take just under 2½ hours; at Lancaster, you can change for Morecambe, about 10 minutes away. There are some direct trains from Leeds to Lancaster (about 2 hr.) and Manchester (just under 1 hr.). From Liverpool it's about 1¼ hours, with at least one change.

Lancaster is 1¼ hours north of Liverpool by road and about 1 hour northwest of Manchester, with direct National Express buses from the latter (1½ hr.). For public transport in the area, see www.lancashire.gov.uk.

VISITOR INFORMATION   **Blackpool Tourist Information Centre,** Festival House, Promenade (www.visitblackpool.com; ✆ **01253/478222**), is open Monday to Saturday 9am to 5:30pm, Sunday 10am to 4pm.

Lytham St. Annes Tourist Information Centre, 67 St. Annes Rd. (www.visit-lythamstannes.co.uk; ✆ **01253/725610**), is open Monday to Saturday 10am to 5pm.

Morecambe Visitor Information Centre, Old Station Buildings, Marine Road Central (www.citycoastcountryside.co.uk; ✆ **01524/582808**), is open Monday to Saturday 9:30am to 5pm (plus Apr–Oct Sun 10am–4pm).

SPECIAL EVENTS   Lancashire's tacky take on the Northern Lights, the **Blackpool Illuminations** (www.visitblackpool.com/site/illuminations), bedeck the resort's promenade from late August or early September to November each year, featuring hundreds of neon figures (illuminated using green electricity, some from on-site wind turbines). Of course, this is a cynical ploy to extend the resort's season past summer.

Blackpool is a mecca for ballroom dancers and their fans, with five festivals a year (www.blackpooldancefestival.com; ✆ **01253/625252**); the longest-running and most famous is the 8-day Blackpool Dance Festival each May, which featured in the Jennifer Lopez movie *Shall We Dance?*

Exploring the Area
BLACKPOOL ★

A bit like Las Vegas with a Victorian twist, this unremittingly tacky resort is centered on the theme park **Pleasure Beach** (see below). Beyond that, Blackpool has a promenade served by antique electric trams, 7 miles of rather insipid beaches (with donkeys to ride), three piers, and a surfeit of cheap restaurants, guesthouses, and amusement arcades. Indeed, Blackpool is said to have more hotel and B&B rooms than all of Portugal.

The resort does have its charm, if you approach it in the right frame of mind. Depending on your tastes, central "attractions" are the landmark **Blackpool Tower** (see below), a **Madame Tussauds** waxworks museum (www.madametussauds.com/blackpool; ✆ **0871/282-9200**), the **Sea Life** aquarium (www.visitsealife.com/Blackpool; ✆ **01253/621258**), and **Sandcastle Waterpark** (www.sandcastle-waterpark.co.uk; ✆ **01253/343602**)), which includes some Aztec-themed slides.

Not far south of Blackpool, **Lytham St. Annes** is a genteel alternative to the larger resort, formed by the merging of two neighboring towns and globally famed for its golf. Of its four courses and links, the Royal Lytham & St. Annes (www.royallytham.org) is a host of the **British Open** (www.opengolf.com).

Blackpool Tower ★ ☺ ENTERTAINMENT COMPLEX   Built in 1894 as a half-size version of Paris's Eiffel Tower, this famous structure houses a Victorian ballroom, a circus, the **Blackpool Tower Eye** "observation experience" with its 4-D cinema, the **Blackpool Tower Dungeon,** with live actors, a scary ride, shows, and special effects, and an indoor adventure playground.

Promenade. www.theblackpooltower.com. ✆01953/622242. Admission and opening times vary by attraction (combined tickets available); see website.

Great Promenade Show   A rare oasis of culture in Blackpool, this outdoor exhibition stretching just over a mile along the seafront features artworks commissioned from established and emerging artists to celebrate the resort's natural and man-made attractions. One, *Desire,* is inspired by kiss-me-quick and holiday romances and casts a shadow of a broken heart on the ground; another, *The Frankenstein Project,* refers back to Victorian Blackpool's freak shows; and yet others come to life at night.

New South Promenade. Free admission. Open 24 hr.

Pleasure Beach ★★ ☺THEME PARK   Dating back to 1896, this large theme park is now home to 125-plus rides and attractions, from world-famous white-knuckle thrillers including the Pepsi Max Big One and Valhalla to gentler rides for youngsters, some of the latter in the new-in-2011 Nickelodeonland. There's a surprisingly chic in-park hotel (p. 601).

Ocean Boulevard. www.blackpoolpleasurebeach.com. ✆ **0871/222-1234.** Admission 1-day unlimited ride wristband £32 adults, £27 children 2–11, or various passes available. Easter–Nov, with hours varying by season; see website.

Stanley Park ★★   This congenial and historic spot east of the Promenade offers up a golf course and crazy golf, a boating lake, tennis courts, bowling greens, a playground, and an Art Deco cafe hosting live jazz on Sundays, as well as being home to **Blackpool Zoo** (www.blackpoolzoo.org.uk; ✆ **01253/830830**) and **Blackpool Model Village & Gardens** (www.blackpoolmodelvillage.com; ✆ **01253/763827**), with its miniature buildings and model railway.

Southeast of center, next to Blackpool Victoria Hospital. www.blackpool.gov.uk. ✆**01253/478478.** Free admission. Daily dawn–dusk.

OTHER LANCASHIRE HOTSPOTS

Most of the rest of Lancashire couldn't be more different from Blackpool, with the highlight being the **Forest of Bowland** ★★★ (www.forestofbowland.com), an Area of Outstanding Natural Beauty and vast outdoor playground popular with walkers and cyclists, dotted with pretty villages. The Forest is home to the majority of the **Ribble Valley,** with a sculpture trail from Brungerley Bridge to Crosshills Quarry that forms part of the 73-mile **Ribble Way** ★, following the River Ribble from Longton west of Preston through Ribchester and Clitheroe into North Yorkshire (p. 645). Alternatively, you might discover the area via the award-winning **Ribble Valley Food Trail** ★★ (www.ribblevalleyfoodtrail.com) championing local produce, including meat from traditional Lancashire breeds, pies and pastries, ice cream, and handmade chocolate.

Just east of the Ribble Valley market town of Clitheroe, **Pendle Hill** looms over "witch country." At the foot of the hill, St. Mary's churchyard in the unspoiled village of **Newchurch-in-Pendle** has a grave said to be that of local witch Alice Nutter, carved with a skull and crossbones, while the west side of the church tower bears a carving described as the "Eye of God," claimed to ward off evil. Learn all about the Pendle witches at the **Pendle Heritage Centre** (p. 598), the starting point for the 45-mile **Pendle Witch Trail** ★ following the route taken by the "witches" through the Ribble Valley and the Trough of Bowland—a wild beauty spot—to stand trial in **Lancaster** ★, Lancashire's county town. The trial took place within medieval **Lancaster Castle** (see below). Otherwise, like Durham (p. 659), this is a pleasant little city with one of the U.K.'s top universities and a handful of small-scale sights, including the **City Museum and King's Own Royal Regiment Museum** (www.lancashire.gov.uk; ✆ **01524/64637**) and the **Lancaster Maritime Museum** (same website; ✆ **01524/382264**). But one of the best things to do, especially on a fine day, is head up to **Williamson Park** with its Edwardian Butterfly House for great views over Morecambe Bay to the Lake District (p. 603).

Lancaster flows seamlessly into **Morecambe** ★, a resort described in 1930s' ads as "the Sunset Coast" for its setting on a seemingly infinite bay to rival any seascape in the world. Between the days when it was known as the "Brighton of the North" or even the "Naples of the North," attracting the likes of Noel Coward, Wallace Simpson, and Coco Chanel, and its rating as number 3 in the 2003 book *Crap Towns: The 50 Worst Places to Live in the UK,* it underwent a slow but painful decline and lost both its piers and its pleasure beach. The reopening of its Art Deco Midland Hotel (p. 601) in 2008 seemed to bespeak great things to come, but change is still at snail's pace, not least in the restoration of the long-abandoned **Winter Gardens** (www. thewintergardensmorecambe.co.uk), the magnificent red-brick pavilion that once housed a theatre, ballrooms, and baths—the setting for scenes in the 1960 Laurence Olivier movie *The Entertainer.*

If that all makes Morecambe sound unappealing, it's far from the truth: Despite the lack of a pier, the town offers a rare taste of the real, unreconstructed British seaside resort, with a pale-sand, child-friendly beach, a handful of fun rides, a quirky outsize sculpture of Eric Morecambe—the much-loved comedian who changed his name from John Bartholomew in honor of his hometown—and little to do beyond slurp ice creams or buy a bag of fish and chips or some bay-caught cockles or potted shrimps, and sit on the seafront gazing out at the ocean on which Chanel is said to have landed her seaplane after flying up from Antibes.

Bowland Wild Boar Park ★★ ☺ A focal point within the gorgeous Trough of Bowland, this attraction has boar, longhorn cows, deer, llamas, and goats (some of which you can feed), pedal tractors and tractor rides for children, but best of all lots of wooded countryside in which visitors are free to ramble and picnic. The cafe serves home-cooked food including the park's own wild boar meat.

Chipping. www.wildboarpark.co.uk. ✆ **01995/61554.** Admission adults £5, children 3–15 £4.50. Daily mid-Feb–Nov 10:30am–5pm; rest of year 11am–4pm.

Brockholes ★★ ☺ NATURE RESERVE Opened in 2011, this "unreserved reserve" on an old quarry site includes one of Britain's largest strips of ancient woodland and is one of the best spots in the country for spotting birds, especially breeding waders—wildlife hides allow you to get up close. The site also boasts Britain's first floating visitor center, on a pontoon, family nature activities, walking trails and guided walks, and even tai chi sessions. Note that signing up for Wildlife Trust membership helps this free attraction to cover its costs.

Beside junction 31 of the M6. www.brockholes.org. ✆ **01772/877140.** Free admission (car parking £4 for up to 5 hr.). Apr–Oct daily 10am–5pm; rest of year daily 10am–4pm.

Camelot ★ This theme park has rides for all ages, most of them with a medieval theme, and also hosts jousting tournaments, wizardry displays, and flying displays in its birds-of-prey and animal center. The on-site Best Western Park Hall Hotel (www. lavenderhotels.co.uk; ✆ **0845/450-1320**) with its swimming pools offers themed rooms and Camelot breaks.

Chorley. www.camelotthemepark.co.uk. ✆ **01257/453044.** Admission £26 for anyone over 1m/3ft. 4in. tall. Easter–Oct; see website for the days and times.

Clitheroe Castle Museum ★★ ☺ High on a hill, this museum within the former steward's house beside Clitheroe's Norman landmark has been newly revamped to create galleries that take you on a journey through 350 million years of local history, heritage, and geology, and not always by expected means—past exhibits have included a sound installation by a contemporary classical composer. Younger visitors get a rucksack, map, and magnifying glass.

Clitheroe. www.lancashire.gov.uk. ✆ **01772/534061.** Admission £3.65, accompanied children free. Apr–Oct daily 11am–5pm; Nov–Mar noon–4pm.

Lancaster Castle & Judges' Lodgings ★★ CASTLE   Officially owned by the Duke of Lancaster (the Queen), Lancaster Castle—still home to the local courts—was where the Pendle witches (p. 596) were brought to trial and imprisoned, and today's tours take you into the grand jury room, courts, and dungeons. Exhibits also touch the subject of convict transportation, as many hundreds of people were sentenced to deportation in these courts. You can also see the neighboring Judges' Lodgings (on Church Street), the one-time town-house residence of castle-keeper and notorious witchhunter Thomas Covell, with period furniture, plus a small museum of childhood.

Castle Parade, Lancaster. www.lancastercastle.com. ✆ **01524/64998.** Castle tour £5 adults, accompanied children free; Judges' Lodgings £3, £2 children 5–15. Castle tours daily 10:30am– 4pm; Judges' Lodgings July–Sept Mon–Fri 10am–4pm, Sat–Sun noon–4pm; Easter–June and Oct Mon–Fri 1–4pm, Sat–Sun noon–4pm.

Museum of Lancashire ★   Reopened in late 2011 after a £1.7 million revamp, the regional museum, set in the old court house in Lancashire's administrative center, boasts eight new interactive and child-friendly galleries covering Roman times, the Iron Age, and Edwardian Britain. Other displays include Lancashire at Play, focusing on local humor, music, entertainment, and seaside holidays, and Lancashire Goes to War, which features a World War I trench.

Stanley St., Preston. www.lancashire.gov.uk. ✆ **01772/534075.** Free admission. Tues–Sat plus public holiday Mon 10:30am–5pm; Sun noon–5pm.

Pendle Heritage Centre ★★   The starting point for the Pendle Witch Trail (p. 596), these former farm buildings include a museum about both the witches and the 15th-century farm itself, an art gallery and craft shop, a walled garden with 18th-century plants and another small museum on its creation, a woodland walk taking you to the cruck-framed barn housing farm animals, a tearoom serving traditional Lancashire fare, and a tourist information desk.

Park Hill, Barrowford. www.htnw.co.uk/phc.html. ✆ **01282/677150.** Admission £4.40 to whole site (separate tickets available), £2.65 children 5–15. Daily 10am–4pm.

WWT Martin Mere Wetland Centre ★★ ☺ NATURE RESERVE   Great for a family outing in nature, this reserve offers visitors the chance to stroll through waterfowl gardens and hand-feed their inhabitants, see aerial displays of wild ducks, geese, and swans, visit a beaver enclosure, attend otter and flamingo talks, follow the nature trail and/or reedbed walk, let off steam in the adventure play area, and even try a canoe safari.

Fish Lane, Burscough. www.wwt.org.uk/visit-us/martin-mere. ✆ **01704/895181.** Admission £10.45 adults, £5.10 children 4–16. Daily Nov–Feb 9:30am–5pm (to 5:30pm rest of year).

Where to Eat
VERY EXPENSIVE

Northcote ★★ ☺ MODERN BRITISH   A top-notch place for Lancashire produce, this long-standing restaurant with guest rooms on the edge of the Trough of

Bowland offers up food as brave and beautiful as the landscape—think native lobster dab with mushy peas, lemon jelly, and sea lettuce; and grouse Wellington with sweet and sour turnip purée, roast pear, and grouse parfait. Vegetarians are well catered for with their own gourmet menu. If the prices are likely to curb your appetite, come at lunchtime and eat from the seasonal menu (£26 for three courses and coffee). Alternatively, there's an afternoon tea and lounge menu including cream teas, sandwiches, and salads, but advance reservations are essential and at weekends it's only available to those staying in one of the 14 very comfortable **guest rooms** (£220–£270 including English breakfast). The restaurant also warmly welcomes children and will happily provide smaller versions of dishes or simpler alternatives; if you stay, connecting rooms/sofabeds are available. There are also renowned Lancashire breakfasts open to all.

There are four Ribble Valley Inns associated with Northcote, two in Lancashire: The **Three Fishes** (www.thethreefishes.com; ℘ **01254/826888**) at Mitton and **The Clog and Billycock** (www.theclogandbillycock.com; ℘ **01254/201163**) at Pleasington. Both are very child-friendly and both focus on local seafood but also offer wonderful "Length of Lancashire" cheeseboards.

Northcote Rd., Langho. www.northcote.com. ℘ **01254/240555.** Reservations recommended (required for afternoon tea Mon–Fri). Main courses £25–£35. AE, DC, MC, V. Mon–Fri 7:45–9:45am, noon–2:30–5:30pm, and 7–9:30pm; Sat 7:45–9:45am, noon–2pm, 3–5:30pm (guests only), and 6:30–9:30pm; Sun 7:45–9:45am, noon–2pm, 3:30–5:30pm (guests only), and 7–9pm.

EXPENSIVE

Inn at Whitewell ★★ ☺ MODERN BRITISH   In the heart of the Forest of Bowland (Area of Outstanding Natural Beauty), this remote 14th-century coaching inn offers food in both its riverside dining room and garden and its several bar areas. The restaurant is more formal, though not off-puttingly so. The starter of crispy slow-roast belly pork with parched peas, parsnip purée, and apple sauce merits the journey here alone, while the filet of local beef served pink with a little cottage pie of braised oxtail and baby onions, celeriac purée, and red-wine jus is just one of several superb main courses. The livelier bar is the place to eat with children, who get small portions from a menu that includes a famous fish pie and locally made Cumberland sausage with champ; prices here average about £13 for a main course. At lunch, the same dishes are complemented by a choice of substantial salads and sandwiches.

The 23 **guest rooms** (£120–£231 double including English breakfasts) are cozy and a bit chintzy, with comfy traditional wool and horsehair mattresses; about half have open fires, while others have four-posters, roll-top tubs, and eccentric Victorian bathing paraphernalia, and/or sofabeds. There's guests-only fishing on the river.

Whitewell, near Clitheroe. www.innatwhitewell.com. ℘ **01200/448222.** Reservations recommended. Main courses £15.40–£27. MC, V. Daily noon–2pm, dinner 7:30–9:30pm.

MODERATE

Food by Breda Murphy ★★★ ☺ MODERN BRITISH   A stop on the Ribble Valley Food Trail (p. 596), this is a little gem of a deli and daytime bistro offering creative modern fare based on local ingredients. The eponymous Irish chef often gives a modern twist to classic British dishes by incorporating influences gleaned from her travels in southeast Asia: Think warm salad of Goosnargh smoked chicken and Bury black pudding with Bramley apple purée and crisp hashbrowns. There are also delicious open sandwiches, nibbles, and children's meals and portions. Just be careful not to overdo it if you want to indulge in a sensational dessert—perhaps warm caramelized pineapple sponge pudding with coconut sorbet. There are also luxurious afternoon teas.

Abbots Court, 41 Station Rd., Whalley. www.foodbybredamurphy.com. (℗ **01254/823446.** Reservations recommended. Main courses £6.25–£16.25. MC, V. Tues–Sat 10am–6pm, plus occasional evenings.

INEXPENSIVE

P Brucciani ★ 🎁☺ LUNCH/SNACKS   This former milk bar retains its original "high-street Deco" styling of wood, chrome, Formica, and Bakelite, etched glass and mirrors, and penny-in-the-slot cubicles in the toilets. Opened in 1939, it was much frowned upon by some locals, who feared it would tarnish Morecambe's genteel Victorian image. Now almost a part of the resort's very fabric, in its prime seafront promenade spot with killer views of the shimmering bay, it's a great place to step back in time, with old-fashioned knickerbocker glories and sundaes but also sandwiches, soups, and the likes of egg and chips or beans on toast, plus great coffee.

217 Marine Road West, Morecambe. (℗ **01524/421386.** Main courses £2.50–£5.50. MC, V. Daily 10am–5pm.

Yorkshire Fisheries ★ FISH & CHIPS   The decor may be wanting in all respects—this is about as basic an eatery as you can imagine, with old wooden paneling and banquette seating—but Blackpool's oldest fish and chip shop is consistently rated its best by locals and visitors alike. Most of the former wouldn't go anywhere else for their haddock or cod and chips, to eat in or—for the full-on British seaside experience—to take to the beach a few minutes' walk away. The secret lies in the fresh, crispy batter, but the friendly staff and fair prices (£5 gets you fish, chips, mushy peas, bread and butter, and tea!) are big draws too.

16–18 Topping St., Blackpool. (℗ **01253/627739.** Main courses about £5. No credit cards. Mon–Sat 11:30am–7pm.

Shopping

Farmers' markets, farm shops, and other local produce outlets are the shopping highlights of Lancashire (for the Ribble Valley Food Trail, which includes shops, see p. 596). Of particular note is the **Bashall Barn Food Visitor Centre ★★** near Clitheroe (www.bashallbarn.co.uk; (℗ **01200/428964**), which brings together a farm shop, ice-cream parlor, coffee shop, and restaurant, with views directly into both working farm buildings and across the countryside to Pendle Hill (p. 596). Next door, the **Bowland Beer Company Ltd.** (www.bowlandbrewery.com; (℗ **01200/443592**) has a visitor center where you can watch the brewer at work and taste his wares.

Lancaster is also a good spot for food shopping, with a farmers' market on the second Wednesday of each month plus the **Port of Lancaster Smokehouse** (www.polsco.co.uk; (℗ **01524/751493**), offering smoked fish including salmon from the River Lune and Manx kippers, Morecambe Bay shrimps, fresh game in season, specialist cheeses, and more.

Entertainment & Nightlife

Blackpool is still alive and kicking as an entertainment hub, especially in summer, which sees a lot of traditional variety shows. Cultural venues include the **Grand Theatre** (www.blackpoolgrand.co.uk; (℗ **01253/743338**) and the **Winter Gardens** (www.wintergardensblackpool.co.uk; (℗ **01253/625252**), both impressive historic buildings with populist programming. The **Arena** at the Pleasure Beach (p. 596) hosts ice-skating spectaculars and other glitzy shows.

In terms of nightlife, the mood is boisterous—the resort is a popular hen- and stag-night choice, and the transvestite show bar **Funny Girls** (www.funnygirlsonline. co.uk; © **0844/247-2665**) a favorite venue. Blackpool also has the U.K.'s biggest nightclub, **Syndicate** (http://blackpool.thesyndicate.com; © **01253/753222**), with a revolving dance floor. Since World War II, the resort has been known as a safe haven for gay communities, and since the 1990s it's been actively promoted as a gay tourist destination, so there are plenty of gay-friendly venues plus a dedicated radio station (www.gayradiouk.com).

For up-to-date listings, consult www.blackpoolevents.co.uk.

Where to Stay
VERY EXPENSIVE
For rooms at **Northcote** and the **Inn at Whitewell,** see p. 598 and p. 599.

Midland ★   It's all about the history at this Art Deco classic in the middle of Morecambe's promenade—that and the sea views, which are worth the extra money and are really the point of staying here. The reopening of the hotel led the *Guardian*, in 2008, to declare Morecambe the U.K.'s top coastal holiday destination—a turn-around for the once-neglected resort. Seeing it now, you may be amazed that the cruiser-liner-like building was allowed to rot for decades. All praise goes to the developers for seamlessly incorporating iconic features such as the sweeping staircase and Eric Gill frescoes into the new venue. Rooms are spacious and stylish in a Pop Arty way, with ingenious bathrooms (it may take you a while to find the toilet). There's a slight starkness to them, as with many design hotels, but with nothing beyond your window but the sparkling water, you probably won't mind. The top floor is occupied by suites with private terraces, some with an open-air Jacuzzi. The light-flooded **restaurant** with its bay views offers a largely local menu including Morecambe Bay shrimps and scallops, but as in the hotel as a whole, service can be slow and distracted.

Marine Rd. West, Morecambe, Lancashire LA4 4BU. http://englishlakes.co.uk. © **01524/424-000.** 44 units. £94–£276 double; £174–£348 suite. Rates include English breakfast. MC, V. Free parking. **Amenities:** Restaurant; bar; access to leisure club (at nearby sister hotel); room service. *In room:* TV, hair dryer, Wi-Fi (free).

EXPENSIVE
Big Blue Hotel ★ ☺   Situated at Blackpool Pleasure Beach itself, with some of the theme park's rides as a backdrop but with mercifully effective soundproofing, this is a surprising boutique-style option behind a rather ugly facade. Naturally, it's family-friendly, too, with reasonably priced rooms for up to four featuring a separate children's sleeping area complete with bunkbeds and an "entertainment area" with a TV and PlayStation connection (games and consoles can be rented from reception). Deluxe doubles have lounge areas with fireplaces and fabrics by Designers Guild; suites have separate lounges and coffee-makers.

Pleasure Beach, Blackpool FY4 1ND. www.bigbluehotel.com. © **0871/222-4000.** 157 units. £91–£132 double; from £224 suites. Rates include breakfast (some promotional rates are room-only). AE, MC, DV, V. Free parking. **Amenities:** Restaurant; bar; health club; room service. *In room:* TV/DVD (some), hair dryer, children's entertainment area (some), MP3 docking station (suites), Wi-Fi (free).

MODERATE

Red Pump Inn ★★ 🎁 For a warm welcome and peace and quiet, you could do little better than this superb, award-winning B&B deep in the Ribble Valley, with three comfortable rooms with great views of Pendle Hill or Longridge Fell, handmade wooden furniture, and flat-screen TVs. The emphasis is on taking it easy, so the fabulous Lancashire breakfast is generally served between 9 and 9:45am, though you can take it earlier or later if you wish; choose from local bacon, eggs, and black pudding (blood sausage), with heart-shaped fried bread and homemade flat skinless sausages, smoked salmon and scrambled eggs on malted bloomer, or porridge with golden syrup.

Clitheroe Rd., Bashall Eaves, Lancashire BB7 3DA www.theredpumpinn.co.uk. ℂ **01254/826-227.** 3 units. £70–£95 double. Rates include English breakfast. MC, V. Free parking. **Amenities:** Restaurant; bar. *In room:* TV, Wi-Fi (free).

THE LAKE DISTRICT

by Louise McGrath

One of the most beautiful parts of Great Britain, the Lake District is characterized by its stunning mountain and lake scenery. Whether you come for hikes, camping, and watersports, or to follow the trail of Lake poets like William Wordsworth, there's a diverse range of activities. Some visitors delve into Beatrix Potter's world, others enjoy lake cruises and first-class dinners at country hotels.

CITIES & TOWNS **Kendal's** former mill yards bustle with shops and its museums introduce Lakeland life. Boat trips from **Bowness** and **Windermere** ferry visitors around England's largest natural lake; at its northern end **Ambleside** is a popular base for walkers. Wordsworth fans visit his homes in **Rydal** and **Grasmere,** while flower-filled **Hawkshead** is in Beatrix Potter country. **Coniston,** dominated by the "Old Man" mountain, remembers Ruskin the writer, who lived nearby at Brantwood house. Lively **Keswick** presents year-round productions at its Theatre by the Lake.

COUNTRYSIDE Take a boat trip on **Windermere, Coniston, Derwentwater,** or **Ullswater** to explore the length and depth of the lakes, and see the granite fells rising up around you. Footpaths and cycle routes lead along the water's edge, through **Grizedale Forest,** and to the summit of England's highest peak, **Scafell Pike,** while roads snake across **Honister Pass,** offering dramatic valley vistas below. Venture to more isolated lakes like **Haweswater** to spot peregrine falcons and golden eagles.

EATING & DRINKING Herdwick lamb, **Cumberland sausages,** and **venison** are regularly on the menus, so the region might seem a meat-lover's paradise. But you'll find **fresh salmon, scallops** from Morecambe Bay, **artisan bread, chutneys,** and **vegetarian cafes** from Kendal to Keswick. Pick up Cumbrian produce at farm shops and Staveley Mill Yard, and sample local ales in pubs or direct from local **microbreweries** in Coniston and Keswick.

MOUNTAINS & LAKES With its miles of mountains, forest, and lakes, it's easy to see why **Lake District National Park** inspired the Lake poets. The park opens the way for windsurfing on the lakes, fell-walking on **England's highest peaks,** and technical climbing up sheer rock faces. But visitors should tread carefully across mountain, moor, lakeshore, and estuary, being mindful of the delicate **wildlife** habitats and important heritage sites, such as Hardknott **Roman** Fort.

THE best TRAVEL EXPERIENCES IN THE LAKE DISTRICT

○ **Taking a trip across the water:** A boat trip across Derwentwater to Hawes End, followed by an hour-long walk up Catbells Fell for spectacular lake and fell views. See p. 625.

○ **Visiting Rydal Mount:** Go at lunchtime when it's quieter, then a tour of Dove Cottage near Grasmere, ending the afternoon with tea and gingerbread. See p. 617.

○ **Taking to the waters on Coniston:** A boat trip followed by a few hours in Ruskin's house and garden at Brantwood. See p. 620.

○ **Climbing Helvellyn:** It's only The Lake District's third-highest mountain but Striding Edge narrow ridge can be both tricky and exhilarating. See p. 620.

○ **Witnessing Borrowdale's breathtaking scenery:** Zigzag up to Honister Pass and stop at Honister Slate Mine to tackle the leg-wobbling Via Ferrata ladder system up the mountainside. See p. 624.

KENDAL

270 miles NW of London; 72 miles NW of Leeds; 64 miles NW of Bradford; 9 miles SE of Windermere

The River Kent winds through a rich valley of limestone hills, known as fells, and through Kendal, known as the "Gateway to the Lake District." Many visitors bypass Kendal on their way to the central Lakes, but this bustling town boasts some of the most intriguing museums in the region.

Visit the interactive **Kendal Museum** to learn about the town's past, especially its ruined **castle,** where Catherine Parr, the last wife of Henry VIII, was allegedly born. Other worthy visits include the Quaker Museum and Abbott Hall.

Kendal once relied on the woolen industry; today its mill yards are filled with shops, while a former brewery is a vibrant arts center. The town is also famous for its sweet mint cake, which hikers take on long walks through the surrounding limestone fells.

Essentials

GETTING THERE   Trains from London's Euston Station do not go directly to Kendal; Virgin Trains operates up to nine direct trains each day from London Euston to Oxenholme Lake District station about 1½ miles away. One-way tickets cost from £32. (If you're planning on making several journeys by train, it is worth investing in a personal or family railcard. After a couple of journeys it pays for itself.) From here, you'll be able to take a taxi or board one of the local trains that leave for Kendal approximately every hour and take just 4 minutes (total trip time from London to Kendal: 3½ hr.).

To get to Kendal from London by bus, take one of the daily **National Express** buses (trip time: 7½ hr.). £30 single/£42.40 return. Local buses are operated mainly by **Stagecoach** and travel to Bowness, Windermere, Ambleside, Penrith, Keswick, and Ulverston. Northwest Explorer ticket £10 per day, West Cumbria day ticket £4.70, local town day tickets £2.25-2.80 Megabus (www.megabus.com) offers some

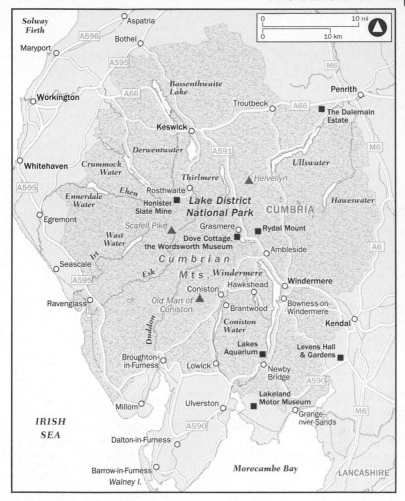

Solway Firth
Aspatria
A596
Bothel
Maryport
A595
Workington
Bassenthwaite Lake
A66
Troutbeck
A66
Penrith
The Dalemain Estate
M6
Keswick
Derwentwater
A591
M6
Ullswater
Whitehaven
Crummock Water
Thirlmere
Helvellyn
A595
Ehen
Rosthwaite
Ennerdale Water
Honister Slate Mine
Lake District National Park
CUMBRIA
Haweswater
Egremont
Scafell Pike
Grasmere
Rydal Mount
Wast Water
Dove Cottage, the Wordsworth Museum
Ambleside
A6
Seascale
Cumbrian
Esk
Mts.
Windermere
Windermere
Irt
A595
Coniston
Hawkshead
Bowness-on-Windermere
Ravenglass
Old Man of Coniston
Brantwood
Kendal
Duddon
Coniston Water
Broughton-in-Furness
Lowick
Lakes Aquarium
Levens Hall & Gardens
Millom
Ulverston
Newby Bridge
A590
Lakeland Motor Museum
M6
IRISH SEA
A590
Grange-over-Sands
Dalton-in-Furness
Barrow-in-Furness
Walney I.
Morecambe Bay
LANCASTER

cheaper tickets but the buses might not be as comfortable *eg London to Carlisle £5 single/£10 return. If driving, take the M1 out of London, and then the M6 to Kendal (trip time: 5 hr.).

VISITOR INFORMATION **Kendal Tourist Information Centre,** Made in Cumbria, 25 Stramongate (www.golakes.co.uk; ℂ **01539/735891**), opens Monday to Saturday 10am to 5pm.

Exploring the Area

Abbot Hall Art Gallery GALLERY   Most visitors arrive at the gallery from Kirkland, first visiting the **Museum of Lakeland Life,** which gives an insight into bygone days. Opt instead for a riverside approach and you'll find the perfect place to pitch up and appreciate Abbott Hall's elegant Georgian facade. Its restored high-ceilinged rooms with ornate cornices and matching period antiques provide an ideal setting for paintings by local 18th-century portrait painter George Romney. The permanent collection also includes 20th-century British works, and there are regular temporary exhibitions by contemporary international artists.

Kirkland. www.abbothall.org.uk. © **01539/722464.** Admission £6.85 adults; free for children 16 and under and full-time students. Mon–Sat 10:30am–5pm (until 4pm Nov–Mar). Closed mid-Dec–mid-Jan.

Kendal Museum ☺ MUSEUM   Kendal Museum might be one of England's oldest museums, but it has refreshed its content with interactive exhibits that bring local history to life. Try on Roman shoes, explore local life 500 years ago via touch-screen computers, then make a medieval-style tiled floor. The natural history section travels from mountaintop to lakeside, and the World Wildlife Gallery displays a vast collection of exotic breeds. Don't miss the Alfred Wainwright exhibition; the fells' best-known visitor, he walked, talked, and wrote with a passion and flair about the Lakes until his death in 1991.

Station Rd. www.kendalmuseum.org.uk. © **01539/815597.** Free admission. Weds–Sat 10:30am–5pm.

Levens Hall & Gardens HISTORIC SITE   Elizabethan pele towers are common in Cumbria, but few are in such a fine setting. Transformed into a mansion in the 1500s by James Bellingham, the house still has many original features, including the oak-paneled entrance hall and Elizabeth I's coat of arms above the drawing room fireplace. After strolling through the 17th-century **topiary garden,** orchard, and herb garden outside, enjoy hot food made from local produce in The Buttery.

8 Levens Park, Levens (4 miles south of Kendal). www.levenshall.co.uk. © **01539/560321.** Admission house and gardens £12 adults, £5 children 5–16, £29 family ticket; gardens only £8.50 adults, £4 children, £21 family ticket. Apr–mid-Oct Sun–Thurs noon–5pm (gardens from 10am). Last admission 4:30pm.

The Quaker Tapestry ★ ⛨ ARTS & CRAFTS   This isn't just any old display of needlework. The embroidered panels, which depict Quaker history, were made by over 4,000 men, women, and children worldwide. They show founding Quaker George Fox, Quaker preacher/missionary Mary Fisher (1623–98), and the Quakers' role as stretcher bearers in World War I, among other contributions to the modern world made by these quiet non-conformists. Vegetarians will love the fresh, healthful options at the adjacent tearooms.

Friends Meeting House, Stramongate, Kendal. www.quaker-tapestry.co.uk. © **01539/722975.** Admission £7.50 adults, £2.50 children 5–16, £2.50 adult with toddler, £16.50 family ticket (2 adults, 2 children). Apr–Dec Mon–Sat 10am–5pm; Meeting House Café closes at 4:30pm.

Sizergh Castle & Garden ☺ CASTLE   A large courtyard leads to Sizergh Castle's entrance, where children can pick up quiz sheets that draw them into the castle's Elizabethan carvings and family portraits of the Strickland family, who have lived here for over 750 years. Chat with the guides to hear tales of priests who were disguised as artists but secretly said Mass during the Reformation. It's worth making time to sit beside the ponds and wildflowers in the rockery garden, and take in the 14th-century pele tower from the wide lawns. *Insider tip:* Come in autumn to see the show of fiery colors climbing the castle walls.

Sizergh, 3½ miles south of Kendal (northwest of interchange A590/591). www.nationaltrust.org.uk/sizergh-castle. © **01539/560951.** Admission house and gardens (including gift aid) £9 adults,

£4.50 children 5–16, £21.80 family ticket (2 adults, 2 children); gardens only £6 adults, £3 children, free early Nov–mid-Mar. House mid-Mar–early Nov Sun–Thurs 1–5pm; shop and gardens Jan–mid-Mar Sat–Sun, Feb half-term week Mon–Fri and early Nov–Dec daily 11am–4pm; mid-Mar–early Nov Sun–Thurs 11am–5pm.

Where to Eat

New Moon Restaurant ★ MODERN BRITISH   The use of regional produce and British cuisine with a twist, along with the contemporary decor and relaxed atmosphere, make this a firm lunch, early supper, and dinner favorite. Tuck into tempura goujons of red mullet, paprika spiced chicken, or veggie options like baked aubergine (eggplant) filled with a casserole of spiced vegetables and mozzarella. If you're really pushing the boat out, enjoy sticky toffee pudding or fruit crumble rounded off with a scoop of Windermere ice cream.

129 Highgate, Kendal. www.newmoonrestaurant.co.uk. ✆ **01539/729254.** Main courses £12.50–£17. MC, V. Tues–Sat 11:30am–2:15pm and 6pm–9:15pm (Sat until 9:30pm).

Wilf's Cafe ★ INTERNATIONAL   Set in Staveley Mill Yard, a few miles north of Kendal, walkers and foodies stop off at Wilf's for relaxing breakfasts, coffee, and a variety of homemade hot meals like veggie chili and Wilf's rarebits.

Mill Yard, Staveley. www.wilfs-cafe.co.uk. ✆ **01539/822329.** Main courses £6.25. MC, V. Daily 9am–5pm (summer weekends from 8:30am).

Shopping

Start out on **Stricklandgate** (home to the Westmorland Shopping Centre; www.westmorlandshopping.com) and explore the **old yards** branching off it. Once the hub of spinning, dyeing, and weaving, today they are home to fashion, gifts, chocolate, and art shops. The liveliest are **Elephant Yard** (www.elephantyard.com), **Blackhall Yard** (www.blackhallyard.co.uk), and **Wainwrights Yard** (www.wainwrightsyard.com).

Foodies shouldn't miss **Low Sizergh Barn** (www.lowsizerghbarn.co.uk; ✆ **01539/560426)**, south of Kendal on the A591, a farm shop with Lakes' produce such as cheese, chutneys, and Cumberland sausage. North of Kendal, former sawmill **Staveley Mill Yard** (www.staveleymillyard.com; ✆ **01539/821234**) is now home to several food producers and Hawkshead Brewery.

Entertainment & Nightlife

The **Brewery Arts Centre,** Highgate (www.breweryarts.co.uk; ✆ **01539/725133**), is one of the best entertainment offerings in the Lake District. Located in a former brewery, there are two cinemas, a theatre, the Grain Store Restaurant, two cafes and a bar. The box office for all attractions is open Monday to Wednesday noon to 8:30pm, Thursday to Saturday 10am to 8:30pm, and Sunday 2pm to 8:30pm.

Where to Stay

Best Western Castle Green Hotel in Kendal ★   Castle Green seems like a rambling country estate, but it once housed offices that have been cleverly converted into comfortable, contemporary bedrooms. All have modernized, tiled, en suite bathrooms, and some also boast garden views. The best guest rooms are the executive studio suites with extra space. Guests enjoy free membership in the hotel's health club, and can wine and dine in the popular on-site **Greenhouse restaurant** and Alexander's pub.

Castle Green Lane, Kendal, Cumbria LA9 6BH. www.castlegreen.co.uk. ✆ **01539/734000.** Fax 01539/735522. 100 units. £102–£150 double; £142–£190 suite. Rates include English breakfast. AE, MC, V. Signposted from the M6, junction 37. **Amenities:** Restaurant; pub; indoor heated pool; health club; room service; solarium; steam room. *In room:* TV, hair dryer.

Bridge House ★   A listed Georgian house, this was once the station master's home. Today it is a homely B&B where guests wake to the smell of homemade bread. There's a double and a twin room available. The owners will collect walking guests from nearby trails and cyclists can leave their bikes in the basement.

Castle Street, Kendal FK14 7DE. www.bridgehouse-kendal.co.uk. ✆ **01539/722041.** 2 units. £70–£80 double. Rates include breakfast. MC, V. Reductions for longer stays. *In room:* TV/DVD, Wi-Fi (free).

WINDERMERE & BOWNESS ★★

274 miles NW of London; 10 miles NW of Kendal; 55 miles N of Liverpool

The largest lake in England is Windermere. Its eastern edge washes up on the town of Bowness (or Bowness-on-Windermere), with the town of Windermere 1½ miles away. From either town, you can climb **Orrest Head** in less than an hour for a panoramic view of the Lakeland. From that vantage point, you can even view **Scafell Pike,** rising to a height of 963m (3,210 ft.)—it's the tallest peak in all of England.

Directly south of Windermere, **Bowness** is an attractive lakeside town with lots of Victorian architecture. An important center for boating and fishing, Bowness has boat rentals of all descriptions to explore the lake.

The location of the towns keep the visitors flooding in, along with an abundance of accommodations, eateries, and pubs. The area is a particular favorite with families who come for the **World of Beatrix Potter, watersports,** and **boat trips** to **Lakeside Aquarium** and **Haverthwaite Steam Train.**

Essentials

GETTING THERE   You can take a TransPennine Express (TPE) train to Windermere from Oxenholme, where Scotland and London trains arrive. One-way tickets from Oxenholme to Windermere cost £4.90, £5 return. Trains from London to Oxenholme from £32 single.

To get to Bowness from Windermere, turn left from the rail terminal and cross the center of Windermere until you reach New Road, which eventually changes its name to Lake Road and leads into Bowness. It's about a 20-minute walk downhill. The Lakeland Experience bus (599) also runs from the Windermere station to Bowness every 20 minutes.

The **National Express** bus link, originating at London's Victoria Coach Station, serves Windermere once a day, with connections also to Preston, Manchester, and Birmingham. Local buses operated mainly by **Stagecoach** go to Kendal, Ambleside, Grasmere, and Keswick. If you're driving from London, head north on the M1 and the M6 past Liverpool until you reach the A685 junction heading west to Kendal. From Kendal, the A591 continues west to Windermere.

VISITOR INFORMATION   **Windermere Tourist Information Centre** is on Victoria Street (www.golakes.co.uk; ✆ **01539/446499**). It's open November through March, Monday to Saturday 9:30am to 5pm and Sunday 10am to 4:30pm, and April through October daily 9:30am to 5pm.

Exploring the Area

Blackwell ★★ ⛪ HISTORIC SITE Tucked away among trees overlooking Windermere, this Arts and Crafts house has been lovingly restored. Built in 1900 by Makay Hugh Baillie Scott (1865–1945) as a holiday home for wealthy industrialist Sir Edward Holt, it slowly fell into disrepair as a post-World War I rental. The Lakeland Arts Trust stepped in to revive the early 20th-century architectural detail and furnish it with period pieces. Admire the contrasting Arts and Crafts style of the hall with its dark-wood paneling featuring intricate foliage carvings and a showy peacock mosaic, and the stark, white drawing room, with cobalt blue fireplace and views over the lake.

Just off the A5074, 2 miles south of Bowness. www.blackwell.org.uk. ℭ **01539/446139.** Admission £7.95 adults, £4.40 children 5–16 or if in full-time education with student card, £19.80 family ticket (2 adults, 4 children). Daily 10:30am–5pm (until 4pm Nov–Mar). Closed first 2 weeks in Jan.

Lake Cruises ★★★ CRUISE England's largest lake (about 11 miles long), Windermere offers the archetypal day out (when the weather is agreeable). The best way to explore the lake is on cruises, which are operated by **Windermere Lake Cruises Ltd** (www.windermere-lakecruises.co.uk; ℭ **01539/443360**). There are round-trip services between Bowness, Ambleside, and Lakeside, and combined tickets can also include tickets for the **Lakes Aquarium** (see below) and steam train ride to Haverthwaite, or the bus to the **Lakeland Motor Museum** (see below). Freedom tickets allow you to use the boat as often as you like, and there are also relaxed cruises of the lake's islands. Seasonal car services operate to Ferry House across from Bowness, a route used regularly by visitors to **Hill Top Farm** (p. 621).

www.windermere-lakecruises.co.uk. ℭ **01539/443360.** Freedom tickets £13 adults, £6.50 children 5–15, £35.50 family ticket (2 adults, 3 children); cruises from £7 adults, £3.50 children 5–15; boat and train £14.50 adults, £8 children, £40 family; boat and aquarium £16.25 adults, £9.35 children, £48.30 family ticket; boat, bus, motor museum, train £20.10 adults, £11.80 children, £55.90 family ticket. Timetable summer approx 9:15am–6:45pm; winter 10am–4pm.

Lakeland Motor Museum ★ MUSEUM Opened in its new custom-made home in 2010, the museum has a vast collection of vintage bicycles, motorcycles, cars, and auto-memorabilia, but pride of place goes to the Campbell Bluebird Collection. Dedicated to the father-and-son team (Sir Malcolm and Donald Campbell) who between them held 21 land and water speed records, it features replicas of several of their vehicles, including the Bluebird K7 in which Donald was tragically killed on nearby Coniston Water during an attempt to break his own water speed record.

Old Blue Mill, Backbarrow. www.lakelandmotormuseum.co.uk. ℭ **01539/530400.** Admission £7.80 adults, £5 children 5–15, £23 family (2 adults, 3 children); combined Windermere Lake Cruises tickets also available. Mid-Feb–early Nov daily 9:30am–5:30pm (early Nov–mid-Feb until 4:30pm).

Lakes Aquarium ☺ AQUARIUM Step into a watery world of red-bellied piranhas, grinning caiman, and leopard tortoises. The aquarium starts with local marine life and travels the world, with an underwater tunnel that brings you face to face with the big fish.

Lakeside. www.lakesaquarium.co.uk. ℭ **01539/530153.** Admission £8.95 adults, £5.95 children 3–15, £7.50 seniors, £19 family ticket (2 adults, 1 child), £23.75 family ticket (2 adults, 2 children), £28.60 family ticket (2 adults, 3 children), £33.35 family ticket (2 adults, 4 children). Save up to 25% by booking online. Daily 9am–4pm (last entry).

World of Beatrix Potter ★★ ☺ ENTERTAINMENT COMPLEX On arrival, you slip through a garden gate and watch a short film about Beatrix Potter, her stories and life as a Lakeland farmer and conservationist. Then you step *into* the tales, following a route past Jemima Puddle-Duck, the Peter Rabbit garden, and Mrs. Tiggy Winkle's kitchen. There is also a shop with official Beatrix Potter merchandise. *Insider tip:* This place is mobbed on summer weekends, so try to come at any other time.

The Old Laundry, Bowness-on-Windermere. www.hop-skip-jump.com. ✆ **01539/488444.** Admission £6.75 adults, £3.50 children 4–16, £5.75 seniors. Easter–Oct daily 10am–5:30pm (to 4:30pm rest of year). Take the A591 to Lake Rd. and follow the signs.

Where to Eat

In addition to the restaurants reviewed here, see "Where to Stay," below, for dining options at hotels.

Francine's Coffee House & Restaurant 🗡 MODERN EUROPEAN The colorful array of hanging baskets provide a warm welcome. Inside, the compact eatery is clean and relaxed with white walls, flowers, and muted lighting. You can start the day with breakfast ciabattas, full English or vegetarian breakfast, or come later for the lunch and dinner set menu. There's also an a la carte menu. Savor dishes like game terrine, Francine's seafood casserole, or wild red Cartmel venison braised with red wine and thyme, rounded off with sticky-toffee pudding. Everything is meticulously presented.

27 Main Rd., Windermere. www.francinesrestaurantwindermere.co.uk. ✆ **01539/444088.** Main courses £11.95–£19.95. MC, V. Tues–Sat 10am–2:30pm and Tues–Sun 6–11pm.

Villa Positano ITALIAN Tucked away in the heart of Bowness, look out for the green canopy that marks the alley entrance to this long-running family favorite. Villa Positano is a lively restaurant, where the buzz of music and conversation is accompanied by classic Italian pasta, pizza, steak, and chicken dishes. In peak season it gets crowded, so book ahead or come early.

Ash St., Bowness. ✆ **01539/445663.** Reservations recommended. Main courses £5.95–£8.95 pizza/pasta; £13.90–£18.90 fish/meat dishes. MC, V. Daily 5:30–10pm.

Shopping

Windermere is the place for sailing and watersports gear. **Windermere Canoe Kayak,** Ferry Nab Road, Bowness (www.windermerecanoekayak.com; ✆ **01539/444451**), sells and rents boats, or bikes if you want to cycle around the lake.

The busy town center of Bowness is packed full of gift, chocolate, jewelry, and swimwear stores. Head to the **World of Beatrix Potter** shop (see above) for toy Peter Rabbits and books, and the **Lakeland** kitchen gadget store in Alexandra Buildings next to the station (www.lakeland.co.uk; ✆ **01539/488100**).

Entertainment & Nightlife

Bowness and Windermere are popular bases for gentle lake cruises (see above) as well as watersports. You can rent canoes from the waterfront at Bowness from **Windermere Canoe Kayak** (see above).

Low Wood Watersports & Activity Centre ★ Just three miles north of Windermere and with a backdrop of Lakeland fells, Low Wood is ideal for sailing, kayaking, waterskiing, wakeboarding, and power-boating. Visitors can book instruction and hire equipment suitable for all ages and abilities.

A591, Windermere. www.elh.co.uk. ✆ **01539/439441.** Apr–Oct open daily.

The oldest pub in Bowness is the **Hole in t' Wall,** Lowside (*©* **01539/443488**), dating back to 1612. The friendly bar room is decorated with a hodgepodge of antiquated farming tools, and a large slate fireplace lends warmth on winter days. There's a good selection of real ales on tap and an eclectic mix of vegetarian, seafood, and local game dishes.

Drive a short distance south of Windermere to Cartmel Fell, situated between the A592 and the A5074, for a pub-lover's dream. The **Mason Arms,** Strawberry Bank (www.masonsarmsstrawberrybank.co.uk; *©* **01539/568486**), is a Jacobean pub with original oak paneling. The pretty garden offers a dramatic view of the Winster Valley beyond, while the pub offers so many beers that there's a 24-page catalog to help you order, and a reasonable menu with various tasty vegetarian options.

Southeast of Windermere, the **Punch Bowl,** off the A5074 in Crosthwaithe (www.the-punchbowl.co.uk; *©* **01539/568234**), is a 16th-century pub with a central room featuring a high-beamed ceiling with minstrel galleries. Outdoors, a stepped terrace on the hillside offers a tranquil retreat. Regional ales are available on tap.

Where to Stay
VERY EXPENSIVE

Cedar Manor Hotel ★ Cedar Manor might have been the 19th-century summer getaway for a wealthy industrialist, but today it is a luxury hotel. Each bedroom is spacious, well-furnished, and individually designed; some have canopied or four-poster beds. The award-winning **Cedar Manor Restaurant,** the perfect place for a candlelit dinner, caters to diners who like rib-eye steak and slow-cooked pork belly as well as for those with an acquired taste for game. Children aged 10 and younger are not allowed in the restaurant for dinner.

Ambleside Rd. (A591), Windermere, Cumbria LA23 1AX. www.cedarmanor.co.uk.*©* **01539/443192.** Fax 01539/445970. 11 units. £120–£210 double; £300–£350 suite. Rates include breakfast. 2-night minimum Sat–Sun. Restaurant £32.95–39.95 per person set menu. AE, MC, V. Free parking. **Amenities:** Restaurant; lounge. *In room:* TV/DVD (in some), fridge (in some), hair dryer, Wi-Fi (free).

Gilpin Lodge ★★★ 🖻 Set in 100 acres of grounds with a croquet lawn and llama paddock, this hotel exudes classical elegance, contemporary style, and an unimposing personal service. Whether you stay in the main house guest rooms or one of the suites, you'll find accommodations individually and tastefully styled. Some suites have private gardens with hot tubs, while the Lake House, opened in 2010, is an individually staffed boutique hotel with just six suites, an indoor pool, and a spa, providing the ultimate luxury retreat. And you don't need to stray far from the hotel as you can **dine** in style, too—after an aperitif in the champagne bar!

Crook Rd., B5284 nr. Windermere, Cumbria LA23 3NE. www.gilpinlodge.co.uk.*©* **01539/488818.** Main House, Orchard, and Garden wings 20 units; Lake House 6 units. Main House £200–£270 double; £310–£380 suite. Lake House £390–£500 per suite. Rates include English breakfast. Lake House also includes afternoon tea and chauffeur to/from Gilpin in the evening. Dinner £40 per person if booked with room, £58 per person for non-guests. 2-night minimum on weekends. AE, MC, V. Free parking. **Amenities:** Restaurant; lounge; bar. *In room:* TV, hair dryer, spa tubs (some), Wi-Fi (free).

Holbeck Ghyll Country House Hotel ★★★ A tranquil oasis overlooking Lake Windermere, this 19th-century former hunting lodge has a high price tag but exudes luxury. Its **restaurant** serves some of the finest cuisine in the area, and rooms are individually designed, most with lake views. All have luxury beds, often crowned by a canopy, while the honeymoon room has a four-poster bed and a bathroom with a double spa tub. A separate lodge contains the hotel's six finest units, all with balcony or patio areas overlooking the lake. *Note:* Children 7 and under are prohibited in the restaurant.

Holbeck Lane (on the A591, 3½ miles northwest of town center), Windermere, Cumbria LA23 1LU. www.holbeckghyll.com. © **01539/432375.** Fax 01539/434743. 21 units. £216–£350 double; £296–£490 suites and cottages. Rates include English breakfast. Restaurant: Dinner £65 per person if not booked with room or for non-guests. Children 16 and under stay half-price in parent's room. AE, DC, MC, V. Free parking. **Amenities:** Restaurant; bar; tennis court; gym; spa; room service. *In room:* TV, kitchenette (in 4 units), hair dryer.

Linthwaite House Hotel ★   This hotel, built in 1900, is surrounded by woodlands and gardens, with a panoramic view of Lake Windermere. As befits its former role as an Edwardian gentleman's residence, it has individually decorated bedrooms, all refurbished with contemporary decor, many with lake views. All are fitted with sumptuous beds and come with tub/shower combinations. The many in-room amenities include bathrobes and satellite TVs. It's worth enjoying lunch or dinner in the hotel **restaurant,** which serves modern British cuisine such as rabbit confit or roast quail with English asparagus salad.

Crook Rd., Bowness-on-Windermere, Cumbria LA23 3JA. www.linthwaite.com. © **01539/488600.** Fax 01539/488601. 27 units. £195–£344 double; £323–£554 suite. Rates include English breakfast. Restaurant dinner and canapés £52; daily noon–2pm lunch, 7–9pm dinner. AE, DC, MC, V. Free parking. **Amenities:** Restaurant; bar; nearby spa; room service. *In room:* TV, hair dryer, CD player, Wi-Fi (free).

The Samling ★★ 🎁   The Samling is set on substantial grounds offering panoramic lake views. It was fashioned from a late-18th-century stone-built manse where Wordsworth used to come to pay his rent on Dove Cottage in neighboring Grasmere. Of the 11 rooms, 5 are located in a converted stable block that's more akin to a ski lodge than a country house. The main-building rooms have more of a traditional British aura, but all are individually styled and spacious. Even if you're not a guest, consider an elegant **set-price dinner** here.

Ambleside Rd., Windermere, Cumbria LA23 1LR. www.thesamling.com. © **01539/431922.** 11 units. £190–£420 per double; £410–£560 suite. Rates include breakfast. Dinner £45 for guests if booked with room; £60 non-guests. AE, DC, MC, V. Free parking. **Amenities:** Restaurant; bar. *In room:* TV, hair dryer, Wi-Fi (in some; free).

EXPENSIVE

The Belsfield ★   You can't fail to notice this hotel overlooking Windermere lake and Bowness Pier. A large, white Victorian mansion set in 6 acres of gardens, it provides guests with a place where they can sit in the summer sunshine and take in the vista. Rooms might not be as stylish as the pricier country houses nearby, but they are comfortable with antique-style furnishings that complement the architecture; several have lake views. What's more, the location is convenient, and facilities include a heated indoor pool, **Moonwaters restaurant,** and a bar and lounge.

Kendal Rd., Bowness, Cumbria LA23 3EL. http://www.corushotels.com/the-belsfield-hotel. © **01539/442448.** 64 units, 3 suites. £84–£180 double; £155–£205 suite. Rates include breakfast. AE, DC, MC, V. **Amenities:** Restaurant; bar; indoor pool and sauna. *In room:* TV, hair dryer, Wi-Fi (free).

MODERATE

Beaumont House   This stone-sided Lakeland villa is on a quiet residential street just off Windermere's commercial center. The property is well looked after and regularly refurbished. Each of the bedrooms contain either an elaborate canopy bed or a four-poster, fitted with a quality mattress. The four-poster beds have proved so popular there are now six of these, all fitted with iPod docking stations. No meals are served other than breakfast, so the owners keep local restaurant menus on hand for their guests to consult.

Holly Rd., Windermere, Cumbria LA23 2AF. www.lakesbeaumont.co.uk. (C) **01539/447075**. Fax 01539/488311. 10 units. £80–£150 double. Rates include English breakfast. MC, V. Free parking. *In room:* TV/DVD (in some), hair dryer.

Fir Trees Guest House ★   One of Windermere's finest guesthouses, Fir Trees provides hotel-like standards at B&B prices. Opposite St. John's Church, halfway between Bowness and Windermere, it is a Victorian house redecorated with antique-style furnishings. Proprietors Bob and Bea Towers offer a warm welcome and beautifully maintained bedrooms, two large enough for families.

Lake Rd., Windermere, Cumbria LA23 2EQ. www.fir-trees.co.uk. (C) **01539/442272.** Fax 01539/442512. 9 units. £68–£96 double. Rates include English breakfast. AE, MC, V. Free parking. *In room:* TV, hair dryer, Wi-Fi (free).

The Wild Boar Inn, Grill & Smokehouse ★   Guests and diners come here for the cozy atmosphere and because it is dog friendly (£10 per dog per night). Most guest rooms have been refurbished and individually styled, some with elaborate French-style beds or velvet headboards; a few have wood-burning stoves. The **restaurant** features an open kitchen where diners can see their wild boar sausages or house-smoked steaks sizzling on the grill. Afterward you can retreat to the quintessentially English bar and sit beside the open fire with one of the 50 whiskies or guest ales available.

Crook Rd., Windermere, Cumbria LA23 3NF. www.elh.co.uk. (C) **0845/850-4604.** 33 units. £98–£260 double. Rates include English breakfast. MC, V. Free parking. **Amenities:** Restaurant, bar. *In room:* TV, hair dryer.

AMBLESIDE

278 miles NW of London; 14 miles NW of Kendal; 4 miles N of Windermere

An idyllic retreat at the north end of Lake Windermere, Ambleside is just a small village, but it's one of the major places to stay in the Lake District, attracting hikers and rock climbers. It's wonderful in warm weather and even through late autumn, when it's fashionable to sport a raincoat.

The town is most renowned for its **plethora of shops** selling outdoor gear, but it also has restaurants to suit all tastes, several lively pubs, and a jazz bar/cinema. But it's not all about eating, drinking, and shopping! There's a gentle walk up to **Stock Ghyll Force** (waterfall) and a steep drive across **Kirkstone Pass** toward Ullswater. Stop en route to take panoramic snapshots of Windermere.

Essentials

GETTING THERE   Take a train to Windermere (see "Windermere & Bowness," earlier in this chapter), and then continue the rest of the way by bus.

Stagecoach has an hourly bus service from Grasmere and Keswick (see "Grasmere & Rydal," below, and "Keswick & Borrowdale," later in this chapter) and from Windermere. All these buses into Ambleside are labeled either no. 555 or 556.

If you're driving from Windermere, continue northwest on the A591.

VISITOR INFORMATION   The **Ambleside Tourist Information Centre** is located at The Hub of Ambleside, Central Buildings, Market Cross (www.golakes. co.uk; ℂ **01539/432582**). It's open Monday to Saturday 9am to 5:30pm, Sunday 9am to 5pm.

Exploring the Area

The Armitt ★ MUSEUM   A bonafide treasure trove of exhibits that together reflect the Lake District, The Armitt's collections span art, photography, personal items, books, and archives of manuscripts to archeological finds, geological specimens, and historical work and domestic items once used by local people. Among its most intriguing items are watercolors by Beatrix Potter of fungi and fossils, letters and documents belonging to philanthropist John Ruskin, a scarf belonging to Dorothy Wordsworth, and Roman relics found around Ambleside.

Rydal Rd., Ambleside. www.armitt.com. ℂ **01539/431212.** Admission £3.50 adults, £1.50 children, £2.80 students and seniors. Mon–Sat 10am–4:30pm.

Stock Ghyll Force NATURAL ATTRACTION   The 15-minute walk to this waterfall is suitable for those who can't manage the more strenuous fell walks. It's a little steep, but once at the top you'll find cascading waterfalls that powered local mills from the 14th century onward. The mills have long since gone, leaving visitors to enjoy the natural force of the water. Like many picturesque places in these parts, spring sees daffodils carpeting the route.

Stock Ghyll Lane.

Where to Eat

In addition to the restaurants reviewed here, see "Where to Stay," below, for other dining options.

Dodd's Restaurant ★ ♟ MODERN EUROPEAN   A rustic restaurant set in the heart of bustling Ambleside, Dodd's serves up modern snacks and light lunches during the day and a full, imaginative menu at night. Begin with nibbles of olives and fresh bread, before trying starters such as potted haddock and smoked carpaccio of beef, mains of roast poussin, rib-eye steak, or risotto, or choose from the range of pizzas and pastas.

Rydal Rd., Ambleside. www.doddsrestaurant.co.uk. ℂ **01539/432134.**. Main courses £7.95–£14.95. DC, MC, V. Daily 12–2:45pm and 5–9pm.

Glass House Restaurant ★ MODERN BRITISH/MEDITERRANEAN   A former saw mill dating back to the 15th century, this restaurant retained the working weir and some of the mill machinery when it was converted in the 1990s. Today, you'll find a split-level combination of medieval and contemporary architecture, with oak interior trim and large windows. The seasonal menu can include main courses like confit duck leg with Cumberland stuffing, and pan-fried sea bass with vegetable noodles.

Rydal Rd., Ambleside. www.theglasshouserestaurant.co.uk. ℂ **01539/432137.** Reservations recommended. Main courses £11–£15. MC, V. Daily 10am–2:30pm and 6:30–9:30pm (peak season weekends until 10pm or 10:30pm).

Rattle Gill Cafe ★ INTERNATIONAL/VEGETARIAN   Tucked down a quiet side street, this cafe offers healthy food at very reasonable prices. The food is homemade daily and can include soup and bread, jacket potatoes, ploughman's lunch (cheese, bread, and pickle), veggie chili, and doorstep sandwiches. There are mini-versions for children, along with beans or spaghetti on toast. Homemade coffee cake or toasted teacake are the perfect accompaniment for a cup of fairtrade coffee or tea.

2 Bridge St., Ambleside. www.rattlegillcafe.co.uk. ℂ **01539/434403.** Main courses £6–£6.50. MC, V. Thurs–Mon 10am–5pm.

Shopping

You can often pick up a bargain on last season's breathable jackets or gortex boots in one of Ambleside's outdoor clothing and equipment shops. You'll also find maps, guidebooks, walking poles, camping equipment, and climbing gear. Try **Gaynor Sports,** Market Cross (www.gaynors.co.uk; ℂ **01524/734938**), for discount wear; **Edge of the World,** Rydal Road (www.edgeoftheworld.co.uk; ℂ **01539/433033**), for more fashion-conscious sweat tops and T-shirts, boots, and beanies; or **The Climbers Shop,** Compston Road (www.climbers-shop.com; ℂ **01539/432297**), for crampons and other technical equipment.

Entertainment & Nightlife

Ambleside pubs spill onto the streets in the summer months, especially the **Royal Oak,** Market Place (ℂ **01539/433382**), a popular bar with seating at the front entrance and a large umbrella for rainy evenings. The **Golden Rule,** Smithy Brow (ℂ**01539/432257**), boasts a large selection of CAMRA (Campaign for Real Ale) beers. You can relax with a pint in one of the leather chairs or slip into another room for a game of darts. Behind the bar, a small garden provides a serene setting in warm weather.

If pints just aren't enough, then **Zeffirellis,** Compston Road (www.zefirellis.com; ℂ **01539/433845**), might be just the ticket. It has a cinema showing Art House films, live music in the jazz bar, a cafe, a pizzeria, and a vegetarian restaurant all in one spot.

Where to Stay

The Best Western Ambleside Salutation In the heart of Ambleside, this large, white hotel is hard to miss. Its 47 spacious en suite rooms are decorated in soft, neutral colors. The hotel also has its own on-site health club that includes gym equipment with iPod docking stations and a heated indoor pool. After working out, you can have a choice of drinking and dining options, including a range of bar meals in the main lounge, pizzas and ribs in the Pizzeria Cellar Bar, or more formal dining in **Victoria's Restaurant.**

Lake Rd., Ambleside, Cumbria LA22 9BX. www.queenshotelambleside.com. ℂ **01539/432244.** Fax 01539/432721. 47 units. Sun–Thurs £58–£106 double; Fri–Sat £78–£149 double. Discounts available for early-bird room reservations. AE, MC, V. Free parking. **Amenities:** Restaurant; bistro/bar; health club. In room: TV, hair dryer.

The Log House ★ This genuine Norwegian log house was imported by local artist Heaton Cooper on his return from the country in the early 20th century. It has had many roles over the years, but today it has a restaurant, bar, and three guest rooms—all fresh, clean, and white and located in the cabin's roof space. The **restaurant's** modern menu includes entrees such as crayfish and chorizo salad, and confit duck leg, and main courses like Cumbrian beef filet, Herdwick lamb, or grilled sea bass with roasted tomato and cumin compote, all made with seasonal, local produce.

Lake Rd., Ambleside, Cumbria LA22 ODN. www.loghouse.co.uk. ℂ **01539/431077.** 3 units. £82–£93 double. Rates include English breakfast. Weekends and public holidays 2-night minimum stay. MC, V. Free parking. On the left-hand side as you drive into Ambleside from Windermere. **Amenities:** Restaurant; bar. *In room:* TV, hair dryer, Wi-Fi (free).

Rothay Manor Hotel ★★ ☺   At this Regency manor house, the **restaurant** is the star, with ingredients sourced from the best regional suppliers. Savor baked halibut in rosemary butter or duo of Cumbrian fell-bred lamb. Most bedrooms have shuttered French doors opening onto a balcony and a mountain view (two are wheelchair accessible). Classic Rooms have twin, double, or queen beds, while some suites can accommodate large families. There's even a children's "high tea" (6–6:30pm), which is really a dinner, and a playground nearby, as well as croquet and boules on-site.

Rothay Bridge, Ambleside, Cumbria LA22 0EH. www.rothaymanor.co.uk. ✆ **01539/433605.** Fax 01539/433607. 19 units. £175–£275 double; £235–£305 suite. Rates include English breakfast. AE, DC, MC, V. Free parking. Take the A593 ½ mile south of Ambleside. **Amenities:** Restaurant; bar; babysitting; free use of nearby health club; Wi-Fi (free). *In room:* TV, hair dryer.

Waterhead Hotel ★   This town-house hotel has a prized position beside Lake Windermere, and is a good base for exploring the lakes on foot or by car. The **restaurant,** bar, and guest rooms are contemporary and meticulously styled. Guest rooms are spacious, some with lake views. On sunny days you can relax outside on the waterfront lawns or sink into a sofa inside, beside the open fire. Guests can also use the watersports center and spa facilities at sister hotel Low Wood, just a mile along the lake.

Lake Rd., Waterhead, Ambleside, Cumbria LA22 0EP. www.elh.co.uk. ✆ **01539/432566.** Fax 01539/431255. 41 units. £135–£308 double. Rates include English breakfast. AE, MC, V. Free parking. **Amenities:** Restaurant; bar; nearby health club and watersports center. *In room:* TV, hair dryer.

GRASMERE & RYDAL ★★

282 miles NW of London; 18 miles NW of Kendal; 43 miles S of Carlisle

Rydal is just a hamlet, a few houses including Rydal Mount, home to the poet Wordsworth for several years. From the gardens you can spy the nearest lake, Rydal Water, where it is said that the poet used to sit and contemplate the view from a point on the western shore now called Wordsworth's Seat.

Farther along the A591 is **Grasmere,** a pretty village set beside a lake of the same name. Also home to Wordsworth, he called the area "the loveliest spot that man hath ever known." Today visitors pour into the village at any opportunity to visit locations associated with the poet—including his grave in the cemetery of St. Oswald's—and to buy bags of Grasmere gingerbread. The village is also a popular place for walks to the Langdale Pikes to the southwest and Helvellyn to the north. One of the most popular fells in the Lake District, the closest access route from here is straight up and down from the eastern shore of Thirlmere. For a longer, more spectacular hike, drive via Ambleside and Kirkstone Pass to Glenridding (a worthwhile drive in itself for its panoramic lake and fell views). From here you can hike across Striding Edge, a steep and dramatic ridge that leads westwards to the peak of Helvellyn. You can return to Thirlmere if you have transport from there or circle back round Red Tarn and back to Glenridding.

Essentials

GETTING THERE   Take a train to Windermere (see "Windermere & Bowness," earlier in this chapter) and continue the rest of the way by bus.

Stagecoach runs an hourly bus service to Grasmere from Keswick and Windermere. Buses in either direction are marked no. 555 or 556.

If you're driving from Windermere, continue northwest along the A591.

VISITOR INFORMATION   Grasmere tourist information is available at the National Trust shop (www.golakes.co.uk; ✆ **01539/435665**). Daily 9.30am-5pm.

Exploring the Area

Dove Cottage, the Wordsworth Museum ★★ HISTORIC HOME   If
you're on the Wordsworth "trail," then Dove Cottage is a good place to start. A small, white cottage with a tangle of pink roses clinging to the walls, it was the Dove and Olive pub years before it became Wordsworth's home in 1799. He spent a few happy years living here with his writer and diarist sister, Dorothy, and later his wife, Mary. A guided tour introduces visitors to the former drinking room downstairs and the study and compact bedrooms upstairs. After the tour, spend time in the garden where he composed "I Wandered Lonely as a Cloud." In the Wordsworth Museum behind the cottage, you can see manuscripts, paintings, and memorabilia, and maybe catch a special exhibition exploring the art and literature of English Romanticism.

On the A591, south of the village of Grasmere on the road to Kendal. www.wordsworth.org.uk. ✆ **01539/435544.** Admission to Dove Cottage and the adjoining museum £7.50 adults, £4.50 children 5–16, £6.50 students, £17.20 family ticket. March–Oct daily 9:30am–5:30pm; Nov–Feb daily 9:30am–4:30pm (last admission 30 min. before closing). Closed Dec 24–26, mid-Jan–early Feb and Tues mornings during winter.

Rydal Mount ★★ HISTORIC HOME   Delve into the world of William Word-
sworth at this Lakeland house, where he lived from 1813 until his death in 1850. Many of the poet's belongings remain here, including his library and cutlass chair (a type of chair designed for men wearing swords), as well as his beloved daughter Dora's bedroom. Don't miss the attic study, which he added onto the original 16th-century farmer's lake cottage. A descendant of Wordsworth now owns the property, which also has a spectacular 4½-acre garden, landscaped by Wordsworth. Walk among the rare trees and clamber up the terrace steps to the "summer house," where he would sit in contemplation while taking in views of Rydal Water.

Off the A591, 1½ miles north of Ambleside. www.rydalmount.co.uk. ✆ **01539/433002.** Admission to house and gardens £6.75 adults, £5.75 seniors and students, £3.25 children 5–15, £16 family ticket, free for children 4 and under. Mar–Oct daily 9:30am–5pm; Nov–Dec and Feb Wed–Sun 11am–4pm. Closed Dec 25–26 and all of Jan.

Wordsworth Graves & St. Oswald's Church CHURCH   William Word-
sworth died in the spring of 1850 and was buried in St. Oswald's Church graveyard. You can walk here from Dove Cottage, stopping in to see the resting place of the poet, his wife, Mary, and daughter, Dora, along with other family members. Take a peek in the church, where there's a memorial to Wordsworth in the 13th-century nave. Named after a 7th-century Christian king, the church comes to life during the Rush-bearing Festival in July; a procession of parishioners re-enact an age-old custom of strewing rushes and flowers on what was once an earthen floor. Look out for the **Grasmere Gingerbread Shop** (www.grasmeregingerbread.co.uk; ✆ **01539/435428**) by the church gate, famous for its fresh cookies.

Church Stile, Grasmere. Free admission. Daily 9am–5pm.

Where to Eat & Stay
VERY EXPENSIVE
Moss Grove Organic Hotel ★ 🛏   This hotel in the heart of Grasmere focuses
on organic produce (local when possible), sustainability, and being as environmentally

friendly as possible. These days, this doesn't mean "living it rough." Instead you'll find spacious, individually furnished guest rooms, some with beds made from reclaimed wood, and fashionable wallpaper combined with neutral tones. All rooms provide a relaxing space to get away from it all. You can even arrange for organic chocolates and wine to be placed in your room.

Grasmere, Cumbria LA22 9RQ. www.mossgrove.com. (C) **01539/435619.** 11 units. £99–£265 double. £129–£325 suite. Rates include English breakfast. 2-night minimum stay at weekends. Dogs allowed in ground-floor superior room and suite for extra £20 per night. MC, V. Free parking. *In room:* TV, hair dryer; underfloor heating (executive rooms), spa bath, Wi-Fi (free).

The Wordsworth Hotel & Spa ★★   Set next to the churchyard where Wordsworth is buried, this stone Lakeland house was once the Earl of Cadogan's hunting lodge. Today its refurbished bedrooms are luxurious, combining classical style with modern comforts. Expect Egyptian cotton sheets, bathrobes, flat-screen TVs, and Wi-Fi; some rooms have four-poster beds and courtyard, village, or mountain views. Families can book adjoining rooms with twin or single beds. Guests can enjoy a cream tea in the lounge, casual eating by the fireside in the bistro, or Cumbrian classics in the **award-winning restaurant.**

Stock Lane, Grasmere, Cumbria LA22 9SW. www.grasmere-hotels.co.uk. (C) **01539/435592.** Fax 01539/435765. 38 units. £118–£250 double; £218–£398 suite. Rates include English breakfast. Dinner £20 extra per person. AE, DC, MC, V. Free parking. Turn left on the A591 at the GRASMERE VILLAGE sign, and follow the road over the bridge, past the church, and around an S-bend; the Wordsworth is on the right. **Amenities:** Restaurant; bar; heated indoor pool; exercise room; Jacuzzi; sauna; room service. *In room:* TV, hair dryer, Wi-Fi (free).

EXPENSIVE

Swan Hotel   Sir Walter Scott used to come here for a secret drink early in the morning, and Wordsworth mentioned the place in "The Waggoner." In fact, the poet's wooden chair is in one of the rooms. Many bedrooms are in a modern wing, added in 1975, which fits gracefully onto the building's older core (only the shell of the original 1650 building remains). Bedrooms are comfortably furnished, each with twin or double beds; the feature rooms have canopy or four-poster beds. The Walkers Bar is popular with hikers (and their dogs) after a day on the fells, who then clean up for British roasts and steaks in the **Waggoner's restaurant.**

On the A591 (on the road to Keswick, ½ mile outside Grasmere), Grasmere, Cumbria LA22 9RF. www.macdonaldhotels.co.uk/swan. (C) **0844/879-9120.** Fax 01539/435741. 38 units. £89–£179 double. Rates include breakfast. Dogs stay for a supplement of £15 per night. AE, MC, V. Free parking. **Amenities:** Restaurant; bar; spa; room service. *In room:* TV, hair dryer, Wi-Fi (free).

MODERATE

Gold Rill Hotel ★★   This sprawling country-house hotel has the most prized location in Grasmere, alongside the lake yet only a 2-minute walk to the center of the village. Surrounded by well-maintained gardens, the hotel has a heated outdoor pool and a private pier. Each midsize to spacious bedroom is individually furnished, some with king-size beds. For romantic breaks, you can arrange in advance for champagne, strawberries, and fresh flowers to be placed in the room. Guests can enjoy pub lunches or a fine evening dinner here, often prepared with local produce.

Red Bank Rd., Grasmere, Cumbria LA22 9PU. www.gold-rill.com. (C) **01539/435486.** 31 units. £106–£128 double. Rates include English breakfast. MC, V. Free parking. **Amenities:** Restaurant; bar; heated outdoor pool; room service. *In room:* TV, hair dryer.

Lancrigg Vegetarian Country House Hotel ★★ 📷   With an emphasis on vegetarian cooking, Lancrigg also caters to vegans and people with allergies. What's more, the hotel is set in a beautiful, secluded valley that used to attract the Lakes poets to the area for inspiration. The spacious guest rooms are very English in style with floral prints and pastel shades; some have four-poster beds and ample seating areas. In addition to savoring the tasty and healthful culinary creations in the **restaurant,** you can pamper your body with a facial and massage in the spa.

Easedale, Grasmere, Cumbria LA22 9QN. www.lancrigg.co.uk. ℭ **01539/435317.** Fax 01539/435058. 12 units. £110–£170 double. Rates include vegetarian breakfast. Dinner £24 extra per person. AE, MC, V. Free parking. Closed Dec–Jan. **Amenities:** Restaurant; health club & spa. *In room:* TV, hair dryer, Wi-Fi (free).

Oak Bank Hotel Each of the 14 guest rooms in this small hotel have been individually refurbished to a high standard, all with en suite bathrooms. Standard rooms have showers and superior bedrooms have shower-tub combinations. There is one guest room with a super-king or twin beds and a sofa bed, while the Acorn Suite has its own front door, super-king or twin beds, seating area, and a spa bathroom en suite. Oak Bank also has its own award-winning restaurant, where they try to make as much as possible in-house, including breads, pasta, and ice cream. They will also cater for dietary needs.

Broadgate, Grasmere, Cumbria LA22 9TA. www.lakedistricthotel.co.uk. ℭ **01539/435217.** Fax 01539/35685. 14 units. £158 double; from £212 suite. Rates include English breakfast. MC, V. Free parking. **Amenities:** Restaurant. *In room:* TV, hair dryer.

CONISTON & HAWKSHEAD

263 miles NW of London; 19 miles NW of Kendal; 52 miles S of Carlisle

Coniston Water lies in a tranquil wooded valley between Grizedale Forest and the high fells of Coniston Old Man and Wetherlam. Coniston village is famously associated with **John Ruskin;** visit the museum named after him, his grave in the cemetery, and his former house, **Brantwood,** across the lake. It's also a good place for hiking and rock climbing. The **Coniston Old Man** towers in the background at 790m (2,633 ft.), giving mountain climbers one of the finest views of the Lake District.

The pretty village of **Hawkshead** is just 4 miles east of Coniston, but to get there you have to drive around the north side of the lake along the B5285. Hawkshead is home to the 15th-century grammar school where Wordsworth studied for 8 years (it is said he carved his name on a desk that is still there). The main attraction here though is the **Beatrix Potter Gallery,** located in the former offices of her husband. Nearby, in Near Sawrey, is **Hill Top Farm,** former 17th-century home of the author.

Essentials

GETTING THERE Take a train to Windermere (see "Windermere & Bowness," earlier in this chapter) and proceed the rest of the way by boat/bus. Local buses are operated mainly by **Stagecoach,** and for Hawkshead you'll need to catch a connecting bus in Ambleside.

Windermere Lake Cruises Ltd (www.windermere-lakecruises.co.uk; ℭ **01539/443360**) operates a ferry service in summer from Bowness, directly south of Windermere, to Ferry House. From April to September, **Mountain Goat** (www.mountain-goat.com; ℭ **01539/445161**) operates several shuttle buses per day from Ferry House to Hawkshead.

By car from Windermere, proceed north on the A591 to Ambleside, cutting south-west on the B5285 to Hawkshead.

VISITOR INFORMATION   Coniston Tourist Information Centre, Ruskin Avenue (www.conistontic.org; ✆ **01539/441533**), is open from April (or Easter, whichever is earlier) to October, daily 9:30am to 5pm, and from November to March (Easter), daily 10am to 4pm.

Hawkshead Tourist Information Centre, Main Street (✆ **01539/436946**), is open in the summer only (approximately Easter to the beginning of October) daily 8am to 5:30pm.

Exploring the Area

Beatrix Potter Gallery ★ GALLERY   This cream-colored cottage was once the office of Potter's husband, solicitor William Heelis. The interior remains largely unaltered since his day, but for the addition of Beatrix Potter's original illustrations, water-colors, and sketches. You can learn something of her role as a landowner and farmer. She bought acres of land to protect it from development, much of which she donated to the National Trust in her will.

Main St. www.nationaltrust.org.uk/beatrix-potter-gallery. ✆ **01539/436355.** Admission £4.80 adults, £2.40 children 5–17, £12 family ticket. Discount for Hill Top Farm with ticket. Mid-Feb–Mar Sat–Thurs 11am–3:30pm; Apr–end May and early Sept–early Nov Sat–Thurs 11am–5pm; end May–early Sept Sat–Thurs 10:30am–5pm. Last admission 30 min. before closing. Take bus no. 505 from Ambleside and Coniston to the square in Hawkshead, or the boat from Bowness to Ferry House and the shuttle bus to Hawkshead.

Brantwood ★★ ☺ HISTORIC SITE   With acres of garden and views across Coniston Water to the fells, Brantwood is the perfect place for a picnic lunch or coffee in the former stables, now converted into tearooms. The house was made famous by John Ruskin, poet, artist, and critic, and one of the great figures of the Victorian age, a prophet of social reform. He moved to Brantwood in 1872 and lived here until his death in 1900. Visitors today can see Ruskin's memorabilia, including some 200 of his pictures; the visit is made more fun for younger ones with quiz sheets.

Outside, part of the 250-acre estate has nature trails. Look for the Coach House Gallery, which follows the Ruskin tradition of encouraging contemporary craftwork of the finest quality. You may want to visit the graveyard of Coniston's village church, where Ruskin was buried; his family turned down the invitation to have him interred at Westminster Abbey.

East shore of Coniston Water. www.brantwood.org.uk.✆ **01539/441369.** Admission £6.30 adults, £5 students, £1.35 children 5–15, £13.15 family ticket. Mid-Mar–mid-Nov daily 11am–5pm; mid-Nov–Dec Wed–Sun 11am–4:30pm; 2 Jan–Mar Wed–Sun 10:30am–4:30pm. Closed Dec 24–26, 31, and Jan 1.

Coniston Launch ★★ ☺ CRUISE   These are traditional timber boats that operate a circular route calling at Coniston, Waterhead, Torver, and Brantwood. Discounts are offered in combination with admission to Brantwood house (see above) and you can hop-on and hop-off, or choose single fares if you're planning on walking back. Other cruises explore the more tranquil part of the lake to the south, again with cruise or single-fare options for walkers. In the summer they also run special "Swallows and Amazons" and "Campbells on Coniston" cruises.

Coniston Pier/Boat House. www.conistonlaunch.co.uk.✆ **01768/775753.** Northern service £9.50 adults, £4.95 children 5–16, £23 family ticket (including Brantwood £15.30 round-trip for adults, £6.20 children, £35.15 family ticket). Southern service £13.50 round-trip for adults, £6.75 children,

£29 family ticket (including Brantwood £19.30 adults, £8 children, £40.65 family ticket). Northern service mid-Mar–Oct daily 10:45am–3:40pm first/last boats from Coniston; round-trip approx. 50 min.; Nov–mid-Mar daily 10:30am–2:30pm first/last boats from Coniston (late Nov–Dec Sat–Sun only), no sailings Jan; Southern service mid-Mar–Sept 2:45pm from Coniston, round-trip approx. 1¾ hr.

Coniston Water NATURAL ATTRACTION   This is one of the most beautiful lakes, with the Old Man fell rising over it and the waters stretching south from Coniston for around 5½ miles. It's easy to drive along the western shore, with picnic places and lakeside paths dotted along the route, while roads on the eastern side are narrow, becoming clogged with tour buses in peak season. The more relaxing option is to travel by boat, taking in the fells from the water and imagining yourself a character in Arthur Ransome's *Swallows and Amazons,* inspired by Coniston Water.

Gondola HISTORICAL SITE/CRUISE   The romantic option is to cruise the lake in an original Victorian steam-powered yacht. The *Gondola,* launched in 1859 and in regular service until 1937, was rescued and completely restored with upholstered seating by the National Trust. Since 1980, it has become a familiar sight on Coniston Water; sailings to Brantwood run throughout the summer. Service is subject to weather conditions, of course.

Coniston Pier/Boat House. www.nationaltrust.org.uk/gondola. ✆ **01539/432733.** £8.50 round-trip for adults, £4.50 children 5–16, £22 family ticket. Discount vouchers available for Brantwood and Ruskin Museum with ticket. Times vary according to capacity and weather conditions; bookings advisable.

Hill Top Farm ★★ HISTORIC HOME   It's a 2-mile walk from Hawkshead to Near Sawrey, a pretty country village where you can visit Beatrix Potter's former home. If driving, park your car beside the ticket office, but come first thing (before opening if you can), as entry is timed and waiting can be lengthy in peak season. The cottage is a few minutes' walk along the road. Enter through the gate beside the shop where a path leads past a tangle of wild flowers (in the summer) to the entrance. You might have time to explore the herb and vegetable garden before going inside, but don't miss your time slot! Inside, the world of Beatrix Potter comes alive. Almost unchanged, you'll see her paintings and personal items throughout, and guides are on hand to embellish them with a few tales.

Near Sawrey, Hawkshead. www.nationaltrust.org.uk/hill-top. ✆ **01539/436269.** £8 adults, £4 children 5–16, £20 family ticket. Discount at Beatrix Potter Gallery with Hill Top ticket. Mid-Feb–Mar Sat–Thurs 10:30am–3:30pm; Apr–May and early Sept–Oct Sat–Thurs 10:30am–4:30pm; June–early Sept 10am–5pm; last entry 30 min. before closing. Shuttle bus from Hawkshead/Ferry House.

Ruskin Museum MUSEUM   This museum, in the center of the village, is divided into the Coniston Gallery, the Ruskin Gallery, and the new Bluebird wing. The first gives an insight into Coniston's past, delving back thousands of years with displays and computer images of old Coniston. Among the artifacts you'll see a preserved hog, slate from the mines, lace and crafts from the local cottage industry, and Arthur Ransom's dinghy, *Mavis.* The Ruskin Gallery provides insight into John Ruskin through personal possessions and mementos, photographs, busts, letters, and his collection of mineral rocks. The Bluebird wing has numerous exhibits relating to Donald Campbell's *Bluebird,* and eventually it will hold a reconstruction of the fateful boat.

Off Yewdale Rd., Coniston. www.ruskinmuseum.com. ✆ **01539/441164.** £5.25 adults, £2.50 children 6–16, £14 family ticket. Early Mar–mid-Nov daily 10am–5:30pm; mid-Nov–early Mar Wed–Sun 10:30am–3:30pm. Closed Dec 24–26.

LAKE DISTRICT national park ★★★

Despite the reverence with which the English treat the Lake District, it required an act of Parliament in 1951 to protect its natural beauty. Spread over 885 sq. miles of hills, eroded mountains, forests, and lakes, the **Lake District National Park** is the largest and one of the most popular National Parks in the U.K., receiving over 8 million day visitors a year. Lured by Romantic Lake poets' work, visitors arrive to take in the mountains, wildlife, flora, fauna, and secluded waterfalls. Much of the area is privately owned, but landowners work with National Park officers to preserve the landscape and its 1,800 miles of footpaths.

Alas, the park's popularity is now one of its major drawbacks. Hordes of weekend tourists descend, especially in summertime and on public holiday weekends. Despite the crowds, great efforts are made to maintain the trails that radiate in a network throughout the district, preserving the purity of a landscape that includes more than 100 lakes and countless numbers of grazing sheep.

Before setting out to explore the lakes, stop in at the **National Park Visitor Centre** (www.lakedistrict.gov.uk; ℂ **01539/446601**), located on the lakeshore at Brockhole, on the A591 between Windermere and Ambleside. It can be reached by bus or by one of the lake launches from Windermere. Once here, you can pick up useful information and explore 30 acres of landscaped gardens and parklands; lake cruises, exhibitions, and film shows are also offered. Lunches and teas are served in the tearooms.

Tourist information offices within the park are richly stocked with maps and suggestions for several dozen bracing rambles. Regardless of the itinerary you select, you'll spot frequent green-and-white signs, or their older equivalents in varnished pine with Adirondack-style routed letters, announcing FOOTPATH TO . . .

Entertainment & Nightlife

You can rent rowboats and sailing dinghies at **Coniston Boating Centre,** Lake Road, Coniston (www.lakedistrict.gov.uk; ℂ **01539/441366**). **Summitreks** also operates from the lakeside at Coniston Boating Centre, offering qualified instruction in canoeing and windsurfing. You can rent a wide range of equipment from the nearby office at Lake Road (www.summitreks.co.uk; ℂ **01539/441212**). A few miles south of Hawkshead, **Grizedale Forest** has nature and forest trails, mountain-bike cycling routes, a cafe and sculpture trail.

Where to Eat & Stay

Black Bull ENGLISH/INTERNATIONAL   A pub, inn, and brewery, the Black Bull dominates the main crossroads in Coniston. A former coaching inn dating back 400 years, it counts artists and poets among its former clients. It has a microbrewery, the Coniston Brewing Company, which produces several types of ale, bitter, and stout. These make a good accompaniment to the sirloin steak, scampi, and crispy duck on the menu. There are also 15 en suite **guest rooms** (£100–£110 double, with English breakfast), all basic but clean and comfortable, two in small cottages.

Yewdale Rd., Coniston. www.blackbullconiston.co.uk. ℂ **01539/441335.** Fax 01539/441168. Reservations recommended. Main courses £9–£16. MC, V. Daily noon–2:30pm and 6:15–9:30pm.

Buckle Yeat Guest House   You'll pass this pretty 17th-century Lakeland house as you stroll to Hill Top Farm (see above). In the flower-filled front yard, you'll often see a stuffed mannequin of Mr. McGregor, feared by the rabbits in Beatrix Potter's *Tale of Peter Rabbit.* Inside, the decor is traditional, furnished with dark wood antiques and an open log fire where guests can warm themselves with Mr. McGregor, who is brought inside for the winter. Guest rooms are individually decorated but all are light and airy with a comfortable country feel.

Near Sawrey, Hawkshead, Cumbria LA22 0LF. www.buckle-yeat.co.uk. © 01539/436446. 6 units. £80–£90 per double. Rates include English breakfast. MC, V. Free parking. **Amenities:** Lounge; breakfast room. *In room:* TV, hair dryer.

The Drunken Duck Inn ★ MODERN BRITISH   People come to this out-of-the-way family-run inn to feast on its creative menu, which can include Cullen skink, wild mushrooms on toast, or an ale-braised beef brisket. Most of the 17 standard **guest rooms** are above the inn, but all are brightwith quality furnishings (£95–£295 double, including breakfast). Superior and deluxe rooms have more space and king-size beds; some have courtyard and mountain views.

2½ miles north of Hawkshead, off the B5286, Barngates, Cumbria LA22 0NG. www.drunkenduck inn.co.uk. © **01539/436347.** Reservations recommended. Main courses £12.95–£27.50. MC, V. Daily noon–4pm and 6:30–9pm.

Queen's Head ENGLISH/INTERNATIONAL   The Queen's Head is a 17th-century building that serves a special brew, Robinsons Stockport, from old-fashioned wooden kegs. Temptations on the menu can include a winter woodland venison casserole. The pub also rents **14 bedrooms** (£75–£110, including English breakfast); two rooms have four-poster beds, and all have a private bathroom, TV, and phone. There are also two suites, one suitable for families of four (both £100–£130 each).

Main St., Hawkshead. www.queensheadhawkshead.co.uk. © **01539/436271.** Reservations recommended. Main courses £12.50–£24.50. MC, V. Daily noon–2:30pm and 6:15–9:30pm.

Sun Hotel ★   The most attractive pub, restaurant, and hotel in Coniston, this country-house hotel dates from 1902, and the attached inn from the 16th century. Situated on beautiful grounds above the village, 135m (450 ft.) from the town center, it lies at the foot of the Coniston Old Man (p. 619). Each bedroom, ranging in size from small to midsize, is decorated with flair; three are big enough for families. Dogs welcome (on a lead and for an additional £10 per night). In the **restaurant,** main courses (£10–£14) include homely favorites like beef-and-ale pie and several vegetarian options.

Brow Hill (off the A593), Coniston, Cumbria LA21 8HQ. www.thesunconiston.com. © **01539/ 441248.** Fax 01539/441219. 10 units. £100–£110 double. Rates include English breakfast. MC, V. Free parking. **Amenities:** Restaurant; bar. *In room:* TV, hair dryer, Wi-Fi (free).

Side Trips

The best places to visit in the South Lakes include the home of Lord and Lady Cavendish, **Holker Hall** (www.holker.co.uk; © **01539/558328**); the **Laurel and Hardy Museum** in Ulverston (www.laurel-and-hardy.co.uk; © **01229/582292**), and the **South Lakes Wild Animal Park** (www.wildanimalpark.co.uk; © **01229/466086**) in Dalton-on-Furness.

If you continue to the West Lakes, you can enjoy a coast-to-mountain ride on the **Ravenglass & Eskdale Railway** (www.ravenglass-railway.co.uk; © **01229/717171**) and visit haunted **Muncaster Castle** (www.muncaster.co.uk; ☎ **01229/717614**), home to the World Owl Trust. Or you can head for Wasdale Head at the northern end of **Wast Water,** a popular starting point for the trek up **Scafell Pike.** Return to Coniston via the heady, winding roads of **Hardknott and Wrynose Passes.**

KESWICK & BORROWDALE ★★

294 miles NW of London; 31 miles NW of Kendal; 22 miles NW of Windermere

Keswick opens onto Derwentwater, one of the loveliest lakes in the region, and the town makes a good base for exploring the northern half of The Lake District National Park, particularly Borrowdale valley's spectacular mountain views and hiking routes.

Keswick is a busy town with a market charter dating back to the 13th century. The weekly **market** still takes place in the pedestrianized main street, which is dominated by the Moot Hall, a former assembly building now home to the tourist office. The town has several attractions, including the Cumberland Pencil Museum. Above the small town is historic Castlerigg stone circle thought to be some 5,000 years old.

From the town center, it's a short walk to **Friar's Crag,** the classic viewing point on Derwentwater. The walk will also take you past **Theatre by the Lake,** a professional repertory theatre, and the pier with launches that operate regular tours around the lake.

Essentials

GETTING THERE Take a train to Windermere (see "Windermere & Bowness," earlier in this chapter) and proceed the rest of the way by bus. **Stagecoach** has a regular bus service from Windermere, Ambleside, and Grasmere (bus no. 555). If you're driving from Windermere, drive northwest on the A591.

VISITOR INFORMATION **Keswick Tourist Information Centre,** at Moot Hall, Market Square (www.golakes.co.uk and www.keswick.org; ☎ **01768/772645**), is open daily 9:30am to 5:30pm. The center is also the Adventure Hub of England and arranges bookings of outdoor activities for all levels of experience and ability.

Exploring the Area

From Keswick you have easy access to the pick of the peaks, including **Blencathra, Skiddaw, Helvellyn, Scafell,** and **Scafell Pike.** For something easier, try **Catbells,** on the west side of Derwentwater (see below). You can also enjoy the mountains by bicycle or car, heading through Borrowdale and stopping at **Honister Slate Mine** (see below), then down to **Buttermere** village and lake and **Crummock Water** for gentle waterfront strolls. You can return to Keswick via Whinlatter Pass (B292), which passes through **Whinlatter Forest Park.** Stop at the visitor center for gifts and lunch or cycling routes and horse riding. Children will love the **Go Ape!** (www.goape.co.uk; ☎ **0845/643-9215**) high-wire adventure that zips them from tree to tree.

One of the most scenic parts of the Lake District, the valley of **Borrowdale ★★** stretches south of Derwentwater to Seathwaite in the heart of the county. The valley is walled in by fell sides, and it's an excellent center for exploring, walking, and climbing. Many use it as a base for exploring Scafell, England's highest mountain, at 963m (3,210 ft.; see below). The southernmost village in the Borrowdale valley is Seatoller, the terminus for buses to and from Keswick. From here, head west along the B5289 through the Honister Pass and Buttermere Fell, one of the most dramatic drives in the Lake District. The road is lined with towering boulders. The lake village of Buttermere also merits a stopover for its lake-country scenery.

Castlerigg Stone Circle ★ HISTORIC SITE   Set in a privileged location with panoramic views of Helvellyn, High Seat, Skiddaw, and Blencathra, Castlerigg is a Neolithic stone circle dating back to approximately 3000 B.C. In total there are 38 stones, the tallest standing 2.3m (7.55 ft.) high. Now owned by the National Trust and tended by English Heritage, visitors can wander among the stones while pondering their origins and taking in the dramatic backdrop.

Castle Lane, Keswick. www.english-heritage.org.uk. Free Admission. Open 24 hr.

Derwentwater ★★ ☺ CRUISE/NATURAL ATTRACTION   Just half a mile from Keswick's town center, Derwentwater is popular with walkers and other leisure seekers. The **Keswick Launch Company** operates a hop-on hop-off circular service. You can board at Keswick and get off at Hawes End, then follow the paths leading to the summit of **Catbells,** a small fell suitable for younger and less-fit walkers. Your efforts will be rewarded with one of the most spectacular vistas in the Lake District. Either return by the same route or walk along the lake shore and then hop on boats from Low Brandlehow, High Brandlehow, Nichol End, Lodore, and Ashness. The circular route operates in both directions, but don't miss the last boat if you don't want a long hike back to town.

Keswick Launch Co., Lake Rd., Keswick. www.keswick-launch.co.uk. ✆ **01768/772263.** £9 adults, £4.50 children 5–16, £22 family ticket for hop-on hop-off circular route (50 min.); single tickets also available. First/last boats from Keswick: Mid–late Mar and mid–late Nov clockwise daily 10am, 3pm (4pm late Mar–June and Sept–Oct; 5pm Easter holiday and July–Aug); counter-clockwise 9:45am, 3:30pm (4:30pm late Mar–June and Sept–Oct; 5:30pm July–Aug).

Honister Slate Mine ★★★ ☺ HISTORIC SITE   There are several reasons to stop at this slate mine on Honister Pass, not least being the dramatic views into the steep-sided valley below. Mine tours take visitors underground to hear about the centuries-old process of mining and splitting slate. If you're really brave, you can try the Via Ferrata, a system of cables and metal rails that allows nonclimbers a taste of traversing a rock face. The hardiest will want to opt for the zip wire, which whizzes you across a crevasse. Back at base, there's a cafe and a shop selling hand-crafted slate gifts.

Honister Pass, Borrowdale. www.honister-slate-mine.co.uk. ✆ **01768/777230.** Mine tours £9.95–£20 adults, £4.95–£20 children 15 and under, depending on tour; Via Ferrata Classic £30 adults, £20 children 10–15, £95 family ticket (2 adults and 2 children); Via Ferrata and zip wire £35 adults, £25 children 10–15, £115 family ticket; all-day pass packages available. Daily 9am–5pm; tours/Via Ferrata dependent on weather conditions.

Entertainment & Nightlife

Keswick's **Theatre by the Lake** (www.theatrebythelake.co.uk; ✆ 01768/774411) is a 400-seat theatre that produces a year-round program of drama productions. It is best to buy tickets in advance, particularly in the summer months when visitor numbers are high.

You'll find several pubs in the town center, including the **Oddfellows Arms** on Main Street (✆ 0871/223-8000) and **The Dog and Gun** on Lake Road (✆ 01768/773463), both of which serve real ales such as Jennings and Coniston Bluebird. **The George** (www.georgehotelkeswick.co.uk; ✆ 01768/772076) also offers several Jennings beers and is the perfect place to enjoy a pint beside the open fire after a day on the fells.

Where to Eat & Stay

At the **Lakeland Pedlar** ★, Bell Close, Keswick (www.lakelandpedlar.co.uk; ⦿ **01768/774492**), there's a bicycle shop (for rentals, parts, and repairs) upstairs and a vegetarian, reasonably priced, and very tasty cafe downstairs (main courses £5.50–£8.50). Options include breakfasts with vegan bacon-style rashers, homemade soups, Bengali-style veggie curry, aubergine and roasted vegetable Greek-style moussaka, and a substantial children's menu with names they'll like ("pirate" and "skateboarder"). There's a pay parking lot in front of the restaurant.

VERY EXPENSIVE

Armathwaite Hall Country House & Spa ★★ A country hotel with a rich history, it began as a house for Benedictine nuns in the 14th century, and was added to by a series of wealthy landowners until the mid-19th century. Today it's a luxury hotel surrounded by dense woodland bordering Bassenthwaite Lake. Guests arrive via a magnificent entrance hall lined with rich wood paneling. The bedrooms are handsomely furnished, all with views of the courtyard, the gardens, the lake, or the deer park. Four-poster and family rooms are available. The **restaurant** serves flambéed signature dishes.

Bassenthwaite Lake, Keswick, Cumbria CA12 4RE. www.armathwaite-hall.com. ⦿ **01768/776551.** Fax 01768/776220. 43 units. £190–£330 double; £370 suite. Rates include English breakfast. AE, DC, MC, V. Free parking. On the B5291, 7 miles northwest of Keswick, 1½ miles west of Bassenthwaite. **Amenities:** Restaurant; bar; indoor heated pool; tennis court; health club; croquet lawn. *In room:* TV, hair dryer, Wi-Fi (free).

EXPENSIVE

Borrowdale Gates Hotel ★ This 1860 Victorian country house is set in one of the most favored spots of Alfred Wainwright (renowned writer of pictorial guides to the fells). Rooms range from medium to large and are decorated with rich Victorian colors and period reproductions. The cozy public areas, with their antiques and open-log fires, include four lounges, a bar, a restaurant, and dining area, all with garden views. The **restaurant** serves Cumbrian meats, but usually has a fish option too.

Grange-in-Borrowdale, Keswick, Cumbria CA12 5UQ. www.borrowdale-gates.com. ⦿ **0845/833-2524.** Fax 01768/777204. 29 units. £134–£204 double. Rates include English breakfast. Dinner £30 extra per person; £39 for non-guests. AE, MC, V. Free parking. From Keswick, take the B5289 4 miles south to Grange; go over the bridge, and the inn sits on the right, just beyond the curve in the road. **Amenities:** Restaurant; bar. *In room:* TV, hair dryer.

Lodore Falls Hotel ★ This hotel overlooks Derwentwater and the nearby mountains. Built in traditional Lakeland slate over 200 years ago, its tradition of good rooms, food, and service continue today. The interior has been completely modernized, and the well-furnished bedrooms vary in size; it's worth opting for one of the larger ones. With a spa and beauty salon, lounge, cafe, and restaurant, the hotel is the perfect retreat after a day's walking.

Borrowdale Rd. (B5289), Borrowdale, Keswick, Cumbria CA12 5UX. www.lakedistricthotels.net/ lodorefalls. ⦿ **01768/777285.** Fax 01768/777343. 69 units. £180–£262 double; £398 suite. 2-night minimum stay Sat–Sun. Rates include breakfast. MC, V. Free parking. On the B5289 3½ miles south of Keswick. **Amenities:** Restaurant; bar; 2 heated pools (1 indoor, 1 outdoor); tennis court; exercise room; spa; sauna; room service; children's playground. *In room:* TV, hair dryer.

Overwater Hall ★★★ 🎁 Built in the late 18th century, this is a Georgian mansion with a castellated roof added by the Victorians. All the bedrooms, though standard in size, are extremely ritzy, having been furnished with top-quality antiques.

Surprisingly, this hotel permits dogs, but the hotel is so immaculate that you wouldn't know it. Guests can enjoy afternoon tea in the drawing room, and an exquisite set dinner in the **restaurant** each evening.

Overwater, Ireby (2 miles north of Bassenthwaite Lake), Cumbria CA5 1HH. www.overwaterhall. co.uk. ⓒ **01768/776566.** Fax 01768/776921. 13 units. £140–£240 double. 2-night minimum stay Sat–Sun. Rates include English breakfast. 4-course table d'hôte dinner £45 per person. MC, V. Free parking. **Amenities:** Restaurant; bar; lounge; room service. *In room:* TV, hair dryer.

MODERATE

The Pheasant Inn ★ A former 17th-century coaching inn near the northwestern tip of Bassenthwaite Lake, this inn evokes old-fashioned English coziness. Fireplaces warm a moderately eccentric bar area, a fusion of antique and old-fashioned furniture, and individually decorated country-style bedrooms with windows overlooking forest and parkland. Two bedrooms offer sitting areas. Dogs are permitted in the Garden Lodge Rooms (£5 per night supplement). Guests also have free use of the spa facilities at nearby Armathwaite Hall. The **Fell Restaurant** serves a fine daily menu, which can include venison, mackerel, and sea bass, depending on the season.

Bassenthwaite Lake, Cockermouth, Cumbria CA13 9YE. www.the-pheasant.co.uk. ⓒ **01768/776234.** Fax 01768/776002. 15 units. £170–£220 double. Rates include breakfast. 3-course dinner £35 (£30 each for guests staying two or more nights). MC, V. Free parking. Located midway between Keswick and Cockermouth, signposted from the A66. **Amenities:** Restaurant; bar; free use of spa; room service. *In room:* TV (on request), hair dryer.

Skiddaw Hotel ☺ This hotel lies behind an impressive facade and entrance marquee built right onto the sidewalk in Keswick's market square. The owners have refurbished the interior, retaining the best features. Bedrooms are compact and eye-catching, with a range of styles and colors; seven units are large enough for families. The upgraded Summit, Deluxe, and Feature rooms offer extras such as bathrobes, mineral water, and seating areas. One room has a super king-size, four-poster bed. Guests may use the pools and spa at Lodore Falls Hotel (see above), a 10-minute drive away, and golf at Keswick Golf Club during the week.

Main St., Market Sq., Keswick, Cumbria CA12 5BN. www.lakedistricthotels.net/skiddawhotel. ⓒ **01768/772071.** Fax 01768/774850. 40 units. £162–£218 double. Rates include English breakfast. MC, V. 2-night minimum stay Sat–Sun. Limited free on-site parking and free parking permits in adjacent public parking lot. **Amenities:** Restaurant; bar; golf, pool, and spa nearby; sauna; room service. *In room:* TV, hair dryer.

INEXPENSIVE

Edwardene Hotel This 1885 gray-slate house stands in a residential area, about a 3-minute walk from the town center. The three-story gabled house is well maintained with tasteful, comfortable accommodations. These rooms take their names from the Lakeland landscape—Myrtle, Bramble, Heather, Poppy, and so on. Attention to detail is paid by the hospitable owners, and guests assemble on chilly nights in the lounge by the fireplace. Cumberland sausages and free-range eggs are featured at breakfast.

26 Southey St., Keswick, Cumbria CA12 4EF. www.edwardenehotel.com. ⓒ **01768/773586.** 11 units. £90–£90 double; £126 family room. Rates include breakfast. MC, V. Free on-street parking. *In room:* TV, hair dryer.

The Lookout Keswick ★ ✦ Located on the western edge of Keswick, a 3-minute drive to Castlerigg Stone Circle, this 1920s house has been transformed into a pristine B&B. With just three guest rooms it provides a tranquil setting away from the bustle of Keswick town center. Rooms are contemporary, spacious, and neutral, two with mountain views and all with easy chairs, king-size beds, down and feather duvets, and en suite bathrooms. Guests can watch the sunset from the balcony or relax in the garden and listen to the stream.

Chestnut Hill, Keswick CA12 4LS. www.thelookoutkeswick.co.uk. ℂ **01768/780407.** 3 units. £80–£110 double. Rates include breakfast. MC, V. Free parking. *In room:* TV,

Side Trips

Northwest of Keswick on the A591, **Bassenthwaite** is one of the most beautiful of Lakeland villages. It nestles on the edge of Bassenthwaite Lake, the northernmost and only true "lake" in the Lake District, visited yearly by many species of northern European migratory birds. You might also catch sight of **ospreys** at the viewpoint in **Dodd Woods,** at the eastern end of the lake. Many visitors stop at **Mirehouse** (www.mirehouse.com; ℂ **01768/772287**), a historic house and estate with woodland playgrounds and tearooms.

You can also take the A66 from Keswick to the coastal town of **Maryport** in around 35 minutes, home to **Senhouse Roman Museum** (www.senhousemuseum. co.uk; ℂ **01900/816168**). South along the A595 is Whitehaven, once an important port town. Follow its rise and fall at the intriguing **Beacon Museum** (www.the beacon-whitehaven.co.uk; ℂ **01946/592302**) in the renovated harbor and at the **Rum Story** museum on Lowther Street (www.rumstory.co.uk; ℂ **01946/592933**).

PENRITH & ULLSWATER ★

296 miles NW of London; 26 miles E of Keswick

Set in a region of gently rolling fields and dramatic mountain rises, Ullswater is a favorite with those who enjoy spectacular natural beauty. A 9-mile expanse of water stretching from Pooley Bridge to Patterdale, **Ullswater** is the second-largest lake in the district and has always held a special attraction for artists and writers. It was on its shores that William Wordsworth saw his "host of golden daffodils." **Aira Force** waterfall, near the National Trust's Gowbarrow, inspired both Wordsworth and Coleridge with its beauty.

To the northeast of Ullswater is **Penrith.** Once capital of Cumbria, its name comes from the Celtic-derived language Cumbric and possibly means "Ford by the Hill." The namesake hill is marked today by a red-sandstone beacon and tower. Today, Penrith remains best known as a lively market town.

Essentials

GETTING THERE Virgin Trains operates about three trains daily from London's Euston to Penrith Station, this region's main rail junction. A change of trains isn't usually necessary. One-way tickets cost from £24. Once in Penrith, passengers usually take a taxi to Ullswater.

National Express (ℂ **0871/781-8181**) operates one daily bus that leaves from London's Victoria Coach Station at 11pm, arriving in Penrith at 5:30am. **Stagecoach** operates two buses per day that stop at Penrith on their way between Carlisle and Keswick. Passengers need to take a taxi from Penrith to Ullswater.

By car, take the M1 out of London, getting on the M6 to Penrith. The trip should take around 6 hours.

VISITOR INFORMATION **Penrith Tourist Information Centre,** Robinson's School, Middlegate (www.golakes.co.uk and www.visiteden.co.uk; ✆ **01768/867466**), is open daily 10am to 4pm (closed Sun in the off-season).

Exploring the Area

You can enjoy gentle walks to **Aira Force,** a spectacular waterfall set within National Trust-owned woodland on the edge of Ullswater (on the A592). There are also popular hikes up to **Askham Fell and High Street,** once a Roman trade route, and to **Helvellyn** from Glenridding.

Ullswater watersports opportunities include the **Glenridding Sailing Centre** (www.glenriddingsailingcentre.co.uk; ✆ **01768/482541**), which offers sailing, kayaking, and canoeing tuition and boat hire. **Eden Adventure** (www.edenoutdoor adventures.com; ✆ **07525/653099**) also offers canoeing, along with organized hikes, rock climbing, and other outdoor activities. While using this area as a base for outdoor activities, you can also easily explore the many places of historic significance, from the times of the ancient Celts right through to modern day. One noteworthy site is **Long Meg and Her Daughters,** an ancient stone circle near Penrith.

The Dalemain Estate ★ HISTORIC SITE   Despite the Georgian facade that greets visitors as they arrive at the estate, the first building here was a Saxon tower. This is long gone, but the 14th-century Old Hall and the Elizabethan wings remain, including the kitchen, which transformed it into a manor house. Tours pass through Tudor passages, Clifford family portraits and knick-knacks, and grand Georgian rooms. Set on a large estate, Dalemain has a deer park and extensive gardens that are most beautiful when the spring buds bloom.

On the A592, 2 miles north of Ullswater. www.dalemain.com. ✆ **01768/486450.** Admission house and garden £9.50 adults, £9 seniors, free for children 15 and under; garden only £6.50 adults and seniors. Tearooms, garden, and gift shop late Mar–late Oct Sun–Thurs 10:30am–5pm (house 11:30am–4pm); tearoom and gardens only late Oct–mid-Dec Sun–Thurs 11am–4pm. House closed Nov–late Mar; gardens & tearooms closed mid-Dec–late Mar.

Rheged Centre ★   Located just outside Penrith at the junction of the A66/A592, the Rheged Centre is a discovery center with stores selling educational children's toys, outdoor gear, farm produce, candy, books, and locally made paper. It's also a great place to take youngsters as there's an outdoor play park built like a Roman fort with towers and tunnels to explore. Inside they can bury themselves in colored balls in the soft-play area, and try their hand at painting some pottery. With the large-scale 3-D cinema and a varied program of theatre, dance, history exhibitions, and vintage fairs, there's plenty to keep everyone entertained.

Redhills, A66/A592, Penrith. www.rheged.com. ✆ **01768/868000** (cinema bookings ✆ **01768/860014**). Cinema first film £6.50 adults, £5 seniors, £4.80 under-16s, £19.50 family (2 adults, 2 children); second film £3.50 adults, £3 seniors, £2.20 under-16s, £9.50 family.

Penrith Castle CASTLE   The ruined castle dates back to 1399, its construction ordered by William Strickland, then Bishop of Canterbury. For the next 70 years, the castle continued to grow in size and strength until it finally became the royal castle and frequent residence for Richard, Duke of Gloucester.

Across from the train station along Ullswater Rd. www.english-heritage.org.uk. Free admission. Daily 24 hr.

Penrith & Eden Museum MUSEUM   Originally constructed in the 1500s, the museum building was turned into a poor girls' school in 1670. Today, the museum surveys the history, archeology, and geology of Penrith and the Eden Valley, which was a desert millions of years ago. Recently refurbished, it now has the addition of a short film about prehistoric Lakeland stone.

Robinson's School, Middlegate. ℂ **01768/865105.** Free admission. Mon–Sat 10am–5pm (also Sun Apr–Oct 1–4:45pm).

Ullswater Steamers ★★ ☺ CRUISE   The best way to take in the mountain scenery around Ullswater is on the water. Steamers operate between Pooley Bridge in the north, Howtown on the east, and Glenridding in the south. You can take a 1-hour cruise, a round-trip, or buy a one-way ticket and walk back along the east side of the lake.

The Pier House, Glenridding, and Pooley Bridge. www.ullswater-steamers.co.uk. ℂ **01768/482229.** Round-trip tickets £9.50–£12.95 adults, £4.75–£6.50 children 5–15, £26–£32 family ticket. The lower prices are for trips to Howtown. First/last boats: Nov-Jan from Glenridding 9:45am/1:45pm, Howtown 10:20am/2:20pm to Pooley Bridge & 3:10pm to GR, Pooley Bridge 12:10pm/2:45pm; until mid-extra sailing Glenridding 3:55pm, Howtown 4:30pm; mid/end Mar-mid Apr & early May-early Sep Glenridding 9:45am/4:45pm, Howtown 10:15am/5:30pm to GR & 10:25am/5:25pm to GR, Pooley Bridge 9:45am/5:05pm; mid-Apr to early May GR 9:45am/3:15pm, HT 10:15am/4:05 to GR, 10:25am/4:05pm to PB, Pooley Bridge 10:50am/3:40pm.

Glenridding is on the A592 at the southern end of Ullswater. Pooley Bridge is 5 miles from the M6 junction 40 to Penrith.

Shopping

Major shopping areas include the covered **Devonshire Arcade,** with its name-brand stores and boutiques; the pedestrian-only **Angel Lane** and **Little Dockray,** with an abundance of family-run specialty shops; and **Angel Square,** just south of Angel Lane. And you can buy treats and sticky gifts at **The Toffee Shop** on Brunswick Road (www.thetoffeeshop.co.uk; ℂ **01768/862008**), renowned for its handmade fudge and toffees.

Cranston's on Ullswater Road (www.cranstons.net; ℂ **01768/868680**) specializes in the Cumberland sausage, and you can buy them family-sized.

Entertainment & Nightlife

In Penrith itself, the **Foundry 34,** Burrowgate (ℂ **01768/210099**), is popular with the younger crowd for food, drinks, and live music. The older crowd might prefer to explore some of the village pubs around Penrith and Ullswater where there's often food as well as local brews. The **Beehive Inn** (www.thebeehivepenrith.co.uk; ℂ **01768/862081**) is one of the best pubs for families with children; it has a large garden with a play area for children, and it has a good selection of real ales and pub grub. The renovated 18th-century former coaching house, the **George and Dragon** in Clifton (www.georgeanddragonclifton.co.uk; ℂ **01768/865381**), is one for foodies, serving up a range of seasonal, local produce and an impressive array of wines.

In Askham, the **Queens Head,** Lower Green (www.queensheadaskham.com; ℂ **01931/712225**), is a well-established Lakeland pub where you can chat to locals over a pint, while the **Pooley Bridge Inn,** Pooley Bridge, Ullswater (www.pooley bridgeinn.co.uk; ℂ **01768/486215**), is a rustic country inn, restaurant, and bar where you can eat or drink beside an open fire in the winter months or head outdoors in the summer months. It has the added bonus of being by Ullswater lake. At the south end of the lake, hikers make a beeline for the **Ramblers Bar** (© **0800 840 245** for a well-earned pint of local ale after descending from Helvellyn.

Where to Eat & Stay

Brackenrigg Inn ★ ⚡ Since the prices at Sharrow Bay (see below) are a bit stunning, many discerning travelers instead book into this traditional inn and **restaurant** overlooking Ullswater. Accommodations range from smaller, standard doubles to more spacious superior rooms and premium ground-floor suites. There's also a convivial bar with an open fire. Chefs specialize in the market-fresh food of Cumbria, "but without all the fuss."

Watermillock (on the A592), Cumbria CA11 0JN. www.brackenrigginn.co.uk. © **01768/486206.** Fax 01768/486945. 17 units. £70–£140. Discount for children 3–16 staying in parent's room. Rates include breakfast. MC, V. Free parking. **Amenities:** Restaurant; bar. *In room:* TV.

Crookey Cottage ★ Set on the "sunny side" of Patterdale, Crookey Cottage is a former farmhouse that's perfectly located for walkers or those who want the quintessential Lake District experience and a quiet place to get away from it all. Its two cozy guest rooms come with oak furnishings and soft, wool carpets, while breakfast includes homemade bread and eggs fresh from the owner's own chickens.

1 Crookabeck, Patterdale, Penrith, Cumbria CA11 0QT. www.crookeycottage.com. © **01768/482278.** 2 units. £80 double. Rate includes English breakfast. Cash only. Free parking. *In room:* TV/DVD, Wi-Fi (free).

George Hotel A 300-year-old coaching inn built in the heart of town, this hotel welcomed Bonnie Prince Charlie in 1745. The front looks out onto Penrith's main street, full of small specialty shops. The guest rooms, spread over three floors, are individually decorated with light colors and up-to-date furnishings. The owners have upgraded all the bedrooms. The **Devonshire Restaurant** is a relaxed place to dine with a varied menu of fish, meat, and vegetarian options.

Devonshire St., Penrith, Cumbria CA11 7SU. www.lakedistricthotels.net/georgehotel. © **01768/862696.** Fax 01768/868223. 34 units. £86–£206 double; £160–£248 suite. Rates include Cumbrian breakfast. 2-night minimum stay Sat–Sun. MC, V. Free parking. Restaurant daily noon–2:30pm and 6–9pm. Reservations recommended. **Amenities:** Restaurant; bar; free use of nearby gym and indoor pool; room service. *In room:* TV, hair dryer.

YORKSHIRE & THE NORTHEAST

17

by Rhonda Carrier

Roman relics, cathedrals, abbeys, castles, stately homes, museums, and literary shrines are just some of the attractions on offer in Yorkshire and the more northern regions of County Durham, Newcastle, and Gateshead (in the county of Tyne and Wear), and Northumberland. Leeds and Newcastle have embraced their industrial heritage while simultaneously transforming into cutting-edge modern cities. Together with richly historic York, they are also jumping-off points for those wanting to explore the wild and remote beauty that characterizes both the interior of the northeast of England and its incredible shoreline.

CITIES A thoroughly modern British city reawakening from a long slumber, **Newcastle** is as hip and happening a destination as you'll find anywhere in the U.K. It has a reputation for its shopping and nightlife but also a whole array of cutting-edge museums such as the Centre for Life and the Seven Stories children's literature museum, galleries, and other sights.

COUNTRYSIDE The **Yorkshire Dales** is justly revered by walkers. **Malhamdale**—praised by Wordsworth and painted by Turner—is a high-point, especially its circular trail taking in Malham Cove, Malham Tarn (the lake—Britain's highest—that inspired Charles Kingsley's *The Water Babies*), and Gordale Scar. Or head for the **Aysgarth Falls,** where several waterfalls tumble in a scenic series.

EATING & DRINKING Foodies will find gastronomic contentment all over the Northeast, where many excellent restaurants and pubs use **local produce** to stunning effect. But don't miss the chance to try some of Britain's best Asian food, most notably in west Yorkshire, where Bradford and Leeds both offer **Indian restaurants** worth the trip in their own right.

COAST The double whammy of Northumberland's **Alnwick Castle,** which doubled as "Hogwarts" in two Harry Potter movies and hosts lots of medieval-themed events, and **The Alnwick Garden,** one of the world's most exciting contemporary (but also family-friendly) gardens, makes the town of Alnwick much more than just a base for those exploring the Northumberland coast a few minutes' drive away.

THE best TRAVEL EXPERIENCES IN YORKSHIRE & THE NORTHEAST

o **Re-living horrible history:** One of the finest U.K. city-break destinations, York offers up many fascinating layers of a long history: Roman, Saxon, Danish, Norman, medieval, Georgian, and Victorian. The Jorvik Viking Centre takes visitors back to A.D. 975, while the mighty Minster melds architectural elements from different centuries as well as concealing Roman remnants in its Undercroft. See p. 646.

o **Going all "Twilight" in Whitby:** Watched over by the ruins of its abbey, inspiration for Bram Stoker, the former whaling and smuggling port of Whitby is an atmospheric base for exploring a coastline along which wild, windswept bays rub shoulders with traditional family resorts. See p. 652.

o **Pondering time at The Living Museum of the North:** The medieval cathedral city of Durham, a UNESCO World Heritage site with more than 600 listed buildings, is a delight to wander around as well as being ideally placed for exploring the glorious North Pennines and learning about local life at the re-created 19th-century pit village of Beamish. See p. 660.

o **Walking Hadrian's Wall:** The most dramatic sections of one of the world's most famous Roman structures can be viewed by following parts of the Hadrian's Wall Path, while dramatic relics along the length of the wall include the Housesteads Roman Fort and Roman Vindolanda. See p. 672.

o **Being King of the Castle:** A contender for the title of Britain's most stupendous castle, Bamburgh Castle lords it over a wave-battered coastline rich in wildlife and dramatic history. See p. 674.

WEST YORKSHIRE

Leeds: 194 miles N of London; 218 miles S of Edinburgh

Long dismissed for its industrial blight, **Leeds,** Yorkshire's largest city, has moved forward dramatically over the past two decades, with many of its great Georgian and Victorian buildings renovated and complemented by attractive new architecture, and a growing reputation for shopping and nightlife. The large student population, multicultural communities, and gay-friendly vibe keep things fresh and continually evolving. In nearby **Bradford,** high-tech firms, art galleries, museums, and mill shops have displaced many of the textile factories that drew immigrants to work the mills from the mid-19th century, yet it's precisely these generations of Irish, German, Italian, eastern European, Asian, and African-Caribbean immigrants who give the city its distinctive flavor today. West of Bradford lies the literary pilgrimage site of Haworth, once home to the Brontë family, and lesser-known Heptonstall and Hardcastle Crags, the one-time home to poets Ted Hughes and Sylvia Plath.

South of Leeds, meanwhile, the small city of **Wakefield** has become somewhat of an art hotspot since the opening, in 2011, of the Hepworth Art Gallery, joining the nearby Yorkshire Sculpture Park (p. 640).

Essentials

GETTING THERE Frequent **trains** from London's King's Cross to Leeds take about 2½ hours; most are direct (costing around £95 for a round-trip off-peak). You usually need to change at Leeds to reach Bradford—the onward journey takes about 20 minutes. Leeds is just 25 minutes from York (p. 646) by direct rail link; there are also direct trains to Leeds from Manchester (p. 566), taking a little under an hour, and from Birmingham (p. 466), taking about 2 hours.

National Express buses (www.nationalexpress.com; ℂ **0871/781-8181**) from London to Leeds take about 4¼ hours.

Leeds is easily accessible by road from the rest of the country as it's at the crossroads of the north–south M1 and the east–west M62. Leeds to Haworth by road is about 25 miles (45 min.), though Haworth is most idyllically accessed via the scenic **Keighley & Worth Valley Railway** (www.kwvr.co.uk), which runs steam and heritage diesel trains on weekends and some weekdays. The starting point, Keighley, is 25 minutes from Leeds by standard rail. There are also buses from Keighley to Haworth (www.keighleybus.co.uk).

Wakefield is 11 miles south of Leeds, with a train station.

VISITOR INFORMATION Leeds Visitor Centre, The Arcade, Leeds City Train Station (www.visitleeds.co.uk; ℂ **0113/242-5242**), is open Monday 10am to 5:30pm, Tuesday to Saturday 9am to 5:30pm, and Sunday 10am to 4pm.

Bradford Visitor Information Centre, City Hall (www.visitbradford.com; ℂ **01274/433678**), is open Monday 10am to 5pm, and Tuesday to Saturday 9:30am to 5pm.

Haworth Visitor Information Centre, 2–4 West Lane (www.visitbradford.com/bronte-country; ℂ **01535/642329**), is open daily 10am–5pm.

Hebden Bridge Visitor and Canal Centre, Butlers Wharf, New Road (www.hebdenbridge.co.uk; ℂ **01422/843831**), is open in summer Monday to Friday 9:30am to 5:30pm, Saturday 10:15am to 5pm, and Sunday 10:30am to 5pm; in winter Monday to Friday 10am–5pm, Saturday and Sunday 10:30am–4:15pm.

SPECIAL EVENTS Leeds is a great place for big music events, with **Opera in the Park** followed by the poppy **Party in the Park** in the grounds of Temple Newsam each July (www.leeds.gov.uk), then the rock-heavy **Leeds Festival** in Bramham Park in August. The **Leeds International Concert Season** (www.leedsconcertseason.com) comprises 200-plus concerts in and around the city year-round, some by national and international orchestras in the stunning Victorian Town Hall on Saturday nights.

Film buffs flock to Bradford in March or April, when the National Media Museum (p. 639) hosts the annual **Bradford Film Festival,** attracting, to date, such big-screen luminaries as Lord Attenborough, Anthony Minghella, and Alan Parker.

Exploring the Area

LEEDS ★

The Romans set up a small camp called Cambodunum on this spot nearly 2,000 years ago, but the next step toward modern Leeds didn't come until the 7th century, when Northumbrian King Edwin established a residence here. In 1152, **Kirkstall Abbey** (www.leeds.gov.uk/kirkstallabbey; ℂ **0113/2305492**)—now one of the best preserved Cistercian monasteries in the country—was formed, and in 1207 Leeds finally obtained its charter. Industrial advances played a great role in the city's growth, strengthening its position as the focus of the cloth trade in the region, and allowing for the development of the coalfields to the south with the introduction of steam power along with such upstart industries as printing, tailoring, and engineering. The

Yorkshire & Northeast

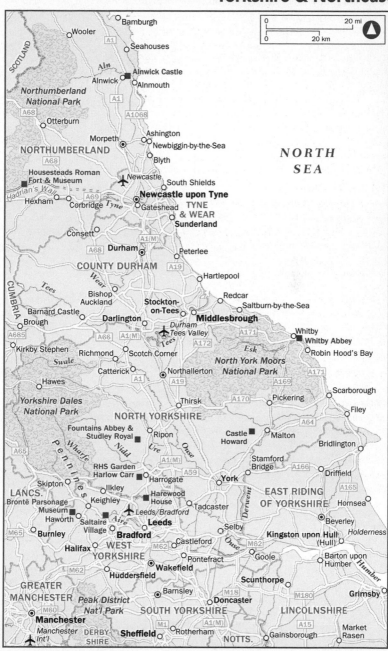

0   20 mi
0   20 km

SCOTLAND

Bamburgh
Wooler
Seahouses
Aln
Alnwick Castle
Alnwick
Alnmouth
Northumberland
National Park
A1
A68
A1068
Otterburn
Morpeth
Ashington
Newbiggin-by-the-Sea
NORTHUMBERLAND
A68
Blyth
Housesteads Roman
Fort & Museum
Newcastle
South Shields
Hadrian's Wall
A69
Newcastle upon Tyne
Hexham
Corbridge *Tyne*
Gateshead
TYNE
& WEAR
Sunderland
Consett
A1(M)
Durham
Peterlee
A68
COUNTY DURHAM
A19
Hartlepool
CUMBRIA
Wear
Tees
Bishop
Auckland
Redcar
Barnard Castle
Stockton-
on-Tees
Saltburn-by-the-Sea
Brough
Darlington
Middlesbrough
A685
A66
A1(M)
Durham
Tees Valley
A171
Whitby
Kirkby Stephen
A172
Whitby Abbey
Richmond
Scotch Corner
Tees
Esk
Robin Hood's Bay
Swale
Catterick
Northallerton
North York Moors
National Park
A169
Hawes
A1
A19
A171
Scarborough
Yorkshire Dales
National Park
Thirsk
A170
Pickering
Filey
NORTH YORKSHIRE
A64
Fountains Abbey &
Studley Royal
Ripon
Castle
Howard
Malton
Bridlington
A65
Pennines
Wharfe
Nidd
Ure
Ouse
A1(M)
Stamford
Bridge
A166
Driffield
RHS Garden
Harlow Carr
Harrogate
A59
York
A165
Skipton
Ilkley
EAST RIDING
OF YORKSHIRE
Hornsea
LANCS.
Keighley
Harewood
House
Tadcaster
Derwent
Brontë Parsonage
Museum
Leeds/Bradford
Beverley
Haworth
Saltaire
Village
Aire
Leeds
Selby
Holderness
M65
Burnley
Bradford
Kingston upon Hull
(Hull)
Halifax
WEST
YORKSHIRE
M62
Castleford
Ouse
M62
Barton upon
Humber
Goole
Humber
M62
Huddersfield
Pontefract
Scunthorpe
Grimsby
GREATER
MANCHESTER
Peak District
Nat'l Park
Wakefield
Barnsley
M18
M180
LINCOLNSHIRE
M60
Doncaster
SOUTH YORKSHIRE
Manchester
M1
A1(M)
A15
Market
Rasen
Manchester
Int'l
DERBY-
SHIRE
Sheffield
Rotherham
Gainsborough
NOTTS.

NORTH
SEA

635

Victorian era saw the glory days of Leeds, which has a surprisingly compact and walkable center with plenty of attractions, many of them free.

Harewood House ★★★ ☺ HISTORIC SITE Resplendent amid stunning Capability Brown gardens with terraces and lakeside and woodland walks, and with a famous Bird Garden with native and exotic species, this 18th-century residence, home to the 7th Earl and Countess of Harewood, boasts a fine Adam interior with superb ceilings and plasterwork, furniture by Thomas Chippendale, and works by Turner and other major British artists. A dressing-up box gets children interested; also on-site is an adventure playground, activity trails, a candy shop, and a fish and chip shop.

Harewood, 8½ miles north of Leeds on the road to Harrogate. www.harewood.org. ℂ **0113/218-1010.** Admission varies by season and what you visit; standard high-season Freedom ticket giving access to everything £15.40 adults, £44 for a family of up to 5. Garden, grounds, and playground Apr–Oct daily 10am–6pm; see website for house, Bird Garden, and so on, and also for winter opening times.

Henry Moore Institute ★ This is one of the largest sculpture galleries in Europe and is named after the greatest British sculptor of the 20th century, who was born in nearby Castleford and studied in Leeds. It hosts changing exhibitions on historical and contemporary sculpture.

74 The Headrow. www.henry-moore.org/hmi. ℂ **0113/246-7467.** Free admission. Thurs–Tues exc public holidays 10am–5:30pm; Wed 10am–9pm.

Leeds Art Gallery ★ Linked to the Henry Moore Institute via a walkway, this venue has one of the best 20th-century British sculpture and painting collections outside London, including more Moore, plus some Hepworth, Calder, and Bacon. Contemporary British art, including Anthony Gormley and Bridget Riley, is also a strong point.

The Headrow. www.leeds.gov.uk/artgallery. ℂ **0113/247-8256.** Free admission. Mon, Tues and Thurs–Sat 10am–5pm; Wed noon–5pm; Sun 1–5pm.

Leeds City Museum ★★ Open since 2008 and boasting four floors of interactive galleries, this venue is strongest in its displays on the city itself: The Leeds Story, showing how it has been shaped by its landscape, people, fashion, housing, music, sport, and even shopping; and the Leeds Arena, with a giant map of the city you can walk on to discover its places of interest and different communities. There are also galleries on Ancient Worlds, Life on Earth, and the spread of African cultures across the globe.

Millennium Sq. www.leeds.gov.uk/citymuseum. ℂ **0113/224-3732.** Free admission. Tues, Wed, and Fri 10am–5pm; Thurs 10am–7pm; Sat, Sun, and public holidays 11am–5pm.

Royal Armouries Museum ★★★ ☺ MUSEUM The U.K.'s national museum of arms, armor, and artillery counts among its dastardly delights some of Henry VIII's armor, various experimental pistols, and weaponry from some of the world's biggest conflicts. It's best to time your visit to catch some of the thrilling combat displays; at weekends and in school holidays there's also a themed play area for those 10 and under and a (well-supervised) crossbow range.

Armouries Dr. www.royalarmouries.org. ℂ **0113/220-1999.** Free admission (charges for some elements). Daily 10am–5pm.

Temple Newsam ★ ☺ HISTORIC SITE Birthplace, in 1545, of the ill-fated Lord Darnley, husband of Mary, Queen of Scots, this grand residence was begun in

Leeds

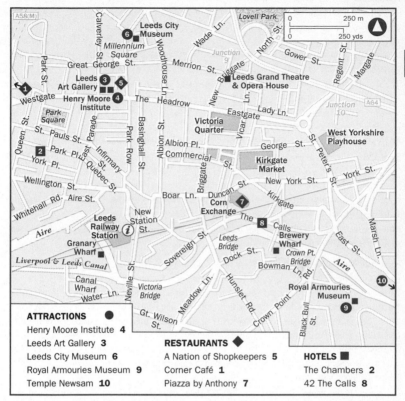

ATTRACTIONS ●

Henry Moore Institute **4**
Leeds Art Gallery **3**
Leeds City Museum **6**
Royal Armouries Museum **9**
Temple Newsam **10**

RESTAURANTS ◆

A Nation of Shopkeepers **5**
Corner Café **1**
Piazza by Anthony **7**

HOTELS ■

The Chambers **2**
42 The Calls **8**

1521 but largely remodeled in the 17th and 18th centuries. Nestled in vast woodland, farmland, and Capability Brown-designed parkland, it's another good spot for a family day out, with priceless works of art and period furniture within, plus Europe's largest working rare breeds farm, a tearoom, and an ice-cream shop on sunny days.

Off Selby Rd., Leeds. www.leeds.gov.uk/templenewsam. ✆ **0113/264-5535.** Admission house and farm £6, £3.70 children 5–16. House Tues–Sun and public holidays 10:30am–5:30pm (to 4pm in winter); farm opens 30 min. earlier.

Thackray Museum ★ ☺   The history of medicine from a child-friendly perspective is told at this interactive museum, where the galleries include Having a Baby, complete with an "empathy belly" to try on, and Plastic Fantastic, allowing you to discover for yourself the best materials for making a wrist splint or hip joint.

Beckett St., 2 miles northeast of center, by St. James's Hospital (with direct buses). www.thackray museum.org. ✆ **0113/244-4343.** Admission adults £7, £5 children 5–16. Daily 10am–5pm.

BRADFORD, BRONTË COUNTRY & AROUND ★

Demonized by Bill Bryson in his *Notes from a Small Island* ("Nowhere on my trip around Britain would I see a more depressing city"), Bradford, a Saxon settlement that grew into the world's wool capital, can be bleak but merits a day's attention if you're in the area. Aside from its great multiethnic eating scene (see below)—Bryson

17

YORKSHIRE & THE NORTHEAST | West Yorkshire

637

concedes that the city has "a thousand excellent Indian restaurants"—Bradford's industrial heritage is the big draw.

Just west of Halifax, **Hebden Bridge** has numerous claims to fame: It has the highest number of lesbians per head in the U.K., was awarded Fair Trade Zone status in 2003, and was named the world's fourth quirkiest place to live by the British Airways magazine in 2005, having built up a population of writers, musicians, artists, photographers, alternative practitioners, and green and New Age activists since the 1970s. American poet Sylvia Plath is buried in the adjoining hilltop village of **Heptonstall,** near the parents and uncle of her husband Ted Hughes, born in neighboring Mytholmroyd. Hughes's former house in Heptonstall is now a residential writing center (www.arvonfoundation.org). However, it's Haworth to the north, once home to the Brontë sisters, that constitutes this area's main literary pilgrimage site.

Bradford Industrial Museum ★ MUSEUM Set in a former spinning mill outside the city center at Eccleshill, this venue depicts how mill life was for local workers and owners in the 1870s, through permanent displays and regular demonstrations, including letterpress demonstrations on Wednesdays. Three terraced mill-workers' cottages have been dressed to reflect three different eras.

Moorside Mills, Moorside Rd. (9 miles west of Bradford), Eccleshill. www.bradfordmuseums.org. ☏ **01274/435900.** Free admission. Tues–Fri 10am–4pm; Sat–Sun 11am–4pm.

Brontë Parsonage Museum ★★ MUSEUM This stone-sided parsonage near the top of the village of Haworth west of Bradford contains the Brontë family's furniture, personal treasures, correspondence, pictures, books, and manuscripts, bearing testament to their residence here from 1820 to 1861—during which time Charlotte wrote *Jane Eyre,* Emily wrote *Wuthering Heights,* and Anne wrote *The Tenant of Wildfell Hall.* The Brontës' father, Patrick, was perpetual curator of the Church of St. Michael, where Charlotte and Emily are now buried in the family vault. *Insider tip:* Avoid visiting in July and August, when the museum gets very crowded. For steam trains to Haworth station, see p. 634.

Church St., Haworth. www.bronte.org.uk. ☏ **01535/642323.** Admission adults £7, £3.60 children 5–15. Apr–Sept daily 10am–5:30pm; Dec, Feb–Mar 11am–5pm.

Cartwright Hall ★ Since 2008 Bradford's civic art venue has devoted its upper galleries to Connect, a permanent exhibition examining the connections between works of art from different cultures and times, across a variety of "universal themes." After touring the displays, enjoy surrounding Lister Park with its Mughal Gardens, boating lake, and adventure playground.

Lister Park. www.bradfordmuseums.org. ☏ **01274/431212.** Free admission. Tues–Fri 10am–4pm; Sat–Sun and public holidays 11am–4pm.

Eureka! The National Children's Museum ★ Paradise for youngsters, this educational charity 8½ miles southwest of Bradford—which celebrated its 20th birthday in 2012—has six interactive galleries, including one for under-5s inspired by the Mojave Desert, complete with soft rocks and boulders to explore. Avoid school holidays, when it gets unpleasantly busy.

Discovery Rd., Halifax. www.eureka.org.uk. ☏ **01422/330069.** Admission adults £9.95, £3.45 children aged 1–2). Tues–Fri 10am–4pm; Sat–Sun10am–5pm (daily 10am–5pm in school holidays).

Hardcastle Crags ★★★ Sylvia Plath's collection *The Colossus* includes a poem about this beautiful valley north of Hebden Bridge, which she describes as "absolute as the ancient world." Miles of woodland walks take you past streams and waterfalls; pick up trail maps in the unique sustainable visitor center in an old cotton mill, where you can also see displays on local social and industrial history.

1½ miles northeast of Hebden Bridge, off the A6033. www.nationaltrust.org.uk. © **01422/844518.** Free admission to valley; mill adults £3.80, children 5–15 £3.80. Countryside accessible daily dawn–dusk; for Gibson Mill visitor center and cafe, see website.

National Media Museum ☺ This venue in the center of Bradford captures the history of photography, film, TV, and the Internet over eight floors of interactive and traditional galleries and through activities for adults and children, including animation workshops, sleepovers, and IMAX screenings.

Pictureville, off Little Horton Lane, Bradford. www.nationalmediamuseum.org.uk. © **0844/856-3797.** Free admission (charges for IMAX cinema and for most activities). Tues–Sun 10am to 6pm, plus Mon school and public holidays.

Peace Museum ★ The U.K.'s only museum devoted to the themes of peace, non-violence, and conflict resolution offers up a unique collection of memorabilia, film, photos, oral history, posters, banners, badges, leaflets, and booklets, plus a program of temporary exhibitions on topics such as the role of sport in bringing together international communities. Note that there are 60 stairs up to the museum and no elevator.

10 Piece Hall Yard. www.peacemuseum.org.uk. © **01274/434009.** Free admission. Thurs–Fri 10am–4pm; 2nd Sat of month 10am–3pm.

Saltaire Village ★★ HISTORIC SITE Reprising the themes of the Bradford Industrial Museum, this UNESCO World Heritage site comprises a restored model factory-community that was developed in the mid-19th century by mill owner and philanthropist Sir Titus Salt. It remains a working village; besides simply strolling around to look at the well-preserved Victorian Italianate architecture, you can visit **Salts Mill** (www.saltsmill.org.uk), which has a local history exhibition and various galleries (one showcasing works by Bradford-born and educated painter and printmaker David Hockney), eateries, and shops. The new visitor center is the starting point for Salts Walks on weekends and public holidays, led by costumed guides.

About 4 miles northwest of Bradford (Salts Mill parking lot is on Victoria St.). www.saltairevillage. info. © **01274/531163.** Free admission. Village open 24 hr.; Salts Mill Mon–Fri 10am–5:30pm, Sat–Sun 10am–6pm; David Hockney exhibition closed Mon–Tues.

WAKEFIELD ★★

Newly on the map by virtue of the addition of a second major art venue, this small city on the edge of the Pennines saw a lot of action during the Wars of the Roses and the Civil War but grew from a market town by virtue of its role as an inland port on the River Calder. In addition to its cultural spaces, it offers up an extreme sports center with an indoor real-snow ski slope, a surf simulator, rock-climbing, a skate park, a cinema, and more (www.xscape.co.uk/yorkshire).

The Hepworth Wakefield ★★ ☺ Beautifully set in a riverside building by modernist architect David Chipperfield, this new-in-2011 art venue is named for local sculptor Barbara Hepworth, to whom the central gallery space is dedicated; many of her works on display have rarely been accessible to the public in the past. Other galleries hold works by significant British artists of the 20th century, including internationally lauded sculptor Henry Moore, born near Wakefield, in Castleford and you can also view the Gott Collection of watercolors, drawings, prints, and letterpress pages devoted to Yorkshire villages, towns, and cities. Gallery trails, explorer backpacks, a packed program of activities and events, and even an outdoor play area with zipwires make the Hepworth a great to visit with children. The cafe-bar is strong on local produce, or you can picnic indoors or beside the river in fine weather.

Gallery Walk, Wakefield. www.hepworthwakefield.org. $\textcircled{C}$ **01924/247360.** Free admission. Tues–Sun 10am–5pm, plus Mon school and public holidays.

National Coal Mining Museum ★★★ ☺ An excellent day out for all the family, this museum offers free tours of one of Britain's oldest working mines, with each visitor provided with a hat, belt, and battery so they can get a feel of working life underground. These can get booked up by noon in summer holidays so you need to arrive early to bag a place. There's also the restored colliery complex Hope Pit, now a science center with interactive models, old mining machinery, some settling ponds where you can witness how water pumped out of the mine is filtered, the pithead baths, where the miners cleaned up after a shift, a restored medical center showing how miners' injuries were treated, an exhibition on miners' home lives, a woodland nature trail, and even some resident ponies to pet (while you learn about their role in coal-mining). Year-round events include changing exhibitions and an underground Santa's grotto, and there's a newly refurbished Mini-Miners play space for under-5s.

Caphouse Colliery, New Rd., Overton, 6 miles from Wakefield (bus no.128 or 232). www.ncm.org. uk. $\textcircled{C}$ **01924/848806.** Free admission. Daily 10am–5pm.

Yorkshire Sculpture Park ★★★ ☺ Another great art site for families, this largely outdoor gallery combines culture with a blast of fresh air within 400 acres of rolling Yorkshire countryside just outside Wakefield. Among the artists you can see represented across the historic estate with its 60 artworks are locally born sculptors Barbara Hepworth and Henry Moore, plus Elizabeth Frink, Antony Gormley, Isamo Noguchi, Sol Lewitt, Eduardo Paolozzi, Sir Anthony Caro, and Andy Goldsworthy. Children are free to touch the artworks, and the grounds are an adventure in themselves, with lakes, woodland, bridges, follies, and historical features including a Greek-style summerhouse, a land-locked boathouse, an obelisk, stepping stones, and a shell grotto. There are also five indoor galleries, plus a restaurant with glorious views and a cafe.

West Bretton, 7 miles outside Wakefield (served by bus no. 96). www.ysp.co.uk. $\textcircled{C}$ **01924/832631.** Free admission (parking £5). Daily 10am–6pm (5pm in winter).

Where to Eat
EXPENSIVE/VERY EXPENSIVE

The **Fourth Floor Café** at Leeds department store Harvey Nichols (p. 642) makes good use of local meat, game, and vegetables in its very good modern British cooking; or try the **Brasserie** in Malmaison hotel (p. 670) for similar fare. For **Weaver's** in Haworth, see p. 644.

Piazza by Anthony ★★ INTERNATIONAL Set within Leeds' old Corn Exchange building with its stunning domed ceiling (especially impressive when lit by twinkling lights at night), this all-day restaurant, informal lunch cantina, champagne bar, bakery, patisserie, chocolaterie, and cheese and artisan-food shop is named for chef Tony Flinn, who once worked at Spain's legendary El Bulli and whose Heston Blumenthal style experimental "molecular gastronomy" is available at his more expensive **Anthony's** (19 Boar Lane, $\textcircled{C}$ **0113/245-5922**). The restaurant at Piazza serves meals from brunch through to dinner, including afternoon tea; the menu is accordingly wide-ranging, with everything from tapas plates and pasta and risotto dishes to steaks. Highlights include cod loin with pig's trotter croquette, beurre noir leeks, and peas; and chorizo and chicken gnocchi with thyme cream and fresh shoots. The same chef has a second patisserie, serving lunches, at Queen Victoria Street in the Victoria Quarter (✆ **0113/244-4222**).

Corn Exchange, Corn Lane. www.anthonysrestaurant.co.uk/piazza. ✆ **0113/247-0995.** Main courses £8.50–£44. AE, DC, MC, V. Mon–Thurs 10am–10pm; Fri–Sat 10am–10:30pm; Sun 10am–9pm.

MODERATE

Leeds has branches of **Sam's Chop House** (p. 572) and **Red Chilli** (p. 573). The latter is in the Electric Press building (www.electricpressuk.com) along with various other bars and eateries.

Corner Café ★★ INDIAN It's worth the 15-minute walk from the center of Leeds to sample the curries at this former transport cafe that began doing Indian food as a sideline and now attracts hordes of loyal locals with its fresh-tasting, generously proportioned curries, including excellent vegetarian options and weekend specials. Standouts are the fish pakora (weekends only), king-prawn shimla, eggplant and mushroom korma, but leave room for the homemade kulfis in weird but wonderful flavors including marmalade. There's also a selection of ales from local microbreweries.

104 Burley Rd., Leeds. www.wix.com/kateghaurimoore/cornercafe. ✆ **0113/234-6677.** Reservations recommended. Main courses £6.95–£9.95. DC, MC, V. Tues–Sat 6–10:30pm.

Fleece Inn & Restaurant ★★ TRADITIONAL BRITISH This super-cozy pub and B&B on the cobbled main street of Haworth counts Branwell Brontë—brother to the famous writers—among its former patrons. You can still rely on it for a true Yorkshire welcome in the company of locals supping award-winning regional cask ales in the stone-flagged bar with its open fire. The relaxed restaurant area is the place to enjoy way-above-average pub food such as thyme and garlic pork belly, crispy crackling, leek mash, sugarsnap peas, and carrots; and splendidly calorific desserts. On weekday lunchtimes you can also get sandwiches, soup, ploughman's lunches, corned beef hash, and jacket potatoes. The rooftop beer garden with its scenic views is popular in the warmer months. The seven **bedrooms** (£70–£105 B&B), all en suite, are clean and handsomely furnished with local pine furniture.

7 Main St., Haworth. www.fleece-inn.co.uk. ✆ **01535/642172.** Reservations recommended. Main courses £7.95–£16.50. MC, V. Mon–Fri noon–3pm and 5–9pm; Sat 10am–8pm; Sun 10–6pm.

Prashad ★★ INDIAN Winner of second place in the TV show *Ramsay's Best Restaurant 2010*, starring celeb chef Gordon Ramsay, this vegetarian restaurant in the heart of Bradford's Asian community outplays a crowded market for Indian restaurant in the "curry capital of the North." Those familiar with south Indian cuisine will be delighted by familiar favorites such as *uttapam* (rice-flour pancakes), *idli sambar* (rice-flour dumplings), and *massala dosa* (rice-flour crepes), all served with spicy lentil soup and coconut and yogurt chutney. But the less familiar offerings won't disappoint: the *pethis* (spice-infused coconut balls fried in a fluffy potato casing) are award-winning, while the Gujarati eggplant and potato curry raises two humble vegetables to a new level. The chili-free "Junior Curry Lover's Meal" (£4.50) contains fritters, *chole* (a chickpea dish), a baby puri, and rice. Note that Prashad is an alcohol-free restaurant.

86 Horton Grange Rd., Bradford. www.prashad.co.uk. © **01274/575893.** Reservations recommended. Main courses £7.95–8.95. MC, V. Tues–Fri 11am–3pm and 6–10:30pm; Sat–Sun 11am–10:30pm.

INEXPENSIVE

A Nation of Shopkeepers ★ INTERNATIONAL   This bohemian bar/restaurant in central Leeds offers good-value eats served by rather distracted hipster staff amid thrift-store decor and twinkling fairylights. A wide range of tastes/moods are catered for on the menu with its traditional and veggie breakfast fry-ups, snacky sharing platters featuring the likes of deep-fried halloumi and vegetable fritters, globally inspired sandwiches and salads, and comfort-food classics including macaroni and cheese; local pies with mash, peas, and gravy; beer-battered fish and chips; and handmade "Boutique Burgers." Sundays see roasts, a quiz with prizes, and a DJ set from 4pm, while other events include live music and visuals by guest local artists. A courtyard with heaters lets you sit outside in most weather.

27–37 Cookridge St., Leeds. www.anationofshopkeepers.com. © **0113/203-1831.** Main courses £3.75–£9.95. MC, V. Sun–Thurs noon–10pm; Fri–Sat noon–9pm.

Shopping

Leeds is shopping central—many people head here to do nothing but that. On the central shopping street of **Briggate** you'll find several department and high-end fashion stores, including the first **Harvey Nichols** branch outside London (www.harveynichols.com; © **0113/204-8888**), and **Louis Vuitton** (www.louisvuitton.com; © **0113/386-3120**), plus high-street stalwarts such as **Zara** and **Topshop.** Fanning out from the top end of Briggate are the famous Victorian glass-roofed **arcades,** housing some of the city's most exclusive and quirky stores. For a full-on bohemian experience, head to **Exchange Quarter** with its cobbled streets lined with independent boutiques, trendy cafes, and piercing parlors. The Kirkgate end of **Call Lane,** a center for stylish nightlife, is fertile ground for vintage and alternative clothes. And on Vicar Lane, don't miss **Kirkgate Market** (www.leeds.gov.uk; © **0113/214-5162**), a vast traditional market held outdoors and within an imposing Edwardian building with ornamental dragons. Daily except Sunday, it includes secondhand clothing on Mondays and a fleamarket on Thursdays. It's on this spot that Michael Marks opened his "penny bazaar" that eventually became the mighty Marks & Spencer empire.

In and around Bradford, look out for **mill shops** selling clothes made from mohair, pure wool, and other local textiles, furniture, and crafts. At Batley southeast of Bradford, **Redbrick Mill** (www.redbrickmill.co.uk) is home to more than 40 cutting-edge interior retailers and houses the sole northern outpost of **Heal's** (www.heals.co.uk; © **01924/464918**), selling furniture and homewares by Philippe Starck, Tom Dixon, and other design luminaries.

Offbeat Hebden Bridge is the place for arts-and-crafts galleries, secondhand bookstores, organic fair-trade delis, and the like. **Innovation** (© **01422/844160**) offers interesting crafts and decorative items, plus a cafe-bar, in a 17th-century mill. The town's **farmers' market,** Lees Yard (© **01422/359034**), on the first and third Sunday of the month, is great for local food and crafts.

Entertainment & Nightlife

Leeds is well known for its music and clubbing scenes, whether you like rock, pop, dance, classical, opera, or jazz. The **Leeds Grand Theatre & Opera House** at 46

New Briggate (www.leedsgrandtheatre.com; ℂ **0844/848-2700**) is an atmospheric venue with an 1878 Victorian facade; it hosts musicals and other shows in addition to performances by the highly regarded Opera North. At the other end of the spectrum, The Cockpit (www.thecockpit.co.uk; ℂ **0113/244-1573**) on Swinegate is an indie institution with one of the best alternative rock nights in the U.K., although it also mixes up metal, punk, emo, pop, and beats.

There's also a vast and endlessly evolving choice of bars and pubs all over the city, from high-concept to bohemian and more traditional, many of them tucked away in old railway arches. Call Lane in the Exchange Quarter is a good place to dip your toe in the water. Gay nightlife finds its focus at Lower Briggate.

Dance, theatre, and film lovers are also well catered for in Leeds. The **West Yorkshire Playhouse,** Quarry Hill (www.wyp.org.uk; ℂ **0113/213-7700**), dubbed "the national theatre of the north," has a wide repertoire, from Shakespeare to comedy and family shows. For up-to-date nightlife and cultural event listings in Leeds, see the monthly *Leeds Guide* (£2; www.leedsguide.co.uk).

Where to Stay

There are three **Roomzzz** apart-hotels (p. 575) in Leeds, one close to the train station.

For the **Fleece Inn** in Haworth, see p. 641.

The Chambers ★★ ☺ An excellent alternative to hotels, whether you're traveling with a family, as a couple, or alone, on business or for pleasure, these plush new serviced apartments have gone down a storm with visitors to Leeds, who appreciate the flexibility they give them, as well as thoughtful touches such as a cosy lounge with an honesty bar and coffee machine and a fridge with free provisions including fresh eggs, plus a Welcome Pack of basics in your apartment on arrival. Some rooms offer wonderful views of the Leeds cityscape, and two of the four penthouses have rooftop Jacuzzis. Rooms range from Studio Apartments to 2-bedroom Penthouses, all with kitchens with dishwasher and washing machine/drier. Some have a balcony or terrace. There's a second Chambers at Riverside West on the banks of the Aire, also central.

30 Park Place, Leeds, West Yorkshire LS1 2SP. www.morethanjustbed.com. ℂ **0113/386-3300.** 58 units. £119 studio apartment; £144–£168 1-bedroom apartment; £240–£420 2-bedroom apartment/penthouse. Parking free for 2-bed apartments, £12 per night for 1-bedroom apartments (subject to availability). AE, MC, DC, V. **Amenities:** Lounge with honesty bar, library, and DVD library; exercise room; courtyard; Wi-Fi (free). *In room:* TVs/DVD players, full kitchen, hair dryer, hot tubs (some), Wi-Fi (free).

42 The Calls ★★ On a cobbled canalside street in the heart of Leeds, this is a very good city-break hotel, with superb staff who greet guests with a complimentary glass of wine, an honesty bar, and fabulous beds. Some of the best breakfasts in the northeast (£15 English, £12 continental) are served here, featuring local produce including a choice of 12 kinds of sausage, Whitby kippers, and toasted crumpets with Yorkshire ham, poached eggs, and mozzarella. The hotel occupies an 18th-century cornmill, so each room is unique: Exposed beams, brickwork, iron girders, and even former mill mechanisms all feature prominently. Some rooms have canal views. The first British "boutique" hotel to open outside London, 42 The Calls has started to show signs of wear and tear, but brand-new ownership was promising a full refurb as this guide went to press.

42 The Calls, Leeds, West Yorkshire LS2 7EW. www.42thecalls.co.uk. © **0113/244-0099.** 41 units. £150–£225 double; £280–£400 suite. AE, DC, MC, V. Parking (nearby) £15. **Amenities:** Bar; concierge; room service (breakfast); babysitting. *In room:* TV, hair dryer, Wi-Fi (free).

Rambles B&B ★★★ ☺

The most alluring option in the Hebden Bridge area, this converted stone barn 20-minutes' walk from the town itself has large grounds traversed by the Pennine Way (p. 538), making it the perfect spot for walkers. With such stunning countryside views, rooms could be an afterthought, but the hostess has created comfy, chintz-free rooms with excellent beds and bedding, flat-screen TVs, and thick fluffy towels. Two of the doubles will take an extra single bed, or there's a new children's room for up to 4 youngsters, with a sensor so parents in the neighboring double (with which it shares a bathroom) will know if the door's been opening, plus a DVD and PlayStation. Scrumptious breakfasts include eggs from the hostess's own chickens and home-baked bread (for a £4 supplement you can get a cooked free-range breakfast, traditional or veggie). This place is a good option for those who don't have their own wheels—for a small fee you can get lifts to and from local transport hubs, restaurants, and so on.

Upper Blackshaw Royd, Blackshaw Head, Hebden Bridge, West Yorkshire HX7 7JU. www.rambles. me.uk. © **07921/500090.** 3 units. Double £55–£60. Rates include continental breakfast. No credit cards. Free parking. **Amenities:** Bicycle storage/washing; clothes- and boot-drying/warming facilities; honesty fridge/box; books, games, and DVDs. *In room:* TV/DVD, hair dryer, PlayStation (children's room), Wi-Fi (free).

Titanic Spa ★★

Set in a former textile mile on the edge of the Pennines, Britain's first eco-spa offers overnight breaks in its one- and two-bedroomed self-catering apartments, although breaks do include lunch on arrival day plus dinner in the bistro so you don't have to cook unless you want to. Spacious and quite luxurious, the apartments all have balconies from which to enjoy the lovely countryside views. Guests get full access to all the spa facilities, including the Heat and Ice Experience (which includes a new-in-2012 herbal-infusion room) and the salt-regulated swimming pool and hydrozone. Treatments include exclusive Decleor massages and facials, while classes including yoga, pilates, and tai chi are available at certain times.

Low Westwood Lane, Linthwaite, West Yorkshire HD7 5UN. www.titanicspa.com. © **0845/410-3333.** 30 units. Overnight breaks £109–£199pppn. Accommodations packages include continental breakfast. AE, MC, DC, V. **Amenities:** Restaurant; swimming pool; health club & spa; DVD library. *In room:* TV/DVD (most apartments), kitchen.

Weaver's ★★★

This "restaurant and bar with rooms" on a cobbled street in Haworth is well worth checking into for the night—not least because staying over allows you to extend your gastronomic pleasure by partaking of a breakfast that might include a Virgin Bloody Mary; kedgeree frittatas; Pennine oatcake with melting Wensleydale cheese, mushroom, and tomato; or bangers (sausages) and onions in a bread cake. The double, twin, and single rooms are eccentrically English in feel, with quirky wall-art; the doubles offer views of the Brontë Parsonage Museum (p. 638), village church, and moors. In the restaurant expect distinctive northern cooking featuring local ingredients: Perhaps spiced pear, with blue Wensleydale, salad leaves, and cracked cobnut dressing, followed by slow-cooked Pennine lamb, "shrugged" from the bone, with hot-pot potato, orange and redcurrant sauce, and a hint of mint.

15 West Lane, Haworth, West Yorkshire BD22 8DU. www.weaversmallhotel.co.uk. © **01535/643822.** 3 units. £90 twin; £110 double. AE, DC, MC, V. Rates include breakfast. **Amenities:** Restaurant. *In room:* TV, hair dryer.

NORTH YORKSHIRE

York: 212 miles N of London; 134 miles NE of Birmingham; 212 miles SE of Edinburgh

The landscape is the star of North Yorkshire, although history never takes a back seat—Romans, Anglo-Saxons, Vikings, medieval monks, kings, craftspeople, hill farmers, wool growers, and mill founders all left their mark. You can see this in bewitching York, in the beguiling former spa town of Harrogate and countryside north of it—rich in historical structures—and in the charming countryside of the Yorkshire Dales and Yorkshire Moors, both walkers' paradises studded with tranquil stone-built towns and villages. With such a stunning interior to explore, the North Yorkshire coast is often overlooked—unjustly.

Essentials

GETTING THERE   Frequent trains from London's King's Cross to York take just under 2 hours, costing around £95 for a round-trip, off-peak. There are also direct trains to York from Manchester, Birmingham, and Edinburgh. Harrogate is just over half an hour from both York and Leeds (p. 634) by direct train.

Daily London–York **National Express** buses (www.nationalexpress.com; ℂ 0871/781-8181) take 5 hours and up; most require a change at Leeds (p. 634). London to Harrogate buses don't normally require a change.

York is 3½ hours north of London by road, not far off the main M1. From Manchester to York it's about 1½ hours, from Birmingham 2 hours 20 minutes, and from Edinburgh 4 hours.

For **Leeds Bradford International Airport,** 31 miles west of York and 12 miles southwest of Harrogate (with buses to and from both), see p. 747. There are also direct trains to York from **Manchester International Airport** (p. 566).

By road, York to Harrogate is 22 miles (40 min.), York to Scarborough 40 miles (1 hr.). Cars are the most convenient option outside the cities, but **local buses** are better than in many areas of the U.K., especially in high season. For buses in the **Dales,** see www.dalesbus.org. The Moorsbus (www.northyorkmoors.org.uk/moorsbus) offers a similar network in the **North York Moors National Park;** there are buses into the park from York, Malton, Scarborough, Middlesbrough, Whitby, Northallerton, and Thirsk. The scenic **Esk Valley Railway** (www.eskvalleyrailway.co.uk) between Middlesbrough and Whitby also takes you into the heart of the park.

Scarborough and **Whitby** both have train stations. Scarborough is 3 to 3½ hours from London King's Cross with a change at York; Whitby is about 4¾ hours from London King's Cross with changes at both Darlington and Middlesbrough, so you're better off getting a bus from Scarborough. But the best way to arrive in Whitby is aboard the **North York Moors Railway** (www.nymr.co.uk) from Pickering, where you can relax in wood-paneled carriages pulled by historic steam engines across an otherworldly landscape.

VISITOR INFORMATION   For the many tourist information centers dotted around the Dales, see www.yorkshiredales.org.uk/touristinformationcentres.htm. For the Moors, see www.northyorkmoors.org.uk/tourist-information-centres-290.

York Visitor Information Centre, 1 Museum St. (www.visityork.org; ℂ **01904/550099**), is open daily 9am to 5:30pm.

Harrogate Tourist Information Office, Royal Baths, Crescent Road (www. harrogate.gov.uk; ℂ **0845/389-3223**), is open April to October Monday to Saturday

9am to 5:30pm, Sunday 10am to 1pm; and November to March Monday to Friday 9am to 5pm, Saturday 9am to 4pm.

Thirsk Tourist Information Centre, 49 Market Place (www.yorkshire.com; © **01845/522755**), is open Monday to Saturday 10am to 4pm (to 5pm in summer).

Scarborough Tourism Bureau, Town Hall, St. Nicholas Street (www.discover yorkshirecoast.com; © 01723/383637), is open daily 9am to 5pm.

The Moors National Park Centre, Lodge Lane, Danby, Whitby (www.north yorkmoors.org.uk; © **01439/772737**), is open March to July and September to October daily 10am to 5pm, August daily 9:30am to 5:30pm, mid-February to March daily 11am to 4pm, November and December Saturday and Sunday 10:30am to 4:30pm. Newly refurbished, this center now has an indoor climbing wall, outdoor play area, and tearoom.

Whitby Moors and Coast Centre, Langborne Road (www.yorkshire.com; © 01723/383636), is open daily 10am to 4:30pm.

SPECIAL EVENTS **The Ebor Festival,** held over 4 days in August, is the highlight of the flat-racing season at the prestigious **York Racecourse** (www.yorkrace course.co.uk). In February, York sees a 9-day **Viking Festival,** organized by Jorvik.

Harrogate's **Great Yorkshire Show** (www.greatyorkshireshow.co.uk), in early July, features cattle parades, sheep-shearing, pole-climbing, and more.

Exploring North Yorkshire

YORK ★★★

Still encircled by its 13th- and 14th-century walls, about 2½ miles long, with four gates, York is a many-layered and picturesque historical tapestry. There was a Roman York (Hadrian came this way), then a Saxon York, a Danish York, a Norman York (William the Conqueror slept here), a medieval York, a Georgian York, and a Victorian York, center of a flourishing rail empire. You can still walk the footpath of the medieval walls and explore much of the 18th-century city; the **Association of Voluntary Guides** (© **01904/550098;** information desk in Visitor Centre; p. 645) runs free guided tours from Exchange Square (10:15am daily, plus 2:15pm and 6:45pm in summer).

Jorvik Viking Centre ★ ☺ ENTERTAINMENT COMPLEX This attraction's "time capsule" ride takes visitors back to this spot as it would have looked in A.D. 97, warts and all: The pig sties, fishmarket, latrines, and other features, populated by animatronic figures, come complete with the requisite sounds and smells. An adjoining museum area has interactive displays, static exhibits, and costumed actors. Continual improvements keep this among York's best attractions, but queues can be long at weekends and in school holidays so pre-book tickets if you can. **Jorvik's** nearby sister attraction, **Dig!** (St. Saviourgate; © **01904/615505**), gives you the chance to plunder excavation pits for clues as to how people lived in Roman, medieval, and Victorian times, accompanied by an archeologist.

Coppergate, York. www.jorvik-viking-centre.co.uk. © **01904/615505.** Admission £9.25 adults, £6.25 children 5–15; joint tickets with Dig! £13.25 adults, £10 children 5–15. Tickets allow unlimited entry for an entire year. Apr–Nov daily 10am–5pm (to 4pm rest of year).

National Railway Museum ★★ ☺ MUSEUM The first national museum built outside London is an original steam-locomotive depot containing more than 100 locomotives, nearly 200 other items of rolling stock, and memorabilia galore that,

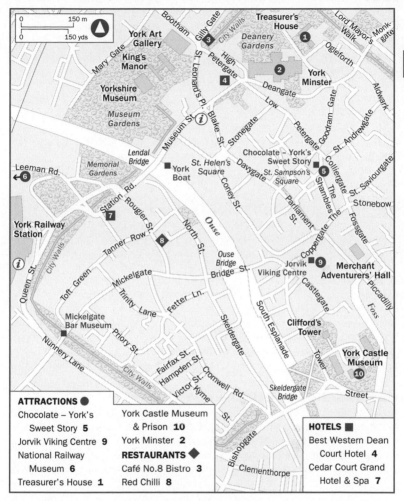

ATTRACTIONS ●

Chocolate – York's
Sweet Story **5**
Jorvik Viking Centre **9**
National Railway
Museum **6**
Treasurer's House **1**

York Castle Museum
& Prison **10**
York Minster **2**

RESTAURANTS ◆

Café No.8 Bistro **3**
Red Chilli **8**

HOTELS ■

Best Western Dean
Court Hotel **4**
Cedar Court Grand
Hotel & Spa **7**

together, trace the history of railways from the early 19th century. A simulator gives you the chance to experience the thrill of hurtling from London to Brighton at up to 765 mph, while special events include the likes of a Wizard Week when you can take a steam ride pulled by "Hogwarts Castle," star of several Harry Potter films. There's also a miniature railway and a railway-themed playground in the grounds.

Leeman Rd. www.nrm.org.uk. ✆ **0844/815-3139.** Free admission (small charges for some activities and events). Daily 10am–6pm.

Treasurer's House ★   Like York Minster a few steps away, this conceals Roman remains—those of a road—in its cellar. You can also tour its 13 period rooms full of antiques, ceramics, textiles, and paintings, the Edwardian servants' attics, and the formal sunken garden. School-holiday activities and a children's guide and quiz/trail make it child-friendly; there are also food events including Edwardian breakfasts.

Minster Yard. www.nationaltrust.org.uk. © **01904/624247.** Admission adults £6.30, children 5–15 £3. Visits by guided tour only 2nd half Feb and all Nov, Sat–Thurs 11am–3pm; self-guided visits Mar–Oct Sat–Thurs 11am–4:30pm.

York Castle Museum & Prison ★ ☺   Occupying the site of York Castle, this is best known for its recreations of entire Victorian and Edwardian streets, but it also has period rooms, a collection of arms and armor, a Costume Gallery, and an exhibition on the building's former history as a jail. An activity guidebook (£2.50) aimed at children 6 and over allows family members to score points, on their own or against each other. You can get joint admission to this and the **Yorkshire Museum** (www.yorkshire museum.org.uk; © **01904/687687**), which holds archeological treasures, plus rare animals, birds, and fossils, within the city's free-to-visit botanical Museum Gardens.

Eye of York. www.yorkcastlemuseum.org.uk. © **01904/687687.** Admission adults £8.50, children under 16 free. Daily 9:30am to 5pm.

York Minster ★★★ CATHEDRAL   York's superb Gothic cathedral—which makes this city an ecclesiastical powerhouse equaled only by Canterbury (p. 240)—traces its origins from the early 7th century, but the present building is from the 13th century, with, like Lincoln's cathedral (p. 554), three 15th-century towers. The central tower is lantern shaped in the Perpendicular style; on a clear day the fit can climb its stone spiral staircase (275 steps) for panoramic views, at an extra charge. Don't miss the medieval stained glass, or, in the Undercroft beneath the central tower, the foundations of the Roman buildings where Emperor Constantine lived while he began his rise to greatness. If visiting with children, ask for a free Safari map to help you discover the animals concealed amidst the carvings in the chapterhouse.

Chapter House St. www.yorkminster.org. © **0844/939-0011.** Admission and guided tour £9 adults, children 15 and under free; tower £6, £3.50 children 8–16. Mon–Sat 9/9:30am–5:30pm; Sun noon–3:45pm

HARROGATE & AROUND ★★★

About 22 miles west of York and 7½ miles north of Harewood House (p. 636), the enchanting Victorian spa town of **Harrogate** is most famous as home, since 1919, to the original **Bettys Café Tea Rooms** (p. 655). Prior to that, in Georgian times, it attracted European nobility and other wealthy visitors to its iron, sulfur, and common-salt rich waters, which continue to be bottled and commercially sold. Despite Dickens's damning description of it as "the queerest place with the strangest people in it leading the oddest lives!," the town continues to be considered one of the U.K.'s most desirable places to live.

Just 4 miles north of Harrogate, charming little **Ripley** ★★★ seems frozen in time, with a fascinating castle, a cozy hotel (p. 658) owned by the same family, a small farm museum, and the **Ripley Store** (© **01423/770044**), looking like something out of a movie set and stocking homemade ice cream, old-fashioned candy, and other local goodies. Carry on up the road north from Ripley to reach Britain's largest monastic ruin, **Fountains Abbey within Studley Royal,** and then the cathedral city of **Ripon.**

Fountains Abbey & Studley Royal ★★ ☺ HISTORIC SITE   Founded on the banks of the Silver Skell by Cistercian monks in 1132, the dramatic ruins of Fountains Abbey now form the breathtaking focal point of the Georgian water gardens of Studley Royal, created around the ruins in the 18th century and dotted with neoclassical statuary and follies. Together they're designated a UNESCO World

Heritage site. The site also comprises a Cistercian corn mill—the last to stand in the U.K., with a children's trail—a medieval deer park populated by three breeds of wild deer, an exhibition on the abbey's history (plus guided tours, some specially for families, with dressing up), and a children's audio tour, trails, play area, and holiday activities and events. There are three stone cottages and two luxury apartments on-site.

Ripon. www.fountainsabbey.org.uk. © **01765/608888.** Admission £9 adults, £4.85 children 5–16. Abbey and water gardens daily Apr–Sept 10am–5pm; rest of year (except Fri Nov–Jan) 10am–4pm; deer park daily during daylight.

Newby Hall & Gardens ★★ ☺ This impressive 17th–18th-century house, designed by Sir Christopher Wren and containing some fine Robert Adam interiors with Chippendale furniture, is often used as a movie location. It's a great spot for a family day out, with fantastic Adventure Gardens designed to include something for all ages, a miniature railway through the lovely gardens, a sculpture park, a woodland discovery walk, and a farm shop.

2 miles off the A1 (Ripon exit; signposted). www.newbyhallandgardens.com. © **0845/450-4068.** Hall and gardens £13.50 adults, £10.50 children 5–15. Apr–Sept Tues–Sun (plus public holiday and July and Aug Mon) 11am–5:30pm.

RHS Garden Harlow Carr ★★ ☺ GARDEN This Royal Horticultural Society garden was created to complement the Yorkshire landscape of which it is a part, with the emphasis on water, stone, and woodland. Seasonal trails, a log maze, woodland dens, and observation beehives make it an unexpectedly fun place to bring children. There's a branch of Bettys Café Tea Rooms (p. 655) on-site.

Crag Lane, Harrogate. www.rhs.org.uk. © **01423/565418.** Admission £8.25 adults, £4.15 children 5–16. Mar–Oct daily 9:30am–6pm (until 4pm in winter).

Royal Pump Room Museum ★ No run-of-the-mill attraction, this museum traces Harrogate's history as a spa town, with displays including Europe's strongest sulfur wells and an exhibition on the town's links with Russian royalty, who came for its waters. There are also general historical displays on the town, some of them centered on Victorian life, and an Egyptian gallery.

Crown Place, Harrogate. www.harrogate.gov.uk. © **01423/556188.** Admission £3.60 adults, £2.10 children 5–15. Mon–Sat 10:30am–5pm; Sun 2–5pm (until 4pm in winter).

Ripley Castle ★★★ ☺ This focal point of the village of Ripley has been inhabited by the Ingilby family for 7 centuries, and Lady and Sir Thomas Ingilby work hard to keep its history alive—children's tours, for instance, bring the castle vividly to life for ages 5 to 16 through tales of Cromwell being kept at gunpoint here, wild boar hunts, and resident ghosts. Secret doors, spiral stairs up to a priest's hole, and lots of armor and weaponry add to the intrigue. Then there are the grounds, with a play trail, treasure hunt, tree-top rope course (www.logheights.co.uk), and deer park.

Ripley. www.ripleycastle.co.uk. © **01423/770152.** Admission castle and gardens £9 adults, £5.50 children 5–16. Gardens daily 9am–5pm (4:30pm in winter); castle for guided tours Apr–Oct daily, Mar and Nov Tues, Thurs and Sat–Sun, Dec–Feb Sat–Sun 11am–3pm; for children's tours see website.

Ripon Cathedral ★ The big draw of Ripon's cathedral is one of the country's oldest Saxon crypts, sole survivor of a church founded on the site by St. Wilfrid in the 7th century, but you can also see some medieval wood-carvings thought to have inspired *Alice in Wonderland* author Lewis Carroll.

Minster Rd., Ripon. www.riponcathedral.info. © **01765/603462.** Free admission. Daily 8:30am–6pm.

Royal Baths ★★ The true highlight of a visit to Harrogate for many people are these restored Victorian Turkish baths, which remain the most complete example of their kind in the U.K., with glorious Moorish arches and screens, glazed brickwork, arabesque painted ceilings, and terrazzo floors. They're still in full working order; visitors can splurge on a treatment or just relax in the steam room, heated chambers, plunge pool, and frigidarium. Pre-booking is advisable.

Parliament St., Harrogate. www.harrogate.gov.uk. © **01423/556746.** Admission £13.50–£19.50; treatments extra. Provides ladies', men's, and mixed sessions; see website for times.

YORKSHIRE DALES NATIONAL PARK ★★

This National Park occupying the western half of North Yorkshire consists of some 700 sq. miles of hills and water-carved valleys filled with dramatic white-limestone crags, fields bordered by dry-stone walls, fast-flowing rivers, isolated sheep farms, and clusters of sandstone cottages. The main Dales are, in the south, **Ribblesdale, Malhamdale, Airedale, Wharfedale,** and **Nidderdale,** and in the north, **Wensleydale, Swaledale,** and **Teesdale.** Harrogate can make for a good base for exploring the park, as can **Grassington,** 26 miles northwest of Harrogate. Grassington, a pretty stone-built village with a cobbled marketplace, is ideal for those who wish to tour **Upper Wharfedale,** one of the most scenic parts of the Dales—the **Dales Way** footpath actually passes through the heart of the village. The **Grassington National Park Centre,** Hebden Road (www.yorkshiredales.org.uk; © **01756/751690**), has information and maps.

There are more National Park centers in the north near Richmond, at **Aysgarth Falls** (another scenic highlight of the Dales, with a series of waterfalls) and at **Reeth,** and also at Malham and Hawes. **Malham,** 12 miles west of Grassington, is good for summer hiking amid some of Britain's most remarkable limestone formations. (***Insider tip:*** Avoid busy June to August in favor of May or Sept.) Malhamdale's scenery was extolled by no less an authority than Wordsworth, and rendered in paint by Turner. Its best walk is a circular 8-mile trail taking in scenic **Malham Cove** (a large rock amphitheatre), **Malham Tarn** (Britain's highest lake, which inspired Charles Kingsley's *The Water Babies*), and **Gordale Scar** (a deep chasm between overhanging limestone cliffs). If that's too strenuous, at least walk the 1 mile north of the village to the cove. The **Park Centre** (© **01729/833200**) has maps and advice.

About 25 miles north of Malham, on the **Pennine Way National Trail** (p. 538), **Hawes** is capital of Wensleydale (of the famed cheese) and England's highest market town.

Bolton Abbey ★★★ ☺ At the southern tip of the National Park, this ruined 12th-century priory is set in beautiful grounds with riverside, woodland, and moorland paths, a river with stepping stones and a beach area, a farm park, and steam train rides from Embsay to the abbey's own station (www.embsayboltonabbeyrailway.org.uk). There's also a ruined hunting lodge to explore, an I-Spy trail for children, and an on-site craftsman, The Bodger, who you can watch at work—and whose woodland products you can purchase. The grounds are dotted with cafes, tea rooms, and refreshment kiosks.

17 miles from Harrogate along the A59. www.boltonabbey.com. © **01756/718000.** Admission £6 per vehicle. Daily 9am–6pm (to 7pm mid-March–May, to 9pm June–Aug); last admission 90 min.–2 hr. ahead of closing times.

Dales Countryside Museum ★ This former train station is given over to displays on the people and landscape of the Yorkshire Dales—past, present, and future—with themes including schooling, home, religion, transport, farming, and local crafts and industries. Hawes National Park tourist information center shares the building.

Station Yard, Hawes. www.yorkshiredales.org.uk/dcm. ⓒ **01969/666210.** Admission adults £4, children free. Feb–Dec daily 10am–5pm.

NORTH YORK MOORS NATIONAL PARK ★★

To the east, the Moors, on the other side of the Vale of York from the Dales, have a wild beauty all their own, especially in summer when purple heather blooms. England's largest expanse of moorland, this is a deeply spiritual landscape dotted with early burial grounds, ancient stone crosses, and ruined abbeys. A 554-sq.-mile section of it has been preserved as a National Park popular among walkers and other lovers of the great outdoors.

If you're heading up from York, don't miss, en route to the Moors, Castle Howard (see below). North of it, the market town of Pickering is one of the gateways to the Moors, which are crisscrossed by an extensive network of public bridle and footpaths. Two noteworthy trails are **Lyke Wake Walk** (www.lykewake.org), a 40-mile east-to-west trek right across the Moors, linking the hamlets of Osmotherly and Ravenscar via the rugged path established by 18th-century coffin bearers. The more challenging **Cleveland Way** (www.nationaltrail.co.uk/ClevelandWay) follows a horseshoe-shaped line along the park's perimeter for 109 miles from Helmsley to Saltburn-by-the-Sea. Local tourist information centers have maps (see above, under "Essentials").

The National Park also embraces a large portion of the North Yorkshire coast, from just north of Scarborough to just past Boulby but circumventing Whitby.

Byland Abbey ★ One of the greatest English monasteries, this ruined early Gothic structure inspired the design of church buildings throughout the North of England—not least the famous rose window of York Minster (p. 648). An on-site museum has interpretation panels and archeological finds from the site. The two-room Byland Abbey Inn offers direct, free access to the abbey for guests.

Byland, Coxwald. www.english-heritage.org.uk. ⓒ **0870/333-1181.** Admission adults £4.40, children 5–15 £2.60. Apr–June and Sept Thurs–Mon 10am–6pm; July and Aug daily 10am–6pm; Oct–Mar Sat and Sun 10am–4pm.

Castle Howard ★★★ ☺ HISTORIC SITE This 18th-century palace designed by Sir John Vanbrugh, of Blenheim Palace (p. 227) fame, occupies dramatic grounds with lakes, fountains, gardens, and an adventure playground. Boat trips on the lake and children's trails and quiz sheets make it a great family bet. Begun in 1699 for the 3rd Earl of Carlisle, Castle Howard has a striking facade topped by a painted and gilded dome, and, inside, a chapel with stunning 19th-century stained-glass windows by Sir Edward Burne-Jones. The many important paintings on display include a portrait of Henry VIII by Holbein and works by Rubens, Reynolds, and Gainsborough. In the grounds, the family mausoleum is by Hawksmoor.

Castle Howard. www.castlehoward.co.uk. ⓒ **01653/648333.** Admission house and gardens £13 adults, £7.50 children 5–16. Apr–Oct daily 10am–5:30pm (house closed 2 wks in Nov and Jan–late March).

The World of James Herriot ★★ ☺ Set in the one-time surgery of Alf Wight, vet and author (under the pseudonym James Herriott) of *All Creatures Great and Small,* this museum is about both Wight's own life and on veterinary science as a whole, with an interactive gallery for children.

THE NORTH YORKSHIRE COAST ★★★

North Yorkshire's 45-mile coastline has an active if waning fishing industry, with some ports doubling as traditional seaside resorts. **Bridlington** and **Filey** in the south are low key, with wide, child-friendly beaches. About 19 miles north of Bridlington, **Scarborough** claims to be the oldest seaside spa in Britain—supposedly located on the site of a Roman signaling station, its mineral springs with medicinal properties were discovered in 1622. Teetering on its headland are the remains of **Scarborough Castle** (see below), and south of that stretches the beach and esplanade, with souvenir stalls, amusement arcades, and fun rides set incongruously against a background of magnificent Victorian facades, some housing hotels that have sadly gone to seed.

About 19 miles up the coast, the village of **Robin Hood's Bay** was once a notorious smugglers' port (it has no link with the eponymous Nottinghamshire outlaw). Tucked into a deep ravine (don't take wheelchairs or buggies), its Lower Bay is a mix of quirky, old-fashioned shops and inns bordering a huge wild beach abounding in rock-pools. Buy fish and chips to eat on the beach or alfresco treats from Picnics on New Road, or a van parks up on the beach to sell farm ice cream, tea and coffee, and rental deckchairs.

Robin Hood's Bay is just shy of this coast's true star, the charming harbor town of **Whitby** ★★★, which began as a religious center in the 7th century, with the original Saxon monastery replaced in the 12th century by **Whitby Abbey** (see below). The town subsequently became a prominent whaling port and eventually an active smugglers' port. Among famous explorers to push off from its beaches were Captain James Cook, who as the king's surveyor circumnavigated the globe twice in ships made by local craftsmen.

Captain Cook Memorial Museum ★   This museum occupies the 17th-century harborside house in which the young James Cook lodged as an apprentice while training as a seaman. The four floors of period rooms include an Orientation Room with maps depicting the known world before Cook's voyages. If you want to learn more about the explorer, ask at the tourist office (p. 645) about the **Captain James Cook Heritage Trail** taking in other North Yorkshire sites, including the **Captain Cook School Room Museum** (www.captaincookschoolroommuseum.co.uk; ℂ **01642/724296**) inland at Great Ayton and the **Captain Cook & Staithes Heritage Centre** (www.captaincookatstaithes.co.uk; ℂ **01947/841454**) up the coast from Whitby.

Grape Lane, Whitby. www.cookmuseumwhitby.co.uk. ℂ **01947/601900.** Admission adults £4.50, children 5–15 £3. March daily 11am–3pm; Apr–Nov daily 9:45am–5pm; most weekends in Feb 11am–3pm; rest of year by appointment.

North Bay Miniature Railway ★ ☺   This historic line, operating since 1931, takes passengers for a 3/4-mile ride along Scarborough's North Bay, with buggies and wheelchairs accommodated. Other attractions run by the railway in the surrounding park are rides on a historic water-chute, and pedal-boating and "water-walking" on the lake, and there's a restaurant, a seafood shack, and the Boatman's Tavern pub on-site.

Northstead Manor Gardens, Scarborough. www.nbr.org.uk. ℂ **01723/368791.** Return train ride adults £3.30, children 3–16 £2.70; see website for other attractions. Daily late March–Oct; rest of year Sat and Sun only; 1st train 10:30am, last train 3pm.

Rotunda, The William Smith Museum of Geology ★ ☺ Set in a landmark building overlooking Scarborough's South Bay, this museum was built in 1829 to hold the fossil collection of William Smith, the "father of English geology" and contains displays on local geology and archeology plus a variety of old scientific instruments. There's a Dino Club for children, plus, in summer, a Dinosaur Coast program of events in the area includes fossil hunts and family fun days.

The Crescent, Scarborough. www.rotundamuseum.co.uk. ℂ **01723/353665.** Admission £4.50 adults, free children 16 and under. Tues–Sun and public holidays 10am–5pm.

RSPB Bempton Cliffs Reserve ★ ☺ Set on the chalk promontory of Flamborough Head between the two resorts of Bridlington and Filey, this reserve offers the scope for bracing clifftop walks to see some of the 200,000 seabirds, including puffins, who inhabit the site from April to August. There are regular birdwatching cruises, some tailored for families.

1mile from Bempton village. www.rspb.org.uk. ℂ **01262/851179.** Admission £3.50 per car. Site open 24 hr.

Scarborough Castle ★ ☺ RUINS This impressive ruin began life as an Iron Age fort before being occupied by the Romans, the Vikings, and finally Henry II. The best time to visit is the summer holidays, when you might catch live-action events, but the awesome coast views from the expansive grounds can be appreciated year-round.

Castle Rd., Scarborough. www.english-heritage.org.uk. ℂ **0870/333-1181.** Admission £4.90 adults, £2.90 children 5–16. Apr–Sept daily 10am–6pm; Oct Thurs–Mon 10am–5pm; Nov–Mar Sat and Sun 10am–4pm.

St. Mary's Church ★ This medieval structure is best known as the final resting place of Anne Brontë, who died in Scarborough in 1849, aged just 28, after being brought from her home in Haworth (p. 638) in the hope that the sea air would revive her health—you can pay homage at her grave, which is overlooked by the castle. The church stands in the ruins of a Roman signal station, built on the castle headland to give warnings of Anglo-Saxon invaders.

Castle Rd., Scarborough. www.stmaryschurchscarborough.co.uk. ℂ **01723-500541.** Free admission. Graveyard open 24 hr.; for church, call in advance.

Whitby Abbey ★★★ ☺ RUINS Looming ominously over the historic port from the East Cliff, this breathtaking ruin replaced a Saxon monastery that occupied the same site. Caedmon, the first identifiable English-language poet, was a monk here, and Bram Stoker was inspired by it in the writing of *Dracula*. The excellent visitor center, which has great features for children, fills you in on this and more.

Abbey Lane, Whitby. www.english-heritage.org.uk. ℂ **0870/333-1181.** Admission £6.20 adults, £3.70 children 5–16. Apr–Sept daily 10am–6pm; Oct Thurs–Mon 10am–4pm (daily in Oct and Feb school holiday); Nov–Mar Sat and Sun 10am–4pm.

Where to Eat
VERY EXPENSIVE
The bistros at the **Hotel du Vin** in both York and Harrogate are good spots for "Home-grown and Local" food with a French slant, including specially selected and aged steaks from a Yorkshire farm.

Lanterna Ristorante ★★ ITALIAN Bringing together Yorkshire ingredients—black pudding and winkles, cuttlefish, and other seafood gleaned from the local fishmarket—with traditional recipes and treats from northern Italy (including white truffles and prosciutto), the Lanterna is Scarborough's culinary landmark. Amid dated but homey Piedmont decor lucky locals including celebrities Alan Ayckbourn and David Hockney feast on the likes of risotto with chickpeas and walnuts, escalopes of veal cooked in butter and white truffles, venison ravioli, and desserts including zabaglione made to order at the table.

33 Queen St., Scarborough. www.lanterna-ristorante.co.uk. ✆ **01723/363616.** Reservations recommended. Main courses £15–£45. MC, V. Mon–Sat 7–9:30pm.

Yorke Arms ★★ MODERN BRITISH   Presided over by one of only six female Michelin-starred chefs in the U.K., this restaurant in an 18th-century coaching house and shooting lodge in a village tucked into the Nidderdale valley offers sensual cooking concocted from seasonal local produce, much of it organic and some home-grown or foraged. The unique dishes include the house "classics" Wensleydale soufflé with sea scallops, vanilla, and tomato; Whitby crab with potage of shellfish, salt cod, and tomato; gnocchi with sweet potato embers, celery velouté, roasted fennel, pine nuts, and young vegetables; and strawberry bavarois with peach, walnut, and thyme pannacotta. If you struggle to choose, give yourself over to the surprise tasting menu, with eight courses paired with recommended wines. Sunday lunches are also unforgettable. Packages combine dinner for two with a night in one of the coolly chic **guest rooms** (£260–£399 double) and full Yorkshire breakfast. There's also a two-bedroom cottage sleeping four.

Ramsgill-in-Nidderdale, 19 miles northwest of Harrogate. www.yorke-arms.co.uk. ✆ **01423/755243.** Reservations recommended. Main courses £23–£32. AE, DC, MC, V. Mon–Sat noon–2pm and 7–9pm; Sun noon–2pm.

EXPENSIVE

York has a branch of **Red Chilli** on George Hudson Street (✆ **01904/733-668**).

Café No.8 Bistro ★★ ☺ INTERNATIONAL   Ultra-handy for York Minster (p. 648), this calm if slightly cramped little spot serves seasonal menus championing local ingredients, including Masham sausages and Ryedale ice cream, but dishes are often given an exotic twist—think Yorkshire beer-battered, peppered parsnip with honey and mustard mayonnaise; and slow-cooked outdoor-reared pork belly with potato purée, autumn vegetables, and star anise infused jus; although lighter dishes such as bruschettas and soups are available in the evening as well as at lunch, and there are good brunches at weekends. If you bag a table in the heated walled garden backing onto the city, you can eat to the chime of the cathedral's bells. Under-10s, who get their own very good menu, eat free with an adult.

8 Gillygate, York. www.cafeno8.co.uk. ✆ **01904/653074.** Reservations recommended. Main courses £6.50–£17.50. MC, V. Mon–Fri noon until late; Sat–Sun 11am until late.

The Magpie Café ★★ ☺ SEAFOOD   Folks flock from far and wide for the traditional fish and chips served in this old-fashioned restaurant on Whitby's harbor, with unforgettable views up to the famous abbey (p. 653). The rest of the menu is almost a distraction, but repeated visits may tempt you to investigate the offerings more fully—Whitby crab and kipper starters, sautéed local squid, or any of the daily fish specials are good starting points. Children get a separate and almost equally vast menu. Fish and chips and many other dishes come in two sizes; order the smallest if you want any chance of tackling a dessert. Limited bookings are taken and you may have to wait for a table—if it's good weather, get a takeout and eat on the quayside instead.

14 Pier Rd., Whitby. www.magpiecafe.co.uk. ℂ **01947/602058.** Main courses £6.95–£22.95. MC, V. Daily 11:30am–9pm.

MODERATE

Bettys Café Tea Rooms ★ ☺ ENGLISH TEA/CONTINENTAL   Don't come to Harrogate without paying at least one visit to the institution that is Bettys (if it's good enough for the Queen…). You can pre-book afternoon tea in the Imperial Room at weekends, served on silver cakestands and accompanied by a classical pianist; otherwise, you have to get in line (usually a long one) for the pleasure of choosing from more than 300 breads, cakes, and chocolates, and about 50 teas and coffees, in the more informal cafe. Part of this, the Montpellier Café Bar, also offers all-day dining, including lunchtime open sandwiches and filled rolls, and dinner sharing plates, light meals, and main courses such as oak-smoked salmon rösti. The children's menu bears such treats as Alpine macaroni with bacon, new potatoes with raclette cheese, toasted sandwiches, and ice-cream shakes.

There are additional Tea Rooms at Harlow Carr Gardens (p. 649), and in York (two branches), Ilkley (west of Harrogate), and Northallerton (north of Thirsk).

1 Parliament St., Harrogate. www.bettys.co.uk. ℂ **01423/814070.** Reservations required (afternoon tea Sat–Sun). Main courses £8.80–£12. AE, DC, MC, V. Daily 8am–9pm.

INEXPENSIVE

Falling Foss Tea Garden ★★ 🎁 ☺ ENGLISH TEA/SNACKS   Five miles outside Whitby, this magical venue is on the woodland grounds of a former gamekeeper's cottage and is a lovely stop-off for walkers doing the coast to coast trail. It's a great spot to bring children, who will love exploring the ancient forest before or after a light lunch, cream tea, or ice cream. They can also paddle in the beck, play Pooh sticks on the footbridge, or use the rustic wooden play area while you relax over a pot of tea. The Hermitage, a hermit's cave carved from stone, is a 5-minute walk through the trees. The homemade cakes and scones, sandwiches, and light snacks are made from mainly local ingredients. This is a garden, not a tearoom, so opening is subject to the weather, though amid the gnarled apple trees there is a yurt with a log burner.

Midge Hall, Sneaton Forest. www.fallingfossteagarden.co.uk. ℂ **07723/477929.** Main courses £3–£5.50. No credit cards. Usually Apr–Oct daily 10:30am–5pm, but call to confirm, especially if raining.

Humble Pie and Mash ★ 🎁 ✦ TRADITIONAL BRITISH   It's not all about fish and chips in Whitby—pies freshly made using free-range meat and organic pastry bring lovers of hearty old-fashioned English grub to this restored 16th-century shop with its open fire, 1940s' chintz, and soundtrack of wartime hits. Best eaten with mash, peas (garden or mushy), and liquor or gravy, the pies include slow-braised stout and leek, and Yorkshire sausage and black pudding, but also come in vegetarian incarnations. With pie meals costing less than £5 and children's prices for pies, sausage and mash, or sausage sandwiches, this is a great place for a budget-conscious but filling family lunch or early supper. Take it easy if you're hoping to fit in one of the scrumptious desserts such as vanilla ice-cream with Belgian chocolate pouring sauce. Note that there's no alcohol license.

163 Church St., Whitby. www.humblepienmash.com. ℂ **07919/074954.** Main courses £4.99. MC, V. Mon–Sat 12:30–8:30pm; Sun 12:30–5pm.

Shopping

York is the region's shopping highlight. Don't miss the cobbled **Shambles;** voted Britain's most picturesque street in the Google Street View awards, it's lined by wooden-framed buildings that lean so far across the narrow alley that some of their roofs almost touch. Once the city's meat-butchering center, it's now home to shops and cafes, many selling jewelry (a highlight of York shopping). York's antiques dealers tend to congregate on or around Gillygate; for independent one-off stores, try Stonegate. On the city outskirts, the **York Designer Outlet** (www.yorkdesigneroutlet. com; © 01904/682720) has more than 100 upper-end brands under one roof, sold tax free and with up to 60% discounts.

York is also a great place to shop for food, with lots of delis and local food stores: Try "liquid deli" **Demijohn,** 11 Museum St. (© 01904/637487), for handmade British wines, spirits, oils, and vinegars bottled to order; **Henshelwoods,** 10 Newgate (© 01904/673877), for award-winning cheese; **Olio and Farina,** 3 Blake St. (© 01904/670885), for Italian specialties; **The Hairy Fig,** 39 Fossgate (© 01904/677074), for "on tap" vinegars, oils, fig vodka, and more; and **The Yorkshire Pantry,** 18 High Petergate (© 01904/675100), for local food and drink, much of it organic and fair trade. York also has a daily open-air **market** with more than 100 stalls.

For more foodie treats try the **Balloon Tree Farmshop and Café,** at Gate Helmsley between York and Bridlington (www.theballoontree.co.uk; © 01759/373023), and, in Harrogate, the award-winning **Weeton's Farm Shop,** 23/24 West Park (www.weetons.com; © 01423/507100) and **Fodder** (www. fodderweb.co.uk; © 01423/546111), the latter based at the Great Yorkshire Showground a couple of miles from the center and unique both in that it ploughs profits back into the community and has its own 80-seat cafe. **Harrogate** is also good for boutiques and designer shops (Parliament Street and Montpellier Quarter) and independent stores (Commercial Street and around).

Entertainment & Nightlife

York is said to have a pub for every day of the year—more per square mile, some claim, than any city in the country—but unlike Leeds the city is lively rather than rowdy, except around the Micklegate area (including Rougier Street). Stick to laidback Goodramgate and the Swinegate area, where you'll find a good mix of traditional pubs and swanky bars appealing to all ages. The Coney Street area is the most upmarket. The oldest pub in town, **Ye Olde Starre Inne,** on Stonegate (© 01904/623063), has a beer garden with Minster views.

Outside York, North Yorkshire tends to be quiet on the nightlife front, although there are many convivial country pubs offering folk and other live music. For culture vultures, Scarborough's **Stephen Joseph Theatre** (www.sjt.uk.com; © 01723/370540) has hosted the premieres of most of the plays of award-winning playwright Alan Ayckbourn, who lives in the town.

Where to Stay
VERY EXPENSIVE
The **Yorke Arms** (p. 654), in the Nidderdale valley, has chic rooms.

Feversham Arms & Verbena Spa ★★★ This haven of luxury in a Moors market town has some suites suitable for families, but it's not the kind of place to bring energetic toddlers, for fear of disturbing the contented guests enjoying cream teas in their bathrobes by the outdoor pool (heated year-round). In any case, you'll want to install yourself in the spa—one of the U.K.'s very best, with a large chill-out area (low-lit by scented candles) and a bar and light meals menu. The "Petite Double" rooms in the older part of the building are cozy, but once you've clocked the poolside or spa suites, you'll sell your soul to upgrade. The **restaurant** is excellent, making half-board a sensible option. Rievaulx Abbey is a pleasant walk away (3 miles), but you'll be loathe to leave the premises.

Helmsley, North Yorkshire YO62 5AG. www.fevershamsmotel.com. ✆ **01439/770766.** 33 units. £180–£280 double; £340–£460 suite. Rates include Yorkshire breakfast (half-board option available). AE, DC, MC, V. Free parking. **Amenities:** Restaurant; bar; outdoor heated pool (year-round); spa; babysitting. *In room:* TV with DVD/CD player, hair dryer, Wi-Fi (free).

Swinton Park ★★★ ☺ Just 22 miles northwest of Harrogate in the heart of the Dales, this family-run home is a great base for exploring the National Park and North Yorkshire, as well as a luxurious destination in its own right. Set in a vast parkland with lakes, gardens, and deer, it offers a spa, a plush **restaurant** offering estate produce (including venison, grouse, trout, and vegetables and herbs from the walled garden), country pursuits galore (fishing, golf, and off-road driving), and a cookery school. Rooms and suites are individually designed and traditional in feel. Families are warmly welcomed, with a games/playroom, outdoor play area and games equipment (bikes, kites, and so on), children's cookery lessons, and an on-site birds-of-prey center with daily flying displays. Family events include Easter-egg hunts and activity days. There's an excellent all-day children's menu, and various suites with sofabeds, including the Turret Suite with circular rooms on three levels.

Masham, North Yorkshire HG4 4JH. www.swintonpark.com. ✆ **01765/680900.** 30 units. £180–£300 double; £310–£380 suite (half-board available). Rates include breakfast (except for Fri–Sat night stays). AE, DC, MC, V. Free parking. **Amenities:** Restaurant; bar; exercise room; outdoor activities; spa; room service; babysitting; Wi-Fi (free, in lobby). *In room:* TV, CD player.

EXPENSIVE

Best Western Dean Court Hotel ★ ☺ Though part of a chain, this York stalwart derives some historical ambience from its occupation of a 19th-century building and its enviable location by the Minster. It's a good option for families: In addition to family rooms, it offers baby-listening via reception, toys and games, a DVD library, practical items such as changing mats, and chefs who "will cook almost anything for youngsters and babies on request!" The most expensive rooms have four-poster beds, but all are comfortable, and staff are very attentive.

Duncombe Place, York, North Yorkshire YO1 7EF. www.deancourt-york.co.uk. ✆ **01904/625082.** 37 units. £145–£240 double. Rates include Yorkshire breakfast. AE, DC, MC, V. Parking £13. **Amenities:** 2 restaurants; bar; room service; babysitting and baby-listening; DVD library. *In room:* TV/DVD, hair dryer, Wi-Fi (free).

Cedar Court Grand Hotel & Spa ★★★ Understated luxury and a successful melding of historical detail (sweeping staircases, mosaic-tiled corridors) with a subtly contemporary feel have garnered the Cedar Court Grand legions of fans since its opening in 2010, when it became York's first five-star hotel. Occupying former railway offices, it evokes, albeit obliquely, the Golden Age of travel, with the emphasis firmly on the leisurely life: There's a **restaurant** serving classic British fare, a whisky and cocktail lounge, a roof terrace for afternoon teas, and a luscious spa and pool in the building's vaults.

Station Rise, York, North Yorkshire YO1 6GD. www.cedarcourtgrand.co.uk.☏ **01904/380038.** 107 units. £129–£399 double; £249–£1,530 suite. AE, DC, MC, V. Parking £20. **Amenities:** Restaurant; bar; indoor swimming pool; gym; spa; room service; babysitting. *In room:* TV, fridge (some), hair dryer, Wi-Fi (free).

MODERATE

There are three atmospheric stone holiday cottages, plus two luxury apartments, at **Fountains Abbey & Studley Gardens** (p. 648), costing £319–£939 for a week's stay. Alternatively, there are two Forest Holidays sites with wooden cabins at Keldy and Cropton about 25 miles west of Scarborough.

Boar's Head ★★ ☺ A cozier, more welcoming hostelry than this former coaching inn in the idyllic, film-set-like village of Ripley is hard to imagine. The decanter of sherry in your room on arrival and the vintage radios reinforce the feeling that you've stepped back in time. Divided between the main building on the village square and an annex across the road (best suited to families), rooms are old-fashioned and homey, with quirky touches such as wooden boats for the bath. Owned by the same family as the village castle (p. 649; guests get free access to the castle and grounds), the inn has a **formal restaurant** and a more relaxed **candlelit bistro** best suited to families; ingredients from the castle's kitchen garden are used to full effect in both.

Ripley, North Yorkshire HG3 3AY. www.boarsheadripley.co.uk.☏ **01423/771888.** 25 units. £100–£150 double. AE, DC, MC, V. Free parking. **Amenities:** 2 restaurants; bar; DVD library; games. *In room:* TV/DVD, Wi-Fi (free).

La Rosa Hotel ★ Super-kitsch seaside fun is offered in this Victorian building in Whitby, with to-die-for sea and abbey views and an enviable history as the place where Lewis Carroll stayed while in town (as a plaque outside attests). Decorated with fleamarket finds and vintage wallpapers, it has an *Alice in Wonderland* vibe, with Carroll's study re-imagined in the Lewis room, but also nods to Bram Stoker, Angela Carter, J. M. Barrie, and everyone from cowgirls to pirates. All rooms are doubles save the attic Crow's Nest, which sleeps six and has a dressing-up box. Continental breakfast comes in a hamper delivered to your room; there's also a retro tearoom. There's no parking, so you'll have to take a chance on finding a paying spot on the street.

The owners extend their green ethos to their **campsite** with vintage caravans 7 miles away, created using recycled, reclaimed, and found objects, with showers in a converted byre, a compost toilet in a shepherds' hut, and an open-air roll-top tub in the orchard.

5 East Terrace, Whitby, North Yorkshire YO21 3HB. www.larosa.co.uk.☏ **01947/606981.** 9 units. £86–£135 double. Rates include continental breakfast. MC, V. **Amenities:** Tearoom. *In room:* TV, DVD (in Crow's Nest).

The Lawrance ★★ 🗲 These stylish serviced apartments in three period buildings in central Harrogate are a boon to everyone from business patrons and local convention-goers to families. Spacious and chic, they boast hand-printed wallpaper, luxurious fabrics, Philippe Starck bathrooms, superb beds and bedding, and state-of-the-art entertainment systems and kitchens. If you don't feel up to struggling out of bed to make breakfast yourself, you can order in a hamper. You can also order a "Grazing Pack" of luxury food items for your arrival, and room service is provided by a local Italian restaurant. At press time, a second Lawrance was slated to open in York.

Kings House, Kings Rd., Harrogate, North Yorkshire HG1 5JW. www.thelawrance.co.uk.☏ **01423/503226.** 19 units. £85–£129 1-bed apartment; £129–£279 2-bed apartment. AE, MC,

DC, V. Parking at most sites (free). **Amenities:** Room service. *In room:* TV/DVD, kitchen, MP3 docking station.

INEXPENSIVE

The Bivouac ★★★ 🎒 ☺   Located on the vast estate belonging to Swinton Park (p. 657), this new-in-2012, sustainable site offers a dose of rustic luxury within six hand-crafted round-wood timber-frame shacks nestled in a patch of woodland, or else in eight canvas yurts in a nearby meadow or in a bunk-barn for up to 12 (groups or individuals). Shacks and yurts are available for 3/4-night weekend or midweek breaks or by the week. Best are the shacks (which sleep up to seven adults), with verandahs for stargazing, wood-burners with cooking ranges, oil-burning lanterns, antique rocking chairs, and handmade and "upcycled" furniture and furnishings, plus a shower room and WC. The yurts, sleeping up to five adults, also have a small wood-burning stove that can be used for cooking, plus a cold-water sink; showers and toilets are a short walk away in the reception building. The bunk-barn, a great option for those walking in the area, has a lockable storage box by each bed. Optional activities on-site include a foraging course, forest school for children, climbing, and arts and crafts, and there's a child-friendly community cafe serving food right through the day. You can also book a masseuse or even join in a wine-tasting evening.

High Knowle Farm, Knowle Lane, Masham, North Yorkshire, HG4 4JZ. www.thebivouac.co.uk. ✆ **01765/535030.** 14 units, plus a 12-bed bunk-barn. Bunk-barn £18 per person per night; shack £430–£730 for 7 nights, yurt £310–£730 for 7 nights. **Amenities:** Cafe; shop; communal toilets and showers; activities; parking; Internet access (at reception). *In-room:* Kitchen facilities, shower room (shacks).

COUNTY DURHAM

Durham: 270 miles N of London; 75 miles N of York; 140 miles S of Edinburgh

The countryside and coast around the famous—and exceedingly pleasant—university city of Durham don't get as many visitors as they deserve, eclipsed as they are by the close proximity of Yorkshire to the south and Northumberland to the north. The rolling hills and waterfalls of the Durham Dales in the North Pennines are particularly worthy of exploration, while the fascinating layers of local history are kept vividly alive at outstanding attractions such as the North of England Lead Mining Museum and Beamish, the Living Museum of the North.

Essentials

GETTING THERE   Durham lies on the main London–York–Edinburgh rail line, with trains from London's King's Cross taking about 2¾ hours (at around £118 for an off-peak round-trip). There are also direct trains from Leeds (p. 634), Manchester (p. 566), and Birmingham (p. 466). Daily **National Express** (www.nationalexpress. com; ✆ **0871/781-8181**) buses to Durham from London take 6 to 7½ hours. London to Durham by car is a straightforward 270-mile run up the M1, then the A1, taking you 4½ hours or more.

VISITOR INFORMATION   **Durham Visitor Contact Centre,** (www.thisis durham.com; ✆ **03000/262626**). Not open to public for face-to-face enquiries.

SPECIAL EVENTS   Durham's **Regatta** (www.durham-regatta.org.uk), dating back to 1834, attracts 600-plus crews to compete over a weekend in June, and also includes street theatre and a fireworks finale on the riverbanks.

Exploring the Area
DURHAM ★★

A pleasant stopover venue for those en route to Northumbria and a charming base for exploring the Durham Dales, this attractive university town is dominated by Britain's largest and best-preserved Norman stronghold, William the Conqueror's Cathedral, while the city center as a whole is a designated conservation area, home to more than 600 listed buildings. With its narrow medieval streets, this is a delightful and compact city to wander around, especially along the river (where you can boat in summertime).

If you are in the area with children, head 6 miles outside Durham to Langley Park, where there's a **Diggerland** theme park.

Durham Castle ★   Like the Cathedral both Norman and a UNESCO-listed World Heritage site, Durham Castle—commissioned by William the Conqueror and home to the Prince Bishops of Durham until 1837—is home to University College, part of the city's highly regarded university, and when the students have gone home for the holidays, visitors can actually stay within its historic walls (p. 663). Alternatively, there are tours most days, lasting 45 minutes, plus two museums on-site: The **Old Fulling Mill Museum of Archaelogy** and the **Oriental Museum** (www.dur. ac.uk/museums), both offering family activities.

Palace Green, Durham. www.dur.ac.uk. ℭ **0191/334-4099.** Tours adults £5, children 5–15 £3.50. Guided tours daily 2pm, 3pm, and 4pm in University term-time; 10am, 11am, and noon, and sometimes also 2pm and 5pm, in University vacations; call to check if making a special trip.

Durham Cathedral ★★★   Breathtaking to view on its hilltop site, this was the first English building with ribbed vault construction and also the first stone-roofed cathedral in Europe—this latter feature was an architectural necessity because it was not only a church and the final resting place of St. Cuthbert from nearby Lindisfarne (p. 673), but also "half Castle 'gainst the Scots." Within it you can see Cuthbert's shrine, cross, and coffin, plus the former monks' dorm with its hammerbeam oak roof. Young visitors are kept engaged by audiovisual displays; those over 1.3m (4 ft. 3 in.) tall can climb the tower for superb views. The cathedral's award-winning Undercroft restaurant champions local produce.

The College, Durham. www.durhamcathedral.co.uk. ℭ **0191/386-4266.** Free admission; tours adults £5, children free. Mon–Sat 7:30am–6pm; Sun 7:45am–5:30pm (till 8pm mid-June–late Aug); call ahead if making special trip. Tours Apr–Oct Mon–Sat 10:30am, 11am, 2pm; call ahead to check.

DURHAM DALES, HERITAGE COAST & BEAMISH ★

Though coal- and iron-mining were the mainstays of the Durham Dales west of the city, the latter are now part of the **North Pennines Area of Outstanding Natural Beauty,** which stretches into Northumberland and Cumbria (p. 671) and has been designated a UNESCO European Geopark for its outstanding geology. Don't miss **Teesdale** with its waterfalls—**High Force,** England's largest, drops 21m (70 ft.).

This is good walking territory: The **Pennine Way** (p. 538) crosses the area, and there's the 90-mile **Teesdale Way** from Middlesbrough in North Yorkshire across County Durham (via Barnard Castle; see below) and into Cumbria, and the 77-mile **Weardale Way** along the River Wear from Roker on the coast near Newcastle. This latter takes you to **Killhope, the North of England Lead Mining Museum** (see below).

The market town of **Stanhope** is the starting point for a scenic ride on the heritage **Weardale Railway** (www.weardale-railway.org.uk) to Wolsingham. Or head to

Hamsterley Forest (www.forestry.gov.uk) with its walking, cycling, and horse-riding routes, bike rental, visitor center, tearoom, and play park. Cyclists should also note that Stanhope is on the **C2C Cycle Route** (Coast to Coast or Sea to Sea national cycle route; www.c2c-guide.co.uk).

Travel 17 miles south of Stanhope to reach the town of **Barnard Castle,** named after its extensive ruined Norman **fortress.** On the way back up to Durham, medieval **Raby Castle** is also worth a stop. Despite being ravaged by mining in the 20th century (as well as impoverished by mine closures in the early 1990s), the **Durham Heritage Coast** (www.durhamheritagecoast.org) offers wild beaches, rugged cliffs, and imposing headlands blessed with rare plants and wildlife, best explored via the coastal path. Focal points are the **Castle Eden Dene National Nature Reserve** (www.naturalengland.org.uk; ℭ **0191/586-0004**), with 12 miles of footpaths through ancient woodlands, and the lively harbor of Seaham, with one of the U.K.'s oldest churches.

The last sight in County Durham as you head north is Beamish, the Living Museum of the North deep in the countryside 12 miles northwest of Durham.

Barnard Castle ★ Set on a rock and affording stunning views over the Tees gorge, Barnard Castle in the town of the same name—derived from the fortress's 12th-century founder Barnard de Balliol—has tactile gardens and a sensory garden with scented plants. Don't miss Richard III's boar emblem carved above the inner ward.

Barnard Castle. www.english-heritage.co.uk. ℭ **01833/638212.** Admission £4.40 adults, £2.60 children 5–15. Apr–Sept daily 10am–6pm; Oct–Mar Sat and Sun 10am–4pm.

Beamish, the Living Museum of the North ★★★ ☺ MUSEUM This vivid open-air re-creation of an early-19th-century pit village includes costumed interpreters acting out daily life in shops, houses, pubs, a farm with real animals, and so on. For children, the stars are a ride on the Pockerley Waggonway-replica locomotives pulling re-created period carriages, the old-fashioned sweet factory, and the coal-fired fish and chip shop. Try to time your visit with one of the busy program of events, including steam fairs and Georgian fairs.

Beamish. www.beamish.org.uk. ℭ **0191/370-4000.** Admission £16 adults, £10 children 5–16 high season; £8 adults, £5 children low season. Apr–Oct daily 10am–5pm; rest of year Tues–Thurs and Sat–Sun 10am–4pm.

Bowes Museum ★ ☺ Northern England's best collection of European fine and decorative arts, held within a magnificent mansion, includes Fashion & Textile and Silver & Metals galleries. Free trails, activity sacks, and dressing-up areas make it a good family bet.

Barnard Castle. www.bowesmuseum.org.uk. ℭ **01833/690606.** Admission £9 adults, free for children. Daily 10am–5pm.

Killhope, The North of England Lead Mining Museum ★★ ☺ MUSEUM Don hard hats to tour a restored 19th-century mine (ages 4 and up), look at a huge working waterwheel and displays about lead mining in the area (Sam Squirrel family backpacks are available for younger visitors), and walk in the surrounding woodland, complete with play park, picnic tables, and wildlife hides, plus changing art works and installations.

Near Cowshill. www.killhope.org.uk. ℭ **01388/537505.** Admission £7 adults, £4 children 4–16. Feb school holiday and Apr–Oct daily 10:30am–5pm.

Raby Castle ★ Surrounded by walled gardens and parkland in which fallow and roe deer roam free, this fine medieval castle—home to Lord Barnard's family since 1626—has interesting medieval, Regency, and Victorian interiors containing European textiles and furniture from the 17th to the 20th centuries and artworks by Van Dyck, Reynolds, and others. Its coachhouse holds a display of carriages.

Staindrop. www.rabycastle.com. ℂ **01833/660202.** Castle, park, and gardens £10 adults, £4.50 children 5–15. Park and garden Easter weekend 11am–5:30pm; May, June, and Sept Sun–Wed; July–Aug Sun–Fri. Castle 14:30pm (by guided tour only Mon–Wed).

Where to Eat
EXPENSIVE
Finbarr's ★★ MODERN BRITISH/EUROPEAN Ranked by many as the best restaurant in town since opening in early 2010, this cozy inn-like building in Durham City's Conservation Area, on the edge of the Flass Vale nature reserve a short walk from the center, conceals a haven of subtle modern chic. The contemporary rustic cooking with the odd, exotic touch features mainly regional produce—standouts are cod cheek and North Sea crab bouillabaisse with braised fennel and Pernod, and *osso bucco* (veal shanks) with parsnip tart and bone marrow. But the highlight is the wonderful Sunday lunches—a bargain at £19.50 for three courses, with children's half-portions available. Finbarr's is also open for breakfast daily.

Waddington St., Flass Vale, Durham. www.finbarrsrestaurant.co.uk. ℂ **0191/370-9999.** Reservations recommended. Main courses £12.50–£25.50. AE, DC, MC, V. Mon–Fri 7–9:30am, noon–2:30pm, and 6–9:30pm; Sat 7–10:30am, noon–2:30pm, and 6–9:30pm; Sun 7:30–10:30am, noon–3pm, and 5–9pm.

Riverside at the Swan ★★★ BRITISH Low-beamed ceilings, candles, and the smell of fabulously good local cooking will lure you into this award-winning restaurant overlooked by Barnard Castle, attracting food lovers from hundreds of miles away. The chargrilled steaks from local farms and the twice-cooked beef are revelations, but you'll also find the irresistible likes of seared filet of sea bass with fresh leek tagliatelle; steamed Shetland mussels; crayfish and crab risotto; and savory Yorkshire blue cheese bread-and-butter pudding with thick-cut chips, sticky onion relish, and crisp dressed salad leaves.

Bridge End, Barnard Castle. www.riverside-restaurant.co.uk. ℂ **01833/637576.** Reservations recommended. Main courses £14.50–£24.50. MC, V. Tues–Sat 6pm–late.

MODERATE
La Spaghettata ★ ☺ 🍴 ITALIAN The lines trailing down the stairs and out the door of this homey restaurant on the street leading up to Durham Cathedral testify to its superiority over the city's many other Italian restaurants in atmosphere, pricing, and portion size, though because it gets so busy, service can suffer. A favorite with Durham's students—perhaps for the penne with vodka, or the kitsch decor with its gaudy *trompe l'oeil* murals and plastic tablecloths—it's also a great spot for a lively meal with children, with half-size pasta dishes available. In addition to good pizzas and pasta dishes, there are intriguing main courses such as grilled salmon with chili, coriander, cherry tomatoes, ginger, and scallions. You can also get food sent upstairs to Fabio's bar, hosting live music, from jazz to dance, until 2am.

66 Saddler St., Durham. www.fabiosdurham.com. ℂ **0191/383-9290.** Main courses £5.50–£12.90. MC, V. Mon–Thurs 5:30–10:30pm; Fri–Sun 11:30am–2pm and 5:30–10:30pm.

INEXPENSIVE

The award-winning Undercroft restaurant at Durham Cathedral (p. 660) serves good cakes, scones, soups, sandwiches, salads, and main courses.

Penny's Tea Rooms LUNCH/SNACKS/AFTERNOON TEA This long-standing tearoom and restaurant is popular with locals and visitors for everything from tea and cakes to home-cooked meals written up on a chalkboard, amid murals picturing local landscapes. A typical day's offerings might include a soup, warm rolls, paninis, jacket potatoes, and the heartier likes of beef and mushroom cobbler, or shepherd's pie with vegetables. Whatever you choose, leave space for an indulgent dessert such as chocolate sponge or plum pie. Vegetarian and gluten- and dairy-free diets are catered for. The owners also offer B&B **rooms.**

4 Market Place, Barnard Castle. ✆ **01833/637634.** Main courses £5–£7.95. MC, V. Sun–Mon 10am–3pm; Tues–Sat 9am–5pm.

Shopping

Durham is the county's shopping focus, notably the beautifully restored Victorian covered **Indoor Market;** its 50 traders selling local produce and goods (Mon–Sat 9am–5pm) include Humbies traditional candy shop, the award-winning Cafe Cenno bistro (with free Wi-Fi), and even a pipe and tobacco shop. The third Thursday of the month also sees the **City of Durham Farmers' Market** in the Market Place, from 9am until about 3:30pm, and there's a twice-yearly (spring and autumn) Continental market. For information on all these, see www.durhammarkets.org.uk. There's also a big Christmas market the first weekend of December, part of a Christmas festival (www.durhamchristmasfestival.com) also including a children's lantern procession and live reindeer).

There are also plenty of interesting one-off shops near the cathedral and around the city center, including fashion emporium **Van Mildert,** at 19–21 Elvet Bridge (www.vanmildert.com; ✆ **0191/384-8508**), with a huge range of desirable labels including Vivienne Westwood and MCQ Alexander McQueen.

Entertainment & Nightlife

Durham is also your best bet for lively nightlife in the county, with the student population ensuring that there's a healthy array of good pubs and clubs, including the recently refurbished classic **Klute** (✆ **0191/386-9859**). On Old Elvet, the **Dun Cow Inn** (✆ **0191/386-9219**) is, in part, a 16th-century alehouse notorious for issuing the Dun Cow Challenge—to have a beer from every pump along the bar. The impossibly narrow 12th-century **Shakespeare Tavern** on Saddler Street (✆ **0191/384-3261**) lays claim to being England's most haunted pub. For **Fabio's** bar above La Spaghettata, see above.

Where to Stay

Durham Castle ★ Durham's famous fortress offers visitors the rare chance to stay in a UNESCO World Heritage site while its student residents are on vacation, offering accommodations in single and twin rooms, some with shared bathroom facilities and others in a medieval gatehouse. There are also two much grander state rooms available year-round, with en suite facilities—the two-room Chaplain's Suite is good for families, while the Bishop's Suite has incredible 17th-century tapestries and a four-poster. Breakfasts are served in the medieval Great Hall. Parking can be tricky:

You can get a permit, subject to availability, to park overnight on Palace Green but must move by 9am. Guests get free castle tours.

Palace Green, Durham DH1 3RN. www.dur.ac.uk/university.college.commercial/acccommodation. (©) **0191/334-4106.** 177 units. £54–£74 double; £150–£200 suite. Rates include continental breakfast. MC, V. Free parking (nighttime only, subject to availability). **Amenities:** Bar/lounge. *In room:* TV (in suites).

Rockliffe Hall ★★ 🛏   Opened to critical and public acclaim in late 2009, Rockliffe Hall offers a large, state-of-the-art spa with a thermal bathing suite, an 18-hole championship golf course, and three restaurants—one with a Michelin-starred chef—on its vast riverside country estate. Within the 19th-century manor, stunning period features including carved stone pillars and fireplaces are beautifully enhanced by slick decor with a contemporary feel. Children are allowed, but you'll feel more comfortable with older children than with energetic toddlers; those 9 and up might like to sign up for the Golf Academy. As a family, you may also prefer to book one of the on-site Woodland Mews cottages, which sleep up to seven.

Hurworth on Tees, Darlington, County Durham DL2 2DU. www.rockliffehall.com.(©) **01325/729999.** 61 units. £270–£430 double; £350–£430 suite. AE, MC, DC, V. Free parking. **Amenities:** 3 restaurants and bars; swimming pool; golf course; health club & spa; room service. *In room:* TV, kitchen (in cottages), hair dryer, Wi-Fi (free).

NEWCASTLE & GATESHEAD

Newcastle: 283 miles N of London; 145 miles NE of Manchester; 121 miles S of Edinburgh

Though distinctive, these cities are physically separated by the River Tyne alone. Seven bridges, including the iconic tilting Gateshead Millennium Bridge or "Winking Eye," link them, and Newcastle and Gateshead are so closely bound that the local tourist board speaks of them as "NewcastleGateshead." Forming the core of the metropolitan county of Tyne & Wear, they have really only appeared on visitors' radars over the past few years, as major investment and development have brought new attractions in their wake.

Essentials

GETTING THERE   By direct train, Newcastle is about 3 hours from London King's Cross (around £120 for a round-trip off-peak). There are also direct trains from Manchester (p. 566), taking about 2½ hours, and from Edinburgh, taking about 1¾ hours. From Newcastle, trains take you directly to Gateshead's Metrocentre mall in less than 10 minutes, or there are ample city buses plus the city's efficient Metro light railway. Daily **National Express** buses (www.nationalexpress.com; (©) **0871/781-8181**) from London to Newcastle take 6½ hours and up.

From London, expect a drive of about 4¾ hours, most of it up the main M1/A1.

Newcastle International Airport (www.newcastleairport.com), 8 miles outside the center (linked by Metro and buses), has connections with many international and U.K. destinations. The city is also 42 miles north of Durham Tees Airport. The North Shields International Passenger Terminal, 8 miles east of the center, links Newcastle with the Netherlands.

VISITOR INFORMATION   **Newcastle Tourist Information Centre,** Central Arcade (www.newcastlegateshead.com; (©) **0191/277-8000**), is open Monday to Friday 9:30am to 5:30pm, Saturday 9am to 5:30pm, Sunday and public holidays 10am to 4pm.

Gateshead Visitor Information Centre, St. Mary's Church, Oakwell Gate, Gateshead Quays (www.newcastlegateshead.com; ✆ **0191/478-4222**), is open Tuesday to Sunday 10am to 4pm.

SPECIAL EVENTS March sees the 6-day **Newcastle Science Fest** (www. newcastlesciencefest.co.uk), with events for all ages at several venues. In June and July, the city's annual 16-day **EAT! festival** (www.eatnewcastlegateshead.com) promotes local produce with special events.

Also in June, Sunderland (19 miles south of Newcastle, with Metro links) hosts the 2-day **Sunderland International Airshow** (www.sunderlandevents.co.uk), with spectacular flying displays over the coast.

Exploring the Area
NEWCASTLE

Tell a local you're on your way to this, one of Britain's most up-and-coming and hip cities, and they'll assume you have shopping or nightlife in mind. But Newcastle is more than the sum of its leisure opportunities. It was founded about 2,000 years ago as a stronghold along Hadrian's Wall (p. 672), the ruin of which you can see at **Segedunum Roman Fort, Baths & Museum** (see below) at Wallsend east of the center (accessible by Metro).

Having grown from a Roman fort into a major port, Newcastle was a key player in the Industrial Revolution, after which, like many such places, it fell into a long decline. Part of its reawakening has come in the form of science—as well as a science fest (see "Special Events," above). To discover the best of the city itself, head for its historic heart, **Grainger Town,** north of Central Station. Here, classical streets built by Richard Grainger around 1840 contain some of Newcastle's finest buildings—Grainger Street, Clayton Street, and Grey Street are well worth a wander, with the latter voted Britain's finest street by BBC Radio 4 listeners in 2005.

But it's along the quayside that you can truly get the measure of this city's transformation, with gleaming new architecture and riverside hotels and restaurants rubbing shoulders with industrial vestiges including Stephenson's High Level Bridge. The **Gateshead Millennium Bridge**—the world's only tilting bridge (to see it when it does, check times on www.gateshead.gov.uk)—allows walkers and cyclists quick access to Gateshead.

Castle Keep ★ Overlooking the Tyne southeast of Grainger Town, this fine Norman ruin is all that is left of the "new castle" after which the city was name, built in 1168–78 by Henry II on the site of an earlier motte-and-bailey castle by William the Conqueror's son, Robert Curthose. You can still see some of the latter, along with remnants of an Anglo-Saxon cemetery and a Roman fort.

Castle Garth. www.castlekeep-newcastle.org.uk. ✆ **0191/232-7938.** Admission £4 adults, free for children 17 and under. Mon–Sat 10am–5pm; Sun noon–5pm.

Centre for Life ★★ ☺ ENTERTAINMENT COMPLEX Newcastle's cutting-edge science village is of most interest to visitors for its wonderful Science Centre, where well-thought-out interactive displays in themed areas, daily science and planetarium shows, a motion ride (with a second, 4-D version in the pipeline at the time of writing), a new Curiosity Zone for all ages, and a new under-7s hands-on zone make for a great family day out.

Discovery Sq. www.life.org.uk. ✆ **0191/243-8210.** Admission £8.25 adults, £6.45 children 2–17. Mon–Sat 10am–6pm; Sun 11am–6pm.

Discovery Museum ★ ☺ MUSEUM A budget alternative to the Centre for Life, this venue includes a science-maze gallery, a British Film Institute Mediatheque, with more than 1,800 films and TV shows from the BFI's National Archive, and various hands-on displays about the history of Newcastle and Tyneside. At the time of writing, work was in progress on a new gallery about the making of modern Tyneside.

Blandford Sq. www.twmuseums.org.uk.✆ **0191/232-6789.** Free admission. Mon–Sat 10am–5pm; Sun 2–5pm.

Great North Museum: Hancock ★★ ☺ This venue opened in 2006 to bring together several pre-existing local collections in one £26-million museum. Highlights are the large-scale, interactive model of Hadrian's Wall (p. 672), the interactive "Living Planet" gallery, with some live-animal tanks and aquariums, and the behind-the-scenes tours.

Barras Bridge. www.twmuseums.org.uk.✆ **0191/222-6765.** Free admission. Mon–Sat 10am–5pm; Sun 1–5pm.

Segedunum Roman Fort, Baths & Museum ★★ ☺ The gateway to Hadrian's Wall as well as its most excavated fort, this UNESCO World Heritage site east of the city center (accessible by Metro) has an interactive museum and a 35-m (115-ft.) viewing tour for getting an overview of the structure and the surrounding area. The highlights are the reconstructed baths with authentic frescoed walls, plunge baths, and replica Roman toilets, and the 80-m (260-ft.) section of Hadrian's Wall west of Segedunum, with a reconstructed section running alongside it, giving an impression of how it might have looked 1,800 years ago. Children get an audioguide designed as a Roman radio show, and there's a new on-site cafe.

Buddle St., Wallsend. www.twmuseums.org.uk. ✆ **0191/236-9347.** Admission adults £4.50, children 16 and under free. Apr–Oct daily 10am–5pm; Nov–Mar Sat–Sun 10am–3pm.

Seven Stories ★★ ☺ ENTERTAINMENT COMPLEX About 20 minutes' walk outside the center, this unique establishment was set up in 2005 to celebrate children's literature through permanent and temporary exhibitions on historic and contemporary authors, as well as storytelling and other activities and events. It also boasts one of the U.K.'s largest independent children's bookstores, plus a family-friendly café.

30 Lime St. www.sevenstories.org.uk. ✆ **0845/271-0777.** Admission £6.50 adults, £5.50 children 4–16. Mon–Sat 10am–5pm; Sun and public holidays 10am–4pm.

Stephenson Railway Museum ★ ☺ On the North Tyneside coast east of Newcastle (past Segedunum Roman Fort; see above), this is home to George Stephenson's "Billy" and other engines from the great age of steam. Visitors can sometimes enjoy rides pulled by heritage diesel engines, and there are family-oriented days and events.

Middle Engine Lane, North Shields. www.twmuseums.org.uk.✆ **0191/200-7146.** Free admission; train rides £2.20, children 5–15 £1.10. Apr–Oct Sat–Sun and public holiday Mon 11am–4pm; daily in school holidays except Christmas.

GATESHEAD & SUNDERLAND

The Millennium Bridge brings you to the foot of the **BALTIC Centre for Contemporary Art,** stunningly set within a former red-brick flour mill on Gateshead Quays, looming over the river. Though it rather eclipses the nearby **Shipley Art Gallery**, the

Newcastle

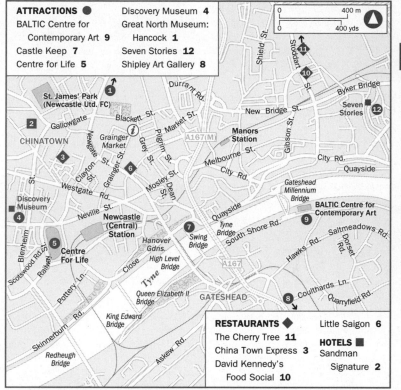

ATTRACTIONS ●

BALTIC Centre for
 Contemporary Art **9**
Castle Keep **7**
Centre for Life **5**

Discovery Museum **4**
Great North Museum:
 Hancock **1**
Seven Stories **12**
Shipley Art Gallery **8**

St. James' Park
(Newcastle Utd. FC)
Gallowgate
CHINATOWN
Blackett St.
Market St.
Durrant Rd.
Grainger
Market
Grey St.
Newgate St.
Pilgrim St.
Clayton St.
Grainger St.
Westgate Rd.
Mosley St.
Dean St.
Melbourne St.
A167(M)
New Bridge St.
Manors
Station
City Rd.
Gibson St.
Stoddart St.
Shield St.
Byker Bridge
Seven
Stories
City Rd.
Quayside
Gateshead
Millennium
Bridge
BALTIC Centre for
Contemporary Art
Quayside
Tyne
Bridge
Swing
Bridge
South Shore Rd.
Hawks Rd.
Saltmeadows Rd.
Dorset Rd.
Discovery
Museum
Neville St.
Newcastle
(Central)
Station
Hanover
Gdns.
High Level
Bridge
Close
Blenheim St.
Scotswood Rd.
Railway St.
Centre
For Life
Pottery Ln.
Tyne
Queen Elizabeth II
Bridge
GATESHEAD
Coulthards Ln.
Quarryfield Rd.
King Edward
Bridge
Skinnerburn Rd.
Redheugh
Bridge
Askew Rd.
Blenheim
A167

0 ——— 400 m
0 ——— 400 yds

RESTAURANTS ◆

The Cherry Tree **11**
China Town Express **3**
David Kennedy's
 Food Social **10**

Little Saigon **6**

HOTELS ■
Sandman
 Signature **2**

17

YORKSHIRE & THE NORTHEAST | Newcastle & Gateshead

latter is well worth a visit. The Shipley has been around since 1907, but this region's cultural renaissance is said to have been kickstarted by the building, in 1998, of the **Angel of the North,** or "Gateshead Flasher" as some locals have dubbed it—Antony Gormley's 20-m (65-ft.) tall steel sculpture of an angel on a hill at the southern edge of Low Fell, overlooking the A1 and A167 into Tyneside, as well as the main rail route. If you don't enter Gateshead via these means, the Angel Bus (no. 21; www. simplygo.com) can take you there. Carry on down to Sunderland for more cutting-edge creativity at the **Northern Gallery for Contemporary Art.**

BALTIC Centre for Contemporary Art ★★ ☺ This major international venue for contemporary visual art, which opened in 2002 and played host to the prestigious Turner Prize in 2011 (the first time it wasn't hosted by a Tate gallery), eschews a permanent collection in favor of an ever-changing roster of exhibitions and events. Arts showcased to date have included pieces by Antony Gormley, Anish Kapoor, and Sam Taylor-Wood. A whole raft of family activities include hands-on sessions and children's tours, and there are free Explorer backpacks. Don't miss the viewing box or the outdoor viewing platform for wonderful views of the Quayside and surrounding cityscape. There's also a cafe-bar and a very good rooftop restaurant, **Six.**

Gateshead Quays, South Shore Rd. www.balticmill.com. © **0191/478-1810.** Free admission. Daily 10am–6pm (from 10:30am Tues).

National Glass Centre ★   This Sunderland venue with its exhibitions, activities, and workshops about glassmaking (including the chance to try it out; pre-booking required) make this a unique choice for a day out. You can take a walk on its roof made of 6-cm thick (2½-in) glass, and there are activities for youngsters.

Liberty Way, Sunderland. www.nationalglasscentre.com. © **0191/515-5555.** Free admission. Daily 10am–5pm.

Northern Gallery for Contemporary Art ★ ☺   Also in Sunderland, this venue offers up temporary exhibitions of new work by artists from around the globe—those displayed here have included Mark Wallinger, Yves Klein, and Anton Corbijn. Work sometimes overspills the building into the surroundings—onto local billboards, for instance. There's an activity space for families and regular family activities.

City Library & Arts Centre, Fawcett St., Sunderland. www.ngca.co.uk. © **0191/561-8487.** Free admission. Mon–Wed 9:30am–7:30pm; Tues–Fri 9:30am–5pm; Sat 9:30am–4pm.

Shipley Art Gallery   Though overshadowed by the BALTIC (see above), this gallery has design and contemporary craft exhibitions that are unrivaled in the Northeast, along with an interesting collection of paintings. The focal point is the Designs for Life gallery showcasing hundreds of objects made around the globe over the last two millennia, from the unique to the mass-produced.

Prince Consort Rd. www.twmuseums.org.uk. © **0191/477-1495.** Free admission. Mon–Sat 10am–5pm; Sun 2–5pm.

WWT Washington Wetland Centre ★★ ☺   Located between Gateshead and Sunderland, these protected wetlands, meadows, and woodlands house ducks, geese, waders, flamingos, cranes, and herons, as well as frogs, bats, and goats. There are family activities galore, plus a wetlands-themed adventure play area for under-5s and an animal-themed sculpture trail.

Pattinson, Washington. www.wwt.org.uk/visit-us/washington. © **0191/416-5454.** Admission £8.45 adults, £4.25 children 4–16. Daily 9:30am–5:30pm (until 4:30pm Nov–Mar).

Where to Eat

The Cherry Tree ★★ ☺ MODERN BRITISH   Newcastle's foremost dining spot opened to critical acclaim in 2008 in the former telephone-exchange building in Jesmond, a 20-minute walk, or £7.50 taxi ride, north of the center. It's worth the detour—and the high prices. The space itself is clean, modern, buzzy, and family friendly. Sunday lunch is a highlight, with traditional roasts sharing the menu with the likes of rock halibut with crushed potatoes, wild mushrooms, and red wine sauce. Children get half-portions or their own menu. Desserts are sensational: Save room for dark-chocolate fondant with blackcurrant and liquorice sorbet, or spiced rice pudding with rum and raisin ice cream and orange shortbread.

9 Osborne Rd., Newcastle. www.thecherrytreejesmond.co.uk. © **0191/239-9924.** Reservations recommended for dinner. Main courses £13.95–£26.50. MC, V. Mon–Wed noon–2:30pm and 5–11:30pm; Sat noon–11:30pm; Sun noon–9pm.

China Town Express 🍴 CHINESE   This is the best option in Newcastle's Chinatown—centered on Stowell Street and also hosting some Korean and Japanese restaurants and shops. As the name suggests, it's canteen-like and no-frills, but for quality, authenticity, and portion sizes, it blows the fancier places in the vicinity out of the water. The salt-and-pepper squid, stewed seafood udon, and Singapore vermicelli are particularly recommended; the chicken's feet are a more acquired taste. No alcohol is served, but there's free green tea in abundance. You may have to wait, as tables can't be booked; takeout is also available.

63–65 Stowell St., Newcastle. © **0191/233-1388.** Main courses £5–£9.50. No credit cards. Daily 11:30am–11pm.

Colmans ★★ ☺ FISH & CHIPS   For award-winning seafood served by four generations of the same family, head to the coast east of Newcastle, to this restaurant and takeaway, proud holder of several national awards. Homemade fishcakes in a secret-recipe batter—featuring cod, crab, lobster, or prawns with Thai spices—may lure you away from straight fish and chips. There's a small, good-value children's menu.

176–186 Ocean Rd., South Shields, 12 miles east of Newcastle. www.colmansfishandchips.com. © **0191/456-1202.** Main courses £5.95–£21.95. MC, V. Daily 11am–7pm.

David Kennedy's Food Social ★★ ☺   Located inside the Biscuit Gallery (see below)—a changing selection of work from which is displayed on its walls—this new restaurant is the brainchild of a former North East Chef of the Year and offers a daily-changing menu of tapas-style dishes based on the freshest local produce. The flexible menu with its "social nibbles" is especially well suited to eating out with family or friends—indeed, you can pre-book "personal feasts," served in a private dining room called The Shed if you desire. Recent menu highlights have included homemade black pudding with fried Belford egg, chorizo, and garlic breadcrumbs; and braised lamb shoulder with *imam bayildi* (Turkish stuffed eggplant), wilted spinach, and chickpea fritter. Set lunch, early-evening, Sunday, and vegetarian menus are all great value.

Shieldfield. www.foodsocial.co.uk. © **0191/260-5411.** Main courses £10.50–£15.50. MC, V. Mon–Fri noon–2pm and 5:30–9pm; Sat noon–3pm and 5:30–10pm; Sun noon–3pm.

Little Saigon ★ VIETNAMESE   Ideally located for those going on to sample some of Newcastle's notoriously boisterous nightlife, or just those who love to people-watch, this is one of the best Asian restaurants in the Northeast, offering fresh-tasting, authentic Vietnamese fare at moderate prices, plus a few more elaborate specials. It's difficult to choose from the long menu of delicious-sounding treats, but sure-fire hits are the starter of soft-shell crabs with seasalt, garlic, and cut chili, and the main course of simmered tamarind king prawn. Lunch, served to 5pm, is particularly good value.

6 Bigg Market, Newcastle. www.littlesaigon.uk.com. © **0191/233-0766.** Reservations recommended. Main courses £6.50–£18.75. MC, V. Sun–Wed 11am–11pm; Thurs–Sat noon–midnight.

Shopping

Newcastle's **Eldon Square** (www.eldon-square.co.uk), one of the U.K.'s biggest city-center shopping complexes, was rather eclipsed by the arrival of Gateshead's **Metrocentre** (www.metrocentre.uk.com), Europe's biggest indoor shopping and leisure center. Combined, they make "NewcastleGateshead" a major shopping destination—and that's not including the boutiques and independent stores of High Bridge and Jesmond. Don't miss the beautifully preserved Edwardian Central Arcade in Grainger Town (p. 665), home to the Tourist Information Centre (p. 664).

If you're in the area for the art and feel inspired to invest, **The Biscuit Factory,** at 16 Stoddart St. (www.thebiscuitfactory.com; © **0191/261-1103**), is the U.K.'s biggest store for original art, selling paintings, drawings, prints, sculpture, photography, ceramics, jewelry, and glass by contemporary artists from around the globe. You can also buy contemporary art by the likes of Damien Hirst and Jake and Dinos Chapman at **Opus Art** (www.opus-art.com; © **0191/232-7389**), in the suburb of Gosforth to the north of the center, open by appointment only.

Newcastle and Gateshead are fantastic for music and theatre lovers. Newcastle's historic **Theatre Royal** (www.theatreroyal.co.uk; © **0844/811-2121**) is regional home to the Royal Shakespeare Company and hosts shows by the National Theatre, Opera North, Rambert Dance, plus West End musicals, comedy, and family shows. Also in Newcastle, the **Metro Radio Arena** (www.metroradioarena.co.uk; © **0844/493-6666**) attracts big-name rock, pop, and comedy acts. The iconic **Sage Gateshead** (www.thesagegateshead.org; © **0191/4434661**) hosts performances by its own chamber orchestra, the Northern Sinfonia, and visiting classical, pop, and jazz artists.

Newcastle is notorious for its social-drinking culture, especially around **Bigg Market** in the center. Other focal points are the Quayside and the area around Central Station with its "Diamond Strip" of upmarket bars. Jesmond is a mixture of the hip and studenty and more upmarket. The Pink Triangle, Newcastle's gay epicenter, is in the Centre for Life/Metro Radio Arena area.

Where to Stay

By far the best-located hotel in Newcastle is the **Malmaison** on the Quayside, with a stunning facade and views over the tilting bridge and toward BALTIC (£99–£125 double). Newcastle's **Hotel du Vin** is a 20-minute walk east of Quayside on City Road (© **0191/229-2200;** doubles about £120–£170).

Sandman Signature ★★ ☺   A popular addition to the Newcastle accommodations scene, with a funky boutique feel, The Sandman occupies a modern building opposite the city's football stadium, a 10-minute walk outside the center and just moments from Chinatown. Its big selling point is its flexibility—standard rooms have very comfortable king-size beds, ergonomic work desks, minifridges and microwaves, while Studios and Suites have fuller kitchens with hotplates but no ovens. Families get their own suites complete with children's bunkbeds, although King Studios and Suites also sleep four on a double pull-out sofabed in addition to a king-size bed. Ask for a room at the back if you're here when a game's on—unless you enjoy the football buzz.

Gallowgate, Newcastle, NE1 4SD. www.sandmansignature.co.uk. © **0191/229-2600.** 175 units. £99–£319 double; £125–£359 suite. AE, MC, DC, V. Parking £6/night. **Amenities:** Restaurant/sports bar; gym; room service; Wi-Fi (free). *In room:* TV, kitchen facilities (varies by room category), hair dryer, iPod docking station, Wi-Fi (free).

Souter Lighthouse Cottages ★ 📖 ☺   Pretty as a picture, these National Trust holiday cottages are on the south side of a complex of buildings attached to the shore-based, clifftop Souter Lighthouse just north of Sunderland (Cottage 1 was originally the lighthouse engineer's home). Available for 2 nights and up, each sleeps four plus a baby/toddler in a cot. Both are fairly modern yet homey in style, with touches of nautical and seabird imagery in the decor and furnishings. Children love the Robinson Crusoe feel of it all, with the old boats on-site and the wild beach at hand, but they do need to be supervised on the grounds as this is a working lighthouse (cottage guests get free guided tours of it).

Whitburn, South Tyneside SR6 7EX. www.nationaltrustcottages.co.uk. ✆ **0844/800-2070.** 2 units. £186–£486 2 nights; £372–£884 7 nights. MC, V. Free parking. Amenities: Walled garden (shared). In cottage: TV, full kitchen (w/dishwasher and washing machine), highchair, travel cot.

NORTHUMBERLAND ★★★

Newcastle: 283 miles N of London; 145 miles NE of Manchester; 121 miles S of Edinburgh

One of Britain's best-kept secrets, this northern county unfurling to the English border with Scotland attracts most visitors to its sections of **Hadrian's Wall** and the ruined Roman forts that dot its length. Few venture north of that historic line to experience the mysteries of the **Kielder Forest & Water Park** with its star-gazing facilities and modern open-air artworks, or to discover the breathtaking castles and beaches of a miraculously unspoilt and wild coastline.

Essentials

GETTING THERE   Newcastle (p. 664) is your major entry point for Northumberland, which is best explored by car (in winter, ideally a 4x4). From Newcastle, regular trains to Hexham take about a half-hour. At Hexham Station, local taxis take visitors to the main Hadrian's Wall sites about 15 miles to the northwest. A more economical option is the **Hadrian's Wall Bus** (AD122), which runs April to October between Newcastle and Carlisle, stopping at visitor attractions, towns, and villages en route (see www.hadrians-wall.org for details).

Kielder Water & Forest Park is 30 miles from Hexham, 52 miles from Newcastle; the Forest Drive is the most scenic way in but the surface is loose chip, and the route closes in winter and inclement weather.

Alnwick lies 35 miles (about 40 min.) north of Newcastle via the main A1, and Bamburgh Castle is another 17 miles (20 min.) north of Alnwick. For local buses, visit www.traveline.org.uk.

VISITOR INFORMATION   **Hexham Tourist Information Centre,** Wentworth Car Park, Wentworth Place (www.visitnorthumberland.com; ✆ **01434/652220**), is open April to October Monday to Saturday 9:30am to 5pm, Sunday 10am to 4pm; November to March Monday to Saturday 10am to 4:30pm.

Once Brewed National Park Centre, Military Road, Bardon Mill (www. northumberlandnationalpark.org.uk; ✆ **0845/155-0236**), is open April to October daily 9:30am to 5pm (Nov–Mar Sat–Sun 10am–3pm).

Tower Knowe Visitor Centre (Kielder Water & Forest Park), Kielder (www. visitkielder.com; ✆ **01434/251000**), is open April to June and September daily 10am to 5pm; July and August daily 10am to 6pm; October daily 10am to 4pm.

Alnwick Tourist Information Centre, 2 The Shambles (www.visitnorthumber land.com; ✆ **01665/511333**), is open April to October Monday to Saturday 9:30am to 5pm, Sunday 10am to 4pm; November to March Monday to Friday 9:30am to 5pm, Saturday 10am to 4pm.

For other National Park Centres, see www.northumberlandnationalpark.org.uk.

Exploring the Area
NORTHUMBERLAND NATIONAL PARK

Covering almost 400 sq. miles of some of the least populated parts of England, this **National Park,** reaching up to the border with Scotland, is noted for its wild landscapes and weather and for its associations with the northern frontier of the ancient

Roman Empire. A buffer zone between the warring English and Scots in the 13th and 14th centuries, these borderlands are most famously home to **Hadrian's Wall** ★★★ (www.hadrians-wall.org), extending 73 miles across the north of England from the North Sea to the Irish Sea. It was built in A.D. 122 by legionnaires after the visit of Emperor Hadrian, who was inspecting far frontiers of the Roman Empire and wanted to construct a dramatic line between the Empire and the barbarians. The western end is accessible from Carlisle in Cumbria, while the eastern end can be reached from Newcastle, where relics include **Segedunum Roman Fort, Baths & Museum** (p. 666).

The historic market town of **Hexham,** 24 miles west of Newcastle, is a good jumping-off point for the Wall's most scenic section—the 10-mile stretch west of Housesteads, which itself lies 2¼ miles northeast of Bardon Mill with its National Park Centre, Once Brewed (see above). Only the lower courses of the wall were preserved intact; the rest were reconstructed in the 19th century using original stones. Sights concentrated in this area include Housesteads Roman Fort & Museum and **Roman Vindolanda** and its sister site, the Roman Army Museum (see below). Within easy walking distance of the museum, **Walltown Crags** (www.english-heritage.org.uk), free to visit, is one of the wall's highest-standing and most impressive sections.

The 84-mile coast-to-coast **Hadrian's Wall Path** (www.nationaltrail.co.uk/hadrianswall) takes you along sections of the wall as well as linking to more than 80 shorter walks, some within the National Park, and, near Housesteads, with the long-distance **Pennine Way** (p. 538), which takes you north into the Cheviot Hills along the Scottish border. Not for the faint-hearted walker, these hills—wrinkled by volcanic pressures, inundated by seawater, scoured by glaciers, silted over by rivers, and thrust upward during a series of geological events—are one of England's most tortuous landscapes.

If you're not a hardened trekker, the area is best visited in the form of **Kielder Water & Forest Park.**

Housesteads Roman Fort & Museum ★★ HISTORIC SITE   Britain's most complete Roman fort, set where Hadrian's Wall climbs to a dramatic escarpment, was a base for 800 soldiers, the remains of whose barracks blocks you can view, together with the commandant's house. The museum, revamped in early 2012 to include an audiovisual exhibition on life in this hilltop settlement, holds a model of what the intact fort would have looked like.

Housesteads Farm, Haydon Bridge. www.english-heritage.org.uk. ☎ **0870/333-1181.** Admission £6 adults, £3.60 children 5–16. Apr–Sept daily 10am–6pm; Oct daily 10am–4pm; Nov–March Sat–Sun 10am–4pm.

Kielder Water & Forest Park ★★★ ☺   This natural playground covering 250 sq. miles contains Europe's largest man-made lake and England's largest working forest, and hosts activities galore including mountain-biking, watersports, forest walking trails, orienteering, and various adventure sports. There are visitor centers at Tower Knowe (see "Visitor Information," above), Kielder Castle, and Leaplish, plus an **Observatory** ★ (www.kielderobservatory.org; ☎ **07805/638469**) running star-gazing sessions—this area has the country's darkest night-skies—a salmon hatchery, and a birds-of-prey center. About half of England's native red squirrels hide out in this wildlife haven, where you may also spot otters, roe deer, and badgers, and the park is dotted with quirky modern art and architecture, including Silvas Capitalis, a wooden head you can climb in and peer out through the eyes.

30 miles northwest of Hexham. www.visitkielder.com. ✆ **01434/220616.** Free admission (car parking at visitor centers £4/day). Open 24 hr.

ALNWICK, THE COAST & HOLY ISLAND

Spectacular, often-deserted beaches (some only accessible on foot), a landscape punctuated by truly breathtaking castles, and a relative lack of crowds make Northumberland's coast one of England's loveliest corners.

Heading up from Newcastle or Hexham, stop just inland to discover **Alnwick,** the gateway to the coast but with several attractions in its own right: Medieval **Alnwick Castle** (see below), **The Alnwick Garden** (see below), and **Barter Books** (www.barterbooks.co.uk; ✆ **01665/604888**), one of Europe's largest secondhand and antiquarian bookstores, set in the former railway station and boasting a model train doing the rounds of the shelves, a children's room, and an honesty cafe in the old waiting room.

From the Coquet Estuary just southeast of Alnwick right up to Berwick-upon-Tweed, this coast is a designated Area of Outstanding Natural Beauty, with stunning beaches plus mud-flats that provide a home for waders, geese, and ducks. Starting at Cresswell, south of the Coquet Estuary, the **Northumberland Coast Path** is a 64-mile section of the North Sea Trail that also takes you as far as Berwick-upon-Tweed. The best-known beach on this stretch is Bamburgh, recognizable as the foreground for many photographs of the impossibly romantic **Bamburgh Castle** (see below), but other great beaches can be found at **Beadnell, Alnmouth,** and **Low Newton by the Sea.** The latter, a picturesque National Trust-owned 18th-century fishing village with cream-washed cottages, looks out to sea across the beach of Newton Haven and Embleton Bay to yet another wonderful fortress, **Dunstanburgh Castle** (see below).

But the jewel in the crown of the Northumberland coast lies farther north, in the form of **Holy Island** or **Lindisfarne** (www.lindisfarne.org.uk), home to a monastery that was established by St. Aidan in 635 and became the main center of learning in Christendom under St. Cuthbert, until Viking raiders destroyed the community in 875 (Cuthbert's shrine is in Durham Cathedral; p. 660). Part of visiting Lindisfarne is the adventure of getting there—this is a tidal island, so check crossing times on the website before driving over the causeway (it's also possible to get there by bus—see the website for details).

Lindisfarne and the other **Farne Islands** are a significant wildlife habitat for, among other creatures, gray seals and puffins. Boat trips (www.farne-islands.com/boat-trips; ✆ **01665/720308**) from the little resort of Seahouses will take you to Inner Farne, the only inhabited island except Lindisfarne (and then only for part of the year, by National Trust bird wardens), and a couple of other islands.

Alnwick Castle ★★★ ☺ CASTLE   Children are thrilled to recognize this medieval castle from the first two Harry Potter movies, where it doubled as "Hogwarts." In addition to family-oriented tours of the structure and grounds, the castle hosts events and activities aplenty, including Knight's Quest, when children can dress as medieval knights, make a dragon-catcher, and master medieval crafts, plus archery, hands-on workshops, falconry displays, Harry Potter-themed magic and wizardry, and historical re-enactments. Combined tickets are available with The Alnwick Garden. The Castle also administers a number of rental cottages in the area (www.alnwickcastlecottages.co.uk).

Alnwick. www.alnwickcastle.com. ✆ **01665/511100.** Admission £14 adults, £7 children 5–16. Apr–Oct daily 10am–6pm.

The Alnwick Garden ★★★ ☺ GARDEN   Set up a decade or so ago by the lady of Alnwick Castle, the Duchess of Northumberland, one of the world's most exciting contemporary gardens occupies once-derelict terrain. Though boasting beautifully landscaped gardens and splendid architecture, it was conceived with families in mind, and younger visitors get lots of opportunities to engage in water-based play, including dodging the jets of the Grand Cascade, the largest water feature of its kind in the country. There's also a Bamboo Labyrinth, rope bridges leading to The Tree-house restaurant (p. 675), and a Poison Garden where you can hear tales of deadly plants (inspiration for the teen novel *The Poison Diaries*).

Denwick Lane, Alnwick. www.alnwickgarden.com. ℂ **01665/511350.** Admission £12 adults, £4 children 5–16, students and over-60s £10.80, family £28; car parking £3.50. Apr–Oct daily 10am–6pm; Nov–Mar daily 10am–4pm; check for changes or weather-related disruptions.

Bamburgh Castle ★★★   Perhaps England's most impressive fortress of all, this seat of the kings of Northumbria sits proud on a volcanic outcrop overlooking the wave-battered coast. It's stunning enough from the outside, but you can go inside to explore 14 public areas (part of the castle houses private apartments) with the help of a new audioguide. There are also live archeological excavations.

Bamburgh. www.bamburghcastle.com. ℂ **01668/214515.** Admission £9 adults, £4 children 5–15. Mid-Feb–Oct daily 10am–5pm; rest of year Sat–Sun 11am–4:30pm.

Dunstanburgh Castle ★   This impressive ruin on its remote headland is accessible only on foot from the pleasant little resort of Craster, making a visit an adventure in itself. Dunstanburgh was built by Earl Thomas of Lancaster, Edward II's most powerful baron, in 1313, but it was John of Gaunt who strengthened it against the Scots by converting the twin-towered gatehouse into the magnificent keep you can still see part of today.

Craster. www.nationaltrust.org.uk. ℂ **01665/576231.** Admission £4 adults, £2.40 for children 5–15. Apr–Sept daily 10am–5pm; Oct daily 10am–4pm; Nov–Mar Sat–Sun 10am–4pm.

Howick Hall Gardens ★ ☺   Another highly rated spot for lovers of horticulture, Howick has a Woodland Garden, a Bog Garden mostly planted from seed collected in the wild, and a family trail in search of red squirrels, herons, and other wildlife. Its annual season starts with a Snowdrop Festival in early February and ends with a brilliant display of autumn colors in mid-November. The teahouse is named Earl Grey to denote the fact that the famous tea blend was created for Charles, 2nd Earl Grey, by a Chinese mandarin to offset the taste of lime in the water at Howick.

Off B1339 east of Alnwick. www.howickhallgardens.org. ℂ **01665/577285.** Admission £6.60 adults, children under 16 free. Feb–late Mar and late Oct–Nov Wed–Sun 10:30am–4pm; late Mar–late Oct daily noon–6pm.

Lindisfarne Castle ★★   Once safely over the causeway to Holy Island, you have to leave your car in the parking lot to discover this 16th-century Tudor fort built to protect the harbor but converted into a private house by Sir Edwin Lutyens in 1903, with a delightful walled garden by Gertrude Jekyll. Don't miss the 19th-century lime kilns on the headland—beautifully preserved and among the largest in the country—or the still-functioning wind indicator within the castle. And look out for the seals that frequently swim below the castle at high tide. There's a children's quiz/trail, but younger visitors must be strictly supervised on the site for reasons of safety.

Holy Island. www.nationaltrust.org.uk. ℂ **01289/389244.** Admission £6.95 adults, £3.50 children 5–17. Mid-Mar–Oct Tues–Sun 10am–3pm or noon–5pm, depending on tides (also Mon when public holidays or in Aug); Nov–mid-Mar two weekends a month 10am–3pm, according to tides (see www.lindisfarne.org.uk).

Lindisfarne Priory ★   Not Holy Island's original monastery but one built by Benedictine monks from Durham (p. 659) in the 12th century, this evocative ruin has a visitor center recounting the site's history, plus stunning views.

Holy Island. www.english-heritage.org.uk. ℭ **0870/333-1181.** Admission £4.90 adults, £2.90 children 5–15. Apr–Sept daily 9:30am–5pm; Oct daily 9:30am–4pm; Nov–Mar Sat–Sun 10am–4pm (daily in Feb school holiday).

Where to Eat
EXPENSIVE

Barn at Beal ★★★ ☺ SNACKS/AFTERNOON TEA/MODERN BRIT-ISH   Overlooking Lindisfarne National Nature Reserve with its sand dunes, mud-flats, and vast skies, this award-winning visitor center set up by a local farmer to educate visitors about agriculture and food fittingly promotes local produce in its restaurant, coffeeshop, and shop selling regional goodies. You can come all day for breakfast, cakes, and snacks, or dinner is served two nights a week: Think seasonal dishes such as pan-fried Beal Farm pheasant-pigeon on chestnut pearl barley risotto, with a sloe gin redcurrant glaze, or wild mushroom kale lasagna with coleslaw, salad and new potatoes. There's a birds-of-prey center and a playground on-site, plus family-friendly walks and trails and a cycle track to the Lindisfarne causeway and beyond. And you can now camp here too.

Beal Farm, Beal. www.barnatbeal.com. ℭ **01289/540044.** Reservations recommended for dinner. Main courses (Fri and Sat eves) £10.95–£17.95. MC, V. Apr–Oct daily 9:30am–6pm; Nov–Mar daily 9:30am–4pm, plus Fri–Sat 7–11pm.

The Treehouse ★ ☺ MODERN BRITISH/EUROPEAN   For the sheer wow factor, this unique restaurant in the treetops at The Alnwick Garden (p. 674) is reached via wooden bridges and has trees growing through the floor, plus a roaring fire in the cooler months. The food is surprisingly sophisticated, with the accent on organic Northumberland meats, crab, and other local seafood, and further regional specialties such as wood pigeon. Menus change seasonally but evening main courses might include guinea fowl breast and pot-roast leg with caraway cabbage, creamed potato, and brandy cream sauce, or poached potato gnocchi with shredded leeks, Northumberland smoked cheese, and chive sauce. Lunch is a substantially cheaper set menu, or you can enjoy hot or cold snacks in the bar. There's also a children's menu. Sunday lunches include traditional roasts, and some evenings see performances of traditional Northumbrian music. You don't need a ticket to the Garden to visit the restaurant.

Denwick Lane, Alnwick. www.alnwickgarden.com. ℭ **01665/511852.** Reservations recommended. Main courses £13.95–£24.95 (dinner). MC, V. Daily noon–2:45pm, plus Thurs–Sun 6:30–11pm.

MODERATE

The Olde Ship Inn ★ TRADITIONAL BRITISH   A fine spot for real ales beside a warming log fire, this traditional pub by the tiny harbor of the resort town of Seahouses is about as nautical as they come. Its wooden floor is made from ships' decking, it has nautical artifacts galore, and there are model fishing boats and a replica of the lifeboat *The Grace Darling*, named after a local lighthousekeeper's daughter who saved 13 people from a shipwreck in Victorian times. There's a casual bar menu including homemade soup, sandwiches, and seafood, plus a lunch and evening menu with traditional favorites such as steak and ale pie and rich desserts including ginger trifle. Evenings, there's also a children's menu; younger guests are welcome in the snug cabin or the beer garden with its harbor and Farne Island views. There are about 20 **guest rooms** and apartments on-site or nearby.

Seahouses. www.seahouses.co.uk. © **01665/720200.** Main courses £9.50–£14.75. MC, V. Mon–Sat 11am–11pm; Sun noon–11pm.

INEXPENSIVE

In northern Northumberland, **Pinnacles in Seahouses,** 17–19 Main St. (© **01665/720708**), serves very good fish and chips in basic surroundings.

Coastline ★ 🎒☺   It's worth going out of your way to visit this huge fish and chip restaurant and takeaway by the beach in southern Northumberland (back toward Newcastle). Its award-winning cod and haddock are both locally caught and sustainably sourced where possible, as well as excellent value. There's also a new in-house ice-cream parlor, **Ciccarelli's**, serving homemade Italian gelato, as well as breakfasts, Italian coffee, and cakes and pastries.

Links Rd., Blyth. http://coastlinefishandchips.co.uk. © **01670/797428.** Main courses £5–£8. MC, V. Summer Mon–Sat 11am–8pm, Sun 11am–7pm; winter Mon–Sat 11am–7pm, Sun 11–5pm; Ciccarelli's summer Mon–Sat 8am–8pm, Sun 8am–7pm; winter Mon–Sat 8am–7pm, Sun 8am–5pm.

Where to Stay

VERY EXPENSIVE

Langley Castle Hotel ★★   West of Hexham, England's only medieval fortified castle to welcome paying guests has atmosphere in spades, with its 14th-century spiral staircase, vast open hearths, and windows set into thick walls, many of which—in guest rooms and the bar—have been turned into quirky seating areas. All rooms are unique; some can accommodate a family of five. The best, the Feature Castle rooms, have unexpectedly luxurious modern bathrooms, some with a spa tub and sauna. Most rooms have a four-poster bed. The newer Castle View rooms, in a converted building, lack the atmosphere of the castle but may be preferred by families—Superior units have living rooms with sofabeds, affording some privacy for parents. Good food is available most of the day, including afternoon tea and a set lunch/"Early Knight" menu from noon to 6pm. Children get their own menu. Guests can tour the turrets, weather permitting.

Langley-on-Tyne, Tynedale, Northumberland NE47 5LU. www.langleycastle.com. © **01434/688888.** 27 units. £149–£275 double; £189 suite. Rates include English breakfast. AE, MC, V. Free parking. **Amenities:** Restaurant; bar; room service; babysitting. *In room:* TV, minibar (some), hair dryer, spa bath and sauna (some), Wi-Fi (free).

Matfen Hall Hotel, Golf & Spa ★★ ☺   In countryside northeast of Hexham and also a handy option for those exploring Newcastle (p. 664) but not wishing to stay in the city, this stately home within its own parkland is home to a Go Ape! adventure course (www.goape.co.uk) for ages 10 and over, so it's a great place to bring active teens or pre-teens (though you don't have to stay on-site to use the course). There's also a bird-of-prey center, an indoor pool, and a children's menu in the Keeper's Lodge "pub restaurant" or family dining (6–7pm) in the Library Print Room Restaurant. But parents aren't forgotten—there's a very good spa. The rooms, some set up for families, come in a variety of guises, from fairly traditional in the old part of the hall to more contemporary in the newer part. If you feel like exploring, ask for a map of local routes, a Matfen Wildlife leaflet, and a packed lunch from the kitchen, or inquire about the Hadrian's Wall Adventure tour.

Matfen, Northumberland NE20 0RH. www.primahotels.co.uk/matfen. ℂ **01661/880-6500.** 53 units. £99–£315 double. Rates include breakfast (half-board available). AE, DC. MC, V. Free parking. **Amenities:** 3 restaurants; bar; golf; indoor pool, health club & spa; adventure course; children's book/DVD/games library. *In room:* TV, DVD (by request), hair dryer.

EXPENSIVE

Chillingham Castle ★ ☺ A good choice for those enraptured by the lovely castles that pepper Northumberland, this 12th-century stronghold in Capability Brown-designed grounds 20 minutes' inland of Bamburgh offers several self-catering apartments (the largest sleeping seven or more), plus ghost tours on certain evenings. There are also daytime tours of the parkland, state rooms, dungeons, and torture chamber, and tours to see the world's only wild cattle (www.chillinghamwildcattle. com). You don't have to stay here to book a tour, but many visitors can't resist the chance to stay in a medieval castle or its former coaching rooms (rooms in the latter are larger but cheaper). The very private Guard Room, for couples, is where the relief watchmen slept. Furnishings are homey rather than plush, with a shabby-chic esthetic. Beware that some guests can find the castle a bit *too* spooky…

Chillingham, Northumberland NE66 5NJ. www.chillingham-castle.com. ℂ **01668/215359.** 8 units. £100–£170 apartment for 2; £200–£340 apartment for 4. MC, V. **Amenities:** Free access to parkland and garden; castle tours (extra charge). *In room:* TV, kitchen.

MODERATE

Coastal Retreats ★★ 🎁 ☺ The Northumberland coast is prime holiday cottage territory, but Coastal Retreats stands out, with all its cottages and beach apartments awarded the English Tourism Council's 5 Stars Self Catering accreditation. The contemporary interiors are professionally designed and include little luxuries such as woolen throws; some have wood-burning stoves. Children are welcomed with dressing-up boxes, Wendy houses (playhouses), games rooms, trampolines, and more—the firm's own Starfish child-friendliness rating system helps find the best option for your family. Leisure club membership is included for those who'd like a swim or some pampering.

Northumberland coast (various addresses). www.coastalretreats.co.uk. ℂ **0191/285-1272.** £470–£1,299 cottage for 4 per week (shorter stays available). MC, V. Free parking. **Amenities:** Vary by cottage but generally include games and toys; games room; health club membership. *In room:* TV/DVD, CD player, books, kitchen, movie library, wood-burning stove (some), Wi-Fi (free).

CARDIFF & THE SOUTH OF WALES

by Nick Dalton & Deborah Stone

This is a land of hills and history, of castles and sandy coves. Yet for every ancient site, there's a modern restaurant serving locally produced organic food. Cardiff, the country's capital, is a vibrant destination, and Swansea, Wales's second city, is hot on its heels. What once was a heartland of the Industrial Revolution now welcomes tourists to the old mining towns as well as to the timeless and beautiful beaches of the Gower Peninsula and Pembrokeshire.

CITIES & TOWNS Cardiff's old docks have been reinvented as the buzzing **Cardiff Bay.** The **Cardiff Bay Barrage** keeps the sea placid, and now the water laps against quaysides alive with restaurants and attractions. It's a perfect counterpoint to the city's fairytale castle, world-class museum, and extensive shopping. To the west is **Swansea,** a sea-front city with its own revamped docks **(the Maritime Quarter),** cool hotels and beaches on **The Mumbles.** At Wales's westernmost point is **St. Davids,** Britain's smallest city, with a beautiful cathedral.

COUNTRYSIDE The **Brecon Beacons National Park,** a wonderland of mountains, waterfalls, and stunning walks, is at the region's heart, but there is so much more. From the stark **Black Mountains** to the meandering valleys near **Rhayader** with their astonishing collection of **Victorian dams,** there's a beauty spot at every turn. There are walks along rivers, in forests, and up **Pen y Fan,** the south's highest peak.

EATING & DRINKING This is a major food area, whether it's **Welsh lamb** grazed on lush hillsides or the **bounty of the sea.** Sophisticated restaurants are springing up all over, and boutique producers even extend to the **ice creams** of Cadwaladers, Gianni's, and Joe's. And **Welsh cakes,** a flat, sugary treat, are as good as ever.

COAST The dazzling beaches on the west coast (**Newgale** near St. Davids is jaw-dropping) and the **Gower's** fine sands get all the publicity, but there are special places all around the coastline; drive down a tiny lane and chances are you'll find a hidden spot. Resort towns are interspersed with extraordinary **castles,** and there are clifftop walks and boat trips, watersports, and fishing villages. And the **Pembrokeshire Coast Path**

offers a 186-mile walk that in early summer 2012 became part of the 870-mile Wales Coast Path from one end of the country to the other.

THE best TRAVEL EXPERIENCES IN CARDIFF & THE SOUTH OF WALES

○ **Hitting the beach:** Here are some of the world's most stunning stretches of sand: Almost anywhere on the Gower Peninsula (especially Three Cliffs Bay; p. 707); Pembrokeshire (the desert island feel of lovely Barafundle Bay; p. 711); craggy cliff-backed Mwnt, near Cardigan, with its sandy beach and crystal-clear sea (p. 717); and the dunes and soft white sand of Dyfi National Nature Reserve (p. 718).

○ **Going underground:** You appreciate the hard life of the coal miner when you see the bleak mountainside entrance of the Big Pit, especially when it's covered in snow. The underground tour, a light strapped to your helmet, takes your breath away. Go down the pit, too, at Rhondda Heritage Park (also coal) and Dolaucothi gold mine. See p. 692.

○ **Storming the castle:** Whether it's Cardiff (a Victorian fairytale reconstruction of an ancient site; p. 682), Caerphilly (Britain's second largest castle; p. 685), the impressive Norman fortress of Pembroke (p. 711), or others, the castles of Wales are all magnificent and wildly different from one another.

○ **Exploring the countryside:** It's easy to get away from it all here, up mountains, by lakes, on hills, in valleys, and on coastal cliffs. Stroll along rushing rivers, or drive down remote roads with extraordinary scenery featuring gently undulating pastures, magical forests, and picturesque peaks around every turn.

○ **Watching the wildlife:** Whether it's a relaxing trip out to spot dolphins in Cardigan Bay (p. 717), to see nesting cliff birds near Whitesands Bay (p. 715), or watching red kites circling overhead just about everywhere, there's plenty going on.

CARDIFF ★

155 miles W of London; 110 miles SW of Birmingham; 40 miles SE of Swansea

From the exciting, arty waterfront of **Cardiff Bay** to the growing number of smart shops in the heart of the city, and from the fairytale fantasy of **Cardiff Castle** to the Aladdin's cave of the **National Museum and Gallery,** this is a city that combines new and old to great effect. Once you take in the outskirts (the even more fairytale **Castell Coch,** the rural delights of **St. Fagans: National History Museum,** Newport's Roman remains, and the seaside of Penarth), you've got a real holiday before even venturing farther afield. This is Europe's youngest capital city, designated as such only in 1955, although it has long been the country's leading urban center. Even though its roots can be traced back to 600 B.C., when the Celts invaded, the Cardiff of today is vibrant. The Victorian indoor market rubs shoulders with the twin, upmarket malls of St. David's 1 and 2, traditional pubs sit next to modern bars, and you'll find some very cool hotels.

Essentials

GETTING THERE   Trains (First Great Western) from London Paddington arrive at Central Station on Wood Street every half-hour during the day, costing around about £40 one-way; the journey takes 2 hours. There are also regular services from cities such as Bristol, Birmingham, Edinburgh, and Glasgow.

National Express (www.nationalexpress.com; ✆ **0871/781-8181**) has frequent buses from London (a 3½-hr. journey) and from other cities.

Cardiff International Airport (www.tbicardiffairport.com; ✆ **01446/711111**) is 12 miles west of the city. **Eastern Airways** (www.easternairways.com; ✆ **0870/366-9100**) has 11 flights a week from Newcastle. **Flybe** (www.flybe.com; ✆ **0871/700-2000**) has up to four flights a day from Glasgow and six from Edinburgh. Flybe also has two daily flights connecting Cardiff with Paris. **KLM** (www.klm.com; ✆ **0871/231-0000**) flies daily between Cardiff and Amsterdam; **Aer Lingus** (www.aerlingus.com; ✆ **0871/718-5000** from U.K.) has two daily flights connecting Cardiff with Dublin (with connections to and from New York and Boston). Spanish low-cost airline Vueling (www.vueling.com; ✆ **0906/7547541**) has a service to Barcelona three days a week.

Cardiff Bus (www.cardiffbus.com; ✆ **0871/200-2233**) operates bus X91 between the airport and bus station (in front of the rail station) hourly from around 7am to 7pm Monday to Friday; Saturdays from around 6am, Sundays 10am. A one-way trip is £3.60 (children £2.40).

VISITOR INFORMATION **Cardiff Tourist Information Centre,** at the Old Library, the Hayes (www.visitcardiff.com; ✆ **029/2087-3573**), is in the heart of the city. Hours are Monday to Saturday 9:30am to 5:30pm, Sunday 10am to 4pm (July–Aug daily 9:30am–7pm). The Cardiff Bay office, the Tube, on Harbour Drive (✆ **029/2046-3833**), is open daily 10am to 6pm.

GETTING AROUND Don't expect to use a car while you're here. Many of the places you'll want to visit are within walking distance of one another, and there's a good bus service, even to sights on the outskirts, although Sunday services are less frequent. One of your main journeys will be between city and Bay, which are connected by the Baycar bendy-bus every few minutes. The **Valley Lines Day Explorer** rail ticket (www.arrivatrains.co.uk), available from any station, gives unlimited travel on trains and buses around Cardiff, and up to Merthyr Tydfil for £10 adults, £5 children. Buses cost £1.60 (children £1.10). The **Cardiff Bus** office (**Bws Caerdydd** in Welsh), across from the bus station in Wood Street (www.cardiffbus.com; ✆ **029/2066-6444**), has full route details. It's open Monday to Friday 8:30am to 5:30pm, Saturday 9am to 4:30pm. Taxi fares range from around £7 to £15. There are taxi stands at the rail and bus station and at St. David's Hall. Hotels and restaurants will call taxis for you, or contact **Capital Cabs** (www.capitalcabs.co.uk; ✆ **029/2077-7777**).

A good way to get an overall view of the city is a hop-on hop-off open-top bus tour by **City Sightseeing** (www.city-sightseeing.com; ✆ **029/2047-3432**). Tours start outside Cardiff Castle. Adults pay £10.50, children ages 5 to 15 £5.50. Tour times change from month to month.

[FastFACTS] CARDIFF

Area Code   The area code for Cardiff is **029**.

Dentist   For emergencies, contact **Parade Dental Practice,** 23 The Parade (www. parade-dentists.co.uk; ✆ **029/2048-1486**).

South Wales

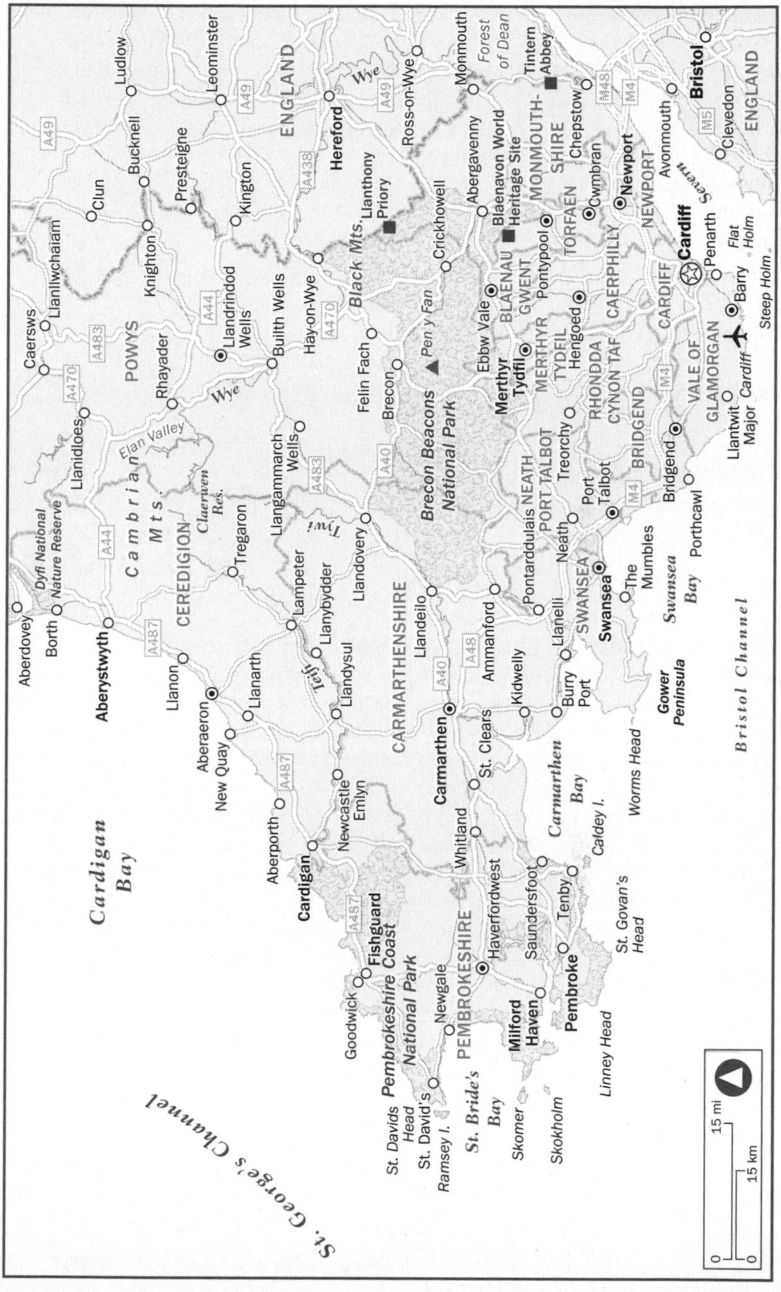
Cardigan Bay
St. George's Channel
Bristol Channel
St. Bride's Bay
Carmarthen Bay
Swansea Bay
Severn
Aberdovey
Borth
Dyfi National Nature Reserve
Aberystwyth
Llanon
Aberaeron
New Quay
Llanarth
Aberporth
Cardigan
Newcastle Emlyn
Llandysul
Llanybydder
Lampeter
Tregaron
Teifi
Goodwick
Fishguard
Pembrokeshire Coast National Park
St. Davids Head
St. David's
Ramsey I.
Newgale
PEMBROKESHIRE
Haverfordwest
Milford Haven
Pembroke
Skomer
Skokholm
Linney Head
Saundersfoot
Tenby
Caldey I.
St. Govan's Head
Whitland
St. Clears
Carmarthen
CARMARTHENSHIRE
Kidwelly
Burry Port
Llanelli
Llandeilo
Ammanford
Pontarddulais
Llandovery
Tywi
Llangammarch Wells
Gower Peninsula
Worms Head
Swansea
SWANSEA
The Mumbles
Neath
NEATH PORT TALBOT
Port Talbot
Porthcawl
Bridgend
BRIDGEND
Treorchy
RHONDDA CYNON TAF
Llantwit Major
Cardiff
VALE OF GLAMORGAN
Barry
Steep Holm
Flat Holm
Penarth
CARDIFF
Cardiff
CAERPHILLY
Hengoed
MERTHYR TYDFIL
Merthyr Tydfil
Ebbw Vale
BLAENAU GWENT
Pontypool
TORFAEN
Cwmbran
Newport
NEWPORT
Blaenavon World Heritage Site
Abergavenny
MONMOUTH-SHIRE
Chepstow
Tintern Abbey
Monmouth
Forest of Dean
Ross-on-Wye
Hereford
Llanthony Priory
Black Mts.
Crickhowell
Pen y Fan
Brecon Beacons National Park
Brecon
Felin Fach
Hay-on-Wye
Builth Wells
Llandrindod Wells
Rhayader
Wye
Elan Valley
Claerwen Res.
Cambrian Mts.
CEREDIGION
Llanidloes
Caersws
Llanllwchaiam
POWYS
Knighton
Clun
Bucknell
Presteigne
Kington
Ludlow
Leominster
ENGLAND
Avonmouth
Bristol
Clevedon
A49
A483
A470
A44
A487
A40
A48
A438
M4
M5
M48
0
15 mi
15 km

Doctor   For emergencies, dial ☏ **999** and ask for an ambulance. Doctors are on 24-hour call. A full list of doctors is posted at all post offices.

Drugstores (Pharmacies)   **Boots the Chemist** has various stores in town. The main prescription dispensing service is at 5 Wood St. (www.boots.com; ☏ **029/2037-7043**), open Monday to Friday 8am to 6:30pm, Saturday 9am to 6pm.

Emergencies   For police, fire service, or ambulance, dial ☏ **999.**

Hospitals   The main hospital is the **University Hospital of Wales** (also known as the Heath Hospital), Heath Park (☏ **029/2074-7747**).

Internet Access   Wi-Fi is free in an increasing number of bars, coffee shops, and hotels. Or you can use **McDonald's,** 12–14 Queen St. (Sun–Thurs 5am–midnight; Fri–Sat open 24 hr.).

Maps   **Cardiff Tourist Information Centre,** the Old Library, The Hayes (☏ **029/2087-3573**), has a selection, and lots of free brochures.

Police   **Central Cardiff Police Station** is at King Edward VII Avenue, Cathays Park (☏ **029/2022-2111**).

Post Office   The main post office is at 45–46 Queens Arcade, Queen Street, (Mon–Sat 9am–5:30pm).

Exploring the City

Bute Park ★ PARK   Once the playground of the fabulously rich Bute family, this Capability Brown-designed park extends from the back of their home, Cardiff Castle. There are gardens, an arboretum, open spaces, and the River Taff runs right through it.

Castle St./North Rd. ☏ **029/2068-4000.** Free admission. Daily dawn to dusk. Bus: 32 or 62.

Cardiff Castle ★★★ CASTLE   If you only have time for one thing, take a guided tour of this fantasyland. There's been a fort here since Roman times, and the 12th-century Norman keep is still intact, with fabulous views from its tower. But what's now known as Cardiff Castle was built in Victorian times in Gothic style by the 3rd Marquess of Bute, reputedly the richest man in the world as owner of South Wales's coal mines, the railway that took the coal to the docks, and the docks themselves. Exquisite wall paintings depict fables, fairytales, and Biblical stories. Highlights include the banqueting hall with minstrels' gallery where the Queen and Prince Charles have dined; the ladies' sitting room, cheekily decorated like a harem; and the rooftop garden. Best of all is the nursery with painted wall tiles depicting nursery rhymes and fairy stories. The last tour starts an hour before closing; though you have to stick with a guide for the castle itself, you can wander freely around the grounds, walls, keep, and military museum. The tours get busy so arrive, book, and then explore.

Castle St. www.cardiffcastle.com. ☏ **029/2087-8100.** Admission £11 adults, £9 students and seniors, £7.95 children 5–16. Mar–Oct daily 9am–6pm; Nov–Feb daily 9am–5pm. Last admission 1 hr. before closing. Closed Dec 25–26 and Jan 1. Bus: 32 or 62.

Cathays Park ★ PARK   Behind the National Museum and City Hall, this is a small oasis of calm, home to the Temple of Peace, which houses the Welsh Book of Remembrance. Within the park are Alexandra Gardens and the Welsh National War Memorial, a circular court of columns and sculptures dating from 1928.

Civic Centre. www.cardiff.ac.uk. ☏ **029/2087-1847.** Free admission. Daily dawn to dusk. Bus: 32 or 62.

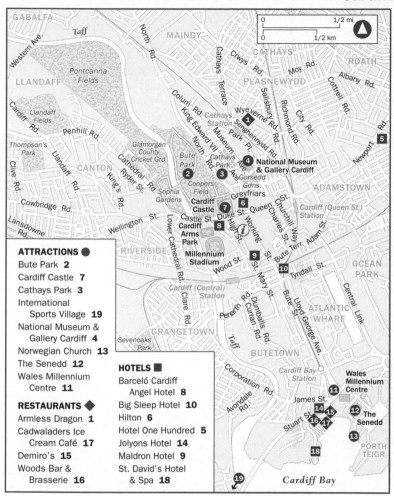

ATTRACTIONS ●

Bute Park **2**
Cardiff Castle **7**
Cathays Park **3**
International
  Sports Village **19**
National Museum &
  Gallery Cardiff **4**
Norwegian Church **13**
The Senedd **12**
Wales Millennium
  Centre **11**

RESTAURANTS ◆

Armless Dragon **1**
Cadwaladers Ice
  Cream Café **17**
Demiro's **15**
Woods Bar &
  Brasserie **16**

HOTELS ■

Barceló Cardiff
  Angel Hotel **8**
Big Sleep Hotel **10**
Hilton **6**
Hotel One Hundred **5**
Jolyons Hotel **14**
Maldron Hotel **9**
St. David's Hotel
  & Spa **18**

National Museum & Gallery Cardiff ★★ ☺ MUSEUM In the grand tradition of British museums, this magnificent, domed building has a bit of everything: One of the biggest collections of Impressionist paintings outside Paris, a wealth of Monets, Manets, Van Goghs, and Cezannes; big names from other movements including the Pre-Raphaelites; even a Rodin bronze. But this is a full-fledged family attraction, with an "Evolution of Wales" section that takes you from the Big Bang to dinosaur skeletons, an animatronic woolly mammoth to the hands-on Clore Discovery Centre.

Cathays Park, Civic Centre. www.museumwales.ac.uk. ✆ **029/2039-7951.** Free admission except for special exhibitions (prices vary). Tues–Sun and public holidays 10am–5pm. Bus: 32 or 62.

Exploring Cardiff Bay

In 1999, the Barrage was built (basically a massive sea wall) across the bay, creating a vast freshwater lake accessible to vessels only via a lock. It is a mecca for sailing and other watersports, its shores full of attractions. **Cardiff Bay** ★★, the redeveloped area of the old docks of Tiger Bay, is about 1½ miles from town. **Cardiff Bay Visitor Centre,** the Tube, Harbour Drive (www.visitcardiff.com; ✆ **029/2046-3833**), open 10am to 6pm, is an attraction in itself. It looks like a beached submarine and has films, exhibitions, a scale model of the city, and lots of free information. The **Waterbus** (www.cardiffcats.com; ✆ **07940/142409**) costs £2.50 one-way, £5 round-trip (children 2–14 half-price) and leaves the city's Taff Mead Embankment every few minutes. It stops at Mermaid Quay for Bay attractions, and at the Barrage for the beach resort of Penarth on its 30-minute tour. The Barrage (www.cardiffharbour.com) is open daily (free admission), for windy strolls and bicycle rides from Bay attractions to Penarth. There's even a windswept cafe. Pont y Werin, a 140-m (460-ft.) footbridge, with 20-m (66-ft.) lifting section to let boats through, now crosses the mouth of the Taff, providing a second link to the Penarth side, completing a 6.2-mile circular Bay Trail (www.cardiffharbour.com has a downloadable map).

International Sports Village WATERSPORTS/SPORTS   A waterfront complex that includes International White Water (an Olympic standard rafting course, open to all levels), Cardiff International Pool (an Olympic-sized swimming pool, with flumes and a lazy river), and the temporary Ice Arena (known as Planet Ice, and home to the Cardiff Devils Ice Hockey team). Nearby is the Water Activity Centre (rowing, sailing, windsurfing). Work on a £200 million ice area and indoor real-snow ski slope in the Sports Village (including two hotels, one of them 6-star) is due to start in spring 2013 for completion by summer 2014.

www.visitcardiffbay.info. Cardiff International White Water, Watkiss Way. (www.ciww.com, ✆ **029/2082-9970**) Mon, Tues, Sat 8am–5pm, Wed–Fri 9am–8pm, Sun 9am–4pm; rafting £45–50 per person for 2 hours. Cardiff International Pool, Olympian Drive (www.leisurecentre.com, ✆ **029-2072/9090**). Mon–Fri 6am–10pm , Sat.7am–6:30pm, Sun 8am–8:30pm; adults £3.95, under 16s £2.95. Planet Ice, Empire Way (www.planet-ice.co.uk, ✆ **029-2038/2001**). Varying daily public sessions Mon–Fri starting at 10am, 1pm and 4pm, plus 7:30pm Fri. Sat–Sun 11am–4pm session. Prices from £5.40 (£7.40 with skates). Also skating lessons. Bus: Baycar, 7, 8, or 35.

Norwegian Church CHURCH   This white, clapboard church by the sea wall was built to serve the Norwegian seamen of the old docks; it's where *Charlie and the Chocolate Factory* author Roald Dahl, a local boy of Norwegian descent, was christened. Today it's an arts center and cafe worth a swift look, and nice for a coffee and Norwegian cake or snack at the outdoor tables gazing over the water.

Harbour Drive. www.norwegianchurchcardiff.com. ✆ **029/2045-4899.** Free admission. Daily 9am–5pm. Bus: Baycar, 7, 8, or 35.

The Senedd ARCHITECTURE/GOVERNMENT BUILDING   This is the modernistic home of the Welsh Assembly, opened by the Queen in 2006. Visitors can take a free tour of the eco-friendly building (after airport-style security screening) and watch debates from the gallery under a wonderful, undulating wooden ceiling.

www.assemblywales.org. ✆ **0845/010-3300.** Free admission. Assembly term time Mon and Fri 9:30am–4:30pm, Tues–Thur 8am to end of business; recess Mon–Fri 9:30am–4:30pm. All year Sat, Sun and bank holidays 10:30am–4:30pm. Recess is late July to late Sept, early Dec to early Jan and various other holiday periods. Bus: Baycar, 7, 8, or 35.

The **National St. David's Day Parade** (www.stdavidsday.org) is a March celebration of Wales's patron saint, featuring musicians and dancers in national or historical dress as well as medieval re-enactments. The parade, in the afternoon, has a finale at the National Museum, but there are events late into the evening. Cardiff Bay is host to many free festivals (www.cardiff-festival.com) from **Cardiff International Food &** **Drink Festival,** which snakes around the waterfront featuring the best of Welsh creations plus produce from the rest of the world, to **WOW on the Waterfront,** a celebration of dance and music (both in July). The **Harbour Festival** (Aug public holiday) is one of the most popular, a weekend of family fun, food, and music along a nautical theme, with water-based activities and visits to tall ships at anchor.

Wales Millennium Centre ENTERTAINMENT COMPLEX The building that's the face of Cardiff Bay is an iconic arts hall with giant poetry cut into its copper roof. The auditorium, like a red-rock canyon from the American West, is stunning. Welsh stone, wood, metal, and glass have been used, and Welsh artists have produced fixtures, and public art. There's often a free lunchtime lobby concert, which you can watch from a cafe-bar. A tour gets you among giant sets, racks of costumes, and dressing rooms. See "Entertainment & Nightlife," below, for information on the performing arts here.

Bute Place. www.wmc.org.uk. © **0870/040-2000.** Free admission to lobby; backstage tours £5.50 adults, £4.50 children 5–15. Daily from 10am. Bus: Baycar, 7, 8, or 35.

Exploring Beyond the City

Penarth is the delightful timewarp seaside resort across Cardiff Bay (walkable from the Barrage). The high street dives down the hill to a mostly elegant promenade, and the beach (part rocky, part sandy). There's a pier where the paddle steamers MV *Balmoral* and PS *Waverly* call in summer. Kiosks sell chips (fries) with gravy, and Joe's ice cream from Swansea. **Piersons** is an old-style hotel with a modern flourish while **Mediterraneo,** in an old boat house, is a chic Italian seafood restaurant.

Caerleon Roman Baths & Amphitheatre HISTORIC SITE One of the most important Roman sites in Britain, this is where the Second Augustan Legion (5,500 men) built a township, fortress, and barracks. The remains of the huge bathhouse are preserved in a modern hall, with walkways above them. Along the road, on the site of the fortress, is the National Roman Legion Museum (free), full of pottery, coins, and artifacts. The amphitheatre, around the corner in the middle of a field, has stone banks encompassing the arena, once alive with pageantry and bloodlust. Now it's a great place to picnic, and in the summer there are often plays and living history enactments.

High St., Caerleon, Newport. www.cadw.cymru.gov.uk. © **01633/422518.** Admission to baths: £2.90 adults, £2.50 children 5–15. Apr–Oct daily 9:30am–5pm; Nov–Mar Mon–Sat 9:30am–5pm, Sun 11am–4pm. Amphitheatre: free, accessible all year.

Caerphilly Castle ★★ CASTLE Crossing the bridge over the moat around the biggest medieval castle in Wales you are left breathless at the sheer size of the 30-acre fortress. One tower leans at what looks like a dangerously drunken angle, but it only adds to the impressiveness of this 13th-century wonder built on three man-made islands and surrounded by artificial lakes created by damming the Nant y Gledr stream. It still looks as impregnable now as it did then with its concentric walls-within-walls design. You can wander into the Great Hall but there's no fancy interior, even though it was restored by the 3rd Marquess of Bute.

On the A469, at Caerphilly. www.cadw.cymru.gov.uk. © **029/2088-3143.** Admission £4 adults, £3.60 children 15 and under. Mar–June and Sept–Oct daily 9:30am–5pm; July–Aug daily 9:30am–6pm; Nov–Feb Mon–Sat 10am–4pm, Sun 11am. Bus: 26 from Cardiff leaves for Caerphilly each hour (also bus no. 71 or 72). Caerphilly train with several departures daily from Central Station in Cardiff.

Castell Coch ★★★ CASTLE   The most beautiful castle in Wales looks like the fantasy fortress in *Chitty Chitty Bang Bang* in its tree-lined hillside position. You can even see it from the ramparts of Cardiff Castle, which is fitting as both were holiday homes for the fabulously rich 3rd Marquess of Bute. He presided over the flamboyant Victorian rebuild of a medieval castle ruin to create a *Harry Potter*-esque fantasy that clings to the mountainside and is approached through a thick forest overlooking a gorge in the Taff Valley. Like its city cousin, the interior is a sumptuous Arts and Crafts-style interpretation of medieval decor. Scenes from Aesop's Fables decorate the walls and ceilings of the living rooms, while the bedrooms are each an individual fantasy. There are spiral staircases and even a working portcullis and drawbridge.

Tongwynlais. www.cadw.cymru.gov.uk. © **029/2081-0101.** Admission £3.80 adults, £3.40 children 15 and under. Apr–June, Sept, Oct daily 9:30am–5pm; July–Aug daily 9:30am–6pm; Nov–Feb daily 10am–4pm (Bus: 132 from Cardiff leaves every 30 min. (60 min. on Sun) for Tongwynlais, a half-mile away.

Dr Who Experience ★★★ ATTRACTION   A flashing, crashing homage to the science-fiction hero who has been scaring TV audiences for almost half a century. This attraction, which opened in spring 2012, is in a purpose-built home next to the new BBC studios on Cardiff Bay where the series is filmed. There is interactive fun along with an ever-changing collection of costumes, from historic outfits to those that are whisked back for more filming, along with monsters (daleks, cybermen, and the like) plus touches of alien-hunting spin-off Torchwood (now a joint U.S.–U.K. production).

Porth Teigr, Cardiff Bay. www.drwhoexperience.com. © **0844/801 2279.** Admission £15 adults, £11 children 16 and under, family ticket £46 (about 15% discount for advance bookings). Wed–Mon 10am–5pm (daily in school holidays). Timed tickets; last entry 2:30pm. Bus: Baycar, 7, 8, or 35.

Dyffryn Gardens GARDEN   Only several miles from the city but deep in the Vale of Glamorgan, these Edwardian gardens cover 55 acres. Centerpoint is a collection of gardens, all clipped hedges, lovely brickwork, and formal planting, but there are also neat lawns, seasonal planting, and an arboretum with trees from around the world. There's been intensive effort to restore the 1906 glory of leading designer Thomas Mawson. A tearoom sits on the banks of a stream.

St. Nicholas, Vale of Glamorgan. www.dyffryngardens.org.uk. © **029/2059-3328.** £6.50 adults (£5 Nov–Feb), £2.50 (£2) children 5–15. Mar–Oct daily 10am–6pm; Nov–Feb daily 10am–4pm.

Llandaff Cathedral ★ CATHEDRAL   You can feel the history creeping up on you at one of the oldest Christian sites in Britain, where there was a community as far back as the 6th century. The current cathedral dates from the start of the 12th century, and accumulated classic features down the centuries: From the West Front (a medieval work of art) through Italian Temple touches from the 1700s to Sir Jacob

Epstein's aluminum statue *Christ in Majesty*, part of the rebirth following a World War II bomb. The cathedral sits at the western edge of the city, on a green with a village atmosphere surrounded by timbered buildings.

Cathedral Rd. www.llandaffcathedral.org.uk. © **029/2056-4554.** Free admission. Daily 7am–7pm. Call for times of services. Bus: 25, 33, 33A, or 62.

St. Fagans: National History Museum ★★ MUSEUM This wonderful open-air museum has more than 40 historic Welsh buildings from around the country, restored to their former glory, on the 100-acre grounds of St. Fagans Castle. It's so beautifully laid-out that you really do feel as though you're skipping down country lanes, walking through a century-old village, or exploring the Middle Ages. There's a farm, school, chapel, and ironmongers, as well as Celtic huts with fires burning, and shields and swords for children to wield. Craftspeople, such as the potter, are at work and native breeds of farm animals graze in the fields. You'll find it to be less a museum than an exploration, before you return to the main building with its galleries devoted to history, textiles, agriculture, and costumes. The castle is actually a 16th-century mansion built inside a Norman castle wall, with formal gardens, now restored.

St. Fagans. www.museumwales.ac.uk. © **029/2057-3500.** Free admission, but charge for parking. Daily 10am–5pm. Bus: 32 or 320, leaving from the bus station in Cardiff every hour during the day.

Where to Eat
MODERATE
Armless Dragon WELSH About 1 mile north of the main streets, the Dragon is known for the best in Welsh produce. "Taste of Wales" dishes include an antipasto of cured ham, lava bread, quail eggs, cockles, olives, and oatcakes. Starters include pan-fried pigeon breast with beetroot risotto, or homemade Glamorgan sausages with leeks and truffle oil. Among the mains are seared Brecon venison with pistachio and pine nut crust, roast garlic mash, and wild mushroom and sherry sage reduction.

97 Wyeverne Rd. www.armlessdragon.co.uk. © **029/2038-2357.** Reservations recommended. Main courses £12–£18. MC, V. Tues–Fri noon–2pm; Tues–Thurs 7–9pm; Fri–Sat 7–9:30pm. Closed Dec 25–26.

Woods Bar & Brasserie ★ MODERN BRITISH/CONTINENTAL In the old Pilotage Building down by the dock, this is a glass-fronted haven of modernity. For starters, try the pressed terrine of pig's brawn, pork jelly, sauce gribiche, and sourdough toasts. Main courses include pan-fried gilthead bream, boulanger potatoes with fennel, lava bread fritter, and cockle and lemon butter.

Pilotage Building, Stuart St., Cardiff Bay. www.woods-brasserie.com. © **029/2049-2400.** Reservations required. Main courses £9–£22.50; fixed-price 2-course pre-opera dinner £16.95. AE, DC, MC, V. Mon–Sat noon–2pm and 5:30–10pm; Sun noon–3pm.

INEXPENSIVE
Cadwaladers Ice Cream Café BRITISH On the quayside at Cardiff Bay, this is one of a growing number of eateries from the family ice-cream company started in Criccieth, North Wales in 1927. The bright, lively place is perfect for that Willy Wonka moment, with wild concoctions such as Dragon's Breath and Chocolate Porridge. There's also coffee and cakes, grilled bruschetta, brioche-style ham, leek pies (for lunch or a pre-theatre snack), and even alcoholic ice-cream cocktails.

Mermaid Quay, Cardiff Bay. www.cadwaladersicecream.co.uk. © **029/2049-7598.** Ice cream and dishes £2–£8. MC, V. Daily from 10am; closing varies from 5pm in winter to 10pm in summer.

Demiro's ITALIAN/SPANISH/WELSH This looks like a traditional Italian restaurant, all deep red with classical statues and big mirrors, but it actually has side-by-side Italian, Welsh, and Spanish menus. Will it be chicken cooked in the wood-burning oven or homemade faggots (an offal meatball) with peas and mash? At a basic level, there are great thin-crust pizzas but you can splash out on local steak and lamb. And there are nice views on to the Wales Millennium Centre and over the Bay.

Mermaid Quay, Cardiff Bay. www.demiros.com. ✆ **029/2049-1882.** Main courses £8–£20. AE, MC, V. Sun–Thurs noon–10pm; Fri–Sat until 10:30pm.

Shopping

Cardiff offers the joys of mainstream shopping on a grand scale. **Queen Street,** the main shopping thoroughfare (car-free), has many major chain stores. A number of nearby streets are also part of the traffic-free zone, and include everything from sophisticated arcades to a traditional indoor market. Of the varied arcades from Victorian and Edwardian times, the oldest is the Royal Arcade, connecting The Hayes and St. Mary Street. It dates from 1858 and still has some original Victorian storefronts. The Morgan Arcade, completed in 1899, runs parallel. Both are a wealth of elegant columns, flagstone floors, and mostly upmarket stores.

The extension to the **St. David's** indoor mall continues the arcade tradition with its limestone-rich Grand Arcade, which is 240m (800 ft.) long, ending at the classic department store John Lewis, the biggest branch outside London. St. David's (www.stdavidscardiff.com; ✆ **029/2036-7600**), with entrances on Queen Street, The Hayes, and various other streets, is the city's leading mall with more than 100 shops, plus its own restaurant quarter, East Side. The **Capitol Shopping Centre,** also on Queen Street, is another indoor complex.

Cardiff Central Market, St. Mary Street, is a classic Victorian indoor market, all iron pillars and glass roof with a wrought-iron balcony around the upper level. It's the place to buy local meat, cheese, laverbread (seaweed), and sugary Welsh cakes, as well as books, records, and much more. On Sunday mornings the Riverside Farmers' Market takes place on the embankment of the River Taff.

Cardiff's shopping streets are filled with grandiose buildings, many of them Edwardian; a good example is the **James Howell** department store on St. Mary Street (part of the House of Fraser chain), all designer fashion on the inside but Corinthian and Ionic columns outside. **Spiller's Records,** an old haunt of the Manic Street Preachers, claims to be the world's oldest record shop, selling discs since 1894, although it has moved from The Hayes to Morgan Arcade. **Jacob's Antiques Centre,** West Canal Wharf (✆ **029/2039-0939**), near the rail station, is a red-brick warehouse with 50-plus stalls selling vintage clothes, bric-a-brac, furniture, and books.

Entertainment & Nightlife
THE PERFORMING ARTS

The **Wales Millennium Centre** ★★★ (www.wmc.org.uk; ✆ **029/2063-6464**) is a £100 million giant on the banks of Cardiff Bay with poetry in enormous letters cut out of its copper facade. Its 1,900-seat auditorium (along with the Weston Studio) is home to a clutch of arts groups, including the Welsh National Opera and the Dance Company of Wales. The Centre, opened by the Queen in 2004, attracts major international companies, but also puts on everything from stand-up comedy to the musical *Mamma Mia!* Some tickets are below £10, others approaching £50.

St. David's Hall (or *Neuadd Dewi Sant* in Welsh), The Hayes (www.stdavidshall.co.uk; ✆ 029/2087-8444), dates back to the early 1980s, and is a modernist venue that vies with the Wales Millennium Centre for the title of Cardiff's leading concert hall. It is a constant host to ballets and orchestras, interspersed with more mainstream concerts. The adjoining **New Theatre** (www.newtheatrecardiff.co.uk; ✆ 029/2087-8889) actually dates from 1906 (it has hosted the likes of Sarah Bernhardt and Jelly Roll Morton) and puts on musicals and pantomimes. **Cardiff International Arena** (www.livenation.co.uk/cardiff; ✆ 029/2022-4488) is a large indoor venue on Mary Ann Street and hosts major music and comedy acts.

LIVE MUSIC, COMEDY & NIGHTCLUBS

Clwb ifor Bach (the **Welsh Club**), 11 Womanby St. (www.clwb.net; ✆ 029/2023-2199), focuses on home-grown acts, and still gets those who have made the leap to international stardom (such as Super Furry Animals) back for low-key shows. There are three floors and in addition to live music you'll also find hip-hop, dance, electronica, and more. Admission ranges from £3 to £10, and the club is open most nights, usually from 7:30pm to either 2 or 3am.

The Glee Club, Mermaid Quay (www.glee.co.uk; ✆ 0871/472-0400), at Cardiff Bay, is a large comedy club with acts generally appearing Thursday to Saturday. It can take up its seats to present the coolest of live music, both modern and from times past, on most other evenings. Admission from £9 to £20. Entry varies, usually between 7:30 and 8pm.

CARDIFF'S pubs

As a capital city, and one with docks and a working-class heritage, Cardiff has plenty of pubs, many of which are historic sites in themselves. The **City Arms**, 10 Quay St. (✆ 029/2022-5258), is a warm, traditional place near the Millennium Stadium, which attracts rugby fans and anyone looking for the real Cardiff. The nearby **Horse & Groom,** on Womanby Street (✆ 0871/432-9005), is Cardiff's smallest, oldest pub. The **Goat Major,** on the High Street (✆ 029/2033-7161), is fabulously traditional, with beams on the outside and dark wood panels coating the inside, a backdrop to the black leather sofas. The **Owain Glyndwr,** 10 St. John's Sq. (✆ 029/2033-9303), is near the castle and another small, friendly backstreet pub.

The Bay has glossy, modern bars such as **Salt,** with its balcony, on Mermaid Quay (www.saltcardiff.com; ✆ 029/2049-4375), home to a young, cocktail-quaffing crowd. But look beneath the surface and you find the pubs of yesteryear, such as **The Packet,** on Bute Street (✆ 029/2046-5513), a hotel for sailors in Victorian times, with its original rope-clad pillars and majestic mahogany-bar backdrop. The **White Hart**, 64 James St. (✆ 029/2047-2561), is the oldest pub in the Docks area, dating back to 1855, and is a lively locals haunt.

Most of the pubs serve Cardiff-brewed Brains' beers, not least the **Yard Bar & Kitchen,** 42 St. Mary St. (www.yardbarkitchen.co.uk; ✆ 029/2022-7577). It's a smart bar and restaurant in old brewery buildings on the edge of the Old Brewery Quarter, a traffic-free cluster of mostly chain eateries and bars. Visit www.sabrain.com for a full list of pubs selling delights such as SA amber ale and the rich dark Rev. James, named after a beer-brewing vicar from Victorian times.

The Globe, 125 Albany Rd. (www.globecardiffmusic.com; ☎ 07590/471888), has live music 7 nights a week, from new names to established stars such as Colin Blunstone, singer with 1960s' heroes The Zombies. Tickets tend to be £10 to £15. Doors open around 7pm.

Oceana, Greyfriars Road (www.oceanaclubs.com; ☎ 0845/296-8588), is Cardiff's biggest nightclub, with seven themed rooms, from Tahiti to New York to Monte Carlo, where you can dance, slump on sofas, or sip cocktails from 10 different bars. Prices start at £5, rising to £15 for special events. Hours are 9pm until 3 or 4am.

GAY CLUBS

The **Wow Club,** 48 Charles St. (www.wowclubcardiff.com; ☎ 029/2066-6247), opened at the end of 2011 on the site of the Exit Club, the city's longest-running gay club, which had hosted DJs 7 days a week for almost 20 years. The Wow premiered with Wednesday, Friday, Saturday, and Sunday opening from 10pm until as late as 4:30am, with plenty of DJs and cheap drinks. **Club X,** 35 Charles St. (www.club xcardiff.net; ☎ 07523/904775), is Exit's main contender with DJs playing house, club classics, and electronica. It's open Friday to Sunday 8pm until 6am; entry is £10 (free on Fridays before 10pm).

Where to Stay

EXPENSIVE

Hilton ★★★ ☺ This is a delightful, friendly, and modern place in a perfect position across the road from the castle and museum, and around the corner from the shops. The rooms are large, sleek-but-comfy, and many have fantastic views. The stainless-steel swimming pool is a joy. The **Razzi restaurant,** serving modern British and Welsh cuisine (such as salt-marsh lamb with bubble and squeak), spills out into a glass extension opposite the castle, and manages to be both sophisticated and child-friendly, with an excellent children's menu. The new Metropole bar is a hip place to meet and has live acoustic music at weekends.

Kingsway, Cardiff CF10 3HH. www.hilton.co.uk/cardiff. ☎ 029/2064-9200. 197 units. £99–£350 double; £159–£850 suite. AE, DC, MC, V. Valet parking £17. **Amenities:** Restaurant; 2 bars; pool; health club; sauna; room service; shop. *In room:* A/C, TV, hair dryer, Wi-Fi (£15 per 24 hr. but free in public areas).

St. David's Hotel & Spa ★★★ ⚑ This landmark is on a promontory at the tip of Cardiff Bay giving it watery views from every room. The glass atrium is as impressive as the sail-like roof. And there's five-star service to match. The rooms are big, stylishly furnished in a pale, interesting way, and have floor-to-ceiling windows leading on to balconies. The Marine Spa has been voted one of Britain's best, and there's a glorious pool. The **Tempus bar and restaurant** is a place for a seaview cocktail, afternoon tea, or a meal, while the **Tides Grill** offers alfresco dining.

Havannah St., Cardiff Bay, Cardiff CF10 5SD. www.thestdavidshotel.com. ☎ 029/2045-4045. Fax 029/2048-7056. 142 units. £95–£190 double; £169–£540 suite. AE, DC, MC, V. Parking £8. **Amenities:** 2 restaurants; bar; indoor heated pool; exercise room; spa; concierge; room service; babysitting. *In room:* A/C, TV/DVD/CD player (in some), minibar, hair dryer.

MODERATE

Barceló Cardiff Angel Hotel ★ The elegant Victorian Angel Hotel, across from Cardiff Castle, was *the* place to stay in South Wales when it was first built. Over the years, it has attracted everybody from Greta Garbo to The Beatles to prime ministers. The Angel is still good—and it has regained some of its old prestige following a restoration. It's a world of neo-Doric decor, *trompe l'oeil* ceilings, Waterford crystal chandeliers, and hand-stippled faux-marble columns. As befits a hotel of this age, its guest rooms come in a wide variety of styles and sizes.

Castle St., Cardiff CF10 1SZ. www.barcelo-hotels.co.uk. ℂ **029/2064-9200.** Fax 029/2039-6212. 106 units. £65–£200 double; £125–£300 suite. AE, DC, MC, V. Parking £5. **Amenities:** Restaurant; bar; concierge; room service. *In room:* A/C, TV, hair dryer, Wi-Fi (£12 per 24 hr.).

Jolyons Hotel ★★ ♟ This former seamen's lodge on Cardiff Bay's oldest terrace has been turned into a delightful boutique hotel. There are only a few bedrooms, each individually furnished. The place is modern and stylish inside, but with a rustic, slate-floored bar with a log stove and red-leather sofas. Most of the bedrooms have views of the bay, and most come with king-size beds. Some of the bathrooms have whirlpool tubs and one has a "wet room." A **sister hotel**, Jolyon's at No 10 (www.jolyons10.com), in Cathedral Road, now offers similar style in the city.

5 Bute Crescent, Cardiff Bay, Cardiff CF10 5AN. www.jolyons.co.uk. ℂ **029/2048-8775.** Fax 029/2048-8775. 7 units. £75–£150 double. AE, MC, V. Rates include Welsh breakfast. **Amenities:** Bar; room service. *In room:* TV, hair dryer, Wi-Fi (free).

Llanerch Vineyard ★ Now here's a thing. Not only a working vineyard 10 miles from Cardiff, but also one with luxury rooms. There are five in a lovely old farmhouse (all with king-size beds and two with views across the vines), seven smart studios in an adjoining building (with vines growing around the doors), and two cottages ideal for families in converted stables. The vineyard, which produces Cariad label whites, is open for tours, there are woodland walks, and a bistro with conservatory and terrace (open 10am–5pm Mon–Sat and for Sunday lunch) serves Welsh cheeses, Welsh rarebit topped with sticky leeks, and other local-tinged dishes. The bar is open daily.

Hensol, Vale of Glamorgan CF72 8GG. www.llanerch-vineyard.co.uk. ℂ **01443/222716.** 14 units. Studios £75–£85; rooms £85–£95. Rates include breakfast. AE, MC, V. Leave the M4 at jct. 34 and follow signs for Hensol. **Amenities:** Restaurant; bar. *In room:* TV/DVD, hair dryer, Wi-Fi (free).

Maldron Hotel Opened in summer 2011, this is the largest hotel in the heart of Cardiff. The new tower is one of the city's tallest buildings and has great views from the 10th and 11th floors, especially if you have a superior corner room with floor-to-ceiling windows. There are family rooms with an extra bed and the option of another. Decor is cool and modern, neutrals augmented with a touch of purple here, lime green there. There's a decent bar with city views, and the **Stir** restaurant (2 courses £15).

St. Mary St., Cardiff CF10 1GD. www.maldronhotelcardiff.com. ℂ **029/2066-8866.** Fax 029/2057-4657. 216 units. £79–£149 double. AE, MC, V. Parking £8. **Amenities:** Bar. *In room:* TV, hair dryer, Wi-Fi (free).

INEXPENSIVE

Big Sleep Hotel ★ ♪ This place is part of a small chain of cool budget hotels partly owned by actor John Malkovich. What was a 1960s' office block is a great place to stay at great prices. Decor is sleek and modern, location is good (right by the St. David's shopping mall), there's a decent bar, and you even get a continental breakfast.

Bute Terrace, Cardiff CF10 2FE. www.thebigsleephotel.com. ℂ **029/2063-6363.** Fax 029/2063-6364. 81 units. From £29 double, £35 family, Mon–Thurs £35–£69 double, £99 suite. Rates include continental breakfast. AE, MC, V. Parking £6. **Amenities:** Bar. *In room:* TV, hair dryer, Wi-Fi (£7.50 per day).

Hotel One Hundred 🛏 A bargain boutique B&B just a 10-minute walk from town. The classic Victorian town house hides rooms that are decorated in a flamboyant modern manner, complete with fluffy duvets and iPod docks. There's a comfy TV room and you can relax with a drink in the pretty decked garden.

100 Newport Rd., Cardiff CF24 1DG. www.hotelonehundred.com. ✆ **029/2048-2379.** 7 units. £70–£100 double. Rates include continental breakfast (cooked breakfast £5). MC, V. Free parking. **Amenities:** Breakfast room; honesty bar; lounge; garden. *In room:* TV/DVD, hair dryer. Wi-Fi (free).

THE WELSH VALLEYS: THE WORLD OF COAL

165 miles W of London; 29 miles NE of Cardiff

The Welsh Valleys are the home of the coal industry. Or at least they were, until the pits that were left were closed in the 1980s. But despite the hardship that followed, the locals never gave up and have reinvented the brooding, often bleak, area as a mecca for industrial-heritage tourism. Pits have been turned into museums and even the most daunting landscape, littered with slag heaps, has risen in a new clanking, grinding glory. The area around **Blaenavon** (on the edge of the Black Mountains, southeast of Abergavenny) is one of the best. It's a short drive from Cardiff but might as well be in another world, in another century. You'll come across towns such as Merthyr Tydfil, which in 1845 had a population of 40,000 due to its iron and steel industry. Here the **Cyfarthfa Castle Museum** remembers the 1966 Aberfan disaster, when 20 houses and a school were buried in a slag-heap slide killing 144 people, mostly children.

Essentials

GETTING THERE By rail, Abergavenny (45 min., £12 one-way) and Merthyr Tydfil (1 hr., £5 one-way) have connections to Cardiff. Train times are irregular but frequent. The **Stagecoach** X43 bus from Brecon stops at both towns, but it's good to have a car and it's an easy drive from Cardiff and the M4.

VISITOR INFORMATION There's an area tourist office at the Blaenavon Ironworks (www.blaenavontic.com; ✆ **01495/792615**), which has seasonal opening, but the Blaenavon World Heritage Centre (see below) is best for information.

Exploring the Area

Big Pit ★★★ ☺ HISTORIC SITE This is also called the National Coal Museum, but the Big Pit is truly what it is: A former coal mine that sits on a sweeping mountainside. It's what Wales was all about: Hard work and dirt, and you can see it from the inside. After a multimedia presentation, you're given a hardhat and lamp and taken 92m (300 ft.) down the mineshaft in a real, clanking pit cage for a 50-minute tour. It's all authentic, and your guide is a real miner who remembers the place being closed by Prime Minister Margaret Thatcher in the 1980s. The tunnels, including underground stables for pit ponies, are dark and atmospheric. Above ground is a well-designed museum in the pithead baths, a number of old buildings to explore, and a cafe. It's all the more impressive in the bleak midwinter, with the landscape covered in snow. It's one of the country's must-see attractions, and it's free.

Blaenavon. www.museumwales.ac.uk. ✆ **01495/790311.** Free admission. Daily 9:30am–5pm; tours 10:30am–3:30pm. From town follow museum signs.

Blaenavon Heritage Railway ★ ☺ RAILWAY   Built to transport coal from the Big Pit (see above), this is the highest and steepest standard-gauge railway in England and Wales reaching the country's highest station, Whistle Halt (400m/1,307 ft.). It's not a long ride, but there is plenty to see: Mountain ponies, peregrine falcons, red kites, and lots of hardy sheep. Five minutes from the main station, Furnace Sidings, are Garn Lakes, a lovely spot for picnics. The Whistle Inn at the end of the line has a beer garden. There are events throughout the year, including Santa Specials.

Blaenavon. www.pontypool-and-blaenavon.co.uk. (✆ **01495/792263.** Tickets £7 adults, £4 children 5–15. Apr–Sept departures on weekends and some weekdays from around 11:30am–4:30pm, and other dates for events. From town follow signs.

Blaenavon World Heritage Site ★★★ HISTORIC SITE   This is the official name for one of the most impressive Industrial Revolution sites in Europe. The town of Blaenavon and its surroundings were awarded UNESCO World Heritage status in 2000. **Blaenavon World Heritage Centre,** in the restored St. Peter's School, gives an overview of the industrial landscape, with its interactive displays. It is also the start of various walks, and has a gift shop and cafe. The rather bleak valley setting is home to Europe's best-preserved 18th-century ironworks (which was fired by the local coal). Seeing what's left of the five furnaces is enough to make you feel humbled. It wasn't even the biggest ironworks in Wales, but in 1789 it was the most advanced in the world. There are plenty of places to wander, such as the restored workers' cottages. The site includes the marvelous Big Pit museum and the Pontypool and Blaenavon Railway, which are attractions in their own right (see reviews, above).

Church Rd., Blaenavon. www.world-heritage-blaenavon.org.uk. (✆ **01495/742333.** Free admission. Centre Apr–Sept Tues–Sat 9am–5pm (until 4pm Oct–Mar). Ironworks daily Apr–Oct 10am–5pm; Nov–Mar Fri–Sat 9:30am–4pm, Sun 11am–4pm. Follow signs from the A465 northwest of Cardiff, outside Pontypool.

Rhondda Heritage Park ☺ HISTORIC SITE   In the Rhondda Valley, heart of Welsh coal mining, the Lewis Merthyr Colliery at Trehafod has been transformed into a family history attraction. There's a reconstructed village street, including shops and homes, showing how life was lived from Victorian times up to the 1950s. Admission is free but you pay for the Black Gold Tour, an audiovisual presentation and tour of the pithead buildings followed by an underground trip. You get a helmet lamp but only go down a few feet, and the train ride finale is a Disney-esque vibrating carriage with runaway train film backdrop (great fun for children). There's also Energy Zone, a giant adventure playground, open April to September, a cafe, and a gift shop.

Coed Cae Rd., Trehafod, Pontypridd. www.rhonddaheritagepark.com. (✆ **01443/682036.** Free admission; Black Gold Tour £5.60 adults, £4.30 children 3–15. Daily 9am–4:30pm. Closed Dec 24–early Jan and Mon Oct–Easter. Btw. Pontypridd and Porth, just off the A470, near jct 32 of the M4.

Where to Eat

This is far from the most attractive part of Wales and therefore isn't a place to base yourself. Stay instead down in Cardiff, or up in the Brecon Beacons. For lunch, the **Heritage Café** (✆ **01495/742339**) at the Blaenavon World Heritage Centre, with its big windows and mountain views, is decent enough, with healthful options and some seasonal fare. And the **Whistle Inn** (✆ **01495/790403**) above Garn Lakes, by the railway, offers pub grub. There are also various cafes in Blaenavon.

ABERGAVENNY & THE BLACK MOUNTAINS

163 miles W of London; 31 miles NE of Cardiff

Traditionally viewed as the gateway to the Brecon Beacons (although it is outside the National Park), **Abergavenny** is more closely associated with the Black Mountains, an entity unto themselves yet which occupy a large, eastern edge of the park. Sitting on the River Usk, Abergavenny is possibly the finest market town in Wales and increasingly a foodie destination. It is a popular weekend getaway. There's history, too, with a Norman castle tucked away in the backstreets, a classic Norman church, and a good museum. It's also a hub for mountain drives and walks. Outside town, the **Black Mountains** offer some of the most dramatic scenery in the Brecons, bald peaks, dizzying drives, and walks along the River Gavenny, River Usk, and Brecon and Abergavenny Canal.

Abergavenny is a good base for a range of **outdoor activities,** including pony trekking, hill walking and climbing, golfing, hang gliding, and fishing. You can also take a boat out for a day or longer on the canal, which passes near the town. To get a feel for the area's remoteness and hill farms, the single-lane roads, and the meandering river valleys, a car is essential.

Essentials

GETTING THERE   By rail, Abergavenny is linked to Newport (Arriva Trains Wales; £8 one-way , 19 miles to the southwest, from where there are connections to London (2½ hr.) and Cardiff. There are also trains from Abergavenny to Shrewsbury and Hereford across the border.

There are regular buses (www.stagecoachbus.com; ☏ **01633/485118**): The X43 from Brecon (£4.50 return), and the X4, which passes through Abergavenny on its Hereford-Cardiff route.

Abergavenny is a short drive along the A4042 from the M4, which links Cardiff and London.

VISITOR INFORMATION   Abergavenny's Civic Society has laid out a **Town Trail,** marking buildings and other points of interest with brass plaques. The **Tourist Information Centre** is at the bus station on Monmouth Road (www.visit abergavenny.co.uk; ☏ **01873/853254**). It's open daily 10am to 5pm.

Exploring Abergavenny

Abergavenny Castle, on Castle Street, is one of the best examples of a motte-and-bailey castle in Britain. Although much has disappeared, including the bailey (courtyard with outbuildings), the restored keep still sits on the motte (man-made mound), giving a good impression of what it would have been like in the 12th century. Admission is free, and it's open daily from dawn to dusk. **Abergavenny Museum** (www. abergavennymuseum.co.uk; ☏ **01873/854282**) is in the castle keep, which was rebuilt as the Marquess of Abergavenny's hunting lodge in 1818. There are archeological finds (relics from the Roman fort of Gobannium) and lots of Welsh life, with displays housing the contents of a farmhouse kitchen, a saddler's, and a grocer's. Admission is free. The museum is open March to October, Monday to Saturday 11am to 1pm and 2 to 5pm, Sunday 2 to 5pm; and November to February, Monday to Saturday 11am to 1pm and 2 to 4pm.

walking TALL

This area has more good hikes than you can shake a walking stick at. **Offa's Dyke Path** (www.offasdyke.demon.co.uk) is a 177-mile hike from Chepstow to Prestatyn on the north coast of Wales, but little more than a third follows the 8th-century earthwork, which protected the English from marauding Celts. There is, however, a particularly good stretch between the Llanthony Valley and Hay-on-Wye. Take the Offa's Dyke Flyer (linked to the Beacons Bus, p. 699) from Hay to Llanthony and walk back. The **Usk Valley Walk** (www.uskvalleywalk. org.uk) is a 48-mile walk that starts at Brecon and mostly follows the Monmouthshire and Brecon Canal towpath, with diversions through woods and across fields, down to Abergavenny, where it follows the River Usk down to Caerleon, with occasional forays into the hills.

St. Mary's Priory Church, Monk Street (www.stmarys-priory.org; ℂ 01873/ 853168), was the church to a priory set up by the first Norman lord of Abergavenny in the early 12th century. It's now one of the biggest parish churches in Wales. It has suffered much through the centuries: From (it is believed) Cromwell's rampaging troops, leaving the tombs wrecked, to injudicious restoration. There's still plenty to see, including the Norman font, carved 14th- and 15th-century monastic choir stalls, and some still outstanding tombs. It's open daily 9am to 7pm year-round.

Llanthony Priory (www.cadw.gov.uk; open daily; free admission) is a peaceful ruin in a quiet valley just north of Abergavenny in the foothills of the Black Mountains. It's an idyllic spot for a picnic or for a beer at the Llanthony Priory Hotel (see "Where To Eat & Stay," below). Talgarth, on the A479 at the northern edge of the Black Mountains, is an attractive town where you can still catch a cattle market (some Tues and Fri), and where Tower House, one of only two fortified houses in Wales, serves as the **tourist office** (ℂ 01874/712226). Nearby is the **Pwll-y-Wrach Nature Reserve** with its waterfalls and springtime carpet of bluebells, where you may see otters, and the Woodland Trust's **Park Wood,** on a ridge above town.

Exploring Hay-on-Wye

For a small town Hay has a huge reputation, not least for its eccentricity: It is twinned with Timbuktu, and once declared independence from Britain. Hay (once half in England) is famed for having more secondhand bookstores than anywhere else in the world, but it was the **Hay Festival** (www.hayfestival.com), launched in 1987, that put it on the international map. During the 10 days of the literary festival, starting the last week in May and attracting authors from around the globe, it becomes an arty city of 150,000. Events and hotels get booked up fast, but you can still have a charming day here, thanks to the food marquees and setting. Mostly Hay is a leisurely delight although a second festival, **Crunch** (www.artfestivalathay.org; ℂ 01497/821762), in mid-November, is growing, with its indie music, arts discussions, and comedy, focused on the Globe at Hay venue on Newport Street. Around town, the bookstores are interspersed with bric-a-brac emporia and organic food stores, and you can stroll along the River Wye. The Bailey Walk follows the river more than a mile on the town side to The Warren, a beauty spot where you can have a

LIFE ON THE canal

The **Monmouthshire and Brecon Canal** is one of the most picturesque in Britain and follows the course of the River Usk for much of its 32 miles. Walking or cycling along the towpath is a rural delight, and you can spot herons, kingfishers, and buzzards. The canal starts in Brecon and heads southeast to Abergavenny and through or near other market towns—Talybont, Llangynidr, and Crickhowell. **Goytre Wharf** (www.goytrewharf.com; ℭ **01873/881069**) at Llanover, just south of Abergavenny, off the A4042, combines a British Waterways Heritage Centre, aqueduct, shops, cafe, bar, children's play areas, woodland walk, canoe rental, and holiday narrowboat rental. At Llanfoist, just north of Abergavenny, **Beacon Park Boats** (www.beaconparkboats.com; ℭ **01873/858277**) has luxury narrowboats for short breaks and longer, heading toward Brecon. *The Owl* canal boat has a four-poster bed, log fire, and hot tub plus a full-size roll-top bath.

paddle and a picnic. Hay also has the remains of a Norman castle, now, predictably, a secondhand bookstore. The Offa's Dyke Path and easy Wye Valley Walk run through town; you can pick up a Walk Pack from the tourist office near the parking lot on Oxford Road.

The biggest bookstore is the **Hay Cinema Bookshop,** Castle Street (www.haycinemabookshop.co.uk; ℭ **01497/820071**), in the former cinema, with 200,000 volumes from 50p to £1,000 or more. **Boz Books,** 13A Castle St. (www.bozbooks.demon.co.uk; ℭ **01497/821277**), features many first editions by Charles Dickens and other 19th-century authors, as well as Dylan Thomas.

The **Old Black Lion,** Lion Street (www.oldblacklion.co.uk; ℭ **01497/820841**), parts of which date back to the 1300s, near the Lion Gate of the town wall, serves smart bar food and has an oak-beamed restaurant dating from the 1600s. The sophisticated cuisine features everything from Moroccan lamb with couscous and an apricot-and-fig compote to peppered venison casserole. There are also 10 bedrooms, from £45 per person, including breakfast.

Exploring Tintern

This is a small, rather lovely village a few miles southeast of Abergavenny, in a mystical wooded setting near Chepstow. Despite the antiques and bookstores, pubs and cafes, its real attraction, just down the hill, takes your breath away. **Tintern Abbey** ★★ (www.cadw.wales.gov.uk; ℭ **01291/689251**) is in ruins, but is spine-tinglingly beautiful. Only the second Cistercian abbey in Britain, it was founded in 1131, became one of the most important monasteries in Wales, and survived until Henry VIII's dissolution of the monasteries. The towering remains, mostly from the 13th century, are easily visible from outside but you get the true feel of scale once you stand in their midst. Parking is free (quite something at Welsh monuments), and you can walk along the river and up into the hills to see it in its full glory. That's what Wordsworth did when he wrote the poem *Composed A Few Miles Above Tintern Abbey,* and he knew a thing or two about views. Admission is £3.80 for adults and £3.40 for children 5 to 16. It's open March to June, September and October, daily 9:30am to 5pm; July and August, daily 9:30am to 6pm; and November to February, Monday to Saturday 10am to 4pm, Sunday 11am to 4pm; closed at all other times.

Shopping

Abergavenny is market heaven (www.abergavennymarket.co.uk; ✆ **01873/735811**): The Tuesday market has more than 200 stalls inside and outside the market hall, heaped with local produce and much more. But there's also an indoor-only market each Friday, a growing indoor/outdoor affair each Saturday, a big fleamarket each Wednesday (an excellent place to find vinyl records and old comic books), an antiques market, (3rd Sun each month), and a crafts market (2nd Sat each month). For good local food, visit **Rawlings,** 19 Market St. (www.rawlingsbutchers.co.uk; ✆ **01873/856773**), which is the place for sausages. Try the award-winning Traditional Pork or the hot, spicy Welsh Dragon. Out of town on the A40 near Crickhowell are two foodie treats. The **Black Mountains Smokery** (www.smoked-foods.co.uk; ✆ **01873/811566**) is renowned for its hot and cold smoked fish, meat, and cheese, while the **Welsh Venison Centre** (www.beaconsfarmshop.co.uk; ✆ **01874 730929**) on Middleton Farm sells its own venison and lamb as well as other local meats, deli products, eggs, and juices.

Where to Eat & Stay

Llangoed Hall Hotel ★★★ This manor house dates back to 1632, and was revamped by Edwardian architect Clough Williams-Ellis into a grand country house in 1919. Its setting in the Wye Valley, overlooking the Black Mountains, is entrancing. The bedrooms are all very different with antiques and fine fabrics, eight with four-posters. Activities on site include fly fishing, clay-pigeon shooting, and croquet, and there's a snooker table in the library. The **restaurant** is a divine space in pale blue, serving Welsh black beef and Radnorshire lamb with vegetables from the gardens.

Llyswen, Brecon, Powys LD3 0YP. www.llangoedhall.com. ✆ **01874/754525.** Fax 01874/754545. 23 units. £210–£350 double; £385–£400 suite. Rates include Welsh breakfast. AE, DC, MC, V. On the A470, 2 miles northwest of Llyswen. **Amenities:** Restaurant; room service. *In room:* TV, hair dryer.

Llanthony Priory Hotel ★★ Staying here is a fabulous, fairytale experience. Originally part of the 12th-century priory, its four rooms are in the tower, reached by a stone spiral staircase. The rooms have no en suite facilities, but some have four-poster beds. The **dining room,** with vaulted ceiling and log fire, serves local produce (main courses from £9.50) and the Undercroft Bar, in the priory cellar, serves real ales. The Offa's Dyke Path passes by, and there is pony trekking nearby.

Llanthony, Abergavenny, Monmouthshire NP7 7NN. www.llanthonyprioryhotel.co.uk. ✆ **01873/890487.** 4 units. £80 (midweek), £175 (weekends) double. Rates include breakfast. AE, MC, V. Free parking. Head north on A465 for Skirrid Mountain Inn, turn left just past inn and continue 5 miles. **Amenities:** Restaurant; bar. *In room:* No phone.

Penydre Farm ☺ A great place for families. This working farm has four cottages (sleeping 4–6) in converted barns and stables facing a meadow with donkeys, geese, and a pig that children can visit. There's a little lawn outside each with a table and chairs, a play area, and a laundry room. The 200-year-old farmhouse is also a B&B, with country-chic rooms and breakfast at the long, ancient kitchen table. There is also a small camping and caravan site with showers and toilets. And it's just along the street from the Skirrid pub (below). The farm is part of the Abergavenny Farm Holiday Group (www.afhg.co.uk) that brings together 11 farms with rooms.

Llanvihangel Crucorney, Abergavenny. Monmouthshire. NP7 8DH. www.penydre.co.uk. ✆ **01873/890246.** 8 units. Cottages £150–£250 (3 nights); double B&B £70 (discount for more than 1 night). B&B rates include full Welsh breakfast. No credit or debit cards. Free parking. Just off the A465, 5 miles north of Abergavenny. **Amenities:** Farm; play area; laundry room. *In room:* TV/DVD, cottages have kitchens, hair dryer.

Skirrid Mountain Inn ★★　This is the oldest pub in Wales and arguably the oldest in Britain; with its stone-walled interior, it feels as ancient as a castle. The Skirrid was first noted in 1110 and has doubled as a courthouse with hangings taking place from the magnificent oak beamed stairs (wood believed to be salvaged from a Royal Navy ship). There are three antiques-filled bedrooms (two with four-posters), a simple menu (including Welsh sirloin steak, £12.95, and Hereford chicken in a cider sauce, £8.95), and a bar with regular guest beers.

Llanvihangel Crucorney, Abergavenny, Monmouthshire NP7 8DH. www.skirridmountaininn.co.uk. ✆ **01873/890258.** 3 units. £90 double. Rates include full Welsh breakfast. AE, MC, V. Free parking. Just off the A465, 5 miles north of Abergavenny. **Amenities:** Restaurant; bar. *In room:* TV.

Walnut Tree Inn ★　The Walnut was making a name for itself 40 years ago, before the great British food revival. The menu changes seasonally (and daily) but might feature halibut with spiced mussel and clam broth or roasted hare with salsify. It's open Tuesday to Saturday (main courses £15–£25). Two cottages, Ivy Cottage and Old Post Office Cottage, are accessible through the garden, each sleeping four, with king-size beds, terraces, and gardens. There are also links with Abergavenny's equally charming Angel hotel, whose proprietor is co-owner here.

Llandewi Skirrid, Abergavenny, Monmouthshire NP7 8AW. www.thewalnuttreeinn.com. ✆ **01873/852797.** Fax: 01873/859764. 2 units. £180 for 2 people, £220 for 3 people, £260 for 4 people. Rates include breakfast supplies. AE, MC, V. Free parking. On the B4521, 3 miles east of Abergavenny. **Amenities:** Restaurant. *In room:* TV, hair dryer.

BRECON BEACONS

140 miles W of London; 20 miles N of Cardiff

The Brecon Beacons is a **National Park,** but it isn't simply a rural wilderness as you might expect from the name; it's a lively region of villages and small towns—including the pretty town of Brecon itself—plus plenty of outdoor activities. The Brecon Beacons is the only U.K. National Park to include an area of such geological importance that it has been granted UNESCO Global Geopark status. And quite stunning it is, too: Open, grassy peaks and dense, forested valleys.

The Fforest Fawr Geopark (Fforest Fawr is Welsh for Great Forest) is the range of mountains between the central Beacons and the Black Mountain to the west and is home to stunning natural attractions such as the **National Showcaves Centre for Wales,** Craig-y-Nos Country Park, spectacular waterfalls, and brooding reservoirs, as well as the highest mountain in southern Britain (Pen y Fan, 886m/2,906 ft.) and the wilderness area of the Black Mountain.

However, the National Park extends farther to the west, taking in the mountain clifftop castle of Carreg Cennon, near the market town of Llandeilo, and going as far east as the Black Mountains (different from the Black Mountain) between Abergavenny and Hay-on-Wye, and as far south as Pontypool and the outskirts of Merthyr Tydfil.

The Brecons are the great outdoors, a place where you can not only walk but also cycle (there are plenty of places to rent bikes), go pony trekking, and explore the historic villages and towns that dot the area. You will be amazed by the different scenery around every twist and turn of the road.

Brecon Beacons

Essentials

GETTING THERE   There is a bus, the T4 (www.stagecoachbus.com; ✆ **01633/ 485118**) between Cardiff and Brecon, via Merthyr Tydfil, which takes 1½ hours an costs about £4.50 one way.

On summer Sundays and public holidays, the **Beacons Bus** network brings visitors from Cardiff (with a bike trailer) and other towns and cities such as Swansea and Hereford to Brecon, then tours the area before heading home (www.travelbrecon beacons.info; £8 all-day ticket). There are trains from Cardiff to Merthyr Tydfil, and connections from the Midlands to other stations. If you're driving from Cardiff, head north on the A470.

VISITOR INFORMATION   The **Tourist Information Centre,** in Brecon Cattle Market (www.brecon-beacons.com; ✆ **01874/622485**), is open daily, summer 9:30am to 5:30pm; winter, Monday to Friday 9:30am to 5pm and weekends 9:30am to 4pm. If you're looking for a good base, **Brecon Beacons Holiday Cottages** (www.breconcottages.com; ✆ **01874/676446**) has more than 300 properties, sleeping 2 to 10-plus, from old farm buildings to places in the heart of Brecon and other towns.

Exploring the Area

Brecon is a busy little market town at the meeting of the Usk and Honddu rivers, and the perfect base for exploring the area. Georgian buildings line the narrow streets, which are home to traditional butchers and greengrocers as well as more mode-ish cafes. The town was established around a castle and priory built by William the Conqueror's half-brother Bernard de Newmarch in 1093. The castle is now the Castle of Brecon hotel, and it's worth popping into the gardens where there are some ruins. The priory, on Priory Hill, was renamed **Brecon Cathedral** (www.brecon cathedral.org.uk; ✆ **01874/623857**) in 1923. It has an imposing tower, a heritage center in the tithe barn next door, and the lovely **Pilgrim Tea Room** in the grounds. The cathedral is open daily 8am to 6:30pm (free).

The **South Wales Borderers Museum** at The Barracks (www.rrw.org.uk; ✆ **01874/613310**) is a real boys' toys place, with the finest collection of weapons in Wales. There's also the Zulu War Room, recounting the battles in which the regiment fought, including Rorke's Drift, which was turned into the 1964 movie *Zulu* with Michael Caine. It's open year-round Monday to Friday 10am to 5pm (also Apr–Sept Sat and public holidays 10am–4pm); £4 adults, children free. **Penpont** (www. penpoint.com; ✆ **01874/636202**) is a Grade I listed house on the River Usk, just west of Brecon, that has been in the same family since it was built around 1666. Set in a huge working estate, there are also lovely gardens, with a walled garden, rose garden, and maze as well as organic farm shop.

Brecon Beacons National Park ★★★ NATIONAL PARK Start at the **National Park Visitor Centre** (www.breconbeacons.org; ✆ **01874/623366**), a few miles south of Brecon on the A470 at Libanus. It's an attraction in itself with a 3-D model of the area which reminds you of the importance of getting a map if you're heading into the hills. There's a cafe with a Taste of Wales menu, a picnic area (with views of Pen y Fan), and walks on Mynydd Illtyd Common. The center is open year-round daily from 9:30am to 5:30pm (July–Aug), to 5:30pm (March–June, Sept, Oct), and to 4pm (Nov–Feb). There are also visitor centers in other towns.

While it's not a National Park in the same way as you find in the U.S. (an area of wilderness with few developments), the 519 sq. miles of landscape is controlled and access is encouraged, although, if you didn't know you'd say it was simply an area of awe-inspiring countryside. Just driving through the scenery is a treat. Narrow, winding roads dip down beside rivers and then head up and over treeless ridges. Walking, however, gets you into the heart of things, and there are trails for all abilities. Note that it can be a harsh environment with weather changing quickly, so take care. A good way to explore is to sign up for one of the guided walks run by the Park authority.

Much of the Beacons is formed from limestone, creating some of the most outstanding caves in Europe. Most are hidden, open only to experts, but the **National Showcaves Centre for Wales,** Abercraf (www.showcaves.co.uk; ✆ **01639/730284**), opens up this world to the public, including children. A series of caves winds through the hillside, revealing underwater rivers, pools, waterfalls, and stalactites and stalagmites. There's Cathedral Cave (two big waterfalls cascading into a lake to the sound of classical music), Bone Cave (a spooky place where 42 human Bronze Age skeletons were excavated), and the Dan-yr-Ogof caves, with their winding paths passing countless stalactites and stalagmites. You can easily spend a day here, particularly if you have children, who will love the life-size dinosaur models, museum, fossil collection, shire horses, special breeds farm, standing stones, play barn, and picnic area. Tours last 2½ hours. The complex is open April to October, daily from 10am to 3pm (later in high season); £13.50 adults, £7.50 children 3 to 16.

Waterfall Country is the area on the southern edge of the park, between the villages of Hirwaun, Ystradfellte, and Pontneddfechan. There are many walks, but opposite the tourist office in Pontneddfechan (with an exhibition on the area, maps, and hiking gear) is a path that climbs steeply up alongside the splashing river. The walk (a joy for energetic youngsters) takes you past a number of falls, until you emerge on a grassy plateau with picnic tables. Halfway up, follow the River Hepste a short distance to Sgwd Gwladys, "lady falls" a wide, low fall with a path behind the water. A few miles to the west is **Henrhyd** waterfall (follow the signs at Coelbren on the A4221), which, with its 24-m (80-ft.) drop, is the highest in South Wales. Again

ADVENTURE FOR amateurs

The Brecon Beacons is a place for all sorts of adventure activities, yet you don't need to be a young, fit outdoors person to take part. Take caving, for instance. Four of the five longest caving systems in Britain are in the National Park, including Ogof Draenen, which, at 43 miles is the longest. Yet anyone can experience the thrill of crawling beneath the ground, even children, at any time of year. **Adventure Britain** (www.adventure britain.com; ✆ **01639/700388**) takes small groups into Porth-Yr-Ogof (nearly a mile and a half long), near Pontneddfechan. Absolute beginners as young as 10 can take part. After being kitted out with a semi-waterproof suit, wellies, and hard hat with a light, a several-hour session with laconic local guides starts with crossing the foaming River Mellte that runs through the cave. Clamber onto a slippery rock and it's a commando crawl for 6m (20ft) through "the Wormhole," a space so shallow that you have to hold your head sideways. From that point on, there's nowhere to stand upright until you leave after experiencing "the Toilet" (a drop through a hole in the rock followed by a crawl along a tunnel in knee-deep water), "the Letterbox" (a slit so tight that a guide has to push you in), and lots of other tight crawl spots. You end up wet but elated, having done something you

never thought you would be able to. A half-day session is £55 pp, with a family group starting at £200. The adventure level depends on the least-able participant. Adventure Britain also does gorge walking (a family-friendly activity that involves swimming and sliding down rapids, climbing waterfalls, and jumping into pools), canyoning (a high adrenalin adult version of gorge walking), rock climbing, kayaking, and canoeing.

The **Wye Valley Canoe Centre** (www. wyevalleycanoes.co.uk; ✆ **01497/ 847213**) is an excellent place to learn to paddle a reassuringly stable, two-person Canadian canoe. In Glasbury (behind the River Café, see p. 703) and five miles from the book town of Hay-on-Wye, the river is largely placid for the several-hour paddle to Hay. On the meandering stretch you're likely to see kingfishers, swans, and red kites. Half-day hire and a lift back to base costs £20 per person.

There's walking everywhere but if you are worried about getting lost on what can be inhospitable terrain, it's possible to employ a guide. **Kevin Walker Mountain Activities** (www.mountainacts.co.uk; ✆ **01874/658784**) offers guiding (about £200 a day for up to four people), as well as hill skills courses, and multi-day walking.

you can walk behind the water after a beautiful walk from the parking lot taking you across the River Nant Llech, up steep steps, and along a narrow path. For good waterfalls information, visit the independent website www.brecon-beacons.com.

Try the several-hour hike up **Pen y Fan** (from the parking lot at Storey Arms, on the A470). There's also the steam-powered narrow-gauge **Brecon Mountain Railway,** from Merthyr (www.breconmountainrailway.co.uk; ℂ **01685/384854**). One of the most stunning sights is **Carreg Cennen Castle** (www.cadw.wales.gov.uk; ℂ **01558/822291**), near Trapp at the park's western tip, sitting at the top of a limestone crag with a 90-m (295-ft.) drop on one side. Explore the **Monmouthshire and Brecon Canal** from Brecon's canal basin, by hiring an electric boat (carries six) from **Beacon Park Boats** (www.beaconparkdayboats.co.uk; ℂ **01873/858277**). Have lunch at a waterside pub then take your boat across the **Brynich Aqueduct.** For walkers and cyclists there's the 55-mile **Taff Trail** (www.tafftrail.org.uk), which links Brecon with Cardiff. It's mostly traffic-free, including a stretch along the canal and past Talybont Reservoir, and can be joined in many places. There's golf at Cradoc's 18-hole championship course with views over Pen y Fan, fly fishing for trout and salmon in the Usk (see www.breconbeacons.org), and riding at the **Cantref Riding Centre** (www.cantref.com; ℂ **01874/665223**), off the A40 east of Brecon, with options including day rides into the hills. There's also pheasant shooting on the **Glanusk Estate** (www.glanuskestate.com; ℂ **01873/810414**) and clay-pigeon shooting at **Woodland Park** (www.wpshoot.co.uk; ℂ **0781/1189413**).

Entertainment & Nightlife

In the evening it's generally a restaurant or a pub, or both. **Theatr Brycheiniog** (www.brycheiniog.co.uk; ℂ **01874/611622**) in Brecon is the region's arts hub with a rolling selection of music, dance, drama, and spoken word (sometimes in Welsh), and a bar-restaurant, Tipple 'n' Tiffin.

Where to Eat & Stay

Brecon Castle Hotel   This isn't a castle but an inn built in 1809, on the site of a Norman castle on a bluff in the midst of town, with views over the roofs to the mountains. Family-run, it has an old-school vibe. The rooms are charming and all different, and there is a modern annex and self-catering options. The oak-floored Regency-feel **Beacons View restaurant** looks as it might have 200 years ago. Food is modern Welsh, dishes such as roast venison steak (from the nearby Welsh Venison Centre) with roast beetroot, and a licorice and port jus (mains £10.50–£18.50).

Castle Sq., Brecon, Powys LD3 9DB. www.breconcastle.co.uk. ℂ **01874/624611.** Fax 01874/623737. 38 units. £75–£150 double. Rates include breakfast. AE, MC, V. Free parking. **Amenities:** Restaurant; bar. *In room:* TV, Wi-Fi (free) in main hotel.

Felin Fach Griffin ★★   A splendid pub with rooms that combines history (the rooms upstairs are in a space that was once the village dancehall) with boutique flair. The restaurant, a disparate collection of oak tables and chairs, an open fire, and even a room with an Aga stove, is warm and well-regarded (a Michelin Bib Gourmand). There's game from the nearby Welsh Venison Centre, local beef, plenty of fish, greens from the kitchen garden, and you might find yourself with an amuse bouche of carrot and coriander soup served in an espresso cup. Mains £13–£20. Some bedrooms have mountain views, a couple have four-posters, all have Welsh blankets, local art, flowers, and homemade biscuits. Breakfast in the library includes eggs from the pub's hens, fruit from the garden, and Usk Valley apple juice.

Felin Fach, Brecon Powys LD3 0UB. www.eatdrinksleep.ltd.uk. © **01874/620111.** Fax 01685/377088. 7 units. £120–£155 double. Rates include breakfast. AE, MC, V. Free parking. **Amenities:** Restaurant; bar. *In room:* TV, hair dryer, Wi-Fi (free).

Nant Ddu Lodge ★ ☺ This 19th-century shooting lodge is now a modern, bright hotel, bistro, and spa in the heart of the National Park, between Merthyr Tydfil and Brecon. The Lodge snuggles against a wooded hillside; the rooms (including family options) are full of country chic and have mountain views. The spa has an indoor pool, gym, and sauna. Food, proudly Welsh with lots of lamb, steak, and fish (main courses £13–£18), is served in the **bistro and bar.**

Cwm Taf, Merthyr Tydfil CF48 2HY. www.nant-ddu-lodge.co.uk. © **01685/379111.** Fax 01685/377088. 31 units. £95–£105 double. Rates include buffet breakfast. AE, MC, V. Free parking. **Amenities:** Bistro; bar; indoor pool; exercise room; spa. *In room:* TV/DVD, hair dryer, Wi-Fi (free).

River Cafe ★ An offshoot of the adjoining Wye Valley Canoe Centre, this cool, calm spot by the A438 bridge over the river at Glasbury is now very much its own place, serving visitors to the festival in Hay, five miles away, as well as active types (it's on the Sustrans national cycle trail and the Wye Valley Walk). It's a sleek coffee bar combined with modern Italian restaurant, with lovely river views from inside and on the deck. The menu changes daily depending on season and local availability; you might find crab pappardelle or whole grilled sea bass alongside lasagna and spag bol. Upstairs are four airy rooms with views, including one for families. The restaurant is open from 9am to 11:30pm Wednesday to Saturday, and until 5:30pm on Sundays.

The Boat House, Glasbury-on-Wye, Herefordshire HR3 5NP. www.therivercafeglasbury.co.uk. © **01497/847007.** 4 units. £70–£80 double. Rates include English breakfast. AE, MC, V. Free parking. **Amenities:** Restaurant; bar. *In room:* TV, hair dryer, Wi-Fi (free).

SWANSEA ★

190 miles W of London; 82 miles W of Bristol; 40 miles W of Cardiff

Walk or cycle the 5-mile arch of Swansea Bay on a sunny day and you might think you've been transported to California, it's so laid-back. The sea is central to Wales's second city, from its early shipbuilding history and later prominence as a port to its new role as a major tourist attraction thanks to the newly developed (and quite superb) maritime quarter. That said, stand in Swansea on a murky day looking at rows of terraced housing climbing up its hillside and you can understand why the nation's greatest poet, Dylan Thomas, described it as an "ugly, lovely town." Whether you get sunshine or rain, there are a few must-dos: The **National Waterfront Museum** and the **Dylan Thomas Centre.** And do cycle or walk around the bay on the promenade, which follows an old tram route from the Marina to Mumbles pier.

Essentials

GETTING THERE First Great Western trains arrive from London, via Cardiff, every hour. It's about 1 hour (£8) from Cardiff one-way, 3 hours (£42 and up, oneway) from London. **National Express** (www.nationalexpress.com; © **0871/781-8181**) operates buses from London (from £12.50), Manchester (from £40), and Birmingham (from £35),, and can involve a connection in Cardiff.

From Cardiff, it's an easy drive west along the M4.

VISITOR INFORMATION The **Swansea Tourist Information Centre,** Plymouth Street (www.visitswanseabay.com; © **01792/468321**), is open year-round

Monday to Saturday 9:30am to 5:30pm. From Easter to September, it's also open Sunday 10am to 4pm.

GETTING AROUND   Swansea has a good bus network, with buses leaving the bus station at the Quadrant Shopping Centre. Bus nos. 4, X12, X13, 25, and 404 go to the rail station (information: www.firstgroup.com; ✆ **0870/608-2608**).

Exploring the Area

The Maritime Quarter on South Dock is where historic buildings have found new glory, where yachts and old sailing ships bob happily, and where new apartments, shops, restaurants, and coffee bars have produced a vibrant area between the sea and the heart of town. The **National Waterfront Museum** ★★ (www.waterfront museum.co.uk; ✆ **01792/638950**) is a state-of-the art building in which you could happily spend hours, a wonderful example of how a waterfront warehouse can be turned into a contemporary treasure trove. It explores how industrialization shaped Wales and the people who live here. Huge screens show what life used to be like, and there's a big collection of industrial equipment such as mine trucks, engines, carriages, and so forth. It is open daily 10am to 5pm, with free admission.

The **Dylan Thomas Centre,** Somerset Place (www.dylanthomas.com; ✆ **01792/ 463980**), pays tribute to the poet who was born in the city with its free Man and Myth exhibition. It sells four "Dylan Thomas Trails" (£1.50 each), which direct you to his spots including his birthplace, 5 Cwmdonkin Dr. (www.5cwmdonkindrive.com; ✆ **01792/405331**). Ex-U.S. president Jimmy Carter, a Thomas fan, opened the attraction in 1995 and has just recorded an introduction for the audiovisual tour. It is also possible to stay in the house. The Dylan Thomas Centre also holds many literary events. It is open daily 10am to 4:30pm, and has an excellent shop, cafe, and restaurant. The **Dylan Thomas Theatre,** Gloucester Place (www.dylanthomastheatre.org. uk; ✆ **01792/473238**), is the modern home of Swansea Little Theatre, with which Thomas performed in the 1930s. Panels in the foyer tell his story. **Swansea Museum,** Victoria Road (www.swansea.gov.uk; ✆ **01792/653763**), is irresistibly old-fashioned. It's the oldest public museum in Wales with glass cabinets full of artifacts, an Egyptian mummy, and countless other objects. **The Tramshed** features Swansea's last double-decker street tram, and there are boats (tug, lightship) in the dock behind. It's open (free) Tuesday to Sunday 10am to 5pm, in season.

Glynn Vivian Art Gallery ★ 🎒 GALLERY   This gem contains the work of 20th-century Welsh artists Augustus John, his sister Gwen John, and others. It was founded in 1911 by Richard Glynn Vivian, who made his fortune in copper, and was tireless in his travels and collecting. A highlight is Alfred Janes's 1964 portrait of Dylan Thomas.

Alexandra Rd. www.swansea.gov.uk. ✆ **01792/516900.** Free admission. Tues–Sun 10am–5pm.

Mumbles WALKWAY   Once a fishing village, then a Victorian seaside resort, and now an upmarket haunt of the new breed of wealthy Welsh, Mumbles is a stirring 4-mile walk along Swansea Bay. It has half a dozen highly rated restaurants and several boutiques, but at heart it is still a jolly seaside village with gift shops, cafes, and pubs, as well as a pier and a wonderful beach. There's a branch of Swansea's finest, Joe's Ice Cream. **Oystermouth Castle** stands guard amid beautiful parkland. The park and woodland walks are open year-round while the castle (www.swansea.gov.uk) opens sporadically in the summer. On the way here you'll also find Clyne Gardens

Swansea

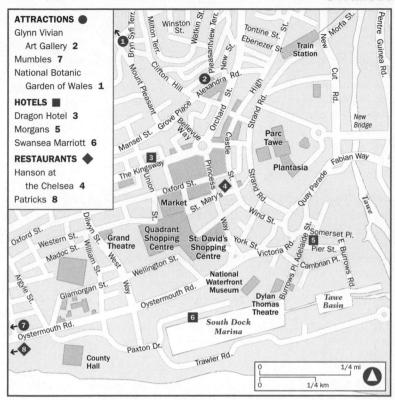

ATTRACTIONS ●
Glynn Vivian
  Art Gallery **2**
Mumbles **7**
National Botanic
  Garden of Wales **1**
HOTELS ■
Dragon Hotel **3**
Morgans **5**
Swansea Marriott **6**
RESTAURANTS ◆
Hanson at
  the Chelsea **4**
Patricks **8**

Map labels: Bryn Syfi Terr., Milton Terr., Winston St., Watkin St., Pleasantview Terr., Tontine St., St., New St., Ebenezer St., Morfa St., New, Pentre Guinea Rd., Train Station, Clifton Hill, Mount Pleasant, Alexandra Rd., New St., High, Cut Rd., New Bridge, Grove Place, Bellevue Way, Orchard St., Strand St., Parc Tawe, Fabian Way, Mansel St., Castle, Princess, Plantasia, Quay Parade, Tawe, The Kingsway, Union, Oxford St., St. Mary's, St., Strand Rd., Market, Way, Wind St., Somerset Pl., Dilwyn St., William St., West Way, Western St., Madoc St., Grand Theatre, Quadrant Shopping Centre, St. David's Shopping Centre, York St., Victoria Rd., Burrows Pl., Adelaide St., Pier St., Cambrian Pl., E. Burrows Rd., Oxford St., Wellington St., National Waterfront Museum, Argyle St., Glamorgan St., Oystermouth Rd., Dylan Thomas Theatre, Tawe Basin, South Dock Marina, Paxton Dr., County Hall, Trawler Rd., 1/4 mi, 1/4 km

18

CARDIFF & THE SOUTH OF WALES

Swansea

(daily, dawn to dusk with free admission), a park known for its rhododendron displays.

National Botanic Garden of Wales ★ GARDEN   This is a garden that is growing into itself; it only opened in 2000, transforming a 568-acre Regency estate into a treasure trove of flowers and wildlife at a cost of £45 million. At its heart is a Great Glasshouse, the largest single-span greenhouse in the world, blending in with the rolling Tywi Valley. It has the best collection of Mediterranean climate zone plants in the northern hemisphere. Expect to spend a full day here; after exploring the themed gardens you can stroll among the lakes, streams, marsh, semi-natural wood-land, and meadows. The garden is 20 miles northwest of Swansea.

Middleton Hall, Llanarthne. www.gardenofwales.org.uk. ⓒ **01558/668768.** Admission £8.50 adults, £7 seniors, £4.50 children 5–16, £21 family ticket. Daily Apr–Sept 10am–6pm (last admission 5pm); Oct–Mar 10am–4:30pm (last admission 3:30pm).

Where to Eat

Hanson at the Chelsea ★ SEAFOOD   Ritz-trained Andrew Hanson brings an innovative menu and bistro style to what used to be the Chelsea Café. A large black-board heavy with daily fish specials dominates the simple, comfy surroundings. There are set menus and a la carte, but there might be a modern take on classics (fish in tempura batter with chips) or a local flourish (baked hake filet with risotto, Welsh cheese crumble, and chive beurre blanc) alongside classy meat dishes.

17 St. Mary's St. Ⓒ **01792/464068.** Main courses (dinner) £15-£20. Set lunch £12.95 2 courses. AE, MC, V. Daily noon–2:15pm; Mon–Sat 7–9:30pm.

Patricks ★ MODERN WELSH   This is what Mumbles is all about: A relaxed, airy seafront restaurant, with dishes such as parsley-crusted hake filet and a cockle beurre blanc, that reflect the ethos of using local produce. They even have a greenhouse and raised beds for micro-herbs and fresh shoots. Lunch dishes (all £10.50) feature the likes of salt and vinegar sea bream filet, hand-cut chips, and tartare sauce. A children's menu offers slimmed-down versions of main dishes. This is a **"restaurant with rooms,"** 16 of them (£115–£175 double).

638 Mumbles Rd. www.patrickswithrooms.com. Ⓒ **01792/360199.** Main courses £17–£25. AE, MC, V. Daily noon–2:20pm; Mon–Sat 6:30–9:50pm.

Entertainment & Nightlife

In addition to the **Dylan Thomas Theatre** (see above), there is the **Grand Theatre,** Singleton Street (www.swansea.gov.uk; Ⓒ **01792/475715**), next to the Quadrant Shopping Centre. It is a Victorian delight that has been refurbished and redeveloped into a multimillion-pound complex, and hosts international opera, ballet, and drama companies, along with dates from top touring entertainers.

Wind Street (rhyming with "dined") is the nightlife hub, a cobbled street full of pubs, bars, and shops. Try **The Bank Statement,** 57–58 Wind St. (www.jd wetherspoon.co.uk; Ⓒ **01792/455477**), one of the chain of low-price, good-beer pubs that pride themselves on taking over unwanted old buildings; here it's in a Victorian bank. More self-consciously trendy is the **No Sign Wine Bar,** 56 Wind St. (Ⓒ **01792/465300**).

Nearby streets (none as busy) also have decent offerings. The **Exchange,** 10 Strand (Ⓒ **01792/462896**), offers glimpses of Ireland, with live music and generous amounts of Celtic *joie de vivre*. The **Potters Wheel,** 85–86 Kingsway (www.jd wetherspoon.co.uk; Ⓒ **01792/465113**), a member of the same chain as the Bank Statement, offers food and drink in a setting that's evocative of turn-of-the-20th-century Wales.

Where to Stay

Dragon Hotel   Right in the heart of the city, the Dragon has been around for 50 years but has blossomed after a £3.5 million refit. It has understated, modern style in the rooms and the smart **brasserie** (2-course dinner £17). There are also excellent health facilities with an 18-m (60-ft.) pool, gym, and beauty treatments. The lounge has its own snack menu. The breakfast buffet is £14.

The Kingsway, Swansea SA1 5LS. www.dragon-hotel.co.uk. Ⓒ **01792/657100.** Fax 01792/456044. 106 units. £78–£149 double. AE, DC, MC, V. Free parking. **Amenities:** Restaurant; bar; indoor pool; exercise room; room service. *In room:* AC, TV, hair dryer, Wi-Fi (£8.20 for 24 hr.).

Morgans ★★   This boutique hotel occupies the grandiose, Grade II-listed former Port Authority building. The decor really does use the setting well: Rich and heady with a sumptuous Morgans Bar and Champagne Bar, plus the upstairs **restaurant** with its high, curving ceiling and wood floor. Room prices are realistic, and even a 3-course dinner costs only £18 Monday to Friday, with £10 bottles of wine available.

You can, however, choose to pay a lot more for the best rooms, which truly are huge, with large beds and 106-cm (42-in) TVs. Over the road, next to the Dylan Thomas Centre, is Morgans Townhouse, a Georgian house with rooms but not room service.

Somerset Place, Swansea SA1 1RR. www.morganshotel.co.uk. ☏ **01792/484848.** 42 units. £65–£250 double. AE, DC, MC, V. Free parking. **Amenities:** Restaurant; bar; concierge; room service. *In room:* TV/DVD, hair dryer, Wii (in main hotel), Wi-Fi (free).

Swansea Marriott ★★   Right on the marina with panoramic views over the bay, this is the safe, international option. Even if it's not the most inspiring building to look at, inside it's everything you expect from the upmarket chain. Rooms are a decent size, and modern in a way that would never offend. There's a good pool, with views over the gardens, a gym, and **the Bayside Grill restaurant.**

Maritime Quarter, Swansea SA1 3SS. www.swanseamarriott.co.uk. ☏ **01792/642020.** Fax 01792/650345. ☏ 800/228-9290 in U.S. and Canada. 119 units. £101–£180 double. AE, DC, MC, V. Free parking. **Amenities:** Restaurant; bar; indoor heated pool; exercise room; Jacuzzi; sauna; concierge; room service. *In room:* A/C, TV, hair dryer, Wi-Fi (£7.50 per day).

GOWER PENINSULA

The Gower (in Wales it's often just "Gower") pokes out from South Wales at the edge of Swansea. Its coastline starts just past Mumbles, the seaside village at the end of Swansea Bay. Britain's first Area of Outstanding Natural Beauty, with a breathtakingly beautiful coastline, Gower is all about beaches. Some are huge (Rhossili is 3 miles long); some are almost exotically picturesque (Three Cliffs Bay is magical); others are simply unspoiled, clean, and sandy, providing everything you need for a beach getaway. There are plenty of outdoor activities here. Walking along the coast path is spectacular, or you can walk across the peninsula following the 35-mile Gower Way. There's also pony-trekking down to the sea, and watersports. Inland there are woods to tramp across, including **Park Wood,** near the **Gower Heritage Centre** at Parkmill (see below), and at **Millwood,** near Penrice, where wild daffodils grow. To the north, there's a huge network of dunes at **Whitford Burrows** and **Llanrhidian Sands.**

Essentials

GETTING THERE   For train information see Swansea (above), because Gower starts just outside the city. By road, from Swansea follow Mumbles Road.

VISITOR INFORMATION   The **Mumbles Tourist Information Centre,** on Mumbles Road (www.mumblesinfo.org.uk; ☏ 01792/361302), is open year-round, Monday to Saturday, 10am to 5pm (4pm winter).

GETTING AROUND   Gower has a good bus network; the **Gower Explorer** will get you to Llangennith, Oxwich, Port Eynon, and Rhossili. **First Cymru** goes to Oystermouth, Mumbles, Bishopston, and Pennard. For details on both, visit www.traveline-cymru.info or call ☏ **0871/200-2233.**

Exploring the Area

Three Cliffs Bay ★★★ is possibly the most beautiful beach in Wales: Fantastic sand, caves, rock pools, a ruined castle, and the unique three-pyramid rock formation (with a natural arch), which gives it its name. It can take 30 minutes to walk from the Southgate parking lot, or you can scramble down the cliffs. Then there's the river

(Pennard Pill) to cross at the start of the beach. There are stepping stones but once the tide races in they are of little use, and swimming is too dangerous except at low tide. This is a beach for those with a sense of adventure and who shun shops and cafes. You just need to time your visit so the tide is going out. If it's in, you can explore Pennard Warren, sand dunes leading up to the unmanned ruins of Pennard Castle. **Tor Bay,** separated from Three Cliffs by the Great Tor headland, is another picturesque, sandy beach, with dunes filling the valley behind it. There's always sand, even at high tide. The best access is from Penmaen village, where there is parking and a 1-mile footpath.

Oxwich Bay lacks the magnificence of other Gower beaches, but is a lot easier to access. There's parking, plus beach shops and cafes to complement the 2½ miles of sand, safe swimming, and dunes. But it becomes crowded. If you want peace, walk east to Nicholaston Burrows; it's calmer and the dunes are bigger. The ruins of Oxwich Castle (really a 16th-century mock fortified manor) are at Oxwich Point, to the west.

Port Eynon Bay is another family spot, with parking at Horton, minutes from the beach. It was once smugglers' territory as you might guess from the Smugglers Gift Shop and Smugglers Haunt Restaurant. In summer there is also a surf shop and fish and chip shop. It has three beaches. **The Sands,** also known as Slade Bay, is farthest east, has rock pools and firm sand, and can be reached over the cliffs from Oxwich Bay. You can also walk 15 minutes across a field from the village of Slade, or via the coastal path from Horton. **The Cove,** also a mix of sand and rocks, is nearer the parking lot. To the far west the beach becomes rockier and near the Youth Hostel (see "Where to Stay," below) is **Salt House Mere,** a small, stony cove.

Rhossili Bay ★★ can be reached by a wonderful 4-mile cliff walk from Port Eynon past Culver Hole, Paviland Cave, Mewslade, and Fall Bay, or you can park and walk down the cliff steps. Either way, the view over the majestic 3-mile beach and the mighty Atlantic is quite something. **Worm's Head** is a rocky island (about a half-mile long) shaped by the sea; if the tide's just gone out you'll have time to walk across the causeway. Rhossili is Gower's best surf beach, the power of the waves proved by the skeletons of two wrecked ships. Walk along the beach to Llangennith Burrows (big dunes), and at low tide you can walk to Burry Holms, a tiny island with the ruins of a medieval monastic settlement.

Away from the coast (close to Parkmill on the A4118) you'll find **Parc le Breos (Giant's Grave),** a Stone Age burial chamber. The remains of at least four people have been found here. A passage and four chambers are in a cairn 21m (70 ft.) long. Parkmill, more a wooded valley than a village, is home to **Gower Heritage Centre** (www. gowerheritagecentre.co.uk; ☎ **01792/371206**), a former mill with animal park, museum, adventure playground, crafts workshops, and tearooms (adults £5.90, children 3 and up £4.90). Nearby is the **Gower Inn,** a stone pub with large garden, the **Parc-Le-Breos Riding Centre,** and several walks in Forestry Commission woods.

Where to Eat

Maes-yr-Haf ★ MODERN WELSH   This is a delight at the end of the footpath down to Three Cliffs Bay (see above). A starter of ravioli of cockle and laverbread, crispy bacon, and buttered Gower leeks, and main courses such as best end of Welsh lamb, marsh samphire, lamb crackling, broad bean, and mint makes the most of local produce. The place, cool and modern in natural materials, is a **"restaurant with guest rooms."** The five bedrooms have large TVs (£100–£140 double with breakfast).

Parkmill, Gower. www.maes-yr-haf.com. © **01792/371000.** Main courses £15–£21. AE, DC, MC, V. Tues–Sun noon–2pm; Tues–Sat 7–9pm. Follow the A4118 from Swansea.

The Welcome to Town MODERN WELSH This "country bistro" is in a charming white-painted building in the heart of the Gower, but only 10 miles from Swansea. Chef proprietor Ian Bennett, who has worked for the Roux Brothers at the famed Waterside Inn in Bray, Berkshire, comes up with dishes such as roast best end of Welsh lamb with wild garlic polenta, glazed spring vegetables, and sauce caisson, and seared hand-dived scallops with curry salt, braised scallions, and crispy chicken skin.

Llanrhidian, Gower. www.thewelcometotown.co.uk. © **01792/390015.** Main courses £20–£25. AE, DC, MC, V. Tues–Sun noon–2pm; Tues–Sat 7–9:30pm. In winter, hours and days are reduced; check website. Follow the B4295 from Swansea.

Where to Stay

Fairyhill ★ This divine, stone 18th-century manor is in grounds with lawns, woods, lake, and a fishing stream. There's a lounge with log fire and the rooms are airy and luxurious in country style. The gardens supply vegetables to go with seafood for dishes such as filet of Gower sea bass, green beans, crushed potatoes, laverbread, and lovage velouté (a white sauce with herbs). Two courses are £35, 3 courses £45.

Reynoldston, Gower, Swansea SA3 1BS. www.fairyhill.net. © **01792/390139.** Fax 01792/391358. 8 units. £180–£280 double. Rates include full Welsh breakfast. AE, MC, V. Outside Reynoldston, off the A4118 11 miles from Swansea. No children under 8. **Amenities:** Restaurant; bar; room service. *In room:* TV/DVD, CD player, iPod docking station, Wi-Fi (free).

The Old Rectory ☺ The National Trust owns large areas of land here and also a number of cottages. This is the Trust at its best. It stands on a terrace above the dreamlike expanse of Rhossili Bay with views of sand and sea all the way to Worm's Head. The main building is from 1850 with outbuildings that are possibly medieval. Inside it is warmly luxurious thanks to wood-burning stoves. There's a sitting room, study, dining room, big kitchen, and three double bedrooms (one king-size), a single, and a cot. It's great for families, and the village is a 10-minute walk.

Rhossili, Gower, Swansea SA3 1PL. www.nationaltrustcottages.co.uk. © **01834/842881.** Sleeps 8. £510–£1,436 for 3 nights (3-night min). AE, MC, V. **Amenities:** TV, kitchen, pay phone.

Port Eynon Youth Hostel ★★ ☺ 👜 If this were a boutique hotel it would cost a fortune to stay here in this beach-side setting. When the tide's in, it almost licks the back door of this old stone lifeboat station. When it's out you can jump onto the sands after your breakfast coffee behind the lounge's picture window. Like many Youth Hostels it's been given a makeover with en suite facilities, and has three double rooms, two family rooms, and a couple of small dorms.

Old Lifeboat House, Port Eynon, Swansea SA3 1NN. www.yha.org.uk. © **0845/371-9135.** 28 beds. From £18.40 adults (plus £3 non-YHA members), £14 children 17 and under. Follow hostel sign down unpaved road behind dunes. AE, MC, V. **Amenities:** Lounge, common room, self-catering kitchen.

LAUGHARNE TO PEMBROKE

Laugharne: 20 miles W of Swansea; Pembroke: 45 miles W of Swansea

To the west of Swansea and Cardiff you'll find a very different Wales. The coast gets wilder and you increasingly find yourself away from it all. **Laugharne** (pronounced *Larne*) is a peaceful estuary town, known as the spot where Dylan Thomas lived and worked. **Pembroke** is a historic town, with an impressive castle. They are quaint and as charming as they come, albeit in a very different manner. But don't be fooled into thinking that this region is quiet and sparsely populated. Between Laugharne and Pembroke is the other face of coastal Wales, the jolly seaside experience of **Tenby** with busy beaches and ice-cream kiosks. Yet Tenby, Wales's busiest resort town, is pretty with brightly painted town houses, even a fort. There's a big choice of caravan parks nearby, and areas of beauty with smart hotels and cottages to stay in. Unspoiled beaches abound, from open expanses to hidden coves. There are plenty of festivals too: **Pembrokeshire Fish Week** (www.fishweek.co.uk) takes place each June, with cookery demos and snorkeling safaris. **Laugharne Weekend** (www.thelaugharne weekend.com) is in March—you might find U.S. rocker Patti Smith reading her poetry.

Essentials

GETTING THERE   From Swansea, there are trains to Tenby (Arriva Trains Wales, 1½ hr., £13 one-way) and Pembroke (which takes another 30 min.; £13 one-way); from Cardiff the journey takes another hour and is about £9 more.

VISITOR INFORMATION   Tourist information offices are in a number of towns, most open year-round with varying hours (see www.visitpembrokeshire for a list). The Tenby office is in the central Gateway Complex (✆ 01834/842402); Pembroke, on Commons Road (✆ 01646/622388); and Carmarthen, on Lammas Street (www.discovercarmarthenshire.com; ✆ 01267/231557).

GETTING AROUND   A car is best, but there are other options. An 8-day **Explore South Wales Pass** (www.arrivatrainswales.co.uk) gives rail travel for 4 days and bus travel for 8 days as far north as Aberystwyth for £60 (half-price for ages 5–25, free children 4 and under) and includes discounts for attractions. The **Coastal Cruiser** bus runs between Pembroke and several popular beaches, and there is a network of other services across to Carmarthenshire. A **West Wales Rover** ticket (£6 adults, £3 accompanied children), sold on buses, allows all-day travel in Pembrokeshire, Carmarthenshire, and up into Cardiganshire. Services are by varied companies, so local council websites are the best places for info (www.pembrokeshire.gov.uk and www.carmarthenshire.gov.uk). For times and routes, see www.traveline-cymru.org.uk.

Exploring the Area

Laugharne sits on the River Taf estuary, with Georgian buildings and pretty cottages, a ruined castle, and the **Dylan Thomas Boathouse** ★ (www.dylanthomasboat house.com; ✆ 01994/427420). This is where the poet and author spent the last 4 years of his life, before dying in 1953 during a trip to America. The boathouse is a museum with family rooms full of his possessions, and on the river path you can peer through the window of a shed where he wrote *Under Milk Wood,* which has the feel that he's likely to return from the pub at any moment. There is a tearoom with home-made cakes and estuary views. Admission is £4 for adults, £3 for seniors, £1.95 for children 7 to 16, and free for children 6 and under (daily May–Oct 10am–5:30pm and Nov–Apr 10:30am–3:30pm). Thomas is buried at the **Parish Church of St. Martin,** on the road into town, his grave marked by a wooden cross. **Laugharne Castle** (www.cadw.wales.gov.uk; ✆ 01443/336000) has a waterfront position; it's pleasing to walk among the Tudor ruins.

   Tenby is a proper seaside town in the nicest possible way. It juts into the sea with a harbor in the middle and long beaches either side: North Beach is near the quay, and South Beach is backed by dunes. The medieval town with its 13th-century walls, castle ruins, and narrow, winding streets rolls right down to the water. Up above are dolled-up hotels and guesthouses, smart shops, and restaurants that veer from the stylish to burger bars. By the quay there are stalls selling their catch and places for coffee.

Tenby Museum & Art Gallery, Castle Hill (www.tenbymuseum.org.uk; $\mathcal{C}$ 01834/842809), opened in 1878 to display naturalist and archeological collections, but now also features work by Augustus and Gwen John, and other Welsh artists. It is open daily 10am to 5pm (closed weekends Nov–Mar). Admission is £4 for adults, £2 for children 5 to 15. The **Tudor Merchant's House,** Quay Hill (www. nationaltrust.org.uk; $\mathcal{C}$ 01834/842279), is a 15th-century home with Tudor furnishings. It's open April to October, Wednesday to Monday 11am to 5pm (daily mid-July–Aug). Admission is £3 adults and £1.50 children under 16.

Boat trips leave the quay regularly for the 20-minute journey to **Caldy Island ★**, settled by Celtic monks in the 6th century. Once there you are free to wander among the trees and flowers or see the chapel, church, priory, and lighthouse. Children love the wild feel. There is island-made perfume, chocolate, and shortbread to buy, and a Post Office selling specially franked covers. Relax in the tea gardens, or picnic on the beach in Priory Bay. Boats run from Easter to late October, Monday to Friday 10am to 3pm, plus Saturdays from May to September. Round-trips are £11 adults, £6 children 14 and under. Visit www.caldey-island.co.uk or call $\mathcal{C}$ **01834/844453.**

Just east of Tenby is the pretty village of **Saundersfoot,** with its central quay and beaches on either side, a lively place full of pubs and fish and chip shops. West of Tenby are a couple of the country's most enchanting beaches. **Manorbier** was home for a short time to playwright George Bernard Shaw, and novelist Virginia Woolf was a regular visitor. **Manorbier Castle** (www.manorbiercastle.co.uk; $\mathcal{C}$ 01834/871394) provides a backdrop (part of it is a holiday rental), and a stream runs down through the flat stones on the beach to the reddish sands. **Barafundle Bay,** south of Pembroke, is one of Wales's natural wonders, like something out of *Pirates of the Caribbean,* a little beach backed by rocks and greenery, and only accessible by steep steps down after a clifftop walk from Stackpole Quay, where there is a parking lot and cafe (www.nationaltrust.org.uk/stackpole; $\mathcal{C}$ 01646/661359).

Pembroke is the county town with shops, restaurants, and inns along one main charming street. It received its charter around 1090 and was built around **Pembroke Castle** (www.pembroke-castle.co.uk; $\mathcal{C}$ 01646/684585), a fortress on a rocky spur above town. The town walls formed the castle's outer ward, and the 14-mile system can still be viewed as a fortified town. The castle, on the banks of the River Pembroke, has been impressively restored. Its round keep is 23m (75 ft.) high with walls 5.5-m (18-ft.) thick, and topped by a dome. There are towers, battlements, passageways, and oak-beamed halls, which children love. The castle is where the Tudor dynasty began; it was the birthplace of Henry VII. Admission is £4.75 adults, £3.75 children 5 to 15. It is open March and October daily 10am to 5pm; April to September daily 9:30am to 6pm; and November to February daily 10am to 4pm.

Where to Eat

Blue Ball BRITISH   This is a restaurant that uses wild garlic and samphire, smokes its own fish, cheese, and meat, and has its own boat for fishing. You might find a whole grilled Tenby lobster with thermidor sauce and an orange and avocado salad, or black bream or sea bass. Much comes as a surprise on the daily specials board depending on what's been found or caught, but the menu does feature local dishes such as faggots. The setting is nice, too, tucked away in the town wall.

Upper Frog St., Tenby. www.theblueballrestaurant.co.uk. © **01834/843038.** Main courses £10.50– £27.50. AE, MC, V. Tues–Sat 6pm–9pm (Sat 9:30pm), but can vary in winter.

Lamphey Court Hotel ★ WELSH/BRITISH   This smart hotel, between Pembroke and the sea, has two options. The formal Georgian Restaurant is open on Friday and Saturday. The Conservatory is open daily for lunch, and is especially lovely when you can sit out on the patio. Both serve local food, including lobster from nearby Freshman Bay, River Teifi salmon, and lamb from Pembrokeshire's Preseli Hills.

Lamphey Court Hotel, Lamphey. www.lampheycourt.co.uk. © **01646/672272.** Reservations required. Main courses £17–£25. AE, DC, MC, V. Georgian Restaurant Fri–Sat 7–9:30pm. Conservatory daily noon–2:30pm.

Stackpole Inn GASTROPUB   This delight, a 15-minute walk from Barafundle Bay, has won many accolades, including Best Gastropub in Wales at the Great British Pub Awards 2011. The menu features dishes such as slow braised Welsh beef featherblade with Welsh bacon, champ, local cabbage, and a rich sticky gravy, and daily specials. The dining room has beamed ceilings, stone walls, and a wood-burning stove, and there are tables on the lawn. Welsh beers (including Double Dragon) are backed up by guest ales from around the U.K. Four soft, white **guest rooms** in a separate building offer a smart place to stay (£90 double).

Jasons Corner, Stackpole. www.stackpoleinn.co.uk. © **01646/672324.** Main courses £10–£18. AE, MC, V. Mon–Fri noon–2:30pm and 6:30–11pm; Sat noon–11pm; Sun noon–3pm.

Entertainment & Nightlife

Nightlife here isn't sophisticated. Tenby has more than a dozen pubs, such as the simple **Buccaneer Inn,** on Julian Street (© **01834/842273**), and the more boisterous **Sun,** on the High Street (© **01834/845941**). There are several brash nightclubs: **Sands,** in the adjoining resort of Saundersfoot (© **01834/813728**); and **Jammo's** (© **01834/845279**) and **DJ's** (© **01834/849400**) in Penally.

Where to Stay

Atlantic Hotel   This grand old hotel looks out over the sea from Tenby's clifftop seafront, with sweeping views of South Beach, Caldey Island, and Castle Hill. There are stylish but unfussy rooms, an indoor pool, the old-world charm of **Carrington's restaurant** (3 courses £25), and a comfy lounge. There are sea-facing gardens from which you can walk down to the beach.

The Esplanade, Tenby, Dyfed SA70 7DU. www.atlantic-hotel.uk.com. © **01834/842881.** 42 units. £120–£180 double. Rates include full English breakfast. AE, MC, V. Free parking. **Amenities:** Restaurant; bar; indoor pool; whirlpool bath; steam room. *In room:* TV, hair dryer, Wi-Fi (free).

Bluestone ☺   Eco-friendly yet quaintly upmarket, this modern village sits in Pembrokeshire Coast National Park. Lodges, cottages, and studios (2–8 beds) are built from local sustainable materials and have solar panels. Yet the village heart looks like an historic hamlet, with a butcher's, baker's, and a pub along with spa, restaurants, and sports club. There's a children's club, high ropes course, and cycle hire, but beaches are a drive away. There's also **Blue Lagoon** (www.bluelagoonwales.com), an indoor/outdoor water park heated by the resort's biomass plant, which is open to the public but Bluestone guests get in free.

Canaston Wood Narberth, Pembrokeshire SA67 8DE. www.bluestonewales.com. ✆ **01834/888367.** 350 units. 3-night weekend and 4-night midweek stays from £225 double. **Amenities:** Restaurants; shops; activities; water park. *In room:* TV/DVD, hair dryer, Wi-Fi (free, in lodges and around resort).

The Grove ★ A beautiful 15th-century house, in the countryside just outside Tenby, that has neo-Gothic Arts & Crafts and Georgian additions and is now a luxury hotel and restaurant. There are nine bedrooms and three suites, half of them in the house, half in outbuildings. All are individually furnished, not least the John Sheddon room, with a king-size four-poster, ceramic fireplace, and cast-iron bath. The restaurant, with its wood-clad walls, is charmingly country house and serves a modern British £45 3-course dinner with dishes such as pollock with Carmarthen ham, oca tubers, chorizo cream, and radiccio, including contributions from the kitchen garden.

Molleston, Narberth, Pembrokeshire SA67 8BX. www.thegrove-narbeth.co.uk. ✆ **01834/860915.** 12 units. £180–£260 double; £250–£290 suite; £190–£380 cottages. Rates include breakfast (weekly non-B&B cottage rates available). AE, MC, V. **Amenities:** Restaurant. *In room:* TV/DVD, hair dryer, Wi-Fi (free).

Hurst House on the Marsh ★ A Grade II listed 16th-century building that used to be a dairy farm but is now a boutique hotel. Guest rooms in the house have antiques, high-tech entertainment, and REN toiletries. There are suites and mezzanine rooms in outbuildings, plus a two-bedroom cottage with wood-burning stove. The restaurant has the air of Spain: Tiled floors, olive trees, views over the kitchen garden and marshland. Modern Welsh dishes feature in the main menu (£34.50 for three courses) and tasting menu (£55). There's also a neat spa and hair salon.

East Marsh, Laugharne, Carmarthenshire SA33 4RS. www.hurst-house.co.uk. ✆ **01994/427417.** 17 units. £175–£1350 double. Rates include breakfast. AE, MC, V. Free parking. **Amenities:** Restaurant; bar; spa; salon. *In room:* TV, hair dryer, Wi-Fi (free).

Manorbier Youth Hostel ☺ Wales has some wonderful Youth Hostels in idyllic locations, and this is one of the best: a striking modern building above Manorbier Beach. It's almost on the coastal path, with cliff walks over to other bays and beaches. The place is simple but classy with en suite rooms ideal for families, as well as the option of good meals and fair trade coffee, or self-catering.

Manorbier, Dyfed SA70 7TT. www.yha.org.uk. ✆ **0870/770-5954.** 69 beds. £10–£18.40 adults (plus £3 non-members). Take the B4585 toward Manorbier, then follow YHA signs. **Amenities:** Restaurant; TV lounge.

THE WILD SOUTHWEST

St. Davids: 95 miles NW of Cardiff, 60 miles W of Swansea

After Pembroke you find yourself at the southern tip of the long west coast. This is the trendy holiday spot for Brits who race down the M4 from London, although the motorway ends just after Swansea and the rest of the journey can take as long again. No part of the county is more than 12 miles from the sea. Here you'll find Britain's smallest city, **St. Davids,** with its tiny cathedral. There's also the sweep of St. Bride's Bay with beaches, cliffs, and awesome sunsets. After St. David's, the coast wiggles north past Fishguard (where ferries arrive and depart for Ireland) and gets ever more rugged until **Poppit Sands** at the River Teifi, across from Cardigan. All this is on the 186-mile Pembrokeshire Coastal Path, part of the **Pembrokeshire Coast**

National Park. The region is dotted with holiday homes and cottages as well as hotels; it's full of visitors but also good for those who want to get away from it all. From the westernmost tip there really is nothing between you and the U.S., but the weather can be delightfully balmy: You're not far north of Cornwall down in England.

Essentials

GETTING THERE Trains can get you as far as Haverfordwest (the region's hub), and Milford Haven, with occasional trains to Fishguard Harbour. The line runs along the south coast, via Swansea and Cardiff, with a line coming down from Birmingham and the Midlands. There's a Cardiff–Haverfordwest train (Arriva Trains Wales; about £22 one-way) every couple of hours and the shortest journey time is around 2 hours 20 minutes. By road, the A40 heads to Haverfordwest, with smaller roads radiating out.

VISITOR INFORMATION The **National Park Visitor Centre** (Oriel y Parc) in High Street, St. Davids, (www.pembrokeshirecoast.org.uk; ℂ **01437/720392**), is a modern gallery and exhibition space devoted to the area. It is open daily Easter to October 9:30am to 5:30pm, November to Easter 10am to 4:30pm.

GETTING AROUND See Laugharne to Pembroke "Essentials" for bus details (p. 710).

Exploring the Area

ST. BRIDE'S BAY This great curve of coast, 30 miles from Wooltack Point stretching to St. Davids, is southwest of Haverfordwest. Here are attractive seaside towns with hills rising up behind them, and beaches bookended by cliffs. There's picturesque **Little Haven** and busy **Broad Haven** with its wide beach, seafront shops, cafes, and pubs. The beach at **Druidston** is sandy and unspoiled, but parking is limited to the coast road, so arrive early. Access is along two paths to the clifftops then a steep climb (there's an excellent hotel, the Druidstone: See "Where to Stay" below).

Access to sandy **Nolton Haven** is easier, with parking, shops, and cafes. And then you come to the pride of St. Bride's: **Newgale ★★★**, a beach that will stay with you forever. It's where the A487 from Haverfordwest to St. Davids hits the coast, plunging down the hill into a heavenly vista with cliffs rising at either end. The flat, perfect sand stretches for 3 miles and the road squeezes between it and the Sands cafe, a pub, a couple of shops, and a busy campsite. There's pay parking (free for cafe users). No matter how many times you come, it's always different thanks to the undulating western light; sometimes in the morning the cliffs are shrouded in sea mist, sunlight filtering through the haze, but by late afternoon the skies can be awash with gold.

ST. DAVIDS St. Davids is thought to be the birthplace of the patron saint of Wales. Dewi Sant (later St. David), a Celtic religious leader in the 6th century, set up a small monastic community here. The wooden church was burned or torn down several times until the Normans built one of stone. The town grew up around the church. Today, with its ornately carved roof and a Norman nave, **St. Davids Cathedral** (www.stdavidscathedral.org.uk; ℂ **01437/720199**) is a magnificent example of medieval religious architecture. It sits in a rural spot on the edge of town and contains what are said to be the bones of St. David. The nave is a place of medieval beauty, and the 15th century choir stalls have lighthearted carvings. Admission is free, daily from 8:30am to 6:30pm. In August there are free tours (although a £4 donation is suggested).

wales COAST PATH

In May 2012 the final stretch of the 870-mile Wales Coastal Path opened, creating the first continuous path around any country in the world. The Pembrokeshire Coastal Path, which waltzes across clifftops amid wonderful scenery, joined up with a footpath that goes from Chepstow in the south to the outskirts of Chester on the English border in the north, taking in the rocky headlands of Anglesey and the gentle shoreline of the River Dee, the beaches of the Gower and the sweep of Cardigan Bay, the seaside town promenade of Llandudno and the Cardiff Bay waterfront, encompassing 18 medieval castles, 12 National Nature Reserves, and 41 Blue Flag beaches. There are maps and full information, including the five top short walks in each of eight regions and details of attractions along the way, at www.ccw.gov.uk.

The **Bishop's Palace** ruins (www.cadw.wales.gov.uk; ✆ **01437/720517**) stand across the meadow and river, with gatehouse, battlements, and curtain walls. An outstanding sight is the elegant parapet that runs along both main walls. The site is open April to June and September, October daily 9:30am to 5pm; July and August daily 9:30am to 6pm; and November to March Monday to Saturday 9:30am to 4pm, Sunday from 11am. Admission is £3.20 for adults, £2.80 for children 5 to 15.

WHITESANDS ★★ This is a splendid beach, 2 miles northwest of St. Davids (take the A487, then the B4583). Access is free, but there's a £2 parking charge. Swimming is largely safe, and there are dunes to play in, beach shops, and cafes. Whitesands is also considered to have some of Britain's best surfing, and there are exhibitions with participants from as far away as California. From here you can take boat trips out to the RSPB reserve of Ramsey Island.

POPPIT SANDS ★ This is the final beach in Pembrokeshire before Cardigan (Ceredigion), and one of the few accessible beaches in the area. It is flat expanse of sand at the mouth of the Teifi, backed by dunes, with striking views of Cardigan's cliffs. To find it, turn off the A487 just south of Cardigan onto the B4546 and meander through village lanes (including St. Dogmaels, where the Pembrokeshire Coast Path officially starts/ends) until you arrive at the shore where you'll find people cramming cars onto the verge to escape the parking fee. It is a wonderful, if windy, spot, and you might also see seals and dolphins. There's a cafe selling homemade cakes.

Where to Eat

Cwtch ★★★ 🎒 ☺ MODERN WELSH Smart, hip, and family-friendly, Cwtch (pronounced *cutch,* which means snug) is a gem. The grown-up menu is great value and there's a children's menu tempting older children rather than assuming everyone under 16 wants chicken nuggets. At £9 for 2 courses they are slimmed-down adult dishes such as pork belly with apple sauce, or (for a £1.50 surcharge) a 4-oz. Welsh Black rib-eye, followed by white-chocolate and lemon curd cheesecake. The place is artily informal, the brainchild of a former ad exec, with slate and wood floors, and blackboards detailing fish specials.

22 High St., St. Davids. www.cwtchrestaurant.co.uk. ✆ **01437/720491**. 3-course menu £32. MC, V. Daily Apr–Sept from 6pm; Oct–Mar Tues–Sat from 6pm. Last sitting 9:30pm.

Sands Cafe ★ INTERNATIONAL   It's *the* place at big Newgale beach, smart and modern yet with the friendliness of a local cafe and a clientele that ranges from surfer dudes to parents with babies. Sands has a deck and even a lawn overlooking water meadows. Food includes fish and chips alongside baguettes (crab and so forth), and homemade hummus with pita bread. Ice cream is Gianni's, made with organic milk from Caerfai Farm, a renowned producer near St. Davids.

Newgale (where the A487 from Haverfordwest to St. Davids dips down to the sea), St. Bride's Bay. www.newsurf.co.uk. ℂ **01437/729222.** Main courses £5–£10. MC, V. Daily 9:30am–5pm in winter, with extended hours in busier seasons.

Where to Stay

Druidstone ★★ 🎒 ☺   This family haven sits in wild gardens on the cliff above Druidston Haven beach. It's part hotel, part holiday home; some of the rooms have en suite, some not. There are self-catering cottages converted from outbuildings that sleep 6–12. It's been run by the same couple since 1972 and has that post-hippie feel, sometimes with arty events (the owners are chummy with reformed pop-folk-rockers Stackridge, the first band George Martin worked with after The Beatles). Breakfast is a treat (St. Bride's Bay mackerel, organic black pudding); there's food served in the cellar bar, a restaurant with an ever-changing menu (main courses £9–£20); and children's high tea. A perfect place for a family get-together.

Broad Haven, Haverfordwest, Pembrokeshire SA62 3NE. www.druidstone.co.uk. ℂ **01437/781221.** Fax 01437/720025. 18 units, inc. 7 cottages. £110–£180 double; cottages £420–£1,260 per week. Rates include breakfast. AE, MC, V. **Amenities:** Restaurant; bar. *In room:* TV, hair dryer.

Warpool Court Hotel   The best views don't always come cheap, and the panorama from this country house is enough to make you pay out. The Warpool sits high on the St. Davids' Peninsula, just outside town, and its 15 acres of gardens gaze loftily over sea and coast. The least expensive rooms are modest and don't benefit from the scenery outside. But for your money you do get secluded gardens and views over one of the most beautiful coastal stretches in Wales. Two-course dinner is £33.50.

St. Davids, Pembrokeshire SA62 6BN. www.warpoolcourthotel.com. ℂ **01437/720300.** Fax 01437/720676. 25 units. £120–£340 double. Rates include breakfast. AE, DC, MC, V. **Amenities:** Restaurant; bar; covered heated pool (Easter–Oct only); outdoor tennis court (lit); babysitting. *In room:* TV, hair dryer, Wi-Fi (free, in most rooms).

MID-WALES: COAST & COUNTRY

Aberystwyth is 240 miles from London, 115 miles north west of Cardiff This isn't the best-known stretch of coast, but it does have its gems. Start at Cardigan and you pass the jolly seaside town of New Quay and the stylish fishing village of Aberaeron. As you edge into mid-Wales you reach the big town of Aberystwyth and eventually wind up on the dunes at the edge of the Dovey estuary, with views of the North Wales mountains in the distance. Head inland and you quickly get into the wild country of hills and valleys and the little city of Lampeter with its university.

Essentials

GETTING THERE   There are hourly trains from Birmingham New Street Station to Aberystwyth (Arriva Trains Wales; from £26 one-way; trip around 3 hours; a connecting service from London makes it nearly 5 hours).

Arriva (www.arrivabus.co.uk) operates the Express 40 Aberystwyth–Carmarthen bus service, roughly hourly, which takes around 2 hours and costs £8.50 one-way. It passes through Aberaeron, from where the hourly Express 50 service connects with New Quay. A few buses continue from Carmarthen to Cardiff, a journey time of around 4-plus hours.

Arriva also operates other buses in the area.

VISITOR INFORMATION   **Aberystwyth Tourist Information Centre,** Terrace Road (www.ceredigion.gov.uk; ✆ **01970/612125**), is open year-round, generally 9:30am to 5:30pm. Offices are also at Aberaeron, New Quay, and Cardigan.

GETTING AROUND   The Arriva bus services (see "Getting There," above) are the best option. See p. 710 (Laugharne) for details of the Rover ticket.

Exploring the Area

MWNT ★★★   This is a classic Welsh beach, not least because of the meandering, hedge-lined lanes that lead to the clifftop parking lot several miles north of Cardigan on the B4548. One person hauling a caravan can cause gridlock and lots of standing around with hands on hips and cars reversing into farmers' fields. But when you get here the view from the grassy, windswept National Trust pay parking lot is awesome: A sandy beach with crashing waves, sheltered by rock faces on three sides. Steps descend past a snack kiosk (with homemade Welsh cakes) to friendly, sometimes crowded, sands. Children adore the place, running into the water, playing beach cricket, dashing back up the steps (past people carrying canoes down) for an ice cream.

NEW QUAY ★   This seaside resort tumbles down the hillside into a little quay and a lovely curving beach. Ice-cream stalls, gift shops, and pubs jostle for attention with green hills all around. Dylan Thomas lived in a cottage across the bay and his classic *Under Milk Wood* is believed to be based on the town and the people. Thomas drank in the **Blue Bell,** and there's a Dylan Thomas Trail around places thought to feature in the book. The beach, between a slipway and stone pier, gets busy but is soft, sandy, and safe. **Cardigan Bay Marine Wildlife Centre** (www.cbmwc.org; ✆ **01545/ 560032**) occupies a listed, seafront building. It's free and has information on bottle-nose dolphins, gray seals, porpoises, and other local wildlife. The charitable trust runs trips on its Dolphin Survey boat that give a real insight into the bay's inhabitants. The center is open April to November, daily 10am to 5pm. Two-hour boat trips cost £18 for adults, £10 for children 11 and under. A path from town takes you onto the cliffs for spectacular views, especially from the National Trust's Craig Yr Adar (Bird Rock). There you'll see many types of gulls, kestrels, and often seals and dolphins. Afterwards there are plenty of fish and chip options, including the Mariner and Captain's Rendezvous, all within a few yards of one another.

ABERAERON   The main road runs through Aberaeron like many towns, but hidden away to one side is the delightful quayside. It's like something in western France, but with gaily-painted Georgian buildings. There are friendly pubs, good fish and chip shops, and the quayside Harbourmaster Hotel (see "Where to Eat & Stay" below), which puts together the lively Cardigan Bay Seafood Festival each July.

ABERYSTWYTH   This university town has a bohemian, bookish feel. Little horse-shoe-shaped North Beach is dark and shingly, hemmed in by tall Edwardian B&B-type places. A seafront stroll takes you past the John Nash-designed college building and up to the ruins of the castle built by Edward I during his conquest of Wales (open all times; free). As you round the small, rocky headland the view opens out with a long, blustery promenade and the more attractive South Beach, which ends at a little

Dolaucothi Gold Mine

Arrive here and you know you're in a real mine, old buildings and discarded machinery in a quarry-like setting criss-crossed by narrow-gauge rail tracks. Children can pan for gold, play in the activity room, and run about, but the real action is below ground. Here you can tour tunnels that date back to Roman times, and which were used well into the last century. The mine is at Pumsaint, Llanwrda (www.nationaltrust.org.uk; (C) **01558/650177**). Admission is £3.60 adults, £1.80 children 5 to 15, and £9 family ticket; underground tour is £3.80 adults, £1.90 children, and £9.50 family ticket. Daily mid-March to October 11am to 5pm (6pm July–Aug).

quayside. The Cliff Railway, from 1896, creeps up 130-m (465-ft.) Constitution Hill, at the far end of North Beach, to a cafe and picnic area. In town, **Ceredigion** (Cardigan) **Museum** on Terrace Road (www.ceredigion.gov.uk) is housed in the Coliseum, a former Edwardian music hall. It's free and has an engaging collection of reconstructed rooms, farming implements, and other local bits and pieces. Shopping is unremarkable, but the **Ultracomida** deli, 31 Pier St. (www.ultracomida.co.uk; (C) **01970/630686**), has a curious Spanish–Welsh–French edge, with lots of local cheese; the little restaurant behind the shop serves tapas/deli dishes Monday to Saturday (10am–4:30pm); on Friday and Saturday (7–9pm) there's a dinner menu with cross-cultural dishes such as Ceredigion lamb chops marinated in harissa and olive oil, with olive-oil mash (£11 for two courses, £15 with Welsh and French cheeses).

BORTH A little seaside town just north of Aberystwyth (from where you can get a train), Borth has one long road running along the beach, although in places the views are blotted out by buildings. Leave the car at the parking area at the T-junction, and cross over to the 2-mile stretch of sand. When the tide's in it is a narrow strip of stones against the sea wall, but when it's out it's really out. It's a trifle windswept but a great place for games. Drive out the other side for one of the real delights of the coast. The road ends amid the giant, white sand dunes of the **Dyfi National Nature Reserve** ★★★ at Ynyslas, at the mouth of the River Dyfi (Dovey), with Aberdyfi (Aberdovey) across the water. You can park on the hard sand, and the feel is California cool. There's a modern, wooden building across a meandering boardwalk with a cafe and toilets.

LAMPETER It looks like an unassuming country town, but Lampeter boasts the oldest university college in Wales, the University of Wales Trinity St. David. After Oxford and Cambridge, it's the oldest degree-awarding institution in England and Wales. The student population adds an extra dimension to what has been a market town since medieval times, and which still has regular cattle markets and a horse fair.

Where to Eat & Stay

Gwesty Cymru MODERN WELSH This restaurant with rooms is on the seafront at North Beach. The old building is awash with slate, chrome, and glass, and serves up Welsh and other dishes with a contemporary touch. Starters include Llanilar wild rabbit pie, with bacon and rocket mash and a port sauce, while mains (£13–£18) might be rump of Welsh lamb or a Welsh Black sirloin steak. Eight **guest rooms** have oak furniture, contemporary oil paintings on the walls, and luxury bathrooms.

19 Marine Terrace, Aberystwyth, Cardigan SY23 2AZ. www.gwestycymru.com. © **01970/612252.**
£87–£140 double. Rates include breakfast. AE, MC, V. Limited free parking. **Amenities:** Restaurant, bar. *In room:* TV, hair dryer. Wi-Fi (free).

Harbourmaster Hotel 🏆 A Georgian harbormaster's house that is now a smart hotel. There are seven rooms, reached by the original spiral staircase; two doubles in a cottage and four super-cool doubles (including the John & Henry with roof terrace) in an old warehouse. The **restaurant and bar,** in the warehouse, serves a casual lunch (pizzas, Welsh beef burger) and a set evening menu (2 courses £25) with dishes such as filet of hake, crab wonton, warm Jerusalem artichoke salad, and truffle vinaigrette. The restaurant is open noon to 2:30pm and 6:30 to 9pm; bar food is served all day.

Quayside, Aberaeron, Cardigan SA46 OBT. www.harbour-master.com. © **01686/628200.** 13 units. £120–£250 double. Rates include breakfast. MC, V. Free parking on street. **Amenities:** Restaurant, bar; free bike hire. *In room:* TV/DVD, hair dryer, Wi-Fi (free) in hotel, broadband (free) in warehouse.

Hive on the Quay MODERN WELSH In an old stone wharf building, the Hive is a bright and breezy cafe and restaurant with a conservatory and spills out onto brightly painted tables on the quay itself. At lunch it serves light fare: Ciabatta, salads, and tapas-style dishes. Come evening and you've got grilled sardines with salsa verde, salted cod cakes with rouille, and coca (a thick, crispy Catalan pizza). And then you have the famed Hive honey ice cream; there is a separate ice-cream counter outside.

Cadwgan Place, Aberaeron. www.hiveonthequay.co.uk. © **01545/570445.** Main courses £8.50–£12.50. AE, MC, V. Daily 9am–9pm (brunch, lunch noon–3pm, afternoon teas, dinner from 6pm).

ELAN VALLEY: WONDER OF THE DAMS

Rhayader is 75 miles north west of Cardiff The Elan Valley, in the heart of Wales, is a beautiful spot. It twists and turns following the gurgling River Elan. Hillsides rise up, layer upon layer; mostly they are open and littered with sheep, while forests roll into the hazy distance. It is an ancient and remote landscape, and yet it was tamed by the Victorians. More than 100 years ago they built a series of **mighty dams** to create a supply of drinking water for the multitudes toiling in England's industrial cities. Now, one moment you see a little river, but around the bend it becomes a vast lake, held in check by massive stone dams. They look brutal in their strength but are topped by delicate architecture such as little turrets like the decoration on a cake. The symmetry of man and nature here is astonishing, and quite beautiful.

Essentials

GETTING THERE About half a dozen single-coach trains (Arriva Trains Wales; about £11 one-way) each day make their way up from Swansea to Llandrindod Wells, about 5 miles from Rhayader. The journey takes 2 hours-plus. Buses (www.veolia-transport.co.uk; © **01597/852000**) connect with Rhayader roughly hourly and take about 30 minutes. By car, Rhayader is about 70 miles north of Brecon on the A470.

VISITOR INFORMATION The **Elan Valley Visitor Centre** (www.elanvalley.org.uk; © **01597/810880**), off the B4518 3 miles southwest of Rhayader, is open late March to early November, 10am to 5:30pm.

A car really is the best way to see the Elan Valley. Walking is the only alternative, and hikers can take the Elan Valley Trail up from Rhayader.

Exploring the Area

Rhayader is the oldest town in mid-Wales, dating back to the 5th century. It's a small, pretty place, with tea shops, country stores, and a riverside picnic area. It's also a good base for exploring the Elan Valley. The **Rhayader Town Trail** (www.rhayader. co.uk) takes you along the river, past the remains of a 12th-century wooden castle, and Smithfield Market, where livestock sales still take place, There are a number of pubs (**Lamb & Flag, Crown, Bear's Head**), all of which serve food.

The **Elan Valley** is a remarkable place, a valley with three Victorian dams, creating five reservoirs, which were built so that there would be drinking water for the burgeoning city of Birmingham. **Elan Valley Visitor Centre** is signed off the B4518 out of Rhayader. It's a Victorian pumping station, on the banks of the River Wye, and features an exhibition on the creation of the reservoirs, a cafe, picnic area, and shop. The lowest dam, **Caban Coch,** appears like the gray wall of a science-fiction citadel upriver. **Pen-y-Gareg** dam is equally impressive from downriver as you walk along, a sloping edifice of rock towering above the stream. Farther on is **Craig Gogh**, perhaps the most impressive, a curving edifice 317m (1,040 ft.) above sea level. It's topped with a narrow road that you can still drive across and park; in the middle is a domed tower in "Birmingham Baroque" style, topped by a wind-vane in the shape of a fish.

The **Elan Valley Trail** is a surfaced path that follows the old Elan Valley Railway route. It starts in Rhayader and goes 8 miles up valley, but there are also walks from the Visitor Centre (leaflets with maps cost 30p). The Elan Valley Estate (managed by Wales Water) covers 70 sq. miles and has 80 miles of public rights of way.

Where to Eat & Stay

Elan Valley Cottages ✒ The Elan Valley Trust has three cottages. The most attractive is the Llannerch y Cawr Longhouse overlooking the Dôl y Mynach reservoir, just off the B4518 valley road, a couple of miles from the Visitor Centre. It's Grade II listed and dates back to the 16th century, when it would have housed people in one end, cattle in the other. It still has original stone flooring, spiral staircase, and wooden beams. It is divided into two sections, one sleeping six, the other four.

Elan Valley Estate www.wales-holidays.co.uk. ✆ **01686/628200.** 3 units, each sleeping 4–6. Longhouse £211–£434 for 3 nights (minimum stay); other properties up to £698. AE, MC, V. **Amenities:** Firewood, central heating, pay phone.

NORTH WALES

by Donald Strachan

I f the south is Wales's heart, the north keeps watch over its soul. North Wales is home to the country's most dramatic crags and mightiest castles, many within the boundary of the Snowdonia National Park. Along the shoreline of Anglesey and the Lleyn Peninsula, you'll find a coast that's perfect for leisure, but that can turn wild and windswept at a moment's notice. The sheltered valleys of Denbighshire hold top-class restaurants and reminders of Wales's industrial past.

SIGHTSEEING One highlight of any trip to North Wales is a ride aboard one of the little steam trains. On the **Welsh Highland** and **Ffestiniog** narrow-gauge lines that once served slate and copper mines, you can ride old-fashioned, wood-paneled carriages through the heart of Snowdonia. At **Portmeirion,** architect Clough Williams-Ellis built a fantasy, pastel-colored village on a magical estuary, where you can roam—or even stay overnight. The once-fashionable Victorian resort of **Llandudno** is enjoying a comeback.

EATING & DRINKING The coasts and pastures of the Welsh North nurture everything from the Black breed of cattle that produces uniquely succulent **beef** to Menai **mussels** and **shellfish** caught in Cardigan Bay. Fine restaurants with rooms, such as Tyddyn Llan in Llandrillo, Tan-y-Foel in Snowdonia, and Venetia in Abersoch, are run by skillful chefs who know how to put the bounty to best use. Anglesey is home of Halen Môn, the sea salt of choice for the world's top chefs.

OUTDOOR ACTIVITIES Mountain peaks, spectacular lakes and brooding cliffs, and valleys with tiny towns seemingly carved from granite—all these make up Snowdonia National Park. It's here that you'll find the best of the area's hiking trails, on **Snowdon** and **Cader Idris,** as well as through the gnarled **Aberglaslyn Gorge.** There's also serene coastal walking around Anglesey and the Lleyn, surfing at **Porth Neigwl,** and extreme mountain biking in the pine forests at **Coed y Brenin.** You need never sit down.

HISTORY It was in the North that many of the key 13th-century battles for Welsh independence were fought—and lost. Victorious English King Edward I subsequently built his "Iron Ring" of castles, the finest of which are mighty **Caernarfon** and **Beaumaris.** (Compare the ruinous state of native castles such as **Dolwyddelan.**) At **Conwy,** built around another of Edward's great castles, the fine Elizabethan town house **Plas Mawr** testifies to the later wealth of the region's merchants. The servant's floor at stately home **Erddig** is like a domestic Victorian time capsule.

THE best TRAVEL EXPERIENCES IN NORTH WALES

o **Hiking up the Aberglaslyn Gorge as the Welsh Highland Railway puffs past:** Between Beddgelert and Pont Croesor, the most famous stretch of this recently rebuilt narrow-gauge line cuts through terrain that's been a beauty spot since the 1800s. See p. 725.

o **Standing on Yr Wyddfa, Mount Snowdon's 1,085-m (3,560-ft.) peak:** Whether you've arrived on the rack railway or hiked any of the trails to the summit, the view over the Snowdonia range is equally spectacular. See p. 725.

o **Enjoying the tranquil comforts of 21st-century Beaumaris:** The more you encounter fragments of life here from centuries past, the more you discover that it wasn't always so genteel—although the cuisine at the Loft drags you right back to the present. See p. 735.

o **Riding the "great little trains":** Originally built to carry slate and copper from mine to port, the Ffestiniog and Welsh Highland steam railways now rattle through some of Snowdonia's most breathtaking scenery. See p. 730 and p. 733.

o **Driving and dining by the Ceiriog:** This little-visited valley twists an idyllic, 15-mile path from rolling terrain around Chirk to the Berwyn Mountains and the fringes of Snowdonia. The most beautiful stretch, around Llanarmon, is also home to one of Denbighshire's best restaurants. See p. 745.

SNOWDONIA ★★★

Llanberis: 105 miles SW of Manchester, 7 miles SE of Caernarfon; Betws-y-Coed: 16 miles E of Llanberis, 44 miles SW of Liverpool

More than just the roof of Wales and the tallest British peaks south of Scotland, the giant mountains of the 823-sq. mile **Snowdonia National Park** have also long been places of myth. Legend has it that dragons, faithful hounds, and even (in the original tales) King Arthur have all lived around here, but the principal attraction for visitors is the endless miles of hiking trails and epic scenery. Paths up **Mount Snowdon,** through the **Aberglaslyn Gorge,** and on the flanks **Cader Idris** are accessible to fit walkers of all experience levels.

Snowdonia also has a long history as a mining center, and the **National Slate Museum** in Llanberis and the **Llechwedd Slate Caverns** outside Blaenau Ffestiniog transport you back to an earlier, industrial era in the life of these beautiful but harsh mountains.

Essentials

GETTING THERE   There's no sizable town in the National Park, just a collection of small places—including **Betws-y-Coed, Llanberis, Beddgelert,** and **Capel Curig**—any of which can be a base. There's also no major railway line that stops in Snowdonia itself. The nearest major station is Bangor, 9 miles north of Llanberis. From Monday through Saturday, buses run approximately hourly throughout the day from Bangor to Llanberis, taking about 45 minutes each way. The minor **Conwy Valley** rail line between Llandudno and Blaenau Ffestiniog passes through

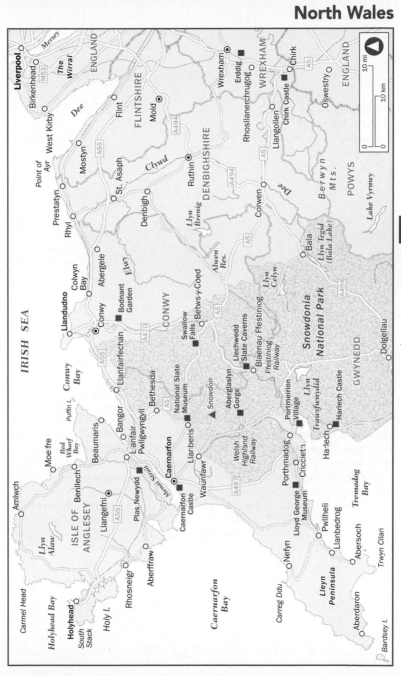

Betws-y-Coed and **Dolwyddelan,** but it runs just four trains each way daily. There are also regular buses from Llandudno and Porthmadog to towns in the park.

The best routes to Snowdonia by car from England are the A55 North Wales coastal road and the slower, but more scenic, A5 from the Midlands, through Llangollen, a spectacular route first laid down by engineer Thomas Telford between 1815 and 1830. Equally scenic, but slower still is the A458/A470 via Welshpool and Dolgellau.

VISITOR INFORMATION   The major information point for Snowdonia is the **Betws-y-Coed Information Centre,** Royal Oak Stables (✆ **01690/710426**), open from Easter to October, daily 9:30am to 5:30pm, and in the off season daily 9:30am to 4:30pm, with a lunchtime closure between 12:30 and 1pm. There are smaller offices at Canolfan Hebog, Beddgelert (✆ **01766/890615;** daily Easter–Oct, Fri–Sun rest of the year); at Stryd Fawr, Harlech (✆ **01766/780658;** daily Easter–Oct, closed rest of the year); and at Eldon Square, Dolgellau (✆ **01341/422888;** daily Easter–Oct, Thurs–Mon rest of the year). The **Llanberis Tourist Information Centre** (www.visitsnowdonia.info; ✆ **01286/870765**) is inside the Electric Mountain Visitor Centre (see below). It's open from Easter to the end of September, Friday to Tuesday from 10am to 4pm. The official National Park website www.eryri-npa.gov.uk is packed with planning information. There's also a free official app, Enjoy Snowdonia, available for iOS and Android systems.

Exploring Snowdonia

LLANBERIS ★ & AROUND

The romantic ruins of **Dolbadarn Castle,** subject of an iconic painting by J. M. W. Turner, overlook Llyn Padarn, a half-mile east of Llanberis; the castle is a relic of the time when the Llanberis Pass was crucial to any conquering army. You can take a look around the meager yet dramatic ruins for free; follow the marked trail opposite the marked parking-lot entrance.

Electric Mountain ★ ☺ FACTORY TOUR   A rare chance to see inside one of the most technologically advanced power stations in Britain, on a 1¼-hour escorted bus and walking tour. Dinorwic incorporates a massive hydroelectric system harnessing the waters of a pair of nearby lakes, with its turbines concealed a ¾-mile below the mountains so as not to spoil the natural beauty. The tour includes access to the vast turbine and generator halls. Reservations are advised, a day ahead if possible, and you must come in appropriate footwear (no sandals, high-heels, or flip-flops).

Electric Mountain Visitor Centre, Llanberis. www.electricmountain.co.uk. ✆ **01286/870636.** Tour £7.75 adults, £4 children ages 4–15. Tours run Easter–Oct daily, with varying frequency (up to half-hourly 9:30am–4:30pm during peak periods). Tours depart from Electric Mountain Visitor Centre, beside the A4086 at Llanberis.

National Slate Museum ★ MUSEUM   While surrounded by so much tranquility and natural beauty, you could easily forget that Snowdonia was, until recently, a place of toil and hardship. The courtyard here once echoed to the industrial din of crushing, hammering, and splitting—this great gray building housed the workshops that kept nearby Dinorwic Quarry running. The impressive museum chronicles the methods, machinery, and men that dug 90,000 tons of slate a year from the mountainside. Particularly poignant are the relocated quarrymen's cottages, each dressed authentically at important moments in Snowdonia's industrial past, including 1969—when Dinorwic closed.

SNOWDONIA'S best HIKES

Mount Snowdon ★★★ As long as the weather's in your favor, make an attempt on the summit your first priority—the peak so loved by such English Romantic poets as Wordsworth and Shelley remains literally the high-point of a trip to North Wales. On a clear day, you'll see every country of the British Isles, and every wrinkle and fold in the National Park below. Although there are trails that, given the wrong conditions, would challenge an experienced alpine hiker, summer months offer tracks that any fit traveler can attempt. The most popular route is the **Llanberis Path,** which slowly winds its way from Llanberis past cascades, across open sheep-grazing moorland, and then finally up to the peak via a dizzying view down into the Llanberis Pass. A fit child of 10 can handle the trail. The same goes for the **Rhyd Ddu Path** that rides Snowdon's western flank to the top. The best way to reach the trailhead is from Caernarfon for the first train of the day on the **Welsh Highland Railway** (p. 733). Get off at Rhyd Ddu station, just after one of the most glorious stretches of the line along the shore of Llyn Cwellyn. Check the timetable before setting off to confirm the time of the day's last return train. Both of these paths require about 5 hours for the return journey. Of course, the view from the top is the same if you ascend via the **Snowdon Mountain Railway** (see below); aim to get an early start so you encounter fewer people at the summit, and pay a cheaper ticket price. Whichever route you attempt (there are three further maintained trails), be sure to plan properly: The website www.eryri-npa.gov.uk/visiting/walking/snowdon-walks should be your first stop. We recommend you pack Ordnance Survey 1:25,000 *Explorer* map OL17, which covers Snowdon and is available everywhere locally.

Beddgelert ★★ This well-kept little mountain village is our other favorite spot in Snowdonia, and the jumping-off point for some of Snowdonia's best gentle walks. Its name (literally, "Gelert's grave") comes from the faithful dog of 13th-century Prince Llywelyn, slain by his master for having been falsely suspected of killing his child. The classic local trek heads past **Gelert's Grave** (mythical rather than genuine) into the **Aberglaslyn Gorge** ★★★, a stunning steep-sided trail constantly soundtracked with the rushing water of the River Glaslyn. The area was a favorite of well-to-do Victorians who first popularized Snowdonia as a leisure destination. Alternatively, a 2-hour circuit takes you northeast along the shores of **Llyn Dinas** and back to the village. With a little more time, you can link the two into a half-day hike by looping around Cwm Bychan. It's all relatively easy hiking, but as with everywhere in Snowdonia you need to be fit and sure-footed.

Cader Idris ★★ The more limited range in Southern Snowdonia offers spectacular coastal views on some easily navigable hiking trails. The only official route up to Pen y Gadair is the ⓣ **Nant Pony Path** that heads to the 893-m (2,927-ft.) summit from the roadside ⓣ Nant parking lot, about 3 miles southwest of Dolgellau. Allow 5 hours for the summit round-trip.

Insider tip: The less energetic can still get a taste of Snowdonia's majesty—from the car. The drive from Betws-y-Coed to Porthmadog passes through two of the most panoramic parts, along the shore of **Llyn Gwynant** ★★★ and then through the Aberglaslyn Gorge (see above). Take the A5 westbound from Betws, turning onto the A4086 at Capel Curig, then the A498 as the road divides at the foot of the Llanberis Pass. Driving time, at a relaxed pace with photo stops, is around an hour.

Llanberis. www.museumwales.ac.uk/en/slate. ©**01286/870630.** Free admission. Easter–Oct daily 10am–5pm; Nov–Easter Sun–Fri 10am–4pm. In Padarn Country Park, ½ mile east of Llanberis.

Snowdon Mountain Railway ★★ ☺TOUR   The fast route up Snowdon runs from Llanberis to within a few paces of the summit, at 1,085m (3,560 ft.). The only rack-and-pinion train in Britain, it is also the country's steepest train ride. The final stretch affords views over classic glacial landscape features like U-shaped troughs and hanging valleys, as well as a frightening look down into the Llanberis Pass with the Glyderau peaks beyond. Trains run to the summit between May and October, a 2½-hour round-trip which includes 30 minutes at the roof of Wales. You can usually get most of the way up between late March and the end of April. It's closed in winter. *Insider tip:* If you book by phone at least a day in advance for a 9am departure, ticket prices are £6 cheaper per person.

Llanberis. www.snowdonrailway.co.uk. © **0844/493-8120.** Round-trip £25 adults, £18 children; single fare £18/£15. Trains run April–Oct daily. Station is at southeast edge of Llanberis, by the A4086.

19 BETWS-Y-COED TO BLAENAU FFESTINIOG

Betws-y-Coed was once an isolated Snowdonia village, surrounded by tumbling rivers, waterfalls, and mountains, nestled in the tree-lined valley of the River Conwy. There's still an alpine feeling about the place, but it gets busy in summer these days. However, as a base it's well located for exploring Snowdonia, and is well stocked with affordable B&Bs.

The town is known for its bridges, most notably **Waterloo Bridge ★** at the village's southern end, the cast-iron construction of Thomas Telford in 1815. The most popular local beauty spot is the **Swallow Falls ★**, beside the A5, 2 miles west of the center. It comprises a series of waterfalls strung together, creating a mist. Drop a £1 coin into a tollbooth to get access to the path anytime you want, night or day.

Standing lonely on a ridge, **Dolwyddelan Castle,** about a mile south of the hamlet of Dolwyddelan (www.cadw.wales.gov.uk; © **01690/750366**), was the birthplace in 1173 of Llywelyn the Great, according to tradition. It was certainly his royal residence, looking out on the rugged grandeur of Moel Siabod peak. A medieval road from the Vale of Conwy ran just below the west tower, which made this a strategic site to control passage. To enter, adults pay £2.80, children and seniors £2.40; a family ticket costs £8. It's open April to September, Monday to Saturday 10am to 5pm, Sunday from 11:30am to 4pm; off-season hours are Monday to Saturday 10am to 4pm, Sunday from 11:30am to 4pm.

The mining village of Blaenau Ffestiniog is the eastern terminus for the scenic, 13½-mile **Ffestiniog Railway ★★**, linking it with the slate port of Porthmadog. See p. 730.

Llechwedd Slate Caverns ★ ☺ FACTORY TOUR/NATURAL ATTRACTION   There are 25 miles of tunnels and mine chambers buried in the great gray hill above Blaenau Ffestiniog, many of them still part of a working slate mine that opened in 1846. At Llechwedd, you can don hard hats to make two separate but complementary half-hour visits underground. The **Deep Mine** takes you 122m (400 ft.) below ground on a self-guided visit helped by eerie audio commentaries emanating from the darkness, and ends at a giant subterranean lake. The **Miners' Tramway** starts with a ride about a half-mile into the slate mountain, and continues with a more didactic talk on the geology of the mine and the working life of the 19th-century miner. On a wet day in high season, arrive early to minimize waiting times.

Blaenau Ffestiniog. www.llechwedd-slate-caverns.co.uk. ℂ **01766/830306.** One tour £10 adults, £9 seniors, £8 children 3–15; 2 tours £16.50 adults, £15 seniors, £12.50 children. Apr–Sept daily 10am–5:15pm; Oct–Mar daily 10am–4:15pm. Beside the A470, 1 mile north of Blaenau Ffestiniog.

SOUTHERN SNOWDONIA ★

Less visited than the heart of Snowdonia, the southern area of the park, where the mountains almost fall into Cardigan Bay, is no less dramatic. Quaint **Dolgellau** is the main base around here. This tiny, slate-gray town has historic links with the Quaker movement—many from Dolgellau emigrated to what's now the Welsh Tract of Pennsylvania in the 1680s. It is also the jumping-off point for hiking on **Cader Idris ★★**; see "Snowdonia's Best Hikes," above.

Harlech Castle ★ CASTLE   If you were selecting a castle to live in, you'd be hard-pressed to find one with a view to match Edward I's great coastal pile. Built in the 1280s as one of the English king's imperial fortresses (p. 733), and despite brief occupation during Owain Glyndr's rebellion in 1404–09, its shell and gatehouse in particular are remarkably intact.

Castle Sq., Harlech. www.cadw.wales.gov.uk. ℂ **01766/780552.** Admission £3.80 adults, £3.40 children 5–15. Mar–Oct daily 9:30am–5pm (until 6pm July–Aug); Nov–Feb Mon–Sat 10am–4pm, Sun 11am–4pm.

Mawddach Trail ★★ ☺ MULTI-USE TRAIL   Dolgellau is the start of one of Britain's best flat cycling and walking trails. The Mawddach Trail follows an abandoned railway line that was closed in 1965—in Victorian times it had carried rich folk from the industrialized English northwest to the fashionable resort of Barmouth. The 9-mile route follows the most photogenic estuary in Wales, before crossing the ¾-mile Barmouth railway bridge for blistering views. The trail is well marked and easy to follow; Dolgellau's tourist office (see p. 724) has a map. You can rent bikes for both adults and children at **Dolgellau Cycles,** Smithfield Street (www.dolgellaucycles. co.uk; ℂ **01341/423332**). Reserve ahead of time in high season.

Dolgellau–Barmouth. No phone. Free admission. Open 24 hr.

Where to Eat & Stay

Among a glut of B&Bs in Betws-y-Coed, our favorite is **Oakfield House,** Holyhead Road, Betws-y-Coed LL24 0BY (www.oakfieldhousebandb.co.uk; ℂ **01690/710450**), a handsome villa beside the A5 at the western fringe of the village. Completely refitted in 2011, rooms are comfortable and spacious, with flat-screen TVs (and DVD players) and free Wi-Fi. Doubles cost £70 per night; a family room costs £110.

Bryn Tyrch Inn ★ 🍴   A renovation project completed in 2011 has upgraded this cozy, informal roadside inn at the heart of Snowdonia to an ideal base for discerning hikers. Rooms, generally compact to midsize, are decked out with comfortable, traditional beds, light-wood furniture, and muted color schemes, giving them a slightly luxurious, Scandinavian feel. There are walking trails from (literally) the front door.

The **restaurant** is known for casting a wide net of culinary influence. Daily specials might include a Mediterranean tapas sharing plate, a crayfish and chorizo risotto, or a braised shoulder of lamb with colcannon. Main courses range from £13 to £18. It's open for dinner daily (except Jan) and lunches on weekends all year, and also midweek during high season.

Capel Curig, Conwy LL24 0EL. www.bryntyrchinn.co.uk. ℂ **01690/720223.** 11 units. £80–£95 double. Rates include breakfast. 2-night minimum stay at weekends (except Dec). Closed 2 weeks in Jan. MC, V. Free parking. **Amenities:** Restaurant; bar. *In room:* TV, hair dryer, CD player, Wi-Fi (free).

Mountain bikers of all abilities will find suitable riding in North Wales. The technical forest trails at **Coed y Brenin** ★ (www.forestry.gov.uk/wales; © **01341/ 440747**), 6 miles north of Dolgellau beside the A470, include the legendary, off-piste, expert-only Pink Heifer, as steep and wild as you'll find in the U.K. (and you won't find it on any official trail map; Google it). **Coed Llandegla Forest** ★ (www.coedllandegla.com;

© **01978/751656**), beside the A525, 9 miles west of Wrexham, has marked trails suited to all abilities, including family groups. Rent equipment locally from **OnePlanet Adventure,** Ruthin Road, Llandegla (www.oneplanet adventure.com; © **01978/751656;** closed Mon). The essential website for mountain biking in Wales is www. mbwales.com.

Castle Cottage ★★ This elegant restaurant with rooms maintains high standards across the board. Rooms inside the petite, 400-year-old cottage are decorated in stylish creams, with maroon notes, exposed wood beams, and handmade light-oak furniture. Decor across all is to a similar, high standard, but a couple of "Superior" units are small; if you value space, book an Executive.

The **award-winning restaurant** is also open to non-guests (reservations are essential). There's a determined focus on local ingredients—expect Welsh lamb and Cardigan Bay seafood to appear—but with an open mind to combinations from farther afield. A three-course dinner costs £40 per person.

Y Lech, Harlech, Gwynedd LL46 2YL. www.castlecottageharlech.co.uk. © **01766/780479.** 7 units. £130–£175 double. Extra bed £15–£25. Rates include breakfast. MC, V. Limited free parking. **Amenities:** Restaurant; bar; Wi-Fi (free). *In room:* TV/DVD, CD player/library, hair dryer, MP3 docking station.

Tan-y-Foel ★★★ A converted 16th-century farmhouse is the best hotel around Betws-y-Coed, opening onto a panoramic sweep of the Conwy Valley. Interior decor skips you forward 5 centuries, with vibrant fabrics and modern wall art scattered liberally. Rooms are moderate to spacious, each furnished in contrasting, Scandinavian-influenced styles. Our favorite is no. 9, a loft hideaway decorated in rich browns with valley views.

Chef Janet Pitman offers a **3-course, limited-choice dinner** (£49 per person), personally created daily using the best seasonal ingredients alongside produce from the hotel garden. Dinner reservations are essential, for both guests and non-guests, and vegetarian options are not available.

Capel Garmon, Llanrwst, Conwy LL26 0RE. www.tyfhotel.co.uk. © **01690/710507.** Fax 01690/710681. 6 units. £115–£245 double. Rates include breakfast. MC, V. Free parking. From Betws-y-Coed, take the A470, heading north to Llanrwst, turning at the signpost for Capel Garmon. No children 11 and under. **Amenities:** Restaurant; bar. *In room:* TV/DVD, hair dryer, CD player/library, Wi-Fi (free).

THE LLEYN PENINSULA ★ & PORTMEIRION ★

Porthmadog: 266 miles NW of London, 20 miles S of Caernarfon; Pwllheli: 14 miles W of Porthmadog; Abersoch: 28 miles SW of Caernarfon, 6 miles SW of Pwllheli

Separating Cardigan Bay and its northern arm, Tremadog Bay, from Caernarfon Bay, the gentle western **Lleyn Peninsula** thrusts out like a giant claw into the Irish Sea. The peninsula has a large Welsh-speaking population, and Welsh feeling is traditionally strong—Plaid Cymru, Wales's nationalist political party, was founded in Pwllheli in 1925. The main reasons to visit the Lleyn are great food, top-class accommodations, and glorious solitude. Aside from small coastal centers like **Pwllheli, Criccieth,** and **Abersoch,** there's very little here—in a splendid way. The peninsula is crisscrossed by small roads and walking trails, where out of season you'll be unlikely to meet anyone at all.

The Lleyn's main tourist center of **Porthmadog** is a terminus for two of Wales's "great little trains," the **Ffestiniog Railway** (see below) and the **Welsh Highland Railway** (p. 733), and close to the pastel-colored architectural wonderland "village" of **Portmeirion.**

Essentials

GETTING THERE   A slow, local rail line connects Pwllheli, Porthmadog, and Criccieth with Aberystwyth (via Machynlleth) and Shrewsbury and Birmingham, in England. (Journey time from Birmingham is a slow, scenic 5 hours; see www.thecambrianline.co.uk.) Buses also pull into Porthmadog every hour from Bangor. Porthmadog is well connected by road with Caernarfon and Snowdonia, via the A487. The main peninsula roads, the A499 and A497, converge at Pwllheli.

VISITOR INFORMATION   The **Tourist Information Centre,** High Street, Porthmadog (www.visitsnowdonia.info; ℂ **01766/512981**), is open from Easter to October, daily 9:30am to 5pm. Off-season hours are Monday to Saturday 10am to 3:30pm. In Pwllheli, there's a seasonal **Tourist Information Centre,** at Min y Don, Station Square (ℂ **01758/613000**), usually open Easter to September 5 days each week (currently closed Thurs and Fri, but exact days can change), between 9:30am and 5pm. **Abersoch** has a small helpful tourist office, High Street (www.abersoch andllyn.co.uk; ℂ **01758/712929**), open Easter to September daily between 10:30am and 2 or 3pm.

Exploring the Lleyn Peninsula & Portmeirion

The peninsula takes its name from an Irish tribe, the Celtic Legine, or Laigin, who didn't have very far to go from home to invade the country of fellow Celts. They were followed by missionaries and pilgrims in the Christian era. The Lleyn's main town, now a resort, **Porthmadog** was named after a "Celtification" of the English name of its builder, William Madocks, a mining mogul who built the town from scratch between 1808 and 1811. At its peak in 1873, 105,500 tonnes (116,000 tons) of slate quarried at Blaenau Ffestiniog (p. 726) were shipped from its harbor across the world.

Now in ruins, **Criccieth Castle** (www.cadw.wales.gov.uk; ℂ **01766/522227**), built as a Welsh stronghold, commands a fine view of Tremadog Bay. During its years as an active fortress, it changed hands—Welsh to English and back and forth—until it was finally sacked and burned in 1404 by Owain Glyndwr, never to rise again as a fortification. Admission is £3.20 for adults, £2.80 for seniors, students, and children 5 to 15. A family ticket goes for £9.20. It's open April through October, daily from 10am to 5pm, and November through March, Friday and Saturday 9:30am to 4pm and Sunday 11am to 4pm. Monday through Thursday in winter, the castle exhibition is closed, but you can enjoy the view from the site for free (10am–4pm).

The pretty port-resort of **Abersoch** ★ is the best base for exploring the farther-flung, emptier reaches of the peninsula. Surfers should make for **Porth Neigwl,** "Hell's Mouth" beach; for a surf report, check www.westcoastsurf.co.uk/surfreport. htm. Serious bird-watchers and solitude-seekers, on the other hand, should book a day trip to **Bardsey (Ynys Enlli)** ★. The tiny islet has been a place of pilgrimage since Christianity first came to North Wales in the 3rd or 4th century, and there was probably a monastery here by the 6th century. Today it is home to a thousands-strong colony of Manx shearwater and other species of coastal bird. Day trips operated by **Bardsey Boat Trips** (www.bardseyboattrips.com; ℭ **07971/769895**) depart from Porth Meudwy, Aberdaron, regularly in season. Trips cost £30 for adults, £20 children, and allow you about 3½ hours to roam Bardsey. For more about the island, see www.enlli.org.

Ffestiniog Railway ★★ RAILWAY   Ride near the front, with the window wedged down, for the full "age of steam" ambience (and odor) on Wales's most famous narrow-gauge heritage railway. The tiny steam engine pulls its wood-paneled carriages (with antique booth seating) the majestic 13½ miles from Porthmadog to Blaenau Ffestiniog several times a day for most of the year. The railway was built in 1832 to carry Blaenau's slate down to the port at Porthmadog.

The route climbs quickly away from the Traeth Bach estuary, clinging to the hillside and winding through forests of pine and oak, past waterfalls and over picturesque uplands to Blaenau. Journey time is 1¼ hours each way.

Harbour Station, Porthmadog. www.festrail.co.uk. ℭ **01766/516024.** Day ticket £20 adults, £18 seniors; half-way round-trip £12 adults, £11 seniors; one child 3–15 travels free with each paying adult, additional children pay half-fare. See website for timetable.

Lloyd George Museum MUSEUM   This small museum is dedicated to David Lloyd George (1863–1945), Liberal prime minister of Britain between 1916 and 1922, and an early advocate of both Welsh home rule and women's suffrage. Displays and a half-hour film illustrate the political career of the statesman nicknamed the "Welsh wizard." Just behind the museum is Lloyd George's monumental **grave,** on the banks of the babbling River Dwyfor, which was designed by Clough Williams-Ellis of Portmeirion fame (see below). Your entrance ticket also gets you inside **Highgate,** his adjacent boyhood home, preserved in its Victorian state.

Llanystumdwy (2 miles W of Criccieth). www.gwynedd.gov.uk/museums. ℭ **01766/522071.** Admission £5 adults, £4 seniors and children, £15 family ticket. Apr–Sept daily 10:30am–5pm (closed weekends except Easter Apr–May; closed Sun June); Oct Mon–Fri 11am–4pm.

Oriel Plas Glyn-y-Weddw ☺ COMMERCIAL ART GALLERY   This grand Victorian Gothic Revival dower house, shrouded in rhododendron bushes, houses Wales' oldest art gallery. Rooms off the great hall exhibit contemporary Welsh artists working in a variety of media. Prices range from prints at £10 to original artworks at over £2,000. There are also activity packs for children, to help them explore the house and grounds, and a pleasant tearoom and cafe.

Llanberdog (4 miles SW of Pwllheli). www.oriel.org.uk. ℭ **01758/740763.** Free admission. Wed–Mon 10am–5pm; limited opening during Jan.

Portmeirion Village ★ HISTORIC SITE   There's more than a whiff of Disney about this magical, multicolored village by the sea. It took architect Clough Williams-Ellis (1883–1978) over half a century to turn what was an original 1850 manor house and its abandoned estate into a "resort" like no other. His elaborate pastiche, with eclectic architectural influences both indigenous and foreign, wrapped in an Italianate sugar-coating and transplanted onto a wild Welsh estuary probably shouldn't work—but Williams-Ellis's ability to create architecture in harmony with nature ensures that it just does. Wander buildings that veer between Arts and Crafts and neoclassical styles, tour the site on a land train, or lose yourself in acres of sub-tropical garden walks and soak up a place that made a suitably surreal setting for *The Prisoner*, a cult 1960s' TV show. For the full Portmeirion effect, stay in the hotel here (see below).

Portmeirion (2½ miles southeast of Porthmadog). www.portmeirion-village.com.© **01766/772311.** Admission £10 adults, £6 children 4–16 (£5 and £3, respectively, after 3:30pm); entrance ticket includes optional guided tour. Daily 9:30am–7:30pm.

Where to Eat & Stay

Rhiwafallen (p. 734), southwest of Caernarfon, could also serve as a base for exploring the Lleyn.

Gwesty Portmeirion ★★   With one of the most idyllic settings in Wales, this hotel was a simple, early Victorian villa until architect Clough Williams-Ellis converted it into an extraordinary "resort" (see above). Writers such as H. G. Wells and George Bernard Shaw were habitués. Decor is exotic: Fabrics from Kashmir, paintings from Rajasthan, and tiles from Delft. Fourteen units are in the main house (the best with sea views), the rest in adjacent Castell Deudraeth or a cluster of "village houses"—a handful of which received a contemporary makeover in 2012. *Insider tip:* Check the website for offers—especially out of season, which can get very affordable.

Portmeirion, Gwynedd LL48 6ER. www.portmeirion-village.com. © **01766/770000.** Fax 01766/770300. 70 units. £95–£239 double; £189–£307 suite. Rates include breakfast. AE, DC, MC, V. Free parking. Off the A487, 2 miles southeast of Porthmadog. **Amenities:** 2 restaurants; bar; outdoor pool; outdoor tennis court; small spa; room service; babysitting. *In room:* TV (DVD in some), hair dryer, Wi-Fi (free).

Plas Bodegroes ★★   One of Wales' pioneering restaurants-with-rooms is installed inside an understated Georgian manor house. Midsize rooms are elegant and traditional, with just enough modernity injected into them to prevent them feeling stuffy. Our favorites are at the back, overlooking manicured lawns, an avenue of beech trees, and sheep grazing beyond. Units on the top floor have low ceilings—and so are unsuited to tall travelers.

The exceptional fine-dining **restaurant** has been the real draw here for over a quarter-century, and specializes in French-influenced cuisine using the best seasonal Welsh ingredients. Reservations are essential for non-guests; a 4-course dinner costs £45 (Tues–Sat; no children 7 and under), and Sunday lunch costs £20.

Pwllheli, Gwynedd LL53 5TH. www.bodegroes.co.uk. © **01758/612363.** Fax 01758/701247. 11 units. £160–£180 double. Rates include breakfast. DC, MC, V. Free parking. By A497 1½ miles northwest of Pwllheli. Closed Dec–Feb. **Amenities:** Restaurant; bar. *In room:* TV, hair dryer, CD player, Wi-Fi (free).

Venetia ★★ 📷   If you're seeking a sleek, chic, romantic seaside hideaway, there's nowhere better on the Lleyn than Venetia, in the pretty port-resort of Abersoch. Rooms inside the modernized Victorian villa are midsize and stylish, decorated with flashes of exuberance, and dressed with Italian furniture. The best is no. 5, "Cinque," with a hydromassage tub big enough for two.

The Lleyn Peninsula & Portmeirion

The cornerstone of Venetia's growing reputation is its **restaurant,** where locally sourced seafood is prepared expertly with a distinctive Italian accent. Try the likes of Pwllheli scallops with prosciutto and Grana Padano shavings, or Aberdaron crab linguine. Main courses range from £11 to £20. Reservations are essential for non-guests.

Lon Sarn Bach, Abersoch, Gwynedd LL53 7EB. www.venetiawales.com. 𝄐**01758/713354.** 5 units. £80–£148 double. Rates include breakfast. 2-night minimum stay at weekends. AE, MC, V. Limited free parking. Closed Jan–mid-Feb, Tues all year, Mon Sept–May, and Sun Nov–Dec. **Amenities:** Restaurant; bar. *In room:* TV/DVD, hair dryer, MP3 docking station (in some), Wi-Fi (free).

CAERNARFON ★

249 miles NW of London; 68 miles W of Chester; 30 miles SE of Holyhead; 9 miles SW of Bangor

The principal reason to come to **Caernarfon,** at the mouth of the River Seiont, is to see **Caernarfon Castle.** In the 13th century, when King Edward I had defeated the Welsh after long and bitter fighting, he ordered the construction of a fortress on the site of an old Norman castle at the western end of the Menai Strait. From here, his sentinels could command a view of the land around, all the way to the mountains and far out across the bay. Caernarfon is also a great place to begin a journey into the heart of Snowdonia, aboard the historic **Welsh Highland Railway,** one of Wales's scenic train rides.

Essentials

GETTING THERE   There's no regular rail link to Caernarfon; the nearest connection is through Bangor, to which Caernarfon is linked by bus. Buses run between Bangor and Caernarfon, a 25-minute ride, at least every 20 minutes throughout the day.

If you're driving from Bangor, head southwest along the A487; from Porthmadog, head north along the A487, or take a day trip aboard the **Welsh Highland Railway** (see below).

VISITOR INFORMATION   The **Caernarfon Tourist Information Centre** is at Oriel Pendeitsh, Castle Street (𝄐 **01286/672232**). From May through October, it's open daily 9:30am to 4:30pm; November through April, hours are Monday to Saturday 10am to 3:45pm.

Exploring Caernarfon

The Romans maintained a fort at **Segontium** for some 3 centuries. Excavations on the outskirts of Caernarfon beside the A4085 have disclosed foundations of barracks, bath-houses, and other remains. Admission to the site is free; it's open dawn till dusk. Allow about 20 minutes to walk around.

Caernarfon Castle ★ CASTLE   The nearest thing Wales has to a royal palace was described by Dr. (Samuel) Johnson after a visit in 1774 as "an edifice of stupendous majesty and strength"—indeed, this may be the largest structure ever built in Wales. Based either on ancient drawings of Constantinople procured by Edward's architect, the Savoy-born James of St. George, or on his firsthand observations (historians believe Edward I might have visited Constantinople during the Crusades), the walls were patterned after those surrounding ancient Byzantium.

The walls between the Chamberlain Tower and Queen's Tower house the **Museum of the Royal Welch Fusiliers** (www.rwfmuseum.org.uk; 𝄐 **01286/673362**),

EDWARD'S iron RING

Although Edward I (1239–1307) was one of medieval England's most powerful kings, he had more than his share of problems with the Celts. Trouble flared up in the early 1280s when Llywelyn ap Gruffudd (1223–82)—still the only native prince a united Welsh nation has ever had—occupied Caernarfon. The Welsh appeared to have abandoned a tradition of internecine fighting in order to mount an effective insurrection against the English. However, Llywelyn was betrayed and killed in 1282 at the Battle of Orewin Bridge, near Builth Wells, and Edward moved quickly to eradicate his line and to establish an "Iron Ring" of castles designed to keep the locals in check forever. Flint and Rhuddlan,

erected after lesser troubles in the 1270s, were strengthened. Progress at **Caernarfon** (see below) was so rapid that by 1284, Edward I's son, later Edward II, was born inside its Eagle Tower (a "native prince!" his father proclaimed). Coastal castles at **Conwy** (p. 740) and **Harlech** (p. 727) were designed to be equally impregnable, and when the Welsh revolted again, in 1294, Edward ordered Caernarfon's walls to be built even taller. The final link in his imperious chain, **Beaumaris** (p. 735), is the most elegant of royal master mason James of St. George's constructions. All have survived the centuries remarkably intact, and represent the pinnacle of medieval castle-building in Europe.

which traces the history of the regiment's role in war across the globe since 1659. Allow 1½ hours total for your visit.

Caernarfon. www.cadw.wales.gov.uk. ✆ **01286/677617.** Admission (includes museum) £5.25 adults, £4.85 seniors and children 5–15, £15 family ticket. Mar–Oct daily 9:30am–5pm; Nov–Feb Mon–Sat 10am–4pm, Sun 11am–4pm.

Welsh Highland Railway ★★★ 📷 RAILWAY Wales's most spectacular little steam railway plies a course from Caernarfon right into the heart of Snowdonia—and since 2011, out the other side to Porthmadog, too. Historic carriages creek, rattle, and cough their way along the Gwyrfai Valley and the shores of Llyn Cwellyn before striking out into undiluted uplands suited only to sightseers, sheep, and the occasional hardy drover. A few trains a day make the return journey, so if you plan it right you can combine the train with some superlative hill walking: Get off at Rhyd Ddu or Snowdon Ranger for major paths up **Mount Snowdon** (p. 725), or at Beddgelert for the **Aberglaslyn Gorge** (p. 725), also the most memorable stretch of the rail line.

St. Helens Rd., Caernarfon. www.festrail.co.uk. ✆ **01286/677018.** Round-trip tickets £11–£33; one child travels free per adult. Apr–Oct 2–4 trains daily; also weekends Mar and Nov–Dec. See website for timetable.

Where to Eat & Stay

There's little reason to stay in Caernarfon itself—our favorite local accommodations are outside town—but if you're resolved on a room in the center, the **Celtic Royal Hotel,** Bangor Street, Caernarfon, Gwynedd LL55 1AY (www.celtic-royal.co.uk; ✆ **01286/674477**), combines some character with an array of amenities including a heated indoor pool and health club. Double rooms cost £135 per night. For a pint of local ale, our central choice is the **Black Boy Inn,** Northgate Street (www.blackboy-inn.com; ✆ **01286/673604**).

Castell ★ BISTRO/WELSH   Simplicity of flavor is the hallmark of the cooking at this modern bistro inside a historic building on Caernarfon's main square. The decor is unremarkable, but the local produce does the talking. The lunchtime menu features tasty light bites such as sautéed wild mushrooms and poached egg on toast alongside the regular menu. At dinner, it's all about properly executed, bold classics: Think Welsh Black filet steak with a slow roasted tomato.

33 Y Maes, Caernarfon. www.castellcaernarfon.co.uk. © **01286/677970.** Reservations recommended. Main courses £7–£21. MC, V. Daily noon–3pm and 6–9pm.

Rhiwafallen ★★ 🎁   This cozy farmhouse-turned-restaurant with guest rooms is the boutique best-bet within range of Caernarfon. Rooms are dressed vibrantly to reflect contrasting themes; the best, Raspberry, has its own sundeck.

Chic wallpaper and light-wood furniture set off Rhiwafallen's **intimate dining room.** The three-course fixed-price menu (£35) changes seasonally, but diners are guaranteed the finest local produce combined with flair. Expect the likes of twice-cooked pork belly served with truffled potatoes and wilted greens. The restaurant is open for dinner Tuesday to Saturday, and on Sunday for lunch; reservations are essential.

Llandwrog, Caernarfon, Gwynedd LL54 5SW. www.rhiwafallen.co.uk. © **01286/830172.** 3 units. £100–£150 double. Rates include breakfast. AE, MC, V. Free parking. No children 15 and under. **Amenities:** Restaurant; bar. *In room:* TV/DVD, hair dryer.

THE ISLE OF ANGLESEY ★★

Holyhead: 27 miles NW of Caernarfon, 215 miles N of Cardiff; Beaumaris: 26 miles E of Holyhead

This is an island of many names: Ynys Môn to the Welsh, the Romans called it Mona, and these days it's usually just **Anglesey**—"Mother of Wales" and home in the 5th century of St. Dwynwen, Wales's patron saint of lovers, whose "alternative Valentine's" is celebrated each January 25. The scenery differs markedly from the mainland's, with undulating farmland interrupted by occasional crags and dotted with single-story whitewashed cottages. Then there's the 125 miles of silent coastline—with a marked circular coastal path for you to follow.

Its "capital," the little town of **Beaumaris**—named from a distinctly un-Welsh corruption of the French for "beautiful marsh"—is the natural first stop. Visit the **Castle,** then the **Court** and **Gaol,** to glimpse some unsavory but fascinating snapshots of life for those who got on the wrong side of this frontier town over the centuries—most of which were spent cut off from the rest of Wales by the narrow, tidal Menai Strait. More remote is **Holy Island,** home to Anglesey's westernmost point, **South Stack,** and the gateway to Ireland via the **Holyhead** ferry.

Essentials

GETTING THERE & AROUND   Holyhead is the terminus of the North Wales Coast rail line. Trains arrive regularly during the day from Cardiff, Bangor, Llandudno, Chester, and even London. **Llanfair PG** is the isle's other main rail halt. Transfer at Bangor for **Beaumaris:** Bus nos. 53, 56, 57, and 58 connect Bangor and Beaumaris approximately every 30 minutes during the day Monday to Saturday, less often on Sunday. The isle's major transport route, bus no. X4, runs regularly between Bangor and Holyhead via Llangefni.

To Ireland by Ferryboat

Two ferry companies operate between Holyhead (pronounced *Holly*-head) and either the Irish port of Dun Laoghaire (a railway junction 7 miles south of Dublin) or Dublin Port itself. Both companies run a swift and conventional service; journey time is around 2 hours for swift ferries (3¼ hr. for conventional ones), with three to five departures daily. On **Stena Line** (www.stenaline.co.uk; ✆ **0844/770-7070**), only foot passengers can travel on the swift ferry; passengers with cars must use conventional ferries. **Irish Ferries** (www.irishferries.com; ✆ **0870/517-1717**) carries passengers and cars on both services. Round-trips for passengers traveling or returning on the same day are £32 for adults, £16 for children 4 to 15, and £80 for a family day-trip ticket (Stena only). Fares for car passage vary with season and ticket type, but typically cost between £80 and £160 or more each way for a car and one passenger.

The A55 North Wales coastal road crosses the Menai Strait and is Anglesey's main arterial road, linking the Menai Bridge and Holyhead. It becomes a causeway as it approaches Holy Island; the Four Mile Bridge on the B4545 also links Holy Island to Anglesey. Aside from the A55, roads on the isle are slow going—but scenic.

VISITOR INFORMATION Anglesey's main **Tourist Information Centre,** Railway Station, Llanfair PG (www.visitanglesey.co.uk; ✆ **01248/713177**), is open Monday to Saturday 9:30am to 5:30pm, Sunday 9:30am to 4:30pm.

Exploring Anglesey

Visitors cross the strait by one of the two bridges built by celebrated engineers of the 19th century: The **Menai Suspension Bridge ★★**, designed by Thomas Telford and completed in 1826, and the **Britannia Bridge,** originally only a railway bridge, which was the work of Robert Stephenson and opened 24 years later. The Britannia had to be rebuilt after a devastating 1970 fire that destroyed its pitch and timberwork; it now carries both trains and cars on two levels. The bridges are almost side-by-side west of Bangor.

BEAUMARIS ★★

The tiny town of **Beaumaris** is the site of the largest of Edward's "Iron Ring" of castles (p. 733). A small settlement grew up around the castle, developing into a major port and making Beaumaris a trading center until the arrival of the railway in the 1800s. Preserved just as it was in 1614, **Beaumaris Court,** Castle Street (✆ **01248/811691**), hosts a fascinating, if slightly grim, exhibition that highlights the arbitrary and brutal nature of justice in centuries past. Although, timbered interior aside, it looks little different from a modern British courtroom, stories of "burning in the hand," hanging, and transportation thankfully belong to another era. It's open April through September Saturday to Thursday 10:30am to 5pm, and the same hours on October weekends. Admission costs £3.70 for adults, £2.90 for seniors and children. The town's squat Victorian **Gaol ★**, Steeple Lane (✆ **01248/810921**), continues the penitentiary theme. You're free to explore its gloomy corridors and cells, many enhanced with detailed explanations of the prison's harsh regime. Grisly highlights include the prisoner-powered treadwheel (a punishment) and the "luxury" condemned man's cell—two public executions were staged here in the 1800s. Opening hours are the same as for the Court; admission costs £4.50 for adults, £3.50 for seniors and children.

Low-rise turrets and circumnavigating ducks give moated **Beaumaris Castle ★★** (www.cadw.wales.gov.uk; © **01248/810361**) a rather twee appearance. However, in the 14th century the last and most gracefully designed of Edward I's maritime fortresses was a feared outpost of English might. Its formidable and largely intact concentric defenses give you an immediate sense of what it was used for—you'll quickly lose count of how many firing berths there are for defenders. In those days the sea came up to the southern walls, and on certain tides small ships could reach the castle directly; the dock is still visible. Visits are possible March to October, daily from 9:30am to 5pm; and November to February, Monday to Saturday from 10am to 4pm, Sunday 11am to 4pm. Admission is £3.80 for adults and £3.40 for seniors, students, and children 5 to 15; family tickets cost £11. Pause for an ice cream at **Red Boat,** 34 Castle St. (www.redboatgelato.com; © **01248/810022**), where flavors like bara brith (Welsh fruitcake) and crème brûlée are handmade on the premises.

LLANFAIR PG

Its fame is its name: **Llanfairpwllgwyngyllgogerychwyrndrobwllllantysiliogogogoch,** or something like that. It translates as "St. Mary's Church in the Hollow of the White Hazel near a Rapid Whirlpool and the Church of St. Tysilio near the Red Cave." In the 1860s, a local tailor had the foresight to embellish the original (shorter) name as a tourist attraction—and the ruse worked. You can get the longest train-platform ticket in the world from the station here, giving the full name. (On maps and most references it is usually called just "Llanfair PG.") The first Women's Institute in Britain met here in 1915.

A short walk from the station is the **Marquess of Anglesey Column** (© **01248/ 714393**), standing 27m (90 ft.) high on a wooded mount 76m (250 ft.) above sea level. It has a statue of the marquess on top, to which visitors can climb—it's 115 steps up a spiral staircase. The marquess lost a leg while he was second in command to the Duke of Wellington at the Battle of Waterloo and was thereafter called "One Leg." The column is open year-round daily 9am to 5pm, charging £1.50 for adults, 75p for seniors and children.

About a mile southwest of the village with the long name, beside the A4080, is **Plas Newydd ★**, Llanfair PG (www.nationaltrust.org.uk/plasnewydd; © **01248/ 714795**), standing on the shores of the Menai. An ancient manor house, it was converted between 1783 and 1809 into a splendid mansion in the Gothic and neoclassical styles. In the long dining room, there's a *trompe l'oeil* mural by Rex Whistler, and a military museum houses relics and uniforms of the Battle of Waterloo. The beautiful woodland garden and lawns have glorious Snowdonia panoramas. Plas Newydd can be visited only from Easter to October, Saturday to Wednesday 1 to 5pm. The gardens are open from 10am. A combined ticket for both the house and garden costs £9 for adults and £4.45 for children 15 and under; it's £22 for a family ticket.

Beyond Plas Newydd, a mile southwest of Brynsiencyn (follow signs for the Sea Zoo), is the home of family-run **Halen Môn Anglesey Sea Salt ★** (www.halenmon. com; © **01248/430871**). This prized natural salt is found in many of the world's most famous kitchens; it's used by Heston Blumenthal, and goes into President Obama's favorite brand of chocolates, Fran's. You're free to taste the varieties,

Anglesey's Best Beaches

The tiny resort of **Rhosneigr** has an unspoiled, sandy beach that's ideal for low-tide rockpooling (foraging for shells, crabs, and so forth). Strong currents make it a favorite haunt of watersports fanatics. For swimming, especially with young children, you're better off on the sheltered eastern coast. The sands at **Benllech** and **Lligwy** are our favorite family spots.

including salt smoked over local oak chippings, before you buy from the small shop at Halen Môn's tiny headquarters. It's open Monday to Friday 10am to 4:30pm.

HOLY ISLAND ★

The largest town on Anglesey, **Holyhead** is not actually on Anglesey at all but on **Holy Island.** However, the two islands have long been linked. Packet boats between Holyhead and Ireland were recorded as far back as 1573—and the town is now a functional place for those connecting with Dublin (see "To Ireland by Ferry-boat," above).

Holyhead Mountain is the highest point in Anglesey, at 216m (710 ft.). The summit is the site of an ancient hill fort and the ruins of an Irish settlement from the 2nd to the 4th century A.D. On the southwestern side of the mountain is **South Stack ★** (☏ 01407/763900), a lighthouse opened in 1809. The towering surrounding cliffs are home to colonies of razorbill, guillemot, and puffin, and gray seals breed in the caves below. The lighthouse is open Easter to September, daily from 10:30am to 5:30pm, charging £5 for adults and £3 for children—but to reach it be prepared to negotiate 400 steps there, and another 400 back. There's gentler, scenic coastal walking on the heathland nearby. Pack your binoculars.

Where to Eat & Stay

For a scenic seaside pint and a smoked salmon sandwich, the best spot on the island is **The Ship,** Red Wharf Bay (www.shipinnredwharfbay.co.uk; ☏ 01248/852568), a whitewashed inn overlooking a sweeping bay 8 miles northwest of Beaumaris. It's signposted off the A5025. **The Seacroft,** Ravenspoint Rd., Trearddur Bay (www.theseacroft.com; ☏ 01407/860348), is a clapboard bar-grill revamped in 2011 in a vaguely New England style. Mains such as ham hock glazed with Anglesey honey range from £10 to £25, and there are pizzas and burgers for youngsters. Six bright rooms decorated in a fresh, "coastal" style cost between £80 and £110 for a double. It's a 2-minute walk to a sandy beach.

Cennin & Café MooBaaOinc ★ MODERN WELSH Local food celebrity Aled Williams is head chef at this split-level, split-personality eating spot on Beaumaris' main drag. Upstairs, dinner at **Cennin** is a fine-dining affair, with local ingredients taking center-stage in such dishes as roast tenderloin, crispy belly, and cheek bon bon of Anglesey pork served with cabbage. The street-level **Café MooBaaOinc** showcases local produce, too, but employs it in simpler fare such as Welsh Black beef burger with homemade ketchup—and despite the name, it also serves vegetarian dishes. There's also a deli and farm shop selling the produce.

13 Castle St., Beaumaris. www.restaurantcennin.co.uk. ☏ **01248/811230.** Reservations recommended (Cennin). Main courses: Cennin £18–£26; MooBaaOinc £9–£16. Cennin Tues–Sat 6:30–9:30pm (Wed–Sat in winter). MooBaaOinc Wed–Sun 11am–4pm (Tues–Sun in holiday periods).

Cleifiog ★ Inside a whitewashed, seafront building that dates at least to the early 1600s, this refined bed and breakfast offers space and warmth in an elegant setting. Rooms are large—especially the pine-paneled "suite" that looks right across the Menai Strait to Snowdonia's peaks—and the liberal use of rich, country-style fabrics in each evokes the feel of a manor house.

Townsend, Beaumaris, Anglesey LL58 8BH. www.cleifiogbandb.co.uk. ℰ**01248/811507.** 3 units. £90–£110 double. Rates include breakfast. MC, V. 2-night minimum stay on weekends. **Amenities:** Wi-Fi (free). *In room:* TV, hair dryer.

The White Eagle ★ ☺GASTROPUB Amid blissful seclusion in the southeastern corner of Holy Island, this family-friendly gastropub has one of Wales' most idyllic settings. Diners can choose between cozy, drawing room seating; a light-drenched, bustling modern bar area; or a glorious sundeck. The kitchen delivers gastropub fare with a flourish, including classics like a steaming bowl of Menai mussels served Flemish style with fries and crusty bread. There's a fine Welsh cheese menu to finish, plenty of options for children, and also usually six beers on tap, including an exclusive house ale crafted by Conwy brewery.

Rhoscolyn LL65 2NJ (off the B4545, 5 miles southeast of Holyhead). www.white-eagle.co.uk. ℰ **01407/860267.** Reservations recommended. Main courses £10–£20. MC, V. Mon–Fri noon–2:30pm and 6–9pm; Sat–Sun noon–9pm.

Ye Olde Bull's Head Inn & Townhouse ★★ This historic coaching inn has been the best address in Beaumaris for some time; it welcomed such notables as Dr. (Samuel) Johnson and Charles Dickens. Bedrooms in the main building come in an array of types and sizes; styling is traditional and some have four-poster beds. To suit a different mood, better units are in the adjacent **Townhouse,** where decor is sharper and contemporary.

You'll find Anglesey's most creative cooking in exclusive surroundings at the **Loft Restaurant,** under the eaves of the old inn. Expect the likes of loin of Welsh lamb with creamed leek porridge and harissa broad beans. It's open Tuesday through Saturday for dinner (3 courses, £41). There's also a lively **Brasserie,** open daily for lunch and dinner, that turns out well-crafted bistro favorites like roast marinated quail with Puy lentils. Main courses range from £11 to £19.

Castle St., Beaumaris, Anglesey LL58 8AP. www.bullsheadinn.co.uk. ℰ **01248/810329.** Fax 01248/811294. 26 units. £105–£175 double. Rates include breakfast. AE, MC, V. Limited free parking. **Amenities:** 2 restaurants; bar; room service. *In room:* A/C (in Townhouse), TV, hair dryer, MP3 docking station (in Townhouse), Wi-Fi (free).

CONWY ★★

241 miles NW of London; 37 miles E of Holyhead; 22 miles NE of Caernarfon

Pint-size and atmospheric, the market town of **Conwy** has a historical importance that punches well above the weight of its population of 15,000. The **castle, town walls,** and enclosed street-plan were laid down by English King Edward I in the 1200s, when Conwy was a crucial garrison town in the king's campaigns against Welsh rebels. Later history almost forgot this little trading port, until the Victorian era, when Telford's **Conwy Suspension Bridge** and Stephenson's **Tubular Railroad Bridge** spanned the estuary, bringing roads and the railway to its ancient town gates and beyond—in the process connecting North Wales to England's industrial heartland.

Conwy

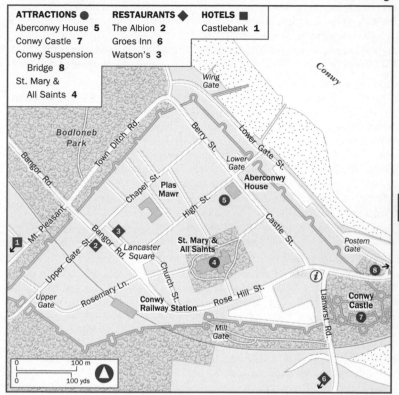

ATTRACTIONS ●
Aberconwy House **5**
Conwy Castle **7**
Conwy Suspension
  Bridge **8**
St. Mary &
  All Saints **4**

RESTAURANTS ◆
The Albion **2**
Groes Inn **6**
Watson's **3**

HOTELS ■
Castlebank **1**

Essentials

GETTING THERE Trains run between Conwy and Chester, Bangor, and northwest England—from London, connect via Chester. Buses from Bangor heading for Llandudno pass through Conwy every 15 minutes during the day Monday to Saturday, and hourly on Sunday.

Motorists from England should head west along the main coastal route, the A55.

VISITOR INFORMATION **Conwy Visitor Centre,** Muriau Building, Rosehill Street ((✆ **01492/577566**), dispenses information about the town and region, and is open Monday to Saturday 10am to 4pm, Sunday 11am to 4pm. Opening is often extended to 5:30pm between Easter and September.

Exploring Conwy

Your first stop should be a walk to the apex of the almost-complete ¾-mile of **Town Walls ★** (free admission), to gain some perspective over Conwy's near-perfect grid of streets.

Aberconwy House HISTORIC SITE The town's only medieval house still standing (and the oldest in Conwy) was completed sometime during the 14th century in the half-timbered English style—although it owes its survival to the stone construction of the first story. Rooms are dressed according to the house's various guises over 6 centuries: As a working base for a Tudor merchant placed strategically close to the quay; as the sometime home of an 18th-century sea captain; and as a temperance (alcohol-free) hotel in the 1890s.

Castle St. www.nationaltrust.org.uk/aberconwy-house. *©01492/592246.* Admission £3.40 adults, £1.70 children 5–16, £8.50 family ticket. Apr–Oct Wed–Mon (July–Aug daily) 11am–5pm.

Conwy Castle ★★ CASTLE   The entire town cowers below Conwy Castle: Edward I had this masterpiece of medieval architecture built after he conquered the last native Prince of Wales, Llywelyn ap Gruffudd. More than any other fortress built for Edward, Conwy Castle provides insight into the clever military architecture of the king's master mason, James of St. George. Separated from the town by a massive ditch, with one entrance through two gates followed by the protection of Outer and Inner Wards, the castle would have been practically impossible to assault head-on— in fact, it was only ever taken by ruse or negotiation in its 700-year history. The wall-walk above the East Barbican is the place to head for the best view of Conwy's 19th-century bridges. Allow an hour to visit.

Castle St. www.cadw.wales.gov.uk. *©01492/592358.* Admission £4.80 adults; £4.30 seniors, students, and children 5–15; £14 family ticket. Mar–June and Sept–Oct daily 9:30am–5pm; July–Aug daily 9:30am–6pm; Nov–Feb Mon–Sat 10am–4pm, Sun 11am–4pm.

Conwy Suspension Bridge ARCHITECTURE   The Conwy estuary is crossed by three bridges that all lead to Conwy. This handsome bridge was built in 1826 by Thomas Telford, whom Romantic poet Robert Southey nicknamed the "Colossus of Roads" (on account of his feat of building the A5 road). It's closed to vehicular traffic now, but you can walk across it. Adjacent is Robert Stephenson's **Tubular Railroad Bridge,** built in 1848, and the only one of its kind still surviving.

Castle St. www.nationaltrust.org.uk/conwy-suspension-bridge. *© 01492/573282.* Admission £1 adults, 50p children 5–15. Daily 11am–5pm.

St. Mary & All Saints CHURCH   Conwy's parish church stands at the town's heart on the site of a 12th-century Cistercian abbey; it's the only structure in town to pre-date the medieval grid, and sections still date from the time of the abbey. The churchyard contains a marked but overgrown grave, containing seven members of the same family, that supposedly inspired William Wordsworth's poem, *We Are Seven.*

Conwy. *©01492/593402.* Free admission. Church: Mon–Fri 9am–5pm. Cemetery: daily dawn to dusk.

Where to Eat

The best pub food for miles around is served outside town at the **Groes Inn,** Tyn-y-Groes (www.groesinn.com; *© 01492/650545*), where you can sense the 16th-century in its restaurant and informal bar. There are plenty of local touches, like the Groes smokie (smoked haddock with Parmesan cheese), gammon steak served with a local farm egg, and Groes Ale, brewed specially for the inn. Main courses cost between £10 and £19. Food is served daily noon to 2pm and 6:30 to 9pm.

Watson's WELSH/INTERNATIONAL   This relaxed bistro in the center combines a commitment to local ingredients with culinary influences from continental Europe. The eclectic menu might include the likes of strips of local seafood in a champagne velouté or shoulder of Welsh lamb with minted hollandaise sauce. The

Reopened in 2012, **The Albion** ★, 6 Uppergate St. (*℃* **01492/582484**), is an original 1920s ale house run as a joint venture between four leading North Wales breweries, including Great Orme and Purple Moose. A careful restoration process ensured that many of the internal Art Deco and Art Nouveau features were preserved.

setting is part of the attraction, inside a quaint old schoolhouse on a quiet Conwy backstreet.

26 Chapel St., Conwy. www.watsonsbistroconwy.co.uk. *℃* **01492/596326.** Reservations recommended. Main courses £10–£17; early-bird dinner menu (5:30–7pm) 2 courses £14.50, 3 courses £17. MC, V. Wed–Sun noon–2pm; Wed–Thurs 6–8:30pm; Fri–Sat 6–9pm.

Where to Stay

Central **Llandudno** (see below), only 20 minutes away by regular bus, offers a wider selection of accommodations.

Castlebank ★ Conwy's best-value central hotel is this converted Victorian villa clinging to a hillside just outside the town walls. You'll find a home-away-from-home thanks to comfortable, traditional decor—think eclectic bric-a-brac, a touch of chintz, and splashes of contemporary styling—and a can-do attitude from the genial host-owners. Rooms are midsize, and individually decorated rather than cookie-cutter: Our favorite is no. 5, with views over the Conwy Estuary.

Mount Pleasant, Conwy LL32 8NY. www.castlebankhotel.co.uk. *℃* **01492/593888.** Fax 01492/596466. 9 units. £75–£90 double; £85–£115 family room. Rates include breakfast. MC, V. Free parking. Closed 3 weeks in Jan. **Amenities:** Restaurant (Fri–Sat only); bar. *In room:* TV/DVD, hair dryer, movie library, Wi-Fi (free).

LLANDUDNO

243 miles NW of London; 43 miles E of Holyhead

This once-fashionable seaside resort of **Llandudno** nestles in a crescent between the giant headlands of the **Great Orme** and the **Little Orme,** named by Vikings who thought they resembled sea serpents when shrouded in mist. The town was mostly built beginning around 1850 by the Mostyn family, after whom many roads, avenues, and sites are named—and is forever linked with the Liddells, whose daughter Alice was the inspiration for Lewis Carroll's *Wonderland.* Although Llandudno has lost some of its prewar luster, its **Promenade** remains one of Britain's most handsome, and there are coastal views from **Marine Drive** and the **Great Orme Tramway.**

The resort's Victorian history lends it a certain cachet that's attracting a new generation of metropolitan weekend-breakers.

Essentials

GETTING THERE **Virgin Trains** has services from London's Euston Station, frequently requiring a change in Chester, the gateway to North Wales. Three trains per day go direct from Euston to Llandudno Junction with no changes, taking 2¾ hours. A standard return costs £80, but you should be able to get it much cheaper if you book ahead. Buses from Llandudno Junction Station to the center (20–30 min.) depart about every 15 minutes, or there's an irregular local train (15 min.). During the day, regular buses also connect Llandudno with Bangor.

If you're driving from England, head across North Wales along the A55.

VISITOR INFORMATION The **Llandudno Tourist Information Centre,** Library Building, Mostyn Street (www.visitllandudno.org.uk; ℂ **01492/577577**), is open daily 9am to 5pm, although closed Sundays from November through March.

Exploring Llandudno

This seaside resort has two **beaches,** the most visited on the northern edge of town, flanking a boardwalk and the Irish Sea, where you'll find the bandstand and traditional *Punch and Judy* shows in summer. Over on the quieter, west side of town, the beach opens onto views of Snowdonia and the Conwy Estuary. It's the place to head at sunset. At the end of the north-shore promenade, a fine Victorian **pier** was built in 1877, jutting 699m (2,295 ft.) into the bay at the base of the Great Orme. You'll get a fine view of it from **Happy Valley,** a former limestone quarry that was turned into lush pleasure gardens in the 1880s.

Great Orme ★ NATURAL ATTRACTION From the summit of this 206m (679-ft.) outcrop, you get a panoramic view along the North Wales coast. Walk up to the top if you're really energetic, but we prefer other means: Take the **Great Orme Tramway ★**, a cable-pulled tram which has been carrying passengers to the summit since 1902. It's closed between late October and late March, during which period you can drive along a cliff-side road, the **Marine Drive,** which winds uphill in a circular route that reaches a point near the summit.

Just above Marine Drive is the ancient **Church of St. Tudno,** named after the 6th-century Celtic saint from whom the town derives its name. The present stone building dates from the 12th century, but the church was founded 600 years earlier on this spot where he preached. Between June and September, there are open-air worship services every Sunday at 11am.

Tramway: Church Walks. www.greatormetramway.com. ℂ **01492/577877.** Round-trip £6 adults, £4 children ages 3–16. Apr–Oct daily 11am–6pm (closes 5pm Oct). **Church:** Great Orme. www.llandudno-parish.org.uk/sttudno.html. ℂ **01492/876624.** Free admission. Apr–Oct daily; Nov–Mar Wed, Sat–Sun.

IN THE CONWY VALLEY

Bodnant Garden ★ PARK/GARDEN The 80-acre hillside grounds of Bodnant Hall have been transformed into a charming mix of multi-tiered, labyrinthine formal gardens and managed wild spaces. Perfumed rose terraces have been carefully designed to afford views over the River Conwy to Snowdonia's foothills beyond. The garden is known for its elegant laburnum arch and a unique, internationally important collection of rhododendrons, first planted here in 1909 (337 hybrids have been registered at Bodnant). April and May are particularly colorful.

Tal-y-Cafn, Conwy. www.nationaltrust.org.uk/bodnant-garden. ℂ **01492/650460.** Admission £8 adults, £4 children 5–16. Mar–Oct daily 10am–5pm; first half of Nov daily 11am–3pm; Jan–Feb daily 11am–3pm (reduced winter opening, half-price admission). Bus: 25 from Llandudno (35 min.).

Where to Eat

For a taste of India's Punjab region, make a reservation at **Jaya,** inside Space (see "Where to Stay," below). For lunch on the go, or a picnic, the award-winning **The**

Llandudno

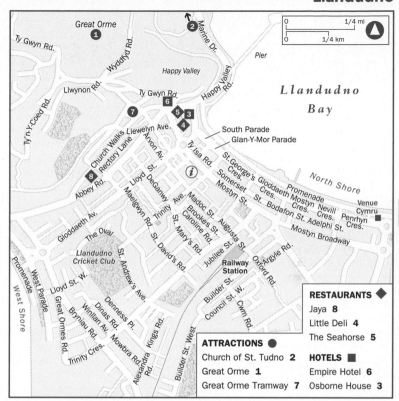

Great Orme ●1

Ty Gwyn Rd.

Marine Dr. ↑ ●2

0   1/4 mi

0   1/4 km

Pier

Happy Valley

Llwynon Rd.

Ty Gwyn Rd.

Happy Valley Rd.

Llandudno Bay

Wyddfyd Rd.

Ty'n-y-Coed Rd.

●7   ●5 ●3

●6   ●4

South Parade

Glan-Y-Mor Parade

Church Walks

Llewelyn Ave.

Rectory Lane

Arvon Ave.

Ty Isa Rd.

St. George's Cres.

Gloddaeth Cres.

North Shore

Promenade

Abbey Rd.

●8

Lloyd St.

DeGanwy

Trinity Ave.

Maelgwn Rd.

St. Mary's Rd.

Madoc St.

Brookes St.

Caroline Rd.

Augusta St.

Somerset St.

Mostyn St.

St. Bodafon St.

Mostyn Cres.

Nevill Cres.

Adelphi St.

Penrhyn Cres.

Venue Cymru ■

Mostyn Broadway

St. David's Rd.

Gloddaeth Ave.

The Oval

Llandudno Cricket Club

St. Andrew's Ave.

Jubilee St.

Argyle Rd.

Oxford Rd.

ⓘ

West Parade

West Shore

Promenade

Lloyd St. W.

Great Ormes Rd.

Denness Pl.

Dinas Rd.

Winllan Av.

Bryniau Rd.

Trinity Cres.

Mowbra Rd.

Kings Rd.

Alexandra Rd.

Builder St. West

Railway Station

Builder St.

Council St. W.

Cwm Rd.

ATTRACTIONS ●
Church of St. Tudno 2
Great Orme 1
Great Orme Tramway 7

RESTAURANTS ◆
Jaya 8
Little Deli 4
The Seahorse 5

HOTELS ■
Empire Hotel 6
Osborne House 3

19

NORTH WALES | Llandudno

Little Deli (see "Shopping," below) sells sandwiches loaded with local produce (£2–£3) and salads (£3–£4).

Enoch's 🏠😊 FISH AND CHIPS   The best fish and chip restaurants combine cooking skill with a commitment to sustainable sourcing and a lack of pretension, all wrapped up in an affordable package. Enoch's ticks every box: You can eat in, surrounded by pleasing nautical decor, and washing your meal down with a glass of wine or local ale; or take it out and feast on the go.

146 Conwy Rd., Llandudno Junction. www.enochs.co.uk. ℂ **01492/581145.** Reservations not accepted. Main courses £7–£14; £5 fish and chips to go. AE, MC, V. Daily 11:30am–8:30pm (until 9:30pm takeaway). On the A547 (Conwy Rd.), a 5-minute walk east of Llandudno Junction rail station; easily accessed from A55, jct. 19.

The Seahorse ★ SEAFOOD/INTERNATIONAL   Traditional, accomplished bistro cuisine and friendly service have brought this family-run restaurant a faithful list of habitués. The Seahorse gained its reputation on the back of its excellent fish cooking. Dishes are catch-dependent, but expect the likes of baked hake and crab thermidor or seared scallops with a lemon and saffron sauce. Lovers of land-roaming food are catered for with such dishes as filet of beef topped with St. Agur cheese.

7 Church Walks. www.the-seahorse.co.uk. ℰ **01492/875315.** Reservations recommended. Fixed-price menu £20 (1 course), £25 (2 courses), £29 (3 courses). AE, MC. Daily 4:30–11pm.

Entertainment & Nightlife

The seafront's most visible public monument is **Venue Cymru,** the Promenade (www.venuecymru.co.uk; ℰ **01492/872000**). It's the place for everything from tours by the Welsh National Opera to plays and rock concerts. Most shows begin at 8pm; tickets usually cost £10 to £45. The **Cottage Loaf,** Market Square (www.the-cottageloaf.co.uk; ℰ **01492/870762**), a traditional tavern with a low-slung ceiling and a summer beer garden, is the best pub in the center, serving four hand-pulled ales.

Shopping

Grumpy's   Junior heaven: Wooden floor-to-ceiling shelves are stacked with old-fashioned candy like lemon bon-bons, rainbow dust, and rhubarb and custards.

102 Mostyn St. www.grumpyssweetshop.com. ℰ **01492/872778.**

The Little Deli ★   Stock up on foodie gifts such as creative homemade jams—including lemon marmalade infused with Brecon gin—and chutneys. The same owners create (and sell) Baravelli artisan chocolates (www.baravelli.com). Closed Sunday.

133 Mostyn St. www.thelittledeli.co.uk. ℰ **01492/872114.**

Mostyn ★   Llandudno's contemporary art space also offers the best craftware shopping in town. Small, handmade ceramics and artisan jewelry (much by local artists) is a specialty. Mostyn also sells art books.

12 Vaughan St. www.mostyn.org. ℰ **01492/879201.**

Where to Stay

Llandudno is popular with weekend visitors from the northwest of England, so book hotels ahead on Friday and Saturday nights.

Empire Hotel ★★   Behind a slightly incongruous neoclassical facade is the best full-service hotel in central Llandudno. Family managed, it is furnished with antiques and fine paintings in the Victorian tradition, but with a subtle contemporary edge. Bedrooms are midsize to spacious and luxuriously furnished. A Victorian annex, "No. 72," contains eight of the establishment's finest rooms, with antiques, touches of silk, and period bathrooms.

Church Walks, Llandudno LL30 2HE. www.empirehotel.co.uk. ℰ **01492/860555.** Fax 01492/860791. 58 units. £105–£135 double. AE, DC, MC, V. Free parking. **Amenities:** 2 restaurants; bar; 2 heated pools (1 indoor, 1 outdoor); exercise room & spa; room service. *In room:* A/C, TV/DVD, fridge, hair dryer, movie library, Wi-Fi (free).

Osborne House ★★★   Sink into opulent Victoriana at this double-fronted 19th-century villa hotel opposite the Promenade. Rooms, all suites, are the size of apartments; classy and fashionable, they are dressed with antiques in a period style, and sport theatrical decor and not a hint of stuffiness about them or the general atmosphere. Beds are large enough to park an SUV in, and the neoclassical grandeur of the dining room makes a candlelit diner here an event. Book way ahead for a weekend stay.

17 North Parade, Llandudno LL30 2LP. www.osbornehouse.com. ℭ **01492/860330.** 7 units. £135–£175 suite. AE, DC, MC, V. Free parking. **Amenities:** Restaurant; bar; room service. *In room:* A/C, TV/DVD, hair dryer, movie library, Wi-Fi (free).

DENBIGHSHIRE ★ & THE NORTHEAST BORDERLANDS

Llangollen: 65 miles SW of Manchester, 55 miles SE of Caernarfon; Wrexham: 34 miles S of Liverpool, 13 miles NE of Llangollen

Away from its developed northern coastline, the historic county of **Denbighshire** is a terrain of rolling, lush grazing pastures, misty hills, and wooded slopes. It's dotted with friendly, workaday market towns that are generally little troubled by tourists—and in sleepy, empty corners like the **Ceiriog Valley,** not even those. One exception is **Llangollen,** whose prime location at a bridge fording the River Dee has attracted visitors since the Regency era—when a trip to see the "Ladies of Llangollen" at their house, **Plas Newydd,** was all the rage. Castles such as the one at **Chirk** also testify that these Welsh borderlands haven't always been so far from the heat of action.

Essentials

GETTING THERE & AROUND   The closest rail hubs are at **Wrexham** and **Rhyl,** and a network of local buses serves the major market towns. However, the only practical way to explore the best of the region—particularly the countryside of southern Denbighshire—is by car.

VISITOR INFORMATION   The main **Tourist Information Centre** is in Llangollen, at Y Capel, Castle Street (www.northwalesborderlands.co.uk; ℭ **01978/860828**). It's open daily 9:30am to 5pm.

Exploring Denbighshire & the Borderlands

The attractive little market town of **Llangollen ★** has retained much of its Victorian character—the High Street straddling the River Dee is a pleasant place to stroll. The most scenic Denbighshire drive follows the B4500 from Chirk up the idyllic, seemingly forgotten **Ceiriog Valley ★★,** as far as the **Pistyll Rhaeadr waterfall,** 4 miles northwest of Llanrhaeadr-ym-Mochnant. At 74m (240 ft.) high, it's the tallest single-drop waterfall in the U.K., and a good jumping off point for woodland and hill walking in the Berwyn Mountains (see also below). Real ale fans should divert for a pint at the traditional **Bridge End Inn ★,** 5 Bridge St., Ruabon (www.mcgivernales.co.uk; ℭ **01978/810881**). It was the first Welsh inn ever to be chosen as pub of the year by Britain's real ale society, and offers several well-chosen beers alongside a choice or two from the on-site microbrewery.

Chirk Castle ★ CASTLE   Perched strategically on a knoll overlooking the lower Ceiriog Valley, the marcher fortress of Chirk was built around 1300 by Roger Mortimer (1287–1330), under the patronage (like many castles in North Wales) of English King Edward I. Mortimer was a key player in the betrayal and killing of Llywelyn ap Gruffudd—still the only native Prince of Wales—in 1282, and Chirk was one of his rewards. The dungeon and Adam Tower date to this period, although the rest of the castle and courtyard have the genteel feel of an Oxford quadrangle—it was converted to serve as the Myddleton family home for 400 years. Views back to the castle from the manicured formal gardens with box-cut yews are sublime.

Chirk (11 miles south of Wrexham). www.nationaltrust.org.uk/chirk-castle. ℂ **01691/777701.** Admission to castle, gardens, and tower: £9 adults, £4.50 children 5–16, £22.50 family; gardens and tower only: £6.50 adults, £3.25 children, £16 family. Apr–Sept daily 11am–5pm, Mar and Oct daily 10am–4pm; gardens and tower only also Nov–mid-Dec and Feb daily 10am–4pm. Bus: 2 from Wrexham (45 min.). Train: Chirk.

North Berwyn Way ★ HIKING TRAIL   This waymarked path is a well-signed but challenging 15-mile walk along the fringe of wild, deserted hills. The path passes abandoned slate quarries where Italian POWs were held during World War II, and Bronze Age burial grounds as it meanders and climbs between Corwen and Llangollen. Take a good map (we recommend *OS Explorer 255: Llangollen and the Berwyns*), supplies, and mountain-ready clothing, because the terrain is empty and unforgiving. Allow a full day to complete the route.

Corwen–Llangollen. www.denbighshirecountryside.org.uk/north_berwyn_way. Open 24 hr.

Plas Newydd HISTORIC HOME   It's easy to see why the so-called "Ladies of Llangollen," Miss Sarah Ponsonby (1755–1832) and Lady Eleanor Butler (1739–1829), so loved their house and gardens, perched on a hill above Llangollen. These celebrities of Regency society lived here, having escaped Ireland together, for nearly 50 years from 1778. The enviable location is complemented by the eccentric Tudor-Gothic house, rich in stained glass and carved oak, much of which was brought as gifts by illustrious visitors such as the Duke of Wellington and William Wordsworth.

Hill St., Llangollen. ℂ **01978/862834.** Admission £5.50 adults, £4.50 seniors and children. Apr–Oct Wed–Sun 10am–5pm.

Where to Eat & Stay

The Hand at Llanarmon ★   You'd be hard pressed to find a more peaceful setting than the tiny village of Llanarmon Dyffryn Ceiriog, in the upper reaches of the unspoiled Ceiriog Valley, where the Hand has established itself as a first-rate eat-and-stay destination for foodies and discerning walkers. All the hotel's simply decorated, midsize units have pleasant rustic touches, but Character Rooms, with bigger beds, period furniture, and decor in keeping with the traditions of this former coaching inn, are worth the extra £20.

Llanarmon DC, Ceiriog Valley, Llangollen LL20 7LD. www.thehandhotel.co.uk. ℂ **01691/600666.** 13 units. £90–£127 double. Rates include breakfast. MC, V. Free parking. **Amenities:** Restaurant; bar; Wi-Fi (free). *In room:* TV, hair dryer.

Tyddyn Llan ★★   This elegant manor in private grounds has been converted into a restaurant and accommodations that splice Georgian exclusivity with modern hospitality. Rooms are individually decorated, some with leather seating and period furniture, others with modern pieces handcrafted in a traditional style.

The **Michelin-starred restaurant** is the real destination here, and usually features an inventive menu stuffed with local ingredients such as Welsh Black beef, local organic pork, or foraged ceps. The two-course fine-dining menu costs £45 (£55 for three courses), and is open to non-guests. Lunch (Fri–Sun) costs £19.50 to £38. Reservations are essential.

Llandrillo, Denbighshire LL21 0ST. www.tyddynllan.co.uk. ℂ **01490/440264.** Fax 01490/440414. 13 units. £150–£240 double; £300 suite. Extra child bed £30. Rates include breakfast. MC, V. Free parking. **Amenities:** Restaurant; bar; babysitting. *In room:* TV/DVD, hair dryer, CD player, movie library, MP3 docking station, Wi-Fi (free). Bus: X94 from Wrexham (70 min.).

PLANNING YOUR TRIP

by Donald Strachan

GETTING THERE

By Plane

London receives most of England's incoming air traffic, and England's principal airport is **London Heathrow** (LHR; www.heathrowairport.com), 17 miles west of the city and boasting five hectic, bustling terminals (Terminals 1 to 5, although Terminal 2 is closed until 2014). This is the U.K. hub of most major airlines, including British Airways, Virgin Atlantic, Qantas, and the North American carriers. **London Gatwick** (LGW; www.gatwickairport.com) is the city's second major airport, with two terminals (North and South), 31 miles south of central London in the Sussex countryside. As with Heathrow, you can fly direct or with a connection to or from pretty much anywhere.

England also has a number of smaller and regional airports. The only two with a significant number of intercontinental connections are **Manchester** (MAN; www.manchesterairport.co.uk), England's third-busiest airport, and **Birmingham** (BHX; www.bhx.co.uk).

Increasingly, however, passengers are flying into England's smaller airports—particularly as budget airlines have proliferated, and even come to dominate short-haul domestic and international routes. **London Stansted** (STN; www.stanstedairport.com), 37 miles northeast of London, is the gateway to a vast array of short-haul destinations in the U.K., continental Europe, and parts of the Middle East. It's also a hub for major budget operator Ryanair. **London Luton** (LTN; www.london-luton.co.uk), anchoring a similarly diverse short-haul network, lies 34 miles northwest of London. Ryanair and easyJet are two of the main users. **London City** (LCY; www.londoncityairport.com), the only commercial airport actually in London itself, is used mainly by business travelers from nearby Docklands and the City, but does have some key intercity links—notably with regular direct flights to New York, Paris, Edinburgh, and Madrid. British Airways and Cityjet are the two major airlines at London City. Outside London, the likes of **Liverpool John Lennon** (LPL; www.liverpoolairport.com), **Leeds Bradford** (LBA; www.leedsbradfordairport.co.uk), and **Newcastle** (NCL; www.newcastleairport.com) are well served by budget and point-to-point airlines offering direct connections to cities and resorts in continental Europe. In Wales, **Cardiff** (CWL; www.tbicardiffairport.com) is the principal airport, with direct flights to/from Orlando, Paris, Seville, and other European destinations.

GETTING INTO LONDON FROM THE AIRPORT

Heathrow Airport

A journey to the heart of London via the Tube on the Piccadilly Line takes 45 to 50 minutes and costs between £2.90 and £5.30—it's cheapest if you travel after 9:30am and use an Oyster Card (p. 78). Trains leave every few minutes, but if you want to plan your connections, use the online journey planner at www.tfl.gov.uk/journey planner. For further Tube information, see chapter 4. Although rail options (see below) are quicker to Paddington Station, unless that is your final destination you still have to continue (probably by Tube or cab), so the Tube can still be your best bet.

The **Heathrow Express** (www.heathrowexpress.com; ✆ **0845/600-1515**) train service runs every 15 minutes daily from 5:10am until 11:40pm between Heathrow and Paddington Station, just west of London's West End. Tickets bought online in advance are £16.50 each way in economy class, rising to £18 if bought from one of the terminal ticket machines, and £23 on the train itself. First-class tickets are £26. Children aged 5 to 15 pay £8.20 to £11.50 standard class, £13 in first class. The trip takes 15 minutes each way between Paddington and Terminals 1 and 3; 21 to 23 minutes from Terminals 4 or 5. The trains have special areas for wheelchairs. From Paddington, you can connect to the Tube, or follow signs to the taxi stand outside.

A better-value, but slower, rail option is the **Heathrow Connect** (www.heathrow connect.com; ✆ **0845/678-6975**). A couple of trains an hour ply the route to Paddington Station via Ealing from Heathrow Terminals 1 and 3, where you make a quick change for a transfer from Terminals 4 or 5. Total journey time is about 25 minutes for Terminals 1 and 3, plus 15 minutes more for Terminals 4 and 5. A single fare to Paddington is £8.50, with children 5 to 15 paying 50% less.

Most expensive of the lot, a **taxi** hailed at one of the airport's official ranks is likely to cost anything from £60 to £85. You can save by booking a fixed-price minicab service in advance from **Addison Lee** (www.addisonlee.com; ✆ **0844/800-6677**). Book online with a credit card or use the company's iPhone app.

Gatwick Airport

The fastest way to central London is via the **Gatwick Express** (www.gatwickexpress. com; ✆ **0845/850-1530**), which departs every 15 minutes, daily between 4:30am and 12:50am. The round-trip fare between Gatwick and Victoria Rail Station is £31 for adults and £15.40 for children aged 5 to 15. (One-way fares cost £18 for adults and £9 for children.) If you book online, you can save about 15% on ticket prices. The travel time each way is 30 minutes Monday to Saturday, and 35 minutes on Sunday. Check the website for regular pre-booking discounts, including 3-for-2 tickets.

Cheaper local trains call at Gatwick several times an hour, connecting either with Victoria or with London Bridge, City Thameslink, Blackfriars, Farringdon, and St. Pancras International. Journeys take 30 to 40 minutes. See www.nationalrail.co.uk.

Roughly hourly **National Express** (www.nationalexpress.com; ✆ **0871/781-8178**) buses link Gatwick with London's Victoria Coach Station. The walk-up fare is £8 single, but that can fall to £4.50 if you book online in advance. Children aged 3 to 14 pay half-price.

A **taxi** from Gatwick to central London costs around £100.

London City Airport

Trains on the **Docklands Light Railway,** known locally as the "DLR," make runs at 10-minute intervals from City Airport to Bank Tube station in the heart of London's financial district. A **taxi** should cost £20 to £40.

Stansted Airport

The **Stansted Express** (www.stanstedexpress.com; ✆ **0845600-7245**) train to Liverpool Street Station runs every 15 minutes from 6am to 11:45pm; the trip takes 45 minutes. If you book online, the cost is £20, or £27 for a round-trip. Tickets cost an extra £1 if bought at the station. If you're heading for the West End, get off at the Express's only interim stop, Tottenham Hale, and switch to the Tube's Victoria Line.

A slower rail route on **National Express East Anglia trains** (www.national expresseastanglia.com; ✆ **0845/600-7245**) is no cheaper but does terminate at Stratford, ideal if you're lodging in East London. Journey time is 1 hour, and trains leave hourly, Monday to Saturday.

By bus, you have several options depending on your final destination in the city. The **National Express A6 Airbus** (www.nationalexpress.com; ✆ **0871/781-8178**) heads for Victoria Bus Station, via the West End 24 hours a day; tickets cost £10 one-way. The half-hourly **National Express A9 Airbus** connects the airport with Stratford station, which lies on the Tube's Jubilee and Central Lines as well as the Overground network. Tickets cost £8. **Easybus** (www.easybus.co.uk) connects Stansted with Baker Street, at bargain rates as low as £2 if you book ahead online. **Terravision** (www.terravision.eu; ✆ **01279/680028**) runs two generally half-hourly services to Victoria and Liverpool Street Stations, respectively. One-way tickets cost £9. Note that because traffic conditions vary, any bus will take between 1 and 2 hours, at the lower end of that range for eastern destinations like Stratford and Liverpool Street.

For a ride to London's West End, a cab will charge around £100.

Luton Airport

Like Stansted, Luton Airport is well served by airbuses. **Greenline** (www.greenline. co.uk; ✆ **0844/801-7261**) service 757 links the airport with Victoria Station via Baker Street and Marble Arch. Fares are £16 for adults, £13 for children aged 5 to 13; a round-trip costs £23 for adults, £18 for children. (easyJet passengers can claim a significant discount by booking online ahead of time.) Buses leave half-hourly for most of the day. **Easybus** (www.easybus.co.uk) follows a similar route, with bargain one-way fares as low as £2 available if you book ahead online, although you're more likely to pay around £10. Buses depart every 20 minutes or so. The **National Express** (www.nationalexpress.com; ✆ **0871/781-8178**) airport bus runs a similar service, with similar frequency; tickets cost around £15 one-way; children get 50% off the full fare. All bus journey times are around 1½ hours, a little less if you get off at Baker Street.

It's quicker if you make for central London by train, although you first have to take the short shuttle bus to Luton Airport Parkway station (£1.50 each way; buses leave every 10 minutes). Both **First Capital Connect** (www.firstcapitalconnect.co.uk; ✆ **0845/026-4700**) and **East Midlands Trains** (www.eastmidlandstrains.co.uk; ✆ **0845/712-5678**) run services to St. Pancras Station. Several direct trains leave every hour, taking between 26 and 37 minutes to reach St. Pancras. One-way tickets cost £12.50; half-price for children 5 to 15. See www.nationalrail.co.uk for timetables and service information. Buy tickets for any of the bus or rail routes into town from the booths in the arrivals hall.

CHANGING AIRPORTS IN LONDON

National Express (www.national express.com; ✆ **0871/781-8178**) buses leave from Heathrow, Gatwick, Stansted, and Luton, circumnavigating the M25 to each of these airports with varying frequencies. Gatwick to Heathrow, for example, costs £25 for adults, £12.25 children, and takes about 1¼ hours. Between Luton and Gatwick airports, the quickest and most frequent service is the train operated by **First Capital Connect** (www.firstcapital connect.co.uk; ✆ **0845/026-4700**). A single fare is £24.50.

By Train

High-speed rail services from Paris and Brussels, via the **Channel Tunnel,** arrive at **St. Pancras International Station.** You can now reach London from Brussels in under 2 hours, and from Paris in 2¼ hours. The London terminus boasts Europe's longest champagne bar, all the Wi-Fi you'll ever need, plus dozens of stores—and saw a major new luxury hotel open in 2011, the **St. Pancras Renaissance London** (p. 180). In the U.K., make reservations for the train by calling **Eurostar** on ✆ **08432/186186;** in North America, book online at www.eurostar.com, or contact **Rail Europe** (www.raileurope.com; ✆ **800/622-8600,** or 800/361-7245 in Canada). International visitors arriving from continental Europe should remember that the validity of the Eurail pass ends at the English Channel. You'll need a separate **BritRail pass** (see below) if you plan to tour the U.K. by train.

GETTING AROUND
By Train

Train travel in Britain is getting faster and more reliable. It is also a great way to get around, gliding through the countryside in a comfy seat with a coffee in your hand. The fastest, best-served routes generally radiate outward from the capital. There are two main lines north from London: The **East Coast Mainline,** which connects King's Cross with York, Newcastle, and Edinburgh, Scotland; and the **West Coast Line,** which connects Euston Station with Birmingham, Manchester, the Lake District, North Wales, and Glasgow, Scotland. London Waterloo has trains to the South Coast and southwestern counties of England. Paddington serves the west, South Wales, and parts of the Midlands. For more information on train connections from London stations, see p. 752. Trains heading north out of the capital are due to get faster still, as work is proposed in 2012 on "HS2," a new high-speed line between London and Birmingham, and eventually onward to Manchester and Leeds. But don't get too excited yet: Opening is scheduled for 2026.

RAIL PASSES   BritRail passes allow unlimited travel in England, Scotland, and Wales on any scheduled train over the whole of the network during the validity of the pass without restrictions. A pass allows you to dodge lines at ticket machines and travel during peak periods without added expense. Passes are also valid on the expensive rail connections from all the key airports. Unless you plan to do lots and lots of travel, they probably aren't the cheapest way to get about—see "Rail Information and Bagging the Cheapest Fares," above—but they are certainly the easiest.

Passes are not available in England or Wales, nor to residents of the U.K.; they are for international visitors only, and you must buy one before you arrive. For comprehensive information, and to buy a pass in your local currency, see www.britrail.com. North Americans can also buy via www.britainontrack.com.

A **BritRail Consecutive** allows you to travel for a consecutive number of days. In the U.S., for example, adults pay $299 for 3 days first class, $375 for 4 days, $535 for 8 days, $799 for 15 days, $1,015 for 22 days, and $1,199 for 1 month. In standard class, fares are $199 for 3 days, $249 for 4 days, $355 for 8 days, $535 for 15 days, $675 for 22 days, and $799 for 1 month. **Seniors** (60 and older) qualify for discounts

RAIL information & BAGGING THE CHEAPEST FARES

Rail travel in Britain can seem baffling, with so many different, independent, private train companies operating on the same set of (state-owned) tracks. However, getting information about times and routes is simple: **National Rail Enquiries** is a one-stop shop with everything you need to know. Go to the website www.nationalrail.co.uk and enter the names of two stations (or towns) and it will give you a list of trains, times, and routes. It also shows fare options, of which there can be many, depending on when you travel and when you book. You can also get the information by phone (*C* **08457/48-49-50** in the U.K., or +44 20/7278-5240 from overseas). The site doesn't actually sell tickets but will connect you to one that does in a click. There are also train schedule apps for virtually every smartphone platform.

The key anomaly about rail travel is this: England has some of the most expensive walk-up rail fares in the world,

but also the cheapest advance-purchase rail tickets in Europe. So, for example, a one-way, walk-up fare at peak times (usually before around 9:15am on weekdays) between London and Manchester costs £148. Be a little savvy, however, book ahead, and travel outside rush hour or on the weekend and you could bag a round-trip on the same route for little more than £20. Advance fares are only available on long-distance routes and from around 12 weeks ahead of your travel dates. If you are able to book in advance, online agents such as **theTrainline.com** and **Quno.com** can bring huge savings. You can pay with a credit card and collect tickets from your departure station. If you're very fortunate, discount reseller **MegaTrain** (www.megatrain.com) may have a seat on your route at an even bigger saving. Alternatively, take all the hassle and planning out of your rail touring with a BritRail pass (see below).

in first-class travel only, and pay $255 for 3 days, $319 for 4 days, $455 for 8 days, $679 for 15 days, $865 for 22 days, and $1,019 for 1 month. Passengers 25 and younger also qualify for a discount. In standard class, rates are $159 for 3 days, $199 for 4 days, $285 for 8 days, $429 for 15 days, $539 for 22 days, and $639 for 1 month. Alternatively, youth holders of a valid Eurail pass are entitled to a 50% discount on regular BritRail pass prices.

More versatile is the **BritRail Flexipass,** allowing you to travel for a fixed number of days during a 2-month period. In first class, it costs $375 for 3 days, $465 for 4 days, $679 for 8 days, and $1,025 for 15 days. In standard class, it costs $249 for 3 days, $315 for 4 days, $455 for 8 days, and $689 for 15 days. One child aged 5 to 15 can travel free with each adult or senior pass when the **BritRail Family Discount** is requested while buying the adult pass; additional children pay half the regular adult fare for their pass. All children 4 and under ride U.K. trains for free. If you plan to stay within the borders of England, the **BritRail England Consecutive** and **BritRail England Flexipass** are both around 20% cheaper than the all-U.K. passes covered above.

For Wales only, the **Explore Wales Pass** allows unlimited travel on all mainline rail services, and almost every bus in the country. It also gives discounted or 2-for-1 entry to many recommended attractions (see chapters 18 and 19) and reduced rates at YHA hostels. The pass costs £89 and gives 4 days of rail travel and 8 days of bus travel within a fixed 8-day period. If you're sticking to one part of the country, there are South Wales and North & Mid-Wales Explorer passes that offer the same deal across a reduced area for £60. Children 5 to 15 are half-price, children 4 and under go free. Tickets can be bought at most rail stations and travel agents throughout Britain, or by calling ✆ **0870/900-0773.** For information, see www.arrivatrains wales.co.uk/explorewalespass.

Train Travel from London to Key Cities

TO	STATION	TRAINS DAILY	MILES	TRAVEL TIME
Bath	Paddington	25	107	1 hr. 29 min.
Birmingham	Euston/Paddington	35	113	1 hr. 25 min.
Bristol	Paddington	46	119	1 hr. 26 min.
Cardiff	Paddington	24	148	2 hr. 1 min.
Chester	Euston	16	179	2 hr. 2 min.
Exeter	Paddington/Waterloo	17	174	2 hr. 11 min.
Leeds	King's Cross	19	185	2 hr. 13 min.
Liverpool	Euston	14	193	2 hr. 8 min.
Manchester	Euston	16	180	2 hr. 7 min.
Newcastle	King's Cross	26	268	2 hr. 50 min.
Oxford	Paddington	37	60	1 hr.
Penzance	Paddington	9	305	5 hr. 25 min.
Portsmouth	Waterloo/Victoria	45	76	1 hr. 37 min.
York	King's Cross	27	188	1 hr. 57 min.

By Bus

In Britain, a long-distance bus is called a "coach" (a "bus" generally denotes shorter-haul, local transport). Coaches are generally the cheapest way to get around the country, but also the slowest. Most sizable towns have a link with the capital and several other major English and Welsh cities, either direct or via a connection. Most services are run by **National Express** (www.nationalexpress.com; ✆ **0871/781-8178**), which uses coaches equipped with reclining seats and toilets. A good budget alternative on some routes is **MegaBus** (www.megabus.com; ✆ **0871/266-3333**), with tickets costing as little as a few pounds. Most buses terminate in London at **Victoria Coach Station,** 164 Buckingham Palace Rd. (✆ **020/7730-3466**), although many offer intermediate stops in the capital. Major cities and towns all have a central bus station. **Traveline** (www.traveline.info; ✆ **0871/200-2233**) is a handy source of integrated service and timetable information.

In Wales, **Arriva Buses Wales** (www.arrivabus.co.uk/wales; ✆ **0844/800-4411**) is one of the main operators, with many local buses in the north and faster services between the north and south. The area around Cardiff is covered by **Cardiff Bus** (www.cardiffbus.com; ✆ **029/2066-6444**). For a full list of bus companies, and comprehensive travel information for Wales, see www.traveline-cymru.info. There are also Traveline smartphone apps for Android and Apple devices.

By Plane

There's rarely any need to take an internal flight within England and Wales. However, **British Airways** (www.ba.com; ✆ **0844/493-0787**) flies to several cities outside London—including Manchester which is served by nine flights per day from London Heathrow, and four flights per day from London Gatwick. London–Manchester flying time is 1 hour. **Flybe** (www.flybe.com; ✆ **0871/700-2000** or 01392/268529) also operates internal flights between London and Newcastle, as well as linking further-flung airports like Exeter, Southampton, Norwich, and Newquay—a flight to the latter can dodge the inevitable high-season traffic jams on roads to Devon and Cornwall.

By Car

This is the way to see the country at its best. Motorways, with a maximum speed of 70 mph, allow you to get from area to area swiftly and simply, then lesser roads and eventually country lanes let you meander through villages, reach distant beaches, experience glorious views, and see everything that's wonderful about England and Wales.

Visitors from overseas should be aware that in Britain traffic travels on the left side of the road, so steering wheels are on the "wrong" side for most. Rental cars are manual, unless you request otherwise, so the gear shift is on your left. Aside from motorways, other roads outside urban areas have a 60 mph speed limit unless sign-posted, and 70 mph on a dual carriageway. The limit decreases depending on size of road, conditions, and locality. Built-up areas generally have a 30 mph limit, although a number of towns are now introducing a 20 mph limit in local streets. Road signs are clear and use international symbols. The *Highway Code* gives full details of signs and driving requirements. It is available from most service stations, many newsstands and bookstores, and can be read online at www.direct.gov.uk/highwaycode.

GETTING THE BEST DEAL ON YOUR RENTAL CAR   The British car-rental market is among the most competitive in Europe. Nevertheless, rentals are expensive, although there are frequent promotional deals, sometimes linked to airlines, and mostly in low season. It's always cheaper to arrange a car in advance; you might also look into a fly/drive deal if you are arriving from overseas by plane.

Car-rental rates vary even more than airline fares. What you pay depends not only on the size of the car, but also where and when you pick it up and drop it off, length of the rental period, where and how far you drive it, whether you get insurance, and a host of other factors. Most companies will rent only to people 23 years and older, and many will not rent to people aged 70 and older.

The big global rental companies all have a presence in England and Wales: **Avis** (www.avis.com), **Budget** (www.budget.com), and **Hertz** (www.hertz.com). You should also check the prices offered by reputable resellers and agents such as **Kemwel** (www.kemwel.com; ✆ **877/820-0668** in North America), **AutoEurope** (www.autoeurope.com; ✆ **888/223-5555** in North America), and **Holiday Autos** (www.holidayautos.co.uk; ✆ **0871/472-5229**). Metasearch engines like **Kayak.com** and **Travelsupermarket.com**, as well as car rental price comparison specialists such as **Carrentals.co.uk**, are always worth consulting.

If booking your rental car direct—or comparing prices using various search variables—a few key questions could save you money:

- Are weekend rates lower than weekday? Find out if the rate is the same for pick-up Friday morning, for instance, as it is for Thursday night.
- Is a weekly rate cheaper than a daily one? If you need the car for 4 days, it might be cheaper to rent it for 5, even if you don't need it for that long.
- Is there a drop-off charge if you do not return the car to the pick-up location? Is it cheaper to pick up the car at the airport compared to a city-center location?

@secret_london	@visitengland
@BBCengland	@samuelpepys
@visitbritain	@londonist
@Number10Gov	@visitwales
@big_ben_clock	@HighwayCodeGB

- Are promotional rates available? If you see an advertised price in a newspaper, in a magazine, or online, ask for that specific rate.
- Are discounts available for members of frequent-flier programs, or trade unions, or organizations such as AARP, AAA, the AA, and so on?
- What is the cost of adding an additional driver's name to the contract?
- How many free miles are included in the price? Free mileage may be negotiable, depending on the length of rental.
- How much does the rental company charge to refill your tank if you return with it less than full? Although rental companies claim these prices are "competitive," fuel is always cheaper in town.

When you reserve a car, or are comparing prices, make sure you find out the total price, including the 20% value-added tax (VAT) and all insurances.

TIPS ON ACCOMMODATIONS

Make reservations as far in advance as possible, even in the quieter months from November to April. Travel to most places in England and Wales peaks between May and October, and during that period, it's hard to come by a moderate or inexpensive hotel room. In a trendy spot such as Pembrokeshire in southwest Wales, or Cornwall in southwest England, it's nigh impossible to find a good hotel room, apartment, or cottage to rent at short notice in the summer. And many of the smaller, boutique hotels around England and Wales can fill up year-round, especially at weekends and in popular city-break or weekend bolthole destinations.

You'll find hotels and other accommodations inside every conceivable kind of building, from 21st-century concrete cubes to medieval inns. In older hotels guest rooms can be smaller than you might expect (if you base your expectation on a modern Radisson, for example), and each room is usually different, sometimes quirkily so. But this is part of the charm. Some rooms may only have a shower, not a bathtub, so if you feel you can't survive without a tub, make that clear when booking. And don't look down on hotel restaurants any more. Several house some of the finest places to eat for miles around, many under the name of celebrated chefs, such as Gordon Ramsay at Claridges in London (p. 183) and Robert Thompson on the Isle of Wight (p. 310). Indeed, the "restaurant with rooms" has become an accommodations category in its own right—and is a particular strong point of rural Wales.

Classification

British hotels are officially graded by stars, and are judged on standards, quality, services, and hospitality. In a one-star hotel, buildings are required to have hot and cold running water in all rooms. All establishments from two stars upward must have

100% en suite (private bathroom) facilities. To achieve four stars or more, hotels must offer room service. Five stars (deluxe) is the highest rating. Star ratings are posted outside the buildings. However, the system is voluntary, and many hotels do not participate—some of our favorite places to stay in England and Wales have no stars at all.

A parallel star system, operated by the AA, awards between one and five stars to guest-house and B&B accommodations. See www.theaa.com/travel/accommodation_restaurants_grading.html for a full explanation of its system.

Bed & Breakfasts

An English bed and breakfast (B&B) often used to be a glum place, little more than a house with rooms, and with guests banished from the premises during the day. Nowadays, though, most are reliable, with rooms that are at worst simple, or decorated to the owners' personal tastes. As in many countries around the world, a new breed has also sprung up, with a boutique-hotel feel. Extravagant or quietly stylish rooms are offered, along with splendid breakfasts, and a decent lounge. Many are run with the care of a small hotel; they simply don't serve lunch or dinner. **Bed & Breakfast Nationwide** (www.bedandbreakfast nationwide.com; ✆ **01255/672377**) is one agency dealing in privately owned bed and breakfasts across the country, from cottages to castles, almost 700 of them.

Breakfast

Most hotels in England and Wales include breakfast in their rates. You might find that breakfast isn't included in big hotels that have a large business clientele, or very upmarket hotels that have an equally upmarket (and pricey) a la carte breakfast. Even then, there is often a rate offered that includes breakfast.

Farmhouses

Farms sometimes have rooms set aside for paying guests, occasionally in the main house, but increasingly in converted barns or cottages. You might still find some that simply offer a visitor a simple room for the night, but more and more they are expanding into full B&B or self-catering territory, with breakfasts often sourced from the farm and surrounding producers. A growing number also offer evening meals, perhaps around a big kitchen table in front of a warming Aga. The settings are often wonderful, deep in the countryside.

Farm Stay UK (www.farmstay.co.uk; ✆ **024/7669-6909**), set up in part by the Royal Agricultural Society of England, and still owned by a consortium of farmers, features more than 1,200 rural retreats including farms, B&Bs, and campsites. Most are open year-round.

Historic Properties

National Trust Holiday Cottages (www.nationaltrustcottages.co.uk; ✆ **0844/800-2070**) is part of Britain's leading conservation group. The National Trust is mainly known for the castles, gardens, and historic homes that you can visit, but it also has over 370 houses and cottages for rent in some of the most beautiful parts of England and Wales. Some of these properties are in remote countryside, others are on the coast. They sleep from 2 to 12 guests, are self-catering, and mostly available year-round, for weekends, short breaks, and longer.

The **Landmark Trust** (www.landmarktrust.org.uk; ☏ **01628/825925**) is a charity that rescues historic buildings and turns them into places to stay. As well as cottages, you'll find castles, country houses, towers, and other odd buildings. There are around 180, such as the Gothic Temple, set in Capability Brown-designed grounds in Buckinghamshire, and Kingswear Castle, dating from 1502, on the water's edge near Dartmouth, Devon. Places sleep from 1 to 16 guests, and are ideal for family get-togethers or group travel.

Welsh Rarebits: Hotels of Distinction (www.rarebits.co.uk; ☏ **01570/470785**) is a collection of over 50 historic hotels across Wales, from Georgian country houses to the Italianate village of Portmeirion (see p. 728), all of them luxury, most of them small and personally run. The same group also offers a portfolio of smaller guest accommodation known as **Great Little Places** (www.little-places.co.uk; ☏ **01570/470785**).

Holiday Cottages & Villages

Many companies around Britain have cottages for rent, and a cottage makes an ideal base for exploring the rural counties of England and Wales. **English Country Cottages** (www.english-country-cottages.co.uk; ☏ **0845/268-0785**) focuses on four- and five-star properties the breadth of the country. **Cottages 4 You** (www.cottages4you.co.uk; ☏ **0845/268-0760**), part of the same company, deals in more modest options, and has over 10,000 properties in the U.K. **Sheepskin Life** (www.sheepskinlife.com; ☏ **01865/764087**) has a much smaller portfolio of luxurious cottages and rural hideaways. In Wales, **Coastal Cottages of Pembrokeshire** (www.coastalcottages.co.uk; ☏ **01437/765765**) is a specialist in the busy south-western getaway spot.

Holiday villages are traditionally basic but jolly spots full of rows of mobile homes or simple chalets, along with bars, amusements, and restaurants. These still exist, but more and more are moving upward in their ambitions, with smarter rooms, luxury mobile homes, and state-of-the-art water parks. They are aimed squarely at family travelers, come packed with facilities, but perhaps lack the character of a cottage or historic property. **Hoseasons** (www.hoseasons.co.uk; ☏ **0844/847-1356**) has mobile homes, timber lodges, and chalets in parks across the country. Some are little more than camping sites, while others have swimming pools, children's clubs, and live entertainment.

Butlins (www.butlins.com; ☏ **0845/070-4734**) is one of the original "holiday camp" companies, popular before international tourism took off, and has reinvented itself. Butlins has three parks, at Minehead (Somerset), Skegness (Lincolnshire), and Bognor Regis (Sussex). The latter is the flagship resort; alongside the many comfortable apartments (all with TVs) and deluxe suites are two hotels, the Shoreline, and the modern-retro Ocean, which opened in 2009. There's an indoor water park, sports (archery and so forth), evening shows, and discos, all included in the price, and a beach outside the gates. It is a great option for a short family break, especially if you take advantage of low off-season rates.

CenterParcs (www.centerparcs.co.uk; ☏ **0844/826-7723**) is a more rural version of the holiday park. Each of the four parks (among them Sherwood Forest in Nottinghamshire) is set in 400 acres of woodland, which visitors negotiate on foot or rental bike. At their heart is the Sub-tropical Swimming Paradise, a balmy, indoor water complex with wave machine, connected to outdoor pool and water chutes.

Many of the historic homes, estates, museums, and castles of England are owned or managed by one of two national heritage organizations, **English Heritage** (EH; www.english-heritage.org.uk) or the **National Trust** (NT; www.nationaltrust.org.uk). If you plan to visit several heritage sites while you are here—and the list includes the likes of Stonehenge, Chartwell, and Fountains Abbey—short-term visitor passes to one or both of the organizations could save you a lot of money. A **National Trust Touring Pass,** for example, offering unlimited entry to NT properties for seven days, costs £23 for one adult, £41 for two adults, and £46 for a family. The 14-day version costs £28/£50/£58. You *must* buy the pass before arriving in the U.K.; see www.nationaltrust.org.uk/visit/overseas-visitors/touring-pass. If you're resident in the U.S., membership of the **Royal Oak Foundation** (www.royal-oak.org; ☏ **800/913-6565**) includes free admission to all Britain's NT sites and properties, plus discounts on National Trust cottages and houses (see "Historic Properties," earlier in this chapter). Annual membership is $55 (families $90). Members of the Heritage Canada Foundation, National Trusts of Australia, and New Zealand Historic Places Trust also receive free admission to all NT properties.

An **English Heritage 9-day Overseas Visitor Pass** costs £23 for one adult, £43 for two adults, and £48 for a family. The 16-day pass costs £27/£52/£56. Order it online at www.english-heritage.org.uk/daysout/overseas-visitor-pass/overseas-visitor-pass and collect it from any staffed EH property.

Chain Hotels

Many U.S. chains, such as Best Western, Hilton, Sheraton, and Travelodge, are found throughout Britain. In addition, Britain has a number of indigenous chains. **Thistle Hotels** (www.thistle.com; ☏ **0871/376-9099** in the U.K., or 0845/305-8379) is a decent chain of moderate to upscale hotels. Increasingly, there are small chains of boutique hotels such as the discreetly stylish **Hotel du Vin** (www.hotelduvin.com; ☏ **0845/365-4438**) and the more outrageously stylish **Malmaison** (www.malmaison.com; ☏ **0845/365-4247**), whose properties include a former church and a prison. Both are part of the same group. **Von Essen** (www.vonessenhotels.co.uk) is a group of some of Britain's finest country-house hotels. At the other end of the scale **Premier Inn** (www.premierinn.com; ☏ **0871/527-8000** in the U.K., or 01582-567890) is the U.K.'s largest hotel chain, offering simple, predictable quality in convenient locations at fair prices.

House Swapping & Peer-to-Peer Accommodation Networks

HomeLink International (www.homelink.org; ☏ **800/638-3841** in the U.S, or 01962/886882 in the U.K.), which costs $119/£115 for a year's membership, is the oldest, largest, and best home-exchange holiday group in the world. An alternative is **Intervac International** (www.intervac-homeexchange.com; ☏ **800/756-HOME** [4663] in the U.S., 0845/260-5776 in the U.K.), which costs $100 annually.

England and Wales are also well represented in online peer-to-peer accommodation networks. **Crashpadder.com** lists everything from spare rooms in locals' homes to whole luxury apartments in central London. Its properties usually represent excellent value. International giants like **AirBnB.com** are also well represented, especially in major English cities; **9flats.com** is another peer-to-peer site worth checking out for U.K. accommodations. **OneFineStay.com** has a small, but special portfolio of apartments in London, serviced in a hotel style.

Youth Hostels

The **Youth Hostels Association** (www.yha.org.uk; ✆ **01629/592700**) has more than 200 hostels in cities, in the countryside, and along the English and Welsh coastline. Hostels used to be known for their stark surroundings, dormitory rooms, and clientele of hardened hikers. However, in recent years they have widened their scope to attract "flashpackers," with new properties, family rooms, good food, and a warm welcome. What haven't changed are the locations, many of which five-star hotels would kill for, not least in Snowdonia, North Wales.

[FastFACTS] ENGLAND & WALES

Area Codes   The country code for Great Britain is **44.** Cities and towns within the country have their own area codes, all of which begin with **0.** (Omit the 0 when dialing from overseas.) The area code for London is **020;** Manchester is **0161.** A full local telephone number is then usually between 6 and 8 digits long.

Business Hours   With many exceptions, business hours are Monday to Friday 9am to 5pm. In general, retail stores are open Monday to Saturday 9am to 6pm, Sunday 11am to 5pm (sometimes noon–6pm). Thursday is often late-night opening in city-center stores; until 8pm or later isn't unusual, sometimes even later in the run-up to Christmas.

Car Rental The main rental companies can be found at almost any airport, but you'll find it cheaper to book a car before you arrive. See "Getting the Best Deal on your Rental Car," above.

Cellphones See "Mobile Phones," below.

Crime See "Safety," below.

Customs **Non-E.U. nationals aged 17 and over** can bring in, duty-free, 200 cigarettes, or 100 cigarillos, or 50 cigars, or 250 grams of smoking tobacco. You can also bring in 4 liters of wine and 16 liters of beer plus either 1 liter of alcohol more than 22% ("spirits") or 2 liters of "fortified" wine at less than 22%. Visitors may also bring in other goods, including perfume, gifts, and souvenirs, totaling £390 in value. (Customs officials tend to be lenient about these general merchandise regulations, realizing the limits are unrealistically low.) For **arrivals from within the E.U.,** there are no limits as long as goods are for your own personal use, or are gifts.

For specifics on what you can take home and the corresponding fees, U.S. citizens should download the free pamphlet *Know Before You Go* at www.cbp.gov. Alternatively, contact the **U.S. Customs & Border Protection (CBP),** 1300 Pennsylvania Ave. NW, Washington, DC 20229 (📞 **877/CBP-5511**), and request the pamphlet. For a clear summary of their own rules, Canadians should consult the booklet *I Declare,* issued by the **Canada Border Services Agency** (www.cbsa-asfc.gc.ca; 📞 **800/461-9999** in Canada, or 204/983-3500). Australians need to read *Guide for Travellers: Know Before You Go.* For more information, call the **Australian Customs Service** at 📞 **1300/363-263,** or download the leaflet from www.customs.gov.au/webdata/resources/files/GuideForTravellers.pdf. For New Zealanders, most questions are answered under "Coming into NZ" at www.customs. govt.nz. For more information, contact the **New Zealand Customs Service** (📞 **0800/428-786,** or 09/927-8036).

Disabled Travelers The best U.K. organization to consult for trip-planning advice is **Tourism for All UK,** Shap Road Industrial Estate, Shap Road, Kendal, Cumbria, LA9 6NZ (www.tourismforall.org.uk; 📞 **0303/303-0146;** from overseas +44(0)1539/814-683). The website also has an invaluable list of relevant organizations to contact for advice relating to specific chronic complaints. The **Royal Association for Disability Rights (RADAR),** 12 City Forum, 250 City Rd., London EC1V 8AF (www.radar.org.uk; 📞 **020/7250-3222**), publishes a number of handy written resources and, for a small fee, sells a key that opens over 8,000 locked public disabled toilets countrywide (£4 inc. U.K. P&P; £6 to anywhere in the world).

Annual guide **Open Britain** (£14) is the country's largest directory of accessible accommodation and travel services. It's widely available in bookstores, and at the usual online retailers worldwide. Companion website OpenBritain.net, launched in 2011, has a handy search facility for accessible accommodation.

For public transportation assistance in the capital, **Transport for London** publishes a deal of accessibility information; visit www.tfl.gov.uk/accessguides for the lowdown on stair-free Underground access, large-print and audio Tube maps, a Tube toilet map, and more. There's also a 24-hour assistance telephone line: 📞 **020/7222-1234.** London's official "black cab" taxis have interiors adapted for those in wheelchairs. In the "Accessible London" section of the **Visit London** website (www.visitlondon.com/access), you'll find links to details of accessible hotels and information about which parts of the transport network are adapted to your needs. Many London hotels, museums, restaurants, buses, Tube stations, and sightseeing attractions have dedicated wheelchair entry, and persons with disabilities are often granted admission discounts. For £1.50, iPhone users can download the **LDN Access app** (www.myukaccess.co.uk), which reviews the accessibility of hotels, restaurants, attractions, and more across the city.

Doctors If you need a non-emergency doctor, your hotel can recommend one, or contact your embassy or consulate. Failing that, try the general-practitioner finder at www. nhsdirect.nhs.uk. North American members of the **International Association for Medical Assistance to Travelers** (**IAMAT;** www.iamat.org; ✆ **716/754-4883,** or 416/652-0137 in Canada) can consult it for lists of approved local doctors. **Note:** U.S. and Canadian visitors who become ill while they're in England and Wales are eligible only for free *emergency* care. For other treatment, including follow-up care, you'll be asked to pay. See also "Insurance," below.

In any medical emergency, immediately call ✆ **999,** or ✆ **112.**

Drinking Laws The legal age for buying alcohol is 18. Those 17 and over may have a glass of beer, wine, or cider with a meal in a pub or restaurant, if it is bought for them by a responsible adult. Children younger than 16 are allowed in pubs only if accompanied by a parent or guardian. Don't drink and drive: Penalties are stiff—not to mention the danger in which you're placing yourself and other road users. Drinking alcohol on **London's public transport network** is forbidden, and on-the-spot fines are issued to transgressors.

Driving Rules See "Getting Around," earlier in this chapter.

Electricity British electricity operates at 240 volts AC (50 cycles), and most overseas plugs don't fit British wall outlets. Always bring suitable transformers and/or adapters, such as world multiplugs—if you plug some American appliances directly into an electrical outlet without a transformer, for example, you'll destroy your appliance and possibly start a fire. Portable electronic devices such as iPods and cellphones (mobiles), however, recharge without problems via USB or using a multiplug. Many long-distance trains have plugs, for the charging of laptops or cellphones.

Embassies & Consulates The **U.S. Embassy** is at 24 Grosvenor Sq., London W1A 1AE (http://london.usembassy.gov; ✆ **020/7499-9000;** Tube: Bond St.). Standard hours are Monday to Friday 8:30am to 5:30pm. However, for passport and visa services relating to U.S. citizens, contact the **Passport and Citizenship Unit,** 55–56 Upper Brook St., London W1A 2LQ (phone number as above, but the preferred method is email: londonpassports@ state.gov). Most non-emergency enquiries require an appointment.

The **High Commission of Canada,** Canada House, 1 Trafalgar Sq., London SW1Y 5BJ (www.canadainternational.gc.ca/united_kingdom-royaume_uni/index.aspx; ✆ **020/7258-6600;** Tube: Charing Cross), handles passport and consular services for Canadians. Hours are Monday to Friday 9:30am to 1pm.

The **Australian High Commission** is at Australia House, Strand, London WC2B 4LA (www.uk.embassy.gov.au; ✆ **020/7887-5776;** Tube: Covent Garden or Temple). Hours are Monday to Friday 9am to 5pm.

The **New Zealand High Commission** is at New Zealand House, 80 Haymarket (at Pall Mall), London SW1Y 4TQ (www.nzembassy.com/uk; ✆ **020/7930-8422;** Tube: Charing Cross or Piccadilly Circus). Hours are Monday to Friday 9am to 5pm.

The **Irish Embassy** is at 17 Grosvenor Place, London SW1X 7HR (www.embassyofireland.co.uk; ✆ **020/7235-2171;** Tube: Hyde Park Corner). Hours are Monday to Friday 9:30am to 5pm.

Emergencies Dial ✆ **999** for police, fire, or ambulance. Give your name and state the nature of the emergency. Dialing ✆ **112** also connects you to the local emergency services anywhere in the E.U.

Family Travel Most high-profile English and Welsh museums have quizzes, events, or entertaining resources for youngsters of any age, and many of the venues you will visit are part of the Kids in Museums program; see www.kidsinmuseums.org.uk. Most accommodations can provide a crib (or "cot") for a baby on request, and if you're renting a car, children under 12 and under 1.35m (4½ ft.) in height must ride in an appropriate car seat.

Consult your car rental company in advance of arrival, but it's the driver's legal responsibility to ensure all child passengers comply (see www.childcarseats.org.uk/law for details). You'll also find babysitting available at most hotels; enquire ahead of time, or at the concierge or reception desk when you arrive.

To locate those hotels, restaurants, and attractions that are particularly child-friendly, refer to the "Kids" icon ☺ throughout this guide. For a list of more family-friendly travel resources, turn to the experts at Frommers.com.

Gasoline   Please see "Car Rental," earlier in this chapter.

Health   Visiting the U.K. doesn't pose any specific health risks. Common drugs widely available throughout the Western world are generally available over the pharmacy counter and in large supermarkets, although visitors from overseas should note the generic rather than brand names of any medicines they rely on. If you're flying into London, pack **prescription medications** in carry-on luggage and carry prescription medications in their original containers, with pharmacy labels—otherwise they won't make it through airport security. Also bring along copies of your prescriptions, in case you lose your pills or run out. Don't forget an extra pair of contact lenses or prescription glasses. The general-purpose painkiller known in North America as acetaminophen is called **paracetamol** in the U.K.

Hospitals   The **NHS Choices** website (www.nhs.uk) has a search facility that enables you to locate your nearest Accident & Emergency department wherever you are in the U.K. In any emergency requiring an ambulance, you should dial ℂ **999.** Emergency care is free for all visitors, irrespective of country of origin.

Insurance   **U.K. nationals** receive free medical treatment countrywide, but visitors from overseas only qualify automatically for free **emergency** care. **U.S. visitors** should note that most domestic health plans (including Medicare and Medicaid) do not provide coverage, and the ones that do often require you to pay for services upfront and reimburse you only after you return home. Try **MEDEX** (www.medexassist.com; ℂ **410/453-6380**) or **Travel Assistance International** (www.travelassistance.com; ℂ **800/821-2828**) for overseas medical insurance coverage. **Canadians** should check with their provincial health plan offices or call **Health Canada** (www.hc-sc.gc.ca; ℂ **866/225-0709**) to find out the extent of their coverage and what documentation and receipts they must take home in case they are treated overseas. **E.U. nationals** (and nationals of E.E.A. countries and Switzerland) should note that reciprocal health agreements are in place to ensure they receive free medical care while in the U.K. However, it is essential that visitors from those countries carry a valid **European Health Identity Card,** or EHIC. At the time of writing, there is also a bilateral agreement in place offering free U.K. healthcare to nationals of **New Zealand.** However, you should always double-check the latest situation before leaving home, with domestic health authorities or online at www.dh.gov.uk/OverseasVisitors.

For information on general traveler's insurance, trip cancellation insurance, and medical insurance while traveling, please visit www.frommers.com/planning.

Internet & Wi-Fi   The availability of the Internet across the U.K. is in a constant state of development. How you access it depends on whether you've brought your own computer or smartphone, or if you're searching for a public terminal. Many hotels have computers for guest use, although pricing can vary from gratis to extortionate. To find a local Internet cafe, start by checking www.cybercaptive.com; it's not especially up-to-date, but is worth a try nevertheless. Although such places have suffered due to the spread of smartphones and free Wi-Fi (see below), they do tend to be prevalent close to popular tourist spots, especially ones frequented by backpackers. Aside from cybercafes, most **hostels** have Internet access, and some **public libraries** allow non-residents to use terminals.

If you have your own computer or smartphone, **Wi-Fi** makes access much easier. Always check before using your hotel's network—some charge exorbitant rates, and free or cheap Wi-Fi isn't hard to find elsewhere, in urban locations at least. Ask locally, or Google "free

Wi-Fi + [town]" before you arrive. To locate free Wi-Fi hotspots, it's worth using the hotspot locator at www.jiwire.com. National chains like **Welcome Break** motorway service stations (www.welcomebreak.co.uk) and **Wetherspoon** pubs (www.jdwetherspoon.co.uk), among many others, offer free Wi-Fi. You will find Wi-Fi on many long-distance trains; ask whether it's free in standard and first class, and calculate whether it's worth upgrading if you want to surf your journey away. There are also **BT Openzone** (www.btopenzone.com) hotspots in many cafes, hotels, and public places across the country (see http://btopenzone. hotspot-directory.com for a searchable directory and map). If you have a subscription to a global wireless ISP like **Boingo** (www.boingo.com), you can use these hotspots for free, or at a reduced rate depending on your subscription package.

Savvy smartphone users from overseas may even find it cheaper and more practical to switch off 3G altogether and call using Wi-Fi in combination with a **Skype** (www.skype. com) account and app.

Legal Aid   If you're visiting from overseas, contact your consulate or embassy (see "Embassies & Consulates," above). They can advise you of your rights and will usually provide a list of local attorneys (for which you'll have to pay if services are used), but they cannot interfere on your behalf in the English legal process. For questions about American citizens who are arrested abroad, including ways of getting money to them, telephone the **Citizens Emergency Center** of the Office of Special Consular Services in Washington, D.C. (✆ **202/647-5225**).

If you're in some sort of substance-abuse emergency, call **Release** (www.release.org.uk; ✆ **0845/450-0215**); the advice line is open Monday to Friday 11am to 1pm and 2 to 4pm. The **Rape and Sexual Abuse Support Centre** (www.rapecrisis.org.uk; ✆ **0808/802-9999**) is open daily noon to 2:30pm and 7 to 9:30pm. **Alcoholics Anonymous** (www.alcoholics-anonymous.org.uk; ✆ **0845/769-7555**) answers its helpline daily 10am to 10pm. For issues related to sexual health and sexually transmitted diseases, call the confidential **Sexual Health Line** at ✆ **0800/567123.**

LGBT Travelers   **Gay News** (www.gayuknews.com) has a comprehensive database of the scene around the country. Local news about gay and lesbian issues is provided by a number of reliable sources, including the **Pink Paper** (www.pinkpaper.com) and **Pink News** (www.pinknews.co.uk). July's annual **Pride London** march and festival (www.pride london.org; ✆ **0844/884-2439**) is the highlight of London's LGBT calendar, while Pride Brighton & Hove (www.brightonpride.org) and Manchester Pride (www.manchesterpride. com) are the main events outside London, on different weekends in August. Manchester-based **Gaydio** (www.gaydio.co.uk) was the U.K.'s first dedicated radio station for lesbian, gay, bisexual, and trans listeners.

For more gay and lesbian travel resources, visit **Frommers.com**.

Mail   An airmail letter from the U.K. to anywhere outside Europe costs 76p for up to 10g (⅓ oz.) and generally takes 5 to 7 working days to arrive; postcards also require a 76p stamp. Within the E.U., letters or postcards under 20g (⅔ oz.) cost 68p. Within the U.K, First Class mail ought to arrive the following working day; Second Class mail takes around 3 days. To find your nearest Post Office, consult the branch finder at www.postoffice.co.uk/branch-finder.

Medical Requirements   Unless you're arriving from an area known to be suffering from an epidemic (particularly cholera or yellow fever), inoculations or vaccinations are not required for entry into the U.K. Also see "Health," above.

Mobile Phones   The three letters that define much of the world's wireless capabilities are **GSM** (Global System for Mobiles), a satellite network that makes for easy cross-border mobile (cell) phone use throughout most of the planet, including the U.K. If you own an unlocked GSM phone, pack it in your hand luggage and pick up a contract-free **SIM-only tariff** when you arrive in the U.K. The SIM card will cost very little, but you will need to load it up with credit to make calls. Tariffs change constantly in response to the market, but in general expect call charges of around 20p per minute, 10p for a text message, and a deal on data that might allow 500MB in a month for about £5. There are phone and SIM card retailers on practically every high street in the country, but not everywhere will sell SIM-only deals to non-residents. Larger branches of supermarket Tesco sell **Tesco Mobile** (www.tescomobile.com) SIMs for 99p that you can top-up in-store with cash or an overseas credit card. Find a convenient branch at www.tesco.com/storelocator. **Three** (www.three.co.uk) offers SIMs for £11.99, with £10 of credit preloaded, which you can top-up further at Three stores, supermarkets, and newsstands (newsagents) across England and Wales. Three SIMs work only in 3G-compatible phones.

There are other options if you're visiting from overseas but don't own an unlocked GSM phone. For a short visit, **renting** a phone may be a good idea, and we suggest renting the handset before you leave home. North Americans can rent from **InTouch USA** (www.intouch usa.us; ℂ **800/872-7626** or 703/222-7161) or **BrightRoam** (www.brightroam.com; ℂ **888/622-3393**). However, handset prices have fallen to a level where you can probably buy a basic U.K. **pay-as-you-go (PAYG) phone** for less than one week's handset rental. Prices at many cellphone retailers start from under £20 for a cheap model, and you can find a basic Android smartphone for around £50. Expect outgoing call charges of approximately 25p per minute to anywhere in the U.K., 10p for text messages (SMS); receiving calls on your local number is free. **Carphone Warehouse** (www.carphonewarehouse.com) has retail branches across the country, and a reliable range of cheap PAYG phones. Buy one, use it while you're here, and recycle it on the way home.

There are several U.K. networks offering a bewildering array of tariffs. Best for reliable countrywide voice and 3G reception are probably **O2** (www.o2.co.uk)—whose cell network is also used by Tesco Mobile—and **Vodafone** (www.vodafone.co.uk). **Orange** (www.orange.co.uk) tends to offer slightly better-value tariffs, while **Three** (www.three.co.uk) usually has the best deals for smartphone users who want data included in their rate—but probably best suits travelers sticking to major towns and cities. Unfortunately, per-minute charges for international calls can be high whatever network you choose, so if you plan to do a lot of calling home use a VoIP service such as **Skype** (www.skype.com) in conjunction with a Web connection. See "Internet & Wi-Fi," above.

If you intend to use your cellphone *solely* to call overseas, and it's unlocked and GSM-compatible, you may find purchasing a specialist **international SIM card** to be the most convenient option. Calls to the U.S., for example, using a SIM card from either **Lyca** (www.lycamobile.co.uk; ℂ **020/7132-0322**) or **Lebara** (www.lebara-mobile.co.uk; ℂ **0870/075-5588,** or 020/7031-0791) cost 5p per minute to both landlines and cellphones. You can buy either at independent phone retailers, and can top-up both brands with vouchers on sale at branches of Tesco, Sainsbury's, the Post Office, and small retailers around the U.K.

For advice on making **international calls,** see "Telephones," later in this section. Mobile coverage is usually very good, although there are still areas where you can't get a signal, and it's as likely to be in a rural area of Suffolk as a Welsh mountain.

Money & Costs   Frommer's lists exact prices in the local currency. The currency conversions quoted above were correct at press time. However, rates fluctuate, so before departing consult a currency exchange website such as www.oanda.com/currency/converter to check up-to-the-minute rates. There's also a smartphone app available for pretty much any mobile device; see www.oanda.com/mobile.

THE VALUE OF THE BRITISH POUND VS. OTHER POPULAR CURRENCIES

UK£	Aus$	Can$	Euro (€)	NZ$	US$
£1	A$1.60	C$1.61	€1.24	NZ$2.07	$1.58

WHAT THINGS COST IN LONDON

	UK£
Taxi from Heathrow to central London	65.00–85.00
Underground from Heathrow to Piccadilly Circus using Oyster Card, off-peak	2.90
Double room at Claridge's (very expensive)	360.00
Double room at the Main House (moderate)	130.00
Double room at Avo (inexpensive)	90.00
Lunch for one at Petersham Nurseries Café (expensive)	25.00
Lunch for one at Tokyo Diner (inexpensive)	11.00
Dinner for one, without wine, at Alain Ducasse (very expensive)	78.00
Dinner for one, without wine, at Pollen Street Social (moderate)	26.00
Dinner for one, without wine, at Mangal I (inexpensive)	13.00
Pint of beer	3.00–4.00
Cup of coffee	1.80–2.50
Admission to national/state museums	Free
Movie ticket	8.00–12.00
Theatre ticket	25.00–85.00

Britain is among the most expensive countries in Europe, but perceptions of value for overseas visitors are at the mercy of exchange rate fluctuations and large regional variations. As capital cities go, London is not as expensive as Tokyo or Oslo, for example, but even an average hotel room can cost £100 a night or more—in many cases, much, much more. A pint of ale in Yorkshire, though, might be up to £1 cheaper than one at a London West End bar. While certain items in England might seem extortionate to an experienced European traveler—such as a cup of coffee, a pizza, or a London Tube fare—everyday clothes cost less than in many neighboring countries. Cellphone charges will seem inexpensive to a visitor from North America, but the same person will shudder at the price of a pair of branded sneakers or an iPod. But with entrance to national state museums costing nothing at all, Britain has more high culture for your buck than anywhere in the world. ATMs are everywhere in U.K. cities—at banks, some fuel stations, motorway rest stops, many supermarkets, and post offices. (Watch out for those inside small shops, however, as they charge users for withdrawing money.) These "cash machines" or "cashpoints" are the easiest way to get cash away from home. The **Cirrus** (www.mastercard.com) and **PLUS** (www.visa.com) networks span the globe; look at the back of your bank card to see which network you're on, and then check online for ATM locations at your destination if you want to be ultra-organized. Be sure you know your personal identification number (PIN) and daily withdrawal limit before you depart. Note that U.K. machines use **4-digit PINs,** so if your bank issues a 6-digit number, contact them before you leave home. Credit cards are accepted just about everywhere, save street markets and tiny independent retailers or street-food vendors. However, North American visitors should note that American Express is accepted far less widely than at home, and Diners only at the very highest of highflying establishments. To be sure of your credit line, and bring a Visa or MasterCard as well.

Britain has been among the world's most aggressive countries in the fight against credit card fraud. As a result, almost everywhere has moved from the magnetic strip credit card to the new system of **Chip and PIN** ("smartcards" with chips embedded in them). Most retailers ask for your 4-digit PIN to be entered into a keypad near the cash register. In restaurants, a server usually brings a hand-held device to your table to authorize payment. If you're visiting from a country where Chip and PIN is less prevalent (such as the U.S.), it's possible that some retailers will be reluctant to accept your (to Brits, old-fashioned) swipe cards. Be prepared to argue your case: swipe cards are still legal and the same machines that read the smartcard chips can also read your magnetic strip. However, do carry some cash with you too, just in case.

For help with currency conversions, tip calculations, and more, download Frommer's convenient Travel Tools app for your mobile device. Go to www.frommers.com/go/mobile and click on the Travel Tools icon.

Newspapers & Magazines   England has some of the best newspapers in the world. Of the quality national newspapers, *The Times* and *Daily Telegraph* generally lean right and the *Guardian* and *Independent* to the left of the political spectrum. All also issue Sunday editions: *The Sunday Times*, *Sunday Telegraph*, *Observer*, and *Independent on Sunday*, respectively. The Monday-to-Saturday *Financial Times* is one of the world's most respected business-oriented news sources. London has two daily papers, both of which are free and mostly available from rail stations: *Metro* appears in the morning (weekdays only, and now in several other cities around the U.K. too); the *Evening Standard* from lunchtime onward, also weekdays only. Most cities and regions have local daily newspapers of their own: Pick up the *Western Mail* in Wales, the *Manchester Evening News* and *Liverpool Echo* in the Northwest, the *Yorkshire Post* in the Northeast, and so on. For coverage of cultural events and nightlife, *Time Out* is London's major listings magazine, and also publishes editions elsewhere, such as Manchester. All of the above are also available, to varying degrees, **online.**

Packing   British weather is notoriously fickle, so although it rains in London much less than in the west of the British Isles, or Manchester—and nowhere close to the levels Britain's almost mythical reputation would have you believe—only the foolhardy visitor heads to the U.K. without some rainwear, even in high summer. On the plus side, winter temperatures rarely stay below freezing for long, and summers can be intermittently muggy, but rarely as hot and humid as southern Europe or the U.S.

Whether you need to find room in your suitcase for formal eveningwear very much depends on where you plan to stay and (especially) dine. Traditional, upscale restaurants in London's West End, for example, still largely expect you to arrive in a collared shirt, non-denim trousers, and "proper" shoes—and the equivalent attire for women. You may feel out of place without similarly formal clothes at a traditional country-house hotel in rural England, too. But anywhere in the country with a contemporary edge, however expensive, will welcome you as you are, even if that means jeans and sneakers.

For more helpful information on packing for your trip, download our Travel Tools app for your mobile device. Go to www.frommers.com/go/mobile and click on the Travel Tools icon.

Passports   To enter the United Kingdom, all U.S. citizens, Canadians, Australians, New Zealanders, and South Africans must have a passport valid through their length of stay. No visa is required. A passport will allow you to stay in the country for up to 6 months. The immigration officer may also want to see proof of your intention to return to your point of origin (usually a round-trip ticket) and of visible means of support while you're in Britain. If you're planning to fly from the United States or Canada to the United Kingdom and then on to a country that requires a visa (India, for example), you should secure that visa before you arrive in Britain.

Passport Offices:

○ **Australia**   Australian Passport Information Service (www.passports.gov.au or ✆ **131-232**).

o Canada Passport Canada, Department of Foreign Affairs and International Trade, Gatineau, QC K1A 1L2 (www.ppt.gc.ca; ℰ **800/567-6868**).

o New Zealand Passport Office, Department of Internal Affairs, P.O. Box 1658, Wellington, 6140 (www.passports.govt.nz; ℰ **0800/22-50-50** in New Zealand or 04/463-9360).

o United States To find your regional passport office, check the U.S. State Department website (travel.state.gov/passport) or call the **National Passport Information Center** (ℰ **877/487-2778**) for automated information.

Petrol See "Getting Around: By Car," earlier in this chapter.

Police Losses, thefts, and other criminal matters should be reported at the nearest police station immediately. You will be given a crime number, which your travel insurer will request if you make a claim. In a non-emergency, you can contact your local police station from anywhere in Britain by dialing ℰ **101.** Always phone ℰ **999** or 112 if the matter is serious or urgent.

Safety Britain has its share of crime, but in general it is one of the safest countries in the world for visitors. Pickpockets are a concern in London and other major cities, but violent crime is relatively rare everywhere. If you are in any doubt about the neighborhood you're in, ask the bar or restaurant you're leaving to phone you a minicab—never get into an unlicensed minicab, especially if you are female. Conceal your wallet or else hold on to your purse, and don't flaunt jewelry or cash. Personal electronic devices like smartphones and iPods are another obvious target for opportunist thieves. In short, it's the same advice you'd follow in your hometown.

In general, Brits practice greater **tolerance** than in most parts of the world. "Live and let live" is the maxim followed by most. As a visitor, you're unlikely to experience overt racial, ethnic, or religious discrimination, or that based on sexual preference. However, the country is by no means some cuddly, tolerant nirvana: You'll know discrimination if you experience it, so take your usual action to deal with it. It is **illegal** for any business offering goods, facilities, or services to discriminate against you because of your race, your religion, or your sexuality.

Senior Travel Britain offers many discounts to senior visitors. Many of the attractions recommended in this book list a separate, reduced entrance fee for seniors. However, even if discounts aren't posted, ask if they're available. Make sure you carry identification that shows your date of birth. Also, mention you're a senior when you make hotel reservations. Some offer discounts—but if you do not ask, they probably won't offer. **BritRail** offers overseas seniors discounted rates on some rail passes around Britain; see "Rail Passes," earlier in this chapter.

If you're heading to Britain from the U.S., members of **AARP,** 601 E St. NW, Washington, DC 20049 (www.aarp.org; ℰ **888/687-2277**), can secure discounts on hotels, airfares, and car rentals. Anyone 50 or older can join.

Smoking Smoking is banned in all indoor public places such as pubs, restaurants, and clubs across England and Wales. The regulations are almost universally observed and strictly enforced. If you wish to smoke, you will usually find temporary companions huddled close to the entrance door. Smoking is allowed in beer gardens and on terraces in bars, and the seats outside coffee shops, which generally means that any nice outdoor areas are effectively off-limits to nonsmokers.

Student Travel Never leave home without your student I.D. card. Visitors from overseas should arm themselves with an **International Student Identity Card (ISIC),** which offers local savings on rail passes, plane tickets, entrance fees, and more. Each country's card offers slightly different benefits (in the U.S., for example, it provides you with basic health and life insurance and a 24-hour helpline). Apply before departing in your country of origin. In the U.S. or Canada, at www.myisic.com; in Australia, see www.isiccard.com.au;

in New Zealand, visit www.isiccard.co.nz. U.K. students should carry their NUS card. If you're no longer a student but are still younger than 26, you can get an **International Youth Travel Card (IYTC),** which entitles you to a more limited range of discounts, as does the **International Teacher Identity Card,** aimed at educators.

Taxes   All prices in the U.K. must be quoted inclusive of any taxes. Since 2011, the national value-added tax **(VAT)** has been 20%. This is included in all hotel and restaurant bills, and in the price of most items you purchase.

If you are permanently resident outside the E.U., VAT on goods can be refunded if you shop at stores that participate in the **Retail Export Scheme**—look for the window sticker or ask the staff. You need to fill out form VAT 407 in store, which the retailer will supply, and show your passport when you make the purchase. Show your receipt and form 407 to customs officials when you leave the U.K. (or at your point of departure from the E.U.) and you then qualify for your refund. Each retailer is allowed to make its own arrangements for processing the refund—some require you to return the countersigned documents to them or an agent, others have an agreement in place with a booth at the airport. Details are posted online at www.hmrc.gov.uk/vat/sectors/consumers/overseas-visitors.htm.

Telephones   To make a call **within the U.K.,** the area codes found throughout this book all begin with "0"; you drop the "0" if you're calling from outside Britain, but you need to dial it along with the rest of the code if you're calling domestically. For calls within the same city or town, the local number is all you need, minus the area code. Dial just the **6- to 8-digit number.** Calling from a cellphone, you need to dial the full number including area code, *no matter where you're calling from.*

Phonecards are often the most economical method for visitors from overseas to make both international and national calls. They are available in several values, and are reusable until the total value has expired. Cards can be purchased from newsstands and small retailers nationwide, and offer call rates of a few pence per minute to English-speaking countries like Australia and the United States. Follow the instructions on the card to make a call from a public payphone. Most payphones now also take **credit cards,** but if your card doesn't have Chip-and-PIN technology embedded (see "Money & Costs," above), you may encounter problems.

To make an **international call** from Britain, dial the international access code **(00),** then the country code, then the area code, and finally the local number. Common country codes are: U.S. and Canada, **1;** Australia, **61;** Ireland, **353;** New Zealand, **64;** and South Africa, **27.** For calling **collect** or if you need an international operator, dial ℭ **155.** Alternatively, call via one of the following long-distance access services: **AT&T USA Direct** (ℭ **0800/890011** or 0500/890011), **Canada Direct** (ℭ **0800/890016**), and **Australia Direct** (ℭ **0800/890061**). For **directory assistance,** dial ℭ **118-118.**

Callers beware: Many hotels routinely add outrageous surcharges onto phone calls made from your room. Inquire before you call. It may be a lot cheaper to use your own calling-card number or to find a phone card.

Time   Britain follows **Greenwich Mean Time** (GMT) between late October and late March. Daylight-saving **British Summer Time** (BST), 1 hour ahead of GMT, is in operation for the rest of the year. London is generally 5 hours ahead of U.S. Eastern Standard Time (EST), although because of different daylight-saving time practices in the two countries, there's a brief period (about a week) in autumn when Britain is only 4 hours ahead of New York or Toronto, and a brief period in spring when it's 6 hours ahead. Sydney is 10 or 11 hours ahead of U.K. time, Auckland 12 or 13 hours ahead.

For help with time translations download our convenient Travel Tools app for your mobile device. Go to www.frommers.com/go/mobile and click the Travel Tools icon.

Tipping   Whether and how much to tip is not without controversy. Visitors from the U.S., in particular, tend to be more generous than locals—and indeed, some Brits resent a heavy tipping culture being "imported."

Tipping in **restaurants** is standard practice, as long as no automatic service charge is added to your bill. Leave 10% to 15% if you were happy with your server. However, be aware that a small number of places do not distribute these tips to staff as perks, but use them to pay their wages. This practice is only possible if you pay by credit or debit card, and unfortunately is perfectly legal. Ask who gets the tip, and if you're unhappy about paying the management's wage bill, have any automatic service charge removed and leave cash for your server to pick up. Earnings usually go into a communal pot to be shared among everyone from the kitchen porter to the sommelier, so there is no need to leave more than one tip per meal.

There's absolutely no need to tip the drivers of London's **black taxicabs:** They charge you extra for each item of luggage, and for standing in traffic. However, if the driver is especially helpful, add a pound or so to say thanks. Minicab drivers, on the other hand, generally earn less, and are always grateful if you are able to top up their rates, provided you're happy with the service.

Tipping in **bars** and **pubs** is practically unheard of, but if you receive table service in an upscale nightclub or wine bar, leave a couple of pounds. In upscale **hotels,** porters expect around £1 per bag. Leave your maid £1 per day if you're happy with the cleaning, but only tip the concierge if they have performed something beyond the call of their regular work. Barbers and **hairdressers** will appreciate an extra pound or two for a good job, but you're not obliged. **Tour guides** may expect £2 for a job well done, although again it's not mandatory. Theatre ushers don't expect tips.

For help with tip calculations, and more, download our convenient Travel Tools app for your mobile device. Go to www.frommers.com/go/mobile and click on the Travel Tools icon.

Toilets   Also known as "loos" or "public conveniences," these are marked by PUBLIC TOILET signs, and are usually free. You also find well-maintained lavatories in all large public buildings, such as museums and art galleries, large department stores, and railway stations (although the latter generally impose a charge). It's not always acceptable to use the lavatories in restaurants and pubs if you're not a customer, but we can't say that we always stick to this rule.

VAT   See "Taxes," above.

Visas   No E.U. nationals require a visa to visit the U.K. Visas are also not required for travelers from Australia, Canada, New Zealand, or the U.S. For nationals of, or visitors from, other countries, check www.ukvisas.gov.uk/en/doineedvisa.

Visitor Information   The U.K. has made a huge investment in placing comprehensive, up-to-date, and inspirational visitor information online, so the Web is the place to begin your research. Start with the umbrella sites: www.visitbritain.com, www.enjoyengland.com (or download the Enjoy England iPhone app), www.visitwales.co.uk, and www.visitlondon.com. Britain is among the world's most active destinations on Facebook; join the conversation at www.facebook.com/LoveUK. Almost any city or region also has its own site—see individual chapters for details. And, of course, there's plenty more—including features and updates—at www.frommers.com/destinations/england.

Individual **Tourist Information Centres** (or "TICs") are found in most tourist destinations around the country. See individual chapters for addresses and contact details. Staff are often the very best people to contact with specific questions, and generally respond promptly to e-mails with excellent insight and the very latest local tips.

There are many blogs about travel around England and Wales. You'll find the "official line" courtesy of a team of bloggers at the **Visit Britain Super Blog** (www.visitbritainsuper blog.com). **Sally Shalam's Britain** (www.sallyshalamsbritain.co.uk) is written by the *Guardian*'s U.K. hotel columnist, and offers an informed, contemporary take on visiting Britain. The best place get to under the capital city's skin is at the magnificent, esoteric **Great Wen** (www.greatwen.com). The **London Review of Breakfasts** (http://londonreviewof breakfasts.blogspot.com) sometimes strays a little further than you'd expect, but still does what it promises. **Bald Hiker** (www.baldhiker.com) follows the ramblings of a northern outdoor enthusiast.

Wi-Fi See "Internet & Wi-Fi," above.

Women Travelers First and foremost, lone women should never ride in **unlicensed taxicabs,** especially at night. Recent high-profile cases have seen this method used by predatory sex attackers. **Journeywoman** (www.journeywoman.com) is an excellent source of tips and ideas for women travelers.

For general travel resources for women, go to Frommers.com.

Index

Hole in t' Wall (Bowness), 611
Holidays, 44
Holkham, 532
Holkham Hall, 532
Holland Park (London), 75
Holly Bush (London), 171
Holst Birthplace Museum
   (Cheltenham), 433–434
Holt, 531
Holyhead, 737
Holyhead Mountain, 737
Holy Island, 673, 737
Holy Trinity Church (Stratford-
   upon-Avon), 456
Honeyclub (Brighton), 272
Honister Slate Mine, 625
Hope and Greenwood
   (London), 161
Horniman Museum (London), 124
Horseback riding, 49
   Dartmoor National Park, 382
Horse Guards (London), 100
Horse Guards Parade
   (London), 100
Horse racing
   Ascot, 206
   Cheltenham, 433
   Chester, 578
   Goodwood (near
      Chichester), 276
   National Horseracing Museum
      (Newmarket), 505
Hospital (London), 115
Hospital of St. Cross
   (Winchester), 292
Hospitals, 761
Hot-air ballooning, Bristol,
   346, 348
Hot Breath (London), 177–178
Hotels, 754–758
Household Cavalry Mounted
   Regiment (London), 100
Household Cavalry Museum
   (London), 100
House of Commons (London), 101
House of Lords (London), 101
House of the Tailor of
   Gloucester, 438
Houses of Parliament (London),
   100–101
Housesteads Roman Fort &
   Museum, 672
Howick Hall Gardens (near
   Alnwick), 674
Hughenden (High Wycombe), 231
Hugh Town, 413
Hunstanton, 532
Hunterian Museum (London), 90
Huntington's Antiques Ltd.
   (Stow-on-the-Wold), 444
Hyde Park (London), 95
Hypocaust (St. Albans), 236

Ice Bar (London), 168
Icknield Way, 511
Ickworth House (Bury St.
   Edmunds), 513–514

Ightham Mote, 258
Ikon Gallery (Birmingham), 471
Ilfracombe, 368
Ilfracombe Tunnels, 369
Imperial War Museum
   Duxford, 506
Imperial War Museum North
   (Manchester), 571
Industrial Revolution, 5
Institute of International
   Education (IIE), 49
Insurance, 761
The Intelligence Trail
   (London), 127
International Antiques and
   Collectors Fair (Newark), 546
International Beatle Week
   (Liverpool), 43
International Convention Centre
   (Birmingham), 475
International Jazz & Blues Festival
   (Birmingham), 468
International Kite Festival
   (Bristol), 44
International Sports Village
   (Watkiss), 684
Internet and Wi-Fi, 761–762
Ip-art (Ipswich), 521
Ipswich, 521–523
Ipswich Museum, 522
Ipswich Regent, 522
Ironbridge, 64, 487–489
Iron Bridge (Ironbridge), 488
Ironbridge Gorge Museums, 488
Island Bar (Birmingham), 476
Isle of Anglesey, 734–738
Isle of Wight, 64, 306–311
Isle of Wight Coastal Path, 309
Isles of Scilly, 412–414
Isobar (St. Ives), 416
Itineraries, suggested, 56–67
   best gardens in 1 week, 65–67
   for families, 63–65
   highlights in 1 week, 56–60
   southern England, 60–63
It's a Green Green World, 45
IWM (Imperial War Museum)
   London, 108

J

Jackfield Tile Museum
   (Ironbridge), 488
Jack the Ripper walk
   (London), 126
James Smith & Sons
   (London), 158
Jam House (Birmingham), 476
Jane Austen Centre (Bath), 339
Jane Austen Festival (Bath), 338
Jane Austen's House Museum
   (Chawton), 294
Jazz Festival (Cheltenham), 434
Jekyll & Hyde (Birmingham), 475
Jericho Tavern (Oxford), 225
Jerwood Gallery (Rye), 263
Jewel House (London), 113–114
Jewel Tower (London), 101
Jewish Museum (London), 120

Jewry Wall Museum
   (Leicester), 558
Jimmy's Farm (Ipswich), 522
Jodrell Bank Centre for
   Astrophysics (near
   Alderley), 580
John F. Kennedy Memorial
   (Runnymede), 205
John Lewis (London), 160
John Mills Theatre (Ipswich),
   522–523
John Milton's Cottage (Chalfont
   St. Giles), 230
John Rylands Library
   (Manchester), 568
Jolly's (Bath), 343
Jolly Sailor (East Looe), 401
Jorvik Viking Centre (York), 646
Jorvik Viking Festival (York), 40
Joy (London), 159
Jubilee Pool (Penzance), 408
The Junction (Cambridge), 503
Jurassic Coast, 317–319
Just Rachel (the Malverns), 480

K

Kabiri (London), 156
Kate Kanzier (London), 158
Keble College (Oxford), 215
Keith Prowse (London), 164
Kelmscott Manor (Burford), 426
Kendal, 604–608
Kendal Museum, 604, 606
Kenilworth Castle, 465–466
Kensington (London), 74
   accommodations, 191
   restaurants, 140–141, 149
Kensington Gardens (London), 95
Kensington Palace (London),
   95–96
Kent, 239–240
   castles and gardens of,
      256–260
Kents Cavern (Torquay), 384
Kenwood House (London), 117
Kersey, 515
Keswick, 624–628
Kettle's Yard (Cambridge), 500
Kielder Water & Forest Park (near
   Hexham), 672–673
Killhope, the North of England
   Lead Mining Museum (near
   Cowshill), 661
King Harry Floating Bridge (near
   St. Just), 403
King's Arms (Oxford), 224
The King's Arms (Colchester), 519
King's College (Cambridge), 498
King's College Chapel
   (Cambridge), 498
King's Cross & St. Pancras
   (London), 77
   accommodations, 180–181
King's Head Public House
   (Aylesbury), 228–229
King's Road (London), 152
Kingston Lacy (Wimborne
   Minster), 314